PRENTICE HALL

WORLD HISTORY

CONNECTIONS TO TODAY

Elisabeth Gaynor Ellis
Anthony Esler

With Senior Consultant
Burton F. Beers

Prentice
Hall

Upper Saddle River, New Jersey
Glenview, Illinois
Needham, Massachusetts

Authors

Elisabeth Gaynor Ellis

Elisabeth Gaynor Ellis is a historian and writer. She is a co-author of *World Cultures: A Global Mosaic.* Ms. Ellis, a former social studies teacher and school administrator, has taught world cultures, Russian studies, and European history. She holds a B.A. from Smith College and an M.A. and M.S. from Columbia University.

Anthony Esler

Anthony Esler is Professor of History at the College of William and Mary. He received his Ph.D. from Duke University and received Fulbright Fellowships to study at the University of London and to travel to Ivory Coast and Tanzania. Dr. Esler's books include *The Human Venture: A World History* and *The Western World: A History,* as well as several historical novels.

Senior Consultant

Burton F. Beers

Burton F. Beers is Professor of History at North Carolina State University. He has taught European history, Asian history, and American history. Dr. Beers has published numerous articles in historical journals and several books, including *The Far East: A History of Western Impacts and Eastern Responses,* with Paul H. Clyde, and *World History: Patterns of Civilization.*

PROGRAM REVIEWERS

AREA SPECIALISTS

Africa
Abraham Kuranga
Department of History
Cincinnati State, Technical
   and Community College
Cincinnati, Ohio

Ancient World
Maud Gleason
Department of Classics
Stanford University
Palo Alto, California

Chicano/a Studies
Shirlene Soto
California State University
Northridge, California

East Asia
Burton F. Beers
Department of History
North Carolina State University
Raleigh, North Carolina

Economics
Richard Roehl
Department of Economics
University of Michigan
Dearborn, Michigan

Richard Sylla
Department of Economics
Stern School of Business
New York University
New York, New York

Medieval Europe
Kathryn Reyerson
Department of History
University of Minnesota
Minneapolis, Minnesota

Modern Europe
Douglas Skopp
Distinguished University Teaching
   Professor of History
State University of New York
Plattsburgh, New York

Religion
William L. Pitts, Jr.
Department of Religion
Baylor University
Waco, Texas

Benjamin Ravid
Department of Near Eastern
   and Judaic Studies
Brandeis University
Waltham, Massachusetts

Michael Sells
Department of Religion
Haverford College
Haverford, Pennsylvania

Thomas Smith
Department of Religious Studies
Loyola University New Orleans
New Orleans, Louisiana

South Asia
David Gilmartin
Department of History
North Carolina State University
Raleigh, North Carolina

Susan Wadley
Department of Anthropology
Syracuse University
Syracuse, New York

Southwest Asia
Linda T. Darling
Department of History
University of Arizona
Tucson, Arizona

Women's History
Lyn Reese
Women in World History Curriculum
Berkeley, California

HISTORICAL MAP CONSULTANT
Gerald A. Danzer
Professor of History
University of Illinois at Chicago
Chicago, Illinois

CONTENT REVIEWERS
David Beaulieu
Former State Human Rights Commissioner
St. Paul, Minnesota

Samuel Chu
Department of History
The Ohio State University
Columbus, Ohio

Susan Douglass
Educational Consultant
Falls Church, Virginia

Shabbir Mansuri
Founding Director, Council on Islamic
   Education
Fountain Valley, California

José Morales
Chair and Assistant Professor, Latin
   American, Caribbean, and Latino
   Studies Program
New Jersey City University
Jersey City, New Jersey

Mark Peterson
Coordinator of Asian Studies
Brigham Young University
Provo, Utah

Charlotte Stokes
Supervisor of Social Studies, K–12
Prince Georges County Public Schools
Prince Georges County, Maryland

Acknowledgments and Illustration Credits begin on page 1046.

ISBN 0-13-009810-8

13 14 15 16 17 18 19 20 21   12 11 10 09

Start Smart

Before you start your study of World History, check out these special pages.

Unit 2   EMPIRES OF THE ANCIENT WORLD 70
1750 B.C.–A.D. 1570

Olmec stone head

v

Viking ship carving

Byzantine Emperor Justinian

Benin bronze

Japanese shrine

Unit 4 EARLY MODERN TIMES 330
1300–1800

*Italian artist
Leonardo da Vinci*

Ocean-going ship

*Catherine the Great,
empress of Russia*

Unit 5 ENLIGHTENMENT AND REVOLUTION 440

1707–1850

American statesman Benjamin Franklin

Early steam engine

South American liberator Simón Bolívar

West African throne

Japanese textile workers

Unit 7 WORLD WARS AND REVOLUTIONS 672
1910–1955

Soldier in World War I

Mexican mural by Diego Rivera

1920s "flapper"

World War II battlefield

First moon landing

Fall of the Berlin Wall

Namibian independence celebration

Honduran folk painting

Assessing Your Skills

 Synthesizing Information

Gather clues from different sources to understand key ideas.

 Comparing Viewpoints

Explore issues by analyzing opinions across time and place.

 Analyzing Primary Sources

Gain insights by examining documents and photographs.

Exploring the Human Drama

 Humanities Link

Experience great literature and arts from around the world.

 Disaster!

See how major disasters affected people's lives.

 You Are There . . .

Travel back in time to become an eyewitness to history.

Taos Pueblo, New Mexico

Virtual Field Trip

Start an Internet activity by visiting sites around the world.

San Martín and O'Higgins cross the Andes, 1817

Why Study History?

See how history is relevant to your life today.

SPECIAL FEATURES

Indira Gandhi

SPECIAL FEATURES/PRIMARY SOURCES

Connections to Today

Explore links between historical events and your world today.

Global Connections

See connections between events in different parts of the world.

Primary Source

Relive history through eyewitness accounts, literature, and documents.

(continued)

PRIMARY SOURCES

(continued)

The Spirits Are Good

The poems in the Book of Songs *offer
a rare look into the everyday lives
of average people in ancient China:*

"The spirits are good,
They will give you many blessings.
The common people are contented,
For daily they have their drink and food.
The thronging herd, the many clans.
All side with you in deeds of power.

To be like the moon advancing to its full,
Like the sun climbing the sky,
Like the everlastingness of the southern
  hills,
Without failing or falling,
Like the pine-tree, the cypress in their
  [foliage]
All these blessings may you receive!"

—*Shih Ching* (Book of Songs)

▶ Primary Sources and Literature

PRIMARY SOURCES: In Text

Middle Eastern market

(continued)

PRIMARY SOURCES

(continued)

"Go, wondrous creature! mount where Science guides;
Go, measure earth, weigh air, and state the tides;
Instruct the planets in what orbs to run,
Correct old Time, and regulate the sun."
—Alexander Pope, *Essay on Man*

MAPS

CHAPTER MAPS

(continued)

MAPS

REFERENCE SECTION MAPS

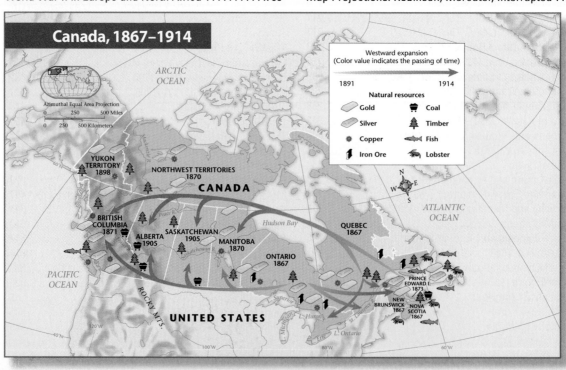

CHARTS AND GRAPHS/SKILLS HANDBOOK

CHARTS AND GRAPHS

CAUSE AND EFFECT

FACT FINDER

UNIT TIME LINES

SKILLS HANDBOOK

Use This Book to Succeed in World History

You can use this book as a tool to master world history. Spend a few minutes to become familiar with the structure of the book and see how you can unlock the secrets of world history.

Reading Focus

- How did Napoleon rise to power?
- How were revolutionary reforms changed under Napoleon?
- How did Napoleon build an empire in Europe?

Vocabul

plebiscite
annex
blockade

Find What Is Important

This book makes it easy to figure out what you really need to know about world history. Each section starts with Reading Focus questions that point out the most important ideas in that section. As you read, notice that the content is organized into several parts with red headings. As you read the paragraphs under the red headings, you can learn the answers to the Reading Focus questions. Later, you will find that the Section Assessment reviews each of these important ideas.

Napoleon's Rise to Power

Napoleon Bonaparte was born in Corsica, a French-ruled island in the Mediterranean. His family were minor nobles, but had little money. At age nine, he was sent to France to be trained for a military career. When the revolution broke out, he was an ambitious 20-year-old lieutenant, eager to make a name for himself.

Napoleon favored the Jacobins and republican rule. However, he found the conflicting ideas and personalities of the revolution confusing. He wrote his brother in 1793: "Since one must take sides, one might as well choose the side that is victorious, the side which devastates, loots, and

Learn in Many Ways

Don't depend just on the main text. Discover world history through all parts of this book—from primary sources to pictures, from charts to activities. Preview each chapter by looking at photographs, a map, and a time line. See connections between main ideas and illustrations. Be transported back through time by reading primary sources. Read stories about real people who have changed the world. Witness grave disasters and relive great moments. Research exciting topics. Act out human dramas. Use all of your senses to explore world history.

Primary Source

The Genius of Leonardo
Italian artist and architect Giorgio Vasari is best known for his engaging book of biographies of Italian artists including Leonardo da Vinci (pictured above):

"Leonardo practiced not one art but all of those that are dependent upon design, and he had great talent for geometry besides being very musical, playing the lute with great ability and being excellent in the art of improvisation. . . . In entertaining, Leonardo was so pleasant that he won everyone's ... ough he may well be ... e owned nothing and to ...ed little, he always kept ...s well as horses."

...iorgio Vasari, *Lives of the ... Eminent Italian Painters, ...Sculptors, and Architects*

Assessment

Source What ...etails did Vasari include ...ardo da Vinci?

Palace of Versailles

Disaster!

CYCLONE RIPS THROUGH CALCUTTA

The storm surge—walls of water pushed by powerful winds—is the deadliest part of a cyclone. Waves start small, but as the

Violent winds and rain struck Calcutta. Breaking waves caused a deafening roar. Then, a monstrous 40-foot wave crashed down on the shore. According to some reports, as many as 300,000 people died and 20,000 boats sank.

Native American Population of Central Mexico

Source: Nicolás Sánchez-Albornoz, *The Population of Latin America*

Portfolio Assessment

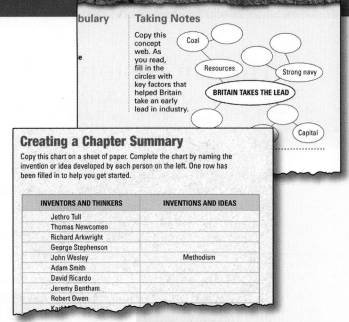

Organize Your Reading

Does so much world history content seem overwhelming? This book has ways to help you organize it. Use the Taking Notes exercise at the beginning of each section to help you take notes as you read. Then, at the end of the chapter, complete the Creating a Chapter Summary graphic organizer. This will help you capture the main ideas of the chapter in a visual way.

Develop Your Skills

Success in world history requires you to master social studies skills. Learn these skills in the Skills Handbook. Practice them by answering questions on maps, pictures, primary sources, charts, and graphs. In each chapter, you can also find an Assessing Your Skills feature, which focuses on analyzing primary sources, synthesizing information, or comparing viewpoints. Then, review your skills by completing the Skills Assessment activities at the end of every chapter.

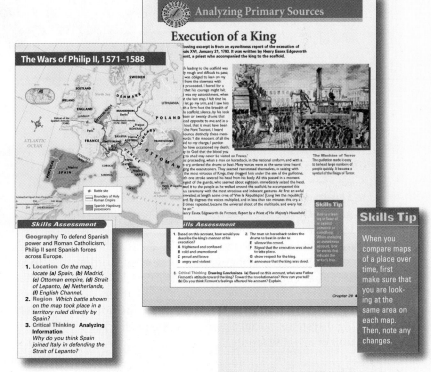

Prepare for Tests

This book will also help you prepare to take tests. To practice for standardized tests, answer the questions at the end of every section and chapter. Pay special attention to the critical-thinking questions. For portfolio assessment, complete activities in each Section Assessment and the portfolio assessment activities in Exploring the Human Drama features. Go to the **phschool.com** Web site to take a practice test for each chapter.

Web Site Self-Test
For practice test questions for Chapter 29, see
www.phschool.com

Human History Is Fascinating and Complex

To make world history easier for you to grasp, this textbook emphasizes nine themes. They can help you focus on the key features of each society and event you read about.

Theme: Continuity and Change

History is the story of change. Some changes can be as quick as a revolution. Others, such as the spread of democratic ideas or the shifting roles of men and women in many nations, may take decades or even centuries. Although change is always taking place, enduring traditions and concerns link people across time and space.

Theme: Geography and History

Geography influences where people settle, how they live, and how goods and ideas travel. Since ancient times, people have dug irrigation canals to water farmlands, and control of waterways or mountain passes has determined the outcome of wars. Today, environmental issues often stir heated debate.

The first moon landing, 1969

Theme: Political and Social Systems

Monarchs, presidents, dictators, tribal councils—each society has a form of government to ensure order and guard against outside threats. Societies around the world have also developed other important institutions to ensure order, including legal systems, social classes, and the most basic unit of all—the family.

Theme: Religions and Value Systems

Today, as in the past, religion exerts a powerful impact on the world. Belief in one God guided the histories of Jews, Christians, and Muslims. Buddhism and Hinduism shaped many Asian cultures. Nonreligious values, such as Greek ideals of beauty and individuality, have also had a wide influence.

Theme: Economics and Technology

Who controls vital resources? How are goods exchanged? What work do people do and how are they paid for that work? Economic questions such as these are often closely linked to technology. From Stone Age farming tools to the printing press to the steam engine to the computer, technology has transformed the world again and again.

Theme: Diversity

The vast diversity of the world's cultures is reflected in many ways, including language, ethnic background, customs, beliefs, and clothing. Such diversity has enriched the human experience. Yet, at the same time, cultural or ethnic differences often lead to bitter conflict.

Theme: Global Interaction

Different parts of the world may interact in many ways—through migration, trade, warfare, or the exchange of ideas. When people traveled by oxcart or sailing ship, interaction was a slow process. Today, communications networks can link all parts of the globe instantly.

Theme: Impact of the Individual

Everyone who ever lived is part of the human story. Yet some people have such an impact on events that we remember them long after they die. For good or ill, individuals such as Confucius, Christopher Columbus, Marie Curie, Stalin, and Mohandas Gandhi have had a lasting influence on our world.

Theme: Art and Literature

Since the days of Stone Age cave paintings, people have created art and literature to express their lives and values. In the Middle Ages, Europeans built soaring cathedrals to the glory of God. Today, novelists and filmmakers from Nigeria to Brazil vividly depict the challenges of modern life.

Are you ready to think thematically? On the next three pages, you will see pictures relating to different themes in world history. Look at the pictures and read the captions. Then, choose *three* of the nine book themes. For each of these themes, skim through the textbook and find a picture or feature that you think reflects that theme. Write a sentence explaining each of your choices.

Theme: Continuity and Change The Chinese system of writing began taking shape nearly 4,000 years ago, when priests used animal bones and tortoise shells to predict the future. Although it has changed greatly over time, this common language continues to link Chinese people across a vast area.

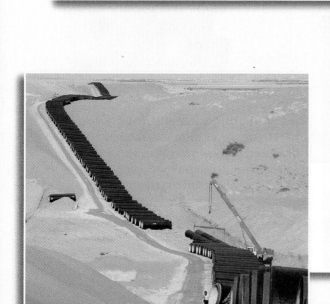

Theme: Geography and History Scarcity of fresh water has influenced settlement patterns, economic activities, and even political events in much of the Middle East. Here, crews assemble pipelines to carry water supplies through the Arabian Desert.

Theme: Political and Social Systems Our modern system of democracy developed largely in England. This painting by William Hogarth shows campaigners trying to win votes for their candidates outside a British tavern in the 1700s.

Theme: Religions and Value Systems According to the Bible, Moses brought the Ten Commandments from God to the Israelites. The Commandments—including "Honor your father and mother" and "You shall not murder"—have provided moral guidance to billions of people.

Theme: Economics and Technology In 1913, American automaker Henry Ford introduced the assembly line. This system allowed Ford to produce automobiles faster and more cheaply and to sell them at a lower price.

Theme: Diversity South Asia has long been home to a wide mix of people, as this ancient Indian painting shows. Today, India has 16 official languages and hundreds of regional languages.

Theme: Global Interaction For more than 200 years, Japan isolated itself from the rest of the world. Then, in 1853, an American expedition demanded that Japan open its ports to foreign trade. Japan quickly became a major world power.

Theme: Impact of the Individual Each country honors its own national heroes. Joan of Arc (left) led a French army to victory against the English. Simón Bolívar (far right) helped liberate several South American nations from Spanish rule. Nelson Mandela (near right) led a long fight against apartheid in South Africa.

Theme: Art and Literature Throughout Africa, skilled craftworkers created elaborate masks like the one shown here (far left) for use in religious and social ceremonies. In the early 1900s, the style of African masks influenced the works of Spanish painter Pablo Picasso (near left).

Explore World History Through the Internet

As you read this book, you will notice many opportunities to make world history come alive by using the Internet. By accessing a Web site designed specifically for Prentice Hall's *World History: Connections to Today* program, you can visit amazing places, develop exciting projects, and even review for tests.

Visit the Prentice Hall World History Web Site

Follow these easy steps to find the Web site that accompanies your book:
- Go to **www.phschool.com**
- Click on the button that says **"Social Studies."**
- Under **"PH@School,"** click on **"World History: Connections to Today."**
  Find the edition of the book you use, and select the student version.
- Select a specific chapter.

Take Virtual Field Trips

Now you can take field trips around the world and across the ages through cyberspace. In every chapter, you will find a Virtual Field Trip feature that highlights a specially selected site on the Internet. Link there via the **phschool.com** Web site to begin your exploration.

Learn Through Internet Activities

Throughout the entire program, you will find activities that are designed to work with the Internet. From doing online research to developing multimedia presentations, these activities use the strength of the Internet to supplement this textbook. Look for the Internet icon on Take It to the Net section and chapter review activities and Exploring the Human Drama portfolio activities.

Prepare for Tests With Web Site Self-Tests

For each chapter, you can take a practice test online at the **phschool.com** Web site. Completing this Web site self-test will give you a quick review of the material and help you identify which areas, if any, you need to study further. You can also use the self-tests to prepare for unit tests, midterms, and finals.

CONTENTS

Learning From Maps

How Will I Use This Skill? Maps are not just for textbooks. They can help you find your way on a bus or in a car. They can help you understand about events in other parts of the world. You can even use them to learn about tomorrow's weather.

Learning the Skill

To learn from a map, you have to look closely at the map's features. Use the map and the information below to learn about the various parts of a map.

Civilizations of the Ancient Middle East

1. **Read the title** The title gives a clue to the main topic of the map. **What is the title of this map?**

2. **Use the scale** You can use the scale of miles and kilometers to calculate the distance between two points. A short distance on a map represents a larger distance on the Earth. For example, one inch may represent 100 miles. **How far is it from Ur to Kish?**

3. **Observe the locator map** The locator map shows which part of the whole Earth is shown on this map. **How does the locator indicate the area shown on the main map?**

4. **Check the compass** The compass shows which direction is north on the map. You can also find the other directions—south, east, and west. Some compasses also show intermediate directions, for example northeast, which is the direction between north and east. **In which direction would you travel to get from the Sinai Peninsula to the Caspian Sea?**

5. **Notice the latitude and longitude lines and numbers** Latitude lines indicate the distance north or south of the equator. Longitude lines show distance east or west from the Prime Meridian, an imaginary line that runs through Greenwich, England. Latitude and longitude are measured in degrees (°). **What desert is located around 30° N latitude?**

6. **Identify bodies of water and other physical features** Maps often show oceans, rivers, mountains, and other physical features. Sometimes, color or shading is used to identify different features. Water, for example, is usually blue. Mountains are indicated by gray shading called relief. **Name three bodies of water shown on this map. Which mountain range is farther north—the Taurus Mountains or the Zagros Mountains?**

7. **Use the key** The key explains colors or symbols used on the map. Here, purple shows Sumer. **How is the Babylonian empire shown?**

8. **Identify political areas** Political areas, such as countries, empires, or cities, can be shown with borders, colors, or other symbols. They may be labeled on the map or in the key. **Describe the location of Mesopotamia.**

Practicing the Skill

Practice learning from maps by recalling the steps you just learned and by answering the following questions based on the map below.

1. What is the title of the map?
2. About how far would you travel to get from Beirut to Riyadh?
3. Study the locator map. What region of Africa is part of the Middle East? What region of Asia is part of the Middle East?
4. In what direction would you travel to get from Ankara to Tehran?
5. Use latitude and longitude to tell the location of the Strait of Hormuz.
6. (a) What are three important rivers in the Middle East? (b) What body of water separates Egypt from Saudi Arabia?
7. (a) A desalinization plant removes the salt from salt water to make it suitable for drinking and watering crops. How are desalinization plants shown on the map? (b) Where are most of them located?
8. (a) Through what countries does the Tigris River flow? (b) Through what countries does the Euphrates River flow? (c) Why do you think leaders from these countries meet to discuss water resources?

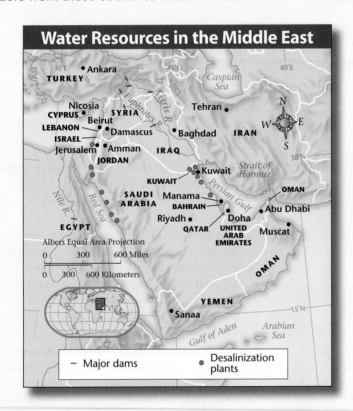

Water Resources in the Middle East

Albers Equal Area Projection

- Major dams
- Desalinization plants

Applying the Skill

Choose a map in your textbook. Based on the skill lesson on these pages, write a series of questions that test understanding of how to read and use the map. Trade with a partner and answer each other's questions. Then, check your partner's answers.

Understanding Charts and Graphs

How Will I Use This Skill? A graph shows numerical facts in picture form. Bar graphs and line graphs allow you to compare things at different times or in different places. You often see this type of graph in newspapers, where it might show a change such as the increase in student enrollment at your school or the average temperature over the last month. Circle graphs, or pie charts, show how a whole thing is divided into parts. The segments in a circle graph represent percentages of the whole, helping you better compare the parts.

Learning the Skill

To interpret a graph, you have to look closely at its features. Use the graphs and the information below to learn how to use various types of graphs.

Bar graph

Travel Times to London

Source: E. J. Hobsbaum, *Industry and Empire*

Circle graph

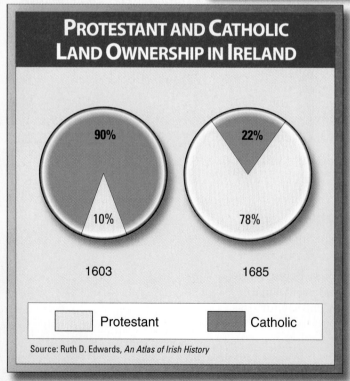

PROTESTANT AND CATHOLIC LAND OWNERSHIP IN IRELAND

Source: Ruth D. Edwards, *An Atlas of Irish History*

1. **Read the title** The title of any kind of graph tells you the main topic of the graph. **What is the title of the bar graph?**

2. **On line and bar graphs, identify the labels** Notice the labels on the bottom and side of the graph. For example, on the bar graph, the bottom, or horizontal axis, refers to hours. **What does the side, or vertical axis, of the bar graph refer to?**

3. **Determine what the bars or lines represent** Graphs use labels or a key to make clearer what the graph is about. On the line graph, for example, the red line represents the amount of steel produced in Germany. **On the bar graph, how are travel times in 1830 shown?**

4. **On circle graphs, identify the parts into which the circle is divided** A circle graph may have labels on the parts to tell you how the circle is divided. Sometimes, however, the graph includes a key to explain the use of color on the graph. For example, on the circle graph, Protestant land ownership in Ireland is shown in beige. **What color is used to show Catholic land ownership?**

5. **Read the graph** Use the title, labels, and colors to understand the meaning of the graph. You can learn from the circle graph that in 1603 Protestants owned 10 percent of the land in Ireland. **What percentage did Protestants own in 1685?**

6. **Interpret the graph** Often, graphs show trends, or tendencies in a given direction. The line graph shows steel production from 1880 to 1910 in three different countries. **(a) Which country had the greatest rise in steel production during this time? (b) Do you think this rise benefited other segments of the nation's economy? Why or why not?**

Line graph

Practicing the Skill

Interpret the graph at right by recalling the steps you just learned and by answering the questions that follow.

1. What is the topic of the graph? How can you tell?
2. What percentage of enslaved Africans was shipped to Portuguese Brazil? To Europe and Asia?
3. To what other parts of the world were enslaved Africans shipped?
4. Can you learn from this graph how many slaves were shipped to North America in 1875? Why or why not?
5. Can you tell from this graph what percentage of enslaved Africans was shipped to the Caribbean? Why or why not?
6. Could this information be presented on a line graph instead of a circle graph? Explain.

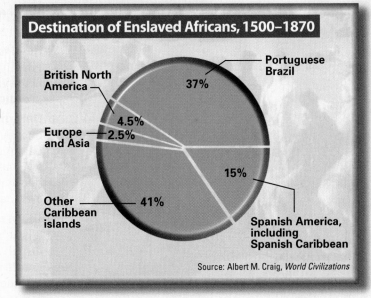

Applying the Skill

Conduct a simple poll among your classmates about a topic related to school, such as the number of hours per day each student spends doing homework or the material used by each student to cover his or her textbooks. Then, create an appropriate graph to display the results of your poll. Be prepared to explain your graph to the class.

Interpreting Visuals

How Will I Use This Skill? In today's fast-paced "information age," we are bombarded with visuals of all kinds. Television, film, the Internet, and print media all carry images that are designed to convey information or influence attitudes. People use drawings, art, photographs, and computer graphics to communicate facts and ideas. Today, literacy means not only the ability to read and write but also the ability to understand and interpret visuals.

Learning the Skill

Use this black-and-white photograph and the following steps to learn some of the methods involved in interpreting visuals.

In the 1950s, children in Europe and other parts of the world were taught they could survive a nuclear attack. This 1954 image was used to advertise a bogus "radiation-resistant" blanket.

1. **Identify the content of the visual** The content of a visual includes all the individual images that make up the larger visual. Be careful to look at both the foreground and background. Note which images seem to have the main importance in the visual. **What are the three main images in this photograph?**

2. **Note the emotional elements** An artist or photographer often tries to convey attitudes and emotions in a visual. **What feelings are conveyed by the boy's position and facial expression?**

3. **Read any text that accompanies the visual** A visual often has a title, caption, or other accompanying text that helps you to interpret it. **When was this photograph produced?**

4. **Determine the purpose of the visual** A visual may be intended to provide information, to persuade, or to entertain. A good starting point for determining the purpose of a visual is to consider the individual or group that produced it. **Who produced this visual? What do you think was its purpose?**

5. **Learn more about the visual or its creator** Sometimes, it is helpful to do some research to better understand the visual or its creator. If you did research on this photograph, you would learn that in the 1950s, the United States and the Soviet Union were engaged in a dangerous rivalry, including a race to build weapons. This rivalry was called the Cold War. Many people feared that a terrible nuclear conflict might erupt at any time. **Does this information refute or confirm your understanding of the picture? Explain.**

6. **React to the visual** React to the visual based on its apparent or intended purpose. If the visual was meant to inform, decide how well it conveys information to you. If it was meant to persuade, consider how effective it might be at influencing the attitudes of those who view it. If it was meant to be entertaining, react to it in those terms. **Do you think this photograph was an effective commercial advertisement that had an influence on people in the 1950s? Why or why not?**

Practicing the Skill

Interpret the visual below by recalling the steps you have just learned and by answering the questions that follow.

Honduran Street Scene
In this colorful folk art painting by Jorge Fermán, one can learn much about the culture of the Central American country of Honduras.

1. **(a)** What are some of the main images in the painting? **(b)** What images provide the background?
2. Do you think the painter portrays village life in Honduras in a favorable or unfavorable way? Explain.
3. How does the painting suggest that Honduras has a tropical climate?
4. What do you think is the purpose of this painting?
5. If you did some research about rural life in Honduras, you would learn that more than 50 percent of the population works in agriculture. Common crops among small farmers are corn, beans, and squash. On large plantations, people grow such cash crops as coffee and cotton. Based on this information, does the painting seem to convey an accurate or inaccurate vision of life in a Honduran village? Explain.
6. **(a)** What emotions does the painting cause you to feel? **(b)** Based on the painting, would you like to visit Honduras? Why or why not?

Applying the Skill

Select a visual in a current newspaper or magazine that appears in print or online. Print out, cut out, or reproduce a copy of the visual and any accompanying text. Use the steps that you have learned in this skill lesson to write an interpretation of the visual.

Analyzing Primary Sources

How Will I Use This Skill? Primary sources include official documents, as well as firsthand accounts of events. They may also include visual evidence, such as a news photograph, a painting by an eyewitness, or a political cartoon. They are a valuable source of information about the past. Historians often use primary sources, but you, too, use them—when you watch an interview on television or listen to a friend tell you about something that happened in school.

Learning the Skill

Use the excerpt, the cartoon, and the steps that follow to learn about analyzing primary sources.

The following excerpt comes from *The Satires*, a series of poems written by Juvenal about life in Rome in the first century A.D. In this excerpt, Juvenal recounts a friend's reasons for moving away from Rome.

66 Since at Rome there is no place for honest pursuits, no profit to be got by honest toil—my fortune is less today than it was yesterday. . . .

What shall I do at Rome? I cannot lie; if a book is bad, I cannot praise it and beg a copy. I know not the motions of the stars . . . no one shall be a thief by my cooperation. . . .

Who, nowadays, is beloved except the confidant of crime? 99

—Juvenal, *The Satires* (tr. Lewis Evans)

This cartoon by Arcadio Esquivel from Costa Rica shows the world being bulldozed. Costa Rica has been more successful than many other countries in balancing the need for development with the need to preserve the environment.

1. **Read the headnote or caption** Often, primary sources are presented with a short introduction about the writer or the document. The headnote with the excerpt above, for example, explains that the excerpt was written by Juvenal. **According to the headnote, when was this primary source written? Why was it written?**

2. **Read the primary source** As you read the primary source, identify unfamiliar words and try to gather the general meaning of the source. **In this excerpt, what is the writer's main point?**

3. **Identify facts and opinions in the written source** A fact can be proved true. An opinion, on the other hand, cannot be proved. Often, you can identify opinion statements by introductory words like "I think" or by strongly positive or negative words, like "gorgeous" or "despicable." Another clue is statements that exaggerate. **Identify an opinion statement in the excerpt.**

4. **Read the source line** You can often get additional information about an excerpt by reading the source line. In this case, for example, you can learn that the excerpt is a translation. **Who translated Juvenal's words?**

5. **Identify bias and evaluate reliability** You have seen that primary sources include both facts and opinions. They may also reveal the bias of the author. These factors affect the reliability of the source. Other factors that affect reliability are the time that may have passed between an event and the author's writing about it and the author's own earlier experiences. Suppose you knew that Juvenal had served in the army, hoping to make his way into government service, but in the end, had not received the promotion he hoped for. **How might that fact affect Juvenal's reliability as a commentator on Roman society?**

6. **Learn from political cartoons** Political cartoons can also be primary sources. They reflect the observations of one artist about events of the time. They often use symbols to represent other things. **(a) In the cartoon on the opposite page, what does the bulldozer represent?** Cartoons also use exaggeration to make their point. **(b) What is exaggerated in this cartoon? (c) Explain the point of view expressed in the cartoon.**

Practicing the Skill

Analyze the primary source below by recalling the steps you have just learned and by answering the questions that follow.

In 1947, India gained independence after hundreds of years as a colony of Great Britain. India's new leader, Jawaharlal Nehru, had worked to bring about independence. He addressed the nation on its first independence day.

66 We are a free and sovereign people today, and we have rid ourselves of the burden of the past. We look at the world with clear and friendly eyes, and at the future with faith and confidence. . . .

Our first and immediate objective must be to put an end to all internal strife and violence, which disfigure and degrade us and injure the cause of freedom. They come in the way of consideration of the great economic problems of the masses of the people which so urgently demand attention.

. . . Production today is the first priority, and every attempt to hamper or lessen production is injuring the nation, and more especially harmful to our laboring masses. . . . 99

—Jawaharlal Nehru, Independence Day speech, August 15, 1947

1. **(a)** Who wrote this document? **(b)** Under what circumstances?
2. **(a)** Identify one fact in Nehru's speech. **(b)** Identify one opinion statement.
3. **(a)** What was Nehru's purpose in giving this speech? **(b)** Do you think his purpose affected the words he spoke? **(c)** Do you think he achieved his purpose?
4. **(a)** Is the speech a reliable source for understanding Nehru's goal for his country? **(b)** Why or why not?

Applying the Skill

Use Internet or library sources to find a primary source that interests you. Remember that it can be either written or visual. Follow the steps outlined on these pages and then write a paragraph analzying the primary source.

Comparing Viewpoints

How Will I Use This Skill? When people describe an idea or event, they usually provide some facts and their own personal viewpoints. A person's viewpoint is shaped by subjective influences such as feelings, prejudices, and past experiences. You often encounter divergent viewpoints, as when two of your friends describe the same event differently, when two politicians recommend different policies, or when two newspapers analyze a news event in different ways. By analyzing and comparing viewpoints, you will be able to better understand issues and form your own viewpoint.

Learning the Skill

Throughout history, people have tried to educate their children. But they have not always agreed on the goals of education. Read the excerpts below and compare the two viewpoints by using the steps that follow.

Henri Christophe, king of Haiti, set up schools for outstanding students of his nation. He believed these schools would help Haiti maintain the freedom it had won fewer than 15 years earlier. In 1817, he wrote:

66 To form good citizens we must educate our children. From our national institutions will proceed a race of men capable of defending by their knowledge and talents those rights so long denied by tyrants. It is from these sources that light will be diffused among the whole mass of the population.99

—King Henri Christophe, 1817

Leo Tolstoy, a Russian aristocrat of the late 1800s, became a famous novelist as a young man. Later, he turned his attention to social issues. In 1902, he wrote:

66 You can take a puppy and feed him, and teach him to carry something, and enjoy the sight of him; but it is not enough to rear and bring up a man, and teach him Greek; he has to be taught to live, that is, to take less from others, and give more.99

—Leo Tolstoy, 1902

---

1. **Identify the authors** It is important always to identify the writer or speaker. **Who are the authors of these two documents, and where and when did they live?**

2. **Make sure that you understand the arguments being made.** Try to identify the main idea and supporting arguments made by each author. **(a) According to Christophe, what is the goal of education? (b) Why does Tolstoy compare raising a puppy to teaching a person Greek?**

3. **Consider the authors' backgrounds** A person's attitudes, beliefs, and past experiences affect that person's viewpoint. By knowing the author's background, you can make judgments about the viewpoint. **How might the backgrounds of Christophe and Tolstoy affect their viewpoints?**

4. **Find common information** If two viewpoints are on the same topic, there should be some points that they agree on. Often, these will be basic facts. **According to both viewpoints, what is true about education?**

5. **Find opinions** Differentiate the opinions from the facts. The opinions represent the author's viewpoint. **Name two words used by Christophe that signal opinions.**

6. **Evaluate the validity of each viewpoint** Evaluate viewpoints by recalling the authors' background and determining if their opinions are based on facts or reasonable arguments. **Are the viewpoints of Christophe and Tolstoy based on reasonable arguments? Explain.**

7. **Draw conclusions** After following the above steps, you are ready to draw conclusions about the viewpoints and the topic that they deal with. **(a) Do you think Tolstoy's view was typical of Russian aristocrats? (b) Why might the king of Haiti have been so concerned about maintaining the freedom of his nation?**

Practicing the Skill

The document and poster below reflect different viewpoints on industry and labor in the Soviet Union during the early 1900s. Compare the two viewpoints by answering the following questions:

1. Who are the authors of the letter?
2. Based on both documents, what was one goal of the Soviet Union?
3. **(a)** According to the poster, what was the general attitude of Soviet workers? **(b)** According to the letter, were most people in the camp treated justly? Explain.
4. Which viewpoint seems more trustworthy to you? Explain.
5. What methods did the Soviet Union use to increase economic production?

This letter protesting prison conditions was written to government leaders of the Soviet Union by former prisoners.

❝ We are prisoners who are returning from the Solovetsky concentration camp because of our poor health. We went there full of energy and good health, and now we are returning as invalids, broken and crippled emotionally and physically. . . . It is difficult for a human being even to imagine such terror, tyranny, violence, and lawlessness. . . . The Unified State Political Directorate [OGPU] without oversight and due process sends workers and peasants there who are by and large innocent. . . .

They die a slow and painful death . . . from hunger, cold, and backbreaking 14–16 hour days. . . . We . . . are asking you to improve the pathetic, tortured existence of those who are there who languish under the yoke of the OGPU's tyranny. . . . To this we subscribe: G. Zheleznov, Vinogradov, F. Belinskii. ❞

—Letter to the Presidium of the Central Executive Committee of the Communist Party, December 14, 1926

КОМСОМОЛ-УДАРНАЯ БРИГАДА ПЯТИЛЕТКИ.

Poster produced by the Soviet government, 1930s.

Applying the Skill

Use the Internet or library resources to find two documents expressing different viewpoints on a major turning point in world history. Some examples are the fall of the Roman empire, the Crusades, the Reformation, and World War I. Make copies of the documents. Then, use the steps that you have learned to write a paragraph comparing the viewpoints.

Synthesizing Information

How Will I Use This Skill? If you want to know whether a movie is worth seeing, you can read a review, watch a television commercial, view a film clip on the Internet, and talk to people who have seen the movie. You can combine the different pieces of evidence to develop a more complete impression of the movie. This process of combining pieces of evidence is called synthesizing. Today and in the future, synthesizing information will help you to become better informed and to make better decisions.

Learning the Skill

Study the three different pieces of information on this page about some developments in the 1400s and early 1500s. Then, follow the steps to learn how to synthesize information.

The caravel, shown above, helped Europeans sail across and into the wind.

Improved Technology Several improvements in technology helped Europeans conquer the vast oceans of the world. Cartographers, or mapmakers, created more accurate maps and sea charts. European sailors also learned to use the astrolabe, an instrument developed by the ancient Greeks and perfected by the Arabs, to determine their latitude at sea.

Along with more reliable navigational tools, Europeans designed larger and better ships. The Portuguese developed the caravel, which combined the square sails of European ships with Arab lateen, or triangular, sails. Caravels also adapted the sternpost rudder and numerous masts of Chinese ships. The new rigging made it easier to sail across or even into the wind. Finally, European ships added more weaponry, including sturdier cannons.

Hardships on the Uncharted Sea

In his journal, Italian sailor Antonio Pigafetta detailed the desperate conditions Magellan's sailors faced as they crossed the Pacific Ocean:

"We remained 3 months and 20 days without taking in provisions or other refreshments and ate only old biscuit reduced to powder, full of grubs and stinking from the dirt which rats had made on it. We drank water that was yellow and stinking. We also ate the ox hides from under the mainyard which we softened by soaking in seawater for several days."

—Journal of Antonio Pigafetta

1. **Focus on a topic** It is usually not very fruitful to synthesize bits of information that have little or nothing in common. The different pieces of information should be on some common topic. **To what common topic do all three bits of information relate?**

2. **Analyze each piece of information** The purpose of synthesizing is to gather evidence on a topic from more than one source. Before you can synthesize, you need to make sure that you understand the main idea and supporting details found in each source. **(a) What is the main idea of the Improved Technology paragraphs? (b) What was the benefit of the caravel? (c) What is the main idea of Pigafetta's firsthand account?**

3. **Look for similarities** Information is more complete and reliable if more than one source provides the same or similar information. Noting and analyzing the similarities will help you reach a more complete understanding of the topic. **Which two sources support the idea that European sailors became better equipped to sail the seas?**

4. **Look for differences** It is also important to look for inconsistent information or other perspectives. **Which sources convey the idea that European sailors still faced hardships at sea?**

5. **Draw conclusions** Our knowledge of a topic becomes more complete when we draw conclusions based on information synthesized from a variety of sources. **Was ocean travel easy or difficult for Europeans in the early 1500s? Explain.**

Practicing the Skill

Study the different pieces of information on this page about developments that occurred between the 1500s and 1700s. Then, answer the following questions:

1. With what general topic do all three pieces of evidence deal?
2. **(a)** What does Las Casas complain about? **(b)** How does the painting show social change in the Americas? **(c)** What is the main idea of the graph?
3. Which two sources emphasize negative effects on Native Americans?
4. Do you think all Europeans were cruel to Native Americans? Explain.
5. Based on the evidence, were the early encounters between Native Americans and Europeans generally harmful or beneficial to the Native Americans? Explain.

A Brutal System

Bartolomé de las Casas, a conquistador turned priest, spoke out against the encomienda system and the treatment of Native Americans:

"It is impossible to recount the burdens with which their owners loaded them [75 to 100 pounds], making them walk [hundreds of miles]. . . . They had wounds on their shoulders and backs, like animals. . . . To tell likewise of the whip-lashings, the beatings, the cuffs, the blows, the curses, and a thousand other kinds of torments to which their masters treated them, while in truth they were working hard, would take much time and much paper; and would be something to amaze mankind."

—Bartolomé de las Casas, *Short Description of the Destruction of the Indies*

Portrait of a Spanish man in the Americas, his wife of Native American ancestry, and their daughter.

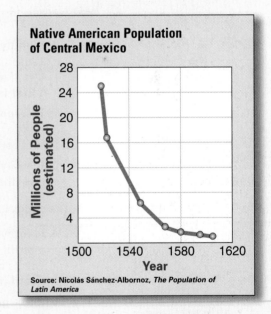

Native American Population of Central Mexico

Source: Nicolás Sánchez-Albornoz, *The Population of Latin America*

This graph shows the impact of diseases from Europe and of fighting against Europeans.

Applying the Skill

Select a current economics topic, such as e-commerce, international trade, or stock market trends. Find three different pieces of information on the topic, including at least one visual. Write questions to analyze and synthesize the information. Trade papers with a partner and answer each other's questions.

Analyzing Cause and Effect

How Will I Use This Skill? **People often try to figure out the causes and effects of things. For example, government officials always conduct an investigation after an airplane accident. Their goals are to identify the causes of the mishap and to then use that knowledge to prevent future accidents. By analyzing causes and effects and by taking appropriate action based on what is learned, you can gain greater control over events and conditions that affect your life.**

Learning the Skill

Read the passage below about a school soccer team. Then, follow the steps to learn how to analyze causes and effects.

A high school soccer team has won the division championship. The team's coach was named coach of the year. The team's colors were blue and gold. All the team members attended practice regularly. Because they passed all their classes, no team members were dropped from the team. As a result of winning the division title, the soccer team competed in the state tournament. The championship game was seen by college coaches on cable television. Several weeks later, a few of those coaches invited some of the players to apply for admission to their colleges and play soccer for them.

---

1. **Identify the central event** Identify the central condition or event whose causes or effects you wish to study. In the introductory paragraph at the top of this page, for example, the central event was airplane accidents. **What is the central event in the soccer story?**

2. **Disregard irrelevant information** Disregard information that has little or nothing to do with the central event. **What information in the story is neither a cause nor an effect of the team's performance?**

3. **Identify possible causes** Causes precede the central event. They are the reasons that the central event or development occurred. In a reading passage, key words that can help you identify causes include *because* and *due to*. **What are the causes of the central event in the soccer story?**

4. **Identify possible effects** Effects come after the central event. They occur as a result of the central event. In a reading passage, key words that indicate effects include *therefore* and *as a result*. **What are the effects of the central event in the soccer story?**

5. **Make generalizations** After investigators find the causes of an accident, they do not think about one plane only. They generalize and consider how the same conditions might cause an accident for other planes. For example, faulty electrical wiring can cause a fire in all planes, not just the one under investigation. **Make a generalization based on the soccer story.**

6. **Make recommendations** By understanding causes and effects, you can recommend actions or make predictions based on what you have learned. **How can any school sports team improve its chances for success?**

Practicing the Skill

By A.D. 1000, East African port cities, such as Mogadishu, Kilwa, and Sofala, were thriving centers of trade. Study the facts below, which are listed in random order, and copy the blank cause-and-effect chart at right. Then, answer the questions below and fill in the chart. (As you work, you may want to consult the world map in the Atlas at the back of this book.)

- Muslim merchants from Arabia and other lands settled in East Africa.
- Africa had gold, ivory, and other valuable resources.
- East African trading cities thrived.
- Mansa Musa ruled an empire in West Africa.
- Favorable winds aided travel between Asia and Africa.
- There were natural harbors along the East African coast.
- Arabic words became part of the Swahili language in East Africa.
- Muslim merchants introduced their religion to East Africa.

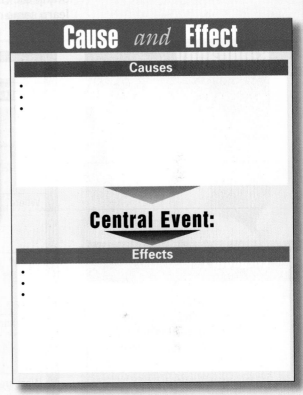

Cause and Effect

Causes
-
-
-

Central Event:

Effects
-
-
-

1. Which of the facts above is the central event whose causes and effects can be determined? Write the central event in the appropriate place on the chart.
2. Which one fact is most probably neither a cause nor an effect of the central event?
3. What three facts were most probably causes of the central event? Write them in the appropriate place on the chart.
4. What three facts about Africa were most probably effects of the central event? Write the three facts in the appropriate place on the chart.
5. In general, what is often a common effect of thriving trade between different lands?
6. In general, if a government wanted to build a profitable center for overseas trade, what do you think would be a good geographic location for the trade center?

Applying the Skill

Suppose that your dentist tells you that you have two cavities. Create a chart identifying probable causes and effects of the cavities. Then, based on the chart, write two generalizations and two recommendations.

Using the Internet

How Will I Use This Skill? By "surfing the Net," you can link to millions of computer sites sponsored by businesses, governments, schools, museums, and individuals all over the world. The Internet provides many services, including information, e-mail, and online shopping. As a student, you may often use the Internet as a valuable research tool.

Learning the Skill

Use the steps below and the computer screen images to help you learn how to use the Internet. For this lesson, assume that you are searching for information on the Crusades, which were a series of holy wars between Christians and Muslims that began in the late 1000s.

A search tool home page

An advanced search page

1. **Begin a search** Sometimes you know the Internet site you want and its URL, or Uniform Resource Locator. At other times, you must use search tools, such as AltaVista, HotBot, and NorthernLight, which are Internet sites that help you find other Internet sites. Some search tools are directories that list sites by category. For example, see the category called "Health" on the home page above. Other search tools are search engines that look for sites based on keywords that you choose and input yourself. Still others provide both a directory and an engine. **What kind of search tool is shown in the sample above?**

2. **Click on a help button** Search tools provide instructions on how to conduct a search. **Where is the help button on the above home page?**

3. **When you use a search engine, type in keywords** The keywords should briefly summarize your topic of choice. Usually, you should not input entire phrases or sentences like "When did the Crusades begin?" Instead, type in the word "Crusades" only. Then, click the search button. **Where is the box in the samples for typing keywords?**

4. **Use Boolean language** Two common Boolean terms are *AND* and *OR*. Use *AND* between two words when you want documents that contain both words. Use *OR* when you want documents that contain either of the words. **If you typed in "Crusades" and "Holy Wars," should you use *AND* or *OR* between them?**

5. **Try an advanced search** After clicking on the advanced search button, you can refine and limit your search. For example, you can specify documents produced only after a certain date or documents only from the **.edu** domain. Limiting the domain in this way will provide sites produced only by schools or other educational sites. The **.org** domain contains only sites produced by organizations. Another common domain is **.gov** which is used by government sites. **To what other domain could you limit your search?**

6. **Evaluate the quality of sites** When the search results page comes up, read the summaries and open those sites that seem to best match your topic. Note when each site was last updated. Note the sponsor or author, too. Universities, museums, libraries, and government agencies are usually the most useful and reliable for social studies research. **Who is the sponsor of the first site on the Crusades in the sample results page?**

7. **Explore, revise, and ask for help** Explore a variety of sites and compare them so you can select the one best suited to your needs. If the results are unsatisfactory, revise your search by typing in new keywords or by using another search tool. Seek guidance from teachers, librarians, and your parents. **What are two other keywords you could try in your search about the Crusades?**

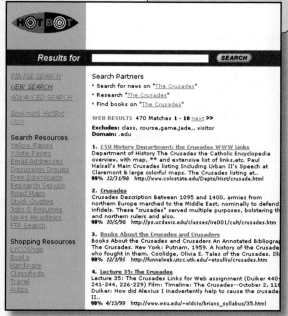
A search results page

Practicing the Skill

Use the Internet to do research on the Mongol empire, especially the Yuan dynasty that the Mongols established in China in 1279. Answer the following questions as you conduct your search:

1. What search tool do you choose? Why?
2. Describe one useful instruction that this search tool provides to users who click on the help button.
3. What keywords and/or Boolean language do you use in your search? Why?
4. How can an advanced search help you?
5. Which site provides the most useful and complete information about the Mongols and the Yuan dynasty? Explain.
6. Revise your search by inputting "Kublai Khan." How are your search results different from those of your earlier search?

Applying the Skill

Use the Internet to search for museum sites that have Native American art and artifacts. You may wish to limit your search to a particular Native American people. You could also limit your search to a particular type of art such as pottery or weaving. Print out your search result pages and circle the descriptions of those sites that you would recommend because they are the most appropriate. For each recommended site, identify the author or sponsor and explain why you recommend it.

Understanding Our Past

Reading Focus

■ How are geography and history linked?

■ How do anthropologists and archaeologists find out about early peoples?

■ How do historians try to reconstruct the past?

Vocabulary

geography
latitude
longitude
prehistory
anthropology
culture
archaeology
artifact
technology
historian

Taking Notes

Make a concept web like the one at right. As you read the section, fill in each blank circle with important information about how experts learn about the past. Add as many circles as needed to complete the web.

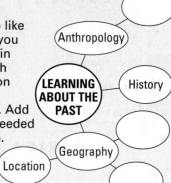

Main Idea Geographers, archaeologists, anthropologists, and historians work to unravel human history.

Primary Source

A View of the Earth

An astronaut describes how world geography looks from space:

"As you eat breakfast you look out the window . . . and there's the Mediterranean area, Greece and Rome. . . . And you go down across North Africa, and out over the Indian Ocean and look up at that great subcontinent of India . . . out over the Philippines and up across that monstrous Pacific Ocean, that vast body of water—you've never realized how big that is before.

You finally come up across the coast of California, and you look for those friendly things, Los Angeles and Phoenix and on across to El Paso. . . . You look down there and you can't imagine how many borders and boundaries you cross, again and again and again, and you don't even see them."

—Russell L. Schweickart, quoted in *The Overview Effect* (White)

Skills Assessment

Primary Source Based on this reading, how is looking at the world from space different from looking at a world map?

Setting the Scene

Austen Layard was sure that the large mounds held hidden secrets. In 1845, he hired workers to dig trenches in what is today Iraq. Day by day, they inched deeper into the hot desert sands.

One morning, Layard's foreman Awad ran toward him, yelling. Layard rushed to see what the diggers had found. He was amazed to see a huge stone head emerging from the sand. Excitement spread through the camp as the diggers unearthed a giant statue. Layard soon realized that they had begun to uncover remains of the Assyrians, known only from stories in the Bible. As Layard and others found additional evidence, they slowly pieced together a picture of these people who had lived some 3,000 years before.

Thanks to the work of scholars like Austen Layard, we know a lot about how people lived in different times and places. Among these scholars are people who study geography—the stage on which all human history takes place.

Geography and History

Geography is the study of people, their environments, and the resources available to them. By showing how people lived in different times and places, geographers have added to our knowledge of human history. Often, geographers must draw conclusions from limited evidence. For example, tons of river mud found in the ruins of an ancient city may indicate that the city was wiped out by a flood. Similarities in language and art in widely separated regions may suggest that there was once contact between the two places.

Five themes sum up the impact of geography on the human story. They are location, place, human-environment interaction, movement, and region.

Location Location tells where a place is on the surface of the Earth. You can locate any place on a map using latitude and longitude. Latitude measures distance north or south of the Equator. Longitude measures distance east or west of the Prime Meridian, an imaginary line that runs north to south through Greenwich, England. For example, you can locate the city of Seoul, South Korea, at 37° N latitude and 127° E longitude. These numbers give its exact location.

Relative location—where one place is located in relation to another—is sometimes more important than exact location. For example, ancient Athens was located on the eastern Mediterranean Sea, near much older civilizations in Egypt and the Middle East. This relative location influenced the Athenians' way of life because they acquired valuable skills and ideas from their neighbors.

Place Geographers describe places in terms of their physical features and human characteristics. Physical features of a place include landforms, bodies of water, climate, soil quality, resources, and plant and animal life. Human characteristics include where most people live and their economic activities, religious beliefs, and languages.

Human-Environment Interaction Since the earliest times, people have interacted with their environment. That is, they have shaped and been shaped by the places in which they lived. Early farmers used water from rivers to irrigate their crops. Much later, European settlers in the Americas cut down trees to clear land for farms. As technology has advanced, we have changed the environment in more complex ways. Today, roads slice through deserts, and canals link distant bodies of water.

Movement The movement of people, goods, and ideas is another key link between geography and history. In early times, people followed herds of deer or buffalo on which they depended for food. In more recent times, people have migrated, or moved, from farms and villages to cities in search of jobs. Others have fled from war or religious persecution.

In ancient times, as today, traders have carried goods from one part of the Earth to another. Ideas also move, carried by people like missionaries or settlers. Today, communications satellites and television cables carry ideas faster and farther than ever before.

Region Geographers divide the world into many types of regions. Some regions are based on physical characteristics, such as location. The Gulf States, for example, are those countries bordering the Persian Gulf. They are part of a larger region of southwestern Asia, which we often call the Middle East. Regions may also be defined by political, economic, or cultural features. Culturally, the Gulf States are part of two larger regions, the Arabic-speaking world and the Muslim world.

Geography Makes a Difference
Geographic features such as landforms, climate, and natural resources have helped to shape a wide variety of human cultures. This reindeer herder in Siberia (below) lives a far different life from that of these rice farmers in Vietnam (left).

Theme: Geography and History Identify two cultural differences shown in these photographs. How might geography contribute to these differences?

How Do We Know?

The search for the human past has led all over the globe and far back to prehistoric times. Prehistory refers to the long period of time before people invented systems of writing. Prehistoric people had no cities, countries, organized central governments, or complex inventions.

Anthropology About 200 years ago, scholars began studying the origins and development of people and their societies. Today we call this field of study anthropology. Modern anthropologists specialize. Some examine the origins of human life. Others focus on the variety of human cultures. In anthropology, culture refers to the way of life of a society that is handed down from one generation to the next by learning and experience.

Archaeology A specialized branch of anthropology is called archaeology (ahr kee AHL uh jee), the study of past people and cultures. Archaeologists find and analyze the material remains of human cultures to learn about prehistoric people and to add to the written records of historical times.

Archaeologists study artifacts, objects made by human beings. Artifacts include tools, weapons, pottery, clothing, and jewelry. By analyzing artifacts and other items, archaeologists draw conclusions about the beliefs, values, and activities of our ancestors. Writer Agatha Christie, who was married to an archaeologist, described how people of the past speak to us through artifacts:

> "'With these bone needles we sewed our clothes.' 'These were our houses, this our bathroom, here our system of sanitation!' . . . 'Here, in this little jar, is my make-up.' 'All these cook-pots are of a very common type. You'll find them by the hundred. We get them from the potter at the corner.'"
> —Agatha Christie, *Come, Tell Me How You Live*

Archaeologists at Work Analyzing ancient artifacts is difficult, but archaeologists have devised many useful techniques. In the 1800s and early 1900s, archaeologists picked a likely site, or place, and began digging. The farther down they dug, the older the artifacts they found. Some long-buried objects crumbled as soon as they were exposed to light and air. Today, scientists have ways to preserve such fragile artifacts.

By studying thousands of items, archaeologists have traced how early people developed new technologies. Technology refers to the skills and tools people use to meet their basic needs. The first stone tools, for example, were crudely made with jagged edges and rough surfaces. Stone tools from later times are smooth and polished, showing improved skills.

Archaeologists today also make detailed maps locating every artifact they find. By analyzing this evidence, they can tell what went on at different locations within a site. Flint chips, for example, might suggest the workplace of a toolmaker.

Technology and the Past Archaeologists use modern technology to study and interpret their findings. Computers can be used to store and sort data or to develop accurate site maps. Aerial photography can reveal patterns of how people used the land. Techniques for measuring radioactivity help chemists and physicists determine the age of objects.

Geologists, or experts on earth science, help archaeologists date artifacts by determining the age of nearby rocks. Botanists and zoologists, experts on plants and animals, examine seeds and animal bones to learn about the diet of early people. Experts on climate determine what conditions early people faced on the plains of Africa or in ice-covered parts of Europe. Biologists analyze human bones as well as bloodstains found on old stone tools and weapons.

You Are There . . .

UNEARTHING THE PAST

Sweat runs down your forehead and into your eyes. It stings. Slowly, you stand up from where you've been kneeling in the dirt and wipe your face. You volunteered to spend your first summer after high school helping archaeologists at a dig in Mexico. Squinting against the bright sun, you wait for your eyes to adjust. . . .

You turn and you see a serene face on an urn that you helped excavate this morning. You feel a sense of pride as you realize that you have helped unearth a piece of the past.

You hear distant murmurs in English and Spanish, and you can pick out an occasional word. Louder are the clink of metal hammers on rock and the crunch of shovels in soft earth. These are the sounds of an archaeological dig.

Paintbrush

Calipers

Toothbrush

Trowel

You gather your tools, lying scattered about you. You use the trowel to dig up an artifact, brushes to gently brush away dirt, and then calipers to measure it. You take great care, because you are unearthing ancient treasure.

Your eyes focus on a pit just in front of you. Archaeologists are examining a burial chamber. They are sketching and mapping the find. Precise records are needed for later analysis.

Portfolio Assessment

The sun dips below the horizon, and you are through for the day. Alone in your tent, you pick up paper and pen and start a letter home. You explain how you have reached your decision about whether to volunteer at another dig next summer.

Historians Reconstruct the Past

While archaeologists have uncovered useful information about the past, most of what goes into a textbook like this one comes from the work of historians. Historians study how people lived in the past. Like archaeologists, historians study artifacts, from clothing and coins to artwork and tombstones. However, they rely even more on written evidence.

About 5,000 years ago, some people in different parts of the world began to keep written records. That event marked the beginning of recorded history. Although these early records are often scanty, they do give us a narrative of events, as well as a number of names and dates. Historians carefully study written evidence, such as letters or tax records. Historians of the recent past also use such evidence as photographs or films.

Historical Detection   Like a detective, the historian must evaluate the evidence to determine if it is reliable. Do records of a meeting between two officials tell us exactly what was said? Who was taking notes? Was a letter writer really giving an eyewitness report or just passing on rumors? Could the letter even be a forgery? The historian tries to find the answers.

Historians then must interpret the evidence, explaining what it means. Often, the historian's goal is to determine the causes of a certain development or event, such as a war or an economic collapse. By explaining why things happened in the past, the historian can help us understand what is going on today and what may happen tomorrow.

Generally, historians try to give a straightforward account of events. Sometimes, though, their personal experiences, cultural backgrounds, or political opinions may affect their interpretations. At times, historians disagree about what the evidence proves. Such differences can lead to lively debates.

The "Great" and the "Small"   The first historians began writing thousands of years ago. These early historians wrote mostly about the deeds of well-known and powerful people such as monarchs, religious leaders, politicians, and generals.

Today, historians still write about famous people whose actions have had wide influence. Yet other historians are studying the lives of ordinary people. How did farmers or workers earn a living? What holidays did they celebrate? What was family life like? The answers to such questions have increased our understanding of the past.

SECTION 1 Assessment

Recall

1. **Define:** **(a)** geography, **(b)** latitude, **(c)** longitude, **(d)** prehistory, **(e)** anthropology, **(f)** culture **(g)** archaeology, **(h)** artifact, **(i)** technology, **(j)** historian.

Comprehension

2. **(a)** What are the five themes of geography? **(b)** Give two examples of how people interact with their environment.
3. How do anthropologists and archaeologists learn about the lives of prehistoric people?
4. What kinds of evidence do historians use to study the past?

Critical Thinking and Writing

5. **Linking Past and Present** Historians and archaeologists have worked to piece together the human story from prehistory up to today. Why do you think it is important for us to understand our past?
6. **Connecting to Geography** How can bodies of water play an important role in shaping human society and economy?

Reading Focus

- What advances did people make during the Old Stone Age?
- How can we learn about the religious beliefs of early people?
- Why was the Neolithic agricultural revolution a turning point in history?

Vocabulary

nomad
glacier
animism
domesticate

Taking Notes

Copy the before-and-after chart shown below. As you read the section, add information about human history under each heading. Save the completed chart to help you recall what you learn in this section.

PEOPLE LEARN TO FARM	
Before	**After**
• Lived in small groups	• Populations grew
•	

Main Idea The change from nomadic to farming life led to the emergence of civilizations.

Setting the Scene A small band of hunters and food gatherers was camped on the shore of Lake Turkana in East Africa. One member of the group picked up a stone and chipped it with another stone to make a sharp, jagged edge. The toolmaker may have used this simple tool to cut meat from a dead animal or to sharpen a stick for digging up edible roots.

The toolmaker left the chipped stone near the lake. Some three million years later, anthropologist Richard Leakey picked it up. "It is a heart-quickening thought," Leakey later said, "that we share the same . . . heritage with the hand that shaped the tool that we can now hold in our own hands."

Very slowly, early people learned to make better tools and weapons from stone, bone, and wood. They also developed new skills. Technological advances like these helped more people to survive.

The Old Stone Age

Historians call the earliest period of human history the Old Stone Age, or Paleolithic age. This long period dates from about 2 million B.C., the time of the first stone toolmakers, to about 10,000 B.C.

African Beginnings Anthropologists have found startling evidence of early human life in East Africa. In 1959, Mary and Louis Leakey found pieces of bone embedded in ancient rock at Olduvai (OHL duh way) Gorge in Tanzania. After careful testing, they concluded that the bone belonged to early hominids, or humanlike primates. In 1974, Donald Johanson found part of a hominid skeleton in Ethiopia. Johanson named his find "Lucy" after a Beatles' song.

Because of such evidence, many scientists think that the earliest people lived in East Africa. Later, their descendants may have migrated north and east into Europe and Asia. In time, people reached the Americas, Australia, and the islands of the Pacific.

Hunters and Food Gatherers Paleolithic people lived in small hunting and food-gathering bands numbering about 20 or 30 people. Everyone contributed to feeding the group. In general, men hunted or fished. Women, with their small children, gathered berries, fruit, nuts, wild grain, roots, or even shellfish. This food kept the band alive when game was scarce. Paleolithic people were nomads, moving from place to place as they followed game animals and ripening fruit.

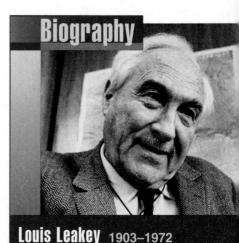

Biography

Louis Leakey 1903–1972

No one who heard Louis Leakey talk about Africa ever forgot it. "He cast a spell," recalled Donald Johanson, "making each listener believe he was speaking only to him or her." Leakey's enthusiasm inspired a whole generation of anthropologists.

Born in Kenya, Leakey began looking for early human remains in East Africa. He and his wife, Mary, found many tools, bones, and other artifacts. Even while working as a spy during World War II, Leakey continued digging in his free time. In later life, he traveled all over the world, lecturing and raising funds for new research projects.

Theme: Impact of the Individual Why might someone devote his or her life to studying human origins?

Art in a Cave
An artist describes seeing cave paintings near Lascaux, France:

"I left the wonderful cave of Lascaux feeling slightly dazed. In such a short time it was not possible to absorb fully the hundreds of painted animals that appeared to prance over the calcite-covered walls and ceilings. Heavy bulls—over sixteen feet long—jostled for space with tiny deer. Leaping cows straddled groups of small ponies, and ibex butted one another like animated bookends. Rounding a sharp corner, I was suddenly confronted by two large black bison, shown rushing away in opposite directions. In the stillness, one could almost hear the animals' stampeding hooves as they hurried to escape capture."
—Douglas Mazonowicz,
Voices From the Stone Age

Skills Assessment

Primary Source How does this artist's description of the Lascaux cave paintings convey a sense of excitement?

People depended wholly on their environment for survival. At the same time, they found ways to adapt to their surroundings. They made simple tools and weapons out of the materials at hand—stone, bone, or wood. At some point, Stone Age people developed spoken language, which let them cooperate during the hunt and perhaps discuss plans for the future.

Still, prehistoric people faced severe challenges from the environment. During several ice ages, the Earth cooled. Thick glaciers, or sheets of ice, spread across parts of Asia, Europe, and North America. To endure the cold, Paleolithic people invented clothing. Wrapped in animal skins, they took refuge in caves or under rocky overhangs during the long winters. They also learned to build fires for warmth and cooking. In this harsh life, only the hardy survived.

Early Religious Beliefs

About 30,000 years ago, people began to leave evidence of their belief in a spiritual world. To them, the world was full of spirits and forces that might reside in animals, objects, or dreams. Such beliefs are known as animism.

In France, Spain, and northern Africa, cave or rock paintings vividly portray animals such as deer, horses, and buffaloes. Some cave paintings show stick-figure people, too. The paintings often lie deep in the caves, far from a band's living quarters. Cave paintings may have been part of animist religious rituals in which hunters sought help from the spirit world for success in an upcoming hunt.

Archaeologists have also found small stone statues that probably had religious meaning. Statues of pregnant women, for example, may have been symbols meant to ensure survival of the band. They suggest that early people worshiped earth-mother goddesses, givers of food and life.

Toward the end of the Old Stone Age, some people began burying their dead with great care. This practice suggests a belief in life after death. They probably believed the afterlife would be similar to life in this world, so they provided the dead with tools, weapons, and other needed goods. Burial customs like these survived in many places into modern times.

The Neolithic Agricultural Revolution

About 11,000 years ago, nomadic bands made a breakthrough that had far-reaching effects. They learned to farm. By producing their own food, they could remain in one place. Farmers thus settled into permanent villages and developed a new range of skills and tools. This change from nomadic to settled farming life ushered in the New Stone Age, or Neolithic age.

The First Farmers No one knows when and how people began to plant seeds for food. Some scholars think that, in the Eastern Hemisphere, farming started in the Middle East and then spread. Others argue that farming developed independently in different regions. No matter which way it occurred, the change had such dramatic effects that historians call it the Neolithic agricultural revolution.

Food-gathering women may have been the first to notice that if seeds were scattered on the ground, new plants would grow the next year. They may also have seen that removing some plants enabled nearby ones to grow stronger. If game animals were scarce, a band might camp at a place where plants grew and begin cultivating them season after season.

The Neolithic revolution included a second feature. People learned to domesticate, or tame, some of the animals they had once hunted. Rather than wait for migrating animals to return each year, hunters rounded them up. Then they herded the animals to good grasslands or penned them in rough enclosures. The animals provided people with a source of protein.

Analyzing Primary Sources

Clues to the Iceman Mystery

In 1991, hikers in the Alps stumbled upon a gruesome sight, a man's head and shoulders sticking out of the ice. Investigators soon discovered that the man had not died recently. In fact, the Iceman, as newspapers called him, had frozen to death more than 5,000 years earlier. Fascinated, scientists studied the Iceman and his belongings.

The Iceman and his possessions were preserved in a pocket of snow (right). The 4½-inch stone-and-wood dagger (below) was found near his body.

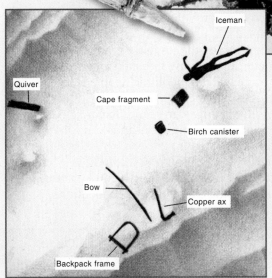

Iceman

Quiver

Cape fragment

Birch canister

Bow

Copper ax

Backpack frame

The Iceman's possessions, such as the bow and quiver shown on this diagram (left), give clues to his occupation. According to researcher Konrad Spindler, "In the high mountains, a shepherd would have to be armed with bow and arrow to defend himself from wild animals and human enemies, and also to secure food for himself."

Scientists were impressed by the complexity of the Iceman's ax. Its copper blade was bound onto a wooden handle with birch gum and leather.

Skills Assessment

1. Based on its size and shape, the dagger that was found with the Iceman might have been used to
   A chop wood for fires.
   B cut up meat or vegetables.
   C kill large animals.
   D carve through solid rock.

2. What conclusion can be made based on the discovery of the copper ax?
   E The Iceman used copper because stone was unavailable in the Alps.
   F People in the Alps knew how to mine and work with copper.
   G The early peoples of the Alps used copper for ornamental purposes.
   H Iron tools replaced copper tools.

3. **Critical Thinking Making Inferences** **(a)** Based on these artifacts, what can you infer about the Iceman's day-to-day life? **(b)** Consider the quality of workmanship of these artifacts. What does this tell you about the Iceman and the culture in which he lived?

Skills Tip

When using an artifact as a primary source, try to determine how that item might have been used at the time it was made.

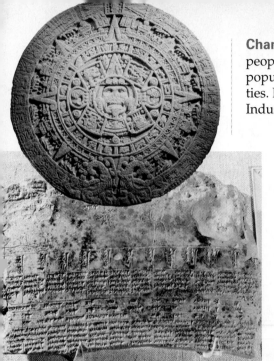

Changing Ways of Life The Neolithic agricultural revolution enabled people to become food producers for the first time. It led to a growth in population, which in turn led to more interaction among human communities. No greater change in the way people lived took place until the Industrial Revolution of the late 1700s.

Like their Paleolithic ancestors, early farmers still divided up the work by gender and age. Still, important differences began to emerge. In settled farming communities, the status of women declined as men came to dominate family, economic, and political life. Heads of families, probably older men, formed a council of elders and made decisions about when to plant and harvest.

When food was scarce, warfare increased, and some men gained prestige as warriors. These elite warriors asserted power over both women and other men. These changes did not mean that women lost all their influence or rights. Rather, they show that village life was reshaping the roles of both women and men.

Settled people had more personal property than their nomadic ancestors. Some people accumulated more possessions than their neighbors, so differences in wealth appeared. Yet big differences among social classes did not exist at this time.

New Technologies To farm successfully, people had to develop new technologies. Like farmers today, they had to find ways to protect their crops and measure out enough seed for the next year's harvest. They also needed to measure time accurately so that they would know when to plant and harvest. Gradually, they created the first calendars. In some places, farmers learned to use animals such as oxen or water buffalo to plow the fields.

Archaeological evidence shows that some villages had separate workshops where villagers made tools, including smooth, polished ax heads and chipped arrowheads. In some parts of the world, Neolithic people learned to weave cloth from animal hair or vegetable fibers.

Inventions did not appear everywhere at the same time. Technologies might travel slowly from one area to another, taking thousands of years to spread across continents. Other technologies may have been invented separately in different parts of the world.

By about 5,000 years ago, the advances made by early farming communities led to a new stage of development—the emergence of civilizations.

Early Calendars
From the Stone Age on, different cultures developed calendars based on the cycles of the sun and the moon. These calendars were created by the Aztecs of Mexico (top) and the Babylonians of the Middle East (bottom).

Theme: Economics and Technology Why was it important for farming societies to create calendars?

SECTION 2 Assessment

Recall
1. **Identify:** **(a)** Paleolithic age, **(b)** Mary and Louis Leakey, **(c)** Neolithic age.
2. **Define:** **(a)** nomad, **(b)** glacier, **(c)** animism, **(d)** domesticate.

Comprehension
3. How did Paleolithic people learn to adapt to their environment?
4. What do burial customs suggest about the beliefs of early peoples?
5. **(a)** What were the key features of the Neolithic agricultural revolution? **(b)** How did it change people's lives?

Critical Thinking and Writing
6. **Recognizing Causes and Effects** **(a)** Why would economic scarcity often lead to increased warfare between farming communities? **(b)** How do you think economic scarcity and warfare changed the status of women in Stone Age societies?
7. **Connecting to Geography** Why would geography probably have played a more important role in the lives of people during the Old Stone Age than it plays in your life today?

Activity
Take It to the NET

Use Internet sources to find out more about prehistoric cave paintings. Then, use the information to write a talk that a tour guide might give to visitors. Include the location of the caves, interesting features about the paintings, and information about the people who made them.

Beginnings of Civilization

Reading Focus

- How did the first cities emerge?
- What are the basic features of civilizations?
- How do cultures spread and change?

Vocabulary

civilization
surplus
polytheistic
artisan
pictogram
scribe
city-state
empire
steppe
cultural diffusion

Taking Notes

As you read, prepare an outline of this section. Use Roman numerals to indicate the major headings of the section, capital letters for the subheadings, and numbers for the supporting details. The sample at right will help you get started.

I. The rise of cities
  A. River valley civilizations
    1.
    2.
II. Features of civilization
  A.
    1.
    2.

Main Idea ▶ The rise of cities was a central feature in the development and spread of civilizations.

Setting the Scene

Perhaps the best-known monuments of the ancient world are the great pyramids of Egypt. More than 100,000 workers labored for years under the hot North African sun to build these giant tombs. Without modern machinery, they fit into place more than two million stone blocks weighing an average of 2½ tons each!

Pyramid building required a society more highly organized and technologically advanced than Neolithic farming villages. In Egypt, as elsewhere, people were taking a giant step from prehistory into history.

The Rise of Cities

The rise of cities was the main feature of civilization. A civilization is a complex, highly organized social order. The first cities emerged after farmers began cultivating fertile lands along river valleys and producing surplus, or extra, food. These surpluses in turn helped populations to expand. As populations grew, some villages swelled into cities.

River Valley Civilizations Cities rose independently in the valleys of the Tigris and Euphrates rivers in the Middle East, the Nile River in Egypt, the Indus River in India, and the Yellow River, or Huang He, in China. Conditions in these river valleys favored farming. Flood waters spread silt across the valleys, renewing the soil and keeping it fertile. The animals that flocked to the rivers to drink were another source of food. In addition, rivers provided a regular water supply and a means of transportation.

Rivers also posed challenges. Farmers had to control flooding and channel waters to the fields. To meet these challenges, cooperation was needed. Early farmers worked together to build dikes, dig canals, and carve out irrigation ditches. Such large-scale projects required leadership and a well-organized government.

Ancient cities were frequently surrounded by high walls. The walls of Babylon were so wide that a chariot could turn around on top of the wall without falling off. Early cities also boasted large temples and palaces and broad avenues used for public ceremonies. Still, most city streets were narrow and tangled, with houses as small as village huts.

Cities in the Americas Unlike the civilizations in Asia, Africa, and Europe, civilizations in the Americas often did not rise in river valleys. Two major civilizations, the Aztecs and Incas, eventually emerged in the highlands of Mexico and Peru.

Did You Know?

The Walls of Jericho

The city of Jericho was tiny—just about the size of eight football fields—but it was home to several thousand people. Jericho, in present-day Jordan, is the oldest city yet found. Archaeologists believe it was first settled a stunning 10,000 years ago. Even more striking is the fact that archaeologists have uncovered a huge wall, 12 feet high and 6 feet thick, that once surrounded the city.

What can we conclude from this great wall? Jericho must have had a powerful government to oversee the building of the wall. We can also conclude that there must have been a very good reason to undertake such a difficult task. One historian put it this way: "The citizens of Jericho felt they had wealth worth defending, and they lived in a world where others would try to take it from them by force."

Theme: Economics and Technology What might be the strategic advantages of a wall 12 feet high and 6 feet thick?

In the Americas, the first cities may have begun as religious centers. There, powerful priests inspired people from nearby villages to build temples to their gods. Villagers would gather at the temples for regular worship. In time, many may have remained permanently, creating cities like those elsewhere.

Features of Civilization

How did civilizations differ from smaller farming societies? What did the early civilizations that rose in different parts of the globe have in common? Historians distinguish eight basic features found in most early civilizations. These eight features are (1) cities, (2) well-organized central governments, (3) complex religions, (4) job specialization, (5) social classes, (6) arts and architecture, (7) public works, and (8) writing.

Organized Governments As cities grew, they needed a steady food supply. To produce large amounts of food and oversee irrigation projects, new forms of government arose. City governments were far more powerful than the councils of elders and local chiefs of farming villages.

At first, priests probably had the greatest power. In time, warrior kings emerged as the chief political leaders. They took over the powers of the old councils of elders and set themselves up as hereditary rulers who passed power from father to son. Almost always, rulers claimed that their right to rule came from the gods. Early Chinese kings took the title "Son of Heaven," and Incan emperors declared that they were sons of the sun itself. Thus, political rulers gained religious power as well.

Government became more complex as rulers issued laws, collected taxes, and organized systems of defense. To enforce order, rulers relied on royal officials. Over time, separate government departments evolved that oversaw functions such as tax collection, irrigation projects, or the military.

Complex Religions Like their Stone Age ancestors, most ancient people were polytheistic, that is, they believed in many gods. People appealed to sun gods, river goddesses, and other spirits that they believed controlled natural forces. Other gods were thought to control human activities such as birth, trade, or war.

In ancient religions, priests and worshipers sought to gain the favor of the gods through complex rituals such as ceremonies, dances, prayers, and hymns. To ensure divine help, people built temples and sacrificed animals, crops, or sometimes other humans to the gods. Sacrifices and other ceremonies required the full-time attention of priests, who had special training and knowledge.

Job Specialization The lives of city dwellers differed from those of their Stone Age ancestors. Urban people developed so many new crafts that a single individual could no longer master all the skills needed to make tools, weapons, or other goods. For the first time, individuals began to specialize in certain jobs. Some became artisans, or skilled craftworkers, who made pottery or finely carved or woven goods. Among the crafts that developed in cities, metalworking was particularly important. People learned to make tools and weapons, first out of copper, then later out of bronze, a more durable mixture of copper and tin.

Cities had other specialists, too. Bricklayers built city walls. Soldiers defended them. Merchants sold goods in the marketplace. Singers, dancers, and storytellers entertained on public occasions. Such specialization made people dependent on others for their various needs.

Social Classes In cities, social organization became more complex. People were ranked according to their jobs. Such ranking led to the growth of social classes. Priests and nobles usually occupied the top level of an

Virtual Field Trip

www.phschool.com
**Harappa and Mohenjo-Daro
Pakistan**

To see other views and artifacts
from these ancient cities, use the
Internet address above to link to an
ancient Indus Valley site.

**Remains of an Ancient
Civilization**

One early civilization emerged in
the Indus River valley. The Indus city
of Mohenjo-Daro included a huge
public water tank (left). Indus Valley
artifacts (below) include stone seals
with writing and a small statue of
a priest-king.

**Theme: Diversity Describe
how these pictures reflect some
of the eight features of civilization.**

ancient society. Next came a small class of wealthy
merchants, followed by humbler artisans. Below
them stood the vast majority of people, peasant
farmers who lived in the surrounding villages and
produced food for the city.

Slaves occupied the lowest social level. Slaves
sometimes came from poor families who sold themselves into slavery to pay their debts. Others were
prisoners captured in war. Because male captives
were often killed, women and children made up
the largest number of these slaves.

Arts and Architecture The arts and architecture of ancient civilizations
expressed the beliefs and values of the people who created them. Temples
and palaces dominated the city scenery. Such buildings reassured people
of the strength and power of their government and religion.

Skilled workers built and decorated massive buildings. In museums
today, you can see statues of gods and goddesses, temple or palace wall
paintings, and furniture and jewelry found in ancient tombs from around
the world. They give ample evidence of the artistic genius of the first
civilizations.

Public Works Closely linked to temples and palaces were vast public
works that strong rulers ordered to be built. Such projects included irrigation systems, roads, bridges, and defensive walls. Although they were costly
in human labor and even lives, such projects were meant to benefit the city,
protecting it from attack and ensuring its food supply.

Writing A critical new skill developed by the earliest civilizations was
the art of writing. It may have begun in temples, where priests needed to
record amounts of grain collected, accurate information about the seasons,
and precise rituals and prayers.

Archaeologists have found masses of ancient writings, ranging from
treaties and tax rolls to business and marriage contracts. The earliest writing
was made up of pictograms, or simple drawings that looked like the objects
they represented. In time, symbols were added. They might stand for
sounds of words or for ideas that could not be expressed easily in pictures.

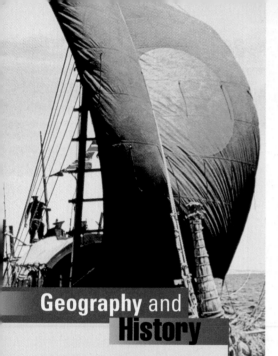

As writing grew more complex, only specially trained people called scribes learned to read and write. Scribes were educated in temple schools and kept records for priests, rulers, and merchants. In only a few societies were women permitted to attend temple schools. As a result, women were generally excluded from becoming scribes, an occupation that could lead to political power.

Spread of Civilization

As ancient rulers gained more power, they conquered territories beyond the boundaries of their cities. This expansion led to the rise of the city-state, a political unit that included a city and its surrounding lands and villages. Rulers, nobles, and priests often controlled the land outside the city and forced peasants to grow crops on it. A large portion of each harvest went to support the government and temples.

The First Empires Rival leaders often battled for power. Sometimes, ambitious rulers conquered many cities and villages, creating the first empires. An empire is a group of states or territories controlled by one ruler. For the conquered people, defeat was painful and often cruel. At the same time, empire building also brought benefits. It helped end war between neighboring communities and created common bonds among people.

Interactions With Nomadic Peoples The first cities were scattered islands in a sea of older, simpler ways of life. Most peoples lived as their Stone Age ancestors had. They hunted, gathered food, or lived in simple farming villages. On some less-fertile lands or on sparse, dry grasslands, called steppes, nomadic herders tended cattle, sheep, goats, or other animals. Because the lands were poor in water and grass, these nomads had to keep moving to find new pasture.

Nomadic cultures were not "civilized," in the sense that they did not exhibit the characteristics of civilization. They built no cities and their governments were simpler than those of settled city-states or empires. However, many nomadic peoples developed sophisticated traditions in oral poetry, music, weaving, jewelry making, animal raising, and other areas of the arts and sciences.

Throughout history, relations between nomads and city dwellers have been complex. At times, the two groups cooperated in political, economic, or military matters. At other times, they have been in conflict, with cities subduing nomadic peoples or nomads overrunning cities. You will read about such encounters in later chapters.

Civilizations and Change

All societies and civilizations change. In fact, history itself might be defined as the story of these changes. Ancient civilizations changed in many ways over the centuries. Among the chief causes of change were shifts in the physical environment and interactions among people.

Environmental Changes Like their Stone Age ancestors, people of early civilizations depended heavily on the physical environment. They needed rain and fertile soil to produce crops. Resources such as stone, timber, or metals were also essential. Changes in the environment could have an immediate impact on people's lives.

At times, sudden, drastic events devastated a community. A tremendous volcano may have wiped out Minoan civilization on the island of Crete in the Mediterranean Sea. Overfarming could destroy soil fertility, or rivers might become too salty. Cities would then suffer famine, and survivors would be forced to move away.

Geography and History

Ancient Travelers

Scientists long thought that ancient peoples tended to stay close to home. But startling new evidence from around the world has cast doubt on this idea.

In Europe, archaeologists found the remains of a sophisticated canoe that is 8,500 years old. In Oceania, we have learned that early people sailed small boats across hundreds, and perhaps thousands, of miles of open ocean. In Asia, scientists have mapped out ancient trade routes that crossed hundreds of miles of some of the most rugged terrain on the planet. These discoveries show that early peoples were much more mobile than anyone had ever imagined.

Theme: Geography and History What might have motivated early peoples to travel?

If people used up nearby timber or ran out of other building resources, they would have to adapt to this scarcity. They might, for example, trade with areas where such resources were available. Or they might use alternate building materials such as reeds.

Interactions Among People An even more important source of change was cultural diffusion, the spread of ideas, customs, and technologies from one people to another. Cultural diffusion occurred through migration, trade, and warfare.

As famine, drought, or other disasters led people to migrate, they interacted with others whose lives differed from their own. As a result, people often shared and adapted customs. Trade, too, introduced people to new goods or better methods of producing them. In ancient times, skills such as working bronze and writing, as well as religious beliefs, passed from one people to another.

Warfare also brought change. Often, victorious armies forced their way of life upon the people they defeated. On other occasions, the victors adopted the ways of a conquered people. Sometimes, nomadic rulers would become absorbed in city life.

Looking Ahead

In the next two chapters, you will read about the earliest civilizations that developed in the river valleys of Africa and Asia. They differed from one another in significant ways, each developing its own culture and traditions. At the same time, the civilizations of Egypt, Mesopotamia, India, and China all fit our definition of a civilization.

Cause and Effect

Long-Term Causes	Immediate Causes
• Silt deposits create fertile soil in river valleys • Neolithic people learn to farm • Hunters and gatherers settle into farming communities	• New technologies improve farming • Food surpluses support rising populations • First cities built in fertile valleys • Farmers cooperate to control flooding and channel water

Rise of River Valley Civilizations

Immediate Effects	Long-Term Effects
• Complex forms of government develop • Arts become more elaborate • Job specialization leads to social classes • Writing is invented	• Government bureaucracies emerge • Early civilizations conquer neighboring lands • Civilizations clash with nomadic peoples

Connections to Today

• Archaeologists mine rich stores of information in Egypt, Middle East, India, and China
• Large cities such as Cairo and Baghdad still flourish in river valley regions

Skills Assessment **Chart** Although river valley civilizations rose in different places, they shared many important features. **How did the rise of civilizations lead to the development of more complex governments?**

Recall
1. **Define: (a)** civilization, **(b)** surplus, **(c)** polytheistic, **(d)** artisan, **(e)** pictogram, **(f)** scribe, **(g)** city-state, **(h)** empire, **(i)** steppe, **(j)** cultural diffusion.

Comprehension
2. How did conditions in some river valleys favor the rise of early civilizations?
3. How were government and religion closely linked in early civilizations?

4. What are three causes of cultural change?

Critical Thinking and Writing
5. **Recognizing Causes and Effects** How did job specialization lead to the emergence of social classes in early civilizations?
6. **Linking Past and Present (a)** Give three examples that show cultural diffusion in today's world. **(b)** Why do you think that cultural changes occur more quickly today than in the past?

Activity
Take It to the NET

Use Internet sources to find out more about how early people learned to measure time. Then, use the information to create a time line about the evolution of time measurement.

Invaders, Traders, and Empire Builders

Reading Focus

- How did early empires arise in Mesopotamia?
- How did ideas and technology spread?
- How did the Persians unite a huge empire?
- What contributions did the Phoenicians make?

Vocabulary

- **codify**
- **criminal law**
- **civil law**
- **tolerance**
- **satrap**
- **barter economy**
- **money economy**
- **colony**
- **alphabet**

Taking Notes

Copy the chart below. As you read, fill in the left-hand column with the names of ancient empires in the Middle East. Fill in the right-hand column with a major contribution of each empire.

EMPIRE	CONTRIBUTION
Babylon	Hammurabi's Code

Main Idea   A series of strong rulers united the lands of the Fertile Crescent into well-organized empires.

Primary Source

The Code of Hammurabi

To establish respect for his laws, Hammurabi began his code with a statement of his authority and principles:

"Then [the gods] Anu and Bel called by name me, Hammurabi, the exalted prince, who feared God, to bring about the rule of righteousness in the land, to destroy the wicked and the evildoers; so that the strong should not harm the weak; so that I should rule over the [people] and enlighten the land, to further the well-being of mankind. Hammurabi, the prince, called of Bel am I, making riches and increase . . . who conquered the four corners of the world [and] made great the name of Babylon. . . . When [the god] Marduk sent me to rule over men, to give the protection of right to the land, I did right and righteousness. . . ."

Skills Assessment

Primary Source   By what authority does Hammurabi claim to issue his legal code?

Setting the Scene

If you had visited the palace of the ancient Assyrian king Assurbanipal (ah soor BAH nuh pahl), you would have found the walls decorated with magnificent carvings. One scene shows Assurbanipal and his queen enjoying a picnic in their lush palace garden. Nearby, musicians entertain the royal couple.

The scene is relaxed and elegant. Look carefully, though, and you will see something startling. Hanging from a tree branch, just behind a harp player, is the head of a defeated king.

In the ancient Middle East, as elsewhere, bloody warfare and advanced culture often went hand in hand. In this section, we will look at the accomplishments of a series of Middle Eastern civilizations across 3,000 years of war and peace.

Ruling a Large Empire

Invasion and conquest were prominent features in the history of the ancient Middle East. Again and again, nomadic peoples or ambitious warriors descended on the rich cities of the Fertile Crescent. While many invaders simply looted and burned, some stayed to rule. Powerful leaders created large, well-organized empires, bringing peace and prosperity to the region.

The First Empire Builder   About 2300 B.C., Sargon, the ruler of neighboring Akkad, invaded and conquered the city-states of Sumer. He built the first empire known to history. His astonishing achievement did not last long, however. Soon after his death, other invaders swept into the wide valley between the rivers, tumbling his empire into ruin.

In time, the Sumerian city-states revived, and their power struggles resumed. Eventually, however, new conquerors followed in the footsteps of Sargon and imposed unity over the Fertile Crescent.

Hammurabi the Lawgiver   About 1790 B.C., Hammurabi (hah moo RAH bee), king of Babylon, brought much of Mesopotamia under his control. He took steps to unite the Babylonian empire. His most ambitious and lasting contribution was his publication of a remarkable set of laws known as the Code of Hammurabi.

Hammurabi was not the author of the code. Most of the laws had been around since Sumerian times. Hammurabi, however, wanted everyone in his empire to know the legal principles his government would follow. He had artisans carve nearly 300 laws on a stone pillar for all to see. On it, he

How Should Society Deal With Lawbreakers?

The question of how to deal fairly and effectively with lawbreakers is as old as society itself. To begin your own investigation, examine the following viewpoints.

Babylon 1790s B.C.

The Code of Hammurabi calls for strict justice:

❝ If a son strike his father, his hands shall be cut off. If a man put out the eye of another man, his eye shall be put out. If he break another man's bone, his bone shall be broken. . . . If a man knock out the teeth of his equal, his teeth shall be knocked out.❞

Italy 1764

Cesare Beccaria was one of the first reformers to argue against torture, capital punishment, and harsh treatment of criminals:

❝ The purpose [of punishment] can only be to prevent the criminal from inflicting new injuries on its citizens and to deter others from similar acts. . . . Such punishments and such methods of inflicting them ought to be chosen, therefore, which will make the strongest and most lasting impression on the minds of men, and inflict the least torment on the body of the criminal.❞

New England 1600

Puritans in colonial New England enforced their laws with stocks, which were both painful and humiliating.

Singapore 1994

In 1994, an American teenager living in Singapore was sentenced to a painful flogging for acts of vandalism. An official defended his country's harsh penalties:

❝ Unlike some other societies which tolerate acts of vandalism, Singapore has its own standards of social order as reflected in our laws. We are able to keep Singapore relatively crime-free. We do not have a situation where acts of vandalism are commonplace, as in cities like New York, where even police cars are not spared.❞

Skills Assessment

1. Which of the following statements summarizes a Puritan view on punishment?

   A Harsh penalties should be avoided.

   B Punishments should not damage a criminal's body.

   C Vandals should get the death penalty.

   D Public humiliation is an effective way to prevent crime.

2. On what point would Beccaria agree with the official from Singapore?

   E Criminals should be put in stocks.

   F Punishments should stop people from committing future crimes.

   G Capital punishment is an acceptable penalty for most crimes.

   H Punishment should be as painful as possible.

3. **Critical Thinking** **Making Decisions** With which of the viewpoints above do you most strongly agree? Explain.

Skills Tip

When expressing a viewpoint, start with a statement of your opinion, and then give strong reasons to support your argument.

Assyrian and Persian Empires

GREECE

Sardis • ASIA MINOR

Black Sea

Danube R.

Halys R.

Cyrus R.

Araxes R.

Caspian Sea

Aral Sea

Jaxartes R.

Oxus R.

Nineveh ▲
Assur ▲

Euphrates R.

Tigris R.

■ Ecbatana

Arius R.

Etymander R.

Mediterranean Sea

Jerusalem •

Babylon ■

Susa ■

Memphis •
EGYPT

Persepolis ■

Persian Gulf

Indus R.

INDIA

N
W · E
S

Red Sea

Nile R.

Thebes •

Albers Equal Area Projection

0   500 Miles
0   500 Kilometers

Tropic of Cancer

Arabian Sea

INDIAN OCEAN

| | Assyrian empire about 625 B.C. | | Persian empire about 500 B.C. | — Great Royal Road |
| ▲ | Assyrian capitals | ■ | Persian capitals | |

Skills Assessment

Geography The Assyrians and Persians built huge empires in the ancient Middle East.

1. **Location** On the map, locate **(a)** Assyrian empire, **(b)** Nineveh, **(c)** Persian empire, **(d)** Asia Minor.
2. **Movement** What land and water routes might a trader have taken to travel from Memphis to Nineveh?
3. **Critical Thinking**
   Making Inferences (a) How many capital cities did the Persian empire have? **(b)** Why do you think the Persians set up so many capitals?

proclaimed that his goals were to "cause justice to prevail in the land / To destroy the wicked and evil / That the strong may not oppress the weak." Hammurabi's Code was the first important attempt by a ruler to codify, or arrange and set down in writing, all of the laws that would govern a state.

Crime and Punishment One section of Hammurabi's Code codified criminal law. This branch of law deals with offenses against others such as robbery, assault, or murder. Earlier traditions often permitted victims of crimes or their families to take the law into their own hands. By setting out specific punishments for specific offenses, Hammurabi's Code limited personal vengeance and encouraged social order.

By today's standards, the punishments in Hammurabi's Code often seem cruel, following the principle of "an eye for an eye and a life for a life." For example, if a house collapsed because of poor construction and the homeowner was killed, the builder of the house could be put to death. Still, such a legal code was more orderly than unrestricted personal vengeance.

Civil Law Another part of Hammurabi's Code involved civil law. This branch of law deals with private rights and matters, such as business contracts, property inheritance, taxes, marriage, and divorce.

Much of Hammurabi's civil code was designed to protect the powerless, such as slaves or women. Some laws, for example, allowed a woman to own property and pass it on to her children. Another law spelled out the rights of a married woman:

"If a woman so hated her husband that she has declared, 'You may not have me,' her record shall be investigated at her city council, and if she . . . was not at fault, that woman, without incurring any blame at all, may take her dowry and go off to her father's house."

—Code of Hammurabi

If the woman were not found blameless, however, the law instructed that she be thrown in the river.

In general, Babylonian civil law gave a husband both legal authority over his wife and a legal duty to support her. The code also gave a father nearly unlimited authority over his children. The Babylonians believed that an orderly household was necessary for a stable empire.

Other Accomplishments Although most famous for his law code, Hammurabi took other steps to unite his empire. He improved irrigation, organized a well-trained army, and had temples repaired. To encourage religious unity across his empire, he promoted the chief Babylonian god, Marduk, over older Sumerian gods.

Warfare and the Spread of Ideas

Later empires shaped the Middle East in different ways. Often, conquerors uprooted the peoples they defeated. By forcing people to move elsewhere, these invaders helped spread ideas. Other conquerors, like the Hittites, brought new skills to the region.

The Secret of Ironworking The Hittites pushed out of Asia Minor into Mesopotamia about 1400 B.C. Although they were less advanced than the peoples of Mesopotamia, they had learned to extract iron from ore. The Hittites heated iron ore and pounded out impurities before plunging it into cold water. The tools and weapons they made with iron were harder and had sharper edges than those made out of bronze or copper. Because iron was plentiful, the Hittites were able to arm more people at less expense.

The Hittites tried to keep this valuable technology secret. But as their empire collapsed about 1200 B.C., Hittite ironsmiths migrated to serve customers elsewhere. The new knowledge thus spread across Asia, Africa, and Europe, ushering in the Iron Age.

Assyrian Warriors The Assyrians, who lived on the upper Tigris, learned to forge iron weapons. By 1100 B.C., they began expanding across Mesopotamia. For 500 years, they earned a reputation for being among the most feared warriors in history.

Historians are unsure why warfare was so central to Assyrian culture. Was it to keep others from attacking or to please their god Assur by bringing peace and order to the region? Whatever the reason, Assyrian rulers boasted of their conquests. One told of capturing Babylon. He proclaimed, "The city and its houses, from top to bottom, I destroyed and burned with fire."

Despite their fierce reputation, Assyrian rulers encouraged a well-ordered society. They were the first rulers to develop extensive laws regulating life within

Contributions of the Fertile Crescent

Wheeled vehicles

Sumerians first used wheeled vehicles to transport goods in trade.

Alphabet

The Phoenician alphabet contained 22 symbols standing for consonant sounds, written in vertical columns from right to left. Later peoples adapted the Phoenician alphabet to produce our 26-letter alphabet.

Ironworking

Hittites learned to extract iron from ore and fashion tools and weapons that were harder than bronze or copper ones. They helped spread their knowledge of iron.

Connections to Today

Ancient civilizations of the Fertile Crescent made breakthroughs in writing, science, and technology. In some form or another, all three of the developments shown are still in use today.

Skills Assessment **Chart** Which technological advance shown on this chart do you think was the most important? Give reasons for your answer.

the royal household. For example, women of the palace were confined in secluded quarters and had to be veiled when they appeared in public. Riches from trade and war loot paid for the splendid palaces in well-planned cities.

At Nineveh (NIHN uh vuh), King Assurbanipal founded one of the first libraries. He ordered his scribes to collect cuneiform tablets from all over the Fertile Crescent. Those tablets have given modern scholars a wealth of information about the ancient Middle East.

Babylon Revived In 612 B.C., shortly after Assurbanipal's death, neighboring people joined forces to crush the once-dreaded Assyrian armies. An aggressive and ruthless king, Nebuchadnezzar (neh buh kuhd NEHZ uhr), revived the power of Babylon. His new Babylonian empire stretched from the Persian Gulf to the Mediterranean Sea.

Nebuchadnezzar rebuilt the canals, temples, walls, and palaces of Babylon. Near his chief palace were the famous Hanging Gardens, known as one of the wonders of the ancient world. The gardens were probably made by planting trees and flowering plants on the steps of a huge ziggurat. According to legend, Nebuchadnezzar had the gardens built to please his wife, who was homesick for the hills where she had grown up.

Under Nebuchadnezzar, the Babylonians pushed the frontiers of learning into new areas. Priest-astrologers were especially eager to understand the stars and planets, which they believed had a great influence on all events on Earth. Their observations of the heavens contributed to the growing knowledge of astronomy.

The Persian Empire

The thick walls built by Nebuchadnezzar failed to hold back new conquerors. In 539 B.C., Babylon fell to the Persian armies of Cyrus the Great. Cyrus and his successors went on to conquer the largest empire yet seen. The Persians eventually controlled a wide sweep of territory from Asia Minor to India, including present-day Turkey, Iran, Egypt, Afghanistan, and Pakistan.

In general, Persian kings pursued a policy of tolerance, or acceptance, of the people they conquered. The Persians respected the customs and religious traditions of the diverse groups in their empire.

Uniting Many Peoples The real unification of the Persian empire was accomplished under the Persian emperor Darius, who ruled from 522 B.C. to 486 B.C. A skilled organizer, Darius set up a government that became a model for later rulers. He divided the Persian empire into provinces, each headed by a governor called a satrap. Each satrapy, or province, had to pay taxes based on its resources and wealth. Special officials, "the Eyes and Ears of the King," visited each province to check on the satraps.

Like Hammurabi, Darius adapted laws from the people he conquered and drew up a single code of laws for the empire. To encourage unity, he had hundreds of miles of roads built or repaired. Roads made it easier to communicate with different parts of the empire. Darius himself kept moving from one royal capital to another. In each, he celebrated important festivals and was seen by the people.

Economic Life To improve trade, Darius set up a common set of weights and measures. He also encouraged the use of coins, which the Lydians of Asia Minor had first introduced. Most

A Money Economy
Persia was the first large empire to create a uniform system of coinage. The Persian coin here depicts the emperor Darius. Today, every country in the world has its own system of coinage.

Theme: Economics and Technology What advantage does a money economy have over a barter economy?

PAST

PRESENT

Phoenician Trade and Colonies

▨	Phoenician colonies about 700 B.C.
→	Phoenician trade routes about 700 B.C.
•	Phoenician towns and trading centers

Azimuthal Equal Area Projection

0   250   500 Miles

0   250   500 Kilometers

BRITAIN

EUROPE

ATLANTIC OCEAN

SPAIN

Cartaea

Abyle

Tipasa

CORSICA

SARDINIA

Tharros

ITALY

Utica

Carthage

Panormos

SICILY

MALTA

GREECE

Oea

AFRICA

Mediterranean Sea

CRETE

Black Sea

ASIA MINOR

CYPRUS

Byblos

Sidon

Tyre

PHOENICIA

PALESTINE

EGYPT

people continued to be part of the barter economy, exchanging one set of goods or services for another. Coins, however, brought merchants and traders into an early form of a money economy. In this system, goods and services are paid for through the exchange of some token of an agreed value, such as a coin or a bill. By setting up a single Persian coinage, Darius created economic links among his far-flung subjects.

A New Religion   Religious beliefs put forward by the Persian thinker Zoroaster (zoh roh AS tuhr) also helped to unite the empire. Zoroaster lived about 600 B.C. He rejected the old Persian gods. Instead, he taught that a single wise god, Ahura Mazda (ah HOO ruh MAHZ duh), ruled the world. Ahura Mazda, however, was in constant battle against Ahriman (AH rih muhn), the prince of lies and evil. Each individual, said Zoroaster, had to choose which side to support.

Zoroaster's teachings were collected in a sacred book, the *Zend-Avesta*. It taught that in the end Ahura Mazda would triumph over the forces of evil:

> "There will come a day, the Judgment Day, when Ahura Mazda will conquer and banish Ahriman . . . when man allies himself with Ahura Mazda and helps him to banish all that is evil, all that is darkness, and all that is death."
> —Zoroaster, *Zend-Avesta*

On the Judgment Day, taught Zoroaster, all individuals would be judged for their actions. Those who had done good would enter paradise. Evil-doers would be condemned to eternal suffering. Two later religions that emerged in the Middle East, Christianity and Islam, stressed similar ideas about heaven, hell, and a final judgment day.*

Phoenician Sea Traders

While powerful rulers subdued large empires, many small states of the ancient Middle East made their own contributions to civilization. The Phoenicians (fuh NEE shuhns), for example, gained fame as sailors and

---

*Today, Zoroastrianism is still practiced by tens of thousands of people, mostly in India. They are known as Parsees, from the word for *Persian*.

Skills Assessment

Geography Although their homeland was small, the Phoenicians established trade and set up colonies throughout the Mediterranean world.

1. **Location** On the map, locate **(a)** Phoenicia, **(b)** Byblos, **(c)** Tyre, **(d)** Cyprus, **(e)** Greece, **(f)** Britain.
2. **Movement** What information on the map supports the claim that the Phoenicians were skilled sailors?
3. **Critical Thinking Drawing Conclusions** *How did geography influence the type of economy that the Phoenicians developed?*

Geography and History

Phoenician Explorers

Did daring Phoenicians sail around Africa? No one knows for sure, but some historians believe that a Phoenician expedition rounded Africa's southern tip about 600 B.C. The only account of this expedition was written by the Greek historian Herodotus, close to 200 years later.

Herodotus gave no description of anything the Phoenicians saw in their travels—with one fascinating exception. The sailors reported that as they rounded Africa, the sun both rose and set on the right side of the ship. Because this unusual phenomenon would occur deep in the Southern Hemisphere, this statement suggests that the Phoenicians did indeed sail completely around Africa.

Theme: Geography and History Plot a course the expedition could have taken, starting in the Red Sea and ending in the Mediterranean.

traders. They occupied a string of cities along the eastern Mediterranean coast, in the area that is today Lebanon and Syria.

Manufacturing and Trade   The coastal land, though narrow, was fertile and supported farming. Still, the resourceful Phoenicians became best known for manufacturing and trade. They made glass from coastal sand. From a tiny sea snail, they produced a widely admired purple dye, called "Tyrian purple" after the city of Tyre. Phoenicians also used papyrus from Egypt to make scrolls, or rolls of paper, for books. The words *Bible* and *bibliography* come from the Phoenician city of Byblos.

Phoenicians traded with people all around the Mediterranean Sea. To promote trade, they set up colonies from North Africa to Sicily and Spain. A colony is a territory settled and ruled by people from another land. A few Phoenician traders braved the stormy Atlantic and sailed as far as England. There, they exchanged goods from the Mediterranean for tin.

The Alphabet   Historians have called the Phoenicians "carriers of civilization" because they spread Middle Eastern civilization around the Mediterranean. Yet the Phoenicians made their own contribution to our world, giving us our alphabet. Unlike cuneiform or hieroglyphics, in which each symbol represents a word or concept, an alphabet contains letters that represent spoken sounds.

Phoenician traders needed a quick, flexible form of writing to record business deals. The wedges of cuneiform were too clumsy, so they developed a system of 22 symbols for consonant sounds. Later, the Greeks adapted the Phoenician alphabet and added symbols for the vowel sounds. From this Greek alphabet came the letters in which this book is written.

Looking Ahead

The Middle East continued to be a vital crossroads, where warriors and traders met, clashed, and mingled. Under Persian rule, scholars drew on 3,000 years of Mesopotamian learning and added their own advances to this rich heritage. In time, the achievements of this culture filtered eastward into India and westward into Europe.

Other conquerors would overwhelm the Persian empire, although different leaders revived Persian power at various times down to the present. The Middle East remained a region where diverse peoples came into close contact. Though these people lived thousands of years ago, some of their beliefs and ideas survived to shape our modern world.

SECTION 4 Assessment

Recall

1. **Identify:** (a) Sargon, (b) Hammurabi, (c) Assurbanipal, (d) Nebuchadnezzar, (e) Cyrus the Great, (f) Darius, (g) Zoroaster.
2. **Define:** (a) codify, (b) criminal law (c) civil law, (d) tolerance, (e) satrap, (f) barter economy, (g) money economy, (h) colony, (i) alphabet.

Comprehension

3. How did Hammurabi build and strengthen an empire?
4. How did the Hittites introduce a new age of technology?

5. Describe two steps Darius took to unite the Persian empire.
6. Why were the Phoenicians called "carriers of civilization"?

Critical Thinking and Writing

7. **Connecting to Geography** How did the geography of the Fertile Crescent help a series of leaders both to conquer and to unify Mesopotamia?
8. **Making Inferences** Why do you think Darius supported the spread of Zoroastrianism throughout the Persian empire?

Activity
Take It to the NET

Use the Internet to research the Seven Wonders of the Ancient World. Then, research a list of possible Wonders of the Modern World. How are these structures similar? How are they different? What do these structures tell you about the cultures that built them?

Reading Focus

- What were the main events in the early history of the Israelites?
- How did the Jews view their relationship with God?
- What moral and ethical ideas did the prophets teach?

Vocabulary

monotheistic
covenant
patriarchal
sabbath
prophet
ethics
diaspora

Taking Notes

Copy this concept web. As you read, fill in the circles with the major beliefs of Judaism. Two circles have been filled in to help you get started.

Torah — JUDAISM — Monotheism

Main Idea The religion of the Israelites was unique in the ancient world because it was monotheistic.

Setting the Scene

"I am the Lord your God, who brought you out of the land of Egypt, out of the house of bondage. You shall have no other gods beside Me." These words—the first of the Ten Commandments—set the Israelites apart from all other people of the Fertile Crescent. Instead of worshiping many gods, the Israelites prayed to one God for guidance and protection. This promise of a unique relationship with God helped shape the history of the Israelites, later known as the Jews. Their early religion evolved into Judaism, one of the world's main faiths.

Early History of the Israelites

Early in their history, the Israelites, or Hebrews, came to believe that God was taking a hand in their lives. As a result, they recorded events and laws in the Torah, their most sacred text.

A Nomadic People According to the Torah, a man named Abraham lived near Ur in Mesopotamia. About 2000 B.C., he and his family migrated, herding their sheep and goats into a region called Canaan.* Abraham is considered the founder of the Israelite nation.

The Book of Genesis tells that a famine later forced many Israelites to migrate to Egypt. There, they were eventually enslaved. In time, Moses led the Israelites in their escape, or exodus, from Egypt. After Moses died, they entered Canaan, the land they believed God had promised them.

The Kingdom of Israel By 1000 B.C., the Israelites had set up a kingdom called Israel. David, a strong and shrewd king, united the feuding Israelite tribes into a single nation.

David's son Solomon turned Jerusalem into an impressive capital, with a splendid temple dedicated to God. Solomon won fame for his wisdom and understanding. He also tried to increase Israel's influence by negotiating with powerful empires in Egypt and Mesopotamia.

Division and Conquest Israel paid a heavy price for Solomon's ambitions. His building projects required such high taxes and so much forced labor that revolts erupted soon after his death about 922 B.C. The kingdom then split into Israel in the north and Judah in the south.

Weakened by this division, the Israelites could not fight off invading armies. In 722 B.C., Israel fell to the Assyrians. In 586 B.C., Babylonian

*Centuries later, under Roman rule, this land became known as Palestine.

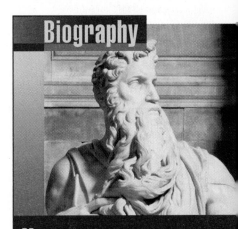

Biography

Moses
c. 1300s B.C.–1200s B.C.

According to the Bible, Moses was a reluctant hero. When God commanded him to free the Israelites from slavery in Egypt, Moses said fearfully, "Who am I that I should go to Pharaoh, and bring the sons of Israel out of Egypt?" When God insisted, Moses protested, "But I am slow of speech and of tongue." Because Moses' brother Aaron was a better public speaker, Moses asked for his help. When they saw the pharaoh, Moses told Aaron what to say, and Aaron did the talking.

Despite Moses' doubts about his abilities as a leader, he accomplished his goal. He finally freed his people from bondage in Egypt.

Theme: Impact of the Individual How did Moses conquer his fears?

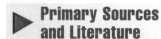

Jews Praying to God
After the Babylonian Captivity, the Jews rebuilt their temple in Jerusalem. Today, the Western Wall is all that remains of the great temple. Here, Jewish men gather at the wall to pray. Above is a morning prayer book.

Theme: Religions and Value Systems Why do you think the Western Wall is sacred to Jews around the world?

▶ **Primary Sources and Literature**

See "Psalm 23" in the Reference Section at the back of this book.

armies captured Judah. Nebuchadnezzar destroyed the great temple and forced many Israelites into exile in Babylon. During this period, called the Babylonian Captivity, the Israelites became known as the Jews.

Years later, when the Persian ruler Cyrus conquered Babylon, he freed the Jews from captivity. Many returned to their homeland, where they rebuilt a smaller version of Solomon's temple. Yet, like other small groups in the region, they continued to live under Persian rule.

A Covenant With God

What you have just read is an outline of Israelite history. To the Israelites, history and faith were interconnected. Each event reflected God's plan for them. In time, their beliefs evolved into the religion we know today as Judaism.

One True God The beliefs of the Israelites differed in basic ways from those of nearby peoples. The Israelites were monotheistic, believing in one true God. At the time, most other people worshiped many gods. A few religious leaders, such as the Egyptian pharaoh Akhenaton, spoke of a single powerful god. However, such ideas did not have the lasting impact that Israelite beliefs did.

The ancient Israelites prayed to God to save them from their enemies. Many other ancient people had also turned to particular gods as special protectors. But they thought of such gods as tied to certain places or people. The Israelites believed in an all-knowing, all-powerful God who was present everywhere.

The Chosen People The Israelites believed that God had made a covenant, or binding agreement, with Abraham:

> "I will make nations of you, and kings shall come forth from you. . . . And I will establish my covenant between me and you and your descendants after you throughout their generations for an everlasting covenant, to be God to you."
> —Book of Genesis

Moses later renewed this covenant. In return for faithful obedience, he said, God would lead the Israelites out of bondage and into the "promised land" of Canaan. Thus, the Israelites and, later, the Jews saw themselves as God's "chosen people."

Teachings on Law and Morality

From early times, the concept of law was central to the Israelites. The Torah set out many laws. Some dealt with everyday matters such as cleanliness and food preparation. Others were criminal laws.

Israelite society was patriarchal, that is, fathers and husbands held great legal and moral authority. The father or oldest male relative was head of the household and arranged marriages for his daughters. Women had few legal rights, although some laws protected them. In early times, a few outstanding women, such as the judge Deborah, won great honor.

The Ten Commandments At the heart of Judaism are the Ten Commandments, a set of laws that Jews believe God gave them through Moses. The first four Commandments stress religious duties toward God, such as keeping the sabbath, a holy day for rest and worship. The rest set out rules for conduct toward other people. They include "Honor your father and mother," "You shall not murder," and "You shall not steal."

An Ethical Worldview Often in Jewish history, spiritual leaders emerged to interpret God's will. These prophets, such as Isaiah and Jeremiah, warned that failure to obey God's law would lead their people to disaster.

The prophets also preached a strong code of ethics, or moral standards of behavior. They urged both personal morality and social justice, calling on the rich and powerful to protect the poor and weak. All people, they said, were equal before God. Unlike many ancient societies in which the ruler was seen as a god, Jews saw their leaders as fully human and bound to obey God's law.

Looking Ahead

More than 2,000 years ago, many Jews left their homeland. This diaspora (dī AS puhr uh), or scattering of people, sent Jews to different parts of the world. Wherever they settled, Jews maintained their identity as a people by living in close-knit communities and obeying their religious laws and traditions. These traditions helped them survive centuries of persecution.

Judaism is considered a major world religion for its unique contribution to religious thought. It also influenced Christianity and Islam, two other monotheistic faiths that rose in the Middle East. Today, Jews, Christians, and Muslims all honor Abraham, Moses, and the prophets, and they all teach the ethical worldview developed by the Israelites. In the west, this shared heritage of Jews and Christians is known as the Judeo-Christian tradition.

Connections to Today

Remembering the Exodus

Every year during the holiday of Passover, Jews retell the story of the Exodus from Egypt as part of an important family celebration called a seder. The storyteller, who is usually one of the adults in the family, explains the key events and symbols of the holiday to the children. The adult identifies with the Israelites who took part in the Exodus by beginning with the words "It is because of what the Lord did for me when I went free out of Egypt."

Special foods eaten during the seder also help Jews feel that they are taking part in the Exodus. A flat bread called matzo recalls how the Jews had to leave Egypt quickly and did not have time to wait for their bread to rise. Grated pieces of horseradish are eaten to symbolize the bitterness of slavery in Egypt.

Theme: Connections to Today Why is it important that the story of the Exodus be told to children as a first-person narrative?

SECTION 5 Assessment

Recall

1. **Identify: (a)** Torah, **(b)** Abraham, **(c)** Moses, **(d)** David, **(e)** Solomon, **(f)** Ten Commandments, **(g)** Judeo-Christian tradition.
2. **Define: (a)** monotheistic, **(b)** covenant, **(c)** patriarchal, **(d)** sabbath, **(e)** prophet, **(f)** ethics, **(g)** diaspora.

Comprehension

3. Why did Israel become divided?
4. How did the beliefs of the Israelites differ from those of other people of Mesopotamia?

5. Describe one Israelite teaching about each of the following: **(a)** family life, **(b)** ethics.

Critical Thinking and Writing

6. **Applying Information** Review what you have read about the Babylonian and Persian empires. Why do you think Nebuchadnezzar and Cyrus the Great treated the Jews differently?
7. **Linking Past and Present** How are the ethical beliefs of the Israelites similar to those commonly accepted in our society?

Activity

Playing a Role
With a partner, act out a conversation between an Israelite parent and child in Egypt or Babylon. The parent should try to explain why, even though they are in exile, the Israelites believe they are the "chosen people."

CHAPTER 2

Review and Assessment

Creating a Chapter Summary

Copy this graphic organizer on a sheet of paper. For each category on the chart, include from one to three facts that describe the characteristics of each civilization. To help you get started, the first row has been partly filled in.

CD-ROM Review For additional review of the major concepts of Chapter 2, see the *Guide to the Essentials of World History* or the *Interactive Student Tutorial CD-ROM*.

CIVILIZATION	LOCATION	GOVERNMENT	RELIGION	CONTRIBUTIONS
EGYPTIAN	• Nile River valley in North Africa	• Strong centralized state • Pharaoh believed to be divine	• Polytheistic • •	• Knowledge of human body from mummification
SUMERIAN				
BABYLONIAN				
PERSIAN				
PHOENICIAN				
ISRAELITE				

Web Site Self-Test For practice test questions for Chapter 2, see **www.phschool.com**.

Building Vocabulary

Review the chapter vocabulary words listed below. Then, use the words and their definitions to create a matching quiz. Exchange quizzes with another student. Check each other's answers when you are finished.

1. **dynasty**
2. **pharaoh**
3. **hieroglyphics**
4. **papyrus**
5. **hierarchy**
6. **cuneiform**
7. **civil law**
8. **barter economy**
9. **monotheistic**
10. **ethics**

Recalling Key Facts

11. Why was the Nile River important to ancient Egyptian civilization?
12. Why did the people of ancient Egypt mummify their dead?
13. How did Egyptians record events?
14. Where did Sumerian civilization develop?
15. Explain the importance of Hammurabi's Code.
16. Why did the Israelites consider themselves to be God's "chosen people"?

Critical Thinking and Writing

17. **Comparing** Compare the view of the afterlife in the Sumerian and Egyptian religions. **(a)** What differences do you see between the two views? **(b)** Why do you think they might have been so different?
18. **Drawing Conclusions** One of Hammurabi's laws states, "If outlaws collect in the house of a wine-seller, and she does not arrest these outlaws and bring them to the palace, that wine-seller shall be put to death." **(a)** What was the purpose of this law? **(b)** Would you consider this a harsh law? **(c)** What similar laws do we have today?
19. **Connecting to Geography** Rivers played a major role in the development of ancient civilizations. Do rivers still play a major role in the world today? Why or why not?

20. **Analyzing Information** **(a)** What rights did women have in Egyptian, Sumerian, and Israelite civilizations? **(b)** How were these rights restricted? **(c)** What do these facts suggest about the status of women in ancient civilizations?

Skills Assessment
Analyzing Primary Sources

In this essay, found on an ancient Sumerian tablet, a young student at a school for scribes describes his school day. Read the essay and answer the questions that follow.

A School for Scribes

"I recited my tablet, ate my lunch, prepared my new tablet, wrote it, finished it. Then they assigned me my oral work, and in the afternoon they assigned me my written work. When school was dismissed, I went home, entered the house, and found my father sitting there. I told my father of my written work, then recited my tablet to him, and my father was delighted. . . . When I awoke early in the morning, I faced my mother and said to her: 'Give me my lunch, I want to go to school.' My mother gave me two rolls and I set out. . . . In school, the monitor in charge of punctuality said to me, 'Why are you late?' Afraid and with pounding heart, I entered before my teacher and made a respectful curtsey."

—quoted in *History Begins at Sumer* (Kramer)

21. What invention of the Sumerians allowed this account to be preserved?
22. What type of schoolwork was assigned to Sumerian students?
23. What seems to be the attitude of the Sumerian student toward **(a)** his father, **(b)** his mother?
24. **(a)** How does the student approach his teacher? **(b)** Why do you think he behaves this way?
25. Would you consider this account a reliable source of information about Sumerian education and family life? Explain.
26. **(a)** Based on what you have read, what role did scribes play in Sumerian society? **(b)** How might this explain the strict discipline of the school described here?
27. Based on this account, compare life at a Sumerian school to life at a modern American high school.

Skills Tip

In evaluating a primary source, you should know whether the writer had firsthand knowledge of the events being described. This will help you determine whether the source is reliable.

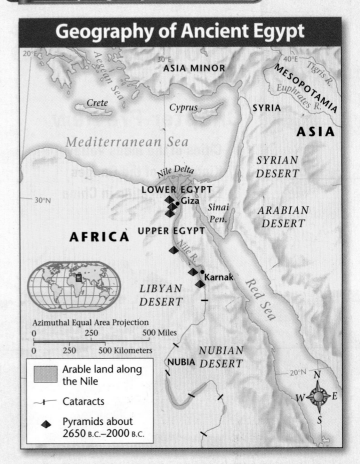

Geography of Ancient Egypt

Azimuthal Equal Area Projection

0   250   500 Miles

0   250   500 Kilometers

- Arable land along the Nile
- Cataracts
- Pyramids about 2650 B.C.–2000 B.C.

Look at the map above and answer the following questions:

28. Describe the location of Lower Egypt.
29. About how far was it from Karnak to Giza?
30. Why did most people in ancient Egypt live near the Nile?
31. Why was travel toward the Nile Delta easier from the northernmost cataract?
32. Based on this map, do you think Egyptian traders would be more likely to travel by the Red Sea or the Mediterranean Sea? Explain.

Skills Assessment
Take It to the NET

Use the Internet to research hieroglyphics. Then, create a cartouche (kar TOOSH) of your name. A cartouche is a hieroglyphic spelling of a name, set within a formal, oval shape. What do the images used in hieroglyphics tell you about the society and environment of ancient Egypt?

Cities of the Indus Valley

Reading Focus

- How has geography influenced India?
- How has archaeology provided clues about Indus Valley civilization?
- What theories do scholars hold about the decline of Indus Valley civilization?

Vocabulary

subcontinent

plateau

monsoon

veneration

Taking Notes

As you read this section, create an outline of the main ideas. Use Roman numerals to indicate the major headings of the section, capital letters for the subheadings, and numbers for the supporting details. The sample at right has been started for you.

I. Geography of the Indian subcontinent
  A. Three regions
    1.
    2.
    3.
  B.
    1.
    2.
II. Indus Valley civilization

Main Idea Archaeologists uncovered the remains of India's first civilization in the Indus River valley.

Setting the Scene
In 1922, archaeologists made a startling discovery in northwestern India. While digging in the Indus River valley, they unearthed bricks, small statues, and other artifacts unlike any they had seen before. The archaeologists soon realized that they had uncovered a "lost civilization"—one that had been forgotten for some 3,500 years. Though later discoveries have added to our knowledge of the cities of the Indus Valley, many mysteries remain.

Geography of the Indian Subcontinent

The Indus Valley is located in the region known as South Asia or the subcontinent of India. A subcontinent is a large landmass that juts out from a continent. The Indian subcontinent is a huge, wedge-shaped peninsula extending into the Indian Ocean. Today, it includes 3 of the world's 10 most populous countries—India, Pakistan, and Bangladesh—as well as the island nation of Sri Lanka (sree LAHNG kah) and the mountain nations of Nepal and Bhutan.

Towering, snow-covered mountain ranges mark the northern border of the subcontinent, including the Hindu Kush and the Himalayas. These mountains limited contacts with other lands and helped India develop a distinct culture, yet the mountains were not a complete barrier. Steep passes through the Hindu Kush served as gateways to migrating and invading peoples for thousands of years.

Regions The Indian subcontinent is divided into three major zones: the well-watered northern plain, the dry triangular Deccan, and the coastal plains on either side of the Deccan.

The northern plain lies just south of the mountains. This fertile region is watered by mighty rivers: the Indus, which gives India its name, the Ganges (GAN jeez), and the Brahmaputra (brahm uh POO truh). These rivers and their tributaries carry melting snow from the mountains to the plains, making agriculture possible. To the people of the Indian subcontinent, rivers are sacred, especially the Ganges. This great importance is reflected in one Indian name for "river": *lok-mata,* or "mother of the people."

The most recognizable feature on any map of India is the Deccan. This triangular plateau, or raised area of level land, juts into the Indian Ocean. The Deccan lacks the melting snows that feed the rivers of the north and provide water for irrigation. As a result, much of the region is arid, unproductive, and sparsely populated.

Geography and History

River of Life

Beginning in an ice cave high in the Himalayas, the Ganges River flows through one of the most heavily cultivated and densely populated regions of the world. By the time it empties into the Bay of Bengal, it has touched the lives of 10 percent of the world's population.

For more than 3,500 years, Indians have drunk from the river, bathed in it, used it for irrigation, and honored it as a giver of life. Considered the most sacred of rivers, the Ganges is central to Hinduism, which teaches that the gods brought the river's water from heaven to purify the ashes of the dead.

Theme: Religions and Value Systems How does the Ganges satisfy the material and spiritual needs of Indians today?

The coastal plains, India's third region, are separated from the Deccan by low-lying mountain ranges, the Eastern and Western Ghats. Rivers and heavy seasonal rains provide water for farmers. From very early times, people used the seas for fishing and as highways for trade.

The Monsoons Today, as in the past, a defining feature of Indian life is the monsoon, a seasonal wind. In October, the winter monsoons blow from the northeast, bringing a flow of hot, dry air that withers crops. In late May or early June, the wet summer monsoons blow from the southwest. These winds pick up moisture over the Indian Ocean and then drench the land with daily downpours.

The monsoon has shaped Indian life. Each year, people welcome the rains that are desperately needed to water the crops. If the rains are late, famine and starvation may occur. Yet, if the rains are too heavy, rushing rivers unleash deadly floods.

Cultural Diversity India's great size and diverse languages made it hard to unite. Many groups of people, with differing languages and traditions, settled in different parts of India. At times, ambitious rulers conquered much of the subcontinent, creating great empires, yet the diversity of customs and traditions remained.

Indus Valley Civilization

The earliest Indian civilization is cloaked in mystery. It emerged in the Indus River valley, in present-day Pakistan, about 2500 B.C. This civilization flourished for about 1,000 years, then vanished without a trace. Only in this century have its once prosperous cities emerged beneath the archaeologists' picks and shovels.

Archaeologists have not fully uncovered many Indus Valley sites. We have no names of kings or queens, no tax records, no literature, no accounts of famous victories. Still, we do know that the Indus Valley civilization covered the largest area of any civilization until the rise of Persia more than 1,000 years later. We know, too, that its cities rivaled those of Sumer.

Well-Planned Cities The two main cities, Harappa and Mohenjo-Daro (moh HEHN joh DAH roh), may have been twin capitals. Both were large, some three miles in circumference. Each was dominated by a massive hill-top structure, probably a fortress or temple. Both cities had huge warehouses to store grain brought in from outlying villages.

The most striking feature of Harappa and Mohenjo-Daro is that they were so carefully planned. Each city was laid out in a grid pattern, with rectangular blocks larger than modern city blocks. All houses were built of uniform oven-fired clay bricks. Houses had surprisingly modern plumbing systems, with baths, drains, and water chutes that led into sewers beneath the streets. Merchants used a uniform system of weights and measures.

From such evidence, archaeologists have concluded that the Indus Valley cities had a well-organized government. Powerful leaders, perhaps priest-kings, made sure that the tens of thousands of city-dwellers had a steady supply of grain from the villages. The rigid pattern of building and

Indus Valley Civilization

Indus Valley civilization, 2500 B.C.–1500 B.C.

HINDU KUSH
Khyber Pass
Bolan Pass
ASIA
Indus R.
Harappa
Mohenjo-Daro
30°N
THAR DESERT
HIMALAYA MTS.
NORTHERN PLAIN
Brahmaputra R.
Ganges R.
VINDHYA MTS.
Narmada R.
INDIA
Arabian Sea
DECCAN PLATEAU
WESTERN GHATS
EASTERN GHATS
Bay of Bengal
15°N
N W E S
Mercator Projection
0   250   500 Miles
0   250   500 Kilometers
75°E
90°E
INDIAN OCEAN

Skills Assessment

Geography The earliest civilization in India developed in the Indus Valley.

1. **Location** On the map, locate **(a)** Himalaya Mountains, **(b)** Deccan Plateau, **(c)** Indus River, **(d)** Ganges River, **(e)** Harappa.
2. **Place** How has India's geography helped to protect the people living in the Deccan Plateau?
3. **Critical Thinking** **Making Inferences** Why do you think the Indus River valley was a more inviting location for the development of a civilization than was the Narmada River valley?

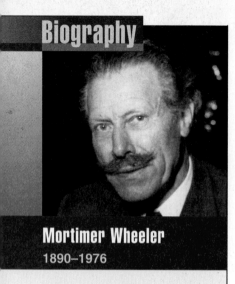
the uniform brick sizes suggest government planners. These experts must also have developed skills in mathematics and surveying to lay out the cities so precisely.

Farming and Trade As in other early civilizations, most Indus Valley people were farmers. They grew a wide variety of crops, including wheat, barley, melons, and dates. They were also the first people to cultivate cotton and weave its fibers into cloth.

Some people were merchants and traders. Their ships carried cargoes of cotton cloth, grain, copper, pearls, and ivory combs to distant lands. By hugging the Arabian Sea coast and sailing up the Persian Gulf, Indian vessels reached the cities of Sumer. Contact with Sumer may have stimulated Indus Valley people to develop their own system of writing.

Religious Beliefs From clues such as statues, archaeologists have speculated about the religious beliefs of Indus Valley people. Like other ancient people, they were polytheistic. A mother goddess, the source of creation, seems to have been widely honored. Indus people also apparently worshiped sacred animals, including the bull. Some scholars think these early practices influenced later Indian beliefs, especially the veneration of, or special regard for, cattle.

Decline and Disappearance

By 1750 B.C., the quality of life in Indus Valley cities was declining. The once orderly cities no longer kept up the old standards. Crude pottery replaced the finer works of earlier days.

We do not know for sure what happened, but scholars have offered several explanations. Damage to the local environment may have contributed to the decline. Possibly too many trees were cut down to fuel the ovens of brick makers. Tons of river mud found in the streets of Mohenjo-Daro suggest that a volcanic eruption blocked the Indus, which flooded the city. Other evidence points to a devastating earthquake.

Scholars think that the deathblow fell about 1500 B.C., when nomadic people arrived in ever larger numbers from the north. The newcomers were the Aryans, whose ancestors had slowly migrated with their herds of cattle, sheep, and goats from what is now southern Russia. With their horse-drawn chariots and superior weapons, the Aryans overran the Indus region. The cities were soon abandoned and eventually forgotten.

SECTION 1 Assessment

Recall
1. **Define: (a)** subcontinent, **(b)** plateau, **(c)** monsoon, **(d)** veneration.

Comprehension
2. Describe two ways in which geography has influenced the people of South Asia.
3. What evidence shows that Indus Valley civilization had a well-organized government?
4. Why do we know so little about Indus Valley civilization?

Critical Thinking and Writing
5. **Linking Past and Present**
   (a) How could natural disasters have contributed to the decline of Indus Valley civilization?
   (b) What environmental problems does the world face today?
6. **Connecting to Geography** What characteristics of rivers might explain why many people in India still consider them sacred?

Activity

Thinking Like an Archaeologist
Imagine that you are an archaeologist digging in the Indus region. Write a "wish list" of three items you would like to uncover to learn more about Indus Valley civilization. Explain what you might learn from the items.

Kingdoms of the Ganges

Reading Focus

- What were the main characteristics of Aryan civilization in India?
- How did expansion lead to changes in Aryan civilization?
- What do ancient Indian epics reveal about Aryan life?

Vocabulary

caste
brahman
mystic
rajah

Taking Notes

Make a concept web like the one below. As you read this section, fill in each blank circle with important information about Aryan civilization. Use the completed web to help you focus on what you learned in this section.

Main Idea Aryan warriors invaded India and developed a new civilization.

Setting the Scene

The Aryans were warlike people. Their hymns praised their warriors as brave heroes and successful looters. In the *Satarudriya,* a poet lauded these warriors with the words:

> "Hail to the lord of thieves . . . hail to the destructive ones
> armed with spears, hail to the lord of plunderers.
> Hail to the archers, to those who stretch the bowstring,
> and to those who take aim."
>
> —*Yajur Veda*

Over the centuries, the Aryans who destroyed and looted the cities of the Indus Valley became the builders of a new Indian civilization. It rose in the northeast along the Ganges River, rather than in the northwest along the Indus.

Aryan Civilization

The Aryans were among many groups of Indo-European people who migrated across Europe and Asia seeking water and pasture for their horses and cattle. The early Aryans built no cities and left no statues or stone seals. Most of what we know about them comes from the Vedas, a collection of prayers, hymns, and other religious teachings. Aryan priests memorized and recited the Vedas for a thousand years before they were written down. As a result, the period from 1500 B.C. to 500 B.C. is often called the Vedic age.*

In the Vedas, the Aryans appear as warriors who fought in chariots with bows and arrows. They loved eating, drinking, music, chariot races, and dice games. These nomadic herders valued cattle, which provided them with food and clothing. Later, when they became settled farmers, families continued to measure their wealth in cows and bulls.

Aryan Society From the Vedas, we learn that the Aryans divided people by occupation. The three basic groups were the Brahmins, or priests; the Kshatriyas (kuh SHAT ree yuhz), or warriors; and the Vaisyas (vīs yuhz), or herders, farmers, artisans, and merchants. At first, warriors enjoyed the highest prestige, but priests eventually gained the most respect. Their power grew because Brahmins claimed that they alone could conduct the ceremonies needed to win the favor of the gods.

---

*Our knowledge about the Aryans is very limited. Historians have re-created a picture of Aryan life from studying their language, but many conclusions are still open to debate.

Primary Source

Hymn to Indra
The Rig Veda *contains this hymn to the war god Indra:*

"The one who made firm the quaking earth; the one who made fast the shaken mountains; the one who measured out wide the atmosphere; the one who propped up heaven: he, O people, is Indra. . . .

The one in whose control are horses, cows, villages, all chariots; the one who has caused to be born the sun, the dawn; the one who is the waters' leader: he, O people, is Indra. . . .

The one without whom people do not conquer; the one to whom, when fighting, they call for help; the one who is a match for everyone; the one who shakes the unshakable: he, O people, is Indra."

—*Rig Veda*

Skills Assessment

Primary Source How can you tell from this source that the Aryans admired military prowess?

Epic Literature

Despite the new written language, the Aryans preserved a strong oral tradition. They continued to memorize and recite ancient hymns, as well as two long epic poems, the *Mahabharata* (muh HAH bah rah tuh) and the *Ramayana* (rah MAH yuh nuh). Like the Sumerian *Epic of Gilgamesh*, the *Mahabharata* and *Ramayana* mix history, mythology, adventure, and religion.

Mahabharata The *Mahabharata* is India's greatest epic. Through the tale's nearly 100,000 verses, we hear echoes of the battles that rival Aryan tribes fought to gain control of the Ganges region. Five royal brothers, the Pandavas, lose their kingdom to their cousins. After a great battle that lasts for 18 days, the Pandavas regain their kingdom and restore peace to India. One episode, known as the *Bhagavad-Gita* (BUHG uh vuhd GEE tuh), reflects important Indian religious beliefs about the immortality of the soul and the importance of duty.

Ramayana The *Ramayana* is much shorter but equally memorable. It recounts the fantastic deeds of the daring hero Rama and his beautiful bride Sita. Sita is kidnapped by the demon-king Ravana. The rest of the story tells how Rama finally rescues Sita with the aid of the monkey general Hanuman.

Like Aryan religion, these epics evolved over thousands of years. Priest-poets added new morals to the tales to teach different lessons. For example, they pointed to Rama as a model of virtue or as an ideal king. Likewise, Sita came to be honored as an ideal woman who remained loyal and obedient to her husband through many hardships.

Looking Ahead

The Aryans were the first of many people to filter into India through passes in the Hindu Kush. Even though scholars recognize that our knowledge of the Aryan migrations is very limited, most accept that Aryan traditions and beliefs formed a framework for later Indian civilization.

Aryan religious beliefs would evolve into major world religions. Just as the Middle East gave rise to three world religions—Judaism, Christianity, and Islam—South Asia was the birthplace of two influential faiths, Hinduism and Buddhism.

▶ **Primary Sources and Literature**

See "The Mahabharata" in the Reference Section at the back of this book.

SECTION 2 Assessment

Recall

1. **Identify:** **(a)** Vedas, **(b)** Brahmins, **(c)** Kshatriyas, **(d)** Vaisyas, **(e)** Sudras, **(f)** Indra.
2. **Define:** **(a)** caste, **(b)** brahman, **(c)** mystic, **(d)** rajah.

Comprehension

3. What do the Vedas tell us about Aryan society and religion?
4. How did Aryan life change as a result of expansion in India?
5. What kinds of lessons do Rama and Sita teach in the epics of the *Ramayana*?

Critical Thinking and Writing

6. **Analyzing Information** Why might epic poems like the *Mahabharata* and *Ramayana* be good vehicles for teaching moral lessons?
7. **Making Generalizations** Based on what you have read about the shift in power from the Aryan warriors to the Brahmins, what generalization could you make about people and their relationship with their gods in Aryan civilization and society?

Activity

Take It to the NET

Use Internet sources to find out more about the moral dilemmas faced by characters in the *Ramayana*. Consider how these dilemmas stem from conflicting obligations. What types of dilemmas might be faced by characters in a modern-day epic?

Early Civilization in China

Reading Focus

- How did geography influence early Chinese civilization?
- How did Chinese culture take shape under the Shang and the Zhou?
- What were key cultural achievements in early China?

Vocabulary

loess
clan
oracle bone
calligraphy
dynastic cycle
feudalism

Taking Notes

Make a chart like this one. As you read the section, add information about China under the Shang to the first column and information about the Zhou under the second column.

SHANG	ZHOU
• Clans controlled most of land	• Mandate of Heaven
•	•

Main Idea Early Chinese people developed a complex civilization and made many advances in learning and the arts.

Setting the Scene In very ancient times, relates a Chinese legend, flood waters rose to the top of the highest hills. Yu, a hard-working official, labored for 13 years to drain the waters:

> "I opened passages for the streams throughout the nine provinces, and conducted them to the sea. I deepened channels and canals, and conducted them to the streams."
> — *Shujing (Book of History)*

While taming the rivers, Yu did not once go home to see his wife and children. As a reward for his selfless efforts, he later became ruler of China.

The legend of Yu offers insights into early China. The ancient Chinese valued the ability to control flood waters and to develop irrigation systems for farming. The legend also shows how highly the Chinese prized devotion to duty. Both of these values played a key role in the development of Chinese civilization.

The Geography of China

The ancient Chinese called their land Zhongguo (JONG goo AW), the Middle Kingdom. China was the most isolated of the civilizations you have studied so far. Long distances and physical barriers separated it from Egypt, the Middle East, and India. This isolation contributed to the Chinese belief that China was the center of the Earth and the sole source of civilization.

Geographic Barriers To the west and southwest of China, high mountain ranges—the Tien Shan and the Himalayas—and brutal deserts blocked the easy movement of people. To the southeast, thick jungles divided China from Southeast Asia. To the north lay the forbidding desert, the Gobi. To the east, the vast Pacific Ocean rolled endlessly.

Despite formidable barriers, the Chinese did have contact with the outside world. They traded with neighboring people and, in time, Chinese goods reached the Middle East and beyond. More often, though, the outsiders whom the Chinese encountered were nomadic invaders. To the Chinese, these nomads were barbarians who did not speak Chinese and lacked the skills and achievements of a settled society. Nomads conquered China from time to time, but they were usually absorbed into the advanced Chinese civilization.

Mt. Everest
In the ancient world, the Himalayas served as one geographic barrier between China and the rest of the world. The range includes the world's highest peak, Mt. Everest, shown here.

Theme: Geography and History Why might a geographic barrier make it easier for a civilization to develop?

Virtual Field Trip

www.phschool.com

**The Tsui Museum of Art
Hong Kong, China**

To see other artworks and artifacts relating to Shang bronzes, use the Internet address above to link to the Tsui Museum of Art.

Shang Bronzes
Bronzework was a high art during the Shang period. These bronze containers were crafted to resemble a snail (left) and a pair of owls (right).

Theme: Art and Literature
What features of the bronzes suggest that the Shang were skilled metalworkers?

Government   Archaeologists have uncovered large palaces and rich tombs of Shang rulers. Shang kings led other noble warriors in battle. From their walled capital city at Anyang, they emerged to drive off nomads from the northern steppes and deserts.

In one Shang tomb, archaeologists discovered the burial place of Fu Hao (FOO HOW), wife of the Shang king Wu Ding. Artifacts show that she owned land and helped to lead a large army against invaders. This evidence suggests that noblewomen had considerable status during the Shang period.

Shang kings probably controlled only a small area. Loyal princes and nobles governed most of the land. They were likely the heads of important clans, or groups of families who claimed a common (often mythical) ancestor. Thus, Shang China probably more closely resembled the city-states of Sumer than the centralized government ruled by the Egyptian pharaohs.

Social Classes   Shang society mirrored that in other early civilizations. Alongside the royal family was a class of noble warriors. Shang warriors used leather armor, bronze weapons, and horse-drawn chariots. The chariots may have come from other Asian peoples.

Early Chinese cities supported a class of artisans and merchants. Artisans produced goods for nobles, including bronze weapons, silk robes, and jade jewelry. Merchants exchanged food and crafts made by local artisans for salt, cowrie shells, and other goods not found in northeastern China.

Peasant Life   Most people in Shang China were peasants. They clustered together in farming villages. Many lived in thatch-roofed pit houses whose earthen floors were dug several feet below the surrounding ground.

Peasants led grueling lives. All family members worked in the fields, using stone tools to prepare the ground for planting or to harvest grain. When they were not in the fields, peasants had to repair the dikes. If war broke out between noble families, men had to fight alongside their lords.

Religious Beliefs

By Shang times, the Chinese had developed complex religious beliefs, many of which continued to be practiced for thousands of years. They prayed to many gods and nature spirits. Chief among them were Shang Di

(SHAHNG DEE) and a mother goddess who brought plants and animals to Earth. The king was seen as the link between the people and Shang Di.

Gods as great as Shang Di, the Chinese believed, would not respond to the pleas of mere mortals. Only the spirits of the greatest mortals, such as the ancestors of the king, could get the ear of the gods. Thus, the prayers of rulers and nobles to their ancestors were thought to serve the community as a whole, ensuring good harvests or victory in war.

At first, only the royal family and other nobles had ancestors important enough to influence the gods. Gradually, other classes shared in these rituals. The Chinese called on the spirits of their ancestors to bring good fortune to the family. To honor their ancestors' spirits, they offered them sacrifices of food and other necessities. When westerners reached China, they mistakenly called this practice "ancestor worship."

The Chinese believed the universe reflected a delicate balance between two forces, yin and yang. Yin was linked to Earth, darkness, and female forces, while yang stood for Heaven, light, and male forces. To the Chinese, these forces were not in opposition. Rather, the well-being of the universe depended on maintaining balance between yin and yang. For example, the king had to make the proper sacrifices to Heaven while at the same time taking practical steps to rule well.

System of Writing

The ancient Chinese also developed a system of writing. Writing, like religious beliefs, was an early development that continued to influence cultures in China throughout history. This system used both pictographs and ideographs, signs that expressed thoughts or ideas.

Consulting the Ancestors Some of the oldest examples of Chinese writing are on oracle bones. On animal bones or turtle shells, Shang priests wrote questions addressed to the gods or the spirit of an ancestor. Priests then heated the bone or shell until it cracked. By interpreting the pattern of cracks, they provided answers or advice from the ancestors.

A Difficult Study Written Chinese took shape almost 4,000 years ago. Over time, it evolved to include tens of thousands of characters. Each character represented a word or idea and was made up of a number of different strokes. In recent years, the Chinese have simplified their characters, but Chinese remains one of the most difficult languages to learn. Students must still memorize up to 10,000 characters to read a newspaper. By contrast, languages based on an alphabet, such as English or Arabic, contain only two dozen or so symbols representing basic sounds.

Not surprisingly, in earlier times, only the well-to-do could afford the years of study needed to master the skills of reading and writing. Working with brush and ink, Chinese scholars turned calligraphy, or fine handwriting, into an elegant art form.

A Force for Unity Despite its complexity, the written language fostered unity. People in different parts of China often could not understand one another's spoken language, but they all used the same system of writing.

The Zhou Dynasty

In 1027 B.C., the battle-hardened Zhou (JOH) people marched out of their kingdom on the western frontier to overthrow the Shang. They set up the Zhou dynasty, which lasted until 256 B.C.

The Mandate of Heaven To justify their rebellion against the Shang, the Zhou promoted the idea of the Mandate of Heaven, or the divine right to rule. The cruelty of the last Shang king, they declared, had so outraged the

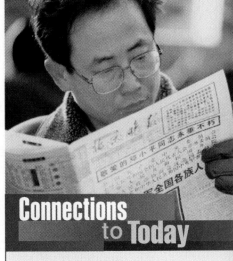

Connections to Today

Digital Chinese
The writing systems in China, Japan, Korea, Vietnam, and Taiwan are all based on a common set of thousands of characters developed in China centuries ago. Over time, each country has modified this system in a different way. These differences have made it difficult for writers in the various countries to communicate clearly with one another.

The computer age has added new communication problems. Since the 1970s, each East Asian country has developed its own code of Chinese characters to input and transmit computer data. The codes are not always compatible, and their differences can corrupt information sent from a computer in one country to that in another. To solve this problem, an international task force is attempting to develop a standard software set of digital Chinese characters.

Theme: Continuity and Change Why might there be so much interest in developing a common Chinese character code for computer communication?

THE DYNASTIC CYCLE IN CHINA

The New Dynasty

Restores peace

Appoints loyal officials

Redistributes land to peasants

Builds canals, irrigation systems, and roads

Repairs defensive walls

After several generations, the new dynasty becomes an aging dynasty

The Aging Dynasty

Neglects government duties

Ignores corrupt officials

Loses control of the provinces

Imposes heavy taxes to pay for luxuries

Allows defensive walls to decay

Problems

Floods, famine, earthquakes

Invasions

Armed bandits in the provinces

Peasant revolts

New dynasty claims the Mandate of Heaven

Aging dynasty loses the Mandate of Heaven

Skills Assessment

Chart The Chinese believed that dynasties could gain or lose the Mandate of Heaven, depending on how wisely the emperor ruled. **According to this flowchart, how did a new dynasty try to repair the problems left by an aging dynasty?**

gods that they had sent ruin on him. The gods then passed the Mandate of Heaven to the Zhou, who "treated the multitudes of the people well." The Chinese later expanded the idea of the Mandate of Heaven to explain the dynastic cycle, or the rise and fall of dynasties. As long as a dynasty provided good government, it enjoyed the Mandate of Heaven. If the rulers became weak or corrupt, the Chinese believed that Heaven would withdraw its support.

Floods, famine, or other catastrophes were signs that a dynasty had lost the favor of Heaven. In the resulting chaos, an ambitious leader might seize power and set up a new dynasty. His success and strong government showed the people that the new dynasty had won the Mandate of Heaven. The dynastic cycle would then begin again.

A Feudal State The Zhou rewarded their supporters by granting them control over different regions. Thus, under the Zhou, China developed into a feudal state. Feudalism (FYOO duhl ihz uhm) was a system of government in which local lords governed their own lands but owed military service and other forms of support to the ruler. (In later centuries, feudal societies also developed in Europe and Japan.)

In theory, Zhou kings ruled China, and for about 250 years, they actually did enjoy great power and prestige. After about 771 B.C., though, feudal lords exercised the real power and profited from the lands worked by peasants within their domains.

Economic Growth During the Zhou period, China's economy grew. Knowledge of ironworking reached China about 500 B.C. As iron axes and ox-drawn iron plows replaced stone, wood, and bronze tools, farmers produced more food. Peasants also began to grow new crops, such as soybeans. Some feudal lords organized large-scale irrigation works, making farming even more productive.

Commerce expanded, too. The Chinese began to use money for the first time. Chinese copper coins had holes in the center so they could be strung on cords. This early form of a cash, or money, economy made trade easier. Merchants also benefited from new roads and canals constructed by feudal lords.

Economic expansion led to an increase in population. People from the Huang He heartland overflowed into central China and began to farm the immense Yangzi basin. Feudal nobles expanded their territories and encouraged peasants to settle in the conquered territories. Toward the end of the Zhou era, China was increasing in area and population, as well as in prosperity.

Chinese Achievements

The Chinese made progress in many areas during the Shang and Zhou periods. For example, astronomers studied the movement of planets and recorded eclipses of the sun. Their findings helped them develop an accurate calendar with 365¼ days. The Chinese also made remarkable achievements in the art and technology of bronzemaking.

Silkmaking By 1000 B.C., the Chinese had discovered how to make silk thread from the cocoons of silkworms. Soon, the Chinese were cultivating both silkworms and the mulberry trees on which they fed. Women did the laborious work of tending the silkworms and processing the cocoons into thread. They then wove silk threads into a smooth cloth that was colored with brilliant dyes. Only royalty and nobles could afford robes made from this luxurious silk.

Silk became China's most valuable export. The trade route that eventually linked China and the Middle East became known as the Silk Road. To protect their control of this profitable trade, the Chinese kept the process of silkmaking a secret.

The First Books Under the Zhou, the Chinese made the first books. They bound thin strips of wood or bamboo together and then carefully drew characters on the flat surface with a brush and ink.

Among the greatest Zhou works is the lovely *Book of Songs.* Many of its poems describe such events in the lives of farming people as planting and harvesting. Others praise kings or describe court ceremonies. The book also includes tender or sad love songs.

Looking Ahead

By 256 B.C., China was a large, wealthy, and highly developed center of civilization. Chinese culture was already dominant in East Asia. Yet the Zhou dynasty was too weak to control feudal lords who ignored the emperor and battled one another in savage wars. Out of these wars rose a ruthless leader who was determined to impose political unity. His triumphs would leave a lasting imprint on Chinese civilization.

Primary Source

The Spirits Are Good
The poems in the Book of Songs *offer a rare look into the everyday lives of average people in ancient China:*

"The spirits are good,
  They will give you many blessings.
  The common people are contented,
  For daily they have their drink and food.
  The thronging herd, the many clans
  All side with you in deeds of power.

To be like the moon advancing to its full,
  Like the sun climbing the sky,
  Like the everlastingness of the southern hills,
  Without failing or falling,
  Like the pine-tree, the cypress in their [foliage]
  All these blessings may you receive!"

—*Shih Ching (Book of Songs)*

Skills Assessment

Primary Source Why might there be so many nature images in this poem?

SECTION 3 Assessment

Recall
1. **Identify: (a)** Zhongguo,
   (b) Shang, **(c)** yin and yang,
   (d) Zhou, **(e)** Mandate of
   Heaven, **(f)** *Book of Songs.*
2. **Define: (a)** loess, **(b)** clan,
   (c) oracle bone, **(d)** calligraphy,
   (e) dynastic cycle, **(f)** feudalism.

Comprehension
3. How did people in China adapt to the environment?
4. What were the characteristics of Shang and Zhou government and social structure?

5. Identify major cultural achievements in early China.

Critical Thinking and Writing
6. **Predicting Consequences** Suppose that you had to learn a language written in unfamiliar characters, rather than in a language using an alphabet you know. Give three examples of how your life and schooling might be different.
7. **Connecting to Geography** How did environmental catastrophes affect Chinese government?

Activity
Take It to the NET
Use Internet sources to learn more about the silkworm. Then, use your information to create a fact sheet about this ancient source of silk. Post your fact sheet on a classroom bulletin board for others to read.

Hinduism and Buddhism

Reading Focus

- In what ways is Hinduism a complex religion?

- What are the major teachings of the Buddha?

- How did Buddhism spread beyond India to become a major world religion?

Vocabulary

atman
moksha
reincarnation
karma
dharma
ahimsa
nirvana
sect

Taking Notes

Copy the partially completed Venn diagram below. As you read about Hinduism and Buddhism, finish the diagram by writing key facts and ideas about the religions under the appropriate headings.

HINDUISM
- No single founder
- Caste system
-

BUDDHISM
- Four Noble Truths
-

• Belief in karma
•

Main Idea Hinduism and Buddhism, two major religions with a wide variety of beliefs, emerged in ancient India.

Setting the Scene

Thousands of years ago, religious teachers in India tried to answer questions about the nature of the universe. Their ideas were later collected into the Upanishads (oo PAN ih shadz). These sacred texts use vivid images to examine complex ideas about the human soul and the connectedness of all life. In one story, a man tries to show his son that the essence of life cannot be seen. He orders the boy to break open the fruit of the banyan, or fig, tree:

"'What do you see?'
'Very tiny seeds, sir.'
'Break one.'
'I have broken it, sir.'
'Now, what do you see?'
'Nothing, sir.'
'My son,' the father said, 'what you do not perceive is the essence, and in that essence the mighty banyan tree exists. Believe me, my son, in that essence is the soul of all that is.'"

—Upanishads

Stories like this one helped people understand the teachings of Hinduism. Hinduism and Buddhism were two major religions that emerged in ancient India. The ethical and spiritual messages of both religions profoundly shaped the civilization of India.

The Beliefs of Hinduism

Unlike most major religions, Hinduism has no single founder and no single sacred text. Instead, it grew out of the overlapping beliefs of the diverse groups who settled India. The process probably began when the Aryans added the gods of the Indus Valley people to their own. Later people brought other gods, beliefs, and practices. As a result, Hinduism became one of the world's most complex religions, with countless gods and goddesses and many forms of worship existing side by side. Despite this diversity, all Hindus share certain basic beliefs.

Many Gods—or One? "God is one, but wise people know it by many names." This ancient proverb reflects a key feature of Hinduism—the belief that all the universe is part of the unchanging, all-powerful spiritual force called brahman. To Hindus, brahman is too complex a concept for most

Shiva
This bronze sculpture portrays the god Shiva crushing a demon into submission. The circle of fire represents the Hindu belief in a cycle of creation, death, and rebirth.
Theme: Diversity Why do you think various cultures use the circle to symbolize continuity?

Read—76-80

Virtual Field Trip

www.phschool.com

**Prince of Wales Museum
of Western India
Mumbai, India**

To view other artworks relating to
Hinduism and Indian history, use
the Internet address above to link to
the Prince of Wales Museum of
Western India.

Bhagavad-Gita
This painting depicts a scene from
the sacred Hindu text *Bhagavad-
Gita*. The furious battle involves
people, gods, goddesses, and
demons.

**Theme: Religions and
Value Systems** Why are sacred
texts central to many religions?

people to understand, so they worship a variety of gods that give a concrete form to brahman.

The most important Hindu gods are Brahma, the Creator; Vishnu, the
Preserver; and Shiva, the Destroyer. Each represents aspects of brahman.
Each of these gods can take many forms, human or animal, and each also
has his own family. Some Hindus, for example, worship Shakti, the powerful wife of Shiva. She is both kind and cruel, a creator and destroyer.

Sacred Texts Over several thousand years, Hindu teachings were recorded in sacred texts such as the Vedas and Upanishads. The *Bhagavad-Gita*, for
example, spells out many ethical ideas central to Hinduism. In that poem,
the god Krishna instructs Prince Arjuna on the importance of duty over
personal desires and ambitions.

The Goal of Life To Hindus, every person has an essential self, or atman
(AHT muhn). But atman is really just another name for brahman. The ultimate goal of existence, Hindus believe, is achieving moksha (MAHK shuh),
or union with brahman. To do that, individuals must free themselves from
selfish desires that separate them from brahman. Most people cannot
achieve moksha in one lifetime, but Hindus believe in reincarnation,
or the rebirth of the soul in another bodily form. Reincarnation allows
people to continue working toward moksha through several lifetimes.

Karma and Dharma In each existence, Hindus believe, a person can
come closer to achieving moksha by obeying the law of karma. Karma
refers to all the actions of a person's life that affect his or her fate in the next
life. To Hindus, all existence is ranked. Humans are closest to brahman.
Then come animals, plants, and objects like rocks or water. People who live
virtuously earn good karma and are reborn at a higher level of existence.
Those who do evil acquire bad karma and are reborn into suffering. In
Indian art, this endless cycle of death and rebirth is symbolized by the
image of the wheel.

To escape the wheel of fate, Hinduism stresses the importance of
dharma (DAHR muh), the religious and moral duties of an individual. These
duties vary according to class, occupation, gender, or age. By obeying one's
dharma, a person acquires merit for the next life. The concepts of karma
and dharma helped ensure the social order by supporting the caste system.

Another key moral principle of Hinduism is ahimsa (uh HIM sah), or nonviolence. To Hindus, all people and things are aspects of brahman and should therefore be respected. Many holy people have tried to follow the path of nonviolence.

Opposition to the Brahmins   About 500 B.C., the teacher Mahavira (muh hah VEE ruh) founded Jainism (JĪN ihz um), a new religion that grew out of Hindu traditions. Mahavira rejected the idea that Brahmin priests alone could perform certain sacred rites. Jain teachings emphasized meditation, self-denial, and an extreme form of ahimsa. To avoid accidentally killing a living thing, even an insect, Jains carried brooms to sweep the ground in front of their feet.

Gautama Buddha: The Enlightened One

In the foothills of the Himalayas, another reformer, Siddhartha Gautama (sihd DAHR tuh go TUH muh), also founded a new religion, Buddhism. His teachings eventually spread across Asia to become the core beliefs of one of the world's most influential religions.

Early Life   Gautama's early life is buried in legend. We know that he was born about 566 B.C. to a high-caste family. According to tradition, his mother dreamed that a radiant white elephant descended to her from heaven. Signs such as this led a prophet to predict that the boy would someday become a wandering holy man. To stop that from happening, Gautama's father kept him in the palace, surrounded by comfort and luxury. Prince Gautama married a beautiful woman, had a son, and enjoyed a happy life.

The Search   One day, as Gautama rode beyond the palace gardens, he saw a sick person, an old person, and a dead body. For the first time, he became aware of human suffering. Deeply disturbed, he bade farewell to his wife and child and left the palace, never to return. He set out to discover "the realm of life where there is neither suffering nor death."

Gautama wandered for years, vainly seeking answers from Hindu scholars and holy men. He fasted and he meditated. One day, he sat under a giant tree, determined to stay there until he understood the mystery of life. For 48 days, evil spirits tempted him to give up his meditations. Then, he suddenly believed that he understood the cause and cure for suffering and sorrow. When he rose, he was Gautama no longer, but the Buddha, the "Enlightened One."

The Buddha
This image of the Buddha in Sri Lanka is carved out of granite. Traditionally, images of the Buddha lying down represent his achievement of nirvana.

Theme: Religions and Value Systems According to Buddhism, how does one achieve nirvana?

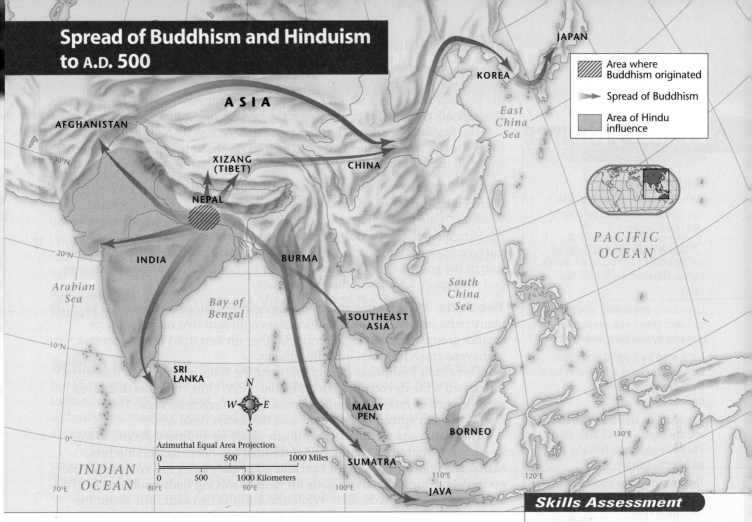

Spread of Buddhism and Hinduism to A.D. 500

ASIA

JAPAN

KOREA

East China Sea

AFGHANISTAN

30°N

XIZANG (TIBET)

CHINA

NEPAL

20°N

INDIA

BURMA

PACIFIC OCEAN

Arabian Sea

Bay of Bengal

South China Sea

SOUTHEAST ASIA

10°N

SRI LANKA

N
W   E
S

MALAY PEN.

BORNEO

130°E

0°

Azimuthal Equal Area Projection

0   500   1000 Miles

0   500   1000 Kilometers

SUMATRA

110°E   120°E

INDIAN OCEAN

70°E   80°E   90°E   100°E

JAVA

Legend	
▨	Area where Buddhism originated
➤	Spread of Buddhism
▥	Area of Hindu influence

Four Noble Truths The Buddha spent the rest of his life teaching others what he had learned. In his first sermon after reaching enlightenment, he explained the Four Noble Truths that stand at the heart of Buddhism:

1. All life is full of suffering, pain, and sorrow.
2. The cause of suffering is the desire for things that are really illusions, such as riches, power, and long life.
3. The only cure for suffering is to overcome desire.
4. The way to overcome desire is to follow the Eightfold Path.

The Buddha described the Eightfold Path as "right views, right aspirations, right speech, right conduct, right livelihood, right effort, right mindfulness, and right contemplation." The first two steps involved understanding the Four Noble Truths and committing oneself to the Eightfold Path. Next, a person had to live a moral life, avoiding evil words and actions. Through meditation, a person might at last achieve enlightenment. For the Buddhist, the final goal is nirvana, union with the universe and release from the cycle of rebirth.

The Buddha saw the Eightfold Path as a middle way between a life devoted to pleasure and one based on harsh self-denial. He stressed moral principles such as honesty, charity, and kindness to all living creatures.

Buddhism and Hinduism Compared Buddhism grew from the same traditions as Hinduism. Both Hindus and Buddhists stressed nonviolence and believed in karma, dharma, moksha, and a cycle of rebirth.

Yet, the two religions differed in several ways. The Buddha rejected the priests, formal rituals, and many gods of Hinduism. Instead, he urged each person to seek enlightenment through meditation. Buddhists also rejected the caste system, offering the hope of nirvana to all regardless of birth.

Skills Assessment

Geography Missionaries and merchants spread Buddhism and Hinduism to many lands of Asia.

1. **Location** On the map, locate (a) India, (b) China, (c) Sri Lanka, (d) Japan.
2. **Movement** How did Buddhism spread to Japan?
3. **Critical Thinking Synthesizing Information** Based on the map and what you have read in this section, which arrows represent the spread of Theravada Buddhism?

Biography

Asoka 304 B.C.(?)–232 B.C.(?)

Asoka's conversion to Buddhism was so complete that he even rejected violence against animals. He gave up hunting and banned the slaughter of animals in royal kitchens.

Asoka made his personal convictions the law of the land. On one pillar he proclaimed a list of protected species. It included several kinds of birds and fish and "all four-footed creatures that are neither useful nor edible." It also declared that "one animal is not to be fed to another."

On certain Buddhist holidays, horses could not be branded and the sale of fish was prohibited. To further emphasize Buddhist respect for life, Asoka also outlawed the burning of forests without good reason.

Theme: Impact of the Individual How did Asoka protect the animals of his kingdom?

back on further conquests. He converted to Buddhism, rejected violence, and resolved to rule by moral example.

True to the Buddhist principle of respect for all life, Asoka became a vegetarian and limited Hindu animal sacrifices. He sent missionaries, or people sent on a religious mission, to spread Buddhism across India and to Sri Lanka. He thus paved the way for the later spread of Buddhism throughout Asia. Although Asoka promoted Buddhism, he preached tolerance for other religions.

Asoka had stone pillars set up across India, announcing laws and promising righteous government. On one, he proclaimed: "All people are my children, and just as I desire for my children that they should obtain welfare and happiness, both in this world and the next, so do I desire the same for all people."

Asoka's rule brought peace and prosperity, and helped unite the diverse people within his empire. Asoka helped his "children" by building hospitals and Buddhist shrines. To aid transportation, he built roads and rest houses for travelers. "I have had banyan trees planted on the roads to give shade to people and animals," he noted. "I have planted mango groves, and I have had [wells] dug and shelters erected along the roads."

Division and Disunity After Asoka's death, Maurya power declined. By 185 B.C., the unity of the Maurya empire was shattered as rival princes again battled for power across the northern plain. In fact, during its long history, India has seldom been united. In ancient times, as today, the subcontinent was home to many peoples and cultures. Although the Aryan north shared a common civilization, fierce local rivalries kept it divided. Meanwhile, distance and cultural differences separated the peoples of the north and the peoples of the Deccan Plateau in the south.

Adding to the turmoil, foreign invaders frequently pushed through mountain passes into northern India. The divided northern kingdoms could not often resist such conquerors.

Kingdoms of the Deccan

Like the northern plain, the Deccan was divided into many kingdoms. Each had its own capital with magnificent temples and bustling workshops. Unlike the peoples of the Aryan north, the peoples of the Deccan were Dravidians with very different languages and traditions. Women, for example, enjoyed a high status and economic power. The Tamil kingdoms, which occupied much of the southernmost part of India, were sometimes ruled by queens.

Over the centuries, Hindu and Buddhist traditions and Sanskrit writings drifted south and blended with local cultures. Deccan rulers generally tolerated all religions as well as the many foreigners who settled in their busy ports.

Trade was important to the Tamil kingdoms. Tamil rulers improved harbors to support overseas trade. Indian merchants sent spices, fine textiles, and other luxuries westward to eager buyers in the Roman empire. As the Roman empire declined, Tamil trade with China increased.

The Tamil kingdoms have left a rich and diverse literature. Tamil poets described fierce wars, heroic deeds, and festive occasions, along with the ordinary routines of peasant and city life.

Golden Age of the Guptas

Although many kingdoms flourished in the Deccan, the most powerful Indian states rose in the north. About 500 years after the Mauryas, the Gupta dynasty again united much of India. Gupta emperors organized a strong central government that promoted peace and prosperity. Under the Guptas, who ruled from A.D. 320 to about 550, India enjoyed a golden age, or period of great cultural achievements.

Peace and Prosperity Gupta rule was probably looser than that of the Mauryas. Much power was left in the hands of individual villages and of city governments elected by merchants and artisans. Faxian (FAH shee EHN), a Chinese Buddhist monk who visited India in the 400s, reported on the mild nature of Gupta rule:

> "The people are very well off, without poll tax or official restrictions. Only those who till the royal lands return a portion of the profit of the land as tax. . . . The kings govern without corporal punishment. Criminals are fined, according to circumstances, lightly or heavily."
> —Faxian, *A Record of Buddhist Kingdoms*

Trade and farming flourished across the Gupta empire. Farmers harvested crops of wheat, rice, and sugar cane. In cities, artisans produced cotton cloth, pottery, and metalware for local markets and for export to East Africa, the Middle East, and Southeast Asia. The prosperity of Gupta India contributed to a flowering in the arts and learning.

Advances in Learning In India, as elsewhere during this period, students were educated in religious schools. However, in Hindu and Buddhist centers, learning was not limited to religion and philosophy. The large Buddhist monastery-university at Nalanda, which attracted students from other parts of Asia, taught mathematics, medicine, physics, languages, literature, and other subjects.

Indian advances in mathematics had a wide impact on the world. Gupta mathematicians devised the simple system of writing numbers that is used today. These numerals are now called "Arabic" numerals because it was Arabs who carried them from India to the Middle East and Europe. Indian mathematicians originated the concept of zero and developed the decimal system of numbers based on 10, which we still use today.

By Gupta times, Indian physicians were using herbs and other remedies to treat illness. Surgeons were skilled in setting bones and in simple surgery to repair facial injuries. Doctors also began vaccinating people against smallpox about 1,000 years before this practice was used in Europe.

Architecture Rajahs sponsored the building of magnificent stone temples. Sometimes, cities grew up around the temples to house the thousands of laborers working there. Hindu temples were designed to reflect cosmic patterns. The ideal shape was a square inscribed in a circle to symbolize eternity.

Buddhists built splendid stupas, large dome-shaped shrines that housed the sacred remains of the Buddha or other holy people. The stupas were ringed with enclosed walkways where Buddhist monks slowly walked, chanting their prayers.

Magnificent Carvings While stupas were quite plain, their gateways featured elaborate carvings that told stories of the life of the Buddha. He

Maurya and Gupta Empires

	Maurya empire about 250 B.C.
	Gupta empire about A.D. 400

BACTRIA
HINDU KUSH
Kabul • GANDHARA
XIZANG (TIBET)
30°N
Indus R.
Brahmaputra R.
HIMALAYA MTS.
Ganges R.
Pataliputra •
Nalanda
MAGADHA
Narmada R.
Ajanta •
DECCAN PLATEAU
KALINGA
Arabian Sea
Bay of Bengal
15°N
N W E S
TAMIL KINGDOMS
INDIAN OCEAN
SRI LANKA
75°E
90°E

Mercator Projection
0   250   500 Miles
0   250   500 Kilometers

Skills Assessment

Geography Maurya and Gupta emperors were able to unite much of India under their rule.

1. **Location** On the map, locate **(a)** Ganges River, **(b)** Indus River, **(c)** Deccan Plateau.
2. **Region** What region of the Indian subcontinent remained separate from both the Maurya and the Gupta empires?
3. **Critical Thinking Connecting to Geography** How did geography limit the northward expansion of both empires?

Daoists, the best government was one that governed the least.

A Blend of Ideas Although scholars kept to Laozi's teachings, Daoism evolved into a popular religion with gods, goddesses, and magical practices. Chinese peasants turned to Daoist priests for charms to protect them from unseen forces. Instead of accepting nature as it was, some Daoist priests searched for a substance to bring immortality. To achieve this goal, they conducted experiments. Sometimes, their work contributed to science and medicine.

Gradually, people blended Confucian and Daoist teachings. Although the two philosophies differed, people took beliefs and practices from each. Confucianism showed them how to behave. Daoism influenced their view of the natural world.

Buddhism in China
Buddhist missionaries built temples, monasteries, and rest houses along their routes between India and China. The golden images of the Buddha (above) are in the Temple of General Peace in China.
Theme: Global Interaction
How did trade aid the spread of Buddhism?

Buddhism in China

By A.D. 100, missionaries and merchants had spread Mahayana Buddhism from India into China. At first, the Chinese had trouble with the new faith. For example, Chinese tradition valued family loyalty, while Buddhism honored monks and nuns who gave up the benefits of family life for a life of solitary meditation.

Despite obstacles such as this, Buddhism became more popular, especially in times of crisis. Its great appeal was the promise of escape from suffering. Mahayana Buddhism offered the hope of eternal happiness and presented Buddha as a compassionate, merciful god. Through prayer, good works, and devotion, anyone could hope to gain salvation. Neither Daoism nor Confucianism emphasized this idea of personal salvation.

By A.D. 400, Buddhism had spread throughout China. Buddhist monasteries became important centers of learning and the arts. Buddhism absorbed many Confucian and Daoist traditions. Chinese Buddhist monks stressed filial piety and honored Confucius.

SECTION 4 Assessment

Recall
1. **Identify: (a)** *Analects*, **(b)** Legalism, **(c)** Daoism.
2. **Define: (a)** philosophy, **(b)** filial piety.

Comprehension
3. Describe the ethical code of conduct that Confucius promoted.
4. **(a)** What kind of government did Legalists favor? **(b)** Why did Daoists disagree with Legalist ideas on government?
5. Why did Buddhism appeal to many people in China?

Critical Thinking and Writing
6. **Recognizing Points of View** "Rewards should be rich and certain so that the people will be attracted by them. Punishments should be severe and definite so that the people will fear them." Which of the philosophers discussed in this section expressed these ideas? Explain.
7. **Comparing** Explain how each of these thinkers believed an orderly society could be achieved: **(a)** Confucius, **(b)** Hanfeizi, **(c)** Laozi.

Activity

Writing a Dialogue
Write a dialogue in which Confucius, Hanfeizi, and Laozi debate their ideas on the nature of the best kind of government and the role that government should play in Chinese society.

Strong Rulers Unite China

Reading Focus

- How did Shi Huangdi unite China?
- How did Han rulers strengthen the economy and government of China?
- Why is the Han period considered a golden age of Chinese civilization?

Vocabulary

monopoly
expansionism
warlord
acupuncture

Taking Notes

Copy this partially completed concept web. As you read the section, add important events and developments to provide examples of how strong rulers united China. Add as many circles as you need to the web.

Wudi improved roads

STRONG RULERS UNITED CHINA

Main Idea Powerful emperors united much of China and encouraged cultural achievements.

Setting the Scene From his base in western China, the powerful ruler of the state of Qin rose to unify all of China. An ancient Chinese poet and historian described how Zheng (JUHNG) crushed all his rivals: "Cracking his long whip, he drove the universe before him, swallowing up the eastern and the western Zhou and overthrowing the feudal lords."

In 221 B.C., Zheng proclaimed himself Shi Huangdi (SHEE hoo ahng DEE), or "First Emperor." Though his methods were brutal, he ushered in China's classical age. Historians call it a classical civilization because it set patterns in government, philosophy, religion, science, and the arts that served as the framework for later cultures.

Shi Huangdi

Shi Huangdi was determined to end the divisions that had splintered Zhou China. He spent 20 years conquering most of the warring states. Then, he centralized power with the help of Legalist advisers. Using rewards for merit and punishments for failure, he built the strong, authoritarian government of the Qin dynasty.

Sima Qian, who served later Chinese emperors as Grand Historian of the court, described a monument that Shi Huangdi had built atop a mountain, with an inscription praising the emperor's accomplishments:

> "A new age is inaugurated by the Emperor;
> Rules and measures are rectified,
> The myriad things set in order, . . .
> And there is harmony between fathers and sons.
> The Emperor in his sagacity, benevolence and justice
> Has made all laws and principles manifest."
> —Sima Qian, quoted in *Records of the Historian*
> (Yang Hsien-yi and Gladys Yang)

Unity Imposed Emperor Shi Huangdi abolished feudalism in China, whereby many local rulers had owed little allegiance to any central government. He replaced the feudal states with 36 military districts and appointed loyal officials to administer them. He then sent inspectors to spy on the local officials and report back to him. Shi Huangdi forced noble families to live in his capital at Xianyang, where he could monitor them. He distributed the lands of the displaced nobles to peasants. Still, peasants had to pay high taxes to support Shi Huangdi's armies and building projects.

Soldier of Shi Huangdi This terra-cotta soldier is one of more than 8,000 that stand guard inside the tomb of Emperor Shi Huangdi. A farmer uncovered the tomb in 1974 while digging a well.

Theme: Impact of the Individual How does the figure symbolize the power and authority of Shi Huangdi?

Qin and Han Empires, 221 B.C.–A.D. 220

CENTRAL ASIA

MANCHURIA

MONGOLIA

GOBI

TAKLA MAKAN DESERT

Great Wall

Great Wall

KUNLUN MTS.

KOREA

XIZANG (TIBET)

Handan

Huang He

Yellow Sea

Xianyang

C H I N A

East China Sea

HIMALAYA MTS.

Chengdu

Yangzi R.

VIETNAM

Si R.

South China Sea

Map Legend
- Qin empire, 221 B.C.–210 B.C.
- Han empire, 206 B.C.–A.D. 220
- Han protectorate
- Silk Road
- Area of silk production during Han

N
W E
S

Azimuthal Equal Area Projection

0   250   500 Miles
0   250   500 Kilometers

To promote unity, the First Emperor standardized weights and measures and replaced the diverse coins of the Zhou states with Qin coins. He also had scholars create uniformity in Chinese writing. Workers repaired and extended roads and canals to strengthen the transportation system. A new law even required cart axles to be the same width so that wheels could run in the same ruts on all Chinese roads.

Crackdown on Dissent Shi Huangdi moved harshly against critics. He jailed, tortured, and killed many who opposed his rule. Hardest hit were the feudal nobles and Confucian scholars who despised his laws. To end dissent, Shi Huangdi approved a ruthless campaign of book burning, ordering the destruction of all works of literature and philosophy. Only books on medicine and agriculture were spared.

The Great Wall Shi Huangdi's most remarkable and costly achievement was the Great Wall. In the past, individual feudal states had built walls to defend their lands against raiders. Shi Huangdi ordered the walls to be joined. Hundreds of thousands of laborers worked for years through bitter cold and burning heat. They pounded earth and stone into a mountainous wall almost 25 feet high topped with a wide brick road. Many workers died in the harsh conditions.

Over the centuries, the wall was extended and rebuilt many times. Eventually, it snaked for thousands of miles across northern China.

While the wall did not keep invaders out of China, it did demonstrate the emperor's ability to mobilize the vast resources of China. In the long run, the Great Wall became an important symbol to the Chinese people, dividing and protecting their civilized world from the nomadic, or wandering, bands north of the wall.

Collapse Shi Huangdi thought his empire would last forever. But when he died in 210 B.C., anger over heavy taxes, forced labor, and cruel policies exploded into revolts. As Qin power collapsed, Liu Bang (LEE oo BAHNG), an illiterate peasant leader, defeated rival armies and founded the new Han dynasty. Like earlier Chinese rulers, Liu Bang claimed that his power was based on the Mandate of Heaven.

The Han Dynasty

As emperor, Liu Bang took the title Gao Zu (GOW DZOO) and set about restoring order and justice to his empire. Although he continued earlier efforts to unify China, he lowered taxes and eased the Qin emperor's harsh Legalist policies. In a key move, he appointed Confucian scholars as advisers. His policies created strong foundations for the Han dynasty, which lasted from 206 B.C. to A.D. 220.

Emperor Wudi The most famous Han emperor, Wudi, took China to new heights. During his long reign from 141 B.C. to 87 B.C., he strengthened the government and economy. Like Gao Zu, he chose officials from Confucian "men of wisdom and virtue." To train scholars, he set up an imperial university at Xian.

Wudi furthered economic growth by improving canals and roads. He had granaries set up across the empire so the government could buy grain when it was abundant and sell it at stable prices when it was scarce. He reorganized finances and imposed a government monopoly on iron and salt. A **monopoly** is the complete control of a product or business by one person or group. The sale of iron and salt gave the government a source of income other than taxes on peasants.

Wudi followed a policy of expansionism by increasing the amount of territory under Chinese rule. He fought many battles to expand China's borders and to drive nomadic peoples beyond the Great Wall. Chinese armies added outposts in Manchuria, Korea, northern Vietnam, Tibet, and Central Asia. Soldiers, traders, and settlers slowly spread Chinese influence across these areas.

Silk Road to the West The emperor Wudi opened up a trade route, later called the Silk Road, that would link China and the west for centuries. During the Han period, new foods such as grapes, figs, cucumbers, and walnuts flowed to China from western Asia. Lucky traders might return to China bearing furs from Central Asia, muslin from India, or glass from Rome. At the same time, the Chinese sent tons of silk westward to fill a growing demand for the prized fabric.

Eventually, the Silk Road stretched for 4,000 miles, linking China to the Fertile Crescent in southwestern Asia. Still, few traders covered the entire distance; instead, goods were relayed in stages from one set of traders to another. At the western end, trade was controlled by various people, including the Persians.

Scholar-Officials Han emperors made Confucianism the official belief system of the state. They relied on well-educated scholars to run the bureaucratic government. A scholar-official was expected to match the Confucian ideal of a gentleman. He would be courteous and dignified and possess a thorough knowledge of history, music, poetry, and Confucian teachings.

Civil Service Examination Han emperors adopted the idea that government officials should win positions by merit rather than through family background. To find the most qualified officials, they set up a system of exams. In time, these civil service exams were given at the local, provincial, and national levels. To pass, candidates studied the Confucian classics, a

Primary Source

Travels on the Silk Road
Faxian, a Chinese Buddhist monk, described a journey crossing the Gobi on the Silk Road in A.D. 399:

"Le Hao, the [chief official] of T'un-hwang, had supplied them with the means of crossing the desert before them, in which there were many evil demons and hot winds. Travelers who encounter them perish all to a man. There is not a bird to be seen in the air above, nor an animal on the ground below. Though you look all round most earnestly to find where you can cross, you know not where to make your choice, the only mark and indication being the dry bones of the dead left upon the sand."

—Faxian, *A Record of Buddhist Kingdoms*

Skills Assessment

Primary Source According to Faxian, what landmarks did travelers use to follow the Silk Road across the Gobi?

collection of histories, poems, and handbooks on customs that Confucius was said to have compiled.

In theory, any man could take the exams. In practice, only those who could afford years of study, such as the sons of wealthy landowners or officials, could hope to succeed. Occasionally, a village or wealthy family might pay for the education of a brilliant peasant boy. If he passed the exams and obtained a government job, he, his family, and his clan all enjoyed immense prestige and moved up in society.

Confucian teachings about filial piety and the superiority of men kept women from taking the civil service exam. As a result, women were closed out of government jobs.

The civil service system had an enormous impact on China for almost 2,000 years. It put men trained in Confucian thought at every level of government and created an enduring system of values. Dynasties rose and fell, but Confucian influence survived.

Collapse of the Han Empire As the Han dynasty aged, signs of decay appeared. Court intrigues undermined emperors who could no longer control powerful warlords, or local military rulers. Weak emperors let canals and roads fall into disrepair. Burdened by heavy taxes and crushing debt, many peasants revolted. Thousands of rebellious peasants abandoned their villages and fled to the mountains. There they joined secret groups of bandits known by colorful names such as the "Red Eyebrows" and the "Green Woodsmen."

In A.D. 220, ambitious warlords overthrew the last Han emperor. After 400 years of unity, China broke up into several kingdoms. Adding to the disorder, invaders poured over the Great Wall and set up their own states. In time, many of these newcomers were absorbed into Chinese civilization.

Achievements of the Han Golden Age

The Han period was one of the golden ages of Chinese civilization. Han China made such tremendous advances in so many fields that the Chinese later called themselves "the people of Han."

Science Han scientists wrote texts on chemistry, zoology, botany, and other subjects. Han astronomers carefully observed and measured movements of the stars and planets, which enabled them to improve earlier calendars and invent better timekeeping devices. One scientist invented a simple seismograph to detect and measure earthquakes.

The scientist Wang Chong disagreed with the widely held belief that comets and eclipses showed Heaven's anger. "On the average, there is one moon eclipse about every 180 days," he wrote, "and a solar eclipse about every 41 or 42 months. Eclipses . . . are not caused by political action." Wang Chong argued that no scientific theories should be accepted unless they were supported by proof.

Medicine Chinese physicians diagnosed diseases, experimented with herbal remedies and other drugs, and developed anesthetics. Some doctors explored the uses of acupuncture. In this medical treatment, the doctor inserts needles under the skin at specific points to relieve pain or treat various illnesses.

Technology In its time, Han China was the most technologically advanced civilization in the world. Cai Lun, an official of the Han court, invented a method for making durable paper out of wood pulp. His basic method is still used to manufacture paper today. The Chinese also pioneered advanced methods of shipbuilding and invented the rudder to steer. Other practical inventions included bronze and iron stirrups, fishing reels, wheelbarrows, suspension bridges, and chain pumps. Some of these ideas

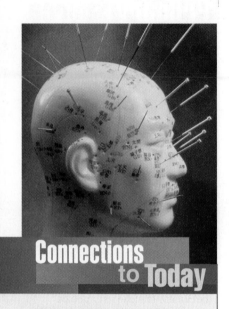

How Acupuncture Works

For more than 2,500 years, Chinese physicians have used acupuncture to ease patients' suffering. There are several ways to explain how acupuncture works.

Traditional Chinese doctors believe that pain and illness are sometimes due to an imbalance of natural energy flow through the body. Equilibrium and good health can be restored by the insertion of needles at the proper points.

Other explanations involve the nervous system. Some doctors think that acupuncture works because the needles block nerves that carry pain. Another possibility is that the needles promote the release of endorphins in the brain. Endorphins are naturally produced substances that inhibit pain.

Theme: Connections to Today Why do you think some patients today are reluctant to undergo acupuncture?

moved west slowly, reaching Europe hundreds of years later.

The Arts The walled cities of Han China boasted splendid temples and palaces amid elegant parks. Although these wooden buildings have not survived, Han poets and historians have described their grandeur. Artisans produced delicate jade and ivory carvings and fine ceramic figures. Bronzeworkers and silkmakers improved on earlier techniques and set high standards for future generations.

In *Lessons for a Woman*, a handbook of behavior written by Ban Zhao (BAHN JOW) around A.D. 100, the proper behavior for women and men was carefully spelled out. Ban Zhao favored equal education for boys and girls. However, she stressed that women should be obedient, respectful, and submissive. "Let a woman modestly yield to others," she advised. "Let her respect others."

Looking Ahead

Shi Huangdi, Gao Zu, Wudi, and later Han rulers forged a vast and varied land into a united China. Han rulers created an empire roughly the size of the continental United States. During this period, Chinese officials established the pattern of government that would survive until 1912. China would undergo great changes. It would break up and be painfully reassembled over and over. On the whole, however, Chinese civilization flourished in a united land. After periods of disunity, a new dynasty would turn to Confucian scholars to revive the days of Han greatness.

Cause *and* Effect

Long-Term Causes	Immediate Causes
• Confucian ideas dominate education • China's isolation permits development without much outside interference • Common system of writing evolves	• Zheng conquers eastern and western Zhou and overthrows feudal lords • Zheng proclaims himself Shi Huangdi ("First Emperor")

Unification of China

Immediate Effects	Long-Term Effects
• Shi Huangdi standardizes weights and measures and money • Roads and canals unify distant provinces • Government cracks down on dissenters • Shi Huangdi supervises work on the Great Wall	• Han dynasty is founded by Liu Bang • China makes advances in government, trade, and transportation • Confucian-educated officials hold most government jobs • Common culture helps China survive upheavals

Connections to Today

- Mainland China remains a large, politically united country
- Chinese still share a common written language

Skills Assessment **Chart** Under Shi Huangdi, most of China united under a single ruler. **How did political unification benefit the Chinese economy?**

SECTION 5 Assessment

Recall
1. **Identify:** (a) Shi Huangdi, (b) Great Wall, (c) Gao Zu, (d) Wudi, (e) Silk Road, (f) Wang Chong, (g) Ban Zhao.
2. **Define:** (a) monopoly, (b) expansionism, (c) warlord, (d) acupuncture.

Comprehension
3. What were three steps Shi Huangdi took to unify China?
4. How did Han emperors further economic growth in China?
5. Describe several of the achievements that helped make the Han period a golden age in Chinese civilization.

Critical Thinking and Writing
6. **Drawing Conclusions** Based on what you know about Confucianism, how do you think the civil service examination system affected the nature of Chinese government?
7. **Comparing** Describe one major difference between Qin government and Han government.

Activity
Take It to the NET

Use Internet sources to find out more about Chinese art during the Qin and Han dynasties. In a scrapbook, collect photocopies of art objects that you find. Write a brief description of each image so that others can learn about Chinese art during these periods.

Early People of the Aegean

Reading Focus

- What civilizations influenced the Minoans?
- How did Mycenaean civilization affect the later Greeks?
- What do the epics of Homer reveal about the Greeks?

Vocabulary

shrine
fresco
strait

Taking Notes

Copy this time line. As you read, fill in the major civilizations and events that occurred.

Trojan War
1250 B.C.

1800 B.C. 1600 B.C. 1400 B.C. | 1200 B.C. 1000 B.C. 800 B.C.

1750 B.C.–1500 B.C.
Minoan civilization
at its height

Main Idea The Minoans and Mycenaeans shaped the first Greek civilizations.

Geography and History

From Egypt to Crete

When Minoan traders sailed the Mediterranean, they often headed for Egypt. Some Egyptian tomb paintings even show Minoan traders offering gifts to the pharaoh. In return, the traders brought valuable items such as linen home to Crete.

Trading goods led to cultural borrowing. Early Greek painting, with its stiff, formal poses, resembles Egyptian art styles. In addition, Egyptian notions of life after death—including a ferry ride across a river to the underworld—may have influenced Greek religious ideas.

Theme: Geography and History How does Egyptian influence on Minoan culture reflect the geographic themes of location and movement?

Setting the Scene Europa, the beautiful daughter of the king of Phoenicia, was gathering flowers when she saw a bull quietly grazing with her father's herds. The bull was actually Zeus, king of the gods, who had fallen in love with her. When Europa reached to place flowers on his horns, he suddenly bounded into the air and carried the weeping princess far across the Mediterranean Sea to the island of Crete. Eventually, Europa married the king of Crete and gave her name to a new continent—Europe.

This Greek legend carries seeds of truth. Crete was the cradle of an early civilization that later influenced Greeks on the European mainland. The people of Crete, however, had absorbed many ideas from the older civilizations of Egypt and Mesopotamia. Europa's journey from Phoenicia to Crete thus suggests the movement of ideas from east to west.

Minoan Civilization

Washed by the warm waters of the Aegean (uh JEE uhn) Sea, Crete was home to a brilliant early civilization. We do not know what the people who built this civilization called themselves. However, the British archaeologist who unearthed its ruins called them Minoans after Minos, a legendary king of Crete. Minoan civilization reached its height, or greatest success, between 1750 B.C. and 1500 B.C.

The success of the Minoans was based on trade, not conquest. Minoan traders set up outposts throughout the Aegean world. From their island home in the eastern Mediterranean, they crossed the seas to the Nile Valley and the Middle East. Through contact with Egypt and Mesopotamia, they acquired ideas and technology that they adapted to their own culture.

The Palace at Knossos The rulers of this trading empire lived in a vast palace at Knossos (NAHS uhs). It housed rooms for the royal family, banquet halls, and working areas for artisans. It also included religious shrines, areas dedicated to the honor of gods and goddesses.

The walls of the palace at Knossos are covered with colorful frescoes, watercolor paintings done on wet plaster. These frescoes tell us much about Minoan society. Leaping dolphins reflect the importance of the sea to the Minoan people. Religious images indicate that the Minoans worshiped the bull and a mother goddess. Other paintings show young men and women strolling through gardens or jumping through the horns of a charging bull. They suggest that women appeared freely in public and may have enjoyed more rights than women in most other ancient civilizations.

A Civilization Disappears By about 1400 B.C., Minoan civilization had vanished. Archaeologists are not sure of the reasons for its disappearance. A sudden volcanic eruption on a nearby island may have rained flaming death on Knossos. An earthquake may have destroyed the palace, followed by a tidal wave that drowned the inhabitants of the island.

However, invaders certainly played a role in the destruction of Minoan civilization. These intruders were the Mycenaeans (mī suh NEE uhnz), the first Greek-speaking people of whom we have a written record.

A Minoan Fresco
These dolphins from the palace at Knossos show the lightness and sense of movement of Minoan frescoes.

Theme: Geography and History Why do you think Minoan artists chose dolphins as a subject?

Rulers of Mycenae

Like the Aryans who swept into India, the Mycenaeans were an Indo-European people. They conquered the Greek mainland before overrunning Crete.

Successful Sea Traders Mycenaean civilization dominated the Aegean world from about 1400 B.C. to 1200 B.C. Like the Minoans, the Mycenaeans were sea traders. They reached out beyond the Aegean to Sicily, Italy, Egypt, and Mesopotamia. The newcomers learned many skills from the Minoans, including the art of writing. They, too, absorbed Egyptian and Mesopotamian influences, which they passed on to later Greeks.

The Mycenaeans lived in separate city-states on the mainland. In each, a warrior-king built a thick-walled fortress from which he ruled the surrounding villages. Wealthy rulers amassed hoards of treasure, including fine gold ornaments that archaeologists have unearthed from their tombs.

The Trojan War The Mycenaeans are best remembered for their part in the Trojan War, which took place around 1250 B.C. The conflict may have had its origins in economic rivalry between Mycenae and Troy, a rich trading city in present-day Turkey. Troy controlled the vital straits, or narrow water passages, that connect the Mediterranean and Black seas. However, Greek legend attributes the war to a more romantic cause. After the Trojan prince Paris kidnapped Helen, the beautiful wife of a Greek king, the Mycenaeans sailed to Troy to rescue her. For the next 10 years, the two sides battled until the Greeks finally seized Troy and burned the city to the ground.

For centuries, most people regarded the Trojan War as purely a legend. Then, in the 1870s, a wealthy German businessman, Heinrich Schliemann (HĪN rihk SHLEE mahn), set out to prove that the legend was rooted in fact. As he excavated the site of ancient Troy, Schliemann found evidence of fire and war dating to about 1250 B.C. Though most of the details remain lost in legend, modern scholars agree that the Trojan War was an actual event.

The Age of Homer

Not long after the fall of Troy, Mycenaean civilization crumbled under the attack of sea raiders. About the same time, another wave of Greek-speaking people, the Dorians, invaded from the north. As Mycenaean power faded, people abandoned the cities, and trade declined. From 1100 B.C. to 800 B.C., Greek civilization seemed to step backward. People forgot many skills, including the art of writing.

We get hints about life during this period from two great epic poems, the *Iliad* and the *Odyssey*. These epics may have been the work of many

Hero of the *Odyssey*
Odysseus was admired for cleverness. Here, he outwits the siren, whose song lures sailors to their doom. He fills his crew's ears with beeswax. Then, he has himself tied to the ship's mast so he can hear the siren's song without endangering the ship.

Theme: Art and Literature Name some fictional heroes of the past and present. What admirable qualities do they possess?

people, but they are credited to the poet Homer, who probably lived about 750 B.C. According to tradition, Homer was a blind poet who wandered from village to village, singing of heroic deeds. Like the great Indian epics, Homer's tales were passed on orally for generations before they were finally written down.

The *Iliad* is our chief source of information about the Trojan War, although the story involves gods, goddesses, and even a talking horse. At the start of the poem, Achilles (uh KIHL eez), the mightiest Greek warrior, is sulking in his tent because of a dispute with his commander. Although the war soon turns against the Greeks, Achilles stubbornly refuses to listen to pleas that he rejoin the fighting. Only after his best friend is killed does Achilles return to battle.

The *Odyssey* tells of the struggles of the Greek hero Odysseus (oh DIHS ee uhs) to return home to his faithful wife, Penelope, after the fall of Troy. On his long voyage, Odysseus encounters a sea monster, a race of one-eyed giants, and a beautiful sorceress who turns men into swine.

The *Iliad* and *Odyssey* reveal much about the values of the ancient Greeks. The heroes display honor, courage, and eloquence, as when Achilles rallies his troops:

> "Every man make up his mind to fight
> And move on his enemy! Strong as I am,
> It's hard for me to face so many men
> And fight with all at once. . . .
> And yet I will!"
>
> —Homer, *Iliad*

For almost 3,000 years, the epics of Homer have inspired European writers and artists.

Looking Ahead

For centuries after the Dorian invasions, the Greeks lived in small, isolated villages. They had no writing and few contacts with the outside world. From this unpromising start, they would develop a civilization that influenced many parts of the world. As they emerged from obscurity, they benefited from the legacy of earlier civilizations. Over time, the stories they heard about Crete and Mycenae underwent changes and became part of the Greek heritage.

SECTION 1 Assessment

Recall

1. Identify: **(a)** Trojan War, **(b)** Heinrich Schliemann, **(c)** Homer.
2. Define: **(a)** shrine, **(b)** fresco, **(c)** strait.

Comprehension

3. How did trade contribute to the development of Minoan and Mycenaean civilizations?
4. What impact did Mycenaean civilization have on later Greeks?
5. What values of the ancient Greeks are found in the poems of Homer?

Critical Thinking and Writing

6. **Connecting to Geography** In addition to location near water, what other geographic features or natural resources would have been important to an early people who made their living as sea traders?
7. **Drawing Conclusions** Do you think the epics of Homer are probably a reliable source of information about the history of the ancient Greeks? Why or why not?

Activity
Take It to the NET

Use the Internet to research ancient Greek myths such as the story of Europa. Then, make a list of five words, like *Europe*, that are derived from these myths. For each word, include an explanation of the connection between the English word and its Greek origin.

The Rise of Greek City-States

Reading Focus

- How did geography influence the Greek city-states?
- What kinds of government did the Greek city-states develop?
- How did Athens and Sparta differ?
- What forces unified the Greek city-states?

Vocabulary

polis
acropolis
monarchy
aristocracy
oligarchy
phalanx
helot
democracy
tyrant
legislature

Taking Notes

Copy this diagram. As you read, fill in both similarities and differences between Athens and Sparta. Parts of these circles have been completed to help you get started.

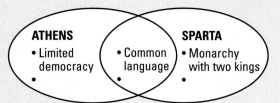

ATHENS
- Limited democracy
-

- Common language
-

SPARTA
- Monarchy with two kings

Main Idea As Greek city-states grew, they developed different types of government, including an early form of democracy.

Setting the Scene "We live around the sea like frogs around a pond," noted the Greek thinker Plato. Indeed, the Mediterranean and Aegean seas were as central to the development of Greek civilization as the Nile was to the Egyptians. The ancient Greeks absorbed many ideas and beliefs from the older civilizations of Mesopotamia and Egypt. At the same time, they evolved their own unique ways. In particular, the Greeks developed new ideas about how best to govern a society.

Geography of the Greek Homeland

As you have read, the earliest civilizations rose in fertile river valleys. There, strong rulers organized irrigation works that helped farmers produce food surpluses needed to support large cities. A very different set of geographic conditions influenced the rise of Greek civilization.

Mountains and Valleys Greece is part of the Balkan peninsula, which extends southward into the eastern Mediterranean Sea. Mountains divide the peninsula into isolated valleys. Beyond the rugged coast, hundreds of rocky islands spread toward the horizon.

   The Greeks who farmed the valleys or settled on the scattered islands did not create a large empire such as that of the Egyptians or Persians. Instead, they built many small city-states, cut off from one another by mountains or water. Each included a city and its surrounding countryside. Greeks fiercely defended the independence of their tiny city-states. Endless rivalry led to frequent wars.

The Seas While mountains divided Greeks, the seas were a vital link to the world outside. With its hundreds of bays, the Greek coastline provided safe harbors for ships. The Greeks became skilled sailors, carrying cargoes of olive oil, wine, and marble around the eastern Mediterranean. They returned not only with grains and metals but also with ideas, which they adapted to their own needs. For example, the Greeks expanded the Phoenician alphabet. The resulting Greek alphabet became the basis for all western alphabets.

   By 750 B.C., rapid population growth was forcing many Greeks to leave their own overcrowded valleys. With fertile land limited, the Greeks expanded overseas. Gradually, a scattering of Greek colonies took root all around the Mediterranean from Spain to Egypt. Wherever they traveled, Greek settlers and traders carried their ideas and culture.

DEVELOPMENT OF THE ALPHABET

Phoenician	Greek	Roman
Ϗ	Λ	A
ϒ	Β	B
Δ	Δ	D
Ψ	Κ	K
Ɩ	Λ	L
ϟ	N	N

Skills Assessment

Chart Our alphabet comes to us from the Phoenicians by way of the Greeks. The word *alphabet* itself comes from the first two Greek letters, *alpha* and *beta*. **Describe how the modern letter A changed over time.**

Geography of Ancient Greece

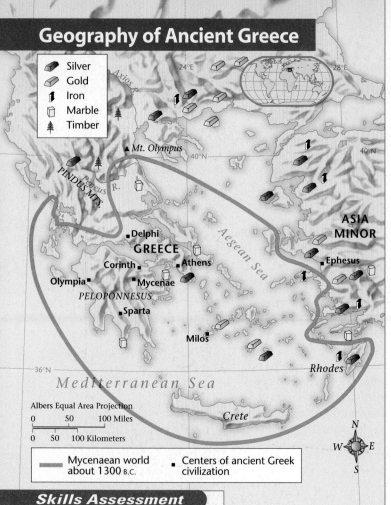

Silver
Gold
Iron
Marble
Timber

Axios R.
24°E
28°E
Peneus R.
PINDUS MTS.
Mt. Olympus
40°N
40°N
Delphi
GREECE
ASIA MINOR
Corinth
Athens
Ephesus
Aegean Sea
Olympia
Mycenae
PELOPONNESUS
Sparta
36°N
Milos
Rhodes
Mediterranean Sea
Crete
N W E S

Albers Equal Area Projection
0   50   100 Miles
0   50   100 Kilometers

Mycenaean world about 1300 B.C.
Centers of ancient Greek civilization

Skills Assessment

Geography Greek civilization was shaped by both rugged mountains and the surrounding seas.

1. **Location** On the map, locate *(a)* Aegean Sea, *(b)* Mediterranean Sea, *(c)* Greece, *(d)* Crete, *(e)* Mycenae, *(f)* Athens, *(g)* Sparta, *(h)* Mt. Olympus.
2. **Region** How did the geography of Greece present obstacles to unity?
3. **Critical Thinking** **Comparing** How did the geography of Greece differ from that of other ancient civilizations?

Governing the City-States

As their world expanded after 750 B.C., the Greeks evolved a unique version of the city-state, which they called the **polis.** Typically, the city itself was built on two levels. On a hilltop stood the **acropolis** (uh KRAHP uh lihs), or high city, with its great marble temples dedicated to different gods and goddesses. On flatter ground below lay the walled main city with its market-place, theater, public buildings, and homes.

The population of each city-state was fairly small, which helped citizens share a sense of responsibility for its triumphs and defeats. In the warm climate of Greece, free men spent much time outdoors in the marketplace, debating issues that affected their lives. The whole community joined in festivals honoring the city's special god or goddess.

Early Governments Between 750 B.C. and 500 B.C., Greeks evolved different forms of government. At first, the ruler of the polis, like those in the river valley empires, was a king. A government in which a king or queen exercises central power is a **monarchy.** Slowly, though, power shifted to a class of noble landowners. They were also the military defenders of the city-states, because only they could afford bronze weapons and chariots. At first these nobles defended the king. In time, they won power for themselves. The result was an **aristocracy,** or rule by a landholding elite.

As trade expanded, a new middle class of wealthy merchants, farmers, and artisans emerged in some cities. They challenged the landowning nobles for power and came to dominate some city-states. The result was a form of government called an **oligarchy.** In an oligarchy, power is in the hands of a small, powerful elite, usually from the business class.

Changes in Warfare Changes in military technology increased the power of the middle class. By about 650 B.C., iron weapons replaced bronze ones. Since iron was cheaper, ordinary citizens could afford iron helmets, shields, and swords. Meanwhile, a new method of fighting emerged. The **phalanx** was a massive formation of heavily armed foot soldiers. It required long hours of drill. Shared training created a strong sense of unity among citizen-soldiers.

By putting the defense of the city-state in the hands of ordinary citizens, the phalanx reduced class differences. The new type of warfare, however, led the two most influential city-states to develop very different ways of life. While Sparta stressed military virtues and stern discipline, Athens glorified the individual and extended political rights to more citizens.

Sparta: A Nation of Soldiers

The Spartans were Dorians who conquered Laconia. This region lies in the Peloponnesus (pehl uh puh NEE suhs), the southern part of Greece. The invaders turned the conquered people into state-owned slaves, called **helots,** and made them work the land. Because the helots greatly outnumbered their rulers, the Spartans set up a brutal system of strict control.

The Spartan government included two kings and a council of elders who advised the monarchs. An assembly made up of all citizens approved major decisions. Citizens were male, native-born Spartans over the age of 30. The assembly also elected five ephors, officials who held the real power and ran day-to-day affairs.

The Rigors of Citizenship   From childhood, a Spartan prepared to be part of a military state. Officials examined every newborn, and sickly children were abandoned to die. Spartans wanted future soldiers or mothers of soldiers to be healthy.

At the age of seven, boys began training for a lifetime in the military. They moved into barracks, where they endured a brutal existence. Toughened by a coarse diet, hard exercise, and rigid discipline, Spartan youths became excellent soldiers. To develop cunning and supplement their diet, boys were even encouraged to steal food. If caught, though, they were beaten severely.

At the age of 20, a man could marry, but he continued to live in the barracks for another 10 years and to eat there for another 40 years. At the age of 30, after further specialized training, he took his place in the assembly.

Women   Girls, too, had a rigorous upbringing. As part of a warrior society, they were expected to produce healthy sons for the army. They therefore were told to exercise and strengthen their bodies—something no other Greek women did.

Like other Greek women, Spartan women had to obey their fathers or husbands. Under Spartan law, though, they had the right to inherit property. Because men were occupied with war, some women took on responsibilities such as running the family's estates.

Sparta and Its Neighbors   The Spartans isolated themselves from other Greeks. They looked down on trade and wealth, forbade their own citizens to travel, and had little use for new ideas or the arts. While other Greeks admired the Spartans' military skills, no other city-state imitated their rigorous way of life. "Spartans are willing to die for their city," some suggested, "because they have no reason to live."

Athens: A Limited Democracy

Athens was located in Attica, just north of the Peloponnesus. As in many Greek city-states, Athenian government evolved from a monarchy into an aristocracy. Around 700 B.C., noble landowners held power and chose the chief officials. Nobles judged major cases in court and dominated the assembly.

Demands for Change   Under the aristocracy, Athenian wealth and power grew. Yet discontent spread among ordinary people. Merchants and soldiers resented the power of the nobles. They argued that their service to Athens entitled them to more rights. Foreign artisans, who produced many goods that Athens traded abroad, were resentful that foreigners were barred from becoming citizens. Farmers, too, demanded change. During hard times, many farmers were forced to sell their land to nobles. A growing number even sold themselves and their families into slavery to pay their debts.

As discontent spread, Athens moved slowly toward democracy, or government by the people. As you will see, the term had a different meaning for the ancient Greeks than it has for us today.

Solon's Reforms   Solon, a wise and trusted leader, was appointed archon (AHR kahn), or chief official, in 594 B.C. Athenians gave Solon a free hand to make needed reforms. He outlawed debt slavery and freed those who had already been sold into slavery for debt. He opened high offices to more citizens, granted citizenship to some foreigners, and gave the Athenian assembly more say in important decisions.

Primary Source

A Spartan Education
An Athenian historian explains the system of education set up by Lycurgus, the Spartan lawgiver:

"Instead of softening the boys' feet with sandals he required them to harden their feet by going without shoes. He believed that if this habit were cultivated it would enable them to climb hills more easily and descend steep inclines with less danger, and that a youth who had accustomed himself to go barefoot would leap and jump and run more nimbly than a boy in sandals. And instead of letting them be pampered in the matter of clothing, he introduced the custom of wearing one garment throughout the year, believing that they would thus be better prepared to face changes of heat and cold."

—Xenophon, *Constitution of the Lacedaemonians*

Skills Assessment

Primary Source Describe the Spartan student dress code. What was its purpose?

Solon introduced economic reforms as well. He encouraged the export of wine and olive oil. This policy helped merchants and farmers by increasing demand for their products.

Although Solon's reforms ensured greater fairness and justice to some groups, citizenship remained limited, and many positions were open only to wealthy landowners. Widespread and continued unrest led to the rise of tyrants, or people who gained power by force. Tyrants often won support of the merchant class and the poor by imposing reforms to help these groups. (Although Greek tyrants often governed well, the word *tyrant* has come to mean a vicious and brutal ruler.)

Later Reforms The Athenian tyrant Pisistratus (pi SIHS truh tuhs) seized power in 546 B.C. He helped farmers by giving them loans and land taken from nobles. New building projects gave jobs to the poor. By giving poor citizens a greater voice, he further weakened the aristocracy.

In 507 B.C., another reformer, Cleisthenes (KLĪS thuh neez), broadened the role of ordinary citizens in government. He set up the Council of 500, whose members were chosen by lot from among all citizens. The council prepared laws for the assembly and supervised the day-to-day work of government. Cleisthenes made the assembly a genuine legislature, or law-making body, that debated laws before deciding to approve or reject them. All male citizens over the age of 30 were members of the assembly.

Limited Rights By modern standards, Athenian democracy was quite limited. Only male citizens could participate in government, and citizenship was severely restricted. Also, tens of thousands of Athenians were slaves without political rights or personal freedom. In fact, it was the labor of slaves that gave citizens the time to participate in government. Still, Athens gave more people a say in decision making than did the other ancient civilizations we have studied.

Women In Athens, as in other Greek city-states, women had no share in public life. The respected thinker Aristotle saw women as imperfect beings who lacked the ability to reason as well as men. "The man is by nature fitter for command than the female," he wrote, "just as an older person is superior to a younger, more immature person."

In well-to-do Athenian homes, women lived a secluded existence. There, they managed the entire household. They spun and wove, cared for their children, and prepared food. Their slaves or children were sent to buy

Athenian Education
Athenians believed that education should teach all arts for the development of well-rounded citizens. This vase painting shows young men learning music and grammar at an Athenian school.

Theme: Continuity and Change How is the ideal of education shown in this painting reflected in American schools today?

food and to fetch water from the public well. Poorer women worked outside the home, tending sheep or working as spinners, weavers, or potters.

Education for Democracy Unlike girls, who received little or no formal education, boys attended school if their families could afford it. Besides learning to read and write, they studied music and memorized poetry. They studied to become skilled public speakers because, as citizens in a democracy, they would have to voice their views. Young men received military training and, to keep their bodies healthy, participated in athletic contests. Unlike Sparta, which put military training above all else, Athens encouraged young men to explore many areas of knowledge.

Forces for Unity

Strong local ties, an independent spirit, and economic rivalry led to fighting among the Greek city-states. Despite these divisions, Greeks shared a common culture. They spoke the same language, honored the same ancient heroes, participated in common festivals, and prayed to the same gods.

Religious Beliefs Like most other ancient people, the Greeks were polytheistic. They believed that the gods lived on Mount Olympus in northern Greece. The most powerful Olympian was Zeus, who presided over the affairs of gods and humans. His children included Aphrodite (af ruh DĪ tee), goddess of love, and Ares, god of war. His daughter Athena, goddess of wisdom, gave her name to Athens.

Greeks honored their gods with temples and festivals. To discover the will of the gods, Greeks consulted the oracles, priests or priestesses through whom the gods were thought to speak. Although religion was important, some Greek thinkers came to believe that the universe was regulated, not by the will of gods, but by natural laws.

View of Non-Greeks As trade and colonies expanded, the Greeks came in contact with people with different languages and customs. Greeks felt superior to non-Greeks and called them *barbaroi*, people who did not speak Greek. The English word *barbarian* comes from this Greek root. These "barbarians" included such people as the Phoenicians and Egyptians, from whom the Greeks borrowed important ideas and inventions. Still, this sense of uniqueness would help the Greeks face a threat from the mightiest power in the Mediterranean world—the Persian empire.

Connections to Today

The Olympic Games

Every four years, in the city-state of Olympia, the Greeks held athletic contests to honor Zeus. Winning athletes, such as wrestlers or discus throwers, would be crowned with a wreath. The Olympic games helped unify the Greek world. Warring city-states would even call a truce so that people could attend the games.

Today, thousands of athletes from around the world compete in the summer and winter Olympics. To honor the Greek origins of the games, relay runners carry a torch from Greece to the host city.

Theme: Global Interaction
Do you think the Olympic games are a force for unity in the world? Why or why not?

SECTION 2 Assessment

Recall
1. **Identify:** **(a)** Peloponnesus, **(b)** Solon, **(c)** Cleisthenes, **(d)** Zeus.
2. **Define:** **(a)** polis, **(b)** acropolis, **(c)** monarchy, **(d)** aristocracy, **(e)** oligarchy, **(f)** phalanx, **(g)** helot, **(h)** democracy, **(i)** tyrant, **(j)** legislature.

Comprehension
3. Identify two ways that geography influenced Greece.
4. **(a)** How did noble landowners gain power in Greek city-states? **(b)** How did the phalanx affect Greek society and government?

5. Describe the system of education in **(a)** Sparta and **(b)** Athens.
6. What cultural ties united the Greek world?

Critical Thinking and Writing
7. **Drawing Conclusions** **(a)** In what ways was Athenian democracy limited? **(b)** Despite such limits, Athens is still admired as an early model of democracy. Why do you think this is so?
8. **Analyzing Ideas** Like the early Chinese, the Greeks felt superior to people outside their own land. How might such an attitude be both a strength and a weakness?

Activity

Creating a Dialogue
Create a dialogue between an Athenian and a Spartan in which they discuss the best form of government and the responsibilities of citizenship.

Victory and Defeat in the Greek World

Reading Focus

■ What impact did the Persian Wars have on Greece?

■ How did Athens enjoy a golden age under Pericles?

■ What were the causes and effects of the Peloponnesian War?

Vocabulary

alliance

direct democracy

stipend

jury

ostracism

Taking Notes

Copy this flowchart. As you read, fill in the boxes with the major events of the many wars in the Greek world. The first box has been completed to help you get started.

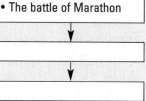

THE WARS OF THE GREEK WORLD

- Athens fights Persia
- Other city-states fight on the side of Athens
- The battle of Marathon

Main Idea Competition among the Greek city-states led to conflict.

Setting the Scene

In 492 B.C., King Darius I of Persia cast an angry eye across the Aegean to the proud Greek city-states. Seeking revenge for a Greek insult, he sent messengers throughout Greece. The messengers demanded gifts of "earth and water"—symbols of submission to Darius I.

Many of the city-states obeyed Darius' demand. After all, the Persian empire was the most powerful in the Mediterranean world. But Athens and Sparta were not so quick to submit. Instead, the Athenians threw Darius' messengers into a well, while the Spartans tossed them into a pit. The Persians, they said, could collect their own earth and water.

The Greek historian Herodotus (hih RAHD uh tuhs) told this story of Greek defiance and pride. Despite their cultural ties, the Greek city-states were often bitterly divided. Yet, when the Persians threatened, the Greeks briefly put aside their differences to defend their freedom.

The Persian Wars

By 500 B.C., Athens had emerged as the wealthiest Greek city-state. But Athens and the entire Greek world soon faced a fearsome threat from outside. The Persians, you will recall, conquered a huge empire stretching from Asia Minor to the border of India. Their subjects included the Greek city-states of Ionia in Asia Minor.

Though under Persian rule, these Ionian city-states were largely self-governing. Still, they resented their situation. In 499 B.C., Ionian Greeks rebelled against Persian rule. Athens sent ships to help them. As Herodotus wrote some years later, "These ships were the beginning of mischief both to the Greeks and to the barbarians."

Victory at Marathon The Persians soon crushed the rebel cities. However, Darius I was furious at Athens' role in the uprising. To keep his anger hot, reported Herodotus, he had a servant whisper to him at every meal, "Master, remember the Athenians."

In time, Darius I sent a huge force across the Aegean to punish Athens for its interference. The mighty Persian army landed near Marathon, a plain north of Athens, in 490 B.C. The Athenians asked for help from neighboring city-states, but received little support.

The Persians greatly outnumbered Athenian forces. Yet the invaders were amazed to see "a mere handful of men coming on at a run without either horsemen or archers." The Persians responded with a rain of arrows, but the Greeks rushed onward. They broke through the Persian line and

Did You Know?

The First Marathon

After the battle of Marathon, the Greeks sent Pheidippides, their fastest runner, to carry home news of the stunning victory. Though exhausted, he sprinted 26.2 miles to Athens. "Rejoice, we conquer," he gasped—then dropped dead. Today, in honor of Pheidippides, marathon runners still cover the same distance that he ran 2,500 years ago.

Theme: Continuity and Change Today, many American communities hold annual marathons. Why do you think such races are popular?

engaged the enemy in fierce hand-to-hand combat. Overwhelmed by the fury of the Athenian assault, the Persians hastily retreated to their ships.

The Athenians celebrated their triumph. Still, the Athenian leader, Themistocles (thuh MIHS tuh kleez), knew the victory at Marathon had bought only a temporary lull in the fighting. He urged Athenians to build a fleet of warships and prepare other defenses.

Renewed Attacks Darius died before he could mass his troops for another attack. But in 480 B.C., his son Xerxes (ZERK seez) sent a much larger force to conquer Greece. By this time, Athens had persuaded Sparta and other city-states to join in the fight against Persia.

Once again, the Persians landed an army in northern Greece. A small Spartan force guarded the narrow mountain pass at Thermopylae (thuhr MAHP uh lee). Led by the great warrior-king Leonidas, the Spartans held out heroically against the enormous Persian force. Herodotus described the heroic stand of the Spartans:

> "Here they defended themselves to the last, such as still had swords using them, and the others resisting with their hands and teeth; till the barbarians who . . . now encircled them upon every side, overwhelmed and buried the remnant that was left beneath showers of missile weapons."
> —Herodotus, *The Persian Wars*

After defeating the Spartans, the Persians marched south and burned Athens. The city was empty, however. The Athenians had withdrawn to safety.

The Greeks now put their faith in the fleet of ships that Themistocles had urged them to build. The Athenians lured the Persian navy into the narrow strait of Salamis. Athenian warships, powered by rowers, drove into the Persian boats with underwater battering rams. On the shore, Xerxes watched helplessly as his mighty fleet sank.

The following year, the Greeks defeated the Persians on land in Asia Minor. This victory marked the end of the Persian invasions. Although fighting continued for years, Greek raiders were on the offensive from this time on. In a brief moment of unity, the Greek city-states had saved themselves from the Persian threat.

Results Victory in the Persian Wars increased the Greeks' sense of their own uniqueness. The gods, they felt, had protected their superior form of government—the city-state—against invaders from Asia.

Athens emerged from the war as the most powerful city-state in Greece. To continue the struggle against Persia, it organized the Delian League, an alliance with other Greek city-states. An **alliance** is a formal agreement between two or more nations or powers to cooperate and come to one another's defense.

From the start, Athens dominated the Delian League. It slowly used its position of leadership to create an Athenian empire. It moved the league treasury from the island of Delos to Athens, using money contributed by other city-states to rebuild its own city. When its allies protested and tried

Persian Wars, 490 B.C.–479 B.C.

MACEDONIA

PERSIAN EMPIRE

Thermopylae
Thebes
Marathon
Salamis · Athens
PELOPONNESUS · ATTICA
Sparta · Delos
LACONIA

Aegean Sea

IONIA

Sardis

Mediterranean Sea

Crete

40°N
36°N
24°E
28°E

Areas settled by Greeks
Route of Xerxes' fleet
Route of Persian army
Battle sites
Athenian empire about 450 B.C.

Alber's Equal Area Projection
0   50   100 Miles
0   50   100 Kilometers

N W E S

Skills Assessment

Geography When the Persian empire attacked Greece, the Greek city-states briefly joined forces to defend their independence.

1. **Location** On the map, locate **(a)** Athens, **(b)** Sparta, **(c)** Marathon, **(d)** Thermopylae, **(e)** Salamis.
2. **Movement** Describe the route of the Persian army toward Athens.
3. **Critical Thinking Making Inferences** Why do you think Xerxes' fleet hugged the coastline instead of sailing directly across the Aegean?

to withdraw from the league, Athens used force to make them remain. Yet, while Athens was enforcing its will abroad, Athenian leaders were championing political freedom at home.

Athens in the Age of Pericles

The years after the Persian Wars were a golden age for Athens. Under the able statesman Pericles (PEHR uh kleez), the economy thrived and the government became more democratic. Because of his wise and skillful leadership, the period from 460 B.C. to 429 B.C. is often called the Age of Pericles.

Political Life Periclean Athens was a direct democracy. Under this system, a large number of citizens take direct part in the day-to-day affairs of government. By contrast, in most democratic countries today, citizens participate in government indirectly through elected representatives.

By the time of Pericles, the Athenian assembly met several times a month. At least 6,000 members had to be present in order to decide important issues. Pericles believed that all male citizens, regardless of wealth or social class, should take part in government. Athens therefore began to pay a stipend, or fixed salary, to men who held public office. This reform enabled poor men to serve in government.

In addition to serving in the assembly, Athenians served on juries. A jury is a panel of citizens who have the authority to make the final judgment in a trial. Unlike a modern American trial jury, which is usually made up of 12 members, an Athenian jury might include hundreds or even thousands of jurors. Male citizens over 30 years of age were chosen by lot to serve on the jury for a year. Like members of the assembly, jurors received a stipend.

Athenian citizens could also vote to banish, or send away, a public figure whom they saw as a threat to their democracy. This process was called ostracism (AHS trah sihzm). To ostracize someone, a citizen wrote that person's name on a piece of pottery. Depending on the number of votes cast, an ostracized individual would have to live outside the city, usually for a period of 10 years.

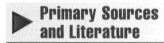

▶ Primary Sources and Literature

See "Thucydides: A History of the Peloponnesian War" in the Reference Section at the back of this book.

The Funeral Oration Thucydides (thoo SIHD uh deez), a historian who lived in the Age of Pericles, recorded a speech given by Pericles at the funeral of Athenians slain in battle. In this famous Funeral Oration, Pericles praised the Athenian form of government. He pointed out that, in Athens, power rested in the hands "not of a minority but of the whole people."

In the Funeral Oration, Pericles stressed not only the rights but also the duties of citizenship. As citizens of a democracy, he said, Athenians bore a special responsibility. "We alone," he stated, "regard a man who takes no interest in public affairs, not as a harmless but as a useless character." Today, Pericles' Funeral Oration is considered one of the earliest and greatest expressions of democratic ideals.

Economic and Cultural Life Athens prospered during the Age of Pericles. With the riches of the Athenian empire, Pericles hired the best architects and sculptors to rebuild the Acropolis, which the Persians had destroyed. Magnificent new temples and colossal statues rose from the ruins of the Acropolis. Such building projects increased Athenians' prosperity by creating jobs for artisans and workers. They also served as a further reminder to both citizens and visitors that the gods had favored the Athenians.

With the help of an educated foreign-born woman named Aspasia, Pericles turned Athens into the cultural center of Greece. Pericles and Aspasia surrounded themselves with thinkers, writers, and artists. Through building programs and public festivals, they supported the arts. In the next section, you will read about Greek contributions to architecture, art, literature, history, and philosophy.

How Should a Society's Leaders Be Chosen?

In his Gettysburg Address, Abraham Lincoln expressed his abiding belief in democracy, which he described as "government of the people, by the people, and for the people." But through the years, not everyone has agreed that democracy is the best form of government. Consider the following viewpoints.

Greece 400s B.C.

In a famous Funeral Oration, Pericles praised the Athenian form of government:

66 Our constitution is called a democracy because power is in the hands not of a minority but of the whole people. . . . When it is a question of putting one person before another in positions of public responsibility, what counts is not membership of a particular class, but the ability the man possesses. 99

United States 1787

Alexander Hamilton, a Caribbean-born statesman who helped shape the Constitution, distrusted ordinary citizens:

66 All communities divide themselves into the few and the many. The first are rich and well-born, the other the mass of the people. . . . The people are turbulent and changing; they seldom judge or determine right. Give therefore to the first class a distinct, permanent share in the government. 99

Algeria 1990s

The Arabic writing on this poster says "Your election equals the restoration of the country's glory."

Chile 1986

Santiago Sinclair, an aide to Chilean military dictator Augusto Pinochet, defended the right of strong leaders to take power into their own hands:

66 Command is voice, conscience, justice. . . . Command guides spirits and unites wills, carrying them to success. . . . 99

Skills Assessment

1. Which writer seems most opposed to choosing leaders in a democratic way?
   A Pericles
   B Hamilton
   C Sinclair
   D the creator of the voting poster

2. With which statement would Pericles agree?
   E Class is more important than ability.
   F The minority should rule.
   G Leaders know best.
   H Power should be shared by all.

3. **Critical Thinking** **Making Decisions** For more than 200 years, people in the United States have been concerned with the way elections are run. If you could change one thing about the American elections, what would it be? Why?

Skills Tip

Someone may express an opinion that is not necessarily what you would expect. A person's background, as well as the time and place in which he or she lived, may have influenced his or her way of thinking.

The Peloponnesian War

The power of Athens contained the seeds of disaster. Many Greeks outside of Athens resented Athenian domination. Before long, the Greek world split into rival camps. To counter the Delian League, Sparta and other enemies of Athens formed the Peloponnesian League. Sparta encouraged oligarchy in the cities of the Peloponnesian League, while Athens supported democracy among its allies.

In 431 B.C., warfare broke out in earnest between Athens and Sparta. The Peloponnesian War soon engulfed all of Greece. The fighting would drag on for 27 years.

Greek Against Greek   Despite its riches and powerful navy, Athens faced a serious geographic disadvantage. Sparta was located inland, so it could not be attacked from the sea. Yet Sparta had only to march north to attack Athens by land.

When Sparta invaded Athens, Pericles allowed people from the surrounding countryside to move inside the city walls. The overcrowded conditions soon led to disaster. A terrible plague broke out, killing at least a third of the population, including Pericles himself. His successors were much less able leaders. Their power struggles quickly undermined the city's democratic government.

As the war dragged on, each side committed savage acts against the other. Sparta even allied itself with Persia, the longtime enemy of the Greeks. Finally, in 404 B.C., with the help of the Persian navy, the Spartans captured Athens. The victors stripped Athenians of their fleet and empire. However, Sparta rejected calls from its allies to destroy Athens, possibly out of respect for the city's role in the Persian Wars.

The Aftermath of War   The Peloponnesian War ended Athenian domination of the Greek world. The Athenian economy eventually revived and Athens remained the cultural center of Greece. However, its spirit and vitality declined. In Athens, as elsewhere in the Greek world, democratic government suffered. Corruption and selfish interests replaced older ideals such as service to the city-state.

For the next century, fighting continued to disrupt the Greek world. Sparta itself soon suffered defeat at the hands of Thebes, another Greek city-state. As Greeks battled among themselves, a new power rose in Macedonia (mas uh DOHN ee yuh), a kingdom to the north. By 359 B.C., its ambitious ruler stood poised to conquer the quarrelsome Greek city-states.

Primary Source

The Plague in Athens
The Greek historian Thucydides describes the unknown plague that struck Athens in 430 B.C.:

"Bodies of dying men lay one upon another, and half-dead people rolled about in the streets and, in their longing for water, near all the fountains. The temples, too, in which they had quartered themselves were full of the corpses of them who had died in them; for the calamity which weighed upon them was so overpowering that men, not knowing what was to become of them, became careless of all law, sacred as well as profane [worldly]. And the customs which they had hitherto observed regarding burial were all thrown into confusion, and they buried their dead each one as he could."

—Thucydides, *A History of the Peloponnesian War*

Skills Assessment

Primary Source What strains would a plague such as this put on a society?

SECTION 3 Assessment

Recall
1. **Identify:** (a) Marathon, (b) Themistocles, (c) Delian League, (d) Pericles, (e) Aspasia.
2. **Define:** (a) alliance, (b) direct democracy, (c) stipend, (d) jury, (e) ostracism.

Comprehension
3. Describe two effects of the Persian Wars.
4. How did Pericles contribute to Athenian greatness?
5. How did the growth of Athenian power lead to war?

Critical Thinking and Writing
6. **Linking Past and Present** Compare Athenian democracy during the Age of Pericles to American democracy today. (a) How are they similar? (b) How are they different?
7. **Recognizing Causes and Effects** (a) What were the reasons that the Athenians and the Spartans formed their rival alliances? (b) Do nations today form alliances with one another for the same reasons? Explain.

Activity

Drawing a Political Cartoon Draw a political cartoon commenting on the causes or effects of the Peloponnesian War. Take the viewpoint of either an Athenian or a Spartan.

The Glory That Was Greece

Reading Focus

- What political and ethical ideas did Greek philosophers develop?
- What were the goals of Greek architects and artists?
- What themes did Greek writers and historians explore?

Vocabulary

logic
rhetoric
tragedy
comedy

Taking Notes

Copy the concept web at right. Include three or four blank circles. As you read, fill in each blank circle with important facts to remember about Greek civilization. Two circles have been completed to help you get started.

Philosophy

GREEK CIVILIZATION

Plato describes ideal government

Main Idea Greek thinkers, artists, and writers explored the nature of the universe and the place of people in it.

Setting the Scene Despite wars and political turmoil, Greeks had confidence in the power of the human mind. "We cultivate the mind," boasted Pericles. "We are lovers of the beautiful, yet simple in our tastes." Driven by curiosity and a belief in reason, Greek thinkers, artists, and writers explored the nature of the universe and the place of people in it.

To later admirers, Greek achievements in the arts represented the height of human development in the western world. They looked back with deep respect on what one poet called "the glory that was Greece."

Greek Philosophers

As you read, some Greek thinkers challenged the belief that events were caused by the whims of gods. Instead, they used observation and reason to find causes for what happened. The Greeks called these thinkers philosophers, meaning "lovers of wisdom."

Greek philosophers explored many subjects, from mathematics and music to logic, or rational thinking. Through reason and observation, they believed, they could discover laws that governed the universe. Much modern science traces its roots to the Greek search for such principles.

Ethical Issues Other Greek philosophers were more interested in ethics and morality. They debated such questions as what was the best kind of government and what standards should rule human behavior.

In Athens, the Sophists questioned accepted ideas. To them, success was more important than moral truth. They developed skills in rhetoric, the art of skillful speaking. Ambitious men could use clever rhetoric to advance their careers. The turmoil of the Peloponnesian War led many young Athenians to follow the Sophists. Older citizens, however, accused the Sophists of undermining traditional values.

Socrates One outspoken critic of the Sophists was Socrates, an Athenian stonemason and philosopher. Most of what we know about Socrates comes from his student Plato. Socrates himself wrote no books. Instead, he lounged around the marketplace, asking his fellow citizens about their beliefs. Using a process we now call the Socratic method, he would pose a series of questions to his students and challenge them to examine the implications of their answers. To Socrates, this patient examination was a way to help others seek truth and self-knowledge. To many Athenians, however, such questioning was a threat to accepted traditions.

Biography

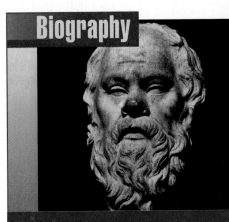

Socrates 469 B.C.–399 B.C.

To most Athenians, Socrates was not an impressive figure. Tradition tells us that his clothes were untidy and he made a poor living. But young men loved to watch him as he questioned citizens, leading them to contradict themselves.

Many Athenians found Socrates annoying—and he knew it. When he was put on trial, he told the jury, "All day long and in all places I am always fastening upon you, stirring you and persuading you and reproaching you. You will not easily find another like me." But Plato had a different view of his teacher. He called Socrates "the wisest, justest, and best of all I have ever known."

Socrates said, "The unexamined life is not worth living." How did his actions support this idea?

When he was about 70 years old, Socrates was put on trial. His enemies accused him of corrupting the city's youth and failing to respect the gods. Standing before a jury of 501 citizens, Socrates offered a calm defense. But the jurors condemned him to death. Loyal to the laws of Athens, Socrates accepted the death penalty. He drank a cup of hemlock, a deadly poison.

Plato   The execution of Socrates left Plato with a lifelong distrust of democracy. He fled Athens for 10 years. When he returned, he set up a school called the Academy. There, he taught and wrote about his own ideas. Like Socrates, Plato emphasized the importance of reason. Through rational thought, he argued, people could discover unchanging ethical values, recognize perfect beauty, and learn how best to organize society.

In *The Republic*, Plato described his vision of an ideal state. He rejected Athenian democracy because it had condemned Socrates. Instead, Plato argued that the state should regulate every aspect of its citizens' lives in order to provide for their best interests. He divided his ideal society into three classes: workers to produce the necessities of life, soldiers to defend the state, and philosophers to rule. This elite class of leaders would be specially trained to ensure order and justice. The wisest of them, a philosopher-king, would have the ultimate authority.

Plato thought that, in general, men surpassed women in mental and physical tasks, but that some women were superior to some men. Talented women, he said, should be educated to serve the state. The ruling elite, both men and women, would take military training together and raise their children in communal centers for the good of the republic.

Aristotle   Plato's most famous student, Aristotle, developed his own ideas about government. He analyzed all forms of government, from monarchy to democracy, and found good and bad examples of each. Like Plato, he was suspicious of democracy, which he thought could lead to mob rule. In the end, he favored rule by a single strong and virtuous leader.

Aristotle also addressed the question of how people ought to live. In his view, good conduct meant pursuing the "golden mean," a moderate course between extremes. He promoted reason as the guiding force for learning.

Aristotle set up a school, the Lyceum, for the study of all branches of knowledge. He left writings on politics, ethics, logic, biology, literature, and many other subjects. When the first European universities evolved some 1,500 years later, their courses were largely based on the works of Aristotle.

Architecture and Art

Plato argued that every object on Earth had an ideal form. The work of Greek artists and architects reflected a similar concern with balance, order, and beauty.

Architecture   Greek architects sought to convey a sense of perfect balance to reflect the harmony and order of the universe. The most famous example of Greek architecture is the Parthenon, a temple dedicated to the goddess Athena. The basic plan of the Parthenon is a simple rectangle, with tall columns supporting a gently sloping roof. The delicate curves add dignity and grace.

Greek architecture has been widely admired for centuries. Today, you can see many public buildings that have adopted various kinds of Greek columns.

Sculpture and Painting   Early Greek sculptors carved figures in rigid poses, perhaps imitating Egyptian styles. By 450 B.C., Greek sculptors had developed a new style that emphasized natural poses. While their work was lifelike, it was also idealistic. That is, sculptors carved gods, goddesses,

Primary Sources and Literature

See "Aristotle: The Politics" in the Reference Section at the back of this book.

Connections to Today

The Parthenon in Danger
The Parthenon has survived nearly 2,500 years. It even withstood being blown up. In 1687, the temple was used to store gunpowder. An explosion damaged the roof and many of the columns.

Today, the Parthenon faces an even greater danger. Air pollution is slowly eating away the ancient marble. Scientists say the temple could be destroyed in a century. International teams are now working to shore up the building. Restorers are using a different-colored stone, so visitors can tell which parts are original.

Theme: Global Interaction
Why do you think people from many different countries are interested in saving the Parthenon?

Virtual Field Trip

www.phschool.com

The Acropolis
Athens, Greece

To see other images of the ancient buildings on the Acropolis, use the Internet address above to link to the Ancient City of Athens.

The Acropolis
The buildings on the Acropolis stand as proud monuments of classical Greek architecture. The most revered temple on the Acropolis is the Parthenon, with its balanced rows of majestic columns.

Theme: Art and Literature
Based on this picture, what kinds of modern buildings were influenced by the style of the Parthenon?

athletes, and famous men in a way that showed individuals in their most perfect, graceful form.

The only Greek paintings to survive are on vases and other pottery. They offer intriguing views of Greek life. Women carry water from wells, warriors race into battle, and athletes compete in javelin contests. Each scene is designed to fit the shape of the pottery.

Poetry and Drama

In literature, as in art, the ancient Greeks developed their own style. To later Europeans, Greek styles were a model of perfection. They admired what they called the "classical style," referring to the elegant, balanced forms of traditional Greek works.

Greek literature began with the epics of Homer, whose stirring tales inspired later writers. In later times, Sappho sang of love and of the beauty of her island home, and Pindar celebrated the victors in athletic contests.

Beginnings of Greek Drama   Perhaps the most important Greek contribution to literature was in the field of drama. The first Greek plays evolved out of religious festivals, especially those held in Athens to honor Dionysus (di uh NĪ suhs), god of fertility and wine. Plays were performed in large outdoor theaters with little or no scenery. Actors wore elaborate costumes and stylized masks. A chorus sang or chanted comments on the action.

Greek dramas were often based on popular myths and legends. Through these familiar stories, playwrights discussed moral and social issues or explored the relationship between people and the gods.

Tragedy   The greatest Athenian playwrights were Aeschylus (EHS kuh luhs), Sophocles (SAHF uh kleez), and Euripides (yu RIHP uh deez). All three wrote tragedies, plays that told stories of human suffering that usually ended in disaster. The purpose of tragedy, the Greeks felt, was to stir emotions of pity and fear. In *The Oresteia* (ohr eh STEE uh), for example, Aeschylus showed a powerful family torn apart by betrayal, murder, and revenge. Audiences saw how pride could cause horrifying misfortune and how the gods could bring down even the greatest heroes.

In *Antigone* (an TIHG uh nee), Sophocles explored what happens when an individual's moral duty conflicts with the laws of the state. Antigone

Alexander and the Hellenistic Age

Reading Focus

- How did Alexander the Great build a huge empire?
- What were the results of Alexander's conquests?
- How did individuals contribute to Hellenistic civilization?

Vocabulary

assassination
assimilate
heliocentric

Taking Notes

Copy this chart. As you read, fill in the chart with examples of contributions made during the Hellenistic period. Parts of the chart have been filled in to help you get started.

ACHIEVEMENTS OF THE HELLENISTIC AGE

| • Art and architecture | • Philosophy | • Mathematics and science | • Medicine |

Main Idea Alexander the Great created a large empire and spread Greek culture throughout the region.

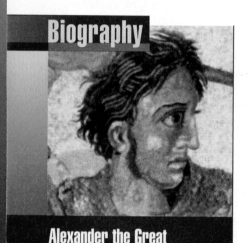

Biography

Alexander the Great
356 B.C.–323 B.C.

As a boy, Alexander had heard tales of Achilles, hero of the *Iliad*. The legendary Greek warrior was all a soldier should be—brave, daring, strong, and almost unbeatable. Alexander saw himself as a second Achilles.

From his tutor, Aristotle, young Alexander acquired a love of learning and the arts, but he was first and foremost a warrior. When Thebes rebelled, he ordered the city to be burned and its inhabitants to be killed or sold into slavery. But he told his soldiers to spare one house—the house where the Greek poet Pindar had once lived.

Theme: Impact of the Individual Why do you think Alexander refused to burn Pindar's house?

Setting the Scene

"He is always taking in more, everywhere casting his net around us, while we sit idle and do nothing!" Demosthenes (dih MAHS thuh neez) was warning his fellow Athenians about Philip II, the king of Macedonia. Bit by bit, Philip was bringing Greece under his rule. "When," asked Demosthenes, "will you Athenians take the necessary action?"

When Athenians finally did take action against Philip, it was too late. Athens and the other Greek city-states lost their independence. Yet the disaster ushered in a new age in which Greek influence spread from the Mediterranean to the borders of India. The architect of this new era was Philip's son, known to history as Alexander the Great.

Alexander the Great

To the Greeks, the rugged, mountainous kingdom of Macedonia was a backward, half-civilized land. The rulers of this frontier land, in fact, were of Greek origin and kept ties to their Greek neighbors. As a youth, Philip had lived in Thebes and had come to admire Greek culture. Later, he hired Aristotle as a tutor to his young son Alexander.

Philip's Dream When Philip gained the throne in 359 B.C., he dreamed of conquering the prosperous city-states to the south. He built a superb army. Through threats, bribery, and diplomacy, he formed alliances with many Greek city-states. Others he conquered. In 338 B.C., when Athens and Thebes joined forces against him, he defeated them at the battle of Chaeronea (kehr uh NEE uh). Philip then brought all of Greece under his control.

Philip had a still grander dream—to conquer the Persian empire. Before he could achieve that plan, though, he was assassinated at his daughter's wedding. Assassination is the murder of a public figure, usually for political reasons. Philip's determined wife, Olympias, then outmaneuvered his other wives and children to put her own son, Alexander, on the throne.

Conquest of Persia Alexander was only 20 years old. Yet he was already an experienced soldier who shared his father's ambitions. With Greece subdued, he began organizing the forces needed to conquer Persia. By 334 B.C., he had enough ships to cross the Dardanelles, the strait separating Europe from Asia Minor.

Persia was no longer the great power it had once been. The emperor Darius III was weak, and the provinces were often in rebellion against him. Still, the Persian empire stretched more than 2,000 miles from Egypt to India.

Empire of Alexander the Great

Legend:
- Macedonia, 336 B.C.
- Alexander's empire at its height, 323 B.C.
- → Route of Alexander, 334 B.C.–323 B.C.
- ○ Towns founded by Alexander and his followers

Albers Equal Area Projection
0 250 500 Miles
0 250 500 Kilometers

Map labels: Danube R., Black Sea, CAUCASUS MTS., Aral Sea, Jaxartes R., Caspian Sea, Oxus R., MACEDONIA, Dardanelles, Troy, Athens, Aegean Sea, ASIA MINOR, Gordium, Mediterranean Sea, Issus, Thapsacus, Tigris R., Euphrates R., Ecbatana, Alexandria, Alexandria, HINDU KUSH, Alexandropolis, Alexandria, Nicaea, Bucephala, Indus R., PERSIA, Tyre, Damascus, Jerusalem, Gaza, PALESTINE, Babylon, *Alexander's death, 323 B.C.*, Susa, Alexandria, Persepolis, Alexandria, Alexandria, Alexandria, Alexandria, Memphis, Nile R., Red Sea, Persian Gulf, Arabian Sea, Tropic of Cancer

Alexander won his first victory against the Persians at the Granicus River. He then moved from victory to victory, marching through Asia Minor into Palestine and south to Egypt. In 331 B.C., he took Babylon, then seized the other Persian capitals. But before Alexander could capture Darius, the Persian emperor was murdered.

Onward to India With much of the Persian empire under his control, the restless Alexander headed farther east. He crossed the Hindu Kush into northern India. There, in 326 B.C., his troops for the first time faced soldiers mounted on war elephants. Although Alexander never lost a battle, his soldiers were tired of the long campaign and refused to go farther east. Reluctantly, Alexander agreed to turn back. After a long, hard march, they reached Babylon, where Alexander began planning a new campaign.

Sudden Death Before he could set out again, Alexander fell victim to a sudden fever. As he lay dying, his commanders asked to whom he left his immense empire. "To the strongest," he is said to have whispered.

In fact, no one leader proved strong enough to succeed Alexander. Instead, after years of disorder, three generals divided up the empire. Macedonia and Greece went to one general, Egypt to another, and most of Persia to a third. For 300 years, their descendants competed for power over the lands Alexander had conquered.

The Legacy of Alexander

Although Alexander's empire soon crumbled, he had unleashed changes that would ripple across the Mediterranean world and the Middle East for centuries. His most lasting achievement was the spread of Greek culture.

Skills Assessment

Geography Alexander's ambitions led him to conquer lands across a wide area.

1. **Location** On the map, locate **(a)** Aegean Sea, **(b)** Arabian Sea, **(c)** Euphrates River, **(d)** Indus River, **(e)** Macedonia, **(f)** Persia.

2. **Region** Locate the map Assyrian and Persian Empires, *which appears in an earlier chapter. Which parts of Alexander's empire had not been part of the Persian empire?*

3. **Critical Thinking Predicting Consequences** *Judging from this map, do you think Alexander's empire would be difficult to keep united? Explain.*

Global Connections

The Seven Wonders of the Ancient World

Around 100 B.C., a Hellenistic traveler named the lighthouse at Alexandria as one of the Seven Wonders of the World. This famous list of awesome structures also included the Hanging Gardens of Babylon and the Colossus, a 100-foot bronze statue on the Aegean island of Rhodes.

Since then, six of the Seven Wonders of the Ancient World have been destroyed, including the Pharos. Only the pyramids of ancient Egypt—the oldest structures on the list—are still standing.

Theme: Arts and Literature
What structures would you include on a list of Seven Wonders of the Modern World?

A Blending of Cultures   Across his far-flung empire, Alexander founded many new cities, most of them named after him. The generals who succeeded him founded still more. Greek soldiers, traders, and artisans settled these new cities. From Egypt to the borders of India, they built Greek temples, filled them with Greek statues, and held athletic contests as they had in Greece. Local people assimilated, or absorbed, Greek ideas. In turn, Greek settlers adopted local customs.

Gradually, a blending of eastern and western cultures occurred. Alexander had encouraged this blending when he married a Persian woman and urged his soldiers to follow his example. He had also adopted many Persian customs, including Persian dress. After his death, a vital new culture emerged which blended Greek, Persian, Egyptian, and Indian influences. This Hellenistic civilization would flourish for centuries.

Alexandria   At the very heart of the Hellenistic world stood the city of Alexandria, Egypt. Located on the sea lanes between Europe and Asia, its markets boasted a wide range of goods, from Greek marble to Arabian spices to East African ivory. A Greek architect had drawn up plans for the city, which would become home to almost a million people. Greeks, Egyptians, Persians, Hebrews, and many others crowded its busy streets. Among the city's marvelous sights was the Pharos, an enormous lighthouse that soared 440 feet into the air.

Alexander and his successors encouraged the work of scholars. The rulers of Alexandria built the great Museum as a center of learning.* The Museum boasted laboratories, lecture halls, and a zoo. Its well-stocked library had thousands of scrolls representing the accumulated knowledge of the ancient world. Unfortunately, the library was later destroyed in a fire.

Opportunities for Women   Paintings, statues, and legal codes show that women were no longer restricted to their homes during the Hellenistic period. More women learned to read and write. Some became philosophers or poets. Royal women held considerable power, working alongside husbands and sons who were the actual rulers. In Egypt, the able and clever queen Cleopatra came to rule in her own right.

Hellenistic Civilization

The cities of the Hellenistic world employed armies of architects and artists. Temples, palaces, and other public buildings were much larger and grander than the buildings of classical Greece. The elaborate new style reflected the desire of Hellenistic rulers to glorify themselves as godlike monarchs.

New Schools of Thought   Political turmoil during the Hellenistic age contributed to the rise of new schools of philosophy. The most influential was Stoicism. Its founder, Zeno, urged people to avoid desires and disappointments by accepting calmly whatever life brought. Stoics preached high moral standards, such as the idea of protecting the rights of fellow humans. They taught that all people, including women and slaves, though unequal in society, were morally equal because all had the power of reason. Stoicism later influenced many Roman and Christian thinkers.

Advances in Learning   During the Hellenistic age, thinkers built on earlier Greek, Babylonian, and Egyptian knowledge. In mathematics, Pythagoras (pih THAG uhr uhs) derived a formula ($a^2 + b^2 = c^2$) to calculate the relationship between the sides of a right triangle. Euclid wrote *The Elements*, a textbook that became the basis for modern geometry.

Using mathematics and careful observation, the astronomer Aristarchus (ar ihs TAHR kuhs) argued that the Earth rotated on its axis and orbited

---

* *Museum* means "house of the Muses." The Muses were nine Greek goddesses who presided over the arts and sciences.

around the sun. This theory of a heliocentric, or sun-centered, solar system was not accepted by most scientists until almost 2,000 years later. Another Hellenistic astronomer, Eratosthenes, (air uh TAHS thu neez), showed that the Earth was round and accurately calculated its circumference.

The most famous Hellenistic scientist, Archimedes (ahr kuh MEE deez), applied principles of physics to make practical inventions. He mastered the use of the lever and pulley. He boasted, "Give me a lever long enough and a place to stand on, and I will move the world." An awed audience watched as he used his invention to draw a ship onto shore.

Medicine About 400 B.C., the Greek physician Hippocrates (hih PAHK ruh teez) studied the causes of illnesses and looked for cures. His Hippocratic oath set ethical standards for doctors. Physicians swore to "help the sick according to my ability and judgment but never with a view to injury and wrong" and to protect the privacy of patients. Doctors today take a similar oath.

Looking Ahead

During the Hellenistic period, Rome emerged as a powerful new state. After its conquest of Asia Minor in 133 B.C., it replaced Greece as the dominant power in the Mediterranean world. Still, by then, the Greeks had already made their greatest contributions.

Greek ideas about law, freedom, justice, and government have influenced political thinking to the present day. In the arts and sciences, Greek works set a standard for later people of Europe. These achievements were especially remarkable because they were produced by a scattering of tiny city-states whose rivalries cost them their freedom. In later chapters, you will see how the Greek legacy influenced the civilizations of Rome and of Western Europe.

Cause *and* Effect

Causes

- Rise of civilizations in Persia, Egypt, and Greece
- Macedonian conquest of Greece
- Growth of Alexander's empire from Greece to northern India
- Growing contacts among kingdoms of eastern Mediterranean and Middle East

Rise of Hellenistic Civilization

Effects

- Learning and arts encouraged by Alexander and his successors
- Alexandria, Egypt, becomes center of trade and learning
- Spread of Greek, Middle Eastern, and Persian religions
- Spread of Christianity

Connections to Today

- Continued practice of Christianity and Judaism in the region
- Alexandria, Egypt, still a center of learning
- Greek architecture still visible in ruins across Middle East

Skills Assessment **Chart** Although Alexander's empire split apart soon after his death, his conquests had an impact that endured for centuries. **How did the conquests of Alexander the Great encourage contact among different Mediterranean civilizations?**

SECTION 5 Assessment

Recall

1. **Identify:** (a) Philip of Macedonia, (b) Stoicism, (c) Pythagoras, (d) Euclid, (e) Archimedes, (f) Hippocrates.
2. **Define:** (a) assassination, (b) assimilate, (c) heliocentric.

Comprehension

3. What was the extent of Alexander's vast empire?
4. How did Alexander's conquests lead to a new civilization?

5. What new ideas did the Stoics introduce?

Critical Thinking and Writing

6. **Defending a Position** Would you agree that Alexander deserved to be called "the Great"? Why or why not?
7. **Ranking** What do you think were the three most important contributions made by Hellenistic scientists and mathematicians? Explain.

Activity

Take It to the NET

Use the Internet to research the lasting effects of Alexander and his ideas on the areas he conquered. Then, create a poster entitled "The Lasting Legacy of Alexander the Great."

Creating a Chapter Summary

Copy this graphic organizer on a sheet of paper. For each period of ancient Greek history, identify the time period and list three or four characteristics and achievements.

MINOAN CIVILIZATION 1750 B.C.–1500 B.C.
1. Traded with other Mediterranean people.
2.

MYCENAEAN CIVILIZATION
1.
2.

GREEK CITY-STATES
1.
2.

HELLENISTIC CIVILIZATION
1.
2.

CD-ROM Review For additional review of the major concepts of Chapter 5, see the *Guide to the Essentials of World History* or the *Interactive Student Tutorial CD-ROM.*

Web Site Self-Test For practice test questions for Chapter 5, see **www.phschool.com**

Building Vocabulary

Write sentences using the chapter vocabulary words listed below; leave blanks where the vocabulary words should go. Exchange your sentences with another student and fill in the blanks in each other's sentences.

1. fresco
2. strait
3. aristocracy
4. tyrant
5. alliance
6. direct democracy
7. jury
8. logic
9. tragedy
10. assimilate

Recalling Key Facts

11. What were the *Iliad* and the *Odyssey?*
12. How did mountains help shape the development of Greek civilization?
13. **(a)** What was the social status of women in Sparta and in Athens? **(b)** How did the status of women change during the Hellenistic period?
14. What were the results of the Persian Wars?
15. What is the Socratic method?
16. What cultures blended to form Hellenistic civilization?

Critical Thinking and Writing

17. **Connecting to Geography** How did the geography and climate of Greece and the Aegean influence the development of Greek civilization?
18. **Analyzing Information** **(a)** How did Athenian culture stress the importance of the individual? Give two examples. **(b)** Do you think there is a relationship between the importance placed on the individual and the development of democracy? Explain.
19. **Recognizing Causes and Effects** **(a)** Identify two immediate and two long-range causes of the Peloponnesian War. **(b)** Why might it be said that all Greeks were losers in this war?
20. **Synthesizing Information** **(a)** How was the form of government outlined in Plato's *Republic* similar to the government of Sparta? **(b)** How was it different?
21. **Linking Past and Present** Reread the description of the Hippocratic oath. **(a)** How did Hippocrates address the question of medical ethics? **(b)** What ethical issues do doctors face today?

The excerpt below is from a pamphlet written by an anonymous Greek calling himself the Old Oligarch. Read the excerpt and answer the questions that follow.

"[The Athenians] have chosen to let the worst people be better off than the good. Therefore, on this account I do not think well of their constitution. But since they have decided to have it so, I intend to point out how well they preserve their constitution and accomplish those other things for which the rest of the Greeks criticize them.

First I want to say this: There the poor and the people generally are right to have more than the highborn and wealthy for the reason that it is the people who man the ships and impart strength to the city. . . .

Everywhere on earth the best element is opposed to democracy. For among the best people there is minimal wantonness [undisciplined behavior] and injustice but a maximum of care for what is good, whereas among the people there is a maximum of ignorance, disorder, and wickedness."

—Old Oligarch, *The Constitution of the Athenians*

22. According to the Old Oligarch, what do the other Greek city-states think about the Athenian political system?
23. According to the Old Oligarch, why is it proper that Athens have a democracy?
24. **(a)** According to the Old Oligarch, who would support democracy in Athens? **(b)** Who would oppose it?
25. This anonymous author chose to call himself the Old Oligarch. **(a)** What was an oligarchy? **(b)** What does the writer's choice of a name indicate about his own social and economic status?
26. What do you think the Old Oligarch means when he refers to the "best" and the "worst" people?
27. Would you consider the Old Oligarch's view of Athenian democracy to be biased? Explain.

Skills Tip

When you analyze a primary source, keep in mind the author's own background. Factors such as age, education, social class, or economic status often influence a person's point of view.

The scene below is from a Greek painting that was created in the 400s B.C. It shows a group of Athenian women preparing a young bride for her wedding. Look at the painting, and then answer the questions that follow.

28. **(a)** What is the subject of this picture? **(b)** Who are the central figures?
29. To what social class would you say these women belonged?
30. What kinds of information about the lives of these women can you get from this painting? Identify at least three details.
31. Based on what you have read about surviving Greek artworks, where would you find this painting?
32. Compare the representations of the human form in Greek painting and Egyptian painting. **(a)** How are the two styles similar? **(b)** How are they different? **(c)** Why might there be some similarities between these two styles of painting?

Use the Internet to research information about the city-states in ancient Greece other than Athens and Sparta. Locate five of these city-states on a blank map of Greece. Then, make a fact sheet that includes two or three facts about each of these five city-states.

Ancient Rome and the Rise of Christianity

509 B.C.–A.D. 476

Chapter Preview

1 The Roman World Takes Shape
2 From Republic to Empire
3 The Roman Achievement
4 The Rise of Christianity
5 The Long Decline

509 B.C.
Romans set up a republic.

218 B.C.
The Carthaginian general Hannibal invades Italy during the Punic Wars between Rome and Carthage.

27 B.C.
The Roman republic ends, and the Roman empire begins under Emperor Augustus.

CHAPTER EVENTS

500 B.C.

300 B.C.

100 B.C.

GLOBAL EVENTS

321 B.C. Chandragupta begins the Maurya dynasty in India.

221 B.C. Shi Huangdi unites much of China.

The Roman Empire at Its Height

At its height, the Roman empire included lands in Europe, Africa, and Asia.

BRITAIN

GERMANY

GAUL

ALPS

Rhine R.

50°N

Danube R.

Black Sea

Roman empire, A.D. 117

40°N

PYRENEES MTS.

SPAIN

CORSICA

Rome

MACEDONIA

Byzantium

ASIA MINOR

Euphrates R.

Tigris R.

New Carthage

SARDINIA

Athens

Antioch

SYRIA

10°W

Carthage
Zama

SICILY

CYPRUS

Damascus

NUMIDIA

Mediterranean Sea

CRETE

ARABIA

30°N

Azimuthal Equal Area Projection

0   250   500 Miles

0   250   500 Kilometers

N
W   E
S

AFRICA

Cyrene

Alexandria

EGYPT

Nile R.

20°N

0°

10°E

20°E

30°E

40°E

Thebes

A.D. 392

Emperor Theodosius makes Christianity the official religion of the Roman empire. The cross and fish were Christian symbols.

A.D. 400s

Roman armies battle Hun and Germanic invaders. In A.D. 476, a Germanic leader seizes Rome.

| A.D. 100 | A.D. 300 | | A.D. 500 |

A.D. 220 In China, warlords overthrow the last Han emperor.

A.D. 350s About this time in Africa, armies from the kingdom of Axum conquer Nubia.

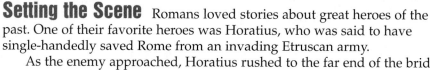

Reading Focus

- How did geography shape the early development of Rome?
- What were the major characteristics of government and society in the Roman republic?
- Why was Rome's expansion in Italy successful?

Vocabulary

republic
patrician
consul
dictator
plebeian
tribune
veto
legion

Taking Notes

At right is a partially completed outline of this section. As you read, finish the outline. Use Roman numerals for major headings, capital letters for subheadings, and numbers for supporting details.

I. Geography and peoples of Italy
  A. Geography
    1. Peninsula
    2.
  B.
II. The Roman republic
  A. The government takes shape
    1.
    2.
  B.

Main Idea   Rome developed a republican form of government based on strong civic virtues and gained control over much of the Italian peninsula.

Setting the Scene   Romans loved stories about great heroes of the past. One of their favorite heroes was Horatius, who was said to have single-handedly saved Rome from an invading Etruscan army.

As the enemy approached, Horatius rushed to the far end of the bridge that led into the city. Standing alone, he held off the attackers while his fellow Romans tore down the bridge behind him. As the last timber fell, Horatius flung himself into the river below. Dodging the spears raining down all around him, he swam safely to the other side.

The story of Horatius is more legend than it is history. Still, it helps us to understand the virtues that the Romans admired. Courage, loyalty, and devotion to duty were the pillars on which Romans would build an empire.

Geography and Peoples of Italy

Rome began as a small city-state in Italy but ended up ruling the entire Mediterranean world. The story of the Romans and how they built a world empire starts with the land where they lived.

Geography   The Italian peninsula looks like a boot, jutting into the Mediterranean Sea. The peninsula is centrally located in the Mediterranean, and the city of Rome is in the center of Italy. That location helped the Romans as they expanded, first in Italy, and then into lands around the Mediterranean.

Because of its geography, Italy was much easier to unify than Greece. Unlike Greece, Italy is not broken up into small, isolated valleys. In addition, the Apennine Mountains, which run like a backbone down the length of the Italian peninsula, are less rugged than the mountains of Greece. Finally, Italy has the advantage of broad, fertile plains, both in the north under the shadow of the Alps, and in the west, where the Romans settled. These plains supported a growing population.

Peoples   The ancestors of the Romans, the Latins, migrated into Italy by about 800 B.C. The Latins settled along the Tiber River in small villages scattered over seven low-lying hills where they herded and farmed. Those villages would in time grow into Rome, the city on seven hills.

The Romans shared the Italian peninsula with other peoples. Among them were Greek colonists whose city-states dotted southern Italy and the Etruscans who lived north of Rome. For a time, the Etruscans ruled much of central Italy, including Rome itself.

Etruscan Helmet
The Etruscans were skilled in metalworking, as is shown by the bronze helmet above. Romans learned much from the other peoples in Italy.

Theme: Diversity What other peoples lived in the Italian peninsula?

The Romans learned much from Etruscan civilization. They adapted the alphabet that the Etruscans had earlier acquired from the Greeks. They also learned to use the arch in building and adapted Etruscan engineering techniques to drain the marshy lands along the Tiber. Etruscan gods and goddesses merged with Roman deities.

The Roman Republic

The Romans drove out their Etruscan ruler in 509 B.C. This date is traditionally considered to mark the founding of the Roman state.

The Romans set up a new government in which some officials were chosen by the people. They called it a **republic,** or "thing of the people." A republic, Romans thought, would keep any individual from gaining too much power.

The Government Takes Shape In the early republic, the most powerful governing body was the senate. Its 300 members were all **patricians,** members of the landholding upper class. Senators, who served for life, made the laws.

Each year, the senators elected from the patrician class two **consuls.** Their job was to supervise the business of government and command the armies. Consuls, however, could serve only one term. They were also expected to consult with the senate. By limiting their time in office and making them responsible to the senate, Rome had a system of checks on the power of government.

In the event of war, the senate might choose a **dictator,** or ruler who has complete control over a government. Each Roman dictator was granted power to rule for six months. Then, he had to give up power. Romans admired Cincinnatus as a model dictator. Cincinnatus organized an army, led the Romans to victory over the attacking enemy, attended victory celebrations, and returned to his farmlands—all within 16 days.

Plebeians Demand Equality At first, all government officials were patricians. **Plebeians** (plih BEE uhnz), the farmers, merchants, artisans, and traders who made up the bulk of the population, had little influence. The efforts of the plebeians to gain power shaped politics in the early republic.

The plebeians' first breakthrough came in 450 B.C., when the government had the laws of Rome inscribed on 12 tablets and set up in the Forum, or marketplace. Plebeians had protested that citizens could not know what the laws were, because they were not written down. The Laws of the Twelve Tables made it possible for the first time for plebeians to appeal a judgment handed down by a patrician judge.

In time, the plebeians gained the right to elect their own officials, called **tribunes,** to protect their interests. The tribunes could **veto,** or block, those laws that they felt were harmful to plebeians. Little by little, plebeians forced the senate to choose plebeians as consuls, appoint plebeians to other high offices, and finally to open the senate itself to plebeians.

A Lasting Legacy Although the senate still dominated the government, the common people had gained access to power and won safeguards for their rights without having to resort to war or revolution. More than 2,000 years later, the framers of the United States Constitution would adapt such Roman ideas as the senate, the veto, and checks on political power.

Ancient Italy About 600 B.C.

Mercator Projection

Legend:
- Greeks
- Etruscans
- Carthaginians

Skills Assessment

Geography The Romans shared the Italian peninsula with other peoples, many of whose ideas they adapted for their own use.

1. **Location** On the map, locate **(a)** Rome, **(b)** Alps, **(c)** Mediterranean Sea, **(d)** Carthage, **(e)** Sicily.
2. **Region** Based on this map, which group do you think had the most influence on the Romans? Explain.
3. **Critical Thinking Comparing** Why was Italy easier to unite than Greece?

Virtual Field Trip

www.phschool.com

**Metropolitan Museum of Art
New York, New York**

To see other artworks and artifacts
relating to ancient Rome, use the
Internet address above to link to
the Metropolitan Museum of Art.

Roman Women
In this wall painting, a woman of the
patrician class is shown playing a
lyre. The girl standing behind her is
probably a servant or slave.

**Theme: Political and Social
Systems** Describe how a
portrait of a plebeian scene might
appear different from the scene
shown here.

Roman Society

The family was the basic unit of Roman society. Under Roman law, the
male head of the household, usually the father, had absolute power in the
family. He enforced strict discipline and demanded total respect for his
authority. His wife was subject to his authority and was not allowed to
administer her own affairs. The ideal Roman woman was loving, dutiful,
dignified, and strong.

Changing Role of Women Roman women played a larger role in society
than did Greek women. In later Roman times, women from all classes ran a
variety of businesses, from small shops to major shipyards. Those who
made their fortunes earned respect by supporting the arts or paying for
public festivals. Most women, though, worked at home, raising their families, spinning, and weaving.

Over the centuries, Roman women gained greater freedom and influence. Patrician women went to the public baths, dined out, and attended
the theater or other public entertainments with their husbands. Some
women, such as Livia and Agrippina the Younger, had highly visible public
roles and exercised significant political influence.

Education Girls and boys alike learned to read and write. Even lower-
class Romans were taught to write, as can be seen from the jokes and other
graffiti that archaeologists found scrawled on walls around the city.

By the late republic, many wealthy Romans were hiring private tutors,
often Greeks, to supervise the education of their children. Under their
guidance, children memorized major events and developments in Roman
history. Rhetoric was an important subject for boys who wanted to pursue
political careers.

Religion Roman gods and goddesses resembled those of the Etruscans
and Greeks. Like the Greek god Zeus, the Roman god Jupiter ruled over the
sky and the other gods. Juno, his wife, like the Greek goddess Hera, protected marriage. Romans also prayed to Neptune, god of the sea, whose

powers were the same as those of the Greek god Poseidon. On the battle-field, they turned to Mars, the god of war.

The Roman calendar was full of feasts and other celebrations to honor the gods and to ensure divine favor for the city. As loyal citizens, Romans joined in these festivals, which inspired a sense of community. Throughout Rome were dozens of temples where statues of the gods were housed. Inside these temples, Romans worshiped and asked for divine assistance.

Expansion in Italy

As Rome's political and social systems evolved at home, its armies expanded Roman power across Italy. Roman armies conquered first the Etruscans and then the Greek city-states in the south. By about 270 B.C., Rome controlled most of the Italian peninsula.

Citizen-Soldiers Rome's success was due to skillful diplomacy and to its loyal, well-trained army. The basic military unit was the legion, made up of about 5,000 men. As in Greece, Roman armies consisted of citizen-soldiers who fought without pay and supplied their own weapons. Roman citizens often made good soldiers because they were brought up to value loyalty, courage, and respect for authority.

To ensure success, Roman commanders mixed rewards with harsh punishment. Young soldiers who showed courage in action won praise and gifts. If a unit fled from battle, however, 1 out of every 10 men from the disgraced unit was put to death.

Conquered Lands Rome generally treated its defeated enemies with justice. Conquered peoples had to acknowledge Roman leadership, pay taxes, and supply soldiers for the Roman army. In return, Rome let them keep their own customs, money, and local government.

To a few privileged groups among the conquered people, Rome gave the highly prized right of full citizenship. Others became partial citizens, who were allowed to marry Romans and carry on trade in Rome. As a result of such generous policies, most conquered lands remained loyal to Rome even in troubled times.

Protection and Unification To protect its conquests, Rome posted soldiers throughout the land. It also built a network of all-weather military roads to link distant territories to Rome. As trade and travel increased, local peoples incorporated Latin into their languages and adopted many Roman customs and beliefs. Slowly, Italy began to unite under Roman rule.

SECTION 1 Assessment

Recall
1. **Identify: (a)** Latins, **(b)** Etruscans, **(c)** Laws of the Twelve Tables, **(d)** Jupiter.
2. **Define: (a)** republic, **(b)** patrician, **(c)** consul, **(d)** dictator, **(e)** plebeian, **(f)** tribune, **(g)** veto, **(h)** legion.

Comprehension
3. Describe two ways that the geography of Italy influenced the rise of Rome.
4. **(a)** What reforms did plebeians win during the early republic? **(b)** How did male and female roles differ in the Roman family?
5. What were two reasons for Rome's success in expanding its power across Italy?

Critical Thinking and Writing
6. **Linking Past and Present** Roman heroes were admired for their courage, loyalty, and devotion to duty. What qualities do American heroes display?
7. **Analyzing Information** Did the Roman republic have a democratic government? Why or why not?

Activity
Writing News Headlines Write a series of newspaper headlines announcing major events in the rise of the Roman republic. Remember that news headlines are usually clear and concise.

From Republic to Empire

Reading Focus

- How did Rome win an empire?
- Why did the Roman republic decline?
- How did Roman emperors promote peace and stability in the empire?

Vocabulary

imperialism
province
latifundia
census

Taking Notes

Copy this concept web. As you read the section, fill in the blank circles with important facts about the decline of the Roman republic. Add more circles if you need them.

THE REPUBLIC DECLINES

Gracchus brothers are killed

Main Idea As Roman power spread around the Mediterranean, the republic ended and the age of the Roman empire began.

Setting the Scene

After gaining control of the Italian peninsula, Rome began to build an empire around the Mediterranean Sea. Expansion created strains and conflicts in Roman society. Addressing plebeians, the Roman tribune Tiberius Gracchus described one of the injustices that he saw in Roman society:

> "The beasts of the field and the birds of the air have their holes and their hiding places, but the men who fight and die for Italy enjoy only the light and the air. . . . You fight and die to give wealth and luxury to others. You are called the masters of the world, but there is not a foot of ground that you can call your own."
>
> —Plutarch, *Parallel Lives*

The effects of territorial expansion gradually weakened and finally crushed the republic. Out of the rubble, though, rose the Roman empire and a new chapter in Rome's long history.

Winning an Empire

Rome's conquest of the Italian peninsula brought it into contact with Carthage, a city-state on the northern coast of Africa. Settled by North Africans and Phoenician traders, Carthage ruled over an empire that stretched across North Africa and the western Mediterranean. As Rome expanded westward, conflict between these two powers became inevitable.

Wars With Carthage Between 264 B.C. and 146 B.C., Rome fought three wars against Carthage. They are called the Punic Wars, from *Punicus*, the Latin word for Phoenician. In the First Punic War, Rome defeated Carthage and won Sicily, Corsica, and Sardinia.

The Carthaginians sought revenge in the Second Punic War. In 218 B.C., the Carthaginian general Hannibal led his army, including dozens of war elephants, on an epic march across the Pyrenees, through France, and over the Alps into Italy. The trek cost Hannibal nearly half his army. However, the Carthaginian general had surprised the Romans who had expected an invasion from the south. For 15 years, Hannibal and his army moved across Italy, winning battle after battle.

The Carthaginians, however, failed to capture Rome itself. In the end, the Romans outflanked Hannibal by sending an army to attack Carthage.

Wars With Carthage
Hannibal crossed the Alps into Italy with an invasion force that included thousands of troops and more than three dozen elephants. From towers on the elephants' backs, soldiers rained arrows and spears on their Roman enemies.

Theme: Impact of the Individual How did Hannibal's invasion route surprise the Romans?

Hannibal returned to defend his homeland, where the Romans defeated him at last. Carthage gave up all its lands except those in Africa.

Nevertheless, many Romans still saw Carthage as a rival and wanted revenge for the terrible destruction that Hannibal's army had brought to Italy. For years, Cato, a wealthy senator, ended every speech he made with the words "Carthage must be destroyed."

Finally, in the Third Punic War, Rome completely destroyed Carthage. Survivors were killed or sold into slavery. The Romans poured salt over the earth so that nothing would grow there again. The Romans were now masters of the western Mediterranean.

Other Conquests "The Carthaginians fought for their own preservation and the sovereignty of Africa," observed a Greek witness to the fall of Carthage; "the Romans, for supremacy and world domination." The Romans were committed to a policy of imperialism, or establishing control over foreign lands and peoples. While Rome fought Carthage in the west, it was also expanding into the eastern Mediterranean. There, Romans confronted the Hellenistic rulers who had divided up the empire of Alexander the Great.

Sometimes to defend Roman interests, sometimes simply for plunder, Rome launched a series of wars in the area. One by one, Macedonia, Greece, and parts of Asia Minor surrendered and became Roman provinces, that is, lands under Roman rule. Other regions, like Egypt, allied with Rome. By 133 B.C., Roman power extended from Spain to Egypt. Truly, the Romans were justified in calling the Mediterranean *Mare Nostrum*, or "Our Sea."

Social and Economic Effects Conquests and control of busy trade routes brought incredible riches into Rome. Generals, officials, and traders amassed fortunes from loot, taxes, and commerce. A new class of wealthy Romans emerged. They built lavish mansions and filled them with luxuries imported from the east. Wealthy families bought up huge estates, called latifundia. As the Romans conquered more and more lands, they forced people captured in war to work as slaves on the latifundia.

The widespread use of slave labor hurt small farmers, who were unable to produce food as cheaply as the latifundia could. The farmers' problems were compounded when huge quantities of grain pouring in from the conquered lands drove down grain prices. Many farmers fell into debt and had to sell their land.

In despair, landless farmers flocked to Rome and other cities looking for jobs. There, they joined a restless class of unemployed people. As the gap between rich and poor widened, angry mobs began to riot.

The new wealth also increased corruption. Greed and self-interest replaced virtues such as simplicity, hard work, and devotion to duty so prized in the early republic.

Attempts at Reform Two young patricians, brothers named Tiberius and Gaius Gracchus (GAY uhs GRAK uhs), were among the first to attempt reform. Tiberius, who was elected a tribune in 133 B.C., called on the state to distribute land to poor farmers. Gaius, elected tribune 10 years later, sought a wider range of reforms, including the use of public funds to buy grain to feed the poor.

The reforms of the Gracchus brothers angered the senate, which saw them as a threat to its power. The brothers, along with thousands of their followers, were killed in waves of street violence set off by senators and their hired thugs.

Connections to Today

Ancient Ruins Under the Sea

Swimming among brightly colored fish, archaeologists are exploring an underwater treasure off the coast of Egypt. In a rare find, they have uncovered remains of the ancient city of Alexandria beneath the waters of the Mediterranean. Divers can swim among sphinxes, columns, and temples—a rich mix of Egyptian, Greek, and Roman artifacts.

Mingled among the ruins created long ago by earthquakes are the wrecks of Roman ships that failed to navigate the dangerous harbor. Cargoes of olive oil and wine are still intact after resting on the sea floor for some 2,000 years.

Theme: Geography and History How did geography contribute to the creation of this archaeological site?

Growth of Roman Power to 44 B.C.

Legend:
- 500 B.C.
- to 264 B.C.
- to 146 B.C.
- to 44 B.C.
- Territory gained from Carthage
- → Hannibal's invasion route

Azimuthal Equal Area Projection

0 — 250 — 500 Miles
0 — 250 — 500 Kilometers

Skills Assessment

Geography Through wars and diplomacy, the Roman republic gradually gained control of lands around the Mediterranean Sea.

1. **Location** On the map, locate **(a)** Spain, **(b)** Gaul, **(c)** Carthage, **(d)** Egypt, **(e)** Macedonia.
2. **Place** During what period did Asia Minor come under Roman control?
3. **Critical Thinking** **Recognizing Causes and Effects** How did Rome gain so much territory between 264 B.C. and 146 B.C?

Decline of the Republic

Unable to resolve its problems peacefully, Rome was plunged into a series of civil wars. At issue was who should hold power—the senate, which wanted to govern as it had in the past, or popular political leaders, who wanted to weaken the senate and enact reforms.

The turmoil sparked slave uprisings and revolts among Rome's allies. Meanwhile, the old legions of Roman citizen-soldiers became professional armies whose first loyalty was to their commanders. Rival generals marched their armies into Rome to advance their ambitions.

Julius Caesar's Rise to Power Out of this chaos emerged Julius Caesar, an ambitious military commander. For a time, Caesar dominated Roman politics with Pompey, another brilliant general. Then, in 59 B.C., Caesar set out with his army to make new conquests. After nine years of fighting, he completed the conquest of Gaul—the area that is now France.

Fearful of Caesar's rising fame, Pompey persuaded the senate to order Caesar to disband his army and return to Rome. Caesar defied the order. Swiftly and secretly, he led his army across the Rubicon River into northern Italy and then headed toward Rome. Once again, civil war erupted across the Roman world.

Caesar crushed Pompey and his supporters. He then swept around the Mediterranean, suppressing rebellions. *"Veni, vidi, vici"*—"I came, I saw, I conquered"—he announced after one victory. Later, returning to Rome, he forced the senate to make him dictator. Although he kept the senate and other features of the republic, he was in fact the absolute ruler of Rome.

Caesar's Reforms Between 48 B.C. and 44 B.C., Caesar pushed through a number of reforms intended to deal with Rome's many problems. He launched a program of public works to employ the jobless and gave public land to the poor. He also reorganized the government of the provinces and granted Roman citizenship to more people. Caesar's most lasting reform was the introduction of a new calendar based on Egyptian knowledge. The Julian calendar, as it was later called, was used in western Europe for over 1,600 years. With minor changes, it is still our calendar today.

Assassination and Civil Wars Caesar's enemies worried that he planned to make himself king of Rome. In order to save the republic, they plotted against him. In March 44 B.C., as Caesar arrived in the senate, his enemies stabbed him to death.

The death of Julius Caesar plunged Rome into a new round of civil wars. Mark Antony, Caesar's chief general, and Octavian, Caesar's grand-nephew, joined forces to hunt down the murderers. The two men soon quarreled, however, setting off a bitter struggle for power. In 31 B.C., Octavian finally defeated Antony and his powerful ally Queen Cleopatra of Egypt.

Roman Empire and Roman Peace

The senate gave the triumphant Octavian the title of *Augustus*, or Exalted One, and declared him *princeps*, or first citizen. Although he was careful not to call himself king, a title that Romans had hated since Etruscan times, Augustus exercised absolute power and named his successor, just as a king would do.

Under Augustus, who ruled from 31 B.C. to A.D. 14, the 500-year-old republic came to an end. Romans did not know it at the time, but a new age had dawned—the age of the Roman empire.

A Stable Government Through firm but moderate policies, Augustus laid the foundation for a stable government. Although he left the senate in place, Augustus created an efficient, well-trained civil service to enforce the laws. High-level jobs were open to men of talent, regardless of their class. In addition, he cemented the allegiance of cities and provinces to Rome by allowing them a large measure of self-government.

Augustus undertook economic reforms, too. To make the tax system more fair, he ordered a census, or population count, to be taken in the empire. He set up a postal service and issued new coins to make trade easier. He put the jobless to work building roads and temples and sent others to farm the land.

The government that Augustus organized functioned well for 200 years. Still, a serious problem kept arising: Who would rule after an emperor died? Romans did not accept the idea of power passing automatically from father to son. As a result, the death of an emperor often led to intrigue and violence.

Bad Emperors and Good Emperors Not all of Augustus' successors were great rulers. Indeed, some were weak and incompetent. Two early emperors, Caligula and Nero, were downright evil and perhaps insane. Caligula, for example, appointed his favorite horse as consul. Nero viciously persecuted Christians and was even blamed for setting a great fire that destroyed much of Rome.

Between A.D. 96 and A.D. 180, the empire benefited from the rule of a series of "good emperors." The emperor Hadrian, for example, codified Roman law, making it the same for all provinces. He also had soldiers build a wall across Britain to hold back attackers from the non-Roman north.

The emperor Marcus Aurelius, who read philosophy while on military campaigns, was close to Plato's ideal of a philosopher-king. His *Meditations* show his Stoic philosophy and commitment to duty: "Hour by hour resolve firmly . . . to do what comes to hand with correct and natural dignity."

The Colosseum
Romans marveled at the shows put on at the Colosseum, ancient Rome's largest stadium. Spectators watched the slaughter of exotic animals, gladiators battling to the death, and mock naval battles, like the one shown above.

The Colosseum was an architectural marvel. Its floor was about the size of a modern football field. As many as 50,000 spectators could crowd onto the Colosseum's marble and wooden benches. There, they were protected from the hot Roman sun by a giant canvas roof.

Theme: Political and Social Systems How does the architectural accomplishment of the Colosseum contrast with what took place there?

The Pax Romana The 200-year span that began with Augustus and ended with Marcus Aurelius is known as the period of the *Pax Romana,* or "Roman Peace." During that time, Roman rule brought peace, order, unity, and prosperity to lands stretching from the Euphrates River in the east to Britain in the west, an area approximately equal in size to the continental United States.

During the Pax Romana, Roman legions maintained and protected the roads, and Roman fleets chased pirates from the seas. Trade flowed freely to and from distant lands in Africa and Asia. Egyptian farmers in the Nile Valley supplied Romans with grain. From other parts of Africa came ivory and gold, as well as lions and other wild animals that were used in public entertainments. From India came spices, cotton, and precious stones. Trade caravans traveled along the great Silk Road, bringing silk and other goods from China.

People too, moved easily within the Roman empire, spreading ideas and knowledge, especially the advances of the Hellenistic east. As you will read, ideas from Greece and Judea would have tremendous impact on Rome and the western world.

Bread and Circuses Throughout the empire, rich and poor alike loved spectacular entertainments. At the Circus Maximus, Rome's largest racecourse, chariots thundered around an oval course, making dangerously tight turns at either end. Fans bet feverishly on their favorite teams—the Reds, Greens, Blues, or Whites—and successful charioteers were hailed as heroes.

Gladiator contests were even more popular. Many gladiators were slaves who had been trained to fight. In the arena, they battled one another, either singly or in groups. Crowds cheered a skilled gladiator, and a good fighter might even win his freedom. But if a gladiator made a poor showing, the crowd turned thumbs down, a signal that he should be killed.

To the emperors who paid for them with the taxes they collected from the empire, these amusements were a way to pacify the city's restless mobs. In much the same spirit, the government provided free grain to feed the poor. Critics warned against this policy of "bread and circuses," but few listened.

During the Pax Romana, the general prosperity hid underlying social and economic problems. Later Roman emperors, however, would face problems that could not be solved with "bread and circuses."

SECTION 2 Assessment

Recall
1. **Identify: (a)** Punic Wars, **(b)** Hannibal, **(c)** Tiberius and Gaius Gracchus, **(d)** Julius Caesar, **(e)** Augustus, **(f)** Hadrian, **(g)** Pax Romana, **(h)** Circus Maximus.
2. **Define: (a)** imperialism, **(b)** province, **(c)** latifundia, **(d)** census.

Comprehension
3. How did Rome build an empire around the Mediterranean Sea?
4. What problems contributed to the decline of the Roman republic?

5. How did Augustus lay the foundation for stable government in the Roman empire?

Critical Thinking and Writing
6. **Analyzing Information** How do you think the founders of the Roman republic would have viewed the government of the Roman empire? Explain.
7. **Predicting Consequences** What were some possible negative consequences of following the policy of "bread and circuses"?

Activity
Creating a Political Cartoon Imagine that you are one of the senators who oppose Julius Caesar. Create a political cartoon that criticizes one of Caesar's policies and shows why you oppose him.

The Roman Achievement

Reading Focus

■ How was Greco–Roman civilization formed?

■ What were some Roman contributions to literature, the arts, and technology?

■ What principles of law did Romans develop?

Vocabulary

satirize
mosaic
engineering
aqueduct

Taking Notes

Make a table like the one below to focus on the cultural achievements of the Romans. Add more information and more rows as you read the section.

LAW	Civil law, law of nations
LITERATURE	Virgil's *Aeneid*
HISTORY	

Main Idea Romans absorbed ideas from other cultures and made great advances in law, literature, engineering, and other areas.

Setting the Scene Marcus Tullius Cicero was a philosopher, politician, and passionate defender of law. As the republic declined, he attacked ambitious men such as Julius Caesar. When Caesar came to power, however, he forgave Cicero, noting that it was "more glorious to have enlarged the limits of the Roman mind than the boundaries of Roman rule."

Romans such as Cicero and Caesar both had a lasting impact. Through war and conquest, Roman generals carried the achievements of Roman civilization to distant lands. Yet the civilization that developed was not simply Roman. Rather, it blended Greek, Hellenistic, and Roman achievements.

Greco-Roman Civilization

In its early days, Rome absorbed ideas from Greek colonists in southern Italy, and it continued to borrow heavily from Greek culture after it conquered Greece. To the Romans emerging from their villages, Greek art, literature, philosophy, and scientific genius represented the height of cultural achievement. Their admiration never wavered, leading the Roman poet Horace to note, "Greece has conquered her rude conqueror."

The Romans adapted Greek and Hellenistic achievements, just as the Greeks had once absorbed ideas from Egypt and the Fertile Crescent. The blending of Greek, Hellenistic, and Roman traditions produced what is known as Greco-Roman civilization. Trade and travel during the Pax Romana helped spread this vital new civilization.

Literature, Philosophy, and History

In the field of literature, the Romans owed a great debt to the Greeks. Many Romans spoke Greek and imitated Greek styles in prose and poetry. Still, the greatest Roman writers used Latin to create their own literature.

Poetry In his epic poem, the *Aeneid*, Virgil tried to show that Rome's past was as heroic as that of Greece. He linked his epic to Homer's work by telling how Aeneas escaped from Troy to found Rome. Virgil wrote the *Aeneid* soon after Augustus came to power. He hoped it would arouse patriotism and help unite Rome after years of civil wars.

Other poets used verse to satirize, or make fun of, Roman society. Horace's satires were gentle, using playful wit to attack human folly. Juvenal and Martial were more biting. Martial's poems were so harsh that he had to use fictitious names to protect himself from retribution.

Primary Source

A Roman Epic
In the opening lines of the Aeneid, *Virgil introduces "the hero" Aeneas and hints at his daring and destiny:*

"I tell about war and the hero who
    first from Troy's frontier,
Displaced by destiny, came . . .
To Italy—a man much travailed on
    sea and land
By the powers above, because of
    the brooding anger of [the
    goddess] Juno,
Suffering much in war until he
    could found a city
And march his gods into Latium,
    whence rose the Latin race,
. . . and the high walls of Rome."

—Virgil, *Aeneid*

Skills Assessment

Primary Source What forces caused Aeneas' suffering and led to his founding of Rome?

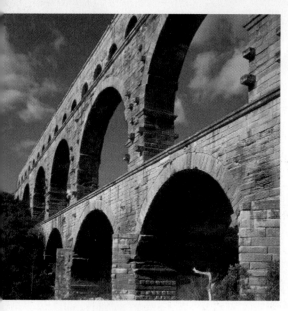

History Roman historians pursued their own theme—the rise and fall of Roman power. Like the poet Virgil, the historian Livy sought to rouse patriotic feeling and restore traditional Roman virtues by recalling images of Rome's heroic past. In his history of Rome, Livy recounted tales of great heroes such as Horatius and Cincinnatus.

Another historian, Tacitus, wrote bitterly about Augustus and his successors, who, he felt, had destroyed Roman liberty. He admired the simple culture of the Germans who lived on Rome's northern frontier and would later invade the empire.

Philosophy Romans borrowed much of their philosophy from the Greeks. The Hellenistic philosophy of Stoicism impressed Roman thinkers like the emperor Marcus Aurelius. Stoics stressed the importance of duty and acceptance of one's fate. They also showed concern for the well-being of all people, an idea that would be reflected in Christian teachings. (See Section 4 of this chapter.)

A Roman Aqueduct
Roman engineers built this aqueduct across the Gardon River in present-day France.

Theme: Economics and Technology Why were aqueducts important to Roman towns?

Art and Architecture

To a large degree, Roman art and architecture were based on Greek and Etruscan models. However, as with literature, the Romans made adaptations to develop their own style.

Art Like the Greeks before them, Roman sculptors stressed realism, portraying their subjects with every wart and vein in place. The Romans also broke new ground, however, by revealing an individual's character. A statue of a soldier, a writer, or an emperor might capture an expression of smugness, discontent, or haughty pride.

Some Roman sculpture was more idealistic. For example, sculptors transformed Augustus, who was neither handsome nor imposing, into a symbol of power and leadership.

Romans beautified their homes with works of art. Examples of these works were preserved in Pompeii, a city buried by the volcanic eruption of Mount Vesuvius in A.D. 79. Artists depicted scenes from Roman literature and daily life in splendid frescoes and mosaics. A mosaic is a picture made from chips of colored stone or glass.

Architecture While the Greeks aimed for simple elegance in architecture, the Romans emphasized grandeur. Immense palaces, temples, and stadiums stood as mighty monuments to Roman power and dignity. The Romans improved on devices such as the column and the arch. Using concrete as a building material, they developed the rounded dome to roof large spaces. The most famous domed structure is the Pantheon, a temple to all the Roman gods, which still stands in Rome.

Technology and Science

The Romans excelled in engineering, which is the application of science and mathematics to develop useful structures and machines. Roman engineers built roads, bridges, and harbors throughout the empire. Roman roads were so solidly built that many of them were still used long after the fall of the empire.

Roman engineers also built many immense aqueducts, or bridgelike stone structures that brought water from the hills into Roman cities. The wealthy had water piped in, and almost every city boasted public baths. Here, people gathered not only to wash themselves but to hear the latest news and exchange gossip.

The Romans generally left scientific research to the Greeks who were by that time citizens of the empire. In Alexandria, Egypt, Hellenistic scientists

Disaster!

Vesuvius Erupts!

One summer day in A.D. 79, the townspeople of Pompeii, a wealthy Roman resort town, felt tremors and heard a low rumble but were not alarmed. Though they lived in the shadow of a huge volcano, no one could remember the last time it had erupted. Within hours, a giant explosion had ripped off the mountaintop. Within two days, the town of Pompeii had disappeared.

Before the eruption, Pompeii was a busy town. Its fanciest homes boasted beautiful mosaic floors and colorful murals.

As ash started to fall, many people tried to flee while others sought safety in their cellars. Still, most people suffocated and were buried in the ash. Rain hardened the ash, forming perfect molds of people and preserving articles of everyday living.

With little warning, Mt. Vesuvius exploded. Gas and hot, liquid rock burst through the cone, shooting ash and whole rocks into the air. Spectacular lightning bolts and clouds of ash filled the sky.

This is a cast of the body of a child who was entombed in the hardened ash.

Portfolio Assessment

INTERNET Use the Internet or other research sources to learn about a recent volcanic eruption. Use the information you find to write articles about the event for the front page of a newspaper. You may want to use pictures or diagrams to illustrate the articles.

Law and Government
Knowledge of the laws and legal procedures of Rome was helpful in pursuing a career in government. Many Roman officials, such as the senator depicted in this sculpture, had argued cases in court and served as judges.

Theme: Continuity and Change Today, many American government officials are lawyers. How do you think this affects the quality of government?

exchanged ideas freely. It was there that astronomer-mathematician Ptolemy (TAHL uh mee) proposed his theory that the Earth was the center of the universe, a mistaken idea that was accepted in the western world for nearly 1,500 years.

The Greek doctor Galen advanced the frontiers of medical science by insisting on experiments to prove a conclusion. Galen compiled a medical encyclopedia summarizing what was known at the time. It remained a standard text for more than 1,000 years.

Although the Romans did little original research, they did put science to practical use. They applied geography to make maps, and medical knowledge to help doctors improve public health. Like Galen, they collected knowledge into encyclopedias. Pliny the Elder, a Roman scientist, compiled volumes on geography, zoology, botany, and other topics, all based on other people's works.

Roman Law

"Let justice be done," proclaimed a Roman saying, "though the heavens fall!" Probably the greatest legacy of Rome was its commitment to the rule of law and to justice. During the Roman empire, the rule of law fostered unity and stability. Many centuries later, the principles of Roman law would become the basis for legal systems in Europe and Latin America.

Two Systems During the republic, Rome developed a system of law, known as the civil law, that applied to its citizens. As Rome expanded, however, it ruled many foreigners who were not covered under the civil law. Gradually, a second system of law, known as the law of nations, emerged. It applied to all people under Roman rule, citizens and noncitizens. Later, when Rome extended citizenship across the empire, the two systems merged.

Common Principles As Roman law developed, certain basic principles evolved. Many of these principles are familiar to Americans today. An accused person was presumed innocent until proven guilty. The accused was allowed to face the accuser and offer a defense against the charge. Guilt had to be established "clearer than daylight" through evidence. Judges were allowed to interpret the laws and were expected to make fair decisions.

SECTION 3 Assessment

Recall
1. **Identify:** (a) Greco-Roman civilization, (b) Virgil, (c) Livy, (d) Pantheon, (e) Galen, (f) civil law, (g) law of nations.
2. **Define:** (a) satirize, (b) mosaic, (c) engineering, (d) aqueduct.

Comprehension
3. How did Greek culture influence the development of Roman civilization?
4. How did Romans use technology to improve life in the empire?
5. What principles of law did Romans develop?

Critical Thinking and Writing
6. **Linking Past and Present** Give two examples of how the principles of law developed by Rome affect life in the United States today.
7. **Analyzing Primary Sources** The Roman poet Horace said of Roman civilization: "Greece has conquered her rude conqueror." (a) What did he mean by this? (b) Give three examples that support his statement.

Activity
Take It to the NET

Roman art often depicted scenes of daily life. Find Internet sites with information about Roman clothing, foods, entertainment, and other aspects of daily life. Use printouts of the sites you visit to create a portfolio on Roman life.

The Rise of Christianity

Reading Focus

- What was Rome's policy toward different religions in the early empire?
- What were the major teachings of Jesus, and how were they spread?
- How did the early Christian Church develop?

Vocabulary

messiah
apostle
martyr
bishop
diocese
patriarch
pope
heresy

Taking Notes

Copy the partially completed flowchart at right. As you read, finish the flowchart by writing in the main events in the rise of Christianity. Add more boxes as needed.

| Romans tolerate various religions |
| Jesus preaches his ideas |
| Followers of Jesus spread Christianity |
| |
| |

Main Idea A new religion, Christianity, emerged in the Roman empire. It gradually spread and became the official religion of the empire.

Setting the Scene Early in the Pax Romana, a new religion, Christianity, sprang up in a distant corner of the Roman empire. At first, Christianity was just one of many religions practiced in the empire. But despite many obstacles, the new faith grew rapidly, and by A.D. 395, it had been declared the official religion of the Roman empire.

As it gained strength and spread through the empire, Christianity reshaped Roman beliefs. And when the Roman empire fell, the Christian Church took over much of its role, becoming the central institution of western civilization for nearly 1,000 years.

Religious Diversity in the Early Empire

Within the culturally diverse Roman empire, a variety of religious beliefs and practices coexisted. Jupiter, Mars, Juno, and other traditional Roman gods remained important to some people. However, a growing number of people were looking elsewhere for spiritual fulfillment.

Mystery Religions Some turned to mystery religions that emphasized secret rituals and promised special rewards. One of the most popular of these was the cult of Isis, which originated in Egypt and offered women equal status with men. Others worshiped the Persian god Mithras, who championed good over evil and offered life after death. Mithraism was especially favored by Roman soldiers.

Religious Toleration Generally, Rome tolerated the varied religious traditions. As long as citizens showed loyalty by honoring Roman gods and acknowledging the divine spirit of the emperor, they were allowed to worship other gods as they pleased. Because most people at the time were polytheistic, they were content to worship the Roman gods along with their own.

Divisions in Judea By 63 B.C., the Romans had conquered Judea, where most Jews of the time lived. As you have learned, the Jews were devoted to their monotheistic traditions. To avoid violating the Jewish belief in one god, the Romans excused Jews from worshiping Roman gods.

Among the Jews themselves, however, religious ferment was creating deep divisions. During the Hellenistic age, many Jews absorbed Greek customs and ideas. Concerned about the weakening of their religion, Jewish conservatives rejected these influences and called for strict obedience to Jewish laws and traditions.

Global Connections

A Jewish-Greek Connection

During Roman times and before, many Jews left their homeland in Judea. They settled in lands around the Mediterranean and elsewhere.

Many of those who migrated began to speak Greek instead of Hebrew, and two Greek words became an important part of Jewish history. The Greek word *diaspora*, which means "scattering," refers to the fact that some Jews migrated and settled in various parts of the world. The Greek word *synagogue*, "a bringing together," was used for the places where Jews gathered to read the sacred Torah. Meeting in synagogues helped Jews share ideas, hold their community together, and preserve traditions. Today, synagogues can be found in most major cities throughout the world.

Theme: Global Interaction
How did synagogues help Jewish culture survive the diaspora?

Jesus Healing a Woman
Jesus promised everlasting life to all who followed his teachings. This Roman mural depicts Jesus miraculously healing an afflicted woman.

Theme: Religions and Value Systems Which social classes were most attracted to Christianity? Why?

While most Jews were reluctantly willing to live under Roman rule, others, called Zealots, were not. They called on Jews to revolt against Rome and reestablish an independent state. Some Jews believed that a messiah, or anointed king sent by God, would soon appear to lead the Jewish people to freedom.

Jewish Revolt In A.D. 66, discontent flared into rebellion. Roman forces crushed the rebels, captured Jerusalem, and destroyed the Jewish temple. When revolts broke out again in the next century, Roman armies leveled Jerusalem. Thousands of Jews were killed in the fighting, and many others were enslaved and transported to various parts of the empire. Faced with the destruction that resulted from the rebellions, growing numbers of Jews decided to leave Judea.

Although they were defeated in their efforts to regain political independence, Jews survived in scattered communities around the Mediterranean. Over the centuries, Jewish rabbis, or scholars, extended and preserved the religious law, as set forth in the Talmud. Commitment to learning Jewish law and traditions enabled the Jews to survive over the centuries.

Jesus and His Message

As turmoil engulfed the Jews in Palestine, a new religion, Christianity, rose among them. Its founder was a Jew named Jesus.

Almost all that we know about the life of Jesus comes from the Gospels, the first four books of the New Testament of the Bible. These accounts were attributed by early Christians to Matthew, Mark, Luke, and John, four followers of Jesus. *Gospel* comes from the Old English word for "good news."

Life of Jesus Jesus was born about 4 B.C. in Bethlehem, near Jerusalem. According to the Gospels, he was a descendant of King David of Israel. An angel, the Gospels say, told Jesus' mother, Mary, that she would give birth to the messiah. "He will be great," said the angel, "and will be called the Son of the Most High God."

Growing up in the small town of Nazareth, Jesus worshiped God and followed Jewish law. As a young man, he may have worked as a carpenter, the occupation of Mary's husband Joseph. At the age of 30, the Gospels relate, he began preaching to villagers near the Sea of Galilee. To help him in his mission, he recruited twelve close followers, known as the apostles, from the Greek word meaning "a person sent forth." Chief among these was one called Peter.

Large crowds gathered to hear Jesus' teachings, especially when word spread that he had performed miracles of healing. Jesus often used parables, or short stories with simple moral lessons, to communicate his ideas. After three years, he and his disciples, or loyal followers, went to Jerusalem to spread his message there.

The Message Jesus' teachings were firmly rooted in Jewish tradition. Jesus believed in one God and accepted the Ten Commandments. He preached obedience to the laws of Moses and defended the teachings of the Jewish prophets.

At the same time, Jesus preached new beliefs. According to his followers, he called himself the Son of God. Many people believed he was the messiah whose appearance Jews had long predicted. Jesus proclaimed that his mission was to bring spiritual salvation and eternal life to anyone who would believe in him.

In the Sermon on the Mount, Jesus summed up his ethical message, which echoed Jewish ideas of mercy and sympathy for the poor and helpless:

"Blessed are the meek, for they shall inherit the earth.
  Blessed are those who hunger and thirst for righteousness,
    for they shall be satisfied.
  Blessed are the merciful, for they shall obtain mercy.
  Blessed are the pure in heart, for they shall see God.
  Blessed are the peacemakers, for they will be called sons of God."
                                        —Gospel According to Matthew

Jesus emphasized God's love and taught the need for justice, morality, and service to others. According to Jesus, a person's major responsibilities were to "love the Lord your God with all your heart" and to "love your neighbor as yourself." Jesus emphasized the importance of forgiveness. "Love your enemies," he told his followers. "If anyone hits you on one cheek, let him hit the other one, too."

Death on the Cross Some Jews welcomed Jesus to Jerusalem. Others, however, regarded him as a dangerous troublemaker. Jewish priests, in particular, felt that he was challenging their leadership. To the Roman authorities, Jesus was a revolutionary who might lead the Jews in a rebellion against Roman rule.

Jesus was betrayed by one of his disciples, the Gospels state. Arrested by the Romans, he was tried and condemned to be crucified. In crucifixion, a Roman method of execution, a person was nailed to or hung on a cross and left to die.

Jesus' disciples were thrown into confusion. But then rumors spread through Jerusalem that Jesus was not dead at all. His disciples, the Gospels say, saw and talked with Jesus, who had risen from the dead. They say Jesus commanded them to spread his teachings, and that he then ascended into heaven.

Spread of Christianity

Following Jesus' death, the apostles and other disciples spread Jesus' message and helped establish Christian communities. First, they preached only among the Jews of Judea. Slowly, some Jews accepted the teaching that Jesus was the messiah, or the Christ, from the Greek for "the anointed one." These people became the first Christians. For a time, Christianity remained a sect within Judaism.

Gradually, disciples of Jesus began to preach in Jewish communities throughout the Roman world. According to tradition, Peter established Christianity in the city of Rome itself. However, it was Paul, a Jew from Asia Minor, who played the most influential role in the spread of Christianity.

Work of Paul Paul had never seen Jesus. In fact, he had been among those who persecuted Jesus' followers. Then one day, Paul had a vision in which Jesus spoke to him. Immediately converting to the new faith, Paul made an important decision. He would spread the teachings of Jesus beyond Jewish communities to gentiles, or non-Jews.

Paul's missionary work set Christianity on the road to becoming a world religion. A tireless traveler, Paul journeyed around the Mediterranean and set up churches from Mesopotamia to Rome. In long letters to the Christian communities, he explained difficult doctrines, judged disputes, and expanded Christian teachings. These letters are part of the New Testament. In his writings, Paul emphasized the idea that Jesus had sacrificed his life out of love for humankind. Paul promised that those

 Primary Sources and Literature

See "St. Paul: First Letter to the Corinthians" in the Reference Section at the back of this book.

Spread of Christianity to A.D. 476

Legend:
- Christian areas, A.D. 325
- Christian areas added by A.D. 476
- Boundary of Roman empire, A.D. 476
- → Paul's first journey
- - -▶ Paul's second journey
- - -▶ Paul's third journey
- ····▶ Paul's journey to Rome

Map labels: BRITAIN, GERMANY, ATLANTIC OCEAN, GAUL, EUROPE, Milan, SPAIN, Rome, ITALY, SARDINIA, Philippi, Thessalonica, Constantinople, ASIA MINOR, GALATIA, GREECE, Ephesus, Black Sea, Caspian Sea, Corinth, Athens, Colossae, Antioch, SYRIA, Carthage, SICILY, CRETE, Mediterranean Sea, Jerusalem, Alexandria, AFRICA, EGYPT, Red Sea

Azimuthal Equal Area Projection
0   250   500 Miles
0   250   500 Kilometers

Skills Assessment

Geography Aided by the work of Paul and other missionaries, Christianity gradually spread across the Roman empire.

1. **Location** On the map, locate **(a)** Jerusalem, **(b)** Asia Minor, **(c)** Antioch, **(d)** Constantinople, **(e)** Alexandria.
2. **Movement** In what areas did Paul travel on his first journeys?
3. **Critical Thinking Connecting to Geography** How was the Mediterranean Sea important in the spread of Christianity?

who believed Jesus was the son of God and followed his teachings would achieve salvation, or eternal life.

Persecution Rome's tolerant attitude toward religion did not extend to Christianity. Roman officials suspected Christians of disloyalty to Rome because they refused to make sacrifices to the emperor or to honor the Roman gods. When Christians met in secret to avoid persecution, rumors spread that they were engaged in evil practices.

In times of trouble, persecution increased. Roman rulers like Nero used Christians as scapegoats, blaming them for social or economic ills. Over the centuries, thousands of Christians became martyrs, people who suffer or die for their beliefs. According to tradition, both Peter and Paul were killed in Rome during the reign of Nero.

Reasons for Christianity's Appeal Despite the attacks, Christianity continued to spread. The reasons were many. Jesus had welcomed all people, especially the humble, poor, and oppressed. They found comfort in his message of love. Equality, human dignity, and the promise of a better life beyond the grave were very attractive teachings.

As they did their work, Christian missionaries like Paul added ideas from Plato, the Stoics, and other Greek thinkers to Jesus' message. Educated Romans, in particular, were attracted to a religion that incorporated the discipline and moderation of Greek philosophy.

The work of missionaries such as Paul was made easier by the unity of the Roman empire. Christians traveled along Roman roads and across the Mediterranean Sea, which was protected by Roman fleets. Early Christian documents were usually written in Greek or Latin, languages that many people in the empire understood.

Even persecution brought new converts. Observing the willingness of Christians to die for their religion, people were impressed by the strength of Christians' belief. "The blood of the martyr is the seed of the [Christian] Church," noted one Roman.

Triumph The persecution of Christians finally ended in A.D. 313, when the emperor Constantine issued the Edict of Milan. It granted freedom of worship to all citizens of the Roman empire. In making his decision, Constantine was influenced by his mother, who was a devout Christian. Some 80 years later, the emperor Theodosius (thee uh DOH shuhs) made Christianity the official religion of the Roman empire.

The Early Christian Church

Early Christian communities shared a common faith in the teachings of Jesus and a common way of worship. Only gradually did the scattered communities organize a structured Church.

Patterns of Life and Worship A person fully joined the Christian community by renouncing evil in the rite of baptism. Christians believed that through baptism their sins were forgiven by the grace of God. Members of the community were considered equals, and they addressed each other as "brother" or "sister." Each Sunday, Christians gathered for a ceremony of thanksgiving to God. The baptized ate bread and drank wine in a sacred meal called the Eucharist. They did this in memory of Jesus, whose last supper was described in the Gospels. Justin, an early Christian philosopher and martyr, tried to explain the Eucharist in a letter to the Roman emperor and senate:

> "And this food is called among us the Eucharist. . . . For not as common bread and common drink do we receive these; but in like manner as Jesus Christ our Savior, having been made flesh by the Word of God . . . so likewise we have been taught that the food which is blessed by the prayer of his word, and from which our blood and flesh by transformation are nourished, is the flesh and blood of that Jesus who was made flesh."
>
> —*First Apology of Justin*

Role of Women Women often led the way to Christianity. Many welcomed its promise that in the Church "there is neither Jew nor Greek . . . neither slave nor free . . . neither male nor female." In early Christian communities, women served as teachers and administrators. Even when they were later barred from any official role in the Church, they still worked to win converts across the Roman world.

Structure of the Church Each Christian community had its own priest. Only men were allowed to become members of the Christian clergy. Priests came under the authority of a bishop, a Church official who was responsible for all Christians in an area called a diocese (dī uh sihs). Bishops traced their spiritual authority to the apostles, and through the apostles, to Jesus himself. In the early Christian Church, all bishops were considered equal successors of the apostles.

Gradually, the bishops of the most important cities in the Roman empire gained greater authority. The bishops of Rome, Antioch, Alexandria, Jerusalem, and Constantinople gained the honorary title of patriarch, and exercised authority over other bishops in their area. Except for Rome, the cities in which patriarchs resided were all in the eastern empire. The Christian Church thus developed into a hierarchy, or organization in which officials are arranged according to rank.

A Sacred Meal
Christians gathered frequently to celebrate the sacred meal of the Eucharist. The gilded plate and chalice shown here held the bread and wine of the Eucharist.

Theme: Religions and Value Systems Why did Christians consider the Eucharist so important?

Divisions in the Church As the rituals and structure of the Church became more defined, divisions began to arise. A major divisive force was rivalry among the patriarchs. In the Latin-speaking west, bishops of Rome, who came to be called popes, began to claim greater authority over all other bishops. In the Greek-speaking east, the patriarchs felt that the five patriarchs should share spiritual authority as equals.

Another source of disunity was the emergence of heresies, or beliefs said to be contrary to official Church teachings. To end disputes over questions of faith, councils of Church leaders met to decide official Christian teachings. The Church also sent out missionaries both within the Roman empire and beyond to convert people to Christianity.

Theology and Scholarship Early Christians produced an abundance of works on Judeo-Christian theology. The word *theology* was borrowed from Greek philosophy and literally means "talk or discourse about God."

Two leading scholars of the early Christian Church were Clement and Origen. Both lived and worked as teachers in the Egyptian city of Alexandria, a major center of learning in the Roman world. And, like most Christian scholars of their time, they both wrote in Greek.

Origen was most respected for his intellectual achievements. Though he fully accepted the traditions of the Gospels, he also believed that he and other Christians could reach a deeper understanding of Jesus' teachings through reflection. Several of his works, such as *On Prayer* and *On First Principles,* exerted a lasting influence on Christianity.

Perhaps the greatest of the early Church scholars was Augustine, who was bishop of Hippo in North Africa. He combined Greco-Roman learning, especially the philosophy of Plato, with Christian doctrine. Shocked by the sack of Rome in 410, Augustine wrote *The City of God*. In this work, Augustine said the City of God was the community of those who loved God and would one day live with him in heaven. Those whose minds and hearts were set only on worldly things lived outside the City of God.

Looking Ahead

While the Christian Church was growing in strength and influence, Roman power was fading. When the western Roman empire finally collapsed, the Church inherited many of its functions. The Church preserved and spread not only Christian teachings but also the achievements of Greco-Roman civilization. In this way, the foundation was laid for the future development of western civilization.

SECTION 4 Assessment

Recall
1. Identify: **(a)** Jesus, **(b)** Gospels, **(c)** Paul, **(d)** Edict of Milan.
2. Define: **(a)** messiah, **(b)** apostle, **(c)** martyr, **(d)** bishop, **(e)** diocese, **(f)** patriarch, **(g)** pope, **(h)** heresy.

Comprehension
3. What was Rome's policy toward most of the religions in the empire?
4. **(a)** Describe three basic teachings of Jesus. **(b)** Why did many people find Jesus' ideas attractive?
5. What beliefs and practices did early Christians have in common?

Critical Thinking and Writing
6. **Synthesizing Information** How do you think the geography of the Roman empire and Rome's extensive road system helped Christianity to spread?
7. **Making Inferences** Some emperors persecuted Christians for their refusal to make sacrifices to the emperor or to honor Roman gods. Why do you think emperors considered this refusal a threat to the empire?

Activity
Take It to the NET

Use Internet sources to find information about the life and career of Origen or Augustine. Use the information to write a brief biographical sketch of the person you have chosen.

The Long Decline

Reading Focus

- How did Roman emperors try to end the crisis in the empire?
- How did Hun invasions contribute to the decline of Rome?
- How did economic and social problems lead to the fall of Rome?

Vocabulary

inflation
mercenary

Taking Notes

Copy the partially completed cause-and-effect chart below. As you read, fill in two more categories of causes. Then, add individual causes under the appropriate categories.

Military	Political		
• German invasions			
•			

DECLINE OF ROME

Main Idea Foreign invasions, along with political, social, and economic problems, led to the fall of the Roman empire.

Setting the Scene More than 1,500 years ago, the western half of the Roman empire stumbled into ruin. At the time, the spectacle of decline and defeat left Romans stunned. Some looked for reasons for the decay. The Roman historian Ammianus Marcellinus pointed to declining values. "Centers of learning," he wrote, "are now filled with ridiculous amusements . . . and the libraries are closed forever like so many graves." Marcellinus witnessed moral decay among Romans of all classes. Of the powerful, he complained that they "fall away into error and vice." Of the lower classes, he reported that "some spend the whole night in the wine shops . . . or else they play at dice." He was also alarmed about external threats to the empire, such as the invading Huns, who he feared could "force their way through all obstacles."

The end of Roman greatness did not occur overnight. Decay had set in centuries before the final fall. In the late 200s, for example, the empire was divided into two parts, each ruled by a co-emperor. A complex combination of problems led to the decline and fall of the western Roman empire.

Crisis and Reforms

After the death of the emperor Marcus Aurelius in 180, the golden age of the Pax Romana ended. For the next 100 years, political and economic turmoil rocked the Roman empire.

Struggles for Power During this period, a disruptive political pattern emerged. Again and again, emperors were overthrown by political intriguers or ambitious generals who seized power with the support of their troops. Those who rose to the imperial throne in this way ruled for just a few months or years until they, too, were overthrown or assassinated. In one 50-year period, at least 26 emperors reigned. Only one died of natural causes. Political violence and instability, rather than order and efficiency, thus became the rule.

Economic and Social Problems At the same time, the empire was shaken by disturbing social and economic trends. High taxes to support the army and the bureaucracy placed heavy burdens on business people and small farmers. Farmland that had been overcultivated for too many years lost its productivity.

Many poor farmers left their land and sought protection from wealthy landowners. Living on large estates, they worked for the landowners and

Sharing Power
Co-emperors Diocletian and Maximian shared the responsibility of ruling and defending the empire. Both established mobile imperial courts so that they could move swiftly to wherever a crisis broke out.

Theme: Political and Social Systems How do you think the division of the empire might have hastened Rome's decline?

Invasions of the Roman Empire to A.D. 500

Western Roman empire

Eastern Roman empire

★ Major battle sites

Azimuthal Equal Area Projection

0   250   500 Miles

0   250   500 Kilometers

farmed small plots for themselves. Although technically free, they were not allowed to leave the land.

Emperor Diocletian   In 284, the emperor Diocletian (DĪ uh KLEE shuhn) set out to restore order. To make the empire easier to govern, he divided it into two parts. He kept control of the wealthier eastern part himself but appointed a co-emperor to rule the western provinces. The co-emperor was responsible to Diocletian, who retained absolute power.

Diocletian tried to increase the prestige of the emperor by surrounding himself with elaborate ceremonies. He wore purple robes embroidered with gold and a crown encrusted with jewels. Anyone who approached the throne had to kneel and kiss the hem of the emperor's robe.

Diocletian also took steps to end the empire's economic decay. To slow inflation, or the rapid rise of prices, he fixed prices for goods and services. Other laws forced farmers to remain on the land. In cities, sons were required to follow their fathers' occupations. These rules were meant to ensure steady production of food and other goods.

Emperor Constantine   In 312, the talented general Constantine gained the throne. As emperor, Constantine continued Diocletian's reforms. More important, he took two steps that changed the course of European history.

First, as you have read, Constantine granted toleration to Christians. By doing so, he encouraged the rapid growth of Christianity within the empire and guaranteed its future success.

Second, he built a new capital, Constantinople, on the Bosporus, the strait that connects the Black and Mediterranean seas. By making his capital there, Constantine made the eastern portion of the empire the center of power. The western Roman empire was in decline, but the eastern Roman empire, which had more people and greater resources, would prosper for centuries to come.

Mixed Results The reforms of Diocletian and Constantine had mixed results. They revived the economy. And by increasing the power of government, they helped hold the empire together for another century. Still, the reforms failed to stop the long-term decline. In the end, internal problems combined with attacks from outside to bring the empire down.

Foreign Invasions

For centuries, Rome had faced attacks from the Germanic peoples who lived east of the Rhine and north of the Danube rivers. When Rome was powerful, the legions on the frontiers were successful in holding back the invaders. Some of the Germanic peoples who lived along the borders learned Roman ways and became allies of the Romans.

Impact of the Huns As early as A.D. 200, wars in East Asia set off a chain of events that would eventually overwhelm Rome, thousands of miles to the west. Those wars sent the Huns, a nomadic people, migrating across Central Asia. By 350, the Huns reached eastern Europe. These skilled riders fought fierce battles to dislodge the Germanic peoples in their path. The Visigoths, Ostrogoths, and other Germanic peoples crossed into Roman territory seeking safety.

Men armed with spears moved in bands along with women and children, carts and herds, hoping to settle on Roman land. With the empire in decline, Roman legions were hard pressed to halt the invading peoples. Under pressure from attacks, the Roman empire surrendered first Britain, then France and Spain. It was only a matter of time before foreign invaders marched into Italy and took over Rome itself.

Rome Defeated In 378, when a Roman army tried to turn back the Visigoths at Adrianople, it suffered a stunning defeat. Roman power was fading. New waves of invaders were soon hammering at Rome's borders, especially in the west. In 410, the Visigoth general Alaric overran Italy and plundered Rome. Meanwhile, the Vandals moved through Gaul and Spain into North Africa. Gradually, other Germanic peoples occupied more and more of the western Roman empire.

For Rome, the worst was yet to come. Starting in 434, the Hun leader Attila embarked on a savage campaign of conquest across much of Europe. Christians called Attila the "scourge of God" because they believed his attacks were a punishment for the sins of humankind. Attila died in 453. Although his empire collapsed soon after, the Hun invasion sent still more Germanic peoples fleeing into the Roman empire.

Finally, in 476, Odoacer (oh doh AY suhr), a Germanic leader, ousted the emperor in Rome. Later, historians referred to that event as the "fall" of Rome. By then, however, Rome had already lost many of its territories, and Roman power in the west had ended.

Causes of the Fall of Rome

The passing of Rome's power and greatness was a major turning point in the history of western civilization. Why did Rome "fall"? Modern historians identify a number of interrelated causes.

Military Causes Perhaps the most obvious cause of Rome's fall was the Germanic invasions. Still, these attacks were successful in part because Roman legions of the late empire lacked the discipline and training of past Roman armies. To meet its need for soldiers, Rome hired mercenaries, or foreign soldiers serving for pay, to defend its borders. Many were German warriors who, according to some historians, felt little loyalty to Rome.

Primary Source

Admiration for the Germans
The eagles above, crafted by Visigoth artisans, give evidence of Germanic cultural pursuits. Although most Romans viewed the Germans simply as barbaric invaders, the Roman historian Tacitus admired Germanic culture:

"No nation indulges more profusely in entertainments and hospitality. To exclude any human being from their roof is thought impious; every German, according to his means, receives his guest with a well-furnished table. When his supplies are exhausted, he who was . . . the host becomes the guide and companion to further hospitality, and without invitation they go to the next house. It matters not; they are entertained with like cordiality. No one distinguishes between an acquaintance and a stranger, as regards the rights of hospitality. It is usual to give the departing guest whatever he may ask for, and a present in return is asked with as little hesitation."

—Tacitus, *Germania*

Skills Assessment

Primary Source What did a German host do after he ran out of food and drink for his guest?

Why Did Rome Fall?

Although historians often cite 476 as the official date of the fall of Rome, the Roman empire had been in trouble for centuries. The illustration, the quotation, and the graphic organizer on this page all give clues to why Rome declined.

Hun Warrior

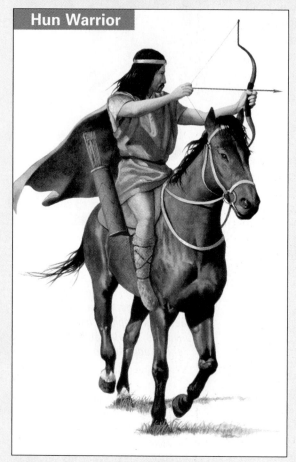

Hun warriors struck fear in the hearts of their enemies. Swooping down on horseback, they shot arrows great distances with deadly accuracy. The Huns were among the many groups of invaders who defeated weakened Roman legions.

Corruption in Rome

"Rome is still looked upon as the queen of the earth, and the name of the Roman people is respected and venerated. But the magnificence of Rome is defaced by the [stupidity] of a few, who never recollect where they are born, but fall away into error and [corruption]. . . . The Romans have even sunk so far, that not long ago, when [there was a famine] and the foreigners were driven from the city, [scholars] were expelled instantly, yet the followers of actresses and all their ilk were [allowed] to stay. . . . "

—Ammianus Marcellinus,
The Luxury of the Rich in Rome

The Decline and Fall of Rome

Military Causes
- Germanic invasions
- Weakened Roman legions

Political Causes
- Oppressive government
- Corrupt officials
- Divided empire

The Decline and Fall of Rome

Social Causes
- Erosion of traditional values
- Self-serving upper class
- "Bread and circuses"

Economic Causes
- Heavy taxes
- Population decline

Skills Tip

Graphic organizers show information in an easy-to-read format. Read the information in the boxes and trace the arrows to determine the main idea of the graphic organizer.

Skills Assessment

1. What type of cause shown in the graphic organizer does the Hun warrior illustrate?
   A social cause
   B political cause
   C economic cause
   D military cause

2. According to Ammianus Marcellinus, Rome's greatness was threatened by
   E Romans who wanted only amusements.
   F an increase in interest in liberal studies.
   G invasion by the Huns.
   H a shrinking population of foreigners.

3. **Critical Thinking Synthesizing Information** According to one historian, Rome's decline and fall were a result of its prosperity and power. He said that we should not concern ourselves with why the Roman empire fell, but with why it lasted as long as it did. Using the information above, explain why you agree or disagree with this idea.

Political Causes Political problems also contributed to Rome's decline. First, as the government became more oppressive and authoritarian, it lost the support of the people. Growing numbers of corrupt officials undermined loyalty, too. So did frequent civil wars over succession to the imperial throne. Again and again, rival armies battled to have their commanders chosen as emperor. Perhaps most important, dividing the empire at a time when it was under attack may have weakened it beyond repair. The richer eastern Roman empire did little to help the west.

Economic Causes Economic problems were widespread in the empire. Heavier and heavier taxes were required to support the vast government bureaucracy and huge military establishment. At the same time, reliance on slave labor discouraged Romans from exploring new technology. The wealth of the empire dwindled as farmers abandoned their land and the middle classes sank into poverty. Some scholars have suggested that climatic change was yet another reason for reduced agricultural productivity. In addition, the population itself declined as war and epidemic diseases swept the empire.

Social Causes For centuries, worried Romans pointed to the decline in values such as patriotism, discipline, and devotion to duty on which the empire was built. The need to replace citizen soldiers with mercenaries testified to the decline of patriotism. The upper class, which had once provided leaders, devoted itself to luxury and self-interest. Besides being costly, providing "bread and circuses" may also have undermined the self-reliance of the masses.

Did Rome Fall? Although we talk of the "fall" of Rome, the Roman empire did not disappear from the map in 476. An emperor still ruled the eastern Roman empire, which later became known as the Byzantine empire and lasted for another 1,000 years.

The phrase "the fall of Rome" is, in fact, shorthand for a long, slow change from one way of life to another. Roman civilization survived the events of 476. In Italy, people continued to live much as they had before, though under new rulers. Many still spoke Latin and obeyed Roman laws.

Over the next centuries, however, German customs and languages replaced much of Roman culture. Old Roman cities crumbled, and Roman roads disappeared. Still, the Christian Church preserved elements of Roman civilization. In later chapters, you will read how Roman and Christian traditions gave rise to medieval civilization in western Europe.

SECTION 5 Assessment

Recall
1. **Identify: (a)** Diocletian, **(b)** Constantine, **(c)** Huns, **(d)** Visigoths, **(e)** Alaric, **(f)** Attila, **(g)** Odoacer.
2. **Define: (a)** inflation, **(b)** mercenary.

Comprehension
3. **(a)** Describe the crisis that afflicted the Roman empire after the Pax Romana ended. **(b)** List two ways in which Diocletian tried to ease the crisis.
4. How did the invasion of the Huns weaken the Roman empire?
5. What social problems contributed to the decline of the Roman empire?

Critical Thinking and Writing
6. **Linking Past and Present** Imagine that the United States government in Washington no longer existed. What would be the effects on **(a)** your life, **(b)** your state, **(c)** the United States?
7. **Recognizing Causes and Effects** What were the causes and effects of the division of the Roman empire into two parts?

Activity

Creating a Booklet
Create an illustrated booklet explaining why the Roman empire fell. You may wish to use pictures, maps, cartoons, and graphic organizers to illustrate your booklet.

Creating a Chapter Summary

On a sheet of paper create a time line like the one started here. Add other important dates and events. Use the time line to review the events and developments that you have learned about in this chapter.

Romans drive out Etruscan king

264 B.C.

Fall of western Roman empire

500 B.C.

Punic Wars begin

A.D. 476

CD-ROM Review For additional review of the major concepts of Chapter 6, see the *Guide to the Essentials of World History* or the *Interactive Student Tutorial CD-ROM.*

Web Site Self-Test For practice test questions for Chapter 6, see **www.phschool.com.**

Building Vocabulary

Review the chapter vocabulary words listed below. Then, use the words and their definitions to create a matching quiz. Exchange quizzes with another student. Check each other's answers when you are finished.

1. republic
2. dictator
3. plebeian
4. imperialism
5. census
6. satirize
7. aqueduct
8. messiah
9. heresy
10. mercenary

Recalling Key Facts

11. How did tribunes protect plebeian interests in the Roman republic?
12. What were the results of the wars between Rome and Carthage?
13. How did Augustus' rise to power mark a significant change in Rome's form of government?
14. What were the major characteristics of the Pax Romana?
15. What were the important principles of Roman law?
16. How did Christianity spread through the Roman empire?

17. Describe three reasons for the fall of the Roman empire.

Critical Thinking and Writing

18. **Connecting to Geography** **(a)** How did geographic conditions make it easier to unite Italy than to unite Greece? **(b)** How did both Greece and Rome benefit from their location on the Mediterranean Sea?
19. **Making Decisions** Imagine that you were a Roman senator living at the time of Cato. Would you have supported his call to destroy Carthage? Why or why not?
20. **Linking Past and Present** "History," said Cicero, "illuminates reality, vitalizes memory, provides guidance in daily life, and brings us tidings of antiquity." **(a)** How did the work of Roman historians like Livy and Tacitus illustrate Cicero's idea? **(b)** Do you think Cicero's views on the value of history are still valid today? Why or why not?
21. **Solving Problems** **(a)** Describe two policies that Rome might have followed to restore its strength in the later years of the empire. **(b)** Do you think it would have been possible for the Romans to follow such policies? Why or why not?

The excerpt below is from a letter sent by Emperor Trajan to Pliny the Younger, one of his governors. After reading the excerpt, answer the questions that follow.

> "The method you have pursued, my dear Pliny, in sifting the cases of those denounced to you as Christians is extremely proper. . . . No search should be made for these people; when they are denounced and found guilty they must be punished, with the restriction, however, that when the party denies himself to be a Christian and shall give proof that he is not (that is, by adoring our gods), he shall be pardoned on the ground of repentance, even though he may have formerly incurred suspicion. Information without the accuser's name subscribed [affixed] must not be admitted in evidence against anyone, as it is introducing a very dangerous precedent and by no means agreeable to the spirit of the age."

—quoted in Pliny the Younger, *Letters*

22. Based on this letter, why do you think Trajan supported the persecution of Christians?
23. Why do you think Trajan felt the need to write this letter to Pliny?
24. **(a)** How could a person accused of being a Christian be pardoned? **(b)** Do you think many Christians avoided punishment in this way? Explain.
25. What kind of evidence does Trajan declare to be inadmissible evidence?
26. Based on this letter, do you think Trajan was strongly committed to the policy of persecution? Why or why not?

INFLUENTIAL ROMAN EMPERORS

Leader Years in Office	Major Policies
Augustus 31 B.C.–A.D. 14	Ended civil war; reformed government; established empire
Nero A.D. 54–A.D. 68	Persecuted Christians after fire destroyed much of Rome
Vespasian A.D. 69–A.D. 79	Authorized building projects in Rome; reorganized government finance
Hadrian A.D. 117–A.D. 138	Built Hadrian's Wall in Britain; codified Roman law
Marcus Aurelius A.D. 161–A.D. 180	Helped unify empire economically; made legal reforms
Constantine A.D. 306–A.D. 337	Ended persecution of Christians; called Nicaea council to settle Church disputes; built new capital of Constantinople

Study the table above and then answer the following questions:

27. Which emperor's reign was the longest? Which was the shortest?
28. How did the religious policies of Nero and Constantine differ?
29. Which emperor built a structure to help keep invaders out of Britain?
30. How did Constantine reduce the importance and power of the city of Rome?
31. Which emperor had the longest reign?

Skills Tip

When you use a table, be sure to read the title and the headings first.

Use the Internet to research the territorial expansion of the Roman empire. Then, create a map of the empire at its height. Draw present-day national boundaries on the map to show which nations were once part of the Roman empire.

Civilizations of the Americas 1400 B.C.–A.D. 1570

Chapter Preview

1 Civilizations of Middle America
2 The World of the Incas
3 Peoples of North America

1400 B.C.

The Olmecs establish the first American civilization. Remains of their culture include giant heads carved in stone.

850 B.C.

Construction takes place on a huge temple in Chavín de Huantar.

A.D. 300

The Mayas begin to build elaborate cities, which include enormous pyramids such as the Temple of the Magician, shown here.

CHAPTER EVENTS

1400 B.C.

1000 B.C.

A.D. 400

GLOBAL EVENTS

1027 B.C. The Zhou dynasty is founded in China.

A.D. 392 Christianity becomes the official religion of the Roman empire.

Trade Routes in the Americas

Early civilizations throughout the Americas traded a wide variety of goods.

Trade routes

SIBERIA

Bering Strait

NORTH AMERICA

ROCKY MTS.

GREAT PLAINS

MISSISSIPPI R.

APPALACHIAN MTS

W. SIERRA MADRE

E. SIERRA MADRE

Gulf of Mexico

Yucatán Peninsula

CENTRAL AMERICA

Caribbean Sea

ATLANTIC OCEAN

PACIFIC OCEAN

Amazon R.

SOUTH AMERICA

ANDES MTS.

Atacama Desert

Brazilian Highlands

Robinson Projection

0   1000   2000 Miles

0   1000   2000 Kilometers

N W E S

0° Equator

A.D. 900s

The Anasazis build pueblo towns and create elaborately decorated pottery, such as these clay mugs.

A.D. 1200

The Mississippian center of Cahokia thrives.

A.D. 1400s

The Aztec empire expands across Mexico, from the Gulf of Mexico to the Pacific Ocean.

A.D. 800

A.D. 1200

A.D. 1600

A.D. 800 Pope Leo III crowns Charlemagne emperor of the Romans.

A.D. 1556 Akbar begins his rule of Mughal India.

Chapter 7 **155**

Civilizations of Middle America

Reading Focus

- How did geography affect the development of cultures in the Americas?

- What were the main features of Olmec and Mayan civilizations?

- How did the Aztec culture develop?

Vocabulary

global warming

plains

chinampas

tribute

Taking Notes

As you read this section, prepare an outline of the contents. Use Roman numerals to indicate major headings. Use capital letters for the subheadings and numbers for the supporting details. The sample at right will help you get started.

I. Civilizations of Middle America
A. Geography of the Americas
   1. Earth grows warmer
   2. Agricultural revolution
B. Olmecs develop first American civilization

Main Idea Climate and geography contributed to the rise of several powerful civilizations in Middle America.

Setting the Scene

The Aztecs of Middle America evolved a complex system of religious beliefs. Their religions, like those of many other people, included a belief that the world and all of its inhabitants would someday come to a fiery end.

According to the Aztec Legend of the Suns, the universe had been created and destroyed four times in the past. People living under the First Sun had been destroyed by jaguars. Next, people living under the Second Sun were swept away by wind. People living under the Third Sun perished in the fire and ash of volcanoes, while those people who lived under the Fourth Sun had been swallowed by water. The Fifth Sun represented the time of the Aztec empire:

> "This is our Sun, the one in which we now live. And here is its sign, how the Sun fell into the fire, into the divine hearth . . . . And as the elders continue to say, under the Sun there will be earthquakes and hunger, and then our end shall come."
> —quoted in *Seeds of Change* (Viola)

The Legend of the Suns reflects the important role of the sun in Aztec religion. It also suggests a feeling of helplessness in the face of the harsh forces of nature. Despite this sense of impending doom, the Aztecs were able to create a remarkable civilization. In order to do so, they built on the achievements of earlier peoples. To understand more about these early American civilizations, we must go far back in time to the arrival of the first people in the Americas.

Geography of the Americas

Perhaps as early as 30,000 years ago,* according to some scholars, small family groups of Paleolithic hunters and food gatherers reached North America from Asia. This great migration took place during the last ice age. At that time, so much water froze into thick ice sheets that the sea level dropped, exposing a land bridge between Siberia and Alaska, in the area now known as the Bering Strait. Many historians believe that hunters followed herds of bison and mammoths across this land bridge. Other migrating people may have paddled small boats and fished along the coasts.

Geography and History

When Were the Americas First Settled?

For many years, scientists believed that human migration to the Americas from Siberia began about 11,500 years ago. But recent finds challenge that view.

In New Mexico, fingerprints were found preserved in clay at least 13,000 years old. In Virginia, stone tools more than 15,000 years old were found.

Based on such finds, archaeologists are beginning to question when the first people migrated to the Americas from Asia, and even if they may have come from other places as well.

Theme: Geography and History A skeleton found in Brazil is believed to be 11,500 years old. How would this information contradict the theory that people first migrated from Siberia to Alaska 11,500 years ago?

---

*Scholars disagree about exactly when the first people reached the Americas. They have proposed dates ranging from 70,000 to 10,000 years ago.

Global Warming About 10,000 B.C., the Earth's climate grew warmer. As the ice melted, water levels rose, covering the land bridge under the Bering Strait. The global warming—or worldwide temperature increase—along with the hunting skills of the first Americans, may have killed off large game animals like the mammoth. People adapted by hunting smaller animals, fishing, and gathering fruit, roots, and shellfish. These nomadic hunter-gatherers slowly migrated eastward and southward across the Americas.

Regions What lands did the first Americans explore and settle? The Americas are made up of the two continents of North America and South America. Within these two geographic regions is a cultural region that historians call Middle America. Middle America includes Mexico and Central America and was home to several early civilizations.

Great mountain chains form a spiny backbone down the western Americas. In North America, the Rocky Mountains split into the East and West Sierra Madre of Mexico. The towering Andes run down the length of South America. The continents are drained by two of the world's three longest rivers, the Amazon of South America and the Mississippi of North America.

The first Americans adapted to a variety of climates and resources. Far to the north and the south, people learned to survive in icy, treeless lands. Closer to the Equator, people settled in the hot, wet climate and thick vegetation of the Amazon rain forests. Elsewhere, hunters adapted to deserts like the Atacama of Chile, woodlands like those in eastern North America, and the fertile plains, or rolling flatlands, of both continents.

The Agricultural Revolution In the Americas, as elsewhere, the greatest adaptation occurred when some people learned to cultivate plants and domesticate animals. Archaeologists think that farming was partly a response to the disappearance of the large mammals. With fewer animals to hunt, people came to depend more on other food sources. In Mexico, or perhaps farther south, Neolithic people began cultivating a range of crops, from corn and beans to sweet potatoes, peppers, tomatoes, and squash. These changes took place slowly between about 8500 B.C. and 2000 B.C.

Early American farmers learned to domesticate animals. In South America, domesticated animals include the llama and other creatures valued for their wool. However, the Americas had no large animals such as oxen or horses that were capable of bearing heavy loads or pulling wagons. This lack of draft animals would limit development in some areas.

In the Americas, as in Africa and Eurasia, the agricultural revolution helped to cause other changes. Farming people settled into villages. Populations expanded. Some villages grew into large religious centers and then into the great cities of the first American civilizations.

Legacy of the Olmecs

The earliest American civilization emerged in the tropical forests along the Mexican Gulf Coast. The Olmec civilization lasted from about 1400 B.C. to 500 B.C.

Geography of the Americas

Land bridge about 18,000 B.C.

Mayan civilization, A.D. 300–A.D. 900

Aztec empire, A.D. 1200s–A.D. 1521

Incan empire, A.D. 1400s–A.D. 1535

Lambert Equal Area Projection

0   1000   2000 Miles

0   1000   2000 Kilometers

Archaeologists know very little about the Olmecs. However, rich tombs and temples suggest that a powerful class of priests and aristocrats stood at the top of Olmec society. The Olmecs did not build true cities. Rather, they built ceremonial centers made up of pyramid-shaped temples and other buildings. People came from nearby farming villages to work on the temples or attend religious ceremonies.

The most dramatic remains of the Olmec civilization are the giant carved stone heads found in the ruins of a religious center at La Venta. No one knows how the Olmecs moved these colossal 40-ton stones from distant quarries without wheeled vehicles or draft animals.

Through trade, Olmec influence spread over a wide area. The grinning jaguars and serpents that decorate many Olmec carvings appear in the arts of later peoples. The Olmecs also invented a calendar and used carved inscriptions as a form of writing. But their most important legacy may have been the tradition of priestly leadership and religious devotion that became a basic part of later Middle American civilizations.

The World of the Mayas

Among the peoples influenced by the Olmecs were the Mayas. Between A.D. 300 and 900, Mayan city-states flourished from the Yucatán in southern Mexico through much of Central America.

Scientists have recently determined how Mayan farming methods allowed them to thrive in the tropical environment. Mayan farmers cleared the dense rain forests and then built raised fields that caught and held rainwater. They also built channels that could be opened to drain excess water. This complex system produced enough native corn, called maize, and other crops to support rapidly growing cities.

Temples and Palaces Towering pyramid temples dominated the largest Mayan city of Tikal (tee KAHL), in present-day Guatemala. Priests climbed steep temple stairs to perform sacrifices on high platforms, while ordinary people watched from the plazas far below. Some temples also served as burial places for nobles and priests. The Mayan pyramids remained the tallest structures in the Americas until 1903, when the Flatiron Building, a skyscraper, was built in New York City.

Tikal also boasted large palaces and huge stone pillars covered with elaborate carvings. The carvings, which usually record events in Mayan history, preserve striking images of haughty aristocrats, warriors in plumed headdresses, and captives about to be sacrificed to the gods.

Much of the wealth of Tikal and the other Mayan cities came from trade. Along roads made of packed earth, traders carried valuable cargoes of honey, cocoa, cotton cloth, and feathers to exchange with other people across Middle America.

Social Classes Each Mayan city had its own ruling chief. He was surrounded by nobles who served as military leaders and officials who managed public works, collected taxes, and enforced laws. Rulers were usually men, but Mayan records and carvings show that women occasionally governed on their own or in the name of young sons. Priests held great power because only they could conduct the elaborate ceremonies needed to ensure good harvests and success in war.

Mayan Ball Games
Ball courts (PAST) were a key feature of Mayan cities. Spectators watched as two teams competed to drive a solid rubber ball through a stone ring that hung from a wall. Opposing players moved the ball across the court by using their bodies, but not their hands and feet. Players wore protective helmets and padding, but injuries were still common. Today, ball games such as soccer (PRESENT) continue to be popular with players and spectators alike.

Theme: Continuity and Change What modern games are similar to the Mayan ball game? Describe the similarities.

PAST

PRESENT

Most Mayas were farmers. They grew corn, beans, and squash—the basic food crops of Middle America—as well as fruit trees, cotton, and brilliant tropical flowers. Men usually cultivated the crops, while women turned them into food. To support the cities, farmers paid taxes in food and helped build the temples.

Advances in Learning Along with their magnificent buildings and carvings, the Mayas made impressive advances in learning. They developed a hieroglyphic writing system, which has only recently been deciphered. Mayan scribes kept their sacred knowledge in books made of bark. Though Spanish conquerors later burned most of these books, a handful were taken to Europe and survive in European museums.

Mayan priests needed to measure time accurately in order to hold ceremonies at the correct moment. As a result, many priests became expert mathematicians and astronomers. They developed an accurate 365-day solar calendar, as well as a 260-day calendar based on the orbit of the planet Venus. Mayan priests also invented a numbering system and understood the concept of zero.

Decline About A.D. 900, the Mayas abandoned their cities, leaving their great stone palaces and temples to be swallowed up by the jungle. Not until modern times were these "lost cities" rediscovered.

No one knows for sure why Mayan civilization declined. Possibly, frequent warfare forced the Mayas to abandon their traditional agricultural methods. Or overpopulation may have led to overfarming, which in turn exhausted the soil. Heavy taxes to finance wars and temple building may have sparked peasant revolts. Still, remnants of Mayan culture have survived. Today, millions of people in Guatemala and southern Mexico speak Mayan languages and are descended from the builders of this early American civilization.

Roots of Aztec Culture

Long before Mayan cities rose to the south, the city of Teotihuacán (tay oh tee wah KAHN) had emerged in the Valley of Mexico. The Valley of Mexico is a huge oval basin ringed by snowcapped volcanoes, located in the high plateau of central Mexico. From A.D. 100 to A.D. 750, Teotihuacán dominated a large area.

Teotihuacán The city of Teotihuacán was well planned, with wide roads, massive temples, and large apartment buildings. Along the main avenue, the Pyramid of the Sun and the Pyramid of the Moon rose majestically toward the sky. Citizens of Teotihuacán worshiped a powerful nature goddess and rain god, whose images often appear on public buildings and on everyday objects. Teotihuacán eventually fell to invaders, but its culture influenced later peoples, especially the Aztecs.

Arrival of the Aztecs In the late 1200s, bands of nomadic people, the ancestors of the Aztecs, migrated into the Valley of Mexico from the north. According to Aztec legend, the gods had told them to search for an eagle perched atop a cactus holding a snake in its beak. They finally saw the sign on a swampy island in Lake Texcoco. Once settled, the Aztecs shifted from hunting to farming. Slowly, they built the city of Tenochtitlán (tay nawch tee TLAHN), on the site of present-day Mexico City.

As their population grew, the Aztecs found ingenious ways to create more farmland. They built chinampas, artificial islands made of earth piled on reed mats that were anchored to the shallow lake bed. On these "floating gardens," they raised corn, squash, and beans. They gradually filled in parts of the lake and created canals for transportation. Wide stone causeways linked Tenochtitlán to the mainland.

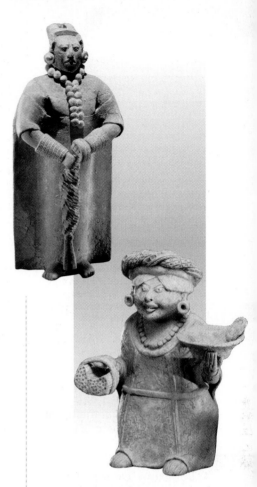

Mayan Society in Art
Mayan potters fashioned clay figurines depicting people at all levels of society. Here, an aristocrat (top) poses in his robes, while a peasant woman (bottom) holds tortillas.

Theme: Art and Literature
How do these figurines suggest that these two people were from different social classes?

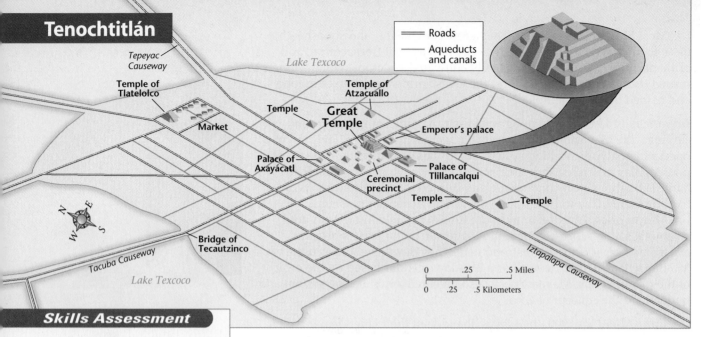

Tenochtitlán

Tepeyac Causeway

Lake Texcoco

Temple of Tlatelolco

Market

Temple

Temple of Atzacuallo

Great Temple

Emperor's palace

Palace of Axayácatl

Ceremonial precinct

Palace of Tlillancalqui

Temple

Temple

Bridge of Tecautzinco

Tacuba Causeway

Lake Texcoco

Iztapalapa Causeway

Roads
Aqueducts and canals

0   .25   .5 Miles
0   .25   .5 Kilometers

Skills Assessment

Geography The Aztec capital, Tenochtitlán, was located in Lake Texcoco and connected to the mainland by causeways. In the center of the city, people gathered at the Great Temple, the emperor's palace, the market, or other public centers.

1. **Location** *On the map, locate (a) Great Temple, (b) market, (c) emperor's palace, (d) Lake Texcoco.*
2. **Interaction** *Give two examples of ways the Aztecs adapted their environment to meet their needs in Tenochtitlán.*
3. **Critical Thinking Analyzing Information** *How does the map suggest that religion played an important role in Aztec life?*

Conquering an Empire In the 1400s, the Aztecs greatly expanded their territory. Through a combination of fierce conquests and shrewd alliances, they spread their rule across most of Mexico, from the Gulf of Mexico on the east to the Pacific Ocean on the west. By 1500, the Aztec empire numbered an estimated 30 million people.

War brought immense wealth as well as power. Tribute, or payment from conquered peoples, helped the Aztecs turn their capital into a magnificent city.

The World of the Aztecs

When the Spanish reached Tenochtitlán in 1519, they were awestruck at its magnificence. The Spanish conqueror Hernán Cortés described the city as it looked then:

> "The city has many squares where markets are held and trading is carried on. There is one square . . . where there are daily more than 60,000 souls, buying and selling, and where are found all the kinds of merchandise produced in these countries, including food products, jewels of gold and silver, lead, brass, copper, zinc, bones, shells, and feathers."
> —Hernán Cortés, quoted in
> *Latin American Civilization* (Keen)

From its temples and royal palaces to its zoos and floating gardens, Tenochtitlán was a city of wonders. It was also the center of a complex, well-ordered empire.

Government and Society Unlike the Mayan city-states, each of which had its own king, the Aztecs had a single ruler. The emperor was chosen by a council of nobles and priests to lead in war. Below him, nobles served as officials, judges, and governors of conquered provinces. They enjoyed special privileges such as wearing luxurious feathered cloaks and gold jewelry. Next came the warriors, who could rise to noble status by killing or capturing enemy soldiers. The majority of people were commoners who farmed the land.

At the bottom of society were the slaves, mostly criminals or prisoners of war. Despite their low status, slaves' rights were clearly spelled out by law. For example, slaves could own land and buy their freedom.

Buying Treasures in an Aztec Market

Thoughts of shopping fill you with excitement. Although Tenochtitlán's market is packed with eager buyers and sellers today, the crowd doesn't bother you. You are a wealthy Aztec noble, and your servants carry you above it all. Carefully, you clutch your bag of cocoa beans; they are very valuable and you will use them to buy what you want.

Thousands of different goods spill out over the vendors' tables. Some are ordinary—food products like tomatoes, chili peppers, or turkeys. Others dazzle you—turquoise masks and fine gold and silver jewelry.

First, you buy a fan made of brilliantly colored feathers. You will give it to your brother, an important government official. It will show his high rank in society.

After shopping for hours, you are ready to go home. Then, a cup carved like a rabbit catches your eye. You could use it to drink chocolate. Only the wealthy can drink this brew made from cocoa beans, so chocolate deserves a special cup. You decide to buy it.

Portfolio Assessment

Write a shopping list for your next trip to the market. Briefly explain why you need each item on the list. Refer to the mural above for ideas.

Protected by Aztec power, a class of long-distance traders ferried goods across the empire and beyond. From the highlands, they took goods such as weapons, tools, and rope to barter for tropical products such as jaguar skins and cocoa beans. They also served as spies, finding new areas for trade and conquest.

Religious Beliefs The priests were a class apart. They performed the rituals needed to please the many Aztec gods and prevent droughts, floods, or other disasters. The chief Aztec god was Huitzilopochtli (wee tsee loh POHKT lee), the sun god. His giant pyramid-temple towered above central Tenochtitlán.

Huitzilopochtli, the Aztecs believed, battled the forces of darkness each night and was reborn each morning. As the Legend of the Suns shows, there was no guarantee that the sun would always win. To give the sun strength to rise each day, the Aztecs offered human sacrifices. Priests offered the hearts of tens of thousands of victims to Huitzilopochtli and other Aztec gods. Most of the victims were prisoners of war, but sometimes a noble family gave up one of its own members to appease the gods.

Other cultures such as the Olmecs and the Mayas had practiced human sacrifice, but not on the massive scale of the Aztecs. The Aztecs carried on almost continuous warfare, using the captured enemy soldiers for a regular source of sacrificial victims. Among the conquered peoples, discontent festered and rebellion often flared up. When the armies from Spain later arrived, they found ready allies among peoples who were ruled by the Aztec empire.

Education and Learning Priests were the keepers of Aztec knowledge. They recorded laws and historical events. Some ran schools for the sons of nobles. Others used their knowledge of astronomy and mathematics to foretell the future. The Aztecs, like the Mayas, had an accurate calendar.

Like many other ancient peoples, the Aztecs believed that illness was a punishment from the gods. Still, Aztec priests used herbs and other medicines to treat fevers and wounds. Aztec physicians could set broken bones and treat dental cavities. They also prescribed steam baths as cures for various ills, a therapy still in use today.

Looking Ahead

The Aztecs developed a sophisticated and complex culture, but their world would not last forever. At the height of Aztec power, word reached Tenochtitlán that pale-skinned, bearded men had landed on the east coast. Later, you will read about the results of the encounter between the Aztecs and the newcomers from far-off Spain.

SECTION 1 Assessment

Recall
1. Identify: **(a)** Olmecs, **(b)** Tikal, **(c)** Teotihuacán, **(d)** Tenochtitlán.
2. Define: **(a)** global warming, **(b)** plains, **(c)** chinampas, **(d)** tribute.

Comprehension
3. How did early people adapt to different environments in the Americas?
4. **(a)** What role did religion play in Olmec and Mayan culture? **(b)** How was Mayan society organized?
5. How did the Aztecs build and control a powerful empire in Mexico?

Critical Thinking and Writing
6. **Connecting to Geography** Explain why a lack of large draft animals might limit agricultural development in some regions.
7. **Analyzing Information** How would archaeologists use evidence such as artwork and public buildings to trace the influence of the Olmecs or similar civilizations on later Middle American people?

Activity
Take It to the NET
Use the Internet to research the migration of people across the land bridge. Then, write a series of diary entries describing the crossing from Siberia into the Americas. Include descriptions of the animal and plant life encountered along the way.

The World of the Incas

Reading Focus

- What were the main achievements of the early peoples of Peru?
- How did Incan emperors extend and maintain their empire?
- How did the Incas live?

Vocabulary

glyph

quipu

alloy

Taking Notes

Copy this flowchart, adding information about each of the successive cultures that inhabited Peru. When possible, indicate how cultures influenced later peoples. Add more boxes as necessary.

CHAVÍN
850 B.C.
Influenced art and religion
of later cultures

Main Idea The Incas built a complex civilization that relied on order and absolute authority.

Setting the Scene The Sapa Inca lifted a golden cup to the rising sun, a gesture to honor his divine ancestor. He then entered the temple, where sunlight glinted off the golden statues along the walls. A priest placed a bundle of fibers on the altar. With a copper mirror, he directed the magical power of the sun's rays to explode the fibers into flame.

Other rituals followed. Priests sacrificed a llama and prayed for success in the coming year. When the ceremonies ended, horns blared the news to the crowds outside the temple. A shout rose: "*Hailli!*"—"Victory!" Reed pipes and flutes echoed the joy as people prepared for a day of feasting and dancing.

This ceremony honoring the sun god took place each year in Cuzco, capital of the Incan empire of Peru. By the early 1500s, the Incas, like the Aztecs, ruled a mighty empire.

Early Peoples of Peru

Western South America includes a wide variety of climates and terrains. The narrow coastal plain is a dry, lifeless desert crossed by occasional river valleys. Further inland, the snow-capped Andes Mountains rise steeply, leveling off into high plateaus that bake by day and freeze at night. East of the Andes lie dense jungles that stretch from Peru into Brazil.

Native American peoples developed many different styles of life across South America. Hunters and gatherers thrived in some regions, while farmers grew root crops in the Amazon rain forests. Thousands of years ago, people settled in fishing villages along the desert coast of Peru. Gradually they expanded inland, farming the river valleys that run up into the highland plateaus. Using careful irrigation, they grew corn, cotton, squash, and beans. On mountain slopes, they cultivated potatoes, eventually producing 700 varieties. In high plateaus, they domesticated the llama and the alpaca. Like the Mayas, they built large ceremonial centers and developed skills in pottery and weaving.

Chavín Through painstaking work at many sites, archaeologists have pieced together a chronology of various cultures that left their mark on the region. The earliest of these was the Chavín (chah VEEN) culture, named for ruins at Chavín de Huantar in the Andes. There, about 850 B.C., people built a huge temple complex. Stone carvings and pottery show that the Chavín people worshiped a ferocious-looking god, part jaguar and part human with grinning catlike features. The arts and religion of the Chavín culture influenced later peoples of Peru.

Peruvian Textile
Artisans among the Paracas, an early people of Peru, produced this cloak around the 500s B.C. Spinners, weavers, and skillful dyers worked together to create this fabric adorned with complex and imaginative designs.

Theme: Art and Literature
What does this fabric suggest about cultural development among the Paracas?

Mochica Between about A.D. 100 and 700, the Mochica people forged an empire along the arid north coast of Peru. The Mochicas were skilled farmers, developing methods of terracing, irrigation, and fertilization of the soil. Their leaders built roads and organized networks of relay runners to carry messages, ideas that the Incas would later adopt.

Remains of Mochica cities and temples dot the land. To build one temple, workers had to produce 130 million sun-dried adobe bricks. The people perfected skills in textile production, goldwork, and woodcarving. They produced remarkable pots decorated with realistic scenes of daily life. On these painted vases, helmeted warriors go into battle, musicians play pipes and drums, and women weave textiles on small portable looms.

Nazca Many other cultures left tantalizing clues to their lives and beliefs. In southern Peru, the Nazca people etched glyphs in the desert. A glyph is a pictograph or other symbol carved into a surface. Nazca glyphs include straight lines that run for miles, as well as giant figures of birds, whales, and other creatures. These figures may have been family symbols or part of an ancient calendar.

For more than 2,000 years, diverse civilizations rose and fell in Peru. Then, in the mid-1400s, the Incas emerged from high in the Andes. Incan armies rapidly conquered an empire that stretched 2,500 miles down the Andes and along the Pacific coast. Like the Romans, who also ruled a diverse empire, the Incas drew heavily on the ideas and skills of the peoples they conquered.

The Incan Empire

Pachacuti, a skilled warrior and leader, was the founder of the Incan empire. In 1438, he proclaimed himself Sapa Inca, or emperor, and set out on a policy of conquest. From a small kingdom in the high mountain valley of Cuzco, he came to dominate an immense empire. Once he had subdued neighboring peoples, he enlisted them in his armies for future campaigns. In this way, he and his son extended Incan rule from Ecuador in the north to Chile in the south.

Government The Sapa Inca exercised absolute power over the empire. Claiming that he was divine, the son of the sun itself, he was also the chief religious leader. Like the pharaohs of ancient Egypt, the Incan god-king owned all the land, herds, mines, and people. Gold, the "sweat of the sun," was his symbol. He lived in splendor, eating from golden plates and dressing in richly embroidered clothes. In fact, the Sapa Inca never wore the same royal garments twice. His queen, the Coya, carried out important religious duties and sometimes governed when the Sapa Inca was absent.

From Cuzco, the Incas ran an efficient government with a chain of command reaching into every village. Nobles ruled the provinces along with local chieftains whom the Incas had conquered. Below them, officials carried out the day-to-day business of collecting taxes and enforcing laws. Specially trained officials kept records on a quipu, a collection of knotted, colored strings. Modern scholars think that quipus noted dates and events as well as statistics on population and crops.

Roads and Runners To unite their empire, the Incas imposed their own language, Quechua (KEHCH wuh), and religion on the people. They also created one of the great road systems of history. It wound more than 12,000 miles through mountains and deserts. Hundreds of bridges spanned rivers and deep gorges. Steps were cut into steep slopes and tunnels dug through hillsides. Even more impressive than the roads that united the Roman empire, the Incan road system was unmatched until modern times.

The roads allowed armies and news to move rapidly throughout the empire. At regular stations, runners waited to carry messages. Relays of

Growing up, Pachacuti did not seem destined to rule the Incan people. True, his father, Viracocha, was their king. But Pachacuti was neither the eldest son—that was Urcon—nor his father's favorite.

Then one day, the army of a powerful neighboring people, the Chancas, swept down on Cuzco. Soon, the battle was going against the Incan army. Viracocha and Urcon fled the field for the safety of a mountain stronghold. But Pachacuti fought on, commanding the army and inspiring his warriors to turn almost certain defeat into a stunning victory. Within days, Pachacuti deposed the shamed Viracocha, denied the throne to Urcon, and seized it for himself.

Theme: Impact of the Individual From what you have read about Pachacuti, what traits and skills must he have had?

Incan Government

People of the Incan empire lived in one of the most highly ordered societies in history. Use the quotation, chart, and diagram below to draw conclusions about the government that created this order.

Incan System of Rule

Leader	Responsibility
The Inca	• Ruled the entire Incan empire
Suyuyuq Apu	• Controlled one of four regions of the empire
Hunu Kamayoq	• Governed a province containing 10,000 families
Waranq Kamayoq	• Acted as head of 1,000 families
Pichqa Pachaq Kamayoq	• Acted as head of 500 families
Pachaq Kamayoq	• Acted as head of 100 families
Pichqa Chunka Kamayoq	• Acted as head of 50 families
Chunka Kamayoq	• Acted as head of 10 families
Pichqa Kamayoq	• Acted as head of 5 families
Pureq	• Acted as head of 1 family

The Incan bureaucracy controlled life, even at the individual family level.

Incan Farming System

Field of the sun god, used for priests

Field of the sick, orphans, widows, and those away on government service

Field of the Inca, used for the state and the community

Field assigned for the needs of the individual families

All land belonged to the community. Farmers grew crops in different fields.

A Sapa Inca's Purpose

In the following quotation, the Inca explains what he believes the sun has ordered Incan rulers to do.

"'Each day that passes,' said our father, the sun, 'I go around the world in order to have a better knowledge of men's needs and to satisfy those needs. Follow my example: Do unto all of them as a merciful father would do to his well-beloved children; for I have sent you on earth for the good of men, that they might cease to live like wild animals. You shall be the kings and lords of all the peoples who accept our law and our rule.'"
—Garcilaso de la Vega, *The Royal Commentaries of the Inca*

Skills Tip

Start by reading the title of the activity to identify its general topic. Then, when you examine each source, ask yourself how the specific information presented relates to the general topic.

Skills Assessment

1. Like the sun god, the Inca was supposed to
   A satisfy his people's needs.
   B act like a favorite child.
   C prevent the division of land by the community.
   D accept the rule of the high priests.

2. How were orphans provided for by Incan society?
   E They became priests of the sun god.
   F They went to live with the Hunu Kamayoq.
   G They received crops from land assigned to them.
   H They were adopted by Incan nobles.

3. **Critical Thinking** **Drawing Conclusions** How might an Incan ruler explain the need to have such an extensive bureaucracy?

Virtual Field Trip

www.phschool.com

Machu Picchu, Peru

To learn more about Machu Picchu, use the Internet address above to link to the Web site of Machu Picchu, Peru.

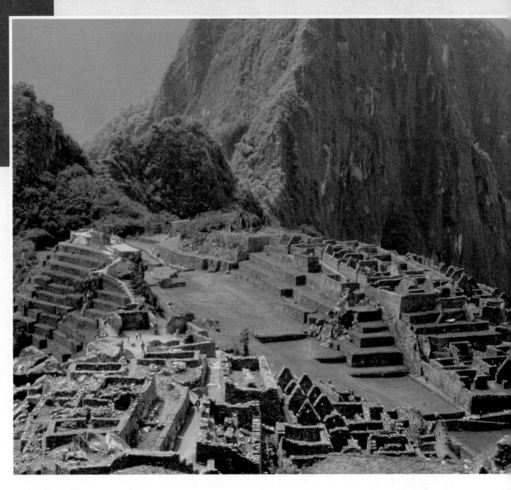

Machu Picchu

Machu Picchu lies some 7,000 feet above sea level. The sturdy walls have withstood centuries of earthquakes. Incan workers cut and fitted the stones together without the aid of mortar. Abandoned for some 300 years, the ruins of Machu Picchu were rediscovered in 1911.

Theme: Economics and Technology How do the ruins of Machu Picchu show that the Incan empire was well organized and technologically advanced?

Global Connections

Finding a Way Across

Like the Romans, the Incas were inventive road builders. But the deep gorges of the Andes presented a formidable obstacle: How can a road cross from one steep canyon wall to another, often high above a rushing river? The Incans built massive stone piers on either side and slung five cables of twisted fiber between them. They attached wooden crosspieces to three cables and made the other two handrails.

When Europeans first saw these flimsy-looking suspension bridges swaying in the wind, they were terrified of them. But they marveled too, knowing no way to improve upon their design.

Theme: Economics and Technology How did the environment affect Incan construction methods?

runners could carry news of a revolt swiftly from a distant province to the capital. The Incas kept soldiers at outposts throughout the empire. Within days of an uprising, they would be on the move to crush the rebels. Ordinary people, though, were restricted from using the roads at all.

Cuzco All roads led through Cuzco. The population was made up of representatives of all the peoples of the empire, each living in a particular part of the city. They wore regional costumes and practiced traditional crafts. In the heart of the city stood the great Temple of the Sun, its interior walls lined with gold. Like Incan palaces and forts, the temple was made of enormous stone blocks, each polished and carved to fit exactly in place. The engineering was so precise that, although no mortar was used to hold the stones together, Incan buildings have survived severe earthquakes.

Daily Life

The Incas strictly regulated the lives of millions of people within their empire. People lived in close-knit communities, called ayllus (Ī LOOZ). Leaders of each ayllu carried out government orders, assigning jobs to each family and organizing the community to work the land. Government officials arranged marriages to ensure that men and women were settled at a certain age.

Farming Farmers expanded the step terraces built by earlier peoples. On steep hillsides, they carved out strips of land to be held in place by stone walls. These terraces kept rains from washing away the soil and made farming possible in places where flat land was scarce.

Farmers had to spend part of each year working land for the emperor and the temples as well as for their own communities. All land belonged to the Inca, but cultivation and crops were allotted to specific groups of people or for particular purposes. The government took possession of each harvest, dividing it among the people and storing part of it in case of famine.

Metalworking The Incas were the best metalworkers in the Americas. They learned to work and alloy, or blend, copper, tin, bronze, silver, and gold. While they employed copper and bronze for useful objects, they used precious metals for statues of gods and goddesses, eating utensils for the aristocracy, and decorations.

Medical Advances The Incas developed some important medical practices, including surgery on the human skull. In such operations, they first cleaned the operating area and then made the patient unconscious with a drug—procedures much closer to the use of modern antiseptics and anesthesia than anything practiced in Europe at that time.

Religion Like other early peoples, the Incas were polytheistic, worshiping many gods linked to the forces of nature. People offered food, clothing, and drink to the guardian spirits of the home and the village. Religion was tied to the routines of life. Each month had its own festival, from the great ripening and the dance of the young maize to the festival of the water. Festivals were celebrated with ceremonies, sports, and games. A powerful class of priests served the gods, celebrating their special festivals and tending to their needs.

Chief among the gods was Inti, the sun god. His special attendants, the "Chosen Women," were selected from each region of the empire. During years of training, they studied the mysteries of the religion, learned to prepare ritual food and drink, and made the elaborate wool garments worn by the Sapa Inca and the Coya. At the end of their training, most of the Chosen Women continued to serve the sun god. Others, however, joined the Inca's court or married nobles.

Looking Ahead

At its height, the Incan civilization, like those of Middle America, was a center of learning and political power. Then, in 1525, the emperor Huayna Capac (wī nah KAH pahk) died suddenly of an unknown plague that swept across the land. As he had not named a successor, civil war broke out between two of his sons. The fighting weakened the empire at a crucial moment. Like the Aztecs to the north, the Incas soon faced an even greater threat from Spanish invaders.

SECTION 2 Assessment

Recall
1. **Identify: (a)** Pachacuti, **(b)** Quechua.
2. **Define: (a)** glyph, **(b)** quipu, **(c)** alloy.

Comprehension
3. Describe one achievement of each of the following early peoples of Peru: **(a)** Chavín, **(b)** Mochica.
4. Describe two ways in which the Incas united their empire.
5. What were some elements of daily life for the Incas?

Critical Thinking and Writing
6. **Connecting to Geography (a)** How did geography pose a challenge to the Incas as they built their empire? **(b)** How did they meet this challenge? **(c)** What does this suggest about the level of government and learning among the Incas?
7. **Recognizing Points of View** For the average Inca, what might be the benefits of the absolute rule of the Sapa Inca? What might be the disadvantages?

Activity
Take It to the NET

Use the Internet to research the ancient Incan city of Machu Picchu. Then, create a museum exhibit describing the discovery of this "lost city" in 1911, as well as the buildings and artifacts found there.

Peoples of North America

Reading Focus

- How did people in the desert southwest adapt to their environment?

- How did the culture of the Mound Builders reflect their contact with other regions?

- How did the diverse regional cultures in the Americas differ from one another?

Vocabulary

pueblo

kiva

potlatch

Taking Notes

Create a table that compares three culture areas in North America. This sample will help you get started.

CULTURE AREA	GEOGRAPHY	WAY OF LIFE	OTHER
ARCTIC	Harsh climate		
NORTHWEST COAST			Shared wealth
EASTERN WOODLANDS		Built villages in forests	

Main Idea Geographic diversity contributed to the growth of a great variety of cultures in North America.

Setting the Scene Climate and natural resources had profound effects on daily life for the first people in North America. A traditional southwest song reflects how the natural world provided beauty as well as the necessities of life:

> "The whole Southwest was a House Made of Dawn. It was made of pollen and of rain. The land was old and everlasting. There were many colors on the hills and on the plain, and there was a dark wilderness on the mountains beyond. The land was tilled and strong and it was beautiful all around."
> —quoted in *The Native Americans: An Illustrated History* (Ballantine)

The impact of the environment stretched far beyond the southwest. Hundreds of cultural groups emerged in the present-day United States and Canada. For centuries, they lived by hunting, fishing, and gathering wild plants. As farming spread north from Middle America, many people raised corn and other food crops. Some people farmed so successfully that they built large permanent settlements. Here, we will look at the earliest of these farming cultures, in the desert southwest and in the Mississippi Valley.

The Desert Southwest

More than 1,000 years ago, fields of corn, beans, and squash bloomed in the desert southwest. The farmers who planted these fields were called the Hohokams, or "Vanished Ones," by their later descendants, the Pimas and Papagos. To farm the desert, they built a complex irrigation system.

The Hohokams lived near the Gila River in present-day Arizona. They may have acquired skills such as irrigation from the civilizations of Middle America. They built temple mounds and ball courts, as the Mayas did. The Hohokams survived until about A.D. 1500, when drought seems to have forced them to leave their settlements.

Anasazi The best-known society of the southwest was that of the Anasazi. They lived in what is today the Four Corners region of Arizona, New Mexico, Colorado, and Utah. Between about A.D. 900 and 1300, the Anasazi built large villages, later called pueblos by the Spanish.

Remains of Pueblo Bonito still stand in New Mexico. The village consisted of a huge complex with 800 rooms that housed about 6,000 people.

Connections to Today

Apartment Living

"Cliff dwellers"—today that term could describe people who live in tall apartment buildings. But it was first used to describe the Anasazi.

Named because it backed up against a sheer cliff, the Cliff Palace was one of the Anasazi's major "apartment buildings." With 217 rooms and 250 residents, it was larger than many modern apartment buildings. In place of brick, its walls were made of carefully cut slabs of stone, fitted tightly together. Rather than flat boards, great logs formed its floors and roofs. There were no elevators, though—its residents reached their rooms by either climbing ladders or mounting steps carved in the stone.

Theme: Continuity and Change Why do you think that the Anasazi and modern city dwellers developed similar types of housing?

Builders used stone and adobe bricks to erect a crescent-shaped compound rising five stories high.

At the center of the great complex was a plaza. There, the Anasazis dug their kiva, a large underground chamber used for religious ceremonies. Paintings on the walls show their concern with weather, including storms that might damage crops.

Cliff Dwellings In the late 1100s, the Anasazi began building housing complexes in the shadow of canyon walls, where the cliffs offered protection from raiders. The largest of these cliff dwellings at Mesa Verde, in present-day Colorado, had over 200 rooms. People had to climb ladders to reach their fields on the flatlands above or the canyon floor below.

In the late 1200s, a long drought forced the Anasazi to abandon their cliff dwellings. Without rain, they could no longer live in large settlements. Attacks by Navajos and Apaches may have contributed further to their decline. Anasazi traditions survived, however, among the Hopis and other Pueblo Indians of the present-day southwestern United States.

The Mound Builders

Far to the east of the Anasazi, in the Mississippi and Ohio valleys, other farming cultures emerged as early as 700 B.C. The Adena and Hopewell people left behind giant earthen mounds. Some mounds were cone-shaped, while others were made in the shape of animals. The Great Serpent Mound in Ohio wriggles and twists for almost a quarter of a mile.

Objects found in Hopewell mounds show that traders extended their influence over a wide area. They brought back shells and shark teeth from the Gulf of Mexico and copper from the Great Lakes region. Skilled artisans hammered and shaped the copper into fine ornaments.

Cahokia By A.D. 800, these early cultures had disappeared, but a new people, the Mississippians, gained influence. As their culture spread, the Mississippians built clusters of earthen mounds and ever larger towns and ceremonial centers.

Their greatest center, Cahokia in present-day Illinois, housed as many as 40,000 people by about A.D. 1200. Cahokia boasted at least 60 mounds. On top of some mounds stood the homes of rulers and nobles. The largest mound probably had a temple on its summit, where priests and rulers offered prayers and sacrifices to the sun. Archaeologists think that this temple mound shows the influence of Middle American civilizations.

Heirs of the Mound Builders The Mississippians left no written records, and their cities had disappeared by the time Europeans reached the area. Still, their traditions survived among the Natchez people, whose ruler, the Great Sun, had absolute power. He and his family lived on the top of pyramid mounds.

Diverse Regional Cultures

Many other groups of Native Americans emerged in North America prior to 1500. Modern scholars have identified 10 culture areas based on the environments in which people lived: the Arctic, Subarctic, Northwest Coast, California, Great Basin, Plateau, Southwest, Great Plains, Eastern Woodlands, and Southeast. In each area, people adapted to geographic conditions that influenced their ways of life.

Legacy of the Mound Builders
The Great Serpent Mound (center) in Ohio shows careful planning in its even curves. Archaeologists have discovered artifacts such as this mica bird's claw (top) and carved frog (bottom) in mounds built by the Adena, Hopewell, and Mississippian peoples.

Theme: Global Interaction Why do scholars think that Mississippian mounds may show the influence of Middle American civilizations?

North American Culture Areas About 1450

Geography As Native Americans spread out to populate North America, they developed a wide variety of cultures. The map shows culture areas in which tribes shared similar environments and ways of life.

1. **Location** On the map, locate **(a)** Northwest Coast culture area, **(b)** Eastern Woodlands culture area, **(c)** Great Basin culture area.
2. **Place** **(a)** Name two tribes in the Great Plains culture area. **(b)** With which culture area are the Cherokees associated?
3. **Critical Thinking Making Inferences** The Navajos lived in the Southwest culture area but spoke a Subarctic language. **(a)** How might this be explained? **(b)** What were some other characteristics of peoples in the Southwest culture area?

Legend:
- Arctic/Subarctic
- Northwest Coast
- California/Great Basin/Plateau
- Southwest
- Great Plains
- Eastern Woodlands
- Southeast

Azimuthal Equal Area Projection

0   500   1000 Miles

0   500   1000 Kilometers

Native American Culture Groups of North America

Arctic/Subarctic

Beavers, Crees, Inuits, Kutchins

Lived as nomadic hunters and food gatherers in cold climate; honored ocean, weather, and animal spirits

California/Great Basin/Plateau

Nez Percés, Pomos, Shoshones

Lived as hunters and gatherers in small family groups; ate mainly fish, berries, acorns

Southwest

Hohokams, Hopis, Navajos, Pueblos

Lived in villages in homes made of adobe; built irrigation systems to grow corn and other crops; honored earth, sky, and water spirits

Southeast

Cherokees, Natchez

Grew corn, squash, beans, and other crops; held yearly Green Corn Ceremony to mark end of year and celebrate harvest

Northwest Coast

Bella Coolas, Coos, Kwakiutls, Tlingits

Lived in villages; benefited from rich natural resources in forests, rivers, and ocean; held potlatches, or ceremonial dinners, where host families gave gifts to guests to show wealth and gain status

Great Plains

Arapahos, Blackfeet, Cheyennes, Comanches, Crows, Lakotas, Mandans, Osages

Lived in tepees; animals hunted by men; crops grown by women; relied on buffalo to meet basic needs of food, shelter, and clothing

Eastern Woodlands

Algonquins, Chippewas, Hurons, Iroquois, Leni-Lenapes, Miamis, Pequots, Shawnees

Lived in farming villages, but also hunted for food; long houses shared by several families; women held social and political power

Here, we will look in greater detail at the distinct ways of life that developed in three regions—the Arctic, the Northwest Coast, and the Eastern Woodlands.

A Frozen World   In the far north, the Inuits* adapted to a harsh climate, using the resources of the frozen land to survive. Small bands lived by hunting and fishing. Seals and other sea mammals provided them with food, skins for clothing, bones for needles and tools, and oil for cooking. They paddled kayaks in open waters or used dog sleds to transport goods across the ice. In some areas, Inuits constructed igloos, or dome-shaped homes made from snow and ice. In others, they built sod dwellings that were partly underground.

A Land of Plenty   The people of the Northwest Coast lived in a far richer environment than the Inuits. Rivers teemed with salmon, and the Pacific Ocean offered other fish and sea mammals. Hunters tracked deer, wolves, and bears in the forests. In this land of plenty, people built large permanent villages with homes made of wood. They traded their surplus goods, gaining wealth that was shared in ceremonies like the potlatch. At this ceremony, which continues in Canada today, a person of rank and wealth distributes lavish gifts to large numbers of guests. By accepting the gifts, the guests acknowledge the host's high status.

The Iroquois League   The Eastern Woodlands, stretching from the Atlantic Coast to the Great Lakes, was home to a number of groups, including the Iroquois. They cleared land and built villages in the forests. While women farmed, men hunted and frequently warred against rival nations.

According to Iroquois tradition, the prophet Dekanawidah (deh kan ah WEE dah) urged rival Iroquois nations to stop their constant wars. In the late 1500s, he became one of the founders of the unique political system known as the Iroquois League. This was an alliance of five nations who spoke the same language and shared similar traditions.

The Iroquois League did not always succeed in keeping the peace. Still, it was the best-organized political group north of Mexico. Member nations governed their own villages but met jointly in a council when they needed to address larger issues. Only men sat on the council, but each clan had a "clan mother" who could name or depose members of the council.

The Iroquois League emerged just at the time when Europeans arrived in the Americas. Encounters with Europeans would take a fearful toll on the peoples of North America and topple the Aztec and Incan empires.

* The Inuits were late immigrants from Siberia. Other Native Americans called them Eskimos, "eaters of raw flesh," but they called themselves the Inuits, the "people."

Primary Source

A Plea for Peace
In about 1570, the prophet Dekanawidah persuaded warring Iroquois nations to form a confederacy:

"I, Dekanawidah, and the confederate lords now uproot the tallest tree and into the cavity thereby made we cast all weapons of war. Into the depths of the earth we cast all weapons of strife. We bury them from sight forever and plant again the tree. Thus shall all Great Peace be established and hostilities shall no longer be known between the Five Nations but only peace to a united people."

—Iroquois Constitution

Skills Assessment

Primary Source What does Dekanawidah believe the Iroquois must do to achieve the Great Peace?

SECTION 3 Assessment

Recall
1. **Identify: (a)** Hohokams, **(b)** Anasazis, **(c)** Mound Builders, **(d)** Inuits, **(e)** Iroquois League.
2. **Define: (a)** pueblo, **(b)** kiva, **(c)** potlatch.

Comprehension
3. How did the Hohokams farm the desert southwest?
4. How do we know about the lives of the Mound Builders and their contacts with other peoples?

5. Give examples of how the environment influenced three early cultures of North America.

Critical Thinking and Writing
6. **Asking Questions** If you were an archaeologist studying the Adena and Hopewell people, what three questions might you ask about the giant mounds they built?
7. **Linking Past and Present** How does environment affect your community?

Activity

Creating a Poster
With a partner, create a poster that expresses the ideas behind the formation of the Iroquois League. Use symbols to represent the five Iroquois nations.

Creating a Chapter Summary

Fill in the missing events and dates on the following time line. Add more events and dates to create a time line that includes the major cultures discussed in this chapter.

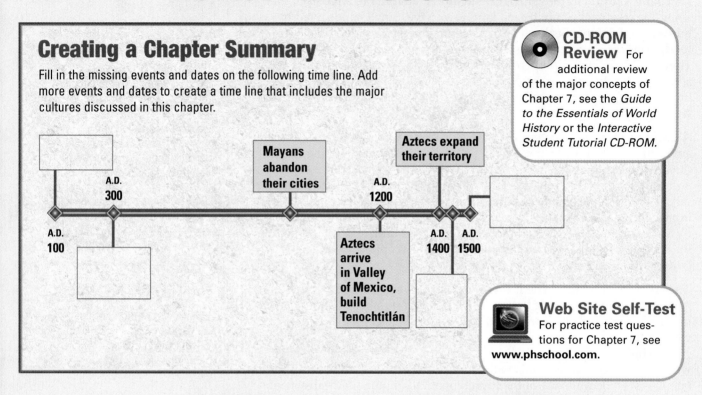

Mayans abandon their cities

Aztecs expand their territory

A.D. 300

A.D. 1200

A.D. 100

Aztecs arrive in Valley of Mexico, build Tenochtitlán

A.D. 1400   A.D. 1500

CD-ROM Review For additional review of the major concepts of Chapter 7, see the *Guide to the Essentials of World History* or the *Interactive Student Tutorial CD-ROM.*

Web Site Self-Test For practice test questions for Chapter 7, see **www.phschool.com.**

Building Vocabulary

Review the vocabulary words listed below. Then, use the words and their definitions to create a matching quiz. Exchange quizzes with another student. Check each other's answers when you are finished.

1. global warming
2. plains
3. chinampas
4. tribute
5. glyph
6. quipu
7. alloy
8. pueblo
9. kiva
10. potlatch

Recalling Key Facts

11. How and when do historians think that people first migrated to the Americas?
12. Name three advances in learning made by the Mayas.
13. Describe the social structure of the Aztec empire.
14. Why did the Incas build an extensive road system?
15. Why did the Anasazis abandon their cliff dwellings?
16. What was the main goal of the Iroquois League?

Critical Thinking and Writing

17. **Analyzing Information (a)** What advances in agriculture did the Mayas, Aztecs, and Incas make? **(b)** Why were these farming methods critical to the development of each of these civilizations?
18. **Predicting Consequences** How do you think the people conquered by the Aztecs might respond to an invasion by a foreign power? Explain.
19. **Synthesizing Information (a)** How were religion and government linked in the Incan empire? **(b)** Identify two other ancient civilizations you have read about in which rulers claimed divine powers.
20. **Comparing** Review the information on the Roman empire in the previous chapter. Then, compare the methods used by the Incas and the Romans to unite and control their diverse, far-flung empires.
21. **Connecting to Geography (a)** Describe the environment of the Northwest Coast. **(b)** How did people adapt to this environment?

Father Bernabe Cobo was a seventeenth-century Spanish missionary who worked with the Indians of Peru. Over the years, Cobo closely observed the Incas. In the excerpt below, Cobo describes the great majesty and splendor of the Sapa Inca. Read the excerpt and answer the questions that follow.

"The multitude of servants that they had in their palace was incredible. They were served all the exquisite, precious, and rare things that the land produced. . . . Serving women brought him all of his food. . . . When he pointed out the dish that he wanted, . . . one of these serving women would take it to him and hold it in her hand while he ate. . . . All leftovers from the meal and whatever the Inca touched with his hands were kept by the Indians in chests; thus, in one chest they placed the little [mats] that they placed before him when he ate; in another, the bones of the poultry and meat left over from his meals; in another, the clothes that he discarded. Finally, everything that the Inca had touched was kept in a hut, . . . and on a certain day each year it was all burned. They said that since the Incas were children of the Sun, whatever they touched had to be burned, . . . and no one was to touch it."

—Bernabe Cobo, *History of the Inca Empire*

22. What is the source of the excerpt?
23. According to Cobo, how was the Inca treated by his subjects?
24. **(a)** What happened to things that the Inca touched? **(b)** Why?
25. Do you think this is a reliable source of information about the Incas? Explain.

Take It to the NET

Use the Internet to research Aztec, Incan, or Mayan art. Then, create a sketch, sculpture, or textile in the artistic style of the civilization you have researched. If you prefer, write a description of a piece of art you have researched, focusing on special features of that civilization's style.

This picture is from an Aztec codex, or book. It is a symbolic representation of the rise of Tenochtitlán, the Aztec capital. Study the picture and review what you have learned about the Aztec empire to answer the following questions:

26. **(a)** Identify two symbols in the top portion of the picture. **(b)** What might they represent?
27. **(a)** What is the bird in the center of the picture? **(b)** What is the bird perched on? **(c)** Why do you think the Aztec artist placed it there?
28. Canals divided Tenochtitlán into four quarters. How did the artist represent the canals?
29. **(a)** What might the symbols at the bottom of the panel represent? **(b)** What do the symbols suggest about Aztec culture?

Skills Tip

Artists often use symbols to represent ideas. Study the symbols and compare them with your own knowledge to identify their meaning.

2 Empires of the Ancient World

Chapter 4

Empires of India and China
(600 B.C.–A.D. 550)

Between 600 B.C. and A.D. 550, strong, unified empires with complex belief systems emerged in India and China. These civilizations set patterns in government, religion, and philosophy that influenced later cultures.

- Hindu beliefs, including the concepts of reincarnation, karma, and dharma, profoundly influenced Indian civilization.
- The Buddha, an Indian religious reformer, sought spiritual enlightenment. His teachings gave rise to a new religion, Buddhism, that spread through Southeast and East Asia.
- Under the Maurya and Gupta dynasties, India developed into a center of trade and had contacts with civilizations in Africa, the Middle East, and Central and Southeast Asia.
- The caste system, the village, and the family influenced many aspects of Indian life.
- The teachings of Confucius, based on ideals of duty and social good, influenced Chinese government and society.
- Legalism and Daoism were two other important philosophies that arose in China.
- Shi Huangdi united China and built a strong authoritarian government, which laid the groundwork for China's classical age.
- Under Han rulers, the Chinese made huge advances in trade, government, technology, and the arts.

Chapter 5

Ancient Greece
(1750 B.C.–133 B.C.)

Despite bitter rivalry, Greek city-states gave rise to a civilization that set a standard of excellence for later civilizations. Greek ideas about the universe, the individual, and government still live on in the world today.

- Through trading contacts, Minoan and Mycenaean culture acquired many ideas from older civilizations of Egypt and Mesopotamia.
- Separated by mountains, the Greek city-states often warred with one another but united to defeat the Persians.
- After the Persian Wars, democracy flourished and culture thrived in Athens under the leadership of Pericles.
- Guided by a belief in reason, Greek artists, writers, and philosophers used their genius to seek order in the universe.
- The conquests of Alexander the Great spread Greek civilization throughout the Mediterranean world and across the Middle East to the outskirts of India.
- Greek culture blended with Persian, Egyptian, and Indian cultures to create the Hellenistic civilization, in which art, science, mathematics, and philosophy flourished.

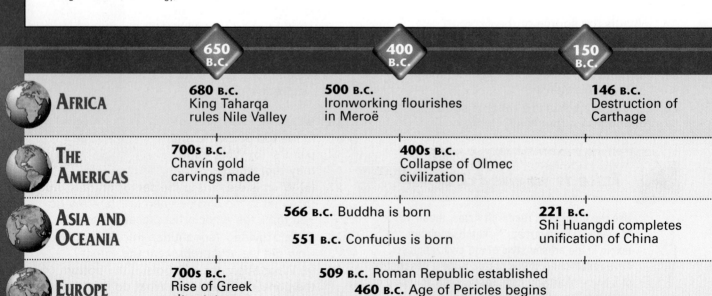

	650 B.C.	400 B.C.	150 B.C.
AFRICA	**680 B.C.** King Taharqa rules Nile Valley	**500 B.C.** Ironworking flourishes in Meroë	**146 B.C.** Destruction of Carthage
THE AMERICAS	**700s B.C.** Chavín gold carvings made	**400s B.C.** Collapse of Olmec civilization	
ASIA AND OCEANIA	**566 B.C.** Buddha is born **551 B.C.** Confucius is born		**221 B.C.** Shi Huangdi completes unification of China
EUROPE	**700s B.C.** Rise of Greek city-states	**509 B.C.** Roman Republic established **460 B.C.** Age of Pericles begins **323 B.C.** Hellenistic age begins	

Chapter 6

Ancient Rome and the Rise of Christianity
(509 B.C.–A.D. 476)

Rome expanded across the Mediterranean to build a huge, diverse empire. In the process, it spread the civilizations of Greece, Egypt, and the Fertile Crescent westward into Europe.

- After the Romans threw out their Etruscan king, they set up a republic. Eventually, commoners were allowed to be elected to the Roman senate.
- Conquest and diplomacy helped the Romans to extend their rule from Spain to Egypt. However, expansion created social and economic problems that led to the decline of the republic and the rule of an emperor.
- During the Pax Romana, Roman emperors brought peace, order, unity, and prosperity to the lands under their control.
- Rome acted as a bridge between the east and the west by borrowing and transforming Greek and Hellenistic achievements to produce Greco-Roman civilization.
- Christianity, which emerged in Roman-held lands in the Middle East, spread quickly throughout the Roman empire. The new faith reshaped Roman beliefs.
- Foreign invasions, the division of the empire, a corrupt government, poverty and unemployment, and declining moral values finally contributed to the downfall of the Roman empire.

Chapter 7

Civilizations of the Americas
(1400 B.C.–A.D.1570)

Four advanced civilizations—those of the Olmecs, the Mayas, the Aztecs, and the Incas—developed in Middle and South America. In North America, diverse culture groups emerged.

- The first settlers in the Americas were nomadic hunters who migrated across a land bridge between Siberia and Alaska and gradually populated two vast continents.
- From about 1400 B.C to 500 B.C., the Olmec civilization flourished along the Mexican Gulf Coast. Their religious, scientific, and architectural contributions influenced later civilizations in Mexico.
- Mayan civilization flourished from southern Mexico through Central America between A.D. 300 and A.D. 900. Its system of city-states supported a complex religious structure.
- In the 1400s, the Aztecs conquered most of Mexico and built a highly developed civilization led by a single ruler.
- By the 1500s, the Incas established a centralized government in Peru, ruled by a god-king and a powerful class of priests.
- Ten culture groups developed in the Arctic, Subarctic, Northwest Coast, California, Great Basin, Plateau, Southwest, Great Plains, Southeast, and Eastern Woodlands. Their diverse ways of life were strongly influenced by geography.

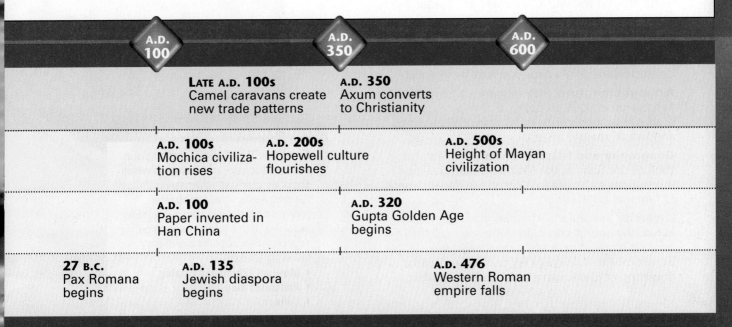

A.D. 100 — A.D. 350 — A.D. 600

LATE A.D. 100s
Camel caravans create new trade patterns

A.D. 350
Axum converts to Christianity

A.D. 100s
Mochica civilization rises

A.D. 200s
Hopewell culture flourishes

A.D. 500s
Height of Mayan civilization

A.D. 100
Paper invented in Han China

A.D. 320
Gupta Golden Age begins

27 B.C.
Pax Romana begins

A.D. 135
Jewish diaspora begins

A.D. 476
Western Roman empire falls

CHAPTER 8

The Rise of Europe

500–1300

Chapter Preview

1 The Early Middle Ages
2 Feudalism and the Manor Economy
3 The Medieval Church
4 Economic Expansion and Change

500s

Germanic tribes such as the Franks dominate Western Europe. This bronze brooch depicts a Frankish warrior.

732

Frankish forces defeat Muslim armies at the battle of Tours.

800

Frankish King Charlemagne is crowned emperor by the pope. Under Charlemagne, much of Western Europe is briefly united.

CHAPTER EVENTS

400 — 600 — 800

GLOBAL EVENTS

527 Justinian rules Byzantine empire.

622 The Muslim prophet Muhammad leaves Mecca.

180 *Chapter 8*

Geography and Resources of Europe

Europe is rich in natural resources. But in the early Middle Ages, many of these resources remained largely untapped.

Map labels:

Faroe Is.
Norwegian Sea
Shetland Is.
SCANDINAVIAN PEN.
URAL MTS.
60°N
60°E
North Sea
JUTLAND PEN.
Baltic Sea
BRITISH ISLES
Volga R.
50°N
NORTHERN EUROPEAN PLAIN
RUHR VALLEY
Vistula R.
Oder R.
Elbe R.
Rhine R.
Ural R.
Don R.
Loire R.
Seine R.
Dnieper R.
50°E
Dniester R.
CARPATHIAN MTS.
Danube R.
40°N
ALPS
Po R.
Garonne R.
Rhône R.
PYRENEES MTS.
DINARIC ALPS
CAUCASUS MTS.
IBERIAN PEN.
Ebro R.
APENNINE MTS.
Adriatic Sea
BALKAN PEN.
Black Sea
Tagus R.
ITALIAN PEN.
BALKAN MTS.
Guadiana R.
Corsica
ASIA
ATLANTIC OCEAN
Balearic Is.
PINDUS MTS.
Azimuthal Equal Area Projection
10°W
Sardinia
0   250   500 Miles
Mediterranean Sea
0   250   500 Kilometers
AFRICA
0°
10°E
Crete
20°E
30°E
40°E

Legend:
- Coal
- Fish
- Furs
- Iron
- Other metals
- Timber

900s

Sailing out of Scandinavia in long ships, Viking raiders plunge much of Europe into disorder. Such invasions contribute to the emergence of European feudalism.

1000s

The European economy begins to recover. The growth of bustling new towns is one sign of revival.

1200s

The Dominican and Franciscan orders of Christian friars are founded.

Timeline: 1000   1200   1400

1100s Feudalism develops in Japan.

1230s Sundiata founds the empire of Mali in West Africa.

The Early Middle Ages

Reading Focus

- Why was Western Europe a frontier land during the early Middle Ages?

- How did Germanic kingdoms gain power in the early Middle Ages?

- How did Charlemagne briefly reunite much of Western Europe?

Vocabulary

medieval

frontier

missi dominici

curriculum

Taking Notes

As you read, prepare an outline of this section. Use Roman numerals to indicate the major headings of the section, letters for the subheadings, and numbers for the supporting details. The sample at right will help you get started.

I. Geography of Western Europe
  A. Location
    1.
    2.
  B.
II. The Germanic kingdoms
  A. The Franks
    1.
    2.
  B.

Main Idea   After the fall of Rome, Germanic tribes divided Western Europe into many small kingdoms.

Setting the Scene   Pope Gregory the Great sat at his desk, thinking about the perils facing Italy. The Lombards were attacking from the north. Once again, Rome might fall to plundering invaders. "Where is the senate?" Gregory wrote. "Where are the people? The bones are all dissolved, the flesh is consumed. . . . The whole mass is boiled away."

Gregory was writing around A.D. 600, as waves of invaders swept across Europe. Trade slowed to a trickle, towns emptied, and learning virtually ceased. During the early Middle Ages,* from about 500 to 1000, Europe was a relatively backward region largely cut off from advanced civilizations in the Middle East, China, and India. Slowly, though, a new European civilization would emerge that blended Greco-Roman, Germanic, and Christian traditions. Much later, it would be called medieval civilization, from the Latin for "middle age."

Geography of Western Europe

Rome had linked its distant European territories with miles of roads and had spread classical ideas, the Latin language, and Christianity to the tribal peoples of Western Europe. But Rome was a Mediterranean power. The Germanic peoples who ended Roman rule in the West shifted the focus of European history to the north.

Location   Europe is relatively small—the second smallest in land area of the seven continents. It lies on the western end of Eurasia, the giant landmass that stretches from present-day Portugal in the west all the way to China in the east. Despite Europe's size, its impact on the modern world has been enormous.

Resources   From about 500 to 1000, this region was a frontier land—a sparsely populated, undeveloped area on the outskirts of a civilization. Still, it had great untapped potential. Dense forests flourished in the north. The region's rich earth was better suited to raising crops than were the dry soils of the Mediterranean. Underground lay mineral resources. Nearby seas provided fish for food and served as transportation routes. Europe's large rivers were ideal for trade, and its mountain streams could turn water wheels.

---

* The period from about 500 to 1450 is known today as the Middle Ages because it came between the fall of Rome and the start of the modern era.

The Germanic Kingdoms

The Germanic tribes who migrated across Europe were farmers and herders. Their culture differed greatly from that of the Romans. They had no cities or written laws. Instead, they lived in small communities governed by unwritten customs. They elected kings to lead them in war. Warrior nobles swore loyalty to the king in exchange for weapons and loot.

The Franks Between 400 and 700, Germanic tribes carved Western Europe into small kingdoms. The strongest kingdom to emerge was that of the Franks. In 486, Clovis, king of the Franks, conquered the former Roman province of Gaul. He ruled his new lands according to Frankish custom but did preserve much of the Roman legacy in Gaul.

Clovis took an important step when he converted to Christianity, the religion of the people in Gaul. Not only did he earn their support, but he also gained a powerful ally in the Christian Church of Rome.

Europe and the Muslim World As the Franks and other Germanic peoples carved up Europe, a new power was emerging across the Mediterranean. The religion of Islam appeared in Arabia in 622. From there, Muslims, or believers in Islam, built a huge empire and created a new civilization, as you will read in Chapter 11.

European Christians were stunned when Muslim armies overran Christian lands from Palestine to North Africa to Spain. When a Muslim army crossed into France, Charles Martel rallied Frankish warriors. At the battle of Tours in 732, Christian warriors triumphed. To them, the victory was a sign that God was on their side. Muslims advanced no farther into Western Europe, although they continued to rule most of Spain.

To European Christians, the Muslim presence was a source of anxiety. Even when Islam was no longer a threat, Christians viewed the Muslim world with hostility. In time, though, medieval Europeans would learn much from Muslims, whose learning in many areas exceeded their own.

The Age of Charlemagne

Around 800, Western Europe had a moment of unity when the grandson of Charles Martel built an empire reaching across France, Germany, and part of Italy. This emperor is known to history as Charlemagne (SHAHR luh mayn), or Charles the Great. Charlemagne towered over most people of his time. He loved battle and spent much of his 46-year reign fighting Muslims in Spain, Saxons in the north, Avars and Slavs in the east, and Lombards in Italy. His conquests reunited much of the old Roman empire.

A Christian Emperor In 800, Pope Leo III called on Charlemagne for help against rebellious nobles in Rome. Frankish armies marched south and crushed the rebellion. On Christmas Day, the pope showed his gratitude by placing a crown on Charlemagne's head and proclaiming him Emperor of the Romans.

The ceremony would have enormous significance. A Christian pope had crowned a German king successor to the Roman emperors. In doing so,

Empire of Charlemagne, 768–843

Kingdom of the Franks, 768

Area conquered by Charlemagne, 768–814

★ Battle sites

— Division of Charlemagne's empire (Treaty of Verdun, 843)

North Sea

ENGLAND

SAXONS

Süntel

SLAVS

Aachen

ATLANTIC OCEAN

Seine R.

Paris

Verdun

Rhine R.

Danube R.

Tours

Loire R.

AVARS

Azimuthal Equal Area Projection

0 150 300 Miles

0 150 300 Kilometers

Roncesvalles

Rhône R.

Po R.

LOMBARDS

CORSICA

Rome

SPAIN

Mediterranean Sea

50°N

40°N

10°W

0°

10°E

Geography Between 700 and 1000, Western Europe was battered by invaders.

1. **Location** On the map, locate **(a)** Byzantine empire, **(b)** Scandinavia, **(c)** Ireland, **(d)** England, **(e)** Cordoba.
2. **Place** **(a)** From where did the Magyars set out? **(b)** Where did the Vikings and Muslims build settlements?
3. **Critical Thinking** **Comparing** How did the Viking invasions differ from those of the Magyars and the Muslims?

he revived the ideal of a united Christian community. He also laid the ground for desperate power struggles between future Roman Catholic popes and German emperors.

The pope's action outraged the emperor of the eastern Roman empire in Constantinople. The eastern emperor saw himself, and not some backward Frankish king, as the sole Roman ruler. In the long run, the crowning of Charlemagne helped widen the split between the eastern and western Christian worlds.

Government Charlemagne tried to exercise control over his many lands and create a united Christian Europe. Working closely with the Church, he helped spread Christianity to the conquered peoples on the fringes of his empire. Missionaries converted many Saxons and Slavs.

Like other Germanic kings, Charlemagne appointed powerful nobles to rule local regions. He gave them land so that they could offer support and supply soldiers for his armies. To keep control of these provincial rulers, he sent out officials called *missi dominici* (MIH see dohm in NEE kee) to check on roads, listen to grievances, and see that justice was done. Charlemagne instructed the *missi* to "administer the law fully and justly in the case of the holy churches of God and of the poor, of wards and of widows, and of the whole people."

Revival of Learning Charlemagne wanted to make his court at Aachen (AH kuhn) a "second Rome." To do so, he set out to revive Latin learning in his empire. Education had declined so much that even supposedly educated clergy were often sadly ignorant. Charlemagne himself could read but not write. Still, as a ruler, he saw the need for officials to keep accurate records and write clear reports.

Charlemagne founded a school at Aachen under the direction of a respected scholar, Alcuin (AL kwihn) of York. Alcuin created a curriculum, or formal course of study, based on Latin learning. It included grammar, rhetoric, logic, arithmetic, geometry, music, and astronomy. Alcuin also hired scholars to copy ancient manuscripts, including the Bible and Latin works of history and science. Alcuin's system would become the educational model for medieval Europe.

After Charlemagne

After Charlemagne died in 814, his empire soon fell apart. His heirs battled for power for nearly 30 years. Finally, in 843, Charlemagne's grandsons drew up the Treaty of Verdun, which split the empire into three regions.

Legacy of Charlemagne   Still, Charlemagne left a lasting legacy. He extended Christian civilization into northern Europe and furthered the blending of German, Roman, and Christian traditions. He also set up strong, efficient governments. Later medieval rulers looked to his example when they tried to strengthen their own kingdoms.

A New Wave of Invasions   Charlemagne's heirs faced new waves of invasions. Despite the Christian victory at Tours, Muslim forces still posed a threat to Europe. In the late 800s, they conquered Sicily, which became a thriving center of Islamic culture. Not until the 900s, when power struggles erupted in the Middle East, did Muslim attacks finally subside.

About 896, a new wave of nomadic people, the Magyars, settled in what is today Hungary. From there, they overran eastern Europe and moved on to plunder Germany, parts of France, and Italy. Finally, after about 50 years, they were pushed back into Hungary.

The Vikings snapped the last threads of unity in Charlemagne's empire. These expert sailors burst out of Scandinavia, a northern region that now includes Norway, Sweden, and Denmark. Starting in the 900s, they looted and burned communities along the coasts and rivers of Europe.

The Vikings were not just destructive raiders. They were also traders and explorers who sailed around the Mediterranean Sea and across the Atlantic Ocean. Vikings opened trade routes that linked northern Europe to Mediterranean lands. Vikings also settled in England, Ireland, northern France, and parts of Russia. Around the year 1000, Leif Erikson set up a short-lived Viking colony on North America.

Did You Know?

The Voyage to Valhalla

According to Viking mythology, Valhalla was a great hall in the grandest palace of Odin, king of the gods. The walls of Valhalla were gold, and its roof was made of battle shields. Vikings believed that if they died heroically in battle, they would spend eternity fighting and then feasting in Valhalla with Odin.

To make the voyage to Valhalla, a Viking hero needed a proper funeral. This included being buried with his weapons, his clothing, and a ship. The servants of Viking warriors were buried with them to serve their masters on the journey and beyond. Sometimes, instead of being buried, the fully stocked ship was cast adrift and burned.

Theme: Religions and Value Systems   How might a Viking's beliefs have affected his behavior in battle?

SECTION 1 Assessment

Recall

1. Identify: **(a)** Clovis, **(b)** Islam, **(c)** Charlemagne, **(d)** Alcuin, **(e)** Treaty of Verdun, **(f)** Vikings.
2. Define: **(a)** medieval, **(b)** frontier, **(c)** *missi dominici*, **(d)** curriculum.

Comprehension

3. What untapped resources did Western Europe possess in the early Middle Ages?
4. How did Clovis increase the power of the Frankish kingdoms?
5. **(a)** What steps did Charlemagne take to improve government and unify his empire? **(b)** What happened to his empire after he died?

Critical Thinking and Writing

6. **Recognizing Points of View** The term *Middle Ages* was coined by Europeans to describe the period from 500 to 1450. Do you think that other civilizations use the same term for that period? Why or why not?
7. **Ranking** List the accomplishments of Charlemagne. Which do you think had the most lasting importance? Why?

Activity
Take It to the NET

The Vikings did not produce much art, but they did decorate many of their possessions with elaborate designs. Use the Internet to find out about Viking ornamentation. Then, draw an example to share with the class. Explain how or where the Vikings might have used the design.

Feudalism and the Manor Economy

Reading Focus

■ How did feudalism shape medieval society?

■ What was feudal life like for nobles and peasants?

■ What was the basis of the manor economy?

Vocabulary

feudalism
vassal
feudal contract
fief
knight
tournament
chivalry
troubadour
manor
serf

Taking Notes

Copy the table below. Then, fill it in as you read. Part of the table has been filled in to help you get started.

	NOBLES	PEASANTS
OBLIGATIONS	• Military service to lord •	
RIGHTS AND BENEFITS		• Protection from lord •
LIVES		

Main Idea A new political and social system, called feudalism, shaped medieval life.

Connections to Today

The Middle Ages Are Alive and Well!

The town is abuzz: Soon the king and queen will be passing by! Peasants crowd the muddy street. Shopkeepers loudly peddle food and drink. Minstrels wander through the crowd, singing and playing instruments. On the outskirts of town, knights in armor prepare to joust.

Scenes like this are common today all over this country at medieval festivals. Professional actors and others dress up in period costumes, pretend to have European accents, and play people from all levels of medieval society. The results are very romanticized and not always accurate. Still, the fairs give thousands of visitors a small taste of medieval life.

Theme: Continuity and Change Do you think a medieval festival would be a good place to learn about the Middle Ages? Why or why not?

Setting the Scene

Count William had just inherited the rich lands of Flanders. The local nobles gathered to pledge loyalty to their new lord. One by one, they knelt before him and took a solemn oath. "I promise on my faith," pledged each lord, "that I will in future be faithful to Count William and will observe my [loyalty] to him completely against all persons in good faith and without deceit."

The count then touched the noble with a small rod. With that gesture, he granted the noble a parcel of land, which included any towns, castles, or people on it.

Although the words might vary, ceremonies like this one took place across Europe during the Middle Ages. In public, before witnesses, great nobles and lesser lords exchanged vows of loyalty and service. Those vows were part of a new political and social system that governed medieval life.

The Emergence of Feudalism

In the face of invasions by Vikings, Muslims, and Magyars, kings and emperors were too weak to maintain law and order. People needed protection for themselves, their homes, and their lands. In response to this basic need for protection, a new system evolved, known as feudalism. Feudalism was a loosely organized system of rule in which powerful local lords divided their landholdings among lesser lords. In exchange, these lesser lords, or vassals, pledged service and loyalty to the greater lord.

Mutual Obligations The relationship between lords and vassals was established by custom and tradition and by an exchange of pledges known as the feudal contract. A lord granted his vassal a fief (FEEF), or estate. Fiefs ranged from a few acres to hundreds of square miles. In addition to the land itself, the fief included peasants to work the land, as well as any towns or buildings on the land.

As part of the feudal contract, the lord promised to protect his vassal. In return, the vassal pledged loyalty to his lord. He also agreed to provide the lord with 40 days of military service each year, certain money payments, and advice.

A Structured Society Everyone had a place in feudal society. Below the monarch were powerful lords, such as dukes and counts, who held the largest fiefs. Each of these lords had vassals, and these vassals in turn had their own vassals. In many cases, the same man was both vassal and lord—vassal to a more powerful lord above him and lord to a less powerful vassal below him.

Because vassals often held fiefs from more than one lord, feudal relationships grew very complex. A vassal who had pledged loyalty to several lords could have serious problems if his overlords quarreled with each other. What was he to do if both demanded his aid? To solve this problem, a vassal usually had a liege lord to whom he owed his first loyalty.

The World of Nobles

For feudal nobles, warfare was a way of life. Rival lords battled constantly for power. Many nobles trained from boyhood for a future occupation as a knight, or mounted warrior.

Achieving Knighthood At the age of seven, a boy slated to become a knight was sent away to the castle of his father's lord. There, he learned to ride and fight. He also learned to keep his armor and weapons in good condition. Training was difficult and discipline was strict. Any laziness was punished with an angry blow or even a severe beating.

With his training finished, the youth was ready to become a knight. Kneeling before an older knight, he bowed his head. The knight struck the young man with his hand or the flat side of his sword and declared something like the following: "In the name of God, Saint Michael, and Saint George, I dub thee knight. Be valiant." After this "dubbing," the young knight took his place beside other warriors.

As feudal warfare decreased in the 1100s, tournaments, or mock battles, came into fashion. A lord would invite knights from the surrounding area to enter contests of fighting skill. Early tournaments were as dangerous as real battles, and captured knights were held for ransom. In time, tournaments acquired more ceremony and ritual.

Castles During the early Middle Ages, powerful lords fortified their homes to withstand attack. Their strongholds included a keep, or wooden tower, ringed by a fence. The keep was separated from the surrounding area by a moat, or water-filled ditch.

The strongholds gradually became larger and grander. By the 1100s, monarchs and nobles owned sprawling stone castles with high walls, towers, and drawbridges over wide moats. Wars often centered on seizing

A Medieval Castle
By the late Middle Ages, some feudal castles had become vast fortresses. This castle at Carcassonne in France, which people still visit today, had a double outer wall to protect it from attack.

Theme: Economics and Technology What do you think was the function of the high turrets, or towers, that surround this castle?

A View of Peasant Life
This French painting from the late Middle Ages presents an idealized picture of farm life in winter. While a peasant takes cattle to market, his family members warm themselves by the fire in their hut.

Theme: Art and Literature
Illustrations like these were created for nobles. Why do you think they might have idealized peasant life?

freely, they also could not be forced off it. In theory, at least, they were guaranteed food, housing, and land.

A Self-Sufficient World The manor was generally self-sufficient. That is, peasants produced almost everything they needed, from food and clothing to simple furniture and tools. Most peasants never ventured more than a few miles from their village. They had no schooling and no knowledge of a larger world outside.

A typical manor included a few dozen one-room huts clustered close together in a village. Nearby stood a water mill to grind grain, a tiny church, and the manor house. The fields surrounding the village were divided into narrow strips. Each family had strips of land in different fields so that good land and bad land were shared evenly.

Peasant Life For most peasants, life was harsh. Men, women, and children worked long hours, from sunup to sundown. During planting season, a man might guide an ox-drawn plow through the fields while his wife walked alongside, goading the ox into motion with a pointed stick. Children helped plant seeds, weeded, and took care of pigs or sheep.

The peasant family ate a simple diet of black bread with vegetables such as peas, cabbage, turnips, or onions. They seldom had meat unless they poached wild game on their lord's manor, at the risk of harsh punishment. If they lived near a river, a meal might include fish. At night, the family and any cows, chickens, pigs, or sheep slept together in their one-room hut.

Like farmers everywhere, European peasants worked according to the season. In spring and autumn, they plowed and harvested. In summer, they hayed. At other times, they weeded, repaired fences, and performed chores. In late winter, when the harvest was exhausted and new crops had not yet ripened, hunger was common. Disease took a heavy toll, and few peasants lived beyond the age of 35.

Still, peasants found occasions to celebrate, such as marriages and births. Welcome breaks came at Christmas and Easter, when peasants had a week off from work. Dozens of other festivals in the Christian calendar brought days off. At these times, people might butcher an animal so that they could feast on meat. There would also be dancing and rough sports, from wrestling to ball games.

SECTION 2 Assessment

Recall
1. **Define:** (a) feudalism, (b) vassal, (c) feudal contract, (d) fief, (e) knight, (f) tournament, (g) chivalry, (h) troubadour, (i) manor, (j) serf.

Comprehension
2. Describe three features of feudal society.
3. (a) What obligations did lords and vassals have under the feudal system? (b) How did the code of chivalry affect medieval ideas about women?

4. (a) What responsibilities did the peasant have toward the lord of a manor? (b) What responsibilities did the lord of the manor have toward the peasants?

Critical Thinking and Writing
5. **Recognizing Causes and Effects** How did the breakdown of central authority in Europe lead to the development of feudalism?
6. **Linking Past and Present** Compare the code of chivalry to ideas about "good sportsmanship" today.

Activity
Take It to the NET

Use the Internet to learn more about the way knights in the early Middle Ages dressed. Make a diagram showing the various items in a knight's armor and add labels to identify them. Display your diagram on a bulletin board.

Reading Focus

- How did the Church and its monks and nuns shape medieval life?
- How did the power of the Church grow?
- How did reformers work for change in the Church?
- What problems did Jewish communities face?

Vocabulary

sacrament
tithe
secular
papal supremacy
canon law
excommunication
interdict
simony
friar
antisemitism

Taking Notes

Copy this concept web. As you read, add information about the role of the Church in medieval times. Add as many circles as you need to complete the web.

Main Idea The Church played a vital role in medieval life and in time grew into a secular power as well.

Setting the Scene Charlemagne waged battle in the name of Christianity. "It is our task," he said, "with the aid of divine goodness, to defend the holy church of Christ everywhere . . . and to strengthen it within through the knowledge of the Catholic faith."

It took centuries for Christian missionaries to spread their faith across Europe. But in time, the medieval Church emerged as the most powerful force in Europe. The Church's teachings and practices shaped the lives of Christian Europeans.

The Church and Medieval Life

During the early Middle Ages, the Church's most important achievement was to Christianize the diverse peoples of Western Europe. In 597, Pope Gregory I sent Augustine to convert the Anglo-Saxons in England. From Britain, later missionaries went back to the continent to spread their faith among Germanic tribes.

Women also spread the faith even at the risk of their own lives. Some women married pagan kings and brought their husbands into the Church. Clothilde, for example, persuaded her husband Clovis, who was king of the Franks, to accept Christianity.

The Parish Priest In manor villages, the priest of the parish, or local region, was usually the only contact people had with the Church. The priest cared for the souls of his parishioners by celebrating the mass and by administering the sacraments, the sacred rites of the Church. Christians believed that faith in Christ and participation in the sacraments would lead them to salvation, or everlasting life with God.

In addition to administering the sacraments, priests preached the Gospels and the teachings of the Church. They guided people on issues regarding values and morality. They offered assistance to the sick and needy.

Christian rituals and faith were part of the fabric of everyday life. Priests married peasants and nobles, baptized their children, and buried the dead in sacred ground.

The Village Church The church was a social center as well as a place of worship. After services, peasants gossiped or danced, although the priest might condemn their rowdy songs or behavior. In the later Middle Ages, some parish priests ran schools.

Primary Source

The Role of the Parish Priest
The English poet Geoffrey Chaucer describes an ideal parish priest:

"Wide was his parish, with houses far asunder,
But he would not be kept by rain or thunder,
If any had suffered a sickness or a blow
From visiting the farthest, high or low,
Plodding his way on foot, his staff in hand,
He was a model his flock could understand,
For first he did and afterward he taught."

—Geoffrey Chaucer,
The Canterbury Tales

Skills Assessment

Primary Source What were some of the duties of this fictional parish priest?

Spread of Christianity in Europe

Mostly Christian, 476

Mostly Christian, added by 1050

Muslim, 1050

⊕ Monastery

Azimuthal Equal Area Projection

0   250   500 Miles

0   250   500 Kilometers

NORWAY
SWEDEN
SCOTLAND
North Sea
IRELAND
DENMARK
ENGLAND
RUSSIA
Canterbury
GERMANY
Bingen
ATLANTIC OCEAN
FRANCE
Cluny
Black Sea
ITALY
PAPAL STATES
SPAIN
CORSICA Assisi
Rome Monte Cassino
Constantinople
Nicaea
SARDINIA
BYZANTINE EMPIRE
SICILY
CRETE
Mediterranean Sea
Baltic Sea

Skills Assessment

Geography Missionaries helped spread Christianity throughout medieval Europe.

1. **Location** *On the map, locate (a) Papal States, (b) Rome, (c) Cluny, (d) Bingen, (e) Assisi.*
2. **Region** *(a) Name three areas of Europe that became Christian between 476 and 1050. (b) Which areas of Europe remained under Muslim control?*
3. **Critical Thinking Understanding Sequence** *What device is used on this map to demonstrate a sequence of events? Explain.*

Villages took pride in their church buildings and decorated them with care. In later medieval times, prosperous communities built stone churches rather than wooden ones. Some churches housed relics, or remains of martyrs or other holy figures. Local people, as well as visitors, might make pilgrimages, or journeys, to pray before the relics.

To support itself and its parishes, the Church required Christians to pay a tithe, or tax equal to a tenth of their income. The tithe had its origins in the Bible. Tithing is still common in many Christian churches today.

Daily life revolved around the Christian calendar, which marked "holy days" such as Easter in addition to changes in the seasons. In medieval times, many holidays were added to the calendar to honor saints.

Views of Women The Church taught that men and women were equal before God. But on Earth, women were viewed as "daughters of Eve," weak and easily led into sin. Thus, they needed the guidance of men. At the same time, the Church offered a view of the ideal woman, as modest and pure as Mary, the mother of Jesus. Many churches were dedicated to the "mother of God" and "queen of heaven." Men and women asked Mary to pray to God on their behalf.

The Church tried to protect women. It set a minimum age for marriage. Church courts could fine men who seriously injured their wives. Yet they often punished women more harshly than men for the same offense.

Monks and Nuns

During the early Middle Ages, both women and men withdrew from worldly life to become nuns and monks. Behind the walls of monasteries and convents, they devoted their lives to spiritual goals.

The Benedictine Rule About 530, a monk named Benedict organized the monastery of Monte Cassino in southern Italy. He drew up a set of rules to regulate monastic life. In time, the Benedictine Rule was used by monasteries and convents across Europe.

Under the Benedictine Rule, monks and nuns took three vows. The first was obedience to the abbot or abbess, who headed the monastery or convent. The second was poverty, and the third was chastity, or purity. Each day was divided into periods for worship, work, and study. Benedict believed in the spiritual value of manual labor, so he required monks to work in the fields or at other physical tasks. As part of their labor, monks and nuns cleared and drained land and experimented with crops.

A Life of Service In a world without hospitals or schools, monasteries and convents often provided basic services. Monks and nuns looked after the poor and sick and sometimes set up schools for children. They gave food and lodging to travelers, especially to Christian pilgrims traveling to holy shrines. Some monks and nuns became missionaries. St. Patrick, for example, was a monk who set up the Irish Church. Later, the Church honored many missionaries by declaring them saints.

Virtual Field Trip

www.phschool.com

Trinity College Library
Dublin, Ireland

To see other pages from this illuminated manuscript, use the Internet address above to link to the *Book of Kells,* Trinity College, Dublin.

The Book of Kells
As monks and nuns copied books, they illuminated, or illustrated, each page. They decorated the letters and framed the text with intricate designs or scenes. This page is from the *Book of Kells,* illuminated by Irish monks on the island of Iona in the 800s.

Theme: Religions and Value Systems Why do you think copiers wanted to make this book so beautiful?

Centers of Learning Monasteries and convents also performed a vital role in preserving the writings of the ancient world. Often, monks and nuns copied ancient works as a form of labor. Once copied, the work might remain unread for centuries. Still, it would be there when later scholars took an interest in ancient learning.

Educated monks and nuns kept learning alive. In Italy, Abbot Cassiodorus wrote useful summaries of Greek and Latin works and taught the classics to other monks. In Britain, the Venerable Bede wrote the earliest known history of England. Bede introduced the use of B.C. and A.D. to date historical events.

Convents Although women could not become priests, many did enter convents. There, capable, strong-minded women could escape the limits of society. In the 1100s, Abbess Hildegard of Bingen composed religious music and wrote books on many subjects. Because of her mystical visions, popes and rulers sought her advice. She spoke her mind freely. "Take care that the Highest King does not strike you down because of the blindness that prevents you from governing justly," she warned one ruler.

In the later Middle Ages, the Church put more restrictions on nuns. It withdrew rights that nuns had once enjoyed, such as preaching the Gospel, and placed most independent convents under the control of church officials. It frowned on too much learning for women, preferring them to accept Church authority. Although women's role within the Church was limited, they made valuable contributions to their faith.

The Power of the Church Grows

In the centuries after the fall of Rome, the Church carved out a unique position in Western Europe. It not only controlled the spiritual life of Christians but gradually became the most powerful secular, or worldly, force in medieval Europe.

The Church and Feudal Society During the Middle Ages, the pope was the spiritual leader of the Roman Catholic Church. As representatives of Christ on Earth, medieval popes eventually claimed papal supremacy, or authority over all secular rulers.

Preserving a Jewish Tradition
Jewish communities in medieval Europe observed their unique customs. This plate belonged to a Jewish family in Spain. On Passover, it was filled with the traditional foods of the Seder, or Passover meal.

Theme: Diversity **In what way is this Seder plate similar to the illuminated manuscript on page 193?**

poverty, humility, and love of God. Soon after, Dominic, a Spanish priest, set up the Dominican order. Its chief goal was to combat heresy by teaching official Roman Catholic beliefs.

Women joined this reform movement by creating new religious groups. One such group was the Beguines (BEHG eenz). Most convents accepted only well-born women whose families gave a dowry, or gift, to the Church. The Beguines welcomed women without the wealth to enter a regular convent. Using funds from selling their weavings and embroidery, they helped the poor and set up hospitals and shelters.

Jews in Europe

Jewish communities existed across Europe. In their homes, Jews preserved the oral and written laws that were central to their faith.

Jews flourished in Spain, where they became known as Sephardim, from the Hebrew word for Spain. The Muslims who conquered Spain in 711 were tolerant of both Jews and Christians. Muslim Spain became a center of Jewish culture and scholarship. There, Sephardic Jews served as officials in Muslim royal courts.

During the Middle Ages, Jewish farmers migrated to other parts of Western Europe. Later, they became known as Ashkenazim, or "German" Jews. For centuries, Christians and Jews lived side by side in relative peace. Early German kings gave educated Jews positions at court. Many rulers in northern Europe valued and protected Jewish communities, although they taxed them heavily.

In the late 1000s, Christian persecution of Jews increased. Many Church leaders charged that Jews were responsible for the death of Jesus. As the Church grew in power, it issued orders forbidding Jews to own land or practice most occupations. Yet popes and rulers still turned to educated Jews as financial advisers and physicians.

In bad times, antisemitism, or prejudice against Jews, worsened. Faced with disasters they could not understand, such as illness or famine, many Christians blamed Jews. People also blamed their economic woes on Jews, as many Jews barred from other professions had become moneylenders. In response to growing persecution, thousands of Jews migrated to Eastern Europe. There, rulers welcomed the newcomers' skills and knowledge. Jewish communities thrived in Eastern Europe until modern times.

SECTION 3 Assessment

Recall
1. **Identify: (a)** Benedictine Rule, **(b)** Cluny, **(c)** Francis of Assisi, **(d)** Dominicans, **(e)** Beguines.
2. **Define: (a)** sacrament, **(b)** tithe, **(c)** secular, **(d)** papal supremacy, **(e)** canon law, **(f)** excommunication, **(g)** interdict, **(h)** simony, **(i)** friar, **(j)** antisemitism.

Comprehension
3. **(a)** Describe three ways in which the Church shaped medieval life. **(b)** How did monks and nuns help build Christian civilization in Europe?
4. How did the Church increase its secular power?

5. What reforms did Francis and Dominic promote?
6. Why were Jewish communities able to flourish in Spain?

Critical Thinking and Writing
7. **Analyzing Information (a)** What views did the Church put forth about women? **(b)** Why do you think important leaders were willing to accept the advice of Hildegard of Bingen?
8. **Identifying Main Ideas** Choose one of the main headings from this section. Write a sentence describing the main idea of the material in that subsection.

Activity
Writing a Letter
Write a letter that Benedict might have sent to a neighboring monastery in the 500s. Explain why you have drawn up a set of rules for the monks at Monte Cassino and why you think it would be worthwhile for other monasteries to follow the Benedictine Rule.

Economic Expansion and Change

Reading Focus

- How did new technologies spark an agricultural revolution?

- How did the revival of trade revolutionize commerce?

- How were guilds linked to the rise of towns and cities?

Vocabulary

charter
capital
partnership
bill of exchange
tenant farmer
middle class
usury
guild
apprentice
journeyman

Taking Notes

Create a diagram like the one shown below. As you read the section, fill in the main causes for the economic recovery in Europe. The first one has been partially filled in for you.

New Technology
- Iron plows
- Windmills

ECONOMIC RECOVERY IN EUROPE

Main Idea During the High Middle Ages, Europe's economy grew, cities and towns expanded, and a middle class arose.

Setting the Scene

The castle of Count William of Flanders was a bustling place. Hundreds of people lived and worked there, from nobles to servants. Such a large castle had many needs, and people came from near and far to supply them. "There began to throng before the gate near the castle bridge, traders and merchants selling costly goods," wrote one medieval chronicler. After that, other merchants came and built inns where visitors could eat and sleep, "and the houses so increased that there grew up a town."

The appearance of new towns was a symbol of Europe's economic recovery. This revival, which lasted from about 1000 to 1300, is called the High Middle Ages.

An Agricultural Revolution

By 1000, Europe's economic recovery was well underway. It had begun in the countryside, where peasants adapted new farming technologies that made their fields more productive. The result was an agricultural revolution that transformed Europe.

New Technologies By the 800s, peasants were using new iron plows that carved deep into the heavy soil of northern Europe. These plows were a big improvement over the old wooden plows, which had been designed for the light soils of the Mediterranean region. Also, a new kind of harness allowed peasants to use horses rather than oxen to pull the plows. Because faster-moving horses could plow more land in a day than could oxen, peasants were able to enlarge their fields and plant more crops.

A peasant might look up and see another new device, a windmill, turning slowly against the sky. Where there were no fast-moving streams to turn a water mill, the power of the wind had been harnessed to grind the peasants' grain into flour.

Expanding Production Other changes brought still more land into use. Feudal lords who wanted to boost their incomes pushed peasants to clear forests, drain swamps, and reclaim wasteland for farming and grazing.

Peasants also adopted the three-field system. They planted one field with grain, a second with legumes, such as peas and beans, and they left the third fallow, or unplanted. The legumes restored soil fertility while adding variety to the peasant diet. Unlike the old two-field system, the new method left only a third of the land unplanted.

Geography and History

Roadblock

The roads to places like Count William's castle in Flanders bustled with travelers. Among them were peasants, carrying farm products to the marketplace.

In those days, wealthy travelers might ride horses, but the farmers walked. Neither riders nor walkers were comfortable on the road, however, because of the ruts, cracks, and potholes. The roads built by the Romans were still in use but had been poorly maintained. Other minor roads had been added since Roman times, but these were little more than narrow tracks. Worse, peasants would dig up the roads for clay to repair their houses. The story goes that one miller dug a deep hole in the middle of a nearby road. When it rained, the hole filled with water and a traveling glovemaker fell in, drowning both himself and his horse!

Theme: Economics and Technology What conditions or developments might lead to the improvement of medieval roads?

Trade in Medieval Europe, 1000–1300

Legend:
- ● Towns holding fairs
- ○ Major commercial centers
- — Major trade routes

Azimuthal Equal Area Projection

0 — 250 — 500 Miles
0 — 250 — 500 Kilometers

Map labels: North Sea, Baltic Sea, Smolensk, Kiev, To China, Caspian Sea, ATLANTIC OCEAN, FLANDERS, Hamburg, Bruges, Lübeck, Danzig, ENGLAND, London, Winchester, Ghent, HOLY ROMAN EMPIRE, Ypres, Lagny, Lille, Tournai, Paris, Provins, Troyes, Bar-sur-Aube, FRANCE, Verona, Lyon, Milan, Turin, Venice, Florence, Genoa, ITALY, Black Sea, NAVARRE, LEÓN, León, Bayonne, Pisa, Siena, Rome, Constantinople, To India, PORTUGAL, CASTILE, ARAGON, Barcelona, Adriatic Sea, Toledo, Valencia, Córdoba, Naples, Cádiz, EMPIRE OF THE ALMOHADS, KINGDOM OF SICILY, Tunis, Mediterranean Sea, Tripoli, Alexandria

All these improvements let farmers produce more food. With more food available, the population grew. Between about 1000 and 1300, the population of Europe doubled.

Trade Revives

Europe's growing population needed goods that were not available on the manor. Peasants needed iron for farm tools. Wealthy nobles wanted fine wool, furs, and spices from Asia. As foreign invasions and feudal warfare declined, traders crisscrossed Europe to meet the growing demand for goods.

New Trade Routes Enterprising traders formed merchant companies that traveled in armed caravans for safety. They followed regular trade routes. Along these routes, merchants exchanged local goods for those from remote markets in the Middle East and further east into Asia.

In Constantinople, merchants bought Chinese silks, Byzantine gold jewelry, and Asian spices. They shipped these goods to Venice on the Adriatic Sea. In Venice, traders loaded their wares onto pack mules and headed north over the Alps and up the Rhine River to Flanders. In Flanders, other traders bought the goods to send on to England and the lands along the Baltic Sea. Northern Europeans paid for the goods with products such as honey, furs, cloth, tin, and lead.

Trade Fairs At first, traders and their customers did business at local trade fairs. These fairs took place each year near navigable rivers or where busy trade routes met.

People from the surrounding villages, towns, and castles flocked to the fairs. Peasants traded farm goods and animals. As they ate and drank, they enjoyed the antics of jugglers, acrobats, or even dancing bears. Still, peasants had no money to buy fine swords, sugar, and silks. The customers for these luxuries were the feudal rulers, nobles, and wealthy churchmen.

New Towns   Trade fairs closed in the autumn when the weather made roads impassable. Merchants might wait out the winter months near a castle or in a town with a bishop's palace. These settlements attracted artisans who made goods that the merchants could sell.

Slowly, these small centers of trade and handicraft developed into the first real medieval cities. Some boasted populations of 10,000, and a few topped 100,000. Europe had not seen towns of this size since Roman times. The richest cities grew up in northern Italy and Flanders—the two ends of the profitable north-south trade route. Both areas were centers of the wool trade and had prosperous textile industries.

To protect their interests, the merchants who set up a new town would ask the local lord, or if possible the king himself, for a charter. This written document set out the rights and privileges of the town. In return, merchants paid the lord or the king a large sum of money, a yearly fee, or both.

Although charters varied from place to place, they almost always granted townspeople the right to choose their own leaders and control their own affairs. Most charters also had a clause, popular with runaway serfs, that declared that anyone who lived in the town for a year and a day was free. "Town air makes free," was a common medieval saying.

A Commercial Revolution

As trade revived, money reappeared, which in turn led to more changes. Merchants, for example, needed money to buy goods so they borrowed from moneylenders. In time, their need for capital, or money for investment, spurred the growth of banking houses.

New Business Practices   To meet the needs of the changing economy, Europeans developed new ways of doing business. For example, many merchants joined together in an organization known as a partnership. Under this setup, a group of merchants pooled their funds to finance a large-scale venture that would have been too costly for any individual trader. This practice made capital available more easily. It also reduced the risk for any one partner in the venture because no one had to invest all his or her capital in the company.

Merchants also developed a system of insurance to help reduce business risks. For a small fee, an underwriter would insure the merchant's shipment. If the shipment was lost or destroyed, the underwriter paid the merchant most of its value. If the goods arrived safely, the merchant lost only the insurance payment.

Europeans adopted other practices from Middle Eastern merchants. Among the most important was the bill of exchange. A merchant deposited money with a banker in his home city. The banker issued a bill of exchange, which the merchant exchanged for cash in a distant city. A merchant could thus travel without carrying gold coins, which were easily stolen.

Social Changes   These new ways of doing business were part of a commercial revolution that transformed the medieval economy. Slowly, they also reshaped medieval society.

For example, the use of money undermined serfdom. Feudal lords needed money to buy fine goods. As a result, many peasants began selling farm products to townspeople and fulfilling their obligations to their lords by paying their rent in cash rather than in labor. By 1300, most peasants in Western Europe were either tenant farmers, who paid rent for their land, or hired farm laborers.

Connections to Today

Taking Care of Business

A medieval merchant visiting the United States today might understand many modern business practices. Like medieval merchants, today's mutual fund investors pool their money to make possible much larger-scale investments than they could make as individuals. The medieval idea of insurance is also alive and well. Today's insurance possibilities are endless—life, business, car, home, jewelry. A famous dancer was even able to insure her legs!

The bill of exchange has echoes in today's automated teller machines, or ATMs. With hundreds of thousands of them in operation internationally, anyone with a bank account can access the money in it instantly, around the corner or halfway across the world.

Theme: Continuity and Change   How is an ATM like a bill of exchange?

Guild Members at Work
All over Europe, artisans in many fields organized craft guilds. These Italian pictures show medieval artisans weaving tapestries (top) and building cabinets (bottom).

Theme: Economics and Technology How do modern factories differ from these medieval workshops?

In towns, the old social order of nobles, clergy, and peasants gradually changed. By 1000, a new class appeared that included merchants, traders, and artisans. They formed a middle class, standing between nobles and peasants.

Nobles and the clergy despised the new middle class. To nobles, towns were a disruptive influence beyond their control. To the clergy, the profits that merchants and bankers made from usury (yoo zhuh ree), or lending money at interest, were immoral.*

During the Middle Ages, the Church forbade Christians to lend money at interest. As a result, many Jews who were barred from other professions became moneylenders. Although money-lenders played an essential role in the growing medieval economy, the need to pay them back led to much resentment and a rise in antisemitism, as you have read.

Role of Guilds

In medieval towns, merchants and artisans formed associations known as guilds. Merchant guilds appeared first. They dominated town life, passing laws and levying taxes. They also decided whether to spend funds to pave the streets with cobblestones, build protective walls, or raise a new town hall.

In time, artisans came to resent the powerful merchants. They organized craft guilds. Each guild represented workers in one occupation, such as weavers, bakers, brewers, or goldsmiths. In some towns, struggles between craft guilds and the wealthier merchant guilds led to riots.

Guild members cooperated to protect their own economic interests. To prevent competition, they limited membership in the guild. No one except guild members could work in any trade. Guilds made rules to protect the quality of their goods, regulate hours of labor, and set prices. Guilds also provided social services. Besides operating schools and hospitals, they looked after the needs of their members. For example, the regulations of a craft guild in the leather-making trade stated:

> "If by chance any of the said trade shall fall into poverty, whether through old age or because he cannot labor or work, and have nothing with which to keep himself, he shall have every week from the said box 7d for his support, if he be a man of good repute."
> —*Ordinances of the White-Tawyers*

Guilds also pledged to provide support for the widows and orphans of their members.

Becoming a Guild Member To become a guild member meant many years of hard work. At the age of seven or eight, a child might become an apprentice, or trainee, to a guild master. The apprentice usually spent seven years learning the trade. The guild master paid no wages, but was required to give the apprentice bed and board.

Few apprentices ever became guild masters unless they were related to one. Most worked for guild members as journeymen, or salaried workers. Journeymen often accused masters of keeping their wages low so that they could not save enough to open a competing shop.

Women and the Guilds Women worked in dozens of crafts. A woman often engaged in the same trade as her father or husband and might inherit his workshop if he died. Because she knew the craft well, she kept the shop

---

*Today, the term *usury* refers to charging excessive interest.

going and sometimes might become a guild master herself. Young girls became apprentices in trades ranging from ribbonmaking to papermaking to surgery.

Women dominated some trades and even had their own guilds. In Paris, they far outnumbered men in the profitable silk and woolen guilds. A third of the guilds in Frankfurt were composed entirely of women.

Town and City Life

Medieval towns and cities were surrounded by high, protective walls. As the city grew, space within the walls filled to overflowing, and newcomers had to settle in the fields outside the walls. To keep up with this constant growth, every few years the city might rebuild its walls farther and farther out.

A typical medieval city was a jumble of narrow streets lined with tall houses. Upper floors hung out over the streets, making those below dim even in daytime. In the largest cities, a great cathedral, where a bishop presided, or a splendid guild hall might tower above humbler residences.

During the day, streets echoed with the cries of hawkers selling their wares and porters grumbling under heavy loads. A wealthy merchant might pass, followed by a procession of servants. At night, the unlit streets were deserted.

Even a rich town had no garbage collection or sewer system. Residents simply flung their wastes into the street. Larger cities might pass laws, such as one requiring butchers to dump their garbage on the edge of town. But towns remained filthy, smelly, noisy, and crowded.

Looking Ahead

By 1300, Western Europe was a different place from what it had been in the early Middle Ages. Although most people had no way of knowing it, slow but momentous changes were sending shock waves through medieval life. Trade, for example, put ideas as well as money into circulation. New riches revised the social structure. In politics, too, new forces were at work.

In the global sphere, the economic revival of the High Middle Ages was bringing Europeans into contact with civilizations much more advanced than their own. From these lands to the east came products, ideas, and technologies that would spark an even greater transformation in how Europeans thought and lived.

Primary Source

City Fun and Games
A Londoner describes some of the sports and pastimes enjoyed by young city dwellers in the 1100s:

"In the holidays, all the summer the youths are exercised in leaping, dancing, shooting, wrestling, casting the stone, and practicing their shields. The maidens . . . dance as long as they can well see. . . .

When the great [swamp] which watereth the walls of the city on the north side, is frozen, many young men play upon the ice . . . some tie bones to their feet and under their heels; and shoving themselves by a little picked staff, do slide as swift as a bird flieth in the air."

—William Fitz-Stephen, quoted in *Source-Book of English History* (Kendall)

Skills Assessment

Primary Source How are the sports described above similar to those enjoyed by young people today? How are they different?

SECTION 4 Assessment

Recall
1. **Identify:** High Middle Ages.
2. **Define:** (a) charter, (b) capital, (c) partnership, (d) bill of exchange, (e) tenant farmer, (f) middle class, (g) usury, (h) guild, (i) apprentice, (j) journeyman.

Comprehension
3. What were two effects of the agricultural revolution that took place during the Middle Ages?
4. What new ways of doing business evolved in the Middle Ages?

5. (a) How did a merchant guild differ from a craft guild? (b) How did guilds improve life for townspeople?

Critical Thinking and Writing
6. **Synthesizing Information** Give three pieces of evidence to support the idea that the High Middle Ages were a time of economic growth.
7. **Comparing** Compare economic life in the early Middle Ages to economic life in the High Middle Ages.

Activity

Creating an Advertisement Imagine that a growing medieval city has hired you to attract people to move there. Create an ad that describes opportunities the city provides for merchants, artisans, and peasants.

Creating a Chapter Summary

On a sheet of paper start a table like the one shown here. Add important facts under each heading to help you review the events you have learned about in this chapter. Part of the table has been filled in to help you get started.

EARLY MIDDLE AGES	HIGH MIDDLE AGES
Feudal society	Rise of middle class
Life centered on manors	Cities develop

 CD-ROM Review For additional review of the major concepts of Chapter 8, see the *Guide to the Essentials of World History* or the *Interactive Student Tutorial CD-ROM.*

Web Site Self-Test For practice test questions for Chapter 8, see www.phschool.com.

Building Vocabulary

Write sentences using the chapter vocabulary words listed below, leaving blanks where the vocabulary words would go. Exchange your sentences with another student and fill in the blanks in each other's sentences.

1. **medieval**
2. **feudalism**
3. **vassal**
4. **fief**
5. **tithe**
6. **secular**
7. **interdict**
8. **charter**
9. **guild**
10. **journeyman**

Recalling Key Facts

11. How did the culture of the Germanic tribes differ from that of the Romans?
12. What happened to Charlemagne's empire after his death?
13. Why was the pope a powerful figure in medieval Europe?
14. What role did monasteries and convents play in the preservation of ancient culture?
15. What social changes were caused by the commercial revolution of the Middle Ages?
16. Describe the typical medieval city.

Critical Thinking and Writing

17. **Connecting to Geography** Compare life on a medieval manor with life on an American farm today. Which do you think would be more self-sufficient? Why?
18. **Predicting Consequences** How do you think the weakening of the feudal system affected the Church? Explain your answer.
19. **Recognizing Causes and Effects** As you have read, antisemitism increased during economic bad times. Why do you think this was so?
20. **Understanding Sequences** Arrange the following developments in the order in which they occurred: new technologies, growth of towns, agricultural revolution, population growth, revival of trade. Then, explain why they occurred in that order.
21. **Making Decisions** If you had been a European peasant during the High Middle Ages, do you think you would have chosen to stay in the countryside or move to a town? Give reasons to support your decision.

Einhard, a medieval monk at the court of Charlemagne, wrote a life of the king. In this letter, quoted by Einhard, Charlemagne instructs one of his lords, Abbot Fulrad, about what to bring to a meeting of nobles. Read the passage and answer the questions that follow.

"[Arrive] so prepared with your men that you may be able to go thence well equipped in any direction which our command shall order, that is with arms and accoutrements [equipment] and other provisions for war in the way of food and clothing. Each horseman is expected to have a shield, lance, sword, dagger, bow, quiver with arrows, and in your cart shall be . . . axes, planes, augers, boards, spades, iron shovels and other utensils which are necessary in any army. In the wagons shall be supplies for three months, together with arms and clothing for six months."

—Einhard, *Life of Charlemagne*

22. What is each horseman expected to bring to the meeting?
23. Why do you think Charlemagne wants the men prepared in the way that he describes?
24. How long might these men be engaged in the king's service?
25. (a) Based on what you have learned about feudalism, what does the lord abbot owe Charlemagne? (b) What do the lord's men owe the lord?
26. Fulrad was both an abbot and a lord. What does this fact suggest about the role of the Church at this time?

Use the Internet to research daily life in early medieval Europe. Then, write a diary entry from the point of view of a medieval European. You might choose to take the role of a lord, noblewoman, knight, monk, nun, serf, or town merchant. Include information about how your status in medieval society affects your tasks, beliefs, and expectations of life.

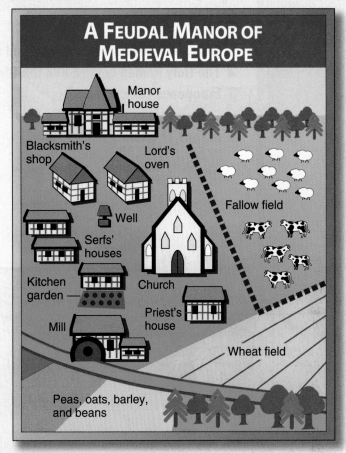

A FEUDAL MANOR OF MEDIEVAL EUROPE

The diagram above represents a medieval manor. Study the diagram and answer the following questions:

27. (a) What kinds of buildings does the diagram show? (b) How many fields are shown?
28. Describe the purpose of: (a) the kitchen garden, (b) the blacksmith's shop, (c) the lord's oven, (d) the mill.
29. How does the diagram show that religion played an important role in manor life?
30. Does this diagram represent a manor before or after the agricultural revolution of the High Middle Ages? How can you tell?
31. How does the diagram support the statement that the medieval manor was self-sufficient?
32. Do you think this diagram represents an actual manor? Give reasons for your answer.

Skills Tip

Some diagrams represent an actual place or object, such as the blueprint of a house. Others give a more general picture of a typical place or object.

Growth of Royal Power in England and France

Reading Focus

■ How did monarchs gain power over nobles and the Church?

■ What traditions of government developed under John and later English monarchs?

■ How did strong monarchs succeed in unifying France?

Vocabulary

exchequer

common law

jury

Taking Notes

Copy this incomplete Venn diagram. As you read, write key facts about royal power in England and France in the appropriate sections. Write common characteristics in the overlapping section.

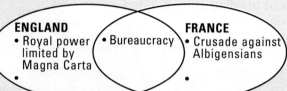

ENGLAND
• Royal power limited by Magna Carta
•

• Bureaucracy

FRANCE
• Crusade against Albigensians
•

Main Idea   In England and France, monarchs expanded royal authority and laid the foundations for united nation-states.

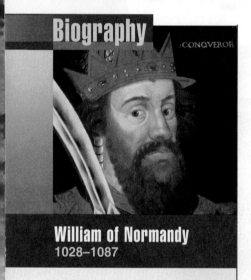

Biography

William of Normandy
1028–1087

From the time he became Duke of Normandy at age seven, William's life and position were in constant danger, mostly from jealous relatives. Four of his guardians were murdered—one in the very room in which William lay sleeping.

As an adult, William did all that he could to get and keep power. At age 20, he led an army to defeat a rebellious cousin. When an abbot condemned his marriage to Matilda of Flanders because they were too closely related, an enraged William burned down a monastery. But when the pope validated the marriage, William had a new abbey built.

Theme: Impact of the Individual How did William's experience as duke prepare him to be king of England?

Setting the Scene

A monarch could not always count on the loyalty of powerful nobles and Church officials. A medieval chronicle tells of the difficulties faced by one English king in the 1100s:

> "King Stephen . . . seized . . . Alexander, bishop of Lincoln, and Roger, the chancellor, his nephew, and he kept them all in prison. . . . They had done homage to him, and sworn oaths, but they . . . broke their allegiance, for every rich man built his castles, and defended them against him."
> —*Anglo-Saxon Chronicle*

During the Middle Ages, monarchs struggled to exert royal authority over nobles and churchmen. Bit by bit over many centuries, they built the framework for what would become the European nation-states of today.

Monarchs, Nobles, and the Church

Feudal monarchs in Europe stood at the head of society, but had limited power. While they ruled their own domains, they relied on vassals for military support. Nobles and the Church had as much—or more—power than the monarch. Both nobles and the Church had their own courts, collected their own taxes, and fielded their own armies. They jealously guarded their rights and privileges against any effort by rulers to increase royal authority.

Monarchs used various means to centralize power. They expanded the royal domain and set up a system of royal justice that undermined feudal or Church courts. They organized a government bureaucracy, developed a system of taxes, and built a standing army. Monarchs strengthened ties with the middle class. Townspeople, in turn, supported royal rulers, who could impose the peace and unity that were needed for trade.

Strong Monarchs in England

During the early Middle Ages, Angles, Saxons, and Vikings invaded and settled in England. Although feudalism developed, English rulers generally kept their kingdoms united.

In 1066, the Anglo-Saxon king Edward died without an heir. A council of nobles chose Edward's brother-in-law Harold to rule. But Duke William of Normandy, a tough, ruthless descendant of the Vikings, also claimed the English throne. The answer to the rival claims lay on the battlefield.

Norman Conquest Duke William raised an army and won the backing of the pope. He then sailed across the English Channel. At the Battle of Hastings, William and his Norman knights triumphed over Harold. On Christmas Day 1066, William the Conqueror, as he was now called, assumed the crown of England.

Although William's French-speaking nobles dominated England, the country's Anglo-Saxon population survived. Over the next 300 years, a gradual blending occurred of Norman French and Anglo-Saxon customs, languages, and traditions.

Growth of Royal Power William exerted firm control over his new lands. Like other feudal monarchs, he granted fiefs to the Church and his Norman lords, or barons, but he kept a large amount of land for himself. He monitored who built castles and where. He required every vassal to swear first allegiance to him rather than to any other feudal lord.

To learn about his kingdom, William had a complete census taken in 1086. The result was the *Domesday Book* (pronounced "doomsday"), which listed every castle, field, and pigpen in England. As the title suggests, the survey was as thorough and inevitable as doomsday, believed to be God's final day of judgment that no one could escape. Information in the *Domesday Book* helped William and later English monarchs build an efficient system of tax collecting.

William's successors continued to increase royal authority. In the area of finance, they created the royal exchequer, or treasury, to collect taxes. Into the exchequer flowed fees, fines, and other dues.

A Unified Legal System In 1154, an energetic, well-educated king, Henry II, inherited the throne. He broadened the system of royal justice. As a ruler, he could not simply write new laws but had to follow accepted customs. Henry found ways to expand customs into law. He then sent out traveling justices to enforce royal laws. The decisions of the royal courts became the foundation of English common law, a legal system based on custom and court rulings. Unlike local feudal laws, common law applied to all of England. In time, people chose royal courts over those of nobles or the Church. Because royal courts charged fees, the exchequer benefited from the growth of royal justice.

Under Henry II, England also developed an early jury system. When traveling justices visited an area, local officials collected a jury, or group of men sworn to speak the truth. (The word *jury* is derived from the French *juré*, meaning "sworn on oath.") These early juries determined which cases should be brought to trial and were the ancestors of today's grand jury. Later, another jury evolved that was composed of 12 neighbors of an accused. It was the ancestor of today's trial jury.

Conflict With the Church Henry's efforts to extend royal power led to a bitter dispute with the Church. Henry claimed the right to try clergy in royal courts. Thomas Becket, the archbishop of Canterbury and once a close friend of Henry's, fiercely opposed the king's move. The conflict simmered for years.

At last, Henry's fury exploded. "What a pack of fools and cowards I have nourished," he cried, "that not one of them will avenge me of this turbulent priest." Four hot-headed knights took Henry at his word. In 1170, they murdered the archbishop in his own cathedral. Henry denied any part in the attack. Still, to make peace with the Church,

FACT FINDER

Evolution of English Government

1066	**Norman Conquest** William of Normandy defeats Anglo-Saxons at Hastings.
1086	***Domesday Book*** William I uses this survey as a basis for taxation.
1160s–1180s	**Common Law** Henry II lays foundation for English legal system.
1215	**Magna Carta** John signs this document limiting royal power and extending rights.
1295	**Model Parliament** Edward I summons Parliament, which includes representatives of common people.

Skills Assessment

Chart Traditions of English government and law evolved during the Middle Ages. **How did the *Domesday Book* benefit William I? How did the Magna Carta affect English government?**

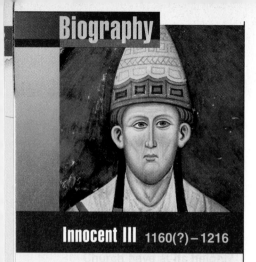

Innocent III 1160(?)–1216

Lotario de' Conti grew up in an influential Roman family. Several of his uncles were leading Church figures, including one pope. Lotario attended the finest schools of Europe, studying theology in Paris and law in Bologna. He became a leading expert on canon law and rose quickly through Church ranks. In 1198, he was elected pope, just one month before he was ordained a priest.

One of Innocent's most lasting achievements was to convene an important Church council in Rome. There, more than 1,000 Church officials established several practices that are still followed by Catholics today, such as regular confession of sins.

Theme: Impact of the Individual How did Innocent's background prepare him to assume the role of pope?

As Holy Roman emperor, Frederick spent little time in Germany. Instead, he pursued his ambitions in Italy. There, he clashed repeatedly and unsuccessfully with several popes. Like his grandfather, Frederick also tried but failed to subdue the cities of northern Italy.

Effects on Germany and Italy While Frederick was embroiled in Italy, German nobles grew more independent. The Holy Roman Empire survived, but it remained fragmented into many feudal states. The German people paid a high price for their emperors' ambitions. Unlike France and England, Germany would not achieve unity for another 600 years.

Southern Italy and Sicily also faced centuries of upheaval. There, popes turned to the French to overthrow Frederick's heirs. A local uprising against French rule in Sicily led to 200 years of chaos as French and Spanish rivals battled for power. The region that had once been a thriving center of culture was left in ruins.

The Height of Church Power

Pope Innocent III, who took office in 1198, embodied the triumph of the Church. As head of the Church, he claimed supremacy over all other rulers. The pope, he said, stands "between God and man, lower than God but higher than men, who judges all and is judged by no one."

Innocent clashed with all the powerful rulers of his day. More often than not, the pope came out ahead. As you have read, when King John of England dared to appoint an archbishop of Canterbury without the pope's approval, Innocent excommunicated the king and placed his kingdom under interdict. Innocent ordered the same punishment for France when Philip II tried unlawfully to annul, or invalidate, his marriage. The Holy Roman emperor Frederick II also felt the wrath of the powerful pope.

In 1209, Innocent, aided by Philip II, launched a brutal crusade, or holy war, against the Albigensians in southern France. The Albigensians wanted to purify the Church and return to the simple ways of early Christianity. Tens of thousands of people were slaughtered in the Albigensian Crusade.

After Innocent's death, popes continued to press their claim to supremacy. During this period, though, the French and English monarchies were growing stronger. In 1296, Philip IV of France successfully challenged Pope Boniface VIII on the issue of taxing the clergy. After Philip engineered the election of a French pope, the papacy entered a period of decline.

SECTION 2 Assessment

Recall

1. **Identify:** (a) Holy Roman Empire, (b) Gregory VII, (c) Henry IV, (d) Concordat of Worms, (e) Frederick II, (f) Innocent III, (g) Albigensian Crusade.
2. **Define:** (a) lay investiture, (b) annul, (c) crusade.

Comprehension

3. Why was the power of German emperors limited?
4. How did conflicts between popes and emperors affect (a) the Holy Roman Empire, and (b) Italy?

5. How did Pope Innocent III assert the power of the Church?

Critical Thinking and Writing

6. **Comparing** (a) How did the political development of the Holy Roman Empire differ from that of England and France? (b) What were the causes of these differences?
7. **Analyzing Primary Sources** Review the words of Innocent III at the beginning of this section. (a) To what does Innocent compare a monarch? (b) What point was he trying to make?

Activity

Making a Map
On an outline map of Europe, label the places that you have read about in this section. Illustrate your map to show what happened in each location.

SECTION 3 Europeans Look Outward

Reading Focus

- What advanced civilizations flourished around the world in 1050?

- What were the causes and effects of the Crusades?

- How did Christians in Spain carry out the Reconquista?

Vocabulary

schism

levy

religious toleration

Taking Notes

As you read, complete the following chart showing the effects that the Crusades had on life in Europe.

THE CRUSADES			
Economy • Encouraged trade	**Monarch** •	**Church** •	**Worldview** •

Main Idea The Crusades stimulated economic and political change in Europe and broadened Europeans' view of the world.

Setting the Scene Nearly 23 weeks after departing France, Count Stephen of Blois reached the city of Antioch in Syria. There, in March 1098, he composed a letter to his wife, Adele. He described the battles he had fought and the riches he had won. Stephen proudly told Adele that he and his fellow knights were "full of fury" and "prepared to die for Christ."

Stephen of Blois was one of thousands of Europeans who took part in a series of wars known as the Crusades. In these wars, which began in 1096, Christians battled Muslims for control of lands in the Middle East. As they streamed eastward over the next 200 years, Western Europeans learned that the world was much larger than they had ever dreamed. Their encounters outside Europe would serve to stimulate the pace of change.

The World in 1050

In 1050, as Western Europe was just emerging from a period of isolation, civilizations were thriving elsewhere. These civilizations are described in detail in other chapters. What follows here is an overview of the world at the time that medieval Europe was first beginning to test its strength.

During Europe's Middle Ages, Islam had given rise to a brilliant new civilization that stretched from Spain to India. Muslim traders and scholars spread goods and ideas even further. Trading caravans regularly crossed the Sahara to West Africa. Arab ships visited East African ports and sailed to India and East Asia.

Although India was politically divided, it was a land of thriving cities. Hindu and Buddhist traditions flourished, and wealthy princes built stunning temples and palaces. Indian mathematicians invented a number system, which Arabs adapted and eventually passed to Europeans.

China had a strong central government. Under the Tang and Song dynasties, China's culture flourished and influenced neighboring peoples. The Chinese made amazing advances in technology, inventing paper, printing, and gunpowder. In dozens of cities, traders used coins and paper money, unknown to medieval Europeans.

In West Africa, the Soninke people were building the great trading empire of Ghana. Its merchants traded goods, especially gold, across the Sahara to North Africa, the Middle East, and even Europe.

Across the Atlantic, in the Americas, the Mayas had cleared rain forests and built cities dominated by towering temples. In Peru, Native Americans were building empires and creating great works of art, including elegant

Global Connections

A Mongol Alliance?

Later during the Crusades, Pope Innocent IV sent a diplomatic mission to the Mongols in Central Asia. The pope hoped that the Mongol khan would halt his invasions of Christian lands, convert to Christianity, and join European Christians in their struggle against the Muslims. In a letter written in Mongol, Arabic, and Latin, the khan rejected the pope's proposal.

The pope's mission failed to win an alliance, but it did bring the Europeans new knowledge about the world. Giovanni da Pian del Carpini, the monk who had led the mission, wrote a text based on his extensive travels. His book on the Mongol empire consisted of chapters on climate, customs, religion, character, history, policy, and tactics.

Theme: Global Interaction
How can increased knowledge of other cultures improve international relations?

Virtual Field Trip

www.phschool.com

University of Calgary
Calgary, Canada

For more images and information about the Reconquista and the history of Spain, use the Internet address above to link to the department of history at the University of Calgary.

The Reconquista
In 1492, the fall of the Muslim city of Granada completed the Christian reconquest of Spain. This Spanish woodcarving shows Granada surrendering to Queen Isabella and King Ferdinand.

Theme: Economics and Technology How were Granada and other medieval towns designed to provide defense?

Increased Power for Monarchs The Crusades helped to increase the power of feudal monarchs. Rulers won new rights to levy, or collect, taxes in order to support the Crusades. Some rulers, including the French king Louis IX, led crusades, which added greatly to their prestige.

The Church Enthusiasm for the Crusades brought papal power to its greatest height. This period of enhanced prestige was short-lived, however. As we have seen, popes were soon involved in bitter clashes with feudal monarchs. Also, the Crusades did not end the split between the Roman and Byzantine churches. In fact, Byzantine resentment against the West hardened as a result of the Fourth Crusade.

A Wider Worldview Contacts with the Muslim world led Christians to realize that millions of people lived in regions they had never known existed. Soon, a few curious Europeans visited far-off places like India and China.

In 1271, a young Venetian, Marco Polo, set out for China with his merchant father and uncle. After many years in China, he returned to Venice full of stories about the wonders of Chinese civilization. Doubting Europeans called Marco Polo the "prince of liars." To them, his tales of a government-run mail service and black stones (coal) that were burned to heat homes were totally untrue.

The experiences of crusaders and of travelers like Marco Polo expanded European horizons. They brought Europe into a wider world from which it had been cut off since the fall of Rome. By the 1400s, a desire to trade directly with India and China led Europeans to a new age of exploration.

The Reconquista in Spain

The crusading spirit continued long after the European defeat at Acre. It flourished especially in Spain, where Christian warriors had been battling Muslims for centuries. Muslims had conquered most of Spain in the 700s. Several tiny Christian kingdoms survived in the north, however. As they slowly expanded their borders, they sought to take over Muslim lands. Their campaign to drive the Muslims from Spain became known as the Reconquista, or "reconquest."

Christian Advances Efforts by Christian warriors to expel the Muslims began in the 700s. Their first real success did not come, however, until 1085, when they recaptured the city of Toledo. During the next 200 years, Christian forces pushed slowly and steadily southward. By 1300, Christians controlled the entire Iberian Peninsula except for Granada. Muslim influences remained strong, though, and helped shape the arts and literature of Christian Spain.

Ferdinand and Isabella In 1469, Isabella of Castile married Ferdinand of Aragon. This marriage between the rulers of two powerful kingdoms opened the way for a unified state. Using their combined forces, the two monarchs made a final push against the Muslim stronghold of Granada. In 1492, Granada fell. The Reconquista was complete.

Isabella and Ferdinand tried to impose unity on their diverse peoples. They joined forces with townspeople against powerful nobles. Isabella was determined to bring religious as well as political unity to Spain.

Under Muslim rule, Spain had enjoyed a tradition of religious toleration, that is, a policy of allowing people to worship as they choose. Christians, Jews, and Muslims lived there in relative peace. Isabella ended that policy of toleration. With the support of the Inquisition, a Church court set up to try people accused of heresy, Isabella launched a brutal crusade against Jews and Muslims. Often, those who refused to convert to Christianity were burned at the stake.

The queen achieved religious unity but at a high price. More than 150,000 people fled Spain. Many of these exiles were skilled, educated people who had contributed much to Spain's economy and culture.

Cause *and* Effect

Long-Term Causes	Immediate Causes
• Growth of strong monarchs • Growth of towns and cities • Growth of representative bodies • Crusades • Increased trade • Population decline	• Economic revival • New technology and agricultural productivity • Development of universities • Wider worldview

Western European Emergence From Isolation

Immediate Effects	Long-Term Effects
• Population growth • End of feudalism • Centralized monarchies • Growth of Italian trading centers • Increased productivity	• Renaissance • Age of Exploration • Scientific Revolution • Western European colonies in Asia, Africa, and the Americas

Connections to Today

• Growth of strong central governments
• Spread of representative government
• Capitalism and powerful business classes
• Influence of Western European culture around the world
• Influence of technology on everyday life

Skills Assessment **Chart** During the late Middle Ages, Europe was emerging from a period of isolation. **How did the Crusades contribute to economic revival?**

SECTION 3 Assessment

Recall
1. **Identify: (a)** Crusades, **(b)** Council of Clermont, **(c)** Saladin, **(d)** Reconquista, **(e)** Ferdinand and Isabella.
2. **Define: (a)** schism, **(b)** levy, **(c)** religious toleration.

Comprehension
3. What advanced civilizations existed around the world at the time of the First Crusade?
4. **(a)** Why did Europeans join the Crusades? **(b)** What were three results of the Crusades?

5. How did Spain achieve political and religious unity?

Critical Thinking and Writing
6. **Analyzing Information** How did the Crusades reflect the growing strength of medieval Europe?
7. **Making Generalizations (a)** How was the Reconquista part of the crusading spirit that appealed to many Europeans? **(b)** How were the goals of Ferdinand and Isabella similar to the goals of other monarchs in Europe?

Activity

Expressing Different Points of View
Write two articles reporting on the First Crusade: one from the point of view of a Christian knight, and another from the point of view of a Muslim living in Jerusalem.

Learning, Literature, and the Arts

Reading Focus

- How did medieval universities advance learning?
- How did "new" learning affect medieval thought?
- What styles of literature, architecture, and art developed in the High Middle Ages?

Vocabulary

scholasticism
vernacular
epic
flying buttress
illumination

Taking Notes

Copy this concept web. As you read, complete the web. Add circles as needed.

Universities — CULTURAL ACHIEVEMENTS — Literature — Epics praise virtues — The arts

Main Idea As economic and political conditions improved, Europeans made notable achievements in learning, literature, and the arts.

Setting the Scene By the 1100s, Europe was experiencing dynamic changes. No longer was everyone preoccupied with the daily struggle to survive. Improvements in agriculture were creating a steadier food supply. The revival of trade and the growth of towns were signs of increased prosperity. Within the towns and cities of medieval Europe, a few people were acquiring wealth. In time, towns contributed a vital spark that ignited the cultural flowering of the High Middle Ages.

Medieval Universities

As economic and political conditions improved in the High Middle Ages, the need for education expanded. The Church wanted better-educated clergy. Royal rulers also needed literate men for their growing bureaucracies. By getting an education, the sons of wealthy townspeople might hope to qualify for high jobs in the Church or royal governments.

Academic Guilds By the 1100s, schools had sprung up around the great cathedrals to train the clergy. Some of these cathedral schools evolved into the first universities. They were organized like guilds with charters to protect the rights of members and set standards for training.

Salerno and Bologna in Italy boasted the first universities. Paris and Oxford soon had theirs. In the 1200s, other cities rushed to organize universities. Students often traveled from one university to another. They might study law in Bologna, medicine in Montpellier, and theology, or religion, in Paris.

Student Life University life offered few comforts. A bell wakened students at about 5 A.M. for prayers. Students then attended classes until 10 A.M., when they had their first meal of the day—perhaps a bit of beef and soup mixed with oatmeal. Afternoon classes continued until 5 P.M. Students usually ate a light supper and then studied until it was time for bed.

Because medieval universities did not have permanent buildings, classes were held in rented rooms or in the choir loft of a church. Students sat for hours on hard benches as the teacher dictated and then explained Latin texts. Students were expected to memorize what they heard.

University of Paris
Students listened as teachers read aloud five logic books and two grammar books, as part of the course of study for a bachelor of arts.

Theme: Economics and Technology Why do you think there was not a book for each student?

A program of study covered the seven liberal arts: arithmetic, geometry, astronomy, music, grammar, rhetoric, and logic. To show that they had mastered a subject, students took an oral exam. Earning a degree as a bachelor of arts took between three and six years. Only after several more years of study could a man qualify to become a master of arts and a teacher.

Women and Education Women were not allowed to attend the universities. This exclusion seriously affected their lives. Without a university education, they could not become doctors, lawyers, administrators, church officials, or professors. They were also deprived of the mental stimulation that was an important part of university life.

An exception was Christine de Pizan (duh pee ZAHN), an Italian-born woman who came to live in the French court. De Pizan was married at 15, but her husband died before she was 25. Left with three children to raise, De Pizan earned her living as a writer, an unusual occupation for a woman of that time.

De Pizan used her pen to examine the achievements of women. In *The City of Ladies*, she questions several imaginary characters about men's negative views of women. She asks Lady Reason, for example, whether women are less capable of learning and understanding, as men insist. Lady Reason replies: "If it were customary to send daughters to school like sons, and if they were then taught the same subjects, they would learn as thoroughly and understand the subtleties of all arts and sciences as well as sons."

Still, men continued to look on educated women as oddities. Women, they felt, should pursue their "natural" gifts at home, raising children, managing the household, and doing needlework, and leave books and writing to men.

Europeans Acquire "New" Learning

Universities received a further boost from an explosion of knowledge that reached Europe in the High Middle Ages. Many of the "new" ideas had originated in ancient Greece but had been lost to Western Europeans after the fall of Rome.

Spread of Learning In the Middle East, Muslim scholars had translated the works of Aristotle and other Greek thinkers into Arabic, and their texts had spread across the Muslim world. In Muslim Spain, Jewish scholars translated these works into Latin, the language of Christian European scholars. By the 1100s, these new translations were seeping into Western Europe. There they set off a revolution in the world of learning.

Philosophy The writings of the ancient Greeks posed a challenge to Christian scholars. Aristotle taught that people should use reason to discover basic truths. Christians, however, accepted many ideas on faith. They believed that the Church was the final authority on all questions. How could they use the logic of Aristotle without undermining their Christian faith?

Christian scholars, known as scholastics, tried to resolve the conflict between faith and reason. Their method, known as scholasticism, used reason to support Christian beliefs. Scholastics studied the works of the Muslim philosopher Averroës (ah VEHR oh eez) and the Jewish rabbi Maimonides (mī MAHN uh deez). These thinkers, too, used logic to resolve the conflict between faith and reason.

The writings of these thinkers influenced the scholastic Thomas Aquinas (uh KWĪ nuhs). In a monumental work, *Summa Theologica*, Aquinas examined Christian teachings in the light of reason. Faith and reason, he concluded, existed in harmony. Both led to the same truth, that God ruled over an orderly universe. He thus brought together Christian faith and classical Greek philosophy.

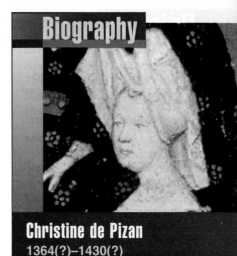

Biography

Christine de Pizan
1364(?)–1430(?)

Christine de Pizan was more educated than most men of her time. Her father, a physician and astronomer in the French court of Charles V, had seen that she received an excellent education. She spoke French, Italian, and possibly Latin as well.

To support her family, De Pizan wrote poems, songs, and ballads. Her work was supported by lords and ladies, by King Charles VI of France, and by his wife, Queen Isabella. Because of her desire to comment on social issues, De Pizan gradually switched her focus to prose. In much of her work, she promoted women's rights and accomplishments. Shortly before her death, she wrote the poem "Hymn to Joan of Arc" to honor a young Frenchwoman who was leading French soldiers to victory over the English.

Theme: Impact of the Individual What was a major theme of De Pizan's writing?

The new Gothic churches soared to incredible heights. Their graceful spires, lofty ceilings, and enormous windows carried the eye upward to the heavens. "Since their brilliance lets the splendor of the True Light pass into the church," declared a medieval visitor, "they enlighten those inside."

Cities all over Europe competed to build grander, taller cathedrals. The faithful contributed money, labor, and skills to help build these monuments "to the greater glory of God."

Art in Stone and Glass As churches rose, stonemasons carved sculptures to decorate them inside and out. The sculptors portrayed scenes from the Bible and other religious themes. They also carved images of everyday life that included lifelike forms of plants and animals. Among the most interesting of their creations were whimsical or frightening images of mythical creatures such as dragons, griffins, and unicorns.

At the same time, other skilled craftworkers created stained-glass windows that added to the brilliant splendor of Gothic churches. The artisans stained small pieces of glass in glowing colors. They then set the pieces in thin lead frames to create pictures depicting the life of Jesus, a biblical event, or other religious themes. Stained glass and carvings served as a religious education for the people, most of whom were illiterate.

Art and Religion
Stained-glass windows depicted biblical or other religious scenes. In the 1100s, a monk wrote that his church was filled with "the most radiant windows" to "illuminate men's minds so that they may travel through it [light] to an apprehension of God's light."

Theme: Art and Literature
How did medieval art help illiterate Christians learn about the Bible?

Illuminated Manuscripts In the 1300s and 1400s, the Gothic style was applied to paintings and illumination, that is, the artistic decoration of books. Since the early Middle Ages, monks, nuns, and other skilled artisans had illuminated books with intricate designs and miniature paintings of biblical scenes and daily life. Characteristics of the new Gothic style included bold, brilliant colors and decorative detail. Some fine examples of Gothic painting appeared in prayer books known as Books of Hours. Artists decorated these prayer books with depictions of towns and castles, knights and ladies in gardens or at banquet, and peasants working in the fields.

SECTION 4 Assessment

Recall
1. **Identify:** (a) Christine de Pizan, (b) Thomas Aquinas, (c) *Song of Roland*, (d) *Poem of the Cid*, (e) Dante Alighieri, (f) Geoffrey Chaucer.
2. **Define:** (a) scholasticism, (b) vernacular, (c) epic, (d) flying buttress, (e) illumination.

Comprehension
3. What subjects were included in the course of study in medieval universities?
4. How did new knowledge pose a challenge to Christian scholars?

5. What were the characteristics of Gothic architecture?

Critical Thinking and Writing
6. **Making Inferences** Why do you think Gothic churches are sometimes referred to as "Bibles in stone"?
7. **Solving Problems** Solve this problem using Roman numerals: MCMLXXX + MMCCCLX. Then, translate and solve the problem using Arabic numerals. How do you think the introduction of Arabic numerals might have affected mathematics in Western Europe?

Activity
Take It to the NET

Use the Internet to learn more about the literature and views of Dante or Chaucer. Then, with a small group of classmates, stage a TV program in which you interview one of the writers. Develop your questions and answers by referring to what you learned in your research.

SECTION 5 · A Time of Crisis

Reading Focus

■ How did the Black Death cause social and economic decline?

■ What problems afflicted the Church in the late Middle Ages?

■ What were the causes, turning points, and effects of the Hundred Years' War?

Vocabulary

epidemic

inflation

longbow

Taking Notes

Copy the chart at right on conditions before and after the Hundred Years' War. As you read, fill in each column with appropriate information.

HUNDRED YEARS' WAR

Before	After
• Castles offered adequate protection	• English hold only Calais in France
•	•

Main Idea — Plague, upheaval in the Church, and war made the 1300s and early 1400s a time of crisis for Europeans.

Setting the Scene In the autumn of 1347, a fleet of Genoese trading ships, loaded with grain, left the Black Sea port of Caffa and set sail for Messina, Sicily. By midvoyage, sailors were falling sick and dying. Soon after the ships tied up at Messina, townspeople, too, fell sick and died. A medieval chronicler described how the people of Messina "drove (the Genoese) in all haste from their city and port." Nevertheless, "the sickness remained and a terrible mortality ensued." Within months, the disease that Europeans called the Black Death was raging through Italy.

To Europeans in the mid-1300s, the end of the world seemed to have come. First, widespread crop failures brought famine and starvation. Then, plague and war deepened the crisis. Europe eventually recovered from these disasters. Still, the upheavals of the 1300s and 1400s marked the end of the Middle Ages and the beginning of the early modern age.

The Black Death

By 1348, the Black Death had reached beyond Italy to Spain and France. From there, it ravaged the rest of Europe. One in three people died—worse than in any war in history.

A Global Epidemic The sickness was bubonic plague, a disease spread by fleas on rats. Bubonic plague had broken out before in Europe, Asia, and North Africa but had subsided. One strain, though, had survived in Mongolia. In the 1200s, Mongol armies conquered much of Asia, probably setting off the new epidemic, or outbreak of rapid-spreading disease.

In the premodern world, rats infested ships, towns, and even the homes of the rich and powerful, so no one took any notice of them. In the early 1300s, rats scurrying through crowded Chinese cities spread the plague, which killed about 35 million people there.

Fleas jumped from those rats to infest the clothes and packs of traders traveling west. As a result, the disease spread from Asia to the Middle East. Terrible reports reached Europe: "India was depopulated," wrote a chronicler. "Mesopotamia, Syria, and Armenia were covered with dead bodies." In Cairo, one of the world's largest cities, the plague at its peak killed about 7,000 people a day.

Social Upheaval In Europe, the plague brought terror and bewilderment, as people had no way to stop the disease. Some people turned to magic and witchcraft for cures. Others plunged into wild pleasures, believing they

Turning Points of the Hundred Years' War

Longbow

During the early years of the war, English armies equipped with the long-bow overpowered their French counterparts equipped with the cross-bow. An English archer could shoot three arrows in the time it took a French archer to shoot one.

Joan of Arc

From 1429 to 1431, Joan's successes in battle rallied the French forces to victory. French armies continued to win even after she was executed by the English.

Cannon

The cannon helped the French to capture English-held castles and defeat England's armies. French cannons were instrumental in defeating English forces in Normandy.

Connections to Today

England, which is now part of the United Kingdom, and France have friendly relations today. Their economies are closely linked in that both nations are members of the European Union. The two cooperate militarily as members of the North Atlantic Treaty Organization.

Skills Assessment **Chart** Changes in leadership and new technology marked some of the major turning points in the Hundred Years' War. **How did technology benefit the English in the early years of the war?**

---

that people could read it themselves rather than rely on the clergy to read it. Czech students at Oxford carried Wycliffe's ideas to Bohemia—what is today the Czech Republic. There, Jan Hus led the call for reforms.

The Church responded by persecuting Wycliffe and his followers and suppressing the Hussites. Hus was tried for preaching heresy—ideas contrary to Church teachings. Found guilty, he was burned at the stake in 1415. The ideas of Wycliffe and Hus survived, however. A century later, other reformers took up the same demands.

The Hundred Years' War

On top of the disasters of famine, plague, and economic decline came a long, destructive war. Between 1337 and 1453, England and France fought a series of conflicts, known as the Hundred Years' War.

Causes As you have read, English rulers had battled for centuries to hold onto the French lands of their Norman ancestors. French kings, for their part, were intent on extending their own power in France. When Edward III of England claimed the French crown in 1337, war erupted anew between these rival powers. Once fighting started, economic rivalry and a growing sense of national pride made it hard for either side to give up the struggle.

English Victories At first, the English won a string of victories—at Crécy in 1346, Poitiers 10 years later, and Agincourt in 1415. They owed much of their success to the longbow wielded by English archers. This powerful new weapon was six feet long and took years to master. But it could discharge three arrows in the time a French archer with his crossbow fired just one, and its arrows pierced all but the heaviest armor.

The English victories took a heavy toll on French morale. England, it seemed, was likely to bring all of France under its control. Then, in what seemed to the French a miracle, their fortunes were reversed.

Joan of Arc and French Victory In 1429, a 17-year-old peasant woman, Joan of Arc, appeared at the court of Charles VII, the uncrowned king of France. She told Charles that God had sent her to save France. She persuaded the desperate French king to let her lead his army against the English.

To Charles's amazement, Joan inspired the battered and despairing French troops to fight anew. In an astonishing year of campaigning, she led the French to several victories and planted the seeds for future triumphs.

Joan paid for success with her life. She was taken captive by allies of the English and turned over to her enemies for trial. The English wanted to discredit her, and they had her tried for witchcraft. She was convicted and burned at the stake. Much later, however, the Church declared her a saint.

The execution of Joan rallied the French, who saw her as a martyr. After Joan's death, the French took the offensive. With a powerful new weapon, the cannon, they attacked English-held castles. By 1453, the English held only the port of Calais in north-western France.

Effects The Hundred Years' War set France and England on different paths. The war created a growing sense of national feeling in France and allowed French kings to expand their power. During the war, English rulers turned repeatedly to Parliament for funds, which helped that body win the "power of the purse." The loss of French lands shattered English dreams of a continental empire, but English rulers soon began looking at new trading ventures overseas.

The Hundred Years' War brought many changes to the late medieval world. The longbow and cannon gave common soldiers a new importance on the battlefield and undermined the value of armored knights. Castles and knights were doomed to disappear because their defenses could not stand up to the more deadly firepower. Feudal society was changing. Monarchs needed large armies, not feudal vassals, to fight their wars.

Looking Ahead

In the 1400s, as Europe recovered from the Black Death, other changes occurred. The population expanded and manufacturing grew. These changes, in turn, led to increased trade. Italian cities flourished as centers of shipping. They sent European cloth to the Middle East in exchange for spices, sugar, and cotton. Europeans developed new technologies. German miners, for example, used water power to crush ore and built blast furnaces to make cast iron.

The recovery of the late Middle Ages set the stage for further changes during the Renaissance, Reformation, and Age of Exploration. As Europe grew stronger over the next few centuries, it would take a more prominent role on the global stage.

Hundred Years' War, 1337–1453

France, 1337
Held by England, 1337
Held by England, 1429
Battle sites
Route of Joan of Arc
Boundary of France, 1453

Skills Assessment

Geography The English and French fought for control of France in the Hundred Years' War.

1. **Location** On the map, locate **(a)** Normandy, **(b)** Poitiers, **(c)** Calais.
2. **Place** What city in northern France was still under English control in 1453?
3. **Critical Thinking Analyzing Information** What regions of France did England gain between 1337 and 1429?

SECTION 5 Assessment

Recall

1. **Identify:** **(a)** Black Death, **(b)** Babylonian Captivity, **(c)** John Wycliffe, **(d)** Jan Hus, **(e)** Hundred Years' War, **(f)** Joan of Arc.
2. **Define:** **(a)** epidemic, **(b)** inflation, **(c)** longbow.

Comprehension

3. What were three effects of the bubonic plague on late medieval Europe?
4. **(a)** Why did reformers criticize the Church? **(b)** How did the Church respond to this criticism?
5. **(a)** How did new technologies affect fighting during the Hundred Years' War? **(b)** What were the results of the war?

Critical Thinking and Writing

6. **Understanding Sequence** Make a step-by-step list showing how the bubonic plague spread from Asia to Europe and resulted in the deaths of millions of Europeans.
7. **Comparing** Compare the effects of the Hundred Years' War on France and on England.

Activity
Take It to the NET

Use the Internet to research the Black Death in Europe, especially its effects on population and the economy. Then, use the information you have found to create graphs showing the decline of Europe's population and economy during the plague years. You might download pictures from the Net to illustrate your graphs.

CHAPTER 9

Review and Assessment

Creating a Chapter Summary

On a separate sheet of paper, copy and complete the following chart showing the major political, economic, cultural, and religious developments of the High Middle Ages.

POLITICAL	ECONOMIC	CULTURAL	RELIGIOUS
Monarchs expanded royal power.	Crusades spurred growth of a money economy.	Universities were established.	Church reached height of its power.

CD-ROM Review For additional review of the major concepts of Chapter 9, see the *Guide to the Essentials of World History* or the *Interactive Student Tutorial CD-ROM.*

Web Site Self-Test For practice test questions for Chapter 9, see **www.phschool.com.**

Building Vocabulary

Review the meaning of the chapter vocabulary words listed below. Then, write a sentence for each word, describing its significance in medieval Europe.

1. **common law**
2. **jury**
3. **lay investiture**
4. **crusade**
5. **schism**
6. **scholasticism**
7. **vernacular**
8. **epidemic**
9. **inflation**
10. **longbow**

Recalling Key Facts

11. List two ways English and French monarchs increased royal power.
12. Why did Holy Roman emperors come into conflict with the Church?
13. **(a)** What was the goal of the Crusades? **(b)** Did they achieve their goal? Explain.
14. **(a)** What steps did Isabella take to bring religious unity to Spain? **(b)** What were the results of her policy?
15. What new knowledge reached Europe in the High Middle Ages?
16. **(a)** What steps did reformers take to end the Babylonian Captivity of the Church? **(b)** What were the results?

Critical Thinking and Writing

17. **Analyzing Information (a)** List four goals of medieval monarchs. **(b)** Explain how one ruler furthered these goals.
18. **Defending a Position** Review the conflict between Gregory VII and Henry IV. Cite two arguments each man might have given to defend his position.
19. **Ranking** List four effects of the Crusades. Then, rank them in order of their importance. Give reasons for your ranking.
20. **Connecting to Geography** Review the map titled "Trade in Medieval Europe" in the last chapter and the map titled "Spread of the Black Death" in this chapter. How might trade routes and the spread of the disease be linked?

21. **Making Inferences** How might the rise of medieval literature written in the vernacular reflect a change in education and literacy rates?
22. **Recognizing Causes and Effects (a)** How did the creation of the Magna Carta affect government in England? **(b)** How do you think the lack of a similar document in France affected the development of government there?

Roger of Wendover, an English monk, describes how King John came to sign the Magna Carta. Read the excerpt and answer the questions that follow.

> *"In Easter week of [1215], the . . . nobles assembled . . . with horses and arms; for they had now induced almost all the nobility of the whole kingdom to join them . . . and when the king learned this, he sent . . . to them to inquire [what] they demanded. The barons then delivered to the messengers a paper, containing in great measure the laws and ancient customs of the kingdom, and declared that, unless the king immediately granted them . . . they would, by taking possession of his fortresses, force him to give them sufficient satisfaction. . . .*
>
> *King John, when he saw that he was deserted by almost all, . . . deceitfully pretended to make peace with the aforesaid barons, and . . . told them that . . . he would willingly grant them the laws and liberties they required."*

—Roger of Wendover, quoted in *Source Book of English History* (Kendall)

23. **(a)** What demands did the nobles make? **(b)** What did they threaten to do if King John did not agree?
24. Do you think Roger of Wendover expected King John to keep his word and honor the Magna Carta? Explain.
25. What was contained in the Magna Carta?
26. What does this excerpt suggest about English royal power in 1215? Explain.

Use the Internet to research medieval Gothic cathedrals. Based on information that you find on the Internet, draw a simple diagram of part of a cathedral. With your diagram, include a description of the technology used to build that section of the cathedral, or an explanation of that section's significance to medieval architects, clergy, and citizens.

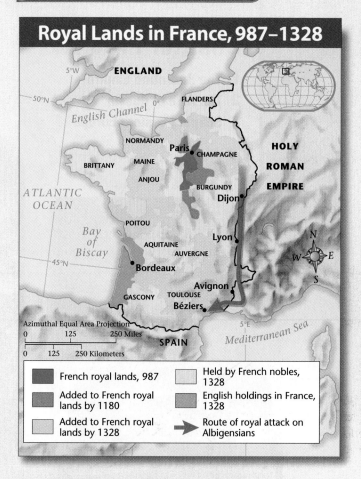

Royal Lands in France, 987–1328

Legend:
- French royal lands, 987
- Added to French royal lands by 1180
- Added to French royal lands by 1328
- Held by French nobles, 1328
- English holdings in France, 1328
- Route of royal attack on Albigensians

Azimuthal Equal Area Projection
0 125 250 Miles
0 125 250 Kilometers

The map above shows the growth of royal lands over a period of several hundred years. Use the map to answer the following questions:

27. Describe the extent of French royal lands in 987.
28. **(a)** Between what years did Anjou become part of French royal lands? **(b)** Between what years did royal lands increase the most?
29. **(a)** Describe the route used by Philip Augustus's army to attack the Albigensians. **(b)** About how many miles did the army travel?
30. In 1328, who controlled **(a)** Normandy? **(b)** Brittany? **(c)** Bordeaux?

Skills Tip

To understand a map, compare the information on the map with what you have read in your textbook.

The Age of Justinian

The Byzantine empire reached its greatest size under the emperor Justinian, who ruled from 527 to 565. Justinian was determined to revive ancient Rome by recovering the provinces that had been overrun by invaders. Led by the brilliant general Belisarius, Byzantine armies reconquered North Africa, Italy, and southern Spain. The fighting exhausted Justinian's treasury and weakened his defenses in the east. In the end, the victories were temporary. Justinian's successors lost the bitterly contested lands.

Hagia Sophia Justinian left a more lasting monument in his buildings. To restore Roman glory, he launched a program to beautify Constantinople. His great triumph was the church of Hagia Sophia ("Holy Wisdom"). Its immense, arching dome improved on earlier Roman buildings. The interior glowed with colored marble and embroidered silk curtains. Seeing this church, the emperor recalled King Solomon's temple in Jerusalem. "Glory to God who has judged me worthy of accomplishing such a work as this!" Justinian exclaimed. "O Solomon, I have surpassed you!"

Code of Laws Justinian is best remembered for his reform of the law. Early in his reign, he set up a commission to collect, revise, and organize all the laws of ancient Rome. The result was the *Corpus Juris Civilis*, or "Body of Civil Law," popularly known as Justinian's Code. This massive collection included laws passed by Roman assemblies or decreed by Roman emperors, as well as the legal writings of Roman judges and a handbook for students.

Justinian's Code had an impact far beyond the Byzantine empire. By the 1100s, it had reached Western Europe. There, both the Roman Catholic Church and medieval monarchs modeled their laws on its principles. Centuries later, the code also guided legal thinkers who began to put together the international law in use today.

Absolute Power Justinian used the law to unite the empire under his control. He ruled as an autocrat, or sole ruler with complete authority. The emperor also had power over the Church. He was deemed Christ's co-ruler on Earth. As a Byzantine official wrote, "The emperor is equal to all men in the nature of his body, but in the authority of his rank he is similar to God, who rules all." Unlike feudal monarchs in Western Europe, he combined both political power and spiritual authority. His control was aided by his wife, Theodora. A shrewd politician, she served as adviser and co-ruler to Justinian and even pursued her own policies.

Changing Fortunes In the centuries after Justinian, the fortunes of the empire rose and fell. Attacks by Persians, Slavs, Vikings, Mongols, and Turks were largely unsuccessful. The empire thus served as a buffer for Western Europe. Beginning in the 600s and 700s, however, Arab armies gained control of much of the Mediterranean world. Constantinople itself withstood their attack, and the Byzantines held onto their heartland in the Balkans and Asia Minor. The empire's greatest strengths came from a strong central government and a prosperous economy.

Peasants formed the backbone of the empire, working the land, paying taxes, and providing soldiers for the military. In the cities of the empire, trade and industry flourished. While Western Europe was reduced to a barter economy, the Byzantine empire preserved a healthy money economy. The bezant, the Byzantine gold coin stamped with the emperor's image, circulated from England to China.

Byzantine Christianity

Christianity was as influential in the Byzantine empire as it was in Western Europe. But religious divisions grew between the two regions.

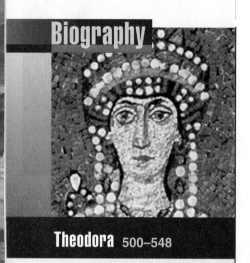

Biography

Theodora 500–548

From humble beginnings as the daughter of a bearkeeper, Theodora rose to become Justinian's adviser and co-ruler. A shrewd, tough, and sometimes ruthless politician, Theodora did not hesitate to challenge the emperor and pursue her own policies.

Her most dramatic act came during a revolt in 532. "Emperor, if you wish to flee, well and good, you have the money, the ships are ready, the sea is clear," calmly spoke Theodora. "But I shall stay," she concluded. "I accept the ancient proverb: Royal purple is the best burial sheet." Theodora's courageous words inspired Justinian to remain in Constantinople and crush the revolt that threatened his power.

Theme: Impact of the Individual How did Theodora affect the outcome of the revolt?

Virtual Field Trip

www.phschool.com

**Byzantine Museum
Athens, Greece**

To see other examples of Orthodox Christian icons, use the Internet address above to link to the Byzantine Museum.

Icons

In this early Byzantine icon, the figures of Christ (right) and a saint stare directly outward, inviting the viewer into a personal relationship. The figures and their golden halos seem to glow because the artist painted on a background of reflecting gold paint. Over the centuries, Byzantine artists tended to use similar styles and techniques.

Theme: Art and Literature
What do you think the artist was trying to accomplish with this icon?

Differences East and West Since early Christian times, differences had emerged over Church leadership. Although the Byzantine emperor was not a priest, he controlled Church affairs and appointed the patriarch, or highest Church official, in Constantinople. Byzantine Christians rejected the pope's claim to authority over all Christians.

Further differences developed. Unlike priests in Western Europe, the Byzantine clergy kept their right to marry. Greek, not Latin, was the language of the Byzantine Church. The chief Byzantine holy day was Easter, celebrated as the day Jesus rose from the dead. In contrast, western Christians placed greater emphasis on Christmas, the birthday of Jesus.

Schism During the Middle Ages, the two branches of Christianity drew farther apart. A dispute over the use of icons, or holy images, contributed to the split. Many Byzantine Christians prayed to images of Christ, the Virgin Mary, and the saints. In the 700s, however, a Byzantine emperor outlawed the veneration of icons, saying it violated God's commandment against worshiping "graven images."

The ban set off violent battles within the empire. From the west, the pope took a hand in the dispute, excommunicating the emperor. Although a later empress eventually restored the use of icons, the conflict left great resentment against the pope.

In 1054, other controversies provoked a schism, or permanent split, between the Eastern (Greek) Orthodox and the Roman Catholic churches. The pope and the patriarch excommunicated each other. Thereafter, contacts between the two churches were guarded and distant. They treated each other as rivals rather than as branches of the same faith.

Crisis and Collapse

By the time of the schism, the Byzantine empire was declining. Struggles over succession, court intrigues, and constant wars undermined its strength. As in Western Europe, powerful local lords gained control of large areas. As the empire faltered, its enemies advanced. The Normans conquered southern Italy. Even more serious, the Seljuk Turks advanced across Asia Minor.

The Rise of Russia

Reading Focus

- How did geography help shape early Russia and the growth of Kiev?
- How did the Mongol conquest affect Russia?
- Why did Moscow emerge as the chief power in Russia?

Vocabulary

steppe

boyar

czar

Taking Notes

Create a time line that shows events in the rise of Russia between the 700s and 1613. The sample on this page will help you get started.

700s	900	1100	1300	1500	1613

Varangians appear

Main Idea In its early years, Russia was influenced by the Slavs, Vikings, Byzantines, and Mongols.

Setting the Scene In Russia, a patriotic monk saw a special meaning in the fall of Constantinople. Moscow, he declared, was a "third Rome," the successor to the Roman and Byzantine empires:

> "The third Rome . . . shines like the sun . . . throughout the whole universe. . . . Two Romes have fallen, and the third one stands, and a fourth one there shall not be."
> —Philotheos, quoted in *Tsar and People* (Cherniavsky)

Moscow had reason to claim itself heir to the Byzantine empire. Over many centuries, Byzantine culture greatly influenced the development of Russian society.

The Geography of Russia

Russia lies on the vast Eurasian plain that reaches from Europe to the borders of China. Although mapmakers use the Ural Mountains to mark the boundary between Europe and Asia, these ancient mountains were long ago worn away to wooded hills. They posed no obstacle to migration.

Three broad zones with different climates and resources helped shape early Russian life. The northern forests supplied lumber for building and fuel. Fur-bearing animals attracted hunters, but poor soil and a cold, snowy climate hindered farming. Farther south, a band of fertile land attracted early farmers. This region—today the country of Ukraine—was home to Russia's first civilization.

A third region, the southern steppe, is an open, treeless grassland. It offered splendid pasture for the herds and horses of nomadic peoples. With no natural barriers, the steppe was a great highway, along which streams of nomads migrated from Asia into Europe.

Russia's network of rivers provided transportation for both people and goods. The Dnieper (NEE puhr) and Volga rivers became productive trade routes. Major rivers ran from north to south, linking the Russians early on to the advanced Byzantine world in the south.

Growth of Kiev

During Roman times, the Slavs expanded into southern Russia. Like the Germanic peoples who pushed into Western Europe, the Slavs had a simple political organization and were organized into clans. They lived in small

Primary Source

The Russians Become Christians

Prince Vladimir of Kiev sent representatives to visit the churches of many lands:

"The envoys reported, 'When we journeyed among the Bulgars, we beheld how they worship in their temple. . . . Their religion is not good. Then we went among the Germans, . . . but we beheld no glory there. Then we went on to Greece, and the Greeks led us to the edifices [buildings] where they worship their God, and we knew not whether we were in heaven or on earth. For on earth there is no such splendor or such beauty, and we are at a loss how to describe it. We know only that God dwells there among men, and their service is fairer than the ceremonies of other nations. For we cannot forget that beauty.'"

—*The Primary Chronicle*

Skills Assessment

Primary Source What impressed the Russians about the Greek Orthodox Church?

villages, farmed, and traded along the rivers that ran between the Baltic and the Black seas.

The Varangians In the 700s and 800s, the Vikings steered their long ships out of Scandinavia. These expert sailors were as much at home on Russian rivers as on the stormy Atlantic. The Vikings, called Varangians by later Russians, worked their way south along the rivers, trading with and collecting tribute from the Slavs. They also conducted a thriving trade with Constantinople.

Located at the heart of this vital trade network was the city of Kiev. In time, it would become the center of the first Russian state. Within a few generations, the Varangians who had settled among the Slavs were absorbed into the local culture. Viking names like *Helga* and *Waldemar* became the Slavic names *Olga* and *Vladimir*.

Byzantine Influences Early on, trade had brought Kiev into the Byzantine orbit. Constantinople later sent Christian missionaries to convert the Slavs. About 863, two Greek monks, Cyril and Methodius, adapted the Greek alphabet so they could translate the Bible into Slavic languages. This Cyrillic (suh RIHL ihk) alphabet became the written script used in Russia and Ukraine to the present.

In 957, Princess Olga of Kiev converted to Byzantine Christianity. But it was not until the reign of her grandson Vladimir that the new religion spread widely. After his own conversion, Vladimir married the sister of a Byzantine emperor. Soon, Greek priests arrived in Kiev to preside over the mass baptisms organized by the prince.

As Byzantine Christianity gained strength in Russia, princes began to see themselves as heirs to many cultural and political aspects of the Byzantine empire. The Russians acquired a written language, and a class of educated Russian priests emerged. Russians adapted Byzantine religious art, music, and architecture. Byzantine domes capped with colorful, carved "helmets" became the onion domes of Russian churches.

Byzantine Christianity set the pattern for close ties between Church and state. Russian rulers, like the Byzantine emperor, eventually controlled the Church, making it dependent on them for support. The Russian Orthodox Church would long remain a pillar of state power.

Yaroslav Kiev enjoyed a golden age under Yaroslav the Wise, who ruled from 1019 to 1054. Like Justinian, he issued a written law code to improve justice. A scholar, he translated Greek works into his language. Yaroslav arranged marriages between his children and some of the royal families of Western Europe.

Kiev declined in the 1100s as rival families battled for the throne. Also, Russian trading cities were hurt because Byzantine prosperity faded. As Russian princes squabbled among themselves, Mongol invaders from central Asia struck the final blow.

Mongol Conquest

In the early 1200s, a young leader united the nomadic Mongols of central Asia. As his mounted bowmen overran lands from China to Eastern Europe, he took the title Genghiz Khan (GEHNG gihz KAHN), "World Emperor."

The Golden Horde Between 1236 and 1241, Batu, the grandson of Genghiz, led Mongol armies into Russia. Known as the Golden Horde, from

Constantinople and Russia
Cyril and Methodius became saints in both the Orthodox and Roman Catholic churches. Modern Russian script is based on the Cyrillic alphabet developed by the two Greek monks.

Theme: Impact of the Individual How does this image, from a church fresco, reflect the contributions of Cyril and Methodius?

Growth of Russia, 1330–1584

Skills Assessment

Geography Between 1300 and 1584, Russian lands grew from a small area around Moscow to a large territory.

1. **Location** On the map, locate **(a)** Black Sea, **(b)** Volga River, **(c)** Danube River, **(d)** Caspian Sea, **(e)** Kulikovo.

2. **Place** During what years did Novgorod come under Russian rule?

3. **Critical Thinking Synthesizing Information** Locate the natural feature many mapmakers consider the boundary between Europe and Asia. In 1584, were Russian lands mostly in Europe or in Asia?

the color of their tents, they looted and burned Kiev and other Russian towns. So many inhabitants were killed, declared a Russian historian, that "no eye remained to weep for the dead." From their capital on the Volga, the Golden Horde ruled Russia for the next 240 years.

The Mongols, although fierce conquerors, were generally tolerant rulers. They demanded regular payments of heavy tribute, and Russian princes had to acknowledge the Mongols as their overlords. But as long as the tribute was paid, the Mongols left Russian princes to rule without much interference.

Mongol Influences Historians have long debated how Mongol rule affected Russia. Peasants felt the burden of heavy taxes. Some fled to remote regions, and others sought protection from Mongol raids by becoming serfs of Russian nobles. Even though the Golden Horde converted to Islam, the Mongols tolerated the Russian Orthodox Church, which grew more powerful during this period. The Mongol conquest brought peace to the huge swath of land between China and Eastern Europe, and Russian merchants benefited from new trade routes across this region.

During the period of Mongol rule, Russians adopted the practice of isolating upper-class women in separate quarters. Beginning in the 1200s, women became totally subject to male authority in the household. Husbands could even sell their wives into slavery to pay family debts.

The absolute power of the Mongols served as a model for later Russian rulers. Russian princes developed a strong desire to centralize their own power without interference from nobles, the clergy, or wealthy merchants. Perhaps most important, Mongol rule cut Russia off from contacts with Western Europe at a time when Europeans were making rapid advances in the arts and sciences.

Moscow Takes the Lead

During the Mongol period, the princes of Moscow steadily increased their power. Their success was due in part to the city's location near important river trade routes. They also used their positions as tribute collectors for the Mongols to subdue neighboring towns. When the head of the Russian Orthodox Church made Moscow his capital, the city became not just Russia's political center, but its spiritual center as well.

As Mongol power declined, the princes of Moscow took on a new role as patriotic defenders of Russia against foreign rule. In 1380, they rallied other Russians and defeated the Golden Horde at the battle of Kulikovo. Although the Mongols continued their terrifying raids, their strength was much reduced.

Ivan the Great A driving force behind Moscow's successes was Ivan III, known as Ivan the Great. Between 1462 and 1505, he brought much of northern Russia under his rule. He also recovered Russian territories that had fallen into the hands of neighboring Slavic states.

Ivan built the framework for absolute rule. He tried to limit the power of the boyars, or great landowning nobles. After he married Sophia-Zoë

Paleologus, niece of the last Byzantine emperor, he adopted Byzantine court rituals to emphasize Russia's role as the heir to Byzantine power. Like the Byzantine emperors, he used a double-headed eagle as his symbol. Ivan and his successors took the title czar, the Russian word for Caesar. "The czar," claimed Ivan, "is in nature like all men, but in authority he is like the highest God."

Ivan the Terrible   Ivan IV, grandson of Ivan the Great, further centralized royal power. He limited the privileges of the old boyar families and granted land to nobles in exchange for military or other service. At a time when the manor system was fading in Western Europe, Ivan IV introduced new laws that tied Russian serfs to the land.

About 1560, Ivan IV became increasingly unstable. He trusted no one and became subject to violent fits of rage. In a moment of madness, he even killed his own son. He organized the *oprichniki* (aw PREECH nee kee), agents of terror who enforced the czar's will. Dressed in black robes and mounted on black horses, they slaughtered rebellious boyars and sacked towns where people were suspected of disloyalty. Their saddles were decorated with a dog's head and a broom, symbols of their constant watchfulness to sweep away their master's enemies.

The czar's awesome power, and the ways he used it, earned him the title "Ivan the Terrible." When he died in 1584, he left a land seething with rebellion. But he had introduced Russia to a tradition of extreme absolute power.

Looking Ahead

Disputes over succession, peasant uprisings, and foreign invasions soon plunged Russia into a period of disorder. This "Time of Troubles" lasted from 1604 to 1613. Finally, the zemsky sobor (ZEHM skee suh BAWR), an assembly of clergy, nobles, and townsmen, chose a new czar, 17-year-old Michael Romanov. His reign established the Romanov dynasty, which would rule Russia until 1917.

In the 1600s, Russia was an emerging power. Like monarchs in France or Spain, the czars expanded national borders and centralized royal control. But Russia developed along far different lines. Byzantine influences had helped establish a strong tradition of autocratic rule. Later Russian rulers were generally more autocratic than western kings and queens. Authoritarian leaders, from Peter the Great and Catherine the Great to Joseph Stalin, would shape Russian history down to this century.

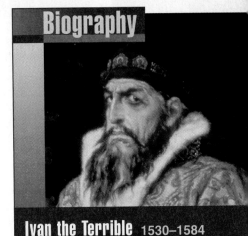

Biography

Ivan the Terrible 1530–1584

"I grew up on the throne," explained Ivan of his unhappy childhood. His father, Vasily, died when Ivan was only three years old. Intelligent, well read, and religious, young Ivan was crowned czar at age 17.

Though Ivan had long been a harsh ruler, his behavior became increasingly unstable after his wife died. Prone to violence, he crushed any opposition, real or imagined. He had thousands of people killed in the city of Novgorod because he feared a plot. Almost every noble family was affected by his murders. "From Adam to this day I have surpassed all sinners," he confessed in his will.

Theme: Impact of the Individual   How did Ivan's reign affect Russia?

SECTION 2 Assessment

Recall
1. **Identify:** (a) Cyril and Methodius, (b) Vladimir, (c) Yaroslav, (d) Genghiz Khan, (e) Golden Horde, (f) "Time of Troubles," (g) Michael Romanov.
2. **Define:** (a) steppe, (b) boyar, (c) czar.

Comprehension
3. Describe how Russia's geography affected the rise of Kiev.
4. How did Mongol rule influence the economy and political structure of Russia?

5. How did Ivan III and Ivan IV establish royal power in Russia?

Critical Thinking and Writing
6. **Recognizing Points of View** Supporters of Ivan III called Moscow "the third Rome." **(a)** Why do you think they wanted to compare Moscow to Rome? **(b)** Do you agree that Moscow was truly the heir to Rome? Why or why not?
7. **Connecting to Geography** How did geography aid the princes of Moscow in gaining power?

Activity
Creating a Chart
Create a chart that summarizes the various cultural, religious, and political influences of the following groups on Russia: Varangians, Byzantines, Mongols.

Shaping Eastern Europe

Reading Focus

- How did geography influence developments in Eastern Europe?

- Why did Eastern Europe become a cultural crossroads with a diverse mix of peoples?

- What threats did the early kingdoms of Europe face?

Vocabulary

ethnic group

diet

Taking Notes

On a sheet of paper begin a concept web like this one. As you read the section, fill in the blank circles with relevant information about Eastern Europe. Add more circles if needed.

Main Idea Ethnic diversity contributed to the varied cultural traditions of Eastern Europe.

Setting the Scene Many times in the past hundred years, people have opened their newspapers to find news about turbulent events in Eastern Europe. In 1914, a political assassination by Serbian nationalists triggered World War I. In 1938 and 1939, German aggression in Czechoslovakia and Poland sparked World War II. In 1989, revolts in Eastern European nations helped topple the Soviet empire. In the 1990s, war again erupted in the Balkans as rival national groups clashed in Bosnia and Kosovo.

The roots of such conflicts lie deep in the history of Eastern Europe. As you will see, it has been a history often marked by war, revolution, and foreign conquest. At the same time, its diverse mix of peoples has enriched the culture of the region.

Geography and History

The Blue Danube

"The Danube is Eastern Europe's great throbbing artery," wrote one journalist. "No other river in Europe . . . flows through as many nations . . . or echoes to as many languages." For more than 2,500 years, the Danube River has been a pathway for armies, goods, and ideas. Greek traders sailed along the lower part of the river as early as 600 B.C. Roman and, later, Ottoman armies built forts along its banks. Some of those fortresses grew into major cities, including Budapest and Belgrade. Today, dams on the 1,800 mile-long "Blue Danube" are a vital source of electric power.

Theme: Geography and History What resources has the Danube provided over the centuries?

The Geography of Eastern Europe

The region known as Eastern Europe is a wide swath of territory lying between German-speaking Central Europe to the west and the largest Slavic nation, Russia, to the east. Many peoples and many nations have flourished in the area over the centuries.

Eastern Europe reaches from the chilly waters of the Baltic Sea, down across the plains of Poland, then through the mountainous Balkans. The Balkan Peninsula, a roughly triangular arm of land, juts southward into the warm Mediterranean. Several geographic features contributed to developments in Eastern Europe. Much of the region lies on the great European plain that links up with the steppes of southern Russia.

The main rivers of Eastern Europe, like the Danube and the Vistula, flow either south into the Black Sea or north into the Baltic Sea. Goods and cultural influences traveled along these river routes. As a result, the Balkans in the south felt the impact of the Byzantine empire and, later, the Muslim Ottoman empire. In contrast, the northern regions bordering Germany and the Baltic Sea forged closer links to Western Europe.

A Diverse Mix of Peoples

Eastern Europe's geography has made it a cultural crossroads. The ease of migration encouraged many different peoples to seek new homes, as well as increased power, in the region. As a result, Eastern Europe now includes a wealth of languages and cultures.

The Balkans In the early Middle Ages, the Slavs spread out from a central heartland in Russia. The West Slavs filtered into present-day Poland and the Czech and Slovak republics. The South Slavs descended into the Balkans and became the ancestors of the Serbs, Croats, and Slovenes.

The Balkans were peopled by other ethnic groups as well. An ethnic group is a large group of people who share the same language and cultural heritage. Waves of Asian peoples migrated into Eastern Europe, among them the Huns, Avars, Bulgars, Khazars, and Magyars. Vikings and other Germanic peoples added to the mix.

Powerful neighboring states exercised strong cultural influences on Eastern Europe. Byzantine missionaries carried Eastern Orthodox Christianity and Byzantine culture throughout the Balkans. German knights and missionaries from the West spread Roman Catholic Christianity to Poland, Hungary, the Czech area, and the western Balkans. In the 1300s, the Ottomans invaded the Balkans, spreading Islam into pockets of that area.

Jewish Settlements In the late Middle Ages, Eastern Europe was a refuge for many Jewish settlers. Western European Christians launched brutal attacks on Jewish communities, particularly during the Crusades and the Black Death. To escape persecution, many Jews fled east. Monarchs in England, France, and Spain also expelled Jews from their lands. (See "Synthesizing Information" on the next page.)

In the 1300s, Polish kings followed a policy of toleration toward Jews. As a result, Jewish villages sprang up in Poland and other sparsely populated areas of Eastern Europe. Jewish merchants and scholars contributed to the economic and cultural development of Poland during this period.

Early Kingdoms

During the Middle Ages, Eastern Europe included many kingdoms and small states. Sometimes, empires absorbed national groups. Alliances or royal marriages might bind others together for a time. To get a sense of these shifting fortunes, we will look at the kingdoms of Poland, Hungary, and Serbia.

Poland Missionaries brought Roman Catholicism to the West Slavs of Poland in the 900s. A century later, the first Polish king was crowned. To survive, Poland often had to battle Germans, Russians, and Mongols.

Poland's greatest age came after Queen Jadwiga (yahd VEE gah) married Duke Wladyslav Jagiello (vwah DIHS wahv yahg YEH loh) of Lithuania in 1386. Poland-Lithuania controlled the largest state in Europe, stretching from the Baltic to the Black Sea. Jadwiga supported a university in Cracow, which became a major center of science and the arts.

Byzantine Cavalry
Although Byzantine civilization influenced many people in Eastern Europe, conflict often erupted. In this illustration from the 1300s, Byzantine knights defeat Bulgar soldiers.

Theme: Political and Social Systems What reasons might the Bulgars have had for fighting the Byzantine empire?

Synthesizing Information

Jewish Migrations in Europe

The late Middle Ages were a time of troubles for the Jews of Europe. Though masters of trade, finance, and learning, Jews were expelled from several of the Christian nations of Western Europe. The map and the time line below show events related to their migrations.

Migrations and Expulsions, 1100–1650

During the early Middle Ages, Jews created economically and intellectually vital communities in Western Europe. Beginning in the 1200s, however, the rulers of several nations formally expelled the Jews from their lands. Many migrated to Poland and other parts of Eastern Europe, where they were allowed to build their own communities.

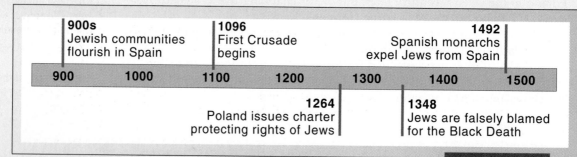

900s Jewish communities flourish in Spain	**1096** First Crusade begins		**1492** Spanish monarchs expel Jews from Spain
900 1000	1100 1200	1300 1400	1500
	1264 Poland issues charter protecting rights of Jews	**1348** Jews are falsely blamed for the Black Death	

Skills Assessment

1. When expelled from France in 1394, Jews migrated to
   A England.
   B Italy and Germany.
   C Spain and Portugal.
   D Poland and Eastern Europe.

2. Which event resulted in a widespread scattering of the Jewish population outside Europe?
   E expulsion from Spain
   F Polish charter
   G Black Death
   H First Crusade

3. **Critical Thinking** **Drawing Conclusions** Based on the evidence provided, where were Jews more likely to settle after 1350? Why?

Skills Tip

Time lines show a sequence of events over time. Follow the dates from left to right to find the chronological order of events.

Unlike Russia or Western Europe, Poland gradually increased the power of its nobles at the expense of the monarch. They met in a *diet,* or assembly, where the vote of a single noble was enough to block the passage of a law. This liberum veto, or "free veto," made it hard for the government to take decisive action.

Without a strong central government, Poland declined. It enjoyed a final moment of glory in 1683 when the Polish king Jan Sobieski (YAHN SAW BYEH skee) broke the Ottoman siege of Vienna. In the next century, however, Poland was gobbled up by ambitious neighbors and disappeared from the map entirely.

Hungary The Magyars raided Europe from the Asian steppes and settled in Hungary. Like the West Slavs of Poland, they adopted Roman Catholic Christianity. During the Middle Ages, the country was much larger than it is today. Hungarian rulers controlled present-day Slovakia, Croatia, and parts of Romania.

Like King John of England, the Hungarian king was forced to sign a charter recognizing the rights of his nobles. Known as the Golden Bull of 1222, it strictly limited royal power.

The Mongols overran Hungary in 1241, killing perhaps as much as half its population. They soon withdrew, so their invasion did not have the same impact it had on Russia. The expansion of the Ottoman Turks, though, ended Hungarian independence in 1526.

Serbia During the 600s, South Slavs settled the mountainous Balkans. Serbs, Croats, Slovenes, and other Slavic peoples in the Balkans had different histories during the Middle Ages. The Serbs accepted Orthodox Christianity. By the late 1100s, they had set up their own state, which reached its height under Stefan Dušan (STEH fahn DOO shahn). Stefan also encouraged Byzantine culture, even modeling his law code on that of Justinian.

Dušan's successors lacked his political gifts, however, and Serbia could not withstand the advance of Ottoman Turks. At the battle of Kosovo in 1389, Serbs fought to the death, a memory still honored by their descendants more than 600 years later.

Looking Ahead

Migration, conquest, dynastic marriages, and missionary activity helped produce a tangle of overlapping claims to territories in Eastern Europe. During the 1600s and 1700s, large empires to the east and west swallowed up much of the region. Yet whenever they had a chance, the peoples of Eastern Europe tried to recover their independence. In later chapters, we will see how the desire to rebuild separate states repeatedly ignited new turmoils.

Connections to Today

Balkan Boiling Pot

Throughout the 1990s, violence exploded in the Balkans. In 1992, Eastern Orthodox Serbs, Bosnian Muslims, and Catholic Croats fought a bloody civil war in Bosnia. In 1998, Christian Serbs and Muslims of Albanian heritage clashed in Kosovo.

The modern-day wars echo ethnic struggles that have gone on for more than 600 years in the Balkans. In 1389, Turkish soldiers from the Ottoman empire defeated Serbs at the Battle of Kosovo and took over the region. Different ethnic groups practicing different religions dispersed throughout the area. Even though they were forced to live together, the different groups have remained fiercely independent. Instead of being a melting pot of cultures, the Balkan region has continued to simmer and occasionally boil over.

Theme: Religions and Value Systems How have religions and ethnic groups affected life in the Balkans?

SECTION 3 Assessment

Recall

1. **Identify:** **(a)** Jadwiga and Wladyslaw Jagiello, **(b)** Jan Sobieski, **(c)** Golden Bull of 1222, **(d)** Stefan Dušan.
2. **Define:** **(a)** ethnic group, **(b)** diet.

Comprehension

3. What role did rivers play in Eastern Europe?
4. How did Eastern Europe become home to many ethnic groups?

5. What relationship did the Ottoman Turks have with the early kingdoms of Eastern Europe?

Critical Thinking and Writing

6. **Comparing** **(a)** How were the histories of Poland, Hungary, and Serbia similar? **(b)** How were their histories different?
7. **Linking Past and Present** Why is Kosovo so important to modern-day Serbs?

Activity
Take It to the NET

Use the Internet to research old Cracow in Poland. Use your information to create a guide to the old part of the city. Then, take your classmates on a virtual tour.

Creating a Chapter Summary

Copy the table shown below. Fill in the spaces under each heading to help you review key facts about the chapter.

	BYZANTINE EMPIRE	RUSSIA	EASTERN EUROPE
IMPORTANT CITIES	Constantinople	Kiev, Moscow	Cracow (Poland), Kosovo (Serbia)
RULERS			
RELIGION			
OTHER CONTRIBUTIONS			

CD-ROM Review For additional review of the major concepts of Chapter 10, see the *Guide to the Essentials of World History* or the *Interactive Student Tutorial CD-ROM.*

Web Site Self-Test For practice test questions for Chapter 10, see **www.phschool.com.**

Building Vocabulary

Use the chapter vocabulary words listed below to create a crossword puzzle. Exchange puzzles with a classmate. Complete the puzzles and then check each other's answers.

1. **autocrat**
2. **patriarch**
3. **icon**
4. **steppe**
5. **boyar**
6. **czar**
7. **ethnic group**
8. **diet**

Recalling Key Facts

9. How was the Byzantine empire an outgrowth of the Roman empire?
10. What important split in Christianity occurred in 1054?
11. What was the Golden Horde?
12. What were the accomplishments of Ivan the Great?
13. What peoples and religions are represented in Eastern Europe?
14. Why did many Jews migrate to Eastern Europe?
15. Why did the kingdom of Poland decline?

Critical Thinking and Writing

16. **Drawing Conclusions** How might European history have been different if the Byzantine empire had fallen after the death of Justinian?
17. **Defending a Position** Autocratic rule helped leaders of Moscow and Russia create a strong central state. Do you think that there is any justification for autocratic rule? Explain.
18. **Linking Past and Present** **(a)** How have long-standing ethnic differences in Eastern Europe influenced events in modern times? **(b)** Do you think that ethnic differences have played a similar role in the growth of American society? Explain.
19. **Synthesizing Information** **(a)** Construct a time line showing events in the Byzantine empire, Russia, and Eastern Europe. **(b)** Identify influences that had a significant impact on the history of all three regions.
20. **Connecting to Geography** Describe the role that bodies of water played in linking the Byzantine empire with Russia and Eastern Europe.

During the reign of Czar Ivan IV, a book called the *Domostroi* was published. The title means "house order." The *Domostroi* contains instructions on all aspects of a noble's home life, including the preparation and serving of food; the treatment of children, guests, merchants, and servants; and the celebration of religious holidays. The author may have been a priest who served at the Kremlin Cathedral of the Annunciation in Moscow. Read the excerpt below and answer the questions that follow.

> "If God send any disease or ailment down upon a person let him cure himself through the grace of God, through tears, prayer, fasting, charity to the poor, and true repentance. Let him thank the Lord and beg His forgiveness, and show mercy and undisguised charity to everybody. . . .
>
> When a sick person is in the house, let the homeowner invite seven or more priests and as many deacons as he can find. They will pray over commemorative beer for health and over frumenty [a kind of pudding] to bring peace of mind.
>
> After someone departs this life, the priest or deacon will cense [perfume with incense] every room, sprinkling it with holy water and making the sign of the cross. Then those in the house, praising God according to the divine liturgy, should at once set up a table so that the priests and monks, along with the rest of the guests and the neighborhood poor, may eat and drink. Then all, contented and replete [full], will go to their homes praising God."
>
> —*Domostroi*

21. **(a)** According to the writer, what should a person do if he or she becomes ill? **(b)** What does this suggest about the author's view of sickness?
22. What does the author say a homeowner should do when someone in the home is ill?
23. What actions should follow the death of a sick person?
24. What does this passage suggest about the role of religious figures in everyday Russian life?
25. Based on this passage, would you say that rituals were important in the Russian Orthodox religion? Explain.

DECLINE OF THE BYZANTINE EMPIRE

EXTERNAL FACTORS	OUTCOMES
Invasions	Normans conquer southern Italy.
	Seljuk Turks advance through Asia Minor.
Crusades	Trade rivalries lead to conflict with Venice.
	Knights capture Constantinople during Fourth Crusade.
Ottoman Attack	Constantinople is captured by Turks.
	Constantinople is transformed into Muslim Istanbul.

This chart summarizes information about the decline of the Byzantine empire. Study the chart and answer the following questions:

26. What was the result of the invasion in southern Italy?
27. Name two results of the Crusades that contributed to the decline of the Byzantine empire.
28. Why did Constantinople become Istanbul?
29. What do the three events listed on the chart have in common?

Skills Tip

When conducting research on the Internet, try to determine if the information seems inaccurate or presents only one point of view. Check facts against sites provided by governments or universities.

Skills Assessment
Take It to the NET

Use the Internet to research a period of Byzantine history—for example, the age of Justinian, the schism, the Crusades, or the fall of Constantinople. Then, write a brief explanation of how the events of that period affected life in the Byzantine empire.

The Muslim World
622–1629

Chapter Preview

1 Rise of Islam
2 Islam Spreads
3 Golden Age of Muslim Civilization
4 Muslims in India
5 The Ottoman and Safavid Empires

750

Abu al-Abbas establishes the Abbassid dynasty.
Over the next several centuries, Muslim merchant ships
travel around the Abbassid empire and beyond.

622

Muhammad journeys from Mecca to Yathrib,
an event that marks the rise of Islam. The Quran,
shown above, is the sacred book of Islam.

1099

Christian crusaders from
Europe capture Jerusalem
from the Muslims.

**CHAPTER
EVENTS**

600 · · 800 · 1000 ·

**GLOBAL
EVENTS**

732 At the battle of Tours,
the Muslim advance into
Europe is stopped.

843 In Europe, the Frankish
empire is split in three by the
Treaty of Verdun.

1000s East African
port cities flourish.

The Muslim World, 1150

Muslim world, 1150

ENGLAND
FRANCE **HUNGARY**
Danube R.
SPAIN **BULGARIA** Constantinople
Black Sea
SELJUKS
Córdoba **BYZANTINE EMPIRE**
Tunis *Mediterranean Sea* Damascus
Fez Jerusalem
MOROCCO Tripoli Cairo
EGYPT

Bukhara Samarkand

Tigris R. *Caspian Sea*
Baghdad **GHAZNAVIDS**
Euphrates R. **ABBASID EMPIRE** **PERSIA**
Indus R. *Ganges R.*
Persian Gulf
ARABIA *Arabian Sea* **INDIA**

ATLANTIC OCEAN
Nile R. *Red Sea*

INDIAN OCEAN

During its early centuries, Islam spread from Arabia across the Middle East and North Africa and into Spain.

N W E S

Robinson Projection
0   500   1000 Miles
0   500   1000 Kilometers

1206
Muslims set up Delhi sultanate in northern India. From atop the tower shown here, Indian Muslims are called to prayer.

1520
Suleiman becomes ruler of the Ottoman empire. During his reign, the empire grows and enjoys a golden age.

1620s
Under Shah Abbas the Great, Persian culture thrives.

1200   **1400**   **1600**

1279 Mongols complete the conquest of China.

1389 Serbs defeat Ottoman forces at the battle of Kosovo.

Rise of Islam

Reading Focus

- How did Muhammad become the prophet of Islam?
- What are the teachings of Islam?
- How did Islam help shape the way of life of its believers?

Vocabulary

oasis
hijra
monotheistic
mosque
hajj
jihad

Taking Notes

Copy this chart. As you read, fill in the first column with key events concerning the emergence of Islam. In the second column, write down some of the basic teachings of Islam.

KEY EVENTS	TEACHINGS

Main Idea Islam arose in the Arabian Peninsula and became one of the world's major religions.

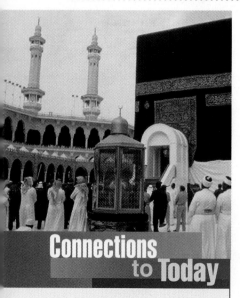

Connections to Today

A Sacred Duty

Today, more than two million Muslims gather each year in Mecca. Every Muslim who is physically and financially able must make a journey there at least once. Muslims believe that Abraham built the Kaaba in Mecca as the first house of worship for God. Today, it is adorned with a black cloth containing religious verses embroidered in gold. Pilgrims wear special clothes: simple garments that erase cultural and class differences so that all stand equal before God. The simple attire also symbolizes the abandonment of the material world for the sake of God.

Theme: Religions and Value Systems Why do Muslims consider Mecca sacred?

Setting the Scene

In the Arabian town of Mecca, the marketplace echoed with the bustle of bargaining. One corner, though, was hushed. There, a husky, black-bearded man spoke to a handful of followers:

> "In the name of God, the Compassionate, the Merciful,
> Praise be to God, Lord of the Universe,
> The Compassionate, the Merciful,
> Sovereign of the Day of Judgment!
> You alone we worship, and to You alone we turn for help."
> —Quran

Some bowed their heads, moved by Muhammad's words. But many merchants scoffed. Muhammad had once been a good merchant himself. Surely, they thought, he had gone mad.

In years to come, Muhammad would be recognized by millions of Muslims as the Prophet. His followers would carry the message of Islam to people on three continents and set off one of the most powerful forces in world history.

The Prophet Muhammad

Islam emerged in the Arabian Peninsula, part of southwestern Asia. Its deserts and trade centers helped shape the early life of Muhammad.

Geographic Setting The Arabian Peninsula is mostly desert, but farming is possible through irrigation or in scattered oases. (See the map in Section 2 of this chapter.) An oasis is a fertile area in a desert, watered by a natural well or spring.

Many Arab clans occupied Arabia at the time of Muhammad. Nomadic herders, called Bedouins (BEHD oo ihnz), used camels to cross the scorching desert in search of seasonal pasturelands. Raids for scarce grazing land led to frequent warfare. The Bedouins would form the backbone of the armies that conquered a huge empire in the 600s and 700s. Bedouins traded with other Arabs who had settled in oasis towns. One of these was Mecca.

Mecca was a bustling market town at the crossroads of two main caravan routes. One route linked southern Arabia to Syria and Palestine on the Mediterranean coast. The other route crossed from Mesopotamia to eastern Africa. Mecca was also a thriving pilgrimage center. Arabs came to pray at the Kaaba, an ancient shrine that Muslims today believe was built by the prophet Abraham. In Muhammad's time, though, the Kaaba housed statues of many local gods and goddesses. The pilgrim traffic brought good profits to the local merchants.

Muhammad's Vision Muhammad was born in Mecca about 570. In his youth, he worked as a shepherd among the Bedouins. Later, he led caravans across the desert and became a successful merchant. When he was about 25, Muhammad married Khadija (kah DEE jah), a wealthy widow who ran a prosperous caravan business. By all accounts, he was a devoted husband and a loving father to his daughters.

Muhammad was troubled by the idol worship and moral ills of society. When he was about 40, he went to a desert cave to meditate. According to Muslim belief, he heard a voice saying, "Recite!" Muhammad replied, "What shall I recite?" The voice explained: "Recite in the name of your God, the Creator, who created man from clots of blood."

Muhammad understood that it was the voice of the angel Gabriel calling him to be the messenger of God. But Muhammad was terrified and puzzled. How could he, an illiterate merchant, become the messenger of God? But Khadija encouraged him to accept the call. She became the first convert to the faith called Islam, from the Arabic word for "submission." Muhammad devoted the rest of his life to spreading Islam. He urged Arabs to give up their false gods and submit to the one true God. In Arabic, the word for god is *Allah.*

The Hijra: A Turning Point At first, few people listened to the teachings of Muhammad. His rejection of the traditional Arab gods angered Meccan merchants who feared neglecting their idols and disrupting the pilgrim trade. In 622, faced with the threat of murder, Muhammad and his followers left Mecca for Yathrib, a journey known as the hijra. Later, Yathrib was renamed Medina, or "city of the Prophet," and 622 became the first year of the Muslim calendar.*

The hijra was a turning point for Islam. In Medina, Muhammad was welcomed by Muslim converts, not only as God's prophet, but also as ruler and lawgiver. As his reputation grew, thousands of Arabs adopted Islam. From Medina, Muslims launched attacks on Meccan caravans and defeated the Meccans in battle.

Finally, in 630, Muhammad returned in triumph to Mecca, where he destroyed the idols in the Kaaba. In the next two years, Muhammad worked to unite the Arabs under Islam. Muhammad died in 632, but the faith that he proclaimed continued to spread. Today, Islam is one of the world's major religions.

Teachings of Islam

Like Judaism and Christianity, Islam is monotheistic, based on belief in one God. The Quran (ku RAHN), the sacred text of Islam, teaches that God is all-powerful and compassionate. It also states that people are responsible for their own actions: "Whoever strays bears the full responsibility for straying." According to the Quran, each individual will stand before God on the final judgment day to face either eternal punishment in hell or eternal bliss in paradise. Muslims recognize no official priests who mediate between the people and God.

---

* The Muslim calendar uses A.H. for dates after the hijra. However, this chapter, like the rest of the book, will continue to use dates based on the Christian Era calendar.

Messenger of God
On several occasions Muhammad heard the angel Gabriel calling him to be the messenger of God. In this miniature painting, an angel's announcement is symbolized by the blowing of a horn.

Theme Religions and Value Systems How did Muhammad respond to God's calling?

One of the holiest sites in the Muslim world is the Dome of the Rock in Jerusalem. It was built in the 690s above a rock from which Muslims believed Muhammad had risen into heaven.

Theme: Religions and Value Systems Why is the city of Jerusalem also sacred to Christians and Jews?

▶ **Primary Sources and Literature**

See "The Quran" in the Reference Section at the back of this book.

Five Pillars All Muslims accept five basic duties, known as the Five Pillars of Islam. The first is a declaration of faith. "There is no god but God, Muhammad is the messenger of God." Muslims believe that God had sent other prophets, including Abraham, Moses, and Jesus, but that Muhammad was the last and greatest prophet. The second pillar is daily prayer. After a ritual washing, Muslims face the holy city of Mecca to pray. Although Muslims may pray anywhere, they often gather in houses of worship called *masjids* or mosques. The third pillar is giving charity to the poor. The fourth is fasting from sunrise to sunset during the holy month of Ramadan. The fifth pillar is the hajj, or pilgrimage to Mecca. All Muslims who are able are expected to visit the Kaaba at least once in their lives.

Some Muslims look on jihad (jee HAHD), or effort in God's service, as another duty. Jihad has often been mistakenly translated simply as "holy war." In fact, it may include acts of charity or an inner struggle to achieve spiritual peace, as well as any battle in defense of Islam.

The Quran To Muslims, the Quran contains the sacred word of God as revealed to Muhammad. It is the final authority on all matters. The Quran not only teaches about God but also provides a complete guide to life. Its ethical standards emphasize honesty, generosity, and social justice. It sets harsh penalties for crimes such as stealing or murder.

Muslims believe that, in its original Arabic form, the Quran is the direct, unchangeable word of God. Because the meaning and beauty of the Quran reside in its original language, converts to Islam learn Arabic. This shared language has helped unite Muslims from many regions.

"People of the Book" Muslims profess faith in the same God as that worshiped by Jews and Christians. The Quran teaches that Islam is God's final and complete revelation, and that the Torah and Bible contain partial revelation from God. To Muslims, Jews and Christians are "People of the Book," spiritually superior to polytheistic idol worshipers. Although some later Muslims overlooked Muhammad's principle of tolerance, in general, the People of the Book enjoyed religious freedom in early Muslim societies.

A Way of Life

Islam is both a religion and a way of life. Its teachings help shape the lives of Muslims around the world. Islamic law governs many aspects of daily life, and Islamic traditions determine ethical behavior and influence family relations.

Sharia Over time, Muslim scholars developed an immense body of law interpreting the Quran and applying its teachings to daily life. This Islamic system of law, called the Sharia, regulates moral conduct, family life, business practices, government, and other aspects of a Muslim community. Like the Quran, the Sharia helped unite the many peoples who converted to Islam.

Unlike the law codes that evolved in the west, the Sharia does not separate religious matters from criminal or civil law. The Sharia applies the Quran to all legal situations.

Impact of Islam on Women Before Islam, the position of women in Arab society varied. In some communities, women took a hand in religion, trade, or warfare. Most women, however, were under the control of a male guardian and could not inherit property. Furthermore, among a few tribes, unwanted daughters were sometimes killed at birth.

Islam affirmed the spiritual equality of women and men. "Whoever does right, whether male or female," states the Quran, "and is a believer, all such will enter the Garden." Women therefore won greater protection under the law. The Quran prohibited the killing of daughters. Inheritance laws guaranteed a woman a share of her parents' or husband's property. Muslim women had to consent freely to marriage and had the right to an education. In the early days of Islam, some Arab women participated actively in public life.

Though spiritually equal, men and women had different roles and rights. For example, the amount of an inheritance given to a daughter was less than that given to a son. A woman could seek a divorce, but it was harder for her to get one than for a man.

As Islam spread, Arabs sometimes absorbed attitudes from the peoples they conquered. In Persian and Byzantine lands, Arabs adopted the practice of veiling upper-class women and secluding them in a separate part of the home. There, they managed the affairs of the household but seldom ventured out. Still, as in other cultures, women's lives varied according to region and class. Veiling and seclusion were not so strictly followed among lower-class city women. In rural areas, peasant women continued to contribute to the economy in many ways.

Islamic Law Court
The Sharia applies Islamic teachings to legal issues. In this Persian painting, a man and woman seek a decision before a judge.

Theme: Political and Social Systems What does this picture suggest about the rights of Muslim women?

SECTION 1 Assessment

Recall
1. **Identify:** (a) Mecca, (b) Bedouins, (c) Kaaba, (d) Khadija, (e) Quran, (f) People of the Book, (g) Sharia.
2. **Define:** (a) oasis, (b) hijra, (c) monotheistic, (d) mosque, (e) hajj, (f) jihad.

Comprehension
3. How did Muhammad become the prophet of Islam?
4. (a) What are the Five Pillars of Islam? (b) How do they help unite Muslims?

5. How do the Quran and Sharia guide the lives of Muslims?

Critical Thinking and Writing
6. **Comparing** In what ways are the religious teachings of Islam similar to those of Judaism and Christianity?
7. **Identifying Main Ideas** Review the three paragraphs that appear in this section under the heading "The Hijra: A Turning Point." For each paragraph, identify the main idea and two details that support the main idea.

Activity
Take It to the NET

Use the Internet to learn more about the hajj, or pilgrimage to Mecca, today. Then, assume the role of a news reporter in Mecca. Write a news article describing the special customs and rites associated with the hajj.

Islam Spreads

Reading Focus

- How did Muslims conquer many lands?
- What movements emerged within Islam?
- Why did the empire of the caliphs decline?

Vocabulary

caliph
minaret
muezzin
sultan

Taking Notes

On a piece of paper, make a time line like the model below. As you read, fill in the time line with major events concerning the spread of Islam and the rise and fall of Muslim empires.

```
        Muslims
        enter Spain
        711

    600      800      1000     1200     1400
```

Main Idea Inspired by Muhammad's teachings, Arab armies spread Islam through parts of three continents.

Setting the Scene The death of Muhammad plunged his followers into grief. The Prophet had been a pious man and a powerful leader. No one else had ever been able to unify the Bedouin tribes. Could his legacy survive without him?

Abu Bakr, an early convert to Islam, was determined to continue the Prophet's work. He sternly told the faithful, "If you worship Muhammad, Muhammad is dead. If you worship God, God is alive."

Despite some bitter struggles, Arab unity did not collapse. Inspired by the teachings of the Prophet, Arab armies surged across the Byzantine and Persian empires. In a stunningly short time, an Arabic empire reached from the Atlantic to the borders of India.

An Age of Conquests

As the first caliph, or successor to Muhammad, Abu Bakr faced an immediate crisis. The loyalty of some Arab tribal leaders had been dependent on Muhammad's personal command. They now refused to follow Abu Bakr and withdrew their loyalty to Islam. Abu Bakr succeeded in reuniting the Arabs, based first and foremost on their allegiance to Islam. Once reunited, the Arabs set out on a remarkable series of military conquests.

From Victory to Victory Under the first four caliphs, Arab armies marched from victory to victory. They conquered great chunks of the Byzantine empire, including the provinces of Syria and Palestine, with the cities of Damascus and Jerusalem. Next, they rapidly demolished the Persian empire. The Arabs then swept into Egypt.

Later Muslim armies conquered even more lands. From Egypt, Muslims dashed west, defeating Byzantine forces across North Africa. In 711, they crossed the Strait of Gibraltar into Spain and pushed north into France. There, in 732, they were defeated at the battle of Tours. The Muslim advance into Western Europe was halted. Even so, Muslims would rule parts of Spain for centuries. Elsewhere, Muslims besieged the Byzantine capital of Constantinople, but failed to take the well-defended city. Later waves of conquests would expand Muslim rule farther into the continents of Asia and Africa.

Reasons for Success Why did the Arabs have such an astonishing series of victories? One reason was the weakness of the Byzantine and Persian empires. These longtime rivals had fought each other to exhaustion. Many people in the Fertile Crescent welcomed the Arabs as liberators from harsh

Geography and History

Desert Warfare

"Fight the enemy in the desert," said one wounded Muslim leader. "There you will be victorious . . . you will have the friendly and familiar desert at your backs. The enemy cannot follow you there."

In response to the geographic conditions of the Arabian Peninsula, Arab soldiers became skilled in the special tactics of desert warfare. They knew how to use horses and camels to cross broad areas quickly and then sweep down to catch their enemies by surprise. The sudden charge of an Arab cavalry overwhelmed unprepared defenders. The elements of surprise and speed, as well as maneuverability, helped the Arabs conquer much of the Byzantine and Persian empires.

Theme: Geography and History Why were Arab soldiers skilled in the tactics of desert warfare?

Byzantine or Persian rule. Bold, efficient fighting methods also contributed to the Arab success. The Bedouin camel and horse cavalry mounted aggressive and mobile offensives that overwhelmed more traditional armies.

Perhaps the key reason for Arab success, however, was the common faith Muhammad had given his people. Islam knitted a patchwork of tribes into a determined, unified state. Belief in Islam and the certainty of paradise for those who fell in battle spurred the Arab armies to victory.

Treatment of Conquered People The advancing Arabs brought many people under their rule. Muslim leaders imposed a special tax on non-Muslims, but allowed Christians, Jews, and Zoroastrians to practice their own faiths and follow their own laws. As Muslim civilization developed, many Jews and Christians played key roles as officials, doctors, and translators. In time, many non-Muslims converted to Islam.

Many nomadic peoples in North Africa and Central Asia chose Islam immediately. Its message was simple and direct, and they saw its triumph as a sign of God's favor. Moreover, Islam had no religious hierarchy or class of priests. In principle, it emphasized the equality of all believers, regardless of race, sex, class, or wealth. In later centuries, Turkish and Mongol converts helped spread Islam far across Asia.

Muslims in Europe For centuries after the battle of Tours, Christian forces fought to reconquer Spain. Only in 1492 did they seize the last Muslim stronghold. In the meantime, Spain flourished as a center of Muslim civilization.

Muslim rulers in Spain presided over brilliant courts, where the arts and learning thrived. In general, they were more tolerant of other religions than Christian rulers of the time. At centers of learning such as the city of Córdoba, rulers employed Jewish officials and welcomed Christian scholars to study science and philosophy. Architects built grand buildings, such as the Alhambra, a fortified palace in Granada. Its lovely gardens, reflecting pools, and finely decorated marble columns mark a high point of Muslim civilization in Spain.

Muslim civilization also thrived in Sicily and other Mediterranean islands seized by Arab forces in the late 800s. Muslim rule lasted briefly. But even after knights from Normandy gained control of Sicily, it remained strongly Arabic in culture. Muslim officials governed the island well, and merchants and farmers helped the economy prosper. Muslim poets, philosophers, and scientists enriched the courts of Norman kings.

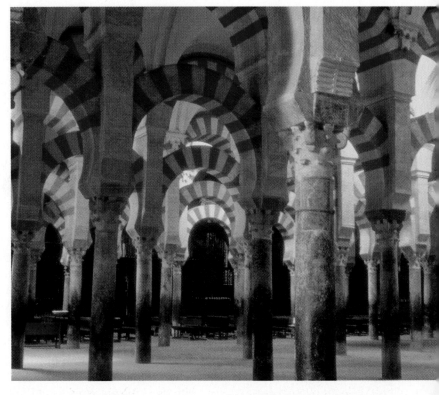

Great Mosque of Córdoba
Córdoba was the cultural center of Muslim Spain. The columns and arches of this mosque in Córdoba show the elaborate nature of Muslim architecture.

Theme: Continuity and Change What earlier civilizations pioneered the use of columns and arches?

Movements Within Islam

Not long after Muhammad's death, divisions arose within Islam over his successor. The split between Sunni (SOO nee) and Shiite (SHEE ite) Muslims had a profound impact on later Islamic history.

Sunni and Shiites The Sunni felt that the caliph should be chosen by leaders of the Muslim community. Although the Sunni agreed that the caliph should be a pious Muslim, they viewed him simply as a leader, not as a religious authority.

Spread of Islam

Boundary of Byzantine empire, 565

Muslim lands
at death of Muhammad, 632

Lands conquered by Muslims
under first four caliphs, 632–661

Lands conquered by Muslims under
Umayyad caliphs, 661–750

Robinson Projection

0   500   1000 Miles

0   500   1000 Kilometers

Skills Assessment

Geography In less than 150 years, Islam spread from Arabia across southwest Asia and North Africa and into Europe.

1. **Location** On the map, locate (a) Arabian Desert, (b) Mecca, (c) Medina, (d) Persia, (e) Cairo, (f) Constantinople, (g) Córdoba.
2. **Region** During what period did Spain come under Muslim rule?
3. **Critical Thinking** **Applying Information** How might the spread of Islam have contributed to Muslim success in trade?

The Shiites, on the other hand, argued that the only true successors to the Prophet were descendants of Muhammad's daughter and son-in-law, Fatima and Ali. The Shiites believed that the descendants of the Prophet were divinely inspired. The Sunni believed that inspiration came from the example of Muhammad as recorded by his early followers.

Ali became the fourth caliph, but he was assassinated in 661 in a struggle for leadership. Later, his son, too, was killed. Many other Shiites died in battle against Sunni, trying to install their candidates for caliph. Shiites grew to admire martyrdom as a demonstration of their faith.

Like the schism between Roman Catholic and Eastern Orthodox Christians, the division between Sunni and Shiite Muslims has survived to the present day. Members of both branches of Islam believe in the same one God, look to the Quran for guidance, and make the hajj. But numerous differences have emerged in such areas as religious practice, law, and daily life. Today, about 90 percent of Muslims are Sunni. Most Shiites live in Iran, Lebanon, Iraq, and Yemen. The Shiite movement itself has split into several different factions.

Sufi A third tradition in Islam emerged with the Sufis, Muslim mystics who sought communion with God through meditation, fasting, and other rituals. Sufis were respected for their piety and miraculous powers.

Like Christian monks and nuns, some Sufis helped spread Islam through missionary work. They carried the faith to remote villages, where they blended local traditions and beliefs into Muslim culture.

Empire of the Caliphs

After the death of Ali, the Umayyad (oh MĪ ad) family set up a dynasty that ruled the Islamic world until 750. From their capital at Damascus in Syria, they directed the spectacular conquests that carried Islam from the Atlantic to the Indus Valley.

Umayyads Even as victories expanded the Arab empire, the Umayyads faced numerous problems. First, they had to adapt from desert life to ruling large cities and huge territories. To govern their empire, the Umayyads often relied on local officials, including educated Jews, Greeks, and Persians. As a result, Byzantine and Persian traditions of government influenced Arab rulers.

While conquests continued, vast wealth flowed into Umayyad hands. When conquests slowed in the 700s, economic tensions increased between wealthy Arabs and those who had less. Many Muslims criticized the court at Damascus for abandoning the simple ways of the early caliphs. Shiites hated the Umayyads because they had defeated Ali and killed his son, dishonoring the Prophet's family. Unrest also festered among non-Arab converts to Islam, who under the Umayyads had fewer rights than Arabs.

Abbassids Discontented Muslims found a leader in Abu al-Abbas, who captured Damascus in 750. Soon after, one of his generals invited members of the defeated Umayyad family to a banquet—and killed them all. Abu al-Abbas then founded the Abbassid dynasty, which lasted until 1258.

The Abbassid dynasty ended Arab dominance and helped make Islam a truly universal religion. Under the early Abbassids, the empire of the caliphs reached its greatest wealth and power, and Muslim civilization enjoyed a golden age.

Splendors of Baghdad The Abbassid caliph al-Mansur chose as the site of his new capital Baghdad, a small market town in present-day Iraq. "It is an excellent military camp," he wrote. "Besides here is the Tigris to put us in touch with lands as far as China and bring us all that the seas yield." Under the Abbassids, Baghdad exceeded Constantinople in size and wealth.

In Baghdad, Persian traditions strongly influenced Arab life, but Islam remained the religion and Arabic the language of the empire. Poets, scholars, philosophers, and entertainers from all over the Muslim world flocked to the Abbassid court. Visitors no doubt felt that Baghdad deserved its title "City of Peace, Gift of God, Paradise on Earth."

Many gardens, dotted with fabulous fountains, gleamed in the sunlight. Above the streets loomed domes and minarets, the slender towers of mosques. Each day, a mosque official called a muezzin climbed to the top of the minaret and called the faithful to prayer. In busy market courtyards, merchants sold goods from Africa, Asia, and Europe. The palace of the caliph echoed with the music of flutes, cymbals, and tambourines, along with the voices of female singers.

The city of Baghdad reached its peak under the reign of caliph Harun al-Rashid, who ruled from 786 to 809. For centuries, in both Europe and the Muslim world, Harun was admired as a model ruler. He was viewed as a symbol of wealth and splendor.

Decline of the Caliphate

Starting about 850, Abbassid control over the Arab empire fragmented. In Spain, Egypt, and elsewhere, independent dynasties ruled separate Muslim states. As the caliph's power faded, civil wars erupted, and Shiite rulers took over parts of the empire. Between 900 and 1400, a series of invasions added to the chaos.

Seljuks In the 900s, the Seljuk Turks migrated into the Middle East from Central Asia. They adopted Islam and built a large empire across the Fertile Crescent. By 1055, a Seljuk sultan, or authority, controlled Baghdad, but he left the Abbassid caliph as a figurehead. As the Seljuks pushed into Asia Minor, they threatened the Byzantine empire. Reports of Seljuk interference with Christian pilgrims traveling to Jerusalem led Pope Urban II, in 1095, to call for the First Crusade.

Crusaders In 1099, after a long and bloody siege, Christian crusaders captured Jerusalem. For 150 years, the city passed back and forth between Muslims and Christians. The Muslim general Salah al-Din, or Saladin, ousted Christians from Jerusalem in 1187. They regained it after his death, holding it until 1244.

Christians also ruled a few tiny states in Palestine, but they were eventually expelled. In the long term, as you read, the Crusades had a much greater impact on Europe than on the Muslim world.

Biography

Harun al-Rashid
763(?) – 809

Many stories and legends recall Caliph Harun al-Rashid's wealth, generosity, and support of learning. Poets, physicians, philosophers, and artists all gathered at his court in Baghdad. One story tells how Harun rewarded a favorite poet with a robe of honor, a splendid horse, and 5,000 dirhams—a vast sum of money.

Harun used his generosity to create closer ties with other rulers. He sent the Frankish king Charlemagne several gifts, including a mechanical clock and an elephant. Harun hoped that the Franks would join him in an alliance against the rival Umayyad caliphate in Spain.

Despite his lavishness and generosity, Harun amassed a great fortune. At his death, he had millions of dirhams, plus huge stores of jewels and gold.

Theme: Impact of the Individual How did Harun help make Baghdad a major center of Muslim culture?

PRESENT

In the Marketplace
In the painting (top), Muslim merchants sell their wares. In cities like Baghdad, merchants sold goods in roofed bazaars containing miles of streets. Today's multilevel shopping mall (bottom) is a modern version of the bazaar.

Theme: Economics and Technology In what businesses are the four bazaar merchants engaged?

of slaves. Many slaves bought their freedom, often with the help of charitable donations or even state funds.

An International Trade Network Merchants were honored in the Muslim world, in part because Muhammad had been a merchant. A traditional collection of deeds and sayings stated:

> "The honest, truthful Muslim merchant will stand with the martyrs on the Day of Judgment. I commend the merchants to you, for they are the couriers of the horizon and God's trusted servants on Earth."
> —Sayings of the Prophet

Between 750 and 1350, merchants built a vast trading network across the Muslim world and beyond, spreading Islam peacefully in their wake. Camel caravans—the "ships of the desert"—crossed the Sahara into West Africa. Muslim traders traveled the Silk Road from China. Monsoon winds carried Arab ships from East Africa to India. Everywhere Muslim traders bought and exchanged goods, creating great fortunes for the most successful.

Trade spread both products and technologies. As you have read, Muslim merchants brought Arabic numerals from India to the western world. Arabs also carried sugar from India and papermaking from China. A common language and a common religion helped this global exchange to grow and thrive.

Extensive trade and a prosperous money economy led Muslims to pioneer new business practices. They set up partnerships, bought and sold on credit, and formed banks to change currency. To transfer money more easily, Muslims invented the ancestors of today's bank checks. We get our word *check* from the Arabic word *sakk*. Bankers developed a sophisticated system of accounting. They opened branch banks in all major cities, so that a check written in Baghdad might be cashed in Cairo.

Manufacturing As in medieval Europe, handicraft manufacturing in Muslim cities was typically organized by guilds. The heads of the guilds, chosen by their members, often had the authority to regulate prices, weights and measures, methods of production, and the quality of the product. Most labor was done by wage workers.

Across the Muslim world, artisans produced a wealth of fine goods. Steel swords from Damascus, leather goods from Córdoba, cotton textiles from Egypt, and carpets from Persia were highly valued. Workshops also turned out fine glassware, furniture, and tapestries.

Agriculture Outside the cities, agriculture flourished across a wide variety of climates and landforms. Muslim farmers cultivated sugar cane, cotton, dyes, medicinal herbs, fruits, vegetables, and flowers that were bought and sold in world markets.

The more arid regions of the Muslim world were basically divided into two kinds of land, "the desert and the sown." Small farming communities faced a constant scarcity of water. To improve farm output, the Abbassids organized massive irrigation projects and drained swamplands between the Tigris and Euphrates. Farmers in Mesopotamia, Egypt, and the Mediterranean coast produced grain, olives, dates, and other crops.

The deserts continued to support independent nomads who lived by herding. Still, nomads and farmers shared economic ties. Nomads bought dates and grain from settled peoples, while farming populations acquired meat, wool, and hides from the nomads.

Art and Literature

As in Christian Europe and Hindu India, religion shaped the arts and literature of the Islamic world. The great work of Islamic literature was the poetic Quran itself. Scholars studied the sacred words of the Quran in Arabic and then produced their own works interpreting its meaning.

Muslim art and literature reflected the diverse traditions of the various peoples who lived under Muslim rule. Muslim artists and writers were also influenced by the skills and styles of the many peoples with whom they came in contact, including Greeks, Romans, Persians, and Indians.

Design and Decoration Because the Quran strictly banned the worship of idols, Muslim religious leaders forbade artists to portray God or human figures in religious art. The walls and ceilings of mosques were decorated with elaborate abstract and geometric patterns. The arabesque, an intricate design composed of curved lines that suggest floral shapes, appeared in rugs, textiles, and glassware. Muslim artists also perfected skills in calligraphy, the art of beautiful handwriting. They worked the flowing Arabic script, especially verses from the Quran, into decorations on buildings and objects of art.

In nonreligious art, some Muslim artists did paint human and animal figures. Arabic scientific works were often lavishly illustrated. Literary works and luxury objects sometimes showed stylized figures. In later periods, Persian, Turkish, and Indian artists excelled at painting miniatures to illustrate books of poems and fables.

Architecture Muslim architects adapted the domes and arches of Byzantine buildings to new uses. In Jerusalem, they built the Dome of the Rock, a great shrine capped with a magnificent dome. Domed mosques and high minarets dominated Muslim cities in the same way that cathedral spires dominated medieval Christian cities.

Poetry Long before Muhammad, Arabs had a rich tradition of oral poetry. In musical verses, Bedouin poets chanted the dangers of desert journeys, the joys of battle, or the glories of their clans. Their most important themes, chivalry and the romance of nomadic life, recurred in Arab poetry throughout the centuries. Through Muslim Spain, these traditions came to influence medieval European literature and music.

Later Arab poets developed elaborate formal rules for writing poetry and explored both religious and worldly themes. The poems of Rabiah al-Adawiyya expressed Sufi mysticism and encouraged the faithful to worship God selflessly without hope of reward. "If I worship Thee in hope of Paradise / Exclude me from Paradise," she wrote in one prayer poem. Other poets praised important leaders, described the lavish lives of the wealthy, sang of the joys and sorrows of love, or conveyed nuggets of wisdom.

Persian Muslims also had a fine poetic tradition. Firdawsi (fihr DOW see) wrote in Persian using Arabic script. His masterpiece, the *Shah Namah*, or *Book of Kings*, tells the history of Persia. Omar Khayyám (kī YAHM),

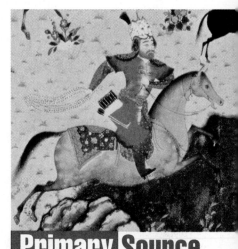

Primary Source

A Hero's Super Powers

Firdawsi's Shah Namah *tells the story of many Persian heroes—among them, Rustam:*

"The tale is told that Rustam had at first
Such strength bestowed by Him who giveth all
That if he walked upon a rock his feet
Would sink therein. Such [power] as that
Proved an abiding trouble, and he prayed
To God in bitterness of soul to [diminish]
His strength that he might walk like other men."

—Firdawsi, *Shah Namah*

Skills Assessment

Primary Source Why was Rustam's strength both an advantage and a disadvantage?

Art of the Muslim World

Throughout the Middle Ages, Muslim artists from Spain to India created paintings, sculptures, and mosaics in many different forms and styles, often borrowing ideas from the local cultures. Some of the artwork reflected religious themes, while other pieces focused on more worldly concerns, such as war, nature, and wealth.

This sixteenth-century painting was created by a Muslim artist from India. As a rule, representations of humans and animals were prohibited in Muslim art. But some people considered images of living creatures harmless if they were small, appeared on everyday objects, or did not cast a shadow.

Muslim artists showed their praise for Allah by decorating mosques with intricate mosaics. This sixteenth-century niche is created from ceramic tiles fitted together in geometric designs and decorated with floral patterns and calligraphy.

Fast Facts

- Calligraphy became a major Muslim art form because it reflected the holiness of the written Quran.

- As a sign of respect, Muhammad's face is never depicted in Muslim art.

- In the Middle Ages, Europeans prized Persian carpets so highly that they used them to cover tables instead of floors.

Portfolio Assessment

INTERNET Use the Internet or library resources to discover other examples of Muslim art. Choose two pieces from different time periods and geographic regions. Using what you have learned here, prepare a presentation comparing the two pieces.

This large sculpture, created by Muslim metalworkers around the year 1000, portrays an ancient mythological figure called a griffin. Arabic inscriptions on the figure wish its owner health and good fortune.

famous in the Muslim world as a scholar and astronomer, is best known to westerners for *The Rubáiyát* (ROO bī yaht). In this collection of four-line poems, Khayyám meditates on fate and the fleeting nature of life:

> "The Moving Finger writes; and having writ,
> Moves on; nor all your Piety nor Wit
> Shall lure it back to cancel half a line,
> Nor all your Tears wash out a word of it."

> —Omar Khayyám, *The Rubáiyát*

Tales Arab writers prized the art of storytelling. Across their empire, they gathered and adapted stories from Indian, Persian, Greek, Jewish, Egyptian, and Turkish sources. The best-known collection is *The Thousand and One Nights*, a group of tales narrated by the fictional princess Scheherezade (shu hehr uh ZAH duh). They include romances, fables, adventures, and humorous anecdotes, many set in the Baghdad of Harun al-Rashid. Later versions filtered into Europe, where millions of children thrilled to "Aladdin and His Magic Lamp" or "Ali Baba and the Forty Thieves."

The World of Learning

"Seek knowledge even as far as China," said Muhammad. Although he could not read or write, his respect for learning inspired Muslims to make great advances in learning.

Centers of Learning Both boys and girls were provided with elementary education. This training emphasized reading and writing, especially study of the Quran. Institutions of higher learning included schools for religious instruction and for the study of Islamic law.

Al-Mamun and later caliphs made Baghdad into the greatest Muslim center of learning. Its vast libraries attracted a galaxy of scholars, who were well paid and highly respected. Other cities, like Cairo, Bukhara, Timbuktu, and Córdoba, had their own centers of learning. In all these places, Muslim scholars made advances in philosophy, mathematics, medicine, and other fields. They preserved the learning of earlier civilizations by translating ancient Persian, Sanskrit, and Greek texts into Arabic.

Philosophy Muslim scholars translated the works of the Greek philosophers, as well as many Hindu and Buddhist texts. Like later Christian thinkers in Europe, Muslim scholars tried to harmonize Greek ideas about reason with religious beliefs based on divine revelation. In Córdoba, the philosopher Ibn Rushd—known in Europe as Averroës—put all knowledge except the Quran to the test of reason. His writings on Aristotle were translated into Latin and influenced Christian scholastics in medieval Europe.

Another Arab thinker, Ibn Khaldun, set standards for the scientific study of history. He stressed the importance of economics and social structure as causes of historical events. He also warned about common sources of error in historical writing. These included bias, exaggeration, and overconfidence in the accuracy of one's sources. Khaldun urged historians to trust sources only after a thorough investigation.

Mathematics Muslim scholars studied both Indian and Greek mathematics before making their original contributions. The greatest Muslim mathematician was al-Khwarizmi (ahl kwah REEZ mee). His work pioneered the study of algebra (from the Arabic word *al-jabr*). In the 800s, he wrote a book that was later translated into Latin and became a standard mathematics textbook in Europe.

Astronomy Like many scholars of the time, al-Khwarizmi made contributions in other fields. He developed a set of astronomical tables based on Greek and Indian discoveries. At observatories from Baghdad to Central

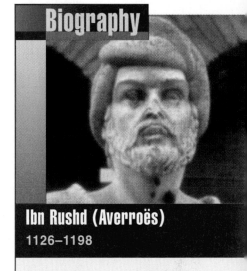

Biography

Ibn Rushd (Averroës)
1126–1198

While growing up in Spain, Muslim scholar Ibn Rushd (known as Averroës to the Christian world) was interested in almost every subject and profession. He first focused on medicine and became chief physician to the Muslim ruler in Spain. Later, he studied astronomy and wrote several important books on the subject. Ibn Rushd also studied law, became a famous judge, and wrote a digest of Islamic law.

Ibn Rushd is best known as a philosopher—both Muslims and Christians have studied his commentaries on Aristotle for centuries. For part of his life, however, Ibn Rushd was forced to live in exile outside Spain because some Muslim religious leaders felt that his writings contradicted the teachings of Islam.

Theme: Impact of the Individual What role did Ibn Rushd play in increasing the knowledge of people during the Middle Ages?

An Arabic Medical Text
At hospitals in Baghdad, Cairo, and Damascus, libraries were well stocked with medical textbooks. This page is from an Arabic textbook on anatomy.

Theme: Economics and Technology Identify three details that suggest that this drawing was based on the study of actual human skeletons.

Asia, Muslim astronomers studied eclipses, observed the Earth's rotation, and calculated the circumference of the Earth to within a few thousand feet. The work of Muslim astronomers and navigators helped pave the way for later explorers like Christopher Columbus.

Medicine Building on the knowledge of the ancient Greeks, Muslims made remarkable advances in medicine and public health. Under the caliphs, physicians and pharmacists had to pass a test before they could practice their profession. The government set up hospitals, with separate wards for women. Injured people could get quick treatment at a facility similar to today's emergency room. Physicians traveled to rural areas to provide health care to those who could not get to a city, while others regularly visited jails.

One of the most original medical thinkers was Muhammad al-Razi, head physician at Baghdad's chief hospital. He wrote many books on medicine, including a pioneering study of measles and smallpox. He also challenged accepted medical practices. Treat the mind as well as the body, he advised young doctors. If a doctor made hopeful comments, he taught, patients would recover faster.

Equally famous was the Persian physician Ibn Sina, known in Europe as Avicenna. By the age of 16, he was already a doctor to the Persian nobility. His great work was the *Canon on Medicine,* a huge encyclopedia of what the Greeks, the Arabs, and he himself had learned about the diagnosis and treatment of disease. The book includes a list of more than 4,000 prescriptions, made with such ingredients as mercury from Spain, myrrh from East Africa, and camphor from India.

Behind these two great names stood dozens of others. Muslim surgeons developed a way to treat cataracts, drawing fluid out of the lenses with a hollow needle. For centuries, surgeons around the world used this method to save patients' eyesight. Arab pharmacists were the first to mix bitter medicines into sweet-tasting syrups and gums.

Knowledge Moves West Over time, Muslim scholars helped knowledge move into Christian Europe. The two main routes of entry were through Spain and through Sicily. Christian European scholars were reintroduced to achievements of Greco-Roman civilization. They studied Muslim philosophy, art, and science. Eventually, European physicians began to attend Muslim universities in Spain and to translate Arabic medical texts. For 500 years, the works of Avicenna and al-Razi were the standard medical textbooks at European schools.

SECTION 3 Assessment

Recall
1. **Identify:** (a) Omar Khayyám, (b) Averroës, (c) Muhammad al-Razi, (d) Avicenna.
2. **Define:** (a) social mobility, (b) arabesque, (c) calligraphy.

Comprehension
3. How did new business methods encourage trade and industry?
4. How did the teachings of Islam influence the arts?
5. Describe one advance made by Muslim civilization in each of the following areas: (a) mathematics, (b) astronomy, (c) medicine.

Critical Thinking and Writing
6. **Analyzing Primary Sources** Muhammad taught that "the ink of the scholar is holier than the blood of the martyr." (a) What do you think he meant? (b) How might this attitude have contributed to the development of Muslim civilization?
7. **Comparing** What were the similarities and differences between Muslim society under the Abbassids and European society in the early Middle Ages?

Activity
Take It to the NET

Visit some Internet museum sites that contain descriptions and examples of Muslim art and architecture. Then, make a poster that shows the major characteristics of Muslim art during the Abbassid golden age.

Reading Focus

- What impact did the Delhi sultanate have on India?
- How did Muslim and Hindu traditions clash and blend?
- How did Akbar strengthen Mughal India?

Vocabulary

sultanate

caste

rajah

Taking Notes

Copy the partially completed outline at right. As you read this section, finish the outline. Use Roman numerals to indicate the major headings of the section, capital letters for the subheadings, and numbers for the supporting details.

I. The Delhi sultanate
  A. Origins of the sultanate
    1.
    2.
  B. Effects of Muslim rule
    1.
    2.
II. Muslims and Hindus

Main Idea   Muslim invasions and rule over India led to cultural diffusion as well as bloody clashes between Muslims and Hindus.

Setting the Scene

"The whole of India is full of gold and jewels," advisers told Sultan Mahmud of Ghazni. "And since the inhabitants are chiefly infidels and idolaters, by the order of God and his Prophet, it is right for us to conquer them." In 1001, Mahmud led his armies into northern India. Smashing and looting Hindu temples, Mahmud used the fabulous riches of India to turn his capital into a great Muslim center. Later Muslim invaders did more than loot and destroy. They built a dazzling new Muslim empire in India.

The arrival of Islam brought changes to India as great as those caused by the Aryan migrations 2,000 years earlier. As Muslims mingled with Indians, each civilization absorbed elements from the other.

The Delhi Sultanate

After the Gupta empire fell in about 550, India again fragmented into many local kingdoms. Rival princes battled for control of the northern plain. Despite power struggles, Indian culture flourished. Hindu and Buddhist rulers spent huge sums to build and decorate magnificent temples. Trade networks linked India to the Middle East, Southeast Asia, and China.

Origins of the Sultanate   Although Arabs conquered the Indus Valley in 711, they advanced no farther into the subcontinent. Then about 1000, Muslim Turks and Afghans pushed into India. At first, they were adventurers like Mahmud, who pillaged much of the north. However, in the late 1100s, the sultan of Ghur defeated Hindu armies across the northern plain. He made Delhi his capital. From there, his successors organized a sultanate, or land ruled by a sultan. The Delhi sultanate, which lasted from 1206 to 1526, marked the start of Muslim rule in northern India.

Why did the Muslim invaders triumph? They won on the battlefield in part because Muslim mounted archers had far greater mobility than Hindu forces, who rode slow-moving war elephants. Also, Hindu princes wasted resources battling one another instead of uniting against a common enemy. In some places, large numbers of Hindus, especially from low castes, converted to Islam. In the Hindu social system, you will recall, people were born into castes, or social groups from which they could not change.

Effects of Muslim Rule   Muslim rule brought changes to Indian government and society. Sultans introduced Muslim traditions of government. Many Turks, Persians, and Arabs migrated to India to serve as soldiers

Global Connections

Ibn Battuta: World Traveler

In 1333, the sultan of Delhi was seeking the services of educated foreigners. To fill the position of judge, he hired a scholarly traveler from Morocco. The name of the traveler was Ibn Battuta.

Ibn Battuta was no ordinary traveler. By the time he reached India, he had already visited Egypt, the eastern coast of Africa, Asia Minor, and Central Asia. After eight years in India, he sailed on to Southeast Asia and China. Still later, he trekked across the Sahara to tour West Africa. In all, he logged an estimated 75,000 miles. After finally returning to Morocco, Ibn Battutta dictated an account of his extraordinary travels that has survived to this day.

Theme: Global Interaction
Why was it so rare for people of the time to travel as widely as Ibn Battuta had?

Delhi Sultanate and Mughal Empire

Delhi sultanate about 1300

→ **Route of Tamerlane's invasion, 1398**

Mughal empire, 1526

Lands added to the empire by 1605

Lands added to the empire by 1707

◇ **Taj Mahal**

Skills Assessment

Geography Two Muslim dynasties ruled much of the Indian subcontinent. The Delhi sultanate lasted more than 300 years before the Mughal dynasty replaced it.

1. **Location** On the map, locate **(a)** Delhi, **(b)** Hindu Kush, **(c)** Ganges River, **(d)** Taj Mahal.
2. **Movement** Describe Tamerlane's invasion route into India.
3. **Critical Thinking Linking Past and Present** Use the map of Asia in the Reference Section to identify the present-day countries that now occupy the lands of the Mughal empire.

or officials. Trade between India and the Muslim world increased. During the Mongol raids of the 1200s, many scholars and adventurers fled from Baghdad to India, bringing Persian and Greek learning. The newcomers helped create a brilliant civilization at Delhi, where Persian art and architecture flourished.

Decline In 1398, Tamerlane invaded India. He plundered the northern plain and smashed into Delhi. "Not a bird on the wing moved," reported stunned survivors. Thousands of artisans were enslaved to build Tamerlane's capital at Samarkand. Delhi, an empty shell, slowly recovered. But the sultans no longer controlled a large empire, and northern India again fragmented, this time into rival Hindu and Muslim states.

Muslims and Hindus

At its worst, the Muslim conquest of northern India inflicted disaster on Hindus and Buddhists. The widespread destruction of Buddhist monasteries contributed to the drastic decline of Buddhism as a major religion in India. During the most violent onslaughts, many Hindus were killed. Others may have converted to escape death. In time, though, relations became more peaceful.

Hindu-Muslim Differences The Muslim advance brought two utterly different religions and cultures face to face. Hinduism was an ancient religion that had evolved over thousands of years. Hindus recognized many sacred texts and prayed before statues representing many gods and goddesses. Islam, by contrast, was a newer faith with a single sacred text. Muslims were devout monotheists who saw the statues and carvings in Hindu temples as an offense to the one true god.

Hindus accepted differences in caste status and honored Brahmans as a priestly caste. Muslims taught the equality of all believers before God and had no religious hierarchy. Hindus celebrated religious occasions with music and dance, a practice that many strict Muslims condemned.

Interactions Eventually, the Delhi sultans grew more tolerant of their subject population. Some Muslim scholars argued that behind the many Hindu gods and goddesses was a single god. Hinduism was thus accepted as a monotheistic religion. Although Hindus remained second-class citizens, as long as they paid the non-Muslim tax, they could practice their religion. Some sultans even left rajahs, or local Hindu rulers, in place.

During the Delhi sultanate, a growing number of Hindus converted to Islam. Some lower-caste Hindus preferred Islam because it rejected the caste system. Other converts came from higher castes. They chose to adopt Islam either because they accepted its beliefs or because they served in the Muslim government. Indian merchants were attracted to Islam in part because of the strong trade network across Muslim lands.

Cultural Blending During this period, too, Indian Muslims absorbed elements of Hindu culture, such as marriage customs and caste ideas. A new language, Urdu, evolved as a marriage of Persian, Arabic, and Hindi. Local artisans applied Persian art styles to Indian subjects. Indian music and dance reappeared at the courts of the sultan.

governn
partner:
himself

Akt
includir
Indian l
eration.
a firm f

Akt
governn
He mod
weights

Akbar':
ruler th
wife, N
judgme:
the mos

The
the reig
died at
he criec
tomb bu
Persian
in clear
Taj Mah

Sha
for him:
the thro
years la

Looki

In the la
and res
heavy t
will rea
foothol

SECTI

Recall
1. **Ident**
   (c) M
   (e) Ta
2. **Defin**
   (c) ra

Compr
3. (a) W
   Delhi
   India
   affec
4. How
   and N
5. What
   to st

Virtual Field Trip

www.phschool.com

Prince of Wales Museum of Western India
Mumbai, India

To see more artworks from the Mughal period, as well as other periods in Indian history, use the Internet address above to link to the Prince of Wales Museum of Western India.

Akbar the Great
As ruler of the Mughal empire, Akbar tried to promote harmony among the diverse peoples of India. Here, Akbar enjoys a performance of traditional Hindu dance.

Theme: Diversity How does this picture reflect Akbar's policy of toleration?

An Indian holy man, Nanak, sought to blend Islamic and Hindu beliefs. He preached "the unity of God, the brotherhood of man, the rejection of caste, and the futility of idol worship." His teachings led to the rise of a new religion, Sikhism, in northern India. (See the chart in the Chapter Review and Assessment.) The Sikhs later organized into military forces that clashed with the powerful Mughal rulers of India.

Mughal India

In 1526, Turkish and Mongol invaders again poured through the mountain passes in India. At their head rode Babur (BAH buhr), who claimed descent from Genghiz Khan and Tamerlane. Babur was a military genius, poet, and author of a fascinating book of memoirs.

Babur Founds a Dynasty Just north of Delhi, Babur met a huge army led by the sultan Ibrahim. "I placed my foot in the stirrup of resolution and my hands on the reins of confidence in God," recalled Babur. His force was small but had cannons, which he put to good use:

> "The sun had mounted spear-high when the onset began, and the battle lasted till midday, when the enemy was completely broken and routed. By the grace and mercy of Almighty God, this difficult affair was made easy to me, and that mighty army . . . was crushed in the dust."
> —Babur, *Memoirs*

In no time, Babur swept away the remnants of the Delhi sultanate and set up the Mughal dynasty, which ruled from 1526 to 1857. (*Mughal* is the Persian word for "Mongol.") Babur and his heirs conquered an empire that stretched from the Himalayas to the Deccan Plateau.

Akbar the Great The chief builder of the Mughal empire was Babur's grandson Akbar. During his long reign, from 1556 to 1605, he created a strong central government, earning the title Akbar the Great.

Akbar was a leader of unusual abilities. Although a Muslim, he won the support of Hindu subjects through his policy of toleration. He opened

SECTION 1 Early Civilizations of Africa

Reading Focus

- How did geography affect cultural development and the migration of peoples?
- What were the achievements of the kingdom of Nubia?
- How did outside influences lead to change in North Africa?

Vocabulary

savanna
desertification
outpost

Taking Notes

Copy this concept web. As you read the section, complete the circles with important facts to remember about desertification. Add as many circles as you need.

Loss of cropland

DESERTIFICATION

Diverse cultures

Migration

Main Idea Africa's geographic features had a major impact on the development of societies.

Do
or
"India ha
commen
1970s. "F
Should a
weaken
mind as

India
Akbar t
found i

66 O Go
every
be a n
Chris
It is Y

Italy 1
Giusep
unite Ita
that bin

66 A nat
broug
geog
assig
the sa
er to
unde
It is n
show
purit

Ski
1. Who
dive
A Al
B M
C H
D M

3. Criti
dive
and

Shown twice actual size

Did You Know?

The Tsetse Fly

The tsetse fly carries one of Africa's most troublesome diseases—sleeping sickness. Flies pass on the deadly disease by biting humans and large animals. Some people have abandoned their villages in heavily infested areas. In other regions, people have stopped raising horses and cattle because of the pests. Many tourists arrange their trips to avoid the tsetse fly.

How can Africans overcome this menace? Tsetse flies are attracted to moving vehicles, dark colors, and perfume and after-shave. Using this knowledge, scientists have built traps. A dark blue cloth, treated to smell like ox breath—irresistible to the tsetse fly—acts as a lure. The cloth is also treated with insecticide, to kill the flies.

Theme: Economics and Technology How might African economies be affected by eliminating the tsetse fly?

Setting the Scene

As the sun rose above the east bank of the Nile, workers hurried to the construction site. They had only a few hours to work in comfort before the sun turned the desert into a furnace. Still, as long as King Taharqa (tuh HAHR kuh) was determined to turn the old mud-brick temple into a magnificent monument, their work would continue. An ancient inscription explains how the monument was "built of good white sandstone, excellent, hard, . . . the house being of gold, the columns of gold, the inlays thereof being of silver."

About 680 B.C., Taharqa commanded the Nile Valley from Nubia to the Mediterranean. By that time, Nubia was already 3,000 years old. Along with Egypt, it stood as one of the world's early civilizations.

The Geography of Africa

After Asia, Africa is the second largest continent, covering one fifth of all the Earth's land surface. Its geography is immensely varied. However, certain geographic features, such as distinct climate zones, have had a major impact on its development.

Climate Zones Many outsiders, misled by movies, imagine Africa as a continent covered with thick jungles. In fact, tropical rain forests cover less than five percent of the land, mostly along the Equator. Thick trees and roots make this region unsuitable for farming.

Africa's largest and most populated climate zone is the savanna, or grassy plain, which stretches north and south of the forest zone. Although the savanna has good soil, irregular patterns of rainfall sometimes cause long, deadly droughts. In parts of the savanna, the tsetse fly infects people and cattle with sleeping sickness. But in other parts, cattle herding is a common occupation.

The savanna belts trail off into increasingly dry steppe zones and then into two major deserts. The blistering Sahara in the north is the world's largest desert. Although the Sahara did become a highway for migration and trade, its size and harsh terrain limited movement. The Kalahari and Namib in the south are smaller but equally forbidding. Finally, along the Mediterranean coast of North Africa and at the tip of southern Africa lie areas of fertile farmland. These varied regions also offer a variety of mineral resources, such as salt, gold, iron, copper, diamonds, and oil, all of which have spurred trade.

Movement In addition to deserts and rain forests, other geographic features have acted as barriers to easy movement of people and goods. Africa has an enormous coastline, but few good natural harbors. In addition, much of the interior is a high plateau. As rivers approach the coast, they cascade through a series of rapids and cataracts that hinder travel between the coast and the interior.

Despite geographic barriers, people did migrate within Africa and to neighboring lands. The Great Rift Valley of East Africa served as one interior corridor. Many rivers were navigable in the interior of the continent. The Red Sea and Indian Ocean linked East Africa to the Middle East and other Asian lands, while North Africa was a part of the Mediterranean world.

Resources Mineral resources spurred trade among various African regions. Salt, gold, iron, and copper were particularly valuable to early trade. In later centuries, diamonds and oil would also gain importance.

Migration of Peoples

Archaeologists have uncovered evidence that the Great Rift Valley of East Africa was the home of the earliest people. Gradually, their descendants spread to almost every corner of the Earth.

The Changing Sahara In Africa, as elsewhere, Paleolithic people developed skills as hunters and food gatherers. By 5500 B.C., Neolithic farmers had learned to cultivate the Nile Valley and to domesticate animals. As farming spread across North Africa, Neolithic villages even appeared in the Sahara, which was then a well-watered zone. Ancient rock paintings show a Sahara full of forests and rivers.

About 2500 B.C., a climate change slowly dried out the Sahara. As the land became parched, the desert spread. This process of desertification has continued to the present, devouring thousands of acres of cropland and pastureland each year. Desertification has also encouraged migration, as people are forced to seek new areas to maintain their ways of life.

The Bantu Migrations Over thousands of years, migrations contributed to the rich diversity of peoples and cultures. Scholars have traced these migrations by studying language patterns. They have learned that West African farmers and herders migrated to the south and east between about 1000 B.C. and A.D. 1000. Like the Indo-European peoples of Europe and Asia, these West African peoples spoke a variety of languages that derived from a common root language. We call this root language Bantu.

As people migrated across Africa, they adapted to its many climates and developed a diversity of cultures. While some were nomadic cattle herders, others cultivated grain or root crops. In several regions, farming people built great empires.

The Nile Kingdom of Nubia

While Egyptian civilization was developing, another African civilization took shape on a wide band of fertile land among the cataracts of the upper Nile. The ancient kingdom of Nubia, also called Kush, was located in present-day Sudan.

Bantu Migrations

Bantu migration route
(Color value indicates the passage of time)

1000 B.C.   A.D. 1000

Skills Assessment

Geography Over a period of 2,000 years, Bantu peoples migrated to southern Africa. Today, as many as one third of Africans speak a Bantu language.

1. **Location** On the map, locate **(a)** Lake Victoria, **(b)** Orange River, **(c)** Lake Nyasa.
2. **Movement (a)** Where did Bantu peoples originate? **(b)** About when did Bantu-speaking peoples reach the Orange River?
3. **Critical Thinking Solving Problems** How have scientists learned about the Bantu migrations?

Nubian Carvings
Conquest and trade provided Nubia with opportunities to learn about Egyptian culture. Many traditions and beliefs were adapted to become part of Nubian civilization.

Theme: Art and Literature
How do these Nubian carvings reflect the influence of Egyptian art?

From time to time, ambitious Egyptian pharaohs subdued Nubia, but the Nubians always regained their independence. As a result of conquest and trade, Nubian rulers adopted many Egyptian traditions. They modeled palaces and pyramids on Egyptian styles. About 750 B.C., the Nubian king Piankhi (pee AHNG kee) conquered Egypt. For a century, Nubian kings ruled Egypt. But their armies could not match the iron weapons of the invading Assyrians. The Nubians retreated south from Egypt.

The Furnaces of Meroë By 500 B.C., Nubian rulers moved their capital to Meroë (MEHR uh wee). Meroë commanded both the north-south Nile route and the east-west route from the Red Sea into the savanna and North Africa. Along this wide trade network, Nubia sent gold, ivory, animal skins, perfumes, and slaves to the Mediterranean world and the Middle East.

Equally important, Meroë was rich in iron ore. Its furnaces, fueled by large quantities of timber, produced iron. Today, giant heaps of iron waste remain as evidence of ancient Meroë's industry.

Splendor and Decline Although Nubia absorbed much from Egypt, it later followed an independent course. Nubians worshiped their own gods including Apedemak, a lion-headed warrior god. At Meroë, artistic styles reflected a greater sense of freedom than did Egyptian styles. Nubians also created their own system of writing, using an alphabet instead of hiero-glyphics. Unfortunately, the Nubian alphabet has yet to be deciphered.

After the joint reign of King Natakamani and Queen Amanitere in the first century A.D., Nubia's golden age dimmed. Finally, about A.D. 350, armies from the kingdom of Axum on the Red Sea overwhelmed Nubia. King Ezana of Axum boasted, "I burnt their towns, both those built of brick and those built of reeds, and my army carried off their food and copper and iron . . . and destroyed the statues in their temples." As you will read later, Axum would make its own mark on this region beyond the Nile.

North Africa

Early African civilizations had strong ties to the Mediterranean world. At the opposite end of the Mediterranean from Nubia and Axum, Carthage rose as a great North African power. Like Nubia, its wealth came from trade. Founded by Phoenician traders, Carthage came to dominate trade in the western Mediterranean and North Africa. Between 800 B.C. and 146 B.C., it forged an empire that stretched from the Maghreb (present-day Tunisia, Algeria, and Morocco) to southern Spain and Sicily. Carthage also established outposts, or distant military stations, in England and France.

As Rome expanded, territorial and trade rivalries erupted between the two powers, resulting in the Punic Wars. Despite the efforts of Hannibal, Rome eventually crushed Carthage. Trade, however, continued.

Roman Rule The Romans built roads, dams, aqueducts, and cities across North Africa. They developed its farmlands and imported lions and other fierce animals to do battle with gladiators. North Africa also provided soldiers for the Roman army. One of them, Septimius Severus, later became emperor of Rome.

Under Roman rule, Christianity spread to the cities of North Africa. St. Augustine, the most influential Christian thinker of the late Roman empire, was born in present-day Algeria. From A.D. 395 to A.D. 430, Augustine was bishop of Hippo, a city near the ruins of ancient Carthage.

Camels and Trade By A.D. 200, camels had been brought to North Africa from Asia. These hardy "ships of the desert" revolutionized trade across the Sahara. Camels could carry loads of up to 500 pounds and could plod 20 or 30 miles a day, often without water. Although daring traders had earlier made the difficult desert crossing in horse-drawn chariots, camel caravans created new trade networks.

Spread of Islam Further changes came in the 600s, when Arab armies carried Islam into North Africa. At first, the Arabs occupied the cities and battled the Berbers in the desert. Later, Berbers and Arabs joined forces to conquer Spain. Islam replaced Christianity as the dominant religion of North Africa, and Arabic replaced Latin as its language.

North Africa benefited from the blossoming of Muslim civilization. Cities like Cairo, Fez, and Marrakesh were famed for their mosques and libraries. Linked into a global trade network, North African ports did a busy trade in grain, wine, fruit, ivory, and gold. Along with their goods, Muslim traders from North Africa carried Islam into West Africa.

SECTION 1 Assessment

Recall
1. **Identify:** (a) Taharqa, (b) Bantu, (c) Piankhi, (d) Meroë, (e) St. Augustine.
2. **Define:** (a) savanna, (b) desertification, (c) outpost.

Comprehension
3. (a) What geographic barriers hindered movement in Africa? (b) Describe two examples of migration in Africa.
4. How did Nubia prosper?
5. Describe one way each of the following influenced North Africa: (a) the growth of the Roman empire, (b) the spread of Islam.

Critical Thinking and Writing
6. **Linking Past and Present** (a) What effects did desertification have on African peoples? (b) How might life in the United States today be affected if well-watered areas began to turn into desert?
7. **Connecting to Geography** Explain the link between geography and the introduction of camel caravans.

Activity
Take It to the NET

Search on the Internet for Lepcis Magna, an archaeological site on the Mediterranean coast of North Africa. Write a paragraph about the city's history and its link to Septimius Severus.

Kingdoms of West Africa

Reading Focus

- Why were gold and salt important in early Africa?
- How did the rulers of Ghana, Mali, and Songhai build strong kingdoms?
- How did other West African kingdoms develop?

Vocabulary

surplus
commodity
mansa
oba

Taking Notes

Copy and complete the time line below. As you read, add entries for the establishment of kingdoms mentioned in this section. One has been included as an example.

```
550      800      1050     1300     1550
         Ghana
```

Main Idea Between about A.D. 800 and A.D. 1600, several powerful kingdoms won control of the Sahara trade and built prosperous cities in West Africa.

Setting the Scene In the early 1500s, the scholar Hassan ibn Muhammad—known in the West as Leo Africanus—described the commercial wealth and bustling markets of the West African city of Timbuktu:

> "Here are many shops of . . . merchants, and especially such as weave linen and cotton cloth. And here do the Barbary (North African) merchants bring the cloth of Europe. All the women of this region, except maidservants, go with their faces covered and sell all the necessary foods."
> —Hassan ibn Muhammad, quoted in
> *Ancient African Kingdoms* (Shinnie)

Timbuktu stood at one end of a trade network that reached north to Cairo and then across the Mediterranean Sea to Italy. Between about 800 and 1600, several powerful kingdoms in turn won control of the prosperous Sahara trade. Among the richest of these West African states were Ghana, Mali, and Songhai.

Trading Gold and Salt

As the Sahara dried out, you will recall, some Neolithic people migrated southward into the savanna. There, farmers grew beans, melons, and cereal grains. By A.D. 100, settled farming villages were expanding, especially along the Senegal and Niger rivers and around Lake Chad.

Villagers traded any surplus, or excess, food they produced. Gradually, a trade network linked the savanna to forest lands in the south and then funneled goods across the Sahara to civilizations along the Mediterranean and in the Middle East.

Two products, gold and salt, dominated the Sahara trade. Gold was plentiful in present-day Ghana, Nigeria, and Senegal. Men dug the gold-bearing soil from pits. Women then washed the soil to extract the gold dust. The precious metal was stuffed into hollow feather quills for safe travel to the markets of North Africa and Europe.

In return, West Africans received an equally important commodity, or valuable product, salt. People need salt in their diet to prevent dehydration, especially in hot, tropical areas. The Sahara had an abundance of salt. At Taghaza, in the central Sahara, people even built homes of salt blocks. But in the savanna, several hundred miles south, salt was scarce. A block of salt was easily worth its weight in gold.

Geography and History

The Salt Trade

The camel changed the Saharan salt trade. For centuries, trade was limited because the horses that transported the salt were not suited to desert travel. However, about A.D. 300, the Berbers, an Arabic people of North Africa, began using camels to carry their goods. When the caravans reached Ghana, merchants would pay one pound of gold dust for one pound of salt. The salt trade began to thrive.

Now, more than 1,000 years later, the salt trade still exists. As late as 1975, workers in Taghaza (now called Taoudenni) were living in salt huts and mining several thousand tons of salt per year. Small caravans of camels carrying salt still arrive in Timbuktu today.

Theme: Continuity and Change Why are camels still used in the salt trade in today's technological age?

As farming and trade prospered, cities developed on the northern edges of the savanna. Strong monarchs gained control of the most profitable trade routes and built powerful kingdoms.

Gold Wealth of Ghana

By A.D. 800, the rulers of the Soninke people had united many farming villages to create the kingdom of Ghana.* Ghana was located in the broad "V" made by the Niger and Senegal rivers. From there, the king controlled gold-salt trade routes across West Africa. The two streams of trade met in the marketplaces of Ghana, where the king collected tolls on all goods entering or leaving his land. So great was the flow of gold that Arab writers called Ghana "land of gold."

Capital and King The capital of Ghana was Kumbi Saleh, made up of two separate, walled towns, some six miles apart. The first town was dominated by the royal palace, surrounded by a complex of domed buildings. Here, in a court noted for its wealth and splendor, the king of Ghana presided over elaborate ceremonies. To the people, he was a semidivine figure who dispensed justice and kept order.

In the second town of Kumbi Saleh, prosperous Muslim merchants from north of the Sahara lived in luxurious stone buildings. Lured by the gold wealth of Ghana, these merchants helped make Kumbi Saleh a bustling center of trade.

Influence of Islam Muslim merchants, settled in their own communities throughout the kingdom, brought their Islamic faith to Ghana. Islam spread slowly at first. The king employed Muslims as counselors and officials, gradually absorbing Muslim military technology and ideas about government. Muslims also introduced their written language, coinage, business methods, and styles of architecture. In time, a few city dwellers adopted Islam, but most of the Soninke people continued to follow their own traditional beliefs.

About 1050, the Almoravids (al MOR uh veedz), pious Muslims of North Africa, launched a campaign to spread their form of Islam. They eventually overwhelmed Ghana, but were unable to maintain control over such a distant land. In time, Ghana was swallowed up by a rising new power, the West African kingdom of Mali.

The Kingdom of Mali

Amid the turmoil of Ghana's collapse, the Mandinka people on the upper Niger suffered a bitter defeat by a rival leader. Their king and all but one of his sons were executed. According to tradition, the survivor was Sundiata. By 1235, he had crushed his enemies, won control of the gold trade routes, and founded the empire of Mali.

Mali is an Arab version of the Mandinka word meaning "where the king dwells." The **mansas,** or kings, expanded their influence over both the gold-mining regions to the south and the salt supplies of Taghaza. Where caravan routes crossed, towns like Timbuktu mushroomed into great trading cities.

The greatest emperor of Mali was Mansa Musa (MAHN sah MOO sah), who came to the throne in about 1312. He expanded Mali's borders westward to the Atlantic Ocean and pushed northward to conquer many cities. During Mansa Musa's 25-year reign, he worked to ensure peace and order in his empire. "There is complete and general safety throughout the land,"

---

* *Ghana,* meaning ruler, was the name used for the kingdom by Arab traders. The modern nation of Ghana is not located on the site of the ancient kingdom, but lies several hundred miles to the south.

The Gold Trade
This gold scorpion was probably used as a weight by West African merchants. Along with salt, gold dominated the Sahara trade and was a mainstay of the West African economy.

Theme: Economics and Technology Why might someone choose to make a weight from so valuable a material as gold?

Biography

Sundiata (?)–1255

During the early 1200s, a tyrant named Sumanguru ruled in western Africa. According to legend, Sumanguru feared a royal Mandinka family. He killed 11 brothers in the family. But he spared the life of one brother, Sundiata, who appeared to be sickly and already near death. Sundiata survived and recruited an army. In 1235, Sundiata defeated Sumanguru and quickly persuaded other Mandinka chiefs to surrender to his rule.

History tells us that over the next two decades, Sundiata expanded his power. He founded the empire of Mali, which lasted for 200 years. Sundiata became a great hero, and West Africans have told stories about his exploits for hundreds of years.

Theme: Impact of the Individual Why did West Africans tell stories about Sundiata long after his death?

Traveling With Mansa Musa

Despite the blistering heat of the Sahara, your heart is light. As a minor official, you feel honored to be a part of the *hajj*—or pilgrimage—of your emperor, Mansa Musa. Although there are still many miles between you and the holy city of Mecca, you know that the people of Mali will sing songs about this trip for generations to come.

You began the 4,800-mile trip in Niani, the capital of Mali. Musa's caravan followed the Niger River to Timbuktu, then headed toward the salt mines of Taghaza. Now, you are near the Egyptian city of Cairo. After visiting Mecca, your party must return to Mali. The hajj will take over a year.

Africa

Cairo

Taghaza

Mecca

Timbuktu

Niger R.

Niani

Musa's enormous caravan snakes along as far as the eye can see. You travel with thousands of people and camels, as well as enough food and supplies for months.

It seems as if you have been riding a camel forever. Although it can be a mean-tempered beast, your camel is the best form of transportation through this vast desert.

Musa dazzles everyone with Mali's wealth. At each city and oasis, Musa showers gifts of gold on local leaders and gives alms to the poor. He can afford to be generous, because the caravan boasts 100 camels heavily laden with gold. Five hundred slaves each carry a golden staff.

Portfolio Assessment

Write a song to commemorate the great pilgrimage of Mansa Musa. Be sure to add details about your journey and the impression Musa made on the people he met.

commented Ibn Battuta when he visited Mali. "The traveler here has no more reason to fear thieves than the man who stays at home."

Mansa Musa converted to Islam and based his system of justice on the Quran. At the same time, he did not adopt all customs associated with some nearby Muslim societies. For example, women in Mali wore no veils and were not secluded within the home.

In 1324, Mansa Musa fulfilled one of the Five Pillars of Islam by making the hajj, or pilgrimage to Mecca. Through his pilgrimage, Mansa Musa showed his devotion to Islam. He also forged new diplomatic and economic ties with other Muslim states. The movement of wealth, people, and ideas increased Mali's renown. By the 1400s, Timbuktu had become a leading center of learning. The city drew some of the best scholars from all over the Muslim world.

A New Empire in Songhai

In the 1400s, disputes over succession weakened Mali. Subject peoples broke away, and the empire shriveled. By 1450, the wealthy trading city of Gao (GOW) had emerged as the capital of a new West African kingdom, Songhai (SAWNG hī).

Two Great Leaders Songhai grew up on the bend of the Niger River in present-day Niger and Burkina Faso. Between 1464 and 1492, the soldier-king Sonni Ali used his powerful army to forge the largest state that had ever existed in West Africa. Sonni Ali brought trade routes and wealthy cities like Timbuktu under his control. Unlike the rulers of Mali, he did not adopt the practices of Islam. Instead, he followed traditional religious beliefs.

Soon after Sonni Ali's death, though, the emperor Askia Muhammad set up a Muslim dynasty. He further expanded the territory of Songhai and improved the government. Askia Muhammad set up a bureaucracy with separate departments for farming, the army, and the treasury.

Like Mansa Musa, Askia Muhammad made a pilgrimage to Mecca that led to increased ties with the Muslim world. Scholars and poets from Muslim lands flocked to his court at Gao. In towns and cities across Songhai, Askia Muhammad built mosques and opened schools for the study of the Quran.

Invaders From the North Songhai prospered until about 1586, when disputes over succession led to civil war. Soon after, the ruler of Morocco sent his armies south to seize the West African gold mines. The invaders used gunpowder weapons to defeat the disunited forces of Songhai.

Like the Almoravids in Ghana, however, the Moroccans were not able to rule an empire across the Sahara. With the downfall of Songhai, this part of West Africa splintered into many small kingdoms.

Other Kingdoms of West Africa

In the period from 500 to 1500, other kingdoms flourished in various parts of West Africa. The fertile northern lands of modern-day Nigeria were home to the Hausa people, who had probably migrated there when the Sahara dried out. They were successful at both farming and trading.

Walled City-States of the Hausa By the 1300s, the Hausa had built a number of clay-walled cities. While these city-states remained independent of one another, in time they expanded into thriving commercial centers. In the cities, cotton weavers and dyers, leatherworkers, and other artisans produced goods for sale. Merchants traded with Arab and Berber caravans from north of the Sahara. Hausa goods were sold as far away as North Africa and southern Europe.

Kano was the most prosperous Hausa city-state. Its walls, 14 miles in circumference, protected a population of more than 30,000. Kano's greatest

Virtual Field Trip

www.phschool.com

The British Museum London, England

To see other examples of Benin bronzework, use the Internet address above to link to the British Museum.

Benin Bronzes

The forest kingdom of Benin was famous for its sculptures, such as this depiction of a queen mother. Benin artisans used a lost-wax process to create sculptures of bronze and brass. In this process, the sculptor formed a wax model inside a clay shell and then poured molten metal into the shell. The melting wax ran out, leaving behind a finished metal sculpture.

Theme: Political and Social Systems How does this casting suggest that the subject was an important person in Benin?

king, Muhammad Rumfa, was a Muslim, as were many merchants and officials. The Hausa developed a written language based on Arabic.

Many Hausa rulers were women, such as Amina of the city-state of Zaria. In the 1500s, she conquered Kano and expanded the boundary of Zaria as far as the Niger River. Under Amina, the Hausa came to dominate many Saharan trade routes.

The Forest Kingdom of Benin South of the savanna, Benin (beh NIN) rose in the rain forests of the Guinea coast. The forest peoples carved out farming villages and traded pepper, ivory, and, later, slaves to their neighbors in the savanna.

The rulers of Benin organized their kingdom in the 1300s, probably building on the achievements of earlier forest cultures. An oba, or king, was both a political and a religious leader. Still, much power was spread among other figures, including the queen mother and a council of hereditary chiefs. A three-mile-long wall surrounded the capital, Benin City. Its broad avenues were dotted with tidy homes and a great palace.

The palace, in particular, was decorated with elaborate brass plaques and sculptures. According to tradition, artisans from Ife (EE fay), an earlier forest society, had taught the people of Benin how to cast bronze and brass. Benin sculptors developed their own unique style for representing the human face and form. Their works depicted warriors armed for battle, queen mothers with upswept hairstyles, and the oba himself.

Looking Ahead

Later Benin bronzeworks showed helmeted and bearded Portuguese merchants. These newcomers began to arrive in growing numbers in the 1500s. At first, Benin benefited from the new trade with European countries. However, increasing contacts with Europe opened the door to a booming slave trade that would have far-reaching consequences for all of West Africa.

SECTION 2 Assessment

Recall

1. **Identify:** (a) Almoravids, (b) Sundiata, (c) Sonni Ali, (d) Askia Muhammad, (e) Amina.
2. **Define:** (a) surplus, (b) commodity, (c) mansa, (d) oba.

Comprehension

3. How did the gold-salt trade develop between West Africa and North Africa?
4. How did Mansa Musa, Sonni Ali, and Askia Muhammad change their kingdoms?

5. What were the achievements of the (a) Hausa city-states, (b) kingdom of Benin?

Critical Thinking and Writing

6. **Recognizing Causes and Effects** (a) Describe two short-term effects of Mansa Musa's hajj. (b) What do you think was the most important long-term effect?
7. **Drawing Conclusions** What might historians learn about the kingdom of Benin by studying its sculpture?

Activity

Creating a Map
Research the pilgrimages of Mansa Musa and Askia Muhammad. On a map, trace the routes of the pilgrimages. What regions and kingdoms did each ruler visit during his pilgrimage? Label each of these regions.

Trade Routes of East Africa

Reading Focus

- How did religion influence the development of Axum and Ethiopia?

- What effects did trade have on city-states in East Africa?

- What have archaeologists discovered about Great Zimbabwe?

Taking Notes

Copy this table. As you read, fill in the columns with trade goods from Africa, Asia, and Europe and the Mediterranean that passed through the markets of Axum and the East African coast.

AFRICA	ASIA	EUROPE AND THE MEDITERRANEAN
		Linen cloth
Hides, skins, and animal products		
		Copper
	Cotton cloth and silk	
	Porcelain, china, and glassware	

Main Idea Religion and trade played an important role in Ethiopia and East African city-states.

Setting the Scene

According to Ethiopian tradition, the first emperor of Ethiopia was the son of the Israelite king Solomon and Makeda, the queen of Sheba. An ancient chronicle described how Makeda decided to journey to Jerusalem after hearing of Solomon's wisdom. "Learning is better than treasures of silver and gold," she said. The queen spent six months at Solomon's court, gathering knowledge to bring back to her people.

According to the chronicle, when Makeda was about to return to Sheba, Solomon gave her a ring and a blessing:

"May the peace of God be with thee. While I was sleeping . . . I had a vision. The sun which before my eyes was shining upon Israel, moved away. It went and soared above Ethiopia. It remained there. Who knows but that thy country may be blessed because of thee? Above all keep the truth which I have brought thee. Worship God."

—*The Glory of Kings*

The subsequent East African kingdom of Ethiopia was proud of its ancient Jewish roots and Christian traditions of Byzantine origin. In later centuries, other kingdoms across Africa were becoming part of the Islamic world, but Ethiopia remained Christian through its Coptic church.

Axum and Its Successors

About A.D. 350, as you will recall, King Ezana of Axum conquered and absorbed the ancient Nile kingdom of Nubia. Located to the southeast of Nubia, Axum extended from the mountains of present-day Ethiopia to the sun-bleached shores of the Red Sea. The peoples of Axum were descended from African farmers and from traders who brought Jewish religious traditions through Arabia. This merging of cultures introduced another religion to Axum. It also gave rise to a unique written and spoken language, Geez.

A Trade Network The kingdom of Axum profited from the strategic location of its two main cities, the port of Adulis on the Red Sea and the upland capital city of Axum. From about 200 B.C. to A.D. 400, Axum commanded a triangular trade network that connected Africa to India by way of the Arabian Sea and to the Mediterranean world.

From the interior of Africa, traders brought ivory, animal hides, rhinoceros horn, and gold to the markets of Axum. Goods from farther south along the African coast came to the harbor of Adulis. There, too, markets offered iron, spices, precious stones, and cotton cloth from India and other lands beyond the Indian Ocean. Ships bore these goods up the Red Sea, where they collected linen cloth, brass, copper, iron tools, wine, and olive oil from Europe and countries along the Mediterranean.

The Spread of Christianity In these great centers of international trade, Greek, Egyptian, Arab, and Jewish merchants mingled with traders from Africa, India, and other regions. As elsewhere, ideas spread along with goods. In the 300s, Axum's great king, Ezana, converted to Christianity. As the new religion took hold among the people, Christian churches replaced older temples.

At first, Christianity strengthened the ties between Axum, North Africa, and the Mediterranean world. Axum's other African neighbors, however, were not Christian. In the 600s, Islam began spreading across Africa. Many African rulers embraced this new faith, creating strong cultural ties across much of the continent. Axum was now isolated from its own trade network—by distance from Europe and by religion from many former trading partners. Civil war and economic decline combined to weaken Axum, and the kingdom slowly declined.

Ethiopia, a Christian Outpost Though Axum's political and economic power faded, its cultural and religious influence did not vanish. This legacy survived among the peoples of the interior uplands, in what today is Ethiopia. Protected by rugged mountains, descendants of the Axumites were able to maintain their independence for centuries. Their success was due in part to the unifying power of their Coptic Christian faith, which gave them a unique sense of identity and helped establish a culture distinct from that of neighboring peoples.

During the reign of King Lalibela in the early 1200s, Christian monks built a number of remarkable churches. They were carved into the solid rock of the mountains. According to Ethiopian chronicles, the builders had divine help:

> "Angels joined the workers, the quarry men, the stone cutters, and the laborers. The angels worked with them by day and by themselves at night. The men . . . doubted whether the angels were doing this work because they could not see them, but Lalibela knew, because the angels, who understood his virtue, did not hide from him."
>
> —The Ethiopian Royal Chronicles

Despite their isolation, Ethiopian Christians kept ties with the Holy Land. Some made pilgrimages to Jerusalem. Ethiopians also were in touch with Christian communities in Egypt. Still, Ethiopians saw their country as a Christian outpost. Over time, Ethiopian Christians absorbed many local customs. They adapted traditional East African drum music and dances that are still used in church services today.

The kings of Ethiopia claimed descent from the Israelite king Solomon and the queen of Sheba. This belief was recorded in an ancient Ethiopian book called *The Glory of Kings* and reinforced by observing Jewish holidays and dietary laws. One group of Ethiopians practiced Judaism rather than Christianity. These Ethiopian Jews, known as the Falasha, survived in the mountains of Ethiopia until recent years, when they were evacuated to Israel during a famine.

East African City-States

While Axum declined, a string of commercial cities—including Kilwa, Mogadishu, Mombasa, and Sofala—gradually rose along the East African coast. Since ancient times, Phoenician, Greek, Roman, and Indian traders had visited this coast. Under the protection of local African rulers, Arab and

Primary Source

Trade in Mogadishu
In 1331, the North African scholar Ibn Battuta visited East Africa. His account of his travels provides the only eyewitness description of Mogadishu during this period:

"Among the customs of the people of this town is the following: when a ship comes into port, it is boarded from . . . little boats. Each [boat] carries a crowd of young men, each carrying a covered dish, containing food. Each one of them presents his dish to a merchant on board, and calls out, 'This man is my guest.' . . . Not one of the merchants disembarks except to go to the house of his host. . . .

When a merchant has settled in his host's house, the latter sells for him what he has brought and makes his purchases for him. Buying anything from a merchant below its market price or selling him anything except in his host's presence is disapproved of by the people of Mogadishu."

—*Les Voyages d'Ibn Batoutah*

Skills Assessment

Primary Source How did the people of Mogadishu control trade?

Persian merchants set up Muslim communities beginning in the A.D. 600s. Later, Bantu-speaking peoples migrated into the region and adopted Islam. Port cities, as well as offshore islands like Lamu and Zanzibar, were ideally located for trade with Asia. As a result, Asian traders and immigrants from as far away as Indonesia soon added to the rich cultural mix.

Growth of Trade Early mariners detected the annual monsoon winds, which could carry sailing vessels northeast to India in summer and back to Africa in winter. On the East African coast, many rulers saw the advantages of encouraging trade. Ivory, leopard skins, iron, copper, pearls, and gold came from the interior of Africa as well as from the coastal regions. From India, Southeast Asia, and China came cotton cloth, silk, spices, porcelain, china, glassware, and swords. A thriving slave trade also developed. Vessels from Arabia, Persia, and even China might be docked near African cities.

Trade helped local rulers build strong city-states. A Muslim visitor described Kilwa as "one of the most beautiful and well-constructed towns in the world." Its royal palace stands on cliffs that today overlook the modern city. The complex of courtyards and large rooms runs for two acres. Built of coral and cut stone, the structure is evidence of the city's splendor.

African Kingdoms and Trading States, 1000 B.C. – A.D. 1600

Mercator Projection

| Egypt, 712 B.C.–525 B.C. |
| Nubia, 1000 B.C.–A.D.150 |
| Axum, 900 B.C.–A.D. 600 |
| Ghana, A.D. 800–A.D.1000 |
| Mali, A.D.1200–A.D.1450 |
| Ethiopia, A.D.1270–A.D.1550 |
| Songhai, A.D.1450–A.D.1600 |
| Major trade routes |

A Blend of Cultures International trade created a rich and varied mix of cultures in the East African city-states. Bantu-speaking Africans, Arabs, and other Middle Easterners mingled in the streets with people from Southeast Asia, India, and China. With the spread of Islam, Middle Eastern influences grew stronger. Marriages between African women and non-African Muslim men furthered the spread of Muslim culture. An African wife's traditional property rights allowed her husband to settle and own land, creating opportunities for these non-African men. Their children often gained positions of leadership.

Both private houses and palaces show strong Arab and Middle Eastern influences in the East African cities. Additionally, the blend of cultures gave rise to a new language. Known as Swahili, it fused many Arabic words onto a Bantu base and was written in Arabic script.

Great Zimbabwe

To the south and inland from the coastal city-states, massive stone ruins sprawl across rocky hilltops near the great bend in the Limpopo River. The looming walls, great palace, and cone-shaped towers testify that these structures were part of the powerful and prosperous capital of a great inland empire. Today, these impressive ruins are known as Great Zimbabwe, which means "great stone buildings."

Europeans who came upon these ruins in the 1800s thought they were the work of the ancient Phoenicians. In fact, the builders were a succession of Bantu-speaking peoples who settled in the region between 900 and 1500. The newcomers brought improved farming skills, iron, and mining methods. On the relatively fertile land, they produced enough food to support a growing population.

Skills Assessment

Geography From 1000 B.C. in Nubia to the A.D. 1400s and 1500s in Songhai, Africans built strong trading kingdoms in East Africa and West Africa. Many of the kingdoms developed because of profitable trade with other lands.

1. **Location** On the map, locate (a) Indian Ocean, (b) Nile River, (c) Axum, (d) Ghana, (e) Malindi.
2. **Region** (a) What was the major hub of West Africa? (b) Which cities were most likely to trade directly with India?
3. **Critical Thinking Drawing Conclusions** Explain why West and East Africa saw a series of kingdoms develop within the same general areas, rather than in different places.

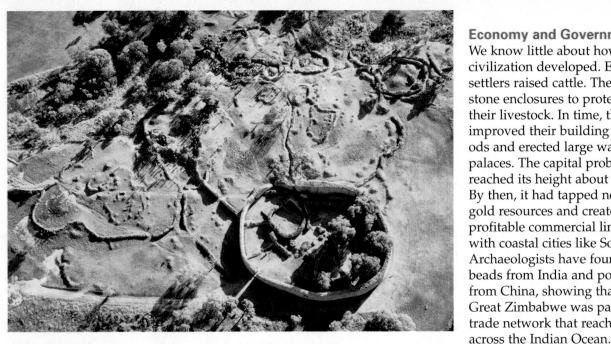

Economy and Government

We know little about how this civilization developed. Early settlers raised cattle. They built stone enclosures to protect their livestock. In time, they improved their building methods and erected large walls and palaces. The capital probably reached its height about 1300. By then, it had tapped nearby gold resources and created profitable commercial links with coastal cities like Sofala. Archaeologists have found beads from India and porcelain from China, showing that Great Zimbabwe was part of a trade network that reached across the Indian Ocean.

Great Zimbabwe

The ruins of Great Zimbabwe suggest a rich and varied society. This aerial view of the stone structures shows the extent of the empire's capital.

Theme: Economics and Technology Which of the structures appears to have been most significant in the capital? Explain your answer.

Besides controlling trade, Zimbabwe was a center for manufacturing. Artisans turned gold and copper into beautiful jewelry and made iron tools for everyday use. Weaving cotton into cloth seems to have been an important craft.

Very little is known about the government in Great Zimbabwe. Some scholars have suggested, however, that the ruler was a god-king who presided over a large court. He may have shared authority with a powerful queen mother as well as nine queens, each of whom had her own court. Below the king, a central bureaucracy may have ruled an inner ring of provinces, while appointed governors had authority in more distant villages.

Decline By 1500, Zimbabwe was in decline. Some scholars suggest that overfarming had exhausted the soil. In addition, civil war and dwindling trade probably contributed to the breakup of Zimbabwe. By then, Portuguese traders were pushing inland to find the source of gold that they were able to buy in cities along the coast. They failed to discover the gold mines, and their intrusion helped undermine later small states that formed in the region.

SECTION 3 Assessment

Recall

1. **Identify:** (a) queen of Sheba, (b) Ezana, (c) Geez, (d) Lalibela, (e) Falasha, (f) Swahili, (g) Great Zimbabwe.

Comprehension

2. What religious traditions came together in Ethiopia?

3. (a) Why did Axum become a key trading center for three continents? (b) How did trade encourage a blending of cultures in East African city-states such as Kilwa, Mombasa, and Mogadishu?

4. (a) What evidence suggests that Great Zimbabwe was a center of trade? (b) What do historians think were the reasons that Great Zimbabwe declined?

Critical Thinking and Writing

5. **Analyzing Information** Why did Ethiopia become increasingly isolated from its neighbors over the centuries?

6. **Making Inferences** Why might the language of Swahili have emerged in the East African city-states?

Activity

Take It to the NET

Research African beadmaking between 10,000 B.C. and A.D. 1200. Write a paragraph about the impact of shell, stone, clay, metal, and glass beads on Africa's trade networks and cultures.

Reading Focus

- How did the interaction of people and the environment lead to diverse societies?

- How did government, family, and religion hold African societies together?

- How did artistic and literary traditions reflect the values of African societies?

Vocabulary

slash-and-burn agriculture

nuclear family

patrilineal

matrilineal

lineage

griot

Taking Notes

As you read, prepare an outline of this section. Use Roman numerals to indicate the major headings of the section, capital letters for the subheadings, and numbers for the supporting details. The sample at right has been started for you.

I. People and the environment
A. Hunting and food gathering
   1. Lived in Africa's fringe areas
   2.
B. Herding and fishing

Main Idea   The process of adapting to the land contributed to the development of many different cultures in Africa.

Setting the Scene
At harvest time, the Kikuyu (kee KOO yoo) people of East Africa offered prayers of thanksgiving to their traditional gods. A modern writer recorded one ancient prayer:

> "Mwene-Nyaga, you who have brought us rain and have given us good harvest, let people eat grain of this harvest calmly and peacefully. . . . Guard us against illness of people or our herds and flocks so that we may enjoy this season's harvest in tranquility."
>
> —Jomo Kenyatta, *Facing Mount Kenya*

In West African mosques, Muslims recited a different prayer: "Praise be to God, Lord of the Universe, the Compassionate, the Merciful."

Differing religious traditions contributed to the diversity of the vast continent of Africa. At the same time, religious beliefs formed deep bonds that united individual societies.

People and the Environment

Over thousands of years, Bantu-speaking peoples migrated across Africa. With them, they carried farming skills and knowledge of ironworking to its many regions. Wherever these people settled, they adapted to local environments and absorbed ideas from the peoples they encountered. Trade or other contacts brought additional changes. As a result, the ways of life of African societies varied greatly from place to place.

Hunting and Food Gathering   Bantu migrations pushed many hunting and food-gathering peoples of Africa to fringe areas. The Khoisan people, for example, adapted to the harsh conditions of the Kalahari Desert by gathering roots and herbs and hunting small game.

Because food was scarce, hunting-gathering people lived in small bands numbering only about 20 or 30. Their knowledge of the natural world, however, was unmatched by city dwellers or farming villagers. They could track animals across long distances and identify the food and healing properties of many different plants.

Herding and Fishing   In parts of the savanna free from the tsetse fly, some peoples raised herds of cattle. Because grazing areas were limited, these societies were often nomadic. To protect their herds against raiders, these peoples perfected skills in warfare.

Along the coasts and rivers, fish was the basic food for some people. Most fishing peoples used nets. They traded any surplus fish for grain, animal skins, and other products made by people who lived inland. Some fishing areas had enough food resources to support large populations.

Settled Farming Societies Farming communities raised a variety of crops from grains to root crops like yams or tree crops like bananas. Most farming peoples practiced a method that is today called slash-and-burn agriculture. They cleared forest and brush land with iron axes and hoes, then burned the remains, using the ash for fertilizer. Because the land lost its fertility within a few years, villagers would move on to clear other land. Eventually, after giving the soil time to renew its fertility, they might return to the abandoned fields.

Forms of Village Government

Farming peoples generally lived in tightknit communities and helped one another in tasks such as clearing the land, planting, and harvesting. Both men and women planted, but they usually were responsible for different crops. Political patterns varied, depending in part on the size of the communities. However, village governments often had similar features.

Sharing Power In these pre-urban societies, power was usually shared among a number of people rather than centralized in the hands of a single leader. In some villages, a chief had a good deal of authority, but in many others, elders made the major decisions. In some places, especially in parts of West Africa, women took the dominant role in the marketplace or acted as official peacemakers in the village.

Villages often made decisions by a process known as consensus. In open discussions, people whose opinions were valued voiced their views before

African Masks
Many societies in Africa used masks in political, religious, and social rituals. Carved masks might be elaborately decorated with paint or items such as shells to show the authority of the wearer or to represent a particular spiritual force.

Theme: Art and Literature
What kinds of artistic skills would be needed to create these masks?

a general agreement was reached. The opinions of older women and men usually held the greatest weight.

Villages within a large kingdom like that of Songhai had to obey decisions made at a distant court. These villagers had to pay taxes and provide soldiers to the central government.

The Kingdom of Kongo The kingdom of Kongo, which flourished about 1500 in central Africa, illustrates one of the many forms of government organization in Africa. It consisted of many villages grouped into districts and provinces and governed by officials appointed by the king. Each village had its own chief, a man chosen on the basis of the descent of his mother's family.

The king of Kongo might seem to have absolute power, but actually that power was limited. The king was chosen by a board of electors and had to govern according to traditional laws. Unlike rulers of West African states, who maintained strong standing armies, kings of Kongo could only call upon men to fight in times of need. Through local governors, the king collected taxes either in goods or in cowrie shells, a common African currency.

Family Patterns

In Africa, as elsewhere, the family was the basic unit of society. Patterns of family life varied greatly. In hunting-and-gathering societies, for example, the nuclear family was typical, with parents and children living and working together as a unit. In other African communities, people lived in joint families. Several generations shared the same complex of houses.

Lines of Descent Family organization varied in other ways. Some families were patrilineal. In these families, important kinship ties and inheritance were passed through the father's side. Other families were matrilineal, with inheritance traced through the mother's side. In a patrilineal culture, a bride would move to her husband's village to become part of his family. In a matrilineal culture, the husband joined his wife's family.

Matrilineal cultures also forged strong ties between brothers and sisters. Brothers were expected to protect their sisters, and sisters made their sons available to help their brothers whenever needed.

Wider Ties Each family belonged to a lineage, or group of households who claimed a common ancestor. Several lineages formed a clan that traced its descent to an even more remote and often legendary ancestor. Belonging to a particular family, lineage, or clan gave people a sense of community.

An individual's place in society was also determined by a system of age grades. An age grade included all girls or boys born in the same year. Each age grade had particular responsibilities and privileges. In the older age grades, children began to take part in village activities, which created social ties beyond the family.

Religious Beliefs

Across Africa, religious beliefs were varied and complex. Like Hindus or ancient Greeks and Romans, village Africans worshiped many gods and goddesses. They identified the forces of nature with divine spirits and tried to influence those forces through rituals and ceremonies.

Many African peoples believed that a single, unknowable supreme being stood above all the other gods and goddesses. This supreme being was the creator and ruler of the universe and was helped by the lesser spirits, who were closer to the people. Like the Chinese, many African peoples believed that the spirits of their ancestors could help, warn, or punish their descendants on Earth. Just as Christians in medieval Europe called on the saints, people in Africa turned to the spirits of their departed ancestors.

The Griots of Africa

As historians, poets, and musicians, the griots of West Africa have captivated their audiences for centuries. They are greatly respected for their knowledge, wisdom, and honesty. Becoming a griot takes years of training. Here is part of a speech by a modern griot from Guinea.

"I am a griot. It is I, Djeli Mamoudou Kouyate, son of Bintou Kouyate and Djeli Kedian Kouyate, master in the art of eloquence. Since time immemorial the Kouyates have been in the service of the Keita princes of Mali; we are vessels of speech, we are the repositories which harbor secrets many centuries old. The art of eloquence has no secrets for us; without us the names of kings vanish into oblivion, we are the memory of mankind; by the spoken word we bring to life the deeds and exploits of kings for younger generations.

I derive my knowledge from my father, Djeli Kedian, who also got it from his father; history holds no mystery for us. . . .

I know the list of all the sovereigns who succeeded to the throne of Mali. I know how the black people divided into tribes, for my father bequeathed to me all his learning; I know why such and such is called Kamara, another Keita, and yet another Sibibe or Traore; every name has a meaning, a secret import.

I teach kings the history of their ancestors so that the lives of the ancients might serve them as an example, for the world is old, but the future springs from the past.

My word is pure and free of all untruth; it is the word of my father; it is the word of my father's father. I will give you my father's words just as I received them; royal griots do not know what lying is. When a quarrel breaks out between tribes it is we who settle the difference, for we are the depositories of oaths which the ancestors swore.

Listen to my word, you who want to know . . . . To acquire my knowledge I have journeyed all round Mali. . . . Everywhere I was able to see and understand what my masters were teaching me, but between their hands I took an oath to teach only what is to be taught and to conceal what is to be kept concealed."

—Djeli Mamoudou Kouyate, *Through African Eyes* (Clark)

From Generation to Generation History—and the lessons to be learned from it—becomes lively stories in the mouth of the griot. Here, children listen to the stories of their people.

Skills Assessment

1. From whom did Kouyate learn to be a griot?
   A the ruler of Mali
   B his mother
   C his father
   D his grandfather

2. Kamara, Keita, Sibibe, and Traore are
   E griots.
   F Kouyate's ancestors.
   G tribes of Mali.
   H rulers of Mali.

3. **Critical Thinking** **Analyzing Information** **(a)** According to Kouyate, for what two special tasks besides relating history are griots responsible? What purposes do these tasks serve? Why might griots be especially well equipped to handle these tasks? **(b)** Does Kouyate relate everything he knows to everyone who hears him? How do you know? What might be the reason for this?

Skills Tip

In an excerpt, dots indicate where something has been left out. Three spaced dots (. . .) usually indicate that part of a sentence has been omitted. A period followed by three spaced dots (. . . .) usually indicates the omission of the last part of a sentence.

Christianity and Islam, as you have seen, influenced peoples in some parts of Africa. Converts often associated the God of Christians and Muslims with their traditional supreme being. In this way, Christianity and Islam absorbed many local practices and beliefs.

Artistic and Literary Traditions

In art and architecture, African traditions extend far back in time to the ancient rock paintings of the Sahara. The pyramids of Egypt and Nubia, the rock churches of Ethiopia, and the palace of Great Zimbabwe bear lasting witness to the creative power of these early civilizations. Sadly, many wooden buildings and works of art have not survived.

Arts   African artists created works in ivory, wood, and bronze. Sometimes, their work was decorative. Artisans wove and dyed cloth, inscribed jugs and bowls, and shaped bracelets and neck ornaments simply for beauty. Much art, though, served social and religious purposes.

Art strengthened bonds within the community and linked both the makers and the users of the work. Patterns used to decorate textiles, baskets, swords, and other objects had important meanings. Often, they identified an object as the work of a particular clan or the possession of royalty.

In Africa, as elsewhere, much art was closely tied to religion. Statues and other objects were used in religious ceremonies. In many rituals, leaders wore impressively carved wooden masks decorated with cowrie shells or grass. Once the mask was in place, both the wearer and the viewers could feel the presence of the spiritual force it represented.

Literature   African societies preserved their histories and values through both oral and written literature. Ancient Egypt, Nubia, and Axum left written records of their past. Later, Arabic provided a common written language in parts of Africa influenced by Islam. African Muslim scholars gathered in cities like Timbuktu and Kilwa as well as in North African cities. Documents in Arabic offer invaluable evidence about law, religion, and history.

Oral traditions date back many centuries. In West Africa, griots (GREE ohs), or professional poets, recited ancient stories. They preserved both histories and traditional folk tales in the same way that the epics of Homer or Aryan India were passed orally from generation to generation.

Histories praised the heroic deeds of famous ancestors or kings. Folk tales, which blended fanciful stories with humor and sophisticated word play, taught important moral lessons. Oral literature, like religion and art, thus encouraged a sense of community and common values.

Connections to Today

Kente Cloth

Centuries ago, the Asante people of Ghana developed a colorful, intricately designed cloth called kente. Once the apparel of Asante royalty, today kente designs represent the philosophy, moral values, and code of conduct in Ghanaian culture. Some designs symbolize good omens and spiritual rebirth, while others may represent family unity, cooperation, or sharing.

In recent years, many Americans have begun wearing kente cloth as a celebration of their African heritage. Traditionally the garb of joyous occasions, imported kente is used in a wide variety of items, from shirts to neckties to backpacks.

Theme: Religions and Value Systems **Why might the people in this picture have chosen to wear kente cloth?**

SECTION 4 Assessment

Recall
1. **Identify:** **(a)** Khoisan people, **(b)** Kongo.
2. **Define:** **(a)** slash-and-burn agriculture, **(b)** nuclear family, **(c)** patrilineal, **(d)** matrilineal, **(e)** lineage, **(f)** griot.

Comprehension
3. List three examples of how the environment influenced African societies.
4. What types of institutions and traditions held African societies together?

5. How was art connected to religion in African cultures?

Critical Thinking and Writing
6. **Analyzing Information** How might a matrilineal line of descent allow women to exercise greater authority in village affairs?
7. **Predicting Consequences** **(a)** Describe the process of slash-and-burn agriculture. **(b)** What might be some dangers of the extensive use of slash-and-burn agriculture?

Activity

Retelling a Tale
Find an African folk tale and read it. Then, retell it without using the book. Based on this experience, write two or three sentences describing the challenges that a griot faces.

Creating a Chapter Summary

Copy this chart on a sheet of paper. For each kingdom listed, fill in the row by naming the kingdom's characteristics. To help you get started, one row has been filled in.

KINGDOM	ERA	RULER	RELIGION	ECONOMIC BASE
NUBIA				
AXUM				
GHANA				
MALI				
HAUSA				
BENIN	1300s	Oba, queen mother, and council	Unknown	Farming, pepper, ivory
GREAT ZIMBABWE				
SONGHAI				

CD-ROM Review For additional review of the major concepts of Chapter 12, see the *Guide to the Essentials of World History* or the *Interactive Student Tutorial CD-ROM.*

Web Site Self-Test For practice test questions for Chapter 12, see **www.phschool.com.**

Building Vocabulary

Write sentences using the vocabulary words listed below, leaving blanks for the vocabulary words. Exchange your sentences with another student, and complete each other's sentences.

1. savanna
2. desertification
3. outpost
4. commodity
5. oba
6. nuclear family
7. patrilineal
8. matrilineal
9. lineage
10. griot

Recalling Key Facts

11. How do ancient rock paintings help scholars determine that the Sahara was a well-watered zone during the Neolithic age?
12. Into what present-day countries did the empire of Carthage extend?
13. How did the Hausa come to dominate Saharan trade routes under Amina's rule?
14. Why did Ethiopia's roots embrace both Jewish and Christian traditions?
15. How did the Khoisan people adapt to their environment?

Critical Thinking and Writing

16. **Drawing Conclusions** From what you have learned about African religions, why do you think many Africans found it easy to accept the monotheism of Christianity or Islam?
17. **Linking Past and Present** **(a)** Describe three traditions that created social bonds in African communities. **(b)** How are these traditions similar to the traditions that create bonds in your community? How are they different?
18. **Analyzing Information** Reread Setting the Scene, including the selection from *The Glory of Kings* in Section 3. **(a)** What reason does Makeda give for going to Jerusalem? **(b)** According to Solomon, what is the great lesson he has taught Makeda? **(c)** Would you consider *The Glory of Kings* a reliable source of historical information? Explain.
19. **Connecting to Geography** Look at the maps in this chapter. **(a)** Into which areas did Bantu-speaking peoples migrate? **(b)** Why might certain climate zones act as barriers?

In the 1000s, the Spanish Arab geographer al-Bakri wrote an encyclopedia of the entire world he knew about. Here, he describes the ceremonies when the king of ancient Ghana held court. Read the passage and answer the questions that follow.

> "The king adorns himself . . . with necklaces and bracelets, and when he sits before the people he puts on a high cap decorated with gold and wrapped in turbans of fine cotton. The court of appeal is held in a domed pavilion around which stand ten horses with gold embroidered trappings. Behind the king stand ten pages holding shields and swords decorated with gold, and on his right are the sons of the secondary kings of his country, all wearing splendid garments and with their hair mixed with gold. On the ground around him are seated his ministers, whilst the governor of the city sits before him. . . . The royal audience is announced by the beating of a drum which they call 'deba' made out of a long piece of hollowed-out wood. When the people have gathered, those who profess the same religion as the king draw near upon their knees, sprinkling dust upon their heads as a sign of respect, whilst the Muslims clap hands as their form of greeting."

—al-Bakri, *Book of Roads and Kingdoms*

20. How does this passage reflect the image of Ghana as a "land of gold"?

21. What details show the importance of the king's audience?

22. How does al-Bakri's description illustrate the people's view of their king as a semidivine figure?

23. How do the Muslims at court differ from the followers of the king's own religion?

24. Would you consider this a reliable source of information about the ancient kingdom of Ghana? Why or why not?

Skills Tip

Secondary sources are accounts by people who did not directly witness the events they are describing. In reading a secondary source, be aware of what sources of information the writer used.

The sculpted panel above depicts a family at work in an African agricultural village. Look at the panel and answer the following questions:

25. What economic and social activities are depicted in this sculpture?

26. How does the sculpture depict a nuclear family?

27. How does the picture reflect the importance of family in African societies?

28. What seems to be the principal source of food for this family?

29. What does this picture suggest about the family's living conditions?

Skills Assessment
Take It to the NET

Use the Internet to research the history of Swahili and the countries in which it is commonly spoken today. Then, create a simple map that indicates concentrations of Swahili-speaking peoples. Compare your map to the Bantu Migrations map in this chapter. Using both maps, prepare a brief oral report that explains the development of the Swahili language.

Two Golden Ages of China

Reading Focus

- How did Tang and Song rulers ensure Chinese unity and prosperity?
- How did Chinese society reflect Confucian traditions?
- What were the literary and artistic achievements of Tang and Song China?

Vocabulary

usurp
tributary state
land reform
gentry
pagoda

Taking Notes

On a sheet of paper, copy this Venn diagram. As you read, add information about the Tang and Song. Include information that applies to both dynasties in the intersecting parts of the circles. Part of the diagram has been filled out to help you get started.

TANG
- Conquered Vietnam, Tibet, Korea

Well-ordered society

SONG
- Ruled less territory

Main Idea The Tang and Song dynasties restored culture and prosperity to China.

Setting the Scene

Many people in China had reason to distrust Empress Wu Zhao (woo jow). From humble beginnings, she had risen to a position of influence with the emperor. After his death, she had ruthlessly taken power into her own hands, unseating her own sons from the throne. She had even declared herself "Son of Heaven," the age-old title of China's emperors. No other woman had ever dared do such a thing!

Now, rival princes and Confucian scholars were raising the banner of revolt against her. The poet Lo Binwang wrote a declaration condemning the empress as a "vile character" who had usurped, or illegally taken over, the throne. "Rise, rise, all men!" Lo Binwang wrote. "Consider, the orphans of our emperor are left helpless and defenseless while their father's grave is hardly dry!"

When the empress saw the declaration, she demanded to know who wrote it. But, surprisingly, she did not direct her anger at Lo Binwang. Rather, she berated her own ministers for failing to bring such a talented writer into her service! Like other educated Chinese, Wu prized a skilled and brilliant writer, no matter what side he was on.

In the late 600s, Wu Zhao became the only woman to rule China in her own name. Her strong rule helped guide China through one of its most brilliant periods. At a time when Europe was fragmented into many small feudal kingdoms, China remained unified under two powerful dynasties—the Tang and the Song.

The Brilliant Tang

After the Han dynasty collapsed in 220, China remained divided for nearly 400 years. Yet China escaped the decay that disrupted Western Europe after the fall of Rome. Farm production expanded and technology slowly improved. Buddhism spread, while learning and the arts continued. Even Chinese cities survived. Although invaders stormed northern China, they often adopted Chinese civilization rather than demolishing it.

Meanwhile, various dynasties rose and fell in the south. During the brief Sui dynasty (589–618), the emperor Sui Wendi reunited the north and south. But China was not restored to its earlier glory until the emergence of the Tang dynasty in 618.

Building an Empire The first Tang emperor, Li Yuan, was a general under the Sui dynasty. When the Sui began to crumble, his ambitious 16-year-old son, Li Shimin, urged him to lead a revolt. Father and son crushed all rivals and established the Tang dynasty. Eight years later, Li Shimin compelled his aging father to step down and mounted the throne himself, taking the name Tang Taizong. Brilliant general, government reformer, historian, and master of the calligraphy brush, Tang Taizong would become China's most admired emperor.

Later Tang rulers carried empire building to new heights, conquering territories deep into Central Asia. Chinese armies forced the neighboring lands of Vietnam, Tibet, and Korea to become **tributary states.** That is, while these states remained independent, their rulers had to acknowledge Chinese supremacy and send regular tribute to the Tang emperor. At the same time, students from Korea and Japan traveled to the Tang capital to learn about Chinese government, law, and arts.

Government and the Economy Tang rulers, such as Empress Wu Zhao, helped restore the Han system of uniform government throughout China. They rebuilt the bureaucracy and enlarged the civil service system to recruit talented officials trained in Confucian philosophy. They also set up schools to prepare male students for the exams and developed a flexible new law code.

Tang emperors instituted a system of **land reform.** That is, they broke up large agricultural holdings and redistributed the land to peasants. This policy strengthened the central government by weakening the power of large landowners. It also increased government revenues, since the peasants who farmed their own land would be able to pay taxes.

Under the Tang, a system of canals encouraged internal trade and transportation. The Grand Canal linked the Huang He to the Yangzi River. As a result, food grown in the south could be shipped to the capital in the north. At the time, the Grand Canal was the longest waterway ever dug by human labor.

Decline Like earlier dynasties, the Tang eventually weakened. Later Tang emperors lost territories in Central Asia to the Arabs. Corruption, high taxes, drought, famine, and rebellions all contributed to the downward swing of the dynastic cycle. In 907, a rebel general overthrew the last Tang emperor. This time, however, the chaos following the collapse of a dynasty did not last long.

Prosperity Under the Song

In 960, a scholarly general reunited much of China and founded the Song dynasty. The Song ruled 319 years, slightly longer than the Tang; however, the Song controlled less territory than the Tang. In addition, the Song faced the constant threat of invaders in the north. In the early 1100s, the battered Song retreated south of the Huang He. There, the Southern Song continued to rule for another 150 years.

Despite military setbacks, the Song period was a golden age. Chinese wealth and culture dominated East Asia even when its armies did not. Under the Song, the

Technology of Tang and Song China

Mechanical clock, 700s

The Chinese learned of water-powered clocks from Middle Easterners. Mechanical clocks used a complex series of wheels, shafts, and pins, turning at a steady rate, to tell exact time.

Gunpowder, 850

The earliest form of gunpowder was made from a mixture of saltpeter, sulfur, and charcoal, all found in abundance in China. It was first used in fireworks and later in weapons.

Block printing, 700s
Movable type, 1040s

Both printing processes were based on earlier techniques, such as seals (first used in the Middle East). In block printing, a full page of characters was carved onto a wooden block. Movable type was made up of pre-cut characters that were combined to form a page.

Connections to Today

In addition to the advances shown here, the Chinese developed a smallpox vaccine, invented a spinning wheel, and pioneered the use of arches in bridge building. In time, many of these developments traveled westward. Modernized versions of most of these inventions are still widely used today.

Skills Assessment **Chart Explain how one of the inventions shown here could have aided the spread of Chinese civilization to other lands.**

Chinese economy expanded. The center of farming shifted from the wheat fields of the north to the rice paddies of the Yangzi in the south. New strains of rice and improved irrigation methods helped peasants produce two rice crops a year. The rise in productivity created surpluses, allowing more people to pursue commerce, learning, or the arts.

Under both the Tang and Song, foreign trade flourished. Merchants arrived from India, Persia, and Arabia. Chinese merchants carried goods to Southeast Asia in exchange for spices and special woods. Song porcelain has been found as far away as East Africa. To improve trade, the government issued paper money. China's cities, which had been mainly centers of government, now prospered as centers of trade.

Chinese Society

Under the Tang and Song, China was a well-ordered society. At its head was the emperor, whose court was filled with aristocratic families. The court supervised a huge bureaucracy, from which officials fanned out to every part of China. Aside from the court, China's two main social classes were the gentry and the peasantry.

Gentry Most scholar-officials at court came from the gentry, or wealthy landowning class. They alone could afford to spend years studying the Confucian classics in order to pass the grueling civil service exam. When not in government service, the gentry often served in the provinces as allies of the emperor's officials.

The Song scholar-gentry valued learning more than physical labor. They supported a revival of Confucian thought. New schools of Confucian philosophers emphasized social order based on duty, rank, and proper behavior. Although corruption and greed existed among civil servants, the ideal Confucian official was a wise, virtuous scholar who knew how to ensure harmony in society.

Peasants Most Chinese were peasants who worked the land, living on what they produced. Drought and famine were a constant threat, but new tools and crops did improve the lives of many peasants. To add to their income, some families produced handicrafts such as baskets or embroidery. They carried these products to nearby market towns to sell or trade for salt, tea, or iron tools.

Peasants lived in small, largely self-sufficient villages that managed their own affairs. "Heaven is high," noted one Chinese saying, "and the emperor far away." Peasants relied on one another rather than the government. When disputes arose, a village leader and council of elders put pressure on the parties to resolve the problem. Only if such efforts failed did villagers take their disputes to the emperor's county representative.

In China, even peasants could move up in society through education and government service. If a bright peasant boy received an education and passed the civil service examinations, both he and his family rose in status.

Merchants In market towns and cities, some merchants acquired vast wealth. Still, according to Confucian tradition, merchants had an even lower social status than peasants because their riches came from the labor of others. An ambitious merchant therefore might buy land and educate at least one son to enter the ranks of the scholar-gentry.

The Confucian attitude toward merchants affected economic policy. Some rulers favored commerce but sought to control it. They often restricted where foreign merchants could live and even limited the activities of private traders. Still, Chinese trade flourished during Song times.

Status of Women Women had higher status in Tang and early Song times than they did later. Within the home, women were called upon to

The Real Reason Sunglasses Were Invented

Add "sunglasses" to the long list of Chinese inventions. But unlike modern sunglasses, they were not invented to shade people's eyes from the sun. Instead, they had a role to play in the efficient Chinese bureaucracy.

The Chinese made the lenses for their glasses from clear quartz. The lenses were tinted, or darkened, by exposing them to smoke. The lenses were so dark that they kept others from seeing the wearer's eyes. And that is exactly what the Chinese wanted.

The darkened glasses were worn only by judges in Chinese courts to prevent people from reading their eye expressions. If people arguing a case could read the judge's reaction in his eyes, they might alter their statements to sway him.

Theme: Religion and Value Systems Based on this information, what can you conclude about the role of Chinese judges?

Advice for Families in China

During the Tang and Song dynasties, women sometimes enjoyed higher status than they did later. The following excerpt is from a collection of essays offering practical advice to families. A scholar, Yüan Tsai, wrote it in the 1100s, during the Song dynasty. Here, he discusses how to treat daughters and how women want to help family members.

A Tang Woman
This ceramic figurine of a woman kneeling at the imperial court, holding a bamboo flute, dates from the Tang dynasty.

"Without going overboard, people should marry their daughters with dowries appropriate to their family's wealth. Rich families should not consider their daughters outsiders but should give them a share of the property. Sometimes people have incapable sons and so have to entrust their affairs to their daughters' families; even after their deaths, their burials and sacrifices are performed by their daughters. So how can people say that daughters are not as good as sons?

Generally speaking, a woman's heart is very sympathetic. If her parents' family is wealthy and her husband's family is poor, she wants to take her parents' wealth to help her husband's family prosper. If her husband's family is wealthy but her parents' family is poor, then she wants to take from her husband's family to enable her parents to prosper. Her parents and husband should be sympathetic toward her feelings and indulge some of her wishes. When her own sons and daughters are grown and married, if either her son's family or her daughter's family is wealthy while the other is poor, she wishes to take from the wealthy one to give to the poor one. Her sons and daughters should understand her feelings and be somewhat indulgent. But taking from the poor to make the rich richer is unacceptable, and no one should ever go along with it."

—Yüan Tsai, quoted in *Chinese Civilization and Society* (Ebery)

Skills Assessment

1. Yüan would agree that
   A daughters should be allowed to choose their own husbands.
   B sons take better care of their families than daughters.
   C daughters are as good as sons.
   D dowries are not necessary.

2. Yüan suggests that
   E a married daughter should be allowed to help her poor relatives.
   F poor relatives should go to work for rich ones.
   G daughters should have nothing to do with their parents after they are married.
   H sons and daughters should make their own way in the world.

3. **Critical Thinking Making Inferences** What responsibility does Yüan imply that family members have toward one another? Explain.

Skills Tip

As you read a historical document, look for statements that the author assumes everyone in the audience will accept without question. Such assumptions can help you understand the accepted beliefs and values of the author's culture.

**Council of Cultural Affairs
Taipei, Republic of China**

To see other Chinese paintings, use the Internet address above to link to the Council of Cultural Affairs.

Song Landscape Painting
Landscapes painted during the Song dynasty stressed the harmony of nature. In *Travelers Among Mountains and Streams,* painter Fan Kuan balances a towering mountain against the rushing stream below. In the lower right, a tiny line of travelers on horseback emerges from the woods.

Theme: Arts and Literature Why do you think the painter made the human figures so small?

run family affairs. Wives and mothers-in-law had great authority, managing servants and family finances. Still, families valued boys more highly than girls. When a young woman married, she completely became a part of her husband's family. She could not keep her dowry and could never remarry.

Women's subordinate position was reinforced in late Song times when the custom of footbinding emerged. The custom probably began at the imperial court but later spread to the lower classes. The feet of young girls were bound with long strips of cloth, producing a lily-shaped foot about half the size of a foot that was allowed to grow normally. Tiny feet and a stilted walk became a symbol of nobility and beauty.

Footbinding was extremely painful. Yet the custom survived and in time spread to lower classes. Even peasant parents feared that they could not find a husband for a daughter with large feet.

Not all girls in China had their feet bound. Peasants who needed their daughters to work in the fields did not accept the practice. Yet most women did have to submit to footbinding. Women with bound feet often could not walk without help. Thus, footbinding reinforced the Confucian tradition that women should remain inside the home.

Arts and Literature of the Tang and Song

A prosperous economy supported the rich culture of Tang and Song China. The splendid palaces of the emperors were long ago destroyed, but many paintings, statues, temples, and ceramics have survived.

Landscape Painting Along with poetry, painting and calligraphy were essential skills for the scholar-gentry. In both of these crafts, artists sought balance and harmony through the mastery of simple strokes and lines. The Song period saw the triumph of Chinese landscape painting. Steeped in the Daoist tradition, painters sought to capture the spiritual essence of the natural world. "When you are planning to paint," instructed a Song artist, "you must always create a harmonious relationship between heaven and earth."

Misty mountains and delicate bamboo forests dominated Chinese land-scapes. Yet Chinese painters also produced realistic, vivid portraits of emperors or lively scenes of city life.

Other Arts Buddhist themes dominated sculpture and influenced Chinese architecture. The Indian stupa evolved into the graceful Chinese pagoda, a multistoried temple with eaves that curve up at the corners. Chinese sculptors created striking statues of the Buddha. These statues created such a strong impression that, today, many people picture the Buddha as a Chinese god rather than an Indian holy man.

The Chinese perfected skills in making porcelain, a shiny, hard pottery that was prized as the finest in the world. They developed beautiful glazes to decorate vases, tea services, and other objects that westerners would later call "chinaware." Artists also produced porcelain figures of neighing camels, elegant court ladies playing polo, and bearded foreigners fresh from their travels on the Silk Road.

A Flood of Literature Prose and poetry flowed from the brushes of Tang and Song writers. Scholars produced works on philosophy, religion, and history. Short stories that often blended fantasy, romance, and adventure made their first appearance in Chinese literature.

Still, among the gentry, poetry was the most respected form of Chinese literature. Confucian scholars were expected to master the skills of poetry. We know the names of some 200 major and 400 minor Tang and Song poets. Their works touched on Buddhist and Daoist themes as well as on social issues. Many poems reflected on the shortness of life and the immensity of the universe.

Probably the greatest Tang poet was Li Bo (LEE BOW). A zestful lover of life and freedom, he spent most of his life moving from place to place. He wrote some 2,000 poems celebrating harmony with nature or lamenting the passage of time. A popular legend says that Li Bo drowned when he tried to embrace the reflection of the moon in a lake.

More realistic and less romantic were the poems of Li Bo's friend Du Fu. His verses described the horrors of war or condemned the lavishness of the court. A later poet, Li Qingzhao (LEE CHING jow), described the experience of women left behind when a loved one goes off to war. Her poems reflect a time when invasion threatened to bring the brilliant Song dynasty to an end.

Primary Source

Li Bo: Devoted Father
Separated from his children, Li Bo wrote a poem to them:

"This is the tree I myself put in
  When I left you, nearly three
    years past;
A peach tree, level with the eaves,
And I sailing cannot yet turn
    home!

Pretty daughter, P'ing-yang is
    your name,
Breaking blossom, there beside
    my tree,
Breaking blossom, you cannot
    see me
And your tears flow like the
    running stream;

And little son, Po-ch'in you are
    called,
Your big sister's shoulder you
    must reach
When you come there underneath
    my peach,
Oh, to pat and pet you too, my
    child!"

—Li Bo, "Letter to His Two Small Children"

Skills Assessment

Primary Source How do Li Bo's feelings still relate to our lives?

SECTION 1 Assessment

Recall

1. **Identify: (a)** Sui Wendi, **(b)** Tang Taizong, **(c)** Wu Zhao, **(d)** Grand Canal, **(e)** Li Bo.
2. **Define: (a)** usurp, **(b)** tributary state, **(c)** land reform, **(d)** gentry, **(e)** pagoda.

Comprehension

3. In what ways did the rise of the Tang and Song dynasties benefit China?
4. **(a)** Describe the social structure of China under the Tang and Song dynasties. **(b)** How did the social structure reflect Confucian traditions?

5. **(a)** What ideas and traditions shaped Chinese painting? **(b)** What themes did Chinese poets address?

Critical Thinking and Writing

6. **Connecting to Geography** How might a map of China before the Tang dynasty look different from a map of China afterward? Give two examples.
7. **Applying Information** "Distant water cannot put out a nearby fire." How does this saying reflect the nature of village government under the Tang and Song dynasties?

Activity

Preparing a Museum Guide
Find two illustrations of Chinese porcelain or painting from the Tang or Song periods. (If possible, make copies of them.) Then, for each selection, write an entry that might appear in a guide to a museum exhibit. List the date and artist (if known), and briefly describe what the work shows.

The Mongol and Ming Empires

Reading Focus

- How did the Mongols conquer and rule a huge empire?
- What were the effects of Mongol rule on China?
- How did the Ming restore Chinese rule?
- What policies did the Ming pursue with regard to the outside world?

Taking Notes

On a sheet of paper create a flowchart like this one. Add important events as you read this section. Use the chart to help you focus on key events in the section.

```
┌─────────────────────────┐
│ Mongols advance into    │
│ China; cannons used     │
└─────────────────────────┘
            │
            ▼
┌─────────────────────────┐
│ Kublai Khan topples     │
│ Song emperor            │
└─────────────────────────┘
            │
            ▼
┌─────────────────────────┐
│                         │
└─────────────────────────┘
            │
            ▼
┌─────────────────────────┐
│                         │
└─────────────────────────┘
```

Main Idea Mongol armies conquered China, much of Asia, and part of Europe, but in time, the Ming dynasty regained control in China.

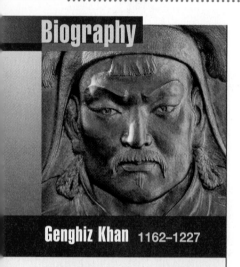

Biography

Genghiz Khan 1162–1227

When Temujin—later known as Genghiz Khan—was a boy, his father was poisoned by a rival Mongol clan. Then, at the age of 15, Temujin was taken prisoner. For the rest of his life, he never forgot the humiliation of being locked in a wooden collar and paraded before his enemies.

Though he regained his freedom, Temujin wandered among drifting clans. He grew up with a reputation for courage and leadership. He took revenge on the clan that had imprisoned him and, in time, became supreme ruler of all the Mongols. Once despised, Genghiz Khan would be admired and feared across two continents.

Theme: Impact of the Individual How might Temujin's experiences have motivated him to unite the Mongol clans?

Setting the Scene

The Mongols were tough, skilled warriors who lived in the saddle. They could travel for days at a time on their shaggy ponies, drinking mare's milk and eating only a few handfuls of grain. They were also considered the most skilled horse riders in the world. An observer described Mongol battle tactics:

> "They keep hovering about the enemy, discharging their arrows first from one side and then from the other. . . . Their horses are so well broken-in to quick changes of movement, that upon the signal given, they instantly turn in any direction, and by these rapid maneuvers many victories have been obtained."
>
> —Marco Polo, *A Description of the World*

About 1200, the Mongols burst out of Central Asia to conquer an empire stretching across Asia and Europe. In the process, they overran Song China and imposed Mongol rule on its people.

Building the Mongol Empire

The Mongols were a nomadic people who grazed their horses and sheep on the steppes of Central Asia. Rival Mongol clans spent much of their time warring with one another. In the early 1200s, however, a brilliant Mongol chieftain united these warring tribes. This chieftain took the name Genghiz Khan, meaning "World Emperor." Under his leadership, Mongol forces triumphantly conquered a vast empire that stretched from the Pacific Ocean to Eastern Europe.

Conquests Genghiz Khan imposed strict military discipline and demanded absolute loyalty. His highly trained, mobile armies had some of the most skilled horsemen in the world. Genghiz Khan had a reputation for fierceness. He could order the massacre of an entire city. Yet he also could be generous, rewarding the bravery of a single fighter.

Mongol armies conquered the Asian steppe lands with some ease, but as they turned on China, they faced the problem of attacking walled cities. Chinese and Turkish military experts taught them to use cannons and other new weapons. The Mongols and Chinese launched missiles against each other from metal tubes filled with gunpowder. This use of cannons in warfare would soon spread westward to Europe.

Genghiz Khan did not live to complete the conquest of China. His heirs, however, continued to expand the Mongol empire. For the next 150 years, they dominated much of Asia. Their furious assaults toppled empires and spread destruction from southern Russia through Muslim lands in the Middle East to China. In China, the Mongols devastated the flourishing province of Sichuan (see CHWAHN) and annihilated its great capital city of Chengdu.

Mongol Rule   Once conquest was completed, the Mongols were not oppressive rulers. Often, they allowed conquered people to live much as they had before—as long as they regularly paid tribute to the Mongols.

Genghiz Khan had set an example for his successors by ruling conquered lands with toleration and justice. Although the Mongol warrior had no use for city life, he respected scholars, artists, and artisans. He listened to the ideas of Confucians, Buddhists, Christians, Muslims, Jews, and Zoroastrians.

The Mongol Peace   In the 1200s and 1300s, the sons and grandsons of Genghiz Khan established peace and order within their domains. Today, many historians refer to this period of order as the *Pax Mongolica,* or Mongol Peace.

Political stability set the stage for economic growth. Under the protection of the Mongols, who now controlled the great Silk Road, trade flourished across Eurasia. According to a contemporary, Mongol rule meant that people "enjoyed such a peace that a man might have journeyed from the land of sunrise to the land of sunset with a golden platter upon his head without suffering the least violence from anyone."

Cultural exchanges increased as foods, tools, inventions, and ideas spread along the protected trade routes. From China, the use of windmills and gunpowder moved westward into Europe. Techniques of papermaking reached the Middle East, and crops and trees from the Middle East were carried into East Asia.

Skills Assessment

Geography   At its height, the Mongol empire was the largest in the world up to that time.

1. **Location**   *On the map, locate (a) Beijing, (b) Hangzhou, (c) Venice, (d) Tibet, (e) Russia.*
2. **Region**   *Describe what happened to the Mongol empire between 1227 and 1294.*
3. **Critical Thinking Linking Past and Present**   *Look at the atlas maps in the Reference Section at the end of this book. What countries would Marco Polo pass through if he made his journey today?*

Mongol Empire

Mongol empire at Genghiz Khan's death, 1227

Mongol empire at its greatest extent, 1294

Boundary of Yuan dynasty of Kublai Khan

Route of Marco Polo, 1271–1295

Robinson Projection

0   500   1000 Miles

0   500   1000 Kilometers

China Under Mongol Rule

Although Genghiz Khan had subdued northern China, the Mongols needed nearly 70 more years to conquer the south. Genghiz Khan's grandson, Kublai (KOO blī), finally toppled the last Song emperor in 1279. From his capital at Cambulac, present-day Beijing, Kublai Khan ruled all of China as well as Korea, Tibet, and Vietnam.

Government Kublai Khan tried to prevent the Mongols from being absorbed into Chinese civilization as other conquerors of China had been. He decreed that only Mongols could serve in the military. He also reserved the highest government jobs for Mongols or for other non-Chinese officials whom he employed. Still, because there were too few Mongols to control so vast an empire, Kublai allowed Chinese officials to continue to rule in the provinces.

Under Mongol rule, an uneasy mix of Chinese and foreign ways developed. Kublai adopted a Chinese name for his dynasty, the Yuan (yoo AHN), and turned Cambulac into a Chinese walled city. At the same time, he had Arab architects design his palace, and many rooms reflected Mongol steppe dwellings.

Kublai Khan was a capable but demanding emperor. He rebuilt and extended the Grand Canal to his new capital, though at a terrible cost in human lives. He also welcomed many foreigners to his court, including the African Muslim world traveler Ibn Battuta.

A Western Visitor The Italian merchant Marco Polo was one of many visitors to China during the Yuan dynasty. In 1271, Polo left Venice with his father and uncle. He crossed Persia and Central Asia to reach China. During his stay in China, he spent 17 years in Kublai's service. He returned to Venice by sea after visiting Southeast Asia and India.

In his writings, Marco Polo left a vivid account of the wealth and splendor of China. He described the royal palace of Kublai Khan, with its walls "covered with gold and silver and decorated with pictures of dragons and birds and horsemen and various breeds of beasts and scenes of battle." Polo also described China's efficient royal mail system, with couriers riding swift ponies along the empire's well-kept roads. Furthermore, he reported that the city of Hangzhou was 10 or 12 times the size of Venice, one of Italy's richest city-states.

As you have read, Marco Polo's book astonished readers in medieval Europe. In the next centuries, Polo's reports sparked European interest in the riches of Asia.

Other Contacts As long as the Mongol empire prospered, contacts between Europe and Asia continued. The Mongols tolerated a variety of beliefs. The pope sent Christian priests to Beijing, while Muslims set up their own communities in China. Meanwhile, some Chinese products moved toward Europe. They included gunpowder, porcelain, and playing cards.

The Ming Restore Chinese Rule

The Yuan dynasty declined after the death of Kublai Khan. Most Chinese despised the foreign Mongol rulers. Confucian scholars retreated into their own world, seeing little to gain from the barbarians. Heavy taxes, corruption, and natural disasters led to frequent uprisings. Finally, Zhu Yuanzhang (DZOO yoo ahn DZUHNG), a peasant leader, forged a rebel army that toppled the Mongols and pushed them back beyond the Great Wall. In 1368, he founded a new Chinese dynasty, which he called the Ming, meaning brilliant.

Ming Porcelain
Ming dynasty artisans created a unique form of blue and white porcelain. Today, collectors have paid over a million dollars for genuine Ming vases like this one.

Theme: Continuity and Change How does this vase build on earlier Chinese achievements?

Voyages of Zheng He

N W E S

PERSIAN EMPIRE

Persian Gulf

ARABIA

Jiddah• •Mecca

Red Sea

Aden•

Ormuz•

1413–1415

1413–1415

Arabian Sea

AFRICA

Mogadishu•

1417–1419

1421–1422

Robinson Projection

0   500   1000 Miles

0   500   1000 Kilometers

20°E   30°E   40°E   50°E   60°E   70°E

Exploration routes

MUGHAL EMPIRE

Calicut•

1413–1415

Bay of Bengal

1413–1415

1405–1407

1413–1415

80°E   90°E

INDIAN OCEAN

•Chittagong

ASIA

MING EMPIRE

Canton•

1405–1407

1417–1419

1413–1415

1409–1411

•Vijaya

South China Sea

Malacca•

1405–1407

EAST INDIES

100°E   110°E   120°E   130°E

1417–1419

PACIFIC OCEAN

30°N

20°N

10°N

Skills Assessment

Geography Between 1405 and 1433, Chinese explorer Zheng He visited many lands bordering the Indian Ocean.

1. **Location** On the map, locate **(a)** East Indies, **(b)** Calicut, **(c)** Malacca, **(d)** Arabia, **(e)** Mogadishu.
2. **Movement** **(a)** Where did Zheng He travel from 1405 to 1407? **(b)** When did he reach the Persian Gulf?
3. **Critical Thinking Synthesizing Information** *Look at the map of African Kingdoms and Trading States in Section 3 of the previous chapter. Besides Mogadishu, what other East African cities might Zheng He have been able to visit?*

Early Ming rulers sought to reassert Chinese greatness after years of foreign rule. The Ming restored the civil service system, and Confucian learning again became the road to success. The civil service exams became more rigorous than ever. A board of censors watched over the bureaucracy, rooting out corruption and disloyalty.

Economic Revival Economically, Ming China was immensely productive. The fertile, well-irrigated plains of eastern China supported a population of more than 100 million. In the Yangzi Valley, peasants produced huge rice crops. Better methods of fertilizing helped to improve farming. In the 1500s, new crops reached China from the Americas, especially corn and sweet potatoes.

Chinese cities were home to many industries, including porcelain, paper, and tools. The Ming repaired the extensive canal system that linked various regions and made trade easier. New technologies increased output in manufacturing. Better methods of printing, for example, led to the production of a flood of books.

Cultural Flowering Ming China also saw a revival of arts and literature. Ming artists developed their own styles of landscape painting and created brilliant blue and white porcelain. Ming vases were among the most valuable and popular Chinese products exported to the West.

Confucian scholars continued to produce classical poetry. At the same time, new forms of popular literature, meant to be enjoyed by the common people, began to emerge. Ming writers composed novels, including *The Water Margin*, about an outlaw gang that tries to end injustice by corrupt officials. Ming writers also produced the world's first detective stories. Performing artists developed a popular tradition of Chinese opera that combined music, dance, and drama.

China and the World

Early Ming rulers proudly sent Chinese fleets into distant waters. The most extraordinary of these overseas ventures were the voyages of the Chinese admiral Zheng He (DZUHNG HEH).

The Voyages of Zheng He In 1405, Zheng He commanded the first of seven expeditions. He departed at the head of a fleet of 62 huge ships and hundreds of smaller ones, carrying a crew of more than 25,000 sailors. The largest ships measured 400 feet long. The goal of each expedition was to promote trade and collect tribute from lesser powers across the "western seas."

Beasts From Across the Sea

Zheng He's voyages from China left a lasting impression on the peoples he visited. But his return to China left an equally power-ful —and totally unexpected— impression on the Chinese.

Wherever Zheng He went, he collected animals to bring back to China. Back in China, they were kept in the imperial zoo.

One of these animals was known to the Chinese as a *qilin*, a legendary beast whose appear-ance was a sign of heaven's favor. People flocked to marvel at this bizarre creature. It stood 15 feet tall, had the body of a deer and the tail of an ox, and was covered with red spots.

Today, we call it the giraffe.

Theme: Global Interaction
Why might Zheng He have collected animals from foreign lands?

Between 1405 and 1433, Zheng He explored the coasts of Southeast Asia and India and the entrances to the Red Sea and the Persian Gulf. He also dropped anchor and visited many ports in East Africa. In the wake of the expeditions, Chinese merchants settled in Southeast Asian and Indian trading centers. The voyages also showed local rulers the power and strength of the Middle Kingdom. Many acknowledged the supremacy of the Chinese empire.

Zheng He set up an engraved stone tablet listing the dates, places, and achievements of his voyages. The tablet proudly proclaimed that the Ming had unified the "seas and continents" even more than the Han and Tang had done:

> "The countries beyond the horizon and from the ends of the earth have all become subjects. . . . We have crossed immense water spaces and have seen huge waves like mountains rising sky-high, and we have set eyes on barbarian regions far away . . . while our sails loftily unfurled like clouds day and night continued their course, crossing those savage waves as if we were walking on a public highway. . . ."
> —Zheng He, quoted in *The True Dates of the Chinese Maritime Expeditions in the Early Fifteenth Century* (Duyvendak)

Turning Inward In 1433, the year Zheng He died, the Ming emperor sud-denly banned the building of seagoing ships. Later, ships with more than two masts were forbidden. Zheng He's huge ships were retired and rotted away.

Why did China, with its advanced naval technology, turn its back on overseas exploration? Historians are not sure. However, some speculate that the fleets were costly and did not produce any profits. Also, Confucian scholars at court had little interest in overseas ventures. To them, Chinese civilization was the most successful in the world. They wanted to preserve its ancient traditions, which they saw as the source of stability. In fact, such rigid loyalty to tradition would eventually weaken China and once again leave it prey to foreign domination.

Fewer than 60 years after China halted overseas expeditions, the explorer Christopher Columbus would sail west from Spain in search of a sea route to Asia. As you will see, this voyage made Spain a major power and had a dramatic impact on the entire world. We can only wonder how the course of history might have changed if the Chinese had continued the explorations they had begun under the Ming.

SECTION 2 Assessment

Recall
1. **Identify:** **(a)** Kublai Khan, **(b)** Marco Polo, **(c)** Zheng He.

Comprehension
2. How did the Mongol conquests promote trade and cultural exchanges?
3. How did Kublai Khan organize Mongol rule in China?
4. How did the Ming emperors try to restore Chinese culture?
5. What was the purpose of Zheng He's overseas expeditions?

Critical Thinking and Writing
6. **Making Inferences** What does Marco Polo's awe at the glories of China suggest about the differ-ences between China and Europe at that time?
7. **Recognizing Causes and Effects** Describe one effect of each of the following on China: **(a)** the rise of the Ming dynasty, **(b)** the Mongol invasion, **(c)** the expulsion of the Mongols.

Activity
Organizing a Debate Organize a debate that might have taken place at the Ming court between Confucian scholars, who want to end overseas voy-ages, and court officials, who want to finance more expeditions by Zheng He.

Korea and Its Traditions

Reading Focus

■ How did geography affect life in the Korean peninsula?

■ How did Korea maintain its unity and independence despite Chinese influence?

■ What were the major achievements of the Choson dynasty?

Vocabulary

celadon

hangul

literacy rate

Taking Notes

Begin a concept web like this one. As you read this section, fill in the blank circles with relevant information about Korea. Add more circles as needed.

Geography

KOREA

Shilla dynasty

Main Idea Korea's history and culture were linked closely to those of China and Japan.

Setting the Scene

For centuries, Korea survived in the shadow of powerful neighbors, China and Japan. Koreans thus came to see their land as a "shrimp among whales." Yet Korea had another name, "Land of the Morning Calm." Whether tossed in turbulent seas or at rest in a calm land, Koreans had their own identity.

As early as Han times, China extended its influence to Korea. Although Koreans absorbed many Chinese traditions, they maintained a separate and distinct culture.

Geography of the Korean Peninsula

Korea is located on a peninsula that juts south from the Asian mainland with its tip pointing toward Japan. At the northern end of the peninsula, mountains and the Yalu River separate Korea from China.

Mountains and Seas An early visitor once compared Korea's landscape to "a sea in a heavy gale." Low but steep mountains cover nearly 70 percent of the Korean peninsula. The most important range is the T'aebaek (TEH BEHK). It runs from the north to the south along the eastern coast, with smaller chains branching off to form hilly areas. Because farming is difficult on the mountains, most people live along the western coastal plains, Korea's major farming region.

Korea has a 5,400-mile coastline with hundreds of good harbors. In addition, the offshore waters feature thousands of islands. Since earliest times, Koreans have depended upon seafood for most of the protein in their diet. Today, South Korea has the third largest fishing industry in the world.

The Impact of Location Korea's location on China's doorstep has played a key role in its development. From its powerful mainland neighbor, Korea received many cultural and technological influences. At various times in history, China extended political control over the Korean peninsula. Throughout its history, Korea has also served as a cultural bridge linking China and Japan. From early times, Koreans adapted and transformed Chinese traditions before passing them on to the Japanese.

Despite these strong ties, the Korean language is not related to Chinese. The earliest Koreans probably migrated eastward from Siberia and northern Manchuria during the Stone Age. They evolved

Mountains of Korea
"Over the mountains, mountains!" says one Korean proverb. This photograph shows a steep ridge in the T'aebaek Range.

Theme: Geography and History How would mountains affect settlement patterns?

Geography of Korea

CHINA

Paektu Mt.

KOREA

Korea Bay

Yalu R.

Taedong R.

Nangnim Range

Imjin R.

Kaesong

T'aebaek Range

Han R.

Sobaek Range

Yellow Sea

Sea of Japan

Korea Strait

JAPAN

East China Sea

Conic Projection

0   100   200 Miles

0   100   200 Kilometers

Kingdoms, A.D. 300–A.D. 600
- Koguryo
- Paekche
- Shilla

Skills Assessment

Geography Korea occupies a peninsula that juts south from China toward the islands of Japan.

1. **Location** *On the map, locate (a) T'aebaek Range, (b) Yalu River, (c) Korea Strait, (d) Koguryo, (e) Paekche, (f) Shilla.*
2. **Region** *Why do most Koreans live along the western coastal plain?*
3. **Critical Thinking Predicting Consequences** *In the 1590s, Japan made plans to invade China. What effect might this have had on Korea?*

their own ways of life before the first wave of Chinese influence reached the peninsula during the Han dynasty. In 108 B.C., the Han emperor Wudi invaded Korea and set up a military colony there. From this outpost, Confucian traditions and Chinese ideas about government, as well as Chinese writing and farming methods, spread to Korea.

Korea United

Between about A.D. 300 and 600, powerful local rulers forged three separate kingdoms: Koguryo (KOH GUH REE OH) in the north, Paekche (PEHK CHEH) in the southwest, and Shilla (SHIL LAH) in the southeast. Although they shared the same language and cultural background, the three kingdoms often warred with one another or with China. Still, Chinese influences continued to arrive. Missionaries spread Mahayana Buddhism, which took root among the rulers and nobles. Korean monks then traveled to China and India to learn more about Buddhism. They brought home the arts and learning of China.

In 668, with the support of the Tang empress Wu Zhao, the Shilla kingdom united the Korean peninsula. Unlike China, Korea had only three dynasties in its history. The Shilla ruled from 668 to 918, the Koryo (KOR EE OH) ruled from 918 to 1392, and the Choson (CHOH SUHN), or Yi, ruled from 1392 to 1910.

Chinese Influence Under the Shilla dynasty, Korea became a tributary state, acknowledging Chinese overlordship but preserving its independence. Over the centuries, Korea came to see its relationship to China in Confucian terms, as that of a younger brother who owed respect and loyalty to an older brother. Koreans also adopted the Confucian emphasis on the family as the foundation of the state.

Confucian ideas affected the rights of women. Early on, Korean women had the right to inherit property. Some upper-class women held public roles. Over time, as Confucian views took root, women's rights became restricted. Women could no longer inherit property, and a woman's position within the family became more subordinate.

At the same time, Koreans adapted and modified Chinese ideas. For example, they adapted the Chinese civil service examination to reflect their own system of inherited ranks. In China, even a peasant could win political influence by passing the exam. In Korea, only aristocrats were permitted to take the test.

Buddhist Influence During the Koryo age, Buddhism reached its greatest influence in Korea. Korean scholars wrote histories and poems based on Chinese models, and artists created landscape paintings following Chinese principles. The Koryo dynasty built their capital at Kaesong (KEH SUNG) following the plan of the Tang capital at Chang'an.

Koreans used woodblock printing from China to produce a flood of Buddhist texts. Later, Korean inventors made movable metal type to print large numbers of books. Koreans improved on other Chinese inventions. They learned to make porcelain from China, but then perfected techniques of making celadon, a porcelain with an unusual blue-green glaze. Korean celadon vases and jars were prized throughout Asia. In the 1200s, when the Mongols overran Korea and destroyed many industries, the secret of making celadon was lost forever.

Choson: The Longest Dynasty

The Mongols occupied Korea until the 1350s. In 1392, the brilliant Korean general Yi Song-gye (EE SUNG KEH) set up the Choson dynasty. In *Songs of the Flying Dragons,* Korea's leading poets held Yi up as a model of virtue and wisdom for future rulers:

> "When you have men at your beck and call,
> When you punish men and sentence them,
> Remember, my Lord, His mercy and temperance.
> If you are unaware of people's sorrow,
> Heaven will abandon you.
> Remember, my Lord, His labor and love."
> —*Songs of the Flying Dragons*

Yi reduced Buddhist influence and set up a government based upon Confucian principles. Within a few generations, Confucianism had made a deep impact on Korean life.

A Korean Alphabet Despite Chinese influence, Korea preserved its distinct identity. In 1443, Korea's most celebrated ruler, King Sejong (SEH JONG) decided to replace the complex Chinese system of writing. "The language of this land," he noted, "is different from China's." Sejong had experts develop hangul, an alphabet using symbols to represent the sounds of spoken Korean.

Although Confucian scholars rejected hangul at the outset, its use quickly spread. Hangul was easier for Koreans to use than the thousands of characters of written Chinese. Its use led to an extremely high literacy rate, or percentage of people who can read and write.

Japanese Invasions In the 1590s, an ambitious Japanese ruler decided to invade China by way of Korea. Japanese armies landed and for years looted and burned across the peninsula. To stop the invaders at sea, the Korean admiral Yi Sun-shin used metal-plated "turtle boats." After six years, the Japanese armies withdrew from Korea. As they left, however, they carried off many Korean artisans to introduce their skills to Japan.

Connections to Today

A Peninsula Divided

Korean unity lasted almost 1,300 years. But today, the Korean peninsula is again divided into hostile camps.

North Korea is a communist country. South Korea is a democracy. Each nation wants to rule the entire peninsula. Both sides have massed soldiers and equipment along the border in preparation for war.

The United States is South Korea's most powerful ally. North Korea maintains close ties to Communist China. As a result, Korea is one of the world's hot spots. The Korean War (1950–1953) was fought there, and there is a constant fear that the troubled Korean Peninsula may be the site of more bloodshed.

Theme: Continuity and Change How is today's division of Korea different from that created by early kingdoms?

SECTION 3 Assessment

Recall
1. **Identify:** (a) Shilla, (b) Koryo, (c) Choson, (d) Yi Song-gye, (e) Sejong.
2. **Define:** (a) celadon, (b) hangul, (c) literacy rate.

Comprehension
3. How did the relative location of the Korean peninsula influence the development of Korean civilization?
4. Give two examples of how Koreans adapted or modified Chinese ideas under the Shilla or Koryo dynasty.

5. (a) How did Confucianism influence Korea during the Choson dynasty? (b) How did Korea preserve its own identity?

Critical Thinking and Writing
6. **Analyzing Literature** Reread the excerpt from *Songs of the Flying Dragons* in this section. How does this poem reflect Confucian influences?
7. **Analyzing Information** Today, Hangul Day is a holiday in South Korea. Why do you think Koreans celebrate the creation of their alphabet?

Activity

Making a Poster
Draw a poster that expresses the relationship between Korea and China during either the Shilla, Koryo, or Choson dynasty. Use symbols to show the exchange of ideas.

The Emergence of Japan

Reading Focus

■ What geographic features influenced the early development of Japan?

■ How did Chinese civilization influence early Japanese traditions?

■ What traditions emerged at the Heian court?

Vocabulary

archipelago

tsunami

selective borrowing

kana

Taking Notes

On a sheet of paper copy this concept web. As you read the section, add circles to the left with more information about the influence of China and circles to the right with more information about Japan's own traditions.

Ideas of government

China's influence

EMERGENCE OF JAPAN

Japanese traditions

Shinto

Main Idea Japan borrowed elements of Chinese civilization but remained free of Chinese control.

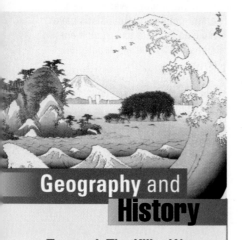

Geography and History

Tsunami: The Killer Wave

Picture an ocean wave seven stories tall—heading right at you. That's what the people on the Japanese island of Honshu faced on June 15, 1896. The huge wave—a tsunami—slammed into 200 miles of Japanese coastline. Whole villages were swept away. Nearly 30,000 people were killed.

Tsunamis begin far out at sea, when an undersea earthquake, landslide, or volcano sets the water in motion. The wave can travel at up to 600 miles per hour. In deep water, the wave is barely noticeable on the surface. But in shallow water, it reaches horrific height, sometimes as much as 100 feet.

Theme: Geography and History How might Japan's geography have increased death tolls from tsunamis?

Setting the Scene Prince Shotoku of Japan's ruling Yamato clan wanted to create an orderly society. In 604, he outlined ideals of behavior for both the royal court and ordinary people. "Harmony should be valued," he wrote, "and quarrels avoided." Shotoku's words reflected a strong Confucian influence about social order. As he stated:

"Everyone has his biases, and few men are far-sighted. Therefore some disobey their lords and fathers and keep up feuds with their neighbors. But when the superiors are in harmony with each other and inferiors are friendly, then affairs are discussed quietly and the right view of matters prevails."

—Prince Shotoku, *Laws*

Like Korea, Japan felt the powerful influence of Chinese civilization early in its history. At the same time, the Japanese continued to maintain their own distinct culture.

Geography: Japan, a Land Apart

Japan is located on an archipelago (ahr kuh PEHL uh goh), or chain of islands, about 100 miles off the Asian mainland and east of the Korean peninsula. Its four main islands are Hokkaido (hoh KĪ doh), Honshu (hahn SHOO), Kyushu (kee oo SHOO), and Shikoku (shee KOH koo).

Land and Sea Japan is about the size of Montana, but four fifths of its land is too mountainous to farm. As a result, most people settled in narrow river valleys and along the coastal plains. A mild climate and sufficient rainfall, however, helped Japanese farmers make the most of the limited arable land. As in ancient Greece, the mountainous terrain at first was an obstacle to unity.

The surrounding seas have both protected and isolated Japan. It was close enough to the mainland to learn from Korea and China, but too far away for the Chinese to conquer. Japan thus had greater freedom to accept or reject Chinese influences than did other East Asian lands. At times, the Japanese sealed themselves off from foreign influences, choosing to go their own way.

The seas that helped Japan preserve its identity also served as trade routes. The Inland Sea was an especially important link among various

Japanese islands. The seas also offered plentiful food resources. The Japanese, like the Koreans, developed a thriving fishing industry.

Ring of Fire Japan lies in a Pacific region known as the Ring of Fire, which also includes the Philippines, Indonesia, and parts of Australia and South America. This region is subject to frequent earthquakes and volcanoes. Underwater earthquakes can launch killer tidal waves, called tsunami (tsoo NAH mee), that sweep over the land without warning, wiping out everything in their path.

The Japanese came to fear and respect the dramatic forces of nature. Today, as in the past, soaring Mount Fuji, with its snowcapped volcanic crater, is a sacred symbol of the beauty and majesty of nature.

Early Traditions

The people we know today as the Japanese probably migrated from the Asian mainland more than 2,000 years ago. They slowly pushed the earlier inhabitants, the Ainu, onto the northernmost island of Hokkaido.

Yamato Clan Early Japanese society was divided into uji, or clans. Each uji had its own chief and a special god or goddess who was seen as the clan's original ancestor. Some clan leaders were women, suggesting that women enjoyed a respected position in society.

By about A.D. 500, the Yamato clan came to dominate a corner of Honshu, the largest Japanese island. For the next 1,000 years, the Yamato Plain was the heartland of Japanese government. The Yamato set up Japan's first and only dynasty. They claimed direct descent from the sun goddess, Amaterasu, and chose the rising sun as their symbol. Later Japanese emperors were revered as living gods. While this is no longer the case, the current Japanese emperor still traces his roots to the Yamato clan.

Shinto Early Japanese clans honored kami, or nature spirits. This worship of the forces of nature became known as Shinto, meaning "the way of the gods." Shinto never evolved into an international religion like Christianity, Buddhism, or Islam. Still, its traditions have survived to the present day. Hundreds of Shinto shrines dot the Japanese countryside. Though simple in design, they are generally located in beautiful, natural surroundings. Shinto shrines are dedicated to special sites or objects such as mountains or waterfalls, ancient gnarled trees, or even oddly shaped rocks.

The Korean Bridge The Japanese language is distantly related to Korean but completely different from Chinese. From early on, Japan and Korea were in continuous contact with each other. Korean artisans and metalworkers settled in Japan, bringing sophisticated skills and technology. Japanese and Korean warriors crossed the sea in both directions to attack each other's strongholds. Some of the leading families at the Yamato court claimed Korean ancestors.

By about A.D. 500, missionaries from Korea had introduced Buddhism to Japan. With it came knowledge of Chinese writing and culture. This opening sparked a sudden surge of Japanese interest in Chinese civilization.

Geography of Japan

▲ Volcano

● Yamato influence

Skills Assessment

Geography Japan is located on an archipelago. In addition to its four main islands, Japan includes over 3,000 smaller islands.

1. **Location** On the map, locate **(a)** Hokkaido, **(b)** Honshu, **(c)** Kyushu, **(d)** Shikoku, **(e)** Mount Fuji.
2. **Interaction** Explain how two geographic features might have influenced Japanese life.
3. **Critical Thinking Drawing Conclusions** Which city was more likely to feel the influence of the Yamato clan—Osaka or Edo? Why?

Reading Focus

- How did feudalism develop in Japan?
- What changes took place under the Tokugawa shoguns?
- What cultural and artistic traditions emerged in feudal Japan?

Vocabulary

shogun
daimyo
samurai
bushido
kabuki
bunraku
haiku

Taking Notes

As you read this section, prepare an outline of Japan's feudal age. Use Roman numerals to indicate major headings, capital letters for the subheadings, and numbers for the supporting details. The sample at right has been started for you.

I. Japanese feudalism emerges
   A. The world of warriors
      1. Daimyo
      2. Samurai
   B. Status of noble-women
      1.
      2.

Main Idea During feudal times, military rulers called shoguns dominated Japanese society and eventually created a strong central government.

Setting the Scene The poet Sogi was one of the leading writers of Japan in the 1400s. In verses like this one, he expresses a sense of uncertainty and despair:

> "To live in the world
> Is sad enough without this rain
> Pounding on my shelter."
> —Sogi, *Haiku*

The 1400s, when Sogi lived, were a time of political intrigue, rebellions, and feudal warfare in Japan. Disorder continued through the following century. Yet, despite the turmoil, a new Japanese culture blossomed.

Japanese Feudalism Emerges

While the emperor presided over the splendid court at Heian, rival clans battled for control of the countryside. Local warlords and even Buddhist temples formed armed bands loyal to them rather than to the central government. As these armies struggled for power, Japan evolved a feudal system. As in the feudal world of medieval Europe, a warrior aristocracy dominated Japanese society.

In theory, the emperor stood at the head of Japanese feudal society. In fact, he was a powerless, though revered, figurehead. Real power lay in the hands of the **shogun,** or supreme military commander. Minamoto Yoritomo was appointed shogun in 1192. He set up the Kamakura shogunate, the first of three military dynasties that would rule Japan for almost 700 years.

The World of Warriors Often the shogun controlled only a small part of Japan. He distributed lands to vassal lords who agreed to support him with their armies in time of need. These great warrior lords were later called **daimyo** (DĪ myoh). They, in turn, granted land to lesser warriors called **samurai,** meaning "those who serve." Samurai were the fighting aristocracy of a war-torn land.

Like medieval Christian knights in Europe, samurai were heavily armed and trained in the skills of fighting. They also developed their own code of values. Known as **bushido** (BOO shee doh), or the "way of the warrior," the code emphasized honor, bravery, and absolute loyalty to one's lord.

Connections to Today

The Martial Arts

Nearly 1,500 years ago, warriors in China, Japan, and Korea learned ways to fight without weapons. These techniques, developed originally by Buddhist monks from India and Tibet, were called the martial, or military, arts.

Today, millions of people around the world learn and practice different forms of martial arts. Discipline—both physical and mental—is a key to success. Those who practice the Korean art of tae kwon do agree to be committed to 11 "tenets," or principles. These include showing respect for teachers, parents, and other elders and always finishing what you begin.

Theme: Continuity and Change Why do you think the martial arts are still popular?

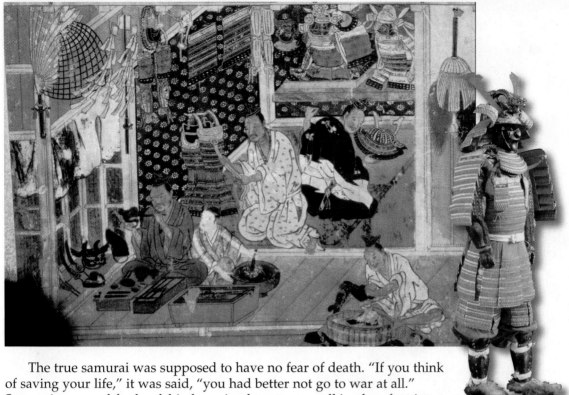

The true samurai was supposed to have no fear of death. "If you think of saving your life," it was said, "you had better not go to war at all." Samurai prepared for hardship by going hungry or walking barefoot in the snow. For a samurai, it was said, "when his stomach is empty, it is a disgrace to feel hungry." A samurai who betrayed the code of bushido was expected to commit *seppuku* (seh POO koo), or ritual suicide, rather than live without honor.

Status of Noblewomen At first, some noblewomen in Japanese feudal society trained in the military arts. A few even became legendary warriors. At times, some noblewomen supervised their family's estates.

As the age of the samurai progressed, however, the position of women declined steadily. When feudal warfare increased, inheritance was limited to sons. Unlike the European ideal of chivalry, the samurai code did not set women on a pedestal. Instead, the wife of a warrior had to accept the same hardships as her husband and owed the same loyalty to his overlord.

Peasants, Artisans, and Merchants Far below the samurai in the social hierarchy were the peasants, artisans, and merchants. Peasants, who made up 75 percent of the population, formed the backbone of feudal society in Japan. Peasant families cultivated rice and other crops on the estates of samurai. Some peasants also served as foot soldiers in feudal wars. On rare occasions, an able peasant soldier might rise through the ranks to become a samurai himself.

Artisans, such as armorers and swordmakers, provided necessary goods for the samurai class. Merchants had the lowest rank in Japanese feudal society. However, as you will see, their status gradually improved.

Mongol Invasions During the feudal age, most fighting took place between rival warlords, but the Mongol conquest of China and Korea also threatened Japan. When the Japanese refused to accept Mongol rule, Kublai Khan launched an invasion from Korea in 1274. After a fleet carrying 30,000 troops arrived, a typhoon wrecked many Mongol ships.

In 1281, the Mongols landed an even larger invasion force, but again a typhoon destroyed much of the Mongol fleet. The Japanese credited their miraculous delivery to the *kamikaze* (kah mih KAH zee), or divine winds. The Mongol failure reinforced the Japanese sense that they were a people set apart who enjoyed the special protection of the gods.

Armor for a Warrior
This painting shows Japanese artisans constructing armor and weapons for a samurai warrior. Unlike the solid steel plates worn by European feudal knights, the samurai's armor was made up of thin strips of steel held together by brightly colored silk cords.

Theme: Economics and Technology What might be the advantages and disadvantages of the type of armor used by a samurai?

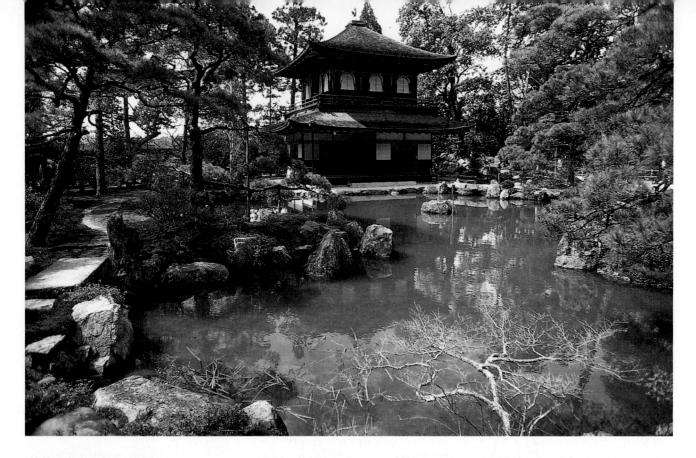

A Zen Buddhist Temple
Zen monks were the leading scholars and artists of feudal Japan. This temple was a Zen monastery and a peaceful retreat for visiting shoguns seeking advice.

Theme: Religions and Value Systems How does the setting of this temple reflect Zen values?

Order and Unity Under the Tokugawas

The Kamakura shogunate crumbled in the aftermath of the Mongol invasions. A new dynasty took power in 1338, but the level of warfare increased after 1450. To defend their castles, daimyo armed peasants as well as samurai, which led to even more ruthless fighting. A popular saying of the time declared, "The warrior does not care if he's called a dog or beast. The main thing is winning."

Gradually, several powerful warriors united large parts of Japan. By 1590, the brilliant general Toyotomi Hideyoshi (hee day YOH shee), a commoner by birth, had brought most of Japan under his control. He then tried, but failed, to conquer Korea and China. In 1600, the daimyo Tokugawa Ieyasu (toh kuh GAH wah ee YAY yah soo) defeated his rivals to become master of Japan. Three years later, he was named shogun. The Tokugawa shogunate ruled Japan until 1868.

Centralized Feudalism The Tokugawa shoguns were determined to end feudal warfare. They kept the outward forms of feudal society but imposed central government control on all Japan. For this reason, their system of government is called centralized feudalism.

The Tokugawas created a unified, orderly society. To control the daimyo, they required these great lords to live in the shogun's capital at Edo (present-day Tokyo) every other year. A daimyo's wife and children had to remain in Edo full time, giving the shogun a powerful check on the entire family. The shogun also forbade daimyo to repair their castles or marry without permission.

New laws fixed the old social order rigidly in place and upheld a strict moral code. Only samurai were allowed to serve in the military or hold government jobs. They were expected to follow the traditions of bushido. Peasants had to remain on the land. Lower classes were forbidden to wear luxuries such as silk clothing.

Women, too, faced greater restrictions under the Tokugawas. One government decree, sent to all villages, stated, "However good-looking a wife may be, if she neglects her household duties by drinking tea or sightseeing or rambling on the hillsides, she must be divorced." Women's freedom to move about, or even travel with their husbands, was strictly regulated.

Economic Growth While the shoguns tried to hold back social change, the Japanese economy grew by leaps and bounds. With peace restored to the countryside, agriculture improved and expanded. New seeds, tools, and the use of fertilizer led to greater output of crops.

Food surpluses supported rapid population growth. Towns sprang up on the lands around the castles of daimyo. Edo grew into a booming city, where artisans and merchants flocked to supply the needs of the daimyo and their families.

Trade flourished within Japan. New roads linked castle towns and Edo. Each year, daimyo and their servants traveled to and from the capital, creating a demand for food and services along the route. In the cities, a wealthy merchant class emerged. In accordance with Confucian tradition, merchants had low social status. Still, Japanese merchants gained influence by lending money to daimyo and samurai. Sometimes, merchants further improved their social position by arranging to marry their daughters into the samurai class.

Zen Buddhism and Japanese Culture

During Japan's feudal age, a Buddhist sect from China won widespread acceptance among samurai. Known in Japan as Zen, it emphasized meditation and devotion to duty.

Zen had seemingly contradictory traditions. Zen monks were great scholars, yet they valued the uncluttered mind and stressed the importance of reaching a moment of "non-knowing." Zen stressed compassion for all, yet samurai fought to kill. In Zen monasteries, monks sought to experience absolute freedom, yet rigid rules gave the master complete authority over his students.

Zen beliefs shaped Japanese culture in many ways. At Zen monasteries, upper-class men learned to express devotion to nature in such activities as landscape gardening. Zen Buddhists believed that people could seek enlightenment, not only through meditation, but through the precise performance of everyday tasks. For example, the elaborate rituals of the tea ceremony reflected Zen values of peace, simplicity, and love of beauty. Zen reverence for nature also influenced the development of fine landscape paintings.

Changing Artistic Traditions

Cities such as Edo and Osaka were home to an explosion in the arts and theater. At stylish entertainment quarters, sophisticated nobles mixed with the urban middle class. Urban culture emphasized luxuries and pleasures and differed greatly from the feudal culture that had dominated Japan for centuries.

Theater In the 1300s, feudal culture had produced Nō plays performed on a square, wooden stage without scenery. Men wore elegant carved masks while a chorus chanted important lines to musical accompaniment. The action was slow. Each movement had a special meaning. Many Nō plays presented Zen Buddhist themes, emphasizing the need to renounce selfish desires. Others recounted fairy tales or the struggles between powerful feudal lords.

In the 1600s, towns gave rise to a popular new form of drama, kabuki (kuh BOO kee). Kabuki was influenced by Nō plays, but it was less refined and included comedy or melodrama. Kabuki plays often portrayed family or historical events. Dressed in colorful costumes, actors used lively and

Creating a Chapter Summary

On a sheet of paper copy the table shown here. Fill in the spaces under each heading to help you review key information about China, Korea, and Japan.

	CHINA	KOREA	JAPAN
PERIODS OR DYNASTIES	Tang, Song, Yuan, Ming		
OUTSIDE INFLUENCES			
TYPE OF SOCIETY			
MAIN ACHIEVEMENTS			

CD-ROM Review For additional review of the major concepts of Chapter 13, see the *Guide to the Essentials of World History* or the *Interactive Student Tutorial CD-ROM.*

Web Site Self-Test For practice test questions for Chapter 13, see **www.phschool.com**.

Building Vocabulary

(a) Classify each of the chapter vocabulary words listed below under *one* of the following themes: Art and Literature, Political and Social Systems, Geography and History.
(b) Choose *one* word in each category and write a sentence explaining how that word relates to the theme.

1. tributary state
2. land reform
3. gentry
4. celadon
5. hangul
6. archipelago
7. tsunami
8. shogun
9. bushido
10. bunraku

Recalling Key Facts

11. Which two dynasties united and ruled China between the 600s and 1200s?
12. What impact did Mongol rule have on Asia?
13. What lands did Zheng He visit?
14. Describe the location of Korea in relation to China and Japan.
15. How has Japan's island status affected its history?
16. How did life in Japan change under the Tokugawas?

Critical Thinking and Writing

17. **Synthesizing Information** Review what you have read about the Mongol empire in this chapter and in earlier chapters. **(a)** How was the Mongol period both destructive and constructive? **(b)** What do you think were the three greatest effects of the Mongol conquests?

18. **Applying Information** Using the information in this chapter and in earlier chapters, construct a time chart of major Chinese dynasties. **(a)** When did each dynasty rise and fall? **(b)** What periods fall between major dynasties? **(c)** Make one generalization about the history of dynasties in China.

19. **Drawing Conclusions (a)** Describe the Japanese practice of selective borrowing. **(b)** How have Americans borrowed from other cultures? Give two examples. **(c)** What are some of the benefits and disadvantages of borrowing from other cultures?

20. **Connecting to Geography (a)** In what ways are the geographies of Japan and Korea similar? **(b)** What similar effects has geography had on these nations?

The following passage is from a 1315 book of regulations for Chinese students. Read the passage, then answer the questions that follow.

"You should concentrate on your book and keep a dignified appearance. You should count the number of times you read an assigned piece. If, upon completion of the assigned number, you still have not memorized the piece, you should continue until you are able to recite it. On the other hand, if you have memorized the piece quickly, you should still go on to complete the assigned number of readings.

Only after a book has been thoroughly learned should you go on to another. Do not read too many things on a superficial level. Do not attempt to memorize a piece without understanding it. Read only those books which expound virtues. Do not look into useless writings."

—Chieng Tuan-li, *A Schedule for Learning*

21. According to the author, how should a student behave while reading a book?

22. What are two key procedures to follow when reading?

23. **(a)** What kinds of books does the author think a student should read? **(b)** What kinds of books does he advise students to avoid? **(c)** What does this suggest about his view of the goal of education?

24. How does this instruction reflect the new school of Confucian thought that emerged during the Song dynasty?

25. Compare the way a Chinese student of the fourteenth century read a book to the way you read a book.

Use the Internet to research an invention or technological discovery from early China during the time period discussed in this chapter. Then, create and deliver a brief presentation about it. You should tell when the item or technique was invented, how it was discovered or created, and whether it is still used today.

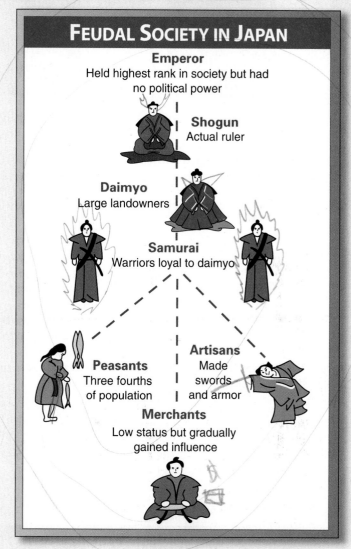

FEUDAL SOCIETY IN JAPAN

Emperor
Held highest rank in society but had no political power

Shogun
Actual ruler

Daimyo
Large landowners

Samurai
Warriors loyal to daimyo

Peasants
Three fourths of population

Artisans
Made swords and armor

Merchants
Low status but gradually gained influence

The organization chart above illustrates the social levels of feudal society in Japan. Study the chart and then answer the following questions:

26. **(a)** Who occupied the highest position in Japanese feudal society? **(b)** How does the chart show this?

27. Who occupied the lowest position in Japanese feudal society?

28. What group made up the largest part of the population?

29. Why does the chart show no lines connecting the peasants, artisans, and merchants?

Skills Tip

Organization charts are usually arranged from highest (top) to lowest (bottom). Connecting lines show relationships between groups.

Chapter 8

The Rise of Europe
(A.D. 500–A.D. 1300)

From 500 to 1000, Europe was a fragmented, largely isolated region. Feudalism, the manor economy, and the Roman Catholic Church were dominant forces during the early Middle Ages.

- Between 400 and 700, Germanic invaders carved Europe up into small kingdoms.
- In the 800s, Charlemagne temporarily reunited much of Europe. He revived learning and furthered the blending of German, Roman, and Christian traditions.
- Feudalism, based on mutual obligations among lords and vassals, gave a strict order to medieval society.
- The Church guided the spiritual lives of Christians and was the most powerful political force in medieval Europe.
- By the 1000s, advances in agriculture and commerce spurred economic revival.

Chapter 9

The High Middle Ages
(A.D. 1050–A.D. 1450)

During the High Middle Ages, economic conditions improved, and learning and the arts flourished. At the same time, feudal monarchs moved to centralize their power, building a framework for the modern nation-state.

- In England and France, long-lasting traditions of royal government evolved.
- In the Holy Roman Empire, conflicts erupted between popes and secular rulers.
- European contacts with the Middle East during the Crusades revived interest in trade and exploration.
- Beginning in the 1300s, famine, plague, and war marked the decline of medieval Europe.

Chapter 10

The Byzantine Empire and Russia (A.D. 330–A.D. 1613)

After the fall of Rome, the Greco-Roman heritage survived in the Byzantine empire. Byzantine civilization shaped the developing cultures of Russia and Eastern Europe.

- The Byzantine empire served as a center of world trade and a buffer between Western Europe, and the Arab empire.
- Traders and missionaries carried Byzantine culture and Eastern Orthodox Christianity to Russia, Eastern Europe, and Ethiopia.
- Czars Ivan III and Ivan IV expanded the Russian empire and laid the foundation for extreme absolute power.
- Invasions and migrations created a mix of ethnic and religious groups in Eastern Europe.
- Jews fleeing the Crusades and the Inquisition migrated further into Eastern Europe and the Middle East.

	A.D. 500	A.D. 700	A.D. 900
AFRICA		**A.D. 600s** Islam spreads to North Africa	**A.D. 800s** Ghana controls gold-salt trade
THE AMERICAS		**A.D. 600s** Mayan civilization thrives	**A.D. 800s** Mississippian civilization flourishes
ASIA AND OCEANIA	A.D. 500s Buddhism introduced to Japan	A.D. 622 Muhammad's hijra from Mecca to Medina	
EUROPE	**A.D. 500s** Byzantine empire reaches height		**A.D. 800** Charlemagne crowned emperor by pope

Chapter 11

The Muslim World
(A.D. 622–A.D. 1629)

The religion of Islam emerged on the Arabian Peninsula in the 600s. Muslim civilization eventually created cultural ties among diverse peoples across three continents.

- Muhammad was the prophet of Islam, a monotheistic religion. Through the Quran, the Five Pillars, and the Sharia, Islam was both a religion and a way of life.
- The Arab empire was ruled by several powerful caliphates. After 850, they were replaced by independent dynasties ruling separate Muslim states.
- Learning, literature, science, medicine, and trade flourished during the golden age of Muslim civilization.
- By the 1500s, the Mughals, Ottomans, and Safavids dominated the Muslim world with powerful empires in India, Eastern Europe, the Middle East, and North Africa.

Chapter 12

Kingdoms and Trading States of Africa (750 B.C.–A.D. 1586)

Despite geographic barriers, many civilizations rose and flourished in Africa. Kingdoms in the west and city-states in the east became important commercial and political centers.

- The Bantu migrations, contacts with Greece and Rome, the spread of Islam, and trade with Asia contributed to Africa's diversity.
- Between 800 and 1600, a succession of powerful West African kingdoms controlled the rich Sahara trade route.
- Indian Ocean trade routes led to the growth of prosperous city-states along the East African coast.
- Art and oral literature fostered common values and a sense of community among the peoples of Africa.

Chapter 13

Spread of Civilizations in East Asia (A.D. 500–A.D. 1650)

After 400 years of fragmentation, China reemerged as a united empire and the most powerful force in East Asia. Although Korea and Japan were heavily influenced by Chinese civilization, each maintained its own identity.

- China expanded and prospered under the powerful Tang and Song dynasties.
- During the 1200s and 1300s, the Mongols ruled much of Asia. After the fall of the Mongols, the Ming restored Chinese culture and later imposed a policy of isolation.
- While maintaining its own identity, Korea served as a cultural bridge linking China and Japan.
- The seas allowed Japan to preserve its unique culture while selectively borrowing religious, political, and artistic traditions from China.
- During the 1100s, Japan created a feudal society that was ruled by powerful military lords.

A.D. **1100** A.D. **1300** A.D. **1500**

A.D. **1000**
East African trading cities prosper

A.D. **1250**
Empire of Mali reaches height

A.D. **1500**
Kongo kingdom flourishes

A.D. **1000s**
Anasazis build pueblo towns

A.D. **1438** Incan empire founded

A.D. **1500** Aztec empire reaches height

A.D. **960**
Song dynasty in China founded

A.D. **1206**
Delhi sultanate founded

A.D. **1368**
Ming dynasty ends Mongol rule

A.D. **1520**
Reign of Suleiman begins

A.D. **1066**
Normans conquer Britain

A.D. **1215**
English Magna Carta signed

A.D. **1389** Ottomans defeat Serbs at Kosovo

A.D. **1462** Reign of Ivan the Great begins

UNIT 4

Early Modern Times

1300–1800

OUTLINE

Themes

As you read about developments that led to the
emergence of modern Europe and the first age of
global interaction, you will encounter the following
unit themes.

Economics and Technology A scientific revolution
enabled explorers to travel the world in search of trade
and riches. Dramatic economic developments, such as
the rise of capitalism, affected all social classes.

Global Interaction Exploration by powerful nations
led to increased competition for trade. The spread of
cultural beliefs and the exchange of material goods
often were accomplished by conquest and by destruction of native cultures.

Political and Social Systems Absolute monarchs
forged modern nation-states with strong central governments. The struggle between monarchs and Parliament
in England was an important step in the development of
modern democracy.

Religions and Value Systems Classical and Christian
humanist ideals shaped the Renaissance. While the
Protestant Reformation shattered the religious unity of
Europe, Christianity continued to spread to new lands.

Unit Theme Activity

For Your Portfolio The chapters in
this unit illustrate changes that led to
the first era of global interaction. As you
read the chapters, prepare a portfolio
project highlighting these developments.
Your project might take one of the
following forms:
- **Chart or other detailed graphic
  organizer**
- **Debate**
- **Diary**

The Palace of Versailles was designed to glorify the power of France and its monarch, Louis XIV. It served as the capital of France and as the royal residence from 1682 until the French Revolution.

Reading Focus

- Why were the Italian city-states a favorable setting for a cultural rebirth?
- What was the Renaissance?
- What themes and techniques did Renaissance artists and writers explore?

Vocabulary

patron

humanism

humanities

perspective

Taking Notes

As you read, prepare an outline of this section. Use Roman numerals to indicate major headings, capital letters for the sub-headings, and numbers for the supporting details. The sample at right will help you get started.

I. The Italian city-states
  A. Why Italy?
    1. Remains of Roman heritage
    2. Prosperous city-states
    3.
  B. Florence and the Medicis
    1.
    2.
II.

Main Idea The Renaissance that began in Italy was characterized by an interest in learning and the arts and a desire to explore the human experience.

Geography and History

The Islands of Venice

One of the world's most remarkable cities was born after the fall of the western Roman empire. As invaders began conquering Italy, refugees fled to the islands in the Adriatic Sea. They drove wooden pilings into the marshy area to make a flat surface so that they could build houses. By Renaissance times, Venetian sailors were bringing back a wealth of trade goods from East and West.

The Grand Canal, an S-shaped waterway, became the main "street." Venetians row from island to island in flat-bottomed boats, called gondolas. Over 150 canals and 400 bridges link the islands into a single, unique city.

Theme: Geography and History How did Venetians adapt to geography?

Setting the Scene

The philosopher Marsilio Ficino smiled with pleasure as he watched the sun cast a golden glow over his native city of Florence. To Ficino, this glow symbolized the revival of art and thought taking place in Italy. Dipping his pen in ink, he began to write. "This century," he wrote, "like a golden age has restored to light the liberal arts, which were almost extinct: grammar, poetry, rhetoric, painting, sculpture, architecture, music." What a glorious time to be alive, he thought.

As Ficino recognized, a new age had dawned in Western Europe. Europeans called it the Renaissance, meaning "rebirth." It began in the 1300s and reached its peak around 1500.

The Italian City-States

The Renaissance began in Italy, then spread north to the rest of Europe. Italy was the birthplace of the Renaissance for several reasons.

Why Italy? The Renaissance was marked by a new interest in the culture of ancient Rome. Because Italy had been the center of the Roman empire, it was a logical place for this reawakening to begin. Architectural remains, statues, coins, and inscriptions—all were visible reminders of Roman grandeur.

Italy differed from the rest of Europe in other ways. Its cities survived the Middle Ages. In the north, city-states like Florence, Milan, Venice, and Genoa grew into prosperous centers of trade and manufacturing. Rome, in central Italy, and Naples, in the south, along with a number of smaller city-states, also contributed to the Renaissance cultural revival.

A wealthy and powerful merchant class in these city-states further promoted the cultural rebirth. These merchants exerted both political and economic leadership, and their attitudes and interests helped to shape the Italian Renaissance. They stressed education and individual achievement. They also spent lavishly to support the arts.

Florence and the Medicis Florence, perhaps more than any other city, came to symbolize the energy and brilliance of the Italian Renaissance. Like the ancient city of Athens, it produced a dazzling number of gifted poets, artists, architects, scholars, and scientists in a short span of time.

In the 1400s, the Medici (MEH dee chee) family of Florence organized a successful banking business. Before long, the family expanded into wool manufacturing, mining, and other ventures. The Medicis ranked among the richest merchants and bankers in Europe. Money translated into cultural and political power. Cosimo de' Medici gained control of the Florentine government in 1434, and the family continued as uncrowned rulers of the city for many years.

Cosimo's grandson Lorenzo, known as "the Magnificent," represented the Renaissance ideal. A clever politician, he held Florence together in the late 1400s during difficult times. He was also a generous patron, or financial supporter, of the arts. Under Lorenzo, poets and philosophers frequently visited the Medici palace. Artists learned their craft by sketching ancient Roman statues displayed in the Medici gardens.

Renaissance Italy, 1505

Duchy of Milan
Republic of Genoa
Republic of Florence
Papal States
Republic of Venice
Kingdoms under Spanish sovereignty
Other city-states

Mercator Projection
0   100   200 Miles
0   100   200 Kilometers

What Was the Renaissance?

The Renaissance was a time of creativity and change in many areas—political, social, economic, and cultural. Perhaps most important, however, were the changes that took place in the way people viewed themselves and their world.

A New Worldview Spurred by a reawakened interest in the classical learning of Greece and Rome, creative Renaissance minds set out to transform their own age. Their era, they felt, was a time of rebirth after what they saw as the disorder and disunity of the medieval world.

In reality, Renaissance Europe did not break completely with its medieval past. After all, monks and scholars of the Middle Ages had preserved much of the classical heritage. Latin had survived as the language of the Church and of educated people. And the mathematics of Euclid, the astronomy of Ptolemy, and the works of Aristotle were well known to late medieval scholars.

Yet the Renaissance did produce new attitudes toward culture and learning. Unlike medieval scholars, who were more likely to focus on life after death, Renaissance thinkers explored the richness and variety of human experience in the here and now. At the same time, there was a new emphasis on individual achievement. Indeed, the Renaissance ideal was the person with talent in many fields.

A Spirit of Adventure The Renaissance supported a spirit of adventure and a wide-ranging curiosity that led people to explore new worlds. The Italian navigator Christopher Columbus, who sailed to the Americas in 1492, represented that spirit. So did Nicolaus Copernicus, a Polish scientist who revolutionized the way people viewed the universe. Renaissance writers and artists, eager to experiment with new forms, were also products of that adventurous spirit.

Humanism At the heart of the Italian Renaissance was an intellectual movement known as humanism. Based on the study of classical culture, humanism focused on worldly subjects rather than on the religious issues that had occupied medieval thinkers. Most humanist scholars were pious

Skills Assessment

Geography At the time of the Renaissance, Italy was made up of numerous republics, kingdoms, and city-states.

1. **Location** On the map, locate (a) Florence, (b) Venice, (c) Rome, (d) Papal States, (e) Duchy of Milan.
2. **Place** (a) In which state was Pisa an important city? (b) Who controlled Corsica and Sicily?
3. **Critical Thinking Making Inferences** Based on this map, why was Venice in a good position to trade with the Muslim world?

Christians who hoped to use the wisdom of the ancients to increase their understanding of their own times.

Humanists believed that education should stimulate the individual's creative powers. They returned to the humanities, the subjects taught in ancient Greek and Roman schools. The main areas of study were grammar, rhetoric, poetry, and history, based on Greek and Roman texts. Humanists did not accept the classical texts without question, however. Rather, they studied the ancient authorities in light of their own experiences.

Francesco Petrarch (PEE trahrk), a Florentine who lived in the 1300s, was an early Renaissance humanist. In monasteries and churches, he found and assembled a library of Greek and Roman manuscripts. Through his efforts and those of others encouraged by his example, the works of Cicero, Homer, and Virgil again became known to Western Europeans. Petrarch also wrote literature of his own. His *Sonnets to Laura,* love poems inspired by a woman he knew only from a distance, greatly influenced later writers.

A Golden Age in the Arts

The Renaissance attained its most glorious expression in its paintings, sculpture, and architecture. Wealthy patrons played a major role in this artistic flowering. Popes and princes supported the work of hundreds of artists. Wealthy and powerful women such as Isabella d'Este of Mantua were important patrons of the arts as well.

Humanist Concerns Renaissance art reflected humanist concerns. Like artists of the Middle Ages, Renaissance artists portrayed religious figures such as Jesus and Mary. However, they often set these figures against Greek or Roman backgrounds. Painters also produced portraits of well-known figures of the day, reflecting the humanist interest in individual achievement.

Perspective
Renaissance artists used perspective to create an illusion of depth. The diagram below shows how the lines in this painting by Antonello da Messina recede from the viewer toward a single vanishing point.

Theme: Arts and Literature
How does the size of objects in this painting add to the sense of depth?

vanishing point

Renaissance artists studied ancient Greek and Roman works and revived many classical forms. The sculptor Donatello, for example, created a life-size statue of a soldier on horseback. It was the first such figure done since ancient times.

New Techniques Roman art had been very realistic, and Renaissance painters developed new techniques for representing both humans and landscapes in a realistic way. Renaissance artists learned the rules of perspective. By making distant objects smaller than those close to the viewer, artists could paint scenes that appeared three-dimensional.

Renaissance painters used shading to make objects look round and real. Painters and sculptors also studied human anatomy and drew from live models. As a result, they were able to portray the human body more accurately than medieval artists had done.

Women Artists Some women overcame the limits on education and training to become professional artists. Sometimes, these women kept their work secret, allowing their husbands to pass it off as their own. Still, a few women artists did gain acceptance. In the 1500s, Sofonisba Anguissola (soh foh NIHZ bah ahn gwee SOH lah), an Italian noblewoman, became court painter to King Philip II of Spain.

Architecture Renaissance architects rejected the Gothic style of the late Middle Ages as cluttered and disorderly. Instead, they adopted the columns, arches, and domes that had been favored by the Greeks and Romans. For the cathedral in Florence, Filippo Brunelleschi (broo nehl LEHS kee) created a majestic dome, which he modeled on the dome of the Pantheon in Rome.

Three Geniuses of Renaissance Art

Renaissance Florence was home to many outstanding painters and sculptors. The three most celebrated Florentine masters were Leonardo da Vinci, Michelangelo, and Raphael.

Leonardo Leonardo da Vinci (dah VIHN chee) was born in 1452. His exploring mind and endless curiosity fed a genius for invention. He made sketches of nature and of models in his studio. He even dissected corpses to learn how bones and muscles work. "Indicate which are the muscles and which the tendons, which become prominent or retreat in the different movements of each limb," he wrote in his notebook.

Today, people admire Leonardo's paintings for their freshness and realism. Most popular is the *Mona Lisa*, a portrait of a woman whose mysterious smile has baffled viewers for centuries. *The Last Supper*, showing Christ and his apostles on the night before the crucifixion, is both a moving religious painting and a masterpiece of perspective. Because Leonardo was experimenting with a new type of paint, much of *The Last Supper* decayed over the years, but it has recently been restored.

Leonardo thought of himself as an artist, but his talents and accomplishments ranged over many areas. His interests extended to botany, anatomy, optics, music, architecture, and engineering. He made sketches for flying machines and undersea boats centuries before the first airplane or submarine was actually built.

Michelangelo Like Leonardo, Michelangelo was a many-sided genius—sculptor, engineer, painter, architect, and poet. As a young man, he shaped marble into masterpieces like the *Pietà*, which captures the sorrow of Mary as she cradles the dead Christ on her knees. Michelangelo's statue of David, the biblical shepherd who killed the giant Goliath, recalls the harmony and grace of ancient Greek tradition.

Primary Source

The Genius of Leonardo
Italian artist and architect Giorgio Vasari is best known for his engaging book of biographies of Italian artists, including Leonardo da Vinci (pictured above):

"Leonardo practiced not one art but all of those that are dependent upon design, and he had great talent for geometry besides being very musical, playing the lute with great ability and being excellent in the art of improvisation. . . . In entertaining, Leonardo was so pleasant that he won everyone's heart. Although he may well be said to have owned nothing and to have worked little, he always kept a servant as well as horses."

—Giorgio Vasari, *Lives of the Most Eminent Italian Painters, Sculptors, and Architects*

Skills Assessment

Primary Source What personal details did Vasari include about Leonardo da Vinci?

A Masterpiece by Michelangelo

Michelangelo spent four years painting biblical scenes on the ceiling of the Sistine Chapel. One of the most dramatic images, the *Creation of Adam*, shows God bringing the first man to life with a touch.

Theme: Religions and Value Systems How does Michelangelo suggest the power of God?

One of Michelangelo's greatest projects was painting a huge mural to decorate the ceiling of the Sistine Chapel in Rome. It was an enormous task, depicting the biblical history of the world, from the Creation to the Flood. For four years, the artist lay on his back on a wooden platform suspended just a few inches below the chapel ceiling. In a poem, Michelangelo later described his ordeal:

> "My stomach is thrust toward my chin
>   My beard curls up toward the sky
>   My head leans right over onto my back . . .
>   The brush endlessly dripping onto my face."
>   —Michelangelo, *Poems*

Michelangelo was also a talented architect. His most famous design was for the dome of St. Peter's Cathedral in Rome. It served as a model for many later structures, including the United States Capitol building in Washington, D.C.

Raphael A few years younger than Leonardo and Michelangelo, Raphael (RAF ee uhl) studied the works of those great masters. His paintings blend Christian and classical styles. He is probably best known for his tender portrayals of the madonna, the mother of Jesus.

In *The School of Athens,* Raphael pictures an imaginary gathering of great thinkers and scientists, such as Plato, Aristotle, Socrates, and the Arab philosopher Averroës. With typical Renaissance self-confidence, Raphael included the faces of Michelangelo, Leonardo—and himself.

Italian Renaissance Writers

Poets, artists, and scholars mingled with politicians at the courts of Renaissance rulers. A literature of "how-to" books sprang up to help ambitious men and women who wanted to rise in the Renaissance world.

Castiglione's Ideal Courtier The most widely read of these handbooks was *The Book of the Courtier*. Its author, Baldassare Castiglione (bahl dahs

SAHR ray kahs steel YOHN ay), describes the manners, skills, learning, and virtues that a member of the court should have. Castiglione's ideal courtier was a well-educated, well-mannered aristocrat who mastered many fields, from poetry to music to sports.

Castiglione's ideal differed for men and women. The ideal man, he wrote, is athletic but not overactive. He is good at games, but not a gambler. He plays a musical instrument and knows literature and history but is not arrogant. The ideal woman offers a balance to men. She is graceful and kind, lively but reserved. She is beautiful, "for outer beauty," wrote Castiglione, "is the true sign of inner goodness."

Machiavelli's Successful Prince Niccolò Machiavelli (mahk ee uh VEHL ee) wrote a different kind of handbook. Machiavelli had served Florence as a diplomat and had observed kings and princes in foreign courts. He also had studied ancient Roman history. In *The Prince,* published in 1513, Machiavelli combined his personal experience of politics with his knowledge of the past to offer a guide to rulers on how to gain and maintain power.

Unlike earlier political writers, such as Plato, Machiavelli did not discuss leadership in terms of high ideals. Instead, *The Prince* looked at real rulers, such as the Medicis, in an age of ruthless power politics. Machiavelli stressed that the end justifies the means. He urged rulers to use whatever methods were necessary to achieve their goals. On the issue of honesty in government, for example, he taught that getting results was more important than keeping promises. He wrote:

> "How praiseworthy it is for a prince to keep his word and live with integrity rather than craftiness, everyone understands; yet . . . those princes have accomplished most who paid little heed to keeping their promises, but who knew how craftily to manipulate the minds of men."
> —Niccolò Machiavelli, *The Prince*

Machiavelli saw himself as an enemy of oppression and corruption. But critics attacked his cynical advice. Some even claimed that he was inspired by the devil. (In fact, the term "Machiavellian" came to refer to the use of deceit in politics.) Later students of government, however, argued that Machiavelli provided a realistic look at politics. His work continues to spark debate because it raises important ethical questions about the nature of government and the use of power.

 Primary Sources and Literature

See "Niccolò Machiavelli: Discourses," in the Reference Section at the back of this book.

SECTION 1 Assessment

Recall
1. Identify: **(a)** Lorenzo de' Medici, **(b)** Francesco Petrarch, **(c)** Leonardo da Vinci, **(d)** Michelangelo, **(e)** Raphael, **(f)** Baldassare Castiglione, **(g)** Niccolò Machiavelli.
2. Define: **(a)** patron, **(b)** humanism, **(c)** humanities, **(d)** perspective.

Comprehension
3. What conditions in Italy contributed to the emergence of the Renaissance?
4. Identify the concerns and attitudes emphasized during the Renaissance.
5. How did Renaissance art reflect humanist concerns?

Critical Thinking and Writing
6. **Making Inferences** Why might powerful rulers and wealthy business people choose to become patrons of the arts during the Renaissance?
7. **Linking Past and Present** In *The Prince,* Machiavelli advised rulers that it "is much safer to be feared than loved." **(a)** What did he mean by that? **(b)** Do you think a political leader today would be wise to follow that advice? Why or why not?

 Activity

Take It to the NET

Use the Internet to learn more about a major artist of the Italian Renaissance. You may choose one of the artists mentioned in this section or another artist such as Fra Angelico, Benvenuto Cellini, Sandro Botticelli, or Titian. Prepare a report on one artwork. Include a copy of the work.

Reading Focus

- Which artists brought the Renaissance to northern Europe?
- What themes did humanist thinkers and other writers explore?
- What impact did the printing revolution have on Europe?

Vocabulary

engraving

vernacular

utopian

Taking Notes

On a sheet of paper begin a table like the one shown here. Add information about the Renaissance under each heading as you read the section.

DUTCH	GERMAN	FLEMISH	ENGLISH	FRENCH	SPANISH
Erasmus	Dürer				

Main Idea The Renaissance slowly spread to northern Europe, where artists and writers experimented with new methods and ideas.

Setting the Scene "Had I not torn myself from Rome, I could never have resolved to leave," wrote Dutch priest Desiderius Erasmus. "There one enjoys sweet liberty, rich libraries, the charming friendship of writers and scholars, and the sight of antique monuments." Inspired by his visit to Italy, Erasmus helped spread the Renaissance to northern Europe.

Unlike Italy, northern Europe recovered slowly from the ravages of the Black Death. Only after 1450 did the north enjoy the economic growth that had earlier supported the Renaissance in Italy.

Artists of the Northern Renaissance

The northern Renaissance began in the prosperous cities of Flanders, a region that included parts of present-day northern France, Belgium, and the Netherlands. Spain, France, Germany, and England enjoyed their great cultural rebirth 100 years later, in the 1500s.

A "German Leonardo" Albrecht Dürer traveled to Italy in 1494 to study the techniques of the Italian masters. Returning home, he employed these methods in paintings and, especially, in engravings. In this form of art, an artist etches a design on a metal plate with acid. The artist then uses the plate to make prints. Many of Dürer's engravings portray the religious upheaval of his age.

Through his art as well as through essays, Dürer helped to spread Italian Renaissance ideas in his homeland. Because of his wide-ranging interests, which extended far beyond art, he is sometimes called the "German Leonardo."

Flemish Painters Among the many artists of Flanders in the 1400s, Jan and Hubert van Eyck (van ĪK) stand out. Their portrayals of townspeople as well as religious scenes abound in rich, realistic details. The van Eycks also developed oil paint. Northern artists used this new medium to produce strong colors and a hard surface that could survive the centuries.

In the 1500s, Pieter Bruegel (PEE tuhr BROY guhl) used vibrant colors to portray lively scenes of peasant life. Bruegel's work influenced later Flemish artists, who painted scenes of daily life rather than religious or classical themes.

In the 1600s, Peter Paul Rubens blended the realistic tradition of Flemish painters like Bruegel with the classical themes and artistic freedom of the Italian Renaissance. Many of his enormous paintings portray pagan figures from the classical past.

Northern Humanists

Like Italian humanists, northern European humanist scholars stressed education and classical learning. At the same time, they emphasized religious themes. They believed that the revival of ancient learning should be used to bring about religious and moral reform.

Erasmus The great Dutch priest and humanist Desiderius Erasmus used his knowledge of classical languages to produce a new Greek edition of the New Testament. He also called for a translation of the Bible into the vernacular, or everyday language of ordinary people. He scorned "those who are unwilling that Holy Scripture, translated into the vernacular, be read by the uneducated . . . as if the strength of the Christian religion consisted in the ignorance of it."

To Erasmus, an individual's chief duties were to be open-minded and of good will toward others. As a priest, he was disturbed by corruption in the Church and called for reform. In *The Praise of Folly*, Erasmus uses humor to expose the ignorant and immoral behavior of many people of his day, including the clergy.

More Erasmus's friend, the English humanist Thomas More, also pressed for social reform. In *Utopia*, More describes an ideal society in which men and women live in peace and harmony. No one is idle, all are educated, and justice is used to end crime rather than to eliminate the criminal. Today, the word utopian has come to describe any ideal society.

Writers for a New Audience

Scholars like More and Erasmus wrote mostly in Latin. In northern towns and cities, the growing middle class demanded new works in the vernacular. This audience particularly enjoyed dramatic tales and earthy comedies.

Rabelais The French humanist François Rabelais had a varied career as a monk, physician, Greek scholar, and author. In *Gargantua and Pantagruel,* he chronicles the adventures of two gentle giants. On the surface, the novel is

Dürer, the "German Leonardo"
Albrecht Dürer, shown in a self-portrait (below right), helped bring the genius of the Italian Renaissance to northern Europe. Many of his finest works were engravings, such as the portrait of a peasant couple (below left).

Theme: Arts and Literature How do these works reflect the Renaissance interest in the individual?

Reading Focus

■ How did abuses in the Church spark widespread criticism?

■ How did Martin Luther challenge Catholic authority and teachings?

■ What role did John Calvin play in the Reformation?

Vocabulary

indulgence

recant

predestination

theocracy

Taking Notes

On a sheet of paper draw a flowchart like the one shown here. As you read this section, add important events and ideas that contributed to the Protestant Reformation.

Church involved in worldly affairs
↓
Tetzel sells indulgences to raise money for new cathedral
↓
↓

Main Idea The ideas of Martin Luther and John Calvin led people to separate from the Roman Catholic Church and form new Protestant churches.

Setting the Scene During the Renaissance, the Church increasingly came under fire. Christians at all levels of society accused the clergy of corruption and worldliness. One peasant even compared the clergy to "wicked wolves." He protested, "Instead of saving the souls of the dead and sending them to Heaven, they gorge themselves at banquets after funerals."

During the Middle Ages, the Church had renewed itself from within. In the 1500s, though, new calls for reform unleashed forces that would shatter Christian unity. This movement is known as the Protestant Reformation.

Abuses in the Church

Beginning in the late Middle Ages, the Church had become increasingly caught up in worldly affairs. Popes competed with Italian princes for political power. They fought long wars to protect the Papal States against invasions by secular rulers. They intrigued against powerful monarchs who tried to seize control of the Church within their lands.

Like other Renaissance rulers, popes maintained a lavish lifestyle. Popes were also patrons of the arts. They hired painters and sculptors to beautify churches.

To finance such projects, the Church increased fees for services such as marriages and baptisms. Some clergy also promoted the sale of indulgences. According to Church teaching, an **indulgence** was a lessening of the time a soul would have to spend in purgatory, a place where souls too impure to enter heaven atoned for sins committed during their lifetimes. In the Middle Ages, the Church had granted indulgences only for good deeds, such as going on a crusade. By the late 1400s, however, indulgences could also be obtained in exchange for money gifts to the Church.

Many Christians protested such practices, especially in northern Europe. Christian humanists such as Erasmus urged a return to the simple ways of the early Christian Church. They stressed Bible study and rejected what they saw as the worldliness of the Church.

Luther's Protest

In 1517, protests against Church abuses erupted into a full-scale revolt. The man who triggered the revolt was a German monk and professor of theology named Martin Luther.

As a young man, Luther prayed and fasted and tried to lead a holy life. Still, he believed he was doomed to eternal damnation. He also grew disillusioned with what he saw as Church corruption and worldliness. At last, an incident in the town of Wittenberg prompted him to take action.

The 95 Theses In 1517, a priest named Johann Tetzel set up a pulpit on the outskirts of Wittenberg. He offered indulgences to any Christian who contributed money for the rebuilding of the Cathedral of St. Peter in Rome. Tetzel claimed that purchase of these indulgences would assure entry into heaven not only for the purchasers but for their dead relatives as well. "Don't you hear the voices of your dead parents and other relatives crying out?" he demanded.

To Luther, Tetzel's actions were the final outrage. He drew up 95 theses, or arguments, against indulgences. Among other things, he argued that indulgences had no basis in the Bible, that the pope had no authority to release souls from purgatory, and that Christians could be saved only through faith. In accordance with the custom of the time, he posted his list on the door of Wittenberg's All Saints Church.

Luther Versus the Church Almost overnight, copies of Luther's 95 Theses were printed and distributed across Europe, where they stirred furious debate. The Church called on Luther to recant, or give up his views. Luther refused. Instead, he developed even more radical new doctrines. Before long, he was urging Christians to reject the authority of Rome. Because the Church would not reform itself, he wrote, it must be reformed by secular authorities.

In 1521, the pope excommunicated Luther. Later that year, the new Holy Roman emperor, Charles V, summoned Luther to the diet, or assembly of German princes, at Worms. Luther went, expecting to defend his writings. Instead, the emperor simply ordered him to give them up. Luther again refused to recant:

> "Unless I am convicted by Scripture and plain reason—I do not accept the authority of popes and councils, for they have contradicted each other—I am captive to the Word of God. I cannot and will not recant anything, for to go against conscience is neither right nor safe."
> —Martin Luther, Speech Before the Diet of Worms

Charles declared Luther an outlaw, making it a crime for anyone in the empire to give him food or shelter. Still, Luther had many powerful supporters. One prince hid him at a castle in Wartburg. Luther remained in hiding for nearly a year. Throughout Germany, in the meantime, thousands hailed him as a hero. They accepted his teachings and, following his lead, renounced the authority of the pope.

Selling Indulgences
This 1517 cartoon shows Johann Tetzel selling indulgences to the people of Wittenberg. A jingle in the upper left corner said, "As soon as the coin in the coffer rings, a soul from purgatory springs."

Theme: Religions and Value Systems Do you think the artist who drew this picture approved of Tetzel's actions? Why or why not?

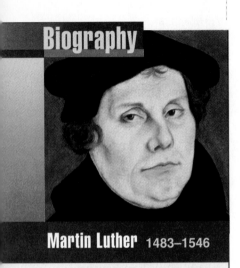

Martin Luther 1483–1546

"I am rough, boisterous, stormy, and altogether warlike," concluded Martin Luther. Luther's strong personality allowed him to take on the powerful Catholic Church. As a monk, Luther closely studied the Bible and came to believe that only its words—and not the pope or the Catholic Church—should dictate a person's actions.

When he appeared at the Diet of Worms, Luther was 37 years old. Though depressed and fearful about the confrontation, he held to his beliefs. According to one report, Luther declared, "Here I stand, I cannot do otherwise." When he refused to retract his statements, an order was given to destroy his books. Yet his influence grew, leading to a division within Christianity and the founding of a new church that took his name.

Theme: Impact of the Individual What inspired Luther's firm stand against the Church?

Luther's Teachings At the heart of Luther's teachings were several beliefs. First, he rejected the Church doctrine that good deeds were necessary for salvation. Instead, Luther argued that salvation was achieved through faith alone.

Second, Luther upheld the Bible as the sole source of religious truth. "The Gospel supplies the world with the salvation of Jesus Christ, peace of conscience, and every blessing," Luther wrote. He denied other authorities, such as Church councils or the pope.

Third, Luther rejected the idea that priests and the Church hierarchy had special powers. Instead, he talked of a "priesthood of all believers." All Christians, he said, had equal access to God through faith and the Bible. Luther translated the Bible into the German vernacular so that ordinary people could study it by themselves. Every town, he said, should have a school so that girls and boys could learn to read the Bible.

Luther called for other practices of the Catholic Church to be modified. He rejected five of the seven sacraments because the Bible did not mention them. He banned indulgences, confession, pilgrimages, and prayers to saints. He simplified the elaborate ritual of the mass and instead emphasized the sermon. And he permitted the clergy to marry. These and other changes were adopted by the Lutheran churches that were set up by Luther's followers.

Spread of Lutheran Ideas

Luther's ideas found a fertile field in northern Germany and Scandinavia. While the new printing presses spread Luther's writings, fiery preachers denounced Church abuses. By 1530, the Lutherans were using a new name, Protestant, for those who "protested" papal authority.

Widespread Support Why did Lutheranism win widespread support? Many clergy saw Luther's reforms as the answer to Church corruption. A number of German princes, however, embraced Lutheran beliefs for more selfish reasons. Some saw Lutheranism as a way to throw off the rule of both the Church and the Holy Roman emperor. Others welcomed a chance to seize Church property in their territory. Still other Germans supported Luther because of feelings of national loyalty. They were tired of German money going to support churches and clergy in Italy.

The Peasants' Revolt Many peasants also took up Luther's banner. They hoped to gain his support for social and economic change.

In 1524, a Peasants' Revolt erupted across Germany. The rebels called for an end to serfdom and demanded other changes in their harsh lives. Luther, however, strongly favored social order and respect for political authority. As the Peasants' Revolt grew more violent, Luther denounced it. With his support, nobles suppressed the rebellion, killing tens of thousands of people and leaving thousands more homeless.

The Peace of Augsburg During the 1530s and 1540s, Holy Roman emperor Charles V tried to force Lutheran princes back into the Catholic Church, but with little success. Finally, after a number of brief wars, Charles and the princes reached a settlement. The Peace of Augsburg, signed in 1555, allowed each prince to decide which religion—Catholic or Lutheran—would be followed in his lands. Most northern German states chose Lutheranism. The south remained largely Catholic.

John Calvin

The most important reformer to follow Martin Luther was John Calvin. Calvin had a logical, razor-sharp mind. His ideas had a profound effect on the direction of the Reformation.

Comparing Viewpoints

What Is the Goal of Education?

Both the Renaissance and the Reformation stressed the importance of education. What is your goal in pursuing an education? Think about the goals of modern-day schools as you compare the following viewpoints.

China 500 B.C.

Chinese philosopher Confucius explained how learning was essential for both the individual and the community:

❝ Extension of knowledge comes from the investigation of things. When things are investigated, knowledge is extended. When knowledge is extended, the will becomes sincere. When the will is sincere, the heart can be set right. When the heart is right, the personal life can be cultivated. When the personal life is cultivated, the community can be regulated. When the community is regulated, the government can be made orderly. And when the government is orderly, there will be peace in the world. ❞

Germany 1524

Protestant reformer Martin Luther called for German communities to set up and pay for Christian schools:

❝ The world has need of educated men and women to the end that men may govern the country properly and women may properly bring up their children, care for their domestics, and direct the affairs of the household. . . . The welfare of the state depends on the intelligence and virtue of its citizens. ❞

United States 1990s

This poster was designed for school guidance counselors.

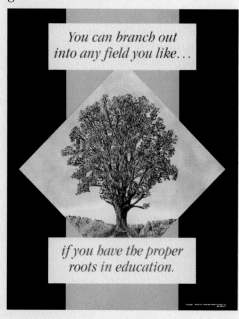

You can branch out into any field you like...

if you have the proper roots in education.

Cuba 1883

José Martí, a poet and political leader, turned away from classical ideas about what should be taught:

❝ The schools teach classes in ancient geography, rules of rhetoric, and similar things of long ago, but in their place there should be courses in health; advice on hygiene; practical counseling; clear and simple studies of the human body, its parts, functions, ways of adjusting one to the other, economizing one's strength, and directing it well so that there will be no reason to restore it later. ❞

Skills Assessment

1. What goal of education is stressed by both Confucius and Luther?
   - **A** gaining knowledge for its own sake
   - **B** making a good living
   - **C** cultivating the personal life
   - **D** contributing to the community

2. Who would be most likely to favor classes in physical education?
   - **E** Confucius
   - **F** Luther
   - **G** Martí
   - **H** the designer of the poster

3. **Critical Thinking** **Making Decisions** Identify a future career for yourself. Which educational theory would be most useful in helping you achieve this goal? Why? Explain why more than one type of education would be helpful.

Skills Tip

It is important to recognize that a writer may express his or her point of view as an absolute truth to convince others of its validity.

Teachings Calvin was born in France and trained as a priest and lawyer. In 1536, Calvin published the *Institutes of the Christian Religion.* In this book, which was read by Protestants everywhere, he set forth his religious beliefs. He also provided advice on how to organize and run a Protestant church.

Like Luther, Calvin believed that salvation was gained through faith alone. He, too, regarded the Bible as the only source of religious truth. But Calvin put forth a number of ideas of his own. He preached predestination, the idea that God had long ago determined who would gain salvation. To Calvinists, the world was divided into two kinds of people—saints and sinners. Calvinists tried to live like saints, believing that only those who were saved could live truly Christian lives.

Calvin's Geneva In 1541, Protestants in the city-state of Geneva in Switzerland asked Calvin to lead their community. In keeping with his teachings, Calvin set up a theocracy, or government run by church leaders.

Calvin's followers in Geneva came to see themselves as a new "chosen people" entrusted by God to build a truly Christian society. Calvinists stressed hard work, discipline, thrift, honesty, and morality. Citizens faced fines or other harsher punishments for offenses such as fighting, swearing, laughing in church, or dancing. Calvin closed theaters and frowned on elaborate dress. To many Protestants, this emphasis on strict morality made Calvinist Geneva seem a model community.

Like Luther, Calvin believed in religious education for girls as well as for boys. Women, he felt, should read the Bible—in private. Calvin also allowed women to sing in church, a practice that many church leaders criticized.

Spread of Calvinism Reformers from all over Europe visited Geneva and then returned home to spread Calvin's ideas. By the late 1500s, Calvinism had taken root in Germany, France, the Netherlands, England, and Scotland. This new challenge to the Roman Catholic Church set off bloody wars of religion across Europe.

In Germany, Calvinists faced opposition not only from Catholics, but from Lutherans as well. In France, wars raged between French Calvinists, called Huguenots, and Catholics. Calvinists in the Netherlands organized the Dutch Reformed Church. To avoid persecution, "field preachers" gave sermons in the countryside, away from the eyes of town authorities.

In Scotland, a Calvinist preacher named John Knox led a religious rebellion. Under Knox, Scottish Protestants overthrew their Catholic queen. They then set up the Scottish Presbyterian Church.

SECTION 3 Assessment

Recall
1. **Identify:** (a) Protestant Reformation, (b) Martin Luther, (c) Peace of Augsburg, (d) John Calvin, (e) Huguenot, (f) John Knox.
2. **Define:** (a) indulgence, (b) recant, (c) predestination, (d) theocracy.

Comprehension
3. Why did many Christians call for Church reform?
4. (a) How did Martin Luther's ideas differ from those expressed by the Catholic Church?

(b) Why did Luther gain wide-spread support?
5. Identify five ideas taught by John Calvin.

Critical Thinking and Writing
6. **Synthesizing Information** How did the Reformation reflect humanist ideas?
7. **Analyzing Information** Why do you think Luther's teachings caused a split in the Catholic Church when earlier reform movements did not?

Activity

Writing an Obituary
Read some obituaries, or death notices, in a current newspaper. Then, using the same style of writing, prepare a brief obituary of Martin Luther. The obituary should list key events in Luther's life and explain why he will be remembered. Try to avoid bias.

Reformation Ideas Spread

Reading Focus

- What ideas did radical reformers support?
- Why did England form a new church?
- How did the Catholic Church reform itself?
- Why did some groups face persecution?

Vocabulary

annul

canonize

compromise

scapegoat

ghetto

Taking Notes

On a sheet of paper draw a Venn diagram like the one shown here. As you read the section, add information from the text.

ENGLISH REFORMATION
- King Henry VIII establishes Church of England

• Widespread persecution

CATHOLIC REFORMATION
- Council of Trent

Main Idea Both the Protestant and Catholic reformations brought sweeping changes to Europe.

Setting the Scene

Henry III, the Catholic king of France, was deeply disturbed by Calvinist reformers in Geneva. "It would have been a good thing," he wrote, "if the city of Geneva were long ago reduced to ashes, because of the evil doctrine which has been sown from that city."

Throughout Europe, Catholic monarchs and the Catholic Church fought back against the Protestant challenge. They also took steps to reform the Church and to restore its spiritual leadership of the Christian world. At the same time, Protestant ideas continued to spread.

Radical Reformers

As the Reformation continued, hundreds of new Protestant sects sprang up. These sects often had ideas that were even more radical than those of Luther and Calvin. A number of groups, for example, rejected infant baptism. Infants, they argued, are too young to understand what it means to accept the Christian faith. Only adults, they felt, should receive the sacrament of baptism. They became known as Anabaptists.

A few Anabaptist sects sought radical social change as well. Some wanted to abolish private property. Others sought to speed up the coming of God's day of judgment by violent means. When radical Anabaptists took over the city of Munster in Germany, even Luther advised his supporters to join Catholics in suppressing the threat to the traditional order.

Most Anabaptists were peaceful. They called for religious toleration and separation of church and state. Despite harsh persecution, these groups influenced Protestant thinking in many countries. Today, the Baptists, Quakers, Mennonites, and Amish all trace their ancestry to the Anabaptists.

The English Reformation

In England, religious leaders such as John Wycliffe had called for Church reform as early as the 1300s. By the 1520s, some English clergy were toying with Protestant ideas. The break with the Catholic Church, however, was the work not of religious leaders but of King Henry VIII. For political reasons, Henry wanted to end papal control over the English church.

Seeking an Annulment At first, Henry VIII stood firmly against the Protestant revolt. The pope even awarded him the title "Defender of the Faith" for a pamphlet that he wrote denouncing Luther.

Henry VIII
Henry VIII wrote love songs, played tennis, and married six times. He was also ruthless to his enemies. He had dozens of people beheaded, including his second and fifth wives.

Theme: Impact of the Individual What impression of Henry do you get from this picture?

In 1527, an issue arose that set Henry at odds with the Church. After 18 years of marriage, Henry and his Spanish wife, Catherine of Aragon, had one surviving child, Mary Tudor. Henry felt that England's stability depended on his having a male heir. He wanted to marry Anne Boleyn, hoping that she would bear him a son. Because Catholic law does not permit divorce, he asked the pope to annul, or cancel, his marriage. Popes had annulled royal marriages before. But the current pope refused. He did not want to offend the Holy Roman emperor Charles V, Catherine's nephew.

Break With Rome   Henry was furious. Spurred on by his advisers, many of whom leaned toward Protestant teachings, he decided to take over the English church. Acting through Parliament, he had a series of laws passed. They took the English church from the pope's control and placed it under Henry's rule. In 1534, the Act of Supremacy made Henry "the only supreme head on Earth of the Church of England." Many loyal Catholics refused to accept the Act of Supremacy and were executed for treason. Among them was Sir Thomas More, the great English humanist. More was later canonized, or recognized as a saint, by the Catholic Church.

At the same time, Henry appointed Thomas Cranmer archbishop. Cranmer annulled the king's marriage. Henry then wed Anne Boleyn, who bore him a second daughter, Elizabeth. In the years ahead, Henry married four more times but had only one son, Edward.

The Church of England   Between 1536 and 1540, royal officials investigated English convents and monasteries. Claiming that they were centers of immorality, Henry ordered them closed. He then confiscated, or seized, their lands and wealth. Henry shrewdly granted some of these lands to nobles and other high-ranking citizens. He thus secured their support for the Anglican Church, as the new Church of England was called.

Despite these actions, Henry was not a religious radical. He rejected most Protestant doctrines. Aside from breaking away from Rome and allowing use of the English Bible, he kept most Catholic forms of worship.

Religious Turmoil   When Henry died in 1547, his 10-year-old son, Edward VI, inherited the throne. The young king's advisers were devout Protestants. Under Edward, Parliament passed new laws that brought the Protestant reforms to England. Thomas Cranmer drew up the *Book of Common Prayer.* It imposed a moderate form of Protestant service, while keeping many Catholic doctrines. Even so, the changes sparked uprisings that were harshly suppressed.

When Edward died in his teens, his half-sister, Mary Tudor, became queen. She was determined to return England to the Catholic faith. Under Queen Mary, hundreds of English Protestants were burned at the stake.

The Elizabethan Settlement   On Mary's death in 1558, the throne passed to Elizabeth. For years, Elizabeth had survived court intrigues, including the religious swings under Edward and Mary. As queen, Elizabeth had to determine the future of the Church of England. Moving cautiously at first, she slowly enforced a series of reforms that later were called the Elizabethan settlement.

The queen's policies were a compromise, or acceptable middle ground, between Protestant and Catholic practices. The Church of England preserved much Catholic ceremony and ritual. It kept the hierarchy of bishops and archbishops, but the queen reaffirmed that the monarch was the head of the Anglican Church. At the same time, Elizabeth restored a version of the *Book of Common Prayer,* accepted moderate Protestant doctrine, and allowed English to replace Latin in church services.

During a long reign, Elizabeth used all her skills to restore unity to England. Even while keeping many Catholic traditions, she made England a firmly Protestant nation. After her death, England faced new religious

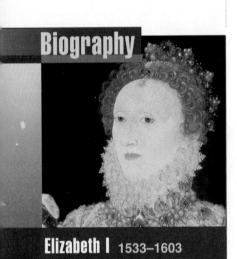

Biography

Elizabeth I 1533–1603

"She takes great pleasure in dancing and music," noted an English observer of Queen Elizabeth I. "In her youth she danced very well and composed measures and music and had played them herself." The normally thrifty queen employed some 50 singers, 40 musicians, and several songwriters to stage concerts for her.

Elizabeth also loved to see plays. She especially enjoyed the works of William Shakespeare, whom she helped to promote. The queen provided financial support and prestige for major acting groups, which led to a flowering of English theater.

Elizabeth's popular 45-year reign inspired other writers of the day. Poet Edmund Spenser dedicated *The Faerie Queene* to Elizabeth.

Theme: Impact of the Individual How did Queen Elizabeth help promote English arts?

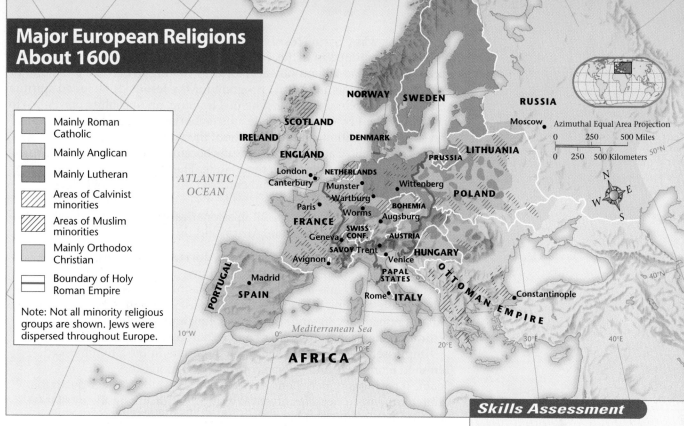

Major European Religions About 1600

Legend:
- Mainly Roman Catholic
- Mainly Anglican
- Mainly Lutheran
- Areas of Calvinist minorities
- Areas of Muslim minorities
- Mainly Orthodox Christian
- Boundary of Holy Roman Empire

Note: Not all minority religious groups are shown. Jews were dispersed throughout Europe.

Azimuthal Equal Area Projection
0   250   500 Miles
0   250   500 Kilometers

Map labels: NORWAY, SWEDEN, RUSSIA, Moscow, SCOTLAND, IRELAND, DENMARK, LITHUANIA, ENGLAND, PRUSSIA, London, Canterbury, NETHERLANDS, Munster, Wittenberg, POLAND, Wartburg, Paris, Worms, BOHEMIA, Augsburg, FRANCE, SWISS CONF., AUSTRIA, Geneva, SAVOY, Trent, HUNGARY, Avignon, Venice, PAPAL STATES, OTTOMAN EMPIRE, Madrid, PORTUGAL, SPAIN, Rome, ITALY, Constantinople, ATLANTIC OCEAN, Mediterranean Sea, AFRICA

Skills Assessment

Geography As a result of the Reformation, Europe was largely divided into Catholic and Protestant lands.

1. **Location** On the map, locate **(a)** England, **(b)** Scotland, **(c)** Wittenberg, **(d)** Worms, **(e)** Geneva.
2. **Region** **(a)** What was the majority religion in France? **(b)** Name one country that was mainly Lutheran.
3. **Critical Thinking** **Predicting Consequences** Based on this map, identify two areas where you think religious conflicts would be least likely to break out. Explain.

storms. But it escaped the endless religious wars that tore apart France and many other European states during the 1500s.

The Catholic Reformation

As the Protestant Reformation swept across northern Europe, a vigorous reform movement took hold within the Catholic Church. The leader of this movement, known as the Catholic Reformation, was Pope Paul III. During the 1530s and 1540s, he set out to revive the moral authority of the Church and roll back the Protestant tide. To end corruption within the papacy itself, he appointed reformers to key posts. They and their successors guided the Catholic Reformation for the rest of the century.

Council of Trent To establish the direction that reform should take, the pope called the Council of Trent in 1545. It met off and on for almost 20 years. The council reaffirmed traditional Catholic views, which Protestants had challenged. Salvation comes through faith and good works, it declared. The Bible, while a major source of religious truth, is not the only source.

The council also took steps to end abuses in the Church. It provided stiff penalties for worldliness and corruption among the clergy. It also established schools to create a better-educated clergy who could challenge Protestant teachings.

The Inquisition To deal with the Protestant threat more directly, Pope Paul strengthened the Inquisition. As you have read, the Inquisition was a Church court set up during the Middle Ages. The Inquisition used secret testimony, torture, and execution to root out heresy. It also prepared the Index of Forbidden Books, a list of works considered too immoral or irreligious for Catholics to read. It included books by Luther and Calvin.

Ignatius of Loyola In 1540, the pope recognized a new religious order, the Society of Jesus, or Jesuits. Founded by Ignatius of Loyola, the Jesuit order was determined to combat heresy and spread the Catholic faith.

Ignatius was a Spanish knight raised in the crusading tradition. After his leg was shattered in battle, he found comfort reading about saints who had overcome mental and physical torture. Vowing to become a "soldier of God," Ignatius drew up a strict program for the Jesuits. It included spiritual and moral discipline, rigorous religious training, and absolute obedience to the Church. Led by Ignatius, the Jesuits embarked on a crusade to defend and spread the Catholic faith throughout the world.

To further the Catholic cause, Jesuits became advisers to Catholic rulers, helping them combat heresy in their lands. They set up schools that taught humanist and Catholic beliefs and enforced discipline and obedience. Daring Jesuits slipped into Protestant lands in disguise to minister to the spiritual needs of Catholics. Jesuit missionaries spread their Catholic faith to distant lands, including Asia, Africa, and the Americas.

Teresa of Avila   As the Catholic Reformation spread, many Catholics experienced renewed feelings of intense faith. Teresa of Avila symbolized this renewal. Born into a wealthy Spanish family, Teresa entered a convent in her youth. Finding convent routine not strict enough, she set up her own order of nuns. They lived in isolation, eating and sleeping very little and dedicating themselves to prayer and meditation.

Impressed by her spiritual life, her superiors in the Church asked Teresa to reorganize and reform convents and monasteries throughout Spain. Teresa was widely honored for her work, and after her death the Church canonized her. Her mystical writings rank among the most important Christian texts of her time.

Results   Did the Catholic Reformation succeed? By 1600, Rome was a far more devout city than it had been 100 years earlier. Across Catholic Europe, piety and charity flourished. The reforms did slow the Protestant tide and even returned some areas to the Catholic Church. Still, Europe remained divided into a Catholic south and a Protestant north.

Widespread Persecution

During this period of heightened religious passion, persecution was widespread. Both Catholics and Protestants fostered intolerance. Catholic mobs attacked and killed Protestants. Protestants killed Catholic priests and wrecked Catholic churches. Both Catholics and Protestants persecuted radical sects like the Anabaptists.

Witch Hunts   Almost certainly, the religious fervor of the times contributed to a wave of witch hunting. Those accused of being witches, or agents of the devil, were usually women, although some men faced similar attacks. Between 1450 and 1750, tens of thousands of women and men died as victims of witch hunts.

Scholars have offered various reasons for this persecution. At the time, most people believed in magic and spirits. They saw a close link between magic and heresy. In addition, during times of trouble, people often look for scapegoats on whom they can blame their problems. People accused of witchcraft were often social outcasts—beggars, poor widows, midwives blamed for infant deaths, or herbalists whose potions were seen as gifts from the devil.

Most victims of the witch hunts died in the German states, Switzerland, and France, all centers of religious conflict. When the wars of religion came to an end, the persecution of witches also declined.

Jews and the Reformation   The Reformation brought hard times to Europe's Jews. For many Jews in Italy, the early Renaissance had been a time of relative prosperity. Unlike Spain, which had expelled its Jews in 1492, Italy allowed Jews to remain. Some Jews followed the traditional trades they had been restricted to in medieval times. They were goldsmiths, artists, traders, and moneylenders. Others expanded into medicine, law, government, and business. Still, pressure remained strong on Jews to convert. By 1516, Venice ordered Jews to live in a separate quarter of the city, which became known as a ghetto. Other Italian cities also forced Jews into walled ghettos.

During the Reformation, restrictions on Jews increased. At first, Luther hoped that Jews would be converted to his teachings. However, when they did not convert, he called for them to be expelled from Christian lands and for their synagogues and books to be burned. In time, some German princes did expel Jews. Others confined Jews to ghettos, requiring them to wear a yellow badge if they traveled outside.

In the 1550s, Pope Paul IV placed added restrictions on Jews. Even Emperor Charles V, who supported toleration of Jews in the Holy Roman Empire, banned them from Spanish colonies in the Americas. After 1550, many Jews migrated to Poland-Lithuania and to parts of the Ottoman empire, where they were permitted to prosper. Dutch Calvinists allowed Jewish families who were driven out of Portugal and Spain to settle in the Netherlands.

Looking Ahead

The upheavals of the Catholic and Protestant reformations sparked wars of religion in Europe until the mid-1600s. At that time, issues of religion began to give way to issues of national power. As you will read, Catholic and Protestant rulers often made decisions based on political interests rather than for purely religious reasons.

Cause *and* Effect

Long-Term Causes	Immediate Causes
• Roman Catholic Church becomes more worldly • Humanists urge a return to simple religion • Strong national monarchs emerge	• Johann Tetzel sells indulgences in Wittenberg • Martin Luther posts 95 Theses • Luther translates the Bible into German • Printing press allows spread of reform ideas • Calvin and other reformers preach against Roman Catholic traditions

Protestant Reformation

Immediate Effects	Long-Term Effects
• Peasants' Revolt • Founding of Lutheran, Calvinist, Anglican, Presbyterian, and other Protestant churches • Weakening of Holy Roman Empire • Luther calls for Jews to be expelled from Christian lands	• Religious wars in Europe • Catholic Reformation • Strengthening of the Inquisition • Jewish migration to Eastern Europe • Increased antisemitism

Connections to Today

• About one fourth of Christians are Protestant
• Religious conflict in Northern Ireland

Skills Assessment **Chart** The Protestant Reformation brought sweeping changes to Western Europe. **Identify one religious and one political effect of the Reformation.**

SECTION 4 Assessment

Recall

1. **Identify:** (a) Henry VIII, (b) Elizabeth I, (c) Council of Trent, (d) Inquisition, (e) Jesuits, (f) Teresa of Avila.
2. **Define:** (a) annul, (b) canonize, (c) compromise, (d) scapegoat, (e) ghetto.

Comprehension

3. Why were the Anabaptists considered radical?
4. Describe the steps by which England became a Protestant country.
5. What were the goals of the Catholic Reformation?

6. Why did persecution increase after the Reformation?

Critical Thinking and Writing

7. **Recognizing Causes and Effects** If the Catholic Church had undertaken reform earlier, do you think that the Protestant Reformation would have occurred? Explain.
8. **Recognizing Point of View** The Protestant term for the Catholic Reformation was the Counter-Reformation. (The prefix *counter* means "against.") How do these two terms reflect different points of view?

Activity

Writing a News Report Prepare a script for a TV news program reporting on King Henry VIII and his break with the Catholic Church. You might wish to include visuals and interviews as well.

The Scientific Revolution

Reading Focus

- How did astronomers change the way people viewed the universe?
- What was the new scientific method?
- What advances did Newton and other scientists make?

Vocabulary

heliocentric
hypothesis
scientific method
gravity

Taking Notes

On a sheet of paper, begin a concept web like this one. As you read this section, fill in the blank circles with information about the Scientific Revolution. Add as many other circles as you need.

(Astronomy) — SCIENTIFIC REVOLUTION — Heliocentric theory

Main Idea A new way of thinking, based on experimentation and observation, changed the way Europeans looked at the world.

Galileo

In addition to his work in astronomy, Galileo made important discoveries about the motion of pendulums and falling objects. This statue honors Galileo.

Theme: Impact of the Individual In this statue, what might be the meaning of the object Galileo holds in his hand?

Setting the Scene In 1609, Galileo Galilei trained his new telescope on the night sky. Its specially ground lens allowed him to view amazing sights. He saw mountains on the moon, fiery spots on the sun, and four moons circling the planet Jupiter. "I did discover many particulars in Heaven that had been unseen and unheard of until this our age," he later wrote. Galileo's observations supported a new view of the universe.

Leaders of the Renaissance and the Reformation looked to the past for models. Humanists turned to ancient classical ideas. Religious reformers were inspired by the Bible and early Christian times. By contrast, the profound change that took place in science in the mid-1500s pointed ahead, toward a future shaped by a new way of thinking about the physical universe. We call that historical change the Scientific Revolution.

Changing Views of the Universe

Until the mid-1500s, European scholars accepted the theory of the ancient Greek astronomer Ptolemy. Ptolemy taught that the Earth was the center of the universe. Not only did this view seem to agree with common sense, it also matched the teachings of the Church. In the 1500s and 1600s, some startling discoveries radically changed the way Europeans viewed the physical world.

A Revolutionary Theory In 1543, Polish scholar Nicolaus Copernicus (koh PER nuh kuhs) published *On the Revolutions of the Heavenly Spheres*. In it, he proposed a heliocentric, or sun-centered, model of the universe. The sun, he said, stood at the center of the universe. The Earth was just one of several planets that revolved around the sun.

Most experts rejected this revolutionary theory. In Europe at the time, all scientific knowledge and many religious teachings were based on the arguments developed by classical thinkers. If Ptolemy's reasoning about the planets was wrong, they believed, then the whole system of human knowledge might be called into question. But in the late 1500s, the Danish astronomer Tycho Brahe (TEE koh BRAH uh) provided evidence that supported Copernicus's theory. Brahe set up an astronomical observatory. Every night for years, he carefully observed the sky, accumulating data about the movement of the heavenly bodies.

After Brahe's death, his assistant, the brilliant German astronomer and mathematician Johannes Kepler, used Brahe's data to calculate the orbits of the planets revolving around the sun. His calculations supported Copernicus's heliocentric view. At the same time, however, they showed that each planet did not move in a perfect circle, as both Ptolemy and Copernicus believed, but in an oval-shaped orbit called an ellipse.

Galileo Scientists of many lands built on the foundations laid by Copernicus and Kepler. In Italy, Galileo Galilei assembled an astronomical telescope. As you have read, he observed the four moons of Jupiter moving slowly around that planet—exactly, he realized, the way Copernicus said that the Earth moved around the sun.

Galileo's discoveries caused an uproar. Other scholars attacked him because his observations contradicted ancient views about the world. The Church condemned him because his ideas challenged the Christian teaching that the heavens were fixed, unmoving, and perfect.

In 1633, Galileo was tried before the Inquisition. Threatened with death unless he withdrew his "heresies," Galileo agreed to state publicly that the Earth stood motionless at the center of the universe. "Nevertheless," he is said to have muttered as he left the court, "it does move."

A New Scientific Method

Despite the opposition of religious authorities, by the early 1600s a new approach to science had emerged. Unlike most earlier approaches, it did not rely on authorities like Aristotle or Ptolemy or even the Bible. It depended instead upon observation and experimentation.

A Step-by-Step Process The new approach to science required scientists to collect and accurately measure data. To explain the data, scientists used reasoning to propose a logical hypothesis, or possible explanation. They then tested the hypothesis with further observation or experimentation. Complex mathematical calculations were used to convert the observations and experiments into scientific laws. After reaching a conclusion, scientists repeated their work at least once—and usually many times—to confirm their findings. This step-by-step process of discovery became known as the scientific method.

Bacon and Descartes The new scientific method was really a revolution in thought. Two giants of this revolution were the Englishman Francis Bacon and the Frenchman René Descartes (ruh NAY day KAHRT). Each devoted himself to the problem of knowledge.

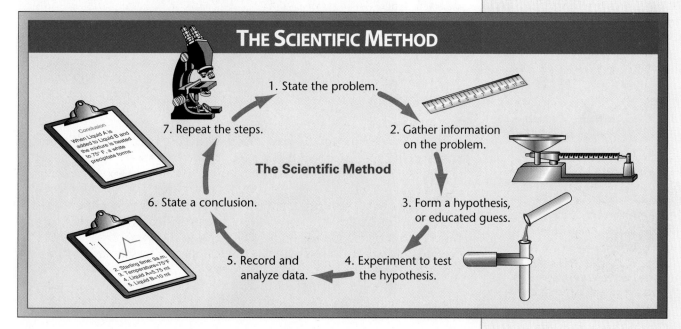

THE SCIENTIFIC METHOD

1. State the problem.
2. Gather information on the problem.
3. Form a hypothesis, or educated guess.
4. Experiment to test the hypothesis.
5. Record and analyze data.
6. State a conclusion.
7. Repeat the steps.

The Scientific Method

Both Bacon and Descartes rejected Aristotle's scientific assumptions. They also challenged the scholarly traditions of the medieval universities that sought to make the physical world fit in with the teachings of the Church. Both argued that truth is not known at the beginning of inquiry but at the end, after a long process of investigation.

Bacon and Descartes differed in their methods, however. Bacon stressed experimentation and observation. He wanted science to make life better for people by leading to practical technologies. Descartes emphasized human reasoning as the best road to understanding. In his *Discourse on Method*, he explains how he decided to discard all traditional authorities and search for provable knowledge. Left only with doubt, he concluded that the doubter had to exist and made his famous statement, "I think, therefore I am."

Newton Ties It All Together

As a student in England, Isaac Newton devoured the works of the leading scientists of his day. By age 24, he had formed a brilliant theory to explain why the planets moved as they did. According to one story, Newton saw an apple fall from a tree. He wondered whether the force that pulled that apple to the Earth might not also control the movements of the planets.

In the next 20 years, Newton perfected his theory. Using mathematics, he showed that a single force keeps the planets in their orbits around the sun. He called this force gravity.

In 1687, Newton published *Mathematical Principles of Natural Philosophy*, explaining the law of gravity and other workings of the universe. Nature, argued Newton, follows uniform laws. All motion in the universe can be measured and described mathematically.

To many, Newton's work seemed to link physics and astronomy, to bind the new science as gravity itself held the universe together. An English poet caught the spirit of what would later be called the Newtonian revolution:

"Nature and Nature's Laws lay hid in night,
God said, Let Newton be! and all was light."
—Alexander Pope, *Epitaphs*

For over 200 years, Newton's laws held fast. In the early 1900s, startling new theories of the universe called some of Newton's ideas into question.

Exploring Human Anatomy
Leonardo da Vinci dissected more than 30 corpses in order to create precise sketches of the human body (PAST). Today, doctors study anatomy with the aid of advanced computer technology (PRESENT).

Theme: Economics and Technology How were anatomical drawings useful to Leonardo? How is computer imaging useful to doctors today?

PAST

PRESENT

Yet Newton's laws of motion and mechanics continue to have many practical uses. Newton also helped develop an important new branch of mathematics—calculus.

Other Scientific Advances

The 1500s and 1600s saw breakthroughs in many branches of science. Some of the most significant advances occurred in chemistry and medicine.

Chemistry Chemistry slowly freed itself from the magical notions of medieval alchemists, who had believed it was possible to transform ordinary metals into gold. In the 1600s, Robert Boyle distinguished between individual elements and chemical compounds. He also explained the effect of temperature and pressure on gases. Boyle's work opened the way to modern chemical analysis of the composition of matter.

Medicine Medieval physicians relied on the ancient works of Galen. Galen, however, had made many errors, in part because he had limited knowledge of human anatomy. During the Renaissance, artists and physicians made new efforts to study the human body. In 1543, Andreas Vesalius published *On the Structure of the Human Body*, the first accurate and detailed study of human anatomy. A French physician, Ambroise Paré, developed a new and more effective ointment for preventing infection. He also developed a technique for closing wounds with stitches.

In the early 1600s, William Harvey, an English scholar, described the circulation of the blood for the first time. He showed how the heart serves as a pump to force blood through veins and arteries. Later in the century, the Dutch inventor Anthony von Leeuwenhoek perfected the microscope and became the first human to see cells and microorganisms. These pioneering scientists opened the way for further advances.

Looking Ahead

The rapid advance in science and technology that began in the 1500s has continued to this day. Thinkers like Bacon, Descartes, and Newton applied the scientific method to the pursuit of knowledge. Their work encouraged others to search for scientific laws governing the universe. Such ideas opened the way to the Enlightenment of the 1700s and a growing belief in human progress.

Did You Know?

A Renaissance Body Snatcher

Gaining firsthand knowledge of anatomy could be a gruesome process. Andreas Vesalius stole bones from a cemetery. Once, he even sneaked out into the countryside at night to steal the almost complete skeleton of an executed criminal.

As his research became more respected, Vesalius gained official permission to examine bodies of executed convicts. At times, executions were even delayed until Vesalius was ready to perform his next autopsy.

Theme: Continuity and Change Do doctors today have to go to the same lengths as Vesalius? Why or why not?

SECTION 5 Assessment

Recall

1. **Identify: (a)** Nicolaus Copernicus, **(b)** Johannes Kepler, **(c)** Galileo Galilei, **(d)** Francis Bacon, **(e)** René Descartes, **(f)** Isaac Newton, **(g)** Robert Boyle.
2. **Define: (a)** heliocentric, **(b)** hypothesis, **(c)** scientific method, **(d)** gravity.

Comprehension

3. Why did some people oppose the heliocentric theory of the universe?
4. How did the scientific method differ from earlier approaches?
5. How did Newton try to explain the workings of the universe?

Critical Thinking and Writing

6. **Making Inferences** Newton wrote, "If I have seen further [than others] it is by standing on the shoulders of giants." **(a)** What do you think he meant? **(b)** Who might be some of the "giants" to whom Newton was referring?
7. **Applying Information** Identify three ways in which your life today might have been different if the Scientific Revolution had never occurred.

Activity
Take It to the NET

Use the Internet to learn more about the life and work of William Harvey. Then, prepare a brief biographical sketch of Harvey. Include a diagram of the circulatory system that he described.

Creating a Chapter Summary

On a sheet of paper make a table like the one shown here. Use it to summarize major events that you have learned about in this chapter. Some cells have been partly filled in to help you get started.

	RENAISSANCE	PROTESTANT REFORMATION	CATHOLIC REFORMATION	SCIENTIFIC REVOLUTION
WHAT IT WAS	• Time of creativity and change			
CAUSES				
IMPORTANT EVENTS		• Luther posts 95 Theses •		
KEY PEOPLE			• Ignatius of Loyola •	

CD-ROM Review For additional review of the major concepts of Chapter 14, see the *Guide to the Essentials of World History* or the *Interactive Student Tutorial CD-ROM.*

Web Site Self-Test For practice test questions for Chapter 14, see **www.phschool.com.**

Building Vocabulary

Write sentences using the chapter vocabulary words listed below, leaving blanks where the vocabulary words would go. Then, exchange your sentences with another student, and fill in the blanks in each other's sentences.

1. patron
2. humanism
3. vernacular
4. utopian
5. indulgence
6. predestination
7. annul
8. ghetto
9. heliocentric
10. hypothesis

Recalling Key Facts

11. **(a)** What was the Renaissance? **(b)** When and where did it begin?
12. What three different kinds of plays did William Shakespeare write?
13. Why did Martin Luther post his 95 Theses?
14. How did the English Reformation occur?
15. What is the scientific method?
16. What did Descartes mean by the statement "I think, therefore I am"?

Critical Thinking and Writing

17. **Connecting to Geography** How did artists translate new techniques of the Renaissance to their landscape paintings?
18. **Comparing** **(a)** Compare and contrast the Renaissance in Italy with the Renaissance in northern Europe. **(b)** How would you account for the differences?
19. **Understanding Sequence** An English author wrote, "The preaching of sermons is speaking to a few of mankind, but printing books is talking to the whole world." How does this statement suggest a relationship between two of the key events discussed in this chapter?
20. **Recognizing Causes and Effects** Why did England escape the kinds of religious wars that tore apart other European nations?
21. **Linking Past and Present** Modern scientists refer to the discoveries of Copernicus as the Copernican Revolution. Why do you think they use that term?

The passage below is from the Council of Trent called by Pope Paul III in 1545 to establish the direction of Catholic reform. Read the passage, then answer the questions that follow.

> "This holy Council cautions all bishops so to live . . . that they can bring together truth and behavior as a kind of constant example of thrift, modesty, and decency, and especially of that holy humility that so strongly commends men to God. Therefore, following the example set by our fathers at the Council of Carthage, it is ordered that bishops shall content themselves not only with modest household furniture and simple food, but with regard to the rest of their manner of living and to their whole house, so that nothing appears that is alien to this holy institution of the Church and that does not show simplicity, zeal for God, and contempt for worldly things."

—Canons and Decrees of the
Holy Council of Trent

22. To what group of people is this passage mainly addressed?
23. (a) What orders are given in the passage? (b) On what authority are these orders given?
24. What does this document imply about the situation in the Church before the Council?
25. How can you tell that the reformers at the Council of Trent looked to the example of the early Christian Church?
26. (a) Do you think the reformers at Trent would agree with Protestant reformers about worldliness in the Church? (b) Do you think they would agree about the subject of papal authority?

Use the Internet to research the invention of the printing press and its effects on Renaissance Europe. Then, write an essay in which you try to persuade the reader that the invention of the Internet either will or will not have a similar effect on world civilization in the future.

Michelangelo sculpted this huge statue of the Israelite prophet Moses for the tomb of Pope Julius II. It stands almost eight feet tall and took years to complete. Study the statue, then answer the following questions:

27. How was this choice of subject typical of the Renaissance?
28. How does the sculpture show Renaissance humanism?
29. How does the sculpture show Michelangelo's attention to anatomical detail?
30. Why would an artist like Michelangelo need the support of a powerful patron like the pope?

Skills Tip

When you study a work of art, use what you know about the period in which it was created. In particular, it is important to understand what themes and topics were of concern to artists of that period.

Reading Focus

- Why did Europeans cross the seas?
- How did Portugal's eastward explorations lead to the development of a trading empire?
- How did Columbus's voyages affect the search for a passage to the Indies?

Vocabulary

cartographer
astrolabe
caravel
scurvy
circumnavigate

Taking Notes

Copy the table below. As you read the section, add information about the explorations of Portugal and Spain in the 1400s and 1500s.

PORTUGAL	SPAIN
• Henry the Navigator sponsors voyages	• Columbus sails for India; reaches Caribbean
•	•

Main Idea A desire to share in the rich spice trade of the East spurred Europeans to explore the oceans.

Setting the Scene Today, we take pepper for granted. To Europeans of past ages, though, this spice was as valuable as gold. Ancient Romans paid as much as $125 for 12 ounces of pepper. During the Middle Ages, the pepper in your local supermarket could have paid a year's rent. By the late 1400s, the desire to share in the rich spice trade of the East spurred Europeans to explore the oceans.

Europeans Explore the Seas

Europeans had traded with Asia long before the Renaissance. The Crusades introduced Europeans to many luxury goods from Asia. Later, when the Mongol empire united much of Asia in the 1200s and 1300s, Asian goods flowed to Europe along complex overland trade routes.

The Black Death and the breakup of the Mongol empire disrupted trade. By the 1400s, though, Europe was recovering from the plague. As its population grew, so did the demand for trade goods. The most valued items were spices, such as cinnamon, cloves, nutmeg, and pepper. People used spices in many ways—to preserve food, add flavor to dried and salted meat, and make medicines and perfumes. The chief source of spices was the Moluccas, an island chain in present-day Indonesia, which Europeans then called the Spice Islands.

The Spice Trade
Voyages of exploration were driven by the desire for access to spices. Nutmeg, cinnamon, cloves, and pepper were among the most prized trade items.

Theme: Economics and Technology Why were spices so costly?

Motives In the 1400s, Muslim and Italian merchants controlled most trade between Asia and Europe. Muslim traders brought prized goods to eastern Mediterranean ports. Traders from Venice and other Italian cities then carried the precious cargoes to European markets. Europeans, however, wanted to gain direct access to the riches of Asia. To do so, the Atlantic powers—first Portugal, then Spain—sought a route to Asia that bypassed the Mediterranean.

The desire for wealth was not the only motive that lured people to sea. Some voyagers were still fired by the centuries-old desire to crusade against the Muslims. The Renaissance spirit of inquiry further fired people's desire to learn more about the lands beyond Europe.

Improved Technology Several improvements in technology helped Europeans conquer the vast oceans of the world. Cartographers, or map-makers, created more accurate maps and sea charts. European sailors also learned to use the astrolabe, an instrument developed by the ancient Greeks and perfected by the Arabs, to determine their latitude at sea.

Along with more reliable navigational tools, Europeans designed larger and better ships. The Portuguese developed the caravel, which combined the square sails of European ships with Arab lateen, or triangular, sails. Caravels also adapted the sternpost rudder and numerous masts of Chinese ships. The new rigging made it easier to sail across or even into the wind. Finally, European ships added more weaponry, including sturdier cannons.

Portugal Sails Eastward

Portugal, a small nation on the western edge of Spain, led the way in exploration. By the 1400s, Portugal was strong enough to expand into Muslim North Africa. In 1415, the Portuguese seized Ceuta (say oo tah) on the North African coast. The victory sparked the imagination of Prince Henry, known to history as Henry the Navigator.

Mapping the African Coast Prince Henry embodied the crusading drive and the new spirit of exploration. He hoped to expand Christianity and find the source of African gold.

At Sagres, in southern Portugal, Henry gathered scientists, cartographers, and other experts. They redesigned ships, prepared maps, and trained captains and crews for long voyages. Henry then sent out ships that slowly worked their way south to explore the western coast of Africa.

Henry died in 1460, but the Portuguese continued their quest. In 1488, Bartholomeu Dias rounded the southern tip of Africa. Despite the turbulent seas, the tip became known as the Cape of Good Hope because it opened the way for a sea route to Asia.

On to India In 1497, Vasco da Gama led four ships around the Cape of Good Hope. After a 10-month voyage, da Gama finally reached the great spice port of Calicut on the west coast of India. The long voyage home took a heavy toll. The Portuguese lost half their ships. Many sailors died of hunger, thirst, and scurvy, a disease caused by a lack of vitamin C in their diets during months at sea. Still, the venture proved highly profitable to the survivors. In India, da Gama had acquired a cargo of spices that he sold at a profit of 3,000 percent.

Da Gama quickly outfitted a new fleet. In 1502, he forced a treaty of friendship on the ruler of Calicut. Da Gama then left Portuguese merchants there to buy spices when prices were low and to store them near the dock until the next fleet could return. Soon, the Portuguese seized key ports around the Indian Ocean to create a vast trading empire.

Columbus Sails to the West

News of Portugal's successes spurred other nations to look for a sea route to Asia. An Italian navigator from the port of Genoa, Christopher Columbus, sought Portuguese backing for his own plan. He wanted to reach the Indies* by sailing west across the Atlantic. Like most educated Europeans, Columbus knew that the Earth was a sphere. A few weeks

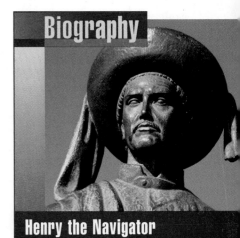

Biography

Henry the Navigator
1394–1460

As a younger son of Portugal's King John I and Queen Philippa, Henry was not destined to rule his nation. This did not stop him, however, from carving out a place in history. During the campaign to conquer Ceuta, in northern Africa, he found his true calling. Inspired by stories of gold beyond the Sahara, he recognized Portugal's need for a sea route to distant lands.

Henry's interest in gaining wealth for Portugal was equaled by his desire to spread Christianity. In 1420, he was made a knight in a religious order. Already the governor of a province in southern Portugal, Henry paid for voyages of exploration with funds provided by the order. Each ship that set out from his court in Sagres bore a red cross on its sails, indicating the dual quest to find new lands and new converts to Christianity.

Theme: Impact of the Individual How might Portugal's history have been different if Henry had been the oldest son?

*The Indies, or East Indies, was the European name for a group of islands in Southeast Asia. Today, they are a part of Indonesia.

Early Voyages of European Exploration, 1487–1609

Explorers for Portugal

- - → Dias, 1487–1488

——→ Da Gama, 1497–1499

Explorers for Spain

- - → Columbus, 1492–1493

——→ Balboa, 1510–1513

-·-·→ Magellan and Elcano, 1519–1522

Explorers for England

——→ Cabot, 1497

Explorers for France

——→ Cartier, 1534–1535

Explorers for the Netherlands

——→ Hudson, 1609

NORTH AMERICA

NEWFOUNDLAND

EUROPE

OTTOMAN EMPIRE

AZTEC EMPIRE

West Indies

SONGHAI

AFRICA

ATLANTIC OCEAN

PACIFIC OCEAN

INCAN EMPIRE

SOUTH AMERICA

Equator

Cape of Good Hope

Strait of Magellan

Cape Horn

Skills Assessment

Geography Beginning in the later 1400s, European nations sent explorers across the oceans in search of riches. New technology, such as the astrolabe and the caravel, made these voyages possible.

1. **Location** On the map, locate **(a)** Ottoman empire, **(b)** West Indies, **(c)** Strait of Magellan.
2. **Movement (a)** What region seems to have been of the most interest to explorers for England and the Netherlands? **(b)** What tool would they have used to determine location during their voyage?
3. **Critical Thinking Making Inferences** Why do you think explorers tended to take similar routes?

sailing west, he reasoned, would bring a ship to eastern Asia. His plan made sense, but Columbus made two errors. First, he greatly underestimated the size of the Earth. Second, he had no idea that two continents lay in his path.

Voyages of Columbus After Portugal refused to help him, Columbus persuaded Ferdinand and Isabella of Spain to finance his "enterprise of the Indies." In 1492, the Catholic rulers had driven the Muslims from their last stronghold in Spain. To strengthen their power, they sought new sources of wealth. Queen Isabella was also anxious to spread Christianity in Asia.

On August 3, 1492, Columbus sailed west with three small ships, the *Pinta*, the *Niña*, and the *Santa María*. Although the expedition encountered good weather and a favorable wind, no land came into sight. Provisions ran low, and the crew became anxious. Finally, on October 12, a lookout yelled, "Land! Land!"

Columbus then spent several months cruising the islands of the Caribbean. Because he thought he had reached the Indies, he called the people of the region Indians. In 1493, he returned to Spain to a hero's welcome. In three later voyages, Columbus remained convinced he had reached the coast of East Asia. Before long, though, other Europeans realized that Columbus had found a route to continents previously unknown to them.

Line of Demarcation Spain and Portugal pressed rival claims to the lands Columbus explored. In 1493, Pope Alexander VI stepped in to keep the peace. He set a Line of Demarcation dividing the non-European world

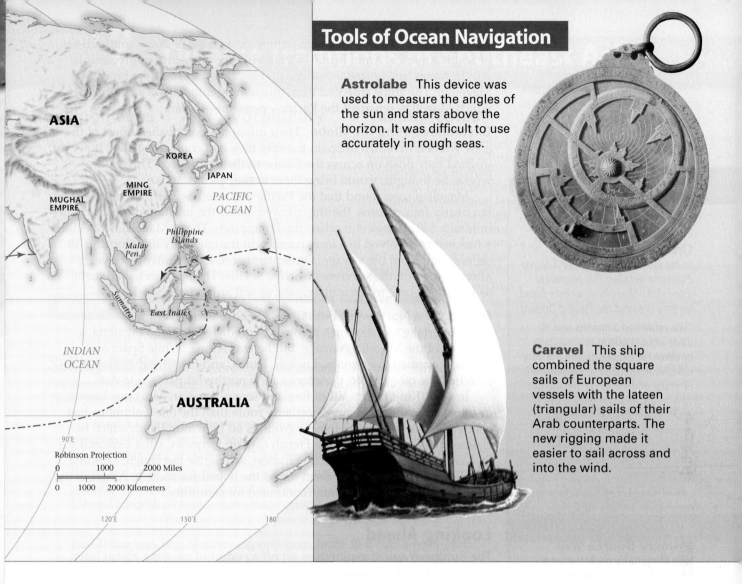

Tools of Ocean Navigation

Astrolabe This device was used to measure the angles of the sun and stars above the horizon. It was difficult to use accurately in rough seas.

Caravel This ship combined the square sails of European vessels with the lateen (triangular) sails of their Arab counterparts. The new rigging made it easier to sail across and into the wind.

Map labels: ASIA, KOREA, JAPAN, MING EMPIRE, MUGHAL EMPIRE, PACIFIC OCEAN, Philippine Islands, Malay Pen., Sumatra, East Indies, INDIAN OCEAN, AUSTRALIA

Robinson Projection
0   1000   2000 Miles
0   1000   2000 Kilometers
90°E   120°E   150°E   180°

into two zones. Spain had trading and exploration rights in any lands west of the line. Portugal had the same rights east of the line.

In 1500, the Portuguese captain Pedro Alvarez Cabral was blown off course as he sailed around Africa. Landing in Brazil, which lay east of the Line of Demarcation, he claimed it for Portugal.

Naming the "New World" In 1507, a German cartographer read reports about the "New World" written by an Italian sailor, Amerigo Vespucci. The mapmaker labeled the region America. The islands Columbus had explored in the Caribbean became known as the West Indies.

The Search Continues

Europeans continued to seek new routes around or through the Americas. In 1513, the Spanish adventurer Vasco Núñez de Balboa, with the help of Native Americans, hacked a passage through the tropical forests of Panama. From a ridge on the west coast, he gazed at a huge body of water that he called the South Sea. On September 20, 1519, a minor Portuguese noble named Ferdinand Magellan set out from Spain with five ships. His crew included men from Europe, Africa, and Southeast Asia.

Perils at Sea As the ships sailed south and west, through storms and calms and tropical heat, Magellan had to put down more than one mutiny. At last, the fleet reached the coast of South America. Carefully, they explored each bay, hoping for one that would lead to the Pacific.

Virtual Field Trip

www.phschool.com

**Angkor Wat
Cambodia**

To learn more about Angkor Wat, use the Internet address above to link to the Web site for Angkor Wat.

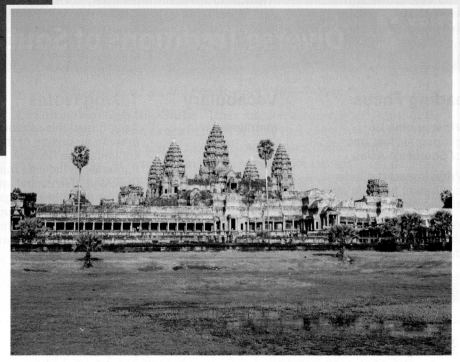

Khmer Temple
Although Angkor Wat lies in ruins today, its intricate carvings suggest the magnificence of the original complex. The central towers represent the peaks of mythical Mount Meru, which was believed to be the home of the gods.

Theme: Religions and Value Systems Why might the builders of Angkor Wat have chosen to represent Mount Meru in their design?

summer and southwest in winter. Between seasons, while waiting for the winds to shift, merchants harbored their vessels in Southeast Asian ports, which became important centers of trade and culture. Soon, an international trade network linked India, Southeast Asia, and China to East Africa and the Middle East.

The key products of Southeast Asia were spices. Only a fraction of the spices traded in the region was destined for markets in Europe. Most cargoes went to East Asia, the Middle East, and East Africa.

Early Traditions The peoples of Southeast Asia developed their own cultures before Indian or Chinese influences shaped the region. At Bang Chiang in Thailand, archaeologists have found jars and bronze bracelets at least 5,000 years old. This evidence is challenging old theories about when civilization began in the region.

Over the centuries, diverse ethnic groups speaking many languages settled in Southeast Asia. Living in isolated villages, they followed their own religious and cultural patterns. Many societies were built around the nuclear family rather than the extended families of India and China.

Women had greater equality in Southeast Asia than elsewhere in Asia. Female merchants took part in the spice trade, gaining fame for their skill in bargaining, finance, and languages. In some port cities, they gained enough wealth and influence to become rulers. Matrilineal descent, or inheritance through the mother, was an accepted custom in Southeast Asia. Women also had some freedom in choosing or divorcing marriage partners. Even after Indian and Chinese influences arrived, women retained their traditional rights.

Impact of India

Indian merchants and Hindu priests filtered into Southeast Asia, slowly spreading their culture. Later, Buddhist monks and scholars introduced Theravada beliefs. Following the path of trade and religion came the influence of writing, law, government, art, architecture, and farming.

Increasing Contacts In the early centuries A.D., Indian traders settled in port cities in growing numbers. They gave presents to local rulers and married into influential families. Trade brought prosperity as merchants exchanged products such as cottons, jewels, and perfume for raw materials such as timber, spices, and gold.

In time, local Indian families exercised considerable power. Also, people from Southeast Asia visited India as pilgrims or students. As these contacts increased, Indian beliefs and ideas won widespread acceptance. Indian influence reached its peak between 500 and 1000.

Islam   Long after Hinduism and Buddhism took root in Southeast Asia, Indians carried a third religion, Islam, into the region. By the 1200s, Muslims ruled northern India. From there, traders spread Islamic beliefs and Muslim civilization throughout the islands of Indonesia and as far east as the Philippines.* Arab merchants, too, spread the new faith. The prevalence of Islam in lands surrounding the Indian Ocean contributed to the growth of a stable, thriving trade network.

New Kingdoms and Empires

The blend of Indian influences with local cultures produced a series of kingdoms and empires in Southeast Asia. Some of these states rivaled those of India.

Pagan   The kingdom of Pagan (pah GAHN) arose in the fertile rice-growing Irrawaddy Valley in present-day Myanmar. In 1044, King Anawrata (ah nuh RAH tuh) united the region. He is credited with bringing Buddhism to the Burman people. Buddhism had reached nearby cultures long before, but Anawrata made Pagan a major Buddhist center. He filled his capital city with magnificent stupas, or dome-shaped shrines, at about the same time that people in medieval Europe were beginning to build Gothic cathedrals.

Pagan flourished for some 200 years after Anawrata's death, but fell in 1287 to conquering Mongols. When the Burmans finally threw off foreign rule, they looked back with pride to the great days of Pagan.

The Khmer Empire   Indian influences also helped shape the Khmer (kuh MEHR) empire, which reached its peak between 800 and 1350. Its greatest rulers controlled much of present-day Cambodia, Thailand, and Malaysia. The Khmer people adapted Indian writing, mathematics, architecture, and art. Khmer rulers became pious Hindus. Like the princes and emperors of India, they saw themselves as god-kings. Most ordinary people, however, preferred Buddhism.

In the 1100s, King Suryavarman II built the great temple complex at Angkor Wat. The ruins that survive today, though overgrown with jungle and pocked by the bullets of recent wars, are among the most impressive in the world. Hundreds of carved figures tell Hindu myths and glorify the king. Although the images of Vishnu, Shiva, and the Buddha reflect strong Indian influence, the style is uniquely Khmer.

Srivijaya   The trading empire of Srivijaya (shree vah JĪ yah), in Indonesia, flourished from the 600s to the 1200s. Srivijaya controlled the Strait of

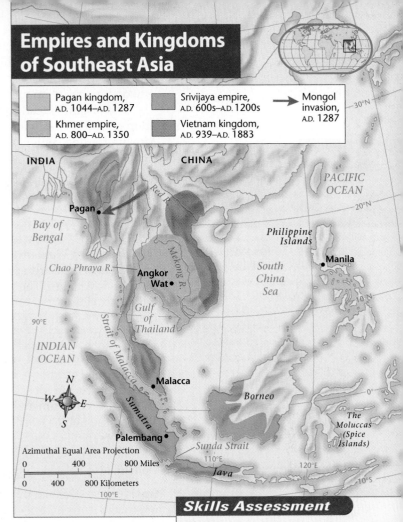

Empires and Kingdoms of Southeast Asia

Pagan kingdom, A.D. 1044–A.D. 1287	Srivijaya empire, A.D. 600s–A.D. 1200s
Khmer empire, A.D. 800–A.D. 1350	Vietnam kingdom, A.D. 939–A.D. 1883

→ Mongol invasion, A.D. 1287

Skills Assessment

Geography   The region we call Southeast Asia consists of both a mainland area and thousands of islands. It was home to numerous ancient and diverse cultures.

1. **Location**   On the map, locate **(a)** Pagan kingdom, **(b)** Angkor Wat, **(c)** the Moluccas, **(d)** Sunda Strait.
2. **Movement**   From which direction did the Mongol invasion take place?
3. **Critical Thinking Understanding Sequence**   During which centuries were these empires and kingdoms most likely to have come into contact with one another?

---

*Today, Indonesia has the largest Muslim population of any nation in the world.

Malacca, which, as you have learned, was vital to shipping. Both Hinduism and Buddhism reached this island empire. As elsewhere in Southeast Asia, however, the local people often blended Indian beliefs into their own forms of worship, based on nature spirits.

Later, Islam spread to Sumatra, Java, and other islands. Local rulers adopted the new religion, which cemented commercial links with other Muslim trading centers around the Indian Ocean.

Vietnam Emerges

In most of Southeast Asia, Indian influence outweighed Chinese influence. Indian traditions spread mostly through trade rather than conquest. China, however, sent military forces to conquer the neighboring state of Annam (now northern Vietnam).

The heart of northern Vietnam was the Red River delta, around present-day Hanoi. There, the river irrigated fertile rice padis, or fields, which provided food for a growing population. The Vietnamese had their own distinct culture. As in other parts of Southeast Asia, women often held positions of authority.

Chinese Domination In 111 B.C., Han armies conquered the region. China remained in control for 1,000 years. During that time, the Vietnamese absorbed Confucian ideas. They adopted the Chinese civil service system and built a government bureaucracy similar to that found in China. Vietnamese nobles learned to speak the Chinese language and read Chinese characters. Unlike the rest of Southeast Asia, where Theravada Buddhism had the strongest impact, Vietnam adopted Mahayana beliefs from China. Daoism also helped shape Vietnamese society.

Resistance Despite these powerful Chinese influences, the Vietnamese preserved a strong sense of their separate identity. In A.D. 39, two noble sisters, Trung Trac and Trung Nhi, led an uprising that briefly drove the Chinese occupiers from the land. They tried to restore a simpler form of government based on ancient Vietnamese traditions. To this day, the Trung sisters are remembered as great martyrs and heroes. Finally in 939, as the Tang dynasty collapsed in China, Vietnam was able to break free from China. The Vietnamese turned back repeated Chinese efforts to reconquer their land, but did remain a tributary state of China.

Biography

Trung Sisters
d. A.D. 42(?)

Although the Chinese conquest of Annam introduced Confucian values, many local traditions continued for centuries. Women remained involved in politics, law, and trade. Still, officials were surprised when sisters Trung Trac and Trung Nhi forged a legacy for themselves as freedom fighters.

The sisters managed to do what no one else could. They forced the conquering Chinese out and established home rule. They did this by recruiting and training over 80,000 men and women to fight. Thirty-six of their generals were women.

After three years, however, the Chinese emperor sent an army against the sisters. According to legend, after a terrible defeat, the Trung sisters drowned themselves to avoid capture.

Theme: Impact of the Individual Why are the Trung sisters still revered in Vietnam today?

SECTION 2 Assessment

Recall
1. **Identify:** (a) Pagan, (b) Anawrata, (c) Khmer, (d) Suryavarman II, (e) Trung sisters.
2. **Define:** (a) matrilineal, (b) stupa, (c) padi.

Comprehension
3. How did geography make Southeast Asia of strategic importance?
4. How did India influence Pagan, the Khmer empire, and Srivijaya?
5. (a) How did China influence Vietnam? (b) How did Vietnam preserve its identity?

Critical Thinking and Writing
6. **Analyzing Information** Women's social status was limited in both India and China. Why do you think Southeast Asian women were able to retain their equality despite strong Indian and Chinese cultural influence?
7. **Comparing** How did the spread of Indian influence through Southeast Asia differ from the spread of Chinese influence through the same region?

Activity

Making a Map
Create a map showing foreign influences in Southeast Asia. First, draw or trace an outline map of the region. Use arrows to show the origins and directions of influences— for example, blue arrows for trade routes, red arrows for invasion routes. Then, show what products or ideas traveled along these routes.

Reading Focus

- How did the Portuguese and the Dutch build empires in the East?
- How did Spain control the Philippines?
- How did the decline of Mughal India affect European traders?

Vocabulary

outpost

sepoy

Taking Notes

Begin a concept web like this one. As you read this section, fill in the blank circles with information about European influence in Southeast Asia and India. Add more circles as necessary.

Main Idea Europeans used military power to build trading empires in Southeast Asia.

Setting the Scene In 1511, a Portuguese fleet commanded by Afonso de Albuquerque (ahl boo KEHR keh) dropped anchor off Malacca, a rich Muslim trading port that controlled the sea route linking India, Southeast Asia, and China. "Have you come in peace or in war?" asked the sultan. "Peace," replied Albuquerque. The true goal of the Portuguese, however, was not peace, but conquest.

The fleet remained at anchor for several weeks. Then they opened fire. The Portuguese quickly took the city, killing its inhabitants and seizing its wealth. On the ruins of a mosque, Albuquerque built a fort. The sultan had fled, thinking the invaders would loot and leave. But when he heard about the fort, he realized that the Portuguese had come to stay.

Portugal was the first European power to gain a foothold in Asia. The Portuguese ships were small in size and number, but the firepower of their shipboard cannons was unmatched. In time, this superior firepower helped them win control of the rich Indian Ocean spice trade and build a Portuguese trading empire in Asia. Before long, however, other European nations would challenge Portugal.

Portugal's Empire in the East

After Vasco da Gama's voyage, the Portuguese, under Albuquerque's command, burst into the Indian Ocean. In 1510, they seized the island of Goa off the coast of India, making it their major military and commercial base. Albuquerque then moved to end Muslim power and turn the Indian Ocean into a "Portuguese lake."

Trading Outposts Albuquerque burned coastal towns and crushed Arab fleets at sea. The Portuguese attacked Aden, at the entrance to the Red Sea, and took Ormuz, gateway to the Persian Gulf. In 1511, Albuquerque took Malacca, massacring the city's Muslims and making the Europeans hated and feared.

In less than 50 years, the Portuguese had built a trading empire with military and merchant outposts, or distant areas under their control, rimming the southern seas. They seized cities on the east coast of Africa so they could resupply and repair their ships. For most of the 1500s, Portugal controlled the spice trade between Europe and Asia.

Impact Despite their sea power, the Portuguese remained on the fringe of Asian trade. They had neither the strength nor the resources to conquer

Primary Source

The Portuguese in India
Afonso de Albuquerque explained to his soldiers why the Portuguese wanted to capture Malacca:

"The king of Portugal has often commanded me to go to the Straits, because . . . this was the best place to intercept the trade which the Moslems . . . carry on in these parts. So it was to do Our Lord's service that we were brought here; by taking Malacca, we would close the Straits so that never again would the Moslems be able to bring their spices by this route. . . . I am very sure that, if this Malacca trade is taken out of their hands, Cairo and Mecca will be completely lost."

—*The Commentaries of the Great Afonso de Albuquerque*

Skills Assessment

Primary Source Why did Portugal want to control Malacca?

Mughal India and European Traders

Before the 1700s, European traders made very little impression on India, which was enjoying one of its greatest periods of strength and prosperity. In 1526, Babur had founded the Mughal dynasty. European merchants were dazzled by India's splendid court and its many luxury goods. There seemed little of value that Europeans could offer to the sophisticated civilization of Mughal India.

Industry and Commerce Besides producing spices, India was the world leader in textile manufacturing. It exported large quantities of silk and cotton cloth, from sheer muslins to elaborate chintzes. Handicrafts and shipbuilding added to the country's wealth.

The Mughal empire was larger, richer, and more powerful than any kingdom in Europe. When Europeans sought trading rights, Mughal emperors saw no threat in granting such concessions. The Portuguese and later the Dutch, English, and French thus were permitted to build forts and warehouses in coastal towns.

Turmoil and Decline When Akbar's successors ended his policy of religious toleration, conflicts rekindled between Hindu and Muslim princes. Years of civil war drained Mughal resources. Rulers then increased taxes, sparking peasant rebellions. Several weak rulers held the throne in the early 1700s. Corruption became widespread, and the central government eventually collapsed.

British-French Rivalry As Mughal power faltered, French and English traders played off rival Indian princes against one another. Both the English and French East India companies made alliances with local officials and independent rajahs. Each company organized its own army of sepoys, or Indian troops.

By the mid-1700s, the British and the French had become locked in a bitter struggle for global power. In 1756, war between Britain and France erupted in Europe. The fighting soon spread, involving both nations' lands in Asia and the Americas.

In India, Robert Clive, an agent of the British East India Company, used an army of British troops and sepoys to drive the French from their trading posts. The Company then forced the Mughal emperor to recognize its right to collect taxes in Bengal in the northeast. By the late 1700s, the Company had become the real ruler of Bengal, able to use its great wealth to spread its influence into other parts of India.

Prized Imports
Indian artisans created products like this hand-painted cotton wall hanging for European markets. Indian cottons became so popular in England that, to protect the English textile industry, Parliament tried to ban them.

Theme: Global Interaction
How does this wall hanging reflect both Indian and European culture?

SECTION 3 Assessment

Recall
1. **Identify:** **(a)** Afonso de Albuquerque, **(b)** Robert Clive.
2. **Define:** **(a)** outpost, **(b)** sepoy.

Comprehension
3. **(a)** How did the Portuguese gain control of the spice trade? **(b)** How were they challenged by the Dutch?
4. **(a)** Why was Spain easily able to conquer the Philippines? **(b)** Why did Spain want to control the islands?

5. **(a)** Why did Mughal power decline? **(b)** What effect did the decline have on France and Britain?

Critical Thinking and Writing
6. **Analyzing Information** How did Europeans build on existing trade networks in the Indian Ocean?
7. **Drawing Conclusions** Some people have argued "to the victors belong the spoils [riches] of the enemy." How do events in this section support this statement?

Activity
Take It to the NET

Use the Internet to learn more about Goa, the Portuguese base in the East. Plan a visit that a modern-day tourist might take to this island. Include historical background that visitors should have, as well as sites that they should see.

Encounters in East Asia

Reading Focus

- How was European trade with China affected by the Manchu conquest?
- What factors led Korea to isolate itself from other nations?
- What attitude did the Tokugawa shoguns have toward foreign traders?

Taking Notes

As you read this section, make a table to show how westerners acted and were received in East Asia. Use this table as a model.

	CHINA	KOREA	JAPAN
WESTERN BEHAVIOR AND ATTITUDES	• Matteo Ricci speaks Chinese • Macartney offends emperor		
RESPONSE TO WESTERNERS	• Restrict trade		

Main Idea China, Korea, and Japan limited contact with western nations.

Setting the Scene

The Europeans who reached Asia in the 1500s often made a poor impression on their hosts. The Italian traveler Niccoló Manucci told how Asians thought that Europeans "have no polite manners, that they are ignorant, wanting in ordered life, and very dirty."

Europeans, by contrast, wrote enthusiastically about China. In 1590, a visitor described Chinese artisans "cleverly making devices out of gold, silver and other metals." He was also impressed with their abilities in handicrafts and gunsmithing, and wrote: "They daily publish huge multitudes of books."

Portuguese ships first reached China by way of the South China Sea during the Ming dynasty. To the Chinese, the Portuguese were "southern barbarians." Like other foreigners, they lacked the civilized ways of the Middle Kingdom.

European Trade With China

The Ming dynasty, you will recall, ended its overseas explorations in the mid-1400s. Confucian officials had little use for foreigners. "Since our empire owns the world," said a Ming document, "there is no country on this or other sides of the seas which does not submit to us."

Strict Limits on Trade Portuguese traders reached China by sea in 1514. To the Chinese, the newcomers had little to offer in exchange for silks and porcelains. European textiles and metalwork were inferior to Chinese products. The Chinese therefore demanded payment in gold or silver.

The Ming eventually allowed the Portuguese a trading post at Macao, near Canton, present-day Guangzhou (gwahng JOH). Later, they let Dutch, English, and other Europeans trade with Chinese merchants, but only under strict limits. Foreigners could trade only at Canton under the supervision of imperial officials. When each year's trading season ended, they had to sail away.

Scholars and Missionaries A few European scholars, like the brilliant Jesuit priest Matteo Ricci, did make a positive impression on Ming China.

China and Foreign Trade This fan shows the harbor in Canton, with European flags flying over warehouses in the background. Strict limits on foreign trade kept Europeans from gaining a foothold in China.

Theme: Economics and Technology How does the scene on this fan suggest the limitations placed on European merchants?

Japanese Screens
Shoguns and daimyo filled their castles with brilliant, multipaneled screen paintings. Many screens depicted the beauties of nature or scenes of everyday life. This screen shows the activities of Japanese and Portuguese sea-farers aboard a large ship.

Theme: Art and Literature
How did the artist create a sense of motion?

Korea and Isolation

Like China, Korea restricted outside contacts in the 1500s and 1600s. Earlier, Korean traders had far-ranging contacts across East Asia. A Korean map from the 1300s accurately outlines lands from Japan to the Mediterranean. Koreans probably acquired this knowledge from Arab traders who had visited Korea.

The Choson dynasty, you will recall, firmly embraced Confucian ideas. Like the Chinese, Koreans felt that Confucian learning was the most advanced in the world. The low status of merchants in Confucianism also led Koreans to look down on foreign traders.

Two other events led the Koreans to turn inward. A Japanese invasion in the 1590s devastated the land of Korea. Then in 1636, the Manchus conquered Korea before overrunning Ming China. When the Manchus set up the Qing dynasty in China, Korea became a tributary state, run by its own government but forced to acknowledge China's supremacy. The two invasions left Korea feeling like "a shrimp among whales."

In response, the Koreans chose isolation, excluding all foreigners except the Chinese and a few Japanese. When European sailors were shipwrecked on Korean shores, they were imprisoned or killed. As a result, Korea became known in the West as the "Hermit Kingdom."

Even though Korea had few contacts with the world for about 250 years, this period was a great age for Korean arts and literature. In one satirical tale, author Pak Chi-won describes a poor scholar who breaks with tradition to become a merchant. Here, Master Ho describes doing business in an isolated country:

> "Our country has no trade with other countries, and . . . everything we use is produced and consumed in the same province. . . . With ten thousand yang, you can buy just about all of one particular item produced in the country. You can buy the whole lot, whether you load it on a cart or on a boat."
>
> —Pak Chi-won, "The Story of Ho"

Japan and Foreign Traders

Unlike the Chinese or Koreans, the Japanese at first welcomed western traders. In 1543, the Portuguese reached Japan. Later came the Spanish, Dutch, and English. They arrived at the turbulent time when strong daimyo were struggling for power. The Japanese quickly acquired western firearms and built castles modeled on European designs. In fact, the new weapons may have helped the Tokugawa shoguns centralize power and impose order.

Japan was much more open to European missionaries than China. Jesuits, like the Spanish priest Francis Xavier, found the Japanese curious and eager to learn about Christianity. A growing number of Japanese adopted the new faith.

The Tokugawa shoguns, however, grew increasingly hostile toward foreigners. After learning how Spain had seized the Philippines, they may have seen the newcomers as agents of an invading force. In addition, Japanese officials disliked the intrigues and competition among Christian missionaries. They also suspected that Japanese Christians—who may have numbered as many as 300,000—owed their allegiance to the pope, rather than to Japanese leaders. In response, the Tokugawas expelled foreign missionaries. They brutally persecuted Japanese Christians, killing many thousands of people.

By 1638, the Tokugawas had barred all western merchants and forbidden Japanese to travel abroad. To further their isolation, they outlawed the building of large ships, thereby ending foreign trade. In order to keep informed about world events, they permitted just one or two Dutch ships each year to trade at a small island in Nagasaki harbor. Through this tiny gateway, a few Japanese did learn about some foreign ideas. They studied Dutch medical texts, for example, which they found to be more accurate than Chinese ones.

Looking Ahead

Japan maintained its policy of strict isolation for more than 200 years. Isolation had a profound effect on Japan. Without outside influence, Japanese culture turned inward. Still, art and literature spread beyond the upper classes. Artists found new ways to interpret traditions.

During this time, internal trade boomed. Cities grew in size and importance, and some merchant families gained wealth and status. By the early 1700s, Edo (present-day Tokyo) had a million inhabitants, more than either London or Paris.

In 1853, Japan was forced to reopen contacts with the western world. Renewed relations unleashed an extraordinary period of change that helped Japan emerge as a major world power.

Global Connections

The Jesuits in Asia

Although Jesuit missionaries in Asia failed to win many converts to Christianity, they succeeded in spreading western ideas and technology. In China, Jesuit priest Matteo Ricci introduced an accurate world map and helped manufacture European-style cannons. Later Jesuits served as heads of the bureau that planned China's official calendar. The Jesuits also translated more than 100 books on science, math, and technology into Chinese. In Japan, Jesuits introduced the printing press.

Cultural influences also flowed in the other direction. The Jesuits introduced Europeans to the works of Confucius.

Theme: Religions and Value Systems What western ideas did the Jesuits introduce in Asia?

SECTION 4 Assessment

Recall
1. **Identify: (a)** Matteo Ricci, **(b)** Manchus, **(c)** Kangxi, **(d)** Qianlong, **(e)** Hermit Kingdom, **(f)** Francis Xavier.

Comprehension
2. **(a)** How was economic prosperity reflected in Qing China? **(b)** How did the Qing restrict trade with other nations?
3. Why did Korea pursue a policy of isolation?
4. Why did the Japanese policy toward trade and foreigners change over time?

Critical Thinking and Writing
5. **Linking Past and Present** Why do some people in the United States today support limited overseas ties?
6. **Making Generalizations (a)** Based on your reading, what generalization might you make about the attitude of European traders to the countries of East Asia? **(b)** What generalization might you make about how East Asians felt toward Europeans? **(c)** What evidence might you give to support each generalization?

Activity

Writing a Dialogue
Write a dialogue between two officials in China, Korea, or Japan. One official should express a willingness to establish relations with European powers. The other should argue in favor of a policy of isolation.

Reading Focus

- What were the results of the first encounters between the Spanish and Native Americans?

- How did Spanish conquistadors conquer the Aztec and Incan empires?

- Why were the Spanish victorious?

Main Idea Various factors enabled the Spanish to conquer the Aztec and Incan empires.

Vocabulary

conquistador

immunity

alliance

civil war

Taking Notes

Copy this diagram. As you read, add other factors that help to explain why the Spanish were able to conquer Native American empires. Add as many boxes as you need.

| Disease weakens Native Americans | | |

EUROPEANS CONQUER NATIVE AMERICANS

Setting the Scene Spanish soldiers who reached the Aztec capital of Tenochtitlán in 1519 were amazed by its size and splendor. From the emperor's palace, reported one soldier, "We had a clear view of the . . . [majestic temples] of the nearby cities, built in the form of towers and fortresses, . . . and others . . . all whitewashed, and wonderfully brilliant."

Within a few years, the Spanish had captured and destroyed the Aztec capital. In its place, they built a new capital, Mexico City, that became the heart of the Spanish empire in the Americas.

First Encounters

In 1492, Christopher Columbus landed in the islands that are now called the West Indies, in the Caribbean. There, he encountered the Taíno people. The Taínos lived in villages and grew corn, yams, and cotton, which they wove into cloth. They were friendly and generous toward the Spanish.

Friendly relations soon evaporated, however. Spanish conquistadors (kahn KEES tuh dohrz), or conquerors, followed in the wake of Columbus. They settled on the islands of Hispaniola (now the Dominican Republic and Haiti), Cuba, and Puerto Rico. They seized the gold ornaments worn by the Taínos, then made them pan for more gold. At the same time, the newcomers forced the Taínos to convert to Christianity.

Meanwhile, a deadly but invisible invader was at work—disease. Europeans unknowingly carried diseases such as smallpox, measles, and influenza to which Native Americans had no immunity, or resistance. These diseases spread rapidly and wiped out village after village. As a result, the Native American population of the Caribbean islands declined by as much as 90 percent in the 1500s. This cycle of disease and death was repeated in many other places across the Western Hemisphere.

The Conquistadors

From Cuba, Spanish explorers probed the coasts of the Americas. They spread stories of empires rich in gold. Attracted by the promise of riches as well as by religious zeal, a flood of adventurers soon followed.

Cortés in Mexico Among the earliest conquistadors was Hernan Cortés. Cortés landed on the coast of Mexico in 1519 with about 600 men, 16 horses, and a few cannons. As he headed inland toward Tenochtitlán, he was helped

www.phschool.com

University of Minnesota Duluth, Minnesota

For more images and information about the Aztecs and the Spanish conquest, use the Internet address above to link to the department of history at the University of Minnesota.

Conquistadors in Mexico
Pedro de Alvarado was one of the Spanish conquistadors who conquered Mexico. This illustration shows Alvarado and his men facing off against a troop of Aztec soldiers.

Theme: Economics and Technology Based on this picture, identify two technological advantages the Spanish had over the Aztecs.

by Malinche (mah LIHN chay), a young Indian woman who served as his translator and adviser. The Spanish called her Doña Marina. Malinche knew both the Mayan and Aztec languages, and she learned Spanish quickly.

From Malinche, Cortés learned that many conquered peoples hated their Aztec overlords. The Aztecs, you will recall, sacrificed thousands of captives to their gods each year. Malinche helped Cortés arrange alliances with these discontented groups. They would help one another fight the Aztecs.

Moctezuma's Dilemma Meanwhile, messengers brought word about the newcomers to the Aztec emperor Moctezuma. He wondered if the leader of the pale-skinned, bearded strangers might be Quetzalcoatl, the god-king who had long ago vowed to return from the east. Moctezuma sent gifts of gold and silver, but urged the strangers not to continue to Tenochtitlán.

Cortés had no intention of turning back. Fighting and negotiating by turns, he led his forces inland toward the capital. At last, they arrived in Tenochtitlán, where they were dazzled by the grandeur of the city.

Fall of Tenochtitlán Moctezuma welcomed Cortés to his capital. However, relations between the Aztecs and Spaniards soon grew strained, and the Aztecs drove the Spanish from the city. Moctezuma was killed in the fighting.

Cortés retreated to plan an assault. In 1521, in a brutal struggle, Cortés and his Indian allies captured and demolished Tenochtitlán. An unknown Aztec lamented, "Broken spears lie in the road; / We have torn our hair with grief. / The houses are roofless now, and their walls are red with blood." On the ruins of Tenochtitlán, the Spanish later built Mexico City.

Pizarro in Peru Cortés's success inspired other adventurers. Among them was Francisco Pizarro. He arrived in Peru in 1532, just after the Incan ruler Atahualpa (ah tah WAHL pah) won the throne from his brother in a bloody civil war. A civil war is fought between groups of people in the same nation.

Helped by Indian allies, Pizarro captured Atahualpa after slaughtering thousands of his followers. The Spanish demanded a huge ransom for the ruler. The Incas paid it, but the Spanish killed Atahualpa anyway.

Despite continuing resistance, the invaders overran the Incan heartland. From Peru, Spanish forces surged across Ecuador and Chile. Before long, Spain added much of South America to its growing empire.

 Primary Sources and Literature

See "Bernal Díaz: The True History of the Conquest of New Spain" in the Reference Section at the back of this book.

Native American Population of Central Mexico

Native American Population of Central Mexico

Millions of People (estimated)

28
24
20
16
12
8
4

1500   1540   1580   1620

Year

Source: Nicolás Sánchez-Albornoz, *The Population of Latin America*

Skills Assessment

Graph Disease and conquest combined to reduce drastically the Native American population. This graph shows what happened to central Mexico's Native Americans after the arrival of the Spanish in 1519. **How did the Native American population change during the period shown on the graph?**

Reasons for Victory

How could a few hundred European soldiers conquer huge Native American empires with populations in the millions? Several reasons explain the amazing Spanish success.

1. Superior military technology was a key factor. The Spaniards' horses frightened some Indians, who had never seen such animals. Spanish muskets and cannons killed Indian soldiers, while metal helmets and armor protected the Spanish from the Indians' arrows and spears.
2. Division and discontent among the Indians aided the Spanish. The Spanish won allies by playing on old hatreds among rival Indian groups. In fact, Indians provided Cortés and Pizarro with much of their fighting power.
3. Disease brought by the Europeans weakened the Aztecs and Incas. As tens of thousands of Indians died, some of the bewildered and demoralized survivors felt that their gods were less powerful than the god of their conquerors.
4. Many Indians believed that the disasters they suffered marked the world's end. To Aztecs, the destruction of Tenochtitlán signaled the end of the reign of the sun god.

Ongoing Resistance   Native Americans continued to resist the invaders, however. For years, Mayas fought Spanish rule. Long after the death of Atahualpa, revolts erupted among the Incas. Throughout the Americas, Indians resisted Europeans by preserving aspects of their own culture, such as language, religious traditions, and clothing.

Looking Ahead

The Spanish seized gold and silver statues and ornaments from the Aztecs and Incas. After depleting these sources, they forced Native Americans to mine silver in Peru and Mexico. In the 1500s and early 1600s, treasure fleets sailed each year to Spain or the Spanish Philippines loaded with gold and silver. As you will read, this flood of wealth created both benefits and problems for the economy of Europe.

SECTION 1 Assessment

Recall

1. Identify: **(a)** Taínos, **(b)** Hernan Cortés, **(c)** Malinche, **(d)** Moctezuma, **(e)** Francisco Pizarro, **(f)** Atahualpa.
2. Define: **(a)** conquistador, **(b)** immunity, **(c)** alliance, **(d)** civil war.

Comprehension

3. How were Native Americans of the Caribbean region affected by their early encounters with Europeans?
4. What methods did Pizarro use to conquer the Incan empire?
5. **(a)** How did divisions within the Aztec and Incan empires help the Spanish? **(b)** What other reasons explain the rapid success of the Spanish conquistadors over Native Americans?

Critical Thinking and Writing

6. **Comparing** Compare the Spanish conquest of the Americas with the Reconquista or the Crusades. **(a)** How were they similar? **(b)** How were they different?
7. **Identifying Main Ideas** Review the three paragraphs under the heading First Encounters. For each paragraph, write a single sentence identifying the main idea of the paragraph.

Activity

Take It to the NET

Use the Internet to research the life of Malinche, whose name means "traitor." Then, write a paragraph explaining why you believe she does or does not deserve this name.

Spanish and Portuguese Colonies in the Americas

Reading Focus

- How did Spain rule its empire in the Americas?
- What were the chief features of colonial society and culture?
- How did Portugal and other European nations challenge Spanish power?

Vocabulary

viceroy
plantation
encomienda
peon
peninsular
creole
mestizo
mulatto
privateer

Taking Notes

Copy this partially completed concept web. As you read, write key facts and ideas about the Spanish empire in the Americas in the appropriate circles. Add as many circles as you need.

Main Idea Native American, African, and European traditions blended to form new cultures in the Americas.

Setting the Scene

Spain was immensely proud of its rich silver mines in the Potosí region of Peru. By the 1540s, tons of Potosí silver filled Spanish treasure ships. Year after year, thousands of Native Americans were forced to extract the rich ore from dangerous shafts deep inside the Andes Mountains. Many Indians died in the terrible conditions, only to be replaced by thousands more.

Scenes such as this were repeated in Mexico, the Caribbean, and other parts of Spain's empire. A flood of Spanish settlers and missionaries followed the conquistadors. Wherever they went, they claimed the land and its people for their king and Church. When there was resistance, the newcomers imposed their will by force. As devout Christians, they thought it was their duty to bring their religion and civilization to the Indians.

From the first, though, Christian Europeans had much to learn from the peoples that they conquered. In the end, a new culture emerged that reflected European, Native American, and African traditions.

Ruling the Spanish Empire

In the 1500s, Spain claimed a vast empire stretching from California to South America. In time, it divided these lands into five provinces. The most important were New Spain (Mexico) and Peru.

Spain was determined to maintain strict control over its empire. To achieve this goal, the king set up the Council of the Indies to pass laws for the colonies. He also appointed viceroys, or representatives who ruled in his name, in each province. Lesser officials and *audiencias*, or advisory councils of Spanish settlers, helped the viceroy rule. The Council of the Indies in Spain closely monitored these colonial officials to make sure they did not assume too much authority.

The Catholic Church To Spain, winning souls for Christianity was as important as gaining land. The Catholic Church played a key role in the colonies, working with the government to convert Native Americans to Christianity. Church leaders often served as royal officials and helped to regulate the activities of Spanish settlers. As Spain's American empire expanded, Church authority expanded along with it.

Franciscan, Jesuit, and other missionaries baptized thousands of Native Americans. In frontier regions, they built mission churches and worked to turn new converts into loyal subjects of the Catholic king of Spain. They forcibly imposed European culture over Native American culture.

They also introduced European clothing, the Spanish language, and new crafts such as carpentry and locksmithing.

The Economy   To make the empire profitable, Spain closely controlled its economic activities, especially trade. Colonists could export raw materials only to Spain and could buy only Spanish manufactured goods. Laws forbade colonists from trading with other European nations or even with other Spanish colonies. The most valuable resources shipped from Spanish America to Spain were silver and gold.

Sugar cane was introduced into the West Indies and elsewhere and quickly became a profitable resource. The cane was refined into sugar, molasses, and rum. Sugar cane, however, had to be grown on plantations, large estates run by an owner or the owner's overseer. Finding the large numbers of workers needed to make the plantations profitable was a major problem.

At first, Spanish monarchs granted the conquistadors encomiendas, the right to demand labor or tribute from Native Americans in a particular area. The conquistadors used this system to force Native Americans to work under the most brutal conditions. Those who resisted were hunted down and killed. Disease, starvation, and cruel treatment caused catastrophic declines in the population.

Bartolomé de las Casas   A few bold priests, like Bartolomé de las Casas, condemned the evils of the encomienda system. In vivid reports to Spain, Las Casas detailed the horrors that Spanish rule had brought to Native Americans and pleaded with the king to end the abuse.

Prodded by Las Casas, Spain passed the New Laws of the Indies in 1542, forbidding enslavement of Native Americans. The laws were meant to end abuses against Native Americans, but Spain was too far away to enforce them. Many Native Americans were forced to become peons, workers forced to labor for a landlord in order to pay off a debt. Landlords advanced them food, tools, or seeds, creating debts that workers could never pay off in their lifetime.

Bringing Workers From Africa   To fill the labor shortage, Las Casas urged colonists to import workers from Africa. Africans were immune to tropical diseases, he said, and had skills in farming, mining, and metalworking. Las Casas later regretted that advice because it furthered the brutal African slave trade. The Spanish began bringing Africans, as slave laborers, to the Americas by the 1530s.

As demand for sugar products skyrocketed, the settlers imported millions of Africans as slaves. They were forced to work as field hands, miners, or servants in the houses of wealthy landowners. Others became peddlers, skilled artisans, artists, and mechanics.

In time, Africans and their American-born descendants greatly outnumbered European settlers in the West Indies and parts of South America. Often, they resisted slavery by rebelling or running away. In the cities, some enslaved Africans earned enough money to buy their freedom.

Colonial Society and Culture

In Spanish America, the mix of diverse peoples gave rise to a new social structure. The blending of Native American, African, and European peoples and traditions resulted in a new American culture.

Social Structure   At the top of colonial society were peninsulares, people born in Spain. (The term *peninsular* referred to the Iberian Peninsula, on which Spain is located.) Peninsulares filled the highest positions in both colonial governments and the Catholic Church. Next came creoles,

A Brutal System
Bartolomé de las Casas, a conquistador turned priest, spoke out against the encomienda system and the treatment of Native Americans:

"It is impossible to recount the burdens with which their owners loaded them, more than [75 to 100 pounds], making them walk [hundreds of miles]. . . . They had wounds on their shoulders and backs, like animals. . . . To tell likewise of the whip-lashings, the beatings, the cuffs, the blows, the curses, and a thousand other kinds of torments to which their masters treated them, while in truth they were working hard, would take much time and much paper; and would be something to amaze mankind."

—Bartolomé de las Casas,
Short Description of the Destruction of the Indies

Skills Assessment

Primary Source How were the conditions Las Casas describes linked to the encomienda system?

American-born descendants of Spanish settlers. Creoles owned most of the plantations, ranches, and mines.

Other social groups reflected the mixing of populations. They included mestizos, people of Native American and European descent, and mulattoes, people of African and European descent. Native Americans and people of African descent formed the lowest social classes.

Cities   Spanish settlers preferred to live in towns and cities. The population of Mexico City grew so quickly that by 1550 it was the largest Spanish-speaking city in the world.

Colonial cities were centers of government, commerce, and European culture. Around the central plaza, or square, stood government buildings and a Spanish-style church. Broad avenues and public monuments symbolized European power and wealth. Cities were also centers of intellectual and cultural life. Architecture and painting, as well as poetry and the exchange of ideas, flourished.

Education   To meet the Church's need for educated priests, the colonies built universities. The University of Mexico was established as early as 1551. A dozen Spanish American universities were busy educating young men long before Harvard, the first university in the 13 English colonies, was founded in 1636.

Women wishing an education might enter a convent. One such woman was Sor Juana Inés de la Cruz. Refused admission to the University of Mexico because she was a girl, Juana entered a convent at the age of 16. There, she devoted herself to study and the writing of poetry. She earned a reputation as one of the greatest poets ever to write in the Spanish language.

Cultural Blending   Although Spanish culture was dominant in the cities, the blending of diverse traditions changed people's lives throughout the Americas. Settlers learned Native American styles of building, ate foods native to the Americas, and traveled in Indian-style canoes. Indian artistic styles influenced the newcomers. At the same time, settlers taught their religion to Native Americans. They also introduced animals, especially the horse, that transformed the lives of many Native Americans.

Africans added to this cultural mix with their farming methods, cooking styles, and crops, including okra and palm oil. African drama, dance, and song heightened Christian services. In Cuba, Haiti, and elsewhere, Africans forged new religions that blended African and Christian beliefs.

The Portuguese Colony in Brazil

A large area of South America remained outside the Spanish empire. By the Treaty of Tordesillas in 1494, Portugal claimed Brazil. (See the map in Section 3.) Portugal issued grants of land to Portuguese nobles, who agreed to develop the land and share profits with the crown. Landowners sent settlers to build towns, plantations, and churches.

The Economy   Unlike Spain's American lands, Brazil offered no instant wealth from silver or gold. Early settlers clung to the coast, where they cut and exported brazilwood, used to produce a precious dye. Before long,

A New Society and Culture
The social structure and culture of Spain's American empire reflected its unique blend of people. This portrait depicts a Spanish man, his Mexican wife, and their mestizo daughter.

Theme: Diversity What were the social classes in Spain's American empire?

Reading Focus

■ What problems did settlers in New France face?

■ What traditions of government evolved in the 13 English colonies?

■ How did competition for power affect Europeans and Native Americans?

Vocabulary

missionary

revenue

compact

Taking Notes

Copy this partially completed table. As you read, fill in key information on the French and English colonies in North America.

	FRENCH COLONIES	ENGLISH COLONIES
LOCATION		East coast of North America
ECONOMY	Based mostly on fishing and fur trading	
GOVERNMENT		
GROWTH		

Main Idea France and England set up colonies and competed for dominance in North America.

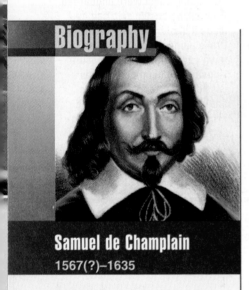

Biography

Samuel de Champlain
1567(?)–1635

Samuel de Champlain was an explorer, geographer, and mapmaker. As founder and first governor of the French colony of Quebec, he is known as the Father of New France, the French colonial empire in North America.

Champlain explored many of the waterways of New France. He especially loved the St. Lawrence River, which he said was "beautiful as the Seine, rapid as the Rhône, and deep as the sea." He helped to make it the main highway for trade through New France and to make himself the force behind the colony's settlement.

Theme: Impact of the Individual Why is Champlain considered the Father of New France?

Setting the Scene In the 1600s, other European powers moved into the Americas and began building settlements. France, the Netherlands, England, and Sweden joined Spain in claiming parts of North America.

At first, the Europeans were disappointed. North America did not yield vast treasure or offer a water passage to Asia, as they had hoped. Before long, though, the English and French were turning large profits by growing tobacco in Virginia, fishing off the North Atlantic coast, and trading fur from New England to Canada.

By 1700, France and England controlled large parts of North America. As their colonies grew, they developed their own governments, different from each other and from that of Spanish America.

Building New France

By the early 1500s, French fishing ships were crossing the Atlantic each year to harvest rich catches of cod off Newfoundland, Canada. Distracted by wars at home, however, French rulers at first paid little attention to Canada—New France, as they called it. Not until 1608 did Samuel de Champlain build the first permanent French settlement in Quebec. Jesuits and other missionaries, hoping to spread Christianity to Native Americans, soon followed. They advanced into the wilderness, trying to convert Native Americans they met.

Slow Growth Helped by Native American allies, French explorers and fur traders traveled inland, claiming vast territory. Soon, France's American empire reached from Quebec to the Great Lakes and down the Mississippi to Louisiana and the Gulf of Mexico.

The population of New France grew slowly. Wealthy landlords owned huge tracts, or areas of land, along the St. Lawrence River. They sought settlers to farm the land, but the harsh Canadian climate attracted few French peasants.

Many who went to New France soon abandoned farming in favor of fur trapping and trading. They faced a hard life in the wilderness, but the soaring European demand for fur ensured good prices. Fishing, too, supported settlers who lived in coastal villages and exported cod and other fish to Europe.

Government Policy In the late 1600s, the French king Louis XIV set out to strengthen royal power and boost revenues, or income from taxes, from his overseas empire. He appointed officials to oversee justice and economic activities in New France. He also sent more settlers and soldiers to North America. The Catholic Louis, however, prohibited Protestants from settling in New France.

By the early 1700s, French forts, missions, and trading posts stretched from Quebec to Louisiana. Yet the population of New France remained small compared to that of the 13 English colonies expanding along the Atlantic coast.

The 13 English Colonies

The English built their first permanent colony at Jamestown, Virginia, in 1607. Its early years were filled with disaster. Many settlers died of starvation and disease. The rest survived with the help of friendly Native Americans. The colony finally made headway when the settlers started to grow and export tobacco, a crop they learned about from the Indians.

In 1620, other English settlers, the Pilgrims,* landed at Plymouth, Massachusetts. They were seeking religious freedom, rather than commercial profit. Before coming ashore, they signed the Mayflower Compact, in which they set out guidelines for governing their North American colony. A compact is an agreement among people. Today, we see this document as an important early step toward self-government. It read:

> "We, whose names are underwritten . . . having undertaken for the Glory of God, and Advancement of the Christian Faith . . . a voyage to plant [a] colony in the [Americas] . . . do enact, constitute, and frame, such just and equal Laws . . . as shall be thought most [fitting] and convenient for the general Good of the Colony."
> —Mayflower Compact

Many Pilgrims died in the early years of the Plymouth colony. Local Indians, however, taught them to grow corn and helped them survive in the new land. Soon, a new wave of Puritan immigrants arrived to establish the Massachusetts Bay Colony.

Growth In the 1600s and 1700s, the English established 13 colonies. Some, like Virginia and New York, were commercial ventures, organized for profit. Others, like Massachusetts, Pennsylvania, and Maryland, were set up as havens for persecuted religious groups.

Geographic conditions helped shape different ways of life in the New England, middle, and southern colonies. In New England, many settlers were farmers who transferred to North America the village life they had enjoyed in England. In parts of the South, there emerged a plantation economy based on tobacco, rice, and other crops.

Like New Spain, the English colonies needed workers to clear land and raise crops. A growing number of Africans were brought to the colonies and sold as slaves. In several mainland colonies, enslaved Africans and their descendants outnumbered people of European descent.

Government Like the rulers of Spain and France, English monarchs asserted control over their American colonies. They appointed royal governors to oversee colonial affairs and had Parliament pass laws to regulate colonial trade. Yet, compared with settlers in the Spanish and French colonies, English colonists enjoyed a large degree of self-government. Each

---

*Pilgrims were a band of English Puritans, a Protestant group, who rejected the practices of the official Church of England.

Primary Source

Pilgrim Courage
Governor William Bradford of Plymouth Colony wrote a first-hand account of its early days, describing what happened after half the Pilgrims had died:

"[Of the 50 left . . . only six or seven were sound. These six or seven] . . . spared no pains night nor day, but with abundance of toil and hazard of their own health, fetched them wood, made them fires, dressed them meat, made their beds, washed their [filthy] clothes, clothed and unclothed them. . . . All this [was done] willingly and cheerfully, without any grudging in the least, showing herein their true love unto their friends and brethren."
—William Bradford, *Of Plymouth Plantation: 1620–1647*

Skills Assessment

Primary Source Why were the "sound" Pilgrims' actions necessary to the survival of Plymouth Colony?

Turbulent Centuries in Africa

Reading Focus

- How did the arrival of Europeans in Africa lead to the Atlantic slave trade?
- How did the slave trade contribute to the rise of new African states?
- What groups battled for power in southern Africa?

Vocabulary

triangular trade

repeal

monopoly

Taking Notes

Copy this partially completed flowchart. As you read, fill in key events in the development of the Atlantic slave trade. Add as many boxes to the chart as you need.

Enslaved Africans taken to Muslim empires

↓

↓

↓

Millions taken from West Africa to the Americas

Main Idea The Atlantic slave trade, the rise of new states, and power struggles created turbulence in Africa.

Setting the Scene

"The first object which saluted my eyes when I arrived on the coast was the sea, and a slave ship which was then riding at anchor and waiting for its cargo. These filled me with astonishment, which was soon converted into terror when I was carried on board." So wrote Olaudah Equiano. In the 1750s, when he was 11 years old, Equiano was seized from his Nigerian village by slave traders. He was then transported as human cargo from West Africa to the Americas.

Enslaved Africans like Equiano formed part of an international trade network that arose during the first global age. Encounters between Europeans and Africans had been taking place since the 1400s. By then, as you have read, Africa was home to diverse societies, and Islam had become an important force in some parts of the continent. As Europeans arrived, they would bring their own influences to Africa.

European Outposts in Africa

In the 1400s, Portuguese ships explored the coast of West Africa, looking for a sea route to India. They built small forts along the West African coast to trade for gold, collect food and water, and repair their ships.

The Portuguese lacked the power to push into the African interior. They did, however, attack the coastal cities of East Africa, such as Mombasa and Malindi, which were hubs of international trade. With cannons blazing, they expelled the Arabs who controlled the East African trade network and took over this thriving commerce for themselves.

The Portuguese, however, gained little profit from their victories. Trade between the interior and the coast soon dwindled. By 1600, the once-prosperous East African coastal cities had sunk into poverty.

Other Europeans soon followed the Portuguese into Africa. The Dutch, the English, and the French established forts along the western coast of Africa. Like the Portuguese, they exchanged muskets, tools, and cloth for gold, ivory, hides, and slaves.

The Atlantic Slave Trade

In the 1500s, Europeans began to view slaves as the most important item of African trade. Slavery had existed in Africa, as elsewhere around the world, since ancient times. Egyptians, Greeks, Romans, Persians, Indians, and Aztecs often enslaved defeated foes. Our word *slave* comes from the large number of Slavs taken from southern Russia to work as unpaid laborers in Roman times.

The Arab empire also used slave labor, often captives taken from Africa. In the Middle East, many enslaved Africans worked on farming estates or large-scale irrigation projects. Others became artisans, soldiers, or merchants. Some rose to prominence in the Muslim world even though they were officially slaves.

European and African Slave Traders   The Atlantic slave trade began in the 1500s, to fill the need for labor in Spain's American empire. In the next 300 years, it grew into a huge and profitable business. Each year, traders shipped tens of thousands of enslaved Africans across the Atlantic to work on tobacco and sugar plantations in the Americas.

Europeans seldom went into the interior to take part in slave raids. Instead, they relied on African rulers and traders to seize captives in the interior and bring them to coastal trading posts and fortresses. There, the captives were exchanged for textiles, metalwork, rum, tobacco, weapons, and gunpowder. The slave trade intensified as the demand for slaves increased in the Americas and as the demand for luxury goods increased in Africa.

Triangular Trade   The Atlantic slave trade formed one part of a three-legged trade network known as the triangular trade. On the first leg, merchant ships brought goods to Africa to be traded for slaves. On the second leg, known as the Middle Passage, the slaves were transported to the West Indies. There, the enslaved Africans were exchanged for sugar, molasses, and other products. On the final leg, these products were shipped to Europe or European colonies in the Americas. The prosperity of port cities such as Nantes in France, Bristol in England, and Salem in Massachusetts thus depended in large part on the slave trade.

Horrors of the Middle Passage   For enslaved Africans, the Middle Passage was a horror. Once purchased, Africans were packed below the decks of slave ships. Hundreds of men, women, and children were crammed into a single vessel. Slave ships became "floating coffins" on which up to half the Africans on board died from disease or brutal mistreatment.

The Slave Trade
Merchants from many lands engaged in the slave trade. Arabs, such as those on the ship below, brought human cargoes out of East Africa. Portuguese traders carried slaves to the Americas from West Africa. A Portuguese soldier is depicted in the delicate ivory carving.
Theme: Global Interaction
Why was there a growing demand for slaves in the Americas?

"TAKE US TO YOUR LEADER . . .
WE'VE COME TO NEGOTIATE A
FREE TRADE AGREEMENT WITH
EARTH."

Connections to Today

The Banana Wars

Governments have been using tariffs to protect their own industries for years. This practice continues today, as the "Banana Wars" between the United States and Europe demonstrate. American multinational companies produce bananas in countries like Honduras and Ecuador. Former European colonies in the Caribbean also produce bananas. European governments decided to let Caribbean bananas come into their countries more cheaply than the bananas produced by American firms, thus taking market share from the American firms. To retaliate, the United States government placed a 100 percent tariff on certain goods from Europe, making them much more expensive. Some 500 years after they began, tariff wars go on.

Theme: Continuity and Change Why do tariff wars develop?

The putting out system separated capital and labor for the first time. From this system controlled by merchants, the next step would be the capitalist-owned factories of the Industrial Revolution of the 1700s, as you will read.

Mercantilism

European monarchs enjoyed the benefits of the commercial revolution. In the fierce competition for trade and empire, they adopted a new economic policy, known as mercantilism, aimed at strengthening their national economies.

Mercantilists supported several basic ideas. They believed that a nation's real wealth was measured in its gold and silver treasure. To build its supply of gold and silver, they said, a nation must export more goods than it imported.

The Role of Colonies Overseas empires were central to the mercantile system. Colonies, said mercantilists, existed for the benefit of the parent country. They provided resources and raw materials not available in Europe. In turn, they enriched a parent country by serving as a market for its manufactured goods.

To achieve these goals, European powers passed strict laws regulating trade with their colonies. Colonists could not set up their own industries to manufacture goods. They were also forbidden to buy goods from a foreign country. In addition, only ships from the parent country or the colonies themselves could be used to send goods in or out of the colonies.

Increasing National Wealth Mercantilists urged rulers to adopt policies to increase national wealth and government revenues. To boost production, governments exploited mineral and timber resources, built roads, and backed new industries. They imposed a single national currency and established standard weights and measures.

Governments also sold monopolies to large producers in certain industries as well as to big overseas trading companies. Finally, governments imposed tariffs, or taxes on imported goods. Tariffs were designed to protect local industries from foreign competition by increasing the price of imported goods.

The Lives of Ordinary People

How did these economic changes affect Europeans? In general, their impact depended on a person's social class. Merchants who invested in overseas ventures acquired wealth. But the price revolution hurt nobles. Their wealth was in land, and they had trouble raising money to pay higher costs for stylish clothing and other luxuries. Some sold off land, which in turn reduced their income. In towns and cities, the wages of hired workers did not keep up with inflation, creating poverty and discontent.

Most Europeans were still peasants. Europe's growing involvement in the world had little immediate effect on their lives. Changes took generations, even centuries, to be felt. For example, tradition-bound peasants were often reluctant to grow foods brought from the Americas. Only in the later 1700s did German peasants begin to raise potatoes. Even then, many complained that these strange-looking tubers tasted terrible.

Within Europe's growing cities, there were great differences in wealth and power. Successful merchants dominated city life. Guilds, too, remained powerful. And as trade grew, another group—lawyers—gained importance for their skills in writing contracts. Middle-class families enjoyed a comfortable life. Servants cooked, cleaned, and waited on them. Other city residents, such as journeymen and other laborers, were not so lucky. They often lived in crowded quarters on the edge of poverty.

Regardless of social class, European families were patriarchal. As husband and father, a man was responsible for the behavior of his wife and children. Women had almost no property or legal rights. A woman's chief roles were as wife and mother. Society stressed such womanly virtues as modesty, household economy, obedience, and caring for the family. Middle-class women might help their husbands in a family business. Peasant women worked alongside their husbands in the fields.

Looking Ahead

In the 1500s and 1600s, Europe emerged as a powerful new force on the world scene. The voyages of exploration marked the beginning of what would become European domination of the globe. In the centuries ahead, competition for empire would spark wars in Europe and on other continents.

European expansion would spread goods and other changes throughout the world. It would also revolutionize the European economy and transform its society. The concept of "the West" itself emerged as European settlers transplanted their culture to the Americas and, later, to Australia and New Zealand.

For centuries, most Europeans knew little or nothing about other lands. Exposure to different cultures was both unsettling and stimulating. As their horizons broadened, they had to reexamine old beliefs and customs.

Cause and Effect

Long-Term Causes	Immediate Causes
• Scientific Revolution • Europeans search for a sea route to Asia	• Columbus and other Europeans arrive in the Americas • Europeans encounter new plants and animals in the Americas

Columbian Exchange

Immediate Effects	Long-Term Effects
• Millions of Native Americans die from diseases • Enslaved Africans sent to the Americas • American foods introduced into Europe	• Exchange of ideas, foods, art, and language between Europe and the Americas • Population migration from Europe to the Americas • Growth of capitalism

Connections to Today

• Multicultural societies in the Americas
• Worldwide reliance on staples such as corn and potatoes

Skills Assessment Chart The arrival of Columbus in the Americas set off a global exchange of people, goods, and ideas. **Based on the chart, name one immediate and one long-term effect of the Columbian Exchange.**

Recall
1. **Identify: (a)** Columbian Exchange, **(b)** commercial revolution, **(c)** putting out system.
2. **Define: (a)** inflation, **(b)** capitalism, **(c)** entrepreneur, **(d)** joint stock company, **(e)** mercantilism, **(f)** tariff.

Comprehension
3. How did the voyages of Columbus lead to global exchanges of goods and ideas?
4. Explain how each of the following contributed to economic changes in Europe: **(a)** the price revolution, **(b)** capitalism, **(c)** mercantilism.

5. How did the economic changes of the 1500s and 1600s affect the lives of ordinary people?

Critical Thinking and Writing
6. **Linking Past and Present** Global exchanges of goods, ideas, and even diseases continue today. How has modern technology quickened the speed with which global exchanges occur? Provide examples to support your answer.
7. **Inferring** Do you think the European policy of mercantilism was beneficial or harmful for the people of Africa and the Americas? Explain.

Activity

Creating a Map
Create an illustrated map of the world showing the movement of items in the Columbian Exchange. Label Europe, Asia, Africa, and North and South America. Create symbols to stand for products and use arrows to indicate the direction in which they traveled.

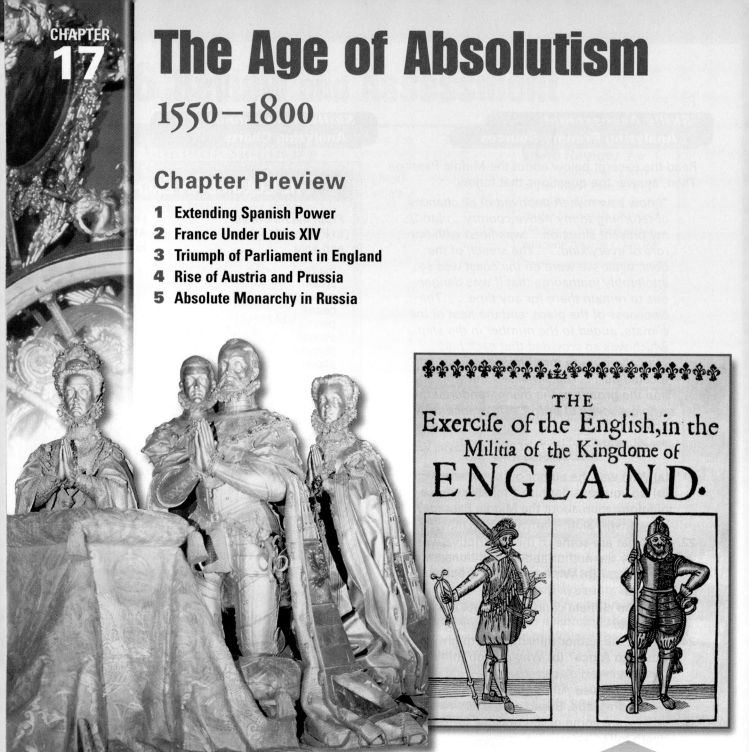

CHAPTER
17

The Age of Absolutism
1550–1800

Chapter Preview

1 Extending Spanish Power
2 France Under Louis XIV
3 Triumph of Parliament in England
4 Rise of Austria and Prussia
5 Absolute Monarchy in Russia

THE
Exercise of the English, in the
Militia of the Kingdome of
ENGLAND.

1556
Philip II (second from right) becomes king of Spain. Under Philip, Spain is the wealthiest and most powerful state in Europe.

1618
Religious conflict between German Protestants and Catholics sparks the Thirty Years' War.

1642
The English Civil War begins, pitting the king's troops (left) against the armies of Parliament (right).

CHAPTER EVENTS

1550   1600   1650

GLOBAL EVENTS

1556 Akbar the Great becomes emperor of India.

1607 British colonists found Jamestown.

European Nation-States, 1700

By 1700, powerful European monarchs had set aside the feudal past and built strong, centralized nation-states. Most of these rulers held absolute power.

Major European monarchies

North Sea

SWEDEN

Baltic Sea

Moscow

RUSSIA

ENGLAND
London

Berlin

PRUSSIA

POLAND

Paris

Rhine R.

Vistula R.

Dnieper R.

FRANCE

Prague

50°N

ALPS

Vienna

AUSTRIA

PYRENEES MTS.

Danube R.

Black Sea

ATLANTIC OCEAN

Madrid

SPAIN

40°N

Rome

OTTOMAN EMPIRE

10°W

0°

Mediterranean Sea

Azimuthal Equidistant Projection

0   250   500 Miles

0   250   500 Kilometers

1697
Czar Peter the Great of Russia tours Europe to study western technology and ideas.

1715
King Louis XIV of France dies. The palace of Versailles, shown here, is a symbol of his 72-year reign.

1795
Russia, Prussia, and Austria complete the partition of Poland.

1700

1750

1800

1680s Asante kingdom is organized in West Africa.

1754 The French and Indian War erupts in North America.

1793 The emperor of China rejects British trade.

Extending Spanish Power

Reading Focus

- How did Spanish power increase under Charles V and Philip II?

- How did the arts flourish during Spain's golden age?

- Why did the Spanish economy decline in the 1600s?

Vocabulary

absolute monarch

divine right

armada

Taking Notes

As you read this section, prepare an outline of the contents. Use Roman numerals to indicate major headings. Use capital letters for the sub-headings and numbers for the supporting details. The example will help you get started.

I. Charles V and the Hapsburg Empire
  A. Wearing two crowns
    1. Spain
    2. Holy Roman Empire and Netherlands
  B. An empire divided
    1.
    2.
II.

Main Idea Philip II extended Spain's power and helped establish a golden age.

Global Connections

Cartloads of Silver and Gold

Old Spanish shipping records tell a tale about amazing wealth: "On 22 March 1595, ships from the Indies . . . began to discharge and deposit with the Chamber of Commerce 332 cartloads of silver, gold, and pearls of great value." This was the haul for *just one day*—and the flow of riches continued for *years!*

A major part of this wealth enriched the royal family. Most of the rest went into the hands of private traders. For Spain, American silver and gold financed a golden age of art, literature—and power.

Theme: Economics and Technology What impact could wealth from the Americas have on the arts in Renaissance Spain?

Setting the Scene

"It is best to keep an eye on everything," Philip II of Spain often said—and he meant it. As king of the most powerful nation in Europe, he gave little time to pleasure. Instead, he plowed through a mountain of paperwork each day, making notes on even the most trivial matters. Once the Spanish ambassador to England wrote about an unfamiliar kind of insect he had seen in London. "Probably fleas," Philip scribbled on the letter.

Philip's determination to "keep an eye on everything" extended far beyond trivia. It helped him build Spain into a strong centralized state. By the late 1500s, he had concentrated all power into his own hands. Over the next 200 years, other European monarchs would pursue similar goals.

Charles V and the Hapsburg Empire

By the 1500s, Spain had shaken off the feudal past and emerged as the first modern European power. Under Queen Isabella and King Ferdinand, Spain had expelled the last Muslim rulers and enforced religious unity. In 1492, Isabella financed Columbus's voyage across the Atlantic, leading to the Spanish conquest of the Americas.

Wearing Two Crowns In 1519, Charles V,* grandson of Ferdinand and Isabella, inherited a huge empire. The new king faced a nearly impossible challenge. He not only inherited the crown of Spain but was also the heir of the Austrian Hapsburgs. The sprawling Hapsburg empire included the Holy Roman Empire and the Netherlands.

Ruling two empires involved Charles in constant warfare. As a devout Catholic, he fought to suppress the Protestant movement in the German states. After years of religious warfare, however, Charles was forced to allow the German princes to choose their own religions.

His greatest foe was the Ottoman empire. Under Suleiman, Ottoman forces advanced across central Europe to the walls of Vienna, Austria. Although Austria held firm, the Ottomans occupied much of Hungary. Ottoman naval forces also challenged Spanish power in the Mediterranean.

An Empire Divided Perhaps the Hapsburg empire was too scattered and diverse for any one person to rule. Exhausted and disillusioned, Charles V gave up his titles and entered a monastery in 1556. He divided his empire,

* Within Spain, the king was known as Charles I. However, historians usually refer to him as Charles V, his title as ruler of the Austrian Hapsburg empire.

leaving the Hapsburg lands in central Europe to his brother Ferdinand, who became Holy Roman emperor. He gave Spain, the Netherlands, southern Italy, and Spain's overseas empire to his 29-year-old son Philip.

Philip II and Divine Right

Like his father, King Philip II was hard-working, devout, and ambitious. During his 42-year reign, he sought to expand Spanish influence, strengthen the Catholic Church, and make his own power absolute. Thanks in part to silver from the Americas, he made Spain the foremost power in Europe.

Unlike many other monarchs, Philip devoted much time to government work. He seldom hunted, never jousted, and lived as sparsely as a monk. His isolated, somber palace outside Madrid reflected the King's character. Known as the Escorial (ehs KOHR ee uhl), it served as a church, a residence, and a tomb for members of the royal family.

As did Ferdinand and Isabella, Philip further centralized royal power, making every part of the government responsible to him. He reigned as an absolute monarch, a ruler with complete authority over the government and the lives of the people. Like other European rulers, Philip asserted that he ruled by divine right. That is, he believed that his authority to rule came directly from God.

Partly as a result of the concept of divine right, Philip saw himself as the guardian of the Roman Catholic Church. The great undertaking of his life was to defend the Catholic Reformation and turn back the rising Protestant tide in Europe. Within his own lands, Philip enforced religious unity. He turned the Inquisition against Protestants and other people thought to be heretics.

The Wars of Philip II

Philip fought many wars as he attempted to advance Spanish Catholic power. At the battle of Lepanto in 1571, Spain and its Italian allies soundly defeated an Ottoman fleet in the Mediterranean. Although Christians hailed this as a great victory, the Ottoman empire remained a major power in the Mediterranean region.

Revolt in the Netherlands During the last half of his reign, Philip battled Protestant rebels in the Netherlands. At the time, the region included 17 provinces that are today Belgium, the Netherlands, and Luxembourg. It was the richest part of Philip's empire. Protestants in the Netherlands resisted Philip's efforts to crush their faith. Protestants and Catholics alike opposed high taxes and autocratic Spanish rule, which threatened local traditions of self-government.

In the 1560s, riots against the Inquisition sparked a general uprising in the Netherlands. Savage fighting raged for decades. In 1581, the northern, largely Protestant provinces declared their independence from Spain and became known as the Dutch Netherlands. They did not gain official recognition, however, until 1648. The southern, mostly Catholic provinces of the Netherlands remained part of the Spanish empire.

Invading England By the 1580s, Philip saw England's Queen Elizabeth I as his chief Protestant enemy. First secretly, then openly, Elizabeth had supported the Dutch against Spain. She even encouraged English captains,

Philip II of Spain
From 1556 to 1598, Philip II ruled the wealthiest, most powerful nation in Europe. Devoted to his family and to the Catholic Church, Philip could also be ruthless toward his enemies.

Theme: Impact of the Individual What impression of Philip II does this painting give you? Explain.

Successes and Failures

Louis XIV ruled France for 72 years, far longer than any other monarch. During his reign, French culture, manners, and customs replaced those of Renaissance Italy as the standard for European taste. In both foreign and domestic affairs, however, many of Louis's policies were costly failures.

Wars of Louis XIV Louis XIV poured vast resources into wars to expand French borders. At first, he did gain some territory. His later wars were disastrous, though, because rival rulers joined forces to check French ambitions. Led by the Dutch or the English, these alliances fought to maintain the balance of power, a distribution of military and economic power that would prevent any one nation from dominating Europe.

In 1700, Louis's grandson Philip V inherited the throne of Spain. Louis declared that France and Spain "must regard themselves as one." But neighboring powers led by England were determined to prevent this union. The War of the Spanish Succession dragged on until 1713, when an exhausted France signed the Treaty of Utrecht. Philip remained on the Spanish throne, but France agreed never to unite the two crowns.

The King as Warrior
Although Louis XIV is best remembered for his extravagant court, he also expanded France's military might. This painting depicts Louis as a gallant warrior.

Theme: Impact of the Individual What symbols does this artist use to glorify Louis XIV?

Persecution of the Huguenots Louis saw France's Protestant minority as a threat to religious and political unity. In 1685, he revoked the Edict of Nantes. More than 100,000 Huguenots fled France.

The persecution of the Huguenots was perhaps the king's most costly blunder. The Huguenots had been among the most hard-working and prosperous of Louis's subjects. Their loss was thus a serious blow to the French economy, just as the expulsion of Muslims and Jews had hurt Spain.

Looking Ahead

Louis XIV outlived his sons and grandsons. When he died in 1715, his five-year-old great-grandson inherited the throne as Louis XV. Although France was then the strongest state in Europe, years of warfare had drained the treasury. The prosperity nurtured by Colbert evaporated under the burden of bad harvests, heavy taxes, and other problems.

Louis XV was too weak a king to deal with such problems. He devoted his days to pleasure, ignoring the growing need for reform. He often quoted an old proverb, "After us, the deluge." As you will read, the deluge came during the reign of the next king.

SECTION 2 Assessment

Recall

1. **Identify: (a)** St. Bartholomew's Day Massacre, **(b)** Edict of Nantes, **(c)** *Fronde*, **(d)** Versailles, **(e)** War of the Spanish Succession.

2. **Define: (a)** intendant, **(b)** levée, **(c)** balance of power.

Comprehension

3. **(a)** What were the effects of the French wars of religion? **(b)** How did Henry IV rebuild French unity?

4. Describe how Louis XIV strengthened the power of the monarchy.

5. How did Louis's persecution of the Huguenots harm France?

Critical Thinking and Writing

6. **Comparing** How were the ideas of Louis XIV about monarchy similar to those of Philip II of Spain?

7. **Applying Information** On his deathbed, Louis XIV told his heir, "I have loved war too well; do not copy me in this, nor in the lavish expenditures I have made." Why do you think Louis gave this advice?

Reading Focus

- How did the Tudors and Stuarts differ in their relations with Parliament?
- How did the English Civil War lead to the rise of the Commonwealth?
- What were the causes and results of the Glorious Revolution?

Vocabulary

dissenter
habeas corpus
limited monarchy

Taking Notes

Create a flowchart that shows the events in England that ultimately led to the strengthening of Parliament. Use this chart as a model, and add boxes as needed.

> Tudors consult with and control Parliament
>
> ↓
>
> James asserts claim to absolute power and clashes with Parliament
>
> ↓
>
> [ ]
>
> ↓
>
> [ ]

Main Idea During the 1600s, the British Parliament asserted its rights against royal claims to absolute power.

Setting the Scene "The most high and absolute power in the realm consists in the Parliament," wrote an English statesman in the 1560s. He was voicing a tradition that had roots in the Middle Ages. But in 1603, a monarch with far different ideas took the throne of England. "Kings are called gods," declared James I, "because they sit upon God's throne on Earth." Before long, James was on a collision course with Parliament.

In the 1600s, while Louis XIV perfected royal absolutism in France, England developed in a different direction. In this section, we will look at why and how Parliament asserted itself against royal power.

The Tudors and Parliament

From 1485 to 1603, England was ruled by the Tudor dynasty. Although the Tudors believed in divine right, they shrewdly recognized the value of good relations with Parliament. As you have read, when Henry VIII broke with the Roman Catholic Church, he turned to Parliament to legalize his actions. Parliament approved the Act of Supremacy, making the monarch head of the Church of England.

A constant need for money also led Henry to consult Parliament frequently. Although he had inherited a bulging treasury, he quickly used up his funds fighting overseas wars. To levy new taxes, the king had to seek the approval of Parliament. Members of Parliament tended to vote as Henry's agents instructed. Still, they became accustomed to being consulted on important matters.

Like her father, Elizabeth I both consulted and controlled Parliament. Her advisers conveyed the queen's wishes to Parliament and forbade discussion of certain subjects, such as foreign policy or the queen's marriage. Her skill in handling Parliament helped make "Good Queen Bess" a popular and successful ruler.

The Early Stuarts

Elizabeth died in 1603 without a direct heir. The throne passed to her relatives the Stuarts, the ruling family of Scotland. The Stuarts were neither as popular as the Tudors nor as skillful in dealing with Parliament. They also inherited problems that Henry and Elizabeth had long suppressed. The result was a "century of revolution" that pitted the Stuart monarchs against Parliament.

The Royal Challenge The first Stuart monarch, James I, had agreed to rule according to English laws and customs. Soon, however, he was lecturing Parliament about divine right. "I will not be content that my power be disputed upon," he declared. Leaders in the House of Commons fiercely resisted the king's claim to absolute power.

James repeatedly clashed with Parliament over money and foreign policy. He needed funds to finance his lavish court and wage wars. When members wanted to discuss foreign policy before voting funds, James dissolved Parliament and collected taxes on his own.

James also found himself embroiled in disputes with dissenters, Protestants who differed with the Church of England. One group, called Puritans, sought to "purify" the church of Catholic practices. Puritans called for simpler services and a more democratic church without bishops. James rejected their demands, vowing to "harry them out of this land or else do worse."

A positive result of the king's dispute with the Puritans was his call for a new translation of the Bible. The King James version that appeared in 1611 has had a lasting influence on English language and literature.

Parliament Responds In 1625, Charles I inherited the throne. Like his father, Charles behaved like an absolute monarch. He imprisoned his foes without trial and squeezed the nation for money. By 1628, though, his need to raise taxes forced Charles to summon Parliament. Before voting any funds, Parliament insisted that Charles sign the Petition of Right. It prohibited the king from raising taxes without the consent of Parliament or from imprisoning anyone without just cause.

Charles did sign the petition, but he then dissolved Parliament in 1629. For 11 years, he ignored the petition and ruled the nation without Parliament. During that time, he created bitter enemies, especially among Puritans. His Archbishop of Canterbury, William Laud, tried to force all clergy to follow strict Anglican rules, dismissing or imprisoning dissenters. Many people felt that the archbishop was trying to revive Catholic practices.

In 1637, Charles and Laud tried to impose the Anglican prayer book on Scotland. The Calvinist Scots revolted. To get funds to suppress the Scottish rebellion, Charles finally had to summon Parliament in 1640. When it met, however, Parliament launched its own revolt.

The Long Parliament The 1640 Parliament became known as the Long Parliament because it lasted on and off until 1653. Its actions triggered the greatest political revolution in English history. In a mounting struggle with the king, Parliament tried and executed his chief ministers, including Archbishop Laud. It further declared that the Parliament could not be dissolved without its own consent and called for the abolition of bishops.

Charles lashed back. In 1642, he led troops into the House of Commons to arrest its most radical leaders. They escaped through a back door and soon raised their own army. The clash now moved to the battlefield.

The English Civil War

The civil war that followed lasted from 1642 to 1649. Like the *Fronde* that occurred about the same time in France, the English Civil War posed a major challenge to absolutism. But while the forces of royal power won in France, in England the forces of revolution triumphed.

Cavaliers and Roundheads At first, the odds seemed to favor the Cavaliers, or supporters of Charles I. Many Cavaliers were wealthy nobles, proud of their plumed hats and fashionably long hair. Well trained in dueling and warfare, the Cavaliers expected a quick victory. But their foes proved to be tough fighters with the courage of their convictions. The

Virtual Field Trip

www.phschool.com

Cromwell Museum
Huntington, England

To see other images relating to the career of Oliver Cromwell, use the Internet address above to link to the Cromwell Museum.

A Victory for Parliament
The Battle of Marston Moor was a turning point in the English Civil War. Though wounded in the neck, Oliver Cromwell (center, on horse) rallied his troops to defeat the forces of King Charles I.

Theme: Continuity and Change How would a modern battle scene differ from this one?

forces of Parliament were composed of country gentry, town-dwelling manufacturers, and Puritan clergy. They were called Roundheads because their hair was cut close around their heads.

The Roundheads found a leader of genius in Oliver Cromwell. A Puritan member of the lesser gentry, Cromwell was a skilled general. He organized the "New Model Army" for Parliament into a disciplined fighting force. Inspired by Puritan chaplains, Cromwell's army defeated the Cavaliers in a series of decisive battles. By 1647, the king was in the hands of parliamentary forces.

Execution of a King Eventually, Parliament set up a court to put the king on trial. It condemned him to death as "a tyrant, traitor, murderer, and public enemy." On a cold January day in 1649, Charles I stood on a scaffold surrounded by his foes. "I am a martyr of the people," he declared.

Showing no fear, the king told the executioner that he himself would give the sign for him to strike. After a brief prayer, Charles knelt and placed his neck on the block. On the agreed signal, the executioner severed the king's head with a single stroke.

The execution sent shock waves throughout Europe. In the past, kings had occasionally been assassinated or died in battle. But for the first time, a ruling monarch had been tried and executed by his own people. The parliamentary forces had sent a clear signal that, in England, no ruler could claim absolute power and ignore the rule of law.

The Commonwealth

After the execution of Charles I, the House of Commons abolished the monarchy, the House of Lords, and the official Church of England. It declared England a republic, known as the Commonwealth, under the leadership of Oliver Cromwell.

Challenges to the Commonwealth The new government faced many threats. Supporters of Charles II, the uncrowned heir to the throne, attacked England by way of Ireland and Scotland. Cromwell led forces into Ireland to crush the uprising. He then took harsh measures against the Irish Catholic majority. In 1652, Parliament passed a law exiling most Catholics to barren

Our Puritan Heritage

Decades before the Puritans gained power in England, a group of settlers tried their hand at building a Puritan society across the Atlantic. Massachusetts Bay was a new colony without any traditions of established churches, strong government, or historic communities. The Puritans knew that to assure survival of their beliefs and culture, they would have to educate their children in their own ways. That was one reason the Puritans built schools, including Harvard College.

Eventually, the colonies became the United States. Over time, the rest of the country adopted the Puritan tradition of establishing public schools to help train children to become good citizens of their community. A literate, well-informed citizenry has continued to be a major aim of American schools to this day.

Theme: Political and Social Systems What other institutions help to train American children to be good citizens?

land in the west of Ireland. Any Catholic found disobeying this order could be killed on sight.

Squabbles also splintered forces within the Commonwealth. One group, called Levellers, thought that poor men should have as much say in government as the gentry, lawyers, and other leading citizens. "The poorest he that is in England hath a life to live as the greatest he," wrote one Leveller. In addition, female Levellers asserted their right to petition Parliament.

These Leveller ideas horrified the gentry who dominated Parliament. Cromwell and his generals suppressed the Levellers, as well as more radical groups who threatened property ownership. As the challenges to order grew, Cromwell took the title Lord Protector in 1653. From then on, he ruled through the army.

Puritan Society Under the Commonwealth, Puritan preachers tried to root out godlessness and impose a "rule of saints." The English Civil War thus ushered in a social revolution as well as a political one.

Parliament enacted a series of laws designed to make sure that Sunday was set aside for religious observance. Anyone over the age of 14 who was caught "profaning the Lord's Day" could be fined. To the Puritans, theaters were "spectacles of pleasure too commonly expressing mirth and levity." So, like John Calvin in Geneva, Cromwell closed all theaters. Puritans also frowned on lewd dancing, taverns, and gambling.

Puritans felt that every Christian, rich and poor, must be able to read the Bible. To spread religious knowledge, they encouraged education for all people. By mid-century, families from all classes were sending their children to school, girls as well as boys.

Puritans pushed for changes in marriage to ensure greater fidelity. In addition to marriages based on business interests, they encouraged marriages based on love. As in the past, women were seen mainly as caretakers of the family, subordinate to men. When some radical Protestant groups allowed women to preach sermons, most Puritans were shocked.

Although Cromwell could not accept open worship by Roman Catholics, he believed in religious freedom for other Protestant groups. He even welcomed Jews back to England, after more than 350 years of exile.

End of the Commonwealth Oliver Cromwell died in 1658. Soon after, the Puritans lost their grip on England. Many people were tired of military rule and strict Puritan ways. In 1660, a newly elected Parliament invited Charles II to return to England from exile.

England's "kingless decade" ended with the restoration of the monarchy. Yet Puritan ideas about morality, equality, government, and education endured. In the following century, these ideas would play an important role in shaping the United States of America.

From Restoration to Glorious Revolution

In late May 1660, cheering crowds welcomed Charles II back to London. One supporter wrote:

> "This day came his Majesty, Charles the Second to London, after a sad and long exile . . . with a triumph of above 20,000 horse and [soldiers], brandishing their swords, and shouting with inexpressible joy; the ways strewd with flowers, the bells ringing, the streets hung with tapestry."
>
> —John Evelyn, *Diary*

With his charm and flashing wit, young Charles II was a popular ruler. He reopened theaters and taverns and presided over a lively court in the manner of Louis XIV. Charles restored the official Church of England but tolerated other Protestants such as Presbyterians, Quakers, and Baptists.

Synthesizing Information

The Struggle Between King and Parliament

In England, a battle for power raged between king and Parliament during the 1600s. The monarchy was abolished and then restored. The picture, the source, and the time line depict a few highlights of that struggle.

Restoration: Charles II in Triumph

King Versus Parliament

James I and Divine Right (1603)

"Kings are called gods because they sit upon God's throne on earth."

English Bill of Rights (1689)

"1. That . . . suspending of laws . . . by regal authority, without consent of Parliament is illegal.
4. That levying money for or to the use of the crown . . . without grant of Parliament . . . is illegal."

1603 Stuart rule begins	**1629** Charles I dissolves Parliament	**1649** Parliament orders execution of Charles I; Cromwell rules	**1688** Glorious Revolution	**1689** Parliament passes Bill of Rights

1600 — 1620 — 1640 — 1660 — 1680 — 1700

1640 Long Parliament meets   **1642** English Civil War   **1660** Parliament restores Stuart rule; Charles II is crowned

> **Skills Tip**
>
> On a time line, equal intervals of time should be represented by an equal amount of space.

Skills Assessment

1. In which of the following years did Parliament seem to have the most power?
   A 1629
   B 1640
   C 1660
   D 1689

2. The person who painted the picture of Charles II probably
   E favored the monarchy.
   F fought for Cromwell.
   G supported Parliament.
   H disliked the new king.

3. **Critical Thinking Applying Information** (a) What advice would you give to an English monarch in the 1600s who wanted to keep his or her throne? (b) What advice would you give to a member of Parliament in the 1600s who wanted the monarchy to continue?

Chapter 17 **425**

Although Charles accepted the Petition of Right, he shared his father's faith in absolute monarchy and secretly had Catholic sympathies. Still, he shrewdly avoided his father's mistakes in dealing with Parliament.

A New Clash With Parliament   Charles's brother, James II, inherited the throne in 1685. Unlike Charles, James flaunted his Catholic faith. He further angered his subjects by suspending laws at whim and appointing Catholics to high office. Many English Protestants feared that James would restore the Roman Catholic Church.

In 1688, alarmed parliamentary leaders invited James's Protestant daughter, Mary, and her Dutch Protestant husband, William III of Orange, to become rulers of England. When William and Mary landed with their army late in 1688, James II fled to France. This bloodless overthrow of a king became known as the Glorious Revolution.

English Bill of Rights   Before they could be crowned, William and Mary had to accept several acts passed by Parliament in 1689 that became known as the English Bill of Rights. The Bill of Rights ensured the superiority of Parliament over the monarchy. It required the monarch to summon Parliament regularly and gave the House of Commons the "power of the purse." A king or queen could no longer interfere in Parliamentary debates or suspend laws. The Bill of Rights also barred any Roman Catholic from sitting on the throne.

The Bill of Rights also restated the traditional rights of English citizens, such as trial by jury. It abolished excessive fines and cruel or unjust punishment. It affirmed the principle of habeas corpus. That is, no person could be held in prison without first being charged with a specific crime.

Later, the Toleration Act of 1689 granted limited religious freedom to Puritans, Quakers, and other dissenters, though not yet to Catholics. Still, only members of the Church of England could hold public office.

► **Primary Sources and Literature**

See "The English Bill of Rights" in the Reference Section at the back of this book.

Looking Ahead

The Glorious Revolution did not create democracy, but a type of government called limited monarchy, in which a constitution or legislative body limits the monarch's powers. English rulers still had much power, but they had to obey the law and govern in partnership with Parliament. In the age of absolute monarchy elsewhere in Europe, the limited monarchy in England was radical enough.

SECTION 3 Assessment

Recall

1. Identify: (a) James I, (b) Charles I, (c) Petition of Right, (d) Cavalier, (e) Roundhead, (f) Oliver Cromwell, (g) Leveller, (h) English Bill of Rights.
2. Define: (a) dissenter, (b) habeas corpus, (c) limited monarchy.

Comprehension

3. (a) How did Tudor monarchs handle Parliament? (b) Why did the early Stuarts clash with Parliament?
4. (a) Explain two causes of the English Civil War. (b) Why did many people welcome the return of the monarchy?
5. Describe two results of the Glorious Revolution.

Critical Thinking and Writing

6. Analyzing Information (a) How might Puritan teachings have led some women to seek greater liberties? (b) Why do you think many men were upset by the idea of women speaking in public?
7. Linking Past and Present Which aspects of Commonwealth society are part of American society today? Which are not?

Activity

Drawing a Political Cartoon
Draw a political cartoon that might have appeared in England in 1649 about the execution of Charles I. Take the point of view of either a Roundhead or a Cavalier.

Reading Focus

- What were the causes and results of the Thirty Years' War?
- How did Austria and Prussia emerge as great powers?
- How did European diplomats try to maintain a balance of power?

Vocabulary

elector
mercenary
depopulation

Taking Notes

On a sheet of paper, copy the chart shown at right. As you read this section, add events that occurred before and after the Peace of Westphalia.

PEACE OF WESTPHALIA	
Before	**After**
• Thirty Years' War	• Germany divided into many states
• Frederick becomes Holy Roman emperor	•

Main Idea Two great empires, Austria and Prussia, rose out of the ashes of the Thirty Years' War.

Setting the Scene

Year after year, war ravaged the German states of central Europe. Bodies of victims littered fields and roads. As the Thirty Years' War dragged on, almost every European power was sucked into the conflict. "We have had blue coats and red coats and now come the yellow coats," cried the citizens of one German town. "God have pity on us!"

Finally, two great German-speaking powers, Austria and Prussia, rose out of the ashes. Like Louis XIV in France, their rulers perfected skills as absolute monarchs.

The Thirty Years' War

The French philosopher Voltaire noted that, by early modern times, the Holy Roman Empire was neither holy, nor Roman, nor an empire. Instead, it was a patchwork of several hundred small, separate states. In theory, these states were under the authority of the Holy Roman emperor, who was chosen by seven leading German princes called electors. In practice, the emperor had little power over the many rival princes. Religion further divided the German states. The north was largely Protestant, and the south was Catholic. This power vacuum sparked the Thirty Years' War.

The War Begins The war had both religious and political causes. It began in Bohemia, the present-day Czech Republic. Ferdinand, the Hapsburg king of Bohemia, sought to suppress Protestants and to assert royal power over local nobles. In May 1618, a few rebellious Protestant noblemen tossed two royal officials out of a castle window in Prague. This act sparked a general revolt, which Ferdinand moved to suppress. As both sides sought allies, what began as a local conflict widened into a general European war.

The following year, Ferdinand was elected Holy Roman emperor. With the support of Spain, Poland, and other Catholic states, he tried to roll back the Reformation. In the early stages of the war, he defeated the Bohemians and their Protestant allies. Alarmed, Protestant powers like the Netherlands and Sweden sent troops into Germany.

Before long, political motives outweighed religious issues. Catholic and Protestant rulers shifted alliances to suit their own interests. At one point, Catholic France joined Lutheran Sweden against the Catholic Hapsburgs.

The Thirty Years' War Begins

In an act known as the Defenestration of Prague, rebellious nobles in Bohemia tossed two royal officials out of a castle window. Both men survived, but the defiant act sparked the terrible Thirty Years' War.

Theme: Diversity What opposing groups do the men shown in this picture represent?

Europe After the Thirty Years' War

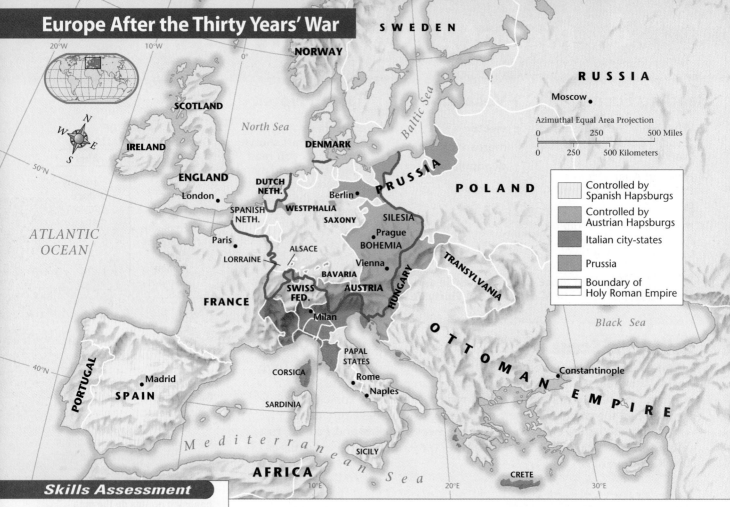

Geography After the Thirty Years' War, the Peace of Westphalia redrew the map of Europe.

1. **Location** On the map, locate **(a)** Poland, **(b)** Sweden, **(c)** Spanish Netherlands, **(d)** Westphalia.
2. **Region** **(a)** In 1648, who controlled Bohemia? **(b)** What lands did the Spanish Hapsburgs control?
3. **Critical Thinking Drawing Conclusions** How can you tell from the map that the Holy Roman Empire was not a strong, unified state?

A Brutal Conflict The fighting took a terrible toll. Roving armies of mercenaries, or soldiers for hire, burned villages, destroyed crops, and killed without mercy. A novel of the time describes episodes of nightmare violence, such as the plundering of a village by marauding soldiers:

> "For one of [the peasants] they had taken they thrust into the baking oven and there lit a fire under him, . . . as for another, they put a cord around his head and twisted it so tight with a piece of wood that the blood gushed from his mouth and nose and ears. In a word each had his own device to torture the peasants."
>
> —Jacob von Grimmelshausen, *Simplicissimus*

Murder and torture were followed by famine and disease. Wolves, not seen in settled areas since the Middle Ages, stalked the deserted streets of once-bustling villages. The war led to severe depopulation, or reduction in population. Although exact population statistics do not exist, historians estimate that as many as one third of the people in the German states may have died as a result of the war.

Peace at Last Finally, in 1648, the exhausted combatants accepted a series of treaties, known as the Peace of Westphalia. Because so many powers had been involved in the conflict, the war ended with a general European peace and an attempt to settle other international problems as well.

France emerged a clear winner, gaining territory on both its Spanish and German frontiers. The Hapsburgs were big losers because they had to accept the almost total independence of all the princes of the Holy Roman Empire. The Netherlands and the Swiss Federation (present-day Switzerland) won recognition as independent states.

The Thirty Years' War left Germany divided into more than 360 separate states, "one for every day of the year." These states still formally acknowledged the leadership of the Holy Roman emperor. Yet each state had its own government, coinage, state church, armed forces, and foreign policy. Germany, potentially the most powerful nation in Europe, thus remained fragmented for another 200 years.

Hapsburg Austria

Though weakened by war, the Hapsburgs still wanted to create a strong united state. They kept the title of Holy Roman emperors, but focused their attention on expanding their own lands. To Austria, they added Bohemia, Hungary, and, later, parts of Poland and Italy.

Unity and Diversity Uniting these lands proved difficult. Divided by geography, they also included diverse peoples and cultures. By the 1700s, the Hapsburg empire included Germans, Magyars, Slavs, and others. In many parts of the empire, people had their own languages, laws, assemblies, and customs.

The Hapsburgs did exert some control over these diverse peoples. They sent German-speaking officials to Bohemia and Hungary and settled Austrians on confiscated lands in these provinces. The Hapsburgs also put down revolts in Bohemia and Hungary. Still, the Hapsburg empire never developed a centralized system like that of France.

Maria Theresa In the early 1700s, the emperor Charles VI faced a new crisis. He had no son. His daughter, Maria Theresa, was intelligent and capable, but no woman had yet ruled Hapsburg lands in her own name. Charles persuaded other European rulers to recognize his daughter's right to succeed him. When he died, however, many ignored their pledge.

The greatest threat came in 1740, when Frederick II of Prussia seized the rich Hapsburg province of Silesia. Maria Theresa set off for Hungary to appeal for military help from her Hungarian subjects. The Hungarians were ordinarily unfriendly to the Hapsburgs. But she made a dramatic plea before an assembly of Hungarian nobles. According to one account, the nobles rose to their feet and shouted, "Our lives and blood for your Majesty!" She eventually got further help from Britain and Russia.

During the eight-year War of the Austrian Succession, Maria Theresa was not able to force Frederick out of Silesia. Still, she did preserve her empire and win the support of most of her people. Equally important, she strengthened Hapsburg power by reorganizing the bureaucracy and improving tax collection. She even forced nobles and clergy to pay taxes and tried to ease the burden of taxes and labor services on peasants. As you will read, many of her reforms were later extended by her son and successor, Joseph II.

The Rise of Prussia

While Austria was molding a strong Catholic state, Prussia emerged as a new Protestant power. In the 1600s, the Hohenzollern (HOH uhn tsahl ern) family ruled scattered lands across north Germany. After the Peace of Westphalia, ambitious Hohenzollern rulers united their lands by taking over the states between them. Like absolute rulers elsewhere, they set up an efficient central bureaucracy and reduced the independence of their nobles, called Junkers (YOON kerz).

To achieve their goals, Prussian rulers like Frederick William I forged one of the best-trained armies in Europe. Great emphasis was placed on military values. One Prussian military leader boasted, "Prussia is not a state which possesses an army, but an army which possesses a state."

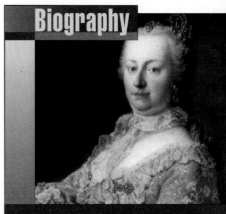

Frederick William won the loyalty of the Junkers by giving them positions in the army and government. By 1740, Prussia was strong enough to challenge its rival Austria.

Frederick II Frederick William made sure that, from an early age, his son Frederick was trained in the art of war:

> "His tutor must take the greatest pains to imbue my son with a sincere love for the soldier's profession and to impress upon him that nothing else in the world can confer upon a prince such fame and honor as the sword."
> —Frederick William, quoted in *The Heritage of World Civilizations* (Craig)

In fact, young Frederick preferred playing the flute and writing poetry. Frederick William despised these pursuits and treated the young prince so badly that he tried to flee the country. Discovering these plans, Frederick William put his son in solitary confinement. A friend who had helped Frederick was beheaded while the 18-year-old prince was forced to watch.

Military Successes Frederick's harsh military training did have an effect. After becoming king in 1740, Frederick II lost no time in using his army. As you read, he boldly seized Silesia from Austria, sparking the War of the Austrian Succession. In several later wars, Frederick made brilliant use of his disciplined army, forcing all to accept Prussia as a great power. His exploits earned him the name Frederick the Great.

Keeping the Balance of Power

By 1750, the great powers of Europe included Austria, Prussia, France, England, and Russia. They formed various alliances to maintain the balance of power. Though nations sometimes switched partners, two rivalries persisted. Prussia battled Austria for control of the German states, while Britain and France competed for overseas empire.

On occasion, European rivalries ignited a worldwide conflict. The Seven Years' War, which lasted from 1756 until 1763, was fought on four continents. Prussia, Austria, Russia, France, and Britain battled in Europe. Britain and France also fought in India and Africa. In North America, the French and Indian War also involved Native American nations. The Treaty of Paris ending the wars gave Britain a huge empire.

SECTION 4 Assessment

Recall
1. **Identify:** (a) Peace of Westphalia, (b) Maria Theresa, (c) War of the Austrian Succession, (d) Frederick the Great, (e) Seven Years' War.
2. **Define:** (a) elector, (b) mercenary, (c) depopulation.

Comprehension
3. What impact did the Thirty Years' War have on the German states?
4. (a) What two major powers emerged in Europe at the end of the Thirty Years' War? (b) How were the goals of these two nations similar?

5. (a) Why did European nations seek a balance of power? (b) What methods did they use?

Critical Thinking and Writing
6. **Linking Past and Present** Westphalia was the first modern peace conference. (a) Why was such a conference needed? (b) How do nations try to settle disputes today?
7. **Making Inferences** "Prussia is not a state which possesses an army, but an army which possesses a state." What values do you think would be emphasized in such a state?

Activity

Mentoring a Monarch
Both Louis XIV and Frederick William wrote instructions for training their sons to rule. With a partner, create a list of eight to ten rules for a successful absolute monarch in the 1600s and 1700s.

Absolute Monarchy in Russia

Reading Focus

- How did Peter the Great try to make Russia into a modern state?
- What steps did Peter take to expand Russia's borders?
- How did Catherine the Great strengthen Russia?

Vocabulary

westernization
boyar
warm-water port
partition

Taking Notes

As you read this section, make a Venn diagram to compare events in the reigns of Peter the Great and Catherine the Great. Use this diagram as a model, and add more information.

PETER
- Visited western countries

- Adopted western ideas

CATHERINE
- Established port on the Black Sea

Main Idea Czar Peter the Great and his successor, Catherine the Great, strengthened Russia and expanded Russian territory.

Setting the Scene

Along the Dutch waterfront, curious observers noticed that Peter Mikhailov was no ordinary man. For one thing, he stood almost seven feet tall. He had a booming laugh but also a furious temper. By day, he dressed in shabby clothes and worked as a shipyard carpenter. At night, he was entertained by royalty. For Peter Mikhailov was none other than Peter the Great, czar of Russia. His mission was to learn all he could about the more advanced nations of Western Europe.

In the early 1600s, Russia was still a medieval state, untouched by the Renaissance and Reformation and largely isolated from Western Europe. As you have read, the "Time of Troubles" had plunged the state into a period of disorder and foreign invasions. The reign of the first Romanov czar in 1613 restored a measure of order. Not until 1682, however, did a czar emerge who was strong enough to regain the absolute power of earlier czars. Peter the Great pushed Russia on the road to becoming a great modern power.

Peter the Great

Peter, just 10 years old when he came to the throne, did not take control of the government until 1689. Though he was not well educated, the young czar was immensely curious. He spent hours in the "German quarter," the Moscow suburb where many Dutch, Scottish, English, and other foreign artisans and soldiers lived. There, he heard of the advanced technology that was helping Western European monarchs forge powerful empires.

Journey to the West In 1697, Peter set out to study western technology for himself. He spent hours walking the streets of European cities, noting the manners and homes of the people. He visited factories and art galleries, learned anatomy from a doctor, and even had a dentist teach him how to pull teeth. In England, Peter was impressed by Parliament. "It is good," he said, "to hear subjects speaking truthfully and openly to their king."

Returning to Russia, Peter brought along a group of technical experts, teachers, and soldiers he had recruited in the West. He then embarked on a policy of westernization, that is, the adoption of western ideas, technology, and culture. But persuading fellow Russians to change their way of life proved difficult. To impose his will, Peter became the most autocratic of Europe's absolute monarchs.

Peter Westernizes Russia
As part of his program of westernization, Peter the Great ordered Russian nobles to shave their beards and dress in western style. Those who refused had to pay a special "beard tax."

Theme: Continuity and Change How is the noble in this cartoon reacting to Peter's beard policy?

Expansion of Russia, 1689–1796

ARCTIC OCEAN

DENMARK
SWEDEN
Berlin
Baltic Sea
PRUSSIA
St. Petersburg
Vienna
Warsaw
Novgorod
AUSTRIA
Moscow
Perm
Odessa
Sibir
URAL MTS.
RUSSIA
Tomsk
Turukhansk
SIBERIA
Yakutsk
Nizhiye Kolymsk
Bering Sea
Petropavlovsk
Okhotsk
Sea of Okhotsk
Constantinople
Sevastopol
Azov
Black Sea
CAUCASUS MTS.
Yeniseysk
Krasnoyarsk
Irkutsk
Amur R.
OTTOMAN EMPIRE
Mediterranean Sea
Aral Sea
Caspian Sea
Ural R.
Volga R.
Don R.
Dnieper R.
Dniester R.
Danube R.
Vistula R.
Elbe R.
Sea of Japan

Azimuthal Equal Area Projection
0   500   1000 Miles
0   500   1000 Kilometers

Russia, 1689	Austria, 1796
Land added by Peter the Great by 1725	Prussia, 1796
Land added by Catherine the Great by 1795	Trade routes
Land added by 1796	Bering's exploration route, 1725–1729

Skills Assessment

Geography During the 1600s and 1700s, Russia expanded both eastward and westward to become the largest nation in the world.

1. **Location** On the map, locate **(a)** Sweden, **(b)** Baltic Sea, **(c)** St. Petersburg, **(d)** Black Sea, **(e)** Siberia, **(f)** Bering Sea.
2. **Place** Why were ports on the Black Sea more appealing to Russia than those on the Baltic?
3. **Critical Thinking Predicting Consequences** How might this map look different if Peter the Great had not modernized Russia?

Autocrat and Reformer   At home, Peter pursued several related goals. He wanted to strengthen the military, expand Russian borders, and centralize royal power. To achieve his ends, he brought all Russian institutions under his control, including the Russian Orthodox Church. He forced the haughty boyars, or landowning nobles, to serve the state in civilian or military jobs.

Under Peter, serfdom spread in Russia, long after it had died out in Western Europe. By tying peasants to land given to nobles, he ensured that nobles could serve the state. Further, he forced some serfs to become soldiers or labor on roads, canals, and other government projects.

Using autocratic methods, Peter pushed through social and economic reforms. He imported western technology, improved education, simplified the Russian alphabet, and set up academies for the study of mathematics, science, and engineering. To pay for his sweeping reforms, Peter adopted mercantilist policies, such as encouraging exports. He improved the waterways and canals, developed mining and textile manufacturing, and backed new trading companies.

Some changes had a symbolic meaning. As you read, after returning from the West, Peter insisted that boyars shave their beards. He also forced them to replace their old-fashioned robes with Western European clothes. To end the practice of secluding upper-class women in separate quarters, he held grand parties at which women and men were expected to dance together. Russian nobles resisted this radical mixing of the sexes in public.

Peter had no mercy for any who resisted the new order. When elite palace guards revolted, he had over 1,000 of the rebels tortured and executed. As an example of his power, he left their rotting corpses outside the palace walls for months.

Expansion Under Peter

From his earliest days as czar, Peter worked to build Russian's military power. He created the largest standing army in Europe and set out to extend Russian borders to the west and south.

Search for a Warm-Water Port Russian seaports, located along the Arctic Ocean, were frozen over in the winter. To increase Russia's ability to trade with the West, Peter desperately wanted a warm-water port—one that would be free of ice all year round.

The nearest warm-water coast was located along the Black Sea. To gain control of this territory, Peter had to push through the powerful Ottoman empire. In the end, Peter was unable to defeat the Ottomans and gain his warm-water port. However, the later Russian monarch Catherine the Great would achieve that goal before the century ended.

War With Sweden In 1700, Peter began a long war against the kingdom of Sweden. At the time, Sweden dominated the Baltic region. Early on, Russia suffered humiliating defeats. A Swedish force of only 8,000 men defeated a Russian army five times its size. Undaunted, Peter rebuilt his army along western lines. In 1709, he defeated the Swedes and won land along the Baltic Sea.

Peter's City On land won from Sweden, Peter built a magnificent new capital city, St. Petersburg. Seeking to open a "window on the West," he located the city on the swampy shores of the Neva River near the Baltic coast. He forced tens of thousands of serfs to drain the swamps. Many thousands died, but Peter got his city. He then invited Italian architects and artisans to design great palaces in western style. Peter even planned the city's parks and boulevards himself.

Just as Versailles became a monument to French absolutism, St. Petersburg became the great symbol of Peter's desire to forge a modern Russia. A hundred years later, Russia's best-known poet, Alexander Pushkin, portrayed Peter as a larger-than-life ruler, determined to tame nature no matter what the cost:

> "Here we at Nature's own behest
> Shall break a window to the West,
> Stand planted on the ocean level;
> Here flags of foreign nations all
> By waters new to them will call
> And unencumbered we shall revel."
> —Alexander Pushkin, *The Bronze Horseman*

Toward the Pacific Russian traders and raiders also crossed the plains and rivers of Siberia, blazing trails to the Pacific. Under Peter, Russia signed a treaty with Qing China, defining their common border in the east. The treaty recognized Russia's right to lands north of Manchuria.

In the early 1700s, Peter hired the Danish navigator Vitus Bering to explore what became known as the Bering Strait between Siberia and Alaska. Russian pioneers crossed into Alaska and migrated as far south as California. Few Russians moved east of the Ural Mountains at this time, but on a map, Russia was already the largest country in the world, as it still is today.

Legacy of Peter the Great

When Peter died in 1725, he left behind a mixed legacy. He had expanded Russian territory, gained ports on the Baltic Sea, and created a mighty army. He had also ended Russia's long period of isolation. From the 1700s on, Russia would be increasingly involved in the affairs of Western Europe. Yet

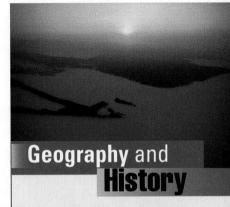

Geography and History

Being "Sent to Siberia"

Russia's absolute monarchs needed a place to exile both criminals and political opponents for long periods of time. What place was better than the arctic region of Siberia to the north? Siberia had an extremely inhospitable climate—temperatures could average –59°F in winter—and it was far away from everything Russian. There was little chance for escape, as it was almost impossible to survive the vast, frozen, sparsely populated region. In fact, approximately 10 to 15 percent of the exiles never made it to Siberia. They died along the way.

Exiles started with a trickle in the early 1600s, but by the early 1800s, the number grew to 2,000 a year. After a revolt in 1825, the czar sent 150,000 people off to their freezing fate. Today, the expression "sent to Siberia" still implies that a person is being punished or has become an outcast.

Theme: Geography and History Why was Siberia chosen as a place for exile?

many of Peter's ambitious reforms died with him. Nobles, for example, soon ignored his policy of service to the state.

Like earlier czars, Peter the Great had brandished terror to enforce his absolute power. His policies contributed to the growth of serfdom, which served only to widen the gap between Russia and the West that Peter had sought to narrow.

Catherine the Great

Peter died without naming a successor, setting off power struggles among various Romanovs. Under a series of ineffective rulers, Russian nobles reasserted their independence. Then, a new monarch took the reins of power firmly in hand. She became known to history as Catherine the Great.

A German princess by birth, Catherine had come to Russia at the age of 15 to wed the heir to the Russian throne. She learned Russian, embraced the Russian Orthodox faith, and won the loyalty of the people. In 1762, her mentally unstable husband, Czar Peter III, was murdered by a group of Russian army officers. Whether or not Catherine was involved in the assassination plot, she certainly benefited from it. With the support of the military, she ascended the Russian throne herself.

An Efficient Ruler Catherine proved to be an efficient, energetic empress. She reorganized the provincial government, codified laws, and began state-sponsored education for boys and girls.

Like Peter the Great, she embraced western ideas. At court, she encouraged French language and customs, wrote histories and plays, and organized court performances. As you will read in the next chapter, she was also a serious student of the French thinkers who led the intellectual movement known as the Enlightenment.

A Ruthless Absolute Monarch Like other absolute monarchs, Catherine could be ruthless. She granted a charter to the boyars outlining important

The Wealth of Catherine the Great
Catherine the Great (pictured above) enjoyed the splendor of being an absolute monarch. The ornate horse-drawn carriage was a gift from one of the Russian nobles who had conspired in the murder of her husband.

Theme: Political and Social Systems Compare this picture to pictures of the French court at Versailles in this chapter. Why do you think great displays of wealth were important to absolute monarchs?

rights, such as exemption from taxes. At the same time, she allowed them to increase their stranglehold on the peasants. When peasants rebelled against the harsh burdens of serfdom, Catherine took firm action to repress them. As a result, conditions grew worse for Russian peasants. Under Catherine, even more peasants were forced into serfdom.

Like Peter the Great, Catherine was determined to expand Russia's borders. After a war against the Ottoman empire, she finally achieved Peter's dream of a warm-water port on the Black Sea. She also took steps to seize territory from neighboring Poland.

Partition of Poland As you have read, Poland had once been a great European power. However, Polish rulers were unable to centralize their power or diminish the influence of the Polish nobility. The divided Polish government was ill prepared to stand up to the increasing might of its neighbors Russia, Prussia, and Austria.

In the 1770s, Catherine the Great, Frederick the Great, and Emperor Joseph II of Austria hungrily eyed Poland. To avoid fighting one another, the three monarchs agreed to partition, or divide up, Poland. At the first partition, in 1772, Catherine took part of eastern Poland, where many Russians and Ukrainians lived. Frederick and Joseph nibbled at Polish territory from the west.

Poland was partitioned again in 1793 and a third time in 1795. By the time Austria, Prussia, and Russia had taken their final slices, the independent kingdom of Poland had vanished from the map. Not until 1919 would a free Polish state reappear.

Looking Ahead

By the mid-1700s, absolute monarchs ruled four of the five leading powers in Europe. Britain, with its strong Parliament, was the only exception. As these five nations competed with one another, they often ended up fighting to maintain the balance of power.

At the same time, new ideas were in the air. Radical changes would soon shatter the French monarchy, upset the balance of power, and revolutionize European societies. In the next unit, you will read about how the Enlightenment, the French Revolution, the rise of Napoleon Bonaparte, and the Industrial Revolution would transform Europe.

Primary Source

An Empress Writes Her Epitaph
Catherine the Great wrote her own epitaph, or gravestone inscription. Her words show how she wished to be remembered:

"When she had ascended the throne of Russia, she wished to do good and tried to bring happiness, freedom, and prosperity to her subjects.
She forgave easily and hated no one.
She was good-natured and easygoing; she had a cheerful temperament, republican sentiments, and a kind heart.
She had friends.
Work was easy for her; she loved sociability and the arts."
—Catherine the Great, *Memoirs*

Skills Assessment

Primary Source What image of herself was Catherine trying to create? Do you think this image was accurate?

SECTION 5 Assessment

Recall
1. **Identify: (a)** Peter the Great, **(b)** St. Petersburg, **(c)** Vitus Bering, **(d)** Catherine the Great.
2. **Define: (a)** westernization, **(b)** boyar, **(c)** warm-water port, **(d)** partition.

Comprehension
3. **(a)** List three goals of Peter the Great. **(b)** Explain one reform that Peter undertook to achieve each goal.
4. Why did Peter seek to expand Russian territory?
5. Describe how two policies of Catherine the Great strengthened Russia.

Critical Thinking and Writing
6. **Comparing** Compare the goals and policies of Peter the Great to those of *one* of the following monarchs: **(a)** Louis XIV of France, **(b)** Frederick II of Prussia, **(c)** Maria Theresa of Austria.
7. **Drawing Conclusions** Peter the Great said of the English Parliament, "It is good to hear subjects speaking truthfully and openly to their king." Based on what you have read, do you think Peter followed this idea in his own kingdom? Give a reason to support your answer.

Activity
Take It to the NET

Use the Internet to learn about the city of St. Petersburg today. Then, write a commentary that Peter the Great might make on the city if he were to see it today. Tell how he would react to a statue such as *The Bronze Horseman* or to the Hermitage Museum.

The Enlightenment and the American Revolution

1707–1800

Chapter Preview

1 Philosophy in the Age of Reason
2 Enlightenment Ideas Spread
3 Britain at Mid-Century
4 Birth of the American Republic

1707

The Act of Union unites England and Scotland. This British flag uses symbols from each country's flag to show unity.

1721

Johann Sebastian Bach publishes his Brandenburg Concertos. Bach composes music for the harpsichord, shown here, and for many other instruments.

1740

Frederick II begins his reign in Prussia.

CHAPTER EVENTS

1700

1720

1740

GLOBAL EVENTS

1736 Qianlong begins a 60-year reign as emperor of China.

North America, 1783

The American Revolution transformed maps of North America as the United States became an independent nation.

United States territory	Russian territory	Claimed by U.S. and Spain
British territory	Spanish territory	Claimed by Russia, Spain, and Great Britain
French territory	Claimed by U.S. and Great Britain	

ALASKA

Yukon R.
Mackenzie R.
Saskatchewan R.
Hudson Bay
CANADA
St. Lawrence R.
Quebec
Halifax
Boston
New York
Philadelphia
Snake R.
Missouri R.
Mississippi R.
Ohio R.
CALIFORNIA
Colorado R.
LOUISIANA
UNITED STATES
ATLANTIC OCEAN
Rio Grande
New Orleans
Charleston
NEW SPAIN
FLORIDA
Gulf of Mexico
BAHAMAS (Br.)
HISPANIOLA
BELIZE
CUBA
PUERTO RICO
Mexico City
JAMAICA
GUADELOUPE (Fr.)
MARTINIQUE (Fr.)
Caribbean Sea
MOSQUITO COAST
SOUTH AMERICA

PACIFIC OCEAN

Tropic of Cancer

Azimuthal Equal Area Projection
0   500   1000 Miles
0   500   1000 Kilometers

Arctic Circle
60°N
40°W
40°N
20°N
140°W   120°W   100°W   80°W   60°W

N W E S

1759
The *philosophe* Voltaire, shown here, publishes *Candide*. The novel mocks French society.

1762
Jean-Jacques Rousseau publishes *The Social Contract*.

1781
The British army surrenders to the Americans after the Battle of Yorktown. This painting shows American and French officers planning the siege.

1760   1780   1800

1763 The Treaty of Paris is signed by France and Great Britain.

1789 Parisians storm the Bastille.

Philosophy in the Age of Reason

Reading Focus

- How did scientific progress promote trust in human reason?
- How did the social contract and separation of powers affect views on government?
- How did new ideas affect society and the economy?

Vocabulary

natural law

social contract

natural right

philosophe

physiocrat

laissez faire

Taking Notes

Make a table like the one here. Add information about each thinker as you read this section.

THINKER	WORKS AND IDEAS
Hobbes	• Wrote *Leviathan* •
Locke	
Montesquieu	
Voltaire	
Diderot	
Rousseau	
Wollstonecraft	
Smith	

Main Idea Enlightenment thinkers tried to apply reason and the laws of nature to human society.

Smallpox Vaccinations In this painting, Edward Jenner vaccinates a child against smallpox. The smallpox vaccine was one of many scientific developments of the 1700s.

Theme: Art and Literature What elements of the painting suggest that smallpox was a major problem before Jenner developed his vaccine?

Setting the Scene By the early 1700s, European thinkers felt that nothing was beyond the reach of the human mind. The following lines by the English poet Alexander Pope celebrated the successes of humans—the "wondrous creature"—in the Scientific Revolution:

> "Go, wondrous creature! mount where Science guides;
>   Go, measure earth, weigh air, and state the tides;
>   Instruct the planets in what orbs to run,
>   Correct old Time, and regulate the sun."
>   —Alexander Pope, *Essay on Man*

Progress and Reason

The Scientific Revolution of the 1500s and 1600s had transformed the way people in Europe looked at the world. In the 1700s, other scientists expanded European knowledge. Joseph Priestley and Antoine Lavoisier (ahn TWAHN lah vwah ZYAY), for example, built the framework for modern chemistry. Edward Jenner developed a vaccine against smallpox, a disease whose path of death spanned the centuries.

Scientific successes convinced educated Europeans of the power of human reason. If people used reason to find laws that governed the physical world, why not use reason to discover natural laws, or laws that govern human nature? Using the methods of the new science, reformers set out to study human behavior and solve the problems of society. Thus, the Scientific Revolution led to another revolution in thinking, known as the Enlightenment. Through the use of reason, insisted Enlightenment thinkers, people and governments could solve every social, political, and economic problem. Heaven could be achieved here on Earth.

Two Views of the Social Contract

In the 1600s, two English thinkers, Thomas Hobbes and John Locke, set forth ideas that were to become key to the Enlightenment. Both men lived through the upheavals of the English Civil War. Yet they came to very different conclusions about human nature and the role of government.

Hobbes Thomas Hobbes set out his ideas in a work titled *Leviathan.* In it, he argued that people were naturally cruel, greedy, and selfish. If not strictly controlled, they would fight, rob, and oppress one another. Life in the "state of nature"—without laws or other control—would be "solitary, poor, nasty, brutish, and short."

To escape that "brutish" life, said Hobbes, people entered into a social contract, an agreement by which they gave up the state of nature for an organized society. Hobbes believed that only a powerful government could ensure an orderly society. For him, such a government was an absolute monarchy, which could impose order and compel obedience.

Locke John Locke had a more optimistic view of human nature. People were basically reasonable and moral, he said. Further, they had certain natural rights, or rights that belonged to all humans from birth. These included the right to life, liberty, and property.

In *Two Treatises of Government,* Locke argued that people formed governments to protect their natural rights. The best kind of government, he said, had limited power and was accepted by all citizens. Thus, unlike Hobbes, Locke rejected absolute monarchy.

Locke then set out a radical idea. A government, he said, has an obligation to the people it governs. If a government fails its obligations or violates people's natural rights, the people have the right to overthrow that government. This right to revolution would echo across Europe and around the world in the centuries that followed.

Separation of Powers

In the 1700s, France saw a flowering of Enlightenment thought. An early and influential thinker was the Baron de Montesquieu (MON tehs kyoo). Montesquieu studied the governments of Europe, from Italy to England. He read all he could about ancient and medieval Europe and learned about Chinese and Native American cultures. His sharp criticism of absolute monarchy opened the doors for later debate.

In 1748, Montesquieu published *The Spirit of the Laws.* In it, he discussed governments throughout history and wrote admiringly about Britain's limited monarchy. Montesquieu felt that the British had protected themselves against tyranny by dividing the various functions and powers of government among three separate branches: the legislative, executive, and judicial. (In fact, he had misunderstood the British system, which did not separate powers in this way.) Still, he felt that the separation of powers was the best way to protect liberty. Montesquieu also felt that each branch of government should be able to serve as a check on the other two, an idea that we call checks and balances.

The *Philosophes* and Society

In France, a group of Enlightenment thinkers applied the methods of science to better understand and improve society. They believed that the use of reason could lead to reforms of government, law, and society. These thinkers were called *philosophes,* which means "lovers of wisdom." Their ideas soon spread beyond France and even beyond Europe.

Voltaire Defends Freedom of Thought Probably the most famous of the *philosophes* was François-Marie Arouet, who took the name Voltaire. "My trade," said Voltaire, "is to say what I think," and he did so throughout his long, controversial life. Voltaire used biting wit as a weapon to expose the abuses of his day. He targeted corrupt officials and idle aristocrats. With his pen, he battled inequality, injustice, and superstition. He detested the slave trade and deplored religious prejudice.

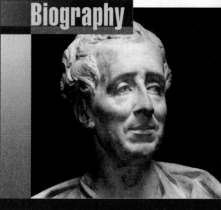

Biography

Montesquieu 1689–1755

Born to wealth, Charles Louis de Secondat inherited the title Baron de Montesquieu. Like many other reformers, his privileged status did not keep him from becoming a voice for democracy. His *Persian Letters* ridiculed the French elite. In *The Spirit of the Laws,* he advanced the idea of separation of powers—a foundation of modern democracy.

Montesquieu's belief in democracy did not mean that he considered all people equal. For example, he held a common view of his time that men were superior to women. However, he thought that women would make good government officials. According to Montesquieu, women's "weakness" would make them "gentle" rulers, thus benefiting the people.

Theme: Impact of the Individual What reforms did Montesquieu promote?

Comparing Viewpoints

What Limits Should There Be on Freedom of Speech?

"I do not agree with a word that you say, but I will defend to the death your right to say it." Whether or not Voltaire said these exact words, he passionately believed in this idea. But his idea has not been universally accepted. To consider whether there should be limits on freedom of speech, examine these viewpoints.

England 1643

John Milton, Puritan writer, expressed views about freedom of expression that later influenced Enlightenment thinkers:

❝ Give me liberty to know, to utter, and to argue freely according to conscience, above all liberties. ❞

China 1957

Mao Zedong led a government in China based on the ideals of the communist philosopher Karl Marx:

❝ What should our policy be toward non-Marxist ideas? As far as unmistakable counterrevolutionaries and saboteurs of the socialist cause are concerned, the matter is easy. We simply deprive them of their freedom of speech. ❞

Canada 1985

The criminal code of Canada outlaws public remarks against religious, racial, or ethnic groups:

❝ Everyone who, by communicating statements other than in private conversation, willfully promotes hatred against any identifiable group is guilty of . . . an indictable offense and is liable to imprisonment for a term not exceeding two years. ❞

United States 1942

Uncle Sam silences an American who is careless in his speech during World War II. "Loose talk" could reveal important secrets to the enemy, costing American lives.

QUIET!

LOOSE TALK CAN COST LIVES

Skills Assessment

1. Who seems to support complete freedom of speech, free from all restrictions?
   A John Milton
   B Uncle Sam
   C Mao Zedong
   D Karl Marx

2. According to Canadian law, freedom of speech
   E does not apply to immigrants.
   F is everyone's right.
   G should be limited under certain circumstances.
   H exists only in public situations.

3. **Critical Thinking** **Analyzing Information** (a) Study the poster. What does it seem to say about freedom of speech? (b) Should freedom of speech ever be limited? If so, under what conditions?

Skills Tip

Before comparing points of view, you must identify the main idea of each separate point of view. Then, look for ways in which the views are the same or different.

Voltaire's outspoken attacks offended both the French government and the Catholic Church. He was imprisoned and forced into exile. Even as he saw his books outlawed and even burned, he continued to defend the principle of freedom of speech.

The *Encyclopedia* Another *philosophe*, Denis Diderot (dee DROH), labored for some 25 years to produce a 28-volume *Encyclopedia*. As the editor of this huge work, Diderot did more than just gather articles on human knowledge. His purpose was "to change the general way of thinking" by explaining the new ideas on topics such as government, philosophy, and religion. Diderot's *Encyclopedia* included articles by leading thinkers of the day, including Montesquieu and Voltaire.

In their *Encyclopedia* articles, the *philosophes* denounced slavery, praised freedom of expression, and urged education for all. They attacked divine-right theory and traditional religions. Critics raised an outcry. The French government argued that the *Encyclopedia* was an attack on public morals, and the pope threatened to excommunicate Roman Catholics who bought or read the volumes.

Despite these and other efforts to ban the *Encyclopedia*, as many as 20,000 copies were printed between 1751 and 1789. When translated into other languages, it helped spread Enlightenment ideas throughout Europe and across the Atlantic to the Americas.

Rousseau The most controversial *philosophe*, Jean-Jacques Rousseau (ZHAHN ZHAHK roo SOH), was a strange, difficult man. Coming from a poor family, he never felt comfortable in the glittering social world of Enlightenment thinkers.

Rousseau believed that people in their natural state were basically good. This natural innocence, he felt, was corrupted by the evils of society, especially the unequal distribution of property. This view was later adopted by many reformers and revolutionaries.

In 1762, Rousseau set forth his ideas about government and society in *The Social Contract*. Rousseau felt that society placed too many limitations on people's behavior. He believed that some controls were necessary, but that they should be minimal. Additionally, these controls should be imposed only by governments that had been freely elected.

Rousseau put his faith in the "general will," or the best conscience of the people. The good of the community as a whole, he said, should be placed above individual interests. Thus, unlike many Enlightenment thinkers who put the individual first, Rousseau felt that the individual should be subordinate to the community.

Rousseau has influenced political and social thinkers for more than 200 years. Woven through his work is a profound hatred of all forms of political and economic oppression. His bold ideas would help fan the flames of revolt in years to come.

Women and the Enlightenment The Enlightenment slogan "free and equal" did not apply to women. Women did have "natural rights," said the *philosophes*. But unlike the natural rights of men, these rights were limited to the areas of home and family.

By the mid-1700s, a small but growing number of women protested this view. They questioned the notion that women were by nature inferior to men and that men's domination of women was therefore part of "nature's plan." Germaine de Staël in France and Catharine Macaulay and Mary Wollstonecraft in Britain argued that women were being excluded from the social contract itself. Their arguments, however, were ridiculed and often sharply condemned.

Wollstonecraft was a well-known British social critic. She accepted that a woman's first duty was to be a good mother. At the same time, however,

Primary Source

The *Encyclopedia*
Diderot's Encyclopedia *contains this passage on the concept of liberty:*

"The first state that man acquires by nature and that is esteemed the most precious of all his possible possessions is the state of liberty. He can neither exchange himself for another, nor sell himself, nor be enslaved, for all men are naturally born free. . . .

By virtue of this state, all men hold from nature itself the power to do what seems right to them and to regulate their actions and their property at will, provided they do not act against the laws of the government. . . ."

—Diderot, Encyclopedia,
or Classified Dictionary of the
Sciences, Arts, and Occupations

Skills Assessment

Primary Source What arguments does Diderot offer against slavery?

she felt that a woman should be able to decide what is in her own interest and should not be completely dependent on her husband. In 1792, Wollstonecraft published *A Vindication of the Rights of Woman*. In it, she called for equal education for girls and boys. Only education, she argued, could give women the tools they needed to participate equally with men in public life.

New Economic Thinking

Other thinkers known as physiocrats focused on economic reforms. Like the *philosophes*, physiocrats looked for natural laws to define a rational economic system.

Laissez Faire Physiocrats rejected mercantilism, which required government regulation of the economy to achieve a favorable balance of trade. Instead, they urged a policy of laissez faire (LEHS ay FAIR), allowing business to operate with little or no government interference. Unlike mercantilists, who called for acquiring gold and silver wealth through trade, the physiocrats claimed that real wealth came from making the land more productive. Extractive industries, they said, such as agriculture, mining, and logging, produced new wealth. Physiocrats also supported free trade and opposed tariffs, or taxes on trade.

Adam Smith British economist Adam Smith greatly admired the physiocrats. In his influential work, *The Wealth of Nations*, he argued that the free market should be allowed to regulate business activity. Smith tried to show how manufacturing, trade, wages, profits, and economic growth were all linked to the market forces of supply and demand. Wherever there is a demand for goods or services, he said, suppliers will seek to meet it. They do so because of the profits and other economic rewards they can get from fulfilling the demand.

Smith was a strong supporter of laissez faire. He believed that the marketplace was better off without any government regulation. At the same time, however, he argued that government had a duty to protect society, administer justice, and provide public works.

Adam Smith's ideas would gain increasing influence as the Industrial Revolution spread across Europe and beyond. His emphasis on the free market and the law of supply and demand would help to shape immensely productive economies in the 1800s and 1900s.

Germaine de Staël
Madame de Staël argued that women had been excluded from the ideals of the Enlightenment. She wrote a number of books, including an analysis of Rousseau.

Theme: Diversity According to the *philosophes*, how were natural rights different for men and for women?

SECTION 1 Assessment

Recall

1. Identify: (a) Thomas Hobbes, (b) John Locke, (c) Baron de Montesquieu, (d) Voltaire, (e) Denis Diderot, (f) Jean-Jacques Rousseau, (g) Mary Wollstonecraft, (h) *The Wealth of Nations.*

2. Define: (a) natural law, (b) social contract, (c) natural right, (d) *philosophe*, (e) physiocrat, (f) laissez faire.

Comprehension

3. How did the achievements of the Scientific Revolution contribute to the Enlightenment?

4. Explain the views of Thomas Hobbes, John Locke, and the Baron de Montesquieu.

5. How did the *philosophes* influence ideas on society and the economy?

Critical Thinking and Writing

6. Defending a Position Rousseau put the common good over the interest of the individual. Do you agree with that position? Explain.

7. Predicting Consequences Suppose that Mary Wollstonecraft encountered another important *philosophe*. What course might their conversation follow?

Activity

Creating a Cartoon
Draw a cartoon to illustrate the ideas of one or more of the *philosophes* you read about in this section. Write a brief caption to accompany your cartoon.

Enlightenment Ideas Spread

Reading Focus

- What roles did censorship and salons play in the spread of new ideas?
- How did *philosophes* influence enlightened despots?
- How did the Enlightenment affect arts and literature?
- Why were the lives of the majority unaffected?

Vocabulary

censorship

salon

enlightened despot

baroque

rococo

Taking Notes

On a sheet of paper draw a concept web to help you record information from this section. The web at right has been started for you. Add more circles as needed.

Main Idea Enlightenment ideas spread across Europe and prompted some rulers to make reforms.

Setting the Scene

Paris, the heart of the Enlightenment, drew many intellectuals and others eager to debate the new ideas. Reforms proposed one evening became the talk of the town the next day. Even an enemy of the Enlightenment admitted that "an opinion launched in Paris was like a battering ram launched by 30 million men."

From France, Enlightenment ideas flowed across Europe and beyond. Everywhere, thinkers examined traditional beliefs and customs in the light of reason and found them flawed. Even absolute monarchs experimented with Enlightenment ideas, although they drew back when changes threatened the established way of doing things.

The Challenge of New Ideas

The ideas of the Enlightenment spread quickly through many levels of society. Educated people all over Europe eagerly read not only Diderot's *Encyclopedia* but also the small, cheap pamphlets that printers churned out on a broad range of issues. More and more, they saw the need for reform to achieve a just society.

During the Middle Ages, most Europeans had accepted without question a society based on divine-right rule, a strict class system, and a belief in heavenly reward for earthly suffering. In the Age of Reason, such ideas seemed unscientific and irrational. A just society, Enlightenment thinkers taught, should ensure social justice and happiness in this world.

Censorship Government and church authorities felt they had a sacred duty to defend the old order. They believed that the old order had been set up by God. To protect against the attacks of the Enlightenment, they waged a war of censorship, or restricting access to ideas and information. They banned and burned books and imprisoned writers.

Philosophes and writers like Montesquieu and Voltaire sometimes disguised their ideas in works of fiction. In the *Persian Letters*, Montesquieu uses two fictional Persian travelers, named Usbek and Rica, to mock French society. The hero of Voltaire's humorous novel *Candide*, published in 1759, travels across Europe and even to the Americas and the Middle East in search of "the best of all possible worlds." Voltaire slyly uses the tale to expose the corruption and hypocrisy of European society.

Salons The new literature, the arts, science, and philosophy were regular topics of discussion in salons, informal social gatherings at which writers,

Global Connections

An American *Philosophe*

Benjamin Franklin first traveled to Europe when he was just 18. There, he wrote in his *Autobiography*, "... I spent little upon myself except ... in books. I had improved my knowledge, ... though I had by no means improved my fortune. But I had made some very ingenious acquaintance, whose conversation was of great advantage to me, and I had read considerably."

Franklin's activities in Europe gave him firsthand exposure to Enlightenment ideas. He carried this new knowledge back to the American colonies, where he helped to create a country based on those ideas—the United States.

Theme: Global Interaction How was the transmission of ideas across the Atlantic different in Franklin's time than it is today?

Salons provided a way for people to gather and share ideas. Today, many people do this without ever meeting—through the Internet.

Every day, millions of people use the Internet to exchange ideas easily. In "chat rooms," people send messages instantly, even if the recipient is on the other side of the world. In "newsgroups," people submit thoughts on a given topic and respond to the comments of others.

Many discussions on the Internet lack the serious-minded tone of a salon conversation. And because participants meet only through computers, there is no way to be sure who is on the other end of the line. But the popularity of the Internet shows that people will find a way to gather and discuss their ideas, even in a "virtual" living room.

Theme: Continuity and Change How does a "virtual" salon compare to the salons of the 1700s?

artists, *philosophes*, and others exchanged ideas. The salon originated in the 1600s, when a group of noblewomen in Paris began inviting a few friends to their homes for poetry readings. By the 1700s, some middle-class women began holding salons. In the drawing rooms of these *salonières* (sah lohn YAIR), middle-class citizens could meet with the nobility on an equal footing to discuss and spread Enlightenment ideas.

One of the most respected salons was run by Madame Geoffrin. In her home on the Rue St. Honoré, she brought together the brightest and most talented people of her day. The young musical genius Wolfgang Amadeus Mozart played for her guests, and Diderot was a regular at her weekly dinners for philosophers and poets.

Enlightened Despots

Discussions of Enlightenment ideas also enlivened the courts of Europe. *Philosophes* tried to persuade European rulers to adopt their ideas. If they could "enlighten" the ruling classes, they thought, they could bring about reform. Some monarchs did accept Enlightenment ideas. They became enlightened despots, or absolute rulers who used their power to bring about political and social change.

Frederick the Great As king of Prussia from 1740 to 1786, Frederick II exerted extremely tight control over his subjects. Still, he saw himself as the "first servant of the state," with a duty to work for the common good.

Frederick admired Voltaire's work and lured the *philosophe* to Berlin to develop a Prussian academy of science. When Frederick was not busy fighting wars, he had swamps drained and forced peasants to grow new crops such as the potato. He had seed and tools distributed to peasants who had suffered in Prussia's wars. Frederick also tolerated religious differences, welcoming victims of religious persecution. "In my kingdom," he said, "everyone can go to heaven in his own fashion."

Frederick's reforms were directed mainly at making the Prussian government more efficient. He reorganized the civil service and simplified laws. But a "rationalized" bureaucracy also meant a stronger monarchy—and more power for Frederick himself.

Catherine the Great Catherine II of Russia read the works of the *philosophes* and exchanged letters with Voltaire and Diderot. She praised Voltaire as someone who had "fought the united enemies of humankind: superstition, fanaticism, ignorance, trickery."

Catherine, who became empress in 1762, toyed with Enlightenment ideas. Early in her reign, she made some limited reforms in law and government. She granted nobles a charter of rights and criticized the institution of serfdom. Still, like Frederick in Prussia, Catherine intended to give up no power. In the end, her political contribution to Russia was not reform but an expanded empire.

Joseph II The most radical of the enlightened despots was the Hapsburg emperor Joseph II, son and successor of Maria Theresa. An eager student of the Enlightenment, Joseph traveled in disguise among his subjects to learn of their problems. His efforts to improve their lives won him the nickname the "peasant emperor."

Maria Theresa had begun to modernize Austria's government. Joseph continued her reforms. Despite opposition, he granted toleration to Protestants and Jews in his Catholic empire. He ended censorship and attempted to bring the Catholic Church under royal control. He sold the property of many monasteries and convents and used the proceeds to build hospitals. Joseph even abolished serfdom. Like many of his other reforms, however, this measure was canceled after his death.

Virtual Field Trip

www.phschool.com

**Utah Museum of Fine Arts
Salt Lake City, Utah**

For more information about the works of Elisabeth Vigée LeBrun, use the Internet address above to link to the Web site of the Utah Museum of Fine Arts.

Enlightenment Painters
During the 1700s, many artists began painting very personal, detailed scenes. In *The Marquise de Peze and the Marquise de Rouget with Her Two Children*, French artist Elisabeth Vigée LeBrun shows the relationships between mothers and young children.

Theme: Art and Literature
What elements of this painting identify its style as rococo rather than baroque?

The Arts and Literature

In the 1600s and 1700s, the arts evolved to meet changing tastes. As in earlier periods, artists and composers had to please their patrons, the men and women who commissioned works from them or gave them jobs.

Courtly Art In the age of Louis XIV, courtly art and architecture were either in the Greek and Roman tradition or in a grand, complex style known as baroque. Baroque paintings were huge, colorful, and full of excitement. They glorified historic battles or the lives of saints. Such works matched the grandeur of European courts.

By the mid-1700s, architects and designers developed the rococo style. Unlike the heavy splendor of the baroque, rococo art was personal, elegant, and charming. Furniture and tapestries featured delicate shells and flowers. Portrait painters showed noble subjects in charming rural settings, surrounded by happy servants and pets.

Middle-Class Audiences A new audience, the growing middle class, emerged with its own requirements. Successful merchants and prosperous town officials wanted their portraits painted, but without frills. They liked pictures of family life or realistic town or country scenes. Dutch painters such as Rembrandt van Rijn (REHM brant van RĪN) conferred great dignity on merchants and other ordinary, middle-class subjects.

Trends in Music New kinds of musical entertainment evolved during this era. Ballets and operas—plays set to music—were performed at royal courts. Before long, opera houses sprang up from Italy to England to amuse the paying public. The music of the period followed ordered, structured forms well suited to the Age of Reason.

Among the towering musical figures of the era was Johann Sebastian Bach. A devout German Lutheran, Bach wrote complex and beautiful religious works for organ and choirs. Another German-born composer, George Frederick Handel, spent much of his life in England. There, he wrote *Water Music* and other pieces for King George I, as well as many operas. His most celebrated work, the *Messiah*, combines instruments and voices. Today, it is a standard at Christmas and Easter concerts.

The Great Mozart

Wolfgang Amadeus Mozart died when he was just 35 years old. His musical genius, however, has lived for centuries. Today, his work is celebrated around the world.

Mozart wrote the opera *The Magic Flute* during the last year of his life. Here, the high priest is passing judgment on a kidnapper. Mozart's operas are famous for their outstanding arias (solos), recitatives (sung dialogues), and ensembles (group singing).

Mozart was a prolific composer. He wrote operas, symphonies, piano concertos, string quartets, and scores of other works, including church music. In all, he composed more than 600 pieces of music.

Mozart's music is admired throughout the world today. It can be playful, serious, uplifting, or somber. Many of his melodies are instantly recognized. People use his music in everything from car commercials to Internet greeting cards.

Fast Facts

- Mozart was a child prodigy. He played the harpsichord at age 4 and began to compose music at age 5. A year later, he performed for the empress of Austria.

- Mozart's father, Leopold, was an accomplished musician. He took his young son on performing tours throughout Europe. Wolfgang never attended school.

Portfolio Assessment

Listen to a recording of one of Mozart's compositions. Then, write a journal entry in which you tell how the music affected you. What feelings did it evoke? What images did it bring to mind? Explain why you think Mozart's music is held in such high regard.

In 1762, a six-year-old prodigy, Wolfgang Amadeus Mozart, burst onto the European scene to gain instant celebrity as a composer and performer. Over the next three decades, his brilliant operas, graceful symphonies, and moving religious music helped define the new style of composition. Although he died in poverty at age 35, his musical legacy thrives today.

The Novel By the 1700s, literature developed new forms and a wide new audience. Middle-class readers, for example, liked stories about their own times told in straightforward prose. One result was an outpouring of novels, or long works of prose fiction. English novelists created many popular works. Daniel Defoe wrote *Robinson Crusoe*, an exciting tale about a sailor shipwrecked on a tropical island. In *Pamela*, Samuel Richardson used a series of letters to tell a story about a servant girl. This technique was adopted by other authors of the period.

Lives of the Majority

Most Europeans were untouched by either courtly or middle-class culture. They remained what they had always been—peasants living in small rural villages. Their culture, based on centuries-old traditions, changed slowly.

Peasant life varied across Europe. Villages in Western Europe were relatively more prosperous than those in Eastern Europe. In the West, serfdom had largely disappeared. Instead, some peasants worked their own patches of land. Others were tenants of large landowners, paying a yearly rent for the land they farmed. Still others were day laborers who hired themselves out to work on other people's farms.

In central and Eastern Europe, however, serfdom was firmly rooted. In Russia, it spread and deepened in the 1700s. Peasants owed labor services to their lords and could be bought and sold with the land.

Despite advances, some echoes of serfdom survived in Western Europe. In France, peasants still had to provide free labor, repairing roads and bridges after the spring floods just as their ancestors had done. In England, country squires had the right to hunt foxes across their tenants' lands, tearing up plowed and planted fields.

By the late 1700s, radical ideas about equality and social justice seeped into peasant villages. While some peasants eagerly sought to topple the old order, others resisted efforts to bring about change. In the 1800s, war and political upheaval, as well as changing economic conditions, would transform peasant life in Europe.

SECTION 2 Assessment

Recall

1. **Identify:** (a) *Candide*, (b) Joseph II, (c) Johann Sebastian Bach, (d) George Frederick Handel, (e) Wolfgang Amadeus Mozart, (f) Daniel Defoe.
2. **Define:** (a) censorship, (b) salon, (c) enlightened despot, (d) baroque, (e) rococo.

Comprehension

3. Explain how each of the following affected the spread of new ideas: (a) censorship, (b) salons.
4. What were the goals of enlightened despots?

5. How did the Enlightenment affect (a) arts and literature, (b) the lives of the majority?

Critical Thinking and Writing

6. **Analyzing Information** (a) What did Frederick II mean when he said, "In my kingdom, everyone can go to heaven in his own fashion"? (b) How did his actions reflect that idea?
7. **Making Inferences** How did the Enlightenment bring together ideas of both the Renaissance and the Reformation?

Activity
Take It to the NET

Search the Internet for information about salons in the 1700s. Identify types of people who attended salons in the 1700s, and create a list of people you would invite to a modern salon. Explain your choices.

Reading Focus

- What influences spurred Britain's rise to global power?
- How did the growth of constitutional government reflect conditions in politics and society?
- How did George III reassert royal power?

Vocabulary

constitutional government
cabinet
prime minister
oligarchy

Taking Notes

As you read this section, make an outline of the information. Use Roman numerals for the main headings. Use capital letters for the subheadings, and use numbers for the supporting details. The outline at right has been started for you.

I. Rise to global power
  A. Geography
    1. Location good for trade
    2. From outposts to empire
  B. Success in war
    1. Won Nova Scotia and Newfoundland
    2.

Main Idea Britain's island location, colonial possessions, and powerful navy contributed to its rise to world power.

A Powerful Navy
By the mid-1700s, Britain controlled territories in North America, South America, Asia, and the Pacific. These scattered holdings required a strong navy, including men-of-war like the one shown here.

Theme: Political and Social Systems How might a strong navy benefit trade?

Setting the Scene Supporters of mercantilism found success in England. In the mid-1600s, a mercantilist wrote, "Foreign trade is . . . the honor of the kingdom, the noble profession of the merchant, . . . the means of our treasure, the sinews of our wars, the terror of our enemies."

Over the next century, Britain embraced mercantilism and built a colonial and commercial empire that reached around the world. At the same time, Britain developed a constitutional monarchy, a political system somewhere between the absolute monarchies of Europe and later democracies.

Rise to Global Power

Why did Britain, a small island kingdom on the edge of Europe, rise to global prominence in the 1700s? Here, we can look at a few reasons for the nation's success.

Geography Location placed England in a position to control trade during the Renaissance. In the 1500s and 1600s, English merchants sent ships across the world's oceans and planted outposts in the West Indies, North America, and India. From these tiny settlements, England would build a global empire.

Success in War In the 1700s, Britain was generally on the winning side in European conflicts. Each victory brought valuable rewards. With the Treaty of Utrecht, France gave Britain Nova Scotia and Newfoundland in North America. Britain also monopolized the slave trade in Spanish America. The slave trade brought enormous wealth to British merchants, who invested their profits in other ventures. In 1763, the Treaty of Paris ending the French and Indian War and the Seven Years' War brought Britain all of French Canada. The British East India Company also pushed the French out of India.

Unlike its European rivals, Britain had no large standing army. Instead, it built up its fleet. By 1763, Britain had developed a more powerful navy than its greatest rival, France. With superior naval power, it could protect its growing empire and trade.

A Favorable Business Climate England offered a more favorable climate to business and commerce than did its European rivals. Although England followed mercantilist policies, it put fewer restrictions on trade than France. Also, while British nobles, like most other nobles in Europe, looked down on trade, some did engage in business activities.

Union With Scotland At home, England expanded by merging with its neighbor, Scotland. In 1707, the Act of Union joined the two countries in the United Kingdom of Great Britain. The United Kingdom also included Wales. The union brought economic advantages to both lands. Free trade between the two created a larger market for farmers and manufacturers. Many Scots, however, resented the union. On two occasions, they supported the claims of Stuart princes who sought to regain the British throne. Eventually, though, growing prosperity made the union more acceptable.

Ireland England had controlled Ireland since the 1100s. In the 1600s, English rulers tried to subdue Catholic Ireland by sending Protestants from England and Scotland to settle there. They gave Protestant settlers title to Irish Catholics' lands. The Irish fiercely resisted Protestant rule. Uprisings led to increased repression. Catholics were forbidden to own weapons, marry non-Catholics, or teach.

Growth of Constitutional Government

In the century following the Glorious Revolution, three new political institutions arose in Britain: political parties, the cabinet, and the office of prime minister. The appearance of these institutions was part of the evolution of Britain's constitutional government—that is, a government whose power is defined and limited by law. The British constitution is not a single document. Instead, it consists of all acts of Parliament over the centuries. It also includes documents such as the Magna Carta and Bill of Rights, as well as unwritten traditions that protect citizens' rights.

Political Parties Two political parties emerged in England in the late 1600s—Tories and Whigs. Tories were generally landed aristocrats who

Skills Assessment

Geography During the 1600s in Ireland, England gave Irish lands to English and Scottish settlers. In Scotland, failed rebellions in 1715 and 1745–1746 marked the end of armed resistance to English control.

1. **Location** On the map, locate **(a)** Irish Sea, **(b)** Dublin, **(c)** Edinburgh, **(d)** London.
2. **Region** What percentage of land in Ireland was owned by Catholics in 1603? In 1685?
3. **Critical Thinking Drawing Conclusions** How might it benefit England economically to join with its neighbors?

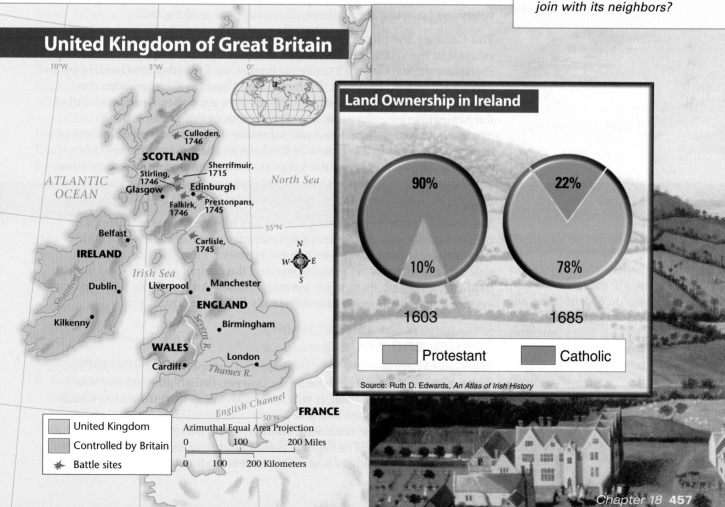

United Kingdom of Great Britain

Culloden, 1746
SCOTLAND
Sherrifmuir, 1715
Stirling, 1746
Glasgow
Edinburgh
Falkirk, 1746
Prestonpans, 1745
ATLANTIC OCEAN
North Sea
Belfast
IRELAND
Carlisle, 1745
Irish Sea
Dublin
Liverpool
Manchester
Shannon R.
Kilkenny
ENGLAND
Severn R.
Birmingham
WALES
London
Cardiff
Thames R.
English Channel
FRANCE

United Kingdom
Controlled by Britain
★ Battle sites

Azimuthal Equal Area Projection
0   100   200 Miles
0   100   200 Kilometers

Land Ownership in Ireland

90%
10%
1603

22%
78%
1685

Protestant   Catholic

Source: Ruth D. Edwards, *An Atlas of Irish History*

Birth of the American Republic

Reading Focus

- What were the chief characteristics of the 13 English colonies?

- How did growing discontent lead to the American Revolution?

- How did the new constitution reflect the ideas of the Enlightenment?

Vocabulary

popular sovereignty
Loyalist
federal republic

Taking Notes

On a sheet of paper draw a time line to show important dates leading up to the emergence of the United States government. Use the time line shown here to help you get started.

French and Indian War ends	Boston Massacre		
1763	1770	1776	1789

Main Idea Colonial opposition to British trade and tax policies led to independence and the founding of the United States of America.

Setting the Scene

Early in 1776, English colonists in North America eagerly read the newly published *Common Sense*. The pamphlet called on them to declare their independence from Britain. Its author, Thomas Paine, a recent immigrant from England, wrote with passion tempered by reason. "In the following pages," he declared, "I offer nothing more than simple facts, plain arguments, and common sense."

In *Common Sense*, Paine echoed the themes of the Enlightenment. He rejected ancient prejudice and tyranny, while appealing to reason, natural laws, and the promise of freedom. He wrote:

"'Tis repugnant to reason, to the universal order of things, to all examples from former ages, to suppose that this Continent can long remain subject to any external power."
—Thomas Paine, *Common Sense*

Colonists hotly debated Paine's arguments. As resentment of British policies grew, however, many came to agree with his radical ideas.

The 13 English Colonies

By 1750, a string of 13 prosperous colonies stretched along the eastern coast of North America. They were part of Britain's growing empire. Colonial cities such as Boston, New York, and Philadelphia were busy commercial centers that linked North America to the West Indies, Africa, and Europe. Colonial shipyards produced many vessels used in that global trade.

Britain applied mercantilist policies to its colonies. In the 1600s, Parliament had passed the Navigation Acts to regulate colonial trade and manufacturing. For the most part, these acts were not rigorously enforced. Smuggling was common and was not considered a crime by the colonists. Even prominent colonists might gain part of their wealth from smuggled goods.

By the mid-1700s, too, the colonies were home to diverse religious and ethnic groups. Social distinctions were more blurred than in Europe, although government and society were dominated

Colonial Unity

Benjamin Franklin created this political cartoon at the beginning of the French and Indian War. The segmented snake represents Britain's colonies in North America.

Theme: Political and Social Systems How does this cartoon suggest Franklin's attitude toward colonial involvement in the war?

JOIN, or DIE.

by wealthy landowners and merchants. In politics as in much else, there was a good deal of free discussion. Colonists felt entitled to the rights of English citizens, and their colonial assemblies exercised much control over local affairs.

Although the ways of life between the colonists of New England and those in the south differed, they all shared common values, respect for individual enterprise, and a growing self-confidence. Many also had an increasing sense of their own destiny separate from Britain.

Growing Discontent

After 1763, relations between Britain and the 13 colonies grew strained. The Seven Years' War and the French and Indian War in North America had drained the British treasury. King George III and his advisers thought that the colonists should help pay for the war and for troops still stationed along the frontier. Britain began to enforce the long-neglected laws regulating colonial trade, and Parliament passed new laws to increase the taxes paid by the colonies.

The British measures were not burdensome, but colonists bitterly resented what they saw as an attack on their rights. "No taxation without representation," they protested. Because they had no representatives in Parliament, they believed, Parliament had no right to tax them. Parliament did repeal some of the hated measures, such as a tax on all paper, but in general, it asserted its right to impose taxes on the colonies.

Early Clashes A series of violent clashes intensified the crisis. In March 1770, British soldiers in Boston opened fire on a crowd that was pelting them with stones and snowballs. Colonists called the death of five protesters the "Boston Massacre." In December 1773, a handful of colonists hurled a cargo of recently arrived British tea into the harbor to protest a tax on tea. The incident became known as the Boston Tea Party. When Parliament passed harsh laws to punish Massachusetts for the destruction of the tea, other colonies rallied to oppose the British response.

As tensions increased, fighting spread, representatives from each colony gathered in Philadelphia. There, they met in a Continental Congress to decide what action to take. Members included some extraordinary men. Among the participants were the radical yet fair-minded Massachusetts lawyer John Adams, who had defended at trial the British soldiers involved in the Boston Massacre; Virginia planter and soldier George Washington; and political and social leaders from all 13 colonies.

Declaring Independence The Congress set up a Continental Army, with George Washington in command. In April 1775, the crisis exploded into war. Although many battles ended in British victories, they showed that the Patriots were determined to fight at any cost. In 1776, the Second Continental Congress took a momentous step, voting to declare independence from Britain. Thomas Jefferson of Virginia was the principal author of the Declaration of Independence, a document that clearly reflects the ideas of John Locke.

The Declaration claimed that people had the right "to alter or to abolish" unjust governments—a right to revolt. It also emphasized the principle of popular sovereignty, which states that all government power comes from the people. Jefferson carefully detailed the colonists' grievances against Britain. Because the king had trampled colonists' natural rights, he argued, the colonists had the right to rebel and set up a new government that would protect them. Aware of the risks involved, on July 4, 1776, American leaders adopted the Declaration, pledging "our lives, our fortunes, and our sacred honor" to creating and protecting the new United States of America.

Primary Source

Inspiring Words
The Declaration of Independence stands as one of the most important documents in all of history. It still serves as inspiration for people around the world. Here is one of its most moving passages:

"We hold these truths to be self-evident, that all men are created equal, that they are endowed by their Creator with certain unalienable Rights, that among these are Life, Liberty and the pursuit of Happiness. That to secure these rights, Governments are instituted among Men, deriving their just powers from the consent of the governed; That whenever any Form of Government becomes destructive of these ends it is the Right of the People to alter or to abolish it, and to institute new Government, laying its foundation on such principles and organizing its powers in such form, as to them shall seem most likely to effect their Safety and Happiness."

—Declaration of Independence

Skills Assessment

Primary Source How does this excerpt reflect the ideas of John Locke?

The French Revolution and Napoleon

1789–1815

Chapter Preview

1 On the Eve of Revolution
2 Creating a New France
3 Radical Days
4 The Age of Napoleon Begins
5 The End of an Era

1793

During the Reign of Terror, which begins in 1793, the guillotine is used to execute thousands of French citizens.

1789

After a battle with royal troops, Parisians capture the Bastille on July 14, 1789.

1799

Napoleon overthrows the Directory.

CHAPTER EVENTS

1790   1795   1800

GLOBAL EVENTS

1789 The United States Constitution is ratified.

1793 China rejects British trade offer.

Revolutionary France at War, 1793

Legend:
- France, 1793
- Allied countries against France
- Boundary of Holy Roman Empire

By 1793, the French Revolution had plunged France into a general European war that would last on and off for more than 20 years and transform Europe.

Map labels:
IRELAND, GREAT BRITAIN, North Sea, KINGDOM OF DENMARK AND NORWAY, SWEDEN, Baltic Sea, PRUSSIA, NETHERLANDS, HANOVER, PRUSSIA, PRUSSIA, SAXONY, POLAND, RUSSIAN EMPIRE, AUSTRIAN NETHERLANDS, Seine R., Rhine R., Elbe R., Oder R., Vistula R., PRUSSIA, BAVARIA, ATLANTIC OCEAN, 50°N, Loire R., FRANCE, SWISS CONFED., AUSTRIA, HUNGARY, ALPS, Rhône R., Po R., VENETIAN REPUBLIC, Danube R., OTTOMAN EMPIRE, PORTUGAL, SPAIN, Ebro R., PYRENEES MTS., Tagus R., KINGDOM OF SARDINIA, PAPAL STATES, Tiber R., Adriatic Sea, 40°N, 10°W, 0°, Mediterranean Sea, 10°E, 20°E, KINGDOM OF NAPLES

Azimuthal Equal Area Projection
0 150 300 Miles
0 150 300 Kilometers

N W E S

1804

In a magnificent ceremony, Napoleon crowns himself emperor of the French.

1812

Napoleon invades Russia.

1815

Napoleon abdicates after British and Prussian forces defeat him at Waterloo. The Duke of Wellington is the victorious British general.

Timeline: 1805 — 1810 — 1815

1804 Haiti declares independence from France.

1812 The United States declares war on Britain.

On the Eve of Revolution

Reading Focus

- What was the social structure of the old regime?
- Why did France face economic troubles in 1789?
- Why did Louis XVI call the Estates General?
- Why did a Paris crowd storm the Bastille?

Vocabulary

bourgeoisie
deficit spending

Taking Notes

As you read this section, create a chart to identify causes of the French Revolution. Use the incomplete chart below as a model. Add more arrows for causes if you need them.

THE FRENCH REVOLUTION

Main Idea Social unrest, economic troubles, and the desire for political reforms led to the French Revolution.

Setting the Scene On April 28, 1789, unrest exploded at a Paris wallpaper factory. A rumor had spread that the factory owner was planning to cut wages even though bread prices were soaring. Enraged workers vandalized the owner's home. Later, they stopped some nobles returning from an afternoon at the racetrack. They forced the nobles to shout: "Long live the Third Estate [the common people]!"

Riots like these did not worry most nobles. They knew that France faced a severe economic crisis but thought that financial reforms would ease the problem. Then, rioters would be hanged, as they deserved.

The nobles were wrong. The crisis went deeper than government finances. Reform would not be enough. By July, the hungry, unemployed, and poorly paid people of Paris had taken up arms. Their actions would push events further and faster than anyone could have foreseen.

The Old Regime

In 1789, France, like the rest of Europe, still clung to an outdated social system that had emerged in the Middle Ages. Under this *ancien regime,* or old order, everyone in France belonged to one of three classes: the First Estate, made up of the clergy; the Second Estate, made up of the nobility; or the Third Estate, the vast majority of the population.

The Clergy In the Middle Ages, the Church had exerted great influence throughout Christian Europe. In 1789, the French clergy still enjoyed enormous wealth and privilege. The Church owned about 10 percent of the land, collected tithes, and paid no direct taxes to the state. High Church leaders such as bishops and abbots were usually nobles who lived very well. Parish priests, however, often came from humble origins and might be as poor as their peasant congregations.

The First Estate did provide some social services. Nuns, monks, and priests ran schools, hospitals, and orphanages. But during the Enlightenment, *philosophes* targeted the Church for reform. They criticized the idleness of some clergy, Church interference in politics, and its intolerance of dissent. In response, many clergy condemned the Enlightenment for undermining religion and moral order.

The Nobles The Second Estate was the titled nobility of French society. In the Middle Ages, noble knights had defended the land. In the 1600s, Richelieu and Louis XIV had crushed the nobles' military power but given them other rights—under strict royal control. Those rights included top jobs in government, the army, the courts, and the Church.

At Versailles, ambitious nobles competed for royal appointments while idle courtiers enjoyed endless entertainments. Many nobles, however, lived far from the center of power. Though they owned land, they had little money income. As a result, they felt the pinch of trying to maintain their status in a period of rising prices.

Many nobles hated absolutism and resented the royal bureaucracy that employed middle-class men in positions that once had been reserved for the aristocracy. They feared losing their traditional privileges, especially their freedom from paying taxes.

The Third Estate In 1789, the Third Estate numbered about 27 million people, or 98 percent of the population. It was a diverse group. At the top sat the bourgeoisie (boor zhwah ZEE), or middle class. The bourgeoisie included prosperous bankers, merchants, and manufacturers. It also included the officials who staffed the royal bureaucracy, as well as lawyers, doctors, journalists, professors, and skilled artisans.

The bulk of the Third Estate—9 out of 10 people in France—were rural peasants. Some were prosperous landowners who hired laborers to work for them. Others were tenant farmers or day laborers.

The poorest members of the Third Estate were urban workers. They included apprentices, journeymen, and others who worked in industries such as printing or clothmaking. Many women and men earned a meager living as servants, stable hands, porters, construction workers, or street sellers of everything from food to pots and pans. A large number of the urban poor were unemployed. To survive, some turned to begging or crime.

Discontent From rich to poor, members of the Third Estate resented the privileges enjoyed by their social "betters." Wealthy bourgeois families could buy political office and even titles, but the best jobs were still reserved for nobles. Urban workers earned miserable wages. Even the smallest rise in the price of bread, their main food, brought the threat of greater hunger or even starvation.

The Old Regime
In this cartoon, a priest and a noble stand on a stone crushing a peasant. The stone represents burdensome taxes and feudal dues. Taken together, the pie graphs below show inequalities among France's three estates.

Theme: Political and Social Systems Why did the Third Estate consider the distribution of land unfair?

First Estate

Second Estate

Third Estate

Population and Land Ownership in France, 1789

Population by Estate

98%

1.5%

0.5%

Land Owned by Estate

70%

20%

10%

Peasants were burdened by taxes on everything from land to soap to salt. Though they were technically free, many owed fees and services that dated back to medieval times, such as the corvée (kohr vay), which was unpaid labor to repair roads and bridges. Peasants were also incensed when nobles, hurt by rising prices, tried to reimpose old manor dues. Also, only nobles had the right to hunt wild game. Peasants were even forbidden to kill rabbits that ate their crops.

In towns and cities, Enlightenment ideas led people to question the inequalities of the old regime. Why, people demanded, should the first two estates have such great privileges at the expense of the majority? It did not meet the test of reason! Throughout France, the Third Estate called for the privileged classes to pay their share.

Economic Troubles

Economic woes added to the social unrest and heightened tensions. One of the causes of the decline was a mushrooming financial crisis that was due in part to years of **deficit spending,** that is, a government's spending more money than it takes in.

The Burden of Debt Louis XIV had left France deeply in debt. Wars like the Seven Years' War and the American Revolution strained the treasury even further. Costs generally had risen in the 1700s, and the lavish court soaked up millions. To bridge the gap between income and expenses, the government borrowed more and more money. By 1789, half its tax income went just to pay interest on this enormous debt.

To solve the financial crisis, the government would have to increase taxes, reduce expenses, or both. However, the nobles and clergy fiercely resisted any attempt to end their exemption from taxes.

Poor Harvests Other economic troubles added to the financial crisis. A general economic decline had begun in the 1770s. Then, in the late 1780s, bad harvests sent food prices soaring and brought hunger to poorer peasants and city dwellers.

Hard times and lack of food inflamed these people. In towns, people rioted, demanding bread. In the countryside, peasants began to attack the manor houses of the nobles. Arthur Young, an English visitor to France, witnessed the violence:

> "Everything conspires to render the present period in France critical: the [lack] of bread is terrible; accounts arrive every moment from the provinces of riots and disturbances, and calling in the military, to preserve the peace of the markets."
> —Arthur Young, *Travels in France During the Years 1787–1789*

Failure of Reform The heirs of Louis XIV were not the right men to solve the economic crisis that afflicted France. Louis XV, who ruled from 1715 to 1774, pursued pleasure before serious business and ran up more debts. His grandson, Louis XVI, was well-meaning but weak and indecisive. He wisely chose Jacques Necker, a financial wizard, as an adviser. Necker urged the king to reduce extravagant court spending, reform government, and abolish burdensome tariffs on internal trade. When Necker proposed taxing the First and Second estates, however, the nobles and high clergy forced the king to dismiss the would-be reformer.

As the crisis deepened, the pressure for reform mounted. Finally, the wealthy and powerful classes demanded that the king summon the Estates General before making any changes. French kings had not called the Estates General for 175 years, fearing that nobles would use it to recover the feudal powers that they had lost under absolute rule. To reform-minded nobles, the Estates General seemed to offer a chance to carry out changes

---

Bread Riots in France

The British embassy in Paris sent regular reports to London. The excerpts below describe the effects of rising bread prices:

"November 27, 1788
The price of bread has again been raised . . . the consequences of which has already been felt in the instance of more than 40 bakers having been obliged to shut up shop. In the provinces these discontents have still risen higher. . . . The public magazines of wheat have been broken open and pillaged.

December 11, 1788
Bread has again been raised. . . . The distress of the poor is already very great as may be conceived, and the unusual severity of the weather is at this moment peculiarly unfortunate for them; nor on this account, is it very surprising that robberies should be frequent, which at present is the case in an alarming degree. It is by no means safe to walk the streets late in the evening."

—O. Browning, *Dispatches from Paris*

Skills Assessment

Primary Source What were the effects of the rising prices?

Virtual Field Trip

www.phschool.com

WebMuseum
Paris, France

To see other David paintings of the French Revolution and Napoleonic era, use the Internet address above to link to the WebMuseum.

The Tennis Court Oath In this painting, Jacques Louis David captures the moment when delegates at the National Assembly took the Tennis Court Oath.

Theme: Continuity and Change Why did the Third Estate want to change the voting system used in the Estates General?

like those that had come with the Glorious Revolution in England. They hoped that they could bring the absolute monarch under the control of the nobles and guarantee their own privileges.

Louis XVI Calls the Estates General

As 1788 came to a close, France tottered on the verge of bankruptcy. Bread riots were spreading, and nobles, fearful of taxes, were denouncing royal tyranny. A baffled Louis XVI finally summoned the Estates General to meet at Versailles the following year.

The Cahiers In preparation, Louis had all three estates prepare *cahiers* (kah YAY), or notebooks, listing their grievances. Many cahiers called for reforms such as fairer taxes, freedom of the press, or regular meetings of the Estates General. In one town, shoemakers denounced regulations that made leather so expensive they could not afford to make shoes. Some peasants demanded the right to kill animals that were destroying their crops. Servant girls in the city of Toulouse demanded the right to leave service when they wanted and that "after a girl has served her master for many years, she receive some reward for her service."

The cahiers testified to boiling class resentments. One called tax collectors "bloodsuckers of the nation who drink the tears of the unfortunate from goblets of gold." Another one of the cahiers condemned the courts of nobles as "vampires pumping the last drop of blood" from the people. Another complained that "20 million must live on half the wealth of France while the clergy . . . devour the other half."

The Tennis Court Oath Delegates to the Estates General from the Third Estate were elected, though only propertied men could vote. Thus, they were mostly lawyers, middle-class officials, and writers. They were familiar with the writings of Voltaire, Rousseau, and other *philosophes*. They went to Versailles not only to solve the financial crisis but also to insist on reform.

The Estates General convened in May 1789. From the start, the delegates were deadlocked over the issue of voting. Traditionally, each estate had met and voted separately. Each group had one vote. Under this system, the First and Second estates always outvoted the Third Estate two to one.

This time, the Third Estate wanted all three estates to meet in a single body, with votes counted "by head."

After weeks of stalemate, delegates of the Third Estate took a daring step. Claiming to represent the people of France, they declared themselves to be the National Assembly. They then invited delegates from the other estates to help them write a constitution, a document that describes the basic rules and laws of government.

A few days later, the National Assembly found its meeting hall locked and guarded. Fearing that the king planned to dismiss them, the delegates moved to a nearby indoor tennis court. As curious spectators looked on, the delegates took their famous Tennis Court Oath. They swore "never to separate and to meet wherever the circumstances might require until we have established a sound and just constitution."

When reform-minded clergy and nobles joined the Assembly, Louis XVI grudgingly accepted it. But royal troops gathered around Paris, and rumors spread that the king planned to dissolve the Assembly.

Suspicion and rumor continued to poison the atmosphere as the crisis deepened in early July. The king, who had brought back Necker to deal with the financial crisis, again dismissed the popular minister. Food shortages were also getting worse because of the disastrous harvest of 1788.

Storming the Bastille

On July 14, 1789, Paris seized the spotlight from the National Assembly meeting in Versailles. The streets buzzed with rumors that royal troops were going to occupy the capital. More than 800 Parisians assembled outside the Bastille, a grim medieval fortress used as a prison for political and other prisoners. The crowd was demanding weapons and gunpowder believed to be stored there.

The commander of the Bastille refused to open the gates and opened fire on the crowd. In the battle that followed, many people were killed. Finally, the enraged mob broke through the defenses. They killed the commander and five guards and released a handful of prisoners, but found no weapons.

When told of the attack, Louis XVI asked, "Is it a revolt?" "No, sire," replied a noble. "It is a revolution." The storming of the Bastille quickly became a symbol of the French Revolution. Supporters saw it as a blow to tyranny, a step toward freedom. Today, the French still celebrate July 14 as Bastille Day, the French national holiday.

SECTION 1 Assessment

Recall

1. Identify: (a) *ancien regime*, (b) Jacques Necker, (c) cahiers, (d) Tennis Court Oath, (e) National Assembly, (f) Bastille.
2. Define: (a) bourgeoisie, (b) deficit spending.

Comprehension

3. Why were members of the Third Estate discontented with conditions under the old regime?
4. What economic troubles did France have in 1789?
5. What issues arose when Louis XVI called the Estates General in 1789?

6. What was the significance of the storming of the Bastille?

Critical Thinking and Writing

7. Understanding Sequence List key decisions and events of 1788 and 1789 in the order in which they occurred. Briefly explain the significance or effects of each decision and event in your list.
8. Defending a Position Suppose that you are Jacques Necker. Write a paragraph or two explaining how your economic reform program will benefit France.

Activity

Writing a Cahier
Imagine that you belong to one of the following groups in 1789 France: nobles, high clergy, parish priests, bourgeoisie, peasants, urban workers. Write a cahier describing who you are and what you think is the chief problem facing the nation.

Reading Focus

- How did popular revolts contribute to the French Revolution?
- What moderate reforms did the National Assembly enact?
- How did foreign reaction to the revolution help lead to war?

Vocabulary

faction
émigré
republic

Taking Notes

As you read this section, prepare an outline following this model. Use Roman numerals for major headings, capital letters for subheadings, and numbers for supporting details.

  I. Revolts in Paris and the provinces
    A. The Great Fear
      1. Inflamed by famine and rumors
      2.
    B. Paris in arms
  II. Moderate reforms

Main Idea The National Assembly instituted political and social reforms in the moderate first stage of the revolution.

Setting the Scene Excitement, wonder, and fear engulfed France as the revolution unfolded at home and spread abroad. Today, historians divide this revolutionary era into four phases. The moderate phase of the National Assembly (1789–1791) turned France into a constitutional monarchy. Then, a phase (1792–1793) of escalating violence led to a Reign of Terror (1793-1794). There followed a period of reaction against extremism, known as the Directory (1795–1799). Finally, the Age of Napoleon (1799–1815) consolidated many revolutionary changes. In this section, you will read about the moderate start of the French Revolution.

Revolts in Paris and the Provinces

The political crisis of 1789 coincided with the worst famine in memory. Starving peasants roamed the countryside or flocked to the towns, where they swelled the ranks of the unemployed. As grain prices soared, even people with jobs had to spend up to 80 percent of their income on bread.

The Great Fear In such desperate times, rumors ran wild and set off what was later called the "Great Fear." Tales of attacks on villages and towns spread panic. Other rumors asserted that government troops were seizing peasant crops.

Inflamed by famine and fear, peasants unleashed their fury on nobles who were trying to reimpose medieval dues. Defiant peasants attacked the homes of nobles, set fire to old manor records, and stole grain from storehouses. The violent attacks died down after a period of time, but they clearly demonstrated peasant anger with an unjust regime.

Paris in Arms Paris, too, was in turmoil. As the capital and chief city of France, it was the revolutionary center. A variety of factions, or small groups, competed to gain power. Moderates looked to the Marquis de Lafayette, the aristocratic "hero of two worlds" who had fought alongside George Washington in the American Revolution. Lafayette headed the National Guard, a largely middle-class militia organized in response to the arrival of royal troops in Paris. The Guard was the first group to don the tricolor—a red, white, and blue badge which was eventually adopted as the national flag of France.

Paris in Arms
In this engraving, an angry mob of men and women march through the streets of Paris.
Theme: Geography and History Why do you think Paris was the center of the French Revolution?

The American Revolution and the French Revolution

The Marquis de Lafayette and Thomas Paine were leading figures in both the American and French revolutions. Lafayette, a French nobleman and military commander, helped the Americans defeat the British at Yorktown. He admired the American Declaration of Independence and American democratic ideals. With these in mind, Lafayette wrote the first draft of the French Declaration of the Rights of Man and the Citizen.

Thomas Paine was a famous American patriot and writer whose ideas in *Common Sense* had a great influence on the American Revolution. During the French Revolution, Paine moved to France. There, he defended the ideals of the revolution and was elected to serve in the revolutionary government.

Theme: Political and Social Systems How did the American Revolution influence the French Revolution?

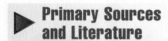

Primary Sources and Literature

See the "Declaration of the Rights of Man and the Citizen" in the Reference Section at the back of this book.

A more radical group, the Paris Commune, replaced the royalist government of the city. It could mobilize whole neighborhoods for protests or violent action to further the revolution. Newspapers and political clubs—many even more radical than the Commune—blossomed everywhere. Some demanded an end to the monarchy and spread scandalous stories about the royal family and members of the court.

Moderate Reforms

Peasant uprisings and the storming of the Bastille stampeded the National Assembly into action. On August 4, in a combative all-night meeting, nobles in the National Assembly voted to end their privileges. They agreed to give up their old manorial dues, exclusive hunting rights, special legal status, and exemption from taxes.

An End to Special Privilege "Feudalism is abolished," announced the proud and weary delegates at 2 A.M. As the president of the Assembly later observed, "We may view this moment as the dawn of a new revolution, when all the burdens weighing on the people were abolished, and France was truly reborn."

Were the votes on the night of August 4 voluntary? Both contemporary observers and modern historians note that the nobles gave up nothing that they had not already lost. In the months ahead, the National Assembly turned the reforms of August 4 into law, meeting a key Enlightenment goal—the equality of all citizens before the law.

Declaration of the Rights of Man In late August, as a first step toward writing a constitution, the Assembly issued the Declaration of the Rights of Man and the Citizen. The document was modeled in part on the American Declaration of Independence, written 13 years earlier. All men, the French declaration announced, were "born and remain free and equal in rights." They enjoyed natural rights to "liberty, property, security, and resistance to oppression." Like the writings of Locke and the *philosophes,* the constitution insisted that governments exist to protect the natural rights of citizens.

The Declaration further proclaimed that all male citizens were equal before the law. Every Frenchman had an equal right to hold public office "with no distinction other than that of their virtues and talents." In addition, the Declaration asserted freedom of religion and called for taxes to be levied according to ability to pay. Its principles were captured in the enduring slogan of the French Revolution, "Liberty, Equality, Fraternity."

Uncertain and hesitant, Louis XVI was slow to accept the reforms of the National Assembly. Parisians grew suspicious as more royal troops arrived. Nobles continued to enjoy gala banquets while people were starving. By autumn, anger again turned to action.

Women March on Versailles On October 5, thousands of women streamed down the road that led from Paris to Versailles. "Bread!" they shouted. They demanded to see the king.

Much of the crowd's anger was directed at the queen, Marie Antoinette. Ever since she had married Louis in 1770, she had come under attack for being frivolous and extravagant. She eventually grew more serious and even advised the king to compromise with moderate reformers. Still, she remained a source of scandal. Early in the revolution, the radical press spread the story that she had answered the cries of hungry people for bread by saying, "Let them eat cake." Though the story was untrue, it helped inflame feelings against the queen.

The women refused to leave Versailles until the king met their most important demand—to return to Paris. Not too happily, the king agreed. The next morning, the crowd, with the king in tow, set out for the city. At the head of the procession rode women perched on the barrels of seized cannons. They told bewildered spectators that they were bringing Louis XVI, Marie Antoinette, and their son back to Paris. "Now we won't have to go so far when we want to see our king," they sang. Crowds along the way cheered the king, who now wore the tricolor.

In Paris, the royal family moved into the Tuileries (TWEE luh reez) palace. For the next three years, Louis was a virtual prisoner.

The National Assembly Presses Onward

The National Assembly soon followed the king to Paris. Its largely bourgeois members worked to draft a constitution and to solve the continuing financial crisis. To pay off the huge government debt—much of it owed to the bourgeoisie—the Assembly voted to take over and sell Church lands.

Reorganizing the Church In an even more radical move, the National Assembly put the French Catholic Church under state control. Under the Civil Constitution of the Clergy, issued in 1790, bishops and priests became elected, salaried officials. The Civil Constitution ended papal authority over the French Church and dissolved convents and monasteries.

Reaction was swift and angry. Many bishops and priests refused to accept the Civil Constitution. The pope condemned it. Large numbers of French peasants, who were conservative concerning religion, also rejected the changes. When the government punished clergy who refused to support the Civil Constitution, a huge gulf opened between revolutionaries in Paris and the peasantry in the provinces.

Constitution of 1791 The National Assembly completed its main task by producing a constitution. The Constitution of 1791 set up a limited monarchy in place of the absolute monarchy that had ruled France for centuries. A new Legislative Assembly had the power to make laws, collect taxes, and decide on issues of war and peace. Lawmakers would be elected by tax-paying male citizens. Still, only about 50,000 men in a population of more than 27 million could qualify as candidates to run for the Assembly.

To make government more efficient, the constitution replaced the old provinces with 83 departments of roughly equal size. It abolished the old provincial courts, and it reformed laws. The middle-class framers of the constitution protected private property and supported free trade. They compensated nobles for land seized by the peasants, abolished guilds, and forbade urban workers to organize labor unions.

Women March on Versailles
As famine gripped Paris, poor mothers did not have enough food for their children. On October 5, 1789, thousands of women decided to bring Louis XVI to Paris, where he could no longer ignore their suffering.

Theme: Continuity and Change Based on this painting, in what ways do you think the march challenged traditional roles of women?

REFORMS OF THE NATIONAL ASSEMBLY

Political	Social and Economic	Religious
• Proclaimed all male citizens equal before the law • Limited the power of the monarchy • Established the Legislative Assembly to make laws • Granted all tax-paying male citizens the right to elect members of the Legislative Assembly	• Abolished special privileges of the nobility • Announced an end to feudalism • Called for taxes to be levied according to ability to pay • Abolished guilds and forbade labor unions • Compensated nobles for lands seized by peasants	• Declared freedom of religion • Took over and sold Church lands • Placed the French Catholic Church under control of the state • Provided that bishops and priests be elected and receive government salaries

Skills Assessment

Chart The National Assembly produced the Declaration of the Rights of Man and the Citizen, the Civil Constitution of the Clergy, and the Constitution of 1791. These documents brought far-reaching change to France. **Which reforms in the chart were due to the Civil Constitution of the Clergy?**

To moderate reformers, the Constitution of 1791 seemed to complete the revolution. Reflecting Enlightenment goals, it ended Church interference in government and ensured equality before the law for all male citizens. At the same time, it put power in the hands of men with the means and leisure to serve in government.

Louis's Failed Flight Meanwhile, Marie Antoinette and others had been urging the king to escape their humiliating situation. Louis finally gave in. One night in June 1791, a coach rolled north from Paris toward the border. Inside sat the king disguised as a servant, the queen dressed as a governess, and the royal children.

The attempted escape failed. In a town along the way, Louis's disguise was uncovered by someone who held up a piece of currency with the king's face on it. A company of soldiers escorted the royal family back to Paris, as onlooking crowds hurled insults at the king. To many, Louis's dash to the border showed that he was a traitor to the revolution.

Reaction Outside France

Events in France stirred debate all over Europe. Supporters of the Enlightenment applauded the reforms of the National Assembly. They saw the French experiment as the dawn of a new age for justice and equality. European rulers and nobles, however, denounced the French Revolution.

Widespread Fears European rulers increased border patrols to stop the spread of the "French plague." Fueling those fears were the horror stories that were told by émigrés (EHM ih grayz)—nobles, clergy, and others who had fled France and its revolutionary forces. Émigrés reported attacks on their privileges, their property, their religion, and even their lives. "Enlightened" rulers turned against French ideas. Catherine the Great of Russia burned Voltaire's letters and locked up her critics.

In Britain, Edmund Burke, who earlier had defended the American Revolution, bitterly condemned revolutionaries in Paris. He predicted all too accurately that the revolution would become more violent. "Plots and assassinations," he wrote, "will be anticipated by preventive murder and preventive confiscation." Burke warned: "When ancient opinions and rules of life are taken away . . . we have no compass to govern us."

Threats From Abroad The failed escape of Louis XVI brought further hostile rumblings from abroad. In August 1791, the king of Prussia and the emperor of Austria—who was Marie Antoinette's brother—issued the Declaration of Pilnitz. In this document, the two monarchs threatened to intervene to protect the French monarchy. The declaration may have been mostly bluff, but revolutionaries in France took the threat seriously and prepared for war. The revolution was about to enter a new, more radical phase of change and conflict.

War at Home and Abroad

In October 1791, the newly elected Legislative Assembly took office. Faced with crises at home and abroad, it would survive for less than a year. Economic problems fed renewed turmoil. Assignats, the revolutionary currency, dropped in value, which caused prices to rise rapidly. Uncertainty about prices led to hoarding and additional food shortages.

Internal Divisions   In Paris and other cities, working-class men and women, called sans-culottes* (sanz kyoo LAHTZ), pushed the revolution into more radical action. By 1791, many sans-culottes demanded a republic, or government ruled not by a monarch, but by elected representatives.

Within the Legislative Assembly, several hostile factions competed for power. The sans-culottes found support among radicals in the Legislative Assembly, especially the Jacobins. A revolutionary political club, the Jacobins were mostly middle-class lawyers or intellectuals. They used pamphleteers and sympathetic newspaper editors to advance the republican cause. Opposing the radicals were moderate reformers and political officials who wanted no more reforms at all.

War on Tyranny   The radicals soon held the upper hand in the Legislative Assembly. In April 1792, the war of words between French revolutionaries and European monarchs moved onto the battlefield. Eager to spread the revolution and destroy tyranny abroad, the Legislative Assembly declared war first on Austria, then on Prussia, Britain, and other states. The great powers expected to win an easy victory against France, a land divided by revolution. In fact, however, the fighting that began in 1792 lasted on and off until 1815.

---

*Sans-culottes means "without culottes," the fancy knee breeches worn by upper-class men. Shopkeepers, artisans, and other working-class men wore trousers, not culottes.

SECTION 2 Assessment

Recall

1. **Identify:** **(a)** Great Fear, **(b)** tricolor, **(c)** Legislative Assembly, **(d)** Declaration of Pilnitz, **(e)** Jacobins.
2. **Define:** **(a)** faction, **(b)** émigré, **(c)** republic.

Comprehension

3. What role did the people of Paris play in the French Revolution?
4. Describe one reform that the National Assembly enacted through each of the following documents: **(a)** the Declaration of the Rights of Man and the Citizen, **(b)** the Civil Constitution of the Clergy, **(c)** the Constitution of 1791.
5. **(a)** Why did some people outside France react negatively to the French Revolution? **(b)** How did these feelings lead to war?

Critical Thinking and Writing

6. **Comparing**   Compare the women's march on Versailles to the storming of the Bastille in terms of goals and results.
7. **Defending a Position**   The Declaration of the Rights of Man has been called the "death certificate" of the old regime. Do you agree? Why or why not?

Activity
Take It to the NET

Use the Internet to research the life of Marie Antoinette. Then, write a feature article about her as it might appear in a popular magazine of today. Include interesting details about her family, friends, and habits that would appeal to your readers.

Radical Days

Reading Focus
- Why did radicals abolish the monarchy?
- How did the excesses of the Convention lead to the Directory?
- What impact did the revolution have on women and daily life?

Vocabulary
suffrage
nationalism
secular

Taking Notes
On a sheet of paper, make a time line like the one begun here. The time line should extend from August 1792 to July 1794. Add dates and important events as you read this section.

August 1792	September 1792	January 1793	July 1794
Mob invades royal palace	September massacres		

Main Idea A radical phase of the revolution led to the monarchy's downfall and a time of violence known as the Reign of Terror.

Did You Know?

The Origin of Madame Tussaud's Wax Museum

In the 1780s, Marie Tussaud ran two wax museums in Paris and was art tutor to the sister of Louis XVI. During the revolution, she was imprisoned as a royalist. Even so, the leaders of the revolution admired her art skills. Tussaud escaped the guillotine by agreeing to make wax models of the revolutionaries and their victims, such as Louis XVI and Marie Antoinette, shown above.

After the revolution, Tussaud took her collection to London. There she established the wax museum that still bears her name. Today, tourists from around the world marvel at the realistic sculptures of the famous and infamous in Madame Tussaud's Wax Museum.

Theme: Art and Literature
How did Tussaud's art skills save her life?

Setting the Scene Someone who had left Paris in 1791 and returned in 1793 could have gotten lost. Almost 4,000 streets had new names. Louis XV Square was renamed the Square of the Revolution. King-of-Sicily Street, named for the brother of Louis XVI, had become the Rights of Man Street.

Renaming streets was one way that Jacobins tried to wipe out all traces of the old order. In 1793, the revolution entered a radical phase. For a year, France experienced one of the bloodiest regimes in its long history as determined leaders sought to extend and preserve the revolution.

The Monarchy Abolished

Dismal news about the war heightened tensions. Well-trained Prussian forces were cutting down raw French recruits. Royalist officers deserted the French army, joining émigrés and others hoping to restore the king's power.

Outbreaks of Violence Battle disasters quickly inflamed revolutionaries who thought the king was in league with the invaders. On August 10, 1792, a crowd of Parisians stormed the Tuileries and slaughtered the king's guards. The royal family fled to the Legislative Assembly.

A month later, citizens attacked prisons that held nobles and priests accused of political offenses. These prisoners were killed, along with many ordinary criminals. Historians disagree about the people who carried out the "September massacres." Some call them bloodthirsty mobs. Others describe them as patriots defending France from its enemies. In fact, most were ordinary citizens fired to fury by real and imagined grievances.

The French Republic Backed by Paris crowds, radicals took control of the Assembly. Radicals called for the election of a new legislative body called the National Convention. Suffrage, the right to vote, was to be extended to all male citizens, not just to property owners.

The Convention that met in September 1792 was a more radical body than earlier assemblies. It voted to abolish the monarchy and declare France a republic. Deputies then drew up a new constitution for France. The Jacobins, who controlled the Convention, set out to erase all traces of the old order. They seized lands of nobles and abolished titles of nobility.

Death of the King and Queen During the early months of the Republic, the Convention also put Louis XVI on trial as a traitor to France. The king was convicted by a single vote and sentenced to death. On a foggy morning

Analyzing Primary Sources

Execution of a King

The following excerpt is from an eyewitness report of the execution of King Louis XVI, January 21, 1793. It was written by Henry Essex Edgeworth de Firmont, a priest who accompanied the king to the scaffold.

"The path leading to the scaffold was extremely rough and difficult to pass; the King was obliged to lean on my arm, and from the slowness with which he proceeded, I feared for a moment that his courage might fail; but what was my astonishment, when arrived at the last step, I felt that he suddenly let go my arm, and I saw him cross with a firm foot the breadth of the whole scaffold; silence, by his look alone, fifteen or twenty drums that were placed opposite to me; and in a voice so loud, that it must have been heard at the Pont Tourant, I heard him pronounce distinctly these memorable words: 'I die innocent of all the crimes laid to my charge; I pardon those who have occasioned my death; and I pray to God that the blood you are going to shed may never be visited on France.'

The Machine of Terror
The guillotine made it easy to behead large numbers of people quickly. It became a symbol of the Reign of Terror.

He was proceeding, when a man on horseback, in the national uniform, and with a ferocious cry, ordered the drums to beat. Many voices were at the same time heard encouraging the executioners. They seemed reanimated themselves, in seizing with violence the most virtuous of Kings, they dragged him under the axe of the guillotine, which with one stroke severed his head from his body. All this passed in a moment. The youngest of the guards, who seemed about eighteen, immediately seized the head, and showed it to the people as he walked around the scaffold; he accompanied this monstrous ceremony with the most atrocious and indecent gestures. At first an awful silence prevailed; at length some cries of 'Vive la République! [Long live the republic!]' were heard. By degrees the voices multiplied, and in less than ten minutes this cry, a thousand times repeated, became the universal shout of the multitude, and every hat was in the air."

—Henry Essex Edgeworth de Firmont, *Report by a Priest of His Majesty's Household*

Skills Assessment

1. Based on this account, how would you describe the king's manner at his execution?
   A frightened and confused
   B cold and unemotional
   C proud and brave
   D angry and violent

2. The man on horseback orders the drums to beat in order to
   E silence the crowd.
   F signal that the execution is about to take place.
   G show respect for the king.
   H announce that the king is dead.

3. **Critical Thinking Drawing Conclusions (a)** Based on this account, what was Father Firmont's attitude toward the king? Toward the revolutionaries? How can you tell? **(b)** Do you think Firmont's feelings affected his account? Explain.

Skills Tip

Bias is a leaning in favor of or against someone or something. When analyzing an eyewitness account, look for words that indicate the writer's bias.

The middle-class and professional people of the bourgeoisie were the dominant force during this stage of the French Revolution. The Directory held power from 1795 to 1799.

Weak but dictatorial, the Directory faced growing discontent. Peace was made with Prussia and Spain, but war with Austria and Great Britain continued. Corrupt leaders lined their own pockets but failed to solve pressing problems. When rising bread prices stirred hungry sans-culottes to riot, the Directory quickly suppressed them. Another threat to the Directory was the revival of royalist feeling. Many émigrés were returning to France, and they were being welcomed by devout Catholics, who resented measures that had been taken against the Church. In the election of 1797, supporters of a constitutional monarchy won the majority of seats in the legislature.

As chaos threatened, politicians turned to Napoleon Bonaparte, a popular military hero who had won a series of brilliant victories against the Austrians in Italy. The politicians planned to use him to advance their own goals—a bad miscalculation! Before long, Napoleon would outwit them all to become ruler of France.

Women in the Revolution

As you have seen, women of all classes participated in the revolution from the very beginning. Working-class women protested and fought in street battles. In Paris and elsewhere, women formed their own political clubs. A few women, like Jeanne Roland, were noted leaders. Roland supported the revolution through her writings, her salon, and her influence on her husband, a government minister.

Rights for Women Many women were very disappointed when the Declaration of the Rights of Man did not grant equal citizenship to women. Olympe de Gouges (oh LAMP duh GOOZH), a journalist, demanded equal rights in her *Declaration of the Rights of Woman.* "Woman is born free," she proclaimed, "and her rights are the same as those of man." Therefore, Gouges reasoned, "all citizens, be they men or women, being equal in the state's eyes, must be equally eligible for all public offices, positions, and jobs." After opposing the Terror and accusing certain Jacobins of corruption, Gouges was sent to the guillotine.

Women did gain some rights for a time. The government made divorce easier, a move that was aimed at weakening Church authority. Government officials also allowed women to inherit property, hoping to undermine the tradition of nobles leaving large estates to their oldest sons. These reforms and others did not last long after Napoleon gained power.

Setbacks As the revolution progressed, women's right to express their views in public came under attack. In 1793, a committee of the National Convention declared that women lacked "the moral and physical strength necessary to practice political rights." Women's revolutionary clubs were banned and violators were arrested.

Women were imprisoned and sent to the guillotine. Among the many women who became victims of the Terror were republicans like Gouges and moderates like Roland. As she mounted the steps to the guillotine, Roland cried, "O liberty, what crimes are committed in your name!"

Changes in Daily Life

By 1799, the 10-year-old French Revolution had dramatically changed France. It had dislodged the old social order, overthrown the monarchy, and brought the Church under state control.

New symbols such as the red "liberty caps" and the tricolor confirmed the liberty and equality of all male citizens. The new title "citizen" applied to people of all social classes. Titles were eliminated. Before he was executed, Louis XVI was called Citizen Capet, from the name of the dynasty that had ruled France in the Middle Ages. Elaborate fashions and powdered wigs gave way to the practical clothes and simple haircuts of the sans-culottes. To show their revolutionary spirit, enthusiastic parents gave their children names like Constitution, Republic, or August Tenth.

Nationalism Revolution and war gave the French people a strong sense of national identity. In earlier times, people had felt loyalty to local authorities. As monarchs centralized power, loyalty shifted to the king or queen. Now, the government rallied sons and daughters of the revolution to defend the nation itself.

Nationalism, a strong feeling of pride in and devotion to one's country, spread throughout France. The French people attended civic festivals that celebrated the nation and the revolution. A variety of dances and songs on themes of the revolution became immensely popular.

By 1793, France was a nation in arms. From the port city of Marseilles (mahr SAY), troops marched to a rousing new song. It urged the "children of the fatherland" to march against the "bloody banner of tyranny." This song, "La Marseillaise" (mahr say EHZ), would later become the French national anthem. The second verse and chorus appear at right.

Social Reform Revolutionaries pushed for social reform and religious toleration. They set up state schools to replace religious ones and organized systems to help the poor, old soldiers, and war widows. With a major slave revolt raging in the colony of St. Domingue (Haiti), the government also abolished slavery in their Caribbean colonies.

The Convention tried to de-Christianize France. It created a secular, or nonreligious, calendar with 1793 as the Year I of the new era of freedom. It banned many religious festivals, replacing them with secular celebrations. Huge public ceremonies boosted support for republican and nationalist ideals.

The Arts In the arts, France adopted a grand classical style that echoed the grandeur of ancient Rome. A leading artist of this period was Jacques Louis David (dah VEED). He immortalized on canvas such stirring events as the Tennis Court Oath and, later, Napoleon's coronation. David helped shape the way future generations pictured the French Revolution.

Primary Source

La Marseillaise
The stirring lyrics of "La Marseillaise" inspired French soldiers to defend their country and the ideals of the revolution:

"Sacred love of the fatherland
  Guide and support our vengeful
    arms.
  Liberty, beloved liberty,
  Fight with your defenders;
  Fight with your defenders.
  Under our flags, so that victory
  Will rush to your manly strains;
  That your dying enemies
  Should see your triumph and glory.

To arms, citizens!
  Form up your battalions.
  Let us march, let us march!
  That their impure blood
  Should water our fields."

—"La Marseillaise"

Skills Assessment

Primary Source Which of the above lines seem most nationalistic? Explain.

SECTION 3 Assessment

Recall
1. **Identify:** (a) Committee of Public Safety, (b) Maximilien Robespierre, (c) Directory, (d) Olympe de Gouges, (e) "La Marseillaise," (f) Jacques Louis David.
2. **Define:** (a) suffrage, (b) nationalism, (c) secular.

Comprehension
3. Why did radical revolutionaries oppose the monarchy?
4. How did the Reign of Terror cause the National Convention to be replaced by the Directory?

5. Describe one effect of the French Revolution on each of the following: (a) women, (b) daily life.

Critical Thinking and Writing
6. **Analyzing Primary Sources** Robespierre wrote, "Terror is nothing but prompt, severe, inflexible justice." Explain why you agree or disagree with Robespierre.
7. **Predicting Consequences** How do you think French nationalism affected the war between France and the powers of Europe?

Activity

Presenting a Poster
Create a poster that might have been used to support or oppose *one* of the following: the goals of the Jacobins; the abolition of the monarchy; the policies of the Committee of Public Safety; French nationalism; equal rights for women.

The Age of Napoleon Begins

Reading Focus

■ How did Napoleon rise to power?

■ How were revolutionary reforms changed under Napoleon?

■ How did Napoleon build an empire in Europe?

Vocabulary

plebiscite

annex

blockade

Taking Notes

Begin a concept web like this one. As you read, fill in the blank circles with relevant information about Napoleon. Add as many circles as you need.

Main Idea Napoleon rose to power in France and built a vast empire that included much of Europe.

Setting the Scene "He was like an expert chess player, with the human race for an opponent, which he proposed to checkmate." Thus did Madame Germaine de Staël (STAHL), a celebrated writer and intellectual, describe Napoleon Bonaparte. Napoleon himself expressed a more humble view of his rise to power. "Nothing has been simpler than my elevation," he once observed. "It is owing to the peculiarities of the time."

From 1799 to 1815, Napoleon would dominate France and Europe. A hero to some, an evil force to others, he gave his name to the final phase of the revolution—the Age of Napoleon.

Napoleon's Rise to Power

Napoleon Bonaparte was born in Corsica, a French-ruled island in the Mediterranean. His family were minor nobles, but had little money. At age nine, he was sent to France to be trained for a military career. When the revolution broke out, he was an ambitious 20-year-old lieutenant, eager to make a name for himself.

Napoleon favored the Jacobins and republican rule. However, he found the conflicting ideas and personalities of the French Revolution confusing. He wrote to his brother in 1793: "Since one must take sides, one might as well choose the side that is victorious, the side which devastates, loots, and burns."

Early Successes During the turmoil of the revolution, Napoleon rose quickly in the army. In December 1793, he drove British forces out of the French port of Toulon (too LOHN). He then went on to win several dazzling victories against the Austrians, capturing most of northern Italy and forcing the Hapsburg emperor to make peace. Hoping to disrupt British trade with India, he led a colorful expedition to Egypt in 1798. The Egyptian campaign proved to be a disaster, but Napoleon managed to hide stories of the worst losses from his admirers in France.

Success fueled his ambition. By 1799, he moved from victorious general to political leader. That year, he helped overthrow the weak Directory and set up a three-man

FACT FINDER

The Rise of Napoleon

1769	Born on island of Corsica
1785	Becomes officer in French army
1793	Helps capture Toulon from British; promoted to brigadier general
1795	Crushes rebels opposed to the National Convention
1796–1797	Becomes commander in chief of the army of Italy; wins victories against Austria
1798–1799	Loses to the British in Egypt and Syria
1799	Overthrows Directory and becomes First Consul of France
1804	Crowns himself emperor of France

Skills Assessment

Chart Napoleon's successes on the battlefield helped him become emperor. **Where and when did Napoleon experience a military setback? Did that setback affect his rise to power? Explain.**

governing board known as the Consulate. Another constitution was drawn up, but Napoleon soon took the title First Consul. In 1802, he had himself named consul for life.

A Self-made Emperor   Two years later, Napoleon had acquired enough power to assume the title Emperor of the French. He invited the pope to preside over his coronation in Paris. During the ceremony, however, Napoleon took the crown from the pope's hands and placed it on his own head. By this action, Napoleon meant to show that he owed his throne to no one but himself.

At each step on his rise to power, Napoleon had held a plebiscite (PLEHB ih sīt), or ballot in which voters say yes or no. Each time, the French strongly supported him. To understand why, we must look at his policies.

France Under Napoleon

During the consulate and empire, Napoleon consolidated his power by strengthening the central government. Order, security, and efficiency replaced liberty, equality, and fraternity as the slogans of the new regime.

Reforms   To restore economic prosperity, Napoleon controlled prices, encouraged new industry, and built roads and canals. To ensure well-trained officials and military officers, he set up a system of public schools under strict government control.

At the same time, Napoleon backed off from some of the revolution's social reforms. He made peace with the Catholic Church in the Concordat of 1801. The Concordat kept the Church under state control but recognized religious freedom for Catholics. Revolutionaries who opposed the Church denounced the agreement, but Catholics welcomed it.

Napoleon won support across class lines. He encouraged émigrés to return, provided that they took an oath of loyalty. Peasants were relieved when he recognized their right to lands they had bought from the Church and nobles during the revolution. The middle class, who had benefited most from the revolution, approved Napoleon's economic reforms and the restoration of order after years of chaos. Napoleon also made jobs "open to

The Coronation
David depicted the splendor and power of the new French emperor in the painting *Napoleon Crowning the Empress Josephine*. Years later, Napoleon would divorce Josephine and marry an Austrian princess.

Theme: Impact of the Individual   How did Napoleon emphasize his personal power at the coronation ceremony?

French territory

States ruled by Napoleon's family

States under French influence

French allies, 1812

★ Battle sites, 1800–1815

→ Route of Napoleon's invasion of Russia

Azimuthal Equal Area Projection

0   250   500 Miles

0   250   500 Kilometers

Skills Assessment

Geography Napoleon won a vast empire in Europe. But resistance in Spain and a disastrous invasion of Russia would turn the tide against him.

1. **Location** *On the map, locate (a) Spain, (b) Moscow, (c) Waterloo.*
2. **Place** *What part of the Italian peninsula was French territory?*
3. **Critical Thinking Drawing Conclusions** *Do you think the spread of nationalism would weaken or strengthen Napoleon's power? Explain.*

all talent," a popular policy among those who remembered the old aristocratic monopoly of power.

Napoleonic Code Among Napoleon's most lasting reforms was a new law code, popularly called the Napoleonic Code. It embodied Enlightenment principles such as the equality of all citizens before the law, religious toleration, and advancement based on merit.

But the Napoleonic Code undid some reforms of the French Revolution. Women, for example, lost most of their newly gained rights and could not exercise the rights of citizenship. Male heads of households regained complete authority over their wives and children. Again, Napoleon valued order and authority over individual rights.

Building an Empire

From 1804 to 1814, Napoleon furthered his reputation on the battlefield. He successfully faced down the combined forces of the greatest European powers. He took great risks and even suffered huge losses. "I grew up on the field of battle," he once said, "and a man such as I am cares little for the life of a million men." By 1810, his Grand Empire reached its greatest extent.

As a military leader, Napoleon valued rapid movements and made effective use of his large armies. He developed a new plan for each battle, so opposing generals could never anticipate what he would do next. His enemies paid tribute to his leadership. Napoleon's presence on the battlefield, said one, was "worth 40,000 troops."

The Grand Empire As Napoleon created a vast French empire, he redrew the map of Europe. He annexed, or added outright, some areas to France, including the Netherlands, Belgium, and parts of Italy and Germany. He also abolished the tottering Holy Roman Empire and created a 38-member Confederation of the Rhine under French protection. He cut Prussian territory in half, turning part of old Poland into the Grand Duchy of Warsaw.

Napoleon controlled much of Europe through forceful diplomacy. One tactic was to put friends and relatives on the thrones of Europe. For example, after unseating the king of Spain, he placed his own brother, Joseph

Bonaparte, on the throne. He also forced alliances on European powers from Madrid to Moscow. At various times, the rulers of Austria, Prussia, and Russia reluctantly signed treaties with the "Corsican upstart," as his enemies called him.

In France, Napoleon's successes boosted the spirit of nationalism. Great victory parades filled the streets of Paris with cheering crowds. The people celebrated the glory and grandeur that Napoleon had won for France.

France Versus Britain Britain alone remained outside Napoleon's European empire. With only a small army, Britain relied on its sea power to stop Napoleon's drive to rule the continent. In 1805, Napoleon prepared to invade England. But at the Battle of Trafalgar, fought off the southwest coast of Spain, British admiral Horatio Nelson smashed a French fleet.

With an invasion ruled out, Napoleon struck at Britain's lifeblood, its commerce. He waged economic warfare through the Continental System, which closed European ports to British goods. Britain responded with its own blockade of European ports. A blockade involves shutting off ports to keep people or supplies from moving in or out. During their long struggle, both Britain and France seized neutral ships suspected of trading with the other side. British attacks on American ships sparked anger in the United States and eventually triggered the War of 1812.

In the end, Napoleon's Continental System failed to bring Britain to its knees. Although British exports declined, its powerful navy kept open vital trade routes to the Americas and India. Meanwhile, trade restrictions created a scarcity of goods in Europe, sent prices soaring, and intensified resentment against French power.

Cause *and* Effect

Long-Term Causes	Immediate Causes
• Corrupt, inconsistent, and insensitive leadership • Prosperous members of Third Estate resent privileges of First and Second estates • Spread of Enlightenment ideas	• Huge government debt • Poor harvests and rising price of bread • Failure of Louis XVI to accept financial reforms • Formation of National Assembly • Storming of Bastille

The French Revolution

Immediate Effects	Long-Term Effects
• Declaration of the Rights of Man and the Citizen adopted • France adopts its first written constitution • Monarchy abolished • Revolutionary France fights coalition of European powers • Reign of Terror	• Napoleon gains power • Napoleonic Code established • French public schools set up • French conquests spread nationalism • Revolutions occur in Europe and Latin America

Connections to Today

• French law reflects Napoleonic Code
• France is a democratic republic

Skills Assessment **Chart** The French Revolution was a major turning point. Its impact spread far beyond France. **How did Napoleon spread the ideas of the French Revolution?**

SECTION 4 Assessment

Recall
1. **Identify:** **(a)** Consulate, **(b)** Concordat of 1801, **(c)** Napoleonic Code, **(d)** Confederation of the Rhine, **(e)** Battle of Trafalgar, **(f)** Continental System.
2. **Define:** **(a)** plebiscite, **(b)** annex, **(c)** blockade.

Comprehension
3. Describe Napoleon Bonaparte's rise to power.
4. **(a)** What revolutionary reforms were undone by Napoleon? **(b)** How did Napoleon preserve some of the principles of the Enlightenment?

5. **(a)** How did Napoleon come to dominate most of Europe? **(b)** Why did his efforts to subdue Britain fail?

Critical Thinking and Writing
6. **Analyzing Information** What opinions do you think each of the following had of Napoleon? **(a)** royalists, **(b)** Catholic priests, **(c)** soldiers, **(d)** republicans.
7. **Making Decisions** Suppose you were a French voter in 1803. How would you have voted on the plebiscite to make Napoleon emperor? Explain your reasons.

Activity
Take It to the NET
Use the Internet to research one of the battles identified on the map in this section. Make a map that shows the terrain of the battle site, and the positions, strengths, and movements of the opposing forces. Write a paragraph or two explaining the outcome.

Reading Focus

- What challenges threatened Napoleon's empire?
- What events led to Napoleon's downfall?
- What were the goals of the Congress of Vienna?

Vocabulary

guerrilla warfare
abdicate
legitimacy

Taking Notes

On a sheet of paper, make a flowchart like the partially completed one at right. As you read this section, add events that led to the downfall of Napoleon. Add as many boxes as you need.

DOWNFALL OF NAPOLEON

Nationalism spurs opposition to French rule

↓

↓

↓

Waterloo

Main Idea Napoleon was finally defeated, but revolutionary ideals and the postwar peace settlement affected Europe for many years.

Setting the Scene Napoleon watched the battle for the Russian city of Smolensk from a chair outside his tent. As fires lit up the walled city, he exclaimed:

"It's like Vesuvius erupting. Don't you think this is a beautiful sight?"

"Horrible, Sire," replied an aide.

"Bah!" snorted Napoleon. "Remember, gentlemen, what a Roman emperor said: 'The corpse of an enemy always smells sweet.'"

In 1812, Napoleon pursued his dream of empire by invading Russia. The campaign began a chain of events that eventually led to his downfall. Napoleon's final defeat brought an end to the era of the French Revolution.

Challenges to Napoleon's Empire

Under Napoleon, French armies spread the ideas of the revolution across Europe. They backed liberal reforms in the lands they conquered. In some places, they helped install revolutionary governments that abolished titles of nobility, ended Church privileges, opened careers to men of talent, and ended serfdom and manorial dues. The Napoleonic Code, too, was carried across Europe. French occupation sometimes brought economic benefits as well, by reducing trade barriers and stimulating industry.

Impact of Nationalism Napoleon's successes, however, contained the seeds of defeat. Although nationalism spurred French armies to success, it worked against them, too. Many Europeans who had welcomed the ideas of the French Revolution nevertheless saw Napoleon and his armies as foreign oppressors. They resented the Continental System and Napoleon's effort to impose French culture.

From Rome to Madrid to the Netherlands, nationalism unleashed revolts against France. In the German states, leaders encouraged national loyalty among German-speaking people to counter French influence.

Resistance in Spain Resistance to foreign rule bled French occupying forces in Spain. In 1808, Napoleon replaced the king of Spain with his own brother, Joseph Bonaparte. He also introduced reforms that sought to undermine the Spanish Catholic Church. But many Spaniards remained loyal to their former king and devoted to the Church. When the Spanish resisted the invaders, well-armed French forces responded with brutal repression. Far from crushing resistance, however, the French reaction further inflamed Spanish nationalism. Efforts to drive out the French intensified.

Spanish patriots conducted a campaign of guerrilla warfare, or hit-and-run raids, against the French. (In Spanish, *guerrilla* means "little war.") Small bands of guerrillas ambushed French supply trains or troops before melting into the countryside. These attacks kept large numbers of French soldiers tied down in Spain, when Napoleon needed them elsewhere. Eventually, the British sent an army under Arthur Wellesley, later the Duke of Wellington, to help the Spanish fight France.

War With Austria Spanish resistance encouraged Austria to resume hostilities against the French. In 1805, at the Battle of Austerlitz, Napoleon had won a crushing victory against an Austro-Russian army of superior numbers. Now, in 1809, the Austrians sought revenge. But once again, Napoleon triumphed—this time at the battle of Wagram. By the peace agreement that followed, Austria surrendered lands populated by more than three million subjects.

The next year, after divorcing his wife Josephine, Napoleon married the Austrian princess Marie Louise. By marrying the daughter of the Hapsburg emperor, he and his heirs could claim kinship with the royalty of Europe.

Defeat in Russia Napoleon's alliance with the Austrian royal family was especially disturbing to Czar Alexander I of Russia. The Russians were also unhappy with the economic effects of Napoleon's Continental System. Yet another cause for concern was that Napoleon had enlarged the Grand Duchy of Warsaw that bordered Russia on the west. These and other issues led the czar to withdraw Russia from the Continental System. Napoleon responded to the czar's action by assembling his Grand Army.

In 1812, more than 400,000 soldiers from France and other countries invaded Russia. To avoid battles with Napoleon, the Russians retreated eastward, burning crops and villages as they went. This "scorched earth" policy left the French hungry and cold as winter came. Napoleon entered Moscow in September. He realized, though, that he

Resistance in Spain
Spanish artist Francisco Goya stressed raw human emotions. Goya's *The Third of May, 1808* shows French soldiers executing Spanish prisoners. His drawing *And They Are Like Wild Beasts* depicts a furious battle between Spanish women and the French.

Theme: Art and Literature How did Goya emphasize nationalism in these artworks?

was not able to feed and supply his army through the long Russian winter. In October, he turned homeward.

The 1,000-mile retreat from Moscow turned into a desperate battle for survival. Russian attacks and the brutal Russian winter took a terrible toll. Philippe Paul de Ségur, an aide to Napoleon, described the grim scene as the remnants of the Grand Army returned:

> "In Napoleon's wake [was] a mob of tattered ghosts draped in . . . odd pieces of carpet, or greatcoats burned full of holes, their feet wrapped in all sorts of rags. . . . [We] stared in horror as those skeletons of soldiers went by, their gaunt, gray faces covered with disfiguring beards, without weapons . . . with lowered heads, eyes on the ground, in absolute silence."
> —*Memoirs of Philippe Paul de Ségur*

Only about 10,000 soldiers of the once-proud Grand Army survived. Many died. Others deserted. French general Michel Ney sadly concluded: "General Famine and General Winter, rather than Russian bullets, have conquered the Grand Army." Napoleon rushed to Paris to raise a new force to defend France. His reputation for success had been shattered.

Downfall of Napoleon

The disaster in Russia brought a new alliance of Russia, Britain, Austria, and Prussia against a weakened France. In 1813, they defeated Napoleon in the Battle of the Nations at Leipzig.

Exile and Return The next year, Napoleon abdicated, or stepped down from power. The victors exiled him to Elba, an island in the Mediterranean. They then recognized Louis XVIII, brother of Louis XVI, as king of France.

The restoration of Louis XVIII did not go smoothly. The Bourbon king agreed to accept the Napoleonic Code and honor the land settlements made during the revolution. However, many émigrés rushed back to France bent on revenge. An economic depression and the fear of a return to the old regime helped rekindle loyalty to Napoleon.

As the victorious allies gathered in Vienna for a general peace conference, Napoleon escaped his island exile and returned to France. Soldiers flocked to his banner. As citizens cheered Napoleon's advance, Louis XVIII fled. In March 1815, the emperor of the French entered Paris in triumph.

Battle of Waterloo Napoleon's triumph was short-lived. His star soared for only 100 days, while the allies reassembled their forces. On June 18, 1815, the opposing armies met near the town of Waterloo in Belgium. British forces under the Duke of Wellington and a Prussian army commanded by General Blücher crushed the French in an agonizing day-long battle. Once again, Napoleon was forced to abdicate and to go into exile on St. Helena, a lonely island in the South Atlantic. This time, he would not return.

Legacy of Napoleon Napoleon died in 1821, but his legend lived on in France and around the world. His contemporaries as well as historians have long debated his legacy. Was he "the revolution on horseback," as he claimed? Or was he a traitor to the revolution?

No one, however, questions Napoleon's impact on France and on Europe. The Napoleonic Code consolidated many changes of the revolution. The France of Napoleon was a centralized state with a constitution. Elections were held with expanded, though limited, suffrage. Many more citizens had rights to property and access to education than under the old regime. Still, French citizens lost many rights promised so fervently by republicans during the Convention.

On the world stage, Napoleon's conquests spread the ideas of the revolution. He failed to make Europe into a French empire. Instead, he sparked

Geography and History

The Battle of Waterloo

Waterloo—to this day it symbolizes utter defeat. But on the morning of the battle, Napoleon felt certain of victory. "This whole affair will not be more serious than swallowing one's breakfast," he said.

But both weather and terrain conspired against him. First, he held off his attack until the rain-soaked ground could dry. (Cannonballs just stick in mud; they can do more damage bouncing along dry ground.) These lost hours gave the enemy time to move in more troops. Second, Napoleon ordered a frontal attack against an enemy positioned on an upward slope. The crest of its ridge helped shield the opposition from French artillery barrages. At Waterloo, more than 20,000 French soldiers died, and Napoleon suffered his final defeat.

Theme: Geography and History How did geography help defeat Napoleon at Waterloo?

Disaster!

Napoleon's Retreat From Moscow

"My greatest and most difficult enterprise," said Napoleon in June 1812 as he eagerly took on the challenge of conquering Russia. A few months later, he would see things differently, and so would his troops. After a disheartening defeat, Napoleon had to hurry back to Paris to squelch rumors that he had been killed, leaving his shrinking army to face the long, brutal winter in Russia.

Fast Facts

- Russian soldiers set Moscow ablaze to avoid handing it over intact to Napoleon's army.
- When the Grand Army retreated from Moscow in October, the line of French troops stretched for more than 50 miles.
- French troops experienced temperatures as low as −40° F.

As French troops stumbled their way through blinding snow, they grew desperate for shelter. Soldiers resorted to building huts using the frozen corpses of their fallen comrades, stacking them like logs to create walls.

Russian forces harassed the retreating French army throughout November.

The Grand Army of France was forced to follow the same path retreating from Moscow that it used to get there. As the army passed over an old battlefield, one observer commented, "It was covered with the debris of helmets . . . wheels, weapons, rags of uniforms—and 30,000 corpses half-eaten by wolves."

Napoleon's Troops in Russia

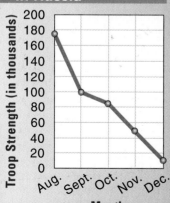

Month

Source: Charles Joseph Minard, 1861

Starting with 422,000 troops in June, Napoleon lost almost half of his forces to fighting, desertion, and famine by August. Grand Army troop strength continued to fall drastically from August through December.

Portfolio Assessment

INTERNET Use the Internet or library resources to learn about another disastrous march in history. Some such marches were the Trail of Tears in North America in 1838–1839, the Long March in China in 1934–1935, or the Bataan Death March in the Philippines in 1942. Write a news story in which you include a map of the route and statistics on loss of life.

Europe After the Congress of Vienna, 1815

Skills Assessment

Geography At the Congress of Vienna, European leaders redrew the map of Europe in order to contain France and keep a balance of power.

1. **Location** On the map, locate **(a)** German Confederation, **(b)** Netherlands, **(c)** Vienna.
2. **Region** Name three states that were in the German Confederation.
3. **Critical Thinking Recognizing Causes and Effects** Why did the Congress enlarge some of the countries around France?

nationalist feeling across Europe. The abolition of the Holy Roman Empire would eventually help in creating a new Germany. Napoleon also had a dramatic impact across the Atlantic. In 1803, his decision to sell France's vast Louisiana Territory to the American government doubled the size of the United States and ushered in an age of American expansion.

The Congress of Vienna

After Waterloo, diplomats and heads of state again sat down at the Congress of Vienna. They faced the monumental task of restoring stability and order in Europe after years of revolution and war.

Gathering of Leaders The Congress met for 10 months, from September 1814 to June 1815. It was a brilliant gathering of European leaders. Diplomats and royalty dined and danced, attended concerts and ballets, and enjoyed parties arranged by their host, Emperor Francis I of Austria.

While the entertainment kept thousands of minor players busy, the real work fell to Prince Clemens von Metternich of Austria, Czar Alexander I of Russia, and Lord Robert Castlereagh (KAS uhl ray) of Britain. Defeated France was represented by Prince Charles Maurice de Talleyrand.

Goals of the Congress The chief goal of the Vienna decision makers was to create a lasting peace by establishing a balance of power and protecting the system of monarchy. Each of the leaders also pursued his own goals. Metternich, the dominant figure at the Congress, wanted to restore the *status quo* (Latin for "the way things are") of 1792. Alexander I urged a "holy alliance" of Christian monarchs to suppress future revolutions. Lord Castlereagh was determined to prevent a revival of French military power.

The aged diplomat Talleyrand shrewdly played the other leaders against one another to get defeated France accepted as an equal partner.

Balance of Power The peacemakers also redrew the map of Europe. To contain French ambitions, they ringed France with strong countries. In the north, they added Belgium and Luxembourg to Holland to create the kingdom of the Netherlands. To prevent French expansion eastward, they gave Prussia lands along the Rhine River. They also allowed Austria to reassert control over northern Italy. This policy of containment proved fairly successful in maintaining the peace.

Restoration of Monarchs To turn back the clock to 1792, the architects of the peace promoted the principle of legitimacy, restoring hereditary monarchies that the French Revolution or Napoleon had unseated. Even before the Congress began, they had put Louis XVIII on the French throne. Later, they restored "legitimate" monarchs in Portugal, Spain, and the Italian states.

Problems of the Peace To protect the new order, Austria, Russia, Prussia, and Great Britain extended their wartime alliance into the postwar era. In the Quadruple Alliance, the four nations pledged to act together to maintain the balance of power and to suppress revolutionary uprisings.

The Vienna statesmen achieved their immediate goals, but they failed to foresee how powerful new forces such as nationalism would shake the foundations of Europe. They redrew national boundaries without any concern for national cultures. In Germany, they created a loosely organized German Confederation with Austria as its official head. But many Germans who had battled Napoleon were already dreaming of a strong, united German nation. Their dream would not come true for more than 50 years, but the story of German unification began in this period.

Looking Ahead

Despite clashes and controversies, the Congress created a framework for peace. Its decisions influenced European politics for the next 100 years. Europe would not see war on a Napoleonic scale until 1914.

The ideals of the French Revolution were not destroyed at Vienna. In the next decades, the French Revolution would inspire people in Europe and Latin America to seek equality and liberty. The spirit of nationalism ignited by Napoleon also remained a powerful force.

Biography

Prince Clemens von Metternich 1773–1859

As Austria's foreign minister, Metternich used a variety of means to achieve his goals. In 1809, when Napoleon seemed vulnerable, Metternich favored war against France. In 1810, after France had crushed Austria, he supported alliance with France. When the French army was in desperate retreat from Russia, Metternich became the "prime minister of the coalition" that defeated Napoleon. At the Congress of Vienna, Metternich helped create a new European order and made sure that Austria had a key role in it. He would skillfully defend that new order for more than 30 years.

Theme: Impact of the Individual Why did Metternich's policies toward France change?

SECTION 5 Assessment

Recall
1. **Identify:** (a) Joseph Bonaparte, (b) Duke of Wellington, (c) Marie Louise, (d) scorched earth policy, (e) Waterloo, (f) Clemens von Metternich, (g) Quadruple Alliance.
2. **Define:** (a) guerrilla warfare, (b) abdicate, (c) legitimacy.

Comprehension
3. What challenges did Napoleon face in: (a) Spain, (b) Austria?
4. How did the defeat in Russia lead to Napoleon's downfall?
5. What were the chief goals of the Congress of Vienna?

Critical Thinking and Writing
6. **Linking Past and Present** The powers of Europe used the Quadruple Alliance to protect the postwar order. How do international alliances and organizations help provide order in the world today?
7. **Connecting to Geography** Review the map on the preceding page. (a) What two states were the leading powers in the German Confederation? (b) How do you think this affected future attempts to unify Germany?

Activity
Take It to the NET

Use the Internet to research the Congress of Vienna. Imagine that you have recently returned from attending the Congress and are writing an editorial about its decisions. Explain how the agreements will affect your nation.

19 Review and Assessment

Creating a Chapter Summary

On a sheet of paper, make a time line to recall the chief events of the French Revolution and Napoleonic era. Use the model shown here as a guide for getting started.

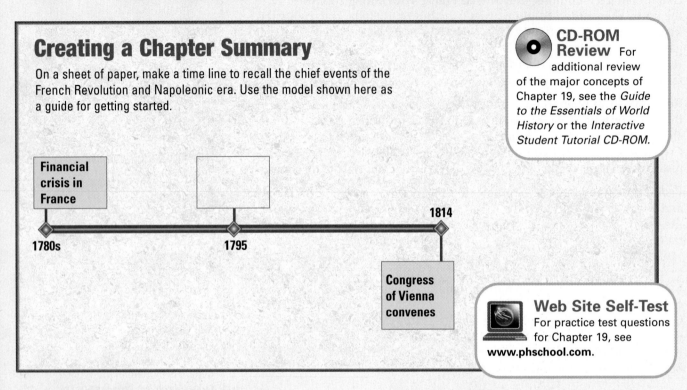

CD-ROM Review For additional review of the major concepts of Chapter 19, see the *Guide to the Essentials of World History* or the *Interactive Student Tutorial CD-ROM.*

Web Site Self-Test For practice test questions for Chapter 19, see **www.phschool.com.**

Building Vocabulary

Use these vocabulary words and their definitions to create a matching quiz. Exchange quizzes with another student. Check each other's answers when you are finished.

1. bourgeoisie
2. deficit spending
3. émigré
4. republic
5. suffrage
6. nationalism
7. plebiscite
8. annex
9. abdicate
10. legitimacy

Recalling Key Facts

11. Why was there discontent with the old regime in France?
12. Why did a crowd storm the Bastille?
13. What was the slogan of the French Revolution?
14. What was the Reign of Terror?
15. List the reforms that Napoleon made as leader of France.
16. **(a)** How did Napoleon build an empire in Europe? **(b)** What were two reasons for his downfall?
17. How did the Congress of Vienna try to restore the balance of power in Europe?

Critical Thinking and Writing

18. **Synthesizing Information** A French noble wrote this on the causes of the revolution: "The most striking of the country's troubles was the chaos in its finances, the result of years of extravagance. . . . No one could think of any remedy, except to search for fresh funds." **(a)** What did the noble mean by "chaos in its finances"? **(b)** How were fresh funds raised? **(c)** How did this lead to revolution?

19. **Connecting to Geography** **(a)** How did the geography of the Russian empire work against Napoleon's Grand Army? **(b)** Do you think geography can affect the outcome of modern warfare? Explain.

20. **Analyzing Primary Sources** Review the words of "La Marseillaise," which appears in Section 3. How does the song express some of the ideals of the French Revolution?

21. **Comparing** Review the English Civil War. **(a)** How were the English Civil War and the French Revolution similar? **(b)** How were they different?

Read the excerpt below from an eyewitness account of the battle at Waterloo. Then answer the questions that follow.

"Our division, which had stood upwards of 5000 men at the commencement of the battle, had gradually dwindled down into a solitary line of skirmishers. . . . Presently a cheer which we knew to be British commenced far to the right, and made everyone prick up his ears; it was Lord Wellington's long-wished-for orders to advance. . . . [To] people who had been so many hours enveloped in darkness, in the midst of destruction, and naturally anxious about the result of the day, the scene which now met the eye conveyed a feeling of more exquisite gratification than can be conceived. . . . The French were flying in one confused mass. British lines were seen in close pursuit, and in admirable order, as far as the eye could reach to the right, while the plain to the left was filled with Prussians."

—Captain J. Kincaid,
Adventures in the Rifle Brigade

22. What nationality is the writer?
23. What evidence is given that the French fought fiercely?
24. Why do the soldiers cheer?
25. How does the writer feel about victory?
26. How does this battle differ from the guerrilla warfare fought against the French in Spain?

Skills Assessment
Take It to the NET

Use the Internet to research one of the symbols of the French Revolution or the French republic, such as the Bastille, the tricolor, or "La Marseillaise." Then, write a brief historical analysis of the symbol. Explain how it originated, what it represented to French citizens during the revolution, and how it continues to be an important symbol to the French people today.

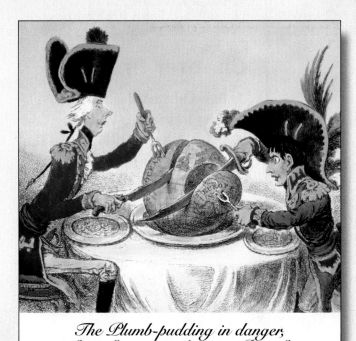

*The Plumb-pudding in danger,
or State Epicures taking un Petit Soup
the great Globe itself and all which it went is too small to
satisfy such insatiable appetites*

In the political cartoon (above), the figure at left represents the British and the figure at right represents Napoleon. Use the cartoon to answer the following questions:

27. What is represented by the meal on the table?
28. Why are the two figures carving the meal?
29. Does the cartoonist portray Napoleon favorably? Explain.
30. How would people of the time have known which nations were represented by the two men in the cartoon?
31. Which of the two sides, if any, does the cartoon favor? Explain.
32. (a) Compose a title for the cartoon. (b) Explain the meaning of the title you created.

Skills Tip

To understand a political cartoon's point of view, first try to figure out the meaning of the cartoon's various figures and symbols.

The Industrial Revolution Begins

1750–1850

Chapter Preview

1 Dawn of the Industrial Age
2 Britain Leads the Way
3 Hardships of Early Industrial Life
4 New Ways of Thinking

CHAPTER EVENTS

1760s
James Watt improves on the steam engine. Watt's engine, shown here, provides a vital source of power.

1800
Robert Owen begins social reforms at New Lanark.

1807
Robert Fulton develops the first successful steamboat, the *Clermont*. Steam power allows the vessel, shown here, to travel against the current without difficulty.

1750

1775

1800

GLOBAL EVENTS

1762 Catherine the Great comes to power in Russia.

1804 Napoleon becomes emperor of France.

Major Centers of Industry in Great Britain, 1825

Lambert Azimuthal Equal Area Projection

0   100   200 Miles
0   100   200 Kilometers

The Industrial Revolution first took hold in Britain, encouraging the growth of cities and factory towns.

Population of urban centers
- • 30,000 or more
- • 80,000 or more
- ● 1,000,000 or more

SCOTLAND

ATLANTIC OCEAN

Glasgow   Edinburgh

Newcastle

Tyne R.

North Sea

Belfast

Irish Sea   Mersey R.   Humber R.

Liverpool   Manchester

IRELAND   ENGLAND

Severn R.   Birmingham

WALES

Thames R.

Bristol

London

55°N

50°N

15°W   10°W   5°W   0°   5°E

1830
The Liverpool-Manchester Railroad opens.

1848
Karl Marx and Friedrich Engels publish *The Communist Manifesto*.

1851
The Great Exhibition is held in London. A display of industrial developments, housed in the Crystal Palace, is shown here.

1825   1850   1875

1847 Liberia, settled by freed African Americans, becomes an independent nation.

Dawn of the Industrial Age

Reading Focus

- Why was the Industrial Revolution a turning point in world history?
- How did an agricultural revolution contribute to population growth?
- What new technologies helped trigger the Industrial Revolution?

Vocabulary

anesthetic

enclosure

smelt

Taking Notes

As you read, create a chart of causes of the Industrial Revolution. This sample will help you get started. Add categories as needed.

Agricultural Revolution	Population Explosion	New Technology	
• Dikes • Fertilizer	• Declining death rates •	• •	

INDUSTRIAL REVOLUTION

Main Idea The Industrial Revolution had an impact on every aspect of life in Western Europe and the United States.

Setting the Scene For thousands of years following the rise of civilization, most people lived and worked in small farming villages. However, a chain of events set in motion in the mid-1700s changed that way of life for all time. Today, we call this period of change the Industrial Revolution.

The Industrial Revolution started in Britain. In contrast with most political revolutions, it was neither sudden nor swift. Instead, it was a long, slow, uneven process in which production shifted from simple hand tools to complex machines. New sources of power replaced human and animal power. In the 250 years since it began, the Industrial Revolution has spread from Britain to the rest of Europe, to North America, and around the globe.

A Turning Point in History

In 1750, most people worked the land, using handmade tools. They lived in simple cottages lit by firelight and candles. They made their own clothes and grew their own food. In nearby towns, they might exchange goods at a weekly outdoor market.

Like their ancestors, these people knew little of the world that existed beyond their village. The few who left home traveled only as far as their feet or a horse-drawn cart could take them. Those bold adventurers who dared to cross the seas were at the mercy of the winds and tides.

With the beginning of the Industrial Revolution, the rural way of life began to disappear. By the 1850s, many country villages had grown into industrial towns and cities. Their inhabitants bought food and clothing in stores that offered a large variety of machine-made goods. Their homes were crowded, multistory apartment buildings.

Industrial-age travelers moved rapidly between countries and continents by train or steamship. Urgent messages flew along telegraph wires. New inventions and scientific "firsts" poured out each year. Between 1830 and 1855, for example, an American dentist first used an anesthetic, or drug that prevents pain during surgery; an American inventor patented the first sewing machine; a French physicist measured the speed of light; and a Hungarian doctor introduced antiseptic methods to reduce the risk of women dying in childbirth.

Still more stunning changes occurred in the next century, creating our familiar world of skyscraper cities and carefully tended suburbs. How and why did these great changes occur? Historians point to a series of interrelated causes that helped trigger the industrialization of the West.

A New Agricultural Revolution

Oddly enough, the Industrial Revolution was made possible in part by a change in the farming fields of Western Europe. The first agricultural revolution took place some 11,000 years ago, when people learned to farm and domesticate animals. About 300 years ago, a second agricultural revolution took place. It greatly improved the quality and quantity of farm products.

Improved Methods of Farming The Dutch led the way in this new agricultural revolution. They built earthen walls known as dikes to reclaim land from the sea. They combined smaller fields into larger ones to make better use of the land and used fertilizer from livestock to renew the soil.

In the 1700s, British farmers expanded on Dutch experiments. Some farmers mixed different kinds of soils to get higher crop yields. Others tried out new methods of crop rotation. Lord Charles Townshend urged farmers to grow turnips, which restored exhausted soil. Jethro Tull invented a new mechanical device, the seed drill, to aid farmers. It deposited seeds in rows rather than scattering them wastefully over the land.

Educated farmers exchanged news of experiments through farm journals. King George III himself, nicknamed "Farmer George," wrote articles about his model farm near Windsor Castle.

Enclosure Movement Meanwhile, rich landowners pushed ahead with enclosure, the process of taking over and fencing off land formerly shared by peasant farmers. In the 1500s, they had enclosed land to gain pastures for sheep and increased wool output. By the 1700s, they wanted to create larger fields that could be cultivated more efficiently.

As millions of acres were enclosed, farm output rose. Profits also rose because large fields needed fewer workers. But such progress had a human cost. Many farm laborers were thrown out of work, and small farmers were forced off their land because they could not compete with large landholders. Villages shrank as cottagers left in search of work.

In time, jobless farmworkers migrated to towns and cities. There, they formed a growing labor force that would tend the machines of the Industrial Revolution.

Changes in Agriculture
New inventions contributed to an agricultural revolution during the 1600s and 1700s. Today, the development of new sources of fuel encourages even more use of machine power in farming.

Theme: Economics and Technology How might agricultural developments increase farm productivity and efficiency?

PAST

This four Wheel Drill Plow, with a Seed and a Manure Hopper, was first Invented in the Year 174[?] and is now in Use with W. Ellis at Little Gaddesden near Hempstead in Hertfordshire, where any perso[n] may View the same. It is so light that a Man may Draw it, but Generally drawn by a pony or little Horfe.

PRESENT

How did a clever Scottish engineer become the "Father of the Industrial Revolution"? After repairing a Newcomen steam engine, James Watt had become fascinated with the idea of improving the device. Within a few months, he knew he had a product that would sell.

Still, Watt lacked the money needed to produce and market it. Fortunately, he found a series of partners, including the shrewd Matthew Boulton. Soon, Boulton could boast, "I have at my disposal what the whole world demands, something which will uplift civilization more than ever by relieving man of all undignified drudgery. I have *steam power.*"

Theme: Impact of the Individual How might the Industrial Revolution have been different if Watt had not found a business partner?

The Population Explosion

The agricultural revolution contributed to a rapid growth of population that continues today. Precise population statistics for the 1700s are rare, but those that do exist are striking. Britain's population, for example, soared from about 5 million in 1700 to almost 9 million in 1800. The population of Europe as a whole shot up from roughly 120 million to about 190 million during the same period. Such growth had never before been seen.

The population boom of the 1700s was due more to declining death rates than to rising birthrates. The agricultural revolution reduced the risk of famine. Because they ate better, women were healthier and had stronger babies. In the 1800s, better hygiene and sanitation, along with improved medical care, further slowed deaths from disease.

New Technology

A third factor that helped trigger the Industrial Revolution was the development of new technology. New sources of energy, along with new materials, enabled business owners to change the ways work was done.

An Energy Revolution From the beginning of human history, the energy for work was provided mostly by the muscles of humans and animals. In time, water mills and windmills were added to muscle power.

During the 1700s, people began to harness new sources of energy. One vital power source was coal, used to develop the steam engine. In 1712, inventor Thomas Newcomen had developed a steam engine powered by coal to pump water out of mines. About 1769, Scottish engineer James Watt improved on Newcomen's engine. Watt's engines would become a key power source of the Industrial Revolution.

Improved Iron Coal was also a vital source of fuel in the production of iron, a material needed for construction of machines and steam engines. The Darby family of Coalbrookdale pioneered new methods of producing iron. In 1709, Abraham Darby used coal to smelt iron, or separate iron from its ore. When he discovered that coal gave off impurities that damaged the iron, Darby found a way to remove the impurities from coal.

Darby's experiments led him to produce better-quality and less expensive iron, and his son and grandson continued to improve on his methods. In the decades that followed, high-quality iron was used more and more widely, especially after the world turned to building railroads.

SECTION 1 Assessment

Recall
1. **Identify:** (a) Charles Townshend, (b) Jethro Tull, (c) Thomas Newcomen, (d) James Watt, (e) Abraham Darby.
2. **Define:** (a) anesthetic, (b) enclosure, (c) smelt.

Comprehension
3. Describe how the Industrial Revolution changed daily life, becoming a turning point in history.
4. Identify three causes of the population explosion in Europe.

5. Explain the impact of each of the following technologies: (a) steam power, (b) improved iron.

Critical Thinking and Writing
6. **Recognizing Causes and Effects** What were the immediate and long-term effects of the agricultural revolution?
7. **Predicting Consequences** How do you think increased population contributed to the Industrial Revolution?

Activity

Creating a Mechanical Drawing
Suppose that you are trying to develop a way to draw water from a well that is faster than pulling up one bucket of water at a time. Draw a sketch of a machine that would speed up the process and require less human labor.

Britain Leads the Way

Reading Focus

- Why was Britain the starting point for the Industrial Revolution?

- What changes transformed the textile industry?

- What new technologies were part of the revolution in transportation?

Vocabulary

capital

factory

turnpike

Taking Notes

Copy this concept web. As you read, fill in the circles with key factors that helped Britain take an early lead in industry.

Main Idea The Industrial Revolution originated in Britain.

Setting the Scene Visitors crowded into London's Crystal Palace in 1851. The immense structure housed the Great Exhibition, a display of the "Works of Industry of all Nations." The palace itself was specially built for the occasion. A vast cavern of glass and iron, it symbolized the triumph of the industrial age.

In the century before the exhibition, Britain had been the first nation to industrialize. Its success became the model for other countries, in Europe and around the world.

Why Britain?

Why did the Industrial Revolution begin in Britain? Historians have identified a number of key factors that helped Britain lead the way.

Resources Britain was a small nation in area. However, it had large supplies of coal to power steam engines. It also had plentiful iron to build the new machines. In addition to natural resources, a labor supply was necessary. Large numbers of workers were needed to mine the coal and iron, build the factories, and run the machines. The agricultural revolution of the 1600s and 1700s freed many people in Britain from farm labor and led to a population boom.

New Technology In the 1700s, Britain had plenty of skilled mechanics who were eager to meet the growing demand for new, practical inventions. Technology was an important part of the Industrial Revolution, but it did not cause it. After all, other societies, such as the ancient Greeks or Chinese, had advanced technology for their time but did not move on to industrialization. Only when other necessary conditions existed, including demand and capital, did technology pave the way for industrialization.

Economic Conditions From the mid-1600s to 1700s, trade from a growing overseas empire helped the British economy prosper. Beginning with the slave trade, the business class accumulated capital, or wealth to invest in enterprises such as shipping, mines, railroads, and factories. Many were ready to risk their capital in new ventures.

At home, the population explosion boosted demand for goods. However, a growing population alone would not have resulted in increased production. General economic prosperity also helped make the new consumer goods affordable to members of every social class.

British Cotton Trade About 1850

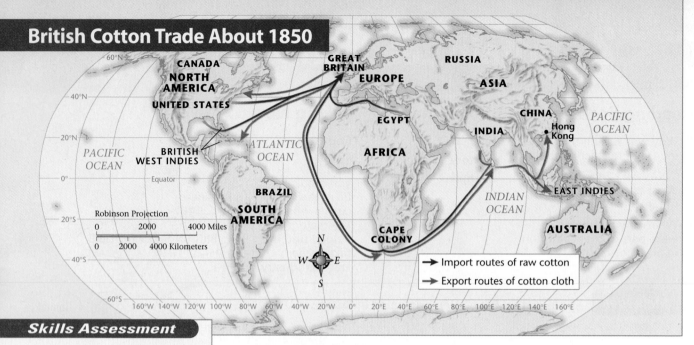

Skills Assessment

Geography As its textile industry grew, Great Britain needed more raw cotton. It also sought out new markets for finished cotton cloth.

1. **Location** On the map, locate **(a)** Great Britain, **(b)** United States, **(c)** British West Indies.
2. **Movement** **(a)** Name two overseas sources that supplied raw cotton to Britain. **(b)** Name two overseas markets to which Britain exported its cotton cloth.
3. **Critical Thinking**
   Predicting Consequences What might have happened to the British cotton industry if Britain had lost control of India?

Political and Social Conditions Britain had a stable government that supported economic growth. It built a strong navy to protect its empire and overseas trade. Although the upper class tended to look down on business people, it did not reject the wealth produced by the new entrepreneurs.

Religious attitudes also played a role. Many entrepreneurs came from religious groups that encouraged thrift and hard work. At the same time, many people focused more on worldly concerns than on the afterlife. Thus, risk takers such as inventors and bankers felt free to devote their energies to material achievements.

Changes in the Textile Industry

The Industrial Revolution first took hold in Britain's largest industry, textiles. In the 1600s, cotton cloth imported from India had become popular. British merchants tried to organize a cotton cloth industry at home. They developed the putting out system, in which raw cotton was distributed to peasant families who spun it into thread and then wove the thread into cloth. Skilled artisans in the towns then finished and dyed the cloth.

Major Inventions Under the putting out system, production was slow. As the demand for cloth grew, inventors came up with a string of remarkable devices that revolutionized the British textile industry. For example, using John Kay's flying shuttle, weavers worked so fast that they soon outpaced spinners. James Hargreaves solved that problem by producing the spinning jenny in 1764, which spun many threads at the same time. A few years later, Richard Arkwright invented the waterframe, which used water power to speed up spinning still further.

The First Factories The new machines doomed the putting out system. They were too large and expensive to be operated at home. Instead, manufacturers built long sheds to house the machines. At first, they located the sheds near rapidly moving streams, which provided water power to run the machines. Later, machines were powered by steam engines.

Spinners and weavers came each day to work in these first factories—places that brought together workers and machines to produce large quantities of goods. Early observers were awed at the size and output of these establishments. One onlooker noted: "The same [amount] of labor is now performed in one of these structures which formerly occupied the industry of an entire district."

Synthesizing Information

Impact of the Railroad

The steam locomotive was one of the key inventions of the Industrial Revolution. The maps, the cartoon, and the graph below all relate to the growth of railroads in Great Britain.

English Cartoon, Early 1800s

Railways in Great Britain

1840

1850

— Railway lines

Travel Times to London

Birmingham

Brighton

Manchester

Hours

1750
1830
1850

Source: E. J. Hobsbaum, *Industry and Empire*

Skills Tip

Bar graphs often show change over time. To determine the amount of change, subtract the smaller measure from the larger one.

Skills Assessment

1. Between 1750 and 1830, travel time from Birmingham to London decreased by about
   A 12 hours.
   B 24 hours.
   C 36 hours.
   D 48 hours.

2. Which of the three pieces of evidence above supports the conclusion that railroads reached more places in 1850 than in 1830?
   E the maps only
   F the graph only
   G the maps and the graph
   H the maps and the cartoon

3. **Critical Thinking** **Drawing Conclusions** **(a)** Based on the evidence provided here, what were some of the benefits and drawbacks of railroads? **(b)** What other positive or negative effects do you think railroads might have had? Give two examples.

Revolution in Transportation

As production increased, entrepreneurs needed faster and cheaper methods of moving goods from place to place. Some capitalists invested in turnpikes, which were privately built roads that charged a fee to travelers who used them. Others had canals dug to link rivers or connect inland towns with coastal ports. Engineers also built stronger bridges and upgraded harbors to help the expanding overseas trade.

On Land   The great revolution in transportation, however, was the invention of the steam locomotive. It was this invention that made possible the growth of railroads. In the early 1800s, pioneers like George Stephenson developed steam-powered locomotives to pull carriages along iron rails. The railroad did not have to follow the course of a river. This meant that tracks could go places rivers did not, allowing factory owners and merchants to ship goods over land.

The world's first major rail line, from Liverpool to Manchester, opened in England in 1830. In the following decades, railroad travel became faster and railroad building boomed. By 1870, rail lines crisscrossed Britain, Europe, and North America.

On Sea   Other inventors applied steam power to improve shipping. In 1807, an American, Robert Fulton, used Watt's steam engine to power the *Clermont* up the Hudson River in New York. Fulton's steamboat traveled at a record-breaking speed of more than five miles an hour!

Designing steamships for ocean voyages was more difficult. The coal needed for the voyage took up much of the cargo space. But by the late 1800s, steam-powered freighters with iron hulls were carrying 10 to 20 times the cargo of older wooden ships.

Looking Ahead

As the Industrial Revolution got under way, it triggered a chain reaction. In response to growing demand, inventors developed machines that could produce large quantities of goods more efficiently. As the supply of goods increased, prices fell. Lower prices made goods more affordable and thus created more consumers who further fed the demand for goods. The Industrial Revolution affected not only how goods were made but also how people lived. It brought a tidal wave of economic and social changes that swept the industrializing nations of the world.

Europe's Canal Boom

People have dug canals since ancient times, but it took the Industrial Revolution to set off a canal-building frenzy in Europe. During the late 1700s and early 1800s, European factories needed an efficient, inexpensive way to receive coal and raw materials and then to ship finished goods to market. The many navigable rivers in Europe did not reach every town and sometimes followed indirect—and lengthy—courses. Canals solved the problem. They connected towns to more distant rivers and provided direct routes from factories to markets.

The canals soon lost some of their importance to railroads, but today Europe is still crisscrossed by a 13,000-mile network of canals and rivers.

Theme: Geography and History How did canals help to advance the Industrial Revolution?

SECTION 2 Assessment

Recall
1. **Identify:** **(a)** John Kay, **(b)** James Hargreaves, **(c)** Richard Arkwright, **(d)** George Stephenson.
2. **Define:** **(a)** capital, **(b)** factory, **(c)** turnpike.

Comprehension
3. Describe four factors that helped bring about the Industrial Revolution in Britain.
4. How did the Industrial Revolution transform the textile industry?
5. How did transportation improve in the early 1800s? Give three examples.

Critical Thinking and Writing
6. **Analyzing Information** Explain how each of the following helped contribute to demand for consumer goods in Britain: **(a)** population explosion, **(b)** general economic prosperity.
7. **Connecting to Geography** Look at the map of the British cotton trade in this section. **(a)** To what continents did Britain export its cotton cloth? **(b)** Explain how advances in transportation, such as the steamboat, contributed to Britain's global cotton trade.

Activity
Take It to the NET

Research connections between mining and transportation. Write a brief explanation of how canals affected the coal industry.

Reading Focus

- What was life like in the new industrial city?
- How did the factory system change the way people worked?
- What benefits and problems did industrialization bring to the working class and the new middle class?

Vocabulary

urbanization
tenement
labor union

Taking Notes

Copy this table. As you read, list the characteristics of the working class and the middle class. Add more entries as needed.

THE WORKING CLASS	THE MIDDLE CLASS
Factory and mine workers	Merchants, inventors, skilled artisans
Tenement housing	

Main Idea The Industrial Revolution created material benefits as well as social problems.

Setting the Scene The Industrial Revolution brought great riches to most of the entrepreneurs who helped set it in motion. For the millions of workers who crowded into the new factories, however, the industrial age brought poverty and harsh living conditions. One observer commented on the disease-ridden neighborhoods and polluted air:

> "The population . . . is crowded into one dense mass of cottages separated by unpaved and almost pestilential streets. This is an atmosphere loaded with the exhalation of a large manufacturing city."
> —J. P. Kay, quoted in *Mill Life at Styal*

In time, reforms would curb many of the worst abuses of the early industrial age in Europe and the Americas, and people at all levels of society would benefit from industrialization. Until then, working people could look forward only to lives marked by dangerous working conditions; unsafe, unsanitary, and overcrowded housing; and unrelenting poverty.

The New Industrial City

The Industrial Revolution brought rapid urbanization, or the movement of people to cities. Changes in farming, soaring population growth, and an ever-increasing demand for workers led masses of people to migrate from farms to cities. Almost overnight, small towns around coal or iron mines mushroomed into cities. Other cities grew up around the factories that entrepreneurs built in once-quiet market towns.

The British market town of Manchester numbered 17,000 people in the 1750s. Within a few years, it exploded into a center of the textile industry. Its population soared to 40,000 by 1780 and 70,000 by 1801. Visitors described the "cloud of coal vapor" that polluted the air, the pounding noise of steam engines, and the filthy stench of its river.

In Manchester, as elsewhere, a gulf divided the urban population. The wealthy and the middle class lived in pleasant neighborhoods. Vast numbers of poor, however, struggled to survive in foul-smelling slums. They packed into tiny rooms in tenements, multistory buildings divided into crowded apartments. These buildings had no running water, only community pumps. There was no sewage or sanitation system, and wastes and garbage rotted in the streets. Cholera and other diseases spread rapidly. In time, reformers pushed for laws to improve conditions in city slums.

▶ Primary Sources and Literature

See "Charles Dickens: Hard Times" in the Reference Section at the back of this book.

**Dunaskin Open Air Museum
Ayrshire, Scotland**

To find more information about iron production during the Industrial Revolution, use the Internet address above to link to the Dunaskin Open Air Museum.

Forging the Anchor
This painting by William James Muler shows workers laboring to make an anchor of iron. The image provides a glimpse of the factory system.

Theme: Art and Literature
How would you describe the artist's opinion of factories?

The Factory System

The heart of the new industrial city was the factory. There, the technology of the machine age imposed a harsh new way of life on workers.

Rigid Discipline The factory system differed greatly from farmwork. In rural villages, people worked hard, but their work varied according to the season. In factories, workers faced a rigid schedule set by the factory whistle. "While the engine runs," said an observer, "people must work—men, women, and children are yoked together with iron and steam."

Working hours were long. Shifts lasted from 12 to 16 hours. Exhausted workers suffered accidents from machines that had no safety devices. They might lose a finger, a limb, or even their lives. Workers were exposed to other dangers, as well. Coal dust destroyed the lungs of miners, and textile workers constantly breathed air filled with lint. If workers were sick or injured, they lost their jobs.

Women Workers Employers often preferred to hire women workers rather than men. They thought women could adapt more easily to machines and were easier to manage than men. More important, they were able to pay women less than men, even for the same work.

Factory work created special problems for women. Their new jobs took them out of their homes for 12 hours or more a day. They then returned to crowded slum tenements to feed and clothe their families, clean, and cope with sickness and other problems. Family life had been hard for poor rural cottagers. In industrial towns, it was even grimmer.

Child Labor Factories and mines also hired many boys and girls. Often, nimble-fingered and quick-moving children changed spools in textile mills. Others clambered through narrow mine shafts, pushing coal carts. Because children had helped with farmwork, parents accepted the idea of child labor. And the wages the children earned were needed to keep their families from starving.

Employers often hired orphans, making deals with local officials who were glad to have the children taken off their hands. Overseers beat children accused of idling. A few enlightened factory owners did provide basic education and a decent life for child workers. More often, though, children, like their parents, were slaves to the machines.

You Are There . . .

Spinning Thread in a Textile Mill

It is your first day at work and you're already exhausted. You wanted to help your family by earning extra money, so you came to Manchester to work with your uncle in a textile mill. You must work on several machines at once, keeping the thread from tangling and breaking. The factory still seems so strange.

The thunder of the spinning mule vibrates through the floor. This machine allows you to make thread faster by yourself than hundreds of people spinning by hand.

It is hard to breathe. Cotton dust flies out of the machines. You hear other workers coughing, their lungs filled with the thick dust.

Children dart in and out, untying knots in the thread. You wince as you see a little boy almost get his hand caught in a machine. The boss gives you a disapproving look, so you try to focus on your own work.

Portfolio Assessment

After a 12-hour day at the mill, you decide to write a letter to your family. In your letter, describe your new job and say whether you want to keep working here in Manchester or go back home to the farm.

Worker Protests
On a hot August day in 1819, workers gathered in St. Peter's Fields in Manchester to hear reformers speak. Suddenly, soldiers attacked the crowd. The incident became known as the Peterloo Massacre.

Theme: Art and Literature
Did the artist who created this cartoon favor the workers or the soldiers? Explain.

In the 1830s and 1840s, British lawmakers looked into abuses in factories and mines. Government commissions heard about children as young as five years old working in factories. Some died; others were stunted in growth or had twisted limbs. Most were uneducated. Slowly, Parliament passed laws to regulate child labor in mines and factories.

The Working Class

In rural villages, farm families had strong ties to a community in which they had lived for generations. When they moved to the new industrial cities, many felt lost and bewildered. In time, though, factory and mine workers developed their own sense of community.

Protests As the Industrial Revolution began, weavers and other skilled artisans resisted the new "labor-saving" machines that were costing them their jobs. Some smashed machines and burned factories. In England, such rioters were called Luddites after a mythical figure, Ned Ludd, who supposedly destroyed machines in the 1780s.

Protests met harsh repression. When workers held a rally in Manchester in 1819, soldiers charged the crowd, killing a dozen and injuring hundreds more. Workers were forbidden to organize in groups to bargain for better pay and working conditions. Strikes were outlawed.

Spread of Methodism Many working-class people found comfort in a new religious movement. In the mid-1700s, John Wesley had founded the Methodist Church. Wesley stressed the need for a personal sense of faith. He urged Christians to improve their lot by adopting sober, moral ways.

Methodist meetings featured hymns and sermons promising forgiveness of sin and a better life to come. Methodist preachers took this message of salvation into the slums. There, they tried to rekindle hope among the working poor. They set up Sunday schools where followers not only studied the Bible but also learned to read and write. Methodists helped channel workers' anger away from revolution and toward social reform.

The New Middle Class

Those who benefited most from the Industrial Revolution were the entrepreneurs who set it in motion. This new middle class came from several sources. Some members were merchants who invested their growing profits in factories. Others were inventors or skilled artisans who developed new technologies. Some rose from "rags to riches," a pattern that the age greatly admired.

Middle-class families lived in solid, well-furnished homes. They dressed and ate well. Middle-class men gained influence in Parliament, where they opposed any effort to improve conditions for workers.

As a sign of their new standard of living, middle-class women were encouraged to become "ladies." They took up "ladylike" activities, such as drawing, embroidery, or playing the piano. A "lady" did not work outside the home or do housework. Instead, the family hired a maid-servant. The family then set about educating its daughters to provide the same type of happy, well-furnished home for their future husbands. Sons gained an education that allowed them to become businessmen.

The new middle class valued hard work and the determination to "get ahead." They had confidence in themselves and often little sympathy for the poor. If they thought of the faceless millions in the factories and mines, they generally supposed the poor to be responsible for their own misery. Some believed the poor were so lazy or ignorant that they could not "work their way up" out of poverty.

Benefits and Problems

Since the 1800s, people have debated whether the Industrial Revolution was a blessing or a curse. The early industrial age brought terrible hardships. Said English writer Thomas Carlyle, "Something [ought] to be done."

In time, "something" would be done. Reformers pressed for laws to improve working conditions. Workers' organizations called **labor unions** won the right to bargain with employers for better wages, hours, and working conditions. Eventually, working-class men gained the right to vote, which gave them political power.

Despite the social problems created by the Industrial Revolution—low pay, unemployment, dismal living conditions—the industrial age did bring material benefits. As demand for mass-produced goods grew, new factories opened, creating more jobs. Wages rose so that workers had enough left after paying rent and buying food to buy a newspaper or visit a music hall. As the cost of railroad travel fell, people could visit family in other towns. Horizons widened; opportunities increased.

Industrialization has spread around the world today. Often, it begins with great suffering. In the end, however, it produces more material benefits for more people.

SECTION 3 Assessment

Recall
1. **Identify:** (a) Luddite, (b) John Wesley, (c) Methodism.
2. **Define:** (a) urbanization, (b) tenement, (c) labor union.

Comprehension
3. Describe life in the new industrial city.
4. (a) What were the main characteristics of factory work? (b) What special problems did factory work create for women?

5. How did the conditions of the early industrial age improve?

Critical Thinking and Writing
6. **Comparing** Compare the life of a farmworker with that of an early factory worker.
7. **Connecting to Geography** Look at the chapter opener map. What geographic feature do many of the industrial centers share? Why do you think this is so?

Activity
Take It to the NET

Search the Internet for information about working conditions during the Industrial Revolution. Draw a political cartoon that illustrates the life of factory workers. Write a caption for your cartoon.

4 New Ways of Thinking

Reading Focus

- What was laissez-faire economics?
- How did the views of utilitarians differ from those of socialists?
- What were the ideas of "scientific socialism," introduced by Karl Marx?

Vocabulary

utilitarianism

socialism

means of production

communism

proletariat

Taking Notes

As you read this section, prepare an outline of its contents. Use Roman numerals to indicate major headings. Use capital letters for subheadings, and use numbers for the supporting details. The example here will help you get started.

I. Laissez-faire economics
  A. Legacy of Adam Smith
    1. Benefits of free market
    2.
  B. Malthus on population
    1. Population outpaces food supply
    2.

Main Idea   The Industrial Revolution fostered new ideas about business and economics.

Biography

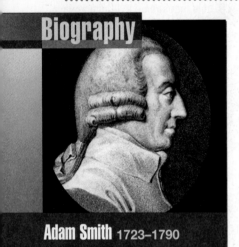

Adam Smith 1723–1790

If anyone fit the image of the "absent-minded professor," it was Adam Smith. He forgot things, spoke awkwardly, and rambled as he walked. "I am a beau in nothing but my books," Smith once said. Still, he had one of history's keenest minds.

At the age of 14, Smith was a student at a university in his native Scotland. There, and later in Paris, he met many influential thinkers of the Enlightenment. He also met local merchants, gaining practical knowledge about business.

Smith spent 10 years writing *The Wealth of Nations*. Published in 1776, it became an instant best-seller. Readers embraced Smith's ideas about laissez-faire and the benefits of capitalism.

Theme: Impact of the Individual How did Smith's education shape his work?

Setting the Scene Everywhere in Britain, Thomas Malthus saw the effects of the population explosion—crowded slums, hungry families, unemployment, and widespread misery. After careful study, in 1798 he published his "Essay on the Principle of Population." Poverty and misery, he concluded, were unavoidable because the population was increasing faster than the food supply. Malthus wrote: "The power of population is [far] greater than the power of the Earth to produce subsistence for man."

Malthus was one of many thinkers who tried to understand the staggering changes taking place in the early industrial age. As heirs to the Enlightenment, these thinkers looked for natural laws that governed the world of business and economics.

Laissez-Faire Economics

During the Enlightenment, physiocrats argued that natural laws should be allowed to operate without interference. As part of this philosophy, they believed that government should not interfere in the free operation of the economy. In the early 1800s, middle-class business leaders embraced this laissez-faire, or "hands-off," approach.

Legacy of Adam Smith The main prophet of laissez-faire economics was Adam Smith, author of *The Wealth of Nations*. Smith asserted that a free market—the unregulated exchange of goods and services—would come to help everyone, not just the rich.

The free market, Smith said, would produce more goods at lower prices, making them affordable by everyone. A growing economy would also encourage capitalists to reinvest profits in new ventures. Supporters of this free-enterprise capitalism pointed to the successes of the industrial age, in which government had played no part.

Malthus on Population Like Smith's book, Thomas Malthus's writings on population shaped economic thinking for generations. Malthus grimly predicted that population would outpace the food supply. The only checks on population growth, he said, were war, disease, and famine. As long as population kept increasing, he went on, the poor would suffer. He thus urged families to have fewer children.

During the early 1800s, many people accepted Malthus's bleak view. It proved to be too pessimistic, however. Although the population boom did continue, the food supply grew even faster. As the century progressed, living conditions for the western world also slowly improved—and then people began having fewer children. By the 1900s, population growth was no longer a problem in the West, but it did continue to afflict many nations elsewhere.

Ricardo on Wages Another influential British economist, David Ricardo, agreed with Malthus that the poor had too many children. In his "iron law of wages," Ricardo pointed out that when wages were high, families had more children. But more children meant a greater supply of labor, which led to lower wages and higher unemployment. Like Malthus, Ricardo did not hold out hope for the working class to escape poverty. Because of such gloomy predictions, economics became known as the "dismal science."

Neither Malthus nor Ricardo was a cruel man. Yet both opposed any government help for the poor. To these supporters of laissez-faire economics, the best cure for poverty was not government relief but the unrestricted "laws of the free market." They felt that individuals should be left to improve their lot through thrift, hard work, and limiting the size of their families.

The Utilitarians

Others adapted laissez-faire doctrines to justify some government intervention. By 1800, Jeremy Bentham was preaching utilitarianism, the idea that the goal of society should be "the greatest happiness for the greatest number" of its citizens. To Bentham, all laws or actions should be judged by their "utility." Did they provide more pleasure (happiness) than pain? He strongly supported individual freedom, which he believed guaranteed happiness. Still, he saw the need for government to become involved under certain circumstances.

Bentham's chief follower, John Stuart Mill, also argued that actions are right if they promote happiness and wrong if they cause pain. He reexamined the idea that unrestricted competition in the free market was always good. Often, he said, it favored the strong over the weak.

Although he believed strongly in individual freedom, Mill wanted the government to step in to improve the hard lives of the working class. "The only purpose for which power can be rightfully exercised over any member of a civilized community, against his will," Mill wrote, "is to prevent harm to others. His own good, either physical or moral, is not a sufficient warrant [cause]." While middle-class business and factory owners were entitled to increase their own happiness, therefore, government should prevent them from doing so in a manner that harmed workers.

Mill further called for giving the vote to workers and women. These groups could then use their political power to win reforms. Utilitarians also worked for reforms in many other areas affecting workers and the poor, from child labor to public health.

Most middle-class people rejected Mill's ideas. Only in the later 1800s were his views slowly accepted. Today's democratic governments, however, have absorbed many ideas from Mill and the other utilitarians.

Emergence of Socialism

While the champions of laissez-faire economics praised individual rights, other thinkers focused on the good of society in general. They condemned the evils of industrial capitalism, which they believed had created a gulf between rich and poor. To end poverty and injustice, they offered a radical solution—socialism. Under socialism, the people as a whole rather than private individuals would own and operate the means of production—the

Overcrowded Conditions
Thomas Malthus warned that population growth could exhaust the food supply, bringing misery to the poor. In *Bishopsgate Street*, artist Gustave Doré captures the squalor and overcrowded conditions of a London slum.

Theme: Political and Social Systems What did Malthus recommend as a solution to the problems of the early industrial age?

farms, factories, railways, and other large businesses that produced and distributed goods.

Socialism grew out of the Enlightenment faith in progress, its belief in the basic goodness of human nature, and its concern for social justice. Socialists wanted to develop a world in which society would operate for the benefit of all members, rather than just for the wealthy. In a socialist society, one reformer predicted:

> "There will be no war, no crime, no administration of justice, as it is called, no government. Besides there will be neither disease, anguish, melancholy, nor resentment. Every man will seek . . . the good of all."
> —William Godwin, "Political Justice"

The Utopians Early socialists tried to build self-sufficient communities in which all work was shared and all property was owned in common. When there was no difference between rich and poor, they felt, fighting between people would disappear. These early socialists were called Utopians, after Thomas More's ideal community. The name implied that they were impractical dreamers. However, the Utopian Robert Owen did set up a model community to put his ideas into practice.

Robert Owen A poor Welsh boy, Owen became a successful mill owner. Unlike most industrialists at the time, he refused to use child labor. He campaigned vigorously for laws that limited child labor and encouraged the organization of labor unions.

Owen insisted that the conditions in which people lived shaped their character. To prove his point, he set up his factory in New Lanark, Scotland, as a model village. He built homes for workers, opened a school for children, and generally treated employees well. He showed that an employer could offer decent living and working conditions and still run a profitable business. By the 1820s, many people were visiting New Lanark to study Owen's reforms.

The "Scientific Socialism" of Karl Marx

In the 1840s, Karl Marx, a German philosopher, condemned the ideas of the Utopians as unrealistic idealism. He put forward a new theory, "scientific socialism," which he claimed was based on a scientific study of history.

As a young man in Germany, Marx agitated for reform. Forced to leave his homeland because of his radical ideas, he lived first in Paris and then settled in London. He teamed up with another German socialist, Friedrich Engels, whose father owned a textile factory in England.

Marx and Engels wrote a pamphlet, *The Communist Manifesto*, which they published in 1848. "A spectre is haunting Europe," it began, "the spectre of communism." Communism is a form of socialism that sees class struggle between employers and employees as unavoidable.

Marxism In *The Communist Manifesto*, Marx theorized that economics was the driving force in history. The entire course of history, he argued, was "the history of class struggles" between the "haves" and the "have-nots." The "haves" have always owned the means of production and thus controlled society and all its wealth. In industrialized Europe, Marx said, the "haves" were the bourgeoisie. The "have-nots" were the proletariat, or working class.

According to Marx, the modern class struggle pitted the bourgeoisie against the proletariat. In the end, he predicted, the proletariat would be triumphant. It would then take control of the means of production and set up a classless, communist society. Such a society would mark the end of the struggles people had endured throughout history, because wealth and power would be equally shared.

Marx despised capitalism. He believed it created prosperity for only a few and poverty for many. He called for an international struggle to bring about its downfall. "Working men of all countries," he urged, "unite!"

Looking Ahead

At first, Marxism gained popularity with many people around the world. Leaders of a number of reform movements adopted the idea that power should be held by workers rather than by business owners. Marx's ideas would never be practiced exactly as he imagined them, however.

Failures As time passed, the failures of Marxist governments would illustrate the flaws in his arguments. Marx claimed that his ideas were based on scientific laws. However, many of the assumptions on which he based his theories were wrong. He predicted that the misery of the proletariat would touch off a world revolution. Instead, by 1900, the efforts of reformers and governments led to improved conditions for the working class. As a result, Marxism lost some of its appeal in the industrially developed countries of Europe and North America.

Marx also predicted that workers would unite across national borders to wage class warfare. Instead, nationalism won out over working-class loyalty. In general, people felt stronger ties to their own countries than to the international communist movement.

Revolutions These failures did not doom the movement instantly. In the late 1800s, Russian socialists embraced Marxism, and the Russian Revolution of 1917 set up a communist-inspired government. For much of the 1900s, revolutionaries around the world would adapt Marxist ideas to their own needs. Independence leaders in Asia, Latin America, and Africa would turn to Marxism. By the 1990s, however, nearly every nation would incorporate elements of free-market capitalism. To many people, Adam Smith's ideas seemed to be of more lasting value than those of Karl Marx.

SECTION 4 Assessment

Recall
1. **Identify:** (a) Thomas Malthus, (b) iron law of wages, (c) John Stuart Mill, (d) Utopians, (e) Karl Marx.
2. **Define:** (a) utilitarianism, (b) socialism, (c) means of production, (d) communism, (e) proletariat.

Comprehension
3. Describe the views of laissez-faire economists (a) Adam Smith, (b) Thomas Malthus, and (c) David Ricardo.
4. Contrast the approaches of utilitarians and socialists to solving economic problems.

5. (a) Describe Karl Marx's view of history. (b) How have events challenged that view?

Critical Thinking and Writing
6. **Linking Past and Present** Choose one economic or political theory discussed in this section. Does that theory seem to apply to the American economy today? Explain.
7. **Applying Information** How might the rise of Methodism and workplace reforms alter Marxist predictions of world revolution?

Activity

Asking Questions
Write five questions you might ask if you were conducting an interview with Robert Owen. Include questions about his goals, how he tried to accomplish them, and whether he succeeded.

Revolutions in Europe and Latin America

1790–1848

Chapter Preview

1 An Age of Ideologies
2 Revolutions of 1830 and 1848
3 Latin American Wars of Independence

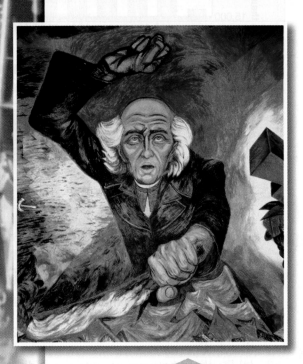

1810
Father Miguel Hidalgo urges Mexicans to fight for independence from Spain.

1804
Haiti declares independence from France.

1819
Simón Bolívar, later known as "The Liberator," seizes Bogota from the Spanish.

CHAPTER EVENTS

1800   1810   1820

GLOBAL EVENTS

1803 United States buys Louisiana from France.

1820 Several thousand British colonists settle in South Africa.

Revolutions in Europe, 1815–1829

Despite the order imposed by the Congress of Vienna, several revolutions erupted in Europe between 1815 and 1829. The spread of revolutionary ideals would ignite new uprisings in 1830 and 1848.

DENMARK

NETHERLANDS

HANOVER

PRUSSIA

Vistula R.

RUSSIA

Rhine R.

Elbe R.

Oder R.

50°N

BAVARIA

SAXONY

Seine R.

AUSTRIAN EMPIRE

Loire R.

Danube R.

FRANCE

SWITZ.

ALPS

LOMBARDY-VENETIA

Po R.

PYRENEES MTS.

Rhône R.

PAPAL STATES

SERBIA

Black Sea

Ebro R.

PORTUGAL

SPAIN

TUSCANY

Adriatic Sea

OTTOMAN EMPIRE

40°N

PIEDMONT-SARDINIA

Tiber R.

ATLANTIC OCEAN

Tagus R.

Mediterranean Sea

KINGDOM OF THE TWO SICILIES

GREECE

30°E

Azimuthal Equal Area Projection

0   150   300 Miles

0   150   300 Kilometers

10°W

0°

10°E

20°E

N W E S

Areas where revolutions occurred

Repression of revolutions

→ French forces

→ Austrian forces

→ Ottoman forces

1830

French revolutionaries battle the king's troops in the streets of Paris.

1848

Revolutions break out across much of Europe.

1830

1840

1850

1839 China and Britain clash in the Opium War.

1850 Taiping Rebellion begins in China.

Chapter 21 **517**

An Age of Ideologies

Reading Focus

- What were the goals of conservatives?
- How did liberalism and nationalism challenge the old order?
- Why was Europe plagued by revolts after 1815?

Vocabulary

ideology
universal manhood suffrage
autonomy

Taking Notes

Copy this chart. As you read this section, list the ideas of conservatism, liberalism, and nationalism.

CONSERVATISM	LIBERALISM	NATIONALISM

Main Idea After 1815, the clash of people with opposing ideologies plunged Europe into an era of turmoil that lasted more than 30 years.

The Conservative Order
Conservatives were determined to preserve the old order. At the heart of that order was the monarchy, symbolized in the Austrian empire by the Hapsburg coat of arms shown here.

Theme: Political and Social Systems What other institutions besides the monarchy were part of the old order?

Setting the Scene A "revolutionary seed" had been planted in Europe, warned Prince Clemens von Metternich. The ideas spread by the French Revolution and Napoleon Bonaparte, he believed, not only threatened Europe's monarchs but also undermined its basic social values:

"Passions are let loose . . . to overthrow everything that society respects as the basis of its existence: religion, public morality, laws, customs, rights, and duties, all are attacked, confounded, overthrown, or called in question."
—*Memoirs of Prince Metternich*

At the Congress of Vienna, the powers of Europe tried to uproot that "revolutionary seed." Other voices, however, kept challenging the order imposed in 1815. The clash of people with opposing ideologies, or systems of thought and belief, plunged Europe into more than 30 years of turmoil.

Conservatives and the Old Order

The Congress of Vienna was a victory for the conservative forces, which included monarchs and their officials, noble landowners, and church leaders. Conservatives supported the political and social order that had existed before the French Revolution. Conservative ideas also appealed to peasants, who wanted to preserve traditional ways.

Conservatives of the early 1800s wanted to turn the clock back to the way things had been before 1789. After all, they had benefited under the old order. They wanted to restore royal families to the thrones they had lost when Napoleon swept across Europe. They supported a social hierarchy in which lower classes were expected to respect and obey their social superiors. Conservatives also backed an established church—Catholic in Austria and southern Europe, Protestant in northern Europe, and Orthodox in eastern Europe.

Conservatives believed that talk about natural rights and constitutional government could lead only to chaos, as it had in France in 1789. If change had to come, they argued, it must come slowly. Conservatives felt that they benefited all people by defending peace and stability. Conservative leaders like Metternich sought to suppress revolutionary ideas. Metternich urged monarchs to oppose freedom of the press, crush protests in their own countries, and send troops to douse the flames of rebellion in neighboring lands.

The Liberal and Nationalist Challenge

Challenging the conservatives at every turn were liberals and nationalists who were inspired by the Enlightenment and the French Revolution. Liberalism and nationalism ignited a number of revolts against established rule.

Liberal Goals Because liberals spoke mostly for the bourgeoisie, or middle class, their ideas are sometimes called "bourgeois liberalism." Liberals included business owners, bankers, and lawyers, as well as politicians, newspaper editors, writers, and others who helped to shape public opinion.

Liberals wanted governments to be based on written constitutions and separation of powers. Liberals spoke out against divine-right monarchy, the old aristocracy, and established churches. They defended the natural rights of individuals to liberty, equality, and property. They called for rulers elected by the people and responsible to them. Thus, most liberals favored a republican form of government over a monarchy, or at least wanted the monarch to be limited by a constitution.

The liberals of the early 1800s saw the role of government as limited to protecting basic rights such as freedom of thought, speech, and religion. They believed that only male property owners or others with a financial stake in society should have the right to vote. Only later in the century did liberals support the principle of universal manhood suffrage, giving all adult men the right to vote.

Liberals strongly supported the laissez-faire economics of Adam Smith and David Ricardo. They saw the free market as an opportunity for capitalist entrepreneurs to succeed. As capitalists and often employers, liberals had different goals from those of workers laboring in factories, mines, and other enterprises of the early Industrial Revolution.

Nationalist Goals For centuries, European rulers had gained or lost lands through wars, marriages, and treaties. They exchanged territories and the people in them like pieces in a game. As a result, by 1815 Europe had several empires that included many nationalities. The Austrian, Russian, and Ottoman empires, for example, each included diverse peoples.

In the 1800s, national groups who shared a common heritage set out to win their own states. Within the diverse Austrian empire, for example, various nationalist leaders tried to unite and win independence for each particular group. Nationalism gave people with a common heritage a sense of identity and the goal of creating their own homeland. At the same time, however, nationalism often bred intolerance and led to persecution of other ethnic or national groups.

Revolts Against the Old Order

Spurred by the ideas of liberalism and nationalism, revolutionaries fought against the old order. During the early 1800s, rebellions erupted in the Balkan Peninsula and elsewhere along the southern fringe of Europe. The Balkans, in southeastern Europe, were inhabited by people of various religions and ethnic groups. These peoples had lived under Ottoman rule for more than 300 years.

The Serb Revolt
In 1804, the Serb leader Karageorge, shown below, led a revolt against Ottoman rule. Ottoman troops crushed this rebellion by 1813, but renewed resistance would eventually lead to Serbian independence.

Theme: Political and Social Systems Why did the Ottoman empire face frequent rebellions in the 1800s?

Independence for Serbia The first Balkan people to revolt were the Serbs. From 1804 to 1813, the Serb leader Karageorge led a guerrilla war against the Ottomans. The bitter struggle was unsuccessful, but it fostered a sense of Serbian identity. A revival of Serbian literature and culture added to the sense of nationhood.

In 1815, Milos Obrenovic led the Serbs in a second, more successful rebellion. One reason for the success was that Obrenovic turned to Russia for assistance. Like the Serbs, the Russian people were Slavic in language and Christian Orthodox in religion. By 1830, Russian support helped the Serbs win autonomy, or self-rule, within the Ottoman empire. The Ottoman sultan later agreed to formal independence. In the future, Russia would continue to defend Serbian interests and affect events in the Balkans.

Independence for Greece In 1821, the Greeks, too, revolted, seeking to end centuries of Ottoman rule. At first, the Greeks were badly divided. But years of suffering in long, bloody wars of independence helped shape a national identity. Leaders of the rebellion justified their struggle as "a national war, a holy war, a war the object of which is to reconquer the rights of individual liberty." They sought help from Western Europeans, who admired ancient Greek civilization.

The Greeks won sympathy in the West. In the late 1820s, Britain, France, and even conservative Russia forced the Ottomans to grant independence to some Greek provinces. By 1830, Greece was independent. The European powers, however, pressured the Greeks to accept a German king, a move meant to show that they did not support revolution. Still, liberals were enthusiastic, and nationalists everywhere saw reasons to hope for a country of their own.

Other Challenges Several other challenges to the Vienna peace settlement erupted in the 1820s. Revolts occurred along the southern fringe of Europe. In Spain, Portugal, and various states in the Italian peninsula, rebels struggled to gain constitutional governments.

Metternich urged conservative rulers to act decisively and crush the dangerous uprisings. In response, a French army marched over the Pyrenees to suppress a revolt in Spain. Austrian forces crossed the Alps to smash rebellious outbreaks in Italy.

Troops dampened the fires of liberalism and nationalism, but could not smother them. In the next decades, sparks would flare anew. Added to liberal and nationalist demands were the goals of the new industrial working class. By the mid-1800s, social reformers and agitators were urging workers to support socialism or other ways of reorganizing property ownership.

SECTION 1 Assessment

Recall
1. **Identify:** (a) conservatives, (b) liberals, (c) nationalists, (d) Karageorge, (e) Milos Obrenovic.
2. **Define:** (a) ideology, (b) universal manhood suffrage, (c) autonomy.

Comprehension
3. What were the goals of conservative leaders?
4. (a) How did the political goals of liberals differ from those of conservatives? (b) How did nationalists threaten the system set up by Metternich?
5. (a) Why did the Serbs and Greeks revolt? (b) Why were there uprisings in Spain, Portugal, and the Italian states?

Critical Thinking and Writing
6. **Applying Information** How did ideologies like liberalism and nationalism contribute to unrest?
7. **Analyzing Information** Why do you think liberals of the early 1800s supported limited voting rights?

Activity
Take It to the NET

On the Internet, find a site that contains some of the writings of Metternich. Print an excerpt that describes one of the key ideas of conservatism. Explain the main idea of the excerpt and explain why Metternich supported this idea.

Revolutions of 1830 and 1848

Reading Focus

- Why did revolutions occur in France in 1830 and 1848?

- How did revolution spread in 1830?

- What were the results of the 1848 revolutions?

Vocabulary

ultraroyalist
recession

Taking Notes

Copy this graphic organizer. As you read, fill in information about conditions before and after the revolutions of 1848.

REVOLUTIONS OF 1848	
Before	**After**
• France is a monarchy	• France is a republic
•	•

Main Idea Revolutions broke out across Europe in 1830 and 1848, but most failed to achieve their goals.

Setting the Scene The quick suppression of liberal and nationalist uprisings in the 1820s did not end Europe's age of revolutions. "We are sleeping on a volcano," warned Alexis de Tocqueville, a liberal French leader who saw widespread discontent. "Do you not see that the Earth trembles anew? A wind of revolution blows, the storm is on the horizon."

In 1830 and 1848, Europeans saw street protests explode into full-scale revolts. As in 1789, the upheavals began in Paris and radiated out across the continent.

The French Revolution of 1830

When the Congress of Vienna restored Louis XVIII to the French throne, he wisely issued a constitution, the Charter of French Liberties. It created a two-house legislature and allowed limited freedom of the press. Still, although Louis was careful to avoid absolutism, the king retained much power.

Sources of Unrest Louis's efforts at compromise satisfied few people. Ultraroyalists, the king's supporters on the far right, despised constitutional government and wanted to restore the old regime. The "ultras" included many high clergy and émigré nobles who had returned to France in the years after the revolution.

The ultras faced bitter opposition from other factions. Liberals wanted to extend suffrage and win a share of power for middle-class citizens like themselves. On the left, radicals yearned for a republic like that of the 1790s. And in working-class slums, men and women wanted what they had wanted in 1789—a decent day's pay and bread they could afford.

The July Revolution When Louis XVIII died in 1824, his younger brother, Charles X, inherited the throne. Charles, a strong believer in absolutism, rejected the very idea of the charter. In July 1830, he suspended the legislature, limited the right to vote, and restricted the press.

Liberals and radicals responded forcefully to the king's challenge. In Paris, angry citizens threw up barricades across the narrow streets. From behind them, they fired on the soldiers and pelted them with stones and roof tiles. Within days, rebels controlled Paris. The revolutionary tricolor flew from the towers of Notre Dame cathedral. A frightened Charles X abdicated and fled to England.

With the king gone, radicals wanted to set up a republic. Moderate liberals, however, insisted on a constitutional monarchy. The Chamber of

Deputies, the lower house of the French legislature, chose Louis Philippe as king. He was a cousin of Charles X and in his youth had supported the revolution of 1789.

The "Citizen King"   The French called Louis Philippe the "citizen king" because he owed his throne to the people. Louis got along well with the liberal bourgeoisie. Like them, he dressed in a frock coat and top hat. Sometimes, he strolled the streets, shaking hands with well-wishers. Liberal politicians and professionals filled his government.

Under Louis Philippe, the upper bourgeoisie prospered. Louis extended suffrage, but only to France's wealthier citizens. The vast majority of the people still could not vote. The king's other policies also favored the middle class at the expense of the workers.

The French Revolution of 1848

In the 1840s, discontent grew. Radicals formed secret societies to work for a French republic. Utopian socialists called for an end to private ownership of property. (See the previous chapter.) Even liberals denounced Louis Philippe's government for corruption and called for expanded suffrage.

Near the end of the decade, discontent was heightened by a recession, or period of reduced economic activity. Factories shut down and people lost their jobs. Poor harvests caused bread prices to rise. Newspapers blamed government officials for some of the problems. As in 1789, Paris was ripe for revolution.

"February Days"   In February 1848, when the government took steps to silence critics and prevent public meetings, angry crowds took to the streets. During the "February Days," iron railings, overturned carts, paving stones, and toppled trees again blocked the streets of Paris. Church bells rang alarms, while women and men on the barricades sang the revolutionary "La Marseillaise." A number of demonstrators clashed with royal troops and were killed.

As the turmoil spread, Louis Philippe abdicated. A group of liberal, radical, and socialist leaders proclaimed the Second Republic. (The First Republic had lasted from 1792 until 1804, when Napoleon became emperor.)

From the start, deep differences divided the new government. Middle-class liberals wanted moderate political reforms. Socialists wanted far-reaching social and economic change that would help hungry workers. In the early days of the new republic, the socialists forced the government to set up national workshops to provide jobs for the unemployed.

"June Days"   By June, however, upper- and middle-class interests had won control of the government. They saw the national workshops as a waste of money, and they shut them down.

Furious, workers took to the streets of Paris, rallying to the cry "Bread or Lead!" This time, however, bourgeois liberals turned violently against the protesters. Peasants, who feared that socialists might take their land, also attacked the rioting workers. At least 1,500 people were killed before the government crushed the rebellion.

The fighting of the "June Days" left a bitter legacy. The middle class both feared and distrusted the left, while the working class nursed a deep hatred for the bourgeoisie.

Louis Napoleon   By the end of 1848, the National Assembly, dominated by members who wanted to restore order, issued a constitution for the Second Republic. It created a strong president and a one-house legislature. But it also gave the vote to all adult men, the widest suffrage in the world at the time. Nine million Frenchmen now could vote, compared with only 200,000 who had that right before.

Art and Revolution

Art became more than an expression of beauty and truth in Europe during the mid-1800s. Many European painters, writers, and composers took an active role in the politics of the time. They used their artistic works to fuel the revolutionary spirit.

French writer Victor Hugo is still revered as a champion of French democracy. His novel *Les Misérables* offers a bleak view of French society in the years leading up to the revolution of 1848. The above poster was created to promote the modern theatrical version of *Les Misérables*.

This painting (above), called *The Uprising*, captures the passion of the French revolutionaries. The painter Honoré Daumier (1808–1879), who was a revolutionary in his own right, used a paintbrush as others might have used a gun or a sword. As a young man, Daumier was imprisoned for drawing caricatures of Emperor Louis Philippe. Daumier's satirical works helped inspire further protests, and much of his work captured the spirit of the revolution he helped to create.

European composers, such as Richard Wagner of Germany (right), also felt the revolutionary spirit and expressed it through their music. The popular music of the day was marked by a new passion and freedom of expression. It seemed to carry the revolutionary and republican spirit through the air.

Portfolio Assessment

INTERNET Using the Internet or library resources, create a display of revolutionary art. You may use works of art, including paintings or drawings. You may choose to illustrate the display with excerpts of revolutionary writings, including poetry, song lyrics, or prose.

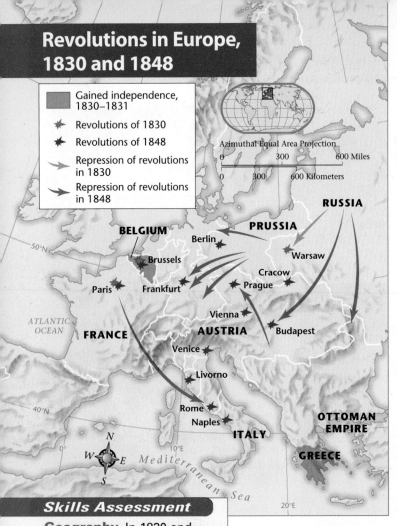

Revolutions in Europe, 1830 and 1848

Legend:
- Gained independence, 1830–1831
- ✦ Revolutions of 1830
- ✦ Revolutions of 1848
- → Repression of revolutions in 1830
- → Repression of revolutions in 1848

Azimuthal Equal Area Projection

0   300   600 Miles
0   300   600 Kilometers

RUSSIA • PRUSSIA • Berlin • Warsaw • Cracow • Prague • BELGIUM • Brussels • Paris • Frankfurt • Vienna • AUSTRIA • Budapest • FRANCE • Venice • Livorno • Rome • Naples • ITALY • OTTOMAN EMPIRE • GREECE • ATLANTIC OCEAN • Mediterranean Sea • 50°N • 40°N • 0° • 10°E • 20°E

Skills Assessment

Geography In 1830 and again in 1848, revolutions in France sparked uprisings throughout Europe. Although most rebellions were quickly crushed, their ideals survived.

1. **Location** On the map, locate *(a)* Paris, *(b)* Warsaw, *(c)* Budapest.
2. **Place** Which countries gained independence in 1830 and 1831?
3. **Critical Thinking Making Inferences** How can you tell from the map that the revolution in Budapest was unsuccessful?

When elections for president were held, the overwhelming winner was Louis Napoleon, nephew of Napoleon Bonaparte. The "new" Napoleon attracted the working classes by presenting himself as a man who cared about social issues such as poverty. At the same time, his famous name, linked with order and past French glory, helped him with conservatives.

Once in office, Louis Napoleon used his position as a steppingstone to greater power. By 1852, he had proclaimed himself emperor, taking the title Napoleon III. (He was the third Napoleon because the son of Napoleon I had died in his youth without ever ruling France.) Thus ended the short-lived Second Republic.

Like his celebrated uncle, Louis Napoleon used a plebiscite to win public approval for his seizure of power. A stunning 90 percent of voters supported his move to set up the Second Empire. Many thought that a monarchy was more stable than a republic. Millions of French hoped that Napoleon III would restore the glory days of Napoleon Bonaparte.

Napoleon III, like Louis Philippe, ruled at a time of rapid economic growth. For the bourgeoisie, the early days of the Second Empire brought prosperity and contentment. In time, however, Napoleon III would embark on foreign adventures that would bring down his empire and end French leadership in Europe.

The Spread of Revolution

In both 1830 and 1848, the revolts in Paris inspired uprisings to break out elsewhere in Europe. As Metternich said, "When France sneezes, Europe catches cold." Most of the uprisings were suppressed by military force. But here and there, rebels did win changes from conservative governments. Even when they failed, revolutions frightened rulers badly enough to encourage reform later in the century.

Belgium The one notable success for Europe's revolutionaries in 1830 took place in Belgium. In 1815, the Congress of Vienna had united the Austrian Netherlands (present-day Belgium) and the Kingdom of Holland under the Dutch king. The Congress had wanted to create a strong barrier to help prevent French expansion in the future.

The Belgians resented the new arrangement. The Belgians and Dutch had different languages, religions, and economic interests. The Belgians were Catholic, while the Dutch were Protestant. The Belgian economy was based on manufacturing; the Dutch, on trade.

In 1830, news of the Paris uprising that toppled Charles X ignited a revolutionary spark in Belgium. Students and workers threw up barricades in Brussels, the capital. The Dutch king turned to the other European powers for help. Britain and France knew that the Belgians were threatening to disrupt the boundaries set up by the Congress of Vienna, but they believed that they would benefit from the separation of Belgium and Holland. They therefore supported Belgian demands for independence. The conservative powers—Austria, Prussia, and Russia—were too busy putting down revolts of their own to help the Dutch king. As a result, in 1831, Belgium became an independent state with a liberal constitution.

Poland Nationalists in Poland also staged an uprising in 1830. But, unlike the Belgians, the Poles failed to win independence for their country.

In the late 1700s, Russia, Austria, and Prussia had divided up Poland. Poles had hoped that the Congress of Vienna would restore their homeland in 1815. Instead, the great powers handed most of Poland to Russia.

In 1830, Polish students, army officers, and landowners rose in revolt. The rebels failed to gain widespread support, however, and were brutally crushed by Russian forces. Some survivors fled to Western Europe and the United States, where they kept alive the dream of freedom.

1848: Another Wave of Rebellion

In 1848, revolts in Paris again unleashed a tidal wave of revolution across Europe. For opponents of the old order, it was a time of such hope that they called it the "springtime of the peoples."

Sources of Discontent Although events in France touched off the revolts, grievances had been piling up for years. Unrest came from many sources. Middle-class liberals wanted a greater share of political power for themselves, as well as protections for the basic rights of all citizens. Workers demanded relief from the miseries of the Industrial Revolution. And nationalists of all classes ached to throw off foreign rule. By 1848, discontent was so widespread that it was only a matter of time before it exploded into full-scale revolution.

Metternich Falls In the Austrian empire, a revolt broke out in Vienna, taking the government by surprise. Metternich, who had dominated Austrian politics for more than 30 years, tried to silence the students who took to the streets. But when workers supported the students, Metternich resigned and fled in disguise. The Austrian emperor then promised reform.

Revolution quickly spread to other parts of the empire. In Budapest, Hungarian nationalists led by Louis Kossuth demanded an independent government. They also called for an end to serfdom and a written constitution to protect basic rights. In Prague, the Czechs made similar demands. Overwhelmed by events, the Austrian government agreed to the reforms.

The gains were temporary. Austrian troops soon regained control of Vienna and Prague. With Russian help, Austrian forces also smashed the rebels in Budapest. Many were imprisoned, executed, or forced into exile.

Revolution in Italy Uprisings also erupted in the Italian states. Nationalists wanted to end domination of Italy by the Austrian Hapsburgs. As elsewhere, nationalist goals were linked to demands for liberal reforms such as constitutional government. Workers suffering economic hardships demanded even more radical changes. From Venice in the north to Naples in the south, Italians set up independent republics. Revolutionaries even expelled the pope from Rome and installed a nationalist government.

Before long, however, the forces of reaction surged back here, too. Austrian troops ousted the new governments in northern Italy. A French army restored the pope to power in Rome. In Naples, local rulers canceled the reforms they had reluctantly accepted.

Turmoil in the German States In the German states, university students passionately demanded national unity and liberal reforms. Economic hard times and a potato famine brought peasants and workers into the struggle. Workers destroyed the machines that threatened their livelihood, while peasants burned the homes of wealthy landowners.

In Prussia, liberals forced King Frederick William IV to agree to a constitution written by an elected assembly. Within a year, though, he dissolved the assembly. Later, he issued his own constitution keeping power in his own hands or those of the upper classes.

THE GREAT SEA SERPENT OF 1848

An Eventful Year
This English cartoon comments on the revolutions of 1848 and the reaction of European rulers.

Theme: Political and Social Systems Based on the cartoon, (a) What ideal caused the revolutions of 1848? (b) How did the revolutions affect Europe's monarchs?

Frankfurt Assembly Throughout 1848, delegates from German states met in the Frankfurt Assembly. "We are to create a constitution for Germany, for the whole land," declared one leader with great optimism.

Divisions soon emerged. Delegates debated endlessly on such topics as whether the new Germany should be a republic or a monarchy, and whether or not to include Austria in a united German state. Finally, the assembly offered Prussia's Frederick William IV the crown of a united Germany. To their dismay, the conservative king rejected the offer because it came not from the German princes but from the people—"from the gutter," as he described it. By early 1849, the assembly was dissolved, under threat from the Prussian military. Outside the assembly, middle-class reformers and workers with radical demands clashed. Conservative forces rallied, dousing the last flames of revolt. Hundreds of people were killed. Many more went to prison. Thousands of Germans left their homeland. Most traveled to the United States, attracted by the young nation's promise of democratic government and economic opportunity.

Looking Ahead

By 1850, rebellion faded, ending the age of liberal revolution that had begun in 1789. Why did the uprisings fail? The rulers' use of military force was just one reason. In general, revolutionaries did not have mass support. In Poland in 1830, for example, peasants did not take part in the uprising. In 1848, a growing gulf divided workers seeking radical economic change and liberals pursuing moderate political reform.

By mid-century, Metternich was gone from the European scene. Still, his conservative system remained in force. In the decades ahead, liberalism, nationalism, and socialism would win successes not through revolution but through political activity. Ambitious political leaders would unify Germany and Italy. Workers would campaign for reforms through unions and the ballot box, as they increasingly won the right to vote.

SECTION 2 Assessment

Recall

1. **Identify:** (a) Charter of French Liberties, (b) Charles X, (c) Louis Philippe, (d) Louis Napoleon, (e) Louis Kossuth, (f) Frankfurt Assembly, (g) Frederick William IV.
2. **Define:** (a) ultraroyalist, (b) recession.

Comprehension

3. Describe one cause and one effect of (a) the French revolution of 1830, (b) the French revolution of 1848.
4. (a) To what lands did revolution spread in 1830? (b) Were these revolutions successful? Explain.

5. Why did most of the revolutions of 1848 fail to achieve their goals?

Critical Thinking and Writing

6. **Identifying Alternatives** Do you think that European rulers could have prevented nationalist revolts by granting autonomy to some groups of people? Why or why not?
7. **Making Decisions** Suppose you had been a conservative adviser to King Frederick William IV of Prussia. Would you have advised the king to accept the crown offered by the Frankfurt Assembly? Explain the reasons for your decision.

Activity
Take It to the NET

In recent years, various ethnic groups have sought independence, just as national groups did in 1830 and 1848. Use the Internet to find news articles about the people of East Timor, Chechnya, Bosnia, or another land where people have struggled to win an independent nation. Write a brief essay describing their struggle.

Latin American Wars of Independence

Reading Focus

- What caused discontent in Latin America?

- How did Haitians, Mexicans, and people in Central America win independence?

- How did the nations of South America win independence?

Vocabulary

peninsular

creole

mestizo

mulatto

truce

Taking Notes

Copy the partially completed table below. As you read, fill in the left column with the names of leaders who led independence movements in Latin America. Fill in the right column with the name of the country or countries that each leader helped liberate.

LEADERS	COUNTRIES
Iturbide	Mexico
San Martín	Argentina, Chile, Peru

Main Idea In the early 1800s, many new nations emerged in Latin America as independence movements freed people from European rule.

Setting the Scene Like many wealthy Latin Americans,* young Simón Bolívar (boh LEE vahr) was sent to Europe to complete his education. There, he became a strong admirer of the ideals of the Enlightenment and the French Revolution.

One afternoon, Bolívar and his Italian tutor sat talking about freedom and the rights that ordinary people should have. Bolívar's thoughts turned to his homeland, held as a colony by Spain. He fell on his knees and swore a solemn oath: "I swear before God and by my honor never to allow my hands to be idle nor my soul to rest until I have broken the chains that bind us to Spain."

In later years, Bolívar would fulfill his oath, leading the struggle to liberate northern South America from Spain. Elsewhere in Latin America, other leaders organized independence movements. By 1825, most of Latin America had been freed from colonial rule.

Sources of Discontent

By the late 1700s, the revolutionary fever that gripped Western Europe had spread to Latin America. There, discontent was rooted in the social, racial, and political system that had emerged during 300 years of Spanish rule.

Ethnic and Social Hierarchy Spanish-born peninsulares dominated Latin American political and social life. Only they could hold top jobs in government and the Church. Many creoles—the European-descended Latin Americans who owned the haciendas, ranches, and mines—bitterly resented their second-class status. Merchants fretted under mercantilist policies that tied the colonies to Spain.

Meanwhile, a growing population of mestizos, people of Native American and European descent, and mulattoes, people of African and European descent, were angry at being denied the status, wealth, and power that were available to whites. Native Americans suffered economic misery under the Spanish, who had conquered the lands of their ancestors. In the Caribbean region and parts of South America, masses of enslaved Africans who worked on plantations longed for freedom.

---

*Latin America refers to the regions in Middle and South America colonized by Europeans, especially the Spanish, French, and Portuguese, whose languages are rooted in Latin. It includes Spanish-speaking countries from Mexico to Argentina, Portuguese-speaking Brazil, and French-speaking Haiti.

The Ruling Class
This is a portrait of Don Tomas Mateo Cervantes, an aristocrat and government official of Cuba in the late 1700s. The portrait was painted by Vincente Escobar, a Cuban of African descent.

Theme: Political and Social Systems How was ethnic background linked to class in Latin America?

Beyond dissatisfaction with Spanish rule, the different classes had little in common. In fact, they distrusted and feared one another. At times, they worked together against the Spanish. But once independence was achieved, the creoles, who had led the revolts, dominated the governments.

Enlightenment Ideas In the 1700s, educated creoles read the works of Enlightenment thinkers. They watched colonists in North America throw off British rule. Translations of the Declaration of Independence and the Constitution of the United States even circulated among the creole elite.

Women actively participated in the exchange of ideas. In some cities, women hosted and attended salons, called tertulias, where independence and revolution were discussed.

During the French Revolution, young creoles like Simón Bolívar traveled in Europe and were inspired by the ideals of "liberty, equality, and fraternity." Despite their admiration for Enlightenment ideas and revolutions in other lands, most creoles were reluctant to act.

Napoleon Bonaparte The spark that finally ignited widespread rebellion in Latin America was Napoleon's invasion of Spain in 1808. Napoleon ousted the Spanish king and placed his brother Joseph on the Spanish throne. In Latin America, leaders saw Spain's weakness as an opportunity to reject foreign domination and demand independence from colonial rule.

Haiti's Struggle for Independence

Even before Spanish colonists hoisted the flag of freedom, revolution had erupted elsewhere in Latin America, in a French-ruled colony on the island of Hispaniola. Haiti, as it is now called, was France's most valued possession in the 1700s.

In Haiti, French planters owned very profitable sugar plantations worked by nearly a half million enslaved Africans. Sugar plantations were labor intensive. The slaves were overworked and underfed. Haiti also had about 25,000 free mulattoes. Many were wealthy, and some also owned slaves. However, they did not have full equality with the French creoles.

A Slave Revolt In the 1790s, revolutionaries in France were debating ways to abolish slavery in the West Indies. However, debating the issue in Paris did not help enslaved Haitians gain their freedom. Embittered by suffering and inspired by the talk of liberty and equality, Haiti's slaves exploded in revolt in 1791.

The rebels were fortunate to find an intelligent and skillful leader in Toussaint L'Ouverture (too SAN loo vuhr TYOOR), a self-educated former slave. Although untrained, Toussaint was a brilliant general. He was also an inspiring commander. On the eve of one crucial battle, he rallied his troops with these stirring words: "We are fighting so that liberty—the most precious of all earthly possessions—may not perish."

The struggle was long and complex. Toussaint's army of former slaves faced many enemies. Some mulattoes joined French planters against the rebels. France, Spain, and Britain each sent armies to Haiti. The fighting took more lives than any other revolution in the Americas.

By 1798, the rebels had achieved their goal; enslaved Haitians had been freed. And even though Haiti was still a French colony, Toussaint's forces controlled most of the island.

Independence In France, meantime, Napoleon Bonaparte rose to power. In 1802, he sent a large army to reconquer Haiti. Toussaint urged Haitians once again to take up arms, this time to fight for full independence from France. The guerrilla forces were aided by a deadly ally, yellow fever, a disease which took a growing toll on the invaders. In April 1802, the French agreed to a truce, or temporary peace.

Geography and History

A Deadly, Microscopic Enemy

French forces in Haiti were up against much more than Toussaint L'Ouverture's brilliant leadership and brave soldiers. They also had to fight an enemy they couldn't see or begin to understand. It was yellow fever.

Soldiers who caught the virus became dizzy and developed high fevers and muscle aches. Their gums would bleed. Many became comatose and eventually died. Historians estimate that of the 33,000 French troops sent to the Caribbean, 29,000 contracted yellow fever within a year.

The source of the disease was the mosquito, so prevalent in tropical Haiti. Mosquitoes can carry the yellow fever virus and transmit it by biting humans.

Might history be different if Haiti were not a tropical island where mosquitoes thrived? Some historians think so. One said simply, "Mosquitoes liberated Haiti."

Theme: Geography and History Why didn't the French take steps to protect themselves from mosquitoes and yellow fever?

Toussaint L'Ouverture on Slavery

In the late 1700s, Toussaint L'Ouverture led a successful revolt in Haiti to eliminate slavery. But Toussaint was haunted by the fear that the French, who still held Haiti as a colony, would try to reestablish slavery. Many French officials, as well as colonists, had already expressed such a desire. Toussaint wrote to the French Directory to oppose any plans to reimpose slavery.

"The attempts on . . . liberty which the colonists propose are all the more to be feared because it is with the veil of patriotism that they cover their detestable plans. We know that they seek to impose some of them on [the French government] by illusory and [deceptive] promises, in order to see renewed in this colony its former scenes of horror. . . . My attachment to France, my knowledge of the blacks, make it my duty not to leave you ignorant either of the crimes which they meditate or the oath that we renew, to bury ourselves under the ruins of a country revived by liberty rather than suffer the return of slavery. . . .

Above, Toussaint L'Ouverture and his army of former slaves battle for independence from France.

Blind as they are! They cannot see how [their] odious conduct . . . can become the signal of new disasters and irreparable misfortunes, and far from making them regain what in their eyes liberty for all has made them lose, they expose themselves to a total ruin and the colony to its inevitable destruction. Do they think that men who have been unable to enjoy the blessing of liberty will calmly see it snatched away? They supported their chains only so long as they did not know any condition of life more happy than that of slavery. But today when they have left it, if they had a thousand lives they would sacrifice them all rather than be forced into slavery again. . . .

But if, to re-establish slavery in [Haiti], this was to be done, then I declare to you it would be to attempt the impossible: we have known how to face dangers to obtain our liberty, we shall know how to brave death to maintain it."

—Toussaint L'Ouverture, quoted in *The Black Jacobins* (James)

Skills Assessment

1. What is the tone of Toussaint's letter?
   - **A** diplomatic
   - **B** peaceful
   - **C** warning
   - **D** friendly

2. What does Toussaint say will happen if the French try to reestablish slavery?
   - **E** The British will take over.
   - **F** The colony will be ruined by war.
   - **G** The blacks will feel resentful.
   - **H** The French will be condemned.

3. **Critical Thinking** **Making Inferences** **(a)** Why do you think Toussaint emphasized that one paragraph in his letter? **(b)** What might you infer about Toussaint himself from this letter?

Skills Tip

Italics in excerpts from old documents may represent underlining or some other form of emphasis in the original document.

Independent Nations of Latin America About 1844

Independent nations with date of independence

*United Provinces of Central America had dissolved by 1841

**Gran Colombia had dissolved by 1830

Azimuthal Equal Area Projection

Latin America About 1790

British

Dutch

French

Portuguese

Spanish

NEW SPAIN
UNITED STATES
Mexico City
BAHAMAS (Br.)
CUBA
HISPANIOLA
West Indies
GUIANAS
Bogotá
NEW GRANADA
BRAZIL
PERU
Lima
LA PLATA
Rio de Janeiro
Buenos Aires

MEXICO 1821
Gulf of Mexico
BAHAMAS (Br.)
HAITI 1804
CUBA (Sp.)
DOMINICAN REPUBLIC 1844
Mexico City
BELIZE (Br.)
JAMAICA (Br.)
PUERTO RICO (Sp.)
GUATEMALA 1839
EL SALVADOR 1839
HONDURAS 1838
NICARAGUA 1838
COSTA RICA 1838
UNITED PROVINCES OF CENTRAL AMERICA*
PANAMA (part of Colombia)
TRINIDAD (Br.)
Caracas
BRITISH GUIANA
DUTCH GUIANA
FRENCH GUIANA
VENEZUELA 1830
Bogotá
COLOMBIA 1819
GRAN COLOMBIA**
Equator 0°
PACIFIC OCEAN
Quito
ECUADOR 1822
PERU 1824
Lima
BRAZIL 1822
La Paz
BOLIVIA 1825
PARAGUAY 1811
Asunción
Rio de Janeiro
20°S
CHILE 1818
ARGENTINA 1816
Buenos Aires
URUGUAY 1828
Montevideo
ATLANTIC OCEAN
Santiago
PATAGONIA
Cape Horn
FALKLAND ISLANDS (Argentine 1820–1833)
80°W   60°W   40°W   20°W   0°
40°S
20°N

Skills Assessment

Geography In the early 1800s, many Latin American nations won independence from European rule.

1. **Location** On the main map, locate **(a)** Mexico, **(b)** Gran Colombia, **(c)** Haiti.
2. **Place** Which nation of South America was once a Portuguese colony?
3. **Critical Thinking** **Synthesizing Information** Why did so many nations of Latin America gain independence by 1830?

Shortly after, the French captured Toussaint and carried him in chains to France. Ten months later, he died there in a cold mountain prison. But Haiti's struggle for freedom continued. In 1804, Haitian leaders declared independence. With yellow fever destroying his army, Napoleon abandoned Haiti. In the following years, rival Haitian leaders fought for power. Finally, in 1820, Haiti became a republic.

Independence for Mexico and Central America

The slave revolt in Haiti frightened creoles in Spanish America. Although they wanted power themselves, most had no desire for economic or social changes that might threaten their way of life. In 1810, however, a creole priest in Mexico, Father Miguel Hidalgo (hih DAHL goh), raised a cry for freedom that would echo across the land.

El Grito de Dolores Father Hidalgo presided over the poor rural parish of Dolores. On September 15, 1810, he rang the church bells summoning the people to prayer. When they gathered, he startled them with an urgent appeal. We do not know his exact words, but his message is remembered: "My children, will you be free? Will you make the effort to recover the lands stolen from your forefathers by the hated Spaniards 300 years ago?" Father Hidalgo's speech became known as "el Grito de Dolores"—the cry of Dolores. It called Mexicans to fight for "Independence and Liberty."

A ragged army of poor mestizos and Native Americans rallied to Father Hidalgo and marched to the outskirts of Mexico City. At first, some creoles supported the revolt. However, they soon rejected Hidalgo's call for an end to slavery and his plea for reforms to improve conditions for Native Americans. They felt that these policies would cost them power.

After some early successes, the rebels faced growing opposition. Less than a year after he issued the "Grito," Hidalgo was captured and executed, and his followers scattered.

José Morelos Another priest picked up the banner of revolution. Father José Morelos was a mestizo who called for wide-ranging social and political reform. He wanted to improve conditions for the majority of Mexicans, abolish slavery, and give the vote to all men. For four years, Morelos led rebel forces before he, too, was captured and shot in 1815.

Spanish forces, backed by conservative creoles, hunted down the surviving guerrillas. They had almost succeeded in ending the rebel movement when events in Spain had unexpected effects on Mexico.

Independence Achieved In Spain in 1820, liberals forced the king to issue a constitution. This move alarmed Agustín de Iturbide (ee toor BEE day), a conservative creole in Mexico. He feared that the new Spanish government might impose liberal reforms on the colonies as well.

Iturbide had spent years fighting Mexican revolutionaries. Suddenly in 1821, he reached out to them. Backed by creoles, mestizos, and Native Americans, he overthrew the Spanish viceroy. Mexico was independent at last. Iturbide took the title Emperor Agustín I. Soon, however, liberal Mexicans toppled the would-be monarch and set up the Republic of Mexico.

Although Mexico was free of Spanish rule, the lives of most people changed little. Military leaders dominated the government and ruled by force of arms. The next 100 years would see new struggles to improve conditions for Mexicans.

New Republics in Central America Spanish-ruled lands in Central America declared independence in the early 1820s. Iturbide tried to add these areas to his Mexican empire. After his overthrow, local leaders set up a republic called the United Provinces of Central America. The union was short-lived. It soon fragmented into the separate republics of Guatemala, Nicaragua, Honduras, El Salvador, and Costa Rica. Like Mexico, the new nations faced many social and economic problems.

Independence in South America

In South America, Native Americans had rebelled against Spanish rule as early as the 1700s. These rebellions had limited results, however. It was not until the 1800s that discontent among the creoles sparked a widespread drive for independence.

A Native American Revolt The strongest challenge to Spanish rule by Native Americans was led by Tupac Amaru, who claimed descent from Incan kings. He demanded that the government end the brutal system of forced Indian labor. Spanish officials rejected the demand for reform. In 1780, Tupac Amaru organized a Native American revolt. A large army crushed the rebels and captured and killed their leader. Still, the revolt did have some positive effects. The Spanish king ordered officials to look into the system of forced labor and eventually abolished it.

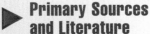

▶ **Primary Sources and Literature**

See "Miguel Hidalgo: Decree of Hidalgo" in the Reference Section at the back of this book.

Connections to Today

Mexican Independence Day

Today, the people of Mexico remember Father Hidalgo's speech as "el Grito de Dolores," which means "the cry of Dolores." Every September 15, the anniversary of the speech, the president of Mexico rings a bell—suggestive of the church bell in Dolores. The president then honors the Grito de Dolores by repeating it.

The next day, September 16, marks the anniversary of the beginning of the fight against the Spanish. It is celebrated as Mexican Independence Day, a national holiday. Schools and businesses shut down, and people throw huge parties. Fireworks light the night sky.

The massive celebration is very different from the event at Dolores that it celebrates, but the spirit of independence is the same.

Theme: Continuity and Change Why is the ringing of bells an important custom of Mexican Independence Day?

Virtual Field Trip

www.phschool.com

The Library of Congress Washington, D.C.

To learn more about the Latin American wars of independence and the history of Chile, use the Internet address above to link to the Library of Congress.

San Martín Crossing the Andes

In this painting, José de San Martín and Bernardo O'Higgins lead their army in a dramatic march over the Andes into Chile. San Martín won independence for Chile when he defeated the Spanish at the battle of Maipú in 1818.

Theme: Geography and History How do you think the successful march across the Andes affected San Martín's army?

Primary Sources and Literature

See "Simón Bolívar: Address to the Congress of Venezuela" in the Reference Section at the back of this book.

Bolívar In the early 1800s, discontent spread across South America. Educated creoles like Simón Bolívar admired the French and American revolutions. They dreamed of winning their own independence from Spain.

In 1808, when Napoleon Bonaparte occupied Spain, Bolívar and his friends saw it as a signal to act. In 1810, Bolívar led an uprising that established a republic in his native Venezuela. Bolívar's new republic was quickly toppled by conservative forces. For years, civil war raged in Venezuela. The revolutionaries suffered many setbacks. Twice Bolívar was forced into exile on the island of Haiti.

Then, Bolívar conceived a daring plan. He would march his army across the Andes and attack the Spanish at Bogotá, the capital of the viceroyalty of New Granada (present-day Colombia). First, he cemented an alliance with the hard-riding *llaneros*, or Venezuelan cowboys. Then, in a grueling campaign, he led an army through swampy lowlands and over the snowcapped Andes. Finally, in August 1819, he swooped down to take Bogotá from the surprised Spanish.

Other victories followed. By 1821, Bolívar had succeeded in freeing Caracas, Venezuela. "The Liberator," as he was now called, then moved south into Ecuador, Peru, and Bolivia. There, he joined forces with another great South American leader, José de San Martín.

San Martín Like Bolívar, San Martín was a creole. He was born in Argentina but went to Europe for military training. In 1816, this gifted general helped Argentina win freedom from Spain. He then joined the independence struggle in other areas. He, too, led an army across the Andes, from Argentina into Chile. He defeated the Spanish in Chile before moving into Peru to strike further blows against colonial rule.

Bolívar and San Martín tried to work together, but their views were too different. In 1822, San Martín stepped aside, letting Bolívar's forces win the final victories against Spain.

Dreams and Disappointments The wars of independence had ended by 1824. Bolívar now worked tirelessly to unite the lands he had liberated into a single nation, called Gran Colombia. Bitter rivalries, however, made that dream impossible. Before long, Gran Colombia split into three independent countries: Venezuela, Colombia, and Ecuador.

Bolívar faced another disappointment as power struggles among rival leaders triggered destructive civil wars. Spain's former South American colonies faced a long struggle to achieve stable governments—and an even longer one for democracy. Before his death in 1830, a discouraged Bolívar wrote, "We have achieved our independence at the expense of everything else." Contrary to his dreams, no social revolution took place. South America's common people had simply changed one set of masters for another.

Independence for Brazil When Napoleon's armies conquered Portugal, the Portuguese royal family fled to Brazil. During his stay in Brazil, the Portuguese king introduced many reforms, including free trade. He encouraged the development of local industries and allowed Brazilian merchants to trade with nations other than Portugal.

When the king returned to Portugal, he left his son Dom Pedro to rule Brazil. "If Brazil demands independence," the king advised Pedro, "proclaim it yourself and put the crown on your own head."

In 1822, Pedro followed his father's advice. A revolution had brought new leaders to Portugal. They planned to abolish the reforms that had benefited Brazil and they demanded that Dom Pedro return to Portugal. Dom Pedro refused to leave and submit to the Portuguese officials. Instead, he became emperor of an independent Brazil. He accepted a constitution that provided for freedom of the press, freedom of religion, and an elected legislature. Brazil remained a monarchy until 1889, when social and political turmoil led it to become a republic.

Cause *and* Effect

Long-Term Causes	Immediate Causes
• European domination of Latin America • Spread of Enlightenment ideas • American and French revolutions • Growth of nationalism in Latin America	• People of Latin America resent colonial rule and social injustices • Revolutionary leaders emerge • Napoleon invades Spain and ousts Spanish king

Independence Movements in Latin America

Immediate Effects	Long-Term Effects
• Toussaint L'Ouverture leads slave revolt in Haiti • Bolívar, San Martín, and others lead successful revolts in Latin America • Colonial rule ends in much of Latin America • Attempts made to rebuild economies	• 18 separate republics set up • Continuing efforts to achieve stable democratic governments and to gain economic independence

Connections to Today

• Numerous independent nations in Latin America
• Ongoing efforts to expand prosperity and democracy in Latin America

Skills Assessment **Chart** The French Revolution and the Napoleonic wars had a lasting impact on Latin America. **What difficulties did Latin Americans face after independence?**

SECTION 3 Assessment

Recall

1. **Identify:** (a) Toussaint L'Ouverture, (b) Miguel Hidalgo, (c) el Grito de Dolores, (d) José Morelos, (e) Tupac Amaru, (f) Simón Bolívar, (g) Dom Pedro.
2. **Define:** (a) peninsular, (b) creole, (c) mestizo, (d) mulatto, (e) truce.

Comprehension

3. How did social structure contribute to discontent in Latin America?
4. (a) What was the first step on Haiti's road to independence?

(b) Why did creoles refuse to support Hidalgo or Morelos?
5. How did successful military campaigns lead to the creation of independent nations in South America?

Critical Thinking and Writing

6. **Comparing** Compare the ways in which Mexico and Brazil achieved independence.
7. **Connecting to Geography** Review the subsection Independence in South America and the map in this section. How does the map show that Bolívar failed to achieve one of his dreams?

Activity

Creating a Poster
Imagine that you are an artist in the service of Bolívar or San Martín. You have been hired to create a poster urging people to join the armies fighting against Spain. Your poster should highlight the goals of the revolutionary armies. It should also be eye-catching and convincing.

UNIT 6

Industrialism and a New Global Age

1800–1914

OUTLINE

Themes

As you read about imperialism and the new global age, you will encounter the following themes.

Diversity Rulers strengthened their nations by incorporating surrounding states and colonies. Conflicts arose as new subjects, often of different ethnic backgrounds, demanded independence. Women struggled to end restrictions on their lives and gain recognition of their rights.

Economics and Technology Developing factory systems, improved transportation and communication, and scientific advances contributed to overseas expansion by European powers. Industrialized nations grew wealthy, often at the expense of colonies.

Impact of the Individual Nationalist leaders in Italy and Germany used warfare and political alliances to forge new nations out of fragmented provinces.

Political and Social Systems In the 1800s, as the middle class grew, democratic rights were extended in Britain, France, and the United States. Urbanization and the impact of industrialization led to major changes in social values.

Unit Theme Activity

For Your Portfolio The chapters in this unit describe the effects of developing technology on national growth. As you read the chapters, prepare a portfolio project showing the significance of industrialization to imperialism. Your project might take one of the following forms:
• Editorial
• Debate
• Time line

The Gateway of India was built in 1911 to honor the visit of King George V and Queen Mary to India. Located on the harbor of Mumbai (Bombay), it combines Indian, Islamic, and Persian styles of art and architecture.

WHY STUDY HISTORY?

Because the Past Has an Impact on Us Today

Most of us take the marvels of our modern world for granted. Without a second thought, we microwave a frozen pizza, watch TV, fly in airplanes, surf the Net. But these "new" inventions did not come about overnight, in a single inspired flash. Instead, over decades, or even centuries, innovators have built on the discoveries and ideas of the past. The process continues today. Our twenty-first-century achievements will serve as building blocks for even more amazing technology in the future.

Architects Defy Gravity

In the 1890s, in Chicago, architects built the 16-story Reliance Building—one of the world's first "skyscrapers" (left). Elevators made it practical for the first time to erect a building of more than 6 stories, and the use of steel made it possible for the frame to carry the weight of the building. Chicagoans of the time marveled at the structure's light and airy facade, composed almost entirely of windows. The Reliance Building is considered the direct ancestor of today's glass-and-steel skyscrapers, such as the Petronas Towers in Kuala Lumpur (right), which rise 88 stories, or 1,453 feet, in the air.

Easing Human Suffering

In 1859, Jean Henri Dunant, a Swiss banker, witnessed a battle during the Italian war for independence. Horrified at the suffering, Dunant helped to organize the International Red Cross to care for battle victims. One of the first groups of Red Cross volunteers, during the Franco-Prussian War in 1870, is shown above at left. Later, the Red Cross expanded its mission to include prevention and relief of human suffering generally. Today, the Red Cross operates in more than 100 countries. In the picture above at right, Red Cross workers join the relief effort in Puebla, Mexico, after a devastating earthquake in 1999.

Trains— Fast and Faster!

The invention of the steam-powered locomotive (above) in the early 1800s revolutionized transportation. Pulled by these massive engines, early railroad trains moved at what seemed startling speed—nearly 40 miles an hour! For more than a century, railroads enjoyed enormous success, carrying tons of freight and millions of passengers each year. Then, in the late 1900s, automobiles and airplanes eroded the popularity of rail travel. Today, thanks to new technology, people are turning once again to the railroad. The reason? High-speed trains, such as the streamlined French "bullet train"(right), now achieve speeds of nearly 200 miles per hour!

Portfolio Assessment

Connecting to Today List three features of modern life that you might research to discover their roots in the past. Describe your plan for conducting the research on one of them.

Life in the Industrial Age 1800–1914

Chapter Preview

CHAPTER EVENTS

Early 1800s
Romanticism shapes western art and literature. Painters such as J.M.W. Turner seek to glorify nature and stir powerful emotions.

1807
First factories open in Belgium, setting off the Industrial Revolution on the European continent.

1839
French inventor Louis Daguerre perfects an effective method of photography.

1790

1815

1840

GLOBAL EVENTS

1819 Simón Bolívar establishes Gran Colombia.

1842 The Treaty of Nanjing gives Britain trading rights in China.

Industrial Growth, 1800–1900

From its beginnings in eighteenth-century Britain, the Industrial Revolution spread through Europe and beyond.

NORTH AMERICA

EUROPE

ASIA

ATLANTIC OCEAN

AFRICA

INDIAN OCEAN

PACIFIC OCEAN

SOUTH AMERICA

AUSTRALIA

Industrializing by 1800
Industrializing by 1850
Industrializing by 1900

Robinson Projection

0   1500   3000 Miles
0   1500   3000 Kilometers

1859
Charles Darwin publishes *On the Origin of Species*. His theory of evolution is denounced by many religious leaders.

1869
Germany legalizes labor unions.

1903
Wilbur and Orville Wright demonstrate the first airplane at Kitty Hawk, North Carolina.

1865

1890

1915

1861 Czar Alexander II emancipates Russian serfs.

1884 European nations carve up Africa at the Berlin Conference.

1914 The Panama Canal opens.

The Industrial Revolution Spreads

Reading Focus

- What industrial powers emerged in the 1800s?

- What impact did new technology have on industry, transportation, and communication?

- How did big business emerge in the late 1800s?

Vocabulary

dynamo

interchangeable parts

assembly line

stock

corporation

cartel

Taking Notes

Copy the diagram below. As you read, fill in the major developments of the Industrial Revolution.

THE SECOND INDUSTRIAL REVOLUTION			
Countries • Belgium • Germany •	**Methods of production**		

Main Idea The second Industrial Revolution was marked by the spread of industry, the development of new technologies, and the rise of big business.

Setting the Scene By the 1880s, steel had replaced steam as the great symbol of the Industrial Revolution. Steel girders could support stronger bridges and taller buildings. Steel rails could carry faster steel railway cars. In huge steel mills, visitors watched with awe as tons of molten metal were poured into giant mixers:

> "At night the scene is indescribably wild and beautiful. The flashing fireworks, the terrific gusts of heat, the gaping, glowing mouth of the giant chest, the quivering light from the liquid iron, the roar of a near-by converter . . . combine to produce an effect on the mind that no words can translate."
> —J. H. Bridge, *History of the Carnegie Steel Company*

The first phase of industrialization had largely been forged from iron, powered by steam engines, and driven by the British textile industry. By the mid-1800s, the Industrial Revolution entered a new phase. New industrial powers emerged. New factories powered by new sources of energy used new processes to turn out new products. And new forms of business organization contributed to the rise of giant new companies. As the twentieth century dawned, this second Industrial Revolution transformed the economies of the western world.

New Industrial Powers

During the early Industrial Revolution, Britain stood alone as the world's industrial giant. To protect its head start, Britain tried to enforce strict rules against exporting inventions.

For a while, the rules worked. Then, in 1807, British mechanic William Cockerill opened factories in Belgium to manufacture spinning and weaving machines. Belgium became the first European nation outside Britain to industrialize. By the mid-1800s, other nations had joined the race, and several newcomers were challenging Britain's industrial supremacy.

The New Pacesetters How were other nations able to catch up to Britain so quickly? First, nations such as Germany, France, and the United States had more abundant supplies of coal, iron, and other resources than did Britain. Also, they had the advantage of being able to follow Britain's lead. Like Belgium, latecomers often borrowed British experts or technology. The first American textile factory was built in Pawtucket, Rhode Island, with plans smuggled out of Britain. American inventor Robert Fulton powered his steamboat with one of James Watt's steam engines.

Two countries in particular thrust their way to industrial leadership. Germany united into a powerful nation in 1871. (See the next chapter.) Within a few decades, it became Europe's leading industrial power. Across the Atlantic, the United States advanced even more rapidly, especially after the Civil War. By 1900, American industry led the world in production.

Uneven Development   Other nations industrialized more slowly, particularly those in eastern and southern Europe. These nations often lacked natural resources or the capital to invest in industry. Although Russia did have resources, social and political conditions slowed its economic development. Only in the late 1800s, more than 100 years after Britain, did Russia lumber toward industrialization.

In East Asia, however, Japan offered a remarkable success story. Although it lacked many basic resources, it industrialized rapidly after 1868. Canada, Australia, and New Zealand also built thriving industries.

Impact   Like Britain, the new industrial nations underwent social changes, such as rapid urbanization. Men, women, and children worked long hours in difficult and dangerous conditions. As you will read, by 1900, these conditions had begun to improve in many industrialized nations.

The factory system produced huge quantities of new goods at lower prices than ever before. In time, workers were buying goods that in earlier times only the wealthy could afford. The demand for goods created jobs, as did the building of cities, railroads, and factories. Politics changed, too, as leaders had to meet the demands of an industrial society.

Globally, industrial nations competed fiercely, altering patterns of world trade. Thanks to their technological and economic advantage, western powers came to dominate the world more than ever before, as you will read.

Skills Assessment

Geography Deposits of raw material such as iron and coal could be the key to a nation's industrial success.

1. **Location** On the map, locate **(a)** Belgium, **(b)** Germany, **(c)** Saar, **(d)** Ruhr.
2. **Interaction** Which American city probably grew because of its location near coal fields?
3. **Critical Thinking Applying Information** Why would you expect Lyon, France, to become a major industrial city?

Centers of Industry, 1871

United States

- • Major industrial cities
- ■ Iron ore deposits
- ▨ Coal fields

Technology and Industry

During the early Industrial Revolution, inventions such as the steam engine were generally the work of gifted tinkerers. They experimented with simple machines to make them better. By the 1880s, the pace of change quickened as companies hired professional chemists and engineers to create new products and machinery. The marriage of science, technology, and industry spurred economic growth.

Steel In 1856, British engineer Henry Bessemer developed a process to purify iron ore and produce a new substance, steel. Steel was lighter, harder, and more durable than iron. Others improved on the Bessemer process, so steel could be produced very cheaply. It rapidly became the major material used in tools, bridges, and railroads.

As steel production soared, industrialized countries measured their success in steel output. In 1880, for example, the average German steel mill produced less than five million metric tons of steel a year. By 1910, that figure had reached nearly fifteen million metric tons.

Chemicals Chemists created hundreds of new products, from medicines such as aspirin to perfumes and soaps. Newly developed chemical fertilizers played a key role in increasing food production.

In 1866, the Swedish chemist Alfred Nobel invented dynamite, an explosive much safer than others used at the time. It was widely used in construction and, to Nobel's dismay, in warfare. Dynamite earned Nobel a huge fortune, which he willed to fund the famous Nobel prizes that are still awarded today.

Electricity In the late 1800s, a new power source—electricity—replaced steam as the dominant source of industrial power. Scientists like Benjamin Franklin had tinkered with electricity a century earlier. The Italian scientist Alessandro Volta developed the first battery about 1800. Later, the English chemist Michael Faraday created the first simple electric motor and the first dynamo, a machine that generates electricity. Today, all electrical generators and transformers work on the principle of Faraday's dynamo.

In the 1870s, the American inventor Thomas Edison made the first electric light bulb. Soon, Edison's "incandescent lamps" illuminated whole cities. The pace of city life quickened, and factories could continue to operate after dark. By the 1890s, cables carried electrical power from dynamos to factories.

New Methods of Production The basic features of the factory system remained the same during the 1800s. Factories still used large numbers of workers and power-driven machines to mass-produce goods. To improve efficiency, however, manufacturers designed products with interchangeable parts, identical components that could be used in place of one another. Interchangeable parts simplified both assembly and repair.

By the early 1900s, manufacturers introduced another new method of production, the assembly line. Workers on an assembly line add parts to a product that moves along a belt from one work station to the next. Like interchangeable parts, the assembly line made production faster and cheaper, lowering the price of goods.

Technology Speeds Transportation and Communication

During the second Industrial Revolution, transportation and communications were transformed by technology. Steamships replaced sailing ships, and railroad building took off. In Europe and North America, rail lines connected inland cities and seaports, mining regions and industrial centers. In

When the Lights Go Out

The role of electric power in our lives has come a long way since the days of Thomas Edison. In December 1998, residents of San Francisco found out just how much their lives depend on electricity. When mistakes during a routine repair led to a widespread power outage, more than one million people were affected for seven hours. Lights and elevators stopped working in skyscrapers, and workers had to carefully make their way down darkened stairways. Others were trapped on trains or stuck in traffic jams caused by nonfunctioning traffic lights. Business slowed when phone systems crashed, computerized cash registers could not ring up sales, and ATM machines went down. With today's linked power grids, such blackouts have the potential to disrupt the lives of millions of people across county and state lines.

Theme: Economics and Technology What economic effects might a power outage have?

Comparing Viewpoints

Is Technology a Blessing or a Curse?

After the second Industrial Revolution, technology began to have an increasing influence on people's lives. Does technology always benefit us, or can it have some harmful effects? Think about the influence of technology as you compare the following viewpoints.

United States 1876

Writer William Dean Howells attended the Centennial Exposition in Philadelphia. He marveled at Machinery Hall, filled with examples of recent American technology:

66 The superior elegance, aptness, and ingenuity of our machinery is observable at a glance. Yes, it is still in these things of iron and steel that the national genius speaks most freely; by and by the inspired marbles, the breathing canvases, the great literature [will be recognized]; for the present America is [expressed] in the strong metals and their infinite uses. 99

India 1955

After India's independence, Prime Minister Jawaharlal Nehru commented on its need for industrial development:

66 There can be no real well-being or advance in material standards in India without the big factory. I shall venture to say that we cannot even maintain our freedom and independence as a nation without the big factory and all it represents. 99

South Africa 1986

This cartoon uses imagery borrowed from the pyramid builders of ancient Egypt to comment on modern technology.

BERRY
THE STAR
Johannesburg
SOUTH AFRICA

CARTOONISTS & WRITERS SYNDICATE http://CartoonWeb.com

Japan 1984

Ikeda Daisaku spoke of the effects of technology from the viewpoint of a Buddhist philosopher:

66 The man who rides in a car all of the time loses the ability to walk long distances vigorously. Even when we employ mechanical devices, we must realize that it is we humans who are at the controls and that whether the machine is a blessing or a curse depends on what is inside us. 99

Skills Assessment

1. The viewpoints most favorable toward technology are expressed by
   A Howells and Daisaku.
   B Nehru and Daisaku.
   C Howells and Nehru.
   D Nehru and the cartoon.

2. Ikeda Daisaku would probably agree with the cartoonist that technology
   E can rule people.
   F expresses the ideals of a nation.
   G is key to economic development.
   H is always destructive.

3. **Critical Thinking Making Decisions** Decide whether you think technology is a blessing or a curse in today's society. Write a short essay explaining your point of view. Be sure to provide several clear examples to support your decision.

Skills Tip

A person's point of view may be influenced by such factors as time and place of birth, historical period, occupation, economic status, religious values, and political opinions.

One View of Big Business
To some critics, the growth of monopolies had a dangerous effect on society. This American cartoon of 1899 shows a monopoly as an octopus-like monster.

Theme: Economics and Technology Do you think this cartoonist favored or opposed government regulation of business? Explain.

gaining control of oil wells, oil refineries, and oil pipelines, he dominated the American petroleum industry.

In their pursuit of profit, ruthless business leaders destroyed competing companies. Then, with the competition gone, they were free to raise prices to any level. Sometimes, a group of large corporations would join forces and form a cartel, an association to fix prices, set production quotas, or control markets. In Germany, a single cartel fixed prices for 170 coal mines. An international shipping cartel of British, German, French, Dutch, and Japanese shippers came close to setting freight rates on the sea lines of the world.

Move Toward Regulation The rise of big business and the creation of such great wealth sparked a stormy debate. Some people saw the Krupps and Rockefellers as "captains of industry and praised their vision and skills. They pointed out that capitalists invested their wealth in worldwide ventures, such as railroad building, that employed thousands of workers and added to general prosperity.

To others, the aggressive magnates were "robber barons." Any effort to destroy competition, critics argued, damaged the free-enterprise system. Reformers called for laws to prevent monopolies and regulate large corporations. By the early 1900s, some governments did move against monopolies. However, the political and economic power of business leaders often hindered efforts at regulation.

Looking Ahead

By the late 1800s, European and American corporations were setting up factories, refineries, and other production facilities around the world. Banks, too, were involved in this global economy. They invested vast sums—the money coming from rich and small depositors—in undertakings such as building ports, railroads, and canals. As western capital flowed into Africa, Asia, and Latin America, western governments became increasingly involved in these areas.

SECTION 1 Assessment

Recall
1. **Identify:** (a) Bessemer process, (b) Alfred Nobel, (c) Michael Faraday, (d) Thomas Edison, (e) Henry Ford, (f) Orville and Wilbur Wright, (g) Guglielmo Marconi, (h) Alfred Krupp.
2. **Define:** (a) dynamo, (b) interchangeable parts, (c) assembly line, (d) stock, (e) corporation, (f) cartel.

Comprehension
3. How did the Industrial Revolution spread in the 1800s?

4. How did technology help industry expand?
5. How did the need for capital lead to new business methods?

Critical Thinking and Writing
6. **Connecting to Geography** "The availability of natural resources is the most important condition for industrialization." Do you agree or disagree? Explain.
7. **Ranking** Which three technological advances in this section do you think were the most important? Explain.

Activity

Drawing a Political Cartoon Draw a political cartoon that might have appeared in a newspaper in the late 1800s. In your cartoon, take a stand for or against the passage of laws to prevent monopolies or regulate big business.

Reading Focus

- What was the impact of medical advances in the late 1800s?
- How had cities changed by 1900?
- How did working-class struggles lead to improved conditions for workers?

Vocabulary

germ theory

urban renewal

mutual-aid society

standard of living

Taking Notes

As you read, prepare an outline of this section. Use Roman numerals to indicate the major headings, capital letters for the subheadings, and numbers for the supporting details. The sample at right will help you get started.

I. Medicine and population
  A. The fight against disease
    1.
    2.
  B. In the hospital
    1.
    2.
II. The life of the cities

Main Idea   The population of cities grew as people moved to urban centers for jobs.

Setting the Scene In the 1870s, a citizen of Berlin, Germany, boasted of his city's rapid growth. "We have already 800,000 inhabitants, next year we shall have 900,000, and the year after that a million." He predicted that Berlin's population would soon rival those of Paris and even London.

The population explosion that had begun during the 1700s continued through the 1800s. Cities grew as rural people streamed into urban areas. By the end of the century, European and American cities had begun to take on many of the features of cities today.

Medicine and Population

Between 1800 and 1900, the population of Europe more than doubled. This rapid growth was not due to larger families. In fact, families in most industrializing countries had fewer children. Instead, populations soared because the death rate fell. People ate better, thanks in part to improved methods of farming, food storage, and distribution. Medical advances and improvements in public sanitation also slowed death rates.

The Fight Against Disease Since the 1600s, scientists had known of microscopic organisms, or microbes. Some scientists speculated that certain microbes might cause specific infectious diseases. Yet most doctors scoffed at this germ theory. Not until 1870 did French chemist Louis Pasteur clearly show the link between microbes and disease. Pasteur went on to make other major contributions, including the development of vaccines against rabies and anthrax and the discovery of a process called pasteurization, named after him, for killing disease-carrying microbes in milk.

In the 1880s, the German doctor Robert Koch identified the bacteria that caused tuberculosis, a respiratory disease that claimed about 30 million human lives in the 1800s. The search for a tuberculosis cure, however, took half a century. By 1914, yellow fever and malaria had been traced to microbes carried by mosquitoes.

As people understood how germs caused disease, they bathed and changed their clothes more often. In western cities, better hygiene caused a marked drop in the rate of disease and death.

FACT FINDER

Average Life Expectancy in Selected Industrial Areas, 1850–1910

Year	Male	Female
1850	40.3 years	42.8 years
1870	42.3 years	44.7 years
1890	45.8 years	48.5 years
1910	52.7 years	56.0 years

Source: E. A. Wrigley, *Population and History* (based on data for parts of Western Europe and the United States)

Skills Assessment

Chart Improved medicine and sanitation played a major role in increasing life expectancy in the industrialized world. **Between 1850 and 1910, how much did life expectancy increase for men? For women?**

In the Hospital In the early 1840s, anesthesia was first used to relieve pain during surgery. The use of anesthetics allowed doctors to experiment with operations that had never before been possible.

Yet, throughout the century, hospitals could be dangerous places. Surgery was performed with dirty instruments in dank operating rooms. Often, a patient would survive an operation, only to die days later of infection. For the poor, being admitted to a hospital was often a death sentence. Wealthy or middle-class patients insisted on treatment in their own homes.

"The very first requirement in a hospital," said British nurse Florence Nightingale, "is that it should do the sick no harm." As an army nurse during the Crimean War, Nightingale insisted on better hygiene in field hospitals. After the war, she worked to introduce sanitary measures in British hospitals. She also founded the world's first school of nursing.

The English surgeon Joseph Lister discovered how antiseptics prevented infection. He insisted that surgeons wash their hands before operating and sterilize their instruments. Eventually, the use of antiseptics drastically reduced deaths from infection.

The Life of the Cities

As industrialization progressed, cities came to dominate the West. City life, as old as civilization itself, underwent dramatic changes.

The Changing City Landscape Growing wealth and industrialization altered the basic layout of western cities. City planners gouged out spacious new squares and boulevards. They lined these avenues with government buildings, offices, department stores, and theaters.

The most extensive urban renewal, or rebuilding of the poor areas of a city, took place in Paris in the 1850s. Georges Haussmann, chief planner for Napoleon III, destroyed many tangled medieval streets full of tenement housing. In their place, he built wide boulevards and splendid public buildings. The project put many people to work, decreasing the threat of social unrest. The wide boulevards also made it harder for rebels to put up barricades and easier for troops to reach any part of the city.

Gradually, settlement patterns shifted. In most American cities, the rich lived in pleasant neighborhoods on the outskirts of the city. The poor crowded into slums near the city center, within reach of factories. Trolley lines made it possible to live in one part of the city and work in another.

Sidewalks, Sewers, and Skyscrapers Paved streets made urban areas much more livable. First gas lamps, then electric street lights, increased safety at night. Cities organized police forces and expanded fire protection.

Beneath the streets, sewage systems made cities healthier places to live. City planners knew that clean water supplies were needed to combat epidemics of cholera and tuberculosis. The massive new sewer systems of London and Paris were costly, but they cut death rates dramatically.

By 1900, architects were using steel to construct soaring buildings. The steel Eiffel Tower became a symbol of Paris. American architects like Louis Sullivan pioneered a new structure, the skyscraper. In large cities, single-family middle-class homes gave way to multistory apartment buildings.

Slums Despite efforts to improve cities, urban life remained harsh for the poor. Some working-class families could afford better clothing, newspapers, or tickets to a music hall. But they went home to small, cramped row houses or tenements in overcrowded neighborhoods.

In the worst tenements, whole families were often crammed into a single room. Unemployment or illness meant lost wages that could ruin a family. High rates of crime and alcoholism were a constant curse. Conditions had improved somewhat from the early Industrial Revolution, but slums remained a fact of city life.

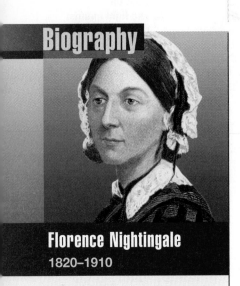

The Lure of the City   Despite their drawbacks, cities attracted millions. New residents were drawn as much by the excitement as by the promise of work. For tourists, too, cities were magnetic centers of action. One reporter described the hustle and bustle of holiday crowds in London:

> "Cyclists of both sexes covered the roads. River steamers and pleasure boats carried their thousands to Kew and the upper reaches of the Thames. The London parks were crowded. The Botanic Gardens and Zoological Gardens formed great attractions, and the flowers of Battersea Park drew large crowds all day."
>
> —*Times* (London), quoted in *Crises in English History, 1066–1945* (Henning)

Music halls, opera houses, and theaters provided entertainment for every taste. Museums and libraries offered educational opportunities. Sports, from tennis to bare-knuckle boxing, drew citizens of all classes. Few of these enjoyments were available in country villages.

Working-Class Struggles

Workers tried to improve the harsh conditions of industrial life. They protested low wages, long hours, unsafe conditions, and the constant threat of unemployment. At first, business owners and governments tried to silence protesters. Strikes and unions were illegal. Demonstrations were crushed.

By mid-century, workers slowly began to make progress. They formed **mutual-aid societies,** self-help groups to aid sick or injured workers. Men and women joined socialist parties or organized unions. The revolutions of 1830 and 1848 left vivid images of worker discontent.

By the late 1800s, most western countries had granted all men the vote. Workers also won the right to organize unions to bargain on their behalf.

The Lure of a City
The photograph of Paris in 1900 (bottom) shows two of its most famous attractions—the Eiffel Tower and a giant Ferris wheel. The city also won worldwide fame for its theaters, music halls, museums, and circuses.

Theme: Continuity and Change   How might this photograph of Paris look different if it were taken today?

Cause *and* Effect

Causes

- Increased agricultural productivity
- Growing population
- New sources of energy, such as steam and coal
- Growing demand for textiles and other mass-produced goods
- Improved technology
- Available natural resources, labor, and money
- Strong, stable governments that promoted economic growth

Industrial Revolution

Immediate Effects	Long-Term Effects
• Rise of factories • Changes in transportation and communication • Urbanization • New methods of production • Rise of urban working class • Growth of reform movements	• Growth of labor unions • Inexpensive new products • Spread of industrialization • Rise of big business • Expansion of public education • Expansion of middle class • Competition for world trade among industrialized nations • Progress in medical care

Connections to Today

- Improvements in world health
- Growth in population
- Industrialization in developing nations
- New energy sources, such as oil and nuclear power
- Mass media and mass entertainment
- Efforts to regulate world trade

Skills Assessment **Chart** The long-term effects of the Industrial Revolution touched nearly every aspect of life. **Identify two social and two economic effects of the Industrial Revolution.**

Germany legalized labor unions in 1869. Britain, Austria, and France followed. Unions grew rapidly. In France, membership grew from 140,000 in 1890 to over a million in 1912.

Pressured by unions, reformers, and working-class voters, governments passed laws to regulate working conditions. Over time, laws were passed outlawing child labor and banning the employment of women in mines. Other laws limited work hours and improved safety. By 1909, British coal miners had won an eight-hour day, setting a standard for workers in other countries.

First in Germany, and then elsewhere, western governments established old-age pensions, as well as disability insurance for workers who were hurt or became ill. These programs protected workers from poverty once they were no longer able to work.

Rising Standards of Living Wages varied throughout the industrialized world, with unskilled laborers earning much less than skilled workers. Women received less than half the pay of men doing the same work. Farm laborers barely scraped by during the economic slump of the late 1800s. Periods of unemployment brought desperate hardships to industrial workers and helped boost union membership.

Overall, though, standards of living for workers did rise. The standard of living measures the quality and availability of necessities and comforts in a society. Families ate more varied diets, lived in better homes, and dressed in inexpensive, mass-produced clothing. Advances in medicine improved health. Some workers moved to suburbs, traveling to work on subways and trams. Still, the gap between workers and the middle class widened.

SECTION 2 Assessment

Recall

1. **Identify:** (a) Louis Pasteur, (b) Robert Koch, (c) Florence Nightingale, (d) Joseph Lister.
2. **Define:** (a) germ theory, (b) urban renewal, (c) mutual-aid society, (d) standard of living.

Comprehension

3. Why did the rate of population growth increase in the late 1800s?
4. Describe three ways that city life changed in the 1800s.

5. What laws helped workers in the late 1800s?

Critical Thinking and Writing

6. **Analyzing Information** What were the advantages and disadvantages of city life in the late 1800s?
7. **Linking Past and Present** By the early 1900s, governments had passed many laws that improved conditions for the working class. What are some laws that regulate working conditions today?

Activity

Writing a Letter
You have moved from a rural village to London or Paris in the late 1800s. Write a letter home describing your feelings about city life. Suggest both positive and negative aspects.

Changing Attitudes and Values

Reading Focus

- What values shaped the new social order?
- How did women and educators seek change?
- How did science challenge existing beliefs?
- What role did religion play in urban society?

Vocabulary

cult of domesticity

temperance movement

women's suffrage

racism

social gospel

Taking Notes

Copy this chart. As you read, list new attitudes and values in the left-hand column. List supporting details in the right-hand column.

CHANGES IN ATTITUDES AND VALUES

1. A new social order	• Upper class—old nobility, new industrialists, and business families
	•
2. Middle-class values	•
3.	•

Main Idea | The Industrial Revolution changed the social order in the western world, and new ideas challenged long-held traditions.

Setting the Scene

"Once a woman has accepted an offer of marriage, all she has . . . becomes virtually the property of the man she has accepted as husband." This advice appeared in an 1859 British publication called *The What-Not or Ladies' Handbook*. But not all women accepted such restrictions. One Italian crusader for women's rights denounced the inferior legal status of women:

> "For her, taxes but not an education; for her, sacrifices but not employment; . . . strong enough to be laden with an array of painful duties, but sufficiently weak not to be allowed to govern herself."
>
> —Anna Mazzoni, *La Liberazione della Donna*

Demand for women's rights was one of many issues that challenged the traditional social order in the late 1800s. By then, the social order itself was changing. In many countries, the middle class increasingly came to dominate society.

A New Social Order

The Industrial Revolution slowly changed the old social order in the western world. For centuries, the two main classes were nobles and peasants. Their roles were defined by their relationship to the land. While middle-class merchants, artisans, lawyers, and officials played important roles, they still occupied a secondary position in society. With the spread of industry, a more complex social structure emerged.

By the late 1800s, Western Europe's new upper class included superrich industrial and business families as well as the old nobility. Wealthy entrepreneurs married into aristocratic families, gaining the status of noble titles. Nobles needed the money brought by the industrial rich to support their lands and lifestyle. By tradition, the upper class held the top jobs in government and the military.

Below this tiny elite, a growing middle class was pushing its way up the social ladder. Its highest rungs were filled with midlevel business people and professionals such as doctors, scientists, and lawyers. With comfortable incomes, they enjoyed a wide range of material goods. Next came the lower middle class, which included teachers, office workers, shopkeepers, and clerks. Even though they earned much smaller incomes, they struggled to keep up with their "betters."

At the base of the social ladder were workers and peasants. In highly industrialized Britain, workers made up more than 30 percent of the population in 1900. In Western Europe and the United States, the number of farmworkers dropped, but many families still worked the land. The rural population was even higher in eastern and southern Europe, where industrialization was limited.

Middle-Class Values

By mid-century, the modern middle class had developed its own way of life. The nuclear family lived in a large house, or perhaps in one of the new apartment houses. Rooms were crammed with large overstuffed furniture, and paintings and photographs lined the walls. Clothing reflected middle-class tastes for luxury and respectability. A strict code of etiquette governed social behavior. Rules dictated how to dress for every occasion, how to give a dinner party, how to pay a social call, when to write letters, and how long to mourn for relatives who died.

Parents strictly supervised their children, who were expected to be "seen but not heard." A child who misbehaved was considered to reflect badly on the entire family. Servants, too, were seen as a reflection of their employers. Even a small middle-class household was expected to have at least a cook and a housemaid.

Courtship and Marriage As in the past, middle-class families had a large say in choosing whom their children married. At the same time, young people had more freedom to choose a marriage partner. The notion of "falling in love" was more accepted than ever before.

Yet most women and men carefully considered the practical side of marriage. Mothers and daughters discussed the "likely prospects" of a possible husband. A young man was expected to court his bride-to-be with tender sentiments, but he also had to convince her father that he could support her in style. Until the late 1800s in most western countries, a husband controlled his wife's property, so marriage contracts were drawn up to protect a daughter's property rights.

The Ideal Home Within the family circle, the division of labor between wife and husband changed. In earlier times, middle-class women had often helped run family businesses out of the home. By the later 1800s, most middle-class husbands went to work in an office or shop. A successful husband was one whose income was enough to keep his wife at home. Women spent their working hours raising children, directing the servants, and perhaps doing religious or charitable service.

Books, magazines, and popular songs supported a cult of domesticity that idealized women and the home. Sayings like "home, sweet home" were stitched into needlework and hung on parlor walls. The ideal woman was seen as a tender, self-sacrificing caregiver who provided a nest for her children and a peaceful refuge for her husband.

This ideal rarely applied to the lower classes. Working-class women labored for low pay in garment factories or worked as domestic servants. Young women might leave domestic service after they married but often had to seek other employment. Despite long days working for wages, they were still expected to take full responsibility for child care and homemaking.

Rights for Women

Some individual women and women's groups protested restrictions on women. Like earlier pioneers Olympe de Gouges and Mary Wollstonecraft, they sought a broad range of rights. Across Europe and the United States, politically active women campaigned for fairness in marriage, divorce, and

Sipping Tea in a Victorian Parlor

You are visiting friends in London. As part of Victorian England's middle class, they think of their home as an island of peace away from the hustle and bustle of the new factories. As you gaze at their lavishly decorated parlor, you are impressed with their good taste.

Heavy velvet drapes and leaded-glass windows make the room quite dark. Pictures, mirrors, and richly colored wallpaper decorate the walls. Almost every surface is covered with knickknacks and flower arrangements. The rest of the house is considered very private, so the parlor is the only room you will see.

You notice that the parlor is crowded with fancy, overstuffed chairs. That is only proper, because everyone should have a fresh seat. It is considered extremely rude for someone to be offered a seat that is still warm.

The butler has just come in to announce another caller. He presents your friend with the visitor's calling card—a small, decorative card that contains the visitor's name. Good manners demand that the lady of the house return the visit, or at least a card, to every caller within three days.

Portfolio Assessment

When you get home from your visit, you decide to redecorate your parlor in the Victorian style. Draw up a floor plan with doorways, windows, and furniture. Write an explanation of how the room will impress your visitors.

property laws. Women's groups also supported the temperance movement, a campaign to limit or ban the use of alcoholic beverages. Temperance leaders argued that drinking threatened family life.

These reformers faced many obstacles. In Europe and the United States, women could not vote. They were barred from most schools and had little, if any, protection under the law. A woman's husband or father controlled her property.

Early Voices Before 1850, some women had become leaders in the union movement. Others, mostly from the middle class, had campaigned for the abolition of slavery. In the process, they realized the severe restrictions on their own lives. In the United States, Elizabeth Cady Stanton and Susan B. Anthony crusaded against slavery before organizing a movement for women's rights.

Many women broke the barriers that kept them out of universities and professions. By the late 1800s, a few brave women overcame opposition to train as doctors or lawyers. Others became explorers, researchers, or inventors, often without recognition. For example, Julia Brainerd Hall worked with her brother to develop an aluminum-producing process. Their company became hugely successful, but Charles Hall received almost all of the credit.

The Suffrage Struggle By the late 1800s, married women in some countries had won the right to control their own property. The struggle for political rights proved far more difficult. In the United States, the Seneca Falls Convention of 1848 demanded that women be granted the right to vote. In Europe, groups dedicated to women's suffrage, or women's right to vote, emerged in the later 1800s.

Among men, some liberals and socialists supported women's suffrage. In general, though, suffragists faced intense opposition. Some critics claimed that women were too emotional to be allowed to vote. Others argued that women needed to be "protected" from grubby politics or that a woman's place was in the home, not in government. To such claims, Sojourner Truth, an African American suffragist, is believed to have replied, "Nobody ever helps me into carriages, or over mudpuddles, or gives me any best place! And ain't I a woman?"

On the edges of the western world, women made faster strides. In New Zealand, Australia, and some western territories of the United States, women won the vote before 1900. There, women who had "tamed the frontier" alongside men were not dismissed as weak and helpless. In Europe and most of the United States, however, the suffrage struggle succeeded only after World War I. (You will read more about the suffrage movement in later chapters.)

Growth of Public Education

By the late 1800s, reformers persuaded many governments to set up public schools and require basic education for all children. Teaching "the three Rs"—reading, writing, and 'rithmetic—was thought to produce better citizens. In addition, industrialized societies recognized the need for a literate work force. Schools taught punctuality, obedience to authority, disciplined work habits, and patriotism. In European schools, children also received basic religious education.

Public Education At first, elementary schools were primitive. Many teachers had little schooling themselves. In rural areas, students attended class only during the times when they were not needed on the farm or in their parents' shops.

By the late 1800s, more and more children were in school, and the quality of elementary education improved. Also, governments began to expand secondary schools, known as high schools in the United States.

In secondary schools, students learned the "classical languages," Latin and Greek, along with history and mathematics.

In general, only middle-class families could afford to have their sons attend these schools, which trained students for more serious study or for government jobs. Middle-class girls were sent to school primarily in the hope that they might marry well and become better wives and mothers.

Higher Education Colleges and universities expanded in this period, too. Most university students were the sons of middle- or upper-class families. The university curriculum emphasized ancient history and languages, philosophy, religion, and law. By the late 1800s, universities added courses in the sciences, especially in chemistry and physics. At the same time, engineering schools trained students who would have the knowledge and skills to build the new industrial society.

Some women sought greater educational opportunities. By the 1840s, a few small colleges for women opened, including Bedford College in England and Mount Holyoke in the United States. In 1863, the British reformer Emily Davies campaigned for female students to be allowed to take the entrance examinations for Cambridge University. She succeeded, but as late as 1897, male Cambridge students rioted against granting degrees to women.

New Directions in Science

As you have seen, science in the service of industry brought great changes in the later 1800s. At the same time, researchers advanced startling theories about the natural world. Their new ideas challenged long-held beliefs.

Atomic Theory A crucial breakthrough in chemistry came in the early 1800s when the English Quaker schoolteacher John Dalton developed modern atomic theory. The ancient Greeks had speculated that all matter was made of tiny particles called atoms. Dalton showed how different kinds of atoms combine to make all chemical substances. In 1869, the Russian chemist Dmitri Mendeleyev (mehn duh LAY ehv) drew up a table that grouped

Public Education
By the late 1800s, poor children often attended elementary school, although many would drop out before high school. Above left, students in a cramped New York City classroom copy their lessons.

Theme: Continuity and Change Why are poor children today more likely to attend high school than the children shown here?

elements according to their atomic weights. Mendeleyev's table became the basis for the periodic table of elements used today.

The Age of the Earth The new science of geology opened disturbing avenues of debate. In *Principles of Geology* (1830–1833), Charles Lyell offered evidence to show that the Earth had formed over millions of years. His successors concluded that the Earth was at least two billion years old and that life had not appeared until long after Earth was formed. These ideas did not seem to agree with biblical accounts of creation.

Archaeology added other pieces to an emerging debate about the origins of life on Earth. In 1856, workers in the Neander valley of Germany accidentally uncovered the fossilized bones of prehistoric people, whom scientists called Neanderthal. Later scholars found fossils of other prehistoric humans and animals. These pioneering archaeologists had limited evidence and often drew mistaken conclusions. But as more discoveries were made around the world, scholars developed new ideas about early human life.

The Darwin Challenge

The most disturbing new idea came from the British naturalist Charles Darwin. In 1859, after years of research, he published *On the Origin of Species.* Darwin argued that all forms of life had evolved into their present state over millions of years. To explain the long, slow process of evolution, he put forward his theory of natural selection.

Theory of Natural Selection Darwin adopted Thomas Malthus's idea that all plants and animals produced more offspring than the food supply could support. As a result, he said, members of each species constantly competed to survive. Natural forces "selected" those with physical traits best adapted to their environment. For example, short-necked giraffes, unable to reach the leaves at the tops of trees, would starve. Longer-necked giraffes, however, would survive and pass the trait on to their offspring. This process of natural selection came to be known as "survival of the fittest."

Over time, said Darwin, natural selection would give rise to entirely new species. He applied this theory to humans. "Man," he declared, "is descended from some less highly organized form." He claimed that humans, like all life forms, were still evolving.

The Darwin Furor Like the ideas of Nicolaus Copernicus and Galileo Galilei in earlier times, Darwin's theory ignited a furious debate between scientists and theologians. To many Christians, the Bible contained the only true account of creation. It told how God created the

Geography and History

A "Living Laboratory"

In 1835, the British ship *Beagle* reached the volcanic Galapagos Islands in the Pacific Ocean, some 600 miles west of South America. The islands were well known for their giant tortoises, which sailors prized as a delicacy. But one crew member, Charles Darwin, was far more interested in how the tortoises, marine and land iguanas, and numerous species of finches survived on the isolated islands.

The specimens he collected and studied helped Darwin develop his theory of evolution. Even today, scientists consider the Galapagos Islands a "living laboratory" for the study of animal life.

Theme: Geography and History Why would the isolation of the Galapagos Islands attract scientists?

world and all forms of life in six days. Darwin's theory, they argued, reduced people to the level of animals and undermined belief in God and the soul.

While some Christians eventually came to accept the idea of evolution, others did not. Controversy over Darwin's theory has continued to the present day, especially in the United States.

Social Darwinism Darwin himself never promoted any social ideas. However, some thinkers used Darwin's theories to support their own beliefs about society. Their ideas became known as Social Darwinism, applying the idea of survival of the fittest to war and economic competition. Industrial tycoons, argued Social Darwinists, were more "fit" than those they put out of business. War brought progress by weeding out weak nations. Victory was seen as proof of superiority.

Social Darwinism encouraged racism, the belief that one racial group is superior to another. By the late 1800s, many Europeans and Americans claimed that the success of western civilization was due to the supremacy of the white race. Karl Pearson, a British mathematician, wrote, "History shows me one way, and one way only, in which a high state of civilization has been produced, namely the struggle of race with race, and the survival of the physically and mentally fitter race." By the end of the century, as you will read, such ideas would be used to justify the global expansion of imperialism, as well as racial discrimination and segregation.

Religion in an Urban Age

Despite the challenge of new ideas, religion continued to be a major force in western society. Christian churches and Jewish synagogues remained at the center of communities. Religious leaders influenced political, social, and educational developments.

The grim realities of industrial life stimulated feelings of compassion and charity. In Europe, Christian labor unions and political parties pushed for reforms. Individuals and church groups tried to help the working poor. Catholic priests and nuns set up schools and hospitals in urban slums. In the United States, Jewish organizations such as B'nai B'rith provided similar social services.

In Europe and the United States, many Protestant churches backed the social gospel, a movement that urged Christians to social service. They campaigned for reforms in housing, health care, and education. By 1878, William and Catherine Booth had set up the Salvation Army in London. It both spread Christian teachings and provided social services.

Comfort for the Poor
Evangeline Booth, daughter of William and Catherine, helped bring the Salvation Army from Britain to the United States and Canada. This picture shows Booth with two slum children.

Theme: Religions and Value Systems How does this picture express the values of groups like the Salvation Army?

SECTION 3 Assessment

Recall

1. **Identify: (a)** atomic theory, **(b)** Charles Lyell, **(c)** natural selection, **(d)** Social Darwinism, **(e)** Salvation Army.
2. **Define: (a)** cult of domesticity, **(b)** temperance movement, **(c)** women's suffrage, **(d)** racism, **(e)** social gospel.

Comprehension

3. **(a)** How did the social order change in industrial nations? **(b)** Describe three values associated with the middle class.

4. **(a)** What were the main goals of the women's movement? **(b)** Why did it face strong opposition?
5. Why did the ideas of Charles Darwin cause controversy?
6. What services did religious organizations provide?

Critical Thinking and Writing

7. **Defending a Position** Why do you think reformers pushed for free public education?
8. **Linking Past and Present** What charitable services do religious organizations perform today?

Activity

Take It to the NET

Use Internet resources to find out about entertaining in a middle-class English home in the 1800s. Then, with two other students, plan a party. Write an invitation, plan a menu, and demonstrate a game that you might play.

A New Culture

Reading Focus

- What themes shaped romantic art, literature, and music?
- How did realists respond to the industrialized, urban world?
- How did the visual arts change?

Vocabulary

romanticism
realism
impressionism

Taking Notes

Copy the diagram below. As you read, fill in the major features of the artistic movements in the 1800s. To help you get started, some answers have been provided.

	GOALS	CHARACTERISTICS	MAJOR FIGURES
ROMANTICISM	• Rebellion against the Enlightenment emphasis on reason •	• Romantic hero in literature •	• Lord Byron • Wordsworth •
REALISM			
IMPRESSIONISM			

Main Idea New artistic styles emerged as a reaction to the Industrial Revolution.

Biography

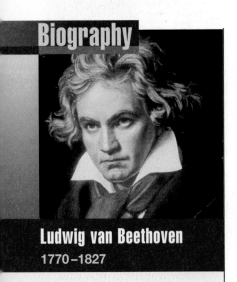

Ludwig van Beethoven
1770–1827

Composer Ludwig van Beethoven wrote from the heart. An accomplished musician by age 12, he agonized over every note of every composition. The result was stunning music that expresses intense emotion. The famous opening of his Fifth Symphony conveys the sense of fate knocking at the door. His Sixth Symphony captures a joyful day in the countryside, interrupted by a violent thunderstorm.

Beethoven's career was haunted by perhaps the greatest tragedy a musician can face. In 1798, he began to lose his hearing. Still, he continued to compose music he could hear only in his mind.

Theme: Impact of the Individual How did Beethoven's music reflect romanticism?

Setting the Scene In the 1800s, many writers turned away from the harsh realities of industrial life to celebrate the natural world. The English poet William Wordsworth described the peace and beauty of sunset:

> "It is a beauteous evening, calm and free,
> The holy time is quiet as a Nun
> Breathless with adoration; the broad sun
> Is sinking down in its tranquillity."
> —William Wordsworth,
> *Complete Poetical Works*

Other writers, however, made the new industrialized, urban society the subject of their work.

The Romantic Revolt Against Reason

Wordsworth was part of a cultural movement called romanticism. From about 1750 to 1850, romanticism shaped western literature and arts. Romantic writers, artists, and composers rebelled against the Enlightenment emphasis on reason and progress. They glorified nature and sought to excite strong emotions in their audiences.

The Romantic Hero Romantic writers created a new kind of hero—a mysterious, melancholy figure who felt out of step with society. "My joys, my grief, my passions, and my powers, / Made me a stranger," wrote Britain's Lord Byron. He himself was a larger-than-life figure equal to those he created. Public interest in his poetry and adventures was so great that moody, isolated romantic heroes came to be described as "Byronic."

The romantic hero often hid a guilty secret and faced a grim destiny. Germany's greatest writer, Johann Wolfgang von Goethe (GEH tuh), wrote the dramatic poem *Faust*. The aging scholar Faust makes a pact with the devil, exchanging his soul for youth. After much agony, Faust wins salvation by accepting his duty to help others. In *Jane Eyre*, British novelist Charlotte Brontë weaves a tale about a quiet governess and her brooding, Byronic employer, whose large mansion conceals a terrifying secret.

Romance of the Past Romantic writers combed history, legend, and folklore. Sir Walter Scott's novels and ballads evoked the turbulent history of Scottish clans or medieval knights. Alexandre Dumas (doo MAH) re-created France's past in novels like *The Three Musketeers*.

Music Romantic composers also tried to stir deep emotions. The passionate music of German composer Ludwig van Beethoven combined classical forms with a stirring range of sound. He was the first composer to take full advantage of the broad range of instruments in the modern orchestra. In all, Beethoven produced nine symphonies, five piano concertos, a violin concerto, an opera, two masses, and dozens of shorter pieces. To many, he is considered the greatest composer of his day.

Other romantic composers wove traditional folk melodies into their works to glorify their nations' pasts. In his piano works, Frederic Chopin (shoh PAN) used Polish peasant dances to convey the sorrows and joys of people living under foreign occupation.

Romanticism in Art Painters, too, broke free from the discipline and strict rules of the Enlightenment. Landscape painters like J.M.W. Turner sought to capture the beauty and power of nature. Using bold brush strokes and colors, Turner showed tiny human figures struggling against sea and storm.

Romantics painted many subjects, from simple peasant life to medieval knights to current events. Bright colors conveyed violent energy and emotion. The French painter Eugène Delacroix (deh luh KRWAH) filled his canvases with dramatic action. In *Liberty Leading the People*, the Goddess of Liberty carries the revolutionary tricolor as French citizens rally to the cause.

The Call to Realism

By the mid-1800s, a new artistic movement, realism, took hold in the West. Realism was an attempt to represent the world as it was. Realists often focused their work on the harsh side of life in cities or villages. Many writers and artists were committed to improving the lot of the unfortunates whose lives they depicted.

Realism in Art
After seeing two men working on a road, Gustave Courbet invited them to pose for him in his studio. In 1849, *The Stone Breakers* became his first important work of realist art.

Theme: Arts and Literature Many critics denounced Courbet's work for being vulgar and unspiritual. Why do you think his work caused such a reaction?

Impressionism
In his many paintings of Rouen Cathedral, Claude Monet showed how light and atmosphere can affect perception. These three paintings show the cathedral at different times of day and in different weather conditions.

Theme: Arts and Literature Why do you think Monet always painted the cathedral from a similar angle?

The Novel The English novelist Charles Dickens vividly portrayed the lives of slum dwellers and factory workers, including children. In *Oliver Twist*, he tells the story of a nine-year-old orphan raised in a grim poorhouse. One day, young Oliver gets up the nerve to ask for extra food:

> "Child as he was, he was desperate with hunger, and reckless with misery. He rose from the table, and advancing on the master, basin and spoon in hand, said somewhat alarmed at his own [boldness]:
> 'Please, sir, I want some more.'"
> —Charles Dickens, *Oliver Twist*

In response to that simple request, Oliver is smacked on the head and sent away to work. Later, he runs away to London. There he is taken in by Fagin, a villain who trains homeless children to become pickpockets. *Oliver Twist* shocked many middle-class readers with its picture of poverty, mistreatment of children, and urban crime. Yet, Dickens's humor and colorful characters made him one of the most popular novelists in the world.

French novelists also portrayed the ills of their time. In *Les Misérables* (LAY mih zehr AHB bluh), Victor Hugo revealed how hunger drove a good man to crime and how the law hounded him ever after. The novels of Émile Zola painted an even grimmer picture. In *Germinal*, Zola exposed class warfare in the French mining industry. To Zola's characters, neither the Enlightenment's faith in reason nor romantic feelings mattered at all.

Drama Norwegian dramatist Henrik Ibsen brought realism to the stage. His plays attacked the hypocrisy he observed around him. *A Doll's House* showed a woman caught in a straitjacket of social rules. In *An Enemy of the People*, a doctor discovers that the water in a local spa is polluted. Because the town's economy depends on its spa, the citizens denounce the doctor and suppress the truth. Ibsen's realistic dramas had a wide influence in Europe and the United States.

Realism in Art Painters also represented the realities of their time. Rejecting the romantic emphasis on imagination, they focused on ordinary subjects, especially working-class men and women. "I cannot paint an angel," said the French realist Gustave Courbet (koor BAY), "because I have never seen one." Instead, he painted works such as *The Stone Breakers*, which shows two rough laborers on a country road. Later in the century, *The Gross Clinic,* by American painter Thomas Eakins, shocked viewers with its realistic depiction of a medical class conducting a dissection.

New Directions in the Visual Arts

By the 1840s, a new art form, photography, was emerging. Louis Daguerre (dah GAYR) in France and William Fox Talbot in England had improved on earlier technologies to produce successful photographs. At first, many photos were stiff, posed portraits of middle-class families or prominent people. Other photographs reflected the romantics' fascination with faraway places.

In time, photographers used the camera to present the grim realities of life. During the American Civil War, Mathew B. Brady preserved a vivid, realistic record of the corpse-strewn battlefields. Other photographers provided vivid evidence of harsh conditions in industrial factories or slums.

The Impressionists Photography posed a challenge to painters. Why try for realism, some artists asked, when a camera could do the same thing better? By the 1870s, a group of painters took art in a new direction, seeking to capture the first fleeting impression made by a scene or object on the viewer's eye. The new movement, known as impressionism, took root in Paris, capital of the western art world.

Since the Renaissance, painters had carefully finished their paintings so that not a brush stroke showed. But impressionists like Claude Monet (moh NAY) and Edgar Degas (day GAH) brushed strokes of color side by side without any blending. According to new scientific studies of optics, the human eye would mix these patches of color.

By concentrating on visual impressions rather than realism, artists achieved a fresh view of familiar subjects. Monet, for example, painted the cathedral at Rouen (roo AHN), France, dozens of times from the same angle, capturing how it looked in different lights at different times of day.

The Postimpressionists Later painters, called postimpressionists, developed a variety of styles. Georges Seurat (suh RAH) arranged small dots of color to define the shapes of objects. The Dutch painter Vincent van Gogh experimented with sharp brush lines and bright colors.

Paul Gauguin (goh GAN) developed a bold, personal style. He rejected the materialism of western life and went to live on the island of Tahiti. In his paintings, people look flat, as in "primitive" folk art. But his brooding colors and black outlining of shapes convey intense feelings and images.

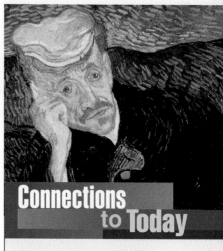

Connections to Today

A Van Gogh at Auction

Vincent van Gogh sold few paintings during his short, unhappy life. In 1890, after several attacks of epilepsy and depression, he began to see the noted doctor Paul-Ferdinand Gachet. Soon after, his doctor became his model. Van Gogh wrote that he had painted Gachet "with the heart-broken expression of our time."

Van Gogh died nearly penniless a year later, but his *Portrait of Dr. Gachet* became one of the most valuable paintings of all time. In 1990, exactly 100 years after it was painted, the portrait sold at an auction in New York for more than $82 million—then an all-time record for any work of art sold at auction.

Theme: Art and Literature
How has the value of Van Gogh's paintings changed?

SECTION 4 Assessment

Recall
1. **Identify: (a)** Lord Byron, **(b)** Johann Wolfgang von Goethe, **(c)** Ludwig van Beethoven, **(d)** Charlotte Brontë, **(e)** Charles Dickens, **(f)** Gustave Courbet, **(g)** Claude Monet, **(h)** postimpressionists.
2. **Define: (a)** romanticism, **(b)** realism, **(c)** impressionism.

Comprehension
3. **(a)** How did romantics respond to the Enlightenment? **(b)** Describe three subjects romantics favored.

4. How did Dickens and Ibsen explore realistic themes?
5. How did photography influence the development of painting?

Critical Thinking and Writing
6. **Recognizing Causes and Effects** In what ways were the new artistic styles of the 1800s a reaction to changes in society?
7. **Defending a Position (a)** What did Courbet mean when he said, "I cannot paint an angel because I have never seen one"? **(b)** Do you agree with his attitude? Explain.

Activity
Take It to the NET

Use the Internet to research one of the artists mentioned in this section. Then, write a review of one of his paintings. Consider such questions as the following: What style is used? What is the artist trying to do? What is your opinion of the work?

Creating a Chapter Summary

Copy this graphic organizer on a piece of paper. Include information about the developments that occurred in each category during the 1800s. Add more circles as needed.

CD-ROM Review For additional review of the major concepts of Chapter 22, see the *Guide to the Essentials of World History* or the *Interactive Student Tutorial CD-ROM.*

Web Site Self-Test For practice test questions for Chapter 22, see **www.phschool.com.**

Building Vocabulary

Review the meaning of the chapter vocabulary words listed below. Then, write a sentence for each word in which you define the word and describe its relationship to life in the Industrial Revolution.

1. **assembly line**
2. **corporation**
3. **cartel**
4. **urban renewal**
5. **standard of living**
6. **cult of domesticity**
7. **temperance movement**
8. **social gospel**
9. **romanticism**
10. **realism**

Recalling Key Facts

11. Which two nations became industrial leaders in the late 1800s?
12. What arguments were made for and against the rise of big business?
13. What kinds of attractions did cities offer their residents?
14. What improvements in working conditions occurred in the late 1800s?
15. Name three characteristics or concerns of romanticism.
16. How did the visual arts change in response to new technology?

Critical Thinking and Writing

17. **Connecting to Geography** How did technology affect the movement of people and goods in the 1800s and early 1900s?
18. **Linking Past and Present** **(a)** How did the second Industrial Revolution differ from the first? **(b)** Some historians believe that we are now in the midst of a "third" Industrial Revolution. Do you agree or disagree? Explain.
19. **Recognizing Points of View** How might each of the following have viewed the Industrial Revolution: **(a)** an inventor, **(b)** an entrepreneur, **(c)** a worker?
20. **Applying Information** Did the lives of women improve as a result of the Industrial Revolution? Why or why not?
21. **Making Inferences** Referring to *Oliver Twist*, Dickens wrote that "to show [criminals] as they really are, for ever skulking uneasily through the dirtiest paths of life . . . would be a service to society." **(a)** What do you think he meant? **(b)** How does his claim reflect the goals of realism?

John Hollingshead was an English journalist who had himself been raised in poverty in London. He wrote this description of city life in 1862. Read the passage and answer the questions that follow.

> *"We are a little too apt to pride ourselves on our national growth and to overlook the quality in the quantity of our population. Thirty millions of people in the United Kingdom, one-tenth of whom belong to London proper . . . show an undoubted advance in capital and prosperity. Taken in detail [however] they show that the spreading limbs of a great city may be healthy and vigorous, while its heart may gradually become more choked and decayed. A vast deal of life that skulks or struggles in London is only familiar to the hard-working clergy, certain medical practitioners, and a few [parish] officers. It burrows in holes and corners at the back of busy thoroughfares. . . . Its records, if truthfully given, have little romance, little beauty, and less variety. Poverty, ignorance, dirt, immorality, and crime are the five great divisions of its history."*
>
> —John Hollingshead, "London Poor"

22. According to the author, what percentage of people in London had experienced an improvement in their standard of living as a result of the Industrial Revolution?

23. What does Hollingshead say are the main problems facing the poor?

24. What does the author mean when he says that "the spreading limbs of a great city may be healthy and vigorous, while its heart may gradually become more choked and decayed"?

25. How does this passage reflect what you have learned about the role of religion in urban society?

26. **(a)** Who do you think was the intended audience for this article? **(b)** Why does Hollingshead say, "We are a little too apt to pride ourselves on our national growth"? **(c)** What effect do you think the author hoped to have on his audience?

27. Do you think Hollingshead's description of London in the 1860s could also apply to cities today? Explain.

STEEL PRODUCTION, 1880–1910

Sources: *European Historical Statistics, 1750–1970,* and *Historical Statistics of the United States*

The graph above shows the amount of steel produced by three major industrialized nations. Look at the graph and answer the following questions:

28. About how much steel did Britain produce in 1880? In 1910?

29. List the three countries shown in the graph in order from highest to lowest steel production in **(a)** 1890, **(b)** 1900.

30. Between 1890 and 1910, which nation had the greatest increase in steel production? The smallest?

31. Based on what you have read, how can you explain Germany's rise in steel production?

Skills Tip

When you analyze a graph, look for increases and decreases, as well as similarities and differences over time.

Skills Assessment
Take It to the NET

Use the Internet to research an invention or breakthrough from the second Industrial Revolution. Then, create and deliver a presentation about it. Include when and how it was discovered or created, its importance at the time it was discovered or created, and whether it is still in use today.

CHAPTER 23

Nationalism Triumphs in Europe

1800–1914

Chapter Preview

1 **Building a German Nation**
2 **Strengthening Germany**
3 **Unifying Italy**
4 **Nationalism Threatens Old Empires**
5 **Russia: Reform and Reaction**

Early 1800s

Nationalism rises in Germany. The folk tales collected by Jacob and William Grimm, such as "Hansel and Gretel" (above), were one attempt to foster a common German heritage.

1814

The Congress of Vienna begins.

1831

Giuseppe Mazzini, shown here, founds a secret society called Young Italy. The society encourages Italian unification.

CHAPTER EVENTS

| 1800 | 1825 | 1850 |

GLOBAL EVENTS

1804 Haiti declares independence from France.

1848 Revolutions take place throughout Europe.

Unification in Europe, 1873

Nationalist movements led to the creation of several new nations across Europe.

ATLANTIC OCEAN

St. Petersburg

UNITED KINGDOM

KINGDOM OF SWEDEN AND NORWAY

DENMARK

NETHERLANDS

BELGIUM

Berlin

GERMANY

RUSSIA

Elbe R.

Rhine R.

Oder R.

Vistula R.

Dnieper R.

Don R.

LUXEMBOURG

SWITZERLAND

FRANCE

Seine R.

Loire R.

Rhône R.

AUSTRIA–HUNGARY

Vienna

Budapest

Dniester R.

ALPS

PO R.

PORTUGAL

SPAIN

PYRENEES MTS.

Ebro R.

Tagus R.

Tiber R.

Rome

ITALY

Adriatic Sea

Danube R.

OTTOMAN EMPIRE

Black Sea

50°N

40°N

10°W

10°E

20°E

30°E

40°E

Mediterranean Sea

N W E S

Azimuthal Equal Area Projection

0   200   400 Miles

0   200   400 Kilometers

1885
Construction begins on the parliament building in Budapest. Although Austria and Hungary have been united under the Dual Monarchy since 1867, each state has its own parliament.

1905
In Russia, the czar's troops, standing in front of the arch, fire on peaceful protesters. The massacre becomes known as Bloody Sunday.

1914
World War I begins.

1875   1900   1925

1898 The Philippines declares independence from Spain.

1903 In North Carolina, the Wright brothers complete the first flight in an airplane.

Building a German Nation

Reading Focus

- What early changes promoted German unity?
- How did Bismarck unify Germany?
- What was the basic political organization of the new German empire?

Vocabulary

chancellor
Realpolitik
annex
kaiser
Reich

Taking Notes

On a sheet of paper, make a flowchart showing the key events that led to a united Germany. Use this flowchart to help you get started. Add more boxes as needed

Main Idea Otto von Bismarck, the chancellor of Prussia, led the drive for German unity.

Setting the Scene The Prussian legislators waited restlessly for Otto von Bismarck to speak. They knew he wanted them to vote more money to build up the Prussian army. Liberal members of the parliament, however, opposed the move. At last, Bismarck rose and dismissed their concerns:

> "Germany does not look to Prussia's liberalism, but to her power. . . . The great questions of the day are not to be decided by speeches and majority resolutions—that was the mistake of 1848 and 1849—but by blood and iron!"
> —Otto von Bismarck, quoted in *Modern and Contemporary European History, 1815–1940* (Schapiro)

Bismarck delivered his "blood and iron" speech in 1862. It set the tone for his policies in the years ahead. Bismarck was determined to build a strong, unified German state, with Prussia at its head.

Steps Toward Unity

In the early 1800s, German-speaking people lived in a number of small and medium-sized states as well as in Prussia and the Austrian Hapsburg empire. Napoleon's invasions unleashed new forces in these territories.

Impact of Napoleon Between 1807 and 1812, Napoleon made important territorial changes in German-speaking lands. He annexed lands along the Rhine River for France. He dissolved the Holy Roman Empire and organized a number of German states into the Rhine Confederation.

At first, some Germans welcomed the French emperor as a hero with enlightened, modern policies. He encouraged freeing the serfs, made trade easier, and abolished laws against Jews. However, not all Germans appreciated Napoleon and his changes. As people fought to free their lands from French rule, they began to demand a unified German state.

Napoleon's defeat did not resolve the issue. At the Congress of Vienna, Metternich pointed out that a united Germany would require dismantling the government of each German state. Instead, the peacemakers created the German Confederation, a weak alliance headed by Austria.

Prussian Leadership In the 1830s, Prussia created an economic union called the *Zollverein* (TSAWL fuh rīn). It dismantled tariff barriers between many German states. Still, Germany remained politically fragmented.

In 1848, liberals meeting in the Frankfurt Assembly again demanded German political unity. They offered the throne of a united German state to Frederick William IV of Prussia. The Prussian ruler, however, rejected the notion of a throne offered by "the people."

Bismarck and German Unity

Otto von Bismarck succeeded where others had failed. Bismarck came from Prussia's Junker (YUNG ker) class, made up of conservative landowning nobles. Bismarck first served Prussia as a diplomat. In 1862, King William I made him **chancellor,** or prime minister. Within a decade, the new chancellor had united the German states under Prussian rule.

Master of *Realpolitik* Bismarck's success was due in part to his strong will. He was a master of *Realpolitik,* or realistic politics based on the needs of the state. Power was more important than principles.

Although Bismarck was the architect of German unity, he was not really a German nationalist. His primary loyalty was to the Hohenzollerns, the ruling dynasty of Prussia. Through unification, he hoped to bring more power to the Hohenzollerns.

Strengthening the Army As chancellor, Bismarck moved first to build up the Prussian army. Despite his "blood and iron" speech, the liberal legislature refused to vote funds for the military. In response, Bismarck strengthened the army with money that had been collected for other purposes. He then was ready to pursue an aggressive foreign policy.

In the next decade, Bismarck led Prussia into three wars. Each war increased Prussian power and paved the way for German unity.

Skills Assessment

Geography In the early 1800s, people living in German-speaking states had local loyalties. By the mid-1800s, however, they were developing a national identity.

1. **Location** On the map, locate *(a)* Prussia, *(b)* Silesia, *(c)* Bavaria, *(d)* Schleswig.
2. **Region** What area did Prussia add to its territory in 1866?
3. **Critical Thinking Analyzing Information** Why do you think Austrian influence was greater among the southern German states than among the northern ones?

Unification of Germany, 1865–1871

Prussia, 1865
Added to Prussia, 1866
Added to form North German Confederation, 1867
Added to form German empire, 1871
Boundary of German empire, 1871
Battle sites
Route of Prussian armies in Austro-Prussian War
Route of German armies in Franco-Prussian War

Azimuthal Equal Area Projection

Analyzing Primary Sources

Crowning the German Emperor

This painting by Anton von Werner shows the coronation of William I (center on the steps) as emperor of the united Germany. The ceremony took place at Versailles in 1871.

Skills Tip

Keep in mind that a painting is an artist's vision of an event. Unlike a photograph of an actual scene, a painting may embellish or exaggerate certain aspects of an event.

Skills Assessment

1. In the painting, William I is saluted by
   A common citizens.
   B the royal court.
   C uniformed men.
   D foreign dignitaries.

2. How is Otto von Bismarck (at center, in white jacket) portrayed?
   E as equal to the emperor
   F as superior to the emperor
   G as unimportant to the coronation
   H as a central part of the coronation

3. **Critical Thinking** **Analyzing Primary Sources** **(a)** What feelings does the painting evoke about the coronation and the union of Germany? Which details support your view? **(b)** Write three questions that the painting raises about the event, then find the answers through further research.

Wars With Denmark and Austria Bismarck's first maneuver was to form an alliance in 1864 with Austria. They seized the provinces of Schleswig and Holstein from Denmark. Prussia and Austria "liberated" the two provinces, which were largely inhabited by Germans, and divided up the spoils.

In 1866, Bismarck invented an excuse to attack Austria. The Austro-Prussian War lasted just seven weeks and ended in a decisive Prussian victory. Prussia then annexed, or took control of, several other north German states.

Bismarck dissolved the Austrian-led German Confederation and created a new confederation dominated by Prussia. He allowed Austria and four other southern German states to remain independent. Bismarck's motives, as always, were strictly practical. "We had to avoid leaving behind any desire for revenge," he later wrote.

The Franco-Prussian War In France, the Prussian victory over Austria worried Napoleon III. A growing rivalry between the two nations led to the Franco-Prussian War of 1870.

Germans recalled only too well the invasions of Napoleon I some 60 years earlier. Bismarck played up the image of the French menace to spur German nationalism. For his part, Napoleon III did little to avoid war, hoping to mask problems at home with military glory.

Bismarck furthered the crisis by rewriting and then releasing to the press a telegram that reported on a meeting between King William I and the French ambassador. Bismarck's editing of the "Ems dispatch" made it seem that William I had insulted the Frenchman. Furious, Napoleon III declared war on Prussia, as Bismarck had hoped.

A superior Prussian force, supported by troops from other German states, smashed the badly organized and poorly supplied French soldiers. Napoleon III, old and ill, surrendered within a few weeks. France had to accept a humiliating peace.

The German Empire

Delighted by the victory over France, princes from the southern German states and the North German Confederation persuaded William I of Prussia to take the title kaiser (KĪ zer), or emperor. In January 1871, German nationalists celebrated the birth of the Second Reich, or empire. They called it that because they considered it heir to the Holy Roman Empire.

A constitution drafted by Bismarck set up a two-house legislature. The Bundesrat, or upper house, was appointed by the rulers of the German states. The Reichstag, or lower house, was elected by universal male suffrage. Because the Bundesrat could veto any decisions of the Reichstag, real power remained in the hands of the emperor and his chancellor.

Primary Source

War and Power
In 1866, Field Marshal Helmuth von Moltke analyzed the importance of Prussia's war against Austria:

"The war of 1866 was entered on not because the existence of Prussia was threatened, nor was it caused by public opinion and the voice of the people; it was a struggle, long foreseen and calmly prepared for, recognized as a necessity by the Cabinet, not for territorial expansion, for an extension of our domain, or for material advantage, but for an ideal end—the establishment of power. Not a foot of land was exacted from Austria. . . . Its center of gravity lay out of Germany; Prussia's lay within it. Prussia felt itself called upon and strong enough to assume the leadership of the German races."

—Helmuth von Moltke, quoted in *Readings in European History* (Robinson)

Skills Assessment

Primary Source Why, according to von Moltke, did Prussia go to war against Austria?

SECTION 1 Assessment

Recall

1. **Identify:** (a) *Zollverein,* (b) Otto von Bismarck, (c) William I.
2. **Define:** (a) chancellor, (b) *Realpolitik,* (c) annex, (d) kaiser, (e) Reich.

Comprehension

3. What territorial and economic changes promoted German unity?
4. Describe the techniques Bismarck used to unify the German states.

5. How did the emperor and his chancellor retain power in the new German government?

Critical Thinking and Writing

6. **Applying Information** Identify three examples of Bismarck's use of *Realpolitik.*
7. **Comparing** How did the nationalism represented by Bismarck differ from that embraced by liberals in the early 1800s?

Activity

Making a Map
Create an illustrated map and time line showing the unification of Germany. Include a legend that explains symbols on your map, such as those used for battle sites.

Strengthening Germany

Reading Focus

- What marked Germany as an industrial giant?
- Why was Bismarck called the Iron Chancellor?
- What policies did Kaiser William II follow?

Vocabulary

Kulturkampf
social welfare

Taking Notes

On a sheet of paper, make a diagram like the one started here. As you read the section, add other causes that led to a strong German nation.

- Plentiful resources for industry
- Educated work force
- •
- •

STRONG GERMAN NATION

Main Idea Germany increased its power by building up its industry and armed forces.

German Industry
The Krupp works was a major German industrial company. This huge cannon was displayed at an international industrial exhibition to demonstrate the might of the house of Krupp and of Germany.

Theme: Economics and Technology What advantages would a cannon like this one offer to an army?

Setting the Scene In January 1871, German princes gathered in the glittering Hall of Mirrors at the French palace of Versailles. They had just defeated Napoleon III in the Franco-Prussian War. The palace of Louis XIV seemed the perfect place to proclaim the new German empire. To the winners as well as to the losers, the symbolism was clear. French domination of Europe, dating from the age of Louis XIV, had ended. Germany, headed by William I and his chancellor, Otto von Bismarck, was now the dominant power in Europe.

The German Industrial Giant

In the aftermath of unification, the German empire emerged as the industrial giant of the European continent. By the late 1800s, German chemical and electrical industries were setting the standard worldwide. German shipping was second only to Britain's among the European powers.

Economic Progress Germany, like Great Britain, possessed several of the factors that made industrialization possible. Germany's spectacular growth was due in part to ample iron and coal resources, the basic ingredients for industrial development. A disciplined and educated work force also helped the economy, and a rapidly growing population—from 41 million in 1871 to 67 million by 1914—provided a huge home market along with a larger supply of industrial workers.

The new nation also benefited from earlier progress. During the 1850s and 1860s, Germans had founded large companies and built many railroads. The house of Krupp boomed after 1871. It became an enormous industrial complex that produced steel and weapons for a world market. Between 1871 and 1914, the business tycoon August Thyssen built a small steel factory of 70 workers into a giant empire with 50,000 employees.

Science, Government, and Industry German industrialists were the first to see the value of applied science in developing new products such as synthetic chemicals and dyes. They supported research and development in the universities and hired trained scientists to solve technological problems in their factories.

The German government promoted economic development. After 1871, it issued a single currency for Germany, reorganized the banking system, and coordinated railroads built by the various German states. When a worldwide depression hit in the late 1800s, Germany raised tariffs to protect home industries from foreign competition. The leaders of the new German empire were determined to maintain economic strength as well as military power.

The Iron Chancellor

As chancellor of the new German empire, Bismarck pursued several foreign-policy goals. He wanted to keep France weak and isolated while building strong links with Austria and Russia. He respected British naval power but did not seek to compete in that arena. "Water rats," he said, "do not fight with land rats." Later, however, he would take a more aggressive stand against Britain as the two nations competed for colonies to expand their overseas empires.

On the domestic front, Bismarck applied the same ruthless methods he had used to achieve unification. The Iron Chancellor, as he was called, sought to erase local loyalties and crush all opposition to the imperial state. He targeted two groups—the Catholic Church and the socialists. In his view, both posed a threat to the new German state.

Campaign Against the Church After unification, Catholics made up about a third of the German population. The Lutheran Bismarck distrusted Catholics—especially the clergy—whose first loyalty, he believed, was to the pope instead of to Germany.

In response to what he saw as the Catholic threat, Bismarck launched the *Kulturkampf,* or "battle for civilization." His goal was to make Catholics put loyalty to the state above allegiance to the Church. The chancellor had laws passed that gave the state the right to supervise Catholic education and approve the appointment of priests. Other laws closed some religious orders, expelled the Jesuits from Prussia, and made it compulsory for couples to be married by civil authority.

Bismarck's moves against the Catholic Church backfired. The faithful rallied behind the Church, and the Catholic Center party gained strength in the Reichstag. A realist, Bismarck saw his mistake and worked to make peace with the Church.

Campaign Against the Socialists Bismarck also saw a threat to the new German empire in the growing power of socialism. By the late 1870s, German Marxists had organized the Social Democratic party, which called for parliamentary democracy and laws to improve conditions for the working class. Bismarck feared that socialists would undermine the loyalty of German workers and turn them toward revolution. He had laws passed that dissolved socialist groups, shut down their newspapers, and banned their meetings. Once again, repression backfired. Workers were unified in support of the socialist cause.

Bismarck then changed course. He set out to woo workers away from socialism by sponsoring laws to protect them. Bismarck made it clear that *Realpolitik* influenced social reform as well as foreign policy:

> "Give the workingman the right to work as long as he is healthy, assure him care when he is sick, and maintenance when he is old . . . then the socialists will sing their siren songs in vain, and the workingmen will cease to throng to their banner."
>
> —Otto von Bismarck, quoted in *Economic Development of Europe* (Ogg and Sharp)

Photography and Daily Life
The invention of photography in the mid-1800s provided artists with a new way to reflect and comment on real life. This photograph is from a series depicting workers at the beginning of the 1900s.

Theme: Art and Literature
What do you think the photographer is trying to say about German workers?

By the 1890s, Germans had health and accident insurance as well as old-age insurance to provide retirement benefits. Thus, under Bismarck, Germany was a pioneer in social reform. Its system of economic safeguards became the model for other European nations.

Bismarck's plan was only partly successful. Although workers benefited from his measures, they did not abandon socialism. In fact, the Social Democratic party continued to grow in strength. By 1912, it had more seats in the Reichstag than were held by any other party. Yet Bismarck's program showed that conditions for workers could be improved without the upheaval of a revolution. Later, Germany and other European nations would build on Bismarck's social policies, greatly increasing government's role in providing for the needs of its citizens.

Kaiser William II

In 1888, William II succeeded his grandfather as kaiser. The new emperor was supremely confident of his abilities and wished to put his own stamp on Germany. In 1890, he shocked Europe by asking the dominating Bismarck to resign. "There is only one master in the Reich," he said, "and that is I."

William II seriously believed that his right to rule came from God. He expressed this view when he said:

> "My grandfather considered that the office of king was a task that God had assigned to him. . . . That which he thought I also think. . . . Those who wish to aid me in that task . . . I welcome with all my heart; those who oppose me in this work I shall crush."
> —William II, quoted in *Europe Since 1815* (Hazen)

Not surprisingly, William resisted efforts to introduce democratic reforms. At the same time, his government provided services, from programs for social welfare, or programs to help certain groups of people, to cheap transportation and electricity. An excellent system of public schools, begun under Bismarck, taught students obedience to the emperor along with reading, writing, and mathematics.

Like his grandfather, William II lavished funds on the German military machine, already the most powerful in Europe. He also launched an ambitious campaign to expand the German navy and win an overseas empire to rival those of Britain and France. You will read in later chapters how William's nationalism and aggressive militarism helped increase tensions on the eve of World War I.

SECTION 2 Assessment

Recall
1. **Identify:** **(a)** house of Krupp, **(b)** August Thyssen, **(c)** Iron Chancellor.
2. **Define:** **(a)** *Kulturkampf,* **(b)** social welfare.

Comprehension
3. How did Germany become an industrial giant in the late 1800s?
4. Why did Bismarck try to crush the Catholic Church and socialists?
5. What policies did William II introduce?

Critical Thinking and Writing
6. **Recognizing Causes and Effects** Why do you think supporters of democratic government had little hope of success in Germany in the late 1800s?
7. **Defending a Position** Were Bismarck's methods justified by his social reforms? Explain.

Activity
Take It to the NET

Use the Internet to research the Krupp family of Germany. Then, write a report explaining their role in the military and industrial history of Germany.

Unifying Italy

Reading Focus

- What were the key obstacles to Italian unity?
- What roles did Count Camillo Cavour and Giuseppe Garibaldi play in the struggle for Italy?
- What challenges faced the new nation of Italy?

Vocabulary

anarchist
emigration

Taking Notes

As you read, make a time line to show events from 1831 to 1871 in Italy. Use the time line shown here to help you get started.

1831	1849	1852	1871
Mazzini founds Young Italy	Mazzini's revolutionary republic in Rome toppled	Cavour becomes prime minister in Sardinia	

Main Idea During the 1800s, influential leaders helped to create a unified Italy.

Setting the Scene

At the Congress of Vienna, Italian nationalists hoped to end centuries of foreign rule and achieve unity. To Metternich, the idea of a unified Italy was laughable. Italy, he was convinced, was a mere "geographic expression."

Although the people of the Italian peninsula spoke the same language, they had not experienced political unity since Roman times. By the early 1800s, though, Italian patriots were determined to build a new, united Italy. As in Germany, unification was brought about by the efforts of a strong state and a shrewd, ruthless politician—Count Camillo Cavour.

Obstacles to Italian Unity

For centuries, Italy had been a battleground for ambitious foreign and local princes. Frequent warfare and foreign rule had led people to identify with local regions. The people of Florence considered themselves Tuscans, those of Venice Venetians, the people of Naples Neapolitans, and so on. But as in Germany, the invasions of Napoleon had sparked dreams of national unity.

The Congress of Vienna, however, ignored the nationalists. At Vienna, Austria took control of much of northern Italy, while Hapsburg monarchs ruled various other Italian states. In the south, a French Bourbon ruler was put in charge of Naples and Sicily.

In response, nationalists organized secret patriotic societies and focused their efforts on expelling Austrian forces from northern Italy. Between 1820 and 1848, nationalist revolts exploded across the region. Each time, Austria sent in troops to crush the rebels.

Mazzini's Young Italy In the 1830s, the nationalist leader Giuseppe Mazzini founded Young Italy. The goal of this secret society was "to constitute Italy, one, free, independent, republican nation." In 1849, Mazzini helped set up a revolutionary republic in Rome, but French forces soon toppled it. Like many other nationalists, Mazzini spent much of his life in exile, plotting and dreaming of a united Italy.

The Tide of Nationalism "Ideas grow quickly," Mazzini once said, "when watered by the blood of martyrs." Although revolution had failed, nationalist agitation had planted seeds for future harvests.

To nationalists like Mazzini, a united Italy made sense not only because of geography, but also because of a common language and history. Nationalists reminded Italians of the glories of ancient Rome and the medieval

Primary Source

First Stirrings of Nationalism

After the failed revolution in northern Italy, many rebels came through Genoa, begging for funds to pay for safe passage to Spain. An impressionable Giuseppe Mazzini described his reaction to the situation:

"He held out a white handkerchief, merely saying, 'For the refugees of Italy.' My mother . . . dropped some money into the handkerchief. . . . That day was the first in which a confused idea presented itself to my mind—I will not say of country or of liberty—but an idea that we Italians could and ought to struggle for the liberty of our country. . . . The idea of an existing wrong on my own country, against which it was a duty to struggle, flashed before my mind on that day for the first time, never again to leave me."

—Giuseppe Mazzini, *Life and Writings*

Skills Assessment

Primary Source How did the man's request influence Mazzini's thinking?

papacy. To others, unity made practical economic sense. It would end trade barriers among the Italian states and stimulate industry.

The Struggle for Italy

After 1848, leadership of the Risorgimento (ree sor jee MEHN toh), or Italian nationalist movement, passed to the kingdom of Sardinia. Its constitutional monarch, Victor Emmanuel II, hoped to join other states to his own, thereby increasing his power.*

Cavour In 1852, Victor Emmanuel made Count Camillo Cavour his prime minister. Cavour came from a noble family but favored liberal goals. He was a flexible, practical, crafty politician, willing to use almost any means to achieve his goals. Like Bismarck in Prussia, Cavour was a monarchist who believed in *Realpolitik*.

Once in office, Cavour moved first to reform Sardinia's economy. He improved agriculture, had railroads built, and encouraged commerce by supporting free trade. Cavour's long-term goal, however, was to end Austrian power in Italy and annex its provinces of Lombardy and Venetia.

Intrigue With France In 1855, led by Cavour, Sardinia joined Britain and France in the Crimean War against Russia. Sardinia did not win territory, but it did have a voice at the peace conference. Sardinia also gained the attention of Napoleon III.

In 1858, Cavour negotiated a secret deal with Napoleon, who promised to aid Sardinia in case it faced a war with Austria. A year later, the shrewd

---

*The kingdom of Sardinia included Piedmont, Nice, and Savoy, as well as the island of Sardinia.

Giuseppe Garibaldi
As leader of a volunteer army (below, right) that fought to unify Italy, Garibaldi told his troops, "I offer hunger, thirst, . . . battles, and death. Let him who loves his country in his heart, and not with his lips only, follow me."

Theme: Impact of the Individual What leadership qualities might someone like Garibaldi have?

Cavour provoked that war. With help from France, Sardinia defeated Austria and annexed Lombardy. Meanwhile, nationalist groups overthrew Austrian-backed rulers in several other northern Italian states. These states then joined with Sardinia.

Garibaldi's Red Shirts Next, attention shifted to the kingdom of the Two Sicilies in southern Italy. There, Giuseppe Garibaldi, a longtime nationalist and an ally of Mazzini, was ready for action. Like Mazzini, Garibaldi wanted to create an Italian republic. He did not, however, hesitate to accept aid from the monarchist Cavour. By 1860, Garibaldi had recruited a force of 1,000 red-shirted volunteers. Cavour provided weapons and allowed two ships to take Garibaldi and his "Red Shirts" south to Sicily.

With surprising speed, Garibaldi's forces won control of Sicily, crossed to the mainland, and marched triumphantly north to Naples. An English volunteer recalled his impression of Garibaldi during one battle:

"I saw Garibaldi, with his red shirt wringing wet with perspiration, his eye sternly gleaming, his face flushed with the heat of conflict. . . . I heard his voice commanding—but it was no longer now the calm, clear voice of quieter times. It was hoarse and guttural, and choked with emotion. For the good general saw his gallant band unfalteringly pouring out their life-blood."
—W. B. Brooke, quoted in *Garibaldi: Great Lives Observed* (Smith)

Unity at Last Garibaldi's success alarmed Cavour, who feared that the nationalist hero would set up his own republic in the south. To prevent this, Cavour urged Victor Emmanuel to send Sardinian troops to deal with Garibaldi. Instead, the Sardinians overran the Papal States and linked up with Garibaldi and his forces in Naples.

In a patriotic move, Garibaldi turned over Naples and Sicily to Victor Emmanuel. Shortly afterward, southern Italy voted to approve the move, and in 1861, Victor Emmanuel II was crowned king of Italy.

Two areas remained outside the new Italian nation: Rome and Venetia. Cavour died in 1861, but his successors completed his dream. In a deal negotiated with Bismarck, Italy acquired Venetia after the Austro-Prussian War. Then, during the Franco-Prussian War in 1870, France was forced to withdraw its troops from Rome. For the first time since the fall of the Roman empire, Italy was a united land.

Challenges Facing the New Nation

Italy faced a host of problems. Like the many states Bismarck cemented into the German empire, Italy had no tradition of unity. Few Italians felt ties to the new nation. Strong regional rivalries left Italy unable to solve critical national issues.

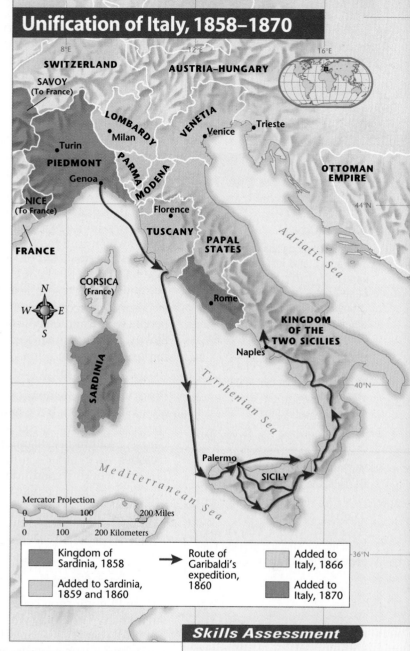

Unification of Italy, 1858–1870

Kingdom of Sardinia, 1858

Added to Sardinia, 1859 and 1860

→ **Route of Garibaldi's expedition, 1860**

Added to Italy, 1866

Added to Italy, 1870

Skills Assessment

Geography By 1871, Italy was a united nation with its capital in Rome. Giuseppe Garibaldi and his Red Shirts played a vital role in achieving unification.

1. **Location** On the map, locate **(a)** Sicily, **(b)** Naples, **(c)** Rome, **(d)** Venetia.
2. **Movement** Describe the route of Garibaldi's expedition in 1860.
3. **Critical Thinking Identifying Main Ideas** *What is the main idea of this map? Explain.*

Divisions The greatest regional differences were between the north and the south. The north was richer and had more cities than the south. For centuries, northern Italian cities had flourished as centers of business and culture. The south, on the other hand, was rural and poor. Its population was booming, but illiterate peasants could wring only a meager existence from the exhausted farmland.

Hostility between Italy and the Roman Catholic Church further divided the nation. Popes bitterly resented the seizure of the Papal States and of Rome. The government granted the papacy the small territory of the Vatican. Popes, however, saw themselves as "prisoners" and urged Italian Catholics—almost all Italians—not to cooperate with their new government.

Turmoil Under Victor Emmanuel, Italy was a constitutional monarchy with a two-house legislature. The king appointed members to the upper house, which could veto bills passed by the lower house. Although the lower house consisted of elected representatives, only a small number of men had the right to vote.

In the late 1800s, unrest increased as radicals on the left struggled against a conservative government. Socialists organized strikes while anarchists, people who want to abolish all government, turned to sabotage and violence. Slowly, the government extended suffrage to more men and passed laws to improve social conditions. Still, the turmoil continued. To distract attention from troubles at home, the government set out to win an overseas empire.

Progress Despite its problems, Italy did develop economically, especially after 1900. Although the nation lacked important natural resources such as coal, industries did sprout up in northern regions. Industrialization, of course, brought urbanization as peasants flocked to the cities to find jobs in factories. As in other countries, reformers campaigned to improve education and working conditions.

The population explosion of this period created tensions. One important safety valve for many people was emigration, or movement away from their homeland. Many Italians left for the United States, Canada, and Latin American nations.

Looking Ahead

Although unification brought great challenges, it also brought increased strength. By 1914, Italy was significantly better off than it had been in 1861. But it was hardly prepared for the great war that broke out in that year and into which it was soon drawn.

SECTION 3 Assessment

Recall

1. **Identify: (a)** Giuseppe Mazzini, **(b)** Risorgimento, **(c)** Victor Emmanuel II, **(d)** Camillo Cavour, **(e)** Giuseppe Garibaldi.
2. **Define: (a)** anarchist, **(b)** emigration.

Comprehension

3. **(a)** What obstacles to unity did Italian nationalists face? **(b)** What conditions favored unity?
4. How did Cavour and Garibaldi work for Italian unity?

5. Describe the problems Italians faced after unification.

Critical Thinking and Writing

6. **Comparing** Compare the goals and methods of Cavour in Italy and Bismarck in Germany. **(a)** How were they similar? **(b)** How were they different?
7. **Analyzing Information (a)** What was the source of conflict between Garibaldi and Cavour? **(b)** How was the conflict resolved?

Activity

Creating a Comic Strip
Create a historical comic strip that illustrates the events leading to Italian unification. Include important historical figures and locations.

Nationalism Threatens Old Empires

Reading Focus

- How did nationalism contribute to the decline of the Austrian empire?
- What were the main characteristics of the Dual Monarchy?
- How did the growth of nationalism affect the Balkans?

Taking Notes

Start a table like the one shown here. As you read this section, add information about the threats and changes that led to the decline of the Hapsburg and Ottoman empires.

HAPSBURGS	OTTOMAN TURKS
• Oldest ruling house in Europe	•
•	•

Main Idea Desires for national independence threatened to break up the Austrian and Ottoman empires.

Setting the Scene The Hapsburgs had controlled the Holy Roman Empire for nearly 400 years when Napoleon invaded the German-speaking states. Austria's center of power now lay in Eastern Europe. Further wars resulted in continued loss of territory to Germany and Italy. Why did nationalism bring new strength to some countries and weaken others?

In Eastern Europe, the Austrian Hapsburgs and the Ottoman Turks ruled lands that included diverse ethnic groups. Nationalist feelings among these subject people contributed to tensions building across Europe.

A Declining Empire

In 1800, the Hapsburgs were the oldest ruling house in Europe. In addition to their homeland of Austria, over the centuries they had acquired the territories of Bohemia and Hungary, as well as parts of Romania, Poland, Ukraine, and northern Italy.

Challenge of Change Since the Congress of Vienna, the Austrian emperor Francis I and Metternich, his foreign minister, had upheld conservative goals against liberal forces. "Rule and change nothing," the emperor told his son. Under Francis and Metternich, newspapers could not even use the word *constitution*, much less discuss this key demand of liberals. The government also tried to limit industrial development, which would threaten traditional ways of life.

Austria, however, could not hold back the changes that were engulfing the rest of Europe. By the 1840s, factories were springing up. Soon, the Hapsburgs found themselves facing the problems of industrial life that had long been familiar in Britain—the growth of cities, worker discontent, and the stirrings of socialism.

A Patchwork of People Equally disturbing to the old order were the urgent demands of nationalists. The Hapsburgs presided over a multinational empire. Of its 50 million people at mid-century, fewer than a quarter were German-speaking Austrians. Almost half belonged to different

The Imperial Hub
Vienna was a glittering, glamorous city that attracted many of the best minds and talents of Europe. Here, Vienna's leading citizens enjoy an evening of gaiety at an imperial ball.

Theme: Political and Social Systems Based on this painting, what generalization might you make about the Hapsburg ruling class?

Virtual Field Trip

www.phschool.com

**Schönbrunn Palace
Vienna, Austria**

To find more information about the Austrian empire, use the Internet address above to link to Schönbrunn Palace.

The Hapsburg Empire
Schönbrunn Palace was the summer home of Hapsburg rulers. The imposing structure and extensive gardens were designed during the 1700s and 1800s to show the power of the Hapsburgs.

Theme: Political and Social Systems Why might the Hapsburgs have wanted a showplace palace?

Slavic groups, including Czechs, Slovaks, Poles, Ukrainians, Romanians, Serbs, Croats, and Slovenes. Often, rival groups shared the same region. The empire also included large numbers of Hungarians and Italians.

The Hapsburgs ignored nationalist demands as long as they could. "Peoples?" Francis I once exclaimed. "What does that mean? I know only subjects." As you have read, when nationalist revolts broke out across the Hapsburg empire in 1848, the government crushed them.

Early Reforms Amid the turmoil, 18-year-old Francis Joseph inherited the Hapsburg throne. He would rule until 1916, presiding over the empire during its fading days into World War I.

An early challenge came when Austria suffered its humiliating defeat at the hands of France and Sardinia in 1859. Francis Joseph realized he needed to strengthen the empire at home. Accordingly, he made some limited reforms. He granted a new constitution that set up a legislature. This body, however, was dominated by German-speaking Austrians. The reforms thus satisfied none of the other national groups that populated the empire. The Hungarians, especially, were determined to settle for nothing less than total self-government.

The Dual Monarchy

Austria's disastrous defeat in the 1866 war with Prussia brought renewed pressure for change from Hungarians within the empire. One year later, Francis Deák (deh AHK), a moderate Hungarian leader, helped work out a compromise that created a new political power known as the Dual Monarchy of Austria-Hungary.

Under the agreement, Austria and Hungary were separate states. Each had its own constitution and parliament. Francis Joseph ruled both, as emperor of Austria and king of Hungary. The two states also shared ministries of finance, defense, and foreign affairs, but were independent of each other in all other areas.

Although Hungarians welcomed the compromise, other subject peoples resented it. Restlessness increased among various Slavic groups, especially the Czechs in Bohemia. Some nationalist leaders called on Slavs to unite, insisting that "only through liberty, equality, and fraternal solidarity" could Slavic peoples fulfill their "great mission in the history of mankind." By the early 1900s, nationalist unrest often left the government paralyzed in the face of pressing political and social problems.

Balkan Nationalism

Like the Hapsburgs, the Ottomans ruled a multi-national empire. It stretched from Eastern Europe and the Balkans to North Africa and the Middle East. There, as in Austria, nationalist demands tore at the fabric of the empire.

In the Balkans, Serbia had won autonomy in 1817, and southern Greece won independence in the 1830s. But many Serbs and Greeks still lived in the Balkans under Ottoman rule. The Ottoman empire was home to other national groups, such as Bulgarians and Romanians. During the 1800s, various subject peoples staged revolts against the Ottomans, hoping to set up their own independent states.

Such nationalist stirrings became mixed up with the ambitions of the great European powers. In the mid-1800s, Europeans came to see the Ottoman empire as "the sick man of Europe." Eagerly, they scrambled to divide up Ottoman lands. Russia pushed south toward the Black Sea and Istanbul, which Russians still called Constantinople. Austria-Hungary took control of the provinces of Bosnia and Herzegovina. This action angered the Serbs, who also had hoped to expand into that area. Meanwhile, Britain and France set their sights on other Ottoman lands in the Middle East and North Africa.

In the end, a complex web of competing interests contributed to a series of crises and wars in the Balkans. Russia fought several wars against the Ottomans. France and Britain sometimes joined the Russians and some-times the Ottomans. Germany supported Austrian authority over the dis-contented national groups. But Germany also encouraged the Ottomans because of their strategic location in the eastern Mediterranean. In between, the subject peoples revolted and then fought among themselves. By the early 1900s, observers were referring to the region as the "Balkan powder keg." The explosion that came in 1914 helped set off World War I.

The Balkans, 1878

- Independent Balkan states
- Ottoman empire

RUSSIA
AUSTRIA–HUNGARY
BOSNIA–HERZEGOVINA (occupied by Austria)
ROMANIA
SERBIA
BULGARIA (autonomous)
MONTENEGRO
EASTERN RUMELIA (administered by Turkey)
Constantinople
ITALY
Black Sea
Adriatic Sea
Aegean Sea
Danube R.
GREECE
Mediterranean Sea
Crete

Azimuthal Equal Area Projection
0   200   400 Miles
0   200   400 Kilometers

40°N
20°E
30°E

Skills Assessment

Geography In the late 1800s, the Balkans had become a center of conflict, as various peoples and empires competed for power.

1. **Location** On the map, locate (a) Black Sea, (b) Ottoman empire, (c) Serbia, (d) Greece, (e) Austria-Hungary.
2. **Place** Which three large seas border the Balkan Peninsula?
3. **Critical Thinking** **Predicting Consequences** Why do you think compet-ing interests in the Balkans led the region to be called a powder keg?

SECTION 4 Assessment

Recall
1. **Identify:** (a) Francis Joseph, (b) Dual Monarchy.

Comprehension
2. Explain how nationalism affected the Austrian empire.
3. (a) How was the Dual Monarchy organized? (b) Why did it fail to end nationalist demands?
4. How did Balkan nationalism contribute to the decline of the Ottoman empire?

Critical Thinking and Writing
5. **Solving Problems** Do you think that either the Hapsburgs or the Ottoman Turks could have built a modern, unified nation from their multinational empires? Explain.
6. **Identifying Alternatives** (a) What actions did Francis Joseph take to maintain power in Austria-Hungary? (b) How else might he have responded to nationalist demands?

Activity

Studying Current Events Research recent develop-ments in the Balkans. Organize your findings into a report that can be pre-sented orally or in writing.

Reading Focus

■ How did conditions in Russia affect progress?

■ Why did czars follow a cycle of absolutism, reform, and reaction?

■ How did the problems of industrialization contribute to the growing crisis and outbreak of revolution?

Vocabulary

colossus
emancipation
zemstvo
pogrom
Duma

Taking Notes

As you read this section, make an outline of the information. Use Roman numerals for the main headings. Use capital letters for the subheadings, and use numbers for the supporting details. The outline has been started for you.

I. Conditions in Russia
  A. Obstacles to progress
    1. Economically undeveloped
    2. Rigid social structure
  B. Serfdom
II. Russian absolutism
  A. Alexander I
    1. Initially open to liberal ideas
    2.

Main Idea Industrialization and reform came more slowly to Russia than to Western Europe.

Setting the Scene Although serfdom had almost disappeared in Western Europe by the 1700s, it survived and spread in Russia. Masters exercised almost total power over their serfs. In the 1800s, a noble who became a revolutionary described the brutal treatment of serfs:

> "I heard . . . stories of men and women torn from their families and their villages, and sold, or lost in gambling, or exchanged for a couple of hunting dogs, and then transported to some remote part of Russia to create a [master's] new estate; . . . of children taken from their parents and sold to cruel masters."
> —Peter Kropotkin, *Memoirs of a Revolutionist*

Reformers hoped to free Russia from autocratic rule, economic backwardness, and social injustice. But efforts to modernize Russia had little success, as czars imprisoned critics or sent them into icy exile in Siberia.

Conditions in Russia

By 1815, Russia was not only the largest, most populous nation in Europe but also a great world power. Since the 1600s, explorers had pushed the Russian frontier eastward across Siberia to the Pacific. Peter the Great and Catherine the Great had added lands on the Baltic and Black seas, and czars in the 1800s had expanded into Central Asia. Russia had thus acquired a huge multinational empire, part European and part Asian.

Other European nations looked on the Russian colossus, or giant, with a mixture of wonder and misgiving. It had immense natural resources. Russia's vast size gave it global interests and influence. But Western Europeans disliked its autocratic government and feared its expansionist aims.

Obstacles to Progress Despite efforts by Peter and Catherine to westernize Russia, it remained economically undeveloped. By the 1800s, czars saw the need to modernize but resisted reforms that would undermine their absolute rule. While the czars wavered, Russia fell further behind Western Europe in economic and social developments.

A great obstacle to progress was the rigid social structure. Landowning nobles dominated society and rejected any change that would threaten their privileges. The middle class was too small to have much influence. The majority of Russians were serfs, laborers bound to the land and to masters who controlled their fates.

Serfdom   Most serfs were peasants. Others might be servants, artisans, or soldiers forced into the czar's army. As industry expanded, some masters sent serfs to work in factories but took much of their pay.

Many enlightened Russians knew that serfdom was inefficient. As long as most people had to serve the whim of their masters, Russia's economy would remain backward. Landowning nobles had no reason to improve agriculture and took little interest in industry.

Russian Absolutism

For centuries, czars had ruled with absolute power, imposing their will on their subjects. The changes brought about by the Enlightenment and the French Revolution had almost no effect on Russian autocracy.

Alexander I   When Alexander I inherited the throne in 1801, however, he seemed open to liberal ideas. The new czar eased censorship and promoted education. He even talked about freeing the serfs.

By the time Napoleon invaded Russia in 1812, Alexander had drawn back from reform. Like earlier czars, he feared losing the support of nobles. At the Congress of Vienna, he joined the conservative powers in opposing liberal and nationalist impulses in Europe.

Revolt and Repression   When Alexander I died in 1825, a group of army officers led an uprising known as the Decembrist Revolt. They had picked up liberal ideas while fighting Napoleon in Western Europe and now demanded a constitution and other reforms. The new czar, Nicholas I, suppressed the Decembrists and cracked down on all dissent.

Nicholas used police spies to hunt out critics. He banned books from Western Europe that might spread liberal ideas. Only approved textbooks were allowed in schools and universities. Many Russians with liberal or revolutionary ideas were judged to be insane and shut up in mental hospitals. Up to 150,000 others were exiled to Siberia.

Nicholas I and Absolutism   To bolster his regime, Nicholas I embraced the three pillars of Russian absolutism symbolized in the motto "Orthodoxy, Autocracy, and Nationalism." *Orthodoxy* referred to the strong ties between the Russian Orthodox Church and the government. *Autocracy* was the absolute power of the state. *Nationalism* involved respect for Russian traditions and suppression of non-Russian groups within the empire.

Still, Nicholas realized that Russia needed to modernize. He issued a new law code and made some economic reforms. He even tried to limit the power of landowners over serfs. But he could see no way to change the system completely without angering Russian nobles and weakening the power of the czar. Before he died, he told his son, "I am handing you command of the country in a poor state."

Reforms of Alexander II

Alexander II came to the throne in 1855 during the Crimean War. The war had broken out after Russia tried to seize Ottoman lands along the Danube. Britain and France stepped in to help the Turks, invading the Crimean peninsula that juts into the Black Sea. The war, which ended in a Russian defeat, revealed the country's backwardness. It had only a few miles of

Russian Serfs
Masters held great power over serfs in Russia, and a large labor supply meant that few landowners invested in machines that could speed up agricultural labor. Here, women clear large stones from a field.

Theme: Economics and Technology How did the continuation of serfdom keep the Russian economy from advancing as quickly as that of Western Europe?

railroads, and the military bureaucracy was hopelessly inefficient. Many felt that dramatic changes were needed.

Emancipation A widespread popular reaction followed. Liberals demanded changes, and students demonstrated for reform. Pressed from all sides, Alexander II finally agreed to reforms. In 1861, he issued a royal decree that required emancipation, or freeing the serfs.

Freedom brought problems. Former serfs had to buy the land they had worked for so long. Many were too poor to do so. Also, the lands allotted to peasants were often too small to farm efficiently or to support a family. As a result, peasants remained poor, and discontent festered.

Still, emancipation was a turning point. Many peasants moved to the cities, taking jobs in factories and building Russian industries. Equally important, freeing the serfs boosted the drive for further reform.

Other Reforms Along with emancipation, Alexander set up a system of local government. Elected assemblies, called zemstvos, were made responsible for matters such as road repair, schools, and agriculture. At the local level, at least, Russians gained some experience of self-government.

The czar also introduced legal reforms based on ideas such as trial by jury. He eased censorship and tried to reform the military. A soldier's term of service was reduced from 25 years to 15, and brutal discipline was limited. Alexander also encouraged the growth of industry in Russia, which still relied almost entirely on agriculture.

A movement to liberate women also swept the urban centers of Russia. Since they were denied education in Russia, hundreds of privileged young women left their homes and families to study abroad in the few universities that would accept them. Many came to support revolutionary goals.

Reaction to Change

Alexander's reforms failed to satisfy many Russians. Peasants had freedom but not land. Liberals wanted a constitution and an elected legislature. Radicals, who had adopted socialist ideas from the West, demanded even more revolutionary changes. The czar, meantime, moved away from reform and toward repression.

Revolutionary Currents In the 1870s, some socialists carried the message of reform to the peasants. They went to live and work among the peasants, sometimes preaching rebellion. These educated young men and women had little success. The peasants scarcely understood them and sometimes turned them over to the police.

The failure of this "Go to the People" movement, combined with renewed government repression, sparked anger among radicals. Some turned to terrorism. A revolutionary group calling itself the People's Will assassinated officials and plotted to kill the czar. Their first attempts failed. Then, on a cold March day in 1881, terrorists hurled two bombs at Alexander's carriage. One struck down several guards. The second killed the leader known to some as the "czar emancipator."

Crackdown Alexander III responded to his father's assassination by reviving the harsh methods of Nicholas I. To wipe out liberals and revolutionaries, he increased the power of the secret police, restored strict censorship, and exiled critics to Siberia. He relied on his adviser and former tutor, Constantine Pobedonostsev (puh beh duh NAWS tsehv), who rejected all talk of democracy and constitutional government as "the lies of hollow and flabby people."

The czar also launched a program of Russification aimed at suppressing the cultures of non-Russian peoples within the empire. Alexander insisted on one language, Russian, and one church, the Russian Orthodox Church.

Global Connections

Freedom for Enslaved Americans

Emancipation was a troublesome issue around the world. For many years, the United States had been divided over slavery. In 1861, civil war erupted, in part over slavery. President Abraham Lincoln issued the Emancipation Proclamation in 1863, declaring the slaves in rebel areas to be free.

Neither Lincoln's action nor four years of bloody fighting settled the question. Finally, in 1865, the Thirteenth Amendment to the United States Constitution abolished slavery throughout the United States.

Even after emancipation, African Americans continued to face great challenges. Former slaves, like former serfs in Russia, had trouble acquiring farm land. Many worked for wages on the farms of former slaveholders, and others left to work in factories.

Theme: Political and Social Systems What settled the issue of slavery in the United States?

Russian Ballet

Although French and Italian in origin, ballet took on a bold, unique form in Russia. Beginning in the eighteenth century, European ballet teachers introduced the classical style to Russia. By the late 1800s, Russian choreographers and dancers had developed an expressive, muscular style that was to rejuvenate and dominate ballet in the twentieth century.

Russian dancer and choreographer Vaslav Nijinsky won worldwide fame while touring with the Ballet Russe in the early 1900s. Many consider him the greatest male ballet dancer of the twentieth century.

The ballet *Firebird*, shown here in a modern production, debuted in Paris in 1910. It was one of the first ballets to be created by a Russian choreographer and inspired by a Russian folk tale.

Twice destroyed by fires, Moscow's ornate Bolshoi ("Big") Theater took on its present form in 1856. Tiers of seats line the opulent interior of the theater, which can seat more than 2,000. Today, the grand theater is considered "the main theater of the country."

Fast Facts

- Until the early 1900s, common people in Russia were thought to be too ignorant to understand and appreciate ballet. Only nobles and people from the wealthy classes attended performances.

- In 1911, Sergey Diaghilev's Ballet Russe began to spread the influence of Russian dance worldwide.

- During World War II, dancers from the Bolshoi traveled from place to place, entertaining Russian troops in the field.

Portfolio Assessment

INTERNET Use the Internet or library resources to find out more about Russian ballet. Then, prepare a presentation on the significance of a particular Russian choreographer or dancer. If possible, include photographs or drawings of the individual you have selected.

Poles, Ukrainians, Finns, Armenians, and many others suffered persecution. The Russification campaign also targeted Jews and Muslims in the empire.

Persecution and Pogroms   Russia had acquired a large Jewish population when it carved up Poland and expanded into Ukraine. Under Alexander III, persecution of Russian Jews increased. The czar limited the number of Jews who were allowed to study in universities and practice professions such as law and medicine. He revived old laws that forced Jews to live in certain restricted areas.

Official persecution encouraged pogroms, or violent mob attacks on Jews. Gangs beat and killed Jews and looted and burned their homes and stores. The police did nothing to stop the violence. Faced with savage persecution, many Jews escaped from Russia. They became refugees, or people who flee their homeland to seek safety elsewhere. Large numbers of Russian Jews went to the United States. Though they often faced prejudice and great hardship there, they were safe from pogroms and official persecution. Jewish immigrants sent joyful news back to Russia: "There is no czar in America!"

Building Russian Industry

Under Alexander III and his son, Nicholas II, Russia finally entered the industrial age. In the 1890s, Count Serge Witte, finance minister to Nicholas, focused on economic development. Witte encouraged railroad building to connect iron and coal mines with factories and to transport goods across Russia. He secured foreign capital to invest in transportation systems and industry. Loans from France helped build the Trans-Siberian Railroad. Begun in the 1890s, it linked European Russia to the Pacific Ocean.

The drive to industrialize increased political and social problems. Government officials and business leaders applauded and encouraged economic growth. Nobles and peasants opposed it, fearing the changes brought by the new ways.

Industrialization also created new social ills as peasants flocked to cities to work in factories. Instead of a better life, they found long hours and low pay in dangerous conditions. In the slums around the factories, poverty, disease, and discontent multiplied.

Radicals sought supporters among the new industrial workers. At factory gates, socialists handed out pamphlets that preached the revolutionary ideas of Karl Marx. Among the revolutionaries of the 1890s was young Vladimir Ulyanov, whose older brother had been executed for plotting to kill Alexander III. Like many revolutionaries, Ulyanov used an alias, or false name—Lenin. In 1917, Lenin would take power in a revolution that transformed Russia.

Turning Point: Crisis and Revolution

War broke out between Russia and Japan in 1904. Nicholas II called on his people to fight for "the Faith, the Czar, and the Fatherland." But despite their efforts, the Russians suffered one humiliating defeat after another.

A Peaceful March   News of the military disasters unleashed pent-up discontent created by years of oppression. Protesters poured into the streets. Workers went on strike with demands for shorter hours and better wages. Liberals called for a constitution and reforms to overhaul the inefficient, corrupt government.

As the crisis deepened, a young Orthodox priest, Father George Gapon, organized a march for Sunday, January 22, 1905. Father Gapon felt certain that the "Little Father," as many Russians called the czar, would help his people if only he understood their sufferings. The parade flowed through

Geography and History

Russia's Long Iron Road

Beginning in the 1890s, Russian workers laid more than 5,000 miles of track to build the Trans-Siberian Railroad, the longest railroad in the world at that time. Siberia's harsh landscape and climate challenged workers. Iron, stone, hardwoods, and food had to be shipped thousands of miles to the crews.

In the chilling winters, many workers died from hypothermia. With no safety devices, some fell to their deaths onto frozen rivers. To lay tracks in some areas, workers had to dynamite permanently frozen soil. These explosions often proved fatal, as did epidemics of bubonic plague, anthrax, and cholera.

Theme: Geography and History What geographic and climatic challenges did the railroad builders face in Siberia?

the icy streets of St. Petersburg toward the czar's lavish Winter Palace. Chanting prayers and singing hymns, workers carried holy icons and pictures of the czar. They also brought a petition for justice and freedom, which was addressed to Nicholas.

Bloody Sunday Fearing the marchers, the czar had fled the palace and called in soldiers. As the people approached, they saw troops lined up across the square. Suddenly, gunfire rang out. Men and women ran and fell. More shots left hundreds dead or wounded in the snow.

A woman stumbling away from the scene of the massacre moaned: "The czar has deserted us! They shot away the orthodox faith." Indeed, the slaughter marked a turning point for Russians. "Bloody Sunday" killed the people's faith and trust in the czar.

The Revolution of 1905 In the months that followed Bloody Sunday, discontent exploded across Russia. Strikes multiplied. In some cities, workers took over local government. In the countryside, peasants revolted and demanded land. Minority nationalities called for autonomy from Russia. Terrorists targeted officials, and some assassins were cheered as heroes by discontented Russians.

At last, the clamor grew so great that Nicholas was forced to announce sweeping reforms. In the October Manifesto, he promised "freedom of person, conscience, speech, assembly, and union." He agreed to summon a Duma, or elected national legislature. No law, he declared, would go into effect without approval by the Duma.

Results of the Revolution The manifesto won over moderates, leaving socialists isolated. These divisions helped the czar, who had no intention of letting strikers, revolutionaries, and rebellious peasants challenge him.

In 1906, the first Duma met, but the czar quickly dissolved it when leaders criticized the government. Nicholas then appointed a new prime minister, Peter Stolypin (stuh LEE pihn). Arrests, pogroms, and executions followed as the conservative Stolypin sought to restore order.

Stolypin soon realized that Russia needed reform, not just repression. To regain peasant support, he introduced moderate land reforms. He strengthened the zemstvos and improved education. These reforms were too limited to meet the broad needs of most Russians, and dissatisfaction still simmered. Stolypin was assassinated in 1911. Several more Dumas met during this period, but new voting laws made sure they were conservative. By 1914, Russia was still an autocracy, simmering with unrest.

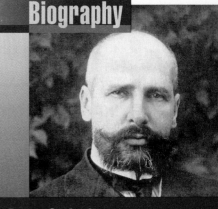

Biography

Peter Stolypin 1862–1911

Violence surrounded Peter Stolypin, who was once described as "a tall stiff man with a dead white face and a dead white beard." As governor and later prime minister, he used harsh measures to silence opposition. On his orders, trials of terrorists were held within 24 hours of arrest; executions were held immediately upon conviction. More than 1,000 suspected terrorists were executed in less than a year. The noose used to hang them came to be known as "Stolypin's necktie."

Stolypin and his family were also the targets of violence. In 1907, his opponents bombed his house, killing many servants and severely injuring his children. Four years later, Stolypin himself was assassinated while attending the theater.

Theme: Impact of the Individual How did Stolypin deal with terrorism?

SECTION 5 Assessment

Recall

1. **Identify: (a)** Decembrist Revolt, **(b)** Alexander II, **(c)** Russification, **(d)** Bloody Sunday, **(e)** October Manifesto, **(f)** Peter Stolypin.
2. **Define: (a)** colossus, **(b)** emancipation, **(c)** zemstvo, **(d)** pogrom, **(e)** Duma.

Comprehension

3. What conditions in Russia posed challenges during the early 1800s?
4. How did Russian czars often react to change?

5. **(a)** What were the causes of the revolution of 1905? **(b)** How did Nicholas II respond?

Critical Thinking and Writing

6. **Analyzing Information** Alexander II declared that it is "better to abolish serfdom from above than to wait until it will be abolished by a movement from below." Explain his statement.
7. **Making Inferences** What does Bloody Sunday suggest about the relationship between the czar and the Russian people?

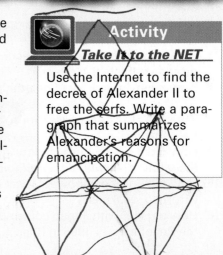

Activity

Take It to the NET

Use the Internet to find the decree of Alexander II to free the serfs. Write a paragraph that summarizes Alexander's reasons for emancipation.

23 Review and Assessment

Creating a Chapter Summary

On a sheet of paper, make a table like the one shown here to list events that led to nationalism in Germany, Italy, Austria, the Balkans, and Russia in the 1800s.

CD-ROM Review For additional review of the major concepts of Chapter 23, see the *Guide to the Essentials of World History* or the *Interactive Student Tutorial CD-ROM*.

GERMANY	ITALY	AUSTRIA	BALKANS	RUSSIA
• German states unite under William I • Empire takes leading role in Europe • Bismarck/Iron Chancellor		• Francis I and Metternich uphold conservative goals •		

Web Site Self-Test For practice test questions for Chapter 23, see **www.phschool.com**.

Reviewing Vocabulary

Review the meaning of the chapter vocabulary words listed below. Then, write a sentence for each word in which you define the word and describe its relation to nationalism in Europe.

1. *Realpolitik*
2. annex
3. Reich
4. *Kulturkampf*
5. anarchist
6. colossus
7. emancipation
8. zemstvo
9. pogrom
10. Duma

Recalling Key Facts

11. What factors aided German economic growth in the late 1800s?
12. How did Bismarck try to persuade workers not to support the socialists?
13. What was the goal of Mazzini's Young Italy society?
14. How did the Hapsburg leaders deal with the ethnic diversity of their empire?
15. How did European powers react to Ottoman weakness?
16. How did war with Japan contribute to the Revolution of 1905 in Russia?

Critical Thinking and Writing

17. **Analyzing Information** Study the painting that appears in the feature in Section 1. **(a)** What is the subject of the painting? **(b)** Where does the scene take place? **(c)** Who seems to be the central figure of the painting? **(d)** What conclusions can you draw from this about the power structure in Germany at the time?
18. **Predicting Consequences** Based on your reading of the chapter, predict the consequences of the following: **(a)** defeat of France in the Franco-Prussian War, **(b)** growth of German nationalism and militarism in the late 1800s, **(c)** failure to satisfy nationalist ambitions in Austria-Hungary, **(d)** weakening of the Ottoman empire.
19. **Connecting to Geography** How did regional differences contribute to continued divisions in Italy after unification?

20. **Linking Past and Present** Is nationalism a force in the world today? Give examples from current events to support your answer.

On January 22, 1905, Father George Gapon led Russian workers to the Winter Palace to deliver a petition to the czar. Unfortunately, Nicholas II had called in soldiers and fled. The result was the massacre known as Bloody Sunday. Read the workers' petition, then answer the questions that follow.

> "We, the workers of the town of St. Petersburg, with our wives, our children and our aged and feeble parents, have come to you, Sire, in search of justice and protection. We have fallen into poverty, we are oppressed, we are loaded with a crushing burden of toil, we are insulted, we are not recognized as men, we are treated as slaves who should bear their sad and bitter lot in patience and silence. . . . Do not refuse to protect your people; raise [Russia] from the grave of arbitrary power, poverty and ignorance; permit it to dispose of its own fate; free it from the intolerable oppression of officials; destroy the wall between yourself and your people—and let it govern the country with you."
>
> —quoted in *Revolution From 1789 to 1906* (Postgate)

21. **(a)** On whose behalf is the petition presented? **(b)** Whom does the petition blame?

22. What hardships does the petition describe?

23. What are the demonstrators' goals?

24. What is the tone of this petition?

25. If Nicholas had stayed to receive this petition, do you think he would have acted differently? Why or why not?

Use the Internet to research the history of the Hapsburgs and their roles in European history. Create a time line that shows major political events relating to the Hapsburgs. Illustrate your time line with copies of photographs or paintings of significant locations, battles, and rulers.

Unification of Italy, 1858–1870

Use the map to answer the following questions:

26. **(a)** When was the largest part of Italy added to the Kingdom of Sardinia? **(b)** When was the last part added?

27. To what country did Corsica belong?

28. In degrees of longitude, approximately how much farther east is Naples than Rome?

29. What body of water lies between Italy and the Ottoman empire?

30. **(a)** Describe the route of Garibaldi's expedition in 1860. **(b)** About how many miles did the expedition travel?

31. Why, in your opinion, was Rome the last area to become part of unified Italy?

Skills Tip

Degrees of longitude tell you how far east or west a point lies from the Prime Meridian.

CHAPTER 24

Growth of Western Democracies 1815–1914

Chapter Preview

1 **Britain Becomes More Democratic**
2 **A Century of Reform**
3 **Division and Democracy in France**
4 **Expansion of the United States**

CHAPTER EVENTS

1832
The Great Reform Act gives more British men the right to vote. The houses of Parliament, shown here, will be the center of a century of political reform.

1845
Ireland's Great Hunger begins, leading to widespread death and disease and mass emigration.

1861
The American Civil War begins. The four-year battle between North and South will lead to the end of slavery in the United States.

1815   1835   1855

GLOBAL EVENTS

1821 Mexico wins independence from Spain.

1858 Britain begins direct rule of India.

Western Democracies, 1900

PACIFIC OCEAN

UNITED STATES

Washington, D.C. ★

ATLANTIC OCEAN

Gulf of Mexico

GREAT BRITAIN GERMANY RUSSIA St. Petersburg ★
London ★ ★Berlin
FRANCE ★Paris Vienna ★ ★Budapest

Black Sea
40°N
Mediterranean Sea
20°N

- Democratic governments
- Autocratic governments

The Industrial Revolution uprooted old ways of life. While Germany and Russia tried to stem the tide of change, Britain, France, and the United States slowly extended democratic rights.

Robinson Projection
0   1000   2000 Miles
0 1000 2000 Kilometers

120°W   100°W   80°W   60°W   40°W   20°W   0°   20°E   40°E

Mr. John Bull-No it does not John I must have one of MY own

THE VOTE

John Bull My umbrella protects us all!

1897
Theodor Herzl organizes the First Zionist Congress for the purpose of founding a Jewish state.

1870
The Franco-Prussian War leads to the fall of Napoleon III and the founding of a new French republic.

1900s
The women's suffrage movement grows in Britain. This 1911 cartoon expresses the determination of British women to win the vote.

1875

1895

1915

1869 The French-built Suez Canal opens in Eygpt.

1889 Brazil becomes a republic.

1893 New Zealand is the first nation to give women the vote.

1910 The Union of South Africa is formed.

Britain Becomes More Democratic

Reading Focus

- Why did reformers seek to change Parliament in the 1800s?
- What values did Queen Victoria represent?
- How did the Liberal and Conservative parties help bring a new era to British politics?

Vocabulary

rotten borough
electorate
secret ballot

Taking Notes

As you read this section, prepare an outline of the contents. Use Roman numerals to indicate major headings. Use capital letters for subheadings, and use numbers for the supporting details. The example at right will help you get started.

I. **Reforming Parliament**
  A. **Pressure for change**
    1. **Religious restrictions on voting**
    2.
    3.
  B. **Reform Act of 1832**
    1.
    2.

Main Idea Throughout the 1800s, political reform gradually expanded suffrage and made Parliament more democratic.

Primary Source

The Need to Reform Parliament

English-born Thomas Paine significantly influenced political thought in Europe and North America:

"What is government more than the management of the affairs of a Nation? It is not, and from its nature cannot be, the property of any particular man or family, but the whole community. . . .

The county of York, which contains near a million souls, sends two county members; and so does the county of Rutland which contains not a hundredth part of that number. The old town of Sarum, which contains not three houses, sends two members; and the town of Manchester, which contains upwards of sixty thousand souls, is not admitted to send any. Is there any principle in these things?"

—Thomas Paine,
Rights of Man, 1791

Skills Assessment

Primary Source Why was representation in Parliament unfair, according to Paine?

Setting the Scene

Charles Egremont, a wealthy young man, is proud to be British. One day, he boasts to strangers that Victoria, the queen of England, "reigns over the greatest nation that ever existed." "Which nation?" asks one of the strangers, "for she reigns over two":

> "Two nations: between whom there is no [communication] and no sympathy; who are as ignorant of each other's habits, thoughts, and feelings, as if they were . . . inhabitants of different planets; who are formed by a different breeding, are fed by a different food, are ordered by different manners, and are not governed by the same laws."
> —Benjamin Disraeli, *Sybil*

What are these "two nations," Egremont wonders. "THE RICH AND THE POOR," the stranger replies.

Egremont is the hero of Benjamin Disraeli's novel *Sybil*. Disraeli, a leading political figure at the time of the Industrial Revolution, had seen both the world of aristocratic luxury and the appalling poverty of factory towns and rural villages. In the 1800s, Disraeli and other political leaders slowly worked to bridge Britain's "two nations" and extend democratic rights. Unlike some of its neighbors in Europe, Britain generally achieved change through reform rather than revolution.

Reforming Parliament

In 1815, Britain was a constitutional monarchy with a parliament and two political parties. Still, it was far from democratic. Although members of the House of Commons were elected, less than five percent of the people had the right to vote. Wealthy nobles and squires, or country landowners, dominated politics and heavily influenced voters. In addition, the House of Lords—made up of hereditary nobles and high-ranking clergy—could veto any bill passed by the House of Commons.

Pressure for Change Long-standing laws kept many people from voting. Catholics and non-Anglican Protestants, for example, could not vote or serve in Parliament. In the 1820s, reformers pushed to end religious restrictions. After fierce debate, Parliament finally granted Catholics and non-Anglican Protestants equal political rights.

An even greater battle soon erupted over making Parliament more representative. During the Industrial Revolution, centers of population shifted.

Some rural towns lost so many people that they had few or no voters. Yet local landowners in these rotten boroughs still sent members to Parliament. At the same time, populous new industrial cities like Manchester and Birmingham had no seats in Parliament at all because they had not existed as important population centers in earlier times.

Reform Act of 1832 By 1830, Whigs and Tories* were battling over a bill to reform Parliament. In the streets, supporters of reform chanted, "The Bill, the whole Bill, and nothing but the Bill!" Their shouts seemed to echo the cries of revolutionaries on the continent.

Parliament finally passed the Great Reform Act in 1832. It redistributed seats in the House of Commons, giving representation to large towns and cities and eliminating rotten boroughs. It also enlarged the electorate, the body of people allowed to vote, by granting suffrage to more men. The Act did, however, keep a property requirement for voting.

The Reform Act of 1832 did not bring full democracy, but it did give a greater political voice to middle-class men. Landowning nobles, however, remained a powerful force in the government and in the economy.

The Chartist Movement The reform bill did not help rural or urban workers. Some of them demanded more radical change. In the 1830s, protesters known as Chartists drew up the People's Charter. This petition demanded universal male suffrage, annual parliamentary elections, and salaries for members of Parliament. Another key demand was for a secret ballot, which would allow people to cast their votes without announcing them publicly.

Twice the Chartists presented petitions with over a million signatures to Parliament. Both petitions were ignored. In 1848, as revolutions swept Europe, the Chartists prepared a third petition and organized a march on Parliament. Fearing violence, the government moved to suppress the march. Soon after, the unsuccessful Chartist movement declined. In time, however, Parliament would pass most of the major reforms proposed by the Chartists.

The Victorian Age

From 1837 to 1901, the great symbol in British life was Queen Victoria. Her reign was the longest in British history. Although she exercised little real political power, she set the tone for what is now called the Victorian age.

Symbol of a Nation's Values As queen, Victoria came to embody the values of her age. These Victorian ideals included duty, thrift, honesty, hard work, and—above all—respectability. Today, we associate most of these qualities with the Victorian middle class. However, people at all levels of society shared these ideals, even if they could not always live up to them.

Victoria herself embraced a strict code of morals and manners. As a young woman, she married a German prince, Albert, and they raised a large family. Albert held a lower rank than Victoria. Still, she treated him with the devotion a dutiful wife was expected to have for her husband. When he died in 1861, Victoria went into deep mourning and dressed in black for the rest of her reign.

Victoria, Queen of England
Although she held little political power, Queen Victoria came to stand for the values of her age. This plate was presented to Victoria on the occasion of her fiftieth year on the throne.

Theme: Political and Social Systems How do the words and images on this plate reflect Britain's sense of optimism and self-confidence?

---

*The Whig party largely represented middle-class and business interests. The Tory party spoke for nobles, landowners, and others whose interests and income were rooted in agriculture.

Two Political Giants
As the leading political figures of Victorian England, Benjamin Disraeli (left) and William Gladstone (right) were often the subjects of caricatures.

Theme: Political and Social Systems Why are political caricatures like these often seen as a sign of a healthy democracy?

A Confident Age Under Victoria, the British middle class—and growing numbers of the working class—felt great confidence in the future. That confidence grew as Britain expanded its already huge empire. Victoria, the empress of India and ruler of some 300 million subjects around the world, became a revered symbol of British might.

As she aged from teenaged monarch to grieving widow to revered national symbol, Victoria witnessed growing agitation for social reform. The queen herself commented that the lower classes "earn their bread and riches so deservedly that they cannot and ought not to be kept back." As the Victorian era went on, reformers continued the push toward greater social and economic justice.

A New Era in British Politics

In the 1860s, a new era dawned in British politics. The old political parties regrouped under new leadership. Benjamin Disraeli forged the Tories into the modern Conservative party. The Whigs, led by William Gladstone, evolved into the Liberal party. Between 1868 and 1880, as the majority in Parliament swung between the two parties, Gladstone and Disraeli alternated as prime minister. Both fought for important reforms.

Expanding Suffrage Disraeli and the Conservative party pushed through the Reform Bill of 1867. By giving the vote to many working-class men, the new law almost doubled the size of the electorate.

In the 1880s, it was the turn of Gladstone and the Liberal party to extend suffrage. Their reforms gave the vote to farmworkers and most other men. By century's end, almost-universal male suffrage, the secret ballot, and other Chartist ambitions had been achieved.

Limiting the Lords In the early 1900s, Liberals in the House of Commons pressed ahead with social reforms. But many bills passed by the Commons met defeat in the House of Lords. In particular, the Lords used their veto power to block any attempt to increase taxes on the wealthy.

In 1911, a Liberal government passed measures to restrict the power of the Lords, including their power to veto tax bills. The Lords resisted. Finally, the government threatened to create enough new lords to approve the law, and the Lords backed down. People hailed the change as a victory for democracy. In time, the House of Lords would become largely a ceremonial body with little power. The elected House of Commons would reign supreme.

SECTION 1 Assessment

Recall
1. **Identify:** (a) Benjamin Disraeli, (b) Chartism, (c) Victoria, (d) William Gladstone.
2. **Define:** (a) rotten borough, (b) electorate, (c) secret ballot.

Comprehension
3. How did the Reform Act of 1832 change Parliament?
4. What middle-class values are associated with the Victorian age?
5. What reforms did the Liberal and Conservative parties achieve?

Critical Thinking and Writing
6. **Drawing Conclusions** Why do you think the Chartists demanded (a) a secret ballot, (b) salaries for members of Parliament?
7. **Analyzing Literature** Reread the excerpt from *Sybil* at the beginning of this section. (a) Restate the stranger's main idea in your own words. (b) Why is Egremont surprised by this view of Britain? (c) Would you consider this novel a reliable source of information about Britain in the early 1800s? Why or why not?

Activity

Take It to the NET

Use the Internet to research the life of Queen Victoria. Then, with a group of classmates, present your findings in a "This Is Your Life" format. Have one student play Victoria and another the host. Other students will play surprise guests who can tell about highlights of Victoria's life.

SECTION 2 A Century of Reform

Reading Focus

- What social and economic reforms benefited British workers and others?
- How did British women work to win the vote?
- What were the goals of Irish nationalists?

Vocabulary

- free trade
- repeal
- capital offense
- penal colony
- absentee landlord
- home rule

Taking Notes

On a sheet of paper, create a concept web like this one. As you read the section, add information to the web. Add as many circles as you need.

Main Idea Parliament passed a wide variety of reform measures, but women's suffrage and the status of Ireland remained difficult issues.

Setting the Scene

Her aristocratic family would have been shocked. Here was Lady Constance Lytton, disguised as a seamstress—and lying in a prison hospital! Lytton had been arrested for taking part in a women's suffrage protest. Now, she refused to eat. Her hunger strike, she vowed, would go on until the British government granted the vote to women. Lytton later recalled:

> "I was visited again by the Senior Medical Officer, who asked me how long I had been without food. I said I had eaten a buttered scone and a banana sent in by friends to the police station on Friday at about midnight. He said, 'Oh, then, this is the fourth day; that is too long, I shall feed you, I must feed you at once.'"
> —Constance Lytton, *Prisons and Prisoners*

In the end, the doctor—with the help of five prison matrons—force-fed Lytton through a tube. Yet the painful ordeal failed to weaken her resolve. "No surrender," she whispered. "No surrender."

Lytton's 1910 hunger strike was part of the long struggle for women's suffrage in Britain. Suffragists were not the only people to fight for change. Between 1815 and 1914, Parliament responded to widespread discontent with a series of social and economic reforms. At the same time, the question of British control over Ireland was becoming a dominant and divisive political issue.

Social and Economic Reforms

During the early and mid-1800s, Parliament passed a wide variety of important new laws. One of the most controversial measures involved the issue of free trade, or trade between countries without quotas, tariffs, or other restrictions.

Free Trade and the Corn Laws In the early 1800s, Britain, like other European nations, taxed foreign imports in order to protect local economies. But supporters of free trade demanded an end to such protective tariffs. Free traders, usually middle-class business leaders, agreed with Adam Smith that a policy of laissez faire would increase prosperity for all. If tariffs were abolished, merchants everywhere would have larger markets in which to sell their goods, and consumers would benefit from open competition.

Punishing Crime
These pictures are from an 1862 study of Britain's new system of reformed prisons. The cell at left reflects the new idea that prisoners should be confined to individual cells instead of milling around a common prison yard. At right, female convicts take care of their children in a prison nursery.

Theme: Political and Social Systems **What does the picture on the left show you about how many prisoners spent their day?**

Some British tariffs were repealed in the 1820s. However, fierce debate erupted over the Corn Laws, which imposed high tariffs on imported grain. (In Britain, "corn" refers to all cereal grains, such as wheat, barley, and oats.) Farmers and wealthy landowners supported the Corn Laws because they kept the price of British grain high. Free traders, however, wanted Parliament to repeal, or cancel, the Corn Laws. They argued that repeal of these laws would lower the price of grain, make bread cheaper for city workers, and open up trade in general.

Parliament finally repealed the Corn Laws in 1846, after widespread crop failures swept many parts of Europe. Liberals hailed the repeal as a victory for free trade and laissez-faire capitalism. However, in the late 1800s, economic hard times led Britain and other European countries to impose protective tariffs on many goods again.

Campaign Against Slavery During the 1700s, Enlightenment thinkers had turned the spotlight on the evils of the slave trade. At the time, British ships were carrying more Africans to the Americas than was any other European country. Under pressure from middle-class reformers, the campaign against the slave trade and slavery slowly took off. In 1807, Britain became the first leading European power to abolish the slave trade.

Banning the slave trade did not end slavery. Although the Congress of Vienna had condemned slavery, it had taken no action. In Britain, liberals preached the immorality of slavery. Finally, in 1833, Parliament passed a law banning slavery in all British colonies. Yet British textile manufacturers still imported cheap cotton produced by enslaved African Americans in the United States.

Crime and Punishment Other reforms were aimed at the criminal justice system. In the early 1800s, more than 200 crimes were punishable by death. Such capital offenses included not only murder but also shoplifting, sheep stealing, and impersonating an army veteran. In practice, some juries refused to convict criminals, because the punishments were so harsh. Executions were public occasions, and the hanging of a well-known murderer might attract thousands of curious spectators. Afterward, instead of receiving a proper burial, the criminal's body might be given to a medical college for dissection.

Victorian reformers began to reduce the number of capital offenses. By 1850, the death penalty was reserved for murder, piracy, treason, and arson. Many petty criminals were instead transported to penal colonies, or special settlements for convicts, in the new British territories of Australia and New

Zealand. In 1868, Parliament ended public hangings. Additional reforms improved prison conditions and outlawed imprisonment for debt.

Victories for the Working Class

"Four [ghosts] haunt the Poor: Old Age, Accident, Sickness and Unemployment," declared Liberal politician David Lloyd George in 1905. "We are going to [expel] them." By the early 1900s, Parliament gradually passed a series of reforms designed to help the men, women, and children whose labor supported the new industrial society.

Working Conditions As you have read, working conditions in the early industrial age were grim and often dangerous. Gradually, Parliament passed laws to regulate conditions in factories and mines. In 1842, for example, mineowners were forbidden to employ women or children under age 10. An 1847 law limited women and children to a 10-hour day. Later in the 1800s, the government regulated many safety conditions in factories and mines—and sent inspectors to see that the laws were enforced. Other laws set minimum wages and maximum hours of work.

Labor Unions Early in the Industrial Revolution, labor unions were outlawed. Under pressure, government and business leaders slowly accepted worker organizations. Trade unions were made legal in 1825. At the same time, though, strikes remained illegal.

Despite restrictions, unions spread, and gradually they won additional rights. Between 1890 and 1914, union membership soared. Besides winning higher wages and shorter hours for workers, unions pressed for other laws to improve the lives of the working class.

Later Reforms During the late 1800s and early 1900s, both political parties enacted social reforms to benefit the working class. Disraeli sponsored laws to improve public health and housing for workers in cities. Under Gladstone, an Education Act called for free elementary education for all children. Gladstone also pushed to open up government jobs based on merit rather than on birth or wealth.

Another force for reform was the Fabian Society, a socialist organization founded in 1883. The Fabians promoted gradual change through legal means rather than by violence. Though small in number, the Fabians had a strong influence on British politics.

In 1900, socialists and union members backed the formation of a new political party, which became the Labour party. ("Labour" is the British spelling of "labor.") The Labour party would grow in power and membership until, by the 1920s, it surpassed the Liberal party as one of Britain's two major parties.

In the early 1900s, Britain began to pass social welfare laws to protect the well-being of the poor and disadvantaged. These laws were modeled on those Bismarck had introduced in Germany. They protected workers with accident, health, and unemployment insurance as well as old-age pensions. One result of such reforms was that Marxism gained only limited support among the British working classes. The middle class hailed reforms as proof that democracy was working.

Votes for Women

In Britain, as elsewhere, women struggled for the right to vote against strong opposition. Just as Parliament had rejected the Chartist demand for universal male suffrage in 1848, so it resisted the demands of the women's suffrage movement 50 years later.

Women themselves were divided on the issue. Some women opposed suffrage altogether. Queen Victoria, for example, called the suffrage struggle

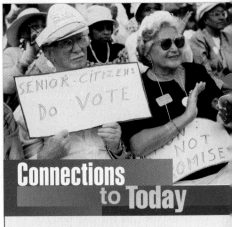

Connections to Today

Your Senior Years: Is Your Future Secure?

The United States created its Social Security system in 1935. It is similar to some of the social reforms Britain introduced years earlier. But Social Security was designed to supplement other pension plans and personal savings. Today, it has become a primary source of retirement income for many older Americans.

Social Security is now facing increasing challenges. The rising cost of living forces retirees to stretch their Social Security benefits more than ever. Also, life expectancies have increased dramatically. In 1900, only 4 percent of the American population was age 65 or over. By the year 2000, that figure was almost 13 percent—and growing. In the future, there will be many more retirees who live longer and healthier lives. These changes will put strains on the Social Security system, and some experts predict that funds will be exhausted by 2032.

Theme: Continuity and Change What might happen if the Social Security system were to run completely out of funding?

Aid for Ireland

Americans from all walks of life rushed to the aid of the starving Irish. Quakers were the first to organize relief efforts. Catholic churches, Jewish synagogues, and women's groups worked to raise funds. The American government encouraged food shipments by announcing that no road or canal tolls would be charged on any supplies headed for Ireland.

The Choctaw people, whose own forced relocation in the 1830s resulted in great hardship and many deaths, identified with the plight of the Irish people. Still recovering from food shortages of their own, the Choctaws contributed over $700—a large sum in the 1840s.

Theme: Global Interaction
How do groups and individuals today respond to disasters around the world?

Then, in 1845, disaster struck. A blight, or disease, destroyed the potato crop. Other crops, such as wheat and oats, were not affected. Yet British landowners continued to ship these crops outside Ireland, leaving little for the Irish except the blighted potatoes. The result was a terrible famine that the Irish called the "Great Hunger."

Witnesses described many "scenes of frightful hunger." One official told of entering what he thought was a deserted village. In one home, he saw "six famished and ghastly skeletons, to all appearances dead . . . huddled in a corner on some filthy straw."

"I approached with horror, and found by a low moaning they were alive—they were in a fever, four children, a woman and what had once been a man. . . . In a few minutes I was surrounded by at least 200 such phantoms, such frightful spectres as no words can describe, either from famine or from fever."
—letter to the *Times* (London), December 24, 1846

In four years, at least one million Irish men, women, and children died of starvation or disease. More than one million emigrated to the United States and Canada. The Great Hunger left a legacy of Irish bitterness toward the English that still exists today.

Struggle for Home Rule Throughout the century, Irish demands for self-rule intensified. In the 1850s, some Irish militants organized the Fenian Brotherhood. Its goal was to liberate Ireland from British rule by force. In the 1870s, moderate Irish nationalists found a rousing leader in Charles Stewart Parnell. He rallied Irish members of Parliament to press for home rule, or local self-government. The debate dragged on for decades.

The "Irish question" disrupted English politics. At times, political parties were so deeply split over the Irish question that they could not take care of other business. As prime minister, Gladstone pushed for reforms in Ireland. He ended the use of Irish tithe money to support the Anglican church and tried to ease the hardships of Irish tenant farmers. New laws prevented landlords from charging unfair rents and protected the rights of tenants to the land they worked.

Finally, in 1914, Parliament passed a home rule bill. But it delayed putting the new law into effect when World War I broke out that year. As you will read, the southern counties of Ireland finally became independent in 1921.

SECTION 2 Assessment

Recall
1. **Identify:** (a) Corn Laws, (b) Fabian Society, (c) Emmeline Pankhurst, (d) Catholic Emancipation Act, (e) Great Hunger, (f) Charles Stewart Parnell.
2. **Define:** (a) free trade, (b) repeal, (c) capital offense, (d) penal colony, (e) absentee landlord, (f) home rule.

Comprehension
3. Describe three social reforms that helped the British working class.
4. What actions did women suffragists take to achieve their goals?

5. (a) Why did Irish nationalists oppose British rule? (b) Describe two reforms that improved conditions in Ireland.

Critical Thinking and Writing
6. **Analyzing Ideas** How is the idea of free trade linked to the principles of laissez faire and competition?
7. **Defending a Position** Do you agree that the tactics used by suffragists like Emmeline Pankhurst were necessary at the time? Why or why not?

Activity

Designing a Poster
Design a poster that an Irish nationalist of the late 1800s or early 1900s might have used in the struggle for home rule. First, decide whether your main goal is to win support from the Irish or to persuade members of the British Parliament.

Reading Focus

- What domestic and foreign policies did Napoleon III pursue?

- What impact did the Dreyfus affair and other challenges have on the Third Republic?

- How did the French government take steps toward reform in the early 1900s?

Vocabulary

provisional

premier

coalition

libel

Taking Notes

On a sheet of paper, draw a time line to show the main events of this section. Use the time line shown here to help you get started.

1848	1860s	1863	1914
Second Empire	Napoleon III eases controls	Napoleon III tries to put Maximilian on throne of Mexico	

Main Idea ▶ Democratic reforms in France took place under the Second Empire of Napoleon III and its successor, the Third Republic.

Setting the Scene The news sent shock waves throughout Paris. An entire French army under the emperor Napoleon III had surrendered to the Prussians at the city of Sedan. Still worse, Prussian forces were now about to advance on Paris. Could the city survive?

Georges Clemenceau (KLEHM uhn soh), a young French doctor who had entered politics, rallied the people of Paris to defend their city and their homeland. "Citizens," he cried, "must France destroy herself and disappear, or shall she resume her old place in the vanguard of nations?" Clemenceau concluded:

> "Each of us knows his duty. We are children of the Revolution. Let us seek inspiration in the example of our forefathers in 1792, and like them we shall conquer. *Vive la France!* [Long Live France!]"
> —Georges Clemenceau, quoted in *Clemenceau and the Third Republic* (Jackson)

For four months, Paris did resist the German onslaught. But finally, in January 1871, the French government at Versailles was forced to accept Prussian surrender terms.

The Franco-Prussian War ended a long period of French domination of Europe that had begun under Louis XIV. Yet the Third Republic rose from the ashes of the Second Empire of Napoleon III. Economic growth, democratic reforms, and the fierce nationalism expressed by Clemenceau all played a part in shaping modern France.

France Under Napoleon III

After the revolution of 1848, Napoleon III set up the Second Empire. His appeal cut across lines of class and ideology. The bourgeoisie saw him as a strong leader who would restore order. His promise to end poverty gave hope to the lower classes. People of all classes were attracted by his name, a reminder of the days when France had towered over Europe. Unlike his famous uncle, however, Napoleon III would bring France neither glory nor an empire.

Limits on Liberty On the surface, the Second Empire looked like a constitutional monarchy. In fact, Napoleon III ruled almost as a dictator, with the power to appoint his cabinet, the upper house of the legislature, and

Napoleon III
This portrait of Emperor Napoleon III suggests his pride and love of pomp. Like many monarchs of his day, Napoleon often had himself painted or photographed in military garb.

Theme: Political and Social Systems Why do you think many monarchs favored military dress?

The Siege of Paris, 1870

Prussian siege line
Prussian batteries
Prussian attacks
French defensive line
French forts
French attacks
City walls

Skills Assessment

Geography For four months, Prussian troops surrounded Paris. In the painting at right, a hot air balloon leaves the city.

1. **Location** *On the map, locate (a) Paris, (b) Seine River, (c) Marne River, (d) Versailles.*
2. **Movement** *In what area did the Prussians launch attacks?*
3. **Critical Thinking Synthesizing Information** *Based on the map, why do you think Parisians made use of hot air balloons during the Prussian siege?*

many officials. Although the assembly was elected by universal male suffrage, appointed officials "managed" elections so that supporters of the emperor would win. Debate was limited, and newspapers faced strict censorship.

In the 1860s, the emperor began to ease controls. He lifted some censorship and gave the legislature more power. On the eve of his disastrous war with Prussia, Napoleon III even issued a new constitution that extended democratic rights.

Economic Growth Like much of Europe, France prospered at mid-century. Napoleon III promoted investment in industry and large-scale ventures such as railroad building and the urban renewal of Paris. During this period, a French entrepreneur, Ferdinand de Lesseps (duh LEHS uhps), organized the building of the Suez Canal to link the Mediterranean with the Red Sea and thus the Indian Ocean.

Workers enjoyed some benefits from economic growth. Napoleon legalized labor unions, extended public education to girls, and created a small public health program. Still, in France, as in other industrial nations, many people lived in great poverty.

Foreign Adventures Napoleon's worst failures were in foreign affairs. In the 1860s, he tried to place Maximilian, an Austrian Hapsburg prince, on the throne of Mexico. Through Maximilian, Napoleon hoped to turn Mexico into a French satellite. But after a large commitment of troops and money, the adventure failed. Mexican patriots resisted fiercely, and the United States protested. After four years, France withdrew its troops. Maximilian was overthrown and shot by Mexican patriots.

Napoleon's successes were almost as costly as his failures. He helped Italian nationalists defeat Austria, gaining Nice (NEES) and Savoy. But this victory backfired when a united Italy emerged as a rival on France's border. And, though France and Britain won the Crimean War, France had little to show for its terrible losses except a small foothold in the Middle East.

War With Prussia At this time, France grew increasingly concerned about the rise of a great rival, Prussia. The Prussian leader Otto von Bismarck shrewdly manipulated French worries to lure Napoleon into war in 1870.

As you have read, the Franco-Prussian War was a disaster for France. After Napoleon III was captured at Sedan, German forces began the four-month siege of Paris. Encircled by Prussian troops, starving Parisians were reduced to catching rats and killing circus animals for food.

Challenges of the Third Republic

After Napoleon's capture, republicans in Paris had declared an end to the Second Empire. They set up a provisional, or temporary, government that evolved into France's Third Republic.

In 1871, the newly elected National Assembly accepted a harsh peace with Germany. France had to surrender the provinces of Alsace and Lorraine and pay a huge sum to Germany. The French burned to avenge their loss.

The Paris Commune In 1871, an uprising broke out in Paris. Rebels set up the Paris Commune. Like the radical government during the French Revolution, its goal was to save the Republic from royalists. Communards, as the rebels were called, included workers and socialists as well as bourgeois republicans. As patriots, they rejected the harsh peace that the National Assembly had signed with Germany. Radicals dreamed of creating a new socialist order.

The National Assembly ordered the Commune to disband. When the Communards refused, the government sent troops to besiege Paris. For weeks, civil war raged. As government troops advanced, the rebels toppled great Paris monuments and slaughtered hostages. Finally, government forces butchered some 20,000 Communards. The suppression of the Paris Commune left bitter memories that deepened social divisions within France.

Government Structure Despite its shaky beginnings, the Third Republic remained in place for 70 years. The new republic had a two-house legislature. The powerful lower house, or Chamber of Deputies, was elected by universal male suffrage. Together with the Senate, it elected the president of the republic. However, he had little power and served mostly as a figurehead. Real power was in the hands of the premier (prih MIR), or prime minister.

Unlike Britain, with its two-party system, France had many parties, reflecting the wide splits within the country. Among them were divine-right royalists, constitutional monarchists, moderate republicans, and radicals. With so many parties, no single party could win a majority in the legislature. In order to govern, politicians had to form coalitions, or alliances of various parties. Once a coalition controlled enough votes, it could then name a premier and form a cabinet.

Multiparty systems and coalition governments are common in Europe. Such alliances allow citizens to vote for a party that most nearly matches their own beliefs. Coalition governments, however, are often unstable. If one party deserts a coalition, the government might lose its majority in the legislature. The government then falls, and new elections must be held. In the first 10 years of the Third Republic, 50 different coalition governments were formed and fell.

Scandals Despite frequent changes of governments, France made economic progress. It paid Germany the huge sum required by the peace treaty and expanded its overseas empire. But in the 1880s and 1890s, a series of political scandals shook public trust in the government.

Le Petit Journal

SUPPLÉMENT ILLUSTRÉ

Le Petit Journal

Le Supplément illustré

Huit pages : CINQ centimes

ABONNEMENTS

Sixième année

DIMANCHE 13 JANVIER 1895

Numero 217

Dreyfus in Disgrace

The cover of this 1895 French magazine shows Alfred Dreyfus being drummed out of the army. By tradition, a disgraced officer stood at attention while his shoulder pads were ripped off and his sword was broken.

Theme: Diversity **How do you think people in France reacted to this magazine cover?**

One crisis erupted when a popular minister of war, General Georges Boulanger (boo lahn ZHAY), rallied royalists and ultranationalists eager for revenge on Germany. Accused of plotting to overthrow the republic, Boulanger fled to Belgium and later committed suicide. In another scandal, a nephew of the president was caught selling nominations for the Legion of Honor, France's highest award. The president was forced to resign.

The Dreyfus Affair

The most divisive scandal began in 1894, when a high-ranking army officer, Alfred Dreyfus, was accused of spying for Germany. At his military trial, neither Dreyfus nor his lawyer was allowed to see the evidence against him. The injustice was rooted in antisemitism. The military elite detested Dreyfus, the first Jew to reach such a high position in the army. Although Dreyfus proclaimed his innocence, he was convicted and condemned to life imprisonment on Devil's Island, a desolate penal colony off the coast of South America.

By 1896, new evidence pointed to another officer, Ferdinand Esterhazy, as the spy. Still, the army refused to grant Dreyfus a new trial.

Deep Divisions The Dreyfus affair, as it was called, scarred French politics and society for decades. Royalists, ultranationalists, and Church officials charged Dreyfus supporters, or "Dreyfusards," with undermining France. Paris echoed with cries of "Long live the army!" and "Death to traitors!" Dreyfusards, mostly liberals and republicans, upheld ideals of justice and equality in the face of massive public anger. In 1898, French novelist Émile Zola joined the battle. In an article headlined *J'Accuse!* (I Accuse!), he charged the army and government with suppressing the truth. As a result, Zola was convicted of libel, or the knowing publication of false and damaging statements. He fled into exile.

Slowly, though, the Dreyfusards made progress. They revealed that the evidence against Dreyfus was forged. In 1906, a French court finally cleared Dreyfus of all charges and restored his honors. That move was a victory for justice, but the political scars of the Dreyfus affair took longer to heal.

Calls for a Jewish State The Dreyfus case reflected the rise of antisemitism in Europe. The Enlightenment and the French Revolution had spread ideas about religious toleration. In Western Europe, some Jews had gained jobs in government, universities, and other areas of life. A few were successful in banking and business, though most struggled to survive in the ghettos of Eastern Europe or slums of Western Europe.

By the late 1800s, however, antisemitism was again on the rise. Antisemites were often members of the lower middle class who felt insecure in their social and economic position. Steeped in the new nationalist fervor, they adopted an aggressive intolerance for outsiders and a violent hatred of Jews.

The Dreyfus case and the pogroms in Russia stirred Theodor Herzl (HEHRT suhl), a Hungarian Jewish journalist living in France. He called for Jews to form their own separate state, where they would have the rights denied to them in European countries. Herzl helped launch modern Zionism, a movement devoted to rebuilding a Jewish state in Palestine. Many Jews had kept alive this dream since the Roman destruction of Jerusalem. In 1897, Herzl organized the First Zionist Congress in Basel, Switzerland.

Reforms in France

Though shaken by the Dreyfus affair, France achieved serious reforms in the early 1900s. Like Britain, France passed laws regulating wages, hours, and safety conditions for workers. It set up a system of free public elementary schools. Creating public schools was also part of a campaign to reduce the power of the Roman Catholic Church, which controlled education.

Separating Church and State   Like Germany, France tried to end Church involvement in government. Republicans viewed the Church as a conservative force that opposed progressive policies. In the Dreyfus affair, it had backed the army and ultranationalists.

The government closed Church schools, along with many convents and monasteries. In 1905, it passed a law to separate church and state and stopped paying the salaries of the clergy. Catholics, Protestants, and Jews enjoyed freedom of worship, but none had any special treatment from the government.

Women's Rights   Under the Napoleonic Code, French women had few rights. Women could not even control their own property. By the 1890s, a growing women's rights movement sought legal reforms. It made some gains, such as an 1896 law giving married women the right to their own earnings.

In 1909, Jeanne-Elizabeth Schmahl founded the French Union for Women's Suffrage. Rejecting the radical tactics used in Britain, Schmahl favored legal protests. Yet even liberal men were reluctant to grant women suffrage. They feared that women would vote for Church and conservative causes. In the end, French women did not win the vote until after World War II.

Looking Ahead

By 1914, France was the largest democratic country in Europe, with a constitution that protected basic rights. France's economy was generally prosperous, and its overseas empire was second only to that of Britain.

Yet the outlook was not all smooth. Coalition governments rose and fell at the slightest pressure. To the east loomed the industrial might of Germany. Many French citizens were itching for a chance to avenge the defeat in the Franco-Prussian War and liberate the "lost provinces" of Alsace and Lorraine. That chance came in 1914, when all of Europe exploded into World War I.

SECTION 3 Assessment

Recall

1. **Identify:** **(a)** Paris Commune, **(b)** Georges Boulanger, **(c)** Alfred Dreyfus, **(d)** Theodor Herzl, **(e)** Jeanne-Elizabeth Schmahl.
2. **Define:** **(a)** provisional, **(b)** premier, **(c)** coalition, **(d)** libel.

Comprehension

3. Describe the government of France during the Second Empire.
4. Explain how each of the following heightened divisions in France: **(a)** the Paris Commune, **(b)** the Dreyfus affair.

5. Describe two reforms enacted in France in the early 1900s.

Critical Thinking and Writing

6. **Comparing** **(a)** How does the French system of political parties differ from the American system? **(b)** How do these differences affect the stability of governments under each system?
7. **Solving Problems** **(a)** What solution did Zionists propose for the problem of widespread anti-semitism? **(b)** Why do you think they felt it was the best solution?

Activity

Drawing a Political Cartoon Draw a political cartoon about one event or development during the reign of Napoleon III. You may focus either on domestic affairs, such as limitations on liberty, or on foreign affairs, such as the Franco-Prussian War.

Expansion of the United States

Reading Focus

■ How did the United States extend its territory?

■ How did American democracy grow before and after the Civil War?

■ What impact did economic growth and social reform have on the United States?

Vocabulary

expansionism

abolitionist

secede

segregation

isolationism

Taking Notes

On a sheet of paper, start a before-and-after chart like the one shown here. As you read this section, list events under the appropriate columns.

| CIVIL WAR | |
Before	After
• Expansion and western settlement • Manifest Destiny • Calls for abolition of slavery	

Main Idea In the United States, the 1800s were a time of changing borders, growing industry, and expanding democracy.

Setting the Scene For many Irish families fleeing hunger, Russian Jews escaping pogroms, or poor Italian farmers seeking economic opportunity, the answer was the same—America! A poem inscribed on the base of the Statue of Liberty expressed the hopes of millions of immigrants:

"Give me your tired, your poor,
  Your huddled masses yearning to breathe free,
  The wretched refuse of your teeming shore.
  Send these, the homeless, tempest-tossed to me.
  I lift my lamp beside the golden door."
      —Emma Lazarus, "The New Colossus"

In the 1800s, the United States was a beacon of hope for many people. The American economy was growing rapidly, offering jobs to newcomers. The Constitution and Bill of Rights held out the hope of political and religious freedom. Not everyone shared in the prosperity or the ideals of democracy. Still, by the turn of the century, Americans were increasingly proud of their status as an emerging world power.

Territorial Expansion

From the earliest years of its history, the United States followed a policy of expansionism, or extending a nation's boundaries. At first, the United States stretched only from the Atlantic coast to the Mississippi River. In 1803, President Thomas Jefferson bought the Louisiana territory from France. In one stroke, the Louisiana Purchase virtually doubled the size of the nation.

Manifest Destiny By 1846, the United States had expanded to include Florida, Oregon, and the Republic of Texas. The Mexican War (1846–1848) added California and the Southwest. With growing pride and confidence, Americans claimed that their nation was destined to spread across the entire continent, from sea to sea. This idea became known as Manifest Destiny. Some expansionists even hoped to absorb Canada and Mexico. In fact, the United States did go far afield. In 1867, it bought Alaska from Russia and in 1898 annexed the Hawaiian Islands.

Settling the West During the 1800s, settlers flocked to newly acquired western lands. The discovery of gold in California drew floods of easterners.

Other people, like the Mormons, sought a place to practice their religion freely. Still others headed west in the spirit of adventure.

The waves of settlers brought tragedy to Native Americans. Following a pattern that began in colonial days, newcomers pushed the Indians off their lands, sometimes by treaty, but more often by force. Some Native American nations resisted the invaders, but they were outgunned and outnumbered. As settlers moved westward, they destroyed the buffalo herds on which the Plains Indians depended. By the 1890s, most surviving Native Americans had been driven onto reservations, usually the least desirable parts of a territory.

Expanding Democracy

In 1800, the United States had the most liberal suffrage in the world, but still only white men who owned property could vote. States slowly chipped away at requirements. By the 1830s, most white men had the right to vote. Democracy was far from complete, however. Women, Native Americans, and free blacks had no vote. Enslaved African Americans had no rights at all.

By mid-century, reformers were campaigning for many changes. Some demanded a ban on the sale of alcoholic beverages. Others called for better treatment of the mentally ill or pushed for free elementary schools. Two crusades, especially, highlighted the limits of American democracy—the abolition movement and the women's rights movement.

Calls for Abolition In the early 1800s, a few Americans demanded an immediate and complete end to slavery. These abolitionists included William Lloyd Garrison, who pressed the antislavery cause through his newspaper, the *Liberator*. Frederick Douglass, who had himself escaped slavery, spoke eloquently in the North about the evils of slavery.

Skills Assessment

Geography Through wars and treaties, the United States expanded its borders to its present size.

1. **Location** *On the map, locate (a) Louisiana Purchase, (b) Florida, (c) Texas, (d) Alaska, (e) Hawaii.*
2. **Region** *Identify three countries that sold territories to the United States.*
3. **Critical Thinking Linking Past and Present** *Compare this map to a map of the present-day United States. How did the area where you live become part of the United States?*

Expansion of the United States, 1783–1898

CEDED BY GREAT BRITAIN (Convention of 1818)

DISPUTED WITH GREAT BRITAIN UNTIL 1842

CANADA

OREGON COUNTRY (Agreement with Great Britain, 1846)

THE UNITED STATES IN 1783

MEXICAN CESSION (Treaty of Guadalupe Hidalgo, 1848)

LOUISIANA PURCHASE (Purchased from France, 1803)

PACIFIC OCEAN

ATLANTIC OCEAN

GADSDEN PURCHASE (Purchased from Mexico, 1853)

TEXAS ANNEXATION (Annexed by Congress, 1845)

FLORIDA CESSION (Treaty with Spain, 1819)

MEXICO

Gulf of Mexico

ALASKA (Purchased from Russia, 1867)

0 400 Miles
0 400 Kilometers

HAWAII (Annexed, 1898)

0 100 Miles
0 100 Kilometers

Albers Conic Equal Area Projection

0 250 500 Miles
0 250 500 Kilometers

A Western-Dominated World

Reading Focus

- What were the causes of the "new imperialism"?

- Why was western imperialism so successful?

- How did governments rule their empires?

Vocabulary

imperialism

protectorate

sphere of influence

Taking Notes

As you read, make an organizer like the model below showing the causes of imperialism in the 1800s. Add as many boxes as you need.

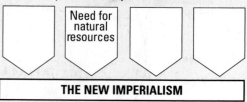

Need for natural resources

THE NEW IMPERIALISM

Main Idea In the late 1800s, industrial nations of the West engaged in imperialism and dominated much of the world.

Setting the Scene When Edward VII inherited the British throne in 1901, his empire extended far beyond Britain. One writer boasted, "The sun never sets" on the British empire. In other words, because the empire circled the globe, the sun always shone on some part of it.

Like Britain, other western powers built overseas empires in the late 1800s. The Industrial Revolution and the growth of science and technology had transformed the West. Armed with new economic and political power, western nations set out to dominate the world.

The New Imperialism and Its Causes

European imperialism did not begin in the 1800s. **Imperialism** is the domination by one country of the political, economic, or cultural life of another country or region. As you have learned, European states won empires in the Americas after 1492, established colonies in South Asia, and gained toeholds on the coasts of Africa and China. Despite these gains, between 1500 and 1800, Europe had little influence on the lives of the peoples of China, India, or Africa.

By the 1800s, however, Europe had gained considerable power. Strong, centrally governed nation-states had emerged, and the Industrial Revolution had greatly enriched European economies. Encouraged by their new economic and military strength, Europeans embarked on a path of aggressive expansion that today's historians call the "new imperialism." Like other key developments in world history, the new imperialism exploded out of a combination of causes.

Economic Interests The Industrial Revolution created needs and desires that spurred overseas expansion. Manufacturers wanted access to natural resources such as rubber, petroleum, manganese for steel, and palm oil for machinery. They also hoped for new markets where they could sell their factory goods. In addition, colonies offered a valuable outlet for Europe's growing population. Lord Frederick Lugard, a British empire builder, tried to justify imperialism in Africa with these words:

> "The necessity that is upon us [is] to provide for our ever-growing population—either by opening new fields for emigration, or by providing work and employment . . . and to stimulate trade by finding new markets."
>
> —Lord Lugard, *The Rise of Our East African Empire*

Political and Military Interests Closely linked to economic motives were political and military issues. Steam-powered merchant ships and naval vessels needed bases around the world to take on coal and supplies. Industrial powers seized islands or harbors to satisfy these needs.

Nationalism played an important role, too. When France, for example, moved into West Africa, rival nations like Britain and Germany seized lands nearby to halt further French expansion. Western leaders claimed that colonies were needed for national security. They also felt that ruling a global empire increased a nation's prestige around the world.

Humanitarian Goals Many westerners felt a genuine concern for their "little brothers" beyond the seas. Missionaries, doctors, and colonial officials believed they had a duty to spread what they saw as the blessings of western civilization, including its medicine, law, and Christian religion.

Social Darwinism Behind the idea of a civilizing mission was a growing sense in the West of racial superiority. Many westerners had embraced the ideas of Social Darwinism. They applied Darwin's ideas about natural selection and survival of the fittest to human societies. European races, they argued, were superior to all others, and imperial conquest and destruction of weaker races were simply nature's way of improving the human species!

The Success of Western Imperialism

In just a few decades, from about 1870 to 1914, imperialist nations gained control over much of the world. Leading the way were soldiers, merchants, settlers, missionaries, and explorers. In Europe, imperial expansion found favor with all classes, from bankers and manufacturers to workers. Western imperialism succeeded for a number of reasons.

Weakness of Nonwestern States While European nations had grown stronger in the 1800s, several older civilizations were in decline, especially the Ottoman Middle East, Mughal India, and Qing China. In West Africa, wars among African peoples and the draining effect of the slave trade had undermined established empires, kingdoms, and city-states. Newer African states were not strong enough to resist the western onslaught.

Western Advantages Europeans had the advantages of strong economies, well-organized governments, and powerful armies and navies. Superior technology and improved medical knowledge also played a role. Quinine and other new medicines helped Europeans survive deadly tropical diseases. And, of course, advances such as Maxim machine guns, repeating rifles, and steam-driven warships were very strong arguments in persuading Africans and Asians to accept western control. As an English writer sarcastically noted: "Whatever happens, we have got the Maxim gun, and they have not."

Resistance Africans and Asians strongly resisted western expansion into their lands. Some people fought the invaders, even though they had no weapons to equal the Maxim gun. As you will read, ruling groups in certain areas tried to strengthen their societies against outsiders by reforming their own Muslim, Hindu, or Confucian traditions. Finally, many western-educated Africans and Asians organized nationalist movements to expel the imperialists from their lands.

Primary Source

"The White Man's Burden"
In the photo above, British writer Rudyard Kipling (front right) is one of several journalists in South Africa. Kipling promoted imperialism in his controversial poem, "The White Man's Burden":

"Take up the White Man's burden—
    Send forth the best ye breed—
Go bind your sons to exile
    To serve your captives' need. . . .
Take up the White Man's burden—
    The savage wars of peace—
Fill full the mouth of Famine,
    And bid the sickness cease;
And when your goal is nearest
    (The end for others sought)
Watch sloth and heathen folly
    Bring all your hope to nought.
                    —Rudyard Kipling,
            "The White Man's Burden"

Skills Assessment

Primary Source Why did Kipling consider imperialism to be beneficial?

The Maxim Gun
Britain's future King Edward VII tries his hand at the Maxim machine gun. Standing next to him is Sir Hiram Maxim, the gun's inventor.

Theme: Economics and Technology Why were European armies often able to defeat African or Asian forces?

Criticism at Home In the West itself, a small group of anti-imperialists emerged. Some argued that colonialism was a tool of the rich. Others said it was immoral. Westerners, they pointed out, were moving toward greater democracy at home but were imposing undemocratic rule on other people. "The new imperialism stood," one English critic protested, "not for a widened and ennobled sense of national responsibility, but for a hard assertion of racial supremacy and material force."

Forms of Imperial Rule

The new imperialism took several forms. In some areas, imperial powers established colonies. Elsewhere, they set up protectorates and spheres of influence.

Colonies France and Britain, the leading imperial powers, developed different kinds of colonial rule. The French practiced direct rule, sending officials and soldiers from France to administer their colonies. Their goal was to impose French culture on their colonies and turn them into French provinces.

The British, by contrast, relied on a system of indirect rule. To govern their colonies, they used sultans, chiefs, or other local rulers. They then encouraged the children of the local ruling class to get an education in Britain. In that way, they groomed a new "westernized" generation of leaders to continue indirect imperial rule and to spread British civilization. Like France and other imperialist nations, however, Britain could still resort to military force if its control over a colony was threatened in any way.

Protectorates In a protectorate, local rulers were left in place but were expected to follow the advice of European advisers on issues such as trade or missionary activity. A protectorate cost less to run than a colony did, and usually did not require a large commitment of military forces.

Spheres of Influence A third form of western control was the sphere of influence, an area in which an outside power claimed exclusive investment or trading privileges. Europeans carved out these spheres in China and elsewhere to prevent conflicts among themselves. The United States claimed Latin America as its sphere of influence.

SECTION 1 Assessment

Recall
1. **Identify:** (a) new imperialism, (b) direct rule, (c) indirect rule.
2. **Define:** (a) imperialism, (b) protectorate, (c) sphere of influence.

Comprehension
3. Describe three causes of the new imperialism.
4. (a) What were three reasons for the success of western imperialism? (b) How did people oppose western imperialism?
5. Describe three different forms of imperial rule.

Critical Thinking and Writing
6. **Analyzing Primary Sources** Review the words of Lord Lugard quoted at the start of this section. Explain why Lugard thought that it was necessary for Britain to pursue a policy of imperialism in Africa.
7. **Recognizing Bias** Western colonial officials and missionaries thought that they had a duty to spread the "blessings of western civilization" to their "little brothers" in Africa and Asia. How was this a biased viewpoint?

Activity
Making a Graphic Organizer
Make a graphic organizer that shows the various reasons for the success of western imperialism. Use the graphic organizers at the start of each section and at the end of each chapter for ideas on how to design your chart.

Reading Focus

- What forces were shaping Africa in the early 1800s?
- How did European contact with Africa increase?
- How did Leopold II start a scramble for colonies?
- How did Africans resist imperialism?

Vocabulary

jihad
missionary
elite

Taking Notes

As you read, create a concept web like the model below that lists examples of African resistance against imperialism. Add as many circles as needed to complete the web.

AFRICANS RESIST IMPERIALISM

Algerians battle French

Main Idea By the end of the 1800s, the imperialist powers of Europe claimed control over most of Africa.

Setting the Scene

In the late 1800s, Britain, France, Germany, and other European powers swept into Africa. Chief Machemba of the Yao people in East Africa wrote in Swahili to a German officer:

> "If it be friendship that you desire, then I am ready for it . . . but to be your subject, that I cannot be. . . . I do not fall at your feet, for you are God's creature just as I am."
> —Chief Machemba, Letter to Herman von Wissman

Though the Yao and others resisted, they could not prevent European conquest. Within about 20 years, the Europeans had carved up the continent and dominated millions of Africans.

Africa in the Early 1800s

To understand the impact of European domination, we must look at Africa in the early 1800s, before the scramble for colonies began. Africa is a huge continent, four times the size of Europe. Across its many regions, people spoke hundreds of languages and had developed varied governments. Some people lived in large centralized states, others in village communities.

North Africa North Africa includes the enormous Sahara and the fertile land along the Mediterranean. Since long before 1800, the region had close ties to the Muslim world. In the early 1800s, much of North Africa remained under the rule of the declining Ottoman empire.

West Africa On the grasslands of West Africa, an Islamic reform movement had brought change. Leaders like Usman dan Fodio preached jihad, a holy struggle, to revive and purify Islam. Under these leaders, several new Muslim states arose, built on trade, farming, and herding.

In the forest regions, strong states like the Asante kingdom had arisen. The Asante traded with Europeans and Muslims and controlled several smaller states. However, these tributary states were ready to turn to Europeans or others who might help them defeat their Asante rulers.

East Africa Islam had long influenced the east coast of Africa, where port cities like Mombasa and Kilwa carried on profitable trade. The cargoes were often slaves. Captives were marched from the interior to the coast to be shipped as slaves to the Middle East. Ivory and copper from Central Africa were also exchanged for goods such as cloth and firearms from India.

The Ivory Trade
East African merchants profited from the ivory trade. For centuries, artists around the world made beautiful ivory carvings. Today, international law severely limits the trade in order to protect declining elephant populations.

Theme: Economics and Technology Besides ivory, what was another source of profits for merchants in East Africa?

Virtual Field Trip

www.phschool.com

David Livingstone National Memorial Blantyre, Scotland

To learn more about the life and work of Dr. David Livingstone, use the Internet address above to link to the David Livingstone National Memorial.

Livingstone and Victoria Falls

After recovering from bouts of malaria and rheumatic fever, Dr. David Livingstone set out in 1853 to explore the Zambesi River valley. On November 17, 1855, he viewed the magnificent site that we know today as Victoria Falls.

Theme: Geography and History Why was exploration of Africa difficult?

Southern Africa In the early 1800s, southern Africa was in turmoil. Shaka, you will recall, united the Zulu nation. His conquests, however, set off mass migrations and wars, creating chaos across much of the region. By the 1830s, the Zulus were also battling the Boers, who were migrating north from the Cape Colony.

The Slave Trade In the early 1800s, European nations began to outlaw the transatlantic slave trade, though it took years to end it. Meanwhile, the East African slave trade, continued to the Middle East and Asia.

Some people in Britain and the United States helped freed slaves resettle in Africa. In 1787, the British organized Sierra Leone in West Africa as a colony for former slaves. Later, some free blacks from the United States settled in nearby Liberia. By 1847, Liberia became an independent republic.

European Contacts Increase

From the 1500s through the 1700s, Europeans traded along the African coast. Difficult geography and diseases kept them from reaching the interior. Medical advances and river steamships changed all that in the 1800s.

Explorers In the early 1800s, European explorers began pushing into the interior of Africa. Daring adventurers like Mungo Park and Richard Burton set out to map the course and sources of the great African rivers such as the Niger, the Nile, and the Congo. These explorers were fascinated by African geography, but they had little understanding of the peoples they met. All, however, endured great hardships in pursuit of their dreams.

Missionaries Catholic and Protestant missionaries followed the explorers. All across Africa, they sought to win people to Christianity. The missionaries were sincere in their desire to help Africans. They built schools and medical clinics alongside churches. They also focused attention on the evils of the slave trade.

Still, missionaries, like most westerners, took a paternalistic view of Africans. They saw them as children in need of guidance. To them, African cultures and religions were "degraded." They urged Africans to reject their own traditions in favor of western civilization.

Livingstone The best known explorer-missionary was Dr. David Livingstone. For 30 years, he crisscrossed Africa. He wrote about the many peoples he met with more sympathy and less bias than did most Europeans. He relentlessly opposed the slave trade, which remained a profitable business for some African rulers and foreign traders. The only way to end this cruel traffic, he believed, was to open up the interior of Africa to Christianity and trade.

Livingstone blazed a trail that others soon followed. In 1869, the journalist Henry Stanley trekked into Central Africa to find Livingstone, who had not been heard from for years. He finally tracked him down in 1871 in what is today Tanzania, greeting him with the now-legendary phrase "Dr. Livingstone, I presume?"

A Scramble for Colonies

Shortly afterward, King Leopold II of Belgium hired Stanley to explore the Congo River basin and arrange trade treaties with African leaders. Publicly, Leopold spoke of a civilizing mission to carry the light "that for millions of men still plunged in barbarism will be the dawn of a better era." Privately, he dreamed of conquest and profit.

Skills Assessment

Geography During the late 1800s, European countries took part in a scramble for Africa. They claimed control of nearly the whole continent by 1914.

1. **Location** On the map, locate **(a)** Algeria, **(b)** Belgian Congo, **(c)** Ethiopia.
2. **Region** In which part of Africa were most of France's colonies located?
3. **Critical Thinking** **Making Inferences** How can you tell from the map that Africans did not willingly accept European domination?

Imperialism in Africa to 1914

Mercator Projection

Legend:
- Belgian
- British
- French
- German
- Italian
- Portuguese
- Spanish
- ★ Outbreaks of anticolonial resistance
- Dates on map indicate year of official colonization

European Colonies in Africa About 1850

European rivals, explained, "We do not want to put anyone in the shade, but we also demand our place in the sun."

Africans Resist Imperialism

Europeans met armed resistance across the continent. The Algerians battled the French for years. Samori Touré fought French forces in West Africa, where he was building his own empire. The British battled the Zulus in southern Africa and the Asante in West Africa. When their king was exiled, the Asante put themselves under the command of their queen, Yaa Asantewaa. She led the fight against the British in the last Asante war. Another woman who became a military leader was Nehanda, of the Shona in Zimbabwe. Although a clever tactician, Nehanda was captured and executed. However, the memory of her achievements inspired later generations to fight for freedom.

In East Africa, the Germans fought wars against people like the Yao and Herero. Fighting was especially fierce in the Maji-Maji Rebellion of 1905. The Germans triumphed only after using a scorched-earth policy. To crush resistance, they burned acres and acres of farmland, leaving thousands of local people to die of starvation.

Ethiopia Survives Successful resistance was mounted by Ethiopia. This ancient Christian kingdom had survived in the highlands of East Africa. But, like feudal Europe, it had been divided up among a number of rival princes who ruled their own domains.

In the late 1800s, a reforming ruler, Menelik II, began to modernize his country. He hired European experts to plan modern roads and bridges and set up a western school system. He imported the latest weapons and European officers to help train his army. Thus, when Italy invaded Ethiopia in 1896, Menelik was prepared. At the battle of Adowa (ah DUH wah), the Ethiopians smashed the Italian invaders. Ethiopia was the only African nation, aside from Liberia, to preserve its independence.

New African Elite During the Age of Imperialism, a western-educated African elite, or upper class, emerged. Some middle-class Africans admired western ways and rejected their own culture. Others valued their African traditions and condemned western societies that upheld liberty and equality for whites only. By the early 1900s, African leaders were forging nationalist movements to pursue self-determination and independence.

Biography

Menelik II 1844–1913

Before becoming emperor of Ethiopia, Menelik II ruled the Shoa region in central Ethiopia. He ensured that he would succeed John IV as emperor by marrying John's daughter. After John died in 1889, Menelik took the throne.

Menelik used profits from ivory sales to buy modern weapons. He then hired European advisers to teach his soldiers how to use the new guns. Menelik's army conquered neighboring lands and won a stunning victory over the Italians at Adowa. European nations rushed to establish diplomatic ties with Ethiopia. Around the world, people of African descent hailed Menelik's victory over European imperialism.

Theme: Impact of the Individual How did Menelik preserve Ethiopian independence?

SECTION 2 Assessment

Recall

1. **Identify:** (a) Asante, (b) Liberia, (c) David Livingstone, (d) Berlin Conference, (e) Boer War, (f) Nehanda, (g) Menelik II.
2. **Define:** (a) jihad, (b) missionary, (c) elite.

Comprehension

3. Describe one development in each region of Africa in the early 1800s.
4. How did European contact with Africa increase?
5. Which European nations were most successful in the scramble for African colonies?

6. Describe two examples of African resistance to European imperialism.

Critical Thinking and Writing

7. **Making Inferences** (a) Why do you think the Europeans did not invite Africans to the Berlin Conference? (b) What might be the effect of this exclusion upon later African leaders?
8. **Connecting to Geography** Review the maps of Africa in this section. Why do you think Britain, France, and Italy were all interested in controlling part of Somaliland?

Activity
Take It to the NET

Use the Internet to find out more about explorer-missionary David Livingstone. Then, prepare a brief biography of him. You may wish to illustrate the biography with a map showing Livingstone's explorations and a chart describing his missionary activities.

European Challenges to the Muslim World

Reading Focus

■ What were sources of stress in the Muslim world?

■ What problems did the Ottoman empire face?

■ How did Egypt seek to modernize?

■ Why were European powers interested in Iran?

Vocabulary

pasha

genocide

concession

Taking Notes

As you read, prepare an outline. Use Roman numerals for major headings, capital letters for subheadings, and numbers for supporting details. The incomplete model below will help you get started.

I. **Stresses in the Muslim world**
   A. **Empires in decline**
      1.
      2.
   B.
   C.
II. **Problems for the Ottoman empire**
   A.

Main Idea   During the 1800s, European nations extended their power into parts of the Muslim world.

Setting the Scene   "Europe is a molehill," said Napoleon Bonaparte in 1797. He felt it offered too few chances for glory. "We must go to the East," he declared. "All great glory has been acquired there." In 1798, he put his thoughts into action by invading Egypt, a province of the Ottoman empire.

Napoleon's Egyptian campaign highlighted Ottoman decline and opened a new era of European contact with the Muslim world. In the early 1800s, European countries were just nibbling at the edges of the Muslim world. Before long, they would strike at its heartlands.

Stresses in the Muslim World

The Muslim world extended from western Africa to Southeast Asia. In the 1500s, three giant Muslim empires ruled much of this world—the Mughals in India, the Ottomans in the Middle East, and the Safavids in Iran.

Empires in Decline   By the 1700s, all three Muslim empires were in decline. The decay had many causes. Central governments had lost control over powerful groups such as landowning nobles, military elites, and urban craft guilds. Corruption was widespread. In some places, Muslim scholars and religious leaders were allied with the state. In other areas, they helped to stir discontent against the government.

Islamic Reform Movement   In the 1700s and early 1800s, reform movements sprang up across the Muslim world. Most stressed religious piety and strict rules of behavior. The Wahhabi movement in Arabia, for example, rejected the schools of theology and law that had emerged in the Ottoman empire. In their place, they wanted to recapture the purity and simplicity of Muhammad's original teachings. An Arab prince led the Wahhabis against Ottoman rule. Although the revolt was crushed, the Wahhabi movement survived. Its teachings are influential in the kingdom of Saudi Arabia today.

Islamic revivals rose in Africa, too. As you have read, Usman dan Fodio led the struggle to reform Muslim practices. In the Sudan, south of Egypt, Muhammad Ahmad announced that he was the Mahdi, the long-awaited savior of the faith. In the 1880s, the Mahdi and his followers fiercely resisted British expansion into the region.

European Imperialism   In addition to internal decay and stress, the old Muslim empires faced western imperialism. Through diplomacy and military threats, European powers won treaties giving them favorable

Constantinople
People from all over the world met and traded at Constantinople. The capital of the Ottoman empire was located on the Bosporus.

Theme: Geography and History Why did Russia hope to gain control of the Bosporus?

trading terms. They then demanded special rights for Europeans residing in Muslim lands. At times, European powers protected those rights by intervening in local affairs. Sometimes, they took over an entire region.

Problems for the Ottoman Empire

At its height, the Ottoman empire had extended across the Middle East, North Africa, and Southeastern Europe. By the early 1800s, however, it faced serious challenges. Ambitious pashas, or provincial rulers, had increased their power. Economic problems and corruption added to Ottoman decay.

Nationalist Revolts As ideas of nationalism spread from Western Europe, internal revolts weakened the multiethnic Ottoman empire. Subject peoples in Eastern Europe, the Middle East, and North Africa threatened to break away. In the Balkans, Greeks, Serbs, Bulgarians, and Romanians gained their independence. Revolts against Ottoman rule also erupted in Arabia, Lebanon, and Armenia. The Ottomans suppressed these uprisings, but another valuable territory, Egypt, slipped out of their control.

European Pressure European states sought to benefit from the slow crumbling of the Ottoman empire. After seizing Algeria in the 1830s, France hoped to gain more Ottoman territory. Russia schemed to gain control of the Bosporus and the Dardanelles. Control of these straits would give the Russians access to the Mediterranean Sea. Britain tried to thwart Russia's ambitions, which it saw as a threat to its own power in the Mediterranean and beyond it to India. And in 1898, the new German empire jumped onto the bandwagon, hoping to increase its influence in the region by building a Berlin-to-Baghdad railway.

Efforts to Westernize Since the late 1700s, several Ottoman rulers had seen the need for reform and looked to the West for ideas. They reorganized the bureaucracy and system of tax collection. They built railroads, improved education, and hired European officers to train a modern military. Young men were sent to the West to study the new sciences and technology. Many returned home with western ideas about democracy and equality.

The reforms also brought better medical care and revitalized farming. These improvements, however, were a mixed blessing. Better living conditions resulted in a population explosion. The growing population increased competition for the best land, which led to unrest.

The adoption of western ideas about government also increased tension. Many officials objected to changes that were inspired by a foreign culture. For their part, repressive sultans rejected reform and tried to rebuild the autocratic power enjoyed by earlier rulers.

Young Turks In the 1890s, a group of liberals formed a movement called the Young Turks. They insisted that reform was the only way to save the empire. In 1908, the Young Turks overthrew the sultan. Before they could achieve their planned reforms, however, the Ottoman empire was plunged into the world war that erupted in 1914.

Massacre of Armenians Traditionally, the Ottomans had let minority nationalities live in their own communities and practice their own religions. By the 1890s, however, nationalism was igniting new tensions, especially between

Turkish nationalists and minority peoples who sought their own states. These tensions triggered a brutal genocide of the Armenians, a Christian people concentrated in the eastern mountains of the empire. Genocide is a deliberate attempt to destroy an entire religious or ethnic group.

The Muslim Turks distrusted the Christian Armenians and accused them of supporting Russian plans against the Ottoman empire. When Armenians protested repressive Ottoman policies, the sultan had tens of thousands of them slaughtered. Over the next 25 years, a million or more Armenians in the Ottoman empire were killed.

Egypt Seeks to Modernize

Egypt in 1800 was a semi-independent province of the Ottoman empire. In the early 1800s, it made great strides toward reform. Its success was due to Muhammad Ali, who was appointed governor of Egypt in 1805.

Muhammad Ali Muhammad Ali is sometimes called the "father of modern Egypt." To strengthen Egypt, he introduced a number of political and economic reforms. He improved tax collection, reorganized the landholding system, and backed large irrigation projects to increase farm output. By expanding cotton production and encouraging the development of local industry, he increased Egyptian participation in world trade.

Muhammad Ali also brought western military experts to Egypt to help him build a well-trained, modern army. He conquered the neighboring lands of Arabia, Syria, and Sudan. Before he died in 1849, he had set Egypt on the road to becoming a major Middle Eastern power.

The Suez Canal Muhammad Ali's successors lacked his skills, and Egypt came increasingly under foreign control. In 1859, a French entrepreneur, Ferdinand de Lesseps, organized a company to build the Suez Canal. This

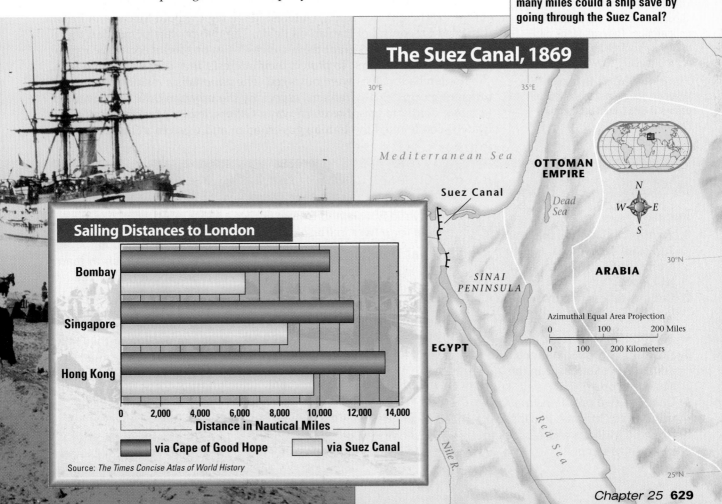

The Suez Canal, 1869

Mediterranean Sea

OTTOMAN EMPIRE

Suez Canal

Dead Sea

SINAI PENINSULA

ARABIA

EGYPT

Red Sea

Nile R.

Azimuthal Equal Area Projection
0   100   200 Miles
0   100   200 Kilometers

Sailing Distances to London

Bombay

Singapore

Hong Kong

0   2,000   4,000   6,000   8,000   10,000   12,000   14,000
Distance in Nautical Miles

■ via Cape of Good Hope   □ via Suez Canal

Source: *The Times Concise Atlas of World History*

100-mile waterway links the Mediterranean and Red seas. (See the map on the previous page.) Europeans hailed its opening in 1869 because it greatly shortened the sea route from Europe to South and East Asia. To Britain, especially, the canal was a "lifeline" to India.

In 1875, the ruler of Egypt was unable to repay loans he had contracted for the canal and other modernization projects. To pay his debts, he was forced to sell his shares in the canal. British prime minister Disraeli quickly bought the shares, giving Britain a controlling interest in the canal.

A British Protectorate   When Egyptian nationalists revolted against foreign influence in 1882, Britain made Egypt a protectorate. In theory, the governor of Egypt was still an official of the Ottoman government. In fact, he followed policies dictated by Britain. Under British influence, Egypt continued to modernize. At the same time, however, nationalist discontent simmered and flared into protests and riots well into the next century.

Iran and the European Powers

Like the Ottoman empire, Iran faced major challenges in the 1800s. The Qajar (kah JAHR) shahs, who ruled Iran from 1794 to 1925, exercised absolute power like the Safavids before them. Still, they did take steps to introduce reforms. The government improved finances, sponsored the building of telegraph lines and railroads, and even experimented with a liberal constitution.

Reform, however, did not save Iran from western imperialism. Both Russia and Britain battled for influence in the area. Russia wanted to protect its southern frontier and expand into Central Asia. Britain was concerned about protecting its interests in India.

For a time, each nation set up its own sphere of influence in Iran. Russia operated in the north and Britain in the south. The discovery of oil in the early 1900s heightened foreign interest in the region. Both Russia and Britain intrigued for control of Iranian oil fields. The two powers persuaded the Iranian government to grant them concessions, or special economic rights given to foreign powers. To protect their interests, they sent troops into Iran.

Iranian nationalists were outraged. The nationalists included two very different groups. Some Iranians, especially the urban middle class, wanted to move swiftly to adopt western ways. Others, led by Muslim religious leaders, condemned the Iranian government and western influences.

The Power of Oil
In the early 1900s, Russia and Britain competed for oil in the Middle East. Today, the vast petroleum deposits in the region are controlled by Middle Eastern countries themselves.

Oil produces enormous wealth for countries in the Middle East. Industrialized nations rely on imported oil to produce electricity, run factories, and fuel vehicles. In the Organization of Petroleum Exporting Countries (OPEC), oil-producing countries of the Middle East and other world regions try to maximize their profits through cooperation. They influence oil prices by controlling how much oil is produced.

Theme: Global Interaction
What do you think happens to oil prices if OPEC cuts production? Explain.

SECTION 3 Assessment

Recall
1. **Identify:** (a) Mahdi, (b) Young Turks, (c) Armenians, (d) Muhammad Ali, (e) Suez Canal, (f) Qajars.
2. **Define:** (a) pasha, (b) genocide, (c) concession.

Comprehension
3. How did European nations take advantage of stresses in the Muslim world?
4. Describe two problems that contributed to Ottoman decline.
5. How did Muhammad Ali seek to modernize Egypt?

6. Why did Russia and Britain compete for power in Iran?

Critical Thinking and Writing
7. **Linking Past and Present** (a) How did Turkish nationalism lead to intolerance of minorities in the Ottoman empire? (b) Describe a present-day example of nationalism's causing intolerance of others.
8. **Solving Problems** Suppose you are an Ottoman government official in the 1800s. Recommend and explain a series of actions that you think will solve the problems afflicting the Ottoman empire.

Activity

Making a Time Line
Conduct research to learn more about Iran in the late 1800s and early 1900s. Then, make a time line that identifies key events in the decline of the Qajar government and the rise of Russian and British influence in the region.

4 The British Take Over India

Reading Focus

- What were the causes and effects of the Sepoy Rebellion?
- How did British rule affect India?
- How did Indians view western culture?
- What were the origins of Indian nationalism?

Vocabulary

sati
sepoy
viceroy
deforestation
purdah

Taking Notes

As you read this section, make a flowchart to show the events that led to increased British control of India. Use the incomplete chart below as a model.

```
British East India Company
gets trading rights
        │
        ▼
British officials introduce
western education and law
        │
        ▼
┌──────────────────────────┐
│                          │
└──────────────────────────┘
        │
        ▼
┌──────────────────────────┐
│                          │
└──────────────────────────┘
```

Main Idea Despite Indian opposition, Britain gradually extended its control over most of India.

Setting the Scene

Ranjit Singh ruled the large Sikh empire in northwestern India during the early 1800s. He had cordial dealings with the British but saw only too well where their ambitions were headed. One day, he was looking at a map of India on which British-held lands were shaded red. "All will one day become red!" he predicted.

Not long after Ranjit Singh's death in 1839, the British conquered the Sikh empire. They added its 100,000 square miles to their steadily growing lands. As Singh had forecast, India was falling under British control.

East India Company and Sepoy Rebellion

In the early 1600s, the British East India Company won trading rights on the fringe of the Mughal empire. As Mughal power declined, the company's influence grew. By the mid-1800s, it controlled three fifths of India.

Exploiting Indian Diversity The British were able to conquer such a vast territory by exploiting the diversity of India. Even when Mughal power was at its height, India was home to many people and cultures. As Mughal power crumbled, India fragmented. Indians with different traditions and dozens of different languages were not able to unite against the newcomers. The British took advantage of Indian divisions by encouraging competition and disunity among rival princes. Where British diplomacy or intrigue did not work, their superior weapons overpowered local rulers.

British Policies The East India Company's main goal in India was to make money, and leading officials often got very rich. At the same time, the company did work to improve roads, preserve peace, and reduce banditry.

By the early 1800s, British officials introduced western education and legal procedures. Missionaries tried to convert Indians to Christianity, which they felt was far superior to Indian religions. The British also pressed for social change. They worked to end slavery and the caste system and to improve the position of women within the family. One law outlawed sati, a Hindu custom practiced mainly by the upper classes. It called for a widow to join her husband in death by throwing herself on his funeral fire.

Causes of Discontent In the 1850s, the East India Company made several unpopular moves. First, it required sepoys, or Indian soldiers in its service, to serve anywhere, either in India or overseas. For high-caste Hindus, however, overseas travel was an offense against their religion. Second, it

Global Connections

"Thank God for Tea!"

The British East India Company made a fortune by importing tea—a drink with a long history. According to legend, a Chinese emperor discovered tea thousands of years ago when windblown leaves fell into a pot of boiling water. Buddhist monks brought the drink to Japan and made it part of their meditation rites. Europeans did not become acquainted with the pleasure of tea until the 1600s—but they caught on quickly.

In England, tea was first used as a medicinal drink only. However, it soon became common to have tea every afternoon. The custom became a regular social event. People invited friends for afternoon tea served with cake, bread, and butter. By the 1800s, tea was considered an essential part of English culture, moving one writer to offer special thanks: "Thank God for tea! What would the world do without tea?—how did it exist? I am glad I was not born before tea."

Theme: Global Interaction
Why did the British East India Company earn huge profits?

Legend:
- British colonies in 1765
- Territory under British rule in 1805
- Territory under British rule in 1858
- Main area affected by Sepoy Rebellion

KASHMIR
PUNJAB
Indus R.
Delhi
RAJPUTANA
NORTHWEST PROVINCES
Brahmaputra R.
30°N
SIND
BIHAR
Ganges R.
ASSAM
BENGAL
Calcutta
Narmada R.
BERAR
Bombay
HYDERABAD
Arabian Sea
ARAKAN
Bay of Bengal
15°N
Goa (Portuguese)
MYSORE
Madras
Andaman Islands
N
W E
S
Pondicherry (French)
CEYLON
Mercator Projection
0 300 600 Miles
0 300 600 Kilometers
INDIAN OCEAN
75°E
90°E

Skills Assessment

Geography Britain controlled all of India by 1858. British officials ruled some areas directly and other areas through local Indian rulers.

1. **Location** On the map, locate **(a)** Punjab, **(b)** Delhi, **(c)** Hyderabad, **(d)** Madras.
2. **Region** Which regions were most greatly affected by the Sepoy Rebellion?
3. **Critical Thinking** **Asking Questions** Write three questions based on information on the map.

passed a law that allowed Hindu widows to remarry. Hindus viewed both moves as a Christian conspiracy to undermine their beliefs.

Then, in 1857, the British issued new rifles to the sepoys. Troops were told to bite off the tips of cartridges before loading them into the rifles. The cartridges, however, were greased with animal fat—either from cows, which Hindus considered sacred, or from pigs, which were forbidden to Muslims. When the troops refused the order to "load rifles," they were sent home without pay.

Rebellion and Aftermath Angry sepoys rose up against their British officers. The Sepoy Rebellion swept across northern and central India. Several sepoy regiments marched off to Delhi, the old Mughal capital. There, they hailed the last Mughal ruler as their leader.

The sepoys brutally massacred British men, women, and children in some places. But the British soon rallied and crushed the revolt. They then took terrible revenge for their earlier losses, torching villages and slaughtering thousands of unarmed Indians.

The Sepoy Rebellion left a bitter legacy of fear, hatred, and mistrust on both sides. It also brought major changes in British policy. In 1858, Parliament ended the rule of the East India Company and put India directly under the British crown. It sent more troops to India, taxing Indians to pay the cost of these occupying forces. While it slowed the "reforms" that had angered Hindus and Muslims, it continued to develop India for Britain's own economic benefit.

British Colonial Rule

After 1858, Parliament set up a system of colonial rule in India. A British viceroy in India governed in the name of the queen, and British officials held the top positions in the civil service and army. Indians filled most other jobs. With their cooperation, the British made India the "brightest jewel" in the crown of their empire.

British policies were designed to fit India into the overall British economy. At the same time, British officials felt they were helping India to modernize. In their terms, modernizing meant adopting not only western technology but also western culture.

An Unequal Partnership Britain saw India as a market and as a source of raw materials. To this end, the British built roads and an impressive railroad network. Improved transportation let the British sell their factory-made goods across the subcontinent and carry Indian cotton, jute, and coal to coastal ports for transport to factories in England. New methods of communication, such as the telegraph, also gave Britain better control of India.

After the Suez Canal opened in 1869, British trade with India soared. But it remained an unequal partnership, favoring the British. The British flooded India with inexpensive, machine-made textiles, ruining India's once-prosperous hand-weaving industry.

Britain also transformed Indian agriculture. It encouraged nomadic herders to settle into farming and pushed farmers to grow cash crops, such as cotton and jute, that could be sold on the world market. Clearing new farmlands led to massive deforestation, or cutting of trees.

Population Growth and Famine The British introduced medical improvements and new farming methods. Better health care and increased food production led to rapid population growth. The rising numbers, however, put a strain on the food supply, especially as farmland was turned over to growing cash crops instead of food. In the late 1800s, terrible famines swept India.

Benefits of British Rule On the positive side, British rule brought peace and order to the countryside. The British revised the legal system to promote justice for Indians regardless of class or caste. Railroads helped Indians move around the country, while the telegraph and postal system improved communication. Greater contact helped bridge regional differences and opened the way for Indians to develop a sense of national unity.

The upper classes, especially, benefited from some British policies. They sent their sons to British schools, where they were trained for posts in the civil service and military. Indian landowners and princes, who still ruled their own territories, grew rich from exporting cash crops.

Different Views on Culture

During the Age of Imperialism, Indians and British developed different views of each other's culture. Both the British and the Indians were divided in their opinions.

Indian Attitudes Some educated Indians were impressed by British power and technology and urged India to follow a western model of progress. These mostly upper-class Indians learned English and adopted western ways. Other Indians felt that the answer to change lay with their own Hindu or Muslim cultures.

In the early 1800s, Ram Mohun Roy combined both views. A great scholar, he knew Sanskrit, Persian, and Arabic classics, as well as English, Greek, and Latin works. Roy felt that India could learn from the West. At the same time, he wanted to revitalize and reform traditional Indian culture.

Roy condemned some traditions, such as rigid caste distinctions, child marriage, sati, and purdah, the isolation of women in separate quarters. But he also set up educational societies that helped revive pride in Indian culture. Because of his influence on later leaders, he is often hailed today as the founder of Indian nationalism.

Western Attitudes The British disagreed among themselves about India. A few admired Indian theology and philosophy. As western scholars translated Indian classics, they acquired respect for India's ancient heritage. Western writers and philosophers borrowed ideas from Hinduism and Buddhism.

However, most British people knew little about Indian achievements and dismissed Indian culture with contempt. In an essay on whether Indians should be taught in English or their own languages, the English historian Thomas Macaulay wrote that "a single shelf of a good European library is worth the whole native literature of India and Arabia."

Cotton: A Valuable Cash Crop
In the 1800s, British officials encouraged Indian farmers to grow cash crops rather than food crops. Today, India is one of the world's largest producers of cotton.
Theme: Global Interaction
How did British policy contribute to famine in India?

Indian Nationalism

During the years of British rule, a class of western-educated Indians emerged. In the view of Macaulay and others, this elite class would bolster British power:

> "We must at present do our best to form a class who may be interpreters between us and the millions whom we govern; a class of persons, Indian in blood and color, but English in taste, in opinions, in morals, and in intellect."
>
> —Thomas Macaulay, quoted in
> *Sources of Indian Tradition* (deBary)

As it turned out, exposure to European ideas had the opposite effect. By the late 1800s, western-educated Indians were spearheading a nationalist movement. Schooled in western ideals such as democracy and equality, they dreamed of ending imperial rule.

Indian National Congress In 1885, nationalist leaders organized the Indian National Congress, which became known as the Congress party. Its members were mostly professionals and business leaders who believed in peaceful protest to gain their ends. They called for greater democracy, which they felt would bring more power to Indians like themselves. The Indian National Congress looked forward to eventual self-rule but supported western-style modernization.

Muslim League At first, Muslims and Hindus worked together for self-rule. In time, however, Muslims grew to resent Hindu domination of the Congress party. They also worried that a Hindu-run government would oppress Muslims. In 1906, Muslims formed the Muslim League to pursue their own goals. Soon, they were talking of a separate Muslim state.

Looking Ahead

By the early 1900s, protests and resistance to British rule increased. Some Indian nationalists urged that Indian languages and cultures be restored. More and more Indians demanded not simply self-rule but complete independence. Their goal finally would be achieved in 1947, but only after a long struggle against the British and a nightmare of bloody conflict between Hindus and Muslims.

British Railroads and Indian Nationalism

The British railway system in India was massive in size and importance. By 1900, 25,000 miles of track crisscrossed the Asian subcontinent, providing easy transportation for tea, cotton, jute, and other goods destined to enrich the British economy.

The vast rail network aided India as well. India had long been divided by geography, cultural differences, and rival rulers. British railroads helped to bridge some of these divisions and promote a sense of nationalism. They enabled Indians to travel across the country. The trains also helped ideas spread by transporting books, newspapers, and letters.

One British official compared the railroad system in India to "the aqueducts of Rome, the pyramids of Egypt, the great wall of China . . . monuments not merely of intelligence and power, but of utility and beneficence."

Theme: Geography and History How did railroads encourage Indian nationalism?

SECTION 4 Assessment

Recall

1. **Identify: (a)** East India Company, **(b)** Sepoy Rebellion, **(c)** Ram Mohun Roy, **(d)** Indian National Congress, **(e)** Muslim League.
2. **Define: (a)** sati, **(b)** sepoy, **(c)** viceroy, **(d)** deforestation, **(e)** purdah.

Comprehension

3. What were the causes and effects of the Sepoy Rebellion?
4. Describe three effects of British colonial rule on India.
5. How did Indians differ in their views on Indian and British culture?
6. How did British rule lead to growing Indian nationalism?

Critical Thinking and Writing

7. **Analyzing Primary Sources** Review the words of Thomas Macaulay, quoted above. What kind of education did Macaulay favor for Indians? Why?
8. **Defending a Position** Do you think that the British were right to pass laws that tried to reform the caste system and end sati? Explain and defend your position.

Activity

Drawing a Political Cartoon
Draw a cartoon that either praises or criticizes a British colonial policy in India. Give your cartoon a title and a caption. Consider using symbolism such as a lion, which is a traditional symbol of Britain.

China and the New Imperialism

Reading Focus

- What trade rights did westerners seek in China?
- What internal problems did Chinese reformers try to solve?
- How did the Qing dynasty come to an end?

Vocabulary

trade surplus
trade deficit
indemnity
extraterritoriality

Taking Notes

As you read, create a concept web, like this partially completed model, to show key events and developments in the decline of Qing China. Add as many circles as you need to finish the web.

Opium War

Boxer Uprising

DECLINE OF QING CHINA

Main Idea During the 1800s, Qing China declined as western powers used diplomacy and war to gain power in East Asia.

Setting the Scene

By the 1830s, British merchant ships were arriving in China loaded with opium to sell to the Chinese. One Chinese official complained bitterly to Britain's Queen Victoria. "I have heard that smoking opium is strictly forbidden in your country," he wrote. "Why do you let this evil drug be sent to harm people in other countries?"

For centuries, Chinese regulations had ensured that China had a favorable balance of trade with other nations. The phrase *balance of trade* refers to the difference between how much a country imports and how much it exports. By the 1800s, however, western nations were using their growing power to gain more influence over East Asia.

The Trade Issue

Prior to the 1800s, Chinese rulers placed strict limits on foreign traders. European merchants were restricted to a small area in southern China. China sold them silk, porcelain, and tea in exchange for gold and silver. Under this arrangement, China enjoyed a trade surplus, exporting more than it imported. Westerners, on the other hand, had a trade deficit with China, buying more from the Chinese than they sold to them.

By the late 1700s, two developments were underway that would transform China's relations with the western world. First, China entered a period of decline. Second, the Industrial Revolution created a need for expanded markets for European goods. At the same time, it gave the West superior military power.

The Opium War During the late 1700s, British merchants began making huge profits by trading opium grown in India for Chinese tea, which was popular in Britain. Soon, many Chinese had become addicted to the drug. Silver flowed out of China in payment for the drug, disrupting the economy.

The Chinese government outlawed opium and executed Chinese drug dealers. They called on Britain to stop the trade. The British refused, insisting on the right of free trade.

The Opium War
The Opium War began when Chinese officials tried to keep British ships from bringing the addictive drug into China. Here, a British warship sinks Chinese junks during the war.

Theme: Economics and Technology How does the picture suggest Britain's superior military technology?

In 1839, Chinese warships clashed with British merchants, triggering the Opium War. British gunboats, equipped with the latest in firepower, bombarded Chinese coastal and river ports. With outdated weapons and fighting methods, the Chinese were easily defeated.

Unequal Treaties In 1842, Britain made China accept the Treaty of Nanjing. Britain received a huge indemnity, or payment for losses in the war. The British also gained the island of Hong Kong. (See the map later in this section.) China had to open five ports to foreign trade and grant British citizens in China extraterritoriality, the right to live under their own laws and be tried in their own courts.

The treaty was the first of a series of "unequal treaties" that forced China to make concessions to western powers. During the mid-1800s, under pressure from the West, China agreed to open more ports to foreign trade and to let Christian missionaries preach in China.

Internal Problems

By the 1800s, the Qing dynasty was in decline. Irrigation systems and canals were poorly maintained, leading to massive flooding of the Huang He valley. The population explosion that had begun a century earlier created a terrible hardship for China's peasants. An extravagant court, tax evasion by the rich, and widespread official corruption added to the peasants' burden. Even the honored civil service system was rocked by bribery scandals.

The Taiping Rebellion As poverty and misery increased, peasants rebelled. The Taiping Rebellion, which lasted from 1850 to 1864, was probably the most devastating peasant revolt in history. The leader, Hong Xiuquan (howng shyoo CHWAHN), was a village schoolteacher. Inspired by religious visions, he set himself up as a revolutionary prophet. He wanted to establish a "Heavenly Kingdom of Great Peace"—the Taiping (tī PIHNG).

Influenced by the teachings of Christian missionaries, Hong endorsed social ideas that Chinese leaders considered radical. These included land reform, community ownership of property, and equality of women and men. Above all, he called for an end to the hated Qing dynasty.

The Taiping rebels won control of large parts of China. They held out for 14 years. However, with the help of loyal regional governors and generals, the government crushed the rebellion in the end.

Effects The Taiping Rebellion almost toppled the Qing dynasty. It is estimated to have caused the deaths of between 20 million and 30 million Chinese. The Qing government survived, but it had to share power with regional commanders. During the rebellion, Europeans kept up pressure on China. Russia seized lands in northern China.

Reform Efforts

By the mid-1800s, educated Chinese were divided over the need to adopt western ways. Most scholar-officials saw no reason for new industries because China's wealth and taxes came from land. Although Chinese merchants were allowed to do business, they were not seen as a source of prosperity.

Scholar-officials also disapproved of the ideas of western missionaries, whose emphasis on individual choice challenged the Confucian order. They saw western technology as dangerous, too, because it threatened Confucian ways that had served China successfully for so long.

The imperial court was a center of conservative opposition. By the late 1800s, the empress Ci Xi (tsee SHYEE) had gained power. A strong-willed ruler, she surrounded herself with advisers who were deeply committed to Confucian traditions.

You Are There . . .

Meeting the Emperor

After years of education, you have finally made it. You are about to be installed as a government official in the service of the emperor. You stand in the throne room known as the Hall of Supreme Harmony. Yet today, there is little harmony. Wars and rebellion have weakened China, and the foreigners are gaining power. Here in Beijing, meanwhile, leaders quarrel over what to do.

The room fell silent when Emperor Guang Xu entered. Now, as he begins the ceremony, you reflect on his recent actions as emperor. You know that he is trying to modernize China. However, conservatives in the government are fighting his reforms.

The Dowager Empress Ci Xi is not present. You have heard that she does not approve of the emperor's reforms. When the ceremony ends, you feel confused. You want to be loyal to your emperor, but you have spent years studying traditional Confucian ways of governing. Should you support reform?

Portfolio Assessment

In your new government post, you can either support or oppose the emperor's reforms. Write a poem explaining your decision. Be sure to include both reasons for and possible consequences of your decision.

Imperialism in China to 1914

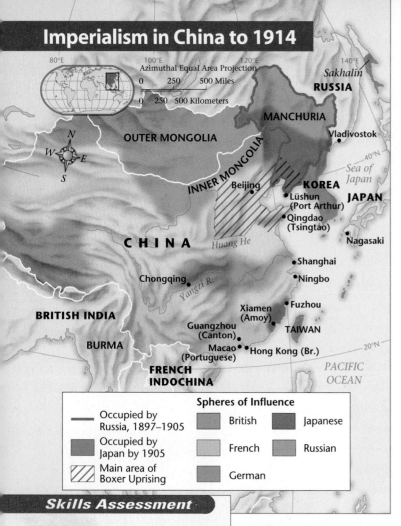

Spheres of Influence

- ——— Occupied by Russia, 1897–1905
- ▨ Occupied by Japan by 1905
- ▨ Main area of Boxer Uprising
- ▨ British
- ▨ French
- ▨ German
- ▨ Japanese
- ▨ Russian

Skills Assessment

Geography The European powers and Japan carved China into spheres of influence.

1. **Location** On the map, locate **(a)** Vladivostok, **(b)** Korea, **(c)** Hong Kong, **(d)** Taiwan.
2. **Place** What river was the center of Britain's sphere of influence?
3. **Critical Thinking** **Recognizing Causes and Effects** Use information on the map to identify causes of the growth of Chinese nationalism.

Self-Strengthening Movement In the 1860s, reformers launched what became known as the "self-strengthening movement." They imported western technology, setting up factories to make modern weapons. They developed shipyards, railroads, mining, and light industry. The Chinese translated western works on science, government, and the economy. However, the movement made limited progress because the government did not rally behind it.

War With Japan Meanwhile, the western powers and nearby Japan moved rapidly ahead. Japan began to modernize after 1868. It then joined the western imperialists in the competition for a global empire.

In 1894, Japanese pressure on China led to the Sino-Japanese War. It ended in disaster for China, with Japan gaining the island of Taiwan off the coast of China. When the two powers met at the peace table, there was a telling difference. Japanese officials were dressed in western clothes, the Chinese in traditional robes.

Spheres of Influence The crushing defeat revealed China's weakness. Western powers moved swiftly to carve out spheres of influence along the Chinese coast. The British took the Yangzi River valley. The French acquired the territory near their colony of Indochina. Germany and Russia gained territory in northern China.

The United States, a longtime trader with the Chinese, did not take part in the carving up of China. It feared that European powers might shut out American merchants. A few years later, in 1899, it called for a policy to keep Chinese trade open to everyone on an equal basis. The imperial powers more or less accepted the idea of an Open Door Policy, as it came to be called. No one, however, consulted the Chinese about the policy.

Hundred Days of Reform Defeated by Japan and humiliated by westerners, the Chinese looked for a scapegoat. Reformers blamed conservative officials for not modernizing China. They urged conservative leaders to stop looking back at China's past golden ages and instead to modernize as Japan had.

In 1898, a young emperor, Guang Xu (gwawng SHYOO), launched the Hundred Days of Reform. New laws set out to modernize the civil service exams, streamline government, and encourage new industries. Reforms affected schools, the military, and the bureaucracy. Conservatives soon rallied against the reform effort. The emperor was imprisoned, and the aging empress Ci Xi reasserted control. Reformers fled for their lives.

The Qing Dynasty Falls

As the century ended, China was in turmoil. Anger grew against Christian missionaries who belittled Chinese thinkers like Confucius. The presence of foreign troops was another source of discontent. Protected by extraterritoriality, foreigners ignored Chinese laws and lived in their own communities.

Boxer Uprising Antiforeign feeling finally exploded in the Boxer Uprising. In 1899, a group of Chinese had formed a secret society, the Righteous

Harmonious Fists. Westerners watching them train in the martial arts dubbed them Boxers. Their goal was to drive out the "foreign devils" who were polluting the land with their un-Chinese ways, strange buildings, machines, and telegraph lines.

In 1900, the Boxers attacked foreigners across China. In response, the western powers and Japan organized a multinational force. It crushed the Boxers and rescued foreigners besieged in Beijing. The empress Ci Xi had at first supported the Boxers but reversed her policy as they retreated.

Aftermath of the Uprising   China once again had to make concessions to foreigners. The defeat, however, forced even Chinese conservatives to support westernization. In a rush of reforms, China admitted women to schools and stressed science and mathematics in place of Confucian thought. More students were sent abroad to study.

China expanded economically, as well. Mining, shipping, railroads, banking, and exports of cash crops grew. With foreign capital, small-scale Chinese industry developed. A Chinese business class emerged, and a new urban working class began to press for rights as western workers had done.

Three Principles of the People   Although the Boxer Uprising failed, the flames of Chinese nationalism spread. Reformers wanted to strengthen China's government. By the early 1900s, they had introduced a constitutional monarchy. Some reformers called for a republic.

A passionate spokesman for a Chinese republic was Sun Yixian* (soon yee SHYAHN). Sun had studied in the West. In the early 1900s, he organized the Revolutionary Alliance. His goal was to rebuild China on "Three Principles of the People." The first principle was nationalism, freeing China from foreign domination. The second was democracy, or representative government. The third was "livelihood," or economic security for all Chinese.

Birth of a Republic   When Ci Xi died in 1908 and a two-year-old boy inherited the throne, China slipped into chaos. In 1911, uprisings in the provinces swiftly spread. Peasants, students, local warlords, and even court politicians helped topple the Qing dynasty.

Sun Yixian hurried home from a trip to the United States. In December 1911, he was named president of the new Chinese republic. From the outset, the republic faced overwhelming problems. For the next 37 years, China was almost constantly at war with itself or fighting off foreign invasion.

*In earlier history books, this name appears as Sun Yat-sen.

Biography

Sun Yixian 1866–1925

Sun Yixian was not born to power. His parents were poor farmers. Sun's preparation for leadership came from his travels, education, and personal ambitions. In his teen years, he lived with his brother in Hawaii and attended British and American schools. Later on, he earned a medical degree.

Sun left his career in medicine to struggle against the Qing government. After a failed uprising in 1895, he went into exile. Sun visited many nations, seeking support against the Qing dynasty. When revolution erupted in China, Sun was in Denver, Colorado. He returned to China to begin his leading role in the new republic.

Theme: Impact of the Individual   How did Sun's background prepare him to lead?

SECTION 5 Assessment

Recall
1. **Identify:** (a) Opium War, (b) Treaty of Nanjing, (c) Taiping Rebellion, (d) Ci Xi, (e) Open Door Policy, (f) Boxer Uprising, (g) Sun Yixian.
2. **Define:** (a) trade surplus, (b) trade deficit, (c) indemnity, (d) extraterritoriality.

Comprehension
3. How did western powers gain greater trading rights in China?
4. (a) What internal problems threatened the Qing dynasty? (b) What were the goals of Chinese reformers?

5. How was the Qing dynasty replaced by a republic?

Critical Thinking and Writing
6. **Making Generalizations** Based on what you have learned about western imperialism in Africa and Asia, what methods did European states use to gain power around the world?
7. **Making Decisions** If you had been a Chinese government official in the 1800s, would you have decided to support or oppose reform efforts designed to westernize China? Explain the reasons for your decision.

Activity

Planning a Debate
Work with a partner to plan a debate between a British merchant and a Chinese government official. The topic is extraterritoriality in China. Each of you should be prepared to present and defend your own position and to criticize the opposing position. Conduct your debate before the class.

Creating a Chapter Summary

On a sheet of paper, create a chart showing the effects of imperialism in the late 1800s and early 1900s. Use the partially completed model below to help you get started. Add as many boxes as you need.

WESTERN IMPERIALISM

Political
• Europeans set up spheres of influence
•
•

Military
•
•
•

Economic
•
•
•

Social
• Britain tries to change Indian caste system
•
•

CD-ROM Review For additional review of the major concepts of Chapter 25, see the *Guide to the Essentials of World History* or the *Interactive Student Tutorial CD-ROM.*

Web Site Self-Test For practice test questions for Chapter 25, see **www.phschool.com.**

Building Vocabulary

Use these words and their definitions to create a matching quiz. When you are finished, exchange quizzes with another student and check each other's answers.

1. imperialism
2. protectorate
3. jihad
4. missionary
5. pasha
6. genocide
7. sepoy
8. viceroy
9. indemnity
10. extraterritoriality

Recalling Key Facts

11. List the four main motives of the new imperialists.
12. How did Ethiopia successfully resist European imperialism?
13. How did the Ottoman empire try to westernize?
14. **(a)** What were the causes of the Sepoy Rebellion? **(b)** What were its effects?
15. Give two main reasons that China's policy of limiting trade with foreigners ended after the 1700s.
16. **(a)** What was the goal of the Boxer Uprising? **(b)** Describe the three principles that guided Sun Yixian.

Critical Thinking and Writing

17. **Linking Past and Present (a)** How did the opening of the Suez Canal in 1869 transform world trade? **(b)** Do you think the canal might be less important today? Why or why not?
18. **Analyzing Information** Western industrial nations set up colonies in Africa and India. In China, however, they established spheres of influence rather than colonies. Why do you think they did not colonize China?
19. **Comparing** In the late 1800s, several nonwestern nations instituted programs of western reforms and modernization. **(a)** Describe the reform efforts of two of the following: Egypt, the Ottoman empire, China. **(b)** Compare the results of these efforts.
20. **Connecting to Geography** Why were the natural resources of African and Asian lands so important to Europeans in the 1800s?
21. **Predicting Consequences** How do you think rivalries between religious groups affected anti-imperialism efforts in India? Explain your answer.

In 1896, Liang Ch'i-ch'ao, an influential Chinese thinker, was unhappy with conditions in China. Read the excerpt below and answer the questions that follow.

> "The age of China as a country is equal to that of India and the fertility of her land is superior to that of Turkey, but her conformity to the defective ways which have accumulated and her incapacity to stand up and reform make her also like a brother of these two countries. . . . Whenever there is a flood or drought, communications are severed, there is no way to transport famine relief, the dead are abandoned to fill the ditches or are disregarded, and nine out of ten houses are emptied. . . . The members of secret societies are scattered over the whole country, waiting for the chance to move. Industry is not developed, commerce is not discussed, the native goods daily become less salable. . . ."
>
> —Liang Ch'i-ch'ao,
> *On the Harm of Not Reforming*

22. According to Liang Ch'i-ch'ao, how is China similar to India and Turkey?
23. What does he say are some of China's most serious problems?
24. What kind of "move" do you think "secret societies" were waiting to make? Explain.
25. What do you think Liang Ch'i-ch'ao wanted Chinese leaders to do?
26. **(a)** What important event occurred in China four years after this was written? **(b)** Based on what you have read, how do you think Liang Ch'i-ch'ao may have felt about this event?

Use the Internet to find primary sources having to do with imperialism in the late 1800s and early 1900s. Select two documents or excerpts of documents and print them out. Explain the meaning of each primary source in your own words.

The cartoon above was published in France in 1904, at the height of the Age of Imperialism. The figure at left is a French soldier. The figure at right is a British soldier. Study the cartoon and answer the following questions:

27. What continent appears on the map?
28. Why are the soldiers in the cartoon ripping the map apart?
29. **(a)** Which part of the continent are the British getting? **(b)** Which part of the continent are the French getting?
30. Why do you think part of the continent was not colored red?
31. How do you think the situation depicted in the cartoon affected relations between Britain and France?
32. How do you think people of the time knew which nations the two figures represented?
33. What prediction about future international relations can you make based on information in the cartoon? Explain.
34. Create an interesting title for the political cartoon. Explain the reason for your choice of title.

Skills Tip

Use information that you already have about a historical topic to help you understand a political cartoon.

New Global Patterns

1800–1914

Chapter Preview

1 Japan Modernizes
2 Southeast Asia and the Pacific
3 Self-Rule for Canada, Australia, and New Zealand
4 Economic Imperialism in Latin America
5 Impact of Imperialism

1840

Britain annexes New Zealand, leading to devastation for the Maori population. This carved figure is an example of Maori art.

1853

American ships commanded by Commodore Matthew Perry arrive in Japan. This woodblock print shows the American "black ships" and Japanese onlookers.

1823

The United States issues the Monroe Doctrine.

**CHAPTER
EVENTS**

1800 • 1825 • • 1850

**GLOBAL
EVENTS**

1804 Haiti declares independence from France.

1818 Shaka begins Zulu conquests.

1845 Potato blight leads to the Great Hunger in Ireland.

Imperialism in Asia, the Pacific, and the Americas, 1900

Industrialized nations competed for control of territories around the world.

Arctic Circle

60°E 80°E 100°E 120°E 140°E 160°E 180° 160°W 140°W 120°W

40°N

PACIFIC OCEAN

Tropic of Cancer
20°N

Caribbean Sea

INDIAN OCEAN

Equator 0°

20°S

Tropic of Capricorn

40°S

Colonial possessions:

- British
- Dutch
- French
- German
- Japanese
- United States
- Russian
- Portuguese

Spheres of influence:

- British
- French
- German
- Japanese
- Russian
- United States
- British and French

N
W · E
S

Robinson Projection

0   1500   3000 Miles
0   1500   3000 Kilometers

1885

The Canadian Pacific Railway opens, linking eastern and western Canada.

1898

The Philippines declares independence from Spain.

1914

The Panama Canal opens, linking the Pacific Ocean and the Caribbean Sea. Construction of the canal, shown here, will lead to greater United States involvement in Latin America.

1875   1900   1925

1871 Germany is unified under Prussian leadership in the Second Reich.

1914 World War I begins.

Japan Modernizes

Reading Focus

- How did discontent in Japanese society and the opening of Japan lead to the Meiji restoration?

- What were the main reforms under the Meiji?

- How did Japanese military strength promote imperialism?

Vocabulary

Diet

zaibatsu

homogeneous society

Taking Notes

Copy this chart. As you read, fill in the major reforms of the Meiji restoration. The sample has been started for you.

REFORMS DURING MEIJI RESTORATION		
Political	**Economic**	**Social**
• Adopted German model of government	•	•
•		

Main Idea During the late 1800s, Japan opened its doors to foreign influence and became a modern industrial power.

Setting the Scene In 1853, the United States displayed its new military might, sending a naval force to make Japan open its ports to trade. Japanese leaders debated how to respond. While some resisted giving up their 215-year-old policy of seclusion, others felt that it would be wiser to learn from the foreigners. One Japanese lord pointed out:

> "There is a saying that when one is besieged in a castle, to raise the drawbridge is to imprison oneself. . . . Even though the Shogun's ancestors set up seclusion laws, they left the Dutch and Chinese to act as a bridge. . . . Might this bridge not now be of advantage to us, . . . providing us with the means whereby we may for a time avert the outbreak of hostilities and then, after some time has elapsed, gain a complete victory?"
> —Ii Naosuke, quoted in *Selected Documents on Japanese Foreign Policy* (Beasley)

In the end, Japan chose to abandon its centuries of isolation and to learn from the West. The country swiftly transformed itself into a modern industrial power and then set out on its own imperialist path.

Discontent in Tokugawa Japan

After the Tokugawa shoguns gained power in 1600, they reimposed centralized feudalism, closed Japan to foreigners, and forbade Japanese to travel overseas. The nation's only window on the world was through Nagasaki, where the Dutch were allowed very limited trade.

For more than 200 years, Japan developed in isolation. Although internal commerce expanded, economic changes introduced severe strains in Japanese society. By the 1800s, shoguns were no longer strong leaders, and corruption was common. Discontent simmered throughout Japan.

Many daimyo suffered financial hardship. Money was needed in a commercial economy, but a daimyo's wealth was in land rather than cash. Daimyo also had the heavy expense of maintaining households in both Edo and their own domains. Lesser samurai were unhappy, too, because they were no longer fighters. Many were bureaucrats. Even though they were noble, they lacked the money to live as well as urban merchants.

Merchants in turn resented their place at the bottom of the social ladder. No matter how rich they were, they had no political power. Peasants, meanwhile, suffered under heavy taxes.

The government responded by trying to revive old ways, emphasizing farming over commerce and praising traditional values. These efforts at reform, however, had scant success. Many groups felt little loyalty to the old system.

Opening Up Japan

While the shogun faced troubles at home, disturbing news reached him from abroad during the 1830s and 1840s. He was alarmed by news of the British victory over China in the Opium War. Even more disturbing was the way in which imperialists had forced China to sign the unequal treaties. Surely, the shogun reasoned, it would not be long before western powers began seeking trading rights in Japan.

External Pressure and Internal Revolt Then, in July 1853, a fleet of well-armed American ships commanded by Commodore Matthew Perry sailed into Tokyo Bay. Perry had a letter from the President of the United States. The letter demanded that Japan open its ports to diplomatic and commercial exchange.

The shogun's advisers debated what to do. As Lord Ii noted, Japan did not have the ability to defend itself against the powerful United States Navy. In the Treaty of Kanagawa in 1854, the shogun agreed to open two Japanese ports to American ships, though not for trade.

The United States soon won trading and other rights, including the right of extraterritoriality and a "most favored nation" clause. European nations demanded and won similar rights. Like the Chinese, the Japanese deeply resented the terms of these unequal treaties, which they found humiliating. Some bitterly criticized the shogun for not taking a strong stand against the foreigners.

Foreign pressure deepened the social and economic unrest. In 1867, discontented daimyo and samurai led a revolt that unseated the shogun and "restored" the 15-year-old emperor to power. He moved from the old imperial capital in Kyoto to the shogun's palace in Edo, which was renamed Tokyo, or "eastern capital."

Tea Ceremony
In Japan, the tea ceremony was developed to provide a peaceful setting for social activity (PAST). Today, the rituals provide a reminder of the nation's cultural heritage, as well as an oasis of calm in an otherwise busy world (PRESENT).

Theme: Continuity and Change Why might people choose to maintain traditions along with modernization?

PRESENT

PAST

Industrialization in Japan

The emperor Meiji wrote a poem to provide inspiration for Japan's efforts to become a modern country: "May our country, / Taking what is good, / and rejecting what is bad, / Be not inferior / To any other." The picture, the song, and the chart on this page relate to Japan's efforts to modernize in the late 1800s.

Clothing Manufacturing in Japan

Japanese manufacturing grew rapidly in the late 1800s. As in Europe and the United States, women played a key role in Japan's industrial revolution. In this 1897 print, women make clothing in a Japanese workshop.

Children's Game

In 1878, a song composed for Japanese children impressed on them the 10 objects that their country should adopt from the West to be truly modern. As they named each object, the children bounced a ball:

"Gas Lamps
Steam Engines
Horse Carriages
Cameras
Telegrams
Lightning Conductors
Newspapers
Schools
[Postal System]
Steamboats"

Investments by Industry in Meiji Japan

Activity	1877	1883	1893
Agriculture	–	1,053,000	2,542,000
Trading	454,000	35,904,000	57,616,000
Manufacturing	–	14,725,000	68,259,000
Railways	–	12,080,000	57,945,000
Banking	24,981,000	75,375,000	111,635,000

All figures are in yen.
Source: S. Uyehara, *The Industry and Trade of Japan*

Skills Tip

In tables containing numbers, a dash is often used to indicate a value of zero or to indicate that no value is given.

Skills Assessment

1. According to the picture, Japanese women
   A adopted western ways.
   B worked long hours.
   C opposed organized labor unions.
   D earned less than men.

2. In which economic activity did the investments increase by about 46 million yen between 1883 and 1893?
   E agriculture
   F trading
   G manufacturing
   H railways

3. **Critical Thinking Evaluating Information** Name two things about modernization in Japan that you cannot learn from the sources on this page. Explain why it would be useful to have that information.

Meiji Restoration The young emperor began a long reign known as the Meiji (MAY jee) restoration. This period, which lasted from 1868 to 1912, was a major turning point in Japanese history. *Meiji* means "enlightened rule." The Meiji reformers, who ruled in the emperor's name, were determined to strengthen Japan. Their goal was summarized in their motto, "A rich country, a strong military."

The new leaders set out to study western ways, adapt them to Japanese needs, and eventually beat westerners at their own game. In 1871, members of the government traveled overseas to learn about western governments, economies, technology, and customs. The government brought experts from western countries to Japan and sent young samurai to study abroad.

Reforms Under the Meiji

The Meiji reformers faced an enormous task. They were committed to replacing the rigid feudal order with a completely new political and social system and to building a modern industrial economy. Change did not come easily. In the end, however, Japan adapted foreign ideas with amazing speed and success.

Government The reformers wanted to create a strong central government, equal to those of western powers. After studying various European governments, they adapted the German model. In 1889, the emperor issued the Meiji constitution. It set forth the principle that all citizens were equal before the law. Like the German system, however, it gave the emperor autocratic power. A legislature, or Diet, was formed, made up of one elected house and one house appointed by the emperor. Additionally, voting rights were sharply limited.

Japan then established a western-style bureaucracy with separate departments to supervise finance, the army, the navy, and education. To strengthen the military, it turned to western technology and ended the special privilege of samurai. In the past, samurai alone were warriors. In modern Japan, as in the West, all men were subject to military service.

Economic Reforms Meiji leaders made the economy a major priority. They encouraged Japan's business class to adopt western methods. The government set up a banking system, built railroads, improved ports, and organized a telegraph and postal system.

To get industries started, the government typically built factories and then sold them to wealthy business families who developed them further. With such support, business dynasties like the Kawasaki family soon ruled over industrial empires that rivaled those of the Rockefellers in the United States or the Krupps in Germany. These powerful banking and industrial families were known as zaibatsu (ZĪ baht soo).

By the 1890s, industry was booming. With modern machines, silk manufacturing soared. Shipyards, copper and coal mining, and steel making also helped make Japan an industrial powerhouse. As in other industrial countries, the population grew rapidly, and many peasants flocked to the growing cities for work.

Social Change The constitution ended legal distinctions between classes, thus providing the opportunity for more people to become involved in nation-building. The government set up schools and a university. It hired westerners to teach the new generation modern technology.

Despite the reforms, class distinctions survived in Japan as they did in the West. Also, although literacy increased and some women gained an education, women in general were still assigned a secondary role in society.

The reform of the Japanese family system, and women's position in it, became the topic of major debates in the 1870s. Reformers wanted women to become full partners in the process of nation-building and to learn skills

Primary Sources and Literature

See "Fukuzawa Yukichi: Autobiography" in the Reference Section at the back of this book.

Virtual Field Trip

www.phschool.com

**Modern Transportation Museum
Osaka, Japan**

To learn more about transportation in Japan after the Meiji restoration, use the Internet address above to link to the Modern Transportation Museum.

A Railway in Japan
One of the most important technological advances that the Meiji borrowed from the West was the steam locomotive. This woodblock print shows a celebration to mark the opening of a Tokyo rail line.

Theme: Continuity and Change How does this picture show the continuity of some Japanese cultural traditions?

that would allow them to live on their own. Although the government agreed to some increases in education for women, it dealt harshly with other attempts at change. After 1898, Japanese women were forbidden any political participation and legally were lumped together with minors.

Amazing Success During the Meiji period, Japan modernized with amazing speed. Its success was due to a number of causes. It was a homogeneous society—that is, it had a common culture and language that gave it a strong sense of identity. Economic growth during Tokugawa times had set Japan on the road to development. Also, the Japanese had experience in learning from foreign nations, such as China.

Like other people faced with western imperialism, the Japanese were determined to resist foreign rule. In fact, in the 1890s, Japan was strong enough to force western powers to revise the unequal treaties. By then, it was already acquiring its own overseas empire.

Growing Military Strength

As with western industrial powers, Japan's economic needs fed its imperialist desires. A small island nation, Japan lacked many basic resources that were essential for industrial growth. Yet, spurred by nationalism and a strong ambition to equal the West, Japan built an empire. With its modern army and navy, it maneuvered for power in East Asia.

Japan Gains Power In 1894, competition between Japan and China led to the Sino-Japanese War. Although China had greater resources, Japan had benefited from modernization. To the surprise of China and the West, Japan won easily. It used its victory to gain treaty ports in China and control over the island of Taiwan, thus joining the West in the race for empire.

Ten years later, Japan successfully challenged Russia, its rival for power in Korea and Manchuria. During the Russo-Japanese War, Japan's armies defeated Russian troops in Manchuria, and its navy destroyed almost an entire Russian fleet. For the first time in modern history, an Asian power humbled a European nation. In the 1905 Treaty of Portsmouth, Japan gained control of Korea as well as rights in parts of Manchuria. This foothold on the East Asian mainland would fuel its ambitions.

Competition for Korea Imperialist rivalries put the spotlight on Korea. Located at a crossroads of East Asia, the Korean peninsula was a focus of competition among Russia, China, and Japan.

Although Korea had long been influenced by its powerful neighbor, it had its own traditions and government. Like China and Japan, Korea had shut its doors to foreigners. It did, however, maintain relations with China and sometimes with Japan.

By the 1800s, Korea faced pressure from outsiders. As Chinese power declined, Russia expanded into East Asia. Then, as Japan industrialized, it too eyed Korea. In 1876, Japan used its superior power to force Korea to open its ports to Japanese trade. Faced with similar demands from western powers, the "Hermit Kingdom" had to accept unequal treaties.

As Japan extended its influence in Korea, it came into conflict with China, which still saw Korea as a tributary state. After defeating China and then Russia, Japan made Korea a protectorate. In 1910, it annexed Korea outright, absorbing the kingdom into the Japanese empire.

Japan Rules Korea Japan ruled Korea for 35 years. Like western imperialists, the Japanese set out to modernize their newly acquired territory. They built factories, railroads, and communications systems. Development, however, generally benefited Japan. Under Japanese rule, Koreans produced more rice than ever before, but most of it went to Japan.

The Japanese were as unpopular in Korea as western imperialists were elsewhere. They imposed harsh rule on their colony and deliberately set out to erase the Korean language and identity. Repression bred resentment. And resentment, in turn, nourished a Korean nationalist movement.

Nine years after annexation, a nonviolent protest against the Japanese began on March 1, 1919, and soon spread throughout Korea. The Japanese crushed the uprising and massacred many Koreans. The violence did not discourage people who worked to end Japanese rule. Instead, the March First Movement became a rallying symbol for Korean nationalists.

Looking Ahead

The Koreans would have to wait many years for freedom. By the early 1900s, Japan was the strongest power in Asia. It continued to expand in East Asia during the years that followed, seeking natural resources and territory. In time, Japanese ambitions to control a sphere of influence in the Pacific would put it on a collision course with several western powers, especially Britain and the United States.

The Russo-Japanese War

The Russo-Japanese War began and ended on the sea. On February 19, 1904, Japanese torpedo boats made a surprise attack on part of the Russian fleet, near Manchuria. Most of those ships were wiped out.

The rest of the Russian navy was based in the Baltic Sea, more than 10,000 miles away. The Russian ships began a slow 15-month journey around Africa. When they chugged into the waters of East Asia on May 27, 1905, the Japanese navy attacked again. Japan's faster ships and more accurate gunnery forced the Russians to surrender within a single day.

Theme: Economics and Technology Why were the Japanese forces able to defeat their opponents so easily?

SECTION 1 Assessment

Recall

1. **Identify:** (a) Matthew Perry, (b) Treaty of Kanagawa, (c) Meiji restoration, (d) Russo-Japanese War, (e) Treaty of Portsmouth.
2. **Define:** (a) Diet, (b) zaibatsu, (c) homogeneous society.

Comprehension

3. (a) What problems did Tokugawa Japan face in the early 1800s? (b) Why did Japan end 200 years of seclusion?
4. (a) List three ways in which Japan modernized. (b) Explain how each of these actions helped strengthen Japan so it could resist western pressure.
5. How did Japan demonstrate its growing military strength?

Critical Thinking and Writing

6. **Connecting to Geography** How did the geographic location of Korea make it desirable to both China and Japan?
7. **Predicting Consequences** What might have happened to Japan if the Meiji reformers had not decided to modernize in the late 1800s? Explain.

Activity

Take It to the NET

Use the Internet to research the opening of Japan by Matthew Perry. Then, write a news article for either an American or a Japanese newspaper describing the event.

Reading Focus

- What impact did European colonization have on Southeast Asia?

- How did Siam maintain its independence?

- How did imperialism spread to the Philippines and other Pacific islands?

Taking Notes

Copy this table. As you read, fill in information on imperialism in Asia and the Pacific. To help you get started, portions of the table have been completed.

REGION	IMPERIALIST POWER	REASONS FOR COLONIZATION
INDONESIA	The Netherlands	
MALAYA		Rubber and tin
INDOCHINA		
SIAM		
HAWAII		
PHILIPPINES		

Main Idea | Western industrialized powers divided up Southeast Asia in pursuit of raw materials, new markets, and converts to Christianity.

Setting the Scene A Vietnamese official, Phan Thanh Gian, faced a dilemma in 1867. The French were threatening to invade. As a patriot, Phan Thanh Gian wanted to resist. But as a devoted follower of Confucius, he was obliged "to live in obedience to reason." And based on the power of the French military, he concluded that the only reasonable course was to surrender. Phan Thanh Gian made his choice with a heavy heart. By avoiding a useless war that would hurt his people, he became a traitor to his king. For that decision, he wrote, "I deserve death."

Leaders throughout Southeast Asia faced the same dilemma during the Age of Imperialism. As they had in Africa, western industrial powers gobbled up the region in their relentless race for raw materials, new markets, and Christian converts.

Europeans Colonize Southeast Asia

Southeast Asia commanded the sea lanes between India and China and had been influenced by both civilizations. From the 1500s through the 1700s, European merchants gained footholds in the region, but most of the area remained independent. This changed in the 1800s. Westerners—notably the Dutch, British, and French—played off local rivalries and used modern armies and technology to colonize much of Southeast Asia.

During the 1600s, the Dutch East India Company gained control of the fabled riches of the Moluccas, or Spice Islands. They then reached out to dominate the rest of Indonesia. The Dutch expected their Southeast Asian colonies to produce profitable crops of coffee and indigo as well as spices.

In the early 1800s, rulers of Burma (present-day Myanmar) clashed with the British, who were expanding eastward from India. In several wars, the Burmese suffered disastrous defeats. They continued to resist British rule, however, even after Britain annexed Burma in 1886.

The British also pushed south through Malaya. The bustling port of Singapore, on the sea route between the Indian Ocean and the China Sea, grew up at the southern tip of the peninsula. Soon, natural resources and profits from Asian trade flowed through Singapore to enrich Britain.

The French, meanwhile, were building an empire on the Southeast Asian mainland. In the early 1800s, French missionaries began winning converts in what is today Vietnam. The region had long been influenced by Confucian traditions. Vietnamese officials tried to suppress Christianity by killing converts and missionary priests.

As with Burma and the British, the Vietnamese misjudged European power. In the 1860s, the French invaded and seized a chunk of Vietnam. Over the next decades, they added more lands, eventually seizing all of Vietnam, Laos, and Cambodia. The French and other westerners referred to these holdings as French Indochina.

By the 1890s, Europeans controlled most of Southeast Asia. They introduced modern technology and expanded commerce and industry. They set up new enterprises to mine tin and harvest rubber, brought in new crops of corn and cassava, and built harbors and railroads. But these changes benefited Europeans far more than the people of Southeast Asia.

Many Chinese migrated to Southeast Asia to escape hardship and turmoil at home and to benefit from growing economic opportunities. Despite persistent local resentment, these communities of "overseas" Chinese formed vital networks in trade, banking, and other economic activities.

Siam Survives

Sandwiched between British-ruled Burma and French Indochina lay the kingdom of Siam—present-day Thailand. King Mongkut, who ruled from 1851 to 1868, did not underestimate western power. Before inheriting the throne, he had studied foreign languages and read widely on modern science and mathematics. He thus had a greater understanding of the West than many other Asian rulers.

Although Mongkut had to accept some unequal treaties, Siam escaped becoming a European colony. He and his son, Chulalongkorn, set Siam on the road to modernization. They reformed government, modernized the army, and hired western experts to train Thais in the new technology. They abolished slavery and gave women some choice in marriage. As Siam modernized, Chulalongkorn bargained to remove the unequal treaties.

In the end, both Britain and France saw the advantage of making Siam a buffer, or neutral zone, between them. In the early 1900s, they guaranteed its independence.

Imperial Powers in the Pacific

In the 1800s, the industrial powers began to take an interest in the islands of the Pacific.* At first, American, French, and British whaling and sealing ships looked for bases to take on supplies. Missionaries, too, moved into the Pacific region and opened the way for political involvement.

In 1878, the United States secured an unequal treaty from Samoa, gaining rights such as extraterritoriality and a naval station. Other nations gained similar agreements. As their rivalry increased, the United States, Germany, and Britain agreed to a triple protectorate over Samoa.

From the mid-1800s, American sugar growers pressed for power in Hawaii. When the Hawaiian queen Liliuokalani (lee lee oo oh kah LAH nee)

*The thousands of islands splashed across the Pacific are known as Oceania. Besides Australia and New Zealand, Oceania includes three regions: Melanesia, Micronesia, and Polynesia. (See the map in the Reference Section at the back of this book.)

Skills Assessment

Geography Spices first attracted Europeans to Southeast Asia. Later, the Industrial Revolution encouraged the search for raw materials and new markets.

1. **Location** On the map, locate **(a)** New Guinea, **(b)** Siam, **(c)** Singapore, **(d)** Philippines, **(e)** Indochina.
2. **Region** Which European countries claimed territory on the mainland?
3. **Critical Thinking** **Making Inferences** According to the map, which countries had the widest variety of resources?

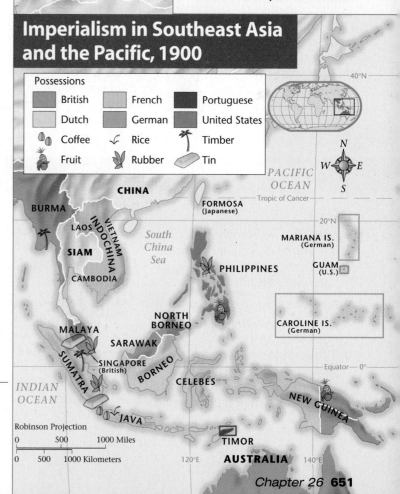

Imperialism in Southeast Asia and the Pacific, 1900

Possessions
- British
- Dutch
- French
- German
- Portuguese
- United States
- Coffee
- Fruit
- Rice
- Rubber
- Timber
- Tin

CHINA
BURMA
LAOS
VIETNAM
INDOCHINA
SIAM
CAMBODIA
FORMOSA (Japanese)
South China Sea
MARIANA IS. (German)
GUAM (U.S.)
PHILIPPINES
CAROLINE IS. (German)
MALAYA
SARAWAK
NORTH BORNEO
SUMATRA
SINGAPORE (British)
BORNEO
CELEBES
NEW GUINEA
INDIAN OCEAN
JAVA
TIMOR
AUSTRALIA
PACIFIC OCEAN
Tropic of Cancer
40°N
20°N
Equator—0°
120°E
140°E

Robinson Projection
0   500   1000 Miles
0   500   1000 Kilometers

tried to reduce foreign influence, American planters overthrew her in 1893. They then asked the United States to annex Hawaii, which it did in 1898. Supporters of annexation argued that if the United States did not take Hawaii, Britain or Japan might do so.

The United States and the Philippines

In the 1500s, Spain had seized the Philippines. Catholic missionaries spread Christianity among the Filipinos, and the Catholic Church gained enormous power and wealth. Many Filipinos accused the Church of abusing its position. By the late 1800s, their anger had fueled strong resistance to Spanish rule. Inspired by leaders such as José Rizal, many Filipinos worked to end Spanish control of the islands.

The United States became involved in the fate of the Philippines almost by accident. In 1898, war broke out between Spain and the United States over Cuba's independence from Spain. During the Spanish-American War, American battleships destroyed the Spanish fleet, which was stationed in the Philippines. Seizing the moment, Filipino leaders declared their independence from Spain. Rebel soldiers threw their support into the fight against Spanish troops.

In return for their help, the Filipino rebels had expected the Americans to recognize their independence. The peace settlement with Spain, however, placed the Philippines under American control.

Bitterly disappointed, Filipino nationalists renewed their struggle. From 1899 to 1901, Filipinos led by Emilio Aguinaldo (ah gee NAHL doh) battled American forces. Thousands of Americans and hundreds of thousands of Filipinos died. In the end, the Americans crushed the rebellion. The United States set out to modernize the Philippines through education, improved health care, economic reform, and construction of dams, roads, railways, and ports. Additionally, the United States promised Filipinos self-rule some time in the future.

Looking Ahead

By 1900, the United States, Britain, France, and Germany had claimed nearly every island in the Pacific. Japan, too, wanted a share of the region. Eventually, it would gain control of German possessions in the Pacific. Japanese territorial expansion would set the stage for a growing rivalry with the United States.

Biography

José Rizal 1861–1896

José Rizal was a pacifist and never fought in any battle himself. Still, he inspired other Filipinos to fight for independence from Spain.

Rizal was a talented man. He was a doctor, sculptor, novelist, and philosopher who spoke many languages fluently. He also wrote two novels that criticized Spanish leaders in the Philippines. The books were banned and even burned. The rulers later arrested Rizal as a revolutionary and had him executed by a firing squad. He is still recognized as a martyr of the cause for independence and a national hero.

Theme: Impact of the Individual Why does Rizal's life make him a national hero?

SECTION 2 Assessment

Recall
1. **Identify:** **(a)** French Indochina, **(b)** Mongkut, **(c)** Liliuokalani, **(d)** Spanish-American War, **(e)** Emilio Aguinaldo.

Comprehension
2. Compare imperialist policies of the Dutch, British, and French.
3. What steps did Siam take to preserve its independence?
4. Describe how the United States acquired each of the following territories in the Pacific: **(a)** Samoa, **(b)** Hawaii, **(c)** Philippines.

Critical Thinking and Writing
5. **Comparing** Compare the partition of Southeast Asia to the partition of Africa during the Age of Imperialism. **(a)** How was it similar? **(b)** How was it different?
6. **Connecting to Geography** Why were the Philippines, Singapore, and Indonesia of strategic value?

Activity
Creating a Time Line Create a time line showing the colonization of Southeast Asia and the Pacific during the Age of Imperialism.

Reading Focus

- How did Canada achieve self-rule?
- How did European settlement change the course of Australian history?
- How did New Zealand emerge as an independent nation?

Vocabulary

indigenous
confederation
dominion

Taking Notes

Copy this Venn diagram. As you read, fill in the information on the similarities and differences between the colonial experiences of Canada and those of Australia. To help you get started, some entries have been made.

CANADA
- Two distinct populations, British and French
-

AUSTRALIA
- Established as penal colony for Britain
-

- Set up government based on British model

Main Idea The British colonies of Canada, Australia, and New Zealand won independence faster and with greater ease than territories in other regions.

Setting the Scene The pattern of imperialism in the British colonies of Australia and New Zealand differed from that in other parts of the world. The indigenous (ihn DIHJ uh nuhs), or original, inhabitants of these regions were relatively few in number, and white settlers quickly subdued and replaced them. Still, the process of "replacement" was as deadly as it had been in the Americas some 200 years earlier.

These two English-speaking colonies, as well as Canada, won independence faster and with greater ease than England's territories in Africa or Asia. One reason was that they, unlike nonwestern peoples, had cultural roots in western-style government. However, western racial attitudes also played a part. Imperialist nations like Britain felt that whites could govern themselves. Nonwhites in places like India were thought to be incapable of shouldering such responsibility.

Canada Achieves Self-Rule

Canada's first European rulers were the French. When France lost Canada to Britain in 1763, thousands of French-speaking settlers remained. After the American Revolution, an estimated 30,000 or more colonists who had remained loyal to Britain fled to Canada. Unlike the French-speaking Catholics, the newcomers were English-speaking and Protestant.

Native Americans formed another strand of the Canadian heritage. In the 1790s, various Native American people still lived in eastern Canada. Others, in the west and the north, remained largely undisturbed by the movement of white settlers.

The Two Canadas To ease ethnic tensions, Britain passed the Canada Act in 1791. It created two provinces: English-speaking Upper Canada (now Ontario) and French-speaking Lower Canada (now Quebec). Each had its own laws, legislature, and royal governor. French traditions and the Catholic Church were protected in Lower Canada, while English traditions and laws guided Upper Canada.

During the early 1800s, unrest grew in both colonies. The people of Upper Canada resented the power held by a small British elite. In Lower Canada, too, people felt that British officials ignored their needs. In 1837, discontent flared into rebellion in both Upper and Lower Canada. "Put down the villains who oppress and enslave our country," cried William Lyon Mackenzie, a leader of the Upper Canada revolt.

Connections to Today

A Quandary for Quebec

Today, travelers to Canada who visit Quebec often feel that they have entered a different country. The French language and culture are evident everywhere, from traffic signs to radio shows.

Many Quebecers want Quebec to become independent. They believe that the cultural differences between French and English speakers are too deep for them to share the same country. They feel allegiance to Quebec rather than to Canada as a whole.

In 1995, a referendum on secession was held in Quebec. The final vote was almost a tie, with 50.5 percent voting against separation and 49.5 percent supporting the idea. Thus, the stage is set for continuing tension.

Theme: Diversity In what ways are Quebecers different from citizens of other Canadian provinces?

Canada, 1867–1914

Westward expansion
(Color value indicates the passing of time)

1891   1914

Natural resources

Gold   Coal

Silver   Timber

Copper   Fish

Iron Ore   Lobster

ARCTIC OCEAN

Azimuthal Equal Area Projection

0   250   500 Miles
0   250   500 Kilometers

YUKON TERRITORY 1898

NORTHWEST TERRITORIES 1870

CANADA

BRITISH COLUMBIA 1871

ALBERTA 1905

SASKATCHEWAN 1905

MANITOBA 1870

ONTARIO 1867

QUEBEC 1867

Hudson Bay

ATLANTIC OCEAN

PACIFIC OCEAN

ROCKY MTS.

UNITED STATES

L. Superior

L. Michigan   L. Huron

L. Erie   L. Ontario

St. Lawrence R.

NEW BRUNSWICK 1867

PRINCE EDWARD I. 1873

NOVA SCOTIA 1867

120°W   100°W   80°W   60°W

40°N   60°N

Mackenzie R.

Peace R.

Fraser R.

Saskatchewan R.

Skills Assessment

Geography By the end of the 1800s, railroads were moving people from one coast of Canada to the other.

1. **Location** On the map, locate **(a)** Quebec, **(b)** Ontario, **(c)** Alberta, **(d)** British Columbia.
2. **Region** Which of the provinces on this map was organized last?
3. **Critical Thinking Drawing Conclusions** What major geographic feature might have provided an obstacle to large-scale migration before the construction of railroads?

The Durham Report The British had learned a lesson from the American Revolution. While they hurried to put down the disorder, they sent an able politician, Lord Durham, to study the causes of the unrest. In 1839, the Durham Report called for the two Canadas to be reunited and given control over their own affairs.

In 1840, Parliament passed the Act of Union, a major step toward self-government. It gave Canada an elected legislature to determine domestic policies. Britain kept control of foreign policy and trade.

Dominion of Canada Like the United States, Canada expanded westward in the 1800s. As the country grew, two Canadians, John Macdonald and George Étienne Cartier, urged confederation, or unification, of all Canada's provinces. Like many Canadians, Macdonald and Cartier feared that the United States might try to dominate Canada. A strong union, they felt, would strengthen the nation against United States ambitions and help Canada develop economically.

Britain finally agreed. In 1867, it passed the British North America Act of 1867, creating the Dominion of Canada. It united four provinces into a dominion, or self-governing nation. Six additional provinces later joined the union.

As a dominion, Canada had its own parliament, modeled on that of Britain. By 1900, Canada had also been granted some control over its own foreign policy. Still, although self-governing, Canada maintained close ties with the British monarchy.

Expansion John Macdonald, Canada's first prime minister, encouraged expansion across the continent. To unite the far-flung regions of Canada, he called for a transcontinental railroad. In 1885, the Canadian Pacific Railway opened, linking eastern and western Canada. Wherever the railroad went, settlers followed. It moved people and products, such as timber and manufactured goods, across the country.

As in the United States, westward expansion destroyed the way of life of Native Americans in Canada. Most were forced to sign treaties giving up their lands. Some resisted. Louis Riel led a revolt of the métis, people of mixed Native American and European descent. Many were French-speaking Catholics who accused the government of stealing their land and trying to destroy their language and religion. Government troops put down the uprising and executed Riel.

Immigration   In the late 1800s and early 1900s, immigration increased as people flooded into Canada from across Europe and Asia. Newcomers from Germany, Italy, Poland, Russia, Ukraine, China, and Japan enriched Canada economically and culturally.

By 1914, Canada was a flourishing nation. Two issues continued to plague it, however. First, French-speaking Canadians were determined to preserve their separate heritage, making it hard for Canadians to create a single national identity. Second, the United States exerted a powerful economic and cultural influence that threatened to dominate its neighbor to the north. Both issues have continued to affect Canada to the present day.

Europeans in Australia

The Dutch in the 1600s were the first Europeans to reach Australia—the world's smallest continent. In 1770, Captain James Cook claimed Australia for Britain. For a time, however, it remained too distant to attract European settlers.

The First Settlers   Like most regions claimed by imperialist powers, Australia had long been inhabited by other people. The first settlers had reached Australia perhaps 50,000 years earlier, probably from Southeast Asia, and spread across the continent. Cut off from the larger world, the Aborigines, as Europeans later called them,* lived in small hunting and food-gathering bands, much as their Stone Age ancestors had. Aborigine groups spoke as many as 250 distinct languages. When white settlers arrived in Australia, the indigenous population suffered disastrously.

A Penal Colony   Events halfway around the world in North America and Britain ended Australia's isolation and brought Europeans to the island continent. During the 1700s, Britain had sent convicts to its North American colonies, especially to Georgia. The American Revolution closed that outlet just when the Industrial Revolution was disrupting British society. Prisons in London and other cities were jammed with poor people arrested for crimes such as stealing food or goods to pawn, agitating against the government, or murder.

To fulfill the need for prisons, Britain made Australia into a penal colony. The first ships, carrying about 700 convicts, arrived in Botany Bay, Australia, in 1788. The men, women, and children who survived the grueling eight-month voyage faced more hardships on shore. Many were city dwellers with no farming skills. Under the brutal discipline of soldiers, work gangs cleared land for the settlement.

Among these first arrivals was Matthew Everingham, who at the age of 14 had been sentenced to seven years in Australia for stealing two books.

Aborigine was a word used by Europeans to denote the earliest people to live in a place. Today, many Australian Aborigines call themselves Koories.

Primary Source

A Convict's Life
Convicts in the Australian penal colonies found that the attitudes of their masters determined the quality of their lives. Here, a son describes his father's life as a shepherd:

"He became a dreadful spectacle . . . weak and helpless as a child. . . . After my father had been out in the bush from sunrise to sunset, he had then to retire for repose to the watchbox, 6 feet by 18 inches, with a small bed and one blanket, where he could lie and gaze upon the starry heavens, and where the wind blew in at one end and out of the other, with nothing to ward off the pitiless storm. . . . Besides this he had to walk four miles [at night] for his rations."

—John Standfield, quoted in
The Fatal Shore (Hughes)

Skills Assessment

Primary Source Why did a convict-shepherd have such a terrible life in Australia?

Geography of Australia and New Zealand

Map Legend:
- Penal settlements
- Coal
- Copper
- Gas
- Gold
- Iron
- Oil
- Other metals
- Sheep
- Silver
- Timber

Mercator Projection

0   300   600 Miles

0   300   600 Kilometers

Skills Assessment

Geography Australia is both a continent and a country. Australia and its neighbor New Zealand feature a great variety of landforms.

1. **Location** On the map, locate **(a)** Great Barrier Reef, **(b)** Great Victoria Desert, **(c)** Central Lowlands, **(d)** Tasmania.

2. **Region** **(a)** In which region was gold found? **(b)** What geographic features did people encounter during the 1851 gold rush?

3. **Critical Thinking** **Drawing Conclusions** How does the map help you conclude that the population of Australia is not evenly distributed?

Despite illness and beatings during the course of his sentence, Everingham continued to have hope for the future:

> "I have now two years and seven months to remain a convict and then I am at liberty to act as a free-born Englishman ought to. . . . I am yet but young, only 19. If my health is spared I shall not be one jot the worse for being transported."
> —Matthew Everingham, quoted in "Children of the First Fleet," *National Geographic*

Everingham later married another convict, Elizabeth Rimes, and stayed in Australia. Their descendants, like those of other convicts and early settlers, carved out farms. Some prospered in their new homeland.

Into the Outback In the early 1800s, Britain encouraged free citizens to emigrate to Australia by offering them land and tools. As the newcomers occupied coastal lands, they thrust aside or killed the Aborigines. After settlers found that sheepherding was suited to the land and climate, a prosperous wool industry grew up in Australia.

In 1851, a gold rush in eastern Australia brought a population boom. Many gold hunters stayed on to become ranchers and farmers. They pushed into the rugged interior known as the Outback, displacing the Aborigines and carving out huge sheep ranches and wheat farms. By the late 1800s, Australia had won a place in a growing world economy.

Achieving Self-Government Like Canada, Australia was made up of separate colonies scattered around the continent. During the Age of Imperialism, Britain worried about interference from other powers. To counter this threat and to boost development, it responded to Australian demands for self-rule. In 1901, Britain helped the colonies unite into the independent Commonwealth of Australia. The new country kept its ties to Britain by recognizing the British monarch as its head of state.

The Australian constitution drew on both British and American models. Like the United States Constitution, it set up a federal system that limited the power of the central government. As in Britain, Australia's executive is a prime minister chosen by the majority party in Parliament. Unlike Britain and the United States, Australia quickly granted women the right to vote. It also was the first nation to introduce the secret ballot.

New Zealand

Far to the southeast of Australia lies New Zealand. In 1769, Captain Cook claimed its islands for Britain. Missionaries landed there in 1814 to convert the local people, the Maoris, to Christianity.

Maori Struggles Unlike Australia, where the Aborigines were spread thinly across a large continent, the Maoris were concentrated in a smaller area. They were descended from seafaring people who had reached New Zealand from Polynesia in the 1200s. The Maoris were settled farmers. They were also determined to defend their land.

Missionaries were followed by white settlers, who were attracted by the mild climate and good soil. These settlers introduced sheep and cattle and were soon exporting wool, mutton, and beef. In 1840, Britain annexed New Zealand.

As colonists poured in, they took over more and more of the land, leading to fierce wars with the Maoris. Many Maoris died in the struggle. Still more perished from disease, alcoholism, and other misfortunes that followed European colonization.

By the 1870s, resistance crumbled. The Maori population had fallen drastically, from 250,000 to less than 50,000. Only in recent years has the Maori population started to grow once more.

Self-Government Like settlers in Australia and Canada, white New Zealanders sought self-rule. In 1907, they won independence, with their own parliament, prime minister, and elected legislature. They, too, preserved close ties to the British empire.

New Zealand pioneered in several areas of democratic government. In 1893, it became the first nation to give suffrage to women. Later, it was in the forefront of other social reforms, passing laws to guarantee old-age pensions and a minimum wage for all workers.

Did You Know?

The Mutiny on the *Bounty*

In 1808, an American ship sailing in the South Pacific unexpectedly came upon Pitcairn Island, about 3,000 miles east of New Zealand. To the American crew's amazement, many of the people on the island spoke English. They also had an unusual story to tell. They were the children of crew members of the *Bounty*, a British trading ship. The crew had mutinied against their harsh captain, William Bligh, more than 20 years before.

Today, the *Bounty* descendants continue to live on Pitcairn Island. The story of that mutiny and its aftermath has been the subject of several books and popular movies.

Theme: Geography and History Why do you think the mutineers stayed in the South Pacific instead of returning to England?

SECTION 3 Assessment

Recall
1. **Identify: (a)** Upper Canada, **(b)** Lower Canada, **(c)** British North America Act, **(d)** Aborigines, **(e)** Maoris.
2. **Define: (a)** indigenous, **(b)** confederation, **(c)** dominion.

Comprehension
3. What steps led to Canadian self-rule?
4. How did the British settle Australia?

5. Why did Maoris fight colonists in New Zealand?

Critical Thinking and Writing
6. **Analyzing Information** Why might young nations like Australia and New Zealand have been willing to grant women the right to vote before European nations did so?
7. **Synthesizing Information** What ethnic tensions did Australia, Canada, and New Zealand face?

Activity
Take It to the NET

Use the Internet to research the British Commonwealth. Then, write a report identifying the member countries and the purpose of the organization.

Economic Imperialism in Latin America

Reading Focus

- What political and economic problems faced new Latin American nations?

- How did Mexico struggle for stability?

- How did the United States influence Latin America?

Vocabulary

regionalism

caudillo

economic dependence

peonage

Taking Notes

Copy this concept web. As you read, fill in the major problems facing Latin American countries during the 1800s. To help you get started, parts of the diagram have been completed.

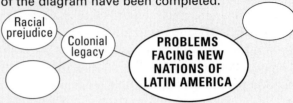

Main Idea The economy of Latin America became dependent on industrialized nations for investment, technology, and manufactured goods.

A City in Brazil
By 1900, the city of Rio de Janeiro, Brazil (below), was a bustling modern seaport. Yet much of the nation's wealth flowed out of the harbor and across the ocean to Europe.

Theme: Global Interaction Why might industrialized nations be eager to invest in Latin American countries?

Setting the Scene The new technology of the Industrial Revolution allowed European nations to import goods from around the world. Meat, which spoiled easily and traditionally required drying before being transported, could now be shipped across the globe in refrigerated vessels. One observer noted: "Great Britain supplies Brazil with its steam and sailing ships, and paves and repairs its streets, lights its cities with gas, . . . carries its mail." These and other developments contributed to the intertwining of nations that might be thousands of miles apart.

During the Age of Imperialism, Latin American nations found their economies increasingly dependent on those of more developed countries. Britain, and later the United States, invested heavily in Latin America.

Lingering Political Problems

Simón Bolívar had hoped to create strong ties among the nations of Latin America. After all, most people shared a common language, religion, and cultural heritage. But feuds among leaders, geographic barriers, and local nationalism shattered that dream of unity. In the end, 20 separate nations emerged.

These new nations wrote constitutions modeled on that of the United States. They set up republics with elected legislatures. During the 1800s, however, most Latin American nations were plagued by revolts, civil war, and dictatorships.

Colonial Legacy Many problems had their origins in colonial rule, as independence barely changed the existing social and political hierarchy. Creoles simply replaced peninsulares as the ruling class. The Roman Catholic Church kept its privileged position and still controlled huge amounts of land.

For most people—mestizos, mulattoes, blacks, and Indians—life did not improve after independence. The new constitutions guaranteed equality before the law, but deep-rooted inequalities remained. Voting rights were limited. Racial prejudice was widespread, and land remained in the hands of a few. Owners of haciendas ruled their great estates, and the peasants who worked them, like medieval European lords.

Instability With few roads and no tradition of unity, the new nations were weakened by regionalism, loyalty to a local area. Local strongmen, called *caudillos,* assembled private armies to resist the central government. At times, popular *caudillos* gained national power. They looted the treasury, ignored the constitution, and ruled as dictators. Power struggles led to frequent revolts that changed little except the name of the leader. In the long run, power remained in the hands of a privileged few who had no desire to share it.

As in Europe, the ruling elite in Latin America were divided between conservatives and liberals. Conservatives defended the old social order, favored press censorship, and strongly supported the Catholic Church. Liberals backed laissez-faire economics, religious toleration, greater access to education, and freedom of the press. Liberals saw themselves as enlightened supporters of progress but often showed little concern for the needs of the majority of the people.

The Economics of Dependence

Under colonial rule, mercantilist policies made Latin America economically dependent on Spain and Portugal. Colonies sent raw materials such as sugar, cotton, or precious metals to the parent country and had to buy manufactured goods from them. Strict laws kept colonists from trading with other countries or building local industries that might compete with the parent country.

After independence, this pattern changed very little. The new republics did adopt free trade, welcoming all comers. Britain and the United States rushed into the new markets, replacing Spain as the chief trading partners with Latin American nations. But the region remained as economically dependent as before.

Economic dependence occurs when less-developed nations export raw materials and commodities to industrial nations and import manufactured goods, capital, and technological know-how. The relationship is unequal because the more developed—and wealthier—nation can control prices and the terms of trade.

Foreign Influence In the 1800s, foreign goods flooded Latin America, creating large profits for foreigners and for a handful of local business people. Foreign investment, which could yield enormous profits, was often accompanied by interference. Investors from Britain, the United States, and other nations might pressure their own governments to take action if political events or reform movements in a Latin American country seemed to threaten their interests.

Economic Growth After 1850, some Latin American economies did grow. With foreign capital, they were able to develop mining and agriculture. Chile exported copper and nitrates, and Argentina expanded livestock and wheat production. Brazil exported coffee and rubber as well as sugar. By the early 1900s, both Venezuela and Mexico were developing important oil industries.

Throughout the region, foreigners invested in modern ports and railroads to carry goods from the interior to coastal cities. As in the United States, European immigrants poured into Latin America. The newcomers helped to promote economic activity, and a small middle class emerged.

Thanks to trade, investment, technology, and migration, Latin American nations moved into the world economy. Yet development was limited. The tiny elite at the top benefited from the economic upturn, but very little trickled down to the masses of people at the bottom. The poor earned too little to buy consumer goods. Without a strong demand, many industries failed to develop.

America provided agricultural goods, natural resources, and cheap labor. Most profits from this global exchange went to the industrialized nations.

The demands of the new world economy disrupted traditional local economies in Africa and Asia. As in Europe before the Industrial Revolution, most people on these continents grew and produced goods by hand for local use. Under colonial rule, they were forced to supply products such as rubber, copper, and coffee needed by the industrial world.

Money Economy Western capitalists developed plantations and mines but relied on a steady supply of local labor to work them. At the same time, colonial rulers introduced a money economy that replaced the old barter system that existed in some countries. To cover the expense of governing their colonies, colonial authorities imposed heavy taxes on their subjects. The only way that people could earn money to pay the taxes was by working on plantations, in mines, or on projects such as railroad building.

Families were disrupted as men left their homes and villages to work in distant mines or cities. In southern and eastern Africa, especially, many men became migrant workers. Their departure shattered families and undermined village life as women were left alone to grow food and support their children. In other parts of the world, such as Japan and Latin America, sons were kept at home to farm while daughters were sent to cities to find work as domestics or in the growing textile industry.

Economic Dependency Mass-produced goods from the industrialized world further disrupted traditional economies. India, for example, was seen by Britain as a great market for its goods. It flooded the subcontinent with cheap, factory-made cloth. The British textile industry flourished. Indian weavers who produced cloth by hand, however, could not compete and were ruined. Elsewhere, too, artisan-run businesses and handicraft industries were destroyed.

Local economies that had once been self-sufficient became dependent on the industrial powers, which bought their raw materials and supplied them with manufactured goods. When the demand and prices for crops or minerals were high, colonies prospered. When demand and prices fell, people suffered. In addition, because many workers were producing export crops rather than food for local consumption, famines occurred in lands that had once fed themselves.

Modernization Colonial rule did bring some economic benefits. Westerners laid the groundwork for modern banking systems. They introduced new technology and built modern communication and transportation networks. Capitalists invested huge sums in railroad building to boost the export economy. Railroads linked plantations and mines to ports, which developers also modernized.

From China to Chile, some local leaders and business people benefited from the new economic system. Countries like Argentina, Brazil, and Chile, for example, used export profits to develop industry, buy modern farm equipment, and promote growth.

Cultural Impact

Like many other peoples in history, Europeans were convinced of their own superiority. During the Age of Imperialism, they also believed that they had a mission to "civilize" the world. Cecil Rhodes, a leading promoter of British imperialism, declared: "The more of the world we inhabit the better it is for the human race. . . . If there be a God, I think what he would like me to do is to paint as much of the map of Africa British red as possible."

Westernization As westerners conquered other lands, they pressed subject people to accept "modern" ways. By this, they meant western ideas,

Biography

Cecil Rhodes 1853–1902

Cecil Rhodes arrived in South Africa at age 17, determined to make his fortune. He got off to a slow start. His first venture, a cotton-farming project, failed. Then Rhodes turned to diamond and gold mining. By the age of 40, he had become one of the richest men in the world.

However, money was not his real interest. "For its own sake I do not care for money," he once wrote. "I want the power." Rhodes strongly supported British imperialism in Africa. He helped Britain extend its African empire by 1,000,000 square miles and had an entire British colony named after himself—Rhodesia (now Zimbabwe). Rhodes also helped promote the policy of the separation of races in southern Africa.

Theme: Impact of the Individual How was Cecil Rhodes's desire for power illustrated by his actions?

government, technology, and culture. Thus, during the Age of Imperialism, modernization and westernization came to be seen as one and the same.*

Many nonwesterners, especially in conquered lands, came to accept a belief in western superiority. The overwhelming successes of the western imperialist nations sapped people's confidence in their own leaders and cultures. To share in the material advantages offered by western society, business and professional people and others who had contact with westerners learned western languages, wore western clothing, adopted western manners, and embraced many western ways.

Other nonwesterners, however, had great misgivings about abandoning their own age-old traditions. They greatly resented—and often strongly resisted—western efforts to force new ways on them.

The new imperialism spread western culture around the world. Still, many regions were able to escape much of its influence. In remote areas of Africa, the Middle East, and Asia, many farming villagers and nomadic herders had virtually no contact with westerners. As a result, their lives continued with relatively few changes.

Westernization and Tradition
In French colonies, local rulers kept their titles while real power was held by colonial officials. In this photo, a French colonial governor (left) meets with the king of Laos (right).

Theme: Continuity and Change What element of the king's clothing shows European influence?

Schools and Hospitals Western culture was often spread by missionaries who built schools and hospitals. They taught children basic literacy and trained young men for jobs in colonial governments.

Western medicine brought many benefits. Missionaries introduced medical breakthroughs such as vaccines and modern methods of hygiene that saved lives. At the same time, however, modern medicine undermined traditional herbalists and local healers, who sometimes possessed useful knowledge of the medicinal value of plants.

Religion Imperialism enabled missionaries to spread their Christian faith across the globe. They had great success in some areas. In southern Africa, for example, Christianity became widespread, although Africans generally adapted its teachings and beliefs to their own traditions. In regions where other world religions or belief systems such as Islam, Hinduism, Buddhism, and Confucianism were deeply rooted, Christian missionaries won fewer converts.

Old and New Ways The pressure to westernize forced colonized people to reevaluate their traditions. In Asia, for example, people were proud of their ancient civilizations. On the other hand, they did work to discourage some customs, such as sati in India or footbinding in China, which they now saw as harmful. In the end, many nonwestern cultures created a complex blend of old and new ways.

As people moved into cities that had become westernized, many still felt the pull of the past. "People come to the city because they want to live

---

*The process of modernization along western lines has continued to the present. In today's world, however, modernization and westernization are often seen as separate and different courses.

European Alliances, 1914

Standing Armies in Europe, 1914

Number of Soldiers (in millions)

ALLIES: Great Britain, France, Russia
CENTRAL POWERS: Austria-Hungary, Germany

Source: *The International Internet Encyclopedia*

Map legend:
- Central Powers
- Allies
- Neutral Nations
- Neutral Nations that later joined the Central Powers
- Neutral Nations that later joined the Allies

Azimuthal Equal Area Projection
0   250   500 Miles
0   250   500 Kilometers

Skills Assessment

Geography By 1914, most of Europe was divided into two armed camps. Millions of troops stood ready for war.

1. **Location** On the map, locate (a) Germany, (b) Austria-Hungary, (c) Serbia, (d) Russia, (e) France, (f) Great Britain.
2. **Region** Why would Germany worry about the alliance between France and Russia?
3. **Critical Thinking** *Synthesizing Information* Based on the map and the graph, which alliance do you think had the greater advantage in 1914?

Eastern Europe In Eastern Europe, Russia sponsored a powerful form of nationalism called Pan-Slavism. It held that all Slavic peoples shared a common nationality. As the largest Slavic country, Russia felt that it had a duty to lead and defend all Slavs. By 1914, it stood ready to support Serbia, a proud young nation that dreamed of creating a South Slav state.

Two old multinational empires particularly feared rising nationalism. Austria-Hungary worried that nationalism might foster rebellion among the many minority populations within its empire. Ottoman Turkey felt threatened by new nations on its borders, such as Serbia and Greece.

In 1912, several Balkan states attacked Turkey. The next year, the new Balkan states fought among themselves over the spoils of war. These brief but bloody Balkan wars raised tensions to a fever pitch. By 1914, the Balkans were the "powder keg of Europe"—a tiny spark might lead to an explosion.

Rivalries Among European Powers

Economic rivalries further poisoned the international atmosphere. Britain felt threatened by Germany's rapid economic growth. By 1900, Germany's new factories were outproducing Britain's older ones. Britain, therefore, had strong economic reasons to oppose Germany in any conflict. The Germans, in turn, thought the other great powers did not give them enough respect.

Imperialism Imperial rivalries also divided European nations. In 1905 and again in 1911, competition for colonies brought France and Germany to the brink of war. Germany wanted to prevent France from imposing a protectorate on Morocco. Although diplomats kept the peace, Germany did gain some territory in central Africa. As a result of the two Moroccan crises, Britain and France began to form closer ties against Germany.

Militarism and the Arms Race The 1800s saw a rise in militarism, the glorification of the military. It grew partly out of Social Darwinism. Echoing the idea of "survival of the fittest," one German militarist called war "a biological necessity of the first importance." Militarists painted war in romantic colors. Young men dreamed of blaring trumpets and dashing cavalry charges—not at all the sort of conflict they would soon face.

With international tensions on the rise, the great powers expanded their armies and navies. The result was an arms race that further increased suspicions and made war more likely. The fiercest competition was the naval rivalry between Britain and Germany. To protect its vast overseas empire, Britain had built the world's most respected navy. As Germany began acquiring overseas colonies, it began to build up its own navy. Suspicious of Germany's motives, Britain in turn increased naval spending.

As readiness for war came to dominate national policy, military leaders came to gain wider influence. On matters of peace and war, governments turned to military leaders for advice. German generals and British admirals enjoyed great respect and got more funds to build up their forces.

A Tangle of Alliances

Distrust led the great powers to sign treaties pledging to defend one another. These alliances were intended to create powerful combinations that no one would dare attack. Gradually, two huge alliances emerged.

The first of these alliances had its origins in Bismarck's day. He knew that France longed to avenge its defeat in the Franco-Prussian War. Sure that France would not attack Germany without help, Bismarck signed treaties with other powers. In 1882, he formed the Triple Alliance with Italy and Austria-Hungary. In 1914, when war did erupt, Germany and Austria-Hungary fought on the same side. They became known as the Central Powers.

A rival bloc took shape in 1894, when France and Russia formed an alliance. In 1904, France and Britain signed an entente (ahn TAHNT), a nonbinding agreement to follow common policies. Though not as formal as a treaty, the entente led to close military and diplomatic ties. Britain later signed a similar agreement with Russia. When war began, these powers became known as the Allies.

Other alliances also formed. Germany signed a treaty with the Ottoman empire, while Britain drew close to Japan. The growth of rival alliance systems increased international tensions. A local conflict could easily mushroom into a general war.

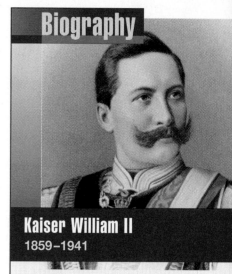

Biography

Kaiser William II
1859–1941

"All the long years of my reign," William II complained, "my colleagues, the monarchs of Europe, have paid no attention to what I have to say." As kaiser, he fought to win respect for himself and his empire.

William's rivalry with other rulers was in many ways a family feud. He and George V of Britain were cousins, grandchildren of Queen Victoria. Czar Nicholas II was another cousin. When war broke out in 1914, the kaiser blamed "George and Nicky.... If my grandmother had been alive, she would never have allowed it!"

Theme: Impact of the Individual How did the kaiser's desire for respect influence his policies?

SECTION 1 Assessment

Recall
1. **Identify:** (a) Hague Tribunal, (b) Pan-Slavism, (c) Central Powers, (d) Allies.
2. **Define:** (a) pacifism, (b) militarism, (c) entente.

Comprehension
3. Identify three peace efforts of the late 1800s and early 1900s.
4. Describe how each of the following served to inflame tensions in Europe: (a) nationalism, (b) imperial rivalries, (c) militarism.

5. (a) Why did European nations form alliances? (b) How did alliances increase fears of war?

Critical Thinking and Writing
6. **Applying Information** Reread Bismarck's statement at the start of this section. Why do you think he made this prediction?
7. **Linking Past and Present** Do you think the idea of going to war excites young people today in the same way that it did 100 years ago? Why or why not?

Activity
Take It to the NET

Use Internet sources to find out about peace efforts today. Then, choose someone whom you would nominate for the Nobel Peace Prize. Write a brief paragraph explaining why you think he or she deserves the honor.

Reading Focus

- How did ethnic tensions in the Balkans spark a political assassination?
- How did conflict between Austria-Hungary and Serbia widen?
- How do historians view the outbreak of World War I?

Vocabulary

ultimatum

mobilize

neutrality

Taking Notes

Copy this flowchart. Include at least five empty boxes. As you read, fill in the chain of events in the summer of 1914 that led to an all-out war.

Francis Ferdinand is assassinated

↓

↓

↓

↓

Britain declares war on Germany

Main Idea The assassination of Archduke Francis Ferdinand ignited the Balkan "powder keg" and sparked World War I.

Setting the Scene Bertha von Suttner devoted her life to peace. Though the daughter of a noble Austrian military family, she wrote a best-selling antiwar novel and organized a peace society. Her tireless work won her the nickname "Peace Bertha." Yet, in April 1913, Suttner wrote in her diary that "the great European disaster is well on its way. If so many seeds have been sown, surely the weeds will sprout up soon and surely so much stockpiled gunpowder will explode."

"Peace Bertha" died on June 20, 1914. Eight days later, an assassin's bullet set off the "gunpowder" and ignited a war that engulfed much of the world for four bloody years.

Assassination in Sarajevo

The crisis began when Archduke Francis Ferdinand of Austria-Hungary announced that he would visit Sarajevo (sar uh YAY voh), the capital of Bosnia. At the time, Bosnia was under the rule of Austria-Hungary. But it was also the home of many Serbs and other Slavs.

Serbian Outrage News of the royal visit angered many Serbian national-ists. They viewed the Austrians as foreign oppressors. Even worse, the date chosen for the archduke's visit, June 28, was a special date in Serbian histo-ry. It was on that date in 1389, Serbia had been conquered by the Ottoman empire. On the very same date in 1912, Serbia had at last freed itself from Turkish rule.

Some members of Unity or Death, a Serbian terrorist group commonly known as the Black Hand, vowed to take action. As one conspirator later recalled, "Our decision was taken almost immediately. Death to the tyrant!"

The Fatal Shots The archduke ignored warnings of anti-Austrian unrest in Sarajevo. On June 28, 1914, he and his wife, Sophie, rode through Sarajevo in an open car. Stationed along the route were several Black Hand conspirators. As the cars passed, one of the conspirators hurled a bomb. It missed the archduke but injured an officer in another car.

Later that day, the archduke asked to visit the wounded officer in the hospital. He did not know that one of the conspirators, Gavrilo Princip (GAHV ree loh PREEN tseep), was still waiting. As the car set out, Princip sprang forward and fired twice into the back seat. Moments later, the arch-duke and his wife were dead.

Connections to Today

A New Balkan Powder Keg?

"Crisis in the Balkans! Threat of War!" Some 80 years after the assassination of Francis Ferdinand, headlines like these flared in the world's newspapers. In 1991, rival-ries among Eastern Orthodox Serbs, Muslim Bosnians, and Catholic Croats led to civil war in Bosnia. More than 250,000 people died, and millions fled their homes. In 1995, American and European troops helped restore peace.

Tensions flared again when Serbia moved to suppress an independence movement by Muslim Albanians in the province of Kosovo. In 1999, the United States and its allies took military action against the Serbian gov-ernment.

Theme: Geography and History Identify two other places where religious or ethnic differences have led to conflict.

propaganda often played up Germa
act. The British and French press cir
against innocent people. Often, thes
completely made up. In Germany, p
sing a "Hymn of Hate" against the l

> "Hate by water and hate by land
> Hate of the head and hate of the
> We love as one, we hate as one;
> We have one foe and one alone—
> ENGLAND!"
> —Ernst Lissauer, "Hymn of

Impact on Women Women playe
of men left to fight, women took ov
economies going. Many women wo
weapons and supplies. Others joine
forces. When food shortages threate
Land Army went to the fields to gr

Nurses shared the dangers of th
aid stations close to the front lines,
especially after a big "push" brougl
English nurse Vera Brittain describe
France, "stopping hemorrhages, rep
serting innumerable rubber tubes"
on the floor."

War work gave women a new s
war, most women had to give up th
they had challenged the idea that w
ing and dangerous jobs. In many cc
United States, women's support for
the right to vote, after decades of st

Collapsing Morale

By 1917, the morale of both troops
was sending 15-year-old recruits to
bankruptcy. Long casualty lists, foc
to win promised victories led to cal

As morale collapsed, troops mu
many soldiers deserted during the
left the front to join in a full-scale r

Revolution in Russia Three year
Stories of incompetent generals anc
dence. In March 1917, bread riots ii
olution that brought down the Rus
about the causes and effects of the

At first, the Allies welcomed th
Russia would institute a democrati
ally. But later that year, when V. I. l
pull Russian troops out of the war.
Brest-Litovsk (brehst lih TAWFSK) w
participation in World War I.

Impact on the War Russia's witl
war. With Russia out of the struggl
on the Western Front. In the spring
to achieve the great breakthrough

The Conflict Widens

The news of his nephew's death shocked the aging Austrian emperor,
Francis Joseph. Still, he was reluctant to go to war. His government in
Vienna, however, saw the incident as an excuse to crush Serbia for good.

A Harsh Ultimatum Austria sent Serbia a sweeping ultimatum, or final
set of demands. To avoid war, said the ultimatum, Serbia must end all anti-
Austrian agitation and punish any Serbian official involved in the murder
plot. It must even let Austria join in the investigation.

Serbia agreed to most, but not all, of the terms of Austria's ultimatum.
This partial refusal gave Austria the opportunity it was seeking. On July 28,
1914, Austria declared war on Serbia.

From Capital to Capital A war between a major power and a small
Balkan state might have been another "summer war," like most European
wars of the past century. But as diplomats sent notes from capital to capital,
larger forces drew the great powers deeper into conflict.

Austria-Hungary might not have pushed Serbia into war at all without
the backing of its longtime ally, Germany. In Berlin, Kaiser William II was
horrified at the assassination of a royal heir. He wrote to Francis Joseph,
advising him to take a firm stand toward Serbia. The kaiser assured the
emperor of Germany's full support. Thus, instead of urging restraint, William II gave Austria a "blank check."

Serbia meanwhile sought help from Russia, the champion of Slavic
nations. From St. Petersburg, Nicholas II telegraphed William II. The czar
asked the kaiser to urge Austria to soften its demands. When this plea
failed, Russia began to mobilize, or prepare its military forces for war.
Germany responded by declaring war on Russia.

Russia, in turn, appealed to its ally France. In Paris, nationalists saw a
chance to avenge France's defeat in the Franco-Prussian War. Though
French leaders had some doubts, they gave Russia the same kind of backing Germany offered Austria. When Germany demanded that France keep
out of the conflict, France refused. Germany then declared war on France.
By early August, the battle lines were hardening.

The Schlieffen Plan Italy and Britain remained uncommitted. Italy chose
to remain neutral for the time being. Neutrality is a policy of supporting
neither side in a war. Britain had to decide quickly whether or not to support
its ally France. Then, Germany's war plans suddenly made the decision for
Britain.

Years earlier, General Alfred von
Schlieffen (SHLEE fuhn) had developed a plan
of attack against France. The Schlieffen Plan
was designed to avoid a two-front war—
against France in the west and Russia to the
east. Schlieffen reasoned that Russia's lum-
bering military would be slow to mobilize.
Under the Schlieffen Plan, Germany first had
to defeat France quickly. Then, it would fight
Russia.

To ensure a swift victory in the west, the
Schlieffen Plan required German armies to
march through Belgium, then swing south
behind French lines. On August 3, Germany
invaded Belgium. However, Britain and other
European powers had signed a treaty guaran-
teeing Belgian neutrality. Outraged by the
invasion of Belgium, Britain declared war on
Germany.

**"Who Killed the Peace of
Europe?"**
One by one, the major powers of
Europe were drawn into war. This
cartoon appeared in an American
newspaper in the summer of 1914.
**Theme: Global
Interaction** What point is this
cartoon making about the events
leading up to the war?

Reading Focus

- How did World War I become a total war?
- What effect did the continuing war have on morale?
- What were the causes and results of American entry into the war?

Main Idea **In their efforts to all their nations'**

Propaganda War
Name-calling is one of the most common techniques of propaganda. Allied propaganda often referred to Germans as Huns, the barbarian tribe who helped destroy Roman civilization.

Theme: Art and Literature How does the picture add to the emotional impact of this propaganda poster?

Virtual Field Trip

www.phschool.com

The Imperial War Museum London, United Kingdom

To see other artworks, artifacts, and documents relating to World War I, use the Internet address above to link to the Imperial War Museum.

Allied Push Toward Victory
In September 1918, American troops pushed German forces back through the Argonne Forest of France. This battle was the last Allied offensive of the war.

Theme: Geography and History What does this picture suggest about the environmental impact of the war?

The United States Declares War

Soon after the Russian Revolution began, however, another event altered the balance of forces. The United States declared war on Germany. Why did the United States exchange neutrality for war in 1917?

Unrestricted Submarine Warfare One major reason involved German submarine attacks on merchant and passenger ships carrying American citizens. Many of these ships were transporting supplies to the Allies. But President Woodrow Wilson insisted that Americans, as citizens of a neutral country, had a right to safe travel on the seas.

In May 1915, a German submarine torpedoed the British liner *Lusitania*. Almost 1,200 passengers were killed, including 128 Americans. Germany justified the attack, arguing that the *Lusitania* was carrying weapons. When Wilson threatened to cut off relations with Germany, though, Germany agreed to restrict its submarine campaign. Before attacking any ship, U-boats would surface and give warning, allowing neutral passengers to escape to the lifeboats. In December 1916, however, Germany announced that it would resume unrestricted submarine warfare. Wilson angrily denounced Germany.

Cultural Ties Many Americans supported the Allies. They felt ties of culture and language to Britain and sympathized with France as another democracy. Still, some German Americans favored the Central Powers. So did many Irish Americans, who resented British rule of Ireland, and Russian Jewish immigrants, who did not want to be allied with the czar.

Zimmermann Note In early 1917, the British intercepted a message from the German foreign minister, Arthur Zimmermann, to his ambassador in Mexico. Zimmermann promised that, in return for Mexican support, Germany would help Mexico "to reconquer the lost territory in New Mexico, Texas, and Arizona." Britain revealed the Zimmermann note to the American government. When the note became public, anti-German feeling intensified in the United States.

Declaring War   In April 1917, Wilson asked Congress to declare war on Germany. "We have no selfish ends to serve," he stated. Instead, he painted the conflict idealistically as a war "to make the world safe for democracy" and as a "war to end war."

First, the United States needed months to recruit, train, supply, and transport a modern army across the Atlantic. By 1918, about two million fresh, confident American soldiers had joined the war-weary Allied troops fighting on the Western Front. Although relatively few American troops got into combat, they proved to be good fighters. Their arrival gave Allied troops a much-needed morale boost. Just as important to the debt-ridden Allies was the financial aid provided by the United States.

The Fourteen Points   Though he had failed to maintain American neutrality, Wilson still hoped to be a peacemaker. In January 1918, he issued the Fourteen Points, a list of his terms for resolving this and future wars. He called for an end to secret treaties, freedom of the seas, free trade, and large-scale reductions of arms. For Eastern Europe, Wilson favored self-determination, the right of people to choose their own form of government. All those issues, he felt, had helped cause the war. Finally, he urged the creation of a "general association of nations" to keep the peace in the future.

Campaign to Victory

A final showdown got underway in early 1918. In March, the Germans launched a huge offensive that pushed the Allies back 40 miles by July. But the effort exhausted the Germans. The Allies then launched a counterattack, slowly driving German forces back across France and Belgium. In September, German generals told the kaiser that the war could not be won.

The German people showed their monarch their frustration as uprisings exploded among hungry city dwellers. German commanders advised the kaiser to step down, as the czar had done. William II did so in early November, fleeing into exile in the Netherlands.

By autumn, Austria-Hungary was also reeling toward collapse. As the government in Vienna tottered, the subject nationalities revolted, splintering the empire of the Hapsburgs.

The new German government sought an armistice, or agreement to end fighting, with the Allies. At 11 A.M. on November 11, 1918, the Great War at last came to an end.

SECTION 4 Assessment

Recall
1. **Identify: (a)** Treaty of Brest-Litovsk, **(b)** Woodrow Wilson, **(c)** *Lusitania*, **(d)** Fourteen Points.
2. **Define: (a)** total war, **(b)** conscription, **(c)** propaganda, **(d)** atrocity, **(e)** self-determination, **(f)** armistice.

Comprehension
3. What measures did wartime governments take to control **(a)** national economies, **(b)** public opinion?
4. What impact did wartime failures have on Russia?

5. **(a)** Why did the United States declare war on Germany? **(b)** What impact did American entry have on the war?

Critical Thinking and Writing
6. **Analyzing Literature** Reread the poem at the beginning of this section. **(a)** To whom is the poem addressed? **(b)** What does it suggest about the effects of trench warfare?
7. **Defending a Position** If you had been a women's suffragist, would you have supported the war effort? Why or why not?

Activity
Take It to the NET

Find five Web sites dealing with World War I. Rank the sites in order from 1 to 5, with 1 being the best. Consider content, images, and interactivity. Review the sites noting URLs, ratings, and a two-sentence description of each site.

Making the Peace

Reading Focus

- What were the costs of the war?
- What issues faced the delegates to the Paris Peace Conference?
- Why were many people dissatisfied with the Treaty of Versailles and other peace settlements?

Vocabulary

pandemic

reparations

collective security

mandate

Taking Notes

Copy this chart. As you read, fill in the left-hand column with issues that faced the world after World War I. In the right-hand column, write how the Paris Peace Conference dealt with each of these issues.

ISSUE	SETTLEMENT
1. Debt	1. German reparations
2.	2. Reduced size of Germany
3. Nationalism	3.
4.	4. League of Nations
5.	5.

Main Idea As Europe struggled to recover from the devastation of war, world leaders met in Paris to craft a peace treaty.

Setting the Scene Just weeks after the war ended, President Wilson boarded a steamship bound for France. He had decided to go in person to Paris, where Allied leaders would make the peace. Wilson was certain that he could solve the problems of old Europe. "Tell me what is right," Wilson urged his advisers, "and I'll fight for it."

Sadly, it would not be that easy. Europe was a shattered continent. Its problems, and those of the world, would not be solved at the Paris Peace Conference, or for many years afterward.

The Costs of War

The human and material costs of the war were staggering. More than 8.5 million people were dead. Double that number had been wounded, many of them handicapped for life. Famine threatened many regions.

The devastation was made even worse in 1918 by a deadly pandemic of influenza. A pandemic is the spread of a disease across an entire country, continent, or—in this case—the whole world. In just a few months, the flu swept around the world, killing more than 20 million people—twice as many as the war itself.

Financial Burdens In battle zones from France to Russia, homes, farms, factories, roads, and churches had been shelled into rubble. The costs of rebuilding and paying off huge national war debts would burden an already battered world.

Shaken and disillusioned, people everywhere felt bitter about the war. The Allies blamed the conflict on their defeated foes and insisted that the losers make reparations, or payments for war damage. The stunned Central Powers, who had viewed the armistice as a cease-fire rather than a surrender, looked for scapegoats on whom they could blame their defeat.

Political Turmoil Under the stress of war, governments had collapsed in Russia, Germany, Austria-Hungary, and the Ottoman empire. Political radicals dreamed of building a new social order from the chaos, as revolutionaries

FACT FINDER

Casualties of World War I

	Deaths in Battle	Wounded in Battle
Allies		
France	1,357,800	4,266,000
British empire	908,371	2,090,212
Russia	1,700,000	4,950,000
Italy	462,391	953,886
United States	50,585	205,690
Others	502,421	342,585
Central Powers		
Germany	1,808,546	4,247,143
Austria-Hungary	922,500	3,620,000
Ottoman empire	325,000	400,000

Source: R. E. Dupuy and T. N. Dupuy, *The Encyclopedia of Military History*

Skills Assessment

Chart World War I resulted in more casualties than any previous war. **Which two nations suffered the most deaths? Why were American casualties relatively low?**

in Russia seemed to be doing. Conservatives warned against the spread of bolshevism, or communism, as it soon came to be called.

Unrest also swept through Europe's colonial empires. African and Asian soldiers had discovered that the imperial powers were not as invincible as they seemed. Colonial troops returned home with a more cynical view of Europeans and renewed hopes for independence.

The Paris Peace Conference

To a weary world, Woodrow Wilson seemed a symbol of hope. His talk of self-determination and democracy raised expectations for a just and lasting peace, even in defeated Germany. Crowds cheered wildly as he rode along the Paris boulevards.

The Big Three   Wilson was one of three strong personalities who dominated the Paris Peace Conference. A dedicated reformer, Wilson was so sure of his rightness that he could be hard to work with. Urging "peace without victory," he wanted the Fourteen Points to be the basis of the peace.

The other Allied leaders at the peace conference had different aims. The British prime minister, David Lloyd George, knew that his people demanded harsh treatment for Germany. He promised to build a postwar Britain "fit for heroes"—a goal that would cost money. The French leader, Georges Clemenceau (KLEHM uhn soh), bore the nickname "the Tiger" for his fierce anti-German war policy. His chief goal was to weaken Germany so that it could never again threaten France. "Mr. Wilson bores me with his Fourteen Points," complained Clemenceau. "Why, God Almighty has only ten!"

Difficult Issues   Crowds of other representatives circled around the "Big Three" with their own demands and interests. The Italian prime minister, Vittorio Orlando, insisted that the Allies honor their secret agreement to give to Italy lands that were once ruled by Austria-Hungary. Such secret agreements violated Wilson's principle of self-determination.

Self-determination posed other problems. Many people who had been ruled by Russia, Austria-Hungary, or the Ottoman empire now demanded national states of their own. The territories claimed by these peoples often overlapped, so it was impossible to satisfy them all.

Faced with conflicting demands, Wilson had to compromise on his Fourteen Points. On one point, though, he stood firm. His dream was to create an international League of Nations. The League would be based on the idea of collective security, a system in which a group of nations acts as one to preserve the peace of all. With the League in place, Wilson felt sure that any mistakes made in Paris could be corrected in time.

The Treaty of Versailles

In June 1919, the peacemakers summoned representatives of the new German Republic to the palace of Versailles outside Paris. The Germans were ordered to sign the treaty drawn up by the Allies.

The German delegates read the document with growing horror. It forced Germany to assume full blame for causing the war. It also imposed huge reparations that would put an already damaged German economy under a staggering burden. The reparations covered not only the destruction caused by the war, but also pensions for millions of Allied soldiers or their widows and families. The total cost of German reparations would come to over $30 billion.

Other clauses were aimed at weakening Germany. The treaty severely limited the size of the once-feared German military. It returned Alsace and Lorraine to France, removed hundreds of square miles of territory from western and eastern Germany, and stripped Germany of its overseas colonies.

Primary Source

Signing the Peace Treaty
A British delegate describes how the German delegates were brought in to sign the Treaty of Versailles:

"Isolated and pitiable, come the two German delegates. Dr. Müller, Dr. Bell. The silence is terrifying. . . . They keep their eyes fixed away from those two thousand staring eyes, fixed up on the ceiling. They are deathly pale. . . . They are conducted to their chairs. Clemenceau at once breaks the silence. 'Messieurs,' he rasps, '[the meeting is open.]' He adds a few ill-chosen words. 'We are here to sign a Treaty of Peace.' The Germans leap up anxiously when he has finished, since they know that they are the first to sign. William Martin, as if a theater manager, motions them [crossly] to sit down again."
—Harold Nicolson,
Peacemaking, 1919

Skills Assessment

Primary Source Do you think Nicolson approved of the way the German delegates were treated? Explain.

Europe, 1914

NORWAY
SWEDEN
North Sea
GREAT BRITAIN
DENMARK
Baltic Sea
RUSSIA
GERMANY
ATLANTIC OCEAN
AUSTRIA-HUNGARY
FRANCE
PORTUGAL
SPAIN
ITALY
ROMANIA
BULGARIA
Black Sea
GREECE
OTTOMAN EMPIRE
Mediterranean Sea

Azimuthal Equal Area Projection
0   250   500 Miles
0   250   500 Kilometers

Europe, 1920

FINLAND
NORWAY
SWEDEN
ESTONIA Moscow
LATVIA
GREAT BRITAIN
DENMARK
Baltic Sea
LITHUANIA
DANZIG
GER.
London
NETH.
Berlin
Warsaw
BELG.
GERMANY
POLAND
RUSSIA
RHINELAND
Paris LUX.
SAAR BASIN
ALSACE LORRAINE
CZECHOSLOVAKIA
Vienna
ATLANTIC OCEAN
FRANCE SWITZ.
AUSTRIA HUNGARY
YUGOSLAVIA
ROMANIA
PORTUGAL
SPAIN
Madrid
ITALY
Rome
BULGARIA
Constantinople
ALBANIA
GREECE
TURK
Mediterranean Sea
DODECANESE (Italy)

Azimuthal Equal Area Projection
0   250   500 Miles
0   250   500 Kilometers

Skills Assessment

Geography The peace treaties that ended World War I redrew the map of Europe.

1. **Location** On the map, locate **(a)** Lithuania, **(b)** Latvia, **(c)** Estonia, **(d)** Poland, **(e)** Yugoslavia.
2. **Region** Which countries lost territory in Eastern Europe?
3. **Critical Thinking Making Inferences** Why do you think the war had no effect on national boundaries in southwestern Europe?

The Germans signed because they had no choice. But German resentment of the Treaty of Versailles would poison the international climate for 20 years—and help spark an even deadlier world war.

Widespread Dissatisfaction

The Allies drew up separate treaties with the other Central Powers. Like the Treaty of Versailles, these treaties left widespread dissatisfaction.

Self-Determination in Eastern Europe Where the German, Austrian, and Russian empires had once ruled, a band of new nations emerged. They included the Baltic states of Latvia, Lithuania, and Estonia. Poland regained independence after more than 100 years of foreign rule.

Three new republics—Czechoslovakia, Austria, and Hungary—rose in the old Hapsburg heartland. In the Balkans, the peacemakers created a new South Slav state, Yugoslavia, dominated by Serbia. Eastern Europe, however, remained a center of conflict, as you will read.

Mandate System European colonies in Africa, Asia, and the Pacific had looked to the Paris Peace Conference with high hopes. Many people from these lands had fought alongside Europeans. Colonial leaders expected that the peace would bring new respect and an end to imperial rule. They took up Wilson's call for self-determination.

However, the leaders at Paris applied self-determination only to parts of Europe. Outside Europe, the victorious Allies added to their overseas empires. The treaties created a system of mandates, territories administered by western powers. Britain and France gained mandates over German colonies in Africa and Ottoman lands in the Middle East. In theory, mandates were to be held and modernized until they were able to "stand alone." In practice, they became European colonies. From Africa to the Middle East and across Asia, colonized peoples felt betrayed by the peacemakers.

Unfulfilled Goals Germany was not the only power dissatisfied by the peace. Italy was angry because it did not get all the lands promised in its secret treaty with the Allies. Japan protested the refusal of western nations to recognize its claims in China. At the same time, China was forced to accept former German holdings. Russia, excluded from the peace talks, resented the reestablishment of a Polish nation and three independent Baltic states on lands that had been part of the Russian empire. All of these discontented nations bided their time. They waited for a chance to revise the peace settlements in their favor.

Hopes for Global Peace The Paris Peace Conference did offer one beacon of hope in the League of Nations. In the aftermath of the war, millions of people looked to the League to ensure the peace. More than 40 nations joined the League. They agreed to negotiate disputes rather than resort to war. Members of the League promised to take common action—economic or even military—against any aggressor state.

Wilson's dream had become a reality. Yet his own Senate refused to ratify the treaty, and the United States never joined the League. Disillusioned with war, the United States chose to play a lone hand in world affairs. As time soon revealed, the League was powerless to prevent war. Still, it was a first step toward something genuinely new—an international organization dedicated to maintaining peace and advancing the interests of all peoples.

Cause *and* Effect

Long-Term Causes	Immediate Causes
• Imperialist and economic rivalries among European powers • European alliance system • Militarism and arms race • Nationalist tensions in Balkans	• Austria-Hungary's annexation of Bosnia and Herzegovina • Fighting in the Balkans • Assassination of Archduke Francis Ferdinand • German invasion of Belgium

World War I

Immediate Effects	Long-Term Effects
• Enormous cost in lives and money • Russian Revolution • Creation of new nations in Eastern Europe • Requirement that Germany pay reparations • German loss of its overseas colonies • Balfour Declaration • League of Nations	• Economic impact of war debts on Europe • Emergence of United States and Japan as important powers • Growth of nationalism in colonies • Rise of fascism • World War II

Connections to Today

• Ethnic tensions in Balkans
• International agreement banning poison gas
• Use of airplanes and submarines for military purposes
• Arab-Israeli conflict

Skills Assessment **Chart** Sparked by old rivalries in Europe, World War I helped shape our world today. **Which effect of the war do you think is most important today? Why?**

SECTION 5 Assessment

Recall

1. **Identify:** (a) David Lloyd George, (b) Georges Clemenceau, (c) League of Nations, (d) Treaty of Versailles.
2. **Define:** (a) pandemic, (b) reparations, (c) collective security, (d) mandate.

Comprehension

3. Describe conditions in Europe after World War I.
4. (a) Identify three issues to be settled at the Paris Peace Conference. (b) How did Woodrow Wilson's goals at the peace talks differ from those of other Allied leaders?

5. How did the peace treaties both follow and violate Wilson's principle of self-determination?

Critical Thinking and Writing

6. **Connecting to Geography** How might the creation of the mandate system affect the map of Africa after World War I?
7. **Making Inferences** Wilson's closest adviser wrote, "Looking at the conference in retrospect, there is much to approve and much to regret." What do you think he might have approved? What might he have regretted?

Activity

Writing an Editorial
Choose *one* of the countries mentioned in this section. Write an editorial about the Paris Peace Conference that might have appeared in a newspaper in that country during or after the peace talks.

Two Revolutions in Russia

Reading Focus

■ Why did revolution occur in Russia in March 1917?

■ Why did Lenin and the Bolsheviks launch the November revolution?

■ How did the Communists defeat their opponents in Russia's civil war?

Vocabulary

proletariat

soviet

commissar

Taking Notes

Copy this partially completed chart on the causes of revolution in Russia. As you read, finish the chart by writing in other causes.

REVOLUTION IN RUSSIA

Main Idea After two revolutions and a civil war, Lenin and the Communist party were the new rulers of Russia.

Geography and History

A Land of Many Nations

Geography had long favored the growth of the Russian empire. The vast plain stretching from Moscow had few natural obstacles to halt the advance of Russian armies. For nearly four centuries, the empire grew steadily. This growth was a mixed blessing, however. In 1897, a census revealed that the Russians were a minority in their own empire. More than half the people under czarist rule were not Russians. The population included Poles, Finns, Ukrainians, Lithuanians, Latvians, Turkic peoples, and other groups.

Nationalism led to the rise of new political parties among these peoples. In addition to social and economic reform, the parties' leaders hoped for some degree of self-rule. Radicals even dreamed of independent nations—a revolutionary idea that contributed to unrest in the Russian empire.

Theme: Geography and History Refer to a modern map of Europe. Name two independent nations of today that were once part of the Russian empire.

Setting the Scene On Easter 1913, Czar Nicholas II gave his wife, Alexandra, a fabulous jeweled egg, made by the famous jewelry firm of Fabergé. The egg's enamel shell held tiny portraits of all the Romanovs who had reigned since Michael Romanov was elected to rule Russia in 1613. Balls, parades, and other festive events celebrated the 300th anniversary of the Romanov dynasty. Everywhere, Russians cheered wildly for the czar and his family.

Czarina Alexandra felt confident that the people loved Nicholas too much to ever threaten him. "They are constantly frightening the emperor with threats of revolution," she told a friend, "and here,—you see it yourself—we need merely to show ourselves and at once their hearts are ours."

Appearances were deceiving. After the Revolution of 1905, Nicholas had failed to solve Russia's basic political, economic, and social problems. Discontent sparked new eruptions. In March 1917, the first of two revolutions would topple the Romanov dynasty and pave the way for even more radical changes.

The March Revolution

In 1914, the huge Russian empire stretched from Eastern Europe to the Pacific Ocean. Unlike industrialized Western Europe, Russia was a backward land dominated by landowning nobles, priests, and an autocratic czar. Much of its majority peasant population endured stark poverty. A small middle class and an urban working class were emerging as Russia began to industrialize.

Long-Term Unrest Under pressure, czars had made some reforms, but too few to ease the nation's crisis. The elected Duma set up after the Revolution of 1905 had no real power. Moderates pressed for a constitution and social change. But Nicholas II, a weak and ineffectual man, blocked attempts to limit his authority. Like past czars, he relied on his secret police and other enforcers to impose his will. Adding to the problems of the government were a corrupt bureaucracy and an overburdened court system.

Revolutionaries hatched radical plots. Some hoped to lead discontented peasants to overthrow the czarist regime. Marxists tried to ignite revolution among the proletariat—the growing class of factory and railroad workers, miners, and urban wage earners. To outwit government spies and informers, revolutionaries worked in secrecy under rigid discipline. A revolution, they believed, would occur, when the time was ripe.

Impact of World War I The outbreak of war in 1914 fired national pride and united Russians. Armies dashed to battle with enthusiasm. But like the Crimean and Russo-Japanese wars, World War I quickly strained Russian resources. Factories could not turn out enough supplies. The transportation system broke down, delivering only a trickle of needed materials to the front. By 1915, many soldiers had no rifles and no ammunition. Badly equipped and poorly led, they died in staggering numbers. In 1915 alone, Russian casualties reached two million.

In a patriotic gesture, Nicholas II went to the front to take personal charge. The decision proved a disastrous blunder. The czar was no more competent than many of his generals. Worse, he left domestic affairs to the czarina, Alexandra. Many Russians already distrusted Alexandra because she was German born. She also knew little about government.

Rasputin Alexandra came to rely on the advice of Gregory Rasputin, an illiterate peasant and self-proclaimed "holy man." Rasputin's powerful personality had helped him gain a widespread reputation as a healer. The czarina, especially, came to believe in his "miraculous" powers after he helped ease the suffering of her son, who suffered from hemophilia, a disorder in which even the smallest injury can result in uncontrollable bleeding.

By 1916, Rasputin's influence over Alexandra had reached new heights and weakened confidence in the government. Officials were appointed or dismissed at his say-so. Those who flattered him won top jobs. Yet Alexandra ignored all warnings about Rasputin. Fearing for the monarchy, a group of Russian nobles killed Rasputin on December 29, 1916.

Collapse of the Monarchy By March 1917,* disasters on the battlefield, combined with food and fuel shortages on the home front, brought the monarchy to collapse. In St. Petersburg (renamed Petrograd during the war), workers were going on strike. Marchers, mostly women, surged through the streets, shouting, "Bread! Bread!" Troops refused to fire on the demonstrators, leaving the government helpless. Finally, on the advice of military and political leaders, the czar abdicated.

Duma politicians then set up a provisional, or temporary, government. Middle-class liberals in the government began preparing a constitution for a new Russian republic. At the same time, they continued the war against Germany. That decision proved fatal. Most Russians were fed up with the war. Troops at the front were deserting in droves. Peasants wanted land. City workers demanded food and an end to the desperate shortages.

Outside the provisional government, revolutionary socialists plotted their own course. In Petrograd and other cities, they set up soviets, or councils of workers and soldiers. At first, the soviets worked democratically within the government. Before long, though, the Bolsheviks, a radical socialist group, took charge. The leader of the Bolsheviks was a determined revolutionary, V. I. Lenin.

Lenin and the Bolsheviks

Vladimir Ilyich Ulyanov (ool YAHN awf) was born in 1870 to a middle-class family. Lenin was the name he adopted when he became a revolutionary. When he was 17, his older brother was arrested and hanged for plotting to kill the czar. The execution branded his family as a threat to the state and instilled in young Vladimir a hatred for the czarist government.

---

* The revolutions of March and November 1917 are known to Russians as the February and October revolutions. In 1917, Russia still used an old calendar, which was 13 days behind the one used in Western Europe. Not until 1918 did Russia adopt the western calendar.

Did You Know?

A Hard Man to Kill

The death of Gregory Rasputin was perhaps even more bizarre than his strange life.

To get rid of him, a group of nobles lured Rasputin to the palace of Prince Felix Yussoupov, where they served him cakes and wine laced with enough cyanide to kill several men. Incredibly, Rasputin was not affected. Next, Yussoupov shot him through the chest with a revolver. Rasputin fell. As the conspirators examined the body, Rasputin sprang to his feet and began to attack Yussoupov! The prince fled.

Then Rasputin attempted his own escape. He bolted outside and ran across the courtyard toward the gate. Another shot hit him, and he fell into the snow. The conspirators then clubbed him unconscious. Flinging Rasputin into the icy Neva River, they watched him sink.

Later, the body of Rasputin—poisoned, shot twice, and badly beaten—was recovered from the river and autopsied. The cause of death? Drowning.

Theme: Impact of the Individual Why did Yussoupov and others go to so much trouble to murder Rasputin?

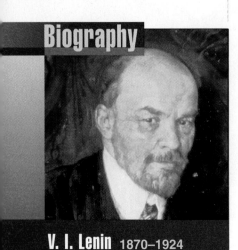
V. I. Lenin 1870–1924

Lenin was the son of a teacher and his wife who lived in a little town on the Volga River. Vladimir lived with his parents and five siblings in a rented wing of a large house. By all accounts it was a happy home. Vladimir excelled at school and looked up to his older brother Alexander. But, when Vladimir was 16, his father died. When he was 17, his beloved brother Alexander was hanged for plotting to kill the czar.

Still reeling from the death of his brother, Vladimir enrolled at Kazan University. There he met other discontented young people. They united to protest the lack of student freedom in the university. Vladimir was expelled within three months for his part in the demonstrations.

Theme: Impact of the Individual How do you think Lenin's early life affected his later political ideas?

Early Career As a young man, Lenin read the works of Karl Marx and participated in student demonstrations. He spread Marxist ideas among factory workers along with other socialists, including Nadezhda Krupskaya (nah DYEZH duh kroop SKĪ uh), the daughter of a poor noble family.

In 1895, Lenin and Krupskaya were arrested and sent to Siberia. During their imprisonment, they were married. After their release, they went into exile in Switzerland. There, they worked tirelessly to spread revolutionary ideas. A rival once described Lenin's total commitment to the cause: "There is no other man who is absorbed by the revolution 24 hours a day, who has no other thoughts but the thought of revolution, and who, even when he sleeps, dreams of nothing but the revolution."

A New View of Marx Lenin adapted Marxist ideas to fit Russian conditions. Marx had predicted that the industrial working class would rise spontaneously to overthrow capitalism. But Russia did not have a large urban proletariat. Instead, Lenin called for an elite group to lead the revolution and set up a "dictatorship of the proletariat." Though this elite revolutionary party represented a small percentage of socialists, Lenin gave them the name Bolsheviks, meaning "majority."

In Western Europe, many leading socialists had come to think that socialism could be achieved through gradual and moderate reforms such as higher wages, increased suffrage, and social welfare programs. The Bolsheviks rejected this approach. To Lenin, reforms of this nature were merely capitalist tricks to repress the masses. Only revolution, he said, could bring about needed changes.

Lenin Returns From Exile In March 1917, Lenin was still in exile. As Russia stumbled into revolution, Germany saw a chance to weaken its enemy by helping Lenin return home. In a special train, it rushed the Bolshevik leader across Germany to the Russian frontier.

On April 16, 1917, Lenin stepped off the train in Petrograd. A crowd of fellow exiles and activists recently released from the czar's prisons met him at the station. Lenin triumphantly addressed the crowd:

"Dear Comrades, soldiers, sailors and workers! I am happy to greet in your persons the victorious Russian revolution, to greet you as the vanguard of the worldwide proletarian army. . . . Any day now the whole of European capitalism may crash. The Russian revolution accomplished by you has prepared the way and opened a new epoch. Long live the worldwide Socialist revolution!"

—V. I. Lenin, quoted in *The Russian Revolution,*
1917 (Sukhanov)

The November Revolution

Lenin threw himself into the work of furthering the revolution. He was assisted by another committed Marxist revolutionary, Leon Trotsky. To the hungry, war-weary Russian people, Lenin and the Bolsheviks promised "Peace, Land, and Bread."

The provisional government, meanwhile, continued the war effort and failed to deal with land reform. In the summer of 1917, the government launched a disastrous offensive against Germany. By November, according to one official report, the army was "a huge crowd of tired, poorly clad, poorly fed, embittered men." Growing numbers of troops mutinied. At the same time, peasants seized land and drove off fearful landlords.

The Bolshevik Takeover Conditions were ripe for the Bolsheviks to make their move. In November 1917, squads of Red Guards—armed factory workers—joined mutinous sailors from the Russian fleet in attacking the provisional government. In just a matter of days, Lenin's forces overthrew a government that no longer had any support.

In Petrograd, members of the government were meeting in a room at the Winter Palace. Suddenly, a young cadet entered the chamber to announce that Bolsheviks were storming the palace. "What are the provisional government's orders?" he asked.

"It's no use," one politician announced. "We give up. No bloodshed!" A moment later, armed rebels flooded into the room. The provisional government had fallen without a struggle.

The Bolsheviks in Charge The Bolsheviks quickly seized power in other cities. In Moscow, it took a week of fighting to blast the local government out of the walled Kremlin, the former czarist center of government. Moscow became the Bolsheviks' capital, and the Kremlin their headquarters.

"We shall now occupy ourselves in Russia in building up a proletarian socialist state," declared Lenin. The Bolsheviks ended private ownership of land and distributed land to peasants. Workers were given control of the factories and mines. A new red flag with an entwined hammer and sickle symbolized union between peasants and workers.

Throughout the land, millions thought they had at last gained control over their own lives. In fact, the Bolsheviks—renamed Communists—would soon become their new masters.

Russian Civil War

After the Bolshevik Revolution, Lenin quickly sought peace with Germany. Russia signed the Treaty of Brest-Litovsk in March 1918, giving up a huge chunk of its territory and its population. The cost for peace was extremely high, but the Communist leaders knew that they needed all their energy to defeat a battery of enemies at home.

Opposing Forces For three years, civil war raged between the "Reds," as the Communists were known, and the "Whites," counterrevolutionaries who remained loyal to the czar. National groups that the czars had conquered also took up arms against the Red Army. Poland, Estonia, Latvia, and Lithuania broke free, but nationalists in Ukraine, the Caucasus, and Central Asia were eventually subdued.

The Allied powers of World War I intervened in the civil war. They hoped that the Whites might overthrow the Communists and support the fight against Germany. Britain, France, and the United States sent forces to help the Whites. Japan seized land in East Asia that czarist Russia had once claimed. The Allied presence, however, did little to help the Whites. The Reds appealed to nationalism and urged Russians to drive out the foreigners. In the long run, the Allied invasion fed Communist distrust of the West.

Turning Points in Russia, 1914–1921

1914

August
World War I begins.

1917

March
Revolution forces the czar to abdicate. A provisional government is formed.

April
Lenin returns to Russia.

July
Russians suffer more than 50,000 casualties in battle against German and Austro-Hungarian forces.

November
A second revolution results in Bolshevik takeover of government.

December
Bolshevik government seeks peace with Germany.

1918

March
Russia signs treaty of Brest-Litovsk, losing a large amount of territory.

July
Civil war between the Reds and Whites begins. The czar and his family are executed.

August
British, American, Japanese, and other foreign forces intervene in Russia.

1921

March
Communist government is victorious. Only sporadic fighting continues.

Skills Assessment **Chart** Between 1914 and 1921, the Russian people struggled through World War I, two revolutions, and civil war. **How did the events of April and July 1917 contribute to revolution later that year?**

Soviet Foreign Policy

Between 1917 and 1939, the Soviet Union pursued two very different goals in foreign policy. As Communists, both Lenin and Stalin wanted to bring about the worldwide revolution that Marx had predicted. But as Russians, they wanted to guarantee their nation's security by winning the support of other countries. The result of pursuing these two different goals was a contradictory and generally unsuccessful foreign policy.

Lenin formed the Communist International, or Comintern. It aided revolutionary groups around the world and urged colonial peoples to rise up against imperialist powers. Yet the Soviet Union also sought to join the League of Nations and to improve relations with western governments.

The Comintern's propaganda against capitalism made western powers highly suspicious of the Soviet Union. In the United States, fear of Bolshevik plots led to the "Red Scare" in the early 1920s. Britain broke off relations with the Soviet Union when evidence revealed Soviet schemes to turn a 1926 strike into a revolution. Even so, the Soviet Union slowly won recognition from western powers and increased trade with capitalist countries. It also joined the League of Nations. However, mistrust still poisoned relations, especially after the Great Purge.

Three Revolutions Compared

Historians often compare the Russian, French, and American revolutions. The American Revolution was in many ways the least radical of the three. American leaders did not order mass executions or seize property. French revolutionaries executed thousands and nationalized the lands of the Church and the aristocracy. In Russia, Stalin seized even the lands of the peasant masses. His policies caused millions of deaths.

All three revolutions had a worldwide impact. The Declaration of Independence and the United States Constitution served as models of democratic government. The French Revolution inspired revolts across Europe. As you will see, the Soviet Union supported revolts in many lands and became a model for other communist governments. Yet today, Russia and most of its allies have abandoned the goals of Lenin and Stalin. Democratic nations, meanwhile, continue to build on the principles preached during the American and French revolutions.

SECTION 2 Assessment

Recall

1. **Identify:** (a) USSR, (b) NEP, (c) Great Purge, (d) Comintern.
2. **Define:** (a) command economy, (b) collective, (c) kulak.

Comprehension

3. (a) How did Lenin make a compromise between the ideas of capitalism and communism? (b) Why did he think that the compromise was necessary?
4. What were the goals and results of Stalin's five-year plans?
5. What were the causes and effects of the Great Purge?

6. How did Soviet foreign policy lead to difficult relations with the West?

Critical Thinking and Writing

7. **Analyzing Information** Review the two charts in this section that show the effects of the five-year plans on industry and agriculture. (a) Were the effects on industry and agriculture similar or different? (b) Explain the reasons for the similar or different results.
8. **Comparing** How did the Soviet command economy under Stalin differ from a capitalist economy?

Activity

Drawing a Political Cartoon
Draw a political cartoon that comments on one of Lenin's or Stalin's policies. Give your cartoon a title and a caption. Try to use symbolism, such as the hammer and sickle.

Reading Focus

- How did Stalin create a totalitarian state?
- How did communism change Soviet society?
- How did state control affect the arts in the Soviet Union?

Vocabulary

totalitarian state
atheism
socialist realism

Taking Notes

Create a chart like this one. Fill in the chart as you read. In the left column, list ways in which people benefited from communist rule. In the right column, list ways in which people suffered.

COMMUNIST RULE	
Benefits	Drawbacks

Main Idea Stalin turned the Soviet Union into a totalitarian state that regulated every aspect of the lives of its citizens.

Setting the Scene From the 1930s until his death in 1953, Stalin tried to boost morale and faith in the communist system by making himself a godlike figure. His propaganda mills described him as a devoted father of the Soviet people. Poets wrote hymns of praise to "Stalin the Wise" and the "Son of Lenin" who was "the unsinking sun of our times." This "cult of personality" was one more pillar to support Stalin's absolute power.

An Age of Totalitarian Control

Marx had predicted that under communism the state would wither away. The opposite occurred under Stalin. He turned the Soviet Union into a totalitarian state. In this form of government, a one-party dictatorship attempts to regulate every aspect of the lives of its citizens. You have already seen, for example, how Stalin imposed central government control over industry and agriculture.

Terror To ensure obedience, Stalin's Communist party used secret police, censorship, violent purges, and terror. Police spies did not hesitate to open private letters or plant listening devices. Nothing appeared in print without official approval. Grumblers or critics were rounded up and sent to brutal labor camps, where many died.

Propaganda Using modern technology, the party bombarded the public with relentless propaganda. Radios and loudspeakers blared into factories and villages. In movies, theaters, and schools, citizens heard about communist successes and the evils of capitalism. Newsreels and newspapers showed bumper harvests and new hydroelectric dams opening up, or proclaimed the misery of workers in the capitalist West. Billboards and posters urged workers to meet or exceed production quotas.

Stalinist propaganda also revived extreme nationalism. Headlines in the Communist party newspaper, *Pravda*, or "Truth," linked enemies at home to foreign agents seeking to restore power to the landowners and capitalists. Supporters of Stalin's aims were often glorified as national heroes. For example, the government put up statues honoring a 14-year-old boy who turned his own father over to the secret police for associating with kulaks.

Forced-Labor Camp
Accused of drawing an anti-Stalin caricature, Russian artist Nikolai Getman was convicted in a seven-minute trial. He spent the next seven years in forced-labor camps, where he painted haunting scenes such as this.

Theme: Art and Literature How does Getman convey the despair of camp life?

Connections to Today

The Russian Orthodox Church

The Russian Orthodox Church survived more than half a century of Communist persecution. Millions of Russians continued to worship, in private and sometimes in public, in defiance of the government's prohibitions.

Today, the Communist government has fallen, and the Church is enjoying a revival. Its membership has swelled to perhaps as many as 50 million people.

Polls of the Russian people indicate that the Orthodox Church surpasses the government and the military as the most respected institution in the country. One Muscovite put it this way: "The Orthodox Church is perhaps the last, lone symbol of Russian national identity to have survived communism more or less intact. People . . . want and need such a symbol."

Theme: Religions and Value Systems Why is the Russian Orthodox Church experiencing a revival today?

War on Religion In accordance with the ideas of Marx, atheism, or the belief that there is no god, became an official state policy. Early on, the Communists targeted the Russian Orthodox Church, which had strongly supported the czars. The party seized religious property and converted churches into offices and museums. Many priests and other religious leaders were killed or died in prison camps.

Other religions were persecuted as well. At one show trial, 15 Roman Catholic priests were charged with "counterrevolutionary activities," such as teaching religion to the young. The state seized Jewish synagogues and banned the use of Hebrew. Islam was also officially discouraged. However, Muslims living in the Soviet Union generally faced fewer restrictions, partly because the Communists hoped to win support among colonized peoples in the Middle East.

The Communists replaced religion with their own ideology. Like a religion, communist ideology had its own "sacred" texts—the writings of Marx and Lenin—and its own shrines, such as the tomb of Lenin. Portraits of Stalin replaced religious icons in Russian homes.

Changes in Soviet Society

The Communists transformed Russian life. They destroyed the old social order of landowning nobles at the top and serfs at the bottom. But instead of creating a society of equals, as they promised, they created a society where a few elite groups emerged as a new ruling class.

The New Elite At the head of society were members of the Communist party. Only a small fraction of Soviet citizens were allowed to join the party. Many who did so were motivated by a desire to get ahead, rather than a belief in communist ideology.

The Soviet elite also included industrial managers, military leaders, scientists, and some artists and writers. The elite enjoyed benefits denied to most people. They had the best apartments in the cities and vacation homes in the country. They could shop at special stores for scarce consumer goods. Good shoes, noted one western visitor, distinguished the elite from the common citizen.

Social Benefits and Drawbacks Although excluded from party membership, most people did enjoy benefits unknown before the revolution. Free education was offered to all. The state also provided free medical care, day care for children, inexpensive housing, and public recreation.

While these benefits were real, the standard of living remained low. As elsewhere, industrial growth led millions of people to migrate to cities. Although the state built massive apartment complexes, housing was scarce. Entire families might be packed into a single room. Bread was plentiful, but meat, fresh fruit, and other foods were in short supply.

Education After the Russian Revolution, the Communists built schools everywhere and required all children to attend. The state supported technical schools and universities as well. Schools served many important goals. Educated workers were needed to build a modern industrial state. In addition to basic skills, schools taught communist values, such as atheism, the glory of collective farming, and love of Stalin.

The Communist party also set up programs for students outside school. These programs included sports, cultural activities, and political classes to train teenagers for party membership. Sometimes, young Communists would be sent to help harvest crops or to participate in huge parades.

Women Long before 1917, women such as Lenin's wife, Krupskaya, worked for the revolution, spreading radical ideas among peasants and workers. Some urged fellow Socialists to pay attention to women's needs.

Virtual Field Trip

www.phschool.com

Virtual Museum of Political Art Vienna, Austria

To see other examples of socialist realism, use the Internet address above to link to the Virtual Museum of Political Art.

Socialist Realism
Bold, heroic images were the trademark of socialist realism. Here, workers and farmers hold aloft the Soviet hammer and sickle. Bright sunbeams suggest a glorious future just ahead.
Theme: Art and Literature
What values did socialist realism try to communicate?

In 1905, Alexandra Kollontai noted "how little our party concerned itself with the fate of women . . . [and] women's liberation." After the revolution, Kollontai became the only high-ranking woman to serve in Lenin's government. She vigorously campaigned for women's rights.

Under the Communists, women won equality under the law. They gained access to education and a wide range of jobs. By the 1930s, many Soviet women were working in medicine, engineering, or the sciences.

By their labor, women contributed to Soviet economic growth. They worked in factories, in construction, and on collectives. Within the family, their wages were needed because men earned low salaries. The government provided day nurseries for children.

The Arts and the State

The Bolshevik Revolution at first meant greater freedom for Russian artists and writers. "Art must serve politics," Lenin had insisted, but he generally did not interfere with artistic freedom. Artists welcomed the chance to experiment with ideas and forms.

Socialist Realism Under Stalin, however, the heavy hand of state control gripped the arts. Stalin forced artists and writers to conform to a style called socialist realism. Its goal was to boost socialism by showing Soviet life in a positive light. Artists and writers could criticize the bourgeois past or even, to a limited degree, point out mistakes under communism. Their overall message, though, had to promote hope in the communist future. Popular themes for socialist-realist artists were peasants, workers, heroes of the revolution, and—of course—Stalin.

Censorship Government controlled what books were published, what music was heard, and which works of art were displayed. Artists who ignored Communist guidelines could not get materials, work space, or jobs.

Under Stalin's totalitarian policies, writers, artists, and composers faced government persecution. The Jewish poet Osip Mandelstam, for example,

Humanities Link

A Revolution in Filmmaking

In the Soviet Union, filmmakers used motion pictures to express revolutionary ideals. "Of all the arts, for us the cinema is the most important," said Lenin, who valued film as a propaganda tool. In 1925, director Sergei Eisenstein's *Battleship Potemkin* went far beyond propaganda. His techniques continue to influence filmmakers around the world.

In the film, sailors on the imperial ship *Potemkin* stage a successful mutiny. In the port city of Odessa, a crowd gathers in support of the mutineers and is fired upon by the czar's soldiers. Eisenstein fictitiously places this dramatic scene on a long flight of steps, where a woman stands among the shadows of the czar's soldiers who have killed her child.

In this dynamic sequence, a baby carriage bounces past murdered and wounded civilians. It evokes the helplessness of the unarmed civilians against armed soldiers. Many later directors from all over the world have copied this image.

Portfolio Assessment

INTERNET   Use the Internet or library resources to find out more about the "golden era of Soviet film," which took place between 1925 and 1930. Then, prepare a class presentation on an important Soviet director or film from this era. Include photographs, drawings, diagrams, or videos that illustrate important aspects of the chosen director or film.

Eisenstein (right) won acclaim for his use of montage, a technique of cutting back and forth between clashing images. *Battleship Potemkin* was the last film over which Eisenstein had full control. After Stalin came to power, censorship was the rule. Eisenstein's last film was banned for criticizing the new leader. It was not shown in the Soviet Union until after Stalin's death.

was imprisoned, tortured, and exiled for composing a satirical verse that was critical of Stalin. Out of fear for his wife's safety, Mandelstam finally submitted to threats and wrote an "Ode to Stalin." Boris Pasternak, who would later win fame for his novel *Doctor Zhivago*, was afraid to publish anything at all during the Stalin years. Rather than write in the favored style of socialist realism, he became a translator of literary works.

Anna Akhmatova (ahk MAH taw vuh), one of Russia's greatest poets, could not publish her works because she had violated state guidelines. Still, she wrote secretly. In "Requiem," she described the ordeal of trying to visit her 20-year-old son, imprisoned during the Stalinist terrors:

"For seventeen long months my pleas,
  My cries have called you home.
  I've begged the hangman on my knees,
  My son, my dread, my own.
  My mind's mixed up for good,
  And I'm no longer even clear
  Who's man, who's beast, nor how much time
  Before the end draws near."
              —Anna Akhmatova, "Requiem"

Despite restrictions, some Soviet writers produced magnificent works. *And Quiet Flows the Don,* by Mikhail Sholokhov, passed the censor. The novel tells the story of a man who spends years fighting in World War I, the Russian Revolution, and the civil war. Sholokhov later became one of the few Soviet writers to win the Nobel Prize for literature.

Looking Ahead

By the time Stalin died in 1953, the Soviet Union had become a military superpower and a world leader in heavy industry. Yet Stalin's efforts exacted a brutal toll. The Soviet people were dominated by a totalitarian system based on terror. Most people in the Soviet Union lived meager lives compared with people in the West.

The Soviet Union was not the only totalitarian state to emerge in the decades after World War I. As you will read, in the 1920s and 1930s, dictators arose in Italy and Germany. They, too, created one-party states and cults of personality to impose dictatorial rule on their people.

SECTION 3 Assessment

Recall

1. **Identify:** (a) *Pravda,* (b) Alexandra Kollontai, (c) Osip Mandelstam, (d) Anna Akhmatova, (e) Mikhail Sholokhov.
2. **Define:** (a) totalitarian state, (b) atheism, (c) socialist realism.

Comprehension

3. What methods did Stalin use to create a totalitarian state?
4. (a) Who made up the new elite in Soviet society? (b) What special privileges did they enjoy?
5. How did the Soviet government make sure that most writers and artists conformed to the style of socialist realism?

Critical Thinking and Writing

6. **Comparing** Compare life under Stalin's rule with life under the Russian czars. (a) Describe two similarities. (b) Describe two differences.
7. **Analyzing Information** One historian has said that socialist realism was "communism with a smiling face." What do you think he meant? (See the Virtual Field Trip in this section.)

Activity

Writing Propaganda
Write two propaganda newspaper articles about Stalin or his policies. One article should be similar to what *Pravda* might have printed. The other article should be similar to what an illegal anti-Stalinist newspaper might have printed.

28 Review and Assessment

Creating a Chapter Summary

Copy the chart below on a sheet of paper. Review what you have learned about communist dictatorship in the Soviet Union by completing the chart. A few entries have been made to help you get started.

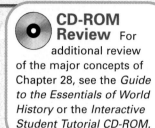

CD-ROM Review For additional review of the major concepts of Chapter 28, see the *Guide to the Essentials of World History* or the *Interactive Student Tutorial CD-ROM.*

COMMUNIST DICTATORSHIP IN THE SOVIET UNION

POLITICAL	ECONOMIC	SOCIAL	CULTURAL	MILITARY
• One party only	• Government makes all decisions			

Web Site Self-Test For practice test questions for Chapter 28, see **www.phschool.com.**

Building Vocabulary

Use the chapter vocabulary words below to create a crossword puzzle. Exchange puzzles with a classmate. Complete the puzzles and then check each other's answers.

1. **proletariat**
2. **soviet**
3. **commissar**
4. **collective**
5. **kulak**
6. **totalitarian state**
7. **atheism**
8. **socialist realism**

Recalling Key Facts

9. How did World War I contribute to the collapse of the Russian monarchy?
10. How and when did the Bolsheviks take power in Russia?
11. What was the final outcome of the Russian civil war?
12. How was the NEP different from "pure communism"?
13. Describe Stalin's policies on agriculture and industry.
14. What was the Great Purge?
15. How did Stalin make use of propaganda?
16. What was the Soviet government's policy toward religion?
17. According to Stalin, what purpose should art serve?

Critical Thinking and Writing

18. **Identifying Alternatives** After the March Revolution, the provisional government of Russia chose a course that led to another revolution. What policies could the provisional government have followed that might have avoided a second revolution?
19. **Comparing** How were the Russian and French revolutions similar or different in terms of **(a)** long-term causes, **(b)** immediate causes, **(c)** effects, **(d)** world reaction?
20. **Synthesizing Information** **(a)** In what ways did Soviet communism conform to the teachings of Marx? **(b)** In what ways did Soviet communism differ from Marxist philosophy?
21. **Linking Past and Present** In the 1990s, the breakup of the Soviet Union led to a revival of religion. Why do you think the Soviets were unsuccessful in their attempt to destroy religion?
22. **Connecting to Geography** Review the map in Section 2. **(a)** How did the Soviet constitution try to satisfy the nationalist aspirations of non-Russians? **(b)** Do you think nationalist leaders in the Soviet Union were satisfied? Explain.

The exerpt below, written by an American news reporter in Russia, is a dramatic eyewitness account of Stalin's brutal campaign against the kulaks. Read the excerpt and then answer the questions that follow.

> "Obliteration of the . . . kulak elements was not only an end in itself, but a means for stampeding the rest of the population into submission to collectivization. . . . A population as large as all of Switzerland's or Denmark's was stripped clean of all their belongings—not alone their land and homes and cattle and tools, but often their last clothes and food and household utensils—and driven out of their villages. They were herded with bayonets at railroad stations, packed indiscriminately into cattle cars and freight cars, and dumped weeks later in the lumber regions of the frozen North, the deserts of Central Asia, wherever labor was needed, there to live or die. Some of this human wreckage was merely flung beyond the limits of their former villages, without shelter or food in those winter months, to start life anew if they could, on land too barren to have been cultivated in the past."

> —Eugene Lyons, *Assignment in Utopia*

23. Who were the kulaks?
24. According to the reporter, what were the reasons for the policy toward the kulaks?
25. What do you think the government did with the confiscated property?
26. Do you think the kulaks prospered in the lands to which they were brought? Explain.
27. **(a)** What part of this account is most probably opinion? Explain. **(b)** What part is most probably fact? Explain.

Skills Assessment
Take It to the NET

Use the Internet to find examples of propaganda such as the Soviet poster on this page. You can look for posters, speeches, film clips, or other types. Print out two examples. For each example, identify the author and the intended audience, and explain the message that is being communicated.

Under the czars, few Russian peasants could read. The Soviet government launched a campaign to increase adult literacy. This Soviet propaganda poster proclaims, "Knowledge Will Break the Chains of Serfdom." Study the poster and answer the following questions:

28. **(a)** What symbol in the poster represents serfdom? **(b)** What symbols represent education?
29. Why do you think the Soviet government wanted people to learn to read?
30. Based on what you have read in this chapter, do you agree or disagree that education broke the "chains of serfdom" for the Russian people? Explain.

Skills Tip

To understand propaganda, try to recognize who the author is and who the intended audience is. Remember that propaganda uses lies, truths, or half-truths to sway opinion.

Nationalism and Revolution Around the World

1910–1939

Chapter Preview

1 **Struggle for Change in Latin America**
2 **Nationalist Movements in Africa and the Middle East**
3 **India Seeks Self-Rule**
4 **Upheavals in China**
5 **Empire of the Rising Sun**

PALESTINE EXHIBITION VIENNA
PALÄSTINA AUSSTELLUNG

1916

Pancho Villa, shown here, invades the United States during the Mexican Revolution. He kills more than a dozen Americans in New Mexico.

1914

New settlement increases the Jewish population of Palestine to 90,000. Leaders promote long-term development of the region's agriculture, as shown in this 1925 poster.

1923

Atatürk begins modernizing Turkey.

CHAPTER EVENTS

1910   1916   1922

GLOBAL EVENTS

1914 World War I begins.

1917 Two revolutions lead to Bolshevik control of Russia.

Major Nationalist Movements, 1910–1939

The end of World War I motivated many people around the world to seek self-government.

ATLANTIC OCEAN

PACIFIC OCEAN

PACIFIC OCEAN

INDIAN OCEAN

MEXICO

TURKEY

IRAN

EGYPT

INDIA

CHINA

JAPAN

NIGERIA

KENYA

SOUTH AFRICA

Robinson Projection

0   1500   3000 Miles

0   1500   3000 Kilometers

1930
Thousands of Indians join Mohandas Gandhi in the Salt March to protest British rule.

1934
Mao Zedong leads the Long March.

1937
The Japanese army captures Nanjing. Here, Japanese soldiers enter the Chinese city, which has been under siege for weeks.

1928

1934

1940

1929 The New York Stock Exchange crashes.

1935 Italy invades Ethiopia.

1939 Germany invades Poland.

Struggle for Change in Latin America

Reading Focus

- What were the causes of the Mexican Revolution?
- What reforms were introduced in Mexico?
- How did nationalism affect Mexico?
- What was the Good Neighbor Policy?

Vocabulary

nationalization

economic nationalism

cultural nationalism

Taking Notes

Copy this diagram. As you read, fill in the major events in Mexican history. To help you get started, one part of the diagram has been completed.

STRUGGLE FOR CHANGE IN MEXICO			
1910s	**1920s**	**1930s**	**1940s**
• Dictator Porfirio Díaz rules • Prosperity for wealthy landowners	•	•	•

Main Idea The desire for lands, better wages, and democratic reforms led to the Mexican Revolution.

Setting the Scene The winds of revolution swept through Mexico between 1910 and 1920. "It is like a hurricane," says a peasant fighter in Mariano Azuela's novel *The Underdogs*. "If you're in it, . . . you're a leaf . . . blown by the wind."

The Mexican Revolution unleashed radical forces. As the revolution spread, Indian peasants battled to end centuries of oppression and to win land. A century after Miguel Hidalgo raised the "cry of Dolores," the Mexican Revolution finally opened the door to social and economic reform.

The Mexican Revolution

By 1910, the dictator Porfirio Díaz had ruled Mexico for almost 35 years, winning reelection as president again and again. On the surface, Mexico enjoyed peace and economic growth. Díaz welcomed foreign investors who developed mines, built railroads, and drilled for oil.

Sources of Discontent Prosperity benefited wealthy landowners, business people, and foreign investors. But most Mexicans were peasants who lived in desperate poverty. Without land or education, they had no hope of improving their situation.

Discontent rippled through Mexico in the early 1900s. Factory workers and miners earning meager wages were restless and angry. And middle-class liberals, who embraced democracy, opposed the Díaz dictatorship.

The Battle Begins The unrest boiled over when Francisco Madero, a liberal reformer, demanded free elections in 1910. After being imprisoned by Díaz, he began to encourage revolt. Faced with rebellion in several parts of the country, Díaz resigned in 1911. "Madero has unleashed a tiger, now let us see if he can control it," declared the dictator as he left Mexico. Díaz's taunt proved well founded. Madero became president of Mexico, but within two years he was murdered.

A Complex Upheaval During the power struggle that followed, several leaders emerged. Among them was Francisco "Pancho" Villa, a hard-riding rebel from the north. He fought mostly for personal power but won the loyalty of his followers. In southern Mexico, Emiliano Zapata led a peasant revolt. Zapata, himself an Indian tenant farmer, understood the misery of peasant villagers. His followers were called Zapatistas.

Fighting flared across Mexico for a decade, killing as many as a million people. Peasants, small farmers, ranchers, and urban workers were drawn

Remembering the Revolution

Zeferino Diego Ferreira was a peasant soldier in Pancho Villa's army. His experiences represent those of the Mexican masses who rallied to the revolutionary cause. Decades later, he shared his memories with an interviewer, who recorded the old man's tales of life as a revolutionary.

Poster of Emiliano Zapata
Zeferino Ferreira displayed a poster like this one on his living room wall. Asked years later what Zapata looked like, he snapped: "It's not important what he looked like. What is important was his politics."

"I was born in 1892. . . . We lived in a little room with no furniture . . . nothing. We slept on the floor. The only thing we had was a box with my mother's clothes in it. . . .

When I was about fourteen years old I got a job in some mines owned by an American company near Tlalpujahua. . . . At that time here in Mexico they didn't pay more than eighteen to twenty-five centavos. . . .

It was there in Tlalpujahua where I first saw firearms. . . . [A] friend of mine talked to me a lot about Villa and finally convinced me to go and join up. . . . My friend and I went north looking for Villa. And, yes, Villa was firing a shot here and there! . . .

In those days at the beginning of the revolution we didn't have many people and we weren't very well armed. You could say we were almost fighting without rifles. . . .

During the revolution I slept for only two hours at night, between two and four o'clock in the morning, and was always leaning against a wall or a rock or on my rifle. Sometimes we didn't have any hope of getting food, so we'd eat a mule, a skunk.

Yes! That was how we went through the revolution. . . .

[Villa] used to tell us: 'We are fighting for the people and we have to respect them.' . . . Villa wasn't like some people say. He was a well-liked person. Yes, he had people shot, but he'd also get his fill and stop the shootings. He was always in the battles. Sometimes he disguised himself but we would recognize him by his horse. Black. Villa never hid away all cozy and warm while his troops fought. He was right there in the middle. He said: 'Where my troops die, I'll die there, too.'

I am glad to have fought in the same cause with Zapata . . . and so many of my dear revolutionary friends who were left behind in the hills, their bones eaten by animals. I wasn't afraid. Just the opposite, I was glad. It's a beautiful thing to fight to realize an ideal."

—Zeferino Diego Ferreira, "The Life Story of a Villista"

Skills Tip

When reading oral history, try to imagine the person talking. This will make the reading "come to life" and help you get the most out of it.

Skills Assessment

1. Which term best describes Villa's peasant army?
   A well equipped
   B professional
   C poor
   D unmotivated

2. According to Ferreira, Villa was
   E a traitor to the peasant cause.
   F brave and decent.
   G seeking money and fame.
   H selfish and cruel.

3. **Critical Thinking Evaluating Information** **(a)** Ferreira spoke of events that had taken place more than 50 years earlier. How reliable do you think he is as a source of information about the Mexican Revolution? **(b)** How might a historian determine the truth of Ferreira's words?

into the violent struggle. Women soldiers called *soldaderas* cooked, tended the wounded, and even fought alongside the men.

Reforms in Mexico

In 1917, voters elected Venustiano Carranza, a conservative, president of Mexico. That year, Carranza reluctantly approved a new constitution. With amendments, it is still in force today.

The Constitution of 1917 addressed three major issues: land, religion, and labor. It permitted the breakup of large estates, placed restrictions on foreigners owning land, and allowed nationalization, or government takeover, of natural resources. Church land was made "the property of the nation." The constitution set a minimum wage and protected workers' right to strike.

Although the constitution gave suffrage only to men, it did give women some protection. Women doing the same job as men were entitled to the same pay. In response to women activists, Carranza also passed laws allowing married women to draw up contracts, take part in legal suits, and have equal authority with men in spending family funds.

Social Change At first, the constitution was just a set of goals to be achieved sometime in the future. But in the 1920s, as the government finally restored order after years of civil war, it began to carry out reforms.

The government helped some Indian communities regain lands that had been taken from them. It supported labor unions and launched a massive effort to combat illiteracy. Schools and libraries were set up.

Dedicated teachers, often young women, worked for low pay. While they taught basic skills, they spread ideas of nationalism that began to bridge the gulf between the regions and the central government. As the revolutionary era ended, Mexico became the first Latin American nation to pursue real social and economic reforms for the majority of its people.

The PRI In 1929, government leaders organized what later became the Institutional Revolutionary Party (PRI). It has dominated Mexican politics ever since. The PRI managed to accommodate all groups in Mexican society, including business and military leaders, peasants, and workers. It backed reform but suppressed opposition. In 1938, the government nationalized foreign oil holdings, part of a program to reduce foreign influence.

Rising Tide of Nationalism

Mexico's move to reclaim its oil fields from foreign investors reflected a growing spirit of nationalism in Latin America. This spirit focused in part on ending economic dependence on the industrial powers, especially the United States.

Economic Nationalism During the 1920s and 1930s, world events affected Latin American economies. After World War I, trade fell off with Europe. The Great Depression that struck the United States in 1929 spread around the world in the 1930s. Prices for Latin American exports plunged as demand dried up. At the same time, the cost of imported consumer goods rose.

Murals
Diego Rivera painted murals with scenes of Mexico's history. The top portion of this mural section depicts people in the Mexican Revolution.

Theme: Art and Literature
How does Rivera show that people from all levels of society were involved in the revolution?

A tide of economic nationalism, or emphasis on domestic control of the economy, swept Latin American countries. They were determined to develop their own economies and end foreign economic control. Local entrepreneurs set up factories to produce goods. They urged their governments to raise tariffs to protect the new industries. Following Mexico's lead, some nations also nationalized resources or took over foreign-owned industries. The drive to create domestic industries had limited success. As in the past, the unequal distribution of wealth hampered economic development.

Cultural Nationalism   By the 1920s, Latin American writers, artists, and thinkers began to reject European influences. Instead, they took pride in their own culture, with its blend of western and Indian traditions.

In Mexico, cultural nationalism, or pride in one's own culture, was reflected in the revival of mural painting, a major art form of the Aztecs. In the 1920s and 1930s, Diego Rivera, José Clemente Orozco (oh RAHS koh), David Alfaro Siqueiros (sih KAY rohs), and other muralists created magnificent works. On the walls of public buildings, they portrayed the struggles of the Mexican people for liberty, first from the Spanish and later during the Díaz era. The murals have been a great source of national pride ever since.

The "Good Neighbor" Policy

During and after World War I, investments by the United States in the nations of Latin America soared, especially as British influence declined. The United States continued to play the role of "international policeman," intervening to restore order when it felt its interests were threatened.

During the Mexican Revolution, the United States supported leaders who it thought would protect American interests. In 1914, it attacked the port of Vera Cruz to punish Mexico for imprisoning several American sailors. In 1916, it invaded Mexico after Pancho Villa killed more than a dozen Americans in New Mexico.

These actions stirred up anti-American feelings, which increased during the 1920s. In Nicaragua, Augusto César Sandino led a guerrilla movement against United States forces occupying his country. Many people in Latin America saw Sandino as a hero.

In the 1930s, President Franklin Roosevelt took a new approach to Latin America and pledged to follow "the policy of the good neighbor." Under the Good Neighbor Policy, the United States withdrew troops stationed in Haiti and Nicaragua. It also lifted the Platt Amendment, which had limited Cuban independence.

SECTION 1 Assessment

Recall

1. **Identify: (a)** Porfirio Díaz, **(b)** Francisco Madero, **(c)** Zapatistas, **(d)** Venustiano Carranza, **(e)** Diego Rivera, **(f)** Good Neighbor Policy.
2. **Define: (a)** nationalization, **(b)** economic nationalism, **(c)** cultural nationalism.

Comprehension

3. Describe three causes of the Mexican Revolution.
4. Explain how the Constitution of 1917 addressed each of these issues: **(a)** land, **(b)** religion, **(c)** labor.

5. Describe how nationalism affected Mexico.
6. How did Franklin Roosevelt change United States policy toward Latin America?

Critical Thinking and Writing

7. **Analyzing Information**   How did world events affect the economies of Latin American nations during the 1920s and 1930s?
8. **Synthesizing Information** **(a)** How did opportunities for women change under the 1917 constitution? **(b)** How did women's lives stay the same?

Activity
Take It to the NET

Use the Internet to research Emiliano Zapata and the Zapatista movement. Then, create a poster publicizing Zapatista goals.

Nationalist Movements in Africa and the Middle East

Reading Focus

- How did Africans resist colonial rule?
- What signs of nationalism developed in Africa?
- How did Turkey and Iran modernize?
- How did European mandates contribute to the growth of Arab nationalism?

Main Idea Following World War I, nationalist sentiment contributed to many changes in Africa and the Middle East.

Vocabulary

apartheid
polygamy

Taking Notes

Copy this table. As you read, fill in the major nationalist developments in Africa and the Middle East. To help you get started, one row of the table has been completed.

NATION	LEADER	PROTESTS AGAINST	RESULTS
KENYA	Jomo Kenyatta	• Loss of land •	• Jailing of nationalist leaders •
SOUTH AFRICA			
EGYPT			
TURKEY			
IRAN			

Primary Source

An African Speaks Out Against Colonialism

Jomo Kenyatta was a leader in Kenya's struggle for independence from British rule. In the following quotation, he dramatizes his view of European colonialism:

"If you woke up one morning and found that somebody had come to your house, and had declared that house belonged to him, you would naturally be surprised, and you would like to know by what arrangement. Many Africans found that, on land that had been in the possession of their ancestors from time immemorial, they were now working as squatters or as laborers."

—Jomo Kenyatta, quoted in
A History of the African People
(July)

Skills Assessment

Primary Source Why was Kenyatta's house comparison an effective device for dramatizing the injustices of colonialism?

Setting the Scene The Kikuyu people of Kenya were outraged. Not only had the British taken their land, but they also treated the Kikuyu like second-class citizens.

The Kikuyu were among many African people who resented colonial rule. During the 1920s and 1930s, a new generation of leaders, proud of their unique heritage, struggled to stem the tide of imperialism and restore Africa for Africans.

Resistance to Colonial Rule

During the early 1900s, Africans felt the impact of colonial rule. In Kenya and Rhodesia, for example, white settlers forced Africans off the best land. The few who kept their land were forbidden to grow the most profitable crops, such as coffee and sisal—only Europeans could grow these. In Kenya, too, the British made all Africans carry identification cards, imposed a tax, and restricted where they could live or travel.

Everywhere, Africans were forced to work on European-run plantations or in mines. The money they earned was needed to pay taxes to the colonial government. Farmers who had kept their land had to grow cash crops, such as cotton, instead of food. This led to famines in some regions. Increasingly, they lost their self-sufficiency and became dependent on European-made goods.

Resistance Opposition to imperialism grew among Africans. Resistance took many forms. Those who had lost their lands to Europeans sometimes squatted, or settled illegally, on European-owned plantations. In cities, workers began to form labor unions, even though such activity was illegal under the law codes imposed by imperialist nations.

Many western-educated Africans criticized the injustice of imperial rule. Although they had trained for professional careers, the best jobs went to Europeans. Inspired by President Woodrow Wilson's call for self-determination, they condemned the system that excluded Africans from political control of their own lands. Some eagerly read Lenin's writings that claimed imperialism was the final stage of a corrupt and dying capitalist society. In Africa, as in other regions around the world, socialism found a growing audience.

Protests Although large-scale revolts were rare, protests were common. In Kenya, the Kikuyu protested the loss of their land, forced labor, heavy taxes, and the hated identification cards. The British jailed the Kikuyu leaders, but protests continued.

In West Africa, women traditionally had controlled the marketplaces and the farmland. In the 1920s, Ibo women in Nigeria denounced British policies that threatened their rights and their economic role. They demanded a voice in decisions that affected them and their business activities. The "Women's War," as it was called, soon became a full-fledged revolt. Women armed with machetes and sticks mocked British troops and shouted down officials who ordered them to disperse.

Racial Segregation and Nationalism in South Africa Between 1910 and 1940, whites strengthened their grip on South Africa. They imposed a system of racial segregation. Their goal was to ensure white economic and political power and social supremacy. New laws, for example, restricted better-paying jobs in mines to whites only. Blacks were pushed into low-paid, less-skilled work. As in Kenya, South African blacks had to carry passes at all times. They were evicted from the best land, which was set aside for whites, and forced to live on crowded "reserves," which were located in dry, infertile areas.

Other laws chipped away at the rights of blacks. In one South African province, educated blacks who owned property had been allowed to vote in local elections. In 1936, the government abolished that right. The system of segregation set up at this time would become even more restrictive after 1948, when apartheid (uh PAHRT tīd) became law.

Yet South Africa was also home to a vital nationalist movement. African Christian churches and African-run newspapers demanded rights for black South Africans. In 1912, educated Africans organized a political party, later known as the African National Congress (ANC). Its members worked through legal means, protesting laws that restricted the freedom of black Africans. Their efforts, however, had no effect on South Africa's white government. Still, the ANC did build a framework for political action in later years.

Rise of Nationalism

During the 1920s, a movement known as Pan-Africanism began to nourish the nationalist spirit. Pan-Africanism emphasized the unity of Africans and people of African descent around the world. Among its most inspiring leaders was Jamaican-born Marcus Garvey. He preached a forceful and appealing message of "Africa for Africans" and demanded an end to colonial rule. Although Garvey never visited Africa, his ideas influenced a new generation of African leaders.

Pan-African Congress Led by African American scholar and activist W.E.B. DuBois (doo BOYS), Pan-Africanists tried to forge a united front. DuBois organized the first Pan-African Congress in 1919. It met in Paris, where the victorious Allies were holding their peace conference. Delegates from African colonies, the West Indies, and the United States called on the Paris peacemakers to approve a charter of rights for Africans. Although the western powers ignored their demands, the Pan-African Congress established cooperation among African and African American leaders.

Négritude French-speaking writers in West Africa and the Caribbean further awakened self-confidence among Africans. They expressed pride in their African roots through the *négritude* movement. Best known among them was the Senegalese poet Léopold Senghor, who celebrated Africa's rich cultural heritage. He fostered African pride by rejecting the negative views of Africa spread by colonial rulers. In his poem "Black Woman," he uses the image of an African woman to reflect on the beauty of Africa. Later, Senghor would take an active role in Senegal's drive to independence, and he would serve as its first president.

Connections to Today

Rekindling Hope in South Africa

Soweto, a poor suburb of Johannesburg, was a harsh symbol of apartheid. Created in the 1930s to house South Africa's black gold miners, it became a center of violent protest against apartheid in the 1970s. Forced into tiny hovels, Soweto's blacks lived lives marked by gunfire and tear gas and midnight visits from the police.

Today, Soweto has changed. In 1989, South Africa held its first all-race elections and began to dismantle apartheid. The new government brought electricity to most residents, built roads, and set up schools and libraries.

Life in post-apartheid Soweto is not perfect. Poverty is still widespread, and crime is a serious problem. Still, Soweto's residents have begun to feel hope for the future.

Theme: Continuity and Change How did the end of apartheid make it possible for Soweto to make social and economic gains?

Egyptian Independence African nationalism brought little political change, except to Egypt. During World War I, Egyptians had been forced to provide food and workers to help Britain. Simmering resistance to British rule flared as the war ended. Western-educated officials, peasants, landowners, Christians, and Muslims united behind the Wafd (WAHFT) party, which launched strikes and riots.

In 1922, the British finally agreed to declare Egypt independent. In fact, however, British troops stayed in Egypt to guard the Suez Canal, and Britain remained the real power behind Egypt's King Faud.

In the 1930s, many young Egyptians were attracted to an organization called the Muslim Brotherhood. This group fostered a broad Islamic nationalism that rejected western culture and denounced widespread corruption in the Egyptian government.

Modernization in Turkey and Iran

Nationalist movements brought immense changes to the Middle East in the aftermath of World War I. The defeated Ottoman empire collapsed in 1918. Its Arab lands, as you have read, were divided up between Britain and France. In Asia Minor, however, Turks resisted western control and fought to build a modern nation.

Atatürk Led by the determined and energetic Mustafa Kemal, Turkish nationalists overthrew the sultan, defeated western occupation forces, and declared Turkey a republic. Kemal later took the name Atatürk, meaning "father of the Turks." Between 1923 and his death in 1938, Atatürk forced through an ambitious program of radical reforms. His goals were to modernize Turkey along western lines and to separate religion from government.

Modernizing Turkey
Atatürk pushed radical reforms to make Turkey a modern nation. One of his changes was the replacement of Arabic with western script. Here, Atatürk reveals the new Turkish alphabet to a crowd in an Istanbul park.

Theme: Impact of the Individual Why do you think Atatürk introduced the new alphabet himself in a public ceremony?

Westernization Atatürk swept away centuries-old traditions when he replaced Islamic law with a new law code based on European models. He discarded the Muslim calendar in favor of the calendar based on western (Christian) traditions and moved the day of rest from Friday, traditional with Muslims, to Sunday, in line with Christian practice.

Like Peter the Great in Russia, Atatürk forced his people to wear western dress. He replaced Arabic script with the western (Latin) alphabet, stating it was easier to learn. He closed religious schools but opened thousands of state schools to prepare young Turks for the challenges of modern society.

Other reforms transformed the lives of women. They no longer had to veil their faces and were allowed to vote. Polygamy—the custom allowing men to have more than one wife—was banned. Given freedom to work outside the home, women became teachers, doctors, lawyers, and even politicians.

Under Atatürk, the government encouraged industrial expansion. The government built roads and railroads, set up factories, and hired westerners to advise on how to make Turkey economically independent.

To achieve his reforms, Atatürk ruled with an iron hand. To many Turks, he was a hero who was transforming Turkey into a strong, modern power. Some Turkish Muslims, how-ever, rejected his secular government. To them, the Quran and Islamic customs provided all needed guidance, from personal concerns such as prayer and behavior to national matters such as government, commerce, and education.

Nationalism and Reform in Iran The success of Atatürk's reforms inspired nationalists in neighboring Iran. They greatly resented the British and Russians, who had won spheres of influence in their land. In 1925, an ambitious army officer, Reza Khan, overthrew the shah. He set up his own Pahlavi dynasty, with himself as shah.

Like Atatürk, Reza Khan rushed to modern-ize Iran and make it fully independent. He built factories, roads, and railroads and strengthened the army. He, too, adopted the western alphabet, forced Iranians to wear western clothing, and set up modern, secular schools. In addition, he moved to replace Islamic law with secular law and encouraged women to take part in public life. Although many wealthy Iranians in cities supported Reza Khan, Muslim religious leaders fiercely condemned his efforts to introduce west-ern ways to the nation.

As Iran modernized, it won better terms from the British company that controlled its oil industry. It persuaded the British to give it a larger share of the profits and insisted that Iranian workers be hired at all levels of the company. In the decades ahead, oil would become a major factor in Iranian economic and foreign affairs.

The Middle East, 1920s

British mandates

French mandates

✡ Jewish settlements

Albers Equal Area Projection

European Mandates and Arab Nationalism

Arab nationalism blossomed after World War I and gave rise to Pan-Arabism. This nationalist movement built on the shared heritage of Arabs who lived in lands from the Arabian Peninsula through North Africa.* It emphasized their common history and language and recalled the golden age of Arab civilization. Pan-Arabism sought to free Arabs from foreign domination and unite them in their own state. The national pact written at the First Arab Students' Conference spoke of this mission:

> "I am an Arab, and I believe that the Arabs constitute one nation. The sacred right of this nation is to be sovereign in her own affairs . . . to liberate the Arab homeland, to unite all its parts and to found [distinctively Arab] political, economic, and social institutions."
> —Arab pledge, quoted in *Arab Nationalism: An Anthology* (Haim)

Betrayal at the Peace Conference The mandates—territories adminis-tered by European nations—set up by the Paris Peace Conference outraged Arabs. During World War I, they had helped the Allies against the Central Powers, especially the Ottomans. In return, they had been promised inde-pendence. Instead, the Allies carved up the Ottoman lands, giving France

Skills Assessment

Geography After the end of World War I, Britain and France received mandates in the former Ottoman empire.

1. **Location** On the map, locate (a) Syria, (b) Palestine, (c) Trans-Jordan, (d) Saudi Arabia, (e) Egypt, (f) Persian Gulf.
2. **Place** (a) Which areas became French mandates after World War I? (b) Which became British mandates?
3. **Critical Thinking Applying Information** Is this map a useful source of information about the origins of conflict in the Middle East? Explain.

* The Arab lands included areas from the Arabian Peninsula through North Africa. Today, this area includes nations such as Syria, Jordan, Iraq, Egypt, Algeria, and Morocco.

Geography and History

Building New Settlements

During the early 1900s, many Jewish settlers in Palestine wanted to develop a new way of life. They organized collective farms, called *kibbutzim*. Members shared belongings, labor, and proceeds. The settlements were communal, with cooking done in a central dining hall. Children were raised in a home, separate from their parents, so that women could join the kibbutz work force.

Together, the settlers, called *kibbutzniks*, introduced new techniques of drainage and irrigation. Their efforts helped Israel become a world leader in agricultural production. The kibbutzniks grew grain, fruit trees, and vegetables. For meat, they raised chickens and cows. Cypress and palm trees were planted to provide shade from the desert sun.

 Theme: Geography and History What were the main characteristics of the kibbutzim?

---

mandates in Syria and Lebanon and Britain mandates in Palestine and Iraq. Later, Trans-Jordan was added to the British mandate.

Arabs felt betrayed by the West—a feeling that has endured to this day. During the 1920s and 1930s, their anger erupted in frequent protests and revolts against western imperialism. A major center of turmoil was the British mandate of Palestine. There, Arab nationalists faced European Zionists, or Jewish nationalists, with dreams of a homeland of their own.

Promises in Palestine Since Roman times, Jews had dreamed of returning to Palestine. In 1897, Theodor Herzl (HER tsuhl) responded to growing antisemitism in Europe by founding the modern Zionist movement. His goal was to rebuild a Jewish state in Palestine, "our ever-memorable historical home." Soon, some Jews, mostly from Eastern Europe, migrated to Palestine. There they joined the small Jewish community that had survived since biblical times.

During World War I, the Allies made two vague sets of promises. First, they promised Arabs their own kingdoms in former Ottoman lands, including Palestine. Then, in 1917, the British issued the Balfour Declaration to win support of European Jews. In it, Britain supported the idea of setting up "a national home for the Jewish people" in Palestine. The declaration noted, however, that "nothing shall be done which may prejudice the civil and religious rights of existing non-Jewish communities in Palestine." Those communities were Arab. The stage was thus set for conflict between Arab and Jewish nationalists.

A Bitter Struggle In the 1930s, antisemitism, primarily in Germany and Eastern Europe, forced many Jews to seek safety in Palestine. Despite great hardships, they set up factories, built new towns, and turned arid desert into irrigated farmland.

At first, some Arabs welcomed the money and modern technical skills that the newcomers brought with them. But as Jews poured into the land of Palestine, tensions between the two groups developed. Sometimes, Jewish settlers bought land from absentee Arab landowners. In the cities, some Jewish factory owners refused to hire Arabs. These tensions were heightened by religious differences between Jews and Arabs. Although most Arabs were Muslim, some were Christian. Angry Arabs staged attacks on Jewish settlements, hoping to oust the Jews. For the rest of the century, Arab nationalists battled Zionists over the land that Arabs called Palestine and Jews called Israel.

SECTION 2 Assessment

Recall

1. **Identify:** **(a)** "Women's War," **(b)** African National Congress, **(c)** Pan-Africanism, **(d)** négritude, **(e)** Pan-Arabism, **(f)** Zionist.
2. **Define:** **(a)** apartheid, **(b)** polygamy.

Comprehension

3. How did Africans resist the impact of colonialism?
4. Describe three examples of the rise of nationalism in Africa.
5. What reforms were introduced in **(a)** Turkey, **(b)** Iran?

6. **(a)** Why were many Arabs angered by decisions made at the Paris Peace Conference after World War I? **(b)** Why did Palestine become a center of conflict?

Critical Thinking and Writing

7. **Synthesizing Information** **(a)** How did nationalist leaders in Africa oppose colonial rule? **(b)** How did colonial powers control African countries?
8. **Drawing Conclusions** How did the Balfour Declaration affect the Middle East?

Reading Focus

■ What sparked the Indian independence movement after World War I?

■ How did Mohandas Gandhi influence the independence movement?

■ What did the Salt March symbolize?

Vocabulary

ahimsa

civil disobedience

Taking Notes

Copy this time line. As you read, fill in the key events in India's move to independence. To help you get started, one part of the time line has been completed.

1900   1910   1920   1930   1940

1858   1914
Britain takes control
of India

Main Idea Mohandas Gandhi and the Congress party led the drive for independence in India.

Setting the Scene

Tensions were running high in Amritsar, a city in northern India. Protests against British rule had sparked riots and attacks on British residents. On April 13, 1919, a large but peaceful crowd jammed into a walled field in the heart of the city. The British commander, General Reginald Dyer, had banned public meetings, but Indians either ignored or had not heard the order. As Indian leaders addressed the crowd, Dyer arrived with 50 soldiers. To clear the field, they opened fire on the unarmed men, women, and children. Within 10 minutes, they had killed 379 people and wounded more than 1,100. The Amritsar massacre was a turning point for many Indians. It convinced them of the evils of British rule.

Moves Toward Independence

The tragedy at Amritsar was linked to broader Indian frustrations after World War I. During the war, more than a million Indians had served overseas, suffering heavy casualties. As thousands died on distant battlefields, Indian nationalists grew angry that they had no freedom at home.

To quiet nationalist demands, the British promised India greater self-government after the war. But when the fighting ended, Britain proposed only a few minor reforms.

Since 1885, the Congress party had pressed for self-rule within the British empire. After Amritsar, it began to call for full independence. But party members were mostly a middle-class, western-educated elite who had little in common with the masses of Indian peasants. In the 1920s, a new leader emerged and united all Indians. Adoring Indians dubbed him Mahatma, or "Great Soul."

Mohandas Gandhi

The new leader was Mohandas Gandhi. Gandhi came from a middle-class Hindu family. At age 19, he went to England to study law. Like thousands of Indians before him, Gandhi went to South Africa. There he joined an Indian law firm. Although Gandhi was more successful financially than many Indians in South Africa, he too faced racial prejudice. For 20 years, Gandhi fought laws that discriminated against Indians in South Africa. In his struggle against injustice, he

Serving the Empire
Large numbers of Indians served in World War I. Here, Indian troops repel an air attack in Mesopotamia.

Theme: Political and Social Systems How did Indian nationalists respond to World War I?

Upheavals in China

Reading Focus

- What were the key challenges to the Chinese republic?

- What leaders emerged in the "new" China?

- How did invasion by Japan affect China?

Taking Notes

As you read this section, prepare an outline of its contents. Use Roman numerals to indicate major headings. Use capital letters for subheadings, and use numbers for the supporting details. The example here will help you get started.

I. The Chinese republic
  A. Internal problems
    1. Yuan Shikai sets up dynasty with himself as emperor
    2.
  B. Foreign imperialism
    1.
    2.

Main Idea   Civil war and foreign invasions plagued the new Chinese republic.

Setting the Scene   Sun Yixian, "father" of the Chinese revolution, painted a grim picture of China after the overthrow of the Qing dynasty. "In comparison with other nations," he wrote, "we have the greatest population and the oldest culture, of 4,000 years' duration." In spite of this, he noted, China was "the poorest and weakest state in the world." Other countries were "the carving knife and the serving dish," and China was "the fish and the meat."

As the new Chinese republic took shape, nationalists like Sun Yixian set the goal of "catching up and surpassing the powers, east and west." But that goal would remain a distant dream as China suffered the turmoil of civil war and foreign invasion.

The Chinese Republic

In China, as you recall, the Qing dynasty collapsed in 1911. Sun Yixian hoped to rebuild China on the Three Principles of the People. But he made little progress. China quickly fell into chaos.

Internal Problems   In 1912, Sun Yixian stepped down as president in favor of a powerful general, Yuan Shikai. Sun hoped that Yuan would restore order and create a strong central government. Instead, the ambitious general tried to set up a new dynasty, with himself as emperor. The military, however, did not support him, and opposition divided the nation. When Yuan died in 1916, China plunged into still greater disorder.

In the provinces, local warlords seized power. As rival armies battled for control, the economy collapsed and millions of peasants suffered terrible hardships. Warlords forced them to pay taxes to support their armies. The constant fighting ravaged the land. Famine and attacks by bandits added to their misery.

Foreign Imperialism   During this period of upheaval, foreign powers increased their influence over Chinese affairs. Foreign merchants, missionaries, and soldiers dominated the ports China had opened to trade. They also exerted influence inland.

In 1915, Japan had begun to put new pressure on its once-powerful neighbor. While the attentions of the western powers were focused on World War I, Japan presented Yuan Shikai with the Twenty-One Demands, which sought to make China a Japanese protectorate. Too weak to resist, Yuan gave in to some of the demands.

Then, in 1919, at the Paris Peace Conference, the victorious Allies gave Japan control over former German possessions in China. That news infuriated Chinese nationalists, who blamed their leaders for "selling out" China in the Treaty of Versailles.

May Fourth Movement On May 4, 1919, student protests erupted in Beijing and later spread to cities across China—a startling event in those days. "China's territory may be conquered," they declared, "but it cannot be given away! The Chinese people may be massacred, but they will not surrender." Students organized boycotts of Japanese goods.

Student protests set off a cultural and intellectual ferment known as the May Fourth Movement. As with earlier reform movements, its goal was to strengthen China. Western-educated leaders blamed the imperialists' successes on China's own weakness. As in Meiji Japan, Chinese reformers wanted to learn from the West and use that knowledge to end foreign domination. Most reformers rejected Confucian traditions, and many turned to western science and ideas such as democracy and nationalism to solve China's problems.

Women played a key role in the May Fourth Movement, just as they had in earlier uprisings. They joined marches and campaigned to end a number of traditional practices, such as arranged marriages, footbinding, and the seclusion of women within the home. Their work helped open doors for women in education and the economy.

The Appeal of Marxism Some Chinese turned to the revolutionary ideas of Marx and Lenin. The Russian Revolution seemed to offer a model of how a strong, well-organized party could transform a nation. And Soviet Russia was more than willing to train Chinese students and military officers to become the vanguard, or elite leaders, of a communist revolution. By the 1920s, a small group of Chinese communists had formed their own political party.

Leaders for a New China

In 1921, Sun Yixian and his Guomindang (gwoh meen DAWNG), or Nationalist, party established a government in south China. Sun planned to raise an army, defeat the warlords, and spread his government's rule over all of China. When western powers ignored pleas for help in building a democratic China, Sun decided "that the one real and genuine friend of the

May Fourth Movement
In 1919, student protests spread across China. Reformers wanted to modernize the nation so that China would be able to expel foreign powers.

Theme: Political and Social Systems Why did some Chinese reformers adopt the ideas of Marx and Lenin?

Empire of the Rising Sun

Reading Focus

■ How did liberal changes affect Japan during the 1920s?

■ How did nationalists react to Japan's problems during the Great Depression?

■ How did the militarists use their power?

Vocabulary

Diet
ultranationalist

Taking Notes

Copy this graphic organizer on a piece of paper. Include facts that describe the causes and effects of the rise of militarism in Japan. To help you get started, part of the graphic organizer has been completed.

Causes
• Unhappiness over loss of tradition
•

↓

RISE OF MILITARISM IN JAPAN

↓

Effects
• Withdrawal from League of Nations
•

Main Idea By the 1930s, the Japanese military dominated a government that emphasized service to the nation and a policy of imperialistic expansion.

Biography

Hirohito 1901–1989

Hirohito became emperor of Japan in 1926. As emperor, according to Japanese tradition, he was a living god and the nation's supreme authority—no one could look at his face or even mention his name. In practice, however, he merely approved the policies that his ministers formulated.

Hirohito was a private man who preferred marine biology to power politics. As a result, his role in Japan's move toward aggression is unclear. Some historians believe that Hirohito did not encourage Japanese military leaders. Others assert that he was actively involved in expansionist policies.

Theme: Impact of the Individual Why was Hirohito given great respect?

Setting the Scene Solemn ceremonies marked the start of Emperor Hirohito's reign. A few honored participants gathered in the Secret Purple Hall. Other high-ranking guests sat in an outer chamber, able to hear but not to see the emperor.

In the hall, the new emperor sat on the ancient throne of Japan. Beside him was his wife, the empress Nagako. With great care, he performed purification rituals that were sacred going back thousands of years. Calling on the spirits of his ancestors, he pledged "to preserve world peace and benefit the welfare of the human race."

The prime minister then made his own brief speech, ending with a ringing cry: "May the Lord Emperor live 10,000 years!" This traditional wish for a long and successful reign echoed across Japan.

In fact, Hirohito reigned from 1926 to 1989—an astonishing 63 years. During those decades, Japan experienced remarkable successes and appalling tragedies. In this section, we will focus on the 1920s and 1930s, when the pressures of extreme nationalism and economic upheaval set Japan on a militaristic and expansionist path that would engulf all of Asia.

Liberal Changes of the 1920s

During the 1920s, Japan moved toward greater democracy. Political parties grew stronger, and elected members of the Diet—the Japanese parliament—exerted their power. By 1925, all adult men had won the right to vote. Western ideas about women's rights had brought a few changes. Overall, however, Japanese women remained subordinate to men, and they would not win suffrage until 1947.

Economic Growth During World War I, the Japanese economy enjoyed phenomenal growth. Its exports to Allied nations soared. Also, while western powers battled in Europe, Japan expanded its influence throughout East Asia. Additionally, it sought further rights in China with the Twenty-One Demands.

By the 1920s, the powerful business leaders known as the zaibatsu strongly influenced politics through donations to political parties. They pushed for policies to favor international trade and their own interests. At the same time, in the spirit of world peace, Japan signed an agreement with the United States and Britain to limit the size of its navy. The government also reduced military spending.

Serious Problems Behind this seeming well-being, Japan faced some grave problems. The economy grew more slowly in the 1920s than at any time since Japan had modernized. Rural peasants enjoyed none of the prosperity of city dwellers. In the cities, factory workers earning low wages were attracted to the socialist ideas of Marx and Lenin. As these workers won the right to vote, many of them elected socialists to the Diet.

In the cities, members of the younger generation were also in revolt against tradition. They adopted western fads and fashions and rejected family authority for the western notion of individual freedom.

During the 1920s, tensions between the government and the military simmered not far below the surface. Conservatives, especially military officers, blasted government corruption, including payoffs by powerful zaibatsu. They also condemned western influences for undermining basic Japanese values of obedience and respect for authority.

The Nationalist Reaction

In 1929, the Great Depression rippled across the Pacific, striking Japan with devastating force. Trade suffered as foreign buyers could no longer afford to purchase Japanese silks and other exports. Unemployment in the cities soared, while in the countryside peasants were only a mouthful from starvation.

A Worsening Crisis Economic disaster fed the discontent of the leading military officials and extreme nationalists, or **ultranationalists.** They condemned politicians for agreeing to western demands to stop overseas expansion. Western industrial powers, they pointed out, had long ago grabbed huge empires. By comparison, Japan's empire was tiny.

Japanese nationalists were further outraged by racial policies in the United States, Canada, and Australia that shut out Japanese immigrants. The Japanese took great pride in their industrial achievements and bitterly resented being treated as second-class citizens in other parts of the world.

As the crisis worsened, nationalists demanded renewed expansion. An empire in Asia, they argued, would provide much-needed raw materials as well as an outlet for Japan's rapidly growing population. They set their sights on the Chinese province of Manchuria. This region was rich in natural resources, and Japanese businesses had already invested heavily there.

The Manchurian Incident In 1931, a group of Japanese army officers provoked an incident that would provide an excuse to seize Manchuria. They set explosives and blew up tracks on a Japanese-owned railroad line. Then, they claimed that the Chinese had committed the act. In "self-defense," the army attacked Chinese forces. Without consulting their own government, the Japanese military forces conquered all of Manchuria and set up a puppet state there that they called Manzhouguo (mahn joh GWOH).

When the League of Nations condemned Japanese aggression against China, Japan simply

Skills Assessment

Geography Between 1918 and 1934, Japan expanded its territory in Asia. From their conquered lands, the Japanese acquired natural resources to fuel their industries.

1. **Location** On the map, locate **(a)** Japan, **(b)** Sakhalin, **(c)** Manchuria, **(d)** Korea, **(e)** Taiwan.
2. **Region** In what regions were Japan's main manufacturing areas located?
3. **Critical Thinking Identifying Main Ideas** Based on this map, which area was the most likely source of raw materials for Japanese industry? Explain.

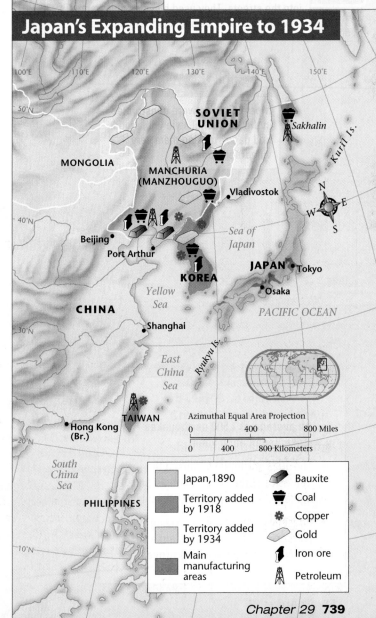

Japan's Expanding Empire to 1934

Japan, 1890
Territory added by 1918
Territory added by 1934
Main manufacturing areas

Bauxite
Coal
Copper
Gold
Iron ore
Petroleum

Azimuthal Equal Area Projection

0   400   800 Miles

0   400   800 Kilometers

Reading Focus

- What issues faced Europe after World War I?
- How did the Great Depression begin and spread?
- How did Britain, France, and the United States try to meet the challenges of the 1920s and 1930s?

Vocabulary

disarmament
overproduction
margin buying
general strike

Taking Notes

On a sheet of paper, make a table like this one. As you read this section, add information about the three democracies in the years after World War I.

	BRITAIN	FRANCE	UNITED STATES
Economic problems			
Political drift to right			

Main Idea Following World War I, the leading democratic powers moved to ensure peace but faced difficult political and economic challenges.

Setting the Scene In his 1929 novel, *All Quiet on the Western Front,* German writer Erich Maria Remarque captured the disillusionment of the World War I generation. The novel's hero, a young German soldier, endures three years of grueling trench warfare. His friends are dead—butchered by bullets, shrapnel, artillery, or poison gas. In the last chapter, he wonders how he can return to civilian life feeling dead inside:

> "Had we returned home in 1916, out of the suffering and the strength of our experience we might have unleashed a storm. Now if we go back we will be weary, broken, burnt out, rootless, and without hope. We will not be able to find our way any more."
> —Erich Maria Remarque, *All Quiet on the Western Front*

The catastrophe of World War I shattered the sense of optimism that had grown in the West since the Enlightenment. Despair gripped survivors on both sides as they added up the staggering costs of the war. Especially among the democracies, economic and political crises only added to the growing pessimism of the 1920s and 1930s.

Postwar Issues

In 1919, three western democracies—Great Britain, France, and the United States—appeared powerful. They had ruled the Paris Peace Conference and boosted hopes for democracy among the new nations of Eastern Europe.

Underlying Problems Beneath the surface, however, postwar Europe faced grave problems. At first, the most pressing issues were finding jobs for returning veterans and rebuilding war-ravaged lands. Many nations also owed huge debts because they had borrowed heavily to pay for the war. In the early postwar years, economic problems fed social unrest and made radical ideas more popular. The Russian Revolution unleashed fears of the spread of communism. Some people saw socialism as the answer to hardships. Others embraced nationalistic political movements.

Other troubles clouded the international scene. As you have read, the peace settlements dissatisfied many Europeans, especially in Germany and among various ethnic groups in Eastern Europe. Finally, Europe lacked strong leaders just when they were most needed. The war had killed many of those who might have helped solve critical problems.

Disillusion in Postwar Europe
German artist Käthe Kollwitz lost a son in World War I. In her 1923 woodcut *The Parents* (below), Kollwitz mirrors the sense of despair that gripped postwar Europe.

Theme: Art and Literature How does this picture make a universal statement about war?

The Pursuit of Peace During the 1920s, diplomats worked hard for peace. Hopes soared in 1925 when representatives from seven European nations signed a series of treaties at Locarno, Switzerland. These treaties settled Germany's disputed borders with France, Belgium, Czechoslovakia, and Poland. The Locarno treaties became the symbol of a new era. "France and Germany Ban War Forever," trumpeted a *New York Times* headline.

The hopeful "spirit of Locarno" was echoed in the Kellogg-Briand Pact of 1928. Almost every independent nation signed this agreement, promising to "renounce war as an instrument of national policy." In this optimistic spirit, the great powers pursued disarmament, the reduction of armed forces and weapons. The United States, Britain, France, Japan, and other nations signed treaties to reduce the size of their navies. However, they failed to agree on limiting the size of their armies.

Despite grumblings about the Versailles treaty, people around the world put great hopes in the League of Nations. From its headquarters in Geneva, Switzerland, the League encouraged cooperation and tried to get members to make a commitment to stop aggression. In 1926, after signing the Locarno agreements, Germany joined the League. Later, the Soviet Union was also admitted.

Obstacles to Peace Although the Kellogg-Briand Pact outlawed war, there was no way of enforcing the ban. The League of Nations, too, was powerless to stop aggressors. It had also been damaged by the American refusal to join. In 1931, the League vigorously condemned Japan's invasion of Manchuria, but to no effect. Noting the League's weakness, ambitious dictators rearmed their military forces and pursued aggressive foreign policies, as you will read.

HAVING AN INSURANCE POLICY DOESN'T MEAN YOU CAN DO WITHOUT FIRE PREVENTION

An End to War?
The Kellogg-Briand Pact raised hopes for an end to war. But not everyone was so optimistic, as this 1929 American cartoon shows.
Theme: Global Interaction Summarize the main idea of this cartoon in your own words.

Recovery and Depression

During the 1920s, Europe made a shaky recovery. Economies returned to peacetime manufacturing and trade. Veterans gradually found jobs. Middle-class families generally enjoyed a rising standard of living, with money to buy new products such as cars, refrigerators, and radios.

The United States emerged from the war as the world's leading economic power. American banks and businesses controlled a global network of trade and finance. American loans and investments backed the recovery in Europe. As long as the American economy was healthy, the global economy remained relatively prosperous.

A Dangerous Imbalance Both the American and the world economy had weak spots, however. One major problem was overproduction, a condition in which production of goods exceeds the demand for them. The war had increased demand for raw materials from Latin America, Africa, and Asia. Improved technology and farming methods also contributed to higher output. After the war, the demand for raw materials dwindled and prices fell. Consumers benefited from the lower prices. But farmers, miners, and other suppliers of raw materials suffered severe hardships.

At the same time, industrial workers won higher wages, which raised the price of manufactured goods. An imbalance emerged. Because farmers' earnings had fallen, they could afford fewer manufactured goods. Despite the slowing demand, factories kept pouring out goods. This imbalance, combined with other problems, undermined industrial economies. By the late 1920s, conditions were ripe for disaster.

France Pursues Security

Like Britain, France emerged from World War I both a victor and a loser. Fighting on the Western Front had devastated northern France. The French had suffered enormous casualties. Survivors felt battered and insecure.

The French economy recovered fairly rapidly, thanks in part to German reparations and to territories gained from Germany, including Alsace and Lorraine. Later, the Great Depression did not hurt France as much as it did some countries. French industry was not as centralized in the hands of big business. Small workshops served local regions and were less affected by global trends.

Coalition Governments Economic swings did occur, adding to an unstable political scene. Political divisions and financial scandals continued to plague the Third Republic. Many parties—from conservatives to communists—competed for power. During the postwar years, France was again ruled by a series of coalition governments.

In 1936, several leftist parties united behind the socialist leader Leon Blum. His Popular Front government tried to solve labor problems and passed some social legislation. But it could not satisfy more radical leftists. Strikes soon brought down Blum's government. Thus, France, like Britain, muddled through a series of crises. Democracy survived, but the country lacked strong leadership that could respond to the clamor for change.

The Maginot Line France's chief concern after the war was securing its borders against Germany. The French remembered with distrust the German invasions of 1870 and 1914. To prevent a third invasion, France built massive fortifications along the border. The Maginot (MA zhee noh) Line, as this defensive "wall" was called, offered a sense of security—a false one. The line would be of little use when Germany again invaded in 1940.

In its quest for security, France strengthened its military and sought alliances with other countries, including the Soviet Union. It insisted on strict enforcement of the Versailles treaty and complete payment of reparations, hoping to keep the German economy weak.

Prosperity and Depression in the United States

The United States emerged from World War I in excellent shape. A late entrant into the war, it had suffered relatively few casualties and little loss of property. It led the world in industrial and agricultural output. American money helped finance the European recovery.

Postwar Issues As you have read, the United States stayed out of the League of Nations. Arguing that membership might lead to involvement in future foreign wars, many Americans insisted that the nation maintain its free hand in foreign affairs. Still, during the 1920s, the United States took a leading role in international diplomacy. It sponsored the Kellogg-Briand Pact, pressed for disarmament, and worked to reduce German reparations.

Fear of bomb-throwing radicals and the Bolshevik Revolution in Russia set off a "Red Scare" in 1919 and 1920. Police rounded up suspected foreign-born radicals, and a number were expelled from the United States.

The "Red Scare" fed growing demands to limit immigration. Millions of immigrants from southern and eastern Europe had poured into the United States between 1890 and 1914. Some native-born Americans sought to exclude these newcomers, whose cultures differed from those of earlier settlers from northern Europe. In response, Congress passed laws limiting immigration from Europe. Earlier laws had already excluded or limited Chinese and Japanese immigration.

Boom and Bust In the boom years of the 1920s, middle-class Americans were enjoying the benefits of capitalism. They stocked their homes with

The Maginot Line

The Maginot Line was a masterpiece of engineering. Most of the line was built underground, with interconnecting tunnels that stretched for miles. Main forts, placed strategically to protect river crossings and crossroads, were located about every three to five miles. These were self-contained underground structures over 20 feet beneath the surface. Large enough to accommodate about 1,200 men, the forts contained barracks, kitchens, infirmaries, storage depots, telephone systems, electrical generating systems, and railways to move supplies. All that could be seen above ground were the barrels of the huge guns and gun placements.

In the end, the line failed to prevent a German invasion. In 1940, German troops simply bypassed the Maginot Line and marched into France.

Theme: Geography and History Look at a map of Europe. What routes could a German army take to bypass the German–French border and invade France?

radios, refrigerators, and automobiles. Most Americans agreed with President Calvin Coolidge that "the business of America is business."

The 1929 stock market crash shattered this mood of prosperity. President Herbert Hoover firmly believed that the government should not intervene in private business matters. However, as hard times got worse, he did try a variety of limited measures to solve the crisis. Nothing seemed to work.

The New Deal In 1932, Americans elected a new President, Franklin D. Roosevelt. "FDR" projected a sense of energy and optimism. Arguing that the government had to take an active role in combating the Great Depression, he introduced the New Deal, a massive package of economic and social programs.

Under the New Deal, the federal government became more directly involved in people's everyday lives than ever before. New laws regulated the stock market and protected bank depositors' savings. Government programs created jobs for the unemployed and gave aid to farmers. A new Social Security system provided old-age pensions and other benefits that major European countries had introduced years earlier.

The New Deal failed to end the Great Depression, but it did ease the suffering for many. Still, some critics fiercely condemned FDR's expansion of the role of government. As a result of the New Deal, many Americans came to expect the government to intervene directly to promote their economic well-being. The debate about the size and role of the federal government continues to this day.

Cause *and* Effect

Long-Term Causes	Immediate Causes
• Worldwide interrelationship of governments and economies • Huge war debts • American loans to Europe • Widespread use of credit • Overproduction of goods • Industrial wages rise as farm earnings fall	• New York stock market crash • Farmers unable to repay loans • Banks demand repayment of loans • American loans to other countries dry up • Without capital, businesses and factories fail

Worldwide Economic Depression

Immediate Effects	Long-Term Effects
• Vast unemployment and misery • Protective tariffs imposed • Loss of faith in capitalism and democracy • Authoritarian leaders emerge	• Rise of fascism and Nazism • Governments experiment with social programs • People blame scapegoats • World War II begins

Connections to Today

• Government monitoring of or control of national economies, banks, credit, and stock markets
• Continuation of social programs
• Monitoring of worldwide economic developments by international agencies

Skills Assessment **Chart** Economists still debate the causes and effects of the Great Depression. **How do governments today deal with the kinds of conditions that caused the depression?**

SECTION 1 Assessment

Recall

1. **Identify: (a)** Locarno treaties, **(b)** Kellogg-Briand Pact, **(c)** IRA, **(d)** Commonwealth of Nations, **(e)** Leon Blum, **(f)** Maginot Line, **(g)** New Deal.
2. **Define: (a)** disarmament, **(b)** overproduction, **(c)** margin buying, **(d)** general strike.

Comprehension

3. **(a)** What steps did the major powers take to protect the peace? **(b)** Why did these moves have limited effects?
4. Explain how each of the following contributed to the outbreak or spread of the Great Depression: **(a)** overproduction, **(b)** margin buying, **(c)** high tariffs.
5. How did the Great Depression affect political developments in the United States?

Critical Thinking and Writing

6. **Understanding Causes and Effects** Why do you think the 1926 general strike in Britain strengthened the Conservative party?
7. **Applying Information** How did Britain and France emerge from World War I as both victors and losers?

Activity

Creating a Political Cartoon Draw a political cartoon that might have appeared in an American or British newspaper in 1932. The cartoon should show how the effects of the Great Depression often undermined confidence in democracy.

civil war, King Victor Emmanuel III asked Mussolini to form a government as prime minister. Without firing a shot, Mussolini thus obtained a "legal" appointment from the king, undermining constitutional democracy.

Mussolini's Italy

At first, Fascists held only a few cabinet posts. By 1925, though, Mussolini had assumed more power and taken the title Il Duce (eel DOO chay), "The Leader." He suppressed rival parties, muzzled the press, rigged elections, and replaced elected officials with Fascist supporters.

In theory, Italy remained a parliamentary monarchy. In fact, it was a dictatorship upheld by terror. Critics were thrown into prison, forced into exile, or murdered. Secret police and propaganda bolstered the regime.

Economic Policy   To encourage economic growth and end conflicts between owners and workers, Mussolini brought the economy under state control. Unlike socialists, though, he preserved capitalism. Under Mussolini's "corporate state," representatives of business, labor, government, and the Fascist party controlled industry, agriculture, and trade. Although production increased, this success came at the expense of workers. They were forbidden to strike, and their wages lagged.

Social Policies   To Fascists, the individual was unimportant except as a member of the state. Men, women, and children were bombarded with slogans glorifying the state and Mussolini. "Believe! Obey! Fight!" loudspeakers blared and posters proclaimed. Men were urged to be ruthless, selfless warriors for the glory of Italy. Women were pushed out of paying jobs. Instead, Mussolini called on women to "win the battle of motherhood." Those who bore more than 14 children were given a medal by Il Duce himself.

Shaping the young was a major Fascist goal. Fascist youth groups toughened children and taught them to obey strict military discipline. Boys and girls learned about the glories of ancient Rome. Young Fascists marched in torchlight parades, singing patriotic hymns and chanting, "Mussolini is always right." By the 1930s, a generation of young soldiers stood ready to back Il Duce's drive to expand Italian power.

What Is Fascism?

Historians still debate the real nature of fascist ideology. Mussolini coined the term, but fascists had no single unifying set of beliefs, as Marxists did. Today, we generally use the term to describe any authoritarian government that is not communist. In the 1920s and 1930s, though, fascism meant different things in different countries.

All forms of fascism, however, shared some basic features. It was rooted in extreme nationalism. Fascists glorified action, violence, discipline, and, above all, blind loyalty to the state. "Fascism conceives of the State as an absolute," declared Mussolini, "in comparison with which all individuals or groups are relative, only to be conceived of in their relation to the State."

Fascists were antidemocratic. They rejected the Enlightenment faith in reason and the concepts of equality and liberty spread by the French Revolution. To them, democracy led to corruption and weakness and put individual or class interests above national goals. Instead, fascists emphasized emotion and the need for the citizen to serve the state.

Fascists also pursued aggressive foreign expansion. Echoing the Social Darwinist idea of "survival of the fittest," Fascist leaders glorified warfare as a necessary and noble struggle for survival.

Compared to Communism   Fascists were the sworn enemies of socialists and communists. While communists had hopes for international change, fascists pursued nationalist goals. Fascists found allies among business

Synthesizing Information

Totalitarianism

In 1922, Benito Mussolini set up a fascist government, making Italy the first totalitarian state in Europe. Shortly afterward, Germany and the Soviet Union also came under totalitarian rule. Use the quotation, the poster, and the photograph to learn about the nature of totalitarianism.

Fascist Propaganda

This propaganda poster celebrates the introduction of new passenger cars for the Italian state railroad. The words say, "State Railroad. The Newest Third-Class Carriages."

Admiring the Leader

"[Only joy at finding such a leader] can explain the enthusiasm [Mussolini] evoked at gathering after gathering, where his mere presence drew the people from all sides to greet him with frenzied acclamations. Even the men who at first came out of mere curiosity and with indifferent or even hostile feelings gradually felt themselves fired by his personal magnetic influence. . . .

The women of the Abruzzi . . . strove to touch his hand as they would to touch a shrine or a relic. . . . The mayor of a little Sicilian village stopped his motor-car and said to him, 'I have nothing to ask of you, but this only. Perhaps you will never again pass over this ground of ours. Dismount that you may touch it with your feet!'"

—Margherita G. Sarfatti, *The Life of Benito Mussolini*
(tr. Frederic Whyte)

Fascist Youth

A company of uniformed Italian boys, shouldering packs and rifles, proudly parades during a military drill.

Skills Tip

When you analyze a work of propaganda, notice how images can convey an emotional impact, even when the words do not.

Skills Assessment

1. What value is reflected in both the photograph and the poster?
   A personal freedom
   B national pride
   C prosperity
   D individuality

2. According to Sarfatti, many Italians greeted Mussolini with
   E petitions for jobs.
   F complaints about his fascist government.
   G calls for him to resign.
   H deep respect.

3. **Critical Thinking Synthesizing Information** (a) How do the quotation, the poster, and the photograph illustrate some of the features of totalitarian states? (b) Based on your reading in the chapter and using the list (from the next page) of six basic features of a totalitarian state, name three additional traits of fascist Italy.

leaders, wealthy landowners, and the lower middle class. Communists won support among urban and agricultural workers.

Despite such differences, these two ideologies had much in common. Both flourished during economic hard times by promoting extreme programs of social change. In Communist Russia as well as Fascist Italy, dictators imposed totalitarian governments in order to bring about social revolutions. In both, a party elite claimed to rule in the name of the national interest.

Totalitarian Rule Mussolini built the first totalitarian state, which became a model for others. Fascist rule in Italy was not as absolute as those of Stalin in the Soviet Union or Adolf Hitler in Germany. Still, all three governments shared these basic features: (1) a single-party dictatorship, (2) state control of the economy, (3) use of police spies and terror to enforce the will of the state, (4) strict censorship and government monopoly of the media, (5) use of schools and the media to indoctrinate and mobilize citizens, and (6) unquestioning obedience to a single leader.

Appeal Given its restrictions of individual freedom, why did fascism appeal to many Italians? First, it promised a strong, stable government and an end to the political feuding that had paralyzed democracy. Mussolini's intense nationalism also struck a chord among most ordinary Italians. He revived national pride, pledging to make the Mediterranean Sea a "Roman lake" once more. Finally, Mussolini projected a sense of power and confidence at a time of disorder and despair.

At first, Il Duce received good press outside Italy, too. Newspapers in Britain, France, and North America applauded the discipline and order of his government. "He got the trains running on time," admirers said. Only later, when Mussolini embarked on a course of foreign conquest, did western democracies protest his actions.

Looking Ahead

Three systems of government competed for influence in postwar Europe. Democracy endured in Britain and France but faced an uphill struggle in hard times. Communism emerged in Russia and won support elsewhere, but many people saw it as a dangerous threat.

In Italy, fascism offered a different formula. Its chest-thumping calls for action, national unity, and dedication to the state ignited patriotic feeling. As the Great Depression spread, other nations—most notably Germany—looked to leaders who preached fascist ideology.

Global Connections

Authoritarian Rule in Eastern Europe

Italy was not the only European nation to embrace authoritarian rule. The newly formed countries of Eastern Europe were in turmoil after World War I. They embraced democracy, but struggled with nationalist sentiments, ethnic tensions, wars, and economic problems. In 1926, General Joseph Pilsudski, a military hero who had helped liberate Poland, used the army to seize control of the country. Eventually every country in Eastern Europe, except Czechoslovakia, turned to some form of authoritarian government.

In the 1930s, President Franklin Roosevelt tried to explain why many nations had rejected democracy. "People . . . have grown tired of unemployment and insecurity," he said. "Finally, in desperation, they chose to sacrifice liberty in the hope of getting something to eat."

Theme: Political and Social Systems What methods might dictators use to reduce ethnic tensions?

SECTION 3 Assessment

Recall
1. **Identify:** **(a)** Black Shirts, **(b)** Il Duce.

Comprehension
2. **(a)** What problems did Italy face after World War I? **(b)** How did these problems help Mussolini win power?
3. Describe two economic or social goals of Mussolini, and explain the actions he took to achieve each goal.
4. **(a)** What values did fascism promote? **(b)** List two similarities and two differences between fascism and communism.

Critical Thinking and Writing
5. **Analyzing Information** Why do you think the Fascists blamed democracy for problems in Italy?
6. **Analyzing Primary Sources** Mussolini said, "Machines and women are the two main causes of unemployment." **(a)** What do you think he meant? **(b)** How did Mussolini's policies reflect his attitude toward women?

Activity

Taking a Poll
Many people today use the word *fascist* in discussing politics. Take a poll of several voters and ask what they think the word means. Then, write a paragraph comparing these definitions with what fascism meant under Mussolini.

Hitler and the Rise of Nazi Germany

Reading Focus

- What problems did the Weimar Republic face?
- How did Hitler come to power?
- What political, social, economic, and cultural policies did Hitler pursue?
- How did Hitler take action against German Jews?

Vocabulary

chancellor
repudiate
concentration camp

Taking Notes

Make a cause-and-effect diagram about the rise of Hitler. This sample will help you get started.

| Versailles Treaty | Inflation | | |

RISE OF HITLER

Main Idea   Under Adolf Hitler, the Nazi government used terror, repression, and one-party rule to establish a totalitarian state.

Setting the Scene   In November 1923, a German army veteran and leader of an extremist party, Adolf Hitler, tried to follow Mussolini's example. His brown-shirted thugs burst into a beer hall in Munich, where a political meeting was set to start. Hitler climbed onto a table and fired his pistol. "The National Socialist revolution has begun!" he shouted.

The coup failed, and Hitler was soon behind bars. But Hitler was a force that could not be ignored forever. Within a decade, he made a new bid for power. This time, he succeeded by legal means.

Hitler's rise to power raises disturbing questions that we still debate today. Why did Germany, which had a democratic government in the 1920s, become a totalitarian state in the 1930s? How could a ruthless, hate-filled dictator gain the enthusiastic support of many Germans?

The Weimar Republic

As World War I drew to a close, Germany tottered on the brink of chaos. Under the threat of a socialist revolution, the kaiser abdicated. Moderate leaders signed the armistice and later, under protest, the Versailles treaty.

In 1919, German leaders drafted a constitution in the city of Weimar (vī mahr). It created a democratic government known as the Weimar Republic. The constitution set up a parliamentary system led by a chancellor, or prime minister. It gave women the vote and included a bill of rights.

Struggles of the Republic   The republic faced severe problems from the start. Politically, it was weak because Germany, like France, had many small parties. The chancellor had to form coalitions that easily fell apart.

The government, led by moderate democratic socialists, came under constant fire from both the left and right. Communists demanded radical changes like those Lenin had brought to Russia. Conservatives—including the old Junker nobility, military officers, and wealthy bourgeoisie—attacked the government as too liberal and weak. They longed for another strong leader like Bismarck or the kaiser. Germans of all classes blamed the Weimar Republic for the hated Versailles treaty, with its war-guilt clause and heavy reparations. In their bitterness, they looked for scapegoats. Many blamed German Jews for economic and political problems.

Inflation   Economic disaster fed unrest. In 1923, when Germany fell behind in reparations payments, France occupied the coal-rich Ruhr Valley. Ruhr Germans turned to passive resistance, refusing to work. To support them,

German Inflation

In 1923, runaway inflation caused prices in Germany to soar. Here, a housewife prepares to light her stove with several million marks.

Theme: Economics and Technology   What does this picture suggest about the price of fuel at the time?

the government printed huge quantities of paper money. This move set off inflation that spiraled out of control. The German mark became almost worthless. An item that cost 100 marks in July 1922 cost 944,000 marks by August 1923. A loaf of bread cost tens of thousands of marks.

Runaway inflation spread misery and despair. Salaries rose by billions of marks, but they still could not keep up with skyrocketing prices. Many middle-class families saw their savings wiped out.

Recovery and Collapse With help from the western powers, the government did bring inflation under control. In 1924, the United States gained British and French approval for a plan to reduce German reparations payments. Under the Dawes Plan, France withdrew its forces from the Ruhr, and American loans helped the German economy recover.

Germany began to prosper. Then, the Great Depression hit, reviving memories of the miseries of 1923. Germans turned to an energetic leader, Adolf Hitler, who promised to solve the economic crisis and restore Germany's former greatness.

Adolf Hitler

Hitler was born in Austria in 1889. When he was 18, he went to Vienna, hoping to enter art school, but he was turned down. Vienna was then the capital of the multinational Hapsburg empire. Austrian Germans made up just one of many ethnic groups. Yet they felt superior to Jews, Serbs, Poles, and other groups. While living in Vienna, Hitler developed the fanatical antisemitism that would later play a major role in his rise to power.

Hitler later moved to Germany and fought in the German army during World War I. Like many ex-soldiers, he despised the Weimar government which he perceived as weak and ineffectual. In 1919, he joined a small group of right-wing extremists. Within a year, he was the unquestioned leader of the National Socialist German Workers, or Nazi, party. Like Mussolini, Hitler organized his supporters into fighting squads. Nazi "Storm Troopers" battled in the streets against their political enemies.

Mein Kampf In 1923, as you have read, Hitler made a failed attempt to seize power in Munich. He was arrested, tried, and found guilty of treason. While in prison, Hitler wrote *Mein Kampf* ("My Struggle"). It would later become the basic book of Nazi goals and ideology.

Mein Kampf reflected Hitler's obsessions—extreme nationalism, racism, and antisemitism. Germans, he said, belonged to a superior "master race" of Aryans, or light-skinned Europeans, whose greatest enemies were the Jews. Hitler viewed Jews not as members of a religion but as a separate race. (He defined a Jew as anyone with one Jewish grandparent.) Echoing a familiar right-wing theme, he claimed that Germany had not lost the war but had been betrayed by a conspiracy of Marxists, Jews, corrupt politicians, and business leaders.

In his recipe for revival, Hitler urged Germans everywhere to unite into one great nation. Germany must expand, he said, to gain *Lebensraum*, or living space, for its people. Slavs and other inferior races must bow to Aryan needs. To achieve its greatness, Germany needed a strong leader, or *Führer* (FYOO ruhr). Hitler was determined to become that leader.

The Road to Power After serving less than a year, Hitler left prison. He soon renewed his table-thumping speeches. He found enthusiastic followers among veterans and lower-middle-class Germans who felt frustrated about their future. The Great Depression played into Hitler's hands. As unemployment rose, Nazi membership grew to almost a million. Hitler's program appealed to workers, the lower middle classes, small-town Germans, and business people alike. He promised to end reparations, create jobs, and defy the Versailles treaty by rearming Germany.

Biography

Adolf Hitler 1889–1945

As a boy, Adolf Hitler became obsessed with reading about Germany's 1871 victory in the Franco–Prussian War. "The great historic struggle would become my greatest spiritual experience," he later wrote. "I became more and more enthusiastic about everything . . . connected with war."

In school, young Hitler was known as a ring leader. One of his teachers recalled, "He demanded of his fellow pupils their unqualified obedience." He failed to finish high school and was later crushed when he was rejected by art school.

After Hitler came to power, he used his elite guard of storm troopers to terrorize his opponents. But when he felt his power threatened, Hitler had storm trooper leaders murdered during the "Night of the Long Knives," June 30, 1934.

Theme: Impact of the Individual Why do you think historians study the upbringing of Hitler?

With the government paralyzed by divisions, both Nazis and Communists won more seats in the Reichstag, or lower house of the legislature. Fearing the growth of communist political power, conservative politicians turned to Hitler. Although they despised him, they believed they could control him. Thus, with conservative support, Hitler was elected chancellor in 1933 through legal, democratic means under the Weimar constitution.

Within a year, Hitler was master of Germany. He suspended civil rights, destroyed the socialists and Communists, and disbanded other political parties. Germany became a one-party state. Nazi flags, with their black swastikas, waved across the country. Like Stalin in Russia, Hitler purged his own party, brutally executing Nazis he felt were disloyal. Nazis learned that Hitler, the Führer, demanded unquestioning obedience.

Hitler's Third Reich

Once in power, Hitler moved to build a new Germany. Like Mussolini, Hitler appealed to nationalism by recalling past glories. Germany's First Reich, or empire, was the medieval Holy Roman Empire. The Second Reich was the empire forged by Bismarck in 1871. Under Hitler's new Third Reich, he boasted, the German master race would dominate Europe for 1,000 years.

Hitler soon repudiated, or rejected, the hated Treaty of Versailles. He began scheming to unite Germany and Austria. "Today Germany belongs to us," sang young Nazis. "Tomorrow, the world."

A Totalitarian State To achieve his goals, Hitler organized an efficient but brutal system of terror, repression, and totalitarian rule. Nazis controlled all areas of German life—from government to religion to education. Elite, black-uniformed SS troops enforced the Führer's will. His secret police, the Gestapo, rooted out opposition.

Few Germans saw or worried about this terror apparatus taking shape. Instead, they cheered Hitler's accomplishments in ending unemployment and reviving German power.

Economic Policy To combat the Great Depression, Hitler launched large public works programs (as did Britain and the United States). Tens of thousands of people were put to work building highways and housing or replanting forests. Hitler also began a crash program to rearm Germany, in violation of the Versailles treaty. Demand for military hardware stimulated business and helped eliminate unemployment.

Nazis March
Militarism was a key element of Nazi ideology. Here, German soldiers march at a Nazi party rally in Nuremberg. The swastika, which the Nazis adopted as a party symbol, actually dates back to ancient times.

Theme: Political and Social Systems Why would mass meetings and marches be important in a totalitarian state?

Aggression, Appeasement, and War

Reading Focus

■ How did dictators and the Spanish Civil War challenge world peace?

■ How did continuing German aggression lead Europe toward war?

■ What factors encouraged the coming of war?

Vocabulary

sanction

appeasement

pacifism

Anschluss

Taking Notes

On a sheet of paper, make a table like the one shown here. As you read this section, complete the table by adding information about how dictators challenged world peace.

JAPAN	ITALY	GERMANY	SPAIN
• 1931 Manchuria seized •	•	•	•

Main Idea During the 1930s, dictators undermined world peace.

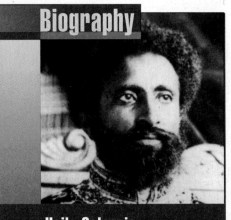

Biography

Haile Selassie 1892–1975

When Tafari Makonnen became emperor of Ethiopia in 1930, he took the name Haile Selassie, which means "Might of the Trinity," to show that his power was conferred by God. The Ethiopian people believed that their leader was descended from King Solomon.

Selassie was exiled during the Italian occupation, but returned after four years. He wanted to modernize his country. Selassie oversaw the writing of a constitution, established a parliament and cabinet, initiated land reforms, and encouraged all adults to vote. He remained in office until 1974, when a military group seized power.

Theme: Impact of the Individual How did Selassie share his power?

Setting the Scene During the 1920s, the western democracies tried to strengthen the framework for peace. In the 1930s, that structure crumbled. Dictators in Spain, Germany, and Italy, along with militarists in Japan, pursued ambitious goals for empire. They scorned peace and glorified war.

Unlike these dictators, leaders of the western democracies were haunted by memories of the Great War. Spurred by voters who demanded "no more war," the leaders of Britain, France, and the United States tried to avoid conflict through diplomacy. During the 1930s, the two sides tested each other's commitment and will.

Dictators Challenge World Peace

Challenges to peace followed a pattern throughout the 1930s. Dictators took aggressive action but met only verbal protests and pleas for peace from the democracies. Mussolini and Hitler viewed that desire for peace as weakness and responded with new acts of aggression. With hindsight, we can see the shortcomings of the democracies' policies. We must remember, however, that these policies were the product of long and careful deliberation. At the time, people strongly believed they would work.

Japan on the Move One of the earliest tests had been posed by Japan. Japanese military leaders and ultranationalists thought that Japan should have an empire equal to those of the western powers. In pursuit of this goal, Japan seized Manchuria in 1931. When the League of Nations condemned the aggression, Japan withdrew from the organization.

Japan's easy success strengthened the militarists. In 1937, Japanese armies overran much of eastern China. Once again, western protests had no effect on the conqueror.

Italy Invades Ethiopia In Italy, Mussolini used his new, modern military to pursue his own imperialist ambitions. He looked first to Ethiopia, in northeastern Africa. Italy's defeat by the Ethiopians at the battle of Adowa in 1896 still rankled.

In 1935, Italy invaded Ethiopia. Although the Ethiopians resisted bravely, their outdated weapons were no match for Mussolini's tanks, machine guns, poison gas, and airplanes. The Ethiopian king Haile Selassie (HĪ lee suh LAS ee) appealed to the League of Nations for help. The League voted sanctions, or penalties, against Italy for having violated international law. But the League had no power to enforce the sanctions, and by early 1936, Italy had conquered Ethiopia.

Hitler's Challenge By then, Hitler, too, had tested the will of the western democracies and found it weak. First, he built up the German military in defiance of the Versailles treaty. Then, in 1936, he sent troops into the "demilitarized" Rhineland bordering France—another treaty violation.

Germans hated the Versailles treaty, and Hitler's successful challenge won him greater popularity at home. Western democracies denounced his moves but took no real action. Instead, they adopted a policy of appeasement, giving in to the demands of an aggressor to keep the peace.

Appeasement and Neutrality The western policy of appeasement developed for a number of reasons. France was demoralized, suffering from political divisions at home. It could not move against Hitler without British support.

The British, however, had no desire to confront the German dictator. Some even thought that Hitler's actions constituted a justifiable response to the terms of the Versailles treaty, which they believed had been too harsh against Germany.

In both Britain and France, many saw Hitler and fascism as a defense against a worse evil—the spread of Soviet communism. Additionally, the Great Depression sapped the energies of the western democracies. Finally, widespread pacifism, or opposition to all war, and disgust with the destruction during the previous war pushed many governments to seek peace at any price.

As war clouds gathered in Europe in the mid-1930s, the United States Congress passed a series of Neutrality Acts. One law forbade the sale of arms to any nation at war. Others outlawed loans to warring nations and prohibited Americans from traveling on ships of warring powers. The fundamental goal of American policy, however, was to avoid involvement in a European war, not to prevent such a conflict.

Rome-Berlin-Tokyo Axis In the face of the democracies' apparent weakness, Germany, Italy, and Japan formed what became known as the Rome-Berlin-Tokyo Axis. The Axis powers agreed to fight Soviet communism. They also agreed not to interfere with one another's plans for expansion. The agreement cleared the way for these anti-democratic, aggressor powers to take even bolder steps.

Axis Leaders
Benito Mussolini (left) and Adolf Hitler (right) were two of the leaders in the Rome-Berlin-Tokyo Axis. Here, they view a parade staged in Mussolini's honor during his 1937 visit to Germany.

Theme: Political and Social Systems What did the Axis powers agree to do?

The Spanish Civil War

In 1936, Spain plunged into civil war. Although the Spanish Civil War was a local struggle, it soon drew other European powers into the fighting.

From Monarchy to Republic In the 1920s, Spain was a monarchy dominated by a landowning upper class, the Catholic Church, and the military. Most Spaniards were poor peasants or urban workers. In 1931, popular unrest against the old order forced the king to leave Spain. A republic was set up with a new, more liberal constitution.

The republican government passed a series of controversial reforms. It took over some Church lands and ended Church control of education. It redistributed some land to peasants, gave women the vote, and ended some privileges of the old ruling class. Spanish public opinion was divided. Leftists demanded more radical reforms. Conservatives, who were backed by the military, rejected change. Although most Spaniards wanted a peaceful democracy, clashes between leftists and rightists created chaos.

Nationalists Versus Loyalists   In 1936, a conservative general named Francisco Franco led a revolt that touched off a bloody civil war. Fascists and supporters of right-wing policies rallied to the banner of Franco's forces, called Nationalists. Supporters of the republic, known as Loyalists, included communists, socialists, and supporters of democracy.

Hitler and Mussolini sent arms and forces to help Franco. Close to 37,000 volunteers from Germany, Italy, the Soviet Union, and the western democracies joined the International Brigades and fought alongside the Loyalists against fascism. The governments of Britain, France, and the United States, however, remained neutral.

A Dress Rehearsal   Both sides committed horrible atrocities. The ruinous struggle took almost one million lives. One of the worst horrors was a German air raid on Guernica, a small Spanish market town that lacked any military value. One April morning in 1937, German bombers streaked over the market square. They dropped their load of bombs and then swooped low to machine-gun anyone in the streets who had survived the first attack. An estimated 1,600 innocent people were killed.

To Nazi leaders, the attack on Guernica was an "experiment" to identify what their new planes could do. To the world, it was a grim warning of the destructive power of modern warfare.

By 1939, Franco had triumphed. Once in power, he created a fascist dictatorship like those of Hitler and Mussolini. He rolled back earlier reforms, killed or jailed enemies, and used terror to promote order.

German Aggression Continues

In the meantime, Hitler pursued his goal of bringing all German-speaking people into the Third Reich. He also took steps to gain "living space" for Germans in Eastern Europe. Hitler, who believed in the superiority of the German, or "Aryan race," thought that Germany had a right to conquer the inferior Slavs to the east. "Nature is cruel," he claimed, "so we may be cruel, too. . . . I have a right to remove millions of an inferior race that breeds like vermin."

Austria Annexed   From the beginning, Nazi propaganda had found fertile ground in Austria. By 1938, Hitler was ready to engineer the Anschluss, or union of Austria and Germany. Early that year, he forced the Austrian chancellor to appoint Nazis to key cabinet posts. When the Austrian leader balked at other demands, Hitler sent in the German army "to preserve order." To indicate his new role as ruler of Austria, Hitler made a speech from the Hofburg Palace, the former residence of the Hapsburg emperors.

The Anschluss violated the Versailles treaty and created a brief war scare. But Hitler quickly silenced any Austrians who opposed him. And since the western democracies took no action, Hitler easily had his way.

The Czech Crisis   Germany's next victim was Czechoslovakia. At first, Hitler insisted that the three million Germans in the Sudetenland—a region of western Czechoslovakia—be given autonomy. The demand set off new alarms among the democracies.

Czechoslovakia was one of only two remaining democracies in Eastern Europe. (Finland was the other.) Still, Britain and France were not willing to go to war to save it. As British and French leaders searched for a peaceful solution, Hitler increased his demands. The Sudetenland, he said, must be annexed to Germany.

At the Munich Conference in September 1938, British and French leaders again chose appeasement. They caved in to Hitler's demands and then persuaded the Czechs to surrender the Sudetenland without a fight. In exchange, Hitler assured Britain and France that he had no further plans to expand his territory.

Aggression in Europe to 1939

Legend:
- Under German control September 1, 1939
- Under Italian control September 1, 1939
- Maginot Line
- German concentration camps, 1939

Azimuthal Equal Area Projection

0 — 250 — 500 Miles
0 — 250 — 500 Kilometers

Map labels: NORWAY, SWEDEN, ESTONIA, LATVIA, LITHUANIA, Danzig, POLISH CORRIDOR, USSR, IRELAND, North Sea, DENMARK, Baltic Sea, GREAT BRITAIN, NETH., Sachsenhausen, GERMANY, Buchenwald, POLAND, BELG., RHINELAND March 1936, LUX., CZECHOSLOVAKIA March 1939, SUDETENLAND September 1938, Mauthausen, Dachau, FRANCE, SWITZ., AUSTRIA March 1938, HUNGARY, ROMANIA, ATLANTIC OCEAN, PORTUGAL, SPAIN, CORSICA, ITALY, YUGOSLAVIA, BULGARIA, Black Sea, SARDINIA, ALBANIA April 1939, GREECE, TURKEY, Mediterranean Sea, SICILY

"Peace for Our Time" Returning from Munich, British prime minister Neville Chamberlain told cheering crowds that he had achieved "peace for our time." To Parliament, he declared that the Munich Pact had "saved Czechoslovakia from destruction and Europe from Armageddon." French leader Edouard Daladier had a different reaction to the joyous crowds that greeted him in Paris. "The fools, why are they cheering?" he asked.

The Czech crisis revealed the Nazi menace. British politician Winston Churchill, who had long warned of the Nazi threat, judged the diplomats harshly: "They had to choose between war and dishonor. They chose dishonor; they will have war."

Europe Plunges Toward War

Just as Churchill predicted, Munich did not bring peace. Instead, Europe plunged rapidly toward war. In March 1939, Hitler gobbled up the rest of Czechoslovakia. The democracies finally accepted the fact that appeasement had failed. At last thoroughly alarmed, they promised to protect Poland, most likely the next target of Hitler's expansion.

Nazi-Soviet Pact In August 1939, Hitler stunned the world by announcing a nonaggression pact with his great enemy—Joseph Stalin, the Soviet dictator. Publicly, the Nazi-Soviet Pact bound Hitler and Stalin to peaceful relations. Secretly, the two agreed (1) not to fight if the other went to war and (2) to divide up Poland and other parts of Eastern Europe.

The pact was based not on friendship or respect but on mutual need. Hitler feared communism as Stalin feared fascism. But Hitler wanted a free hand in Poland. Also, he did not want to fight a war with the western democracies and the Soviet Union at the same time.

Skills Assessment

Geography Between 1936 and 1939, Germany and Italy repeatedly threatened the peace in Europe.

1. **Location** On the map, locate **(a)** Germany, **(b)** Italy, **(c)** Sudetenland, **(d)** Rhineland, **(e)** Albania, **(f)** Dachau.
2. **Region** Locate the region called the Polish Corridor. Why is that an appropriate name for the region?
3. **Critical Thinking Applying Information** **(a)** What example of Italian aggression is not on the map? **(b)** How could the map be changed to show that aggression?

For his part, Stalin had sought allies among the western democracies against the Nazi menace. Mutual suspicions, however, kept them apart. By joining with Hitler, Stalin bought time to build up Soviet defenses. He also saw a chance for important territorial gains.

Invasion of Poland On September 1, 1939, a week after the Nazi-Soviet Pact, German forces invaded Poland. Two days later, Britain and France honored their commitment to Poland and declared war on Germany. World War II had begun. One British poet caught the overwhelming mood of gloom in these lines:

"In the nightmare of the dark
  All the dogs of Europe bark,
  And the living nations wait,
  Each sequestered in its hate."
    —W. H. Auden, "In Memory of W. B. Yeats"

Why War Came

Many factors contributed to the outbreak of World War II. You have learned some of the reasons behind Axis aggression. You have also seen why western democracies adopted a policy of appeasement. Today, historians often see the war as an effort to revise the 1919 peace settlement. The Versailles treaty had divided much of the world into two camps—those who were satisfied with its terms and those who were not. Germany, Italy, Japan, and the Soviet Union all felt betrayed or excluded by the settlement.

Since 1939, people have debated issues such as why the western democracies failed to respond forcefully to the Nazi threat, and whether they could have stopped Hitler if they had responded. Dreading war, the democracies hoped that diplomacy and compromise would right old wrongs and prevent further aggression. They were distracted by their own political and economic problems and misread Hitler's intentions. Most disregarded even Hitler's declared goals in *Mein Kampf.*

Some historians assert that Britain and France could have stopped Hitler in 1936 by aiding Loyalist Spain before Germany was fully rearmed. But neither country was willing to risk war. The devastation of World War I, combined with awareness of the destructive power of modern technology, made the idea of more fighting unbearable. Unfortunately, when war came, it proved to be even more horrendous than anyone had imagined.

SECTION 1 Assessment

Recall
1. **Identify:** **(a)** Haile Selassie, **(b)** Rome-Berlin-Tokyo Axis, **(c)** Guernica, **(d)** Munich Conference, **(e)** Neville Chamberlain, **(f)** Nazi-Soviet Pact.
2. **Define:** **(a)** sanction, **(b)** appeasement, **(c)** pacifism, **(d)** Anschluss.

Comprehension
3. **(a)** How did Japan, Italy, and Germany test the resolve of western democracies before 1937? **(b)** Explain how other countries participated in the Spanish Civil War.

4. Identify major acts of German aggression in 1938 and 1939.
5. How did appeasement lead to the outbreak of war?

Critical Thinking and Writing
6. **Recognizing Causes and Effects** How was the Munich Conference a turning point in the road toward world war?
7. **Analyzing Information** Why do you think some historians call the period between 1919 and 1939 the 20-year armistice?

Activity
Take It to the NET

Use the Internet to find out more about the Munich Conference of 1938. Write a letter to the editor describing your opinion of Prime Minister Chamberlain's actions at the conference.

SECTION 2 | The Global Conflict: Axis Advances

Reading Focus

- What early gains allowed the Axis powers to control much of Europe?
- What were the Battle of Britain and Operation Barbarossa?
- How did Japan respond to growing American involvement?

Vocabulary

blitzkrieg
radar
sonar

Taking Notes

As you read this section, make a time line on a separate sheet of paper. Record key events in the global conflict from 1939 to 1942. The sample on this page will help you get started.

1939	1940	1941	1942
Germany invades Poland			

Main Idea The early years of World War II were marked by Axis victories.

Setting the Scene

"Hitler will collapse the day we declare war on Germany," predicted a confident French general on the eve of World War II. He could not have been more wrong. World War II, the costliest war in history, lasted six years—from 1939 to 1945. It pitted the Axis powers, chiefly Germany, Italy, and Japan, against the Allied powers, which eventually included Britain, France, the Soviet Union, China, the United States, and 45 other nations.

Early Axis Gains

On September 1, 1939, Nazi forces stormed into Poland, revealing the enormous power of Hitler's blitzkrieg, or "lightning war." First, German planes bombed airfields, factories, towns, and cities, and screaming dive bombers fired on troops and civilians. Then, fast-moving tanks and troop transports roared into the country. The Polish army fought back unsuccessfully.

While Germany attacked from the west, Stalin's forces invaded from the east, grabbing lands promised to them under the Nazi-Soviet Pact. Within a month, Poland ceased to exist.

Hitler passed the winter without much further action. Stalin's armies, however, pushed on into the Baltic states of Estonia, Latvia, and Lithuania. Soviet forces also seized part of Finland, which put up stiff but unsuccessful resistance.

The "Phony War" During that first winter, the French hunkered down behind the Maginot Line. Britain sent troops to wait with them. Some reporters referred to this quiet time as the "phony war."

Then, in April 1940, the war exploded into action. Hitler launched a blitzkrieg against Norway and Denmark, both of which soon fell. Next, his forces slammed into the Netherlands and Belgium.

Miracle of Dunkirk By May, German forces were pouring into France. Retreating British forces were soon trapped between the advancing Nazis and the waters of the

Invasion of Poland
World War II was the first war to use airplanes in large-scale attacks. Here, German Stuka dive bombers fly over Poland.

Theme: Economics and Technology How would airplanes be used in wartime?

Faced with this defiance, Hitler ordered his generals to make plans for Operation Sea Lion—the invasion of Britain. In preparation for the invasion, he launched massive air strikes against the island nation.

The London Blitz Beginning on August 12, 1940, German bombers began a daily bombardment of England's southern coast. For a month, the British Royal Air Force valiantly battled the German Luftwaffe. Then, the Germans changed their tactics, turning their attention from military targets in the south to the blitz, or bombing, of London and other cities.

German bombers first appeared over London late on September 7. All through the night, relays of aircraft showered high explosives and firebombs on the sprawling capital. The bombing continued for 57 nights. Much of the city was destroyed, and some 15,000 people lost their lives.

London did not break under the blitz. Defiantly, Parliament continued to meet. Citizens carried on their daily lives, seeking protection in shelters and then emerging when the all-clear sounded to resume their routines. Even the British king and queen chose to support Londoners by joining them in bomb shelters rather than fleeing to the countryside.

Failure of the Blitz German planes continued to bomb London and other cities off and on until June 1941. But contrary to Hitler's hopes, British morale was not destroyed. In fact, the bombing only made the British more determined to turn back the enemy.

Operation Sea Lion was a failure. Hitler turned to a new target—the Soviet Union. The decision to invade Russia helped save Britain. It also proved to be one of Hitler's costliest mistakes.

Operation Barbarossa

In June 1941, Hitler embarked on Operation Barbarossa—the conquest of the Soviet Union.* Hitler made his motives clear. "If I had the Ural Mountains with their incalculable store of treasures in raw materials," he declared, "Siberia with its vast forests, and the Ukraine with its tremendous wheat fields, Germany under National Socialist leadership would swim in plenty." He also wanted to crush communism in Europe and defeat his powerful rival Joseph Stalin.

The German Advance In Operation Barbarossa, Hitler unleashed a new blitzkrieg. About three million Germans poured into the Soviet Union. They caught Stalin unprepared, his army still suffering from the purges that had wiped out many of its top officers.

The Russians lost two and a half million soldiers trying to fend off the invaders. As they were forced back, Russian troops destroyed factories and farm equipment and burned crops to keep them out of enemy hands. But they could not stop the German war machine. By autumn, the Nazis had smashed deep into Russia and were poised to take Moscow and Leningrad.

There, however, the German advance stalled. Like Napoleon's Grand Army in 1812, Hitler's forces were not prepared for the fury of Russia's "General Winter." By early December, temperatures plunged to –4 degrees. Thousands of German soldiers froze to death.

Siege of Leningrad The Russians, meanwhile, suffered appalling hardships. In September 1941, the two-and-a-half-year siege of Leningrad began. Food was soon rationed to two pieces of bread a day. Desperate Leningraders ate almost anything. They boiled wallpaper scraped off walls because its paste was said to contain potato flour. Owners of leather briefcases boiled and ate them—"jellied meat," they called it.

---

*The plan took its name from the Holy Roman emperor Frederick Barbarossa, a medieval Germanic leader who had won great victories in the East.

Although more than a million Leningraders died during the German siege, the survivors struggled to defend their city. Hoping to gain some relief for the exhausted Russians, Stalin urged Britain to open a second front in Western Europe. Although Churchill could not offer much real help, the two powers did agree to work together.

American Involvement Grows

When the war began in 1939, the United States declared its neutrality. Although isolationist feeling remained strong, many Americans sympathized with those who battled the Axis powers. Later, President Roosevelt found ways around the Neutrality Acts to provide aid, including warships, to Britain as it stood alone against Hitler.

The Arsenal of Democracy In early 1941, FDR persuaded Congress to pass the Lend-Lease Act. It allowed him to sell or lend war materials to "any country whose defense the President deems vital to the defense of the United States." The United States, said Roosevelt, would not be drawn into the war, but it would become "the arsenal of democracy," supplying arms to those who were fighting for freedom.

Atlantic Charter In August 1941, Roosevelt and Churchill met secretly on a warship in the Atlantic. The two leaders issued the Atlantic Charter, which set goals for the war—"the final destruction of the Nazi tyranny"— and for the postwar world. They pledged to support "the right of all peoples to choose the form of government under which they will live" and called for a "permanent system of general security."

Japan Attacks

In December 1941, the Allies gained a vital boost when a surprise action by Japan suddenly pitched the United States into the war. From the late 1930s, Japan had been trying to conquer China. Although Japan occupied much of eastern China, the Chinese would not surrender. When war broke out in Europe in 1939, the Japanese saw a chance to grab European possessions in Southeast Asia. The rich resources of the region, including oil, rubber, and tin, would be of immense value in fighting the Chinese war.

Growing Tensions In 1940, Japan advanced into French Indochina and the Dutch East Indies (present-day Indonesia). To stop Japanese aggression, the United States banned the sale to Japan of war materials, such as iron, steel, and oil for airplanes. This move angered the Japanese.

Japan and the United States held talks to ease the growing tension. But extreme militarists such as General Tojo Hideki were gaining power in Japan. They hoped to seize lands in Asia and the Pacific, and the United States was interfering with their plans.

Attack on Pearl Harbor With talks at a standstill, General Tojo ordered a surprise attack on the American fleet at Pearl Harbor, Hawaii. Early on December 7, 1941, Japanese airplanes damaged or destroyed 19 ships, smashed American planes on the ground, and killed more than 2,400 people.

The Eastern Front
In 1941, the German army attacked the Soviet Union. Here, Soviet soldiers crawl through the snow as they try to halt the German advance.

Theme: Geography and History Why was Russia's winter so devastating to the German army?

 Primary Sources and Literature

See "Franklin D. Roosevelt: The Four Freedoms" in the Reference Section at the back of this book.

Virtual Field Trip

www.phschool.com

**USS *Arizona* Memorial
Honolulu, Hawaii**

To learn more about the attack on Pearl Harbor, use the Internet address above to link to the USS *Arizona* Memorial Web site.

Pearl Harbor
On December 7, 1941, Japan attacked the United States naval base at Pearl Harbor, Hawaii. Here, the *Arizona* sinks after being destroyed by Japanese planes.

Theme: Global Interaction
Why did the Japanese attack Pearl Harbor, and how did the United States respond?

The next day, a grim-faced President Roosevelt told the nation that December 7 was "a date which will live in infamy." He asked Congress to declare war on Japan. On December 11, Germany and Italy, as Japan's allies, declared war on the United States.

Japanese Victories   In the long run, the Japanese attack on Pearl Harbor would be as serious a mistake as Hitler's invasion of Russia. But the months after Pearl Harbor gave no such hint. Instead, European and American possessions in the Pacific fell one by one to the Japanese. They captured the Philippines and seized other American islands across the Pacific. They overran the British colonies of Hong Kong, Burma, and Malaya, pushed deeper into the Dutch East Indies, and completed the takeover of French Indochina.

By the beginning of 1942, the Japanese empire stretched from Southeast Asia to the western Pacific Ocean. The Axis powers had reached the high point of their successes.

SECTION 2 Assessment

Recall
1. **Identify: (a)** "phony war," **(b)** Dunkirk, **(c)** Winston Churchill, **(d)** Battle of Britain, **(e)** Operation Barbarossa, **(f)** Lend-Lease Act, **(g)** Pearl Harbor.
2. **Define: (a)** blitzkrieg, **(b)** radar, **(c)** sonar.

Comprehension
3. How did the Axis powers achieve victories in 1939 and 1940?
4. How did Operation Barbarossa affect the Battle of Britain?

5. **(a)** What goals did Japan pursue in Asia? **(b)** Why did General Tojo order a surprise attack on the United States?

Critical Thinking and Writing
6. **Identifying Alternatives** Could the United States have stayed out of the war?
7. **Recognizing Causes and Effects (a)** Describe three technological advances during World War II. **(b)** How did this technology make war more destructive?

Activity

Take It to the NET

Use the Internet to learn more about the attack on Pearl Harbor in 1941. Prepare a radio broadcast giving a first-hand account of the attack and its toll on American ships.

Reading Focus

- How did Germany and Japan treat people in occupied lands?
- How did the Allies turn the tide of war?
- How did the Red Army and the Allied invasion of France undo German plans?

Vocabulary

genocide

collaborator

reparations

Taking Notes

As you read this section, make an outline of its contents. Use Roman numerals for major headings. Use capital letters for subheadings, and use numbers for supporting details. The example at right will help you get started.

I. Occupied lands
  A. Nazi Europe
    1. Slavs considered inferior
    2. Plundered occupied lands
  B. Nazi genocide
  C.

Main Idea In 1942 and 1943, the tide of the war began to turn as Allied forces won key victories.

Setting the Scene World War II was fought on a larger scale and in more places than any other conflict in history. It was also more costly in terms of human life than any previous war. Civilians, as well as soldiers, were targets. In 1941, a reporter visited a Russian town that had been home to 10,000 people before the German invasion. The reporter found a lone survivor: "[She was] a blind old woman who had gone insane. I saw her wandering barefooted around the village, carrying a few dirty rags, a rusty pail, and a tattered sheepskin."

From 1939 until mid-1942, the Axis ran up a string of successes. The conquerors blasted villages and towns and divided up the spoils. Then the Allies won some key victories. Slowly, the tide began to turn.

Occupied Lands

While the Germans rampaged across Europe, the Japanese conquered an empire in Asia and the Pacific. Each set out to build a "new order" in the occupied lands.

Nazi Europe Hitler's new order grew out of his racial obsessions. He set up puppet governments in Western European countries that were peopled by "Aryans" or related "races." The Slavs of Eastern Europe were considered to be an inferior "race." They were shoved aside to provide more "living space" for Germans, whom Hitler considered the ideal "race."

To the Nazis, occupied lands were an economic resource to be plundered and looted. The Nazis systematically stripped conquered nations of their works of art, factories, and other resources. They sent thousands of Slavs and others to work as slave laborers in German war industries. As resistance movements emerged to fight German tyranny, the Nazis took savage revenge, shooting hostages and torturing prisoners.

Nazi Genocide The most savage of Hitler's policies was his program to kill all people he judged "racially inferior," particularly Jews. Other targets included Slavs, Gypsies, and the mentally ill. At first, the Nazis forced Jews in Poland and other countries to live in ghettos and concentration camps. By 1941, however, German leaders had devised plans for the "final solution of the Jewish problem"—the genocide, or deliberate murder, of all European Jews.

To accomplish this goal, Hitler had special "death camps" built in Poland, at places like Auschwitz, Sobibor, and Treblinka. The Nazis

Working on a Deadly Railroad

In Southeast Asia, the Japanese captured tens of thousands of Allied prisoners of war (POWs) and turned them into a slave labor force. Nearly half of the POWs were forced to build a 250-mile rail line linking Siam (Thailand) and Burma (Myanmar). Engineers said the line would take from 2 to 5 years to build. Japanese generals ordered it completed in 18 months.

Geography made the task seem impossible. Not only were there mountains and ravines to cross but also winding rivers to be bridged again and again and a tropical jungle to be braved. Wild animals, deadly snakes, and tropical diseases threatened survival everywhere. Equipped only with pickaxes and shovels, the POWs completed the railway at the cost of thousands of lives.

Theme: Geography and History How did geography contribute to the high death toll in building the Burma-Siam Railway?

shipped Jews from all over occupied Europe to the camps. There, Nazi engineers designed the most efficient means of killing millions of men, women, and children.

As Jews reached the camps, they were stripped of their clothes and valuables. Their heads were shaved. Guards separated men from women and children from their parents. The young, old, and sick were targeted for immediate killing. Within a few days, they were herded into "shower rooms" and gassed. The Nazis worked others to death or used them for perverse "medical" experiments. By 1945, the Nazis had massacred some six million Jews in what became known as the Holocaust. Almost as many other "undesirable" people were killed as well.

Jews resisted the Nazis even though they knew their efforts could not succeed. In October 1944, for example, a group of Jews in the Auschwitz death camp destroyed one of the gas chambers. The rebels were all killed. One woman, Rosa Robota, was tortured for days before she was hanged. "Be strong and have courage," she called out to the camp inmates who were forced by the Nazis to watch her execution.

In some cases, friends, neighbors, or strangers protected Jews. Sugihara Chiune, a Japanese diplomat in Lithuania, saved some 6,000 Jews by writing exit visas until he was ordered home by the Japanese government. Italian peasants hid Jews in their villages, and the nations of Denmark and Bulgaria saved almost all their Jewish populations. Most often, however, people pretended not to notice what was happening. Some were collaborators, helping the Nazis hunt down the Jews or, like the Vichy government in France, shipping tens of thousands of Jews to their death.

The scale and savagery of the Holocaust are unequaled in history. The Nazis deliberately set out to destroy the Jews for no reason other than their religious and ethnic heritage. Today, the record of that slaughter is a vivid reminder of the monstrous results of racism and intolerance.

The Co-Prosperity Sphere As Japan expanded across Asia and the Pacific, it donned the mantle of anti-imperialism. Under the slogan "Asia for Asians," it created the Greater East Asia Co-Prosperity Sphere. Japan's self-proclaimed mission was to help Asians escape western colonial rule. In fact, its real goal was a Japanese empire in Asia.

The Japanese treated the Chinese, Filipinos, Malaysians, and other conquered people with great brutality, killing and torturing civilians throughout East and Southeast Asia. People were shot simply for listening to Allied radio broadcasts. The Japanese seized food crops, destroyed cities and towns, and made local people into slave laborers. Whatever welcome the Japanese had at first met as "liberators" was soon turned to hatred. In the Philippines, Indochina, and elsewhere, nationalist groups waged guerrilla warfare against the Japanese invaders.

The Allied War Effort

After the United States entered the war, the Allied leaders met periodically to hammer out their strategy. In 1942, the Big Three—Roosevelt, Churchill, and Stalin—agreed to finish the war in Europe before turning their attention to Asia.

From the outset, the Allies distrusted one another. Churchill thought Stalin wanted to dominate Europe. Roosevelt felt that Churchill had ambitions to expand British imperial power. Stalin believed that the western powers wanted to destroy communism. At meetings and in writing, Stalin urged Roosevelt and Churchill to relieve the pressure on Russia by opening a second front in Western Europe. Not until 1944, however, did Britain and the United States make such a move. The British and Americans argued that they did not have the resources before then. Stalin saw the delay as a deliberate policy to weaken the Soviet Union.

The Holocaust

As the Allied armies entered territories occupied by Germany, they came upon the concentration camps. The soldiers were horrified by what they saw. General Dwight Eisenhower of the United States insisted on having the camps photographed so others could see the conditions.

After camp inmates were killed, huge ovens like this one were used to cremate their bodies. Between 9 and 12 million people–including about 6 million Jews–died in concentration camps from 1939 to 1945.

These skeletal men were prisoners at Buchenwald camp in Germany. Inmates who escaped execution were used for forced labor. They suffered torture, starvation, and disease.

Children were among the millions of people shipped to the concentration camps. Most suffered the same ghastly fate as their parents.

Skills Tip

Remember that photographs depict real scenes and were also taken for a particular purpose. Knowing this purpose can help you make sense of the photographs.

Skills Assessment

1. Based on the photographs, it can be assumed that
   A families were kept together.
   B conditions were the same in every camp.
   C conditions improved as the war continued.
   D the Nazis cared little about the well-being of their prisoners.

2. The photographs help historians to
   E explain Hitler's motives.
   F document conditions in concentration camps.
   G understand why the Nazis hated Jews.
   H identify the causes of World War II.

3. **Critical Thinking** **Making Inferences** (a) Based on the photographs, what do you think the Nazis thought about the camp inmates? (b) What does the ultimate purpose of the camps seem to have been?

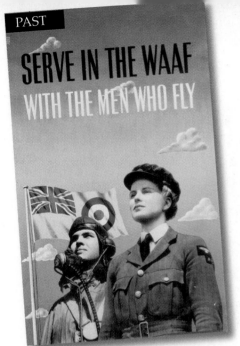

Women in Wartime
Women's military roles have changed dramatically. Although the British and American armies did not allow women to serve in combat positions during World War II, women did serve in auxiliaries such as the Women's Auxiliary Air Force, or WAAF (PAST). Today, women's roles are more active. During Operation Desert Storm in 1991 (PRESENT), women served as soldiers.

Theme: Continuity and Change What reasons might the military have for allowing women to serve as soldiers?

Total War Like the Axis powers, the Allies were committed to total war. Democratic governments in the United States and Britain increased their political power. They directed economic resources into the war effort, ordering factories to stop making cars or refrigerators and to turn out airplanes or tanks instead. Governments rationed consumer goods, from shoes to sugar, and regulated prices and wages. On the positive side, while the war brought shortages and hardships, it ended the unemployment of the depression era.

Under pressure of war, even democratic governments limited the rights of citizens, censored the press, and used propaganda to win public support for the war. In the United States and Canada, many citizens of Japanese descent lost their jobs, property, and civil rights. Japanese Americans and Japanese Canadians even lost their freedom and were forced into internment camps after governments decided that they were a security risk. The British took similar action against German refugees. Some 40 years later, both the United States and Canada apologized for the wartime policy and provided former internees with reparations, or payment for damages caused by the imprisonment.

Women Help Win the War As men joined the military and war industries expanded, millions of women around the world replaced them in essential jobs. Women built ships and planes, produced munitions, and staffed offices. A popular British song recognized women's contributions:

> "She's the girl that makes the thing that drills the hole
> that holds the spring
> That drives the rod that turns the knob that works the
> thingumebob. . . .
> And it's the girl that makes the thing that holds the
> oil that oils the ring
> That works the thingumebob
> THAT'S GOING TO WIN THE WAR!"
> —from *The People's War: Britain, 1939–1945* (Calder)

British and American women served in the armed forces in many auxiliary roles—driving trucks and ambulances, delivering airplanes, decoding messages, and assisting at antiaircraft sites. In occupied Europe, women fought in the resistance. Marie Fourcade, a French woman, directed 3,000 people in the underground and helped downed Allied pilots escape to safety. Many Soviet women played combat roles. Soviet pilot Lily Litvak, for example, shot down 12 German planes before she herself was killed.

Turning Points

During 1942 and 1943, the Allies won several victories that would turn the tide of battle and push back the Axis powers. The first of these turning points came in North Africa and Italy.

El Alamein In Egypt, the British under General Bernard Montgomery finally stopped Rommel's advance during the long, fierce Battle of El Alamein. They then turned the tables on the Desert Fox, driving the Axis forces back across Libya into Tunisia.

Later in 1942, American general Dwight Eisenhower took command of a joint Anglo-American force in Morocco and Algeria. Advancing on Tunisia from the west, he combined with the British forces to trap Rommel's army, which surrendered in May 1943.

World War II in Europe and North Africa

Legend:
- European Axis Powers, 1942
- Maximum extent of Axis control, 1942
- Neutral nations, 1942
- Allied territory, 1942
- → Allied advances
- ■ Concentration camps, 1939–1945

Azimuthal Equal Area Projection

0   300   600 Miles
0   300   600 Kilometers

Invasion of Italy Victory in North Africa let the Allies leap across the Mediterranean into Italy. In July 1943, a combined British and American army landed first in Sicily and then in southern Italy. They defeated the Italian forces there in about a month.

Italians, fed up with Mussolini, overthrew Il Duce. The new Italian government signed an armistice, but the fighting did not end. Hitler sent German troops to rescue Mussolini and stiffen the will of Italians fighting in the north. For the next 18 months, the Allies pushed slowly up the Italian peninsula, suffering heavy losses against stiff German resistance. Still, the Italian invasion was a decisive event for the Allies because it weakened Hitler by forcing him to fight on another front.

The Red Army Resists

Another major turning point in the war occurred in the Soviet Union. After their triumphant advance in 1941, the Germans were stalled outside Moscow and Leningrad. In 1942, Hitler launched a new offensive. This

Skills Assessment

Geography Axis power reached its height in Europe in 1942. Then, the tide began to turn.

1. **Location** On the map, locate **(a)** Vichy France, **(b)** Soviet Union, **(c)** El Alamein, **(d)** Berlin, **(e)** Normandy, **(f)** Anzio.
2. **Movement** Describe the extent of the Axis advance to the east by 1942.
3. **Critical Thinking** **Analyzing Information** How did geography help or hinder Allied advances?

only as far as the city of Stalingrad.

Stalingrad The Battle of Stalingrad was one of the costliest of the war.
Hitler was determined to capture Stalin's namesake city. Stalin was equally
determined to defend it. The battle began when the Germans surrounded
the city. The Russians then encircled their attackers. As winter closed in, a
bitter street-by-street, house-by-house struggle raged. Soldiers fought for
two weeks for a single building, wrote a German officer. Corpses "are
strewn in the cellars, on the landings and the staircases," he said. Trapped,
without food or ammunition and with no hope of rescue, the German commander finally surrendered in early 1943. The battle cost the Germans
approximately 300,000 killed, wounded, or captured soldiers.

Counterattack After the Battle of Stalingrad, the Red Army took the offensive and drove the invaders out of the Soviet Union entirely. Hitler's forces
suffered irreplaceable losses of both troops and equipment. By early 1944,
Soviet troops were advancing into Eastern Europe.

Invasion of France

By 1944, the Allies were at last ready to open a second front in Europe—
with the invasion of France. Eisenhower was made the supreme Allied
commander. He and other Allied leaders faced the enormous task of planning the operation and assembling troops and supplies. To prepare the way
for the invasion, Allied bombers flew constant missions over Germany.
They targeted factories and destroyed aircraft that might be used against
the invasion force. They also bombed a number of German cities.

The Allies chose June 6, 1944—D-Day, they called it—for the invasion
of France. After midnight, Allied planes dropped paratroopers behind
enemy lines. Then, at dawn, thousands of ships ferried 176,000 Allied
troops across the English Channel. From landing craft, the troops fought
their way to shore amid underwater mines and raking machine-gun fire.
They clawed their way inland through the tangled hedges of Normandy.
Finally, they broke through German defenses and advanced toward Paris.
Meanwhile, other Allied forces sailed from Italy to land in southern France.

In Paris, French resistance forces rose up against the occupying
Germans. Under pressure from all sides, the Germans retreated. On August
25, the Allies entered Paris. Within a month, all of France was free.
Attention focused on conquering Germany itself—and defeating Japan.

Primary Source

A Sea of Ships
*As dawn broke on June 6, 1944, a
German artillery officer in Normandy looked out across the
English Channel and made an anxious phone call to Major Block at
divisional headquarters:*

"'There must be 10,000 ships out
there,' I told him. 'It's unbelievable,
fantastic. . . .' Block said, 'Look,
Pluskat, are you really sure? The
Americans and the British together
don't have that many ships.' I just
said, 'Come and look for yourself.'. . .

We watched absolutely petrified, as the armada steadily and
relentlessly approached. . . . [T]hen
the bombardment from the sea
began. The shells screamed like a
thousand express trains. . . . I was
thrown to the ground . . . completely
dazed and unable to speak."

—Werner Pluskat, quoted in
*Nothing Less
Than Victory* (Miller)

Skills Assessment

Primary Source Why were
the German soldiers "absolutely
petrified" as the armada
approached?

SECTION 3 Assessment

Recall
1. **Identify:** **(a)** Holocaust, **(b)**
   Greater East Asia Co-Prosperity
   Sphere, **(c)** Battle of El Alamein,
   (d) Battle of Stalingrad, **(e)** D-Day.
2. **Define:** **(a)** genocide,
   (b) collaborator, **(c)** reparations.

Comprehension
3. **(a)** How did Hitler try to achieve a
   "new order" in Europe? **(b)** How
   did the Japanese treat conquered
   people?
4. How did democratic governments
   mobilize their economies for war?

5. Explain how each of the following
   battles was a turning point in the
   war: **(a)** El Alamein, **(b)** Stalingrad.

Critical Thinking and Writing
6. **Defending a Position** Do you
   think that democratic governments
   should be allowed to limit their
   citizens' freedoms during
   wartime? Defend your position.
7. **Applying Information** Hitler
   translated his hatred of Jews and
   others into a program of genocide. How do ethnic, racial, and
   religious hatreds weaken society?

Activity

Creating a Memorial
Design a memorial com-
memorating the millions
who died in the
Holocaust. Include a brief
description of any sym-
bols you will use in your
memorial.

Toward Victory

Reading Focus

- How was the Pacific war fought?
- How did the Allies defeat Nazi Germany?
- What debates surrounded the defeat of Japan?

Vocabulary

island-hopping
kamikaze

Taking Notes

On a separate sheet of paper, copy the cause-and-effect chart shown here. As you read the section, complete the chart with information about how the Allies won in the Pacific and in Europe.

Europe	Pacific
•	• Island-hopping
	•

ALLIES WIN WORLD WAR II

Main Idea Continued Allied successes led to victory over Germany and Japan in 1945.

Setting the Scene

General Douglas MacArthur stood at the dock on Corregidor in March 1942. A boat waited to evacuate him from the fortified island in the Philippines. Although the United States Army and Filipino defense forces had battled to keep the Japanese out of the island chain, they had not been successful. Thousands of Allied civilians—men, women, and children—were being held in prison camps throughout the islands, and American and Filipino soldiers were under attack on the Bataan peninsula. After reaching Australia, MacArthur pledged his determination to free the Philippines with the words "I shall return."

Allied troops found that the war in Southeast Asia and the Pacific was very different from that in Europe. Most battles were fought at sea, on tiny islands, or in deep jungles.

War in the Pacific

At first, the Japanese won an uninterrupted series of victories. They controlled much of Southeast Asia and many Pacific islands. By May 1942, the Japanese had gained control of the Philippines, killing several hundred American soldiers and some 10,000 Filipino soldiers during the 68-mile Bataan Death March. One survivor described the ordeal as "a macabre litany of heat, dust, starvation, thirst, flies, filth, stench, murder, torture, corpses, and wholesale brutality that numbs the memory." Many Filipino

Storming the Beach
The Pacific war relied on the capture of individual islands. Here, United States Marines land on the island of Iwo Jima.

Theme: Geography and History How was the war in the Pacific different from the fighting in Europe?

miles and instantly killed more than 70,000 people. In the months that followed, many more would die from radiation sickness, a deadly aftereffect from exposure to radioactive materials.

On August 8, the Soviet Union declared war on Japan and invaded Manchuria. Again, Japanese leaders did not respond. The next day, the United States dropped a second atomic bomb, this time on the city of Nagasaki. More than 40,000 people were killed in this second explosion.

Still, the Japanese cabinet argued. Should they surrender or continue to fight? Finally, on August 10, Emperor Hirohito intervened—an action unheard of for a Japanese emperor— and forced the government to surrender. On September 2, 1945, the formal peace treaty was signed on board the American battleship *Missouri*, which was anchored in Tokyo Bay.

An Ongoing Controversy Dropping the atomic bomb brought a quick end to the war. It also unleashed terrifying destruction. Ever since, people have debated whether the United States should have used the bomb.

Why did Truman use the bomb? First, he was convinced that Japan would not surrender without an invasion that would result in an enormous loss of both American and Japanese lives. Truman also may have hoped that the bomb would impress the Soviet Union with American power. At any rate, the Japanese surrendered shortly after the bombs were dropped, and World War II was ended.

Looking Ahead

After the surrender, American forces occupied the smoldering ruins of Japan. In Germany, meanwhile, the Allies had divided Hitler's fallen empire into four zones of occupation. In both countries, the Allies faced difficult decisions about the future. How could they avoid the mistakes of 1919 and build the foundations for a stable world peace?

The Atomic Bomb
President Harry Truman warned the Japanese that if they did not surrender, they would face "a rain of ruin from the air the like of which has never been seen on this Earth." This photo shows the destructive effects of the bomb on Hiroshima. The inset shows a watch stopped by the blast.

Theme: Religions and Value Systems What were some of the arguments for and against dropping the atomic bomb on Japan?

SECTION 4 Assessment

Recall
1. **Identify: (a)** Battle of the Coral Sea, **(b)** Battle of the Bulge, **(c)** V-E Day, **(d)** Harry Truman.
2. **Define: (a)** island-hopping, **(b)** kamikaze.

Comprehension
3. How did the United States fight the war in the Pacific?
4. How did the Allies weaken Germany?
5. How was Japan defeated?

Critical Thinking and Writing
6. **Making Decisions** Suppose that you are President Truman. What information would you want before deciding whether to drop an atomic bomb on Japan?
7. **Making Generalizations** How would you describe the attitudes of the Japanese government and of Hitler toward surrendering to the Allies?

Activity

Writing Headlines
Write a series of newspaper headlines reporting the final months of the war in Europe. Suggest photos or other visuals that might accompany a story for one of the headlines.

Reading Focus

- What issues arose in the aftermath of war?
- Why did the Allies organize the United Nations?
- How did the breakup of the wartime alliance lead to new conflicts?

Vocabulary

containment
satellite

Taking Notes

On a sheet of paper, make a concept web like the one shown here. As you read this section, add information about events that occurred after World War II. Add as many circles as you need.

Main Idea As the war ended, new tensions developed between the United States and the Soviet Union.

Setting the Scene

"Give me ten years and you will not be able to recognize Germany," said Hitler in 1933. His prophecy proved correct—although not in the way he had intended. In 1945, Germany was an unrecognizable ruin. Poland, Russia, Japan, and many other countries also lay in ruins. Total war had gutted cities, factories, harbors, bridges, railroads, farms, homes—and lives. Millions of refugees, displaced by the fighting or liberated from prison camps, wandered the land. Amid the devastation, hunger and disease took large tolls for years after the fighting ended.

Aftermath of War

Even as the Allies celebrated victory, the appalling costs of the war began to emerge. It had killed as many as 75 million people around the world. In Europe, about 38 million people lost their lives, many of them civilians. The Soviet Union suffered the worst casualties, with more than 22 million dead.

Numbers alone did not tell the story of the Nazi nightmare in Europe or the Japanese brutality in Asia. In the aftermath of war, investigation brought new atrocities to light.

Horrors of the Holocaust During the war, the Allies were aware of the existence of Nazi concentration camps and death camps. But only at war's end did they learn the full extent of the inhumanity and misery of the Holocaust. United States general Dwight Eisenhower, who visited the camps, was stunned to come "face to face with indisputable evidence of Nazi brutality and ruthless disregard of every sense of decency."

Walking skeletons stumbled out of the death camps with tales of mass murder. Rudolf Hoess, Nazi commander at Auschwitz, would later admit that he had supervised the killing of some two and a half million people, not counting those who died of disease or starvation.

War Crimes Trials At wartime meetings, the Allies had agreed that Axis leaders should be tried for "crimes against humanity." In Germany, the Allies held war crimes trials in Nuremberg, where Hitler had staged mass rallies in the 1930s. A total of 177 Germans and Austrians were tried, and 142 were found guilty. A handful of top Nazis received death sentences. Others were imprisoned. Similar war crimes trials were held in Japan and Italy. The trials showed that political and military leaders could be held accountable for actions in wartime.

Allied Occupation The war crimes trials served an additional purpose. By exposing the savagery of the Axis regimes, they further discredited the Nazi, fascist, and militarist ideologies that had led to the war.

Yet disturbing questions haunted people then, as now. What made the Nazi horrors possible? Why had ordinary people in Germany, Poland, France, and elsewhere accepted—and even collaborated in—Hitler's "final solution"? How could the world prevent the rise of future dictators?

The Allies tried to address those issues as their troops occupied Germany and Japan. The United States felt that strengthening democracy would ensure tolerance and peace. The western Allies built new governments with democratic constitutions to protect the rights of all citizens. In German schools, for example, Nazi textbooks and courses were replaced with a new curriculum that taught democratic principles.

The United Nations

As in 1919, the World War II Allies set up an international organization to ensure peace. In April 1945, delegates from 50 nations met in San Francisco to draft a charter for the United Nations. The UN would play a greater role in world affairs than did its predecessor, the League of Nations.

Under the UN Charter, each of the member nations had one vote in the General Assembly. A much smaller body called the Security Council was given greater power. Each of its five permanent members—the United States, the Soviet Union (today Russia), Britain, France, and China—had the right to veto any council decision. The goal was to give these great powers the authority to ensure the peace. Often, however, differences among these nations have kept the UN from taking action.

The UN's work would go far beyond peacekeeping. The organization would take on many world problems—from preventing the outbreak of disease and improving education to protecting refugees and aiding nations to develop economically. UN agencies like the World Health Organization and the Food and Agricultural Organization have provided help for millions of people around the world.

FACT FINDER

Casualties of World War II

	Military Dead*	Military Wounded*	Civilian Dead*
Allies			
Britain	389,000	475,000	65,000
France	211,000	400,000	108,000
Soviet Union	7,500,000	14,102,000	15,000,000
United States	292,000	671,000	**
Axis Powers			
Germany	2,850,000	7,250,000	5,000,000
Italy	77,500	120,000	100,000
Japan	1,576,000	500,000	300,000

* All figures are estimates.
** Very small number of civilian dead.
Source: Henri Michel, *The Second World War*

Skills Assessment

Chart World War II resulted in enormous casualties. Because planes carried destruction far beyond the battlefield, civilian deaths reached record numbers. **Which nation suffered the greatest number of both civilian and military casualties?**

The Alliance Breaks Apart

Amid the rubble of war, a new power structure emerged. In Europe, Germany was defeated. France and Britain were drained and exhausted. Two other powers, the United States and the Soviet Union, had brought about the final victory. Before long, these two nations would become superpowers with the economic resources and military might to dominate the globe. They would also become tense rivals in an increasingly divided world.

Growing Differences During the war, the Soviet Union and the nations of the West had cooperated to defeat Nazi Germany. By 1945, however, the wartime alliance was crumbling. Conflicting ideologies and mutual distrust soon led to the conflict known as the Cold War. The Cold War was a state of tension and hostility among nations, without armed conflict between the major rivals. At first, the focus of the Cold War was Eastern Europe, where Stalin and the western powers had very different goals.*

*Stalin was deeply suspicious of other powers. Russia had been invaded by Napoleon's armies and by Germans in World Wars I and II. Also, the United States and Britain had both sent troops into Russia during World War I.

Origins of the Cold War   Stalin had two goals in Eastern Europe. First, he wanted to spread communism into the area. Second, he wanted to create a buffer zone of friendly governments as a defense against Germany, which had invaded Russia during World War I and again in 1941.

As the Red Army had pushed German forces out of Eastern Europe, it had left behind occupying forces. At wartime conferences, Stalin tried to persuade the West to accept Soviet influence in Eastern Europe. He bluntly stated, "Whoever occupies a territory also imposes his own social system. Everyone imposes his own system as far as his armies can reach. It cannot be otherwise."

The Soviet dictator pointed out that the United States was not consulting the Soviet Union about peace terms for Italy or Japan, defeated and occupied by American and British troops. In the same way, Russia would determine the fate of the Eastern European lands overrun by the Red Army on its way to Berlin.

Roosevelt and Churchill rejected Stalin's view, making him promise "free elections" in Eastern Europe. Stalin ignored that pledge. Backed by the Red Army, local communists in Poland, Czechoslovakia, and elsewhere destroyed rival political parties and even assassinated democratic leaders. By 1948, Stalin had installed pro-Soviet communist governments throughout Eastern Europe.

A Divided Europe   Churchill had long distrusted Stalin. As early as 1946, during a visit to the United States, he described Soviet control of Eastern Europe as an "iron curtain" dividing the continent.

In the West, the "iron curtain" became a symbol of the Cold War. It expressed the growing fear of communism. More important, it described the division of Europe into "eastern" and "western" blocs. In the East were the Soviet-dominated, communist countries of Eastern Europe. In the West were the western democracies, led by the United States.

New Conflicts Develop

Like Churchill, President Truman saw communism as an evil force creeping across Europe and threatening countries around the world, including China. To deal with that threat, the United States abandoned its traditional isolationism. After World War I, it had withdrawn from global affairs, but after World War II, the nation took a leading role on the world stage.

Stalin soon showed his aggressive intentions. In Greece, Stalin backed communist rebels who were fighting to overturn a right-wing monarchy supported by Britain. By 1947, however, Britain could no longer afford to defend Greece. Stalin was also menacing Turkey in the Dardanelles, the strait linking the Russian Black Sea coasts and the Mediterranean.

Truman Doctrine   Truman took action. On March 12, 1947, Truman outlined a new policy to Congress: "I believe that it must be the policy of the United States to support free people who are resisting attempted subjugation by armed minorities or by outside pressures."

This policy, known as the Truman Doctrine, would guide the United States for decades. It made clear that Americans would resist Soviet expansion in Europe or elsewhere in the world. Truman soon sent military and economic aid and advisers to Greece and Turkey so that they could withstand the communist threat.

The Truman Doctrine was rooted in the idea of containment, limiting communism to the areas already under Soviet control. George Kennan, the American statesman who first proposed this approach, believed that communism would eventually destroy itself. Stalin, however, saw containment as "encirclement" by the capitalist world that wanted to isolate the Soviet Union.

Primary Source

Curtaining Off Eastern Europe

In 1946, Winston Churchill traveled to Westminster College in Fulton, Missouri, and delivered an address analyzing the Soviet threat in Eastern Europe:

"A shadow has fallen upon the scenes so lately lighted by Allied victory. . . . From Stettin in the Baltic to Trieste in the Adriatic, an iron curtain has descended across the Continent. . . . Warsaw, Berlin, Prague, Vienna, Budapest, Bucharest, and Sofia, all these famous cities and the populations around them lie in what I must call the Soviet sphere, and all are subject . . . not only to Soviet influence but to a very high and, in many cases, increasing measure of control from Moscow. . . . I do not believe that Soviet Russia desires war. What they desire is the fruits of war and the indefinite expansion of their power and doctrines."

—Winston Churchill, speech delivered March 5, 1946

Skills Assessment

Primary Source   What does Churchill believe are Soviet motives for isolating its territories?

Cold War in Europe

Divided Germany, 1945

0 ——— 100 Miles
0 ——— 100 Kilometers

BRITISH ZONE
Berlin •
RUSSIAN ZONE
FRENCH ZONE
AMERICAN ZONE

FINLAND
NORWAY
SWEDEN
ESTONIA
LATVIA
LITHUANIA
North Sea
Baltic Sea
DENMARK
IRELAND
GREAT BRITAIN
ATLANTIC OCEAN
NETH.
Potsdam •
Berlin •
EAST GERMANY
WARSAW
POLAND
SOVIET UNION
BELG.
WEST GERMANY
CZECHOSLOVAKIA
LUX.
FRANCE
SWITZ.
AUSTRIA
HUNGARY
ROMANIA
Yalta •
Black Sea
PORTUGAL
SPAIN
ITALY
YUGOSLAVIA
BULGARIA
ALBANIA
TURKEY
GREECE
Mediterranean Sea

Azimuthal Equal Area Projection
0 ——— 250 ——— 500 Miles
0 ——— 250 ——— 500 Kilometers

NATO nations, 1955 | Warsaw Pact nations, 1955 | Other communist countries | Territory added to Soviet Union

Geography By 1955, western nations had joined to form NATO, and the Soviet Union had formed the Warsaw Pact with its allies. Meanwhile, Germany was divided into communist and noncommunist zones of occupation.

1. **Location** On the main map, locate **(a)** West Germany, **(b)** East Germany, **(c)** Warsaw Pact nations.
2. **Region** Use the inset map to identify the occupation zone in which Berlin was located.
3. **Critical Thinking** **Synthesizing Information** Why would Turkey be a likely location for a Cold War conflict?

The Marshall Plan Postwar hunger and poverty made Western European lands fertile ground for communist ideas. To strengthen democratic governments, the United States offered a massive aid package, called the Marshall Plan. Under it, the United States funneled food and economic assistance to Europe to help countries rebuild. Billions in American aid helped war-shattered Europe recover rapidly.

President Truman also offered aid to the Soviet Union and its satellites, or dependent states, in Eastern Europe. Stalin, however, saw the plan as a trick to win Eastern Europe over to capitalism and democracy. He forbade Eastern European countries to accept American aid, promising help from the Soviet Union in its place.

Divisions in Germany Defeated Germany became another focus of the Cold War. Fearing the danger of a restored Germany, the Soviet Union dismantled factories and other resources in its occupation zone and used them to help rebuild Russia. France, Britain, and the United States, however, decided to unite their zones of occupation, encouraging Germans to rebuild businesses and industries.

Germany thus became a divided nation. In West Germany, the democratic nations allowed the people to write their own constitution and regain self-government. In East Germany, the Soviet Union installed a communist government tied to Moscow.

Berlin Airlift Stalin's resentment at western moves to rebuild Germany as a democracy triggered a crisis over Berlin. The former German capital was occupied by all four victorious Allies, even though it lay deep within the Soviet zone.

In 1948, Stalin tried to force the western Allies out of Berlin by sealing off every railroad and highway into the western sectors of the city. The western powers responded to the blockade by mounting a round-the-clock airlift. For more than a year, cargo planes supplied West Berliners with food and fuel. Their success forced the Soviets to end the blockade. Although the West had won a victory, the crisis deepened hostilities.

Military Alliances   Tensions continued to grow. In 1949, the United States, Canada, and nine Western European countries formed a new military alliance called the North Atlantic Treaty Organization (NATO). Members pledged to help one another if any one of them was attacked.

In 1955, the Soviet Union responded by forming its own military alliance, the Warsaw Pact. It included the USSR and seven satellites in Eastern Europe. Unlike NATO, however, the Warsaw Pact was a weapon used by the Soviets to keep its satellites in order.

The Arms Race   Each side in the Cold War armed itself to withstand an attack by the other. At first, the United States held an advantage in its control of nuclear power. But Stalin's top scientists were under orders to develop an atomic bomb of their own. They succeeded in 1949, and the arms race was on. For four decades, the superpowers spent fantastic sums to develop new, more deadly nuclear and conventional weapons. They invested still more to improve "delivery systems"—bombers, missiles, and submarines to launch these weapons of mass destruction. Soon, the global balance of power became, in Churchill's phrase, a "balance of terror."

The Propaganda War   Both sides participated in a propaganda war. The United States spoke of defending capitalism and democracy against communism and totalitarianism. The Soviet Union claimed the moral high ground in the struggle against western imperialism. Yet linked to those stands, both sides sought world power.

Looking Ahead

In 1945, the world hoped for an end to decades of economic crisis, bloody dictators, and savage war. Instead, it faced new tensions.

The Cold War would last for more than 40 years. Rivalry between the hostile camps would not only divide Europe but also fuel crises around the world. It would strain the resources of the United States and exhaust those of the Soviet Union. Though it would not erupt into large-scale fighting between the two superpowers, many small wars would break out, with the superpowers championing opposite sides. Meanwhile, the spread of ominous new weapons would raise the specter of global destruction.

SECTION 5 Assessment

Recall
1. **Identify: (a)** UN, **(b)** "iron curtain," **(c)** Truman Doctrine, **(d)** Berlin airlift, **(e)** NATO, **(f)** Warsaw Pact.
2. **Define: (a)** containment, **(b)** satellite.

Comprehension
3. How did the Allies try to hold the Axis leaders responsible for the suffering they caused during the war?
4. What was the main purpose of the UN?

5. List two causes of the Cold War.

Critical Thinking and Writing
6. **Recognizing Causes and Effects** Some historians argue that the Cold War began in 1918 when the World War I Allies, including the United States, sent forces to Russia to topple the Bolsheviks. How might they support this position?
7. **Linking Past and Present** Why do people feel it is so important to remember the inhumanity of the Holocaust?

Activity

Creating a Political Cartoon Use Churchill's "iron curtain" image to create a political cartoon about the Cold War. Write a caption for your cartoon.

31 Review and Assessment

Creating a Chapter Summary

Make a flowchart on a separate sheet of paper to show the main events of World War II and its aftermath, as well as related details. Use the chart below to help you get started.

```
┌─────────────────────────────────────────────────────┐
│ Dictators challenge world peace/Japan, Italy, Germany │
└─────────────────────────────────────────────────────┘
                          │
                          ▼
┌─────────────────────────────────────────────────────┐
│ Spanish Civil War/Dress rehearsal                     │
└─────────────────────────────────────────────────────┘
                          │
                          ▼
┌─────────────────────────────────────────────────────┐
│ Appeasement fails/Britain, France                     │
└─────────────────────────────────────────────────────┘
                          │
                          ▼
┌─────────────────────────────────────────────────────┐
│                                                       │
└─────────────────────────────────────────────────────┘
```

CD-ROM Review For additional review of the major concepts of Chapter 31, see the *Guide to the Essentials of World History* or the *Interactive Student Tutorial CD-ROM.*

Web Site Self-Test For practice test questions for Chapter 31, see **www.phschool.com.**

Building Vocabulary

(a) Classify each of the chapter vocabulary words listed below under one of the following themes: economics and technology, global interaction, religions and value systems, geography and history. **(b)** Choose one word in each category and write a sentence explaining how that word relates to the theme.

1. **sanction**
2. **appeasement**
3. **pacifism**
4. **blitzkrieg**
5. **radar**
6. **sonar**
7. **genocide**
8. **collaborator**
9. **island-hopping**
10. **containment**

Recalling Key Facts

11. What happened at the Munich Conference of 1938?
12. What event started World War II? When did it occur?
13. Why was the Battle of Stalingrad important?
14. When and why was the United Nations established?
15. What was the Truman Doctrine?

Critical Thinking and Writing

16. **Linking Past and Present** What lessons does the Holocaust have for us today?
17. **Analyzing Information** Explain the following statement: World War II brought down several dictatorships but increased the power of the world's largest totalitarian state.
18. **Defending a Position** Agree or disagree with the following statement: The western democracies could have prevented World War II. Explain.
19. **Synthesizing Information** **(a)** How did the United States help the Allies before entering World War II? **(b)** Was participation by the United States crucial to winning the war? Explain.
20. **Connecting to Geography** How were Hitler's plans to conquer Europe affected by the geography of **(a)** Britain, **(b)** Russia?

21. **Drawing Conclusions** **(a)** Which battle was most important in the war in Europe? **(b)** Which battle was most important in the war in the Pacific? Explain your answers.

The passage below is from a dispatch filed by Douglas Williams, a reporter for the London *Daily Telegraph*. The report describes Williams's first-hand observation of the evacuation of Dunkirk in May and June of 1940. Read the passage, then answer the questions that follow.

"All day long and during the night evacuation continued. Rescue vessels raced across the Channel loaded with men to the fullest capacity as fast as conditions would permit, steamed back at full speed across the narrow strip of water to return again with undiminished enthusiasm for fresh batches. . . .

Their position at Dunkirk becomes hourly more dangerous as German batteries begin to receive a full [supply] of ammunition from their supply columns. . . .

Parts of the town are in flames, and entire quarters in ruins. Outside, the main roads present scenes of confusion and destruction. Innumerable abandoned motorcars and [trucks] lie ditched in every field, while others set alight blaze fiercely.

Bodies of refugees killed by German machinegun bullets are seen at frequent intervals, and everywhere long lines of soldiers hurry down to the sea and safety.

Yet the work of evacuation continues uninterruptedly with calm efficiency, while a powerful rear-guard fights magnificently to delay the constantly increasing masses of German troops. . . ."

—Douglas Williams,
Dunkirk: May 28–June 4, 1940

22. **(a)** Describe the actions of people involved in the rescue operation. **(b)** According to Williams, what was the attitude of the rescuers?

23. **(a)** Why was the position of the Allied troops at Dunkirk becoming more dangerous? **(b)** How does Williams describe conditions at Dunkirk?

24. How would you describe Williams's point of view?

25. **(a)** How do you think the success of this operation affected British morale? **(b)** An American reporter wrote: "So long as the English tongue survives, the word Dunkirk will be spoken with reverence." What do you think the reporter meant by this?

After World War II, relations between Russia and the western nations deteriorated. The cartoon is a comment on developments in Berlin. Study the cartoon, then answer the following questions:

26. What do the flags stand for?

27. **(a)** What does the bear represent? **(b)** What is the bear doing? Why?

28. Based on what you have learned, why did Russia want to close off Berlin?

Skills Tip

Pay careful attention to symbols in political cartoons. Determine how the cartoonist combines symbols to present a point of view.

Use the Internet to research important events of World War II. Then, create a time line that shows the progression of the war. Use a special color or other design to indicate important dates, such as major turning points.

Chapter 27

World War I and Its Aftermath (1914–1919)

Many forces—including nationalism, militarism, and imperialist rivalries—propelled Europe into World War I. This massive conflict engulfed much of the world for four years and ushered in a new age of modern warfare.

- Two huge alliances emerged in Europe: the Central Powers, dominated by Germany and Austria-Hungary, and the Allies, led by France, Britain, and Russia.
- Although the assassination of Archduke Francis Ferdinand in 1914 ignited World War I, historians agree that all the major powers share blame for the conflict.
- Trench warfare and new weapons contributed to a stalemate on the Western Front.
- In 1917, the United States entered the war, allowing the Allies to achieve victory.
- The Paris Peace Conference imposed heavy penalties on Germany and redrew the map of Eastern Europe.

Chapter 28

Revolution in Russia (1917–1939)

Lenin and his successors transformed czarist Russia into the communist Soviet Union. This experiment in single-party politics and a state-run economy would exert a powerful influence over the modern world for almost 75 years.

- In March 1917, political, social, and economic conditions in Russia sparked a revolution that overthrew the czar and paved the way for more radical changes.
- After leading the Bolsheviks to power in November 1917, Lenin hoped to build a communist state based on the ideas of Marx.
- Lenin's successor, Stalin, imposed "five-year plans" to build industry and increase farm output.
- Stalin created a totalitarian state, employing censorship, propaganda, and terror to ensure personal power and push the Soviet Union toward modernization.

Chapter 29

Nationalism and Revolution Around the World (1910–1939)

Between 1919 and 1939, the desire for democracy and self-determination contributed to explosive struggles in many regions. New leaders in Africa, Latin America, and Asia built liberation movements that would change the world.

- The Mexican revolution opened the door to social and economic reforms.
- African leaders opposed imperialism and reaffirmed traditional cultures.
- Arab Nationalism led to Pan-Arabism, uniting Arabs against foreign domination.
- In India, Gandhi led a campaign of nonviolent resistance to British rule.
- In China, foreigners extended their spheres of influence. Later, communists and nationalists engaged in civil war.
- In the 1920s and 1930s, extreme nationalism and economic upheaval set Japan on a militaristic and expansionist path.

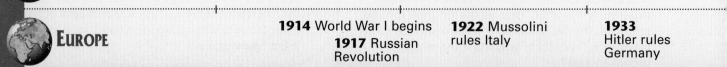

	1910	1920	1930
AFRICA	**1912** African National Congress formed in South Africa	**1919** First Pan-African Congress held in Paris	
THE AMERICAS	**1910** Mexican Revolution begins	**1919** Red Scare in United States	**1929** Stock market crash
ASIA AND OCEANIA	**1911** Civil War in China	**1923** Atatürk begins modernization of Turkey	
EUROPE	**1914** World War I begins **1917** Russian Revolution	**1922** Mussolini rules Italy	**1933** Hitler rules Germany

Chapter 30

Crisis of Democracy in the West
(1919–1939)

After World War I, western nations worked to restore prosperity and ensure peace. At the same time, political and economic turmoil in the 1920s and 1930s challenged democratic traditions and led to the rise of dictators.

- The Great Depression of the 1930s created financial turmoil and widespread suffering throughout the industrialized world.
- Scientific discoveries, new trends in literature and the arts, and social changes all contributed to a sense of uncertainty.
- Unrest in Italy helped Mussolini lead his Fascist party to power in the 1920s.
- In Germany, Hitler rose to power by appealing to extreme nationalism, antisemitism, anti-communism, and resentment of the Treaty of Versailles. In the 1930s, he turned the German state into a totalitarian Nazi dictatorship.
- Three systems of government—democracy, communism, and fascism—competed for influence in postwar Europe.

Chapter 31

World War II and Its Aftermath
(1931–1955)

Between 1939 and 1945, nations all over the globe fought World War II, the largest and most costly conflict in history. The war shifted the balance of world power from Western Europe to the United States and the Soviet Union.

- The Axis powers—Germany, Italy, and Japan—embarked on a course of aggression in the late 1930s. France and Britain first adopted a policy of appeasement but declared war when Hitler invaded Poland.
- During the Holocaust, the Nazis systematically killed more than six million Jews, as well as millions of other people the Nazis considered undesirable.
- The United States, the Soviet Union, and the Allied Powers joined to defeat Germany.
- To force a Japanese surrender, the United States dropped two atomic bombs.
- The Cold War followed World War II, pitting the western democracies, led by the United States, against the communist bloc, dominated by the Soviet Union.

1940   **1950**   **1960**

1935
Italy invades
Ethiopia

1948 South Africa makes apartheid the law of the land

1941
Bombing of
Pearl Harbor

1947
United States announces
Marshall Plan

1930s
Gandhi leads anti-British
protests in India

1945
Japan
surrenders and World War II ends

1949 People's Republic of China established

1939 World War II begins   **1949** NATO formed

1941 Holocaust begins   **1955** Warsaw Pact formed

The World Since 1945: An Overview
1945–Present

Chapter Preview

1 The Changing Political Climate
2 Global Economic Trends
3 Changing Patterns of Life

1969
On July 20, American astronauts become the first people to walk on the moon.

1945
The United Nations is formed. Today, the UN meets in this building in New York City.

1960s
The Green Revolution begins, increasing food production in many developing nations.

CHAPTER EVENTS

1940   1955   1970

The World Economy, 1990s

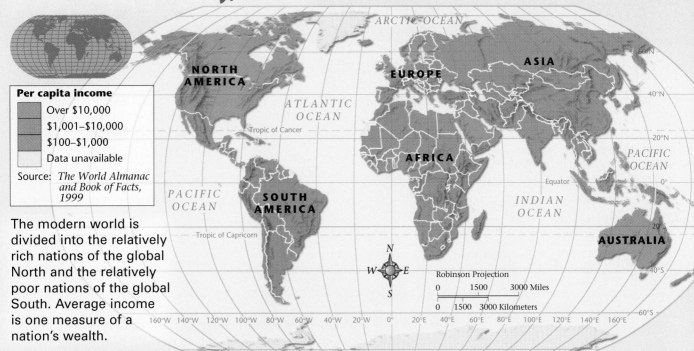

Per capita income

- Over $10,000
- $1,001–$10,000
- $100–$1,000
- Data unavailable

Source: *The World Almanac and Book of Facts, 1999*

The modern world is divided into the relatively rich nations of the global North and the relatively poor nations of the global South. Average income is one measure of a nation's wealth.

1980s
The computer becomes an essential tool in homes and offices. Here, a technician processes data in Senegal.

1991
The global Cold War ends.

2000
A new millennium, or thousand-year period, brings both hopes and fears. The Millennium Dome in Greenwich, England, was built to celebrate the start of this new era in history.

1985   2000   2015

Reading Focus

- How did the end of colonialism and the Cold War shape the world?
- How did new nations try to form stable governments?
- What role have world organizations played?
- What enduring issues face the world today?

Vocabulary

modernization
superpower
ideology
nonaligned
interdependence
summit
terrorism

Taking Notes

As you read this section, make an outline of its contents. Use Roman numerals for major headings. Use capital letters for subheadings, and use numbers for supporting details. This example will help you get started.

I. End to European colonial empires
  A. Nationalism and independence
    1. Nationalist leaders insist on independence
    2.
  B. Different roads to freedom
    1.
  C.

Main Idea After World War II, the Cold War and the decline of European influence shifted the balance of world power.

Connections to Today

The Last Shreds of an Empire

In the great tide of national liberation, Bermuda has gone its own way. It is one of a handful of remaining British colonies, all of them small island remnants of the once-mighty British empire.

A small group of islands that lures half a million visitors per year with soft ocean breezes, Bermuda did experience some political problems. The assassination of the British governor in 1973 and outbreaks of rioting in 1977 delayed independence negotiations. A vote for independence was finally held in August 1995. Prosperous and cautious, the Bermudans voted overwhelmingly to retain their ties to Great Britain.

Theme: Political and Social Systems Why might a colony choose to vote against independence?

Setting the Scene Two centuries ago, the American and French revolutions launched ideals such as the natural rights of all people. In 1972, President Julius Nyerere of Tanzania in East Africa put those ideas in modern terms when he spoke of the goals of new nations that had freed themselves from colonial rule:

> "There is a world-wide movement now—even within the imperialist countries it exists—to put an end to the exploitation [taking advantage] of man by man. This movement will succeed. Eventually, imperialism and racialism will become merely a chapter in the history of man—we shall hear about it in museums."
>
> —Julius K. Nyerere, *Freedom and Development*

The balance of world power changed dramatically after 1945. European influence declined while the United States and the Soviet Union emerged as the world's dominant powers, locked in a tense Cold War. Perhaps the greatest change, however, was the collapse of western overseas empires and the emergence of dozens of new countries.

An End to European Colonial Empires

The postwar decades brought a major turning point in world history. The colonial empires built by western powers during the Age of Imperialism crumbled. In Asia and Africa, people demanded and won freedom. Between 1950 and 1980, more than 50 new nations emerged in Africa alone.

Nationalism and Independence Resistance to colonial rule had begun long before. By the 1930s, nationalist movements had taken root in Africa, Asia, and the Middle East. After World War II, nationalist leaders such as Gandhi in India insisted on independence.

At first, Britain, France, and other powers tried to hold on to their empires. But the war had exhausted their military and financial resources. With subject peoples ready to fight for freedom, many war-weary Europeans had no desire for further conflict.

The Cold War, too, undermined imperialism. The United States backed the right of colonized people to self-determination. Its rival, the Soviet Union, also had long condemned western imperialism. Soon, both sides were seeking allies among emerging nations.

Different Roads to Freedom In most areas, people achieved freedom largely through peaceful means. In a few regions, especially where many whites had settled, colonial rulers were reluctant to leave. Desperate wars of liberation often resulted. France, for example, fought to hold on to Algeria in North Africa and to French Indochina in Southeast Asia. By contrast, it gave up its vast colonial holdings in West Africa without a struggle.

Global Impact Altogether, around 90 new countries emerged during this "great liberation." Some, such as India and Nigeria, were large in area or population. Many others, such as Nepal, Kuwait, and Lesotho, were small.

The new nations of Africa and Asia, as well as the countries of Latin America, became known as the developing world.* Although these nations differed greatly from one another, they shared common goals. All were determined to pursue modernization, which meant building stable governments and developing their countries economically. They followed different paths toward modernization, but many experienced similar challenges.

The needs and goals of developing nations transformed the postwar world. Most joined the United Nations, where they have become an important voice by uniting their interests and often voting as a bloc. Individually and in regional groups, a number of them have played significant roles in global political and economic affairs.

The Cold War Goes Global

The new nations emerged into a world dominated and divided by the Cold War. The United States and Soviet Union emerged as superpowers, nations strong enough to influence the acts and policies of other nations. They competed for influence by offering economic and military aid to developing nations. Each superpower wanted new countries to adopt its ideology, or system of thought or belief—either capitalism or socialism. Many new nations favored socialism, in part because their old colonial rulers had been capitalist. Other nations were attracted by the greater prosperity of the capitalist West.

Nonaligned Nations To avoid superpower rivalry, many new nations chose to remain nonaligned, that is, not allied to either side in the Cold War. The goal of the nonaligned movement was to reduce world tensions and promote economic policies that would benefit developing nations. Giant India, which blended a democratic government with a socialist economy, was a leader in the nonaligned movement.

Hot Spots In Africa, Latin America, and Asia, local conflicts took on a Cold War dimension. Often, the West, led by the United States, supported one side, and the Soviet bloc supported the other. Through such struggles, the superpowers confronted each other indirectly rather than head to head.

Contributing to this tension was the Chinese Communist victory in 1949. When Mao Zedong's forces won control of mainland China, the United States feared that the "red tide" would sweep around the world. American policies, therefore, were designed to stop the communist threat.

On occasion, the Cold War did erupt into "shooting wars," especially in Asia. Both Korea and Vietnam were torn by brutal conflicts in which the United States and the Soviet Union played crucial roles, as you will read.

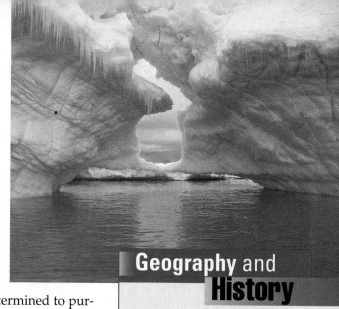

Geography and History

The Coldest Place on Earth

Oddly enough, the coldest place on Earth remained untouched by the Cold War. In 1959, twelve of the world's leading powers—including the United States and the Soviet Union—signed a treaty that made Antarctica a neutral zone of scientific research and cooperation. The continent was now off-limits to military bases, nuclear weapons testing, and radioactive-waste disposal. This treaty was followed in 1991 by a 50-year ban on oil and mineral exploration.

Antarctica is home to as many as 4,000 scientists who may stay for up to a year. Heavily wrapped in special cold-weather gear, they brave temperatures ranging from 32 degrees Fahrenheit to −100 degrees Fahrenheit. These men and women study topics such as global climate changes, ocean life, and geology.

 Theme: Geography and History Why is Antarctica a symbol of international cooperation?

---

*During the Cold War, the term *Third World* was used to refer to these nations with less-advanced technology than that of the First World (the western industrial powers and Japan) or the Second World (the communist bloc nations).

Games for an Interdependent World
Flags of many nations ring the stadium at the 1996 Olympic games in Atlanta, Georgia (above right). Through both the summer and the winter games, the International Olympic Committee works to promote international cooperation.

Theme: Global Interaction
Why are the Olympic games a symbol of interdependence? Why might they also become a source of conflict?

▶ **Primary Sources and Literature**

See *"The Universal Declaration of Human Rights"* in the Reference Section at the back of this book.

developing nations. Many other types of nongovernmental organizations (NGOs) have forged valuable global networks, including the International Olympic Committee and the International Red Cross.

Global Issues

Many issues pose a challenge to world peace. Since the United States first exploded two atomic bombs in 1945, nations have poured resources into building nuclear weapons. The number of nuclear weapons grew from 3 in 1945 to over 50,000 in the 1980s.

Deadly Weapons During the Cold War, efforts to curb the arms race had only limited success. Yet in 1968, many nations signed the Nuclear Non-Proliferation Treaty (NPT), agreeing to halt the spread of nuclear weapons. In 1995, the treaty was renewed, but some nations still refused to sign. Why, they asked, could a few nations like the United States and Russia keep nuclear weapons if they could not? In 1998, for example, India and Pakistan stirred global concerns when they announced successful tests of nuclear weapons.

Even after the Cold War ended, many nations kept spending immense sums on the military. In nations split by ethnic or other conflicts, arms dealers sell weapons, including land mines. Many people have condemned the international arms trade. Others defend the economic right of arms makers to produce and sell their goods on the free market.

Human Rights In 1948, UN members approved the Universal Declaration of Human Rights. According to the document, all people are entitled to basic rights and freedoms "without distinction of any kind, such as race, color, sex, language, property, birth, or other status." Human rights include "the right to life, liberty, and security of person." In 1975, nations signing the Helsinki Accords guaranteed such basic rights as freedom of speech, religion, and the press as well as the rights to a fair trial, to earn a living, and to live in safety.

Despite these documents, human rights abuses, including torture and arbitrary arrest, occurred around the world. At times, the world community pressed countries to stop abuses. Economic pressure, for example, was used to push South Africa to end its system of apartheid.

In some countries, leaders have accused western nations of trying to impose their own ideas about individual freedom. They claim that their cultures value the community over the individual. Chinese leaders, for example, have argued that economic goals, such as improving the standard of living for their people, were more important than individual political freedom.

The Question of Intervention The human rights debate raised tough issues. Does the world community have a duty to step in to end abuses? How can it intervene when the UN Charter forbids any action that violates the independence of a member nation?

The UN and other organizations have a mixed record on intervention. In the 1990s, the UN sent peacekeepers to northern Iraq to protect the Kurds, an ethnic minority suffering brutal government persecution. For complex reasons, the UN was slow to move against Serbs who killed or drove Muslims in Bosnia from their homes. The UN did not intervene when Hutus massacred an estimated one million Tutsis in Rwanda. In 1999, however, NATO forces bombed Serbia to stop its attacks on ethnic Albanians in Kosovo. Ethnic conflicts, especially, have fueled the debate over intervention to protect human rights.

Terrorism Since the 1960s, incidents of terrorism have increased around the world. Terrorism is the deliberate use of violence, especially against civilians, to achieve political goals. Through bombings, kidnappings, airplane hijackings, and shootings, terrorists focus attention on their causes and try to force governments to give in to their demands.

Extremists on both sides of the conflict in Northern Ireland have murdered civilians. A terrorist group killed Israeli athletes at the 1972 Olympic games to push its demands for a Palestinian state. Separate terrorist groups assassinated India's Rajiv Gandhi and bombed United States embassies in Kenya and Tanzania. To combat terrorism, governments have passed tough laws and increased watchfulness.

Some governments have been accused of "state-sponsored terrorism." That is, the government trains and arms extremists to carry out attacks abroad. Human-rights groups have argued that governments even engaged in terrorism at home when they used torture, murder, and illegal arrests against their own citizens.

Deadly Weapons
This Canadian cartoon appeared during the Cold War. It expresses the fears many felt about the arms race between the United States and Soviet Union. Even after the Cold War ended, nuclear arms remained a global concern.

Theme: Global Interaction Do you think this cartoonist favored the Nuclear Non-Proliferation Treaty? Explain.

SECTION 1 Assessment

Recall

1. **Identify:** (a) GATT, (b) International Monetary Fund, (c) NPT, (d) Universal Declaration of Human Rights.
2. **Define:** (a) modernization, (b) superpower, (c) ideology, (d) nonaligned, (e) interdependence, (f) summit, (g) terrorism.

Comprehension

3. (a) Why did European nations lose their colonial empires after World War II? (b) What was one effect of this "great liberation"?
4. Why did political instability plague many developing nations?

5. What two main roles has the UN played in world affairs?
6. Describe one effort nations have made to deal with each of the following issues: (a) the spread of nuclear arms, (b) human rights abuses, (c) terrorism.

Critical Thinking and Writing

7. **Predicting Consequences** Is interdependence likely to make the world more peaceful? Why or why not?
8. **Analyzing Information** (a) Why might lack of experience with representative government be a problem for developing nations? (b) Do you think democracy will help them solve their problems?

Activity

Designing an Invitation Design an invitation to an international conference on nuclear arms, terrorism, or human rights. Your invitation should clearly state the goals of the meeting and who will participate. You may also design a logo relating to the theme of the meeting.

Global Economic Trends

Reading Focus

- In what ways are the global North and South economically interdependent?

- Why have developing nations had trouble reaching their goals?

- How is economic development linked to the environment?

Vocabulary

multinational corporation

privatization

environmentalist

acid rain

global warming

Taking Notes

On a sheet of paper draw a Venn diagram like the one shown here. As you read this section, add more information, including the area where the ovals overlap.

GLOBAL NORTH
- Industrial nations of Europe and North America
- Capitalism

GLOBAL SOUTH
- Nations of developing world

Main Idea The industrial nations of the global North and the developing nations of the global South have become increasingly interdependent.

Setting the Scene "Ours is a time of problems, of gigantic problems," noted Pope Paul VI in 1969. "And every day, if we want to live with open eyes, we have a problem to study, to resolve." Since the 1950s, a deep gulf has divided the world into rich and poor nations. Yet in today's interdependent world, rich and poor nations are closely linked.

The Global North and South

The Cold War created an ideological split between the communist East and the capitalist West. Today, an economic gulf divides the world into two spheres—the relatively rich nations of the global North and the relatively poor nations of the global South.

Rich Nations The global North includes the industrial nations of Europe and North America, as well as Japan and Australia. Most are located in the temperate zone north of the Equator. They control most of the world's wealth. Although pockets of poverty exist, the standard of living in the North is generally high. Most people are literate, earn adequate wages, and have basic health services.

These rich nations have basically capitalist economies. Decisions about what to produce and for whom are generally regulated by the free market, not by the government. The governments of these nations do support economic growth through transportation and communication systems, public education, and social services. They also regulate their economies in various ways, from requiring pure food and drugs to preventing stock market fraud. Still, in the global North, economic success is driven by the free market.

Poor Nations The global South refers to the developing world. Most of these nations lie in Asia, Africa, and Latin America in the zone between the tropics of Cancer and Capricorn. The South has 75 percent of the world's population and much of its natural resources. Some nations have enjoyed strong growth, especially the Asian "tigers," the oil-exporting nations of the Middle East, and several Latin American nations. Overall, though, the global South remains generally underdeveloped and poor. Unlike the nations that industrialized before 1900, newer nations have not had enough time to build up their capital, resources, or industries.

For most people in the developing world, life is a daily struggle for survival. About one billion people worldwide live in extreme poverty—many of them children.

Migration Despite some advances in the developing world, the gap between rich and poor nations is widening. The imbalance has sparked migration of people from poor regions to wealthier ones. Every year, refugees flee poverty or war to seek a better life in Western Europe, North America, and Australia. Millions of others, however, remain close to their homes.

Economic Interdependence

Rich and poor nations are linked by many economic ties. The nations of the global North control much of the world's capital, trade, and technology. But they depend increasingly on low-paid workers in developing states to produce manufactured goods as inexpensively as possible. This shift in labor has led to a loss of manufacturing jobs in many western nations.

Huge multinational corporations, with branches in many countries, have invested in the developing world. They bring new technology to mining, agriculture, transportation, and other industries. Rich nations also provide aid, technical advisers, and loans. At the same time, interdependence has often led to resentment. With its great buying power, the North controls the prices of goods and commodities produced by the South. In addition, multinational corporations remove many profits from developing countries and often limit workers' attempts to seek higher wages.

The Oil Crisis In an interdependent world, events in one country or region can affect people everywhere. A drastic example of this was the oil crisis of the 1970s. All nations use oil for transportation and for products ranging from plastics to fertilizers. This demand has allowed nations with oil resources to seek favorable prices on the world market.

Much of the world's oil comes from the Middle East. In 1973, a political crisis in the region led the Organization of Petroleum Exporting Countries (OPEC) to halt its oil exports and raise oil prices. Shortages and soaring fuel prices set off economic shock waves. Suddenly, industrialized nations realized how much they depended on imported oil. While some efforts were made to find other fuels or to conserve energy use, the energy crisis showed what impact a single vital product could have on the world economy.

The Debt Crisis Another complex economic problem involved the growing debt owed by poor nations to rich ones. Developing nations, needing capital to modernize,

The World of Refugees
By 2000, nearly 20 million refugees around the world had fled poverty and turmoil. Many, like these children from Bosnia (top) and Rwanda (bottom), crowded into refugee camps near their home countries.

Theme: Global Interaction
Based on these pictures, how might you react to living in a refugee camp?

took loans offered by western banks. In the 1980s, however, bank interest rates rose, while the world economy slowed down. As demand for many of their goods fell, poor nations were unable to repay their debts or even the interest on their loans. Their economies stalled as they spent their income from exports on payments to their foreign creditors.

The debt crisis hurt rich nations, too, as banks were stuck with billions of dollars of bad debts. To ease the crisis, the International Monetary Fund, the World Bank, and private banks worked out agreements with debtor nations. Lenders lowered interest rates or gave some nations more time to repay the loans. In some cases, debts were even canceled altogether.

In return, debtor nations had to agree to adopt free-market policies. Many ended governmental supports for industry. They turned instead to privatization, selling off state-owned industries to private investors. Nations hoped that more efficient private enterprises would bring prosperity in the long run. Still, the immediate effects of privatization often hurt the poor.

The Asian Economic Crisis A third economic crisis highlighted the interdependence of the world's financial markets. The trouble began in the late 1990s with a recession in Japan, which had the world's second richest economy. Then, financial crises swept through other successful Asian economies, from South Korea to Singapore. All across the most developed nations of Asia, businesses closed down, workers lost jobs, and poverty spread.

Because all the economies of the world are linked, financial problems spread beyond Asia. Russia, trying to build a new capitalist economy after decades of communism, could not pay its debts. Brazil struggled to stabilize the value of its currency. The century ended with signs of an economic upturn, but the problems created by global financial links remained.

Economic Organizations A number of international economic organizations deal with the economic challenges that face rich and poor countries alike. The World Bank provides funding for major development programs and helps nations get through economic crises. The International Monetary Fund has become a lender of last resort in situations like the Asian financial crisis of the late 1990s.

Such organizations often help with global economic problems. But they have also caused serious social strains by requiring developing nations to abandon inefficient economic systems and end social programs they could not afford. In some cases, the poor in these countries have rioted, rebelled, or even overthrown their governments.

Obstacles to Development

Why have many developing nations been unable to make progress toward modernization? The answers vary from country to country, but many shared problems in five general areas: (1) geography, (2) population and poverty, (3) economic dependence, (4) economic policies, and (5) political instability.

Geography In parts of Africa, Asia, and Latin America, geography has posed an obstacle to development. For example, some of the African countries created since the 1950s are tiny and have few natural resources. Difficult climates, uncertain rainfall, lack of good farmland, and disease have added to the problems of some nations.

Population and Poverty The worldwide population boom that began in the 1700s has continued. Better medical care and increased food supplies have reduced death rates and led to explosive population growth. In the developing world, though, rapid growth is linked to poverty. Each year, the populations of countries like Nigeria and India increase by millions. All those people need food, housing, education, jobs, and medical care. Meeting these needs puts a staggering burden on developing nations.

Health Statistics of Selected Countries, 1999

Country	Population (thousands)	Life Expectancy at Birth (male/female)	Physicians (per 1,000 people)	Infant Mortality (deaths per 1,000)
Angola	10,865	45.6/50.2	*	132
Argentina	36,265	70.9/78.3	2.7	19
Guatemala	12,008	63.4/68.8	*	48
Japan	125,932	76.9/83.3	1.8	4
Jordan	4,435	71.0/74.8	1.6	33
Myanmar	47,305	53.0/56.1	0.3	78
Netherlands	15,731	75.1/81.0	2.4	5
Nigeria	110,532	52.7/54.5	0.2	71
Poland	38,607	68.6/77.2	2.3	13
United States	270,312	72.9/79.6	2.7	6

Source: *World Almanac and Book of Facts*   * Data unavailable

Skills Assessment

Chart Population and poverty can have a critical impact upon a nation's state of health. At right, a doctor in Guatemala treats a poor Indian child. **In which country shown here is life expectancy highest? Which has the fewest physicians per 1,000 people?**

Across the developing world, people are caught in a cycle of poverty. Millions of people die each year from hunger-related illnesses. Children are the most vulnerable. The UN estimates that 35,000 children die each day from malnutrition, disease, and other effects of poverty.

Many developing nations have tried to slow population growth. Few countries, except China, want to force people to limit family size. In farming societies, children are a source of labor. They are seen as an insurance policy to support their parents in old age. Religious traditions often encourage large families. Also, despite education efforts, many people still lack information about or access to family planning.

Economic Dependence Often, economic patterns formed during the Age of Imperialism have survived. Most new nations remained dependent on their former colonial rulers. They sold agricultural products and raw materials to the industrial world. In turn, they relied on the West for manufactured goods, technology, and investment. Also, many new nations had only a single export crop or commodity, such as sugar, cocoa, or copper. Their economies depended on world demand for the product.

As you have read, developing nations borrowed heavily from foreign banks. These funds were intended for development. Once in debt, though, nations had to spend much of their resources to pay interest.

Economic Policies Many newly independent nations saw socialism, rather than capitalism, as a way to modernize quickly. They modeled their economies on those of China or the Soviet Union, rather than on those of their former colonial rulers. Under socialism, the government controls the economy. These nations had little private capital, so only the government could raise the money to finance large-scale development projects.

At first, emerging nations made some gains. But in the long run, socialism often blocked economic growth. Later, like their models China and Russia, many developing nations introduced free-market policies.

Political Instability Political unrest often hindered economic development. El Salvador, Lebanon, Cambodia, and Angola are among the many nations devastated by civil wars. Military dictators or other authoritarian leaders spent huge sums on weapons and warfare instead of on education, housing, or health care. In addition, war created millions of refugees. The loss of their labor further hurt war-torn countries.

Changing Patterns of Life

Reading Focus

■ How are new ways of life replacing old ways?

■ How has modernization affected the lives of women?

■ What are the benefits and limits of modern science and technology?

■ What forces have shaped a new global culture?

Vocabulary

shantytown

fundamentalist

liberation theology

feminist movement

e-commerce

genetic engineering

Taking Notes

On a sheet of paper, draw a concept web to show the changing patterns of life in the past 50 years. Use this web to help you get started. As you read, add as many circles as you need.

Urbanization — CHANGING PATTERNS OF LIFE — New roles for women — Science and technology

Main Idea Forces such as urbanization, religion, and changing roles for women have shaped world societies.

Setting the Scene
"My village is changing," observed Indian writer Prafulla Mohanti. A road was built there in the 1960s to carry iron ore from a nearby mine to a port city some 40 miles away. Since then, Mohanti said, "Nylon, stainless steel, plastic, [and] fizzy drinks have reached the village."

New products and technology are changing villages around the world. At the same time, millions of villagers have migrated to cities, and that has further transformed the lives of people in the developing world.

Old Ways and New

In the western world, industrialization and urbanization began more than 200 years ago during the Industrial Revolution. In the past 50 years, the rest of the world has experienced similar upheavals.

Urbanization Since 1945, people in the developing world have flocked to cities to find jobs and escape rural poverty. Cities offer not only economic opportunities but also attractions such as stores, concerts, and sports.

With no money and few jobs, some newcomers settled in shantytowns. These slums on the outskirts of cities are as crowded and dangerous as European cities were in the 1800s. They lack basic services such as paving, running water, or sewage. Drugs and crime are ever-present threats. Today, millions of people struggle to survive in these conditions.

In the cities, the extended family of rural villages is giving way to the nuclear family. As urban children go to school and learn how to read, they often reject their parents' ways. Without the support of the village and the extended family, older beliefs and values are undermined by such urban values as material wealth, education, and job status. Many villagers who move to cities suffer a sense of stress and isolation.

Westernization In cities, people frequently adopt western fashions and ideas. During the Age of Imperialism, westerners taught that their civilization was superior. Even after independence, many people in emerging nations felt that the way to modernize was to follow western models.

Some early nationalists, such as Mohandas Gandhi, rejected the rush to abandon traditional ways. Today, leaders in some Muslim lands have called for "modernization without westernization." Although they welcome modern technology, they want to preserve older traditions and religious beliefs. They reject western emphasis on material success and the individual, which they think undermines the community and family.

Global Connections

Endangered Languages

Of the 6,700 different languages spoken in the world today, many are spoken only in isolated rural areas or on remote islands among a handful of elderly residents. As families migrate to cities or other countries, their children often grow up speaking a dominant language, such as English, Hindi, or Spanish. In the next century, some linguists predict that 90 to 95 percent of all current languages will disappear. That is an average of more than one language every two weeks. Scholars are now working to preserve oral and written records of many of these disappearing languages.

Theme: Diversity How has migration affected the diversity of languages spoken?

Village Life Despite urbanization, villages are still home to billions of people, mostly in the global South. Their lives vary widely, depending on climate, geographic isolation, and other factors. Still, village life follows similar patterns in much of the world. Many villagers are farmers. Their workday begins at sunrise. Women wash clothes in local streams. Young and old labor in fields or in workshops. Villagers exchange news at tiny shops in the village center and celebrate centuries-old religious festivals.

Westernization and technology are transforming villages. Changes such as roads, clinics, and television can enrich life. But they also weaken traditional cultures and lure young people to abandon villages for cities.

Religious Influences The major world religions and their offshoots still shape modern societies. In recent times, religious revivals have swept many regions. Christian, Muslim, Jewish, Buddhist, and Hindu reformers offer their own solutions to modern problems. Some of these reformers have been called **fundamentalists** because they stress what they see as the fundamental, or basic, values of their faiths. Many have sought political power in order to resist changes which they think undermine their beliefs.

In the West, evangelical Protestant groups emphasize salvation through faith and preaching, offering spiritual guidelines in a rapidly changing world. In the 1960s, the Second Vatican Council gave Roman Catholics more freedom to discuss issues and promoted cooperation with other Christian denominations. In Latin America, some Roman Catholic clergy backed a movement called **liberation theology**. They urged the Church to take a more active role in opposing the social conditions that contributed to poverty. Conservative Catholic forces often oppose such political activities.

In Muslim countries, too, religious reformers have called for social improvements. Some Muslim leaders rejected westernization and secular goals. Instead, they insisted that government and society should be based on strict obedience to the Sharia, or Islamic religious law.

New Rights and Roles for Women

After 1945, women's movements brought changes to both the western and the developing worlds. The UN Charter supported "equal rights for men and women." By 1950, women had won the right to vote in most European nations, as well as in Japan, China, Brazil, and other countries. In most African nations, both women and men won the vote at independence.

A small but growing number of women won elected office. Women headed democratic governments in Britain, Israel, India, Pakistan, the Philippines, and other countries. Still, a report to the UN noted that while women represent half of the world's people, "they perform nearly two thirds of all working hours, receive only one tenth of the world's income, and own less than one percent of world property."

The West In the industrial world, more and more women worked outside the home. By the 1970s, the **feminist movement** sought greater access for women to jobs and promotions, equal pay for equal work, and an end to sexual harassment on the job. Women advanced into high-profile jobs as business owners and executives, astronauts, scientists, and technicians.

Religious Influences
Despite revolutionary changes, religious traditions remain a powerful force throughout the modern world. At top, a Christian woman prays in Kenya. At bottom, Buddhists gather at a temple in Vietnam.

Theme: Religions and Value Systems Besides those represented below, what other religions have millions of followers today?

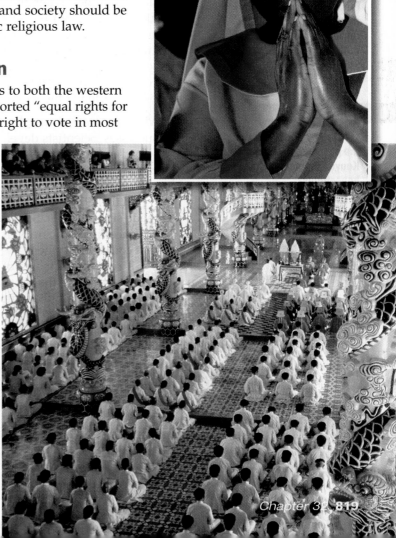

The Western World: An Overview

Reading Focus

- What issues troubled Europe after the Cold War?
- How have recent economic and political trends affected the West?
- How has Europe moved toward greater unity?
- How have social trends changed the West?

Vocabulary

détente
welfare state
recession
service industry
euro

Taking Notes

As you read this section, make an outline of its contents. Use Roman numerals for major headings, capital letters for subheadings, and numbers for supporting details. The model at right will help you get started.

I. Europe: The Cold War and after
  A. The Berlin Wall
    1. Berlin divided into two zones
  B.
II. Economic and political trends
  A.
    1.
    2.
  B. The oil shock

Main Idea   In the years since World War II, various economic, political, and social trends have shaped the western world.

Setting the Scene   Western Europe rebounded out of the rubble of World War II. During the postwar years, standards of living rose dramatically. People earned higher wages, bought homes with central heating and running water, and enjoyed luxuries unheard of in earlier times. Amid these comforts, many other changes were shaping the western world.

Europe: The Cold War and After

For more than 40 years, the Cold War divided Europe into two hostile military alliances. The communist nations of Eastern Europe, dominated by the Soviet Union, formed the Warsaw Pact. The western democracies, led by the United States, formed NATO. The superpowers avoided direct confrontation in Europe, but some issues brought the continent to the brink of war.

The Berlin Wall   Berlin was a focus of Cold War tensions. The city was split into democratic West Berlin and communist East Berlin. In the 1950s, West Berlin became a showcase for West German prosperity. Thousands of low-paid East Germans, discontented with communism, slipped into West Berlin. To stop the exodus, East Germany built a wall in 1961 that separated the two sectors of the city. When completed, the wall was a massive concrete barrier, topped with barbed wire and patrolled by guards.

The Berlin Wall was an ugly symbol of the Cold War and an embarrassment for the Soviets. It showed that workers, far from enjoying a communist paradise, had to be forcibly restrained from fleeing.

The Nuclear Threat   The Cold War triggered an arms race, with both sides producing huge arsenals of nuclear weapons. Critics argued that a nuclear war would destroy both sides. Yet the superpowers claimed that they dared not stop. Each side wanted to have the power to deter the other from launching its nuclear weapons. The result was a "balance of terror."

During the arms race, both superpowers spent huge sums of money on weapons. Such spending meant cutbacks in other areas. In 1953, President Dwight Eisenhower warned Americans about the impact: "Every gun that is made, every warship launched . . . signifies . . . a theft from those who hunger and are not fed, those who are cold and are not clothed."

Disarmament and Détente   To reduce the threat of nuclear destruction, both sides met at disarmament talks. Although mutual distrust often blocked progress, they did sign some agreements, such as the 1963 Nuclear

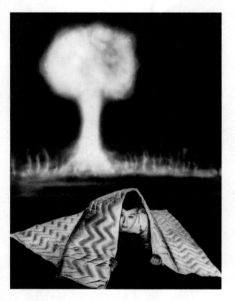

The Nuclear Threat
In Europe and other parts of the world, children were taught they could survive a nuclear attack. In 1954, the image above was used to advertise a bogus "radiation-resistant" blanket.

Theme: Economics and Technology   How did nuclear weapons change the nature of war?

Test Ban Treaty. It banned the testing of nuclear weapons in the atmosphere. Underground testing was still permitted, however.

By the 1970s, American and Soviet leaders promoted an era of détente (day TAHNT), or relaxation of tensions. The two superpowers made new agreements to reduce nuclear stockpiles. Détente ended, however, after the Soviet Union invaded Afghanistan in 1979.

End of the Cold War By the 1990s, as you will read, economic and foreign policy troubles threatened the Soviet Union. A new Soviet leader, Mikhail Gorbachev (mee kah EEL GOR bah chawf), eased the Soviet grip on Eastern Europe. One by one, communist governments collapsed. Communism even fell from power in the Soviet Union, which broke up into separate independent republics.

When the Cold War ended, nations in Western and Eastern Europe sought normal relations. Germany was reunited. The Warsaw Pact dissolved. NATO, originally formed to defend the West against communism, had to redefine its role in a post–Cold War world.

Troublesome Issues As the century neared its end, Europeans faced troublesome issues, new and old. Russia and the nations of Eastern Europe turned to the West for loans and investments to build capitalist economies. Ethnic clashes, especially in the Balkans, created conflicts that threatened the peace of Europe.

The nuclear peril was reduced, but it still remained. The United States, Russia, and other nations still had nuclear weapons. As disarmament talks continued, there were fears that some Russian nuclear materials might end up in the hands of other nations and groups.

NATO's New Role With the Cold War over, NATO allowed Eastern Europe's former communist nations to join the alliance. In 1999, Hungary, Poland, and the Czech Republic entered the organization. Despite Russian protests, several other Eastern European states also sought admission.

In the 1990s, conflict in the Balkans posed new challenges to NATO. When ethnic groups in Bosnia and Kosovo tried to break away from Yugoslavia, war erupted. Europeans witnessed the worst fighting since World War II and were shocked by horrible abuses of human rights. As you will read, NATO members finally sent military forces into both Bosnia and Kosovo. Those moves sparked debate over whether NATO should become Europe's peacekeeper and protector of human rights.

Economic and Political Trends

In the 1950s, Western Europeans recovered quickly from World War II. With Marshall Plan aid, their economies boomed. They rebuilt industries, farms, and transportation networks destroyed by the war.

Meanwhile, right-wing parties were discredited because they had supported fascism. Communists and socialists, who had resisted the Nazis during the war, enjoyed growing support. As a result, postwar governments in France, Italy, and Germany adopted many policies favored by the left.

The Welfare State A major goal of leftist parties was to extend the welfare state. Under this system, a government keeps most features of a capitalist economy but takes greater responsibility for the social and economic needs of its people. The welfare state had its roots in

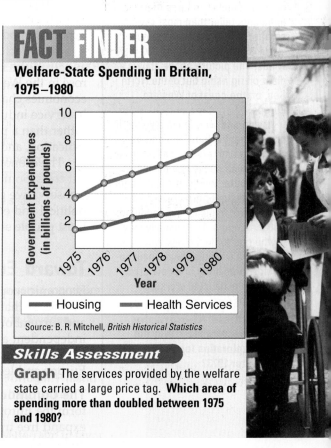

FACT FINDER

Welfare-State Spending in Britain, 1975–1980

Government Expenditures (in billions of pounds) vs. Year

— Housing   — Health Services

Source: B. R. Mitchell, *British Historical Statistics*

Skills Assessment

Graph The services provided by the welfare state carried a large price tag. **Which area of spending more than doubled between 1975 and 1980?**

Canada

After gaining independence, Canada charted its own course but still maintained links with Britain through the Commonwealth of Nations. Canada sided with the Allies in both world wars and became a member of NATO. Through diplomacy, Canada often worked to ease Cold War tensions. Its troops served in UN peacekeeping missions around the world.

Economic Growth Canada is a leading democratic and industrial power. It had a postwar economic boom, due in part to oil and gas deposits found in the western provinces. In 1959, Canada and the United States completed the St. Lawrence Seaway. It opened the Great Lakes to oceangoing ships and linked the interior of both countries to the Atlantic Ocean.

With a population only a tenth that of the United States, Canada has encouraged immigration. Since the 1950s, Canada's population has grown increasingly diverse, with newcomers from Europe, Asia, Africa, Latin America, and the Caribbean.

Quebec Separatism Defining a national identity has remained a challenge for Canada. Quebec's French-speaking people saw themselves as a "distinct society." To protect their culture, Quebec demanded more autonomy within Canada.

Government leaders tried hard to meet those demands. But other provinces resisted any solutions that gave Quebec special treatment. Some Canadians favored separatism. They said that Quebec should separate from Canada and become an independent nation. In the 1990s, Quebec's future remained a subject of heated debate.

United States Influence Another challenge for Canada has been the immense impact of the United States. Although the two nations enjoyed close ties, many Canadians resented their neighbor's cultural domination. Economic competition led to disputes over trade and tariffs. To resolve issues of economic competition, the countries set up the North American Free Trade Association (NAFTA). It created a free trade zone between Canada, the United States, and Mexico.

Other issues between Canada and the United States concerned the environment. Chemical pollution from American smokestacks, for example, contributed to acid rain that fell on northeastern Canada. The two nations agreed to work together for a common solution.

Quebec Separatism
French Canadians are proud of their culture. Some have urged that Quebec separate from Canada. Shown here are separatist buttons and French Canadians waving the blue and white flag of Quebec.

Theme: Diversity Why do you think some Native American Canadians support the idea of separatism?

SECTION 3 Assessment

Recall

1. **Identify:** (a) John F. Kennedy, (b) Richard Nixon, (c) Social Security, (d) Medicare, (e) Ronald Reagan, (f) *Brown* v. *Board of Education of Topeka,* (g) Martin Luther King, Jr., (h) Quebec.
2. **Define:** (a) deficit, (b) surplus, (c) civil rights movement, (d) segregation, (e) separatism.

Comprehension

3. What goals has the United States tried to achieve as a global superpower?
4. (a) How did government policies affect the American economy in the 1980s and 1990s? (b) How did the civil rights movement affect the economy?
5. What issues have challenged Canadians?

Critical Thinking and Writing

6. **Comparing** How is the situation of French-speaking Canadians similar to or different from that of minority groups within the United States?
7. **Linking Past and Present** Describe three ways the civil rights movement helped shape American life today.

Activity
Take It to the NET

On the Internet, find sites that specialize in biographies. From these and other sites, gather information and photographs about the life of Martin Luther King, Jr. Use the information and images to create a brief illustrated biography of King.

The Soviet Union: Rise and Fall of a Superpower

Reading Focus

- What ideas guided Soviet political, economic, and foreign policy?
- Why did the Soviet Union collapse?
- What problems have Russia and the other republics faced since the fall of the Soviet Union?

Vocabulary

dissident
glasnost
perestroika
default

Taking Notes

Copy the before-and-after chart at right. As you read, write key facts about conditions before and after the collapse of the Soviet Union in the appropriate columns.

COLLAPSE OF THE SOVIET UNION

Before	After
• Cold War with the United States	• Attempts to cooperate with the United States
•	•
•	•

Main Idea   After years of Communist rule, the Soviet Union collapsed and was replaced by Russia and other independent republics.

Setting the Scene

"We shall bury you," Soviet leader Nikita Khrushchev (KROOSH chawf) told the West during the Cold War. He later explained that his statement was not a military threat, as many westerners believed. Instead, he said, it was a reference to his belief that capitalism was doomed and that Soviet communism was the wave of the future.

Khrushchev's prediction did not come true. In fact, it was Soviet communism that was doomed. In the 1980s, the Soviet economy began to crumble. Efforts at reform led the Soviet empire to disintegration.

Soviet Government and Economy

After World War II, the Soviet Union emerged as a superpower. Under Stalin, it established a sphere of influence from the Baltic to the Balkans.

Victory, however, brought few rewards to the Soviet people. Stalin continued his ruthless policies. He filled slave labor camps with "enemies of the state" and seemed ready to launch new purges when he died in 1953.

Stalin's Successors   Nikita Khrushchev emerged as the new Soviet leader. In 1956, he shocked top Communist party members when he publicly denounced Stalin's abuse of power. Khrushchev then pursued a policy of de-Stalinization. He did not change Soviet goals but did free many political prisoners and eased censorship. He sought a thaw in the Cold War, calling for a "peaceful coexistence" with the West.

The thaw had limits, though. When discontented Hungarians revolted against communist rule in 1956, Khrushchev sent tanks in to smash them. When critics at home grew too bold, he clamped down. It appeared that a return to Stalinism could happen at any time.

Khrushchev's successor, Leonid Brezhnev (BREHSH nehf) held power from the mid-1960s until he died in

Khrushchev at the UN
Soviet leader Khrushchev was known for strong responses to the West. In 1960 at the UN, he emphasized a point by shaking his fist. *Life* magazine captured the moment and the feeling.

Theme: Global Interaction
How did events in Europe cause the Cold War to heat up?

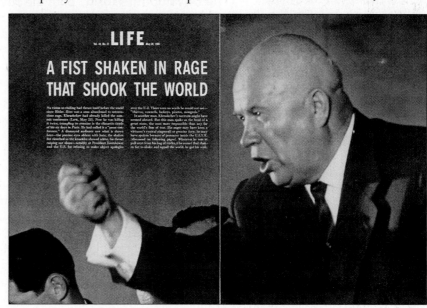

1982. Brezhnev rigorously suppressed **dissidents,** people who spoke out against the government. Critics faced arrest and imprisonment. Some were locked away in insane asylums, a policy once used by czarist Russia.

Some Successes After World War II, the Soviet Union had rebuilt its shattered industries, using factories and equipment stripped from Germany. As in the 1930s, priority was given to industries such as steel, coal, and heavy machinery. The government also poured resources into weapons, science, and technology. In 1957, the Soviets launched *Sputnik I,* the first artificial satellite to orbit the Earth. *Sputnik* was a propaganda victory for the Soviet Union because it suggested technological superiority over the United States.

The Soviets also claimed other successes. Citizens enjoyed benefits such as low rents, cheap bread, free health care, and day care for children. Although wages were low, unemployment was almost nonexistent.

Failure of the Command Economy In general, however, the Soviet economy was plagued by severe problems. Collectivized agriculture remained so unproductive that the Soviet Union frequently had to import grain to feed its people. Nor could the Soviet command economy match the free-market economies of the West in producing consumer goods. Soviet shoes, suits, and television sets were far inferior to those made in the West, and luxuries like clothes washers or automobiles remained rare. People spent many hours of their lives waiting in line to buy food and other goods.

Low output was the result of inefficiencies in central economic planning. A huge bureaucracy, rather than supply and demand, decided what to produce, how much, and for whom. Government planners in Moscow often had little knowledge of the local conditions. Sometimes, factories were forced to shut down because needed supplies never arrived. At the local level, workers set out to meet production quotas, regardless of quality. Because workers had lifetime job security, they had little incentive to produce better-quality goods.

Foreign Policy Issues

Stalin and his successors forcefully asserted Soviet control over Eastern Europe. In 1955, Khrushchev set up the Warsaw Pact, in theory to defend the communist bloc against NATO. In practice, it was used to suppress dissent within Eastern Europe.

The Developing World Both the Soviet Union and the United States sought allies among the developing nations. One way to win and keep allies was to offer military and economic aid. At times, this policy turned local conflicts into Cold War confrontations. In two bitter wars, Soviet-backed governments in North Korea and North Vietnam battled against American-backed governments in South Korea and South Vietnam.

Rivalry With the United States Soviet-American relations swung back and forth between confrontation and détente. In 1961, the building of the Berlin Wall increased Cold War tensions. A year later, Khrushchev tried to build nuclear missile bases in Cuba. That move triggered the dangerous Cuban missile crisis, which you will read about in a later chapter. The crisis brought the two superpowers to the brink of war.

Brezhnev invested in a huge military buildup. In the Brezhnev Doctrine, he asserted that the Soviet Union had a right to intervene militarily in any Warsaw Pact nation. At the same time, however, he also pursued détente and disarmament with the United States.

Détente came to an abrupt end in 1979, after the Soviets invaded Afghanistan to ensure Soviet influence in that neighboring nation. Like the Vietnam War for the United States, the Afghan War drained the Soviet economy and provoked a crisis in morale at home.

Primary Source

Long Lines in the Soviet Command Economy

In the 1970s, Robert Kaiser lived and worked in Moscow as a reporter for the Washington Post. *He witnessed a noteworthy and frustrating result of the Soviet command economy—very long lines:*

"A good shopper will jump into a queue [line] wherever he or she finds it, taking a place and then asking what is being offered for sale at the other end. . . .

The queue is [everywhere] in Soviet life, and it comes in many forms. The queue to buy a private car may be five years long. . . . Mothers will spend an entire day at the Children's World department store hoping to buy an aluminum sled for winter. At the neighborhood bread store, three lines are not uncommon: one to make a selection, another to pay the cashier, a third to exchange the cashier's receipt for the chosen loaf."

—Robert G. Kaiser,
Russia From the Inside

Skills Assessment

Primary Source Why do you think waiting lines for goods were so long in the Soviet Union?

Disaster!

MELTDOWN AT CHERNOBYL

In the **early morning hours of April 26, 1986**, disaster struck near the Ukrainian city of Prypyat. A full-scale nuclear meltdown had taken place in Reactor No. 4 of the Chernobyl nuclear power plant. The meltdown triggered a fire that released radiation-laden gas and dust particles. Countless civilians were contaminated by the radiation.

Radiation Warning Sign

These two children from Kiev, 65 miles southeast of Chernobyl, are being tested for radiation levels. Right now in the Ukraine, Belarus, and Russia, unusually high numbers of children suffer from thyroid cancer. Even children born after the accident are at risk.

The once thriving city of Prypyat is now a ghost town. People living within a 20-mile radius of the plant were evacuated immediately after the accident. The plant and surrounding area are now fenced, and it is still unsafe for humans to live there. Still, with nowhere else to go, hundreds of people have returned to their homes in Prypyat, despite the danger of contamination.

The area surrounding the Chernobyl nuclear power plant was the worst hit by radiation, but much of the Northern Hemisphere was affected, as well.

Radiation Levels

BELORUSSIAN S.S.R.

Dnieper R.
• Savichi

Chernobyl Nuclear Power Plant — Prypyat
Cooling Pond — Chernobyl
Prypyat R.

N
W E
S

Teterev R.
• Ivankov
• Dymer

Kiev Reservoir
Desna R.

0   10 Miles
0   10 Kilometers   UKRAINIAN S.S.R.

• Kiev

☐ Initial evacuation zone
☐ Severe radiation area
☐ Most severe radiation area

Portfolio Assessment

INTERNET Nuclear power is only one alternative form of energy. Using the Internet or library resources, learn more about other energy sources. Create a diagram or model that describes and illustrates how one new alternative energy source works.

From Revolution to Reform in China

Reading Focus

- What were the effects of communist policies in China?
- What challenges did China face during the Cold War?
- How did calls for reform spur renewed repression?
- What challenges face China today?

Vocabulary

collectivization

commune

joint venture

special enterprise zone

Taking Notes

Copy this table. As you read, list developments in the People's Republic of China under Mao Zedong and Deng Xiaoping.

MAO ZEDONG	DENG XIAOPING
• Great Leap Forward	• Joint ventures
•	•

Main Idea After a series of failed reforms in China, Communist leaders introduced elements of capitalism.

Setting the Scene

On October 1, 1999, China celebrated an important anniversary. Exactly 50 years earlier, in 1949, communist leader Mao Zedong had announced the birth of the People's Republic of China. He pledged "to build a new China, independent, . . . prosperous and strong." Under Mao, China experienced a revolution that ranks with Russia's as one of the major social transformations of the 1900s.

Communist Control of China

After World War II, civil war resumed between Mao Zedong's Communist forces and Jiang Jieshi's Nationalists. Battles raged until Mao's forces swept to victory and set up the People's Republic of China (PRC). Jiang Jieshi and his supporters fled to the island of Taiwan. After decades of struggle, China was finally united—with the Communists in control.

Reasons for Victory The Communists triumphed for a number of reasons. Mao won the support of China's huge peasant population. Peasants had long suffered from brutal landlords and crushing taxes. The Communists pledged to redistribute land to poor peasants and end oppression by landlords.

Additionally, many women backed Mao's forces. The Nationalists had made little effort to improve their harsh lives. Women were still seen as inferior to men and often were cruelly mistreated. The Communists rejected the inequalities of the old Confucian order. To point out this break with tradition, Mao said: "Women hold up half the sky."

Mao's armies outfought Jiang's, and while support for the Communists grew, the Nationalists lost popularity. Many educated Chinese saw Jiang's government as morally and politically bankrupt. They hoped that the Communists would build a new China and end foreign domination.

Reorganizing the Economy Once in power, the Communists set out to turn China from a backward peasant society into a modern industrial nation. To build socialism and repair the economy, China nationalized all businesses. The government also drew up five-year plans to develop agriculture and heavy industry. With Soviet help, the Chinese built hydroelectric plants, railroads, and canals.

To boost agriculture, Mao distributed land to peasants. Then he called for **collectivization,** the pooling of peasant land and labor in an attempt to increase efficiency.

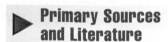

Primary Sources and Literature

See "Mao Zedong: The People's Democratic Dictatorship" in the Reference Section at the back of this book.

Remolding Society   Like Lenin in the Soviet Union, Mao Zedong built a one-party totalitarian state, with the Communist party supreme. Communist ideology replaced Confucian beliefs and traditional religions. The government attacked crime and corruption. It did away with the old landlord and business classes. In their place, peasants and workers were honored as the builders of the new China. Many thousands of landlords and middle-class people were beaten and killed. One official justified the attacks, saying:

> "The freedom we uphold is not the same as that based on the type of democracy advocated by the bourgeoisie. . . . We, on the contrary, hold that there must be democratic liberties among the people, but that no freedom should be extended to counterrevolutionaries: for them we have only dictatorship."
> —Lu Ting-yi, speech delivered May 26, 1956

To increase literacy, the government simplified Chinese characters, making it easier to learn to read and write. Schools were opened for young and old. Reading and writing were mixed with political education. Students learned to praise the "Great Helmsman," Mao Zedong, who could do no wrong.

The Communists also sent health-care workers to remote rural areas. Although many of these "barefoot doctors" had limited training, they did help to reduce disease and teach better hygiene.

Changes for Women   Under China's new constitution, women won equality under the law. They were expected to work alongside men in fields and factories. State-run nurseries were set up to care for the children. These changes weakened the old ideal of the extended family dominated by the oldest male. In China's cities, as elsewhere in the developing world, the nuclear family became increasingly common.

Although Chinese women made real progress, they did not enjoy full equality. Only a few won promotion to top jobs in government and industry. Women were often paid less than men for the same work. Also, after working at paid jobs, they still were responsible for cleaning, cooking, and child care.

Economic Disasters

Although some reforms did result in more access to education and greater equality, people in China paid a heavy cost for Mao's programs. During the 1950s and 1960s, two efforts in particular led to economic disaster and tremendous loss of life.

The Great Leap Forward   In 1958, Mao launched a program known as the "Great Leap Forward." He urged people to make a superhuman effort to increase farm and industrial output. In an attempt to make agriculture more efficient, he created communes. A typical commune included several villages, thousands of acres of land, and up to 25,000 people. It had its own schools, factories, housing, and dining halls. Each commune had production quotas. Communes also mobilized labor brigades to build dams and irrigation systems. Rural communes set up "backyard" industries to produce steel and other products.

The Great Leap Forward was a dismal failure. Backyard industries turned out low-quality, useless goods. The commune system slowed food output. Bad weather and declining food production added to the problems and led to a terrible famine. Between 1959 and 1961, up to 30 million Chinese are thought to have starved to death. In response, China turned to more moderate policies.

The Cultural Revolution   China slowly recovered from the Great Leap Forward. Then, in 1966, Mao launched the Great Proletarian Cultural Revolution. Its goal was to purge China of "bourgeois," or nonrevolutionary, tendencies. He urged young Chinese to experience revolution firsthand, as his generation had.

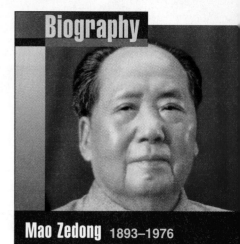

Biography

Mao Zedong 1893–1976

During the mid-1950s, divisions arose within the Communist party in China. In response, Mao launched a campaign under the slogan "Let a hundred flowers bloom, let a hundred thoughts contend." Mao hoped that by offering people the opportunity to openly express their views he would gain more support. When people began to criticize the Communist party, however, Mao ended the campaign. Of the nearly 550,000 Chinese who had spoken out, thousands were executed and hundreds of thousands were exiled to the countryside to "rectify their thinking through labor."

Theme: Impact of the Individual What methods did Mao use to keep power for himself?

In response, teenagers formed bands of Red Guards. Waving copies of the "Little Red Book" of Mao's sayings, Red Guards attacked those they claimed were counterrevolutionaries. They targeted people in authority, from party leaders and factory managers to teachers, writers, and artists. The accused were publicly humiliated or beaten, and sometimes even killed.

The Cultural Revolution convulsed China. Schools and factories closed. The economy slowed, and civil war threatened. Finally, Mao had the army restore order. Many Red Guards were sent to work on communes. They became a lost generation, undereducated and cut off from normal family life and careers. In the end, many became disillusioned with communism.

Red Guards
During the Cultural Revolution, groups of teenagers known as Red Guards responded to Mao's call for renewed revolution. Here, young Red Guards read from Mao's "Little Red Book."

Theme: Impact of the Individual How does this photograph show Mao's importance in communist China?

China and the Cold War

The Communist victory over the Nationalists dominated the Cold War in 1949. After Jiang Jieshi fled to Taiwan, the United States continued to support the Nationalist government. The United States refused to recognize the People's Republic of China, which it saw as an aggressive communist power and a threat to all of Asia.

Relations With the United States For years, the United States tried to isolate China. In 1971, however, China won admission to the United Nations. A year later, United States President Richard Nixon visited Mao in Beijing. Slowly, relations improved. Finally, in 1979, the United States set up formal diplomatic relations with China.

Split With the Soviet Union China and the Soviet Union were uneasy allies in the 1950s. Stalin sent economic aid and technical experts to help China modernize, but he and Mao disagreed on many issues.

Mao had adapted Marxism to Chinese conditions. Marx had predicted that the industrial working class—the proletariat—would lead the revolution. Because China had little industry, however, Mao's revolution relied on peasants rather than factory workers. Stalin rejected Mao's views. Mao, in turn, thought that the Soviets were too conservative and accused them of being too willing to "coexist" with the capitalist powers.

China and the Soviet Union also competed for influence in developing nations. In addition, border disputes triggered tensions between the two. By 1960, border clashes and disputes over ideology led the Soviets to withdraw all aid and advisers from China.

Reform and Repression

Mao Zedong died in 1976. Despite disastrous mistakes, many still saw him as the revolutionary hero who had restored order, ended foreign domination, and made China a world power once again.

After Mao, more moderate leaders controlled China. By 1981, Deng Xiaoping (duhng show PIHNG) had set China on a new path. Deng was a practical reformer, more interested in raising output than in political purity. "I don't care if a cat is black or white," he declared, "as long as it catches mice."

Economic Reforms Deng backed a program called the Four Modernizations, which emphasized agriculture, industry, science, and defense. As part of this plan, Deng introduced economic reforms, including some private ownership of property and free-market policies. In agriculture, the responsibility system replaced the communes. Peasant families were allotted plots of farmland. The government took a share of their crops, but the family could sell the rest on the free market.

Entrepreneurs were allowed to set up their own businesses. Managers of state-run factories were given more freedom but were expected to make their plants more efficient. Deng welcomed foreign capital and technology. Investors from Japan, Hong Kong, Taiwan, and the West organized joint ventures with China, in which foreign companies would organize a business with Chinese firms, with profits shared by both participants. The government also set up special enterprise zones, where foreigners could own and operate industries.

Deng's reforms brought a surge of growth and a better standard of living for some Chinese. They were soon buying motor scooters, televisions, and refrigerators. On the downside, crime and corruption grew. Inequalities increased as a new wealthy class emerged. An economic gap also grew between poor rural farmers in the interior and city dwellers on the coast who were exposed to western influences.

Tiananmen Square Massacre By the late 1980s, some Chinese were demanding greater political freedom as well as economic reform. In Beijing and other cities, students, workers, and others supported a democracy movement like those sweeping Eastern Europe. Deng, however, would not talk about political reform.

In May 1989, tens of thousands of demonstrators occupied Tiananmen Square. They raised banners calling for democracy and brought in a huge plaster statue called the Goddess of Democracy and Freedom. When the demonstrators refused to disperse, the government sent in troops and tanks. Thousands of demonstrators were killed or wounded. Many others were arrested and tortured. Some were put to death.

The crackdown showed that China's Communist leaders were determined to maintain control. To them, order was more important than political freedom. During the 1990s, efforts to persuade China to end human rights violations had limited effects.

Challenges Today

By the mid-1990s, China was a major industrial power. Its economy ranked among the fastest growing in the world, and it was building major trade ties with countries worldwide. Yet even as economic gains continued, the nation faced many unresolved issues.

Population Population growth posed a challenge for the future. Since 1949, China's population has more than doubled, to more than 1.2 billion. Such rapid growth strained the economy. In the 1980s, the government instituted

▶ **Primary Sources and Literature**

See "Harry Wu: The Outlook for China, Human Rights" in the Reference Section at the back of this book.

Population Density
In some Chinese cities, people are likely to use public transportation. Others, such as these Beijing residents, rely on bicycles.

Theme: Economics and Technology Why would the bicycle be a common form of transportation in Chinese cities?

You Are There . . .

Helping Protesters in Tiananmen Square

You are bringing food and supplies to the students in Tiananmen Square. They are protesting government corruption and the lack of democratic reform. As each day passes, the crowd of protesters grows—and tensions mount.

The government has declared military rule, and soldiers are moving into Beijing. In response, crowds of protesters build barricades. A wave of excitement ripples through the square as art students from Beijing University arrive. They have brought a statue that they call the "Goddess of Democracy and Freedom."

Finally, soldiers break through the barricades and march into the city. For 20 minutes, a lone man blocks a column of tanks. Eventually, however, the soldiers occupy Tiananmen Square and force the students out.

Portfolio Assessment

After you return home, you record all you have seen in your diary. In your entry, describe what you saw and how you felt about the demonstration.

a one-child-per-family policy. Parents who had only one child were given rewards, such as better housing or improved medical benefits. Those who had more children faced fines and other penalties.

The campaign to slow the birthrate worked better in cities than in rural areas. Farm families, who wanted children to work the land, often paid fines rather than obey the policy. The one-child policy had a tragic effect in a country that still valued boys over girls. Female infanticide, or the killing of girl babies, increased despite efforts to prevent it.

Economic and Political Issues After Deng Xiaoping died in 1997, Jiang Zemin emerged as China's leader. He continued Deng's economic reforms and had to grapple with the same problems as Deng. Many state-run industries were inefficient, but they could not be closed without risking high unemployment and economic chaos. Cities overflowed with millions of peasants who poured in to seek new opportunities. Inequalities between rich and poor and between urban and rural Chinese continued to grow.

Across China, communist ideology was weakening. From party officials on down, people were more interested in profit than in socialism. Corruption was a growing problem. The government made some efforts to crack down on corruption and other criminal activity.

Human Rights Issues The Communist party maintained its monopoly on power and continued to jail critics. Its human rights abuses, however, brought strong pressure from trading partners such as the United States.

Advocates of western-style human rights did not focus only on the suppression of dissent in China. Some asserted that China used prison labor to produce cheap export goods. Others charged China with imperialistic tyranny in Tibet, where the indigenous culture had been swamped by Chinese immigrants and military suppression of the Tibetan form of Buddhism. At the end of the 1990s, the Chinese government had also cracked down on a new Chinese version of Buddhism, the Falun Gong sect, which claimed millions of members. Political dissidents, human rights advocates, and spokespeople for oppressed Tibet, such as Tibet's exiled religious leader the Dalai Lama, found widespread support in Europe and the United States.

China replied to the charges from the West by declaring that outsiders had no right to tell the Chinese leaders how to run their own domestic affairs. Chinese leaders also denied the right of the West to impose western standards of human rights on other cultures.

Geography and History

Three Gorges Dam

In the mid-1990s, China began construction on the world's largest dam. Located on the Yangzi River, Three Gorges Dam will be 607 feet high and 1.2 miles wide, creating a lake 370 miles long. The dam will cost between $14 billion and $75 billion and will take more than 15 years to complete.

The dam has sparked controversy. Officials say the dam will protect millions from floods and will generate electric power for one of the country's most underdeveloped regions. It will also improve navigation along the river.

Critics argue that the new lake will flood 13 cities and 140 towns, forcing some 1.5 million people to relocate. They point out that the lake will destroy important archaeological treasures in the region. Additionally, many fear that the dam will lead to greater pollution as industrial areas are flooded.

Theme: Economics and Technology
What are the benefits of the dam? What are the costs?

SECTION 2 Assessment

Recall
1. **Identify:** (a) People's Republic of China, (b) five-year plan, (c) Great Leap Forward, (d) Cultural Revolution, (e) "Little Red Book," (f) Four Modernizations, (g) Tiananmen Square.
2. **Define:** (a) collectivization, (b) commune, (c) joint venture, (d) special enterprise zone.

Comprehension
3. How did Mao's economic policies harm China?
4. What major issues did China face during the Cold War?

5. (a) What economic reforms did Deng Xiaoping introduce? (b) What challenges does China face today?

Critical Thinking and Writing
6. **Predicting Consequences** Do you think economic reforms can be successful without political reforms? Explain.
7. **Comparing** Compare Deng's reforms in China to those of Gorbachev in the Soviet Union. (a) How were the reforms similar? (b) How were they different?

Activity
Take It to the NET

Use the Internet to research the Tiananmen Square massacre. Then, write a paragraph explaining the role of students in the 1989 demonstrations in Beijing.

The Asian Tigers

Reading Focus

■ How has China influenced Taiwan and Hong Kong?

■ How did Singapore modernize?

■ Why has Korea remained divided for more than 50 years?

Taking Notes

Create an outline of this section. Use Roman numerals for major headings, capital letters for subheadings, and numbers for the supporting details. Use this sample as a starting point.

I. **Taiwan and Hong Kong**
   A. **Taiwan**
      1. **Ruled by China until 1895**
      2.
   B. **Hong Kong**
      1.

Main Idea — Aggressive economic growth led to world prominence for several nations in East and Southeast Asia.

Setting the Scene

At a university in Taiwan, Professor Xu Wenxing proudly unveiled an invention he had worked on for 10 years. His invention was a computerized fingerprint-recognition device, which was soon put to use. To Xu, however, the most satisfying aspect of his success was that "the technology involved was developed in Taiwan."

Taiwan was one of four small Asian lands that vaulted into the class of "newly industrialized countries" by the 1980s. Besides Taiwan, Hong Kong, Singapore, and South Korea are also known for their aggressive economic growth. The four are often called the "Asian tigers." Although they differ in important ways, all followed similar roads to modernization after 1945. Additionally, all four nations were influenced to some degree by China and by Confucian traditions.

Taiwan and Hong Kong

Both Taiwan and Hong Kong have deep cultural and historical links to China. Both were once part of China. Neither, however, experienced Mao's communist revolution. The island of Taiwan was once ruled by the mainland. Today, the People's Republic still considers it part of China. Hong Kong was returned to China in 1997 after more than a century under British colonial rule.

Taiwan The island of Taiwan was ruled by China until 1895, when it fell to Japan. The Japanese built some industry, providing a foundation for later growth. In 1945, with Japan defeated, Taiwan reverted to China. But when Jiang Jieshi fled the mainland in 1949, he set up his Nationalist government on Taiwan. Despite Jiang's autocratic rule, Taiwan experienced rapid economic growth and enjoyed United States's support.

First, Taiwan set up light industries such as textiles. Later, it developed heavy industry. The Green Revolution of the 1960s, with its new seeds and fertilizers, helped Taiwan's agriculture become more productive. Trade boomed, industrial cities grew, and in time Taiwan's standard of living rose to one of the highest in Asia.

With economic success, the government slowly allowed people more political freedom. Hostility between Taiwan and the mainland eased somewhat as the Cold War ended in the 1990s. Taiwanese businesses took advantage of Deng Xiaoping's economic reforms to invest in companies on the mainland.

Connections to Today

Taiwan: Rebel Province or Independent State?

Since 1949, the People's Republic of China has considered Taiwan a "rebel province" that must be reunited with the parent country. In 1995, the Chinese drove home that point by conducting two months of missile tests and live-fire exercises in the island's waters.

In 1999, Taiwanese President Lee Teng-hui created a new uproar when he insisted that China deal with Taiwan as a separate state. The Chinese responded angrily, renewing their threats of force against Taiwan. In Beijing, the *People's Daily* compared Taiwan's efforts to influence China to "an ant trying to topple a tree."

Theme: Political and Social Systems How do you think reunion with mainland China would affect the lives of the Taiwanese?

Most people in Taiwan welcome closer links with the mainland. Yet some fear Beijing's power over the island's economy. Beijing still wants to reunite Taiwan and China. It sees Taiwan as a province of China, not an independent nation.

Hong Kong   Britain gained the tiny island of Hong Kong after the Opium War. Under British rule, Hong Kong and nearby territories grew into a center of trade. In 1949, millions of refugees from China escaped the revolution by crowding into Hong Kong. They provided labor and capital to help the area develop.

Hong Kong's new prosperity was based largely on trade and light industry, such as textiles and electronics. It also became a world financial center with many foreign banks and a busy stock market. Wealth from these profitable industries helped Hong Kong modernize.

Hong Kong's amazing growth was also due in part to its location on China's doorstep. Hong Kong Chinese built commercial ties to the mainland at a time when the People's Republic was largely isolated from the world community. This gave Hong Kong the chance to buy and sell goods with a market that was unavailable to many other countries.

In 1997, Britain returned Hong Kong to China. The People's Republic of China agreed not to change Hong Kong's social or economic system for 50 years and to allow its people self-government. Still, many Hong Kong residents remained nervous about China's power and use of repressive measures against protests.

Singapore

The smallest Asian tiger is the city-state of Singapore. It sits on a tiny island at the tip of the Malay Peninsula in Southeast Asia. Its 200 square miles have a population of about two million.

In 1819, British empire builder Sir Stamford Raffles leased the island from a local ruler. Raffles recognized its ideal location on the Strait of Malacca, halfway between China and India. He and his successors turned the island's fishing villages into a seaport.

Under British rule, Singapore grew rapidly. The population came to include Malayans, British merchants and sailors, and Chinese and Indian immigrants. All hoped to prosper in the booming city. The British brought in Chinese workers to work in factories that processed tin and rubber from Malaya. In time, the Chinese, with their Confucian tradition, became the dominant ethnic group.

Order and Prosperity   Singapore won independence first from Britain in 1959 and then from nearby Malaya in 1963. For 30 years, Lee Kwan Yew was Singapore's autocratic prime minister. Lee supported a free-market economy. By keeping labor costs low, Lee attracted foreign capital that helped the economy boom. He expanded Singapore's seaport into one of the world's busiest harbors.

The government welcomed skilled immigrants and insisted on education for all its people—in both English and Chinese. It encouraged high-tech industries, manufacturing, finance, and tourism. As Singapore's economy grew, its standard of living rose. The government set up a successful public housing program. Most married couples became homeowners with the help of government loans.

Ongoing Issues   Lee's successors continued his strict policies, allowing little opposition. Critics condemned limits on freedom. In response, the government claimed that order was more important than individual freedoms. Still, it faced demands for more rights from many of its young, well-educated citizens.

Did You Know?

Life in Singapore

Unlike most large Asian cities, Singapore is clean, quiet, and orderly. With low pollution, lush tropical greenery, no traffic jams, and low crime, the city is often described by its citizens as "paradise."

But Singaporeans pay a price for stability. To achieve public order, the government levies—and vigorously enforces—hefty penalties on all sorts of behavior. For example, littering brings a $625 fine, eating on the subway merits a $312 penalty, and failing to flush a public toilet costs the offender $94. The sale of chewing gum is outlawed, as is smoking in public.

Many Singaporeans feel that their nation's prosperity and stability justify these limits on personal freedom. They probably would agree with former Prime Minister Lee Kwan Yew when he said: "When you are hungry, when you lack basic services, freedom, human rights and democracy do not add up to much."

Theme: Political and Social Systems How does Singapore emphasize public order?

Korean War, 1950–1953

USSR

Conic Projection

0   50   100 Miles

0   50   100 Kilometers

Line of farthest North Korean advance, September 1950

UN invasion, September 1950

Line of farthest UN advance, November 1950

Line of farthest Chinese and North Korean advance, January 1951

Armistice line, 1953

Skills Assessment

Geography After North Korean troops stormed across the 38th parallel, the UN sent an army to aid South Korea. Fighting continued for three years, until a cease-fire was signed in 1953.

1. **Location** On the map, locate **(a)** North Korea, **(b)** South Korea, **(c)** 38th parallel, **(d)** Yalu River, **(e)** Inchon.
2. **Movement** How far did UN forces advance into North Korea?
3. **Critical Thinking** **Making Inferences** Based on the map, why do you think the UN advance beyond the 38th parallel worried the Chinese?

Because Singapore depended heavily on trade, its economy was influenced by events elsewhere. Yet it weathered the Asian financial crisis. Over the years, it also faced ethnic tensions between the Chinese majority and Malay and Indian minorities.

Despite such issues, Singapore was often seen as a model of successful development. With few natural resources, it built a booming economy. How did it succeed? Lee Kwan Yew preached "Confucian values," such as hard work, loyalty toward family, and respectful obedience to authority. Lee and others also spoke of a "Confucian model of development." Singapore and the other Asian tigers, they noted, all had stable governments that invested in education. In each, the Confucian ethic shaped attitudes about work. People worked long hours for low wages. They also saved these wages, which enabled banks to invest in further development.

The Two Koreas

The fourth Asian tiger, South Korea, emerged during the Cold War. It occupies the southern half of the Korean peninsula. In 1910, Japan annexed the Korean peninsula, imposing harsh rule on it. After World War II, the Soviet Union and United States agreed to a temporary division of Korea along the 38th parallel of latitude. Before long, North Korea, ruled by Kim Il Sung, became a communist ally of the Soviet Union. In South Korea, the United States backed the authoritarian—but noncommunist—leader, Syngman Rhee.

The Korean War Both leaders wanted to end the division. In early 1950, Kim Il Sung called for a "heroic struggle" to reunite Korea. North Korean troops attacked and soon overran most of the south. The United States then organized a UN force to help South Korea.

UN forces were made up mostly of Americans and South Koreans. They were led by United States general Douglas MacArthur, who had commanded troops in World War I and World War II and headed the occupation of Japan. He landed troops behind enemy lines, drove the invaders back across the 38th parallel, and then pushed northward to the Yalu River, along the border of China. MacArthur's success alarmed China. Mao Zedong sent Chinese troops to help the North Koreans, who again advanced southward.

The Korean War turned into a stalemate. Finally, in 1953, both sides signed an armistice, or end to fighting. The armistice has held for nearly 50 years, but no peace treaty has ever been negotiated. More than a million North Korean and South Korean troops dug in on either side of the demilitarized zone (DMZ), an area with no military forces, near the 38th parallel. At the end of the 1990s, American forces were still in South Korea to help guarantee the peace.

After the war, the two Koreas slowly rebuilt economies destroyed by the fighting and by years of Japanese occupation. Both remained centers of Cold War tensions. The United States funneled aid to South Korea, while the Soviets helped the north.

Analyzing Primary Sources

War Refugees in Korea

The power struggle over North and South Korea played a large part in the Cold War tensions of the late 1940s and 1950s. Those not involved in the politics were drawn in when the Cold War escalated into a hot war between Communist and UN-backed forces in 1950. Civilians, such as K. Connie Kang and her mother, were caught up in the fighting.

"On a cold January night in 1951, when North Korean troops were about to invade Seoul, I rode on the rooftop of the last train bound for Pusan with my mother to escape the oncoming Communists. Bone-chilling wind from Siberia whipped across the 'freedom train,' which was jam-packed with soldiers, the sick, and the injured. There was no room for able-bodied civilians—not even children.

'I don't want to go up there, Mommy,' I protested. 'It's too scary.'

'We will be all right,' Mother assured me, even though I could tell she was scared herself. 'See those fellows on the train? They will secure us.' she said, pointing to the men on top of the train with . . . straw rope in their hands. 'If we don't take this train, we will surely die in the hands of Communists. This is the last train to Pusan.'

Mother climbed very slowly up a small staircase at the back of the coach. When I got up on the top of the train, I was surprised to see how roomy it was. . . . My mother sat beside me and held me by the cord tied around my middle with one hand to make sure I didn't fall off the train. The 'freedom train' traveled all through the night. Not everyone was as fortunate as I on that fateful night. That night several youngsters fell accidentally to their death. Life was cheap. I could have been one of them, had my mother not secured me and grasped the rope tied to my waist through the long trip, her hand nearly frozen under her mittens from the exposure to the biting wind. Whenever my mother caught me dozing off, she pinched me. 'Don't fall asleep. . . . You'll fall off the train if you do,' she said, all the while not once letting go of the rope around my waist."
　　　—K. Connie Kang, *Home Was the Land of Morning Calm*

Fleeing South
Thousands of Korean refugees struggle to board a train heading south out of Seoul to escape the advancing North Korean army.

Skills Assessment

1. Why was Kang forced to ride on top of the train with her mother?
   A They had no money.
   B Only soldiers, the sick, and the injured could ride inside.
   C Passengers heading for Pusan had to ride on top.
   D They had lost their tickets.

2. According to this excerpt, many South Koreans risked the train ride from Seoul because
   E it would soon be winter in Seoul.
   F their homes had been destroyed by bombs.
   G they feared that invading Communists would kill them.
   H there was no food left in Seoul.

3. **Critical Thinking** **Drawing Conclusions** List two conclusions you can draw from the information in the passage.

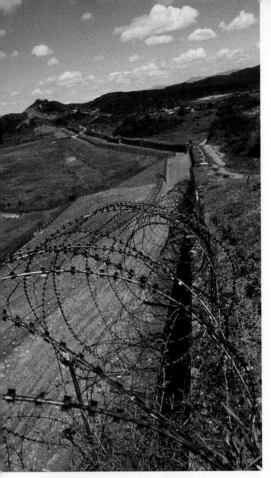

South Korea By the mid-1960s, South Korea's economy had leaped ahead. At first, it exported inexpensive textiles and manufactured goods. Later, it shifted to higher-priced exports such as automobiles and electronics. As in the other Asian tigers, its growth was partly due to low wages, long hours, and other worker sacrifices.

By the 1990s, South Korea was an economic powerhouse. With prosperity, workers won better pay, and the country's standard of living rose greatly. The 1997 Asian financial crisis brought hardships such as business failure and high unemployment. The government undertook difficult economic reforms, and by 2000, the nation's economy was recovering.

For decades after the Korean War, dictators backed by the military ruled in South Korea. By 1987, however, growing prosperity and fierce student protests pushed the government to hold direct elections. Since then, the nation has moved successfully toward democracy.

North Korea Under Kim Il Sung, state-owned industries and collective farms increased output in North Korea. That growth slowed, however, in the late 1960s. Kim's emphasis on self-reliance kept North Korea isolated. Even when its Soviet and Chinese allies undertook economic reforms, North Korea clung to hardline communism.

Propaganda constantly glorified Kim as the "Great Leader." After he died, his son Kim Jong Il, the "Dear Leader," took over. He faced huge problems. Failed government policies and terrible floods destroyed harvests, bringing widespread hunger. During the late 1990s, North Korea had to accept food aid from the United States, South Korea, and other nations to prevent mass starvation. Kim held onto power despite the misery and famine.

Demilitarized Zone
The border between South Korea and North Korea lies in the demilitarized zone, an area in which military forces are prohibited.

Theme: Political and Social Systems Why have tensions remained high between the two nations?

The Nuclear Issue Like several emerging nations, North Korea tried to develop nuclear power for electricity and for weapons. Under intense pressure from the United States, it agreed to end its nuclear weapons program in exchange for oil and other assistance. Yet North Korea continued to threaten South Korea and nearby Japan by testing missiles.

Outlook for Unity Despite differences between the two Koreas, most Koreans want to see their country reunited. After all, they share the same history, language, and culture. Restoring unity is of global interest because of Korea's strategic location in Asia.

SECTION 3 Assessment

Recall

1. **Identify:** (a) Asian tigers, (b) Lee Kwan Yew, (c) Syngman Rhee, (d) Kim Jong Il.

Comprehension

2. Describe how China's strength has affected the development of Taiwan and Hong Kong.
3. How did Singapore's leaders encourage economic growth?
4. (a) How do the economies of South Korea and North Korea differ? (b) How has the North Korean government's policy on isolation affected the nation?

Critical Thinking and Writing

5. **Drawing Conclusions** What characteristic seems to have been most important to the economic success of the "Asian tigers"? Explain.
6. **Linking Past and Present** What conditions existing today in Taiwan, Hong Kong, Singapore, and Korea reflect lingering Cold War tensions?

Activity

Writing a Position Paper In 1950, Kim Il Sung described North Korea's advances on the 38th parallel as the means to "achieve glorious, complete independence." Imagine that you are an official in the South Korean government. Write a position paper reacting to Kim's statement and identifying possible responses.

Southeast Asia and the Pacific Rim

Reading Focus

- How did war affect Vietnam and Cambodia?
- What challenges faced the Philippines and the developing nations of Southeast Asia?
- What factors make the Pacific Rim a vital region?

Vocabulary

domino theory
cease-fire
embargo

Taking Notes

Create a time line that includes major events discussed in this section. The sample below will help you get started.

```
1940   1950   1960   1970   1980   1990   2000
 |      |      |      |      |      |      |
                    1968
               Tet Offensive
```

Main Idea | Southeast Asian nations sought independence in the decades after World War II.

Setting the Scene

Today, Southeast Asia is a key player in the global economy. For decades after the end of World War II, though, the region was shaped by the nationalist drive for independence. Some nations won freedom with little violence. Others faced long wars of liberation against European nations that wanted to reclaim their colonial empires after the war.

War in Vietnam and Cambodia

In mainland Southeast Asia, an agonizing liberation struggle tore apart the region once known as French Indochina. It affected the emerging nations of Vietnam, Cambodia, and Laos. The 30-year conflict had two major phases. First was the battle against the French, dating from 1946 to 1954. Second were the civil war and Cold War conflicts that raged from 1959 to 1975.

In 1946, the French set out to regain Indochina, which Japan had seized during World War II. They faced fierce resistance from guerrilla forces led by Ho Chi Minh. Ho was a nationalist and communist who had fought the Japanese. He and his forces wore down the French and eventually forced them to leave Vietnam.

Vietnam Divided The struggle for Vietnam became part of the Cold War. At an international conference in 1954, western and communist powers agreed to a temporary division of Vietnam. Ho's communists ruled North Vietnam. Ngo Dinh Diem's noncommunist government, supported by the United States, ruled South Vietnam. Cambodia and Laos gained independence.

The agreement called for elections to reunite Vietnam. The elections were never held, however, largely because the Americans and Diem feared that the communists might win. American officials believed in the domino theory. It held that a communist victory in South Vietnam would cause noncommunist governments across Southeast Asia to fall to communism, like a row of dominoes.

American Involvement As the war continued, the United States became increasingly involved. Ho Chi Minh wanted to unite Vietnam under northern rule. He aided the National Liberation Front, communist rebels trying to overthrow Diem in South Vietnam. At first, the United States sent only military advisers and supplies to Diem. Later, it sent troops, turning a local struggle into a major Cold War conflict.

In 1964, the United States began bombing targets in North Vietnam. Eventually, more than 500,000 American troops were committed. At the

Primary Source

Vietnamese Declaration of Independence

Vietnamese nationalists led by Ho Chi Minh proclaimed the Democratic Republic of Vietnam on September 2, 1945. Following is an excerpt from their Declaration of Independence:

"The Declaration of the French Revolution . . . states: 'All men are born free with equal rights, and must always remain free and have equal rights.'. . .

Nevertheless, for more than eighty years, the French imperialists . . . have violated our Fatherland and oppressed our fellow-citizens. They have acted contrary to the ideals of humanity and justice. . . .

For these reasons, we . . . solemnly declare to the world that Vietnam has the right to be a free and independent country. . . . The entire Vietnamese people are determined to . . . sacrifice their lives and property in order to safeguard their independence and liberty."

—Vietnamese Declaration of Independence

Skills Assessment

Primary Source What document does this declaration cite? Why do you think the Vietnamese chose that document?

Tet Offensive, 1968

National Liberation Front base areas

American bases

North Vietnam's final offensive, 1975

CHINA

Tropic of Cancer

Red River

NORTH VIETNAM

Dienbienphu

Hanoi • Haiphong

20°N

LAOS

Gulf of Tonkin

Hainan

Vientiane

N

W E

S

THAILAND

Mekong River

Hue

Danang

Chu Lai

SOUTH VIETNAM

Bangkok

Plei Ku

CAMBODIA

Ho Chi Minh Trail

Gulf of Thailand

Phnom Penh

Câmranh Bay

Mercator Projection

0   200   400 Miles

0   200   400 Kilometers

100°E

Saigon (Ho Chi Minh City)

10°N

MEKONG DELTA

110°E

South China Sea

Skills Assessment

Geography In the Vietnam War, the United States supported South Vietnam in its struggle against communist North Vietnam. Despite this help, the war ended with a North Vietnamese victory.

1. **Location** On the map, locate (a) North Vietnam, (b) South Vietnam, (c) Cambodia, (d) Laos, (e) Saigon, (f) Ho Chi Minh Trail.
2. **Movement** How did North Vietnam's use of the Ho Chi Minh Trail as a supply route help to spread the war beyond Vietnam?
3. **Critical Thinking** **Applying Information** Use the map to describe the "domino theory."

same time, both the Soviet Union and China sent aid—but no troops—to help North Vietnam.

Despite massive American aid, South Vietnam could not defeat the communist guerrillas and their North Vietnamese allies. In 1968, guerrilla forces launched a massive attack on American and South Vietnamese forces. The assault was unexpected because it took place at Tet, the Vietnamese New Year. Although the communists did not capture any cities, the Tet Offensive marked a turning point in public opinion in the United States. It also showed that the North Vietnamese would fight at any cost.

As the fighting continued, the bombing of North Vietnam and growing American casualties on the ground inflamed antiwar opinion in the United States. Under increasing pressure, President Nixon finally arranged a **cease-fire**, or halt in the fighting. He began withdrawing American forces in 1973. Two years later, the North Vietnamese captured Saigon, capital of the south, and reunited the country.

The Communist Victory Why did the communists win? In some ways, the Vietnam War mirrored the civil war in China that brought Mao to power in 1949. Diem and his successors in South Vietnam were unpopular leaders of a corrupt government. Ho Chi Minh was admired as a hero who had fought the Japanese and the French. Many Vietnamese saw the United States as another foreign power seeking to dominate their land. Also, despite American air power and advanced technology, guerrillas fought well in the jungle terrain.

Vietnam Today The communist victors imposed harsh rule on the south. Tens of thousands of Vietnamese fled in small boats. Many of these "boat people" drowned. Survivors landed in refugee camps. Eventually, some were accepted into the United States or other countries.

Vietnam had to rebuild a land destroyed by war. Recovery was slow due to government inefficiency and an American-led **embargo**, or blockage of trade. For years, the country remained mired in poverty and was unable to attract foreign capital.

In the early 1990s, Vietnam introduced some free-market reforms, opening the door to investors. The economy received a further boost after the United States lifted its embargo and restored diplomatic relations. Although Vietnam made some progress, it remained one of the poorest countries in Southeast Asia. The government's monopoly on political power and its complex laws made foreign investment difficult. Vietnam's best hope was the entrepreneurial spirit of its people.

Tragedy in Cambodia During the Vietnam War, fighting spilled over into neighboring Cambodia. North Vietnam sent supplies along the Ho Chi Minh Trail through Cambodia to guerrilla forces in South Vietnam. In 1970, the United States bombed that route and then invaded Cambodia. After the Americans left, Cambodian communist guerrillas called the Khmer Rouge overthrew the government.

Led by Pol Pot, the Khmer Rouge unleashed a reign of terror. To destroy all western influences, they drove people from the cities and forced them to work in the fields. They slaughtered or caused the death of more than a million Cambodians, perhaps a third of the population:

> "There were no more cities. No more markets, stores, restaurants, or cafes. . . . No schools. No books or magazines. No money. No clocks. No holidays and religious festivals. Just the sun that rose and set, the stars at night and the rain that fell from the sky. And work. Everything was work."
>
> —Haing Ngor, *A Cambodian Odyssey*

In 1979, Vietnam invaded and occupied Cambodia. Pol Pot and his forces retreated to remote areas. In the 1990s, the UN helped Cambodia hold elections. The new government, however, soon grew authoritarian. After Pol Pot died in 1998, a number of Khmer Rouge leaders gave up their guerrilla struggle. Cambodia debated whether to put Khmer Rouge leaders on trial.

Challenges for the Philippines

In 1946, the Philippines gained freedom peacefully after almost 50 years of American rule. The United States, however, continued to influence the country through military and economic aid. Although the Filipino constitution set up a democratic government, a wealthy elite controlled politics and the economy. The peasant majority was desperately poor. For a time, the government battled Huks, local communists with strong peasant support.

In 1965, Ferdinand Marcos was elected president. Marcos had promised reform but instead became dictator. He cracked down on free speech and forced opponents into exile. He even had Benigno Aquino (beh NEE nyoh ah KEE noh), a popular rival politician, murdered. Under heavy pressure, Marcos finally held elections in 1986. Voters elected Corazon Aquino, widow of the slain Benigno. Marcos tried to overturn the results, but the people of Manila forced him to leave in what was called the "people power" revolution.

Under Aquino and her successors, the fragile democracy survived. The country enjoyed economic growth during the 1990s. But the government failed to make the major changes needed to improve life for the poverty-stricken majority. With the election of a new president, Fidel Ramos, there was renewed optimism for the future.

Like other developing nations, the Philippines experienced rapid urbanization. Newcomers crowded into the sprawling slums of Manila, the capital. Unrest surfaced in some areas. Natural disasters caused more setbacks. Many enterprising Filipinos left the country to build new lives in the United States and other parts of Asia.

Developing Nations of Southeast Asia

Southeast Asian nations faced many problems after independence. They lacked experience in self-government and were often hampered by complex ethnic and religious conflicts. Demands for political freedom and social justice were frequent. Some government leaders, however, claimed that order and economic development must take priority. All pursued the same goal, modernization, but their paths differed. Here, we will look at the experiences of two developing nations: Indonesia and Myanmar (formerly Burma).

Indonesia Geography posed an obstacle to unity in Indonesia, as in many developing nations. Indonesia includes more than 13,000 islands splashed across 3,200 miles of ocean—a distance equal to the width of the United States. Its large population is ethnically diverse. The Javanese dominate,

Corazon Aquino
The "people power" revolution of 1986 forced Ferdinand Marcos from power in the Philippines. Newly elected president Corazon Aquino, shown above, worked to preserve democracy.

Theme: Political and Social Systems What challenges faced the Philippines during the late 1980s and 1990s?

Aung San Suu Kyi 1945—

Aung San Suu Kyi was living in Britain with her husband and their sons when she decided to go home to Myanmar and oppose the military government. For safety, her family remained in Britain. After the 1990 election, the Myanmar government placed her under house arrest.

In 1991, the government announced that if Suu Kyi traveled to Norway to receive her Nobel Peace Prize, she would not be permitted to return to Myanmar. Her 18-year-old son Alexander accepted the award in her place.

Even after releasing Suu Kyi from house arrest in 1995, the government closely monitored her actions. Still, she resumed her post as general secretary of the opposition party. She gave weekly talks, held press conferences, and wrote speeches.

Theme: Impact of the Individual Why do many people in Myanmar consider Aung San Suu Kyi a hero?

Primary Sources and Literature

See "Aung San Suu Kyi: Freedom From Fear" in the Reference Section at the back of this book.

but about 300 other groups, many with their own languages or dialects, also live in Indonesia. Despite this diversity, about 90 percent of Indonesians are Muslims.

Under authoritarian military rule, Indonesia made great economic progress. It benefited from exporting oil, tin, rubber, spices, and coffee. The rise and fall of world oil prices, however, meant that income was uncertain. Still, the government increased literacy and in the 1990s, introduced economic reforms that attracted more foreign capital.

The 1997 Asian financial crisis shook Indonesia to its roots. Riots erupted against a government accused of massive corruption. President Suharto, who had held power for more than 30 years, was forced to resign. Elections were held for a new government. It faced serious problems such as reforming and restarting the economy, meeting separatist demands, and restoring confidence in government. Meanwhile, many Indonesians sank back into poverty. The spread of religiously motivated violence pitted Muslims against Christians and other minorities.

For years after independence, the authoritarian government suppressed rebellions. In 1965, it crushed what looked like a communist uprising and massacred many suspected communists. Mobs also killed hundreds of thousands of Chinese whose ancestors had settled in Indonesia. Another struggle erupted in East Timor, which Indonesia seized from Portugal in 1975. The East Timorese, who were mostly Catholic, wanted independence. For years, Indonesia brutally suppressed the region. In 1999, under international pressure, it finally allowed a vote on the issue. When the East Timorese chose independence, pro-Indonesia forces unleashed a campaign of terror. Soon after, UN peacekeepers were sent in to restore order.

Myanmar Ethnic tensions have also plagued Burma. The majority, Burmans, long dominated the country. For years, repressive military rulers battled rebel ethnic minorities who wanted autonomy. In 1962, the military government isolated the country, thus limiting trade and foreign investment. It imposed state socialism modeled on Mao's system in China. These policies brought little improvement in the standard of living. In 1989, they renamed the country Myanmar, meaning "the People's Country," which recognized that other groups besides Burmans lived there.

Under mounting pressure, the government held elections in 1990. The opposition party won. It was led by Aung San Suu Kyi (AWNG SAHN SOO SHEE), whose father had helped Burma win independence. The military rejected the election results and jailed, killed, or exiled many opponents. Suu Kyi was held under house arrest. While still a prisoner, she won the Nobel Peace Prize for her "nonviolent struggle for democracy and human rights." Suu Kyi was finally released in 1995 and continued to push for democracy in Myanmar.

Regional Cooperation Demands for political freedom and social justice remained an issue in Southeast Asia. Some government leaders, however, argued that order and economic development must take priority over democracy. To achieve prosperity and improve regional self-reliance, six Southeast Asian countries formed the Association of Southeast Asian Nations (ASEAN) in 1967. Since then, ASEAN has expanded to include most Southeast Asian nations. They have worked to promote economic and cultural cooperation.

The Pacific Rim

In the modern global economy, Southeast Asia and East Asia are part of a vast region known as the Pacific Rim. It includes countries in Asia and the Americas that border the Pacific Ocean.

The Pacific first became an artery for world trade in the 1500s. By the mid-1900s, links across the Pacific had grown dramatically. By the 1990s,

Virtual Field Trip

www.phschool.com

Batik of Indonesia
Jakarta, Indonesia

To learn more about batik, use the Internet address above to link to Batik of Indonesia.

Indonesian Textiles

Batik is made by applying wax and then dye to fabric. The waxed portions of the fabric do not absorb the dye, creating intricate patterns and shapes.

Theme: Art and Literature
What kinds of skills would a batik artist need?

the volume of trade across the Pacific was greater than that across the Atlantic. Some analysts have predicted that the 2000s will be the "Pacific century" because of this region's potential for further growth.

Countries on the Asian Pacific Rim formed a huge market that lured investors, especially multinational corporations. American companies, too, sought a place on the Asian Pacific Rim. With more than 1.2 billion people, China has a fifth of the world's population. Indonesia, with 190 million people, and Japan, with 125 million, are also among the world's most populous nations. Since the 1960s, Japan has dominated the Asian Pacific Rim economically. By the 1990s, however, China was challenging Japan's economic empire.

Pacific Rim countries are enormously diverse. Indian, Hindu, Buddhist, and Confucian traditions, you will recall, helped shape Southeast Asian cultures. Later, Islam took root in some areas, while the Age of Imperialism brought western and Christian influences.

Today, cultural exchanges occur rapidly as radio and television programs are beamed by satellite across Asia. Businesses and tourists aid the exchange of technology and ideas. The development of the Pacific Rim promises to bring the Americas and Asia into closer contact.

SECTION 4 Assessment

Recall

1. **Identify:** (a) Ho Chi Minh, (b) Khmer Rouge, (c) Corazon Aquino, (d) Aung San Suu Kyi, (e) ASEAN.
2. **Define:** (a) domino theory, (b) cease-fire, (c) embargo.

Comprehension

3. Describe the effects of war on (a) Vietnam, (b) Cambodia.
4. What economic and ethnic issues have faced governments in the Philippines and Indonesia?

5. Why is the Pacific Rim seen as an important link in the global economy?

Critical Thinking and Writing

6. **Linking Past and Present** What effects of the Vietnam War can still be seen in the United States today?
7. **Connecting to Geography** How might Indonesia's geographic features affect its ability to create a national identity?

Activity
Take It to the NET

Use the Internet to research the ASEAN Promotion Centre on Trade, Investment, and Tourism. (a) List ASEAN's member countries. (b) Write a paragraph explaining Japan's economic relations with another member country.

CHAPTER 34 Review and Assessment

Creating a Chapter Summary

Copy this diagram on a sheet of paper. In the blank circles, write the names of nations that have communist governments and those that have independent or democratic governments. Add more circles as needed.

CD-ROM Review For additional review of the major concepts of Chapter 34, see the *Guide to the Essentials of World History* or the *Interactive Student Tutorial CD-ROM*.

Web Site Self-Test For practice test questions for Chapter 34, see **www.phschool.com**.

Building Vocabulary

Write a sentence for each of the following terms.

1. zaibatsu
2. gross domestic product
3. trade deficit
4. five-year plan
5. collectivization
6. commune
7. joint venture
8. special enterprise zone
9. domino theory
10. cease-fire

Recalling Key Facts

11. How did the Great Leap Forward affect China?
12. Why did Taiwan create a separate government from that of mainland China?
13. What was the outcome of the war in Vietnam?
14. How did supporters of democracy in the Philippines overturn Ferdinand Marcos's government?
15. How have Southeast Asian nations increased regional cooperation?
16. What is the Pacific Rim? What has happened to trade in this region?

Critical Thinking and Writing

17. **Recognizing Causes and Effects** How might Japan's emergence as an economic superpower threaten some of the values that contributed to that success?
18. **Comparing** How did Deng Xiaoping's reforms in China compare with Mikhail Gorbachev's reforms in the Soviet Union?
19. **Linking Past and Present** How are the effects of the Cold War still felt in Korea today?
20. **Predicting Consequences** What long-term effects might the takeover of Hong Kong by China have on **(a)** Hong Kong, **(b)** China? Explain your answers.
21. **Connecting to Geography** "Five hundred years ago," notes a modern economist, "the world's economic center moved from the Mediterranean to the Atlantic. Today, it has shifted again to the Pacific." Support this statement using details about Asia from this chapter.

China's Cultural Revolution became an assault on intellectuals throughout Chinese society. In the excerpt below, a student describes some of the hardships he endured. Read the excerpt, then answer the questions that follow.

> "When the Cultural Revolution began . . . my family was one of the first in the city to be ransacked. . . . At that time all the funds capitalists had in the banks were frozen. You couldn't withdraw anything. . . . My mother didn't know about that. She went to get some money out. The bank clerks immediately called the Red Guards. They showed up in no time at my home and started to search and ransack our apartment. . . .
>
> The next day, I went to see the Red Guards responsible for ransacking my family. I figured I'd take anything from them: insults, criticism, and everything else. I was going to beg them to allow me to go home to have a look. . . .
>
> I glanced over the rooms. . . . Lots of things were in shreds, smashed and torn. . . . The only thing left to me was the desire to survive. I forgot everything else, even hunger."
>
> —quoted in *Voices From the Whirlwind* (Jicai)

22. Why was the student's home ransacked?
23. What type of damage did the student see?
24. What feelings did the student have after seeing his family's home?

Skills Tip

A critical reader of Internet resources must be able to detect bias. Identify the source of information you are using, such as a university, news organization, or individual.

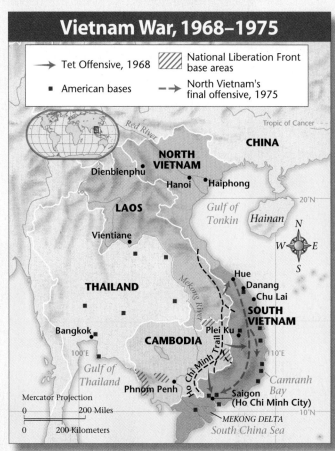

Vietnam War, 1968–1975

→ Tet Offensive, 1968
▨ National Liberation Front base areas
■ American bases
⇢ North Vietnam's final offensive, 1975

Mercator Projection
0 — 200 Miles
0 — 200 Kilometers

Study this map of the Vietnam War. Then, answer the following questions:

25. In what nation did the National Liberation Front have its base areas?
26. What was the starting point for the Tet Offensive?
27. Describe the route of the Ho Chi Minh Trail.
28. What countries provided sites for American bases?
29. Examine the course of the Mekong River. How might different nations have been able to use the river to their advantage during the war?
30. Why do you think the name of the city of Saigon was changed?

Skills Assessment
Take It to the NET

Use the Internet to research diverse opinions about the possibility of reunifying Taiwan and China. Then, write a paragraph explaining whether or not you support reunification.

South Asia and the Middle East

1945–Present

Chapter Preview

1 **Nations of South Asia**

2 **Forces Shaping the Modern Middle East**

3 **Nation Building in the Middle East: Three Case Studies**

4 **The Middle East and the World**

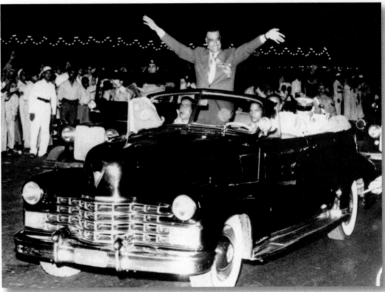

1947
India wins independence from Britain. The subcontinent is divided into Hindu India (top) and Muslim Pakistan (bottom).

1956
Egyptian president Gamal Abdel Nasser (above) nationalizes the Suez Canal, ending British and French control of the vital waterway.

1979
Revolutionaries in Iran oust the shah and declare an Islamic republic.

CHAPTER EVENTS

1940

1955

1970

GLOBAL EVENTS

1941 Nazis begin to implement "Final Solution"

1957 Ghana wins independence.

1966 Cultural Revolution begins in China.

Independence in South Asia and the Middle East

In South Asia and the Middle East, large nations like India and tiny ones like Jordan won independence. Since then, each has charted its own path toward modernization.

Black Sea

Caspian Sea

Mediterranean Sea

Ankara•

TURKEY
1923

LEBANON
1941
Beirut•
SYRIA
1946
•Damascus

Euphrates R.

Tigris R.

•Baghdad

IRAN

ASIA

AFGHANISTAN

•Islamabad

Indus R.

ISRAEL
1948
•Amman
Jerusalem
JORDAN
1946

IRAQ
1932

PAKISTAN
1947

New
Delhi•

NEPAL

Cairo•

KUWAIT
1961
•Kuwait

Persian Gulf

BHUTAN

EGYPT
1922

Red Sea

BAHRAIN
1971
Manama•

QATAR 1971
Riyadh•
Doha•

Abu
•Dhabi
OMAN
1951

UNITED
ARAB
•Muscat
EMIRATES
1971

SAUDI ARABIA
1932

Tropic of Cancer

INDIA
1947

Ganges R.

BANGLADESH
1971
Dhaka•

AFRICA

Arabian
Sea

Bay of
Bengal

Nile R.

YEMEN
1990

Sanaa•

Gulf of Aden

Mercator Projection

| 0 | 400 | 800 Miles |
| 0 | 400 | 800 Kilometers |

INDIAN OCEAN

Dates on map indicate date
of creation or independence

SRI LANKA
1948
•Colombo

1984
Sikh separatists clash with Indian troops at the Golden Temple in Amritsar.

1991
The Persian Gulf War ends an Iraqi invasion of Kuwait. Retreating Iraqi troops set fire to hundreds of Kuwaiti oil wells.

1993
Israeli Prime Minister Yitzhak Rabin (left) and Palestinian leader Yasir Arafat (right) sign a peace accord. Here, American President Bill Clinton joins the two leaders.

1985

2000

2015

1991 The Soviet Union collapses.

1999 Religious unrest increases in East Timor.

Nations of South Asia

Reading Focus

- Why was India partitioned?
- How has India dealt with political, economic, and social change?
- What problems did Pakistan and Bangladesh face?
- How is South Asia linked to world affairs?

Vocabulary

partition
federal system
harijan
deforestation
debt service
cyclone

Taking Notes

On a sheet of paper, make a Venn diagram like this one. As you read, add information about developments in India and Pakistan after winning independence.

INDIA
- World's largest democracy

- Ethnic rivalries

PAKISTAN
- Military leaders seize power

Main Idea After winning independence, Hindu India and Muslim Pakistan pursued separate roads to modernization.

Primary Source

Nehru's Vision of Independence

As the Indian Assembly met to celebrate independence, Prime Minister Jawaharlal Nehru spoke:

"Long years ago we made an [appointment] with destiny, and now the time comes when we shall redeem our pledge, not wholly or in full measure, but very substantially. At the stroke of the midnight hour, when the world sleeps, India will awake to life and freedom. A moment comes, which comes but rarely in history, when we step out from the old to the new, when an age ends and when the soul of a nation long suppressed finds utterance. It is fitting that at this solemn moment we take the pledge of dedication to the service of India and her people and to the still larger cause of humanity."

—Jawaharlal Nehru, "Tryst With Destiny" speech

Skills Assessment

Primary Source What words or phrases did Nehru use to express his optimism about India's future?

Setting the Scene August 15, 1947, was a joyful day in India. Everywhere, crowds gathered to watch parades and fireworks. At the stroke of midnight, power had passed from British colonial rulers into the hands of Indians themselves. This was India's Independence Day.

Three years later, India adopted a new democratic constitution. It set lofty goals for the nation:

"... to secure to all its citizens: JUSTICE, social, economic, and political; LIBERTY of thought, expression, belief, faith and worship; EQUALITY of status and opportunity; and to promote among them all FRATERNITY assuring the dignity of the individual and the unity of the Nation."

—Indian National Constitution

Achieving those goals would be difficult. Most Indians were poor, uneducated, and divided by caste, region, language, and religious and ethnic background. Other nations on the subcontinent faced similar challenges.

Independence and Partition

As you have read, Indian nationalists had demanded independence since the late 1800s. After World War II, Britain finally agreed to these demands. As independence neared, a long-simmering issue surfaced. What would happen to the Muslim minority in a Hindu-dominated India?

Two Nations Muhammad Ali Jinnah, leader of the Muslim League, insisted that Muslims have their own state, Pakistan. Riots between Hindus and Muslims helped persuade Britain to partition, or divide, the subcontinent. Drawing fair borders was impossible because Hindus and Muslims lived side by side. Still, in 1947, British officials hastily created Hindu India and Muslim Pakistan. Pakistan was made up of two widely separated areas in the northern part of the subcontinent that had large Muslim populations.

Tragedy Unfolds In 1947, millions of Hindus and Muslims crossed the borders of India and Pakistan in both directions. During the mass migration, centuries of mistrust—which the British had exploited to keep the population divided—plunged northern India into savage violence. Sikh and Hindu mobs slaughtered Muslims fleeing into Pakistan. Muslims massacred Hindu and Sikh neighbors. An estimated 10 million refugees fled their homes. One million or more, mostly Muslims, may have died.

Horrified at the partition and the violence, Mohandas Gandhi, the "father of the nation," turned once more to satyagraha to restore peace. But on January 30, 1948, he was shot and killed by a Hindu extremist. Jawaharlal Nehru, India's first prime minister, told a stricken nation, "The light has gone out of our lives and there is darkness everywhere." Gandhi's death discredited the extremists and helped to end the worst violence. Still, Hindu-Muslim tensions persisted.

India: World's Largest Democracy

India built on the legacy of British government, including its system of law and government. Today, with a population of about one billion, it is the world's largest democratic nation.

Unity and Diversity To achieve independence, Indians had united behind the Congress party. Still, the new nation was deeply divided. It included hundreds of princely states that had survived British rule. Indians spoke a wide variety of languages and dialects. The majority of Indians were Hindu, but millions of others were Muslim, Sikh, Christian, or Buddhist.

India's constitution set up a federal system, like that of the United States. Under this system, powers are divided between a strong central government and smaller local governments. In time, the government reorganized the princely states into a smaller number of states. It recognized 15 official languages and 35 major regional languages.

The "Nehru Dynasty" For 40 years after independence, members of the Nehru family led India. From 1947 to 1964, Jawaharlal Nehru worked to build a modern, secular state dedicated to promoting social justice. After he died, his daughter Indira Gandhi and, later, his grandson Rajiv Gandhi, served as prime minister. Both were popular, energetic leaders, but at times their highhanded policies eroded goodwill. In the end, both fell victim to violence, as you will read. Today, Sonia Gandhi, the Italian-born widow of Rajiv, has entered the political arena.

Under the "Nehru dynasty," the Congress party dominated Indian politics. In the early 1990s, though, support deepened for the fundamentalist Bharatiya Janata party (BJP). Unlike the Congress party, which wanted to separate religion and government, the BJP called for a government built on Hindu principles. For a few years, the BJP held power. In 1999, the Congress party was returned to power, but it was a shadow of its former self. As the millennium turned, India's political future remained uncertain.

Ongoing Divisions India's size and diversity have contributed to religious and regional divisions. In 1992, the BJP backed calls for the destruction of a mosque in Ayodhya (uh YOHD yuh). Hindu fundamentalists claimed that it stood on a sacred Hindu site seized by Muslim invaders centuries earlier. The BJP wanted a Hindu temple built there. The conflict touched off rioting at Ayodhya and the mosque was destroyed.

Other divisions affected the prosperous Punjab region of northwestern India. There, some Sikhs wanted an independent state. In 1984, these Sikh separatists occupied the Golden Temple in Amritsar. When talks failed to

Partition of India, 1947

India, 1947
Pakistan, 1947
Disputed areas

Mercator Projection
0   300   600 Miles
0   300   600 Kilometers

Skills Assessment

Geography The partition of India created two populous new nations but also led to widespread violence.

1. **Location** *On the map, locate (a) India, (b) East Pakistan, (c) West Pakistan, (d) Kashmir, (e) Afghanistan.*
2. **Movement** *Based on this map, describe the migration of Hindus and Muslims across the India–West Pakistan border in 1947.*
3. **Critical Thinking Linking Past and Present** *Compare this map with the map of Asia in the Reference Section. Identify two changes that have taken place since 1947.*

Geography and History

Scaling Mt. Everest

Its summit soars above 29,000 feet, making Mt. Everest in the Himalayas the highest mountain in the world. On May 29, 1953, Tenzing Norgay of Nepal and Edmund Hillary of New Zealand were the first climbers to reach the top. Since then, some 700 others have risked avalanches, altitude sickness, and blinding snowstorms to reach the "top of the world." More than 150 mountaineers have died in the attempt.

The grueling climb requires sturdy equipment—oxygen tanks, snow tents, thick down suits, and aluminum ladders to cross crevasses—and extreme physical endurance. Explains one veteran climber, "Climbing above 26,000 feet, even with bottled oxygen, is like running on a treadmill and breathing through a straw."

Theme: Economics and Technology What technology has made it possible for climbers to reach the top of Mt. Everest?

At the same time, many nations, including the United States, denounced the military takeover and called for a return to democratic rule.

Economy After independence, Pakistan moved to improve agriculture. It distributed unused lands to landless farmers, experimented with new high-yield crops, and financed irrigation projects. Building dams and clearing land helped boost food production, but at a high cost to the environment. Deforestation, or destruction of forest land, caused terrible floods when monsoon rains were heavy.

To modernize, Pakistan nationalized major industries. More recently, the government has encouraged private or mixed government and private ownership of businesses. Like other developing nations, Pakistan faces an ongoing financial crisis. It has borrowed heavily from lenders such as the World Bank and IMF. Yet debt service, paying interest on loans, takes 40 percent of the nation's budget, leaving little for development.

Some international authorities have urged outright cancellation of the debts of Pakistan and other developing nations. Yet such a move might discourage further foreign investment in nations that desperately need it.

Trials of Bangladesh Since 1971, Bangladesh has struggled to rise out of poverty, but geography often stands in the way. Its large population is crowded on a low-lying coastal plain. The region is subject to devastating floods when monsoon rains are too heavy or to droughts if the rains are too light. Cyclones, fierce circular windstorms, are another frequent threat.

Explosive population growth has strained resources still further. More than 50 million people, many of them women and children, live below the poverty level. Large amounts of foreign aid have brought little relief, in part because various military governments have misused the assistance.

Since the early 1990s, civilian governments have worked to encourage foreign investment. Foreign businesses took advantage of cheap labor costs to make clothes in Bangladesh for export to Japan and the West. However, human rights groups revealed that textile workers, often young children, were treated like slaves. Development in Bangladesh seemed to mirror the miseries of the early Industrial Revolution in the West.

South Asia and the World

India and Pakistan achieved their independence as the Cold War began, and each followed its own path. Nehru welcomed economic aid from both superpowers, but otherwise embraced the nonaligned movement. Pakistan, feeling threatened not only by India but by the Soviet Union to the north, accepted United States military aid. Partly to counter this alliance, Indira Gandhi signed a treaty of friendship with the Soviet Union in the 1970s. With the end of the Cold War in the early 1990s, both India and Pakistan sought aid from the western powers, especially the United States.

Conflict Over Kashmir Fear and mistrust marred relations between India and Pakistan. At independence, border conflicts ignited a war over Kashmir, a princely state in the Himalayas. Its Hindu monarch decided to join India, but its Muslim majority wanted to be part of Pakistan. Since then, Pakistan and India have fought several wars over Kashmir.

In 1999, the border conflict erupted anew. India accused Pakistan of funding groups inside Kashmir who opposed Indian rule and sending troops to fight there. Even after the fighting ended, tensions remained high, especially because India and Pakistan were flexing their muscles on another front, nuclear weapons.

The Nuclear Issue India tested its first nuclear bomb in 1974. India was proud of its new status as a nuclear power. But Pakistan felt threatened. It tried to acquire its own nuclear technology.

In 1998, Pakistan and India both tested nuclear weapons. As the nuclear rivalry raised new fears, leaders of the two nations met. They agreed to "confidence-building measures" to ease tensions and improve relations. Still, both countries faced strong nationalist and religious pressure to use at least the threat of nuclear conflict in future confrontations.

Afghanistan In 1979, Soviet troops invaded Afghanistan. Millions of Afghan Muslims fled into Pakistan. With American aid, Afghan guerrillas based in Pakistan fought against the Soviet puppet government. In time, guerrilla attacks and dissent at home forced the Soviets to withdraw. Conflict raged on for years as rival factions battled for power.

By 2000, a radical Muslim faction, the Taliban, controlled much of Afghanistan. The Taliban government imposed harsh rule. It also harbored Muslim extremists from other countries and was accused of sending militants to stir up fighting between India and Pakistan over Kashmir.

Sri Lanka In the 1970s, ethnic tensions led to guerrilla war in Sri Lanka, an island nation off the southeastern coast of India. Most Sri Lankans were Buddhists who spoke Singhalese. A Tamil-speaking Hindu minority charged the government with discrimination. When efforts to win equality failed, Tamil rebels waged war to set up a separate nation.

India at first favored Tamil separatists. But in the 1980s, Rajiv Gandhi sent troops to smash the rebels. The attempt failed, but outraged Tamil extremists assassinated Gandhi in 1991. Although fighting slowed, tensions remained, with occasional violence.

Cause *and* Effect

Long-Term Causes	Short-Term Causes
• Muslim conquest of northern India in 1100s • British imperialism in India • Nationalists organize the Indian National Congress in 1885 • Muslim nationalists form separate Muslim League in 1906	• World War II weakens European colonial empires • Pressure from Indian nationalists increases • Insistence by Muhammad Ali Jinnah and the Muslim League that Muslims have their own state • Rioting between Hindus and Muslims throughout northern India

Partition of India

Effects

• Violence erupts as millions of Hindus and Muslims cross the border between India and Pakistan
• Gandhi is assassinated by Hindu extremists
• India and Pakistan become centers of Cold War rivalry
• Establishment of the state of Bangladesh

Connections to Today

• Continuing clash between India and Pakistan over Kashmir
• Nuclear arms race as both India and Pakistan refuse to sign Non-Proliferation Treaty

Skills Assessment **Chart** The conflicts that led to the partition of India continue to affect the subcontinent. **How have the long-term effects of the partition spread beyond India and Pakistan?**

SECTION 1 Assessment

Recall
1. **Identify:** (a) Jawaharlal Nehru, (b) Indira Gandhi, (c) Rajiv Gandhi, (d) BJP, (e) Mother Teresa, (f) Zulfikar Ali Bhutto, (g) Kashmir.
2. **Define:** (a) partition, (b) federal system, (c) harijan, (d) deforestation, (e) debt service, (f) cyclone.

Comprehension
3. Why was the Indian subcontinent divided into two nations?
4. (a) What economic goals did India pursue? (b) Why has progress been limited?

5. Describe one problem facing (a) Pakistan, (b) Bangladesh.
6. How did Cold War rivalries affect South Asia? Give two examples.

Critical Thinking and Writing
7. **Applying Information** "The past still clings to us," said Jawaharlal Nehru. Give two examples that support his statement.
8. **Defending a Position** (a) Why would nationalists in India and Pakistan favor development of nuclear weapons? (b) Why did world leaders worry about the arms race in South Asia?

Activity
Take It to the NET

Use the Internet to find out more about a recent flood in Bangladesh. Then, with a partner, prepare an action report outlining local and international efforts to relieve flood victims. You may wish to include an illustrated map of the flood plain.

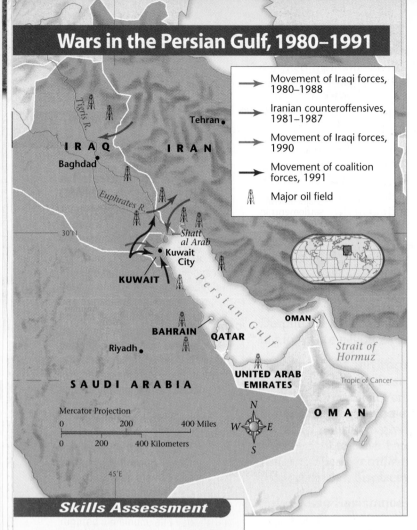

Wars in the Persian Gulf, 1980–1991

Movement of Iraqi forces, 1980–1988

Iranian counteroffensives, 1981–1987

Movement of Iraqi forces, 1990

Movement of coalition forces, 1991

Major oil field

Tigris R.

Tehran

I R A Q   **I R A N**

Baghdad

Euphrates R.

30°N

Shatt al Arab

Kuwait City

KUWAIT

OMAN

BAHRAIN **QATAR**

Riyadh

Strait of Hormuz

UNITED ARAB EMIRATES

Tropic of Cancer

SAUDI ARABIA

O M A N

Mercator Projection

0   200   400 Miles

0   200   400 Kilometers

45°E

N W E S

Skills Assessment

Geography Since 1980, the area around the Persian Gulf has been the site of two wars.

1. **Location** On the map, locate (a) Persian Gulf, (b) Strait of Hormuz, (c) Iraq, (d) Iran, (e) Kuwait, (f) Saudi Arabia.
2. **Movement** Why would the Strait of Hormuz be vital to the world oil trade?
3. **Critical Thinking Drawing Conclusions** Describe two advantages Iraq would gain by taking control of Kuwait.

sect derived from Islam), and others. Maronites held the most power, but local bosses controlled their own districts backed by private armies.

A growing number of Palestinian refugees crossed the border from the occupied territories into Lebanon. Their needs strained resources. Also, the Muslim population began to outnumber Maronites, creating unrest. Adding to the tensions, the PLO developed into an important force in the Palestinian refugee camps. From Lebanon, PLO guerrillas crossed into Israel to attack civilian and military targets. To end the threat to its security, Israel tried to influence events in southern Lebanon.

Years of Violence In 1975, Lebanon was plunged into a seemingly endless civil war. Christian and Muslim militias, bands of citizen soldiers, battled for control of villages and of Beirut, the capital city. Israel invaded the south to clear out PLO bases and advanced almost as far as Beirut. Syria occupied eastern Lebanon.

Lawlessness led to massacres on all sides. As Palestinian refugee camps came under fire, thousands were killed. A UN peacekeeping force tried to restore order, but it withdrew after hundreds of French and American peacekeepers were killed in a series of suicide bombings.

Rebuilding By 1990, Lebanese leaders finally restored some measure of order. The PLO was forced out of southern Lebanon, private armies began to disarm, and the ruined capital slowly rebuilt. Over the following decade, the economic outlook improved, and many Lebanese who had fled their homeland returned. By 2000, Beirut was poised to return to its former status as a leading economic center of the Middle East.

Despite the hopeful outlook, divisions remained. Syria was still a dominant presence and Israeli forces continued to take military action against suspected terrorists in southern Lebanon. The future of this small nation seemed to depend on the prospects for peace among its neighbors.

Two Wars in the Persian Gulf

Border disputes, oil wealth, foreign intervention, and ambitious rulers fed tensions along the Persian Gulf. In 1980, Iraqi dictator Saddam Hussein seized a disputed border region from Iran. Iraqi forces then pushed deeper into Iran, which was embroiled in its recent Islamic revolution. Before long, the Iranians launched a counterattack. They urged young soldiers to spread their revolution to Iraq.

Iraq used its superior weapons, tanks, airplanes, and even poison gas to stop waves of Iranian soldiers. Fighting threatened to spread as both sides attacked international tankers and offshore oil fields in the Persian Gulf. The United States sent naval forces to protect shipping lanes in the Gulf and the Strait of Hormuz. The war dragged on for eight years, ending in a stalemate. For both nations, the human and economic toll was enormous.

A Second Gulf War In 1990, Iraqi troops invaded the oil-rich nation of Kuwait. Saddam Hussein argued that historically the region was part of Iraq. Control of Kuwait would give Iraq not only one of the world's largest oil-producing areas but also access to the Persian Gulf.

The United States saw the invasion as a threat to its ally Saudi Arabia, as well as to oil flow from the Persian Gulf. President George Bush therefore organized a coalition of American, European, and Arab powers to drive Iraqi forces out of Kuwait. In the 1991 Gulf War, American missiles and bombers destroyed targets in Iraq. Then, under the UN banner, coalition forces pushed across the desert to liberate Kuwait. As they retreated, Iraqi troops blew up hundreds of Kuwaiti oil wells.

Unresolved Issues Though defeated and diplomatically isolated, Saddam Hussein held onto power in Iraq. Right after the war, he brutally suppressed revolts by Kurds and Shiites who had suffered under his rule. To protect these minorities, the UN enforced no-fly zones, areas over which Iraqi aircraft were not permitted to fly.

For years after the war, UN economic sanctions kept Iraq from selling oil on the world market and from importing most goods. The goal was to force Saddam Hussein to stop his chemical and nuclear weapons programs. Iraqis suffered severely from the sanctions, but the government generally failed to cooperate with UN weapons monitors.

In the late 1990s, the UN set up an oil-for-food program to help the Iraqi people. It allowed Iraq to sell some oil on the world market and use the profits to buy food and medicines. Still, the standard of living in Iraq fell, setting off an international debate. Some people called for an end to economic sanctions, which they argued were hurting ordinary Iraqis far more than they hurt the government. Others argued that lifting sanctions would reward Saddam Hussein. They insisted that he was still trying to rebuild weapons of mass destruction.

Looking Ahead

By the year 2000, the Middle East remained the focus of many conflicting forces. Nationalist conflicts, clashes between religious and secular goals, and competition for water resources were among many forces that carried the potential for future violence. And the area's vast supplies of oil guaranteed that outside powers would continue to intervene in the region.

At the same time, the region's resources and increasingly educated population could provide the foundation for a peaceful and prosperous future. Much depended on ending the warfare that had torn the Middle East apart for half a century.

SECTION 4 Assessment

Recall

1. **Identify:** (a) PLO, (b) Yasir Arafat, (c) Yitzhak Rabin, (d) Palestinian Authority, (e) Benjamin Netanyahu, (f) Saddam Hussein.
2. **Define:** (a) client state, (b) intifada, (c) unilateral, (d) militia, (e) no-fly zone.

Comprehension

3. How did the Cold War affect the Middle East?
4. (a) Why were the occupied territories a source of conflict? (b) What steps were taken toward peace?

5. Describe one cause of each of the following: (a) the civil war in Lebanon, (b) the Iran-Iraq war, (c) the Persian Gulf War.

Critical Thinking and Writing

6. **Making Decisions** If you had been an Israeli leader in the late 1980s, what response to the intifada would you have favored? Explain your reasons.
7. **Solving Problems** If you were organizing a Middle East peace conference, whom would you invite, and what issues would you put on the table?

Activity

Drawing a Political Cartoon Draw a cartoon about the role of oil in fueling tensions in the Persian Gulf. Take the viewpoint of an Iraqi, a Kuwaiti, a Saudi, or an outside observer. Identify the time period of your cartoon.

Struggles in Southern Africa

Reading Focus

■ What challenges faced Zimbabwe?

■ How did the long struggle to end apartheid lead to a new South Africa?

■ How did the Cold War affect nations of southern Africa?

Taking Notes

Create a table that shows important information about southern Africa. Use this sample as a starting point.

	ZIMBABWE	SOUTH AFRICA	NAMIBIA	ANGOLA	MOZAMBIQUE
NATIONAL LEADERS	Robert Mugabe, Joshua Nkomo				
SOCIAL AND POLITICAL CONFLICTS					
REFORMS					

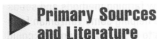 **Main Idea** Nations in southern Africa experienced turmoil as people sought majority rule and equal rights.

Primary Sources and Literature

See "Nelson Mandela: Glory and Hope" in the Reference Section at the back of this book.

Setting the Scene On May 10, 1994, Nelson Mandela stood before a wildly cheering crowd. He had just been inaugurated as South Africa's first president elected by voters of all races. "The time for the healing of wounds has come," he told black and white South Africans.

For almost 350 years, whites had dominated South Africa and had denied blacks the most basic civil rights. Mandela's election marked a new beginning for South Africa. In his inauguration speech, he spoke of the need for a new unity, not of revenge for the losses suffered by black South Africans. The crowd sang "Nkosi Sikelel' iAfrika" (God Bless Africa)—the anthem that had come to symbolize South Africa's struggle for freedom.

Zimbabwe's Road to Majority Rule

During the Age of Imperialism, European nations had carved up southern Africa. In the 1890s, British businessman Cecil Rhodes took control of the region known as Southern Rhodesia. Later, white settlers turned the region into a self-governing British colony. Whites made up only five percent of the population but owned half the land and controlled the government. As the tide of nationalism swept through Africa in the 1960s, white Southern Rhodesians flatly rejected any move to give up power to the black majority. When Britain supported demands for majority rule, conservative whites led by Ian Smith declared independence in 1965.

Armed Struggle In response, nationalist groups waged guerrilla war to achieve majority rule. Among their leaders were Robert Mugabe (moo GAH beh) and Joshua Nkomo (uhn KOH moh). The long struggle caused much suffering. As guerrilla forces won more successes, many whites fled. UN sanctions hurt the economy. Smith finally had to accept a negotiated settlement. In 1980, Southern Rhodesia became the nation of Zimbabwe. It took its name from the ancient kingdom of Great Zimbabwe and the stone structures built there by earlier African peoples.

Rebuilding The new nation faced severe challenges after years of war. International sanctions had further damaged the economy, and droughts caused additional problems. Recovery was also slowed by a power struggle between Mugabe and Nkomo. In the end, Mugabe won and became the elected president of Zimbabwe. He called for a one-party system to promote national unity and tolerated little opposition. In 2000, tensions over land ownership led to renewed violence.

South Africa's Long Struggle

In 1910, South Africa won self-rule from Britain. Freedom, however, was limited to white settlers. Whites, who made up less than 20 percent of the population, controlled vast mineral resources and the most fertile land. Over the next decades, the white-minority government passed racial laws to keep the black majority in a subordinate position.

Afrikaner Nationalism After World War II, thousands of blacks moved to towns and cities. There, as elsewhere in Africa, black nationalism stirred demands for equality. In response, Afrikaners, who were descended from Dutch settlers, demanded severe new limits on blacks.

In 1948, the Afrikaner National party won a majority in a "whites-only" parliament. They then extended the existing system of racial segregation, creating what was known as apartheid, or the separation of the races. Under apartheid, all South Africans were registered by race: Black, White, Colored (people of mixed descent), and Asian. Afrikaners claimed that apartheid would allow each race to develop its own culture. In fact, it was designed to give whites control over South Africa.

Apartheid in Action For nonwhites, apartheid meant a life of restrictions. Blacks were treated like foreigners in their own land. They had to get permission to travel and had to carry passbooks or face arrest. The pass laws were an especially heavy burden for women, who had to get permission from their parents, guardian, or husband, as well as from the authorities, in order to move from one district to another.

Blacks were assigned to "homelands" based on their ethnic group. Homelands were located in arid, unproductive parts of the country. More than 80 percent of South Africa, including cities, mines, and the richest farmland, was reserved for whites. Apartheid laws banned marriages between the races and set up segregated restaurants, beaches, schools, and other facilities. Blacks who worked in factories, mines, and other jobs were paid less than whites for the same work. Low wages and inferior schooling condemned blacks to poverty.

Black Resistance From the beginning, black South Africans protested apartheid. In 1912, an organization, later called the African National Congress (ANC), was set up to oppose white domination. In the 1950s, as Afrikaner nationalists imposed harsh new laws, the ANC organized marches, boycotts, and strikes. As protests continued, government violence increased. In 1960, police gunned down 69 men, women, and children taking part in a peaceful demonstration in Sharpeville, a black township outside Johannesburg. In the wake of the incident, the government outlawed the ANC and cracked down on groups that opposed apartheid.

The massacre at Sharpeville stunned the world. At home, it pushed some ANC activists to shift from nonviolent protest to armed struggle. Some leaders left South Africa to wage the battle for freedom from abroad. Others went underground, including Nelson Mandela.

Mandela's Struggle As a young lawyer, Mandela had helped organize the ANC Youth League. With other league leaders, he mobilized young South Africans to take part in acts of civil disobedience against apartheid laws. As government suppression grew, Mandela joined ANC militants who called for armed struggle against the white-minority government.

In the early 1960s, Mandela was arrested, tried, and condemned to life in prison for conspiracy. "I have cherished the ideal of a democratic and free society," he declared at his trial. It was an ideal Mandela hoped "to live for and to achieve." It was also "an ideal for which I am prepared to die." Mandela spent 27 years in prison, often in isolation. Yet he remained a popular leader and powerful symbol of the struggle against apartheid.

Apartheid and Business
The diamond industry provides great wealth for South Africa. Mined in a rough state (right), diamonds later are cut and polished (left). For decades, white-run companies in South Africa have controlled the world's diamond market.

Theme: Economics and Technology How did white-controlled companies benefit from apartheid?

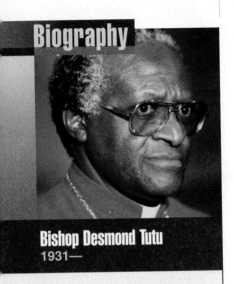

Bishop Desmond Tutu
1931—

Desmond Tutu grew up in the Transvaal region of South Africa, where he attended mission schools as a child. Lacking the money to pursue his dream of attending medical school, he first became a schoolteacher. Later, he took up the study of theology. He was ordained as an Anglican priest in 1961 and was made bishop in 1976.

Tutu used his growing influence to crusade against the brutal laws of apartheid. Although there was the constant threat of violent rebellion, he never wavered from his message of peace and reconciliation. In 1980, Tutu said, "I will never tell anyone to pick up a gun. But I will pray for the man who picks up a gun, pray that he will be less cruel than he might otherwise have been...."

Theme: Impact of the Individual How did people like Desmond Tutu influence South Africa's battle against apartheid?

By the 1980s, demands for an end to apartheid and for Mandela's release intensified. Many countries, including the United States, imposed strict economic sanctions on South Africa. South African athletes were banned from world sports events such as the Olympic games. In 1984, the black Anglican bishop Desmond Tutu won the Nobel Peace Prize for his nonviolent opposition to apartheid.

Toward Reform Foreign boycotts hurt South Africa's economy. Even worse, in 1985, protests and growing violence at home forced the government to impose a state of emergency. Many South African whites questioned the oppressive measures used by the government.

By 1989, a new South African president, F. W. de Klerk, boldly accepted the need for reform. He abandoned apartheid, repealed the hated pass laws, and lifted the ban on the ANC. A year later, he freed Mandela. Over the next four years, Mandela and de Klerk negotiated the terms by which South Africa would move to majority rule. White voters overwhelmingly approved the reforms that would allow "one person, one vote."

Majority Rule In 1994, South Africa held its first multiracial elections. Black, mixed race, and Asian South Africans, young and old, lined up with white voters to cast their ballots. They elected Nelson Mandela as the first president of a new, democratic South Africa. In a speech to supporters, Mandela echoed the African American civil rights leader Martin Luther King, Jr.: "We can loudly proclaim from the rooftops: Free at last!"

The New South Africa

As president, Mandela offered a striking example to other African nations when he welcomed longtime political foes into his government. If he could work with Afrikaners who had once tyrannized the black majority, perhaps other leaders could learn to accept democratic, multiparty systems. "Let us build together," *masakhane*, was Mandela's slogan and guiding policy.

Mandela's government faced the huge challenge of meeting people's high expectations for change. Mandela had promised a better life to the black majority. Delivering on those promises would be difficult. South Africa was a rich country with a strong industrial base. But it could afford only a limited amount of spending for housing, education, and other programs. The gap between blacks and whites remained large.

Even in Mandela's South Africa, whites owned three fourths of the land, black unemployment remained high, and the crime rate made both cities and the shantytowns around them unsafe. But South Africa's first black president did bring both a peaceful transition to democratic rule and soaring international prestige to his country. He also introduced new programs, from public housing to school lunches, making such necessities as pure water and electrical power available to the masses.

In 1999, a second all-race election brought Thabo Mbeki to the presidency. The democratic process seemed to be successful, and people were hopeful for the future. Given the nation's accumulated problems, major changes might take decades rather than years. But a start had been made.

Other Nations of Southern Africa

The colonies of southern Africa were among the last to win independence. From the 1960s to the 1980s, South Africa's white-minority government intervened to prevent neighboring peoples from achieving freedom.

Namibia In 1920, South Africa received German Southwest Africa as a mandate from the League of Nations. After World War II, the UN asked South Africa to prepare the territory for independence. Instead, South Africa backed the oppressive regime run by the white minority.

Reporting on the Election in South Africa

As an American journalist covering South Africa's second all-race elections, you are excited to find that people here feel strongly about exercising their right to vote. Nelson Mandela, the national hero who became president in 1994, has turned down a second term. Which party's candidate will succeed him? All of South Africa holds its breath to see what happens. . . .

When you arrive at the polling station at 8 A.M., you find a line of voters stretching for more than two miles. Because of the enormous turnout, some people will have to wait more than four hours to vote.

Inside the polling station, voters show signs of weariness. The elderly and sick are ushered to the front of the line. Despite the long wait, most people remain patient, knowing their turn will come.

After the station closes, you learn that someone may have tampered with three of the ballot boxes. If this proves to be true, election officials will have to discard hundreds of votes. Despite the problems, you reflect that South Africans have once again demonstrated their commitment to democracy.

Portfolio Assessment

After you return to the United States, your editor asks you to write an article comparing the attitudes toward democracy and elections in South Africa and in the United States.

Virtual Field Trip

www.phschool.com

**Republic of Namibia
Namibia**

For more information about Namibia since independence, use the Internet address above to link to the official Web site of the Republic of Namibia.

Freedom for Namibia
Like many African peoples, Namibians waged a long, armed struggle to win independence. Here, a group of Namibian women celebrate the birth of their nation in 1990.

Theme: Global Interaction
How did the Cold War affect Namibia's struggle for independence?

By the 1960s, the Southwest African People's Organization (SWAPO) had turned to armed struggle to win independence. For years, SWAPO guerrillas battled South African troops. The struggle became part of the Cold War, with the Soviet Union and Cuba lending their support to SWAPO. As the Cold War ground to a halt, an agreement was finally reached to hold free elections. In 1990, Namibia—as the new country was called—celebrated independence.

Portuguese Colonies As Britain and France took steps to meet nationalist demands in their African possessions, Portugal clung fiercely to its colonies in Angola and Mozambique. During the 1960s, the Portuguese dictator António Salazar rejected African demands for freedom. In response, nationalists turned to guerrilla warfare. Portugal responded by sending almost its entire army to defend its last outposts of empire.

After 15 years of fighting, many Portuguese army officers realized that they could not succeed in the struggle. In 1974, an army coup in Portugal toppled the dictatorship of Salazar's successor. The new Portuguese government quickly agreed to withdraw from southern Africa. In 1975, Angola and Mozambique celebrated independence.

Wars Continue Independence did not end the fighting in Angola and Mozambique. Bitter civil wars, fueled by Cold War rivalries, raged for years in both countries. Both South Africa and the United States had seen the struggles for freedom in southern Africa as a threat because some liberation leaders were socialists. To undermine the new governments, South Africa aided rebel groups in both countries that wanted power for themselves.

From 1975 to 1992, rebels in Mozambique starved and killed tens of thousands of civilians. They destroyed schools and health clinics in an effort to overturn the government. The end of the Cold War and South Africa's move to majority rule helped stop the conflict. Although the task of rebuilding was staggering, by the late 1990s, many had confidence that democratic reforms would succeed.

In Angola, a complicated power struggle dragged on for years. The Soviet Union helped one side in the struggle by financing more than 50,000 Cuban troops that went to fight in Angola. South Africa supported a rival group, supplying weapons and troops. The United States, too, tried to undermine the Soviet-backed government. Even after the Cold War ended, the fighting continued between the rival factions in Angola.

Outlook and Gains

Making accurate generalizations about Africa is difficult. Every nation is different. Some nations have rich resources to help finance progress. Others lack resources. Each country has its own set of circumstances and its own history. Despite many setbacks, African nations have made progress. As independent nations, they carved out a place on the world scene and won the power to shape their own future. Within each nation, the process of building a national identity went slowly. But education and urbanization did begin to break the localism of the past.

Education and Health Care As governments set up more schools, literacy rates rose. Every year, more students entered high school. Universities trained a new generation of leaders.

A few countries promoted higher education for women, and great strides were made in providing girls with elementary school education. Relatively few girls, however, went on to high school because they were needed to help their mothers with farm work and household chores. As a result, illiteracy among African women remained high, especially in rural areas.

Most African nations sought to improve health care and created family planning programs. Governments saw that population growth had profound effects on the standards of living.

Economic Opportunity Despite often-depressing economic news, Africa has enormous potential for growth. By the 1990s, many nations had learned from failed policies of the past. With free-market reforms, countries such as Ghana enjoyed economic growth. Other nations expanded mining and manufacturing. Some built factories and expanded communication and transportation networks.

Cultural Influence In literature, film, and the arts, Africans made major contributions to global culture. Writing in African languages produced many writers with large local audiences. Other African writers used western languages to reach a world audience. In music and dance, Africans and members of the "African diaspora"—African-descended citizens of other lands—helped shape the culture of the century. Influential diaspora musical forms included jazz, blues, reggae, and samba.

Global Connections

The Scars of War

After Angola gained independence in 1975, a bitter civil war broke out. Angolans found themselves in the middle of a Cold War battlefield. The Soviet Union offered the Popular Liberation Movement of Angola (MPLA), millions of dollars in arms. It also arranged for thousands of Cuban soldiers to travel to Angola to bolster support. The United States, on the other hand, provided aid to the National Union for the Total Independence of Angola (UNITA), which opposed the MPLA's Marxist policies.

Fighting finally ended in 1991, but the unrest continues. Today, UNITA controls about 70 percent of Angola, including most of the diamond trade, while the MPLA retains the oil-rich regions. Caught between the two are thousands of refugees who still wait for life to return to normal.

Theme: Political and Social Systems How did Angola become a victim of the Cold War?

SECTION 4 Assessment

Recall

1. Identify: (a) Robert Mugabe, **(b)** Joshua Nkomo, **(c)** African National Congress, **(d)** Nelson Mandela, **(e)** F. W. de Klerk, **(f)** Southwest African People's Organization.

Comprehension

2. How did Zimbabwe achieve independence?

3. (a) Identify major events leading to the elimination of apartheid. **(b)** Describe how South Africa has changed since 1989.

4. How did the Cold War affect independence movements in southern Africa?

5. How have African nations worked to improve conditions?

Critical Thinking and Writing

6. Drawing Conclusions Would a country be likely to face greater challenges after independence if it won freedom through fighting or through negotiation? Explain.

7. Identifying Main Ideas Why was the idea of majority rule so important to people in African nations?

Activity

Take It to the NET

Research the history of one of the nations discussed in this section. Create an illustrated time line that shows important dates and events in that nation's history.

Creating a Chapter Summary

Complete the concept web by filling in circles with appropriate information from the chapter. Add more circles as needed.

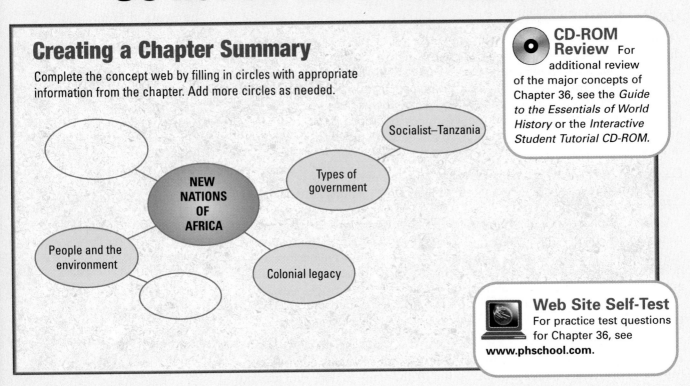

○ **CD-ROM Review** For additional review of the major concepts of Chapter 36, see the *Guide to the Essentials of World History* or the *Interactive Student Tutorial CD-ROM.*

Web Site Self-Test For practice test questions for Chapter 36, see **www.phschool.com**.

Building Vocabulary

For each of the terms below, write a sentence using the term.

1. **one-party system**
2. **mixed economy**
3. **desertification**

Recalling Key Facts

4. How did the colonial legacy affect independence movements in Africa?
5. Compare independence movements in Ghana, Kenya, and Algeria.
6. What role did international organizations play in Africa during the Cold War?
7. What choices did new nations face as they tried to build productive economies?
8. Describe the effects of the population explosion on the African environment.
9. Explain how modernization affected **(a)** cities, **(b)** women, **(c)** religious groups.
10. How has oil affected Nigeria's development?

11. What were Julius Nyerere's goals for Tanzania?
12. How did South Africa overcome apartheid?
13. How did the Cold War affect southern Africa?
14. Describe how education and urbanization have encouraged development in Africa.

Critical Thinking and Writing

15. **Synthesizing Information** How were African nations affected by military dictatorships? Support your answer with examples.
16. **Connecting to Geography** How have subsistence farming and population growth affected desertification in Africa?
17. **Making Inferences** Based on information in this chapter, what types of economic development seem to have been most successful? Explain.
18. **Drawing Conclusions** How has majority rule affected political stability in southern African nations?

In 1998, Catherine Bertini, executive director of the World Food Programme, gave a speech about hunger issues in Africa. Read this excerpt and answer the questions that follow.

> "In Africa, women provide roughly 80 percent of the labor to grow, process, and store food. They account for 60 percent of the labor needed to harvest and market food. They must be involved and benefit from agricultural innovations and reforms, and from food aid and other forms of assistance. . . .
>
> Emphasizing women is done because it is the most efficient way to improve the nutrition of families. . . . Robert Fogel, a Nobel laureate in economics, . . . estimates . . . that almost a third of the growth in per capita income in Britain in the last two centuries can actually be attributed to better nutrition in the workforce. Study after study . . . has shown a clear connection between nutritional status and the productivity and wage earnings of workers. . . ."

—Catherine Bertini, speech delivered February 19, 1998

19. What role do women play in African agriculture?
20. What assistance does Bertini recommend?
21. Why, according to Bertini, must women be at the center of efforts to improve nutrition?
22. **(a)** What economic information does she use to support her point? **(b)** Does this theory seem reasonable? Explain your answer.

Skills Tip

When you read a primary source, pay careful attention to the information used to support the writer's or speaker's opinion.

Use the Internet to research current development projects in one African nation. Create a poster that shows how these projects are supposed to affect your chosen nation.

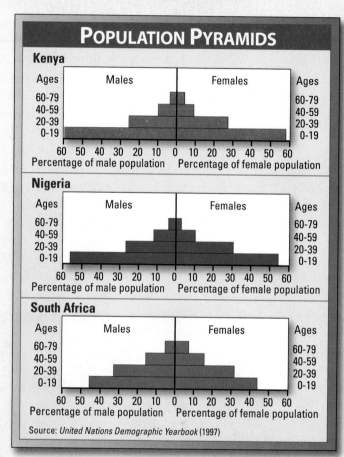

POPULATION PYRAMIDS

Source: *United Nations Demographic Yearbook* (1997)

A population pyramid is a bar graph that shows the percentages of males and females by age group in a particular country. The shape can also tell you whether a population is growing or declining. A wide base indicates growth, and a narrow base indicates decline. Study the graphs and answer the following questions:

23. Which country has the highest percentage of females ages 60–79?
24. Which country has the lowest percentage of males ages 0–19?
25. Which is the largest age group in each of the three countries?
26. How would you explain the great difference in size between age ranges 0–19 and 20–39?
27. According to the population pyramids, which nation seems to be experiencing the fastest rate of growth?

Latin America
1945–Present

Chapter Preview

1 Forces Shaping Modern Latin America
2 Latin America, the United States, and the World
3 Mexico, Central America, and the Caribbean
4 Focus on Argentina and Brazil

1948

The Organization of American States is formed. Its colorful symbol, above, consists of the furled flags of its member nations.

1959

In Cuba, Fidel Castro and his guerrilla army overthrow a corrupt dictator. Later, Castro establishes a communist dictatorship.

CHAPTER EVENTS

1940   1955   1970

GLOBAL EVENTS

1949 The People's Republic of China is founded.

1960s Many African nations gain independence from European rule.

Population Density of Latin America

Latin America is a diverse region that stretches across Mexico, Central America, the Caribbean, and South America. The region's population is very unevenly distributed.

.

Robinson Projection

120°W	
Tropic of Cancer	
MEXICO	Gulf of Mexico
	BAHAMAS
CUBA	DOMINICAN REPUBLIC
JAMAICA	HAITI
	PUERTO RICO (U.S.)
BELIZE	
HONDURAS	Caribbean Sea
GUATEMALA	
EL SALVADOR	NICARAGUA
COSTA RICA	
PANAMA	VENEZUELA
	GUYANA
	SURINAME
	FRENCH GUIANA (Fr.)
COLOMBIA	ATLANTIC OCEAN
Equator	
ECUADOR	
PACIFIC OCEAN	PERU
	BRAZIL
	BOLIVIA
	PARAGUAY
CHILE	
	URUGUAY
ARGENTINA	Tropic of Capricorn

0 — 1000 Miles
0 — 1000 Kilometers

Persons per sq. mi.	Persons per sq. km.
250 +	100 +
100–249	40–99
25–99	10–39
5–24	3–9
0–4	0–2
Data unavailable	Data unavailable

LIBRE

1983
In Argentina, people celebrate the end of military rule and the restoration of democracy.

1992
The Earth Summit, a UN-sponsored conference on the environment, is held in Rio de Janeiro, Brazil. The promotional photograph above points out the significance of the meeting to future generations.

1985 — 2000 — 2015

1980s A global economic slowdown causes many governments to reduce spending.

1999 In southeastern Europe, civil war rages in Kosovo.

Forces Shaping Modern Latin America

Reading Focus

- Why is Latin America a culturally diverse region?
- What conditions contributed to unrest in Latin American countries?
- What forces shaped political, economic, and social patterns in Latin America?

Vocabulary

import substitution
agribusiness
liberation theology

Taking Notes

As you read this section, make an outline of its contents. Use Roman numerals for major headings, capital letters for subheadings, and numbers for supporting details. The model at right will help you get started.

I. A diverse region
   A. Geographic diversity
      1.
      2.
   B. Cultural diversity
II. Sources of unrest
   A. Social structure
      1.
      2.
   B. Population and poverty

Main Idea Latin America's development is influenced by geography, culture, social patterns, and political and economic conditions.

Setting the Scene

For Carolina Maria de Jesus, life in the slums of São Paulo, Brazil, was filled with hardship. Like millions of other poor people, she had moved from the country to the city. To earn money to feed her family, she combed garbage for paper, cans, and other scraps to sell. In her diary, De Jesus described her daily struggle against poverty:

> "July 16. I went to Senhor Manuel, carrying some cans to sell. . . . He gave me 13 [coins]. I kept thinking that I had to buy bread, soap, and milk. . . . The 13 [coins] wouldn't make it. I returned . . . to my shack, nervous and exhausted. I thought of the worrisome life that I led, carrying paper, washing clothes for the children, staying in the street all day long."
> —Carolina Maria de Jesus, *Child of the Dark*

After 1945, Latin American nations faced problems similar to those of other emerging nations—rapid population growth, poverty, illiteracy, political instability, and authoritarian governments. In Latin America, as elsewhere, each country pursued its own course toward modernization.

A Diverse Region

Latin America stretches across an immense region from Mexico, Central America, and the Caribbean through South America. It includes 33 independent countries that range from tiny island nations like Grenada and Haiti to giant Brazil, which is almost as large as the United States.

Skills Assessment

Graph Latin America is a region of ethnic and cultural diversity. **What ethnic group is the largest in each of the following countries? (a) Haiti, (b) Argentina, (c) Peru.**

ETHNIC DIVERSITY IN LATIN AMERICA

Argentina: 15, 85
Brazil: 1, 6, 55, 38
Haiti: 5, 95
Mexico: 1, 9, 60, 30
Peru: 3, 15, 45, 37

Percentage of Population

African | European | Mestizo | Mulatto | Native American | Other

Source: *CIA World Factbook 1998*

Conquest, immigration, and intermarriage made Latin America culturally diverse. After 1492, Europeans imposed their civilization on Native Americans. They later brought millions of Africans to the region. As these populations mingled, they created vital new cultures. Since the late 1800s, immigrants from Europe and Asia have further contributed to the diversity. Today, people of Indian descent are still the majority population in Mexico, Guatemala, Peru, and Bolivia. Brazil has more people of African descent than any other Latin American nation. Although Spanish is the chief language of the region, Portuguese, French, English, Creole, and hundreds of Native American languages and African dialects are also spoken.

Sources of Unrest

For decades after World War II, uprisings and revolutions shook much of Latin America. Although they grew in part out of changes brought by modernization, they also reflected the failure to reform deep-rooted inequalities.

Social Structure Since colonial days, a key feature of Latin America has been the uneven distribution of wealth. In most countries, a tiny elite controlled the land, mines, businesses, and factories. The wealthy few opposed reforms that threatened their economic power. A growing gulf between rich and poor fueled discontent in the postwar era.

Poverty was linked to the social structure that had survived since colonial times. The upper classes were mostly descended from Europeans. The great majority of the population—the urban and rural poor—were mestizos, Native Americans, or people of African descent.

By the mid-1900s, two social classes were emerging as important forces. As cities grew, the middle class and urban working class expanded. They were less tied to particular ethnic groups than the old aristocracy and peasantry. Both had their own hopes for progress and prosperity.

Population and Poverty In Latin America, as elsewhere, the population explosion contributed to poverty. Between 1930 and 1985, for example, the populations of both Brazil and Mexico increased by more than four times. Growth rates in some countries slowed during the 1990s, but economies were still hard pressed to keep pace with population. Overall populations kept rising because a large proportion of the people were young and just starting their own families. Latin America's population reached 400 million in 1990 and exceeded 600 million in 2000.

In rural areas, where most of the people were peasant farmers, population growth put stress on the land. A family might own a small plot for growing food. But most farmers worked for low wages on the estates of wealthy landlords who held the best land. Many had to borrow money from their landlords just to get by from harvest to harvest. Burdened by this so-called debt slavery, they were tied to the land unless they ran away to the cities.

Urbanization Pressure on the land contributed to the great migration that sent millions of peasants to the cities. Today, about 70 percent of all Latin Americans live in cities. Some newcomers found jobs in factories,

Source of Unrest
The gulf between rich and poor contributes to unrest in Latin America. This family lives in a shack near Lima, Peru.

Theme: Political and Social Systems Why do you think poor health is often a problem for people who live in communities such as this?

offices, or stores. Many more survived by working odd jobs such as doing laundry or mending shoes. Others scavenged at the city garbage dump.

In the shantytowns that ringed Latin American cities, people lived in shacks without electricity, sewage, or other services. Yet because they were near urban centers, they were more likely to attend school or have access to health care than were the rural poor. As a result, poor city children were sometimes in a better position to move ahead than rural children.

Politics: Reform, Repression, or Revolution

Most Latin American states had constitutions modeled on those of France or the United States. On paper, they protected the rights of individuals. Yet real democracy seemed difficult to achieve in nations plagued by poverty and inequality.

Competing Ideologies After World War II, various groups pressed for reforms. They included liberals, socialists, students, labor leaders, peasant organizers, and Catholic priests and nuns. Although they differed over how to achieve their goals, all wanted to improve conditions for the poor. Most called for schools, housing, health care, and land reform.

Conservative forces, however, resisted reforms that might undermine their power. These elite groups included the military, the traditional landed aristocracy, and the growing business middle class. They often had strong ties to foreign investors and corporations. Conflict between conservatives and reformers contributed to political instability in many nations.

Military Regimes Military leaders, like *caudillos* of the 1800s, held power in many Latin American nations. They often served conservative interests. However, some supported modest social and economic reforms, in part because a growing number of officers came from the working classes.

In the 1960s and 1970s, as social unrest increased, military governments seized power in Argentina, Brazil, Chile, and elsewhere. Claiming the need to restore order, they imposed harsh regimes. They outlawed political parties, censored the press, and closed universities. In Argentina and Chile, the military imprisoned and executed thousands of dissidents. Others were murdered by illegal "death squads" allied to the government.

Some military rulers tried to solve economic problems by sponsoring capitalism. In Chile, General Augusto Pinochet (pee noh SHAY), who ruled from 1973 to 1990, promoted foreign investment and privatized industry. The Chilean economy did expand. In general, however, most military regimes were unable to solve basic problems.

The Threat of Revolution During the 1960s and 1970s, guerrillas and urban terrorists battled repressive governments in many Latin American countries. Rebel groups used bombings, kidnappings, and assassinations. The leaders of many of these groups supported Marxist goals. Only a socialist revolution, they said, could end inequalities. Marxism won support among peasants, urban workers, and some intellectuals. Other revolutionaries were motivated by nationalism. They condemned economic and cultural domination by the United States.

During the Cold War, the spread of Marxism complicated moderate reform efforts. Conservatives tended to view any effort at reform as a communist threat and often won support from the United States.

Revival of Democracy By the mid-1980s, inflation, debt, and growing protests led repressive leaders to step aside. Argentina, Brazil, Chile, and other countries held multiparty elections to replace military government with civilian government. In the 1990s, the only major nonelected ruler in Latin America was Cuba's Fidel Castro. One former dictator, Augusto Pinochet of Chile, was even arrested in Europe so that he might be put on trial for violation of human rights.

Still, elections alone could not ensure truly democratic government. In Peru, for example, President Alberto Fujimori suspended the nation's constitution to crush antigovernment guerrillas. Since the 1980s, some elected governments have made modest progress, but world economic forces have threatened their successes. Whether stable democratic governments would survive these economic pressures remained to be seen.

▶ **Primary Sources and Literature**

See "Mario Vargas Llosa: Latin America, the Democratic Option" in the Reference Section at the back of this book.

Economic Development

Except during the Great Depression of the 1930s, most Latin American nations experienced economic growth between 1900 and the 1960s. Their economies, though, were influenced by global economic trends and dependence on industrial nations. Many relied on the export of a single crop or commodity, so they were hard hit if harvests failed or demand declined. By the 1960s, Latin America faced growing competition from African and Asian nations seeking to export their crops and commodities.

Industry To reduce dependence on imported goods, many Latin American governments encouraged the development of local industry. This policy was called import substitution. In time, many nations produced consumer goods such as textiles or refrigerators. They also set up auto manufacturing plants, although the parts were mostly imported.

Women in Government
Today, a growing number of women are becoming leaders in government. The billboards shown here advertise a woman running for office in Guadeloupe, a group of Caribbean islands ruled by France.

Theme: Continuity and Change How do the billboards show continuity and change in Latin America?

Efforts to promote industry had mixed success. The middle class prospered, but life did not improve for most people. Many new industries were inefficient and needed government help or foreign capital to survive. Some domestically produced goods were too expensive or too poorly made to compete with imported products. Also, industry did not expand rapidly enough to produce new jobs for a rapidly growing population. Eventually, governments returned to promoting agricultural exports.

Expanding Agriculture Over the past 60 years, large areas of land were opened up for farming through irrigation and clearing of forests. Much of the best farmland belonged to agribusinesses, or giant commercial farms owned by multinational corporations. They used modern technology to develop the land and operate processing plants. In Central America and Brazil, developers cleared tropical forests to provide new farmlands. As you will read, this development had environmental costs.

Commercial agriculture increased the need to import food. Production of some food crops declined as land was turned over to growing crops for export. As a result, more food had to be imported, at a high cost.

Crisis and Reform In the 1980s, Latin American nations were buffeted by economic storms, including high oil costs, rising interest rates, and a worldwide recession. As interest rates rose, nations that had borrowed to develop industry were crushed by a debt crisis.

To combat the crisis, nations like Mexico and Brazil resorted to strong measures. They cut spending on social programs, raised prices on goods, stopped financing local businesses, and opened their markets to foreign companies. Most governments brought their debt payments under control.

In the 1990s, free-trade agreements opened Latin American economies to larger markets. Despite the buffeting of global economic changes, many Latin American nations enjoyed at least some economic growth.

Changing Social Patterns

In Latin America, as elsewhere, urbanization brought social upheaval. City life weakened the extended family of rural villages and often replaced it with the smaller nuclear family. Instead of raising food, family members had to earn cash. The struggle to make a living caused some families to fall apart. In large cities, thousands of abandoned or runaway children roamed the streets. Many were caught up in crime and violence. To support their families, many women took jobs outside the home.

Women Throughout the 1900s, Latin American women worked hard to increase their role in public life and to win equality, including the right to vote. By 1961, women had won the vote throughout the Americas. By the

1990s, women moved into the political arena in small but growing numbers. Both Argentina and Nicaragua had women presidents, and Benedita da Silva became the first black woman elected to the Brazilian congress.

Women's status varied according to class and race. Generally, women were responsible for the home and for child care. Upper-class women had access to education and professional careers and could hire servants to care for their homes and children. Rural women of Indian or African descent faced prejudice and poverty. They lacked schooling and basic health care, and often labored for low pay.

A peasant woman from El Salvador, who began harvesting coffee and cotton at age 16, described the injustices she endured. One problem was the quota system: "They'd give you two and a half sacks as a quota for every day and if you didn't manage it, they didn't pay you anything." Another complaint was unequal treatment: "Men have always been paid 5 colones more than women or children and we all do exactly the same work."

Women struggled to win change. To help their families and communities, some peasant women pushed for schools and health care. In Argentina and elsewhere, women protested human rights abuses by brutal military governments. During the harsh Pinochet years in Chile, women in Santiago organized food kitchens to serve meals to the poor. Others protested violence against women or challenged the subordinate position of women within the family.

Religion The Catholic Church has remained a powerful force throughout Latin America. Traditionally, it was often tied to the conservative ruling class. However, some Church leaders had always spoken up for the poor. During the 1960s and 1970s, many priests, nuns, and church workers crusaded for social justice and an end to poverty. Their movement became known as liberation theology. These activists saw Jesus as a "liberator of the poor." They urged the Church to become a force for reform. Many joined the struggle against oppressive governments. Some became objects of violence themselves. In El Salvador, for example, Archbishop Oscar Romero was assassinated by a right-wing death squad.

Some evangelical Protestant groups won a growing following among the poor. Their message, which emphasized the power of faith, had an especially strong appeal among women, who then brought other family members into the faith.

SECTION 1 Assessment

Recall
1. **Identify:** **(a)** debt slavery, **(b)** Augusto Pinochet, **(c)** Alberto Fujimori, **(d)** Benedita da Silva.
2. **Define:** **(a)** import substitution, **(b)** agribusiness, **(c)** liberation theology.

Comprehension
3. How does the history of Latin America explain its cultural diversity today?
4. Describe four conditions that fed unrest in Latin America.
5. Describe how each of the following has affected Latin America: **(a)** military regimes, **(b)** economic nationalism, **(c)** religion.

Critical Thinking and Writing
6. **Synthesizing Information** Review the Setting the Scene and the picture of Lima, Peru, on the first pages of the section. Use the primary source and the picture to write an editorial commenting on the condition of poor families in Latin America.
7. **Recognizing Causes and Effects** Explain the causes and effects of the debt crisis that afflicted Latin America and other parts of the world in the 1980s.

Activity
Take It to the NET

Use the Internet to find information about urban populations in Latin America. Identify the largest cities in Latin America in order of population, and plot these cities on a map. Write a caption that indicates each city's population and the year the data was gathered.

Latin America, the United States, and the World

Reading Focus

■ How did communist rule affect Cuba?

■ What policies did the United States follow in Latin America?

■ What global issues have linked Latin America to other regions of the world?

Vocabulary

literacy rate

embargo

Taking Notes

Make an organizer like the one shown here to outline relations between the United States and nations of Latin America. Complete the chart as you read. Add as many boxes as you need.

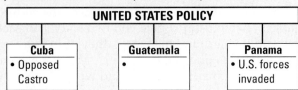

UNITED STATES POLICY		

Cuba	**Guatemala**	**Panama**
• Opposed Castro	•	• U.S. forces invaded

Main Idea Latin American nations have developed policies in response to United States influence, regional issues, and global issues.

Biography

Fidel Castro 1926(?) —

Castro was the son of a wealthy farmer who employed several hundred workers. While studying law at the University of Havana, he and other students took part in a failed attempt to invade the Dominican Republic and overthrow its dictator, Rafael Trujillo. Castro earned his law degree and became a vocal opponent of dictator Fulgencio Batista. In 1953, Castro led an attack on an army barracks. The assault failed and resulted in his imprisonment. After his release, he went into exile in Mexico. In 1956, he returned to Cuba and launched the guerrilla war that eventually led to his victory.

Theme: Impact of the Individual How did Castro demonstrate an ability to overcome failure?

Setting the Scene "The duty of every revolutionary is to make revolution," declared Cuban dictator Fidel Castro in 1962. After bringing about sweeping changes in his island nation, Castro vowed to export communism to other countries in the region. During the Cold War, the threat of communist revolution had a strong influence on United States policy toward Latin America. Meanwhile, Latin American nations tried to limit United States influence in the region. Today, Latin American nations are building new political and economic relations in the global arena.

Communism in Cuba

After the Spanish-American War, Cuba won independence from Spain. However, Cuba was controlled by the United States under the Platt Amendment to the Cuban Constitution until 1935. During this time, American investors bought up Cuban plantations and mills, and the United States became the chief buyer of Cuba's sugar. It continued to support military dictators.

Castro In the 1950s, a young lawyer, Fidel Castro, rallied forces opposed to the corrupt Batista regime. By 1959, Castro had led his tiny guerrilla army to victory. Cubans cheered the rebel as a hero. For many, the joy soon wore off as Castro turned Cuba into a communist state. Castro nationalized foreign-owned sugar plantations and other businesses. He put most land under government control and distributed the rest to peasant farmers.

While Castro imposed harsh authoritarian rule, he did improve conditions for the poor. During the 1960s, Cuba provided basic health care for all, promoted equality for women, and increased the nation's literacy rate, the percentage of a population that can read and write. But communist dictatorship angered middle-class Cubans. Critics were jailed or silenced, and hundreds of thousands fled to the United States.

Cold War Tensions The Cuban Revolution alarmed the United States, especially as Castro turned to the Soviet Union for aid. In 1961, the United States backed a plot by anti-Castro exiles to invade Cuba and overthrow Castro. An invasion force landed at the Bay of Pigs in Cuba but was quickly crushed. The next year, the United States imposed an embargo on Cuba. An embargo is a ban on trade. Castro sought closer ties to the Soviet Union. He let the Soviets build nuclear missile bases in Cuba, just 90 miles from Florida. The threat of nearby Soviet nuclear bases outraged the United States and touched off a dangerous crisis.

In October 1962, President John Kennedy declared a naval blockade of Cuba and demanded that the Soviets remove the weapons. For several days during the Cuban missile crisis, the superpowers stood on the brink of nuclear war. In the end, Soviet leader Nikita Khrushchev backed down. He agreed to remove the missiles from Cuba.

Over the next decades, Castro tried to encourage revolution in other Latin American nations. Cuba also sent troops to Africa to help the socialist government of Angola. In response, the United States continued its efforts to isolate Cuba and undermine Castro. The Soviets, meanwhile, provided massive economic and military aid to Cuba.

Recent Trends When the Soviet Union collapsed in the early 1990s, Cuba lost its chief ally and trading partner. Without Soviet financial aid, Cuba's economy fell into a shambles. In response, Castro encouraged tourism, allowed some features of a market economy, and welcomed foreign investment. At the same time, however, he vowed to preserve communism.

The United States refused to negotiate with Castro, despite the urgings of the United Nations and Latin American leaders, who argued that Cuba no longer posed a threat. Still, as American business people visited the country and baseball teams from the two nations competed, it seemed less and less likely that either Cuban communism or the American embargo would endure for long.

The United States and Latin America

Like powerful nations in many times and places, the United States developed a sphere of influence that included smaller neighboring states. The United States was the leading investor and trading partner for most nations in Latin America. Profits from United States-owned companies flowed from Latin America to the north. At the same time, cultural influences drifted both north and south.

Despite their links, the United States and its neighbors had very different views of one another. The United States saw itself as the defender of democracy and capitalism and the source of humanitarian aid. Many Latin Americans, however, resented that they lived under the shadow of the "colossus of the north."

Intervention During the Cold War, the United States intervened repeatedly in Latin America under the banner of the Monroe Doctrine. It did so to protect its interests and to prevent the spread of communism. The United States backed anti-communist dictators and helped equip and train their soldiers to fight rebel uprisings. It even helped topple leftist leaders.

In 1954, for example, the United States helped Guatemalan soldiers overthrow a popularly elected president, Jacobo Arbenz. This action came after he had enacted land reforms that threatened United States-owned businesses. In the 1970s, after socialist Salvador Allende (ah YEHN day) was elected president of Chile, President Richard Nixon told officials to "make the [Chilean] economy scream." In 1973, the United States quietly lent its support to a military coup that overthrew Allende.

Other United States interventions in Latin America were unrelated to the threat of communism. In 1989, United States forces invaded Panama and overthrew the government of General Manuel Noriega. Noriega was removed from Panama and then tried, convicted, and imprisoned for drug trafficking. In the 1990s, the United States used economic pressure and the threat of military action to force military rulers from power in Haiti.

Many Latin Americans opposed United States economic and military intervention. Although they perhaps admired the wealth and technology of the United States, they often resented its political, economic, and cultural influence in Latin America.

Did You Know?

Escape From Cuba

To flee poverty and political repression, many Cuban *balseros* (rafters) braved 90 miles of open sea to reach the United States. Men, women, and children crossed the Straits of Florida on rickety rafts, small boats, and smugglers' speedboats. Not all survived the trip.

Sun, waves, winds, and even hurricanes imperiled those trying to escape from Cuba. "The weather was so bad that we were lost for the next two days," said one balsero. "We were pushed into the middle of the Atlantic . . . [and] were followed by sharks." The sole survivor of another voyage recalled: "When the raft fell apart, all of us grabbed whatever tire and wood we could."

Theme: Political and Social Systems Why were people willing to risk the voyage from Cuba to Florida?

Cutting Down Lives?

As loggers cut down trees in the Amazon rain forest, medical experts worry. They worry because they know that vital medicines—both discovered and undiscovered—are derived from plants found only in the Amazon and other rain forests. For example, the bark of the cinchona tree produces quinine, which is used for treating malaria. Curare, used by Indians of the Amazon as a dart poison, serves as a muscle relaxant during surgery. A wild Amazonian yam provides a drug that can be used in the treatment of autoimmune diseases and some forms of cancer. One day, the medical experts fear, the loss of plant life in the rain forests and other ecosystems might result in the loss of human life.

Theme: Global Interaction
How might destruction of rain forests lead to loss of human life?

Regional Organizations Despite disagreements, Latin American nations and the United States did work together. The Organization of American States (OAS) was formed in 1948 to promote democracy, economic cooperation, and human rights. Members pledged not to interfere "directly or indirectly, for any reason whatever, in the internal or external affairs of any other State." Although the United States often dominated the OAS, Latin American members did at times pursue an independent line.

The Castro revolution and other Cold War tensions led President Kennedy to launch the Alliance for Progress in 1961. Under this ambitious program, the United States offered billions in loans and investments. In exchange, Latin American governments were to enact genuine reforms. The goals were to promote education and land reform, reduce inequality and poverty, weaken dictatorships, and help countries avoid revolutions.

The alliance produced little progress. Landowners and the business elite in many countries opposed basic reforms. The United States provided aid to Latin America, but never on the scale proposed by Kennedy.

Regional and Global Issues

By the end of the Cold War, many Latin American nations had reduced their dependence on the United States, although it remained their chief trading partner. Increasingly, they were tied to the global economy. Oil-rich Venezuela joined Arab nations in OPEC, while Brazil worked with coffee-exporting nations of Africa to support coffee prices.

Many Latin American nations increased trade and cultural links to European countries. Some exported food or minerals to Asian nations. Japanese investments in Latin America, especially in Brazil, rose rapidly.

Regional Ties In Latin America, as elsewhere around the world, regional trading blocs gained importance in the 1990s. Such groups created larger markets by lowering trade barriers among neighboring countries. In 1993, Mexico linked its economy to those of the United States and Canada through NAFTA. Two years later, a new South American trading bloc, Mercosur, paved the way for increased trade among Argentina, Brazil, Paraguay, and Uruguay. The new groups operated alongside older blocs that linked Andean, Caribbean, or Central American nations. Talks were also underway to create a hemisphere-wide free-trade zone that would be even larger than the expanding European Union.

The Drug Wars Regional cooperation was essential to efforts to control the illegal drug trade. Indians in Colombia, Peru, and Bolivia had for centuries grown coca for their own uses. However, as drug use increased in various parts of the world, criminal gangs, also known as drug cartels, began producing and exporting ever-larger quantities of cocaine and other drugs. By the 1970s, drug lords were reaping huge profits, which they used to bribe government officials. They also hired assassins to kill judges, journalists, and others who spoke out against them.

In the 1980s, the United States declared a "war on drugs." To halt the flow of drugs, the United States pressed governments in Colombia, Peru, and other countries to destroy coca crops and move against the cartels. Governments cooperated, but many Latin Americans argued that the root of the problem was not the supply of drugs but the growing demand for illegal drugs in the United States.

Development Versus the Environment Concerns about the environment also raised some troubling issues for Latin America and the world.

Developing nations insisted that they needed to exploit their land and other resources if they wanted economic growth. "You cannot talk ecology to people who are struggling to survive," said a Brazilian delegate at an international conference on the environment. Developing nations pointed out that western powers had long since cleared many of their forests and mined their lands. What right, they asked, did industrial nations have to tell them to stop developing their resources?

The most widely publicized issue was the rapid destruction of the Amazon rain forest, which occupies more than a million square miles in the heart of Brazil. It is rich in mineral resources needed for economic growth. It also could provide land to millions of landless peasants. Since the 1930s, Brazil has opened more and more of this area to development. By the 1970s and 1980s, vast tracts of forest were being bulldozed and burned for farms, cattle ranches, highways, and even newly planned cities.

Environmentalists argued that deforestation had enormous costs. They called the Amazon rain forest "the lungs of the world" because it plays a key role in absorbing poisonous carbon dioxide from the air and releasing essential oxygen. It has been home to 15 million species of plants and animals, which have been threatened by development. Some forms of plant life might even hold undiscovered cures for diseases.

Another environmental concern was rapid development, which meant disaster for many native peoples. Isolation had protected bands of Native American forest dwellers for centuries. Land-hungry farmers, speculators, and foreign mining companies converged on the forest, threatening these ancient ways of life. Many Indians died of diseases introduced by the newcomers. Others were killed in conflicts provoked by impatient developers moving into the forest.

Migration Latin American immigration to the United States increased rapidly after the 1970s. Poverty, civil war, and repressive governments led many people to flee their homelands. Like earlier immigrants, they sought freedom and economic opportunity.

By the end of the 1990s, the United States had more than 11 million Latin American immigrants. Many immigrants entered the United States legally and eventually became citizens. A large number, however, were illegal immigrants. As a result, pressure increased in the United States to halt illegal immigration, deny services to illegal aliens, and return them to their countries of origin.

SECTION 2 Assessment

Recall

1. **Identify:** **(a)** Fidel Castro, **(b)** Bay of Pigs, **(c)** Cuban missile crisis, **(d)** Salvador Allende, **(e)** Manuel Noriega, **(f)** OAS, **(g)** Alliance for Progress, **(h)** NAFTA, **(i)** Mercosur, **(j)** drug cartel.
2. **Define:** **(a)** literacy rate, **(b)** embargo.

Comprehension

3. What changes did communism bring to life in Cuba?
4. Describe how United States political and economic policies have affected relations with countries of Latin America.

5. How have Latin American nations addressed regional and global issues?

Critical Thinking and Writing

6. **Connecting to Geography** **(a)** What environmental issues face Latin American nations? **(b)** Which of the five themes of geography seems most closely linked to these issues? Explain.
7. **Recognizing Causes and Effects** **(a)** How did the anti-communist stance of the United States affect Cuba? **(b)** How did the collapse of the Soviet Union affect Cuba?

Activity
Take It to the NET

Use the Internet to find recent news articles concerning one Latin American nation's involvement with one of the regional or global issues discussed in this section. Using the news articles, prepare a radio broadcast to deliver to the class.

Mexico, Central America, and the Caribbean

Reading Focus

- What conditions have changed and what conditions have remained the same in Mexico?
- Why did Central American countries suffer civil wars?
- What were the causes of Haiti's political and economic struggles?

Vocabulary

ejido

maquiladora

contra

Taking Notes

Make a table like the one below. Add key information about Mexico, Nicaragua, and two other countries.

	MEXICO	NICARAGUA		
POLITICS				
ECONOMICS	Land redistribution			

Main Idea Although Mexico underwent change with relatively little turmoil, several Central American countries were torn by civil war.

Primary Source

Heading Toward Democracy
Octavio Paz, a Mexican poet, philosopher, and winner of a Nobel Prize for literature, comments on democracy in Latin America:

"Latin American democracy was a late arrival on the scene, and it has been disfigured and betrayed time and time again. It has been weak, hesitant, rebellious, its own worst enemy, all too eager to worship the demagogue, corrupted by money, riddled with favoritism and nepotism. And yet almost everything good that has been achieved in Latin America in the last century and a half has been accomplished under democratic rule, or, as in Mexico, a rule heading toward democracy. A great deal still remains to be done."

—Octavio Paz, *One Earth, Four or Five Worlds: Reflections on Contemporary History*

Skills Assessment

Primary Source Does Paz favor or oppose democracy? Explain.

Setting the Scene Oscar Romero was a conservative member of El Salvador's elite until he became archbishop. Then, he began to condemn government death squads that were killing peasants and students opposed to the government. From his pulpit, he announced, "The church would betray . . . its fidelity to the gospel if it stopped being . . . a defender of . . . every legitimate struggle to achieve a more just society."

Romero's outspoken stance cost him his life. On March 24, 1980, as he said mass, shots rang out. Moments later, Romero lay dead, a victim of the death squads he had denounced. But others took his place, and the protest against injustice continued. As one Salvadoran activist commented, "If you silence a prophet, he will speak out through his people."

In the latter half of the 1900s, El Salvador and other Central American countries were battered by civil wars. To the north, their larger and richer neighbor, Mexico, weathered those decades with relatively less turmoil.

Continuity and Change in Mexico

As you have read, Mexico endured a long, violent revolution in the early 1900s. After the revolution, government officials became committed—at least in theory—to improving conditions for the poor.

The Rural Poor In the 1930s, Mexico's president, Lázaro Cárdenas, had taken steps to fulfill the promises of the Mexican Revolution—especially land reform. He distributed millions of acres of land to peasants. Most was given to *ejidos* (eh HEE dohs), or peasant cooperatives. Some families also received small plots to farm themselves.

Over the years, however, the land reform program proved unsuccessful. Much of the land given to peasants was arid. It needed to be irrigated and fertilized to be productive. As rural populations grew, the land was subdivided and exhausted from overfarming. Presidents after Cárdenas paid less attention to Mexico's rural poor. Instead, they favored agribusinesses that produced cash-earning export crops.

As conditions worsened, many peasants migrated to towns and cities, especially to the capital. The population of Mexico City mushroomed from 1.5 million in 1940 to about 20 million in 1995.

The PRI in Control Since the Mexican Revolution, a single party—the Institutional Revolutionary Party (PRI)—has dominated Mexican politics. It claimed to represent all groups—from workers and peasants to businesindustrial interests and the military. There were some other small political parties, but PRI bosses moved forcefully against any serious opposition.

In part, the PRI held on to power by responding to social ills with reform programs for education, welfare, and health. As a result, the party generally kept discontent from exploding into violence. Yet, in 1968, student protests shook Mexico as they did other western countries. Riot police and the army brutally suppressed the turmoil. The riots and the government's response received worldwide attention because the summer Olympic games were held in Mexico City that year. Despite widespread criticism, the PRI remained in power.

From time to time, the government faced rebel uprisings. One outbreak occurred in Chiapas, a state in southern Mexico which had a large Native American population. Discontent was high there because most Indians had benefited little from the nation's economic growth. In 1994, rebels took up arms and challenged the government. They demanded land reforms and rights for Native Americans. By skillfully using the media, the Chiapas rebels became international heroes. Yet they failed to achieve their goals.

Political Reforms Under pressure from all sides, the PRI made some election reforms in the 1990s. As a result, an opposition candidate was elected mayor of Mexico City, and the PRI lost its majority in the national legislature. The PRI's hold on power was further jeopardized by reports of political corruption, repeated drug scandals, and splits within the party's own ranks. As the 1990s drew to a close, it even seemed possible that, for the first time since the 1920s, Mexico might have a president who was not a member of the PRI.

Economic Ups and Downs After World War II, Mexico pushed ahead with efforts to foster import substitution, reduce foreign influence, and expand agriculture. To promote industry, the government worked closely with private businesses. It invested in building roads, dams, and ports. It also encouraged tourism.

From the 1940s to the early 1980s, both manufacturing and agriculture made huge gains. Mexico's economy became the second largest in Latin America after that of Brazil. This growth turned Mexico from an agricultural society into a mostly urban, industrial society. In the late 1970s, new oil discoveries and rising oil prices spurred an economic boom. Optimistic about the future, Mexico borrowed heavily to fund development projects.

In the 1980s, however, global economic trends worked against Mexico. A worldwide recession, falling oil prices, and rising interest rates plunged the country deeply into debt. Like other debtor nations, Mexico cut spending on social and other programs so that it could make its debt payments. To spur economic recovery, the government reduced barriers to foreign businesses and privatized some industries.

Poverty and Prosperity As the 1900s came to an end, Mexico remained a disturbing mix of prosperity and poverty. *Maquiladoras* (mah kee luh DOHR uhs), or assembly plants owned by multinational corporations, flourished along Mexico's northern border. These plants used cheap Mexican labor to assemble imported parts for cars and electronic goods. Finished products were then exported to the United States, Japan, and elsewhere. The *maquiladoras* provided jobs for many Mexicans—most of them women.

Mexican Democracy
As the 1990s came to an end, it seemed possible that Mexico's government would no longer be dominated by a single party. Above, a husband and wife drop their votes into the ballot box.

Theme: Political and Social Systems Why is it important for a democracy to have at least two major political parties?

Connections to Today

The China-Panama Connection

In the 1970s, the United States hoped for the best when it agreed to give up control of the Panama Canal at the end of the century. But in 1999, some United States leaders were not so optimistic. Senator Trent Lott sounded the alarm that "U.S. naval ships will be at the mercy of Chinese-controlled pilots."

The root of his fear was that the Panamanian government had made a deal with a company based in Hong Kong to run two ports near the canal entrances. Most observers felt that Senator Lott's fears were groundless. After all, the Hong Kong company had an impressive record in managing 19 other ports around the world.

Of more concern, thought some observers, was the fragile Panamanian government. In 1999, Mireya Moscoso took office as president. Her late husband had been elected president three times. He was also deposed by the Panamanian army three times.

Theme: Continuity and Change Why did the change in canal ownership cause some to worry?

Still, environmental problems in the plants, plus the government's refusal to let workers organize, led to labor protests.

Despite economic growth, most Mexicans remained poor. The economy could not produce enough jobs to keep up with rapid population growth. Wealth continued to be unequally distributed. The top 10 percent of the people controlled over 40 percent of the wealth, while the poorest 20 percent earned less than 2 percent of national income.

Links to the United States Mexico has felt the powerful influence of its northern neighbor. In the 1930s, Mexico set out to reduce economic influence through import substitution. Yet the nation continued to rely on investment capital from the United States. In 1995, a $20 billion loan from the United States bailed Mexico out of an economic crisis.

In 1993, Mexico, the United States, and Canada signed NAFTA. Supporters claimed that the free-trade association would boost prosperity by lowering trade barriers, thus opening up a huge regional market. NAFTA did bring some new business and investments to Mexico. At the same time, however, it hurt Mexican manufacturers, who could not compete with a flood of goods from the United States.

Issues such as illegal immigration and drug smuggling created tension between Mexico and the United States. Some employers in the United States, especially commercial farmers, relied on Mexican migrant workers to harvest crops for low wages. But as growing numbers of Mexicans crossed the border illegally, many people in the United States came to resent the newcomers. Despite their differences, both nations cooperated on solving issues of international concern such as environmental problems.

War and Peace in Central America

In Central America, unrest threatened the ruling elite of military, business, and landowning interests. Discontent grew in the cities and among rural Indian communities that had long suffered from poverty and oppression. Fearing the spread of communism, the United States intervened repeatedly in the region.

Nicaragua Along with Mexico and Cuba, Nicaragua was one of three Latin American countries to have a genuine revolution in the twentieth century. From 1936 to 1979, the Somoza family ruled—and looted—Nicaragua. Due to their strong anti-communist stand, they enjoyed United States backing. In the 1970s, various groups opposed to Anastasio Somoza joined forces. They called themselves Sandinistas after Augusto Sandino, a revolutionary of the 1930s. Like Sandino, they were reform-minded nationalists. The Sandinistas included a large number of women and leftist students.

In 1979, the revolutionaries ousted Somoza and set out to reshape Nicaragua. Under Sandinista president Daniel Ortega, they introduced land reform and other socialist policies. Fearing that Nicaragua would become "another Cuba," President Ronald Reagan secretly backed the contras— guerrillas who fought against the Sandinistas. Reagan's pro-contra stance violated OAS policy, sparking bitter debate both within the United States and throughout Latin America.

A long civil war weakened the economy but did not unseat the Sandinistas. Other Central American countries finally helped both sides to reach a compromise and stop the fighting. In 1990, Violeta Chamorro, a moderate, won election as president. The Sandinistas peacefully handed over power but kept control of the army.

Over the next decade, rival political parties competed for power in Nicaragua and the nation's economy stagnated. In the election of 1996, the

Hurricane Strikes!

In October 1998, Hurricane Mitch hovered just off the coast of Honduras for two days, dumping a torrent of rain. Then, Mitch swept across much of Central America. Widespread flooding and mudslides killed thousands, making this hurricane the deadliest Atlantic storm in 200 years.

Fast Facts

- Some regions received up to two feet of rain a day during Hurricane Mitch.

- It has been estimated that it will take more than 15 years for the economies of Central America to recover.

- Earlier deforestation contributed to the devastating mudslides.

The Impact of Hurricane Mitch

Nation	Deaths	Property Loss (estimated)
Honduras	5,657	$3,705 million
Nicaragua	3,045	$969 million
Guatemala	268	$698 million
El Salvador	240	$334 million

Source: Inter-American Development Bank

Hurricane Mitch dealt a devastating social and economic blow to Central America, whose nations were just recovering from decades of civil war.

Firefighters and volunteers dig victims from the mud in Guatemala City, Guatemala. Roaring flood waters and fast-flowing rivers of mud carried away entire villages.

A resident of Mango Bay, Honduras, salvages what he can from his home. Almost 130,000 homes across Central America were destroyed or damaged, leaving an estimated 460,000 people homeless.

Portfolio Assessment

INTERNET Use the Internet or library resources to find out more about a recent hurricane. Then, prepare a class presentation on its impact. If possible, include first-person accounts or photographs of the hurricane you have selected.

Honduras This Week
Tegucigalpa, Honduras

To learn more about culture and current events in Central America, use the Internet address above to link to the online newspaper *Honduras This Week.*

Central American Street Scene

In this colorful folk art painting by Jorge Ferman, one can learn much about the culture of the Central American country of Honduras. Note especially the architecture, costumes, landscape, and plant life in the painting.

Theme: Geography and History What does the painting suggest about the climate and landscape of Central America?

Sandinistas once again failed to win the presidency. Hurricane Mitch, one of the most destructive storms of the century devastated the country in 1998. As the century came to a close, prosperity still lay in the future.

Guatemala Fearing growing communist influence and threats to American interests, the United States helped oust Guatemala's reformist government in 1954. Although the military and landowners regained power, they faced constant challenges from leftist guerrilla movements. During decades of civil war, the government routinely tortured and murdered critics, including student and labor leaders.

The chief victims were the Native American majority, some of whom had taken part in antigovernment actions. An estimated 30,000 died during the 1980s alone. Some were killed fighting for the land they tilled but did not own. Others were shot as military forces exterminated whole villages.

Although a civilian government took power in the mid-1980s, the military remained a powerful force behind the scenes. The United States pressured the government to halt the fighting. In 1996, the 30-year civil war finally ended, when the government and guerrillas signed a peace agreement that recognized the rights of the Guatemalan people.

El Salvador The ruling class of military officials and wealthy landowners was also challenged in El Salvador. Here, as elsewhere in Latin America, reformers and revolutionaries found new support in the Catholic Church. In the 1970s, some Church leaders in Latin America abandoned traditional ties to the elite and instead pressed for reform. Inspired by the ideas of liberation theology, Salvadoran priests preached that God was "a God of justice and love who acts on the side of the poor and oppressed." Archbishop Oscar Romero even proclaimed: "When all peaceful means have been exhausted, the church considers insurrection moral and justified."

During a vicious 12-year civil war, right-wing death squads slaughtered church workers, student and labor leaders, and anyone else thought to sympathize with leftists. In 1980, Archbishop Romero fell victim to the fighting, gunned down as he celebrated mass in a chapel. Meanwhile, the United States pressed the government to make some reforms. However, it also provided weapons and other aid to help the military battle rebel guerrillas.

Finally, in 1991, both sides agreed to a UN-brokered peace. After elections were held, former enemies met in the congress, not in battle. However, problems remained. The civil war had ravaged the economy, which still depended on a single export—coffee. Despite large-scale aid from the International Monetary Fund, El Salvador remained a developing nation with a fragile democracy.

Struggle in Haiti

Like other Latin American countries, the Caribbean nation of Haiti has endured a long history of dictatorial rule and rebellion. Since independence in 1804, a small upper class controlled the economy and ruled over the majority of rural poor.

A Pattern of Dictatorship From 1957 to 1971, Dr. François Duvalier (doo vahl YAY) ruled Haiti. "Papa Doc," as he was called, used his brutal secret police force, the *Tontons Macoutes,* to crush opposition and terrorize the people. After his death, his son, Jean-Claude Duvalier, took over. "Baby Doc" continued to loot the country until he was driven into exile in 1986. A succession of military leaders then ruled the island nation.

In 1990, Haiti held its freest elections ever. Jean-Bertrand Aristide (ar ih STEED), a priest and supporter of liberation theology, won 70 percent of the vote. A hero to the poor, Aristide proclaimed, "Our primary objective is to move from misery to dignified poverty." Just months after Aristide took office, a military coup forced him into exile. The new rulers launched a reign of terror against Aristide's supporters.

An Uncertain Future Aristide returned to Haiti after the threat of United States military action forced Haitian army leaders from power. Upon his return, he optimistically declared, "This is a day on which the sun of democracy rises, never to set." Despite his pledge, Aristide achieved little success in reconciling opposing groups and bringing about meaningful reform. He stepped down in 1996, and a new president was elected.

Haiti's fragile democracy survived but faced many problems. The poorest state in the Western Hemisphere, it lacked adequate roads, electricity, and other services. The government failed to guarantee a peaceful, safe climate, thus discouraging foreign investments and aid. Politically, party rivalries often led to government inaction. Protest demonstrations and soaring crime were further evidence that Haiti faced difficult times ahead.

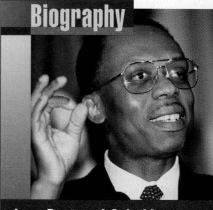

Biography

Jean-Bertrand Aristide
1953—

"Can we continue to find this situation of violence that is imposed on the poor normal?" asked Jean-Bertrand Aristide in a 1982 sermon. "No. We must end this regime," the young priest concluded.

In September 1988, an armed group of Haitian security forces, known as the *Tontons Macoutes,* attacked Aristide and his followers in church. They set fire to the church and killed a number of Aristide's supporters. Aristide escaped, but he was soon forced to resign as a priest. Two years later, Aristide became a presidential candidate—in part, to bring the killers to justice.

Theme: Impact of the Individual Why did Aristide become involved in politics?

SECTION 3 Assessment

Recall
1. **Identify: (a)** Lázaro Cárdenas, **(b)** PRI, **(c)** Chiapas, **(d)** Sandinistas, **(e)** Violeta Chamorro, **(f)** Oscar Romero, **(g)** Jean-Bertrand Aristide.
2. **Define: (a)** *ejido,* **(b)** *maquiladora,* **(c)** contra.

Comprehension
3. **(a)** How has Mexican politics changed in recent years? **(b)** Identify recent developments in the Mexican economy.
4. **(a)** Who were the opposing sides in El Salvador's civil war? **(b)** How did the civil war end?
5. What problems have hindered the development of democracy in Haiti?

Critical Thinking and Writing
6. **Predicting Consequences** How might the collapse of the Soviet Union and the end of the Cold War affect relations between the United States and the nations of Central America?
7. **Identifying Main Ideas** Re-read the subsection Struggle in Haiti. Then, write the main idea of each paragraph in the subsection.

Activity

Writing Political Slogans Write two slogans that a PRI candidate might use during an election campaign in Mexico. Then, write two slogans that a candidate from an opposition party might use. Use one of the slogans to create a campaign poster.

Focus on Argentina and Brazil

Reading Focus

- What challenges has Argentina faced on the road to democracy?

- How did Brazil's government change in the late 1900s?

- What difficulties have limited Brazil's "economic miracle?"

Vocabulary

favela

plebiscite

squatter

Taking Notes

Make a Venn diagram like the one below. Use it to record important facts about recent developments in Argentina and Brazil. In the middle section, list things that are true of both nations.

ARGENTINA
- Facts revealed about the "dirty war"

- Democratic elections restored in 1980s

BRAZIL
- People voted against a monarchy

Main Idea Argentina and Brazil have worked to develop stable governments and strong, modern economies.

Juan and Eva Perón
Despite their authoritarian rule, the charismatic Peróns captured the imagination of working-class Argentinians. Years later, audiences around the world were captivated by *Evita*, a musical play based on the life of Mrs. Perón.

Theme: Impact of the Individual How did the Peróns win popular support?

Setting the Scene One year at Rio de Janeiro's annual carnival parade, a float was based on the story of *Alice's Adventures in Wonderland.* After Alice shrank to tiny size, and then grew very tall, a caterpillar on the float asked her, "Who are you?"

Alice replied: "I no longer know who I am. First, I was small like Brazil, underdeveloped, with many problems. Suddenly I grew, became a giant, a great power, but with many problems."

The caterpillar reassured Alice: "I am a caterpillar, but I turn myself into a butterfly. This could happen to you." The float expressed optimism for Brazil, a nation that has experienced many changes over recent decades.

Brazil is one of a dozen independent nations of South America. Here we will look at the two largest South American republics—Argentina and Brazil. History, geography, and other forces have shaped each country's efforts to develop a stable government and a strong, modern economy.

Dictatorship and Democracy in Argentina

In the early 1900s, Argentina was the largest Spanish-speaking nation in the world and the richest nation in Latin America. It had a fairly stable government dominated by the wealthy elite. Its economy was fed by exports of beef and wheat, mostly to Britain. Argentina attracted millions of immigrants, many of whom worked in the factories of Buenos Aires. Then the Great Depression struck. For the next 50 years, Argentina was plagued by economic crises, social unrest, and military rule.

Perón in Power In 1946, Juan Perón was elected president. He appealed to Argentine nationalism by limiting foreign-owned businesses and promoting import substitution. By boosting wages, strengthening labor unions, and enacting social reforms, Perón won the loyalty of the working classes.

Perón was helped by his glamorous wife Eva Duarte Perón, who had risen from poverty to fame as an actress. As Perón's chief aide, she had clinics built and gave money to the sick and unemployed. To secure more votes for her husband, she helped women gain the right to vote. Meanwhile, she used public funds to enjoy an extravagant lifestyle. "You, too, will have clothes as rich as mine," she promised the poor women of Argentina.

While Juan Perón wooed the urban poor, his authoritarian government stifled opposition. Many educated people fled Argentina. Perón's policies led to a huge debt and soaring inflation. In 1955, Perón was ousted by a military coup and forced into exile.

Military Rule For two decades, the military was in and out of power, and supporters of Perón urged a return to his policies. In 1973, an aging Perón did return, and he was again elected president. His new wife, Isabel, was chosen vice president. When he died the next year, Isabel Perón became president—the first woman head of state in the Western Hemisphere. As she faced economic and political crises, terrorists on the left and on the right disrupted the country. In 1976, the military took power.

To combat leftist guerrillas, the army waged a "dirty war," terrorizing people that they claimed were enemies of the state. They tortured and murdered thousands of citizens. As many as 20,000 people disappeared after being taken from their homes. Week after week, in the Plaza de Mayo in Buenos Aires, mothers marched silently, holding pictures of their children who had disappeared. The "Mothers of the Plaza de Mayo" gained worldwide attention.

In 1982, the military hoped to mask economic troubles by seizing the British-ruled Falkland Islands. Argentina had long claimed these islands, which it called the Malvinas. The military mistakenly believed that Britain would not fight to keep the islands. In a brief but decisive war fought on land, on sea, and in the air, the British recaptured the Falklands. Defeat undermined the power and prestige of Argentina's military, and it was forced to hold free elections.

Democracy Restored In 1983, an elected government restored democracy to Argentina. Despite economic setbacks and scandals of corruption, democratic rule survived. Gradually, more and more facts emerged about the military's "dirty war" against the people. Nearly all who disappeared were murdered—often by being thrown into the ocean from aircraft.

In the 1990s, Argentina's democracy took hold and the economy grew, aided by plentiful natural resources and the highest literacy rate in Latin America. President Carlos Menem was able to cut inflation and enact government financial reforms urged by the International Monetary Fund.

Critics, however, objected to the privatization of government-run industries and noted that unemployment remained high. In some years, one in five adults was jobless. Another persistent problem was that wealth remained concentrated in the hands of a few. In 1999, Argentines elected Fernando de la Rua to the presidency. De la Rua pledged to work for better living conditions for all Argentines.

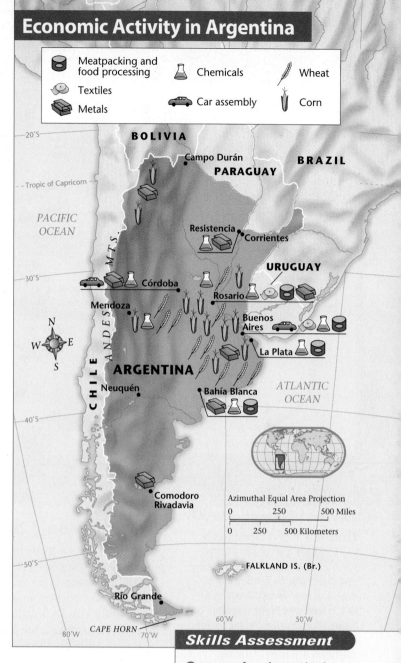

Economic Activity in Argentina

Meatpacking and food processing Chemicals Wheat

Textiles Car assembly Corn

Metals

BOLIVIA
Campo Durán
BRAZIL
PARAGUAY
Tropic of Capricorn
PACIFIC OCEAN
Resistencia
Corrientes
URUGUAY
Córdoba
Mendoza
Rosario
Buenos Aires
La Plata
ARGENTINA
Neuquén
Bahía Blanca
ATLANTIC OCEAN
Comodoro Rivadavia

Azimuthal Equal Area Projection
0   250   500 Miles
0   250   500 Kilometers

FALKLAND IS. (Br.)

Río Grande
CAPE HORN
CHILE
ANDES MTS.

Skills Assessment

Geography Argentina's wide variety of resources and industries has contributed to the nation's economic growth.

1. **Location** On the map, locate (a) Buenos Aires, (b) Falkland Islands, (c) Brazil.
2. **Region** Using latitude and longitude, identify the major agricultural region of Argentina.
3. **Critical Thinking** **Drawing Conclusions** Based on the map, identify one geographic characteristic that is common to most of the major cities in Argentina.

Urbanization in Brazil

1994

22.4% rural

77.6% urban

2025 (estimate)

11.1% rural

88.9% urban

Source: UN Population Division

Skills Assessment

Graph The cityscape above is of São Paulo. Unlike other Latin American countries that have only one major city, Brazil has more than a dozen. **Over the years, have more Brazilians migrated *to* cities or *from* cities? How do you think this pattern affects the Brazilian economy? Explain.**

Brazil's People and Government

Brazil occupies almost half of South America. Its varied landscapes include the mighty Amazon River and the world's largest tropical forest. Northeastern Brazil, however, is an arid plain. Brazil's rich resources include minerals, timber, and rich farmlands that yield cash crops such as coffee and sugar. Geographic conditions have contributed to uneven settlement patterns. About 90 percent of Brazilians live within 200 miles of the Atlantic coast. To draw settlers inland, the government has encouraged development of the interior.

Population Unlike its South American neighbors, Brazil was settled by people from Portugal, not Spain. With a population over 173 million, the nation has more people than any of its Spanish-speaking neighbors. Brazil has a diverse society. Afonso Celso, a noted Brazilian patriot, considered this diversity to be a source of national strength. In his words, "Three elements contributed to the formation of the Brazilian people: the American Indian, the African, and the Portuguese." In the 1900s, many Japanese and Germans settled in Brazil, adding to its cultural mix.

Most Brazilians are Roman Catholic, but a growing number of people embrace evangelical Protestant faiths. Others practice Candomblè, a form of worship that blends African and Christian beliefs.

Rapid population growth and class divisions have contributed to poverty in Brazil. In the cities, where more than 75 percent of Brazilians live, the sharp contrast between rich and poor is seen everywhere. Teeming, garbage-strewn *favelas,* or slums, ring the major cities, which boast luxurious high-rise apartment buildings and wealthy shopping areas. In the *favelas* around São Paulo and Rio de Janeiro, thousands of homeless children survive on the streets without families or education.

Political Instability   Like its neighbors, Brazil has had its share of dictators and military rulers. They pursued modernization under the motto "order and progress."

Between 1930 and 1945, dictator Getúlio Vargas allied himself with the working poor. Like Perón in Argentina, he improved wages and workers' benefits, favored labor unions, and gave women the right to vote. The military eventually toppled Vargas, but they allowed elected presidents to rule Brazil for almost 20 years.

By 1964, economic problems and fear of communism led the military to take over again. The seizure of power was quietly supported by the United States, which was even willing to provide some aid to the military. The assistance was not needed. Backed by the middle and upper classes, the generals ruled with a heavy hand. They tortured and jailed critics, censored the press, and ignored calls for social reform.

In the mid-1980s, though, the military gradually eased their grip on power. In 1989, Brazilians were finally able to vote directly for a president for the first time in 29 years. To determine if Brazil should remain a republic or return to being a monarchy, a plebiscite was held in 1993. A plebiscite is a vote in which people approve or reject a proposal. The people of Brazil voted to keep their republic.

Brazil's "Economic Miracle"

"Brazil is a country of the future, and always will be." This Brazilian saying suggests both the nation's potential and its many setbacks. For more than a century, Brazil has weathered many boom-and-bust cycles.

Early Development   In the early 1900s, the huge demand for Brazilian rubber suddenly fell off, causing economic hardships. Coffee then replaced rubber as the major export. But again and again, declining prices for coffee or natural disasters wreaked havoc on the economy.

In the 1930s, Brazil moved away from dependence on a single export by diversifying its economy. Vargas encouraged industry. He built highways, hydroelectric plants, and schools. During and after World War II, industry continued to expand. In the 1950s, President Juscelino Kubitschek (zhooh suh LEE nuh KOO bih chehk) promised "fifty years of progress in five." He opened up the Amazon forest region to settlers by carving out a new capital, Brasília, hundreds of miles from the Atlantic coast.

Brazil's Economic Miracle
Diversification, modernization, and foreign investments have helped Brazil's economy grow. In the picture, robots assemble cars in a Ford automotive plant in Brazil.

Theme: Economics and Technology Why did Brazil's economy suffer when it relied too much on a single export?

Analyzing Primary Sources

Helping the Street Children of Brazil

Poverty is a widespread problem in Brazil. Of the poor who wander the streets in search of work, food, or shelter, thousands are children. Journalist James Brooke describes Projecto Axé (Project Force), which helps Brazilian street children.

"Salvador, Brazil 1993

'Street children face two choices: death or jail,' said Cesare de Florio La Rocca, director of the program and an immigrant from Italy. 'These youths are beings in development. If we don't act here and now, it will be too late.' . . .

To compete with the lure of street life, which can be fascinating as well as deadly, Mr. La Rocca's social workers offer their own lure, Afro-Brazilian culture. . . .

When Salvador's children show interest, Axé workers offer drumming lessons in the youth corps of the city's internationally known Afro dance and drum groups . . . and culture classes at one of the city's most important Afro-Brazilian religious centers. . . .

Using activities that appeal to children, Axé builds bridges for them to leave a short-term world of the street to a world of plans for the future. 'They are assimilating life habits of discipline and punctuality,' Mr. La Rocca said. 'If a youth goes straight from the street to a job, he will fail.'

Moving beyond cultural activities, Axé offers literacy classes and apprenticeships in a recycled paper workshop and in a silk-screen T-shirt design studio. Each child taking part in activities gets three meals every weekday, bus fare, new clothes, and a spending allowance of $8 a week. In existence for three years, Axé says that last year it helped 768 Axé children reestablish family links and return home. In a measure of growing business interest in the program . . . a local construction company has started taking older Axé boys as apprentice laborers."

—James Brooke, *The New York Times*

Street children wash their clothes in a public fountain in São Paulo, Brazil.

Skills Assessment

1. La Rocca believes that street youths who learn discipline are more likely to
   A hold down a job.
   B survive on the streets.
   C get along with others.
   D commit crimes.

2. Projecto Axé tries to help street children by offering
   E shelter.
   F apprenticeships.
   G family counseling.
   H medical care.

3. **Critical Thinking Analyzing Primary Sources (a)** What point is the photographer trying to make? **(b)** Based on both the primary source and the photograph, what assumptions can you make about the street children and how society views them?

Skills Tip

Photographers sometimes combine two contrasting images in a single frame to convey a message. This technique is called juxtaposition.

Impressive Growth "Power in the world," said one Brazilian leader, "is a great nation that has territory, population, wealth, financial resources, technology, material goods, minerals." Brazil had almost all of these. Under the military, experts ran the economy, which for a time chalked up impressive growth. Brazil began producing everything from steel and cars to shoes. People talked of Brazil's "economic miracle," like those in postwar Germany or Japan. The miracle enriched a few. To most Brazilians, however, it brought little or no benefit.

Economic Challenges In the 1980s, Brazil, like other developing nations, faced a host of economic problems—from inflation fed by higher oil prices to a staggering debt. Population growth and migration strained the government's ability to provide services as millions of people flooded Brazil's major cities. Conditions for the poor worsened when the government cut spending in response to the debt crisis. Despite environmental concerns, economic development of the Amazon region continued.

One of the most persistent economic problems in Brazil was the unequal distribution of land. Less than 3 percent of the population owned more than 50 percent of the land, much of which remained unused. In protest, some Brazilians formed an organization called the Landless Movement. This group urged peasants to become squatters, or people who settle on land that they do not own. Violent clashes erupted between the squatters and the landowners.

In the 1990s, President Fernando Henrique Cardoso, a respected economist, provided strong leadership for Brazil. His policies promoted rapid economic growth and helped to limit inflation. In response to the Landless Movement, he promised to distribute land to nearly 300,000 families. While landowners opposed the president's policy, others accused Cardoso of not doing enough for the poor. Critics of the president also objected to the privatization of state-run industries, and many were very concerned about high unemployment rates.

Looking Ahead

As the 1900s came to an end, Brazil numbered among the top 10 world economies. With ample human and natural resources, this giant of South America was determined to take its place among the world's economic superpowers—and to become the country of the future today.

SECTION 4 Assessment

Recall

1. Identify: (a) Juan Perón, **(b)** Eva Perón, **(c)** Isabel Perón, **(d)** "dirty war," **(e)** Falklands, **(f)** Carlos Menem, **(g)** Getúlio Vargas, **(h)** Brasília.

2. Define: (a) *favela,* **(b)** plebiscite, **(c)** squatter.

Comprehension

3. (a) How have dictatorships affected Argentina? **(b)** What steps did the nation take toward democracy during the 1980s and 1990s?

4. Why did military rulers seize power in Brazil?

5. (a) Describe the Brazilian economic miracle. **(b)** What problems have threatened Brazil's economy since the 1980s?

Critical Thinking and Writing

6. Analyzing Information What benefits and drawbacks might result from building a "cult of personality" around figures like Juan and Eva Perón?

7. Comparing Review the political developments that occurred in Brazil and Argentina between 1945 and the 1980s. Were the political conditions generally similar or different? Explain.

Activity

Staging a Skit
Present a three-act skit that portrays major events in Argentina from the 1940s to today. The first act should present the Peróns. The second act should show Argentina under military rule. The final act should highlight the restoration of democracy.

Creating a Chapter Summary

Make a concept web like the partially completed model below. Fill in the blank circles. Add branches and circles as needed.

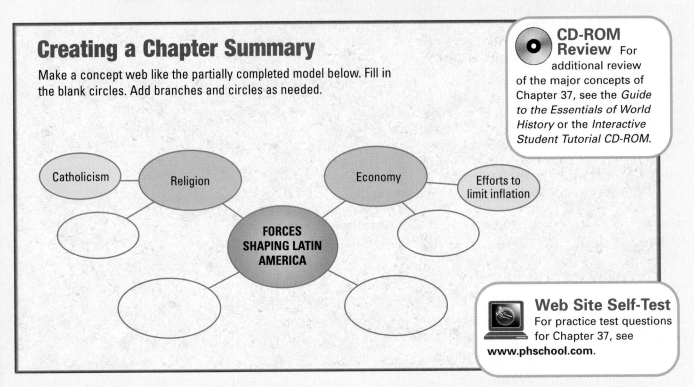

Catholicism — Religion — FORCES SHAPING LATIN AMERICA — Economy — Efforts to limit inflation

CD-ROM Review For additional review of the major concepts of Chapter 37, see the *Guide to the Essentials of World History* or the *Interactive Student Tutorial CD-ROM.*

Web Site Self-Test For practice test questions for Chapter 37, see **www.phschool.com**.

Building Vocabulary

Review the meanings of the terms below. For each term, write a sentence that includes the term.

1. import substitution
2. liberation theology
3. literacy rate
4. embargo
5. squatter

Recalling Key Facts

6. How did the distribution of wealth in Latin America cause problems after World War II?
7. How did military regimes affect nations such as Argentina and Chile?
8. Why did relations between the United States and Cuba worsen after 1959?
9. Describe the *maquiladoras* and their effect on Mexico.
10. (a) Who forced Jean-Bertrand Aristide from power in Haiti? (b) Who returned him to power?
11. What steps did Argentina take toward democratic rule in the 1980s?
12. Has economic growth benefited all Brazilians? Explain.

Critical Thinking and Writing

13. **Drawing Conclusions** How can a wide gap between rich and poor make it difficult for democracy to flourish?
14. **Recognizing Points of View** Environmentalists have called on Brazil to halt destruction of the Amazon rain forest. (a) Why do environmentalists take this view? (b) Why do some people think that it is unfair for developed nations to urge developing nations to protect the environment?
15. **Linking Past and Present** How does Latin America's colonial past help to explain the uneven distribution of land that is common in much of the region today?
16. **Connecting to Geography** (a) How do geography and climate benefit economic growth in Latin America? (b) How do they hinder economic growth?

17. **Making Generalizations** Do you think the general trend in Latin America in the 1980s and 1990s was toward democracy or toward dictatorship? Explain.

Read the news article below about the 1996 visit of Pope John Paul II to Nicaragua. Then, answer the questions that follow.

"MANAGUA, Nicaragua (Feb. 7, 1996)— Pope John Paul on Wednesday hailed Central America's transformation from superpower battleground to peaceful democracy, saying the change showed the hand of God in human history. In impromptu remarks at the end of a joyful open-air Mass celebrated before more than 150,000 cheering supporters in a lakeside plaza, John Paul . . . said, 'Today we can see that you are the master of your own human, Christian, Nicaraguan destiny.' The crowd gathered beneath the tropical blue sky roared 'Pope, Pope, Pope' in approval and thundered its applause. . . . During his 1983 visit, the Pope was forced to shout for silence as Sandinista protesters heckled him during Mass. . . . The Pope said on arriving on Wednesday that his message remained the same as in 1983—one of peace and reconciliation. . . . Analysts say the Sandinistas, now in opposition, have no option but to play the Catholic card if they want to have a chance of winning the presidential election this year in a country where enthusiasm for the Pope has reached fever pitch."

—Reuters Information Service

18. Why do you think the pope called Nicaragua a superpower battleground?
19. **(a)** How did the response to the pope in 1996 differ from the response to him in 1983? **(b)** How can you explain the change?
20. Based on the article, what type of government did Nicaragua have in 1996? Explain.
21. What information in the article is opinion rather than fact?

Skills Tip

Note that a news article can contain both factual reporting and author commentary.

This photograph shows Cuban refugees. Use the photograph and information from the chapter to answer the following questions:

22. What land are the people probably trying to reach?
23. What means of propulsion does the raft rely on?
24. How seaworthy does the raft appear to be? Explain.
25. Why were these people willing to make this voyage?
26. What risks might they face during the voyage from Cuba?

 Skills Assessment

Take It to the NET

Search the Internet to learn more about the Organization of American States. Design a brochure that includes a brief description of the group's history, a list of its current goals, and a diagram of its organizational structure.

Chapter 32

The World Since 1945: An Overview (1945–Present)

Since the end of World War II, the world has changed rapidly. Although we cannot yet determine the long-term impact of events of the recent past, we can identify political, social, and economic trends that have shaped the postwar years.

- The collapse of western colonial empires led to the emergence of nearly 100 new countries, mostly in Africa and Asia.
- Nuclear weapons, terrorism, and human rights are enduring issues in an increasingly interdependent world.
- Complex economic ties link the rich nations of the global North and the poor nations of the global South.
- Urbanization, modernization, women's movements, and technology have brought dramatic social changes.
- Technology has revolutionized medicine and agriculture and helped create a global, westernized popular culture.

Chapter 33

Europe and North America (1945–Present)

Within a framework of growing regional cooperation, Western Europe enjoyed tremendous economic growth after World War II. At the same time, the Cold War pitted the West, led by the United States, against the Soviet Union and its allies.

- In the postwar era, Western European nations expanded social programs and introduced the welfare state. By the 1980s, an economic slowdown forced cuts in social programs.
- The United States led world opposition to communism, pursued economic prosperity, and extended civil rights.
- Efforts to reform inefficiencies in government and the economy led to the collapse of the Soviet Union.
- After shaking off Soviet domination, nations of Eastern Europe faced economic challenges and ethnic conflicts.

Chapter 34

East Asia and Southeast Asia (1945–Present)

China, Japan, and other Asian nations have achieved varying degrees of success in their efforts to modernize. Several of these nations enjoy growing trade and other ties, linking the nations of the Pacific Rim from Asia to the Americas.

- After World War II, Japan introduced democratic reforms and by the 1960s had emerged as an economic superpower.
- Under communist rule, the People's Republic of China achieved modest economic gains while sacrificing individual political freedoms.
- The "Asian tigers"—Taiwan, Hong Kong, Singapore, and South Korea—vaulted into the class of newly industrialized nations.
- Cold War tensions sparked long, devastating conflicts in Korea, Vietnam, and Cambodia.

	1940		**1955**		**1970**

AFRICA

1948 Apartheid is law in South Africa

1957 Ghana gains independence

1966 Civil war begins in Nigeria

THE AMERICAS

1946 Perón becomes president of Argentina

1962 Cuban missile crisis

1954 Brown v. *Board of Education of Topeka*

ASIA AND OCEANIA

1947 India wins independence

1954 French leave Vietnam

1966 Cultural Revolution in China

EUROPE

1945 Labour party gains power in Britain

1956 Hungarian uprising

1957 European Community formed

Chapter 35

South Asia and the Middle East (1945–Present)

In South Asia and the Middle East, nations cast off western rule and set out to modernize. They have often confronted similar challenges—from religious strife and border conflicts to urbanization and population growth.

- Upon achieving independence, India built on the legacy of British rule to create the world's largest democracy.
- Ethnic and religious rivalries have fueled ongoing conflict among people of South Asia.
- When secular governments in the Middle East did not yield promised improvements, some reformers rejected western models and called for a reaffirmation of Islamic values.
- The long Arab-Israeli struggle and other conflicts have focused world attention on the Middle East.

Chapter 36

Africa (1945–Present)

Leaders of new African nations set out to build strong central governments, achieve economic growth, and raise standards of living. They have faced a variety of obstacles, including economic dependency and political instability.

- After independence, a number of new nations experienced military or one-party rule. Many have since introduced multi-party democracy.
- African nations experimented with different economic systems, including socialism and mixed economies.
- After decades of conflict, South Africa abandoned its system of apartheid in the 1990s and made a transition to democratic rule.
- In Africa, as elsewhere, modernization and urbanization have disrupted traditional cultures and ways of life.

Chapter 37

Latin America (1945–Present)

Despite setbacks, Latin American nations have tried to sustain economic growth and overcome a legacy of poverty and social inequality. Marxism, military rule, and the Roman Catholic Church have been continuing influences in the region.

- In the postwar period, poverty and uneven distribution of wealth fed social unrest in many nations.
- Latin America was a focus of Cold War politics, especially after a communist revolution in Cuba in 1959.
- Through trade, investment, and military intervention, the United States was a dominant force in Latin America.
- Although Mexico enjoyed economic gains in agriculture and manufacturing, most people remained in poverty.
- Argentina and Brazil experienced economic growth and long periods of military rule.

1985   **2000**   **2015**

1980s Drought causes famine in parts of Africa

1994 Mandela wins first multiracial election in South Africa

1993 Canada, United States, and Mexico sign NAFTA

2000 Control of Panama Canal shifts to Panama

1979 Revolution in Iran   **1993** Israel and PLO sign peace accord

1997 Hong Kong returned to China

1989 Tiananmen Square massacre in China

1970s Greece restores civilian rule   **1989** Berlin Wall falls

1991 Breakup of Soviet Union

1999 European Union introduces common currency

Reference Section

Contents

PRIMARY SOURCES AND LITERATURE

Instruction of Ptah-hotep

Ptah-hotep, who lived around 2450 B.C. in Egypt, was a vizier, or chief minister, to a pharaoh during the Old Kingdom. In the excerpt below, Ptah-hotep describes some practical rules for behavior that he believes will help his son live a successful life.

Vocabulary Before you read the selection, look up the following words in a dictionary: **arrogant, counsel, venture, council.**

> **Main Idea** In this letter, Ptah-hotep describes rules of behavior that he believes will help his son live a successful life.

Be not arrogant because of your knowledge, and be not puffed up because you are a learned man. Take counsel with the ignorant as with the learned, for the limits of art cannot be reached, and no artist is perfect in his skills. . . .

If you are a leader, commanding the conduct of many, seek out every good aim, so that your policy may be without error. A great thing is truth, enduring and surviving; it has not been upset since the time of Osiris. He who departs from its laws is punished. It is the right path for him who knows nothing. Wrongdoing has never brought its venture safe to port. Evil may win riches, but it is the strength of truth that it endures long. . . .

If you want your conduct to be good, free from every evil, then beware of greed. It is an evil and incurable sickness. No man can live with it; it causes divisions between fathers and mothers, and between brothers of the same mother; it parts wife and husband; it is a gathering of every evil, a bag of everything hateful. A man thrives if his conduct is right. He who follows the right course wins wealth thereby. But the greedy man has no tomb. . . .

If you are a worthy man sitting in the council of his lord, confine your attention to excellence. Silence is more valuable than chatter. Speak only when you know you can resolve difficulties. He who gives good counsel is an artist, for speech is more difficult than any craft. . . .

If you listen to my sayings, then all your affairs will go forward. . . . If the son of a man accepts what his father says, no plan of his will fail. . . . Failure follows him who does not listen. . . .

Egyptian tomb painting

Analyzing Primary Sources

1. Which of the following statements best summarizes the main idea of the fourth paragraph?

   A Speak only when you have something helpful to say.

   B Achieve excellence so that you may council the lord.

   C Remain silent while in the council of the lord.

   D Give good counsel in order to gain wealth.

2. The author wishes his son to listen to his advice so that his son will be

   E greedy.

   F sick.

   G successful.

   H arrogant.

3. **Critical Thinking Making Inferences** What do you think Ptah-hotep means by the phrase "the greedy man has no tomb" (third paragraph)?

Primary Sources and Literature

962 *Reference Section*

The Epic of Gilgamesh

The Sumerian *Epic of Gilgamesh* dates from about 2000 B.C. It is a collection of tales about a hero named Gilgamesh. The main themes of the poem are the unpredictability of the gods and the inevitability of death. These themes may be a reflection of life in Sumer, where the flooding of the Tigris and Euphrates rivers was both unpredictable and devastating.

Vocabulary Before you read the selection, look up the following words in a dictionary: **attain, slough, boon.**

> **Main Idea** In this epic poem, Gilgamesh comes to realize that death is the common lot of all people, even fearless heroes.

Utnapishtim says to him, to Gilgamesh. . . .
"About a plant I will tell thee. . . .
Its thorns will prick thy hands just as does the rose.
If thy hands obtain the plant, thou wilt attain [eternal] life."
No sooner had Gilgamesh heard this, . . .
He tied heavy stones to his feet.
They pulled him down into the deep and he saw the plant.
He took the plant, though it pricked his hands.
He cut the heavy stones from his feet.
The sea cast him up upon its shore.
Gilgamesh says to him, to Urshanabi, the boatman:
"Urshanabi, this plant is a plant apart,
Whereby a man may regain his life's breath. . . .
Its name shall be 'Man Becomes Young in Old Age.'
I myself shall eat it
And thus return to the state of my youth."
Gilgamesh saw a well whose water was cool.
He went down into it to bathe in the water.
A serpent snuffed the fragrance of the plant;
It came up from the water and carried off the plant,
Going back to shed its slough.
Thereupon Gilgamesh sits down and weeps.
His tears running down over his face.
He took the hand of Urshanabi, the boatman:
"For whom, Urshanabi, have my hands toiled?
For whom is being spent the blood of my heart?
I have not obtained a boon for myself.
For the serpent have I effected a boon!"

Sumerian sculpture

Analyzing Literature

1. What does Gilgamesh decide to do after hearing Utnapishtim?

   A seek help from a boatman named Ur-shanabi

   B search for a plant that brings eternal life

   C bathe in a well with cool water

   D battle a serpent who carries away youth

2. At the end of this selection, Gilgamesh weeps because

   E the serpent has shed its skin.

   F he has toiled with his hands for too long.

   G he has failed to find everlasting life and must accept death.

   H he has eaten all of the plant.

3. **Critical Thinking Synthesizing Information** Which physical characteristic of a snake leads the author to choose it as the creature who benefits from the plant?

Psalm 23

The Psalms are a collection of 150 religious hymns. These songs reflect the Israelites' belief in their God as the powerful savior of Israel. Many of the psalms praise the faithfulness of God to each of his people. In this psalm, the speaker describes his faith in God's protection.

Vocabulary Before you read the selection, look up the following words in a dictionary: **righteousness, anoint.**

Main Idea The Twenty-Third Psalm celebrates the Israelites' sense of a special relationship with a loving God.

The LORD is my shepherd, I shall not want;

he makes me lie down in green pastures.
He leads me beside still waters;

he restores my soul.
He leads me in paths of righteousness
for his name's sake.

Even though I walk through the valley of the shadow of death,
I fear no evil;
for thou art with me;
thy rod and thy staff,
they comfort me.

Thou preparest a table before me
in the presence of my enemies;
thou anointest my head with oil,
my cup overflows.

Surely goodness and mercy shall follow me
all the days of my life;
and I shall dwell in the house of the LORD
for ever.

Prayer book in Hebrew

Analyzing Literature

1. The speaker of the Twenty-Third Psalm says that he

   A feels protected by God.

   B feels abandoned by God.

   C fears the anger of God.

   D fears Israel's enemies.

2. According to the speaker, God's strength

   E helps the sheep find water.

   F overcomes the power of death.

   G provides housing and food for the Israelites.

   H builds an army to defeat the enemies of the Israelites.

3. **Critical Thinking Making Generalizations** **(a)** Identify the qualities of God and the Israelites that lead the speaker to compare God to a shepherd. **(b)** How does the Twenty-Third Psalm reflect some of the basic beliefs of Jewish monotheism?

Confucius: *Analects*

The *Analects* are a collection of 497 verses recorded by Confucius' followers long after his death (perhaps in the fourth century B.C.). Confucius' teachings emphasize duty and responsibility as a means of ensuring social order and good government.

Vocabulary Before you read the selection, look up the following words in a dictionary: **homage, bias, induce, piety, incompetent.**

Main Idea In these sayings, Confucius emphasizes that education and self-sacrifice are the keys to becoming a superior person.

The Master said, He who rules by moral force is like the pole-star, which remains in its place while all the lesser stars do homage to it.

The Master said, If out of the three hundred Songs I had to take one phrase to cover all my teaching, I would say 'Let there be no evil in your thoughts.'

Mêng Wu Po asked about the treatment of parents. The Master said, Behave in such a way that your father and mother have no anxiety about you, except concerning your health.

Tzu-kung asked about the true gentleman. The Master said, He does not preach what he practices till he has practiced what he preaches.

The Master said, A gentleman can see a question from all sides without bias. The small man is biased and can see a question only from one side.

The Master said, Yu, shall I teach you what knowledge is? When you know a thing, to recognize that you know it, and when you do not know a thing, to recognize that you do not know it. That is knowledge.

Chi K'ang-tzu asked whether there were any form of encouragement by which he could induce the common people to be respectful and loyal. The Master said, Approach them with dignity, and they will respect you. Show piety towards your parents and kindness towards your children, and they will be loyal to you. Promote those who are worthy, train those who are incompetent; that is the best form of encouragement.

Confucius

Primary Sources and Literature

Analyzing Primary Sources

1. According to the excerpts, which one saying did Confucius pick to best summarize his teachings?

   A Show piety towards your parents and kindness towards your children.

   B Let there be no evil in your thoughts.

   C He does not preach what he practices till he has practiced what he preaches.

   D A gentleman can see a question from all sides without bias.

2. Confucius says that a gentleman

   E is knowledgeable.

   F is respectful and loyal.

   G can understand more than one point of view on a question or issue.

   H can recognize those who are worthy.

3. **Critical Thinking Identifying Main Ideas** Use your own words to describe Confucius' definition of knowledge.

Thucydides: *History of the Peloponnesian War*

This excerpt from Thucydides' *History of the Peloponnesian War* records a speech made by the Athenian leader Pericles in honor of those who died fighting Sparta in the first year of the war (431 B.C.). In the speech, Pericles describes the superior qualities of Athenian democracy as compared with life in Sparta.

Vocabulary Before you read the selection, look up the following words in a dictionary: **extravagance, vainglory, degradation, absorption, aloof, notwithstanding, attainment.**

Main Idea This speech by the Athenian leader Pericles is one of the most famous defenses of democracy of all time.

For our government is not copied from those of our neighbors: we are an example to them rather than they to us. Our constitution is named a democracy, because it is in the hands not of the few but of the many. But our laws secure equal justice for all in their private disputes, and our public opinion welcomes and honors talent in every branch of achievement, not for any sectional reason but on grounds of excellence alone. And as we give free play to all in our public life, so we carry the same spirit into our daily relations with one another. . . .

We are lovers of beauty without extravagance, and lovers of wisdom without unmanliness. Wealth to us is not mere material for vainglory but an opportunity for achievement; and poverty we think it no disgrace to acknowledge but a real degradation to make no effort to overcome. Our citizens attend both to public and private duties, and do not allow absorption in their own various affairs to interfere with their knowledge of the city's. We differ from other states in regarding the man who holds aloof from public life not as 'quiet' but as useless; we decide or debate, carefully and in person, all matters of policy, holding, not that words and deeds go ill together, but that acts are foredoomed to failure when undertaken undiscussed. For we are noted for being at once adventurous in action and most reflective beforehand. Other men are bold in ignorance, while reflection will stop their onset. But the bravest are surely those who have the clearest vision of what is before them, glory and danger alike, and yet notwithstanding go out to meet it. . . . In a word I claim that our city as a whole is an education to Greece, and that her members yield to none, man by man, for independence of spirit, many-sidedness of attainment, and complete self-reliance in limbs and brain.

The Parthenon in Athens

Analyzing Primary Sources

1. Pericles defines democracy as a system based on

   A equal justice for all in their private disputes.

   B the say of many citizens, not just a few.

   C beauty without extravagance and wisdom without unmanliness.

   D free play in public life.

2. According to Pericles, a good citizen

   E participates fully in public debate.

   F is quiet during public debate.

   G acts boldly without discussion.

   H attends exclusively to his own business.

3. **Critical Thinking Synthesizing Information** What does Pericles mean when he states that Athens is "an education to Greece"?

Aristotle: *The Politics*

The Greek philosopher Aristotle (384 B.C.–322 B.C.) was suspicious of democracy, which he thought could lead to mob rule. Instead, Aristotle favored rule by a single strong and virtuous leader. In this excerpt from *The Politics*, Aristotle outlines the forms of government and discusses the strengths and weaknesses of each form.

Vocabulary Before you read the selection, look up the following words in a dictionary: **treatise, constituted, despotic, generic.**

Main Idea In this selection, Aristotle describes the characteristics of an ideal state as well as practical matters relating to the preservation and improvement of government.

First let us consider what is the purpose of a state and how many forms of government there are by which human society is regulated. We have already said, earlier in this treatise . . . that man is by nature a political animal. And therefore men, even when they do not require one another's help, desire to live together all the same, and are in fact brought together by their common interests. . . . Well-being is certainly the chief end of individuals and of states. . . .

The conclusion is evident: governments which have a regard to the common interest are constituted in accordance with strict principles of justice, and are therefore true forms; but those which regard only the interest of the rulers are all defective and perverted forms. For they are despotic, whereas a state is a community of free men. . . .

We call that form of government in which one rules, and which regards the common interest, kingship or royalty; that in which more than one, but not many, rule, aristocracy. It is so called, either because the rulers are the best men, or because they have at heart the best interest of the state and of the citizens. But when the citizens at large administer the state for the common interest, the government is called by the generic name—constitutional government. . . .

Of the above-mentioned forms, the perversions are as follows: of royalty, tyranny; of aristocracy, oligarchy; of constitutional government, democracy. For tyranny is a kind of monarchy which has in view the interest of the monarch only; oligarchy has in view the interest of the wealthy; democracy, of the needy; none of them the common good of all.

Students at an Athenian school

Analyzing Primary Sources

1. According to Aristotle, the form of government known as constitutional government is one in which

   A one rules, and which regards the common interest.

   B the citizens at large administer the state for the common interest.

   C more than one, but not many, rule.

   D the interests of the needy are placed above all.

2. Which of the following does Aristotle describe as the corrupt form of aristocracy?

   E tyranny

   F oligarchy

   G monarchy

   H democracy

3. **Critical Thinking** **Identifying Main Ideas** What do you think Aristotle means when he states that "man is by nature a political animal"?

The Mahabharata

An epic of the ancient Aryans, the *Mahabharata* became a major source of Hindu social and religious doctrine. Indian storytellers still recite segments of the 100,000 stanzas to entertain and instruct village audiences. This excerpt tells of the rewards the god Indra bestows upon a dutiful king, Vasu.

Vocabulary Before you read the selection, look up the following words in a dictionary: **accustomed, celestial, crystalline, garland, lotuses, sustain, renowned.**

Main Idea In this epic, an Indian king is given earthly rule and supernatural gifts as reward for upholding the law of the gods.

Two Hindu gods

Indra said:

May never on earth, O lord of this earth, the Law be confused! Protect it, for the upheld Law holds up all the world. Guard thee this worldly Law, forever on guard and attentive; if yoked to the Law, you shall win the blessed worlds of eternity. You standing on earth have become the dear friend of me standing in heaven—now possess . . . a country beyond all others, with riches and jewels and all good things—Mother Earth, mother of plenty: live on her in the land of the Cedis, king of the Cedis!

The country people are accustomed to the Law, quite content and upright. No lies are spoken there even in jest, let alone in earnest. Sons are devoted to their elders there; they do not divide off from their fathers. Cows are never yoked to the cart, and even lean cows yield plenty. All the classes abide by their own Law, in this land of the Cedis. . . .

This large celestial crystalline chariot in the sky, which it is the God's privilege to enjoy, this airborne chariot will come to you as my gift. Among all mortals you alone shall stand upon a grand and sky-going chariot, and indeed, you will ride there above, like a God come to flesh! And I give you this garland Vaijayanti, woven of lotuses that never fade, which shall sustain you in battle, never hurt by swords. That shall be your mark of distinction here, sovereign of men—grand, rich, unmatched, and renowned as "India's Garland"!

Analyzing Literature

1. What does Indra say will be Vasu's reward for pleasing the gods?

   A Vasu will be given a place among the gods.

   B Vasu will receive jewels and a herd of cattle.

   C Vasu will ride through the skies on a crystal chariot.

   D Vasu will not be required to obey the Law.

2. According to Indra, Vasu will rule

   E Mother Earth.

   F the heavens.

   G his sons.

   H the afterlife.

3. **Critical Thinking Making Inferences** The heroes of epics frequently embody the values of the cultures that produced them. Describe some of the values that King Vasu represents.

Asoka: *Edicts*

During his rule of Maurya India beginning in 268 B.C., Asoka converted to Buddhism, rejected violence, and resolved to rule by moral example. Asoka had stone pillars set up across India announcing laws, or edicts, and describing the just actions of his government. The following are excerpts from several of the pillars.

Vocabulary Before you read the selection, look up the following words in a dictionary: **righteousness, circumspection, disparages, concord, conformity, exhortation, abstention.**

Main Idea The stone pillars set up across India by Asoka announced laws and promised fair and just government.

This world and the other are hard to gain without great love of Righteousness, great self-examination, great obedience, great circumspection, great effort. Through my instruction respect and love of Righteousness daily increase and will increase. . . . For this is my rule—to govern by Righteousness, to administer by Righteousness, to please my subjects by Righteousness, and to protect them by Righteousness.

Whoever honors his own [religion] and disparages another man's, whether from blind loyalty or with the intention of showing his own [religion] in a favorable light, does his own [religion] the greatest possible harm. Concord is best, with each hearing and respecting the other's teachings. It is the wish of the [king] that members of all [religions] should be learned and should teach virtue.

All the good deeds that I have done have been accepted and followed by the people. And so obedience to mother and father, obedience to teachers, respect for the aged, kindliness . . . to the poor and weak, and to slaves and servants, have increased and will continue to increase. . . . And this progress of Righteousness . . . has taken place in two manners, by enforcing conformity to Righteousness, and by exhortation. I have enforced the law against killing certain animals and many others, but the greatest progress of Righteousness . . . comes from exhortation in favor of noninjury to life and abstention from killing living beings.

I have done this that it may endure . . . as long as the moon and sun, and that my sons and my great-grandsons may support it; for by supporting it they will gain both this world and the next.

Sculpture from one of Asoka's pillars

Analyzing Primary Sources

1. This excerpt from the Edicts provides evidence that Asoka

   A was in favor of performing animal sacrifices.

   B wanted to place Buddhism above all other religions.

   C believed in the power of daily religious rituals.

   D sought to promote tolerance of diverse religions.

2. Based on the passage you can tell that Asoka was probably a

   E vegetarian.

   F monk.

   G dictator.

   H judge.

3. **Critical Thinking** **Drawing Conclusions** Which of his actions does Asoka view as the best promotion of Righteousness? Why do you think this is so?

St. Paul:
First Letter to the Corinthians

Around A.D. 51, Paul founded a Christian community in the thriving commercial city of Corinth. After his departure, he wrote two letters to the newly converted Christians to encourage and guide them in their faith. This excerpt from Paul's First Letter to the Corinthians focuses on the importance of love in a Christian life.

Vocabulary Before you read the selection, look up the following word in a dictionary: **prophetic**.

Main Idea In this letter, Paul declares that, for a Christian, love is more important than any other quality.

If I speak in the tongues of men and of angels, but have not love, I am a noisy gong or a clanging cymbal. And if I have prophetic powers and understand all mysteries and all knowledge, and if I have all faith, so as to remove mountains, but have no love, I am nothing. If I give away all I have, and if I deliver my body to be burned, but have not love, I gain nothing.

Love is patient and kind; love is not jealous or boastful; it is not arrogant or rude. Love does not insist on its own way; it is not irritable or resentful; it does not rejoice at wrong, but rejoices in the right. Love bears all things, believes all things, hopes all things, endures all things.

Love never ends; as for prophecies, they will pass away; as for tongues, they will cease; as for knowledge, it will pass away. For our knowledge is imperfect and our prophecy is imperfect; but when the perfect comes, the imperfect will pass away. When I was a child, I spoke like a child, I thought like a child, I reasoned like a child; when I became a man, I gave up childish ways. For now we see in a mirror dimly, but then face to face. Now I know in part; then I shall understand fully, even as I have been fully understood. So faith, hope, love abide, these three; but the greatest of these is love.

Early Christian symbols

Analyzing Primary Sources

1. In his letter to the Corinthians, Paul states that love

   A can be fully understood by people in this life.

   B is a greater virtue than knowledge or faith.

   C has the power to remove mountains.

   D will pass away with an individual's death.

2. According to Paul, people will be able to achieve perfect knowledge when they

   E reach adulthood.

   F love their neighbors.

   G come face to face with God.

   H have prophetic powers.

3. **Critical Thinking Synthesizing Information** What does Paul mean when he says love "endures all things"?

The Quran

The Quran, the holy scriptures of Islam, contains 114 suras, or verses. Muslims believe that the Quran is the actual word of God as revealed to the prophet Muhammad. This excerpt from the Quran tells the faithful what they should do to be righteous and faithful Muslims.

Vocabulary Before you read the selection, look up the following words in a dictionary: **wayfarers, redemption, alms, perchance.**

Main Idea This excerpt from the Quran encourages believers to fast and observe the holy month of Ramadan.

Righteousness does not consist in whether you face towards the east or the west. The righteous man is he who believes in God and the Last Day, in the angels and the Scriptures and the prophets; who for the love of God gives his wealth to his kinsfolk, to the orphans, to the needy, to the wayfarers and to the beggars, and for the redemption of captives; who attends to his prayers and pays the alms-tax; who is true to his promises and steadfast in trial and adversity and in times of war. Such are the true believers; such are the god fearing. . . .

Believers, fasting is decreed for you as it was decreed for those before you; perchance you will guard yourselves against evil. Fast a certain number of days, but if any one of you is ill or on a journey let him fast a similar number of days later on; and for those that can afford it there is a ransom: the feeding of a poor man. He that does good of his own account shall be rewarded; but to fast is better for you, if you but knew it.

In the month of Ramadan the Quran was revealed, a book of guidance with proofs of guidance distinguishing right from wrong. Therefore whoever of you is present in that month let him fast. But he who is ill or on a journey shall fast a similar number of days later on.

God desires your well-being, not your discomfort. He desires you to fast the whole month so that you may magnify Him and render thanks to Him for giving you his guidance.

Pages from the Quran

Analyzing Primary Sources

1. According to the excerpt above, what is one goal of the Quran?

   A It helps the faithful distinguish right from wrong.

   B It helps the faithful guard against evil.

   C It helps the faithful question the will of God.

   D It helps the faithful increase their worldly wealth.

2. The "righteous man" does not have to fast during Ramadan if he

   E gives money to the poor.

   F is ill.

   G believes in God.

   H has not committed evil acts.

3. **Critical Thinking Applying Information** How does this passage from the Quran support the five pillars of Islam?

Murasaki Shikibu:
The Tale of Genji

Murasaki Shikibu's *Tale of Genji* is considered one of the finest works of Japanese literature. The novel provides insight into the court life and mores of tenth-century Japan. In this excerpt, the elaborate rituals associated with Prince Genji's transition from childhood to manhood are described. The passage also reflects the Japanese aristocracy's emphasis on official titles and social ranks.

Vocabulary Before you read the selection, look up the following words in a dictionary: **initiation, zeal, prescribed, loath, homage, chamberlain, obeisance.**

Main Idea This excerpt from the novel describes the royal coming of age ceremony in Heian Japan.

Though it seemed a shame to put so lovely a child into man's dress, he was now twelve years old and the time for his Initiation was come. The Emperor directed the preparations with tireless zeal and insisted upon a magnificence beyond what was prescribed. . . .

Genji arrived at the hour of the Monkey [3 P.M.]. He looked very handsome with his long childish locks, and the Sponsor, whose duty it had just been to bind them with the purple filet, was sorry to think that all this would soon be changed and even the Clerk of the Treasury seemed loath to sever those lovely tresses with the ritual knife. . . .

Duly crowned, Genji went to his chamber and changing into man's dress went down into the courtyard and performed the Dance of Homage, which he did with such grace that tears stood in every eye. . . .

When the courtiers assembled to drink the Love Cup, Genji came and took his place among the other princes. The Minister of the Left came up and whispered something in his ear; but the boy blushed and could think of no reply. A chamberlain now came over to the Minister and brought him a summons to wait upon His Majesty immediately. . . . Then, when he had made him drink out of the Royal Cup, the Emperor recited a poem in which he prayed that the binding of the purple filet might symbolize the union of their two houses; and the Minister answered him that nothing should sever this union save the fading of the purple band. Then he descended the long stairs and from the courtyard performed the Grand Obeisance. Here too were shown the horses from the Royal Stables and the hawks from the Royal Falconry, that had been decreed as presents for the Genji. At the foot of the stairs, the Princes and the Courtiers were lined up to receive their bounties, and gifts of every kind were showered upon them.

Lady Murasaki Shikibu

Analyzing Literature

1. Genji's initiation into manhood is symbolized by

   A his honored position at the Emperor's banquet.

   B the cutting of his hair and changing of his garments.

   C the lining up of the Princes for their gifts.

   D the Emperor's show of affection for the Prince.

2. The importance of the ceremony is reflected in the

   E social rank of the Minister of the Left.

   F performance of the Dance of Homage.

   G elaborate preparations and emphasis on social rank.

   H binding of the hair.

3. **Critical Thinking Linking Past and Present** What kinds of ceremonies do we have today that recognize the transition from childhood to adulthood?

Geoffrey Chaucer:
The Canterbury Tales

In *The Canterbury Tales*, Geoffrey Chaucer presents a portrait of English society in the 1300s. The story involves 29 men and women who tell stories to one another while on pilgrimage to the tomb of Thomas Becket in Canterbury. The detailed descriptions of each character provide a sharp look at three classes of medieval society: clergy, nobles, and common people. In these passages, Chaucer describes a noble knight, a wealthy merchant, and a humble plowman.

Vocabulary Before you read the selection, look up the following words in a dictionary: **sovereign, heathen, motley, estimable, negotiation.**

Main Idea In this poem, Chaucer describes three characters who represent different classes and occupations of medieval society.

There was a *Knight,* a most distinguished man,
Who from the day on which he first began
To ride abroad had followed chivalry,
Truth, honor, generousness, and courtesy.
He had done nobly in his sovereign's war
And ridden into battle, no man more,
As well in Christian as heathen places,
And ever honored for his noble graces. . . .

There was a Merchant with a forking beard
And motley dress; high on his horse he sat,
Upon his head a Flemish beaver hat
And on his feet daintily buckled boots. . . .
He was expert at currency exchange.
This estimable Merchant so had set
His wits to work, none knew he was in debt,
He was so stately in negotiation,
Loan, bargain, and commercial obligation. . . .

[The Plowman] was an honest worker, good and true,
Living in peace and perfect charity. . . .
For steadily about his work he went
To thrash his corn, to dig or to manure
Or make a ditch; and he would help the poor
For love of Christ and never take a penny
If he could help it, and, as prompt as any,
He paid his tithes in full when they were due. . . .

A medieval town

Analyzing Literature

1. What quality do the Knight and the Plowman have in common?

   A wealth

   B bravery

   C honesty

   D sharp wits

2. What conclusion can you draw from these passages?

   E The Knight fought in the Crusades.

   F The Merchant is successful at business.

   G The Plowman is overworked and desperately poor.

   H The Knight and the Merchant look down on the Plowman.

3. **Critical Thinking Applying Information**
   (a) Which of the three characters described in these excerpts represents a class of people who were powerful in early feudal society? **(b)** Which of these characters represents a class that grew more powerful in the High Middle Ages?

Niccolò Machiavelli: *Discourses*

The Florentine writer Niccolò Machiavelli (1469–1527) is best known for his book *The Prince*, in which he describes how a ruler can get and keep power. However, in his book *Discourses on the First Ten Books of Titus Livy*, Machiavelli concludes that the best-governed state is ruled by the people rather than by a ruthless prince.

Vocabulary Before you read the selection, look up the following words in a dictionary: **populace, subservient, licentious, trepidation.**

> **Main Idea** In his *Discourses*, Machiavelli describes methods for establishing and preserving republics.

In short, to bring this topic to conclusion, I say that, just as princely forms of government have endured for a very long time, so, too, have republican forms of government; and that in both cases it has been essential for them to be regulated by laws. For a prince who does what he likes is a lunatic; and a populace which does what it likes is unwise. If, therefore, it be a question of a prince subservient to the laws and of a populace chained up by laws, more virtue will be found in the populace than in the prince; and if it be a question of either of them loosed from control by the law, there will be found fewer errors in the populace than in the prince, and these of less moment and much easier to put right. For a licentious and turbulent populace, when a good man can obtain a hearing, can easily be brought to behave itself; but there is no one to talk to a bad prince, nor is there any remedy except the sword. . . .

When the populace has thrown off all restraint, it is not the mad things it does that are terrifying, nor is it of present evils that one is afraid, but of what may come of them, for amidst such confusion there may come to be a tyrant. In the case of bad princes it is just the opposite: it is present evils that are terrifying, but for the future there is hope, since men are convinced that the evil ways of a bad prince may make for freedom in the end. . . . The reason why people are prejudiced against the populace is because of the populace anyone may speak ill without fear and openly, even when the populace is ruling. But of princes people speak with the utmost trepidation and the utmost reserve.

Analyzing Primary Sources

1. Machiavelli states that the only way to bring an unruly prince under the law is to

   A obtain a hearing.

   B use physical combat.

   C discuss the people's legal rights.

   D choose a tyrant.

2. Machiavelli concludes that the greatest threat posed by an unlawful populace is the

   E rise of a dictator.

   F violence of the mob.

   G loss of a prince.

   H destruction of property.

3. **Critical Thinking Making Inferences**
   (a) According to Machiavelli, what do princely and republican forms of government have in common? **(b)** Why do you think Machiavelli believes that the populace loosed from control is more subject to criticism than a prince loosed from control?

Bernal Díaz: *The True History of the Conquest of New Spain*

Bernal Díaz del Castillo (c. 1492–1581) accompanied Hernan Cortés on his conquest of the Aztecs in present-day Mexico. Díaz wrote his history many years later to refute what he viewed as inaccurate accounts of the conquest. The following excerpt describes a meeting between Cortés and Moctezuma, the Aztec king, in the Aztec city of Tenochtitlán.

Vocabulary Before you read the selection, look up the following words in a dictionary: **oratory, league.**

Main Idea | **This memoir provides an account of the Aztec capital of Tenochtitlán at the time of the Spanish conquest.**

When we climbed to the top of the great [temple] there was a kind of platform, with huge stones where they put the poor Indians to be sacrificed, and an image like a dragon and other evil figures, with a great deal of blood that had been shed that day. Moctezuma, accompanied by two priests, came out from an oratory dedicated to the worship of his cursed idols. . . .

Then Moctezuma took him [Cortés] by the hand and bade him look at his great city and at all the other cities rising from the water, and the many towns around the lake. . . .

There we stood looking, for that large and evil temple was so high that it towered over everything. From there we could see all three of the causeways that led into Mexico. . . .

We saw the fresh water that came from Chapultepec, which supplied the city, and the bridges on the three causeways, built at certain intervals so the water could go from one part of the lake to another, and a multitude of canoes, some arriving with provisions and others leaving with merchandise. We saw that every house in this great city and in the others built on the water could be reached only by wooden drawbridges or by canoe. We saw temples built like towers and fortresses in these cities, all white-washed; it was a sight to see. . . .

After taking a good look and considering all that we had seen, we looked again at the great square and the throngs of people, some buying and others selling. The buzzing of their voices could be heard more than a league away. There were soldiers among us who had been in many parts of the world, in Constantinople and Rome and all over Italy, who said that they had never before seen a market place so large and so well laid out, and so filled with people.

Aztec gold ornament

Analyzing Primary Sources

1. What scene is Bernal Díaz describing in this excerpt?

   A a view of Tenochtitlán's market and sur- roundings from the top of a tall temple

   B an indoor temple with many religious statues

   C a view of Tenochtitlán's temple from the market place

   D a view of the markets in Constantinople and Rome

2. Which of the following best describes the author's view of the Aztecs?

   E generous and busy

   F evil and prosperous

   G loving and kind

   H athletic and loud

3. **Critical Thinking Recognizing Points of View** Which words and phrases in the excerpt above reveal the author's opinion of the Aztec's religion?

King Affonso I:
Letter to King John of Portugal

In 1490, the Portuguese converted the son of a Kongo king to Christianity and then helped him to assume his father's throne. The king, born Nzinga Mbemba, was renamed Affonso. King Affonso soon realized that his relationship with Portugal had extremely negative consequences, as can be seen from his letter in 1526 to King John of Portugal.

Vocabulary Before you read the selection, look up the following words in a dictionary: **comply, jurisdiction, depopulated.**

Main Idea **In this letter, the king of Kongo asks the king of Portugal to end the slave trade.**

African carving of Portuguese soldiers

Sir, Your Highness of Portugal should know how our Kingdom is being lost in so many ways. This is caused by the excessive freedom given by your officials to the men and merchants who are allowed to come to this Kingdom to set up shops with goods and many things which have been prohibited by us. Many of our vassals, whom we had in obedience, do not comply because they have the things in greater abundance than we ourselves. It was with these things that we had them content and subjected under our jurisdiction, so it is doing a great harm not only to the service of God, but to the security and peace of our Kingdoms and State as well.

And we cannot reckon how great the damage is, since the mentioned merchants are taking every day our natives, sons of the land and the sons of our noblemen and vassals and our relatives. The thieves and men of bad conscience grab them wishing to have the things and wares of this Kingdom which they are ambitious of; they grab them and get them to be sold. And so great, Sir, is the corruption and licentiousness that our country is being completely depopulated, and your Highness should not agree with this nor accept it as in your service. And to avoid it we need from those your Kingdoms no more than some priests and a few people to teach in schools, and no other goods except wine and flour for the holy sacrament.

That is why we beg of Your Highness to help and assist us in this matter, commanding your factors that they should not send here either merchants or wares, because *it is our will that in these kingdoms there should not be any trade of slaves nor outlet for them.* Concerning what is referred to above, again we beg of Your Highness to agree with it. . . .

Analyzing Primary Sources

1. Which of the following best describes the author's purpose in writing this letter?

   A to ask the king for money to help in ending the slave trade

   B to inform the king of the abuses taking place and to ask for his help in ending them

   C to inform the king about the extent of trade taking place in the kingdom

   D to ask the king for an explanation for why people are being enslaved

2. What does Affonso request of King John in the last paragraph?

   E that he not send any merchants or wares

   F that he send teachers

   G that he send priests

   H that he pray for Affonso

3. **Critical Thinking Recognizing Causes and Effects** According to King Affonso, how have the Portuguese affected his kingdom and state?

Miguel de Cervantes: *Don Quixote*

In his novel *Don Quixote,* Spanish writer Miguel de Cervantes tells the story of a madman who thinks he is a medieval knight. While Don Quixote's exploits often seem ridiculous, his devotion to the virtues underlying chivalry give his actions dignity. In this famous excerpt, Don Quixote does battle with a group of windmills against the advice of his down-to-earth companion, Sancho Panza.

Vocabulary Before you read the selection, look up the following words in a dictionary: **nigh, leagues, millstone, caitiffs.**

> **Main Idea** **In this excerpt, Don Quixote's devotion to knighthood leads him to attack a windmill, which he sees as a menacing giant.**

Just then they came in sight of thirty or forty windmills that rise from that plain, and no sooner did Don Quixote see them than he said to his squire: "Fortune is guiding our affairs better than we ourselves could have wished. Do you see over yonder, friend Sancho, thirty or forty hulking giants? I intend to do battle with them and slay them. With the spoils we shall begin to be rich, for this is a righteous war. . . ."

"What giants?" asked Sancho Panza.

"Those you see over there," replied his master, "with the long arms; some of them have them well-nigh two leagues in length."

"Take care, sir," cried Sancho. "Those over there are not giants but windmills, and those things that seem to be armed are their sails, which when they are whirled around by the wind turn the millstone."

"It is clear," replied Don Quixote, "that you are not experienced in adventures. Those are giants, and if you are afraid, turn aside and pray whilst I enter into fierce and unequal battle with them."

Uttering these words, he clapped spurs to Rozinante, his steed, without heeding the cries of his squire, Sancho, who warned him that he was not going to attack giants, but windmills. But so convinced was he that they were giants that he neither heard his squire's shouts nor did he notice what they were, though he was very near them. Instead, he rushed on, shouting in a loud voice: "Fly not, cowards and vile caitiffs; one knight alone attacks you!" At that moment a slight breeze arose and the great sails began to move. . . .

He ran his lance into the sail, but the wind twisted it with such violence that it shivered the lance in pieces and dragged both rider and horse after it, rolling them over and over on the ground, sorely damaged.

Analyzing Literature

1. When Don Quixote attacks the giants, he expects

   A to gain great wealth.

   B to fail because he fights alone.

   C Sancho to join him.

   D to be tossed in the air.

2. Don Quixote believes a knight should

   E attack only after being attacked.

   F act boldly when he finds an enemy.

   G seek help before fighting an unequal battle.

   H enter a battle only to gain material wealth.

3. **Critical Thinking Drawing Conclusions** **(a)** What values of chivalry motivate Don Quixote's attack on the windmills? **(b)** How do you think Cervantes feels about Don Quixote and his ideals? Explain.

The English Bill of Rights

When the Catholic king, James II, was forced from the English throne in 1688, Parliament offered the crown to his Protestant daughter Mary and her husband William of Orange. But Parliament insisted that William and Mary submit to a Bill of Rights. This document, a continuation of the struggle between the crown and Parliament, sums up the powers that Parliament had been seeking since the Petition of Right in 1628.

Vocabulary Before you read the selection, look up the following words in a dictionary: **subvert, extirpate, abdicated, prerogative, redress.**

Main Idea This document ensured the superiority of Parliament over the monarchy and spelled out basic rights.

Whereas, the late King James II . . . did endeavor to subvert and extirpate the Protestant religion and the laws and liberties of this kingdom . . . and whereas the said late King James II having abdicated the government, and the throne being vacant. . . .

The said lords [Parliament] . . . being now assembled in a full and free representative [body] of this nation . . . do in the first place . . . declare:

English Houses of Parliament (1800s)

1. That the pretended power of suspending of laws or the execution of laws by regal authority without consent of Parliament is illegal. . . .
4. That levying money for or to the use of the crown by pretense of prerogative without grant of Parliament . . . is illegal;
5. That it is the right of the subjects to petition the king, and all commitments and prosecutions for such petitioning are illegal.
6. That . . . raising or keeping a standing army within the kingdom in time of peace, unless it be with consent of Parliament, is against law. . . .
8. That election of members of Parliament ought to be free. . . .
9. That the freedom of speech and debates or proceedings in Parliament ought not to be challenged or questioned in any court or place out of Parliament. . . .
10. That excessive bail ought not to be required, nor excessive fines imposed, nor cruel and unusual punishments inflicted. . . .
13. And that, for redress of all grievances and for the amending, strengthening, and preserving of the laws, Parliaments ought to be held frequently. . . .

Analyzing Primary Sources

1. Which of the following statements best summarizes these excerpts from the Bill of Rights?

   A The king's powers are limited by the Parliament.

   B The Parliament's powers are limited by the monarch.

   C The Parliament's duty is to amend and preserve laws.

   D The king's powers to raise an army are unlimited.

2. This Bill of Rights required the monarch to

   E raise money for paying the members of Parliament.

   F summon Parliament regularly.

   G cancel laws he or she considered unjust.

   H keep a standing army to defend the country.

3. **Critical Thinking Making Inferences** Why do you think the members of Parliament included item 9? Why do you think this item was important?

John Locke: *Two Treatises on Government*

English philosopher John Locke (1632–1704) published *Two Treatises on Government* in 1690. In the writings, Locke holds that all people possess natural rights, including property and personal freedom. Locke also states that governments hold their power only with the consent of the people. Locke's ideas heavily influenced revolutions in America and France.

Vocabulary Before you read the selection, look up the following words in a dictionary: **promulgated, extempory, inroads, transgress, endeavor, forfeit, devolves.**

Main Idea In this essay, Locke states that the primary purpose of government is to protect the natural rights of the people.

But though men, when they enter into society give up the equality, liberty, and executive power they had in the state of Nature into the hands of society . . . the power of the society or legislative constituted by them can never be supposed to extend farther than the common good. . . . Whoever has the legislative or supreme power of any commonwealth, is bound to govern by established standing laws, promulgated and known to the people, and not by extempory decrees, by [unbiased] and upright judges, who are to decide controversies by those laws; and to employ the force of the community at home only in the execution of such laws, or abroad to prevent or redress foreign injuries and secure the community from inroads and invasion. And all this to be directed to no other end but the peace, safety, and public good of the people. . . .

The reason why men enter into society is the preservation of their property; and the end while they choose and authorize a legislative is that there may be laws made, and rules set, as guards and fences to the properties of all the society, . . .

Whensoever, therefore, the legislative [power] shall transgress this fundamental rule of society, and either by ambition, fear, folly, or corruption, endeavor to grasp themselves, or put into the hands of any other, an absolute power over the lives, liberties, and estates of the people, by this breach of trust they forfeit the power the people had put into their hands for quite contrary ends, and it devolves to the people; who have a right to resume their original liberty, and by the establishment of a new legislative (such as they shall think fit), provide for their own safety and security. . . .

Analyzing Primary Sources

1. Which of the following statements best summarizes the excerpt above?

   A People should give up their fundamental rights in order to establish absolute monarchies.

   B People establish governments in order to set and enforce laws. If a government does not do this, the people may abolish it.

   C Most legislative powers are corrupt.

   D Judges may need to act outside the law.

2. Which of the following groups has the final authority of government in Locke's opinion?

   E the legislature

   F the prince

   G the people

   H the judges

3. **Critical Thinking Making Inferences** According to Locke, what do people give up when they enter into a society? Why do you think people do this?

Jean-Jacques Rousseau:
The Social Contract

In *The Social Contract*, Rousseau (1712–1778) proposes an ideal society formed through a "social contract," and based on the natural will of the people. Rousseau believed that people in their natural state were basically good but were corrupted by the evils of society. The first lines of *The Social Contract*, "Man is born free, but is everywhere in chains," reflect this idea.

Vocabulary Before you read the selection, look up the following words in a dictionary: **indivisible, sovereign.**

> **Main Idea** In consenting to form a government, Rousseau says, individuals choose to give up their self-interest in favor of the common good.

Find a form of association that defends and protects the person and goods of each associate with all the common force, and by means of which each one, uniting with all, nevertheless obeys only himself and remains as free as before. This is the fundamental problem which is solved by the social contract. . . .

[F]irst of all, since each one gives his entire self, the condition is equal for everyone, and since the condition is equal for everyone, no one has an interest in making it burdensome for the others. . . .

If, then, everything that is not the essence of the social compact is set aside, one will find that it can be reduced to the following terms: Each of us puts his person and all his power in common under the supreme direction of the general will; and in a body we receive each member as an indivisible part of the whole.

Instantly, in place of the private person of each contracting party, this act of association produces a moral and collective body, composed of as many members as there are voices in the assembly, which receives from this same act its unity, its common self, its life, and its will. This public person, formed thus by the union of all the others, formerly took the name City, and now takes that of Republic or body politic, which its members call State when it is passive, Sovereign when active, Power when comparing it to similar bodies. As for the associates, they collectively take the name People; and individually are called Citizens as participants in the sovereign authority, and Subjects as subjects to the laws of the State. . . .

Analyzing Primary Sources

1. According to Rousseau, "social contract" provides a solution to the fundamental problem of finding a form of government in which
   A people's differences can be solved peacefully.
   B people remain as free as they were without government.
   C people are not subject to unjust or immoral laws.
   D minorities are protected.

2. The Republic or body politic is defined by Rousseau as the
   E assembly.
   F collective body formed when the social contract is dissolved.
   G collective body formed when private persons enter into the social contract.
   H collective body appointed by the king.

3. **Critical Thinking Drawing Conclusions** Why does Rousseau believe that people are safe putting themselves under the direction of the "general will"?

Declaration of the Rights of Man and the Citizen

The French National Assembly issued this document in 1789 after having overthrown the established government in the early stages of the French Revolution. The document was modeled in part on the English Bill of Rights and on the American Declaration of Independence.

Vocabulary Before you read the selection, look up the following words in a dictionary: **auspices, imprescriptible, indispensable.**

Main Idea This declaration states the natural rights of French citizens and establishes the equality of all citizens before the law.

Therefore the National Assembly recognizes and proclaims, in the presence and under the auspices of the Supreme Being, the following rights of man and of the citizen:

1. Men are born and remain free and equal in rights. Social distinctions may be founded only upon the general good.
2. The aim of all political association is the preservation of the natural and imprescriptible rights of man. These rights are liberty, property, security, and resistance to oppression. . . .
4. Liberty consists in the freedom to do everything which injures no one else. . . .
5. Law can only prohibit such actions as are hurtful to society. . . .
6. Law is the expression of the general will. Every citizen has a right to participate personally, or through his representative, in its formation. It must be the same for all, whether it protects or punishes. All citizens, being equal in the eyes of the law, are equally eligible to all dignities and to all public positions and occupations, according to their abilities, and without distinction except that of their virtues and talents.
7. No person shall be accused, arrested, or imprisoned except in the cases and according to the forms prescribed by law. . . .
9. As all persons are held innocent until they shall have been declared guilty, if arrest shall be deemed indispensable, all harshness not essential to the securing of the prisoner's person shall be severely repressed by law. . . .
11. The free communication of ideas and opinions is one of the most precious of the rights of man. Every citizen may, accordingly, speak, write, and print with freedom. . . .
13. A common contribution is essential for the maintenance of the public [military] forces and for the cost of administration. This should be equitably distributed among all the citizens in proportion to their means.

Paris protesters during the French Revolution

Analyzing Primary Sources

1. Which of the following describes the tax policy set forth in this document?

   A All citizens must pay the same amount of tax.

   B Only citizens in the military must pay taxes.

   C All citizens pay taxes in proportion to their wealth.

   D There should be no taxes imposed on citizens.

2. Which article above specifically protects citizens from police brutality and torture?

   E 5

   F 6

   G 9

   H 11

3. **Critical Thinking Applying Information** Give one real-life example of each of the four natural rights listed under article 2.

Miguel Hidalgo:
Decree of Hidalgo

Father Miguel Hidalgo of Mexico called for freedom from Spanish rule in 1810. The following decree, also issued in 1810 from Guadalajara, Jalisco, was an attempt to gain additional support for the uprising from Native Americans, blacks, and mestizos. In the end, Hidalgo's rebellion failed because creoles feared that more rights for Native Americans and an end to slavery would cost them power. Less than one year after the start of the uprising, Hidalgo was captured and executed, and his followers scattered.

Vocabulary Before you read the selection, look up the following words in a dictionary: **yoke, exactions.**

Main Idea In this decree, Hidalgo calls for an end to slavery and to the heavy taxes imposed on the poor in Mexico.

Miguel Hidalgo

From the happy moment that the valiant American nation took up arms to shake off the heavy yoke that has oppressed it for three centuries, one of the principal objectives has been to extinguish such duties that cannot advance its fortune, especially those which in these critical circumstances do not well serve that end or provide for the real need of the kingdom in meeting the costs of the struggle, so therefore there is now put forward here the most urgent remedy in the following declarations:

1. That all owners of slaves shall give them their freedom before the end of ten days, under penalty of death, which shall be applied to those who violate this article.
2. That from now on the collection of tributes according to [race] shall cease, as shall exactions that are demanded of the Indians.
3. That all legal business, documents, letters and actions can be on common paper, with the requirement of the seal totally abolished.

Analyzing Primary Sources

1. Item 2 of the Decree of Hidalgo calls for an end to
   A slavery.
   B collection of any taxes.
   C collection of taxes based on race.
   D all business transactions with mestizos and Indians.

2. What does "the seal" probably symbolize in item 3 above?
   E approval from Spanish authorities
   F a postage stamp

   G a special type of paper used for legal documents
   H respect for Native American traditions

3. **Critical Thinking Defending a Position** Latin American liberation movements were often based on Enlightenment ideas about natural rights. Describe some of the natural rights Hidalgo could have listed in his decree as explanations for why he wished to abolish slavery, taxes based on race, and the requirement of the seal.

Simón Bolívar: *Address to the Congress of Venezuela*

Encouraged by the revolutions in British North America and France, colonists in Spanish South America soon began to create a force for independence. Simón Bolívar was one of the leaders of this movement. The excerpt below, from Bolívar's Address to the Second National Congress of Venezuela, was given in 1819.

Vocabulary Before you read the selection, look up the following words in a dictionary: **pernicious, inflexible, arduous, erroneous, incentives, succulent.**

Main Idea In this speech, Bolívar offers advice on what type of government to set up in Venezuela.

Subject to the threefold yoke of ignorance, tyranny, and vice, the American people have been unable to acquire knowledge, power, or [civic] virtue. The lessons we received and the models we studied, as pupils of such pernicious teachers, were most destructive. . . .

If a people, perverted by their training, succeed in achieving their liberty, they will soon lose it, for it would be of no avail to endeavor to explain to them that happiness consists in the practice of virtue; that the rule of law is more powerful than the rule of tyrants, because, as the laws are more inflexible, everyone should submit to their beneficent austerity; that proper morals, and not force, are the bases of law; and that to practice justice is to practice liberty. Therefore, Legislators, your work is so much the more arduous, inasmuch as you have to reeducate men who have been corrupted by erroneous illusions and false incentives. Liberty, says Rousseau, is a succulent morsel, but one difficult to digest. . . .

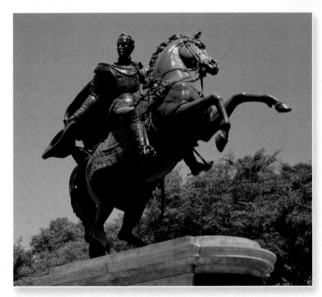

Legislators, meditate well before you choose. Forget not that you are to lay the political foundation for a newly born nation which can rise to the heights of greatness that Nature has marked out for it if you but proportion this foundation in keeping with the high plane that it aspires to attain. Unless your choice is based upon the peculiar . . . experience of Venezuelan people—a factor that should guide you in determining the nature and form of government you are about to adopt for the well-being of the people . . . the result of our reforms will again be slavery.

Simón Bolívar

Analyzing Primary Sources

1. Which statement best summarizes Bolívar's view of the people of Latin America?

   A They have not been well prepared for self-government by their former Spanish rulers.

   B They have been well prepared for self-government by the Spanish.

   C They had been ruled fairly by the Spanish.

   D They have very little desire for self-government.

2. Bolívar states that a government will be most effective if it

   E adheres closely to theories of good government.

   F imitates other successful governments.

   G is molded to fit the character of the nation for which it is built.

   H is based on the rule of law.

3. **Critical Thinking Defending a Position** Would you describe Bolívar as practical or idealistic? Use examples from the excerpt to defend your opinion.

Charles Dickens: *Hard Times*

In *Hard Times*, Charles Dickens protests the dehumanizing conditions of factory life in nineteenth-century England. In this excerpt from the novel, Dickens describes early morning in a fictional factory town named Coketown. (Coke is a form of coal.)

Vocabulary Before you read the selection, look up the following words in a dictionary: **clogs, melancholy, monotony, consign, decomposition, unfathomable, shrouded.**

Main Idea In this excerpt from the novel, Dickens depicts the labor conditions of the early Industrial Revolution.

The Fairy palaces burst into illumination, before pale morning showed the monstrous serpents of smoke trailing themselves over Coketown. A clattering of clogs upon the pavement; a rapid ringing of bells; and all the melancholy mad elephants, polished and oiled up for the day's monotony, were at their heavy exercise again.

Stephen bent over his loom, quiet, watchful, and steady. A special contrast, as every man was in the forest of looms where Stephen worked, to the crashing, smashing, tearing piece of mechanism at which he laboured. Never fear, good people of an anxious turn of mind, that Art will consign Nature to Oblivion. Set anywhere, side by side, the work of God and the work of man; and the former, even though it be a troop of Hands of very small account, will gain in dignity from the comparison.

So many hundred Hands in this Mill; so many hundred horse Steam Power. It is known, to the force of a single pound weight, what the engine will do; but, not all the calculators of the National Debt can tell me the capacity for good or evil, for love or hatred, for patriotism or discontent, for the decomposition of virtue into vice, or the reverse, at any single moment in the soul of one of these its quiet servants, with the composed faces and the regulated actions. There is no mystery in it; there is an unfathomable mystery in the meanest of them, for ever. . . .

The day grew strong, and showed itself outside, even against the flaming lights within. The lights were turned out, and the work went on. The rain fell, and the Smoke-serpents, submissive to the curse of all that tribe, trailed themselves upon the earth. In the waste-yard outside, the steam from the escape pipe, the litter of barrels and old iron, the shining heaps of coals, the ashes everywhere, were shrouded in a veil of mist and rain.

The work went on, until the noon-bell rang. More clattering upon the pavements. The looms, and wheels, and Hands all out of gear for an hour.

A spinning mule

Analyzing Primary Sources

1. What are the "melancholy mad elephants" to which Dickens refers in the excerpt above?

   A factory workers

   B factory owners

   C power looms

   D steam locomotives

2. According to this passage, facts cannot predict

   E the national debt.

   F the potential output of a factory.

   G the amount of work an individual can complete in a day.

   H the capacity of any individual for good or evil.

3. **Critical Thinking** **Making Inferences**
   (a) Why does Dickens refer to the factory workers as "Hands"? **(b)** What seems to be his attitude toward the workers?
   (c) What seems to be his general attitude toward the Industrial Revolution?

Fukuzawa Yukichi: *Autobiography*

In 1858, Fukuzawa Yukichi joined the first Japanese mission to the United States. When he returned home, he wrote articles and books explaining western customs and practices to the Japanese. This selection from his *Autobiography* recalls his impressions of his first days in San Francisco.

Vocabulary Before you read the selection, look up the following words in a dictionary: **inexplicable, revered.**

Main Idea In this autobiography, Fukuzawa Yukichi shows some of the differences between American and Japanese cultures and attitudes.

All of us wore the usual pair of swords at our sides and the [rope] sandals. So attired, we were taken to the modern hotel. There we noticed, covering the interior, the valuable carpets which in Japan only the more wealthy could buy from importers' shops at so much a square inch to make purses and tobacco pouches with. Here the carpet was laid over an entire room—something quite astounding—upon this costly fabric walked our hosts wearing the shoes with which they had come in from the streets!

One evening our hosts said that some ladies and gentlemen were having a dancing party and that they would be glad to have us attend it. We went. To our dismay we could not make out what they were doing. The ladies and gentlemen seemed to be hopping about the room together. As funny as it was, we knew it would be rude to laugh, and we controlled our expressions with difficulty as the dancing went on. These were but a few of the instances of our bewilderment at the strange customs of American society.

When we were taking leave, our host and hostess kindly offered us horses to ride home on. This pleased us, for a chance to ride horseback again was a relief. . . . We touched whip to the horses and rode back to our quarters at a trot. The Americans watched us and exclaimed at the Japanese ability in riding. So neither of us really knew much about the other after all. . . .

Things social, political, and economic proved most inexplicable. One day, on a sudden thought, I asked a gentleman where the descendants of George Washington might be. He replied, "I think there is a woman who is directly descended from Washington. I don't know where she is now, but I think I have heard she is married." His answer was so very casual that it shocked me.

Of course, I knew that America was a republic with a new president every four years, but I could not help feeling that the family of Washington would be revered above all other families. My reasoning was based on the reverence in Japan for the founders of the great line of rulers. . . .

Japanese textile workers

Analyzing Primary Sources

1. Fukuzawa views the dance with
   - **A** fear.
   - **B** horror.
   - **C** reverence.
   - **D** amusement.

2. What conclusion does Fukuzawa come to after the incident with the horses?
   - **E** Americans do not understand the Japanese.
   - **F** Americans do not respect the Japanese.
   - **G** Americans are not as skilled riders as the Japanese.
   - **H** Americans are more skillful riders than the Japanese.

3. **Critical Thinking Recognizing Points of View (a)** Why did Fukuzawa Yukichi expect Americans to treat the descendants of George Washington with respect? **(b)** What does this incident suggest about the differing cultural values of Japan and the United States?

Erich Maria Remarque:
All Quiet on the Western Front

Erich Maria Remarque was wounded five times while serving in the German army during World War I. In 1928, he published *All Quiet on the Western Front*, which is often considered the greatest novel about the war. It follows the narrator, Paul Baumer, from eager recruit to disillusioned veteran. In this passage, Paul is trapped for hours in a foxhole with a French soldier he has just killed.

Vocabulary Before you read the selection, look up the following word in a dictionary: **abstraction**.

> **Main Idea** **In this excerpt from a novel, a young German soldier expresses his horror at killing a man hand-to-hand.**

In the afternoon, about three, he is dead.

I breathe freely again. But only for a short time. Soon the silence is more unbearable than the groans. I wish the gurgling were there again, gasping hoarse, now whistling softly and again hoarse and loud.

It is mad, what I do. But I must do something. I prop the dead man up again so that he lies comfortably, although he feels nothing any more. I close his eyes. They are brown, his hair is black and a bit curly at the sides. . . .

The silence spreads. I talk and must talk. So I speak to him and say to him: "Comrade, I did not want to kill you. If you jumped in here again, I would not do it, if you would be sensible too. But you were only an idea to me before, an abstraction that lived in my mind and called forth its appropriate response. It was that abstraction I stabbed. But now, for the first time, I see you are a man like me. I thought of your hand-grenades, of your bayonet, of your rifle; now I see your wife and your face and our fellowship. Forgive me, comrade. We always see it too late. Why do they never tell us that you are poor devils like us, that your mothers are just as anxious as ours, and that we have the same fear of death, and the same dying and the same agony—Forgive me, comrade; how could you be my enemy? If we threw away these rifles and this uniform you could be my brother just like Kat and Albert. Take twenty years of my life, comrade, and stand up—take more, for I do not know what I can even attempt to do with it now."

German soldiers on their way to the front

Analyzing Literature

1. Why does Paul finally speak to the French soldier?

   A He does not know that the French soldier is dead.

   B He hopes to nurse the French soldier back to life.

   C He wants to brag about his victory over his enemy.

   D He can no longer stand the silence in the foxhole.

2. According to Paul, he can no longer see the French soldier as

   E an abstraction.

   F a human being.

   G a "poor devil."

   H a dead body.

3. **Critical Thinking Recognizing Points of View** **(a)** What does Paul mean by "We always see it too late"? **(b)** How does this passage reflect what you know about the morale of soldiers late in the war?

Mohandas Gandhi: *Hind Swaraj*

Mohandas Gandhi led a successful, peaceful revolution in India against British rule. In the following excerpt from his book *Hind Swaraj* (*Indian Home Rule*), published in 1938, Gandhi explains the ideas behind his nonviolent method of passive resistance in the form of an imaginary conversation between an editor and a reader.

Vocabulary Before you read the selection, look up the following words in a dictionary: **repugnant, breach.**

Main Idea **In this imaginary interview, Gandhi explains the ideas behind his nonviolent method of passive resistance.**

Editor: Passive resistance is a method of securing rights by personal suffering; it is the reverse of resistance by arms. When I refuse to do a thing that is repugnant to my conscience, I use soul-force. For instance, the Government of the day has passed a law which is applicable to me. I do not like it. If by using violence I force the Government to repeal the law, I am employing what may be termed body-force. If I do not obey the law and accept the penalty for its breach, I use soul-force. It involves sacrifice of self.

Everybody admits that sacrifice of self is infinitely superior to sacrifice of others. Moreover, if this kind of force is used in a cause that is unjust, only the person using it suffers. He does not make others suffer for his mistakes. . . . No man can claim that he is absolutely in the right or that a particular thing is wrong because he thinks so, but it is wrong for him so long as that is his deliberate judgment. It is therefore meet [proper] that he should not do that which he knows to be wrong, and suffer the consequence whatever it may be. This is the key to the use of soul-force.

Reader: You would then disregard laws—this is rank disloyalty. We have always been considered a law-abiding nation. You seem to be going even beyond the extremists. They say that we must obey the laws that have been passed, but that if the laws be bad, we must drive out the lawgivers even by force.

Editor: Whether I go beyond them or whether I do not is a matter of no consequence to either of us. We simply want to find out what is right and to act accordingly. The real meaning of the statement that we are a law-abiding nation is that we are passive resisters. When we do not like certain laws, we do not break the heads of law-givers but we suffer and do not submit to the laws.

Mohandas Gandhi

Analyzing Primary Sources

1. What is the goal of passive resistance?
   A to bring about peaceful change
   B to gain support for violence
   C to discover truth
   D to injure wrongdoers

2. The author defines soul-force as
   E weapons used for peaceful purposes.
   F refusal to obey a law that is unjust and accepting the penalty.
   G trying to determine what is right.
   H obeying all laws while working to overthrow the lawmakers.

3. **Critical Thinking Understanding Sequence (a)** According to Gandhi, could soul-force ever be used to support an unjust cause? **(b)** What does Gandhi mean when he says that a person using soul-force "does not make others suffer for his mistakes"?

Nelson Mandela: *Glory and Hope*

Nelson Mandela delivered this speech after having been elected president in South Africa's first multiracial elections in 1994. Knowing that the injustices of apartheid would not be easily erased, Mandela asked the people to work together for peace and justice.

Vocabulary Before you read the selection, look up the following words in a dictionary: **emancipation, covenant, reconciliation.**

Main Idea In this speech, Mandela calls upon black and white South Africans to work together to build a new nation based on justice.

Today, all of us do, by our presence here, and by our celebrations . . . confer glory and hope to newborn liberty.

Out of the experience of an extraordinary human disaster that lasted too long must be born a society of which all humanity will be proud.

Our daily deeds as ordinary South Africans must produce an actual South African reality that will reinforce humanity's belief in justice, strengthen its confidence in the nobility of the human soul and sustain all our hopes for a glorious life for all. . . .

Nelson Mandela (right) with F. W. de Klerk

The time for the healing of the wounds has come. . . .

The time to build is upon us.

We have, at last, achieved our political emancipation. We pledge ourselves to liberate all our people from the continuing bondage of poverty, deprivation, suffering, gender and other discrimination.

We have triumphed in the effort to implant hope in the breasts of the millions of our people. We enter into a covenant that we shall build the society in which all South Africans, both black and white, will be able to walk tall, without any fear in their hearts, assured of the inalienable right to human dignity—a rainbow nation at peace with itself and the world. . . .

We understand it still that there is no easy road to freedom.

We know it well that none of us acting alone can achieve success.

We must therefore act together as a united people, for national reconciliation, for nation building, for the birth of a new world.

Let there be justice for all. Let there be peace for all. Let there be work, bread, water, and salt for all. . . . The sun shall never set on so glorious a human achievement!

Analyzing Primary Sources

1. In this speech, Mandela is celebrating
   A the birth of a new, free nation.
   B decades of peace and justice.
   C the easy road to freedom.
   D the end of violence.

2. Which of the following best summarizes the excerpt?
   E We must find work for all.
   F We must not take the path of violence.

   G We must now finish the work of freedom that we have started.
   H We must correct the injustices of South Africa's past through severe punishments.

3. **Critical Thinking Making Inferences (a)** In addition to political freedom, what further "freedoms" does Mandela call for in his speech? **(b)** What does Mandela mean by "reconciliation"?

Harry Wu: *The Outlook for China, Human Rights*

Primary Sources and Literature

Author and human rights activist Harry Wu was imprisoned in China for 19 years because of his criticisms of the communist regime. The excerpt below is from a speech Wu delivered in 1996.

Vocabulary Before you read the selection, look up the following words in a dictionary: **specter, superstructure, vulcanizing.**

Main Idea **In this speech, Wu describes the system of forced labor camps run by China's communist government.**

Sometimes people ask me, "What are you fighting for?" And my answer is quite simple. I want to see the word *laogai* in every dictionary in every language in the world; I want to see the laogai ended. . . .

The economic boom made possible by capitalism makes profits for both the West and China. But despite the huge profits earned by China's external trade, ordinary people enjoy only a tiny part. The communist government puts most of the profits into upgrading its weapons systems, into internal and external political activities, and into maintaining the nation's political stability. . . .

Today, a specter is hovering over Mainland China—capitalism. Communism is dead; it is no longer believed in by the Chinese in general nor even by the majority of Communist Party members. The "capitalistic" economic boom has made the superstructure of the communist regime appear pretty on the outside, but its pillars are heavily damaged. Looming in front of China are some huge crises.

At the core of the human rights question in China today is China's fundamental machinery for crushing human beings physically, psychologically and spiritually: the laogai camp system, of which we have identified 1,100 camps. It is also an integral part of the national economy. Its importance is illustrated by some basic facts: one third of China's tea is produced in laogai camps; 60 percent of China's rubber vulcanizing chemicals are produced in a single laogai camp in Shanghai; the first and second chain hoist works in the country to receive direct export authority are laogai camps in Zhejiang Province; one of the largest and earliest exporters of hand tools is a camp in Shanghai; an unknown but significant amount of China's cotton crop is grown by prisoners. I could go on and on and on. . . . The laogai is not simply a prison system, it is a political tool for maintaining the Communist Party's totalitarian rule.

Chinese human rights protester

Analyzing Primary Sources

1. What is a laogai?
   - **A** a labor camp for prisoners
   - **B** a warehouse for exports
   - **C** a chemical plant
   - **D** a tea or cotton plantation

2. The damaged "pillars" described by Wu in the third paragraph of this excerpt are a symbol of the
   - **E** non-communist leadership.
   - **F** economy of the country.
   - **G** communist regime's lack of true support by the people.
   - **H** Chinese prison system under the Communist government.

3. **Critical Thinking Synthesizing Information** **(a)** Why do you think the author describes the laogai as "a political tool for maintaining the Communist Party's totalitarian rule"? **(b)** What is the economic role of the labor camps?

Europe: Political

ICELAND
★Reykjavik

Barents Sea

Norwegian Sea

Faroe Is.
(Den.)

Shetland Is.
(Br.)

ATLANTIC
OCEAN

FINLAND

NORWAY

Helsinki★

Oslo★

SWEDEN

St. Petersburg●

Gulf of Bothnia

Stockholm★

Tallinn★

RUSSIA

Scotland

North Sea

ESTONIA

Baltic Sea

Riga★
LATVIA

Moscow★

N.
Ireland

UNITED
KINGDOM

DENMARK

Copenhagen★

LITHUANIA
Vilnius★

Dublin★

IRELAND

NETHERLANDS

RUSSIA

Minsk★

Wales

England

The
Hague★

Amsterdam★

Berlin★

POLAND
Warsaw★

BELARUS

London★

Brussels★
BELGIUM

GERMANY

Kiev★

English Channel

LUXEMBOURG

Prague★
CZECH REP.

UKRAINE

★Paris

SLOVAKIA

MOLDOVA

Bay of
Biscay

FRANCE

LIECHTENSTEIN
Bern★

Vienna★

★Bratislava

Budapest★

Chisinau★

SWITZ.

AUSTRIA

HUNGARY

Ljubljana★

ROMANIA

Bucharest★

SLOVENIA

★Zagreb

Black Sea

PORTUGAL

ANDORRA

SAN
MARINO

CROATIA

Belgrade★

Adriatic Sea

BOSNIA–
HERZEGOVINA

Serbia

BULGARIA

Bosporus

MONACO

ITALY

Sarajevo★ YUGOSLAVIA

Sofia★

Lisbon★

Corsica
(Fr.)

★Madrid

Montenegro

Skopje★
MACEDONIA

Istanbul●

SPAIN

Rome★

VATICAN
CITY

ALBANIA

Tirana★

TURKEY

Ankara★

Sardinia
(It.)

Balearic Is.
(Sp.)

GREECE

Aegean
Sea

Strait of
Gibraltar

Gibraltar●
(Br.)

Mediterranean Sea

Sicily

Athens★

AFRICA

MALTA

Crete

N
W   E
S

★ Capital city

● Major city

Azimuthal Equal Area Projection

0   250   500 Miles

0   250   500 Kilometers

World Atlas

Europe: Physical

30°W · 20°W · 70°N · 10°W · 0° · 10°E · 20°E · 30°E · 40°E · 50°E

Barents Sea

Iceland

Arctic Circle

Norwegian Sea

60°N

Faroe Is.

KJØLEN MTS.

SCANDINAVIAN PENINSULA

Gulf of Bothnia

Shetland Is.

Volga R.

ATLANTIC OCEAN

Baltic Sea

North Sea

JUTLAND PENINSULA

British Isles

50°N

Elbe R.

Thames R.

Ruhr Valley

NORTHERN EUROPEAN PLAIN

Oder R.

Vistula R.

Dnieper R.

English Channel

Seine R.

Rhine R.

Dniester R.

CARPATHIAN MTS.

Don

Bay of Biscay

Loire R.

Rhône R.

ALPS

Po R.

Danube R.

DINARIC ALPS

Black Sea

Garonne R.

PYRENEES

APENNINES

ITALIAN PENINSULA

Adriatic Sea

BALKAN MTS.

Bosporus

IBERIAN PENINSULA

Ebro R.

40°N

Corsica

BALKAN PENINSULA

Tagus R.

Sardinia

Dardanelles

Guadiana R.

Balearic Islands

PINDUS MTS

Aegean Sea

Crete

Strait of Gibraltar

Sicily

30°N

Mediterranean Sea

Land Elevation

Feet		Meters
14,000		4,000
7,000		2,000
1,500		500
700		200
0		0
Below sea level		Below sea level

Icecaps

N W E S

AFRICA

Azimuthal Equal Area Projection

0 · 250 · 500 Miles

0 · 250 · 500 Kilometers

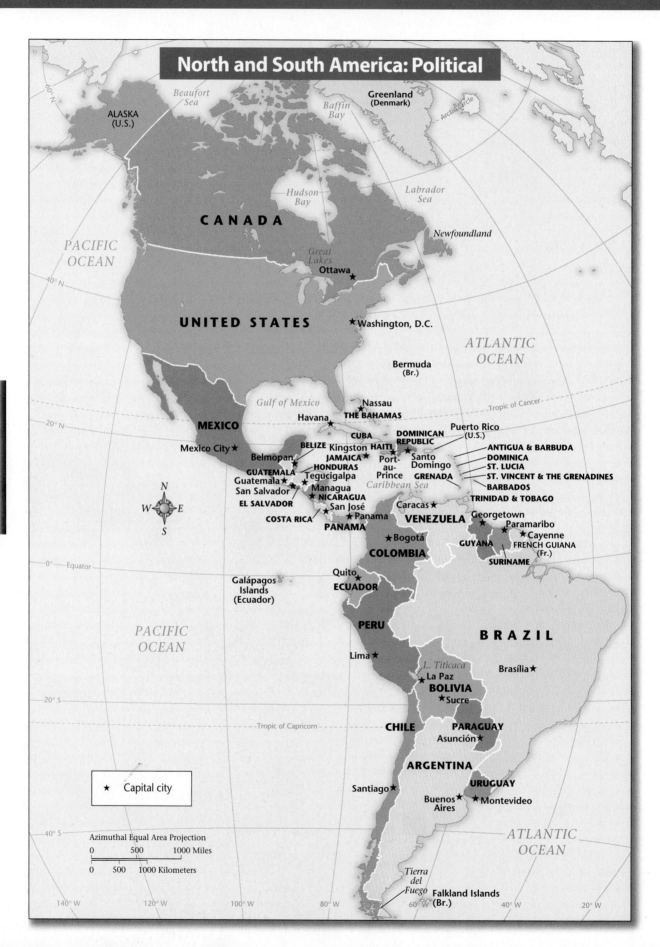

North and South America: Political

World Atlas

ALASKA (U.S.)

Beaufort Sea

Baffin Bay

Greenland (Denmark)

Arctic Circle

PACIFIC OCEAN

Hudson Bay

Great Lakes

Labrador Sea

CANADA

Newfoundland

Ottawa ★

UNITED STATES

★ Washington, D.C.

ATLANTIC OCEAN

Bermuda (Br.)

Gulf of Mexico

Nassau

Tropic of Cancer

MEXICO

Havana

THE BAHAMAS

Mexico City ★

CUBA

DOMINICAN REPUBLIC

Puerto Rico (U.S.)

BELIZE

Kingston **HAITI**

ANTIGUA & BARBUDA

Belmopan

JAMAICA

Port-au-Prince

Santo Domingo

DOMINICA

GUATEMALA

HONDURAS

ST. LUCIA

Guatemala ★

Tegucigalpa

GRENADA

ST. VINCENT & THE GRENADINES

San Salvador ★

Managua

BARBADOS

EL SALVADOR

NICARAGUA

Caribbean Sea

TRINIDAD & TOBAGO

★ San José

COSTA RICA

★ Panama

Caracas ★

Georgetown

Paramaribo

PANAMA

VENEZUELA

★ Bogotá

GUYANA

★ Cayenne

FRENCH GUIANA (Fr.)

COLOMBIA

SURINAME

0° Equator

Quito ★

ECUADOR

Galápagos Islands (Ecuador)

PERU

BRAZIL

Lima ★

L. Titicaca

Brasília ★

La Paz ★

BOLIVIA

★ Sucre

Tropic of Capricorn

CHILE

PARAGUAY

Asunción ★

ARGENTINA

URUGUAY

★ Capital city

Santiago ★

Buenos Aires ★

★ Montevideo

ATLANTIC OCEAN

Azimuthal Equal Area Projection

0   500   1000 Miles

0   500   1000 Kilometers

Tierra del Fuego

Falkland Islands (Br.)

PACIFIC OCEAN

140° W   120° W   100° W   80° W   60° W   40° W   20° W

60° N   40° N   20° N   20° S   40° S

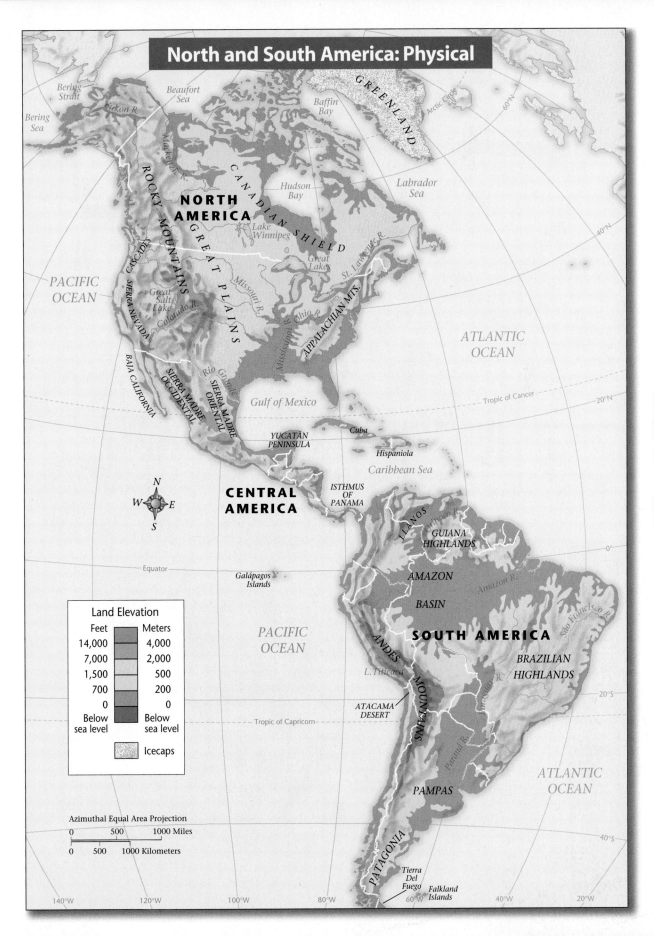

North and South America: Physical

Bering Strait

Bering Sea

Beaufort Sea

Baffin Bay

GREENLAND

Arctic Circle

60°N

Yukon R.

Mackenzie R.

ROCKY MOUNTAINS

CANADIAN SHIELD

NORTH AMERICA

Hudson Bay

Labrador Sea

40°N

GREAT PLAINS

Lake Winnipeg

Great Lakes

St. Lawrence R.

CASCADES

PACIFIC OCEAN

SIERRA NEVADA

Great Salt Lake

Missouri R.

Colorado R.

Mississippi R.

Ohio R.

APPALACHIAN MTS.

ATLANTIC OCEAN

BAJA CALIFORNIA

SIERRA MADRE OCCIDENTAL

Rio Grande

SIERRA MADRE ORIENTAL

Gulf of Mexico

Cuba

Tropic of Cancer

20°N

YUCATÁN PENINSULA

Hispaniola

Caribbean Sea

N W E S

CENTRAL AMERICA

ISTHMUS OF PANAMA

LLANOS

Orinoco R.

GUIANA HIGHLANDS

0°

Equator

Galápagos Islands

AMAZON BASIN

Amazon R.

São Francisco R.

Land Elevation

Feet	Meters
14,000	4,000
7,000	2,000
1,500	500
700	200
0	0
Below sea level	Below sea level
	Icecaps

PACIFIC OCEAN

ANDES MOUNTAINS

L. Titicaca

SOUTH AMERICA

BRAZILIAN HIGHLANDS

20°S

ATACAMA DESERT

Paraná R.

Azimuthal Equal Area Projection

0   500   1000 Miles

0   500   1000 Kilometers

ATLANTIC OCEAN

PAMPAS

40°S

PATAGONIA

Tierra Del Fuego

Falkland Islands

Tropic of Capricorn

140°W   120°W   100°W   80°W   60°W   40°W   20°W

Australia, New Zealand, and Oceania: Political–Physical

ASIA

Philippine
Sea

PALAU ⊛ Koror

Northern
Mariana
Islands
(U.S.)

Guam
(U.S.)

Caroline Islands

MICRONESIA

FEDERATED STATES OF MICRONESIA

Palikir ⊛

Wake Island
(U.S.)

MARSHALL
ISLANDS
Majuro ⊛

Tarawa

Gilbert
Islands

NAURU
Yaren ⊛

M E L A N E S I A

Honiara ⊛
SOLOMON
ISLANDS

New
Hebrides

VANUATU
Port-Vila ⊛

New Caledonia
(Fr.)

KIRIBATI

Line
Islands

Equator

P O L Y N E S I A

Midway Islands
(U.S.)

Tropic of Cancer

Hawaiian
Islands
(U.S.)

PACIFIC OCEAN

N
W E
S

Marquesas
Islands

French Polynesia (Fr.)

Tahiti

Society
Islands

Cook
Islands
(N.Z.)

Tropic of Capricorn

Pitcairn
Island
(Br.)

American
Samoa
(U.S.)

Apia
SAMOA ⊛

TUVALU
Funafuti ⊛

FIJI
ISLANDS
Suva ⊛

Nukualofa ⊛ TONGA

International Date Line

Auckland ●
North
Island
Wellington ⊛
Christchurch ●
NEW
ZEALAND
Dunedin ●
Cook Strait
South
Island
SOUTHERN ALPS
Stewart
Island

Aukland
Islands
(N.Z.)

Tasman
Sea

Brisbane ●

Sydney ●
Canberra ⊛
New
South
Wales
Melbourne ★
Victoria
Bass
Strait
Tasmania
Hobart ★

GREAT DIVIDING RANGE

GREAT BARRIER REEF

Coral
Sea

CAPE
YORK
PENINSULA

Queensland
GREAT
ARTESIAN
BASIN

ARNHEM
LAND
BARKLY
TABLELAND

Darwin ★
Northern
Territory

KIMBERLEY
PLATEAU

GREAT SANDY
DESERT

GIBSON DESERT

Western
Australia

GREAT VICTORIA
DESERT

SIMPSON
DESERT

South
Australia

A U S T R A L I A

NULLARBOR PLAIN

Great
Australian
Bight

Adelaide ★

Murray R.

DARLING RANGE

Perth ★

INDIAN
OCEAN

Arafura Sea

Timor
Sea

Land Elevation

Feet	Meters
14,000	4,000
7,000	2,000
1,500	500
700	200
0	0
Below sea level	Below sea level

⊛ National capital
★ State or territorial capital
● Other city

Mercator Projection

| 0 | 500 | 1000 Miles |
| 0 | 500 | 1000 Kilometers |

15°N

0°

135°W

150°W

165°W

180°

165°E

150°E

135°E

120°E

15°S

30°S

45°S

Understanding Map Projections

Geographers and historians use globes and maps to represent the Earth. A globe is like a small model of the Earth. It shows major geographic features, representing the land-masses and bodies of water accurately. However, a globe is not always convenient to use. A map, on the other hand, which can be printed on a piece of paper or in a book, is a more convenient way to show the Earth. Unfortunately, no map can be an exact picture of the Earth because all maps are flat and the Earth's surface is curved.

Mapmakers have developed many ways of showing the curved Earth on a flat surface. Each of these ways is called a map projection. The three maps on this page show different types of map projections—each with its advantages and disadvantages.

Robinson Projection The Robinson projection shows correct shapes and sizes of land-masses for most parts of the world. They are commonly used today by geographers. You will find numerous Robinson projections in this book. The locator maps that appear with most of the maps in the book are Robinson projections.

Mercator Projection The Mercator projection, one of the earliest projections developed, accurately shows the directions north, south, east, and west. As you can see, the parallels and meridians are straight lines intersecting each other at right angles. This makes it easy to plot distances on the map. As a result, Mercator projections are useful for showing sailors' routes and ocean currents. Sizes become distorted, however, as you move farther away from the equator.

Interrupted Projection The Interrupted projection shows the sizes and shapes of land-masses accurately. However, the interruptions in the oceans make it difficult to measure distances and judge directions across water.

Map Projections

Robinson Projection

Mercator Projection

Interrupted Projection

World Atlas

Skills Assessment

Geography Map projections enable mapmakers to show the curved Earth on a flat page. Each of the projections shown here has its advantages and disadvantages.

1. **Location** On the maps, locate **(a)** North America, **(b)** Africa, **(c)** Australia.
2. **Region** **(a)** On an Interrupted projection, which continent is divided into sections? Why is it divided? **(b)** List three pages in this textbook on which you can find a Robinson projection.
3. **Critical Thinking** **Comparing** Locate Antarctica on the Robinson and Mercator projections. On which map is its size shown more accurately? Explain why this is so.

Glossary

This Glossary defines many important terms and phrases. Some terms are phonetically respelled to aid in pronunciation. See the Pronunciation Key below for an explanation of the respellings. The page number following each definition is the page on which the term or phrase is first discussed in a chapter. All terms that appear in blue type in the text are included in this Glossary.

PRONUNCIATION KEY When difficult terms or names first appear in the text, they are respelled to aid in pronunciation. A syllable in small capital letters receives the most stress. The key below lists the letters used for respelling. It includes examples of words using each sound and shows how they are respelled.

Symbol	Example	Respelling
a	hat	(hat)
ay	pay, late	(pay), (layt)
ah	star, hot	(stahr), (haht)
ai	air, dare	(air), (dair)
aw	law, all	(law), (awl)
eh	met	(meht)
ee	bee, eat	(bee), (eet)
er	learn, sir, fur	(lern), (ser), (fer)
ih	fit	(fiht)
ī	mile	(mīle)
ir	ear	(ir)
oh	no	(noh)
oi	soil, boy	(soil), (boi)
oo	root, rule	(root), (rool)
or	born, door	(born), (dor)
ow	plow, out	(plow), (owt)
u	put, book	(put), (buk)
uh	fun	(fuhn)
yoo	few, use	(fyoo), (yooz)
ch	chill, reach	(chihl), (reech)
g	go, dig	(goh), (dihg)
j	jet, gently, bridge	(jeht), (JEHNT lee), (brihj)
k	kite, cup	(kīt), (kuhp)
ks	mix	(mihks)
kw	quick	(kwihk)
ng	bring	(brihng)
s	say, cent	(say), (sehnt)
sh	she, crash	(shee), (krash)
th	three	(three)
y	yet, onion	(yeht), (UHN yuhn)
z	zip, always	(zihp), (AWL wayz)
zh	treasure	(TREH zher)

A

abdicate give up a high office (p. 490)

abolitionist one who fought for the end of slavery in the United States (p. 609)

absentee landlord one who owns a large estate but does not live there (p. 600)

absolute monarch ruler with complete authority over the government and lives of the people he or she governs (p. 413)

abstract style of art composed of lines, colors, and shapes, usually having no recognizable subject matter (p. 753)

acid rain form of pollution in which toxic chemicals in the air come back to the Earth as rain, snow, or hail (p. 817)

acropolis (uh KRAHP uh lihs) highest and most fortified point within a Greek city-state (p. 106)

acupuncture medical treatment in which needles are inserted under the skin at specific points to relieve pain or treat various illnesses (p. 96)

agribusiness large commercial farm owned by a multinational corporation (p. 938)

ahimsa (uh HIM sah) Hindu belief in nonviolence and a reverence for all life (pp. 78, 732)

alliance formal agreement between two or more nations or powers to cooperate and come to one another's defense (pp. 111, 387)

alloy mix or blend one metal with another (p. 167)

alphabet letters that represent spoken sounds (p. 44)

anarchist someone who wants to abolish all government (p. 580)

anesthetic drug that prevents pain during surgery (p. 498)

animism belief that spirits and forces may live in animals, objects, or dreams (p. 12)

annex add a territory onto an existing state or country (pp. 486, 573)

annul cancel or invalidate (pp. 214, 352)

Anschluss union of Austria and Germany (p. 772)

anthropology study of the origins and development of people and their societies (p. 8)

antisemitism prejudice against Jews (p. 196)

apartheid policy of strict racial separation in South Africa; abolished in 1989 (p. 727)

apostle leader or teacher of a new faith or movement (p. 142)

appeasement policy of giving in to an aggressor's demands in order to keep the peace (p. 771)

apprentice young person learning a trade from a master (p. 200)

aqueduct in ancient Rome, bridgelike stone structure that carried water from the hills into the cities (p. 138)

arabesque intricate design made up of curved lines that suggest floral shapes, used to decorate rugs, textiles, and glassware (p. 263)

archaeology study of past people and cultures (p. 8)

archipelago (ahr kuh PEHL uh goh) chain of islands (p. 316)

aristocracy government headed by a privileged minority or upper class (p. 106)

armada fleet of ships (p. 414)

armistice agreement to end fighting in a war (p. 693)

artifact object made by human beings (p. 8)

artisan skilled craftworker (p. 16)

assassination murder of a public figure, usually for political reasons (p. 120)

assembly line production method that breaks down a complex job into a series of smaller tasks (p. 546)

assimilate absorb or adopt another culture (p. 122)

astrolabe instrument used to determine latitude by measuring the position of the stars (p. 365)

atheism belief that there is no god (p. 714)

atman (AHT muhn) in Hindu belief, a person's essential self (p. 77)

atrocity brutal act committed against innocent people (p. 691)

autocrat ruler who has complete authority (p. 236)

autonomy self-rule (p. 520)

ayatollah title given to a learned Shiite Muslim legal expert (p. 898)

B

balance of power distribution of military and economic power that prevents any one nation from becoming too strong (p. 420)

baroque ornate style of art and architecture popular in the 1600s and 1700s (p. 453)

barter economy system in which one set of goods or services is exchanged for another (p. 43)

bill of exchange issued by a banker in one city to a merchant who could exchange it for cash in a distant city, thus freeing him from traveling with gold, which was easily stolen (p. 199)

bishop high-ranking Church official with authority over a local area, or diocese (p. 145)

blitzkrieg lightning war (p. 775)

blockade shutting off of a port to keep people or supplies from moving in or out (p. 487)

bourgeoisie (boor zhwah ZEE) the middle class (p. 469)

boyar landowning noble in Russia under the czars (pp. 242, 432)

brahman according to Aryan belief, the single spiritual power that resides in all things (p. 57)

bunraku Japanese puppet plays (p. 325)

bushido (BOO shee doh) code of conduct for samurai during the feudal period in Japan (p. 320)

C

cabinet parliamentary advisors to the king who originally met in a small room, or "cabinet" (p. 458)

caliph successor to Muhammad as political and religious leader of the Muslims (p. 256)

calligraphy fancy or stylized handwriting (pp. 63, 263)

canon law body of laws of a church (p. 195)

canonize recognize one as a saint (p. 352)

capital money or wealth (pp. 199, 501)

capital offense crime punishable by death (p. 598)

capitalism economic system in which the means of production are privately owned and operated for profit (p. 404)

caravel improved type of sailing ship in the 1400s (p. 365)

Glossary

cartel association of large corporations formed to fix prices, set production quotas, or divide up markets (p. 550)

cartographer mapmaker (p. 365)

caste in traditional Indian society, unchangeable social group into which a person is born (pp. 57, 267)

cataract waterfall (p. 25)

caudillo military dictator in Latin America (p. 659)

cease-fire halt in fighting (p. 874)

celadon porcelain with an unusual blue-green glaze (p. 314)

censorship restriction on access to ideas and information (p. 451)

census population count (p. 135)

chancellor prime minister (pp. 571, 761, 836)

charter in the Middle Ages, a written document that set out the rights and privileges of a town (p. 199)

chinampas artificial islands made of earth piled on reed mats anchored to a shallow lake bed (p. 159)

chivalry code of conduct for knights during the Middle Ages (p. 189)

circumnavigate travel all the way around the Earth (p. 368)

city-state political unit made up of a city and the surrounding lands (p. 18)

civil disobedience refusal to obey unjust laws (p. 732)

civil law body of law dealing with private rights of individuals (p. 40)

civilization complex, highly organized social order (p. 15)

civil rights movement effort in the 1950s and 1960s to end discrimination and ensure equal rights for all Americans (p. 841)

civil war war fought between two groups of people in the same nation (p. 387)

clan group of families with a common ancestor (p. 62)

client state nation dependent on the support of a stronger power (p. 899)

coalition temporary alliance of various political parties (pp. 605, 838)

codify arrange and set down in writing (p. 40)

collaborator person who cooperates with an enemy (p. 782)

collective large farm owned and operated by peasants as a group (p. 709)

collective security system in which a group of nations acts as one to preserve the peace of all (p. 695)

collectivization pooling of land and labor in an attempt to increase efficiency (p. 862)

colony territory settled and ruled by people from another land (p. 44)

colossus giant (p. 584)

comedy in ancient Greece, play that mocked people or social customs (p. 119)

command economy system in which government officials make all basic economic decisions (p. 708)

commissar communist party official assigned to the army to teach party principles and ensure party loyalty (p. 706)

commodity valuable product (p. 284)

common law system of law that is the same for all people, based on court decisions that have become accepted legal principles (p. 207)

commune community in which property is held in common, living quarters are shared, and physical needs are provided in exchange for work at assigned jobs (p. 863)

communism form of socialism advocated by Karl Marx; according to Marx, class struggle was inevitable and would lead to the creation of a classless society in which all wealth and property would be owned by the community as a whole (p. 512)

compact agreement (p. 395)

compromise acceptable middle ground (p. 352)

concentration camp detention center for civilians who are considered enemies of a state (p. 765)

concession special economic rights given to a foreign power (p. 630)

confederation unification (p. 654)

conquistador (kahn KEES tuh dor) name for the Spanish explorers who claimed lands in the Americas for Spain in the 1500s and 1600s (p. 386)

conscription "the draft," which required all young men to be ready for military or other service (p. 690)

constitutional government government whose power is defined and limited by law (p. 457)

consul in ancient Rome, official from the patrician class who supervised the government and commanded the armies (p. 129)

containment Cold War policy of limiting communism to areas already under Soviet control (p. 793)

contra guerrilla who fought against the Sandinistas in Nicaragua (p. 946)

convoy group of merchant ships protected by warships (p. 688)

corporation business owned by many investors who buy shares of stock and risk only the amount of their investment (p. 549)

covenant binding agreement (p. 46)

creole person in Spain's colonies in the Americas who was an American-born descendant of Spanish settlers (pp. 390, 527)

criminal law branch of law that deals with offenses against others, such as robbery, assault, or murder (p. 40)

crusade holy war (p. 214)

cult of domesticity idealization of women and the home (p. 556)

cultural diffusion spread of ideas, customs, and technologies from one people to another (p. 19)

culture way of life of a society that is handed down from one generation to the next by learning and experience (p. 8)

cuneiform (kyoo NEE uh form) wedge-shaped writing of the ancient Sumerians (p. 36)

curriculum formal course of study (p. 185)

cyclone fierce circular windstorm (p. 886)

czar title of the ruler of the Russian empire (p. 243)

D

daimyo (DĪ myoh) warrior lord directly below the shogun in feudal Japan (p. 320)

debt service paying interest on loans (p. 886)

decimal system system of numbers based on 10 (p. 83)

decipher decode (p. 32)

default fail to make payments (p. 846)

Glossary

deficit gap between what a government spends and what it takes in through taxes and other sources (p. 841)

deficit spending situation in which a government spends more money than it takes in (p. 470)

deforestation the destruction of forest land (pp. 633, 886)

delta triangular area of marshland formed by deposits of silt at the mouth of some rivers (pp. 25, 896)

democracy government in which the people hold ruling power (p. 107)

demotic system of ancient Egyptian writing, simpler than hieroglyphics, that was developed for everyday use (p. 32)

depopulation reduction in population (p. 428)

desalinization process of converting salty sea water into fresh water (p. 890)

desertification process by which fertile or semidesert land becomes desert (pp. 281, 916)

détente easing of tensions between the United States and the Soviet Union in the 1970s (p. 829)

dharma (DAHR muh) in Hindu belief, an individual's religious and moral duties (p. 77)

diaspora (di AS puhr uh) the scattering of people (p. 47)

dictator ruler who has complete control over a government; in ancient Rome, a leader appointed to rule for six months in times of emergency (p. 129)

diet assembly or legislature (pp. 247, 647)

diocese district or region under the care of a bishop (p. 145)

direct democracy system of government in which citizens participate directly in the day-to-day affairs of government rather than through elected representatives (p. 112)

disarmament reduction of armed forces and weapons (p. 747)

dissent different or opposing ideas (p. 81)

dissenter Protestant whose views and opinions differed with those of the Church of England (p. 422)

dissident someone who speaks out against the government (p. 844)

divine right belief that a ruler's authority comes directly from God (p. 413)

domesticate tame animals and crops for the purpose of cultivation (p. 12)

dominion self-governing nation (p. 654)

domino theory belief that if one nation fell to communism, neighboring nations would also fall, like a row of falling dominoes (p. 873)

dowry payment to the bridegroom or his family in an arranged marriage (p. 87)

Duma elected national legislature in Russia (p. 589)

dynamo machine used to generate electricity (p. 546)

dynastic cycle rise and fall of Chinese dynasties according to the Mandate of Heaven (p. 64)

dynasty ruling family (p. 25)

E

e-commerce business and trade conducted over the Internet (p. 820)

economic dependence economic relationship, controlled by a developed nation, in which a less-developed nation exports raw materials to the developed nation and imports manufactured goods, capital, and technological know-how (p. 659)

ejido (eh HEE doh) Mexican peasant cooperative (p. 944)

elector one of seven German princes who would choose the Holy Roman emperor (p. 427)

electorate body of people allowed to vote (p. 595)

elite upper class (p. 626)

emancipation granting of freedom to serfs or slaves (p. 586)

embargo ban on trade (pp. 874, 940)

emigration movement away from one's homeland (p. 580)

émigré (EHM ih gray) person who flees his or her country for political reasons (p. 476)

empire group of states or territories controlled by one ruler (p. 18)

enclosure in England in the 1700s, the process of taking over and fencing off public lands (p. 499)

encomienda right the Spanish government granted to its American colonists to demand labor or tribute from Native Americans (p. 390)

engineering application of science and mathematics to develop useful structures and machines (p. 138)

engraving art form in which an artist etches a design on a metal plate with acid and then uses the plate to make multiple prints (p. 342)

enlightened despot absolute ruler who uses his or her power to bring about political and social change (p. 452)

entente nonbinding agreement to follow common policies (p. 681)

entrepreneur person who assumes financial risks in the hope of making a profit (p. 404)

environmentalist one who raises an alarm about threats to the planet's fragile environment (p. 817)

epic long, narrative poem (p. 222)

epidemic outbreak of a rapidly spreading disease (p. 225)

ethics moral standards of behavior (p. 47)

ethnic cleansing policy of killing or forcibly removing people of certain ethnic groups (p. 852)

ethnic group large group of people who share the same language and cultural heritage (p. 245)

euro common currency used by member nations of the European Union (p. 832)

exchequer treasury (p. 207)

excommunication exclusion from the Roman Catholic Church as a penalty for refusing to obey Church laws (p. 195)

expansionism policy of increasing the amount of territory a government holds (pp. 95, 608)

extraterritoriality right of foreigners to be protected by the laws of their own nation (p. 636)

F

faction small group (p. 473)

factory place in which workers and machines are brought together to produce large quantities of goods (p. 502)

favela Brazilian slum (p. 952)

federal republic government in which power is

divided between the national, or federal, government and the states (p. 463)

federal system system in which powers are divided between a strong central government and local governments (p. 883)

feminist movement sought equal access for women to jobs and promotions, equal pay for equal work, and an end to sexual harassment on the job (p. 819)

feudal contract exchange of pledges between lords and vassals (p. 186)

feudalism (FYOO duhl ihz uhm) loosely organized system of government in which local lords governed their own lands but owed military service and other support to a greater lord (pp. 64, 186)

fief (FEEF) in the Middle Ages, an estate granted by a lord to a vassal in exchange for service and loyalty (p. 186)

filial piety respect for parents (p. 90)

flapper in the United States and Europe in the 1920s, a rebellious young woman (p. 756)

flying buttress stone support on the outside of a building that allowed builders to construct higher walls and leave space for large stained-glass windows (p. 223)

free trade trade between countries without quotas, tariffs, or other restrictions (p. 597)

fresco colorful painting completed on wet plaster (p. 102)

friar monk who traveled throughout Europe's growing towns to preach to the poor (p. 195)

frontier sparsely populated, undeveloped area on the outskirts of civilization (p. 182)

fundamentalist one who stresses the fundamental, or basic, values of his or her faith (p. 819)

G

general strike strike by workers in many different industries at the same time (p. 748)

genetic engineering altering of the chemical code carried by all living things (p. 820)

genocide deliberate attempt to destroy an entire religious or ethnic group (pp. 629, 781)

gentry wealthy, landowning class (p. 304)

geography study of people, their environments, and their resources (p. 6)

germ theory idea that certain microbes might cause specific infectious diseases (p. 551)

ghetto separate section of a city where members of a minority group are forced to live (p. 355)

glacier thick sheet of ice that covered parts of the Earth during the ice age (p. 12)

glasnost policy of openness instituted by Soviet leader Mikhail Gorbachev in the 1980s (p. 846)

global warming worldwide temperature increase (pp. 157, 817)

glyph pictograph or other symbol carved into a surface (p. 164)

golden age period of great cultural achievement (p. 83)

gravity force that tends to pull one mass or object to another (p. 358)

griot (GREE oh) professional storyteller in early West Africa (p. 297)

gross domestic product total value of all goods and services produced by a nation (p. 859)

guerrilla warfare fighting carried on through hit-and-run raids (p. 489)

guild in the Middle Ages, association of merchants or artisans who cooperated to protect their economic interests (p. 200)

H

habeas corpus principle that a person cannot be held in prison without first being charged with a specific crime (p. 426)

haiku form of Japanese poetry that expresses a feeling, thought, or idea in three lines, or 17 syllables (p. 325)

hajj one of the Five Pillars of Islam, the pilgrimage to Mecca that all Muslims are expected to make at least once in their lifetime (p. 254)

hangul alphabet that uses symbols to represent the sounds of spoken Korean (p. 315)

harijan "child of God," Gandhi's term for an untouchable in the caste system (p. 885)

hejab traditional form of dress worn by Muslim women (p. 893)

heliocentric based on the belief that the sun is the center of the universe (pp. 123, 356)

helot member of a class of state-owned slaves in ancient Sparta (p. 106)

heresy religious belief that is contrary to the official teachings of a church (p. 146)

hierarchy (HĪ uhr ahr kee) system of ranking people within a society (p. 35)

hieroglyphics (hi er oh GLIHF ihks) form of picture writing developed by the ancient Egyptians (p. 32)

hijra Muhammad's flight from Mecca to Medina in 622 (p. 253)

historian person who studies how people lived in the past (p. 10)

home rule local self-government (p. 602)

homogeneous society society that has a common culture and language (p. 648)

humanism intellectual movement at the heart of the Italian Renaissance that focused on worldly subjects rather than on religious issues (p. 337)

humanities study of subjects taught in ancient Greece and Rome, such as grammar, rhetoric, poetry, and history (p. 338)

hypothesis possible explanation (p. 357)

I

icon holy image of Christ, the Virgin Mary, or a saint venerated in the Eastern Orthodox Church (p. 237)

ideogram picture that symbolizes an idea or action (p. 32)

ideology system of thought and belief (pp. 518, 807)

illumination artistic decoration in books (p. 224)

immunity natural protection (p. 386)

imperialism domination by one country of the political, economic, or cultural life of another country or region (pp. 133, 618)

import substitution government policy of encouraging local manufacturers to produce goods that would replace imports (p. 937)

impressionism school of painting of the late 1800s and early 1900s that tried to capture fleeting visual impressions (p. 565)

indemnity payment for losses in war (p. 636)

indigenous original or native to a country or region (p. 653)

indulgence in the Roman Catholic Church, pardon for sins committed during a person's lifetime (p. 346)

inflation economic cycle that involves a rapid rise in prices linked to a sharp increase in the amount of money available (pp. 148, 226, 404)

intendant official appointed by French king Louis XIV to govern the provinces, collect taxes, and recruit soldiers (p. 418)

interchangeable parts identical components that can be used in place of one another in manufacturing (p. 546)

interdependence mutual dependence of countries on goods, resources, and knowledge from other parts of the world (p. 809)

interdict in the Roman Catholic Church, excommunication of an entire region, town, or kingdom (p. 195)

intifada mass uprising mounted in 1987 by Palestinians in territory held by Israel (p. 900)

island-hopping method used by Allied forces to recapture some Japanese-held islands in the Pacific while bypassing others (p. 788)

isolationism policy of limited involvement in world affairs (p. 613)

J

janizary elite force of the Ottoman army (p. 273)

jihad in Islam, an effort in God's service (pp. 254, 621)

joint family family organization in which several generations share a common dwelling (p. 87)

joint stock company private trading company in which shares are sold to investors to finance business ventures (p. 404)

joint venture business organized by two parties, with profits shared by both participants (p. 865)

journeyman salaried worker who was employed by a guild master (p. 200)

jury group of people sworn to make a decision in a legal case (pp. 112, 207)

K

kabuki (kuh BOO kee) form of Japanese drama developed in the 1600s (p. 323)

kaiser (KĪ zer) emperor of Germany (p. 573)

kamikaze (kah mih KAH zee) Japanese pilot who undertook a suicide mission (p. 789)

kana in the Japanese writing system, phonetic symbols representing syllables (p. 318)

karma in Hindu belief, all the actions that affect a person's fate in the next life (p. 77)

kibbutz collective farm in Israel (p. 890)

kiva large underground chamber used by the Anasazi for religious ceremonies (p. 169)

knight noble in Europe who served as a mounted warrior for a lord in the Middle Ages (p. 187)

kulak wealthy peasant in the Soviet Union in the 1930s (p. 710)

Kulturkampf Bismarck's "battle for civilization," in which his goal was to make Catholics put loyalty to the state above their allegiance to the Church (p. 575)

L

labor union workers' organization (p. 509)

laissez faire policy allowing business to operate with little or no government interference (p. 450)

land reform breakup of large agricultural holdings for redistribution among peasants (p. 303)

latifundia huge estates bought up by newly wealthy Roman citizens (p. 133)

latitude distance north or south of the Equator (p. 6)

lay investiture creation of bishops by anyone who is not a member of the clergy (p. 213)

legion basic unit of the ancient Roman army, made up of about 5,000 soldiers (p. 131)

legislature lawmaking body (p. 108)

legitimacy principle by which monarchies that had been unseated by the French Revolution or Napoleon were restored (p. 493)

levée morning ritual during which nobles would wait upon King Louis XIV (p. 418)

levy collect (p. 218)

libel knowing publication of false and damaging statements (p. 606)

liberation theology movement in the 1960s and 1970s urging the Roman Catholic Church to take a more active role in changing the social conditions that contributed to poverty and oppression in Latin America (pp. 819, 939)

limited monarchy government in which a constitution or legislative body limits the monarch's powers (p. 426)

lineage group claiming a common ancestor (p. 295)

literacy rate percentage of people who can read and write (pp. 315, 940)

loess fine windblown yellow soil (p. 60)

logic rational thinking (p. 115)

longbow six-foot-long bow that could rapidly fire arrows with enough force to pierce most armor (p. 228)

longitude distance east or west of the Prime Meridian (p. 6)

Loyalist colonist who supported Britain during the American Revolution (p. 462)

M

mandate after World War I, a territory that was administered by a western power (p. 696)

manor during the Middle Ages in Europe, a lord's estate, which included one or more villages and the surrounding lands (p. 189)

mansa title for the king of Mali (p. 285)

maquiladora (mah kee luh DOHR uh) foreign-owned industrial plant in Mexico in which local workers assemble imported parts into finished goods (p. 945)

margin buying paying part of the cost of stocks while borrowing the rest from brokers (p. 748)

martyr person who suffers or dies for his or her beliefs (p. 144)

Glossary

matrilineal term for a family organization in which kinship ties are traced through the mother (pp. 295, 370)

means of production farms, factories, railways, and other large businesses that produce and distribute goods (p. 511)

medieval referring to the Middle Ages in Europe or the period of history in between ancient and modern times (p. 182)

mercantilism policy by which a nation sought to export more than it imported in order to build its supply of gold and silver (p. 406)

mercenary soldier serving in a foreign army for pay (pp. 149, 428)

messiah savior sent by God (p. 142)

mestizo person in Spain's colonies in the Americas who was of Native American and European descent (pp. 391, 527)

middle class new class of people, including merchants, traders, and artisans—who stood between peasants and nobles (p. 200)

militarism glorification of the military (p. 681)

militia band of citizen soldiers (p. 902)

millet in the Ottoman empire, a religious community of non-Muslims (p. 273)

minaret slender tower of a mosque, from which Muslims are called to prayer (p. 259)

missi dominici agents of Emperor Charlemagne who traveled throughout the empire to check the condition of the roads, listen to grievances, and see that justice was done (p. 184)

missionary someone sent on a religious mission (pp. 82, 622)

mixed economy economic system with both private and state-run enterprises (p. 916)

mobilize prepare military forces for war (p. 683)

modernization building a stable government while developing a country economically (p. 807)

moksha (MAHK shuh) in Hindu belief, the ultimate goal of existence, achieving union with brahman (p. 77)

monarchy government in which a king or queen exercises central power (p. 106)

money economy system by which goods and services are paid for through the exchange of a token of agreed value (p. 43)

monopoly complete control of a product or business by one person or group (pp. 95, 401)

monotheistic believing in one God (pp. 46, 253)

monsoon seasonal wind; in India, the winter monsoon brings hot, dry weather and the summer monsoon brings rain (p. 53)

mosaic picture made from chips of colored stone or glass (p. 138)

mosque Muslim house of worship (p. 254)

muezzin mosque official who climbs to the top of a minaret to call the faithful to prayer (p. 259)

mulatto in Spain's colonies in the Americas, person who was of African and European descent (pp. 391, 527)

multinational corporation enterprise with branches in many countries (p. 813)

mummification (muhm mih fih KAY shuhn) practice of preserving the bodies of the dead (p. 29)

mural large wall painting (p. 85)

mutual-aid society self-help group set up to aid sick or injured workers (p. 553)

mystic person who devotes his or her life to seeking spiritual truths (p. 57)

N

nationalism a strong feeling of pride in and devotion to one's country (p. 483)

nationalization takeover of property or resources by the government (p.724)

natural law rule or law that governs human nature (p. 446)

natural right right that belongs to all humans from birth (p. 447)

neutrality policy of supporting neither side in a war (p. 683)

nirvana in Buddhism, union with the universe and release from the cycle of rebirth (p. 79)

no-fly zone area over which Iraqi aircraft were not permitted to fly after the Persian Gulf War (p. 903)

nomad person who moves from place to place in search of food (p. 11)

no man's land empty tract of land where everything has been destroyed by war (p. 687)

nonaligned not allied with either side in a conflict (p. 807)

nuclear family family unit consisting of parents and children (p. 295)

O

oasis fertile area in a desert, watered by a natural well or spring (p. 252)

oba title for the king of Benin (p. 288)

oligarchy government in which ruling power belongs to a few people (pp. 106, 458)

one-party system country that has a single political party (p. 915)

oracle bone bone used by priests in Shang China to predict the future (p. 63)

ostracism used in ancient Greece to banish or send away a public figure who threatened democracy (p. 112)

outpost distant military station (pp. 283, 373)

overproduction condition in which production of goods exceeds the demand for them (p. 747)

P

pacifism opposition to all war (pp. 678, 771)

padi field (p. 372)

pagoda multistoried Buddhist temple with eaves that curve up at the corners (p. 307)

pandemic spread of a disease across a large area, country, continent, or the entire world (p. 694)

papal supremacy authority of medieval popes over all secular rulers (p. 193)

papyrus (puh PĪ ruhs) plant that grows along the banks of the Nile; used by the ancient Egyptians to make a paperlike material (p. 32)

partition divide (pp. 435, 882)

partnership group of merchants who joined together to finance a large-scale venture that would have been too costly for any individual trader (p. 199)

pasha provincial ruler in the Ottoman empire (p. 628)

patriarch in the Byzantine empire, highest church official in a major city (pp. 145, 237)

patriarchal describing a family headed by the father, husband, or oldest male (p. 47)

patrician member of the landholding upper class in ancient Rome (p. 129)

patrilineal term for a family organization in which kinship ties are traced through the father (p. 295)

patron person who provides financial support for the arts (p. 337)

penal colony place where people convicted of crimes are sent (p. 598)

peninsular member of the highest class in Spain's colonies in the Americas (pp. 390, 527)

peon worker forced to labor for a landlord in order to pay off a debt (p. 390)

peonage system by which workers owe labor to pay their debts (p. 661)

perestroika restructuring of the Soviet government and economy in the 1980s (p. 846)

perspective artistic technique used to give drawings and paintings a three-dimensional effect (p. 339)

phalanx in ancient Greece, a massive formation of heavily armed foot soldiers (p. 106)

pharaoh (FAIR oh) title of the rulers of ancient Egypt (p. 25)

philosophe member of a group of Enlightenment thinkers who tried to apply the methods of science to the improvement of society (p. 447)

philosophy system of ideas (p. 89)

physiocrat Enlightenment thinker who searched for natural laws to explain economics (p. 450)

pictogram drawing used to represent a word (p. 17)

plains fertile flatlands (p. 157)

plantation large estate run by an owner or overseer and worked by laborers who live there (p. 390)

plateau raised area of level land (p. 52)

plebeian (plih BEE uhn) member of the lower class in ancient Rome, including farmers, merchants, artisans, and traders (p. 129)

plebiscite ballot in which voters have a direct say on an issue (pp. 485, 953)

pogrom violent mob attack on a Jewish community (p. 588)

polis city-state in ancient Greece (p. 106)

polygamy custom that allows men to have more than one wife (p. 728)

polytheistic believing in many gods (p. 16)

pope head of the Roman Catholic Church (p. 146)

potlatch ceremonial giftgiving by wealthy Native Americans of the Northwest Coast (p. 171)

predestination idea that God long ago determined who will gain salvation (p. 350)

prehistory period of time before writing systems were invented (p. 8)

premier prime minister (p. 605)

prime minister head of the cabinet in a parliamentary government; usually the leader of the largest party in the legislature (p. 458)

privateer pirate (p. 393)

privatization selling off of state-owned industries to private investors (p. 814)

proletariat working class (pp. 512, 702)

propaganda spreading of ideas to promote a certain cause or to damage an opposing cause (p. 690)

prophet spiritual leader believed to be interpreting God's will (p. 47)

protectorate country with its own government but under the control of an outside power (p. 620)

province land outside the city of Rome that was controlled by the Roman government (p. 133)

provisional temporary (p. 605)

psychoanalysis method of studying how the mind works and treating mental disorders (p. 753)

pueblo Southwestern Native American village (p. 168)

purdah isolation of women in separate quarters (p. 633)

Q

quipu knotted strings used by Incan officials for record keeping (p. 164)

R

racism belief that one racial group is superior to another (p. 561)

radar device used to detect the flight of airplanes (p. 776)

rajah elected warrior chief of an Aryan tribe in ancient India; local Hindu ruler in India (pp. 57, 268)

realism artistic movement whose aim was to represent the world as it is (p. 563)

Realpolitik realistic politics based on the needs of the state (p. 571)

recant give up one's views or beliefs (p. 347)

recession period of reduced economic activity (pp. 522, 830)

recognize formally agree to treat a country as a legitimate state with a legitimate government (p. 889)

regionalism loyalty to a local area (p. 659)

Reich German empire (p. 573)

reincarnation in Hinduism, belief in the rebirth of the soul in another bodily form (p. 77)

religious toleration policy of allowing people to worship as they choose (p. 219)

reparation payment for war damages or damages caused by imprisonment (pp. 694, 784)

repeal cancel (pp. 400, 598)

republic system of government in which officials are chosen by the people (pp. 129, 477)

repudiate reject (p. 763)

revenue money taken in through taxes (p. 394)

rhetoric art of skillful speaking (p. 115)

rococo personal, elegant style of art and architecture made popular during the mid-1700s and featuring fancy design in the shape of leaves, shells, and scrolls (p. 453)

romanticism nineteenth-century artistic movement that appealed to emotion rather than reason (p. 562)

rotten borough rural town in England that sent members to Parliament despite having few or no voters (p. 595)

Glossary

S

sabbath holy day for rest and worship (p. 47)

sacrament sacred ritual of the Roman Catholic Church (p. 191)

salon informal social gathering at which writers, artists, and philosophers exchanged ideas; originated in France in the 1600s (p. 451)

samurai member of the warrior class in Japanese feudal society (p. 320)

sanction penalty (p. 770)

satellite dependent state (p. 794)

sati Hindu custom that called for a wife to join her husband in death by throwing herself on his funeral pyre (p. 631)

satirize make fun of (p. 137)

satrap governor of a province in the Persian empire (p. 42)

savanna grassy plain with irregular patterns of rainfall (p. 280)

scapegoat person, group, or thing forced to take the blame for the crimes or mistakes of others (p. 354)

schism permanent division in a church (p. 216)

scholasticism in medieval Europe, school of thought that used logic and reason to support Christian belief (p. 221)

scientific method painstaking method used to confirm findings and to prove or disprove a hypothesis (p. 357)

scribe in ancient civilizations, specially trained person who knew how to read, write and keep records (p. 18)

scurvy disease caused by the lack of vitamin C in someone's diet (p. 365)

secede withdraw (p. 611)

secret ballot votes cast without announcing them publicly (p. 595)

sect small religious group (p. 80)

secular having to do with worldly, rather than religious, matters (pp. 193, 483)

segregation separation of the races (pp. 611, 841)

selective borrowing adopting or adapting some cultural traits but discarding others (p. 318)

self-determination right of people to choose their own form of government (p. 693)

separatism movement advocating that Quebec separate from Canada and become an independent nation (p. 842)

sepoy Indian soldier who served in an army set up by the French or English East India company (pp. 376, 631)

serf in medieval Europe, peasant bound to the lord's land (p. 189)

service industry industry that provides a service rather than a product (p. 830)

shah king (p. 274)

shantytown slum on the outskirts of a city that lacks basic services, such as running water (p. 818)

shogun in Japanese feudal society, supreme military commander who held more power than the emperor (p. 320)

shrine altar, chapel, or other place that is sacred (p. 102)

silt rich soil carried by flooding rivers (p. 24)

simony selling of Church offices (p. 195)

slash-and-burn agriculture farming method in which forest and brush are cut down and burned to create planting fields (p. 294)

smelt melt in order to get the pure metal away from its waste matter (p. 500)

social contract agreement by which people give up their freedom to a powerful government in order to avoid chaos (p. 447)

social gospel movement of the 1800s that urged Christians to do social service (p. 561)

socialism system in which the people as a whole rather than private individuals own all property and operate all businesses (p. 511)

socialist realism artistic style whose goal was to promote socialism by showing Soviet life in a positive light (p. 715)

social mobility ability to move up in social class (p. 261)

social welfare programs to help people in need (p. 576)

sonar device used to detect the path of submarines (p. 776)

soviet council of workers and soldiers set up by Russian revolutionaries in 1917 (p. 703)

special enterprise zone area in China where foreigners can own and operate industries (p. 865)

sphere of influence area in which an outside power claims exclusive investment or trading privileges (p. 620)

squatter person who settles on land he or she does not own (p. 955)

stalemate deadlock in which neither side is able to defeat the other (p. 685)

standard of living measures the quality and availability of necessities and comforts in a society (p. 554)

steppe sparse, dry grassland (pp. 18, 240)

stipend a fixed salary given to public office holders (p. 112)

stock shares in a company (p. 549)

strait narrow water passage (p. 103)

stream of consciousness literary technique that probes a character's random thoughts and feelings (p. 754)

stupa large domelike Buddhist shrine (pp. 83, 371)

subcontinent large landmass that juts out from a continent (p. 52)

suffrage right to vote (p. 478)

sultan Muslim ruler (p. 259)

sultanate land ruled by a sultan (p. 267)

summit conference of leaders and experts from around the world (p. 809)

superpower nation strong enough to influence the acts and policies of other nations (p. 807)

surplus extra or excess (pp. 15, 284, 841)

surrealism artistic movement that attempts to portray the workings of the unconscious mind (p. 753)

T

tariff tax on imported goods (p. 406)

technology tools and skills people use to meet their basic needs (p. 8)

temperance movement campaign to limit or ban the use of alcoholic beverages (p. 558)

tenant farmer someone who would pay rent to a lord in order to farm the land (p. 199)

tenement building multistory building divided into crowded apartments (p. 505)

terrorism deliberate use of random violence, especially against civilians, to achieve political goals (p. 811)

theocracy government run by religious leaders (pp. 350, 898)

tithe payment to a church equal to one tenth of a person's income (p. 192)

tolerance acceptance (p. 42)

total war channeling of a nation's entire resources into a war effort (p. 690)

totalitarian state government in which a one-party dictatorship regulates every aspect of citizens' lives (p. 713)

tournament mock battle in which knights would compete against one another to show off their fighting skills (p. 187)

trade deficit situation in which a country imports more than it exports (pp. 635, 859)

trade surplus situation in which a country exports more than it imports (p. 635)

tragedy in ancient Greece, a play that focused on human suffering and very often ended in disaster (p. 117)

triangular trade colonial trade route among Europe and its colonies, the West Indies, and Africa in which goods were exchanged for slaves (p. 399)

tribune official in ancient Rome who was elected by the plebeians to protect their interests (p. 129)

tributary state independent state that has to acknowledge the supremacy of another state and pay tribute to its ruler (p. 303)

tribute payment that conquered peoples were forced to make to their conquerors (p. 160)

troubadour wandering poet in Europe in the Middle Ages (p. 189)

truce temporary peace (p. 528)

tsunami very large, damaging wave caused by an earthquake or very strong wind (p. 317)

turnpike privately built road that charges a fee to travelers who use it (p. 504)

tyrant in ancient Greece, ruler who gained power by force (p. 108)

U

U-boat submarine (p. 688)

ultimatum final set of demands (p. 683)

ultranationalist extreme nationalist (p. 739)

ultraroyalist émigré noble or member of the clergy in France who opposed constitutional government and favored the restoration of the old regime (p. 521)

unilateral one-sided (p. 901)

universal manhood suffrage right of all adult men to vote (p. 519)

urbanization movement of people from rural areas to cities (p. 505)

urban renewal rebuilding of the poor areas of a city (p. 552)

usurp illegally take over a throne (p. 302)

usury (yoo zhuh ree) practice of lending money with interest (p. 200)

utilitarianism idea that the goal of society should be to bring about the greatest happiness for the greatest number of people (p. 511)

utopia ideal society (p. 343)

V

vassal in medieval Europe, a lord who was granted land in exchange for service and loyalty to a greater lord (p. 186)

veneration special regard (p. 54)

vernacular everyday language of ordinary people (pp. 222, 343)

veto power to block a government action (p. 129)

viceroy representative who ruled one of Spain's provinces in the Americas in the king's name; one who governed in India in the name of the British monarch (pp. 389, 632)

vizier chief minister who supervised the business of government in ancient Egypt (p. 25)

W

war crime act that violates international rules of war (p. 853)

warlord local military ruler (p. 96)

warm-water port port that is free of ice all year (p. 433)

welfare state system in which the government takes responsibility for its citizens' social and economic needs (p. 829)

westernization adoption of western ideas, technology, and culture (p. 431)

women's suffrage right of women to vote (p. 558)

Z

zaibatsu (ZĪ BAHT soo) since the late 1800s, powerful banking and industrial families in Japan (pp. 647, 859)

zemstvo local elected assembly set up in Russia under Alexander II (p. 586)

zeppelin large, gas-filled balloon (p. 688)

ziggurat (ZIHG oo rat) pyramid-temple dedicated to the chief god or goddess of an ancient Sumerian city-state (p. 36)

Glossary

Index

Index

Index

Index

Index

Index

Index

Index

Index

Index

Index

Credits

Illustration Credits

Maps: Mapping Specialists Limited **Features 61, 286** José Morales, S.I. International; **139** Malcolm McGregor; **227, 507** Ben Stahl, Klimt Represents; **375, 740** Richard Courtney, S.I. International; **375, 740** Richard Courtney, S.I. International; **557** Penny Haufe, Klimt Represents; **637** Paul Bachem, Artworks;

Cover: Eiffel Tower, Strasbourg Statue and Obelisk of Luxor, (Paris, France) 1991, Stephen Simpson/ FPG International Corp. **Cover and title page border:** clockwise from top left: Ife Figure. South-Western Nigeria, c.12-15th centuries A.D., Bronze (Nigeria National Museum, Lagos, Nigeria). Photo: John Picton; Heiroglyphs. Bas-Relief, near White Chapel of Karnak dedicated to Amon-Min, ithyphallic god of fertility, limestone (Egypt). Erich Lessing/Art Resource, NY; Zapotec Urn from Monte Alban (Mexico), Charles & Josette Lenars/CORBIS; Detail of Greek translation of discourse by Emperor Nero on the freedom of Greeks, stone. Museo della Civilta Romana, Rome, Italy/Roger-Viollet, Paris/Bridgeman Art Library, London/NY; Queen Elizabeth I (England) Bedfordshire, Woburn Abbey/A.K.G., Berlin/Superstock; Copy of the Aztec Sun Stone Calender c. 16th, Malachite (Mexico) Ian Mursell/ Mexicolore/Bridgeman Art Library, London/NY; Terra-cotta warriors from tomb of Qin Shinuang (China), Christopher Arnesen/Tony Stone Images; Mohandas Gandhi, CORBIS/Hulton-Deutsch Collection; Enconium of Darius I, Acheamenid Period, Archaelogical Museum, Teheran, Iran, SEF/Art Resource, NY **Interior: iv** top: Ministere de la Culture et de la Communication. Direction Regionale des affaires Culturelles de Rhone-Alpes. Service Regional de l'Archeologie; bottom: Scala/Art Resource, NY. **v** top: O. Louis Mazzatenta/NGS Image Collection; middle: C. M. Dixon; bottom: Lee Boltin Picture Library. **vi** top: © University Museum of Cultural Heritage, University of Oslo bottom: Christel Gerstenberg/CORBIS **vii** top: *A Qadi Hears a Case* (detail), Bibliothéque Nationale de France, Paris; middle: © British Museum; bottom: © Copyright 1998 PhotoDisc, Inc. **viii** top: The Science Museum/Science & Society Picture Library; bottom: Hermitage, St. Petersburg, Russia/The Bridgeman Art Library, London/NY **ix** top: SuperStock; middle: The Granger Collection, NY; bottom: Dannielle Hayes/Omni-Photo Communications, Inc. **x** top: The Granger Collection, NY; bottom: Carpenter Center for the Visual Arts, Harvard University, Cambridge, MA **xi** top: Staatliche Museen zu Berlin - PreuBischer Kulturbesitz Museum für Volkerkunde; bottom: Museum of Fine Arts, Boston/Laurie Platt Winfrey, Inc. **xii** top: Culture Pictures, Inc.; bottom: (detail) Photograph © The Detroit Institute of Arts, 1995. Palacio Nacional stairway, Mexico City. © Dirk Bakker, photographer. **xiii** CORBIS **xiv** top: NASA/Science Photo Library /Photo Researchers, Inc.; middle: ©Dan Groshong/CORBIS Sygma **xv** top: ©T. Hegenbart/Black Star; bottom: Mireille Vautier/Woodfin Camp & Associates **xvi** SuperStock **xvii** *Paso de los Andes*, Vilas y Prades, Museo Historico y Militar de Chile **xviii** EddieAdams/Liaison Agency **xxi** (detail) Topkapi Sarayi Museum, Istanbul/Ergun Cagatay/ Tetragon. **xxvi** top: Library of Congress; left: Palace of Versailles, France/SuperStock **xxvii:** Bibliothéque Nationale de France top: Library of Congress **xxviii** NASA/Science Photo Library /Photo Researchers, Inc. **xxix** top,right: ©Dan Groshong/Corbis Sygma; middle: Ray Ellis/Photo Researchers; middle,right: Collection-Academia Sinica, Taipei; photo: Wan-go Weng; bottom: *The Election II - Canvassing for Votes* by William Hogarth, Sir John Soane Museum, London/The Bridgeman Art Library, London/NY **xxx** top: Scala/Art Resource, NY; middle: Ford Motor Company; bottom: SEF/Art Resource,NY **xxxi** top: E T Archive; middle,left:CORBIS; middle: Reuters/CORBIS,Bettmann; middle,right: Dannielle Hayes/Omni-Photo Communications, Inc.; bottom,left: Lee Boltin Picture Library; bottom,right: Picasso Museum, Paris, France/Giraudon, Paris / SuperStock © 2001 Estate of Pablo Picaso/Artists Rights Society (ARS), NY; **xxxviii** ©Hulton Getty/ Liaison Agency **xxxix** Mireille Vautier/Woodfin Camp & Associates **xl** Arcadio Cartoonists & Writers Syndicate,cartoonweb.com **xliii** The Granger Collection, NY **xliv** The ScienceMuseum/Science & Society Picture Library **xlv** *A Spaniard, his Mexican Wife, and their daughter from a series on mixed marriages,* Miguel Cabrera, Museo de America, Madrid/The Bridgeman Art Library, London/NY **xlviii** Walker Art Gallery, Liverpool/The Bridgeman Art Library, London/NY **liv–1** Richard Passmore/Tony Stone Images **2** top: Garrett/National Geographic Society; middle: Collection-Academia Sinica, Taipei, photo: Wan-go Weng; bottom: Arvind Garg/Liaison International **3** top, left: Corel Professional Photos CD-ROM™; top, right: Photofest; bottom: John Elk/Tony Stone Images, Inc. **4** left: Lascaux Caves, France/SuperStock; middle: The Granger Collection, NY; right: Ministere de la Culture et de la Communication. Direction Regionale des affaires Culturelles de Rhone-Alpes. Service Regional de l'Archeologie **5** left: SuperStock; middle: Dorling Kindersley Ltd. courtesy of the Museum of London; right–2: © G. Dagli Orti, Paris, France **7** top: © Geoffrey Clifford/Woodfin Camp & Associates; bottom: Novosti Press/The Image Bank **9** top, right: CORBIS; bottom, left: Brett Houk; bottom, right–4: Corel Professional Photos CD-ROM™; background: Arvind Garg/Liaison Agency **11** CORBIS/Bettmann—UPI **12** Lascaux Caves, France/SuperStock **13** left: Illustration by Peter McCarty from FROZEN MAN by David Getz, 1994, by Peter McCarty. Reprinted by permission of Henry Holt and Company, LLC; middle, left: Bernhard Grobruck/Contrast/Liaison Agency; middle, right: and top, right: CORBIS Sygma **14** bottom: Erich Lessing/Art Resource, NY; top: © George Holton/Photo Researchers, Inc. **17** top: © J. M. Kenoyer/Dept. of Archaeology and Museums, Government of Pakistan; middle: © Jehangir Gazdar/Woodfin Camp & Associates, Inc; bottom: © J. M. Kenoyer/Dept. of Archaeology and Museums, Government of Pakistan **18** The Kon-Tiki Museum, Oslo **21** © Punch-Bill Tidy/Rothco Cartoons **22** top, left: Musée du Louvre, Paris/Giraudon, Paris/SuperStock; left: Courtesy of The Oriental Institute of the University of Chicago; right: Tony Stone Images **23** left: Scala/Art Resource, NY; right: Museum of Israel, Jerusalem—Lauros-Giraudon, Paris/SuperStock **25** Kenneth Garrett/National Geographic Society **27** The Granger Collection, NY **28** Musée du Louvre, Paris/Giraudon, Paris/SuperStock **29** *Mummified Cat,* The Louvre © Photo Réunion des Musées Nationaux **30** left–2: Scala/Art Resource, NY; top, right: Erich Lessing/Art Resource, NY; bottom, right: © Fred J. Maroon/Photo Researchers, Inc. **32** Gary Cralle/The Image Bank **36** The Granger Collection, NY **39** The Granger Collection, NY **41** top and middle: © Michael Holford; bottom: The Metropolitan Museum of Art, Purchase, H. Dunscombe Colt Gift, 1961 (61.62) **42** top: The Granger Collection, NY; bottom: © Kevin Schafer/Peter Arnold, Inc. **45** Scala/Art Resource, NY **46** top: Rafael Macia/Photo Researchers, Inc.; bottom, left: The Jewish Museum, NY/Art Resource, NY **50** top, left: The Victoria and Albert Museum; left: Paolo Koch/Photo Researchers, Inc.; right: The Granger Collection, NY **51** left: *Dragon Head,* late Zhou dynasty. Courtesy of the Freer Gallery of Art, Smithsonian Institution, Washington, D.C. (32.14); right: CORBIS **54** Hulton Getty/Liaison Agency **57** National Museum of India, New Delhi, India/The Bridgeman Art Library, London/NY **59** SuperStock **62** left: *"Fu" Kuang-Ting, Shang Dynasty,* c. 1700 B.C.–1100 B.C. The Lowe Art Museum, The University of Miami/SuperStock; right: National Museum, Beijing, China/Erich Lessing/Art Resource, NY **63** © Dan Groshong/CORBIS Sygma **67** *The Earliest Cities* by Jean-Michel Coblence/CASTERMAN S.S. **68** left: Ministere de la Culture et de la Communication. Direction Regionale des affaires Culturelles de Rhone-Alpes. Service Regional de l'Archeologie; right: Kenneth Garrett/National Geographic Society **69** *Dragon Head,* late Zhou dynasty. Courtesy of the Freer Gallery of Art, Smithsonian Institution, Washington, D.C. (32.14) **70–71** SuperStock **72** top, left: E T Archive; top, right: © British Museum; bottom, left: Ralph Rainer Steffens/Bildarchiv Steffens, Mainz; bottom, right: Laurie Platt Winfrey, Inc. **73** top, right: © The Stock Market; bottom: SuperStock **72–73** National Museum of Scotland **74** left: The Ashmolean Museum/© Copyright Dorling Kindersley; middle: Archaeological Museum, Sarnath/Robert Harding Picture Library; right: Keren Su/Tony Stone Images **75** left: Christie's Images/The Bridgeman Art Library, London/NY; right: CORBIS/Richard A. Cooke **76** Lauros-Giraudon/Art Resource, NY **77** *Krishna's Combat with Indra,* c. 1585–90, Gouache, (detail) Courtesy of the Trustees of the Victorian & Albert Museum **78** W. Hille/Leo de Wys, Inc. **81** © Viren Desai/Dinodia Picture Agency **84** left: Abdullah Khandwani; right: Dorling Kindersley Ltd. **86** SEF/Art Resource, NY **87** Los Angeles County Museum of Art, From the Nasli and Alice Heeramaneck Collection, Museum Associates Purchase **88** © 1983 Steve McCurry/Magnum Photos **90** Bibliothèque Nationale, Paris, France/The Bridgeman Art Library/London/NY **91** The Ashmolean Museum © Dorling Kindersley **92** Chengde, Hubei Province, China/Kurt Scholz/SuperStock **93** O. Louis Mazzatenta/NGS Image Collection **95** Werner Forman/Art Resource, NY **96** Garry Gay/The Image Bank **100** top, left: © Copyright 1998 PhotoDisc, Inc.; left: SuperStock; right: © Peter Connolly, Spalding, Lincolnshire—Trustees of the National Museum of Scotland, Edinburgh **101** left: Lee Boltin Picture Library; right: Giraudon/Art Resource, NY **103** Knossos, Crete/Kurt Scholz/SuperStock **104** C. M. Dixon **107** Vanni/Art Resource, NY **108** Bildarchiv Preussischer Kulturbesitz **109** Stephen Dunn/Allsport **113** Benito/Liaison Agency **115** Alinari/Art Resource, NY **117** © Copyright 1998 PhotoDisc, Inc. **118** top: Martha Swope © Time Inc.; bottom: (detail), The Art Museum, Princeton University. Museum purchase, Caroline G. Mather Fund. Photographer: Bruce White **120** Erich Lessing/Art Resource, NY **122** Private Collection/The Bridgeman Art Library, London/NY **125** © Michael Holford **126** top, left: Paola Koch/Photo Researchers, Inc.; left: CORBIS/Gianni Dagli Orti; right: CORBIS **127** left: McRae Books Srl; right: E T Archive **128** CORBIS/Gianni Dagli Orti **130** *Lady Playing the Cithara* (detail), The Metropolitan Museum of Art, Rogers Fund, 1903 (03.14.5) Photograph © 1986 The Metropolitan Museum of Art **132** Scala/Art Resource, NY **133** © Stephane Compoint/CORBIS Sygma **135** Direzione Generale Musei Vaticani **136** H. M. Herget/NGS Image Collection **138** Paola Koch/Photo Researchers, Inc. **139** bottom, left: CORBIS **140** © Leonard Von Matt/Photo Researchers, Inc. **142** © André Held **143** Masolino da Panicale/E T Archive **145** top: Byzantine Collection, Dumbarton Oaks, Washington, D.C.; bottom: The Metropolitan Museum of Art, The Cloisters Collection, 1950. (50.4) Photograph © 1978 The Metropolitan Museum of Art, NY **147** McRae Books Srl **149** Walters Art Gallery, Baltimore **150** Illustration by Matthew Frey-Wood Ronsaville Harlin, Inc. **154–155** Michael Holford **154** top: M. L. Corvetto/The Image Works; left: Lee Boltin Picture Library **155** right: Trans. no. 3519(2) (Photo by P. Hollembeak/J. Beckett) Courtesy Department of Library Services, American Museum of Natural History **158** top: Otis Imboden © National Geographic Society; bottom: Chris Trotman/Duomo Photography, Inc. **159** top: Lee Boltin Picture Library; bottom: © Justin Kerry **161** top: Museum für Völkerivnde Wien, Foto-Archiv, Foto Nr. 61.240; middle: *La Gran Tenochtitlán*, 1940, (detail) Reproduccion Autorizada Por El Instituto Nacional De Bellas Artes Y Literatura/Banco de Mexico. Photo: Bob Schalkwijk; bottom: National Museum of Anthropology, Mexico City/Werner Forman, Art Resource, NY **163** Museo Nacional de Antropologia y Arqueologia Lima, Peru/Loren McIntyre **164** North Wind Picture Archives **166** M. L. Corvetto/The Image Works **169** top and middle: CORBIS/Richard A. Cooke; bottom: Ohio State Museum/Werner Forman Archive/Art Resource, NY **170** © British Museum **173** The Bodleian Library, Oxford, UK **174** left: Christie's Images/The Bridgeman Art Library, London/NY; right: Bildarchiv Preussischer Kulturbesit **175** left: CORBIS; right: Lee Boltin Picture Library **176–177** SuperStock **178** left: The Granger Collection, NY; bottom, left: Photo: Kim Yong-chui/Korean Cultural Service; right: Korean Cultural Service **179** top, left: AP/Wide World Photos; top, right: Hulton Getty/Liaison

Agency; middle: NASA; bottom: Lisa Quinones/Black Star **180** left: Pierre Belzeaux/Rapho Agence/Photo Researchers, Inc.; right: Giraudon/Art Resource, NY **181** left: SuperStock; right: Bibliothèque Nationale/Archiv für Kunst und Geschichte, Berlin **185** © University Museum of Cultural Heritage—University of Oslo **187** image © Copyright 1998 PhotoDisc, Inc. **188** left: © British Museum **189** Private Collection/The Bridgeman Art Library, London/NY **190** *February* from the Tres Riches Heures du duc de Berry (book of hours) painted by the Flemish [Limbourg, Limburg] Brothers from 1415, Giraudon/Art Resource, NY **193** *Virgin and Child*, miniature from the Book of Kells, Hiberno-Saxon ms., c. A.D. 800, Folio 7V. The Granger Collection, NY **194** top, right: Archiv Gerstenberg; bottom, right: The Pierpont Morgan Library/Art Resource, NY; bottom, left: The Granger Collection, NY; background: © G. Dagli Orti, Paris **195** The Granger Collection, NY **196** © Israel Museum, Jerusalem **200** C. M. Dixon **204** top, left: image © Copyright 1998 PhotoDisc, Inc.; left: *The Siege of Antioch (First Crusade) 1098,* William of Tyre, Bibliothèque Nationale, Paris, France/The Bridgeman Art Library, London, NY; right: Christopher Guy/reproduced by the kind permission of the Dean and Chapter of Worcester **205** *The Entrance of Joan of Arc into Orleans,* Jean-Jacques Sherrer, Musée des Beaux-Arts, Orleans, France/Roger Viollet, Paris/The Bridgeman Art Library, London/NY **206** Philip Mould, Historical Portraits Ltd, London, UK/The Bridgeman Art Library, London, NY **207** image © Copyright 1998 PhotoDisc, Inc. **208** The Royal Collection © 2000 Her Majesty Queen Elizabeth II **209** The Granger Collection, NY **212** © Meyer/Kunsthistorisches Museum, Vienna **214** Scala/Art Resource, NY **218** The Granger Collection, NY **220** Giraudon/Art Resource, NY **221** By permission of The British Library (Harley ms 4431) **223** top: © Agence Top, Paris; bottom: SuperStock **224** Sonia Halliday Photography **227** top, left: *La Ferte Loupiere,* © G. Dagli Orti, Paris **228** top: Froissart's Chronicle, Battle of Janera, 1367 (detail), Bibliothèque Nationale, Paris/The Bridgeman Art Library, London/NY; middle: CORBIS; bottom: Courtesy of the Trustees of British Library, Roy.14.E.IV. **232** top, left: Robert Frerck/Odyssey Productions, Chicago; left: Christel Gerstenberg/CORBIS; right: Bernard Cox/John Bethell PhotoLibrary, St. Albans **233** left, middle: Zamek Krolewski W. Warszawie/Collection of the Royal Castle in Warsaw; right: Hermitage, St. Petersburg, Russia/Bridgeman Art Library, London/NY **235** top, right: Marvin Trachtenberg; bottom: CORBIS/Gianni Dagli Orti; background: Robert Frerck/Odyssey Productions, Chicago **236** Scala/Art Resource, NY **237** Icon of Christ and St. Maenas, Photo Jacqueline Hyde © Réunion des Musées Nationaux **241** © G. Dagli Orti, Paris **243** Archiv für Kunst und

Geschichte, Berlin **245** © Artephot/R. Percheron, Paris **250** top, left: Robert Freck/Odyssey Productions/Chicago; left: Giraudon/Art Resource, NY; right: Private Collection/The Bridgeman Art Library, London/NY **251** left: © D. Banerjeb/Dinodia Picture Agency **251** right: Topkapi Sarayi Museum, Istanbul/Ergun Cagatay/Tetragon **252** Mohamed Lounes/Liaison Agency **253** Courtesy of the Trustees of British Library **254** © M. Reichenthal/The Stock Market **255** *A Qadi Hears a Case,* (detail), Bibliothèque Nationale de France, Paris **257** Robert Freck/Odyssey Productions/Chicago **259** Historical Pictures/Stock Montage, Inc. **261** British Library/The Bridgeman Art Library, London/NY **262** top: (detail), Topkapi Sarayi Museum, Istanbul/Ergun Cagatay/Tetragon, bottom: Joseph Nettis/Photo Researchers, Inc. **263** The Granger Collection, NY **264** top: The Metropolitan Museum of Art, Harris Brisbane Dick Fund, 1939. (39.20) Photograph © 1982 The Metropolitan Museum of Art, NY; middle: British Museum, London/The Bridgeman Art Library, London/NY; bottom: Scala/Art Resource NY **266** By permission of The British Library [1.0. 1379 (Ethé 2296) Folio 34] **269** (detail) Victoria & Albert Museum/The Bridgeman Art Library, London, NY **270** Donato-Toronto Sun, Canada/Rothco Cartoons **273** © Sonia Halliday Photographs **278** top, left: © British Museum; middle: © British Museum; right: Werner Forman/Art Resource, NY **279** Kal Muller/Woodfin Camp & Associates **280** Martin Dohrn-Science Photo Library/Photo Researchers, Inc. **282** (detail), Museum Expedition. Courtesy, Museum of Fine Arts, Boston, MA **285** Lee Boltin Picture Library **288** © British Museum **292** Georg Gerster/Photo Researchers, Inc. **294** left: Lee Boltin Picture Library; right: Robert Harding Picture Library **296** M. & E. Bernheim/ Woodfin Camp & Associates **297** A. Ramsey/Stock, Boston **299** Jean Laure **300** top, left: E T Archive; left: Michael Holford; right: © Copyright 1998 PhotoDisc, Inc. **301** left: Collection of the National Palace Museum. Taiwan, Republic of China; right: Victoria & Albert Museum, London/Art Resource, NY **303** top: Science Museum/ Michael Holford; middle: © Uniphoto, Inc.; bottom: © Jonathan Wallen/Harry N. Abrams, Inc. **305** Werner Forman Archive—Idemitsu Museum of Arts, Tokyo/Art Resource, NY **306** *Travelers Among Mountains and Streams* (detail), Fan K'uan, National Palace Museum, Taiwan, Republic of China **308** James Stanfield/National Geographic Society **310** The Metropolitan Museum of Art, Gift of Robert E. Tod, 1937. (37.191.1) **313** Carmen Redondo/CORBIS **315** Flags of North and South Korea © Copyright 1998 PhotoDisc, Inc. **316** Janette Ostier Gallery, Paris, France/Giraudon, Paris/SuperStock **318** Laurie Platt Winfrey, Inc. **319** E T Archive **320** © 1998 PhotoDisc, Inc. **321** left: Werner Forman/Art Re-

source, NY; right: The Metropolitan Museum of Art, Rogers Fund, 1904. (04.4.2) Photograph by Schecter Lee. Photograph © 1986 The Metropolitan Museum of Art **322** © John Bryson/The Image Bank **324** left: Charles & Josette Lenars/CORBIS; right: Torii Kiyonaga © British Museum; bottom: Stapleton Collection, UK/The Bridgeman Art Library, London/NY **328** left and middle: Giraudon/Art Resource, NY; right: Bernard Cox/John Bethell PhotoLibrary, St. Albans **329** left: Giraudon/Art Resource, NY; middle, left: Robert Harding Picture Library; middle: Lee Boltin Picture Library; right: Werner Forman Archive—Idemitsu Museum of Arts, Tokyo/Art Resource, NY **330–331** Werner Forman/Art Resource, NY **332** top and middle: The Granger Collection, NY; bottom: North Wind Picture Archives **333** top, left: The Granger Collection, NY; left: National Maritime Museum/© Dorling Kindersly Ltd.; top, right: © 1994 Larry Kunkel/FPG International Corp.; middle: The Granger Collection, NY; bottom: Mary Kate Denny/PhotoEdit; top, left: Science Museum, London/The Bridgeman Art Library, London/NY; left: Scala/Art Resource, NY; top, right: Dorling Kindersley Ltd. Courtesy of St. Bride Printing; bottom, right: Courtesy of the Trustees of British Library **335** left: *Mona Lisa,* Leonardo da Vinci, Scala/Art Resource NY; right: Private Collection, Great Britain **336** Richard Elliott/Tony Stone Images **338** *St. Jerome in His Study,* Antonello da Messina, The National Gallery, London **339** Library of Congress **340** *The Creation of Adam,* Michelangelo, Scala/Art Resource, NY **343** left: Library of Congress; right: *Self Portrait,* Albrecht Dürer, SuperStock **344** left: Scala/Art Resource, NY; left: Tom Skudra/Stratford Festival Archives; bottom, right: Clive Barda/Performing Arts Library **347** Mansell Collection/Time Inc. **348** The Granger Collection, NY **349** Cambridge Education Corp. **351** Portrait of Henry VIII, Hans Holbein, the Younger, Belvoir Castle, Leicestershire/The Bridgeman Art Library, London/NY **352** Walker Art Gallery, Liverpool/The Bridgeman Art Library, London/NY **356** Science Museum, London / The Bridgeman Art Library, London/NY **358** left: Windsor Castle, Royal Library/Archiv für Kunst und Geschichte, Berlin; right: CNRI—Science Photo Library/Photo Researchers, Inc. **361** Scala/Art Resource, NY **362** left: The Granger Collection, NY; middle: Index/The Bridgeman Art Library, London/NY; right: The Granger Collection, NY **363** *The Emperor Ch'ien-lung as a Young Man:* The Metropolitan Museum of Art, Rogers Fund, 1942. (42.141.8) Photograph © 1980 The Metropolitan Museum of Art **364** top, left: Barry Runk/Grant Heilman Photography; top, right: Barry L. Runk/Grant Heilman Photography; bottom, left: Felicia Martinez/PhotoEdit; bottom, right: Runk/Schoenberger/Grant Heilman Photography **365** Robert Frerck/Odyssey Productions/Chicago **367** top: Bibliothèque Nationale de Cartes et Plans, Paris/The Bridgeman Art Library, London/NY; bottom: The Science Museum/Science & Society Picture Library **369** Van Bucher/Photo Researchers, Inc. **370** SuperStock **374** George Bernard/Photo Researchers, Inc. **376** By Courtesy of the Board of Trustees of the Victoria & Albert Museum **377** Mr. and Mrs. Rafi Y. Mottahedeh Nelson/Laurie Platt Winfrey, Inc. **378** SuperStock **379** *The Emperor of China Receiving the Embassy of Lord Macarthney,* Birmingham Museum and Art Gallery/The Bridgeman Art Library, London/NY **380** Philadelphia Museum of Art: Given by Mrs. G. Brinton Roberts. Photo, Graydon Wood **384** left: *The Landing of Columbus at San Salvador (Guanahani) in Bahamas, 12 October 1492,* The Granger Collection, NY; right: Lee Boltin Picture Library **385** Douglas Waugh/Peter Arnold, Inc. **387** Biblioteca Nacional, Madrid/The Bridgeman Art Library, London/NY **388** The Granger Collection, NY **391** *A Spaniard, his Mexican wife, and their daughter from a series on mixed marriages,* Miguel Cabrera, Museo de America, Madrid/The Bridgeman Art Library, London/NY **392** left: SuperStock; bottom, right: SuperStock; right: Greg Probst/Tony Stone Images **394** The Granger Collection, NY **395** The Granger Collection, NY **397** *Etow Oh Koam* (detail), Verelst, National Archives of Canada, Ottawa **399** top: Nationalmuseet, Copenhagen/The Bridgeman Art Library, London, NY; bottom: © 1996 North Wind Pictures **400** Jean-Loup Charmet/Science Photo Library/Photo Researchers, Inc. **401** SuperStock **402** left: Local History Museum's Collection, Durban; top: Powell Cotton Museum/Geoff Dann, Dorling Kindersley Media Library **405** *Port of Marseille, France, 1754,* Joseph Vernet, The Granger Collection, NY **406** © Engleman/Rothco **410** top, left: Kremlin Museum, Moscow/The Bridgeman Art Library, London/NY; bottom, left: Archivo Fotographico Oronoz, Madrid; right: The Granger Collection, NY **411** left: State Historical Museum, Moscow, Russia/Leonid Bogdanov/SuperStock; right: Palace of Versailles, France/SuperStock **412** The Granger Collection, NY **413** © Patrimonio Nacional, Madrid **416** Bibliothèque Nationale, Paris/Bulloz **417** Lauros—Giraudon/Art Resource, NY **418** Photographic Bulloz **419** background: Scala/Art Resource, NY; top, right: Adam Woolfitt/Woodfin Camp & Associates; middle: A.K.G., Berlin/SuperStock **420** The Granger Collection **423** *The Battle of Marston Moor,* James Ward, Cromwell Museum, Huntington **425, 427** The Granger Collection, NY **429** Erich Lessing/Art Resource, NY **431** Archiv für Kunst und Geschichte, Berlin **433** Steve Raymer/National Geographic Society **434** top: Kremlin Museum, Moscow/The Bridgeman Art Library, London/NY; bottom, left: Hermitage, St. Petersburg, Russia/The

Bridgeman Art Library, London/NY **438** left: *The Creation of Adam,* Michelangelo, Scala/Art Resource, NY; right: The Granger Collection, NY **439** left: Douglas Waugh/Peter Arnold, Inc.; right: Archivo Fotographico Oronoz, Madrid **440–441** CORBIS/Pablo Corral V **442** top: Yale University Art Gallery; bottom: CORBIS/Gianni Dagli Orti, Paris **443** top: The Granger Collection, NY; middle: Bruce Laurence/Liaison Agency; bottom: Paula Bronstein/Liaison Agency **444** top, left: Giraudon/Art Resource, NY; left: The Admiral's Original Flag Loft, Ltd.; right: Kunsthistorisches Museum, Vienna, Austria/The Bridgeman Art Library, London/NY **445** left: *Voltaire,* Jean-Antoine Houdon, Giraudon /Art Resource, NY; right: *Siege of Yorktown, October 17, 1781,* Giraudon /Art Resource, NY **446** *The First Vaccination,* (detail), Georges-Gaston Melingue, The Granger Collection, NY **447** Art Resource, NY **448** The Granger Collection, NY **450** The Granger Collection, NY **451** SuperStock **453** *The Marquise de Peze and the Marquise de Rouget with her two children,* Eizabeth Vigée-Lebrun, Gift of the Bay Foundation in memory of Josephine Bay Paul and Ambassador Charles Ulrick Bay, Photograph © 1999 Board of Trustees, National Gallery of Art, Washington, D.C. **454** left: Musem der Stadt, Vienna, Austria/E T Archive, London/SuperStock; right: Beth Bergman; bottom: Newberry Library, Chicago/SuperStock **456** Christie's Images, London, UK /The Bridgeman Art Library, London/NY **457** Cheltenham Art Gallery & Museums, Gloucestershire/UK/Bridgeman Art Library, London, NY/ **458** *The Election II—Canvassing for Votes,* William Hogarth, Sir John Soane Museum, London/The Bridgeman Art Library, London/NY **459** *George III,* Studio of Ramsey, The Scottish National Portrait Gallery **460** CORBIS **463** SuperStock **466** top, left: West Point Museum Collections, United States Military Academy, West Point, NY; left: *The Taking of the Bastille, 14th July 1789,* Jean-Pierre Houel, Musée Carnavalet, Paris/The Bridgeman Art Library, London/NY; right: © Jorn Fabricius **467** left: Erich Lessing/Art Resource, NY; right: Victoria & Albert Picture Library **469** Carnavalet/Art Resource, NY **471** *The Tennis Court Oath,* Jacques-Louis David, Musée Carnavalet, Paris, France/The Bridgeman Art Library, London/NY **473** Private Collection/The Bridgeman Art Library, London/NY **475** CORBIS/Gianni Dagli Orti **478** © A. C. Cooper/Madame Tussaud's Wax Museum **479** Bibliothèque Nationale de France **480** Musée des Beaux-Arts, Lille, France/© Erich Lessing/Art Resource, NY **481** top: CORBIS; bottom: Archive Photos **484** West Point Museum Collections, United States Military Academy, West Point, NY **485** *The Coronation of Napoleon by Pope Pius VII,* Jacque-Louis David, Louvre, Paris, France/The Bridgeman Art Library, London/NY **488** The

Granger Collection, NY **489** top: *And They are Like Wild Beasts,* Francisco Goya, The Granger Collection, NY; bottom: *The Third of May, 1808,* Francisco Goya, Giraudon/Art Resource, NY **491** North Wind Picture Archives **493** The Granger Collection **495** The Fotomas Index **496** top, left: Archiv für Kunst und Geschichte, Berlin; left, right: The Granger Collection, NY **497** right: CORBIS **499** top: University of Reading © Rural History Centre; bottom: Arthur C. Smith III/Grant Heilman Photography **500** Huntington Library, Art Collections, and Botanical Gardens, San Marino, California/SuperStock **503** The Science Museum/Science & Society Picture Library **506** *Forging the Anchor,* William James Muler, City of Bristol Museum and Art Gallery, England/Bridgeman Art Library, London/SuperStock **507** top, right: The Science Museum/Science & Society Picture Library **508** Mary Evans Picture Library **510** SuperStock **511** Archiv für Kunst und Geschichte, Berlin **512** New Lanark Conservation Trust **516** left: Photofest; middle: Schalkwijk/Art Resource, NY; right: Dannielle Hayes/Omni-Photo Communications, Inc. **517** *Fighting at the Hotel de Ville, 28th July, 1830,* Jean Victor Schnetz, Musée du Petit Palais, Paris/Giraudon/The Bridgeman Art Library, London/NY **518** Anne S. K. Brown Military Collection, Brown University Library **519** North Wind Picture Archives **520** The Granger Collection, NY **523** left: *The Uprising,* Honore Daumier, The Phillips Collection, Washington, D.C.; top, right: © 1990 CMOL; bottom, right: Rudolf Eichstaedt/Photo Researchers, Inc. **525** Historical Pictures/Stock Montage, Inc. **526** The Granger Collection, NY **527** *Portrait of Don Tomas Mateo Cervantes,* Vincente Escobar, Gift of the Cuban Foundation, The Museum of Arts and Sciences, Daytona Beach, FL **529** CORBIS **532** *Paso de los Andes,* Vilas y Prades, Museo Historico y Militar de Chile **535** Babcock Bequest, Courtesy, Museum of Fine Arts, Boston (14.4187) **536** left: *Voltaire,* Jean-Antoine Houdon Giraudon/Art Resource, NY; right: *The Taking of the Bastille, 14th July 1789,* Jean-Pierre Houel, Musée Carnavalet, Paris/The Bridgeman Art Library, London/NY **537** *Forging the Anchor,* William James Muler, City of Bristol Museum and Art Gallery, England/Bridgeman Art Library, London/SuperStock; right: *Fighting at the Hotel de Ville, 28th July, 1830,* Jean Victor Schnetz, Musée du Petit Palais, Paris/Giraudon/The Bridgeman Art Library, London/NY **538–539** Michael Melford/The Image Bank **540** left: Chicago Historical Society, ICHi-01066; right: John Mead/Photo Researchers, Inc. **541** top, left: Archiv für Kunst und Geschichte, Berlin; top, right: ©Reuters Newmedia Inc./CORBIS; middle: The Granger Collection, NY; bottom: Wernher Krutein/Liaison Agency **542** top: Ford Motor Company; left: *Fisherman Upon A Lee Shore,* Joseph

Turner, Kenwood House, Hampstead, London/Bridgeman Art Library, London/SuperStock; top,right: The Granger Collection, NY; bottom,right: Rebus, Inc. **543** left:Private Collection/Bridgeman Art Library, London/SuperStock right: ©Hulton Getty/Liaison Agency **547** © Berry, 1986 Cartoonists & Writers Syndicate **548** left: Library of Congress; right: Ford Motor Company **549** left: CORBIS; right: Ford Motor Company **550** Library of Congress **551** *The Vaccination,* (detail), Louis Leopold Boilly, Agnew & Sons, London/The Bridgeman Art Library, London/NY **552** The Granger Collection, NY **553** top: Private Collection/The Bridgeman Art Library, London/NY; bottom: The Granger Collection, NY **559** left: The Granger Collection, NY; right: FPG International Corp. **560** top: Sam Fried/Photo Researchers, Inc; bottom: Frans Lanting/Photo Researchers, Inc. **561** Library of Congress **562** ©A.K.G., Berlin/SuperStock **563** *The Stone Breakers,* Gustave Courbert, Staatliche Kunstsammlungen, Dresden, Germany/Bridgeman Art Library, London/SuperStock **564** left: *Rouen Cathedral (The Portal), Harmony in Brown),* Claude Monet, Erich Lessing/Art Resource, NY; middle: *Rouen Cathedral (Gray Day),* Claude Monet, Erich Lessing/Art Resource, NY; right: *Rouen Cathedral (The Portal in Sun),* Claude Monet, ©Photo RMN-Hervé Lewandowski **565** Christie's Images, NY **568** top,left and left: Archiv für Kunst und Geschichte,Berlin; right: CORBIS/Archivo Iconografico, S.A. **569** left: Corel Professional Photos CD-ROM™; right:The Granger Collection, NY **572** Archiv für Kunst und Geschichte,Berlin **574** ©Ullstein-Bilderdienst **575** CORBIS **576** Carpenter Center for the Visual Arts, Harvard University, Cambridge, MA **578** left: Museum of the City of New York/Archive Photos; right: The Granger Collection, NY **581** Museum der Stadt Wien/ET Archive **582** CORBIS/Tim Thompson **585** © 1999 North Wind Picture **587** left: ©Sue Adler/Performing Arts Library; middle: CORBIS/Dean Conger; right: CORBIS/ Bettmann **589** The Granger Collection, NY **592** top,left: The Granger Collection, NY; left: British Information Service; right: CORBIS/Bettmann **593** left: Jewish College Library, London, UK/The Bridgeman Art Library, London/NY; right: The Granger Collection, NY **595** The Royal Collection ©2000 Her Majesty Queen Elizabeth II **596** left,right: Private Collection/The Bridgeman Art Library, London,NY **598** left: Private Collection/The Bridgeman Art Library, London/NY; right: The Stapleton Collection/The Bridgeman Art Library, London/NY **599** John Ficara/Woodfin Camp & Associates **600** The Granger Collection, NY **601** background: Erskine Nicol/ET Archive; **601** top,left: *Fair Lane, Cork - the Ford Family,* 1847, oil on canvas, painted by Rodney Charman, Egan Foundation Collection, Nantucket, Mass. Photo by Terry Pommett **603** Archive Photos **604**

The Balloon, Pierre Puvis de Chavannes © Photo Réunion des Musées Nationaux **606** CORBIS/Bettmann **610, 611, 612** The Granger Collection, NY **615** Private Collection/The Bridgeman Art Library, London/NY **616** top,left: Ulllstein Veroffentlichung nur mit Urhebervermerk; bottom,left: Tony Stone Images; right: The Granger Collection, NY **617** © Jean-Loup Charmet **619** CORBIS/Hulton Deutsch Collection **620** The Granger Collection, NY **621** SuperStock **622** left: image©Copyright 1998 PhotoDisc, Inc.; top,right: Private Collection/The Bridgeman Art Library, London/NY **624** Staatliche Museen zu Berlin - PreuBischer Kulturbesitz Museum für Volkerkunde **625** Ulllstein Veroffentlichung nur mit Urhebervermerk **626** Hulton Getty/Liaison Agency **628** *On the Bosphorous, Istanbul,* (detail), Atkinson Art Gallery, Southport, Lancs/The Bridgeman Art Library, London/NY **629** Archive Photos/Popperfoto **630** Paolo Koch/Photo Researchers, Inc. **633** Henry Wilson **635** E T Archive **637** bottom,left: E T Archive **639** Agence France Presse/ Archive Photos **641** The Granger Collection, NY **642** left: Museum of New Zealand Te Papa Tongarewa (B19095) **642**; right: E T Archive **642** top,left: E T Archive **643** CORBIS/ Bettmann **645** top: Richard Vogel/Liaison Agency; bottom: Reprinted with permission of Iruma City Museum **646** Museum of Fine Arts, Boston/Laurie Platt Winfrey, Inc. **648** Transportation Museum, Tokyo **652** CORBIS **655** The Granger Collection, NY **658** CORBIS/Underwood & Underwood **663** Koninklijk Instituut voor de Tropen, TROPENMUSEUM **664** Rhodes Memorial Museum, USA/The Bridgeman Art Library, London/NY **665** ©Branger-Viollet **666** left: Musee Picasso, Barcelona, Spain/INDEX/ Bridgeman Art Library, London/NY/ ©2001 Estate·of Pablo Picasso/Artists Rights Society(ARS), NY; middle: Werner Forman/Art Resource, NY; right: Picasso Museum, Paris, France/Giraudon, Paris/SuperStock, ©2001 Estate of Pablo Picasso/Artists Rights Society(ARS), NY **670** left: Ford Motor Company; middle: Archiv für Kunst und Geschichte, Berlin; right: The Royal Collection ©2000 Her Majesty Queen Elizabeth II **671** left: Tony Stone Images right: E T Archive **672-673**: US Army Center of Military History **674** top: PECUB, Cartoonists & Writers Syndicate; bottom: Culver Pictures, Inc. **675** top: CORBIS; top inset: Leslie E. Kossoff/AP/ Wide World Photos; bottom: Alain Morvan/The Liaison Agency **676** top,left:National Archives; Culver Pictures; right: Imperial War Museum/ Archive Photos **677** left: Library of Congress; right: Collection of Whitney Museum of American Art **679** Courtesy of the Library of Congress **680** L'Illustration Paris **681** Christel Gerstenberg/CORBIS **683** John McCutchson/The Chicago Tribune, 1914. Photo: Ken Karp **684** Bildarchiv Preussischer Kulturhesitz, Berlin **686** background: COR-

BIS; bottom,left: Culver Pictures, Inc.; bottom,right: René Dazy Collection, Paris **688** top: Smithsonian Institution; middle: Bilderdrenst Suddeutscher Verlag, Munich; bottom: © James A. Bryant **690** The Granger Collection, NY **691** CORBIS **692, 694** National Archives **699** The Imperial War Museum, London **700** top,left: Sovfoto/Novosti; left: *The Storming of the Winter Palace, 7th November, 1917,* Novosti/The Bridgeman Art Library, London/NY; right: Sovfoto/Eastfoto **701** left: The Granger Collection, NY; right: David King Collection **703** Archive für Kunst und Geschichte, London **704** *Lenin and a Manifestation, 1919* (detail), Novosti/The Bridgeman Art Library, London/NY **705** Hulton Getty/Liaison Agency **707** Sovfoto/Novosti **708** AP/Wide World Photos **710** CORBIS/Scheufler Collection **711** The Bettmann Archive/CORBIS **713** *Gulag Prisoners,* Getman/The Jamestown Foundation, Washington, DC. **714** Sovfoto/Novosti **715** Scala/Art Resource,NY **716** top: Sovfoto/Eastfoto; middle: Archiv für Kunst und Geschichte, London; bottom: ITAR-TASS/ Sovfoto **719** Sovfoto/Eastfoto **720** top, left: Photograph © The Detroit Institute of Arts, 1995. Palacio Nacional stairway, Mexico City. © Dirk Bakker, photographer, detail; left: The Central Zionist Archives; right: Irene Hubbell/Root Resources **720** top,left: (detail) Photograph © The Detroit Institute of Arts, 1995. Palacio Nacional stairway, Mexico City. © Dirk Bakker, photographer. **721** CORBIS Sygma **723** The Granger Collection, NY **724** (detail) Photograph © The Detroit Institute of Arts, 1995. Palacio Nacional stairway, Mexico City. © Dirk Bakker, photographer. **727** Julio Donoso/Contact Press Images/PNI **728** Turkish Culture and Information Office, NYC **731** Culver Pictures, Inc. **732** By permission of The British Library (F839) **733** Popperfoto/Archive Photos **735** Roger Viollet/Liaison Agency **738** AP/Wide World Photos **740** inset: CORBIS/ Bettmann **744** top left: © /Topham/The Image Works; middle: *Composition No. 4,* 1920, Fernand Leger, Musee Leger, Biot, France/The Bridgeman Art Library, London/NY, Artists Society(ARS), NY; right: CORBIS **745** left: Private Collection/The Bridgeman Art Library, London/NY; right: The Granger Collection, NY **746** © Elke Walford/Hamburger Kunsthalle, Hamburg **747, 748, 749** The Granger Collection/The Bridgeman Art Library, London/NY **752** Private Collection/The Bridgeman Art Library, London/NY **753** *The Persistence of Memory,* Salvador Dali, The Museum of Modern Art, NY (C) 1996 Demart Pro Arte, Geneva/Artists Rights Society (ARS), NY **755** middle: CORBIS/Frank Driggs; bottom,right: Frank Driggs/Archive Photos; top, right: CORBIS/Bettmann **756** CORBIS **759** left: Italian Government Tourist Board; top: ©by Giancarlo Costa/Ferrovie Dello Stato, 1940 **761** CORBIS **762** Bildarchiv Preussischer Kulturbesitz **763** © Keystone/The Image Works **764** © Topham/The

Image Works **768** top,left: Brown Brothers, NY; right: The Granger Collection, NY; right: Movietone News / CORBIS/Bettmann-UPI **769** left: The Granger Collection, NY; right: CORBIS/Bettmann **770** CORBIS/Bettmann **771** CORBIS/Bettmann-UPI **775** The Granger Collection, NY **777** background: Brown Brothers; right: Hulton Getty/Liaison Agency **779** CORBIS **780** Archive Photos **783** left: Culver Pictures, Inc. **783** top,right: CORBIS/Ira Nowinski; bottom,right: CORBIS/Bettmann-UPI **784** top: The Imperial War Museum London; bottom: © Michael Patrick /Folio. **787** AP/Wide World Photos **788** CORBIS/Bettmann **790** left: Archive Photos; right: AP/Wide World Photos **792** CORBIS/Bettmann **797** The Granger Collection, NY **798** left: Collection of the Whitney Museum of American Art; middle: *Lenin and a Manifestation, 1919* (detail), Novosti/The Bridgeman Art Library, London/NY; right: (detail) Photograph ©The Detroit Institute of Arts, 1995. Palacio Nacional stairway, Mexico City. © Dirk Bakker, photographer. **799** left: *The Persistence of Memory,* Salvador Dali, The Museum of Modern Art, New York (C) 1996 Demart Pro Arte, Geneva/Artists Rights Society (ARS), New York ; right: Archive Photos **800-801** Earth Imaging/Tony Stone Images **802** top,left: Gary Retherford/Photo Researchers, Inc.; top,right: Rogers/Monkmeyer; bottom: Michael Newman/PhotoEdit **803** top: AP/Wide World Photos; middle: SBG; bottom: Agence France Presse/CORBIS **804** top,left: Bob Martin/Sports Illustrated; left: Rudi Von Briel/PhotoEdit; right: NASA/Science Photo Library/Photo Researchers, Inc. **805** left: Marc & Evelyne Bernheim/Woodfin Camp & Associates; right: Hayes Davidson/Nick Wood **807** CORBIS **810** top: Bob Martin/Sports Illustrated; top,left: Carl Yarbrough/Sports Illustrated; bottom,left: Tom Lynn/Sports Illustrated **811** ©Dan Hofoss-Canada/Rothco **813** top: AP/Wide World Photos; bottom: Betty Press/Woodfin Camp & Associates **815** United Nations **816** TOLES © 1992 The Buffalo News. Reprinted with permission of UNIVERSAL PRESS SYNDICATE. All rights reserved. **817** Yousuf Karsh/Woodfin Camp & Associates **819** top: Betty Press/Woodfin Camp & Associates; bottom: Steve Vidler/ SuperStock **821** top: Yagi Studio/SuperStock; middle: CORBIS/Sygma; bottom: Michael Newman/PhotoEdit **822** NASA/LBJ **823** AP/Wide World Photos **825** ABU-The Sunday Observer, Bombay/Rothco Cartoons **826** top,left ©Regis Bossu/CORBIS Sygma; left: Sovfoto/Tass; right: Halstead/Liaison Agency **827** left: CORBIS/Reuters; top,right: 0851 Gamma/Liaison Agency; middle, right: Tony Stone Images; bottom, right: 0851 Gamma/Liaison Agency **828** and **829** ©Hulton Getty/Liaison Agency **830** Georg Gerster/Photo Researchers, Inc. **834** Gamma Presse Images/Liaison Agency **835** Michael Philippot/CORBIS/Sygma

836 ©Thomas Del Braise/The Stock Market **837** left: Lionel Cironneau/ AP/Wide World Photos; right: Regis Bossu/CORBIS Sygma **839** J. Baylor Roberts/National Geographic Society **841** Dan Budnik/Woodfin Camp & Associates **842** left: La Presse/CORBIS Sygma; bottom: ©J.P. Laffont/CORBIS Sygma **843** Carl Mydans/Life Mafgazine ©Time Inc. **845-3** Gerd Ludwig/National Geographic Society **846** Shone/Liaison Agency **847** left: AP/Wide World Photos; right: Swersey/Liaison Agency **849** Dean Conger/CORBIS **850** © Chuck Fishman/Contact Press Images **851** left: Darolle/CORBIS Sygma; right: Vittoriano Rastelli/CORBIS Sygma **856** top,left: ©Fallender/Sipa Press; left: (detail) China Stock/Liu Ligun, artist; right: CORBIS **857** Paul Lowe/Magnum Photos, INC. **858** ©Hulton Getty/Liaison Agency **861** ©The Stock Market/Ken Straiton **863** SuperStock **864** Camera Press/Retna, LTD **865** Lee Foster/Bruce Coleman, Inc. **866** left: ©1989 Stuart Franklin/Magnum Photos, Inc.; background: © Fallender/Sipa Press **869** Naomi Duguid/Asia Access **871** ©Hulton-Deutsch Collection / CORBIS **872** Noboru Hashimoto/CORBIS Sygma **875** Alberto Garcia/Saba **876** ©Stuart Isett/CORBIS Sygma **877** ©Robert Fried www.robertfried-photography.com **880** top,left: Raghu Rai/Magnum Photos; middle,top: Amrit P. Singh; middle,bottom: Alain Evrard/Photo Researchers, Inc.; right: AP/Wide World Photos **881** left: S.Compoint/CORBIS Sygma; right: CORBIS/Reuters **884** Raghu Rai/Magnum Photos **885** Eddie Adams/Liaison Agency **886** © Hillary/Royal Geographic Society **889** ©1997 Richard T. Nowitz **891** Ray Ellis/Photo Researchers **892** Marlene Nelson/Copyright Wasma'a K. Chorbachi **893** Greg English/Sygma **895** Reuters/Kai /Pfaffenbach/ Archive Photos **896** Howard Sochurek/Life Magazine © Time Inc. **897** top: Caputo/Stock, Boston; top,right: Jean-Claude Aunos/Liaison Agency; left: David Turnley/Corbis; bottom,right: Nacerdine Zebar/Liaison Agency; **898** ©1999 Michael Coyne/Black Star **899** D. Wells/Image Works **905** Jagdish Agarwa/Dinodia Picture Agency **906** top,left: Peter Turnley/CORBIS; middle: AP/Wide World Photos; right:. Robert Frerck/ Odyssey Productions/Chicago **907** Reuters /CORBIS/Bettmann **909** Courtesy of the Director, National Army Museum **910** CORBIS / Bettmann-UPI **912** Hulton Getty/Liaison Agency **912** Bas/Rothco Cartoons **913** Reza/Imax/CORBIS Sygma **914** Michael Dwyer/Stock Boston **918** Nik Wheeler / CORBIS **919** ©Marc & Evelyne Bernheim/Woodfin Camp & Associates **920** Bruno Barbey/Magnum **923** AP/Wide World Photos **925** left: Gamma Presse Images/Liaison Agency right: Shahn Kermani/Liaison Agency **926** Joe Traver/Liaison **927** background: Peter Turnley/CORBIS; inset: Noel Quidu/Liaison **928** ©T. Hegenbart/Black Star **932**

top,left: Ary Diesendruck/Tony Stone Images; left: Americas Magazine Oas; right: AP/Wide World Photos **933** left: Alain Mingam/Liaison Agency; middle: Enrique Shore/Woodfin Camp & Associates; right:Antonio Ribeiro/Liaison Agency; **935** Vera Lentz/Black Star **936-937** Courtesy of the artist. **938** ©Daher/Liaison Agency **940** ©P.Robert/CORBIS Sygma **941** CORBIS **942** Mireille Vautier/Woodfin Camp & Associates **945** AP/Wide World Photos **946** Don Goode/Photo Researchers, Inc. **947** background: ©Ilkka Ulimonen/ CORBIS Sygma; middle: AP/Wide World Photos **948** Mireille Vautier/Woodfin Camp & Associates **949** and **950** AP/Wide World Photos **952** Ary Diesendruck/Tony Stone Images **953** ©Les Stone/CORBIS Sygma **954** Ben Gibson/Katz/Woodfin Camp & Associates **957** AP/Wide World Photos **958** left: NASA/SCIENCE Photo Library/Photo Researchers, Inc.; middle: ©Regis Bossu/Corbis Sygma; right Super-Stock **959** left: Marlene Nelson/ Copyright Wasma'a K. Chorbachi; middle: Nik Wheeler/Corbis; right: Mireille Vautier/Woodfin Camp & Associates **960-961** CORBIS/Pablo Corral V **962** Musee du Louvre, Paris/Giraudon, Paris/SuperStock **963** The Oriental Institute Museum **964** The Jewish Museum, NY/Art Resource, NY **965** Bibliotheque Nationale, Paris, France/The Bridgeman Art Library/London/NY **966** ©Copyright 1998 PhotoDisc, Inc. **967** Bildarchiv Preussischer I Kulturbesitz **968** CORBIS **969** Archaeological Museum, Sarnath/Robert Harding Picture Library **970** McRae Books Srl **971** Giraudon/Art Resource, NY **972** E T Archive **973** Bibliotheque Nationale/Archiv für Kunst und Geschichte, Berlin **975** Lee **973** Archaelogical Museum, Sarnath/Robert Harding Picture Library **975** LeeBoltin Picture Library **976** Nationalmuseet, Copenhagen/The Bridgeman Art Library, London **978** British Information Service **981** Private Collection/The Bridgeman Art Library, London/New York **982** Schalkwijk/Art Resource, NY **983** Dannielle Hayes/Omni-Photo Communications, Inc. **984** The Election II-Canvassing for Votes by William Hogarth, Sir John Soane Museum, London/The Bridgeman Art Library, LondonNY **984** The Science Museum/Science & Society Picture Library **985** Museum of Fine Arts, Boston/Laurie Platt Winfrey, Inc. **986** Bildarchiv Preussischer Kulturhesitz, Berlin **987** By permission of The British Library (F839) **988** The Granger Collection, NY **989** Rudi Von Briel/PhotoEdit **990** SuperStock **992** CORBIS/Bettmann-UPI **993** © Chuck Fishman/Contact Press Images **994** Shone/Liaison Agency **996** AP/Wide World Photos **997** ©Stuart Isett/CORBIS Sygma **998** Reuters/CORBIS/Bettmann **999** © Fallender/Sipa Press

Acknowledgements

6 Excerpt from *The Overview Effect* by Frank White. Copyright © 1987, Houghton Mifflin. **55** "The Rig Veda/Hymn to Indra" from *Reading About the World, Volume 1.* Used by permission of Michael Myers, Translator, Washington State University. **65** "The Spirits Are Good" from *The Book of Songs* by Arthur Waley, Translator. Copyright © 1937 by Arthur Waley, Translator. Used by permission of Grove/Atlantic Inc. **67** Excerpt from *The Ramayana*, translated by Kenneth Anderson, aka Krishna Dharma. Copyright © 1998 by Kenneth Anderson, aka Krishna Dharma. Published by Torchlight Publishing, Inc. **80** Excerpt from *The Dhammapada*, edited by Anne Bancroft. Copyright © 1997 Element Books Limited. Used by permission of Element Books Limited and Anne Bancroft, editor. **104** Excerpt from *The Illiad* by Homer; translated by Robert Fitzgerald. Copyright © 1974 by Robert Fitzgerald. Published by Anchor Books/Doubleday. **137** Excerpt from *The Aeneid of Virgil*, translated by C. Day Lewis, reprinted by permission of Oxford University Press, Inc. **191** Excerpt from *The Canterbury Tales* by Geoffrey Chaucer, translated into modern English by Nevill Coghill. Copyright © 1951, 1958, 1960 by Neville Coghill. Reproduced by permission of Penguin Books Ltd. **222** From *The Song of Roland Done into English in the Original Measure*, translated by C. Scott Moncrieff. Copyright © 1919 Chapman & Hall Ltd. Used by permission of the publishers and the executors of the Estate of C. Scott Moncrieff. **287** Excerpt from *Leo Africanus: Description of Timbuktu*, translated by Paul Brians. Copyright © 1998 by Paul Brians, Department of English, Washington State University. **296** Excerpt from *Through African Eyes Volume 1: The Past; the Road to Independence* by Leon E. Clark. Copyright © 1988, 1991 by Leon E. Clark. Published by CITE Books and Distributed by Apex Press. **307** "Letter to His Small Children" from *Li Po and Tu Fu Poems*, translated by Arthur Cooper. Copyright © 1973 by Arthur Cooper. **529** Excerpt from *The Black Jacobins: Toussaint L'Ouverture and the San Domingo Revolution* by C. L. R. James. Copyright © 1963 by Random House, Inc. **579** From "A Foreign Volunteer at the Battle of the Volturno, April 2, 1860" from *Garibaldi: Great Lives Observed*, edited by Denis Mack Smith. Copyright © 1969 by Prentice Hall, Inc. Reprinted by permission of the author. **717** Excerpt from "Requiem," translated by Robin Kemball, Copyright © 1974 by Robin Kemball, from *Selected Poems* by Anna Akhmatova, edited and translated by Walter Arndt. Reprinted by permission of Ardis. **719** From *Assignment in Utopia* by Eugene Lyons. Copyright © 1937, by Harcourt, Brace & World, Inc., and reproduced with their permis-

sion. Published in Great Britain by George G. Harrap & Co. Ltd. Reprinted by permission. **723** Excerpt from "Zeferino Diego Ferreira: The Life Story of a Villista," by Laura Cummings. Copyright © 1999 by University of Arizona *Journal of the Southwest.* **737** Excerpt from *Japanese Imperialism and the Massacre in Nanjing*, translated by Robert P. Gray. Copyright © 1996. **765** "Sophie Yaari Tells Her Story" from *To Save A Life: Stories of Jewish Rescue* by Ellen Land-Weber. Copyright © 1984, 1999 to Ellen Land-Weber. **774** Four lines of "In Memory of W. B. Yeats," from *W. H. Auden: Collected Poems* by W. H. Auden. Copyright © 1940 and renewed 1968 by W. H. Auden. Reprinted by permission of Random House, Inc. and Faber and Faber Limited. **786** From "Major Werner Pluskat, aged 32, 352 Artillery Regiment, 352nd Division" from *Nothing Less Than Victory: An Oral History of D-Day* by Russell Miller. Copyright © 1993 by Russell Miller. Reprinted by permission of Peters Fraser & Dunlop Group, Ltd. **825** "No Time" by Nguyen Sa from *A Thousand Years of Vietnamese Poetry* (ed. Nguyen Ngoc Bich). Copyright © 1962, 1967, 1968, 1969, 1970, 1971, 1972, 1974, by Asia Society, Inc. **833** "A Man's Place" from *The New York Times Magazine*, May 16, 1999 by Claudia Goldin in a conversation moderated by Michael Weinstein. Copyright © 1999, The New York Times Company. **847** Quoted by Alexander Solzhenitsyn in *The New York Times*, January 4, 1997. Copyright © 1997, The New York Times Company. **855** "Liberal Leaders Warn Yeltsin to Protect His People," Reuters Limited, October 6, 1999. Copyright © 1999 Reuters Limited. **859** "The Art and Practice of Japanese Management" by John Micklethwait and Adrian Wooldridge. This article is adapted from *The Witch Doctors*. (c) 1996 by Times Books. **879** From "A Modern Rouge et Noir," translated by Deborah Cao and Lawrence Tedesco from *Voices from the Whirlwind: An Oral History of the Chinese Cultural Revolution*, edited by Feng Jicai. Copyright © 1990 by Foreign Language Press, Beijing, China. Reprinted by permission of the publisher. **901** Excerpt adapted from "A Man is Like a Stalk of Wheat" from *The Yellow Wind* by David Grossman. Copyright © 1988 by David Grossman and Koteret Rashit. English translation copyright © 1988 by Haim Watzman. Reprinted by permission of Farrar, Straus & Giroux, Inc. **910** Excerpt from "Negro Nation of Ghana is Born in Africa" by Thomas F. Brady. Copyright © 1957, The New York Times Company. **939** Excerpt from *Revolution Through Peace* by Dom Helder Camara, translated by Amparo McLean. English translation copyright © 1971 by Harper & Row Publishers, Inc. **954** Excerpt from "For Brazil's Street Children, a Happy Path to Take" by James

Brooke. Copyright © 1993, The New York Times Company. **968** Excerpt from *The Mahabharata*, translated by J. A. B. van Buitenen. Copyright © 1973 by University of Chicago Press. **971** From *The Koran*, translated by N. J. Dawood. Copyright © 1956, 1959, 1966, 1968, 1974 by N. J. Dawood. Published by Penguin Books, Ltd. **973** "The Prolouge" from *The Canterbury Tales* by Geoffrey Chaucer, translated into modern English by Nevill Coghill. Copyright © 1951, 1958, 1960 by Neville Coghill. Reproduced by permission of Penguin Books Ltd. **975** "The True History of the Conquest of New Spain" from *The Bernal Diaz Chronicles*, translated by Albert Idell. Translation copyright © 1956 by Albert Idell. Used by permission of Doubleday, a division of Bantam Doubleday Dell Publishing Group, Inc. **977** Excerpt from *Don Quixote of La Mancha* by Miguel de Cervantes; translated by Walter Starkie. Copyright © 1957 by Macmillan & Co., Ltd., London. Translation copyright © 1964 by Walter Starkie and published by The New American Library. **985** Excerpt from *The Autobiography of Fukuzawa Yukichi*, by Fukuzawa Yukichi, translated by Eiichi Kiyooka. Translation copyright © 1960 by Eiichi Kiyooka. Copyright © 1966 by Columbia University Press. **986** Excerpt from *All Quiet on the Western Front* by Erich Maria Remarque. Copyright © 1929, 1930 by Little, Brown and Company; copyright © renewed 1957, 1958 by Erich Maria Remarque. **991** Excerpt from *Things Fall Apart* by Chinua Achebe. Copyright © 1959 by Chinua Achebe. Published by Doubleday Dell Publishing Group, Inc. Originally published by Heinemann Educational Books, Ltd. **994, 998, 999** "Perestroika" by Mikhail Gorbechev, "Glory and Hope" by Nelson Mandela, and "The Outlook for China: Human Rights" by Harry Wu from *Vital Speeches Of the Day*. Used by permission of The City News. **995** "New Years Address" from *Uncaptive Minds* by Vaclav Havel. Reprinted by permission of Uncaptive Minds, a publication of the Institute for Democracy in Eastern Europe. **996** "Latin America: the Democracy Option" by Mario Vargas Llosa from *Harper's Magazine*. Copyright © 1987 by Harper's Magazine. Reproduced from the June issue by special permission. **997** From *Freedom From Fear and Other Writings* by Aung San Suu Kyi, forwarded by Vaclav Havel, translated by Michael Aris. Translation copyright © 1991 by Aung San Suu Kyi and Michael Aris. Used by permission of Penguin, a division of Penguin Books USA, Inc.

Note: Every effort has been made to locate the copyright owner of material reprinted in this book. Omissions brought to our attention will be corrected in subsequent printings.